DATE DUE

The Measurement of Saving, Investment, and Wealth

Studies in Income and Wealth
Volume 52

National Bureau of Economic Research
Conference on Research in Income and Wealth

The Measurement of Saving, Investment, and Wealth

Edited by Robert E. Lipsey and Helen Stone Tice

 The University of Chicago Press

Chicago and London

ROBERT E. LIPSEY is a professor of economics, Queens College
and the Graduate School and University Center, the City
University of New York. He is also a research associate and
Director, New York Office, of the National Bureau of Economic
Research. HELEN STONE TICE is assistant to the director of the
Bureau of Economic Analysis, U.S. Department of Commerce.

The University of Chicago Press, Chicago 60637
The University of Chicago Press Ltd., London
© 1989 by the National Bureau of Economic Research
All rights reserved. Published 1989
Printed in the United States of America

98 97 96 95 94 93 92 91 90 89   5 4 3 2 1

Library of Congress Cataloging-in-Publication Data

The Measurement of saving, investment, and wealth / edited by
Robert E. Lipsey and Helen Stone Tice.
    p.   cm.— (Studies in income and wealth ; v. 52)
    Bibliography: p.
    Includes index.
    ISBN 0-226-48468-8
    1. Saving and investment. 2. Saving and thrift. 3. Wealth.
I. Lipsey, Robert E.   II. Tice, Helen Stone.   III. Series.
HC106.3.C714   vol. 52
[HC79.S3]
330 s—dc19
[339.4'3]   89-4669
                                            CIP

Contents

Prefatory Note

This volume contains the papers and discussion presented at the Conference on the Measurement of Saving, Investment, and Wealth held in Baltimore, Maryland, 27–28 March 1987. Funds for the Conference on Research in Income and Wealth are provided to the National Bureau of Economic Research by the Bureau of the Census, the Bureau of Economic Analysis, the Bureau of Labor Statistics, and the Statistics Division of the Internal Revenue Service. In addition, the National Science Foundation Program on Measurement Methods and Data Resources provided financing for this conference. We are indebted to all of them for their support. We also thank Robert E. Lipsey and Helen Stone Tice, who served as cochairs of the conference and editors of this volume, and the other members of the initial planning committee, Angus Deaton, John Shoven, and James D. Smith.

Executive Committee, March 1987

Charles R. Hulten, chair	Robert Gillingham
Ernst R. Berndt	Claudia Goldin
Geoffrey Carliner	Zvi Griliches
Christopher K. Clague	Stanley Lebergott
W. Erwin Diewert	Robert P. Parker

Volume Editors' Acknowledgments

Kirsten Foss Davis handled, with her usual skill, the logistics of the conference on which this volume is based. Jane Konkel prepared the papers for the press, and she and Annie Spillane efficiently guided the conference editors through the many stages of the publication process. Henry Peskin and an anonymous referee offered exceptionally insightful comments and suggestions. The editors give their thanks to all of these and to the principal contributors, the authors of the papers and their discussants, all of whom were unusually responsible and helpful.

Introduction

Robert E. Lipsey and Helen Stone Tice

The distinction between current consumption and saving, or putting aside for the future, has been with us for ages. It was the basis for Joseph's solution to the seven lean years he foresaw (Gen. 41:34–36) and for Aesop's fable of the ant and the grasshopper. Yet we still do not seem to have got it right, conceptually or empirically.

This distinction is central to macroeconomics and to the analysis of economic growth. In some theories of economic development, it is the crucial factor or even virtually the only one. It has figured prominently in the policy discussion about changes in U.S. tax laws, about the U.S. budget and trade deficits and possible cures for them, and in the analysis of the slowness of U.S. economic growth relative to that of other countries.

Despite the importance and venerability of the issue, there is probably no other concept for which U.S. official agencies issue annual estimates that differ by more than one-third, as they have done for net household saving. And there is probably no other concept for which reputable scholars claim that the correct measure is close to ten times the officially published one.

The Conference on Research in Income and Wealth has a long tradition of interest in these matters, and the 1987 Conference on the Measurement of Saving, Investment, and Wealth carried on this tradition with two major objectives. One was to look for ways to improve aggregate and sectoral saving and investment estimates, which have long been notorious for the size of discrepancies among different versions, for the size of revisions as new data accumulated, and for major disagreements about concepts. The second was to assess some of the new microdata on household wealth that have been provided by recent surveys, presumably much superior to earlier ones. The two objectives were not entirely independent; it was hoped that the improved survey data might contribute also to solving some of the mysteries in the aggregate saving and wealth data.

Existing statistics on saving have a bad reputation among economists. Despite considerable interest in having accurate measures of saving for policy making and for economic analysis, the official measures of saving are criticized for errors both in concepts and in the statistical realization of those concepts. The data should have improved since 1955, when the Federal Reserve Board's Consultant Committee reported that the federal government's expenditures on statistics of saving were "extraordinarily small . . . not much in excess of $20,000 per year . . . and . . . declining."

The macroeconomic measures most often cited are two components of the national income and product accounts (NIPAs)—personal saving and gross private saving; these measures are derived from the current account as incomes less current expenditures. Alternatively, aggregate saving can be measured from the capital account as the change in net wealth; such measures for nontangible types of saving are presented in the flow of funds accounts (FFAs) for various sectors. Although, in principle, these two approaches should yield the same results, in fact they do not in the United States and in a number of other countries as well; the differences are enormous at times. Part of the conference was therefore devoted to examining these largely statistical differences and attempting to account for them and to reduce them. In addition, some have proposed extensions to the saving concepts used in the "official" NIPA and FFA measures; the conference also considered some of these extensions and the effect of alternative definitions of saving and capital formation on the historical record.

Microeconomic research on household saving behavior has been enriched in recent years by the addition of several new data sets, which provide some types of data not previously available as well as affording a test of the applicability of results obtained from earlier surveys to a period far from the sample period. The conference focused on two of these in particular, the Survey of Income and Program Participation (SIPP), an ongoing survey at the Census Bureau, the first wave of which was carried out in 1984, and the Survey of Consumer Finances (SCF) for 1983, a much larger and more elaborate version of a survey conducted periodically for the Board of Governors of the Federal Reserve System by the Survey Research Center at the University of Michigan. Both of these were examined in detail in papers by those responsible for them, and both of them were used for one or more of the other papers at the conference.

Aside from the review of new microdata sets, the statistical issues we thought of as most in need of discussion and solution were the continuing enormous discrepancies between NIPA and FFA saving estimates and the large discrepancies in international accounts that might have involved errors in the measurement of international saving and investment flows. On the conceptual side, we hoped for a discussion of the suitability of current definitions of saving and investment and particularly for some authoritative estimates of broader alternative concepts. Both the statistical and the conceptual issues had been raised at earlier conferences, and we wished to see the extent to which the current knowledge had improved.

As the reader will see, we made a little progress on the U.S. NIPA-FFA discrepancy but, to our regret, added only fragmentary information on the experience of foreign countries and none on developed countries, many of which must have faced the same problems. We also made some progress in assessing the effect of including consumer durables, government purchases of capital assets, and human capital in investment and including pension assets in personal saving and wealth. On some issues, however, we were not able to make any progress, even though their significance had been established at earlier conferences. The technical problems involved in broadening the investment concept to include expenditures on research and development and the accompanying problems of deflation of such expenditures and rates of depreciation on research and development capital received little attention in the proposals submitted, although there has been a good deal of recent research on these topics. We were also disappointed to receive very few proposals on international aspects of saving and investment measurement.

Historical Background

Since its founding half a century ago, the Conference on Research in Income and Wealth has examined a number of aspects of the measurement of saving, investment, and wealth. Conferences have at times focused on income and its constituents and at others on wealth; other conferences have examined aggregates, and still others have looked at distributional questions. This volume continues this tradition of looking at a number of dimensions of saving and wealth measurement; indeed, almost the only topic that it does not revisit is the measurement of national and sectoral wealth.

The first ten volumes included little on either wealth or saving, the main exceptions being Simon Kuznets's "On the Measurement of National Wealth" in volume 2 and, in volume 3, two papers on methods of estimating the distribution of wealth by C. L. Merwin, Jr., and by Charles Stewart and one on the volume and composition of saving by

Raymond Goldsmith. The assessment of the statistical quality of wealth distributions by Merwin was, in his own words, gloomy. That was not only because of "a paucity of pertinent data" (28) but also because there was little agreement on the definition of wealth or on the unit (families, individuals, estates) to be used for wealth distribution measures and, finally, because he questioned "the intrinsic usefulness of a distribution of wealth, when a distribution of income is contemporaneously available" (29).

The first paper on the distribution of saving, by Dorothy Brady and Rose Friedman, appeared in volume 10. It made use of what were described as the first large studies, done in the mid-1930s, to obtain direct estimates of saving, including data on saving through specific assets and liabilities. Volume 11 included Franco Modigliani's famous paper "Fluctuations in the Saving-Income Ratio," which, aside from its main points, included a plaintive note about the drastic revisions in official estimates of saving, including "its effect on the morale of the econometricians who put confidence in the old estimates."

After that, there was a major shift of the Conference's attention toward wealth. Volumes 12 and 14, covering the 1948 and 1950 meetings, were entirely devoted to wealth measurement. The introduction to the first of these by Morris Copeland referred to the neglect of wealth in the first decade of the Income and Wealth Conference and quoted an unpublished paper by Martin Gainsbrugh at the 1946 Conference characterizing wealth measurement as "the submerged half of the charter originally envisaged for the Conference." Volume 12 was on the measurement of aggregate national wealth and the aggregate wealth of various sectors. Volume 14 included theoretical discussions of the role of wealth and assets in economic behavior and papers on the measurement of both aggregate wealth and assets by type and of the distribution of wealth. The latter were based on estate tax data but did not include the tests of coverage by comparison with aggregates that became standard practice later.

Volume 15 included two papers on the distribution of saving by Janet Fisher and by Dorothy Brady that made extensive use of large-scale surveys of saving and wealth, among which were the prewar surveys of consumer expenditure and the postwar surveys of liquid assets and consumer finances conducted by the Survey Research Center of the University of Michigan, the first of a long line that extends to the present volume. The paper by Janet Fisher included many references to "the family life cycle" and to the fact that average saving rates continued to be positive after age sixty-five and, surprisingly, did not decline greatly from the peak levels. It also included warnings that have become familiar about the probable underrepresentation of the rich elderly population.

The attention of the Conference subsequently shifted to the measurement of capital formation. Volume 19, *Problems of Capital Formation,* edited by Franco Modigliani, considered two major issues. One of these, the calculation of depreciation in current prices, has since been enshrined in the U.S. NIPAs, although the treatment of the real capital gains implied by that estimate of depreciation remains a controversial issue. The other major issue was the treatment of quality change in capital goods in measuring capital formation. That issue, while it has recurred in later conferences, was not part of the current conference.

Volume 22, *A Critique of the National Income and Product Accounts,* edited by Joseph A. Pechman, naturally included some suggestions for expanding the official definition of capital formation. These included the addition of research and development expenditures and consumer durables and also an estimate of government capital formation. All these proposals return in the present Conference in the papers by Boskin, Robinson, and Huber; Holloway; Jorgenson and Fraumeni; and Hendershott and Peek, all supplying some such estimates. Volume 25, *Input, Output, and Productivity Measurement,* edited by John W. Kendrick, included more discussion of capital aggregates, in papers by Richard and Nancy Ruggles and by Daniel Creamer.

The next topic to occupy the Conference at several sessions was the use of consumer surveys as a source of information for social accounting. In volume 26, *The Flow of Funds Approach to Social Accounting,* edited by Vito Natrella, Arthur Broida pointed out the failure to use data from the University of Michigan's SCF in the FFAs and attributed that failure to a judgment that survey data were inaccurate. He included a discussion of the apparent understatements in asset holdings that would be implied in totals calculated from surveys, judging the inaccuracy by comparison with aggregates. That issue is another of the ones that recur in the present conference, only this time with at least some suggestion that it is now the aggregate estimates that should be judged by comparison with the surveys. Volume 29, *Measuring the Nation's Wealth,* included a paper on household wealth by F. Thomas Juster that emphasized the need for surveys overweighted with high-income families to estimate holdings of financial assets, a topic that plays a major role in the discussion at the present conference. The same paper included two suggestions that were more radical and are not repeated here. One was that surveys of tangible assets could better ask for characteristics of the assets, from which the surveyor could estimate value, rather than asking for value directly. The second was that surveys should collect, at the same time, information on individuals' levels of education that would give the survey takers the ability to estimate stocks of educational capital.

The Conference returned to issues of distribution in 1967 in *Six Papers on the Size Distribution of Wealth and Income,* edited by Lee Soltow (vol. 33). Some of the themes of the present conference appeared here, twenty years earlier, mainly in the paper "A Cohort Analysis of Changes in the Distribution of Wealth" by John B. Lansing and John Sonqvist, and in the comments by E. Scott Maynes. One was the difference between results from cross sections and those from following groups of individuals over time and the difficulty of inferring one from the other, an issue explored in the Jianakoplos, Menchik, and Irvine paper at this conference. A second is the unimportance of inheritances as a determinant of the wealth of the great majority of households (excluding the very wealthy), the question discussed here by Hurd and Mundaca. A third is the sensitivity of measures of wealth inequality to chance variability among the very small numbers of the highest-income households reached in a random sample, the problem discussed currently by Curtin, Juster, and Morgan and by McNeil and Lamas at this meeting.

Attention then again shifted to the measurement of aggregates. Volume 34, *Production and Productivity in the Service Industries,* edited by Victor Fuchs, included a paper on the measurement of the real output and productivity of commercial banks. As in the paper by Rymes in the current volume, the author of that paper, John Gorman, appealed to monetary theory to support one proposal for measurement, although, also as in the present volume, the discussants were far from convinced of the value of the method proposed. Volume 35, *Education, Income, and Human Capital,* edited by W. Lee Hansen, was the first Income and Wealth conference to devote attention to investment in human capital, the main subject of the paper by Jorgensen and Fraumeni in this volume. Even the term "human capital" was hardly, if ever, used in the earlier conferences, although some of the ideas were, of course, implied in the discussions of the relation between education levels and income.

In volume 38, *The Measurement of Economic and Social Performance,* edited by Milton Moss, the lead paper by F. Thomas Juster again drew attention to major omissions from the official measures of capital formation, namely investment in consumer durables, in government capital, and in intangible capital assets resulting from research and development, education, and training. He and others at the conference also brought up a relatively new theme: the idea of capital in the form of environmental quality that might be added to or used up and of the capital incorporated in social and political institutions. The stock of consumer durables, proposed earlier as a part of wealth, is estimated in Juster's paper; and, in the paper by Christensen and Jorgenson, methods are outlined for extending the accounting framework to include investment in human capital and research and development, the former of which is accomplished in the paper by Jorgenson and Fraumeni in the present volume. A number of suggestions of the other papers were carried out in the paper "Is Growth Obsolete?" by James Tobin and William Nordhaus.

The 1972 Income and Wealth conference on *The Personal Distribution of Income and Wealth,* edited by James D. Smith (vol. 39), included several papers on wealth distribution, and another conference on distribution was held in 1974, *The Distribution of Economic Well-Being,* edited by Juster (vol. 41). The latter included two papers, one by Lawrence Osman and one by James D. Smith, Stephen Franklin, and Guy Orcutt, dealing with the importance of inheritance in the distribution of wealth, the topic discussed here in the paper by Hurd and Mundaca. Both papers gave only a small role to inheritance in general but did point to exceptions, particularly wealthy young families, for whom the result was predictable, and, more generally, families at the very upper end of the wealth distribution.

The 1975 conference on *New Developments in Productivity Measurement,* edited by John W. Kendrick and Beatrice N. Vaccara (vol. 44), contained no papers specifically devoted to saving or wealth estimation, but several of the papers inevitably bore on the subject because measures of capital input were needed for the measures of productivity. This was the case for the paper by Gollop and Jorgensen on U.S. productivity growth by industry and the international comparison by Christensen, Cummings, and Jorgenson, which form part of the series by Jorgenson and various colleagues that continues into the present volume. Both papers included measures of capital input and of labor quality, the latter reflecting the stock of human capital. Some human capital measures were also included in the paper on international comparisons of agricultural productivity by Yamada and Ruttan.

Volume 45, *The Measurement of Capital,* edited by Dan Usher, returned to some familiar issues, such as rates of depreciation, the widening of the scope of the concept of capital to include research and development and human capital, and estimation of the value of oil and gas reserves. A new proposal was Eisner's suggestion that real capital gains be treated as net investment. Perhaps as a reflection of the oil crisis and the panic over imminent exhaustion of natural resources, there was also a paper by John Soladay, "Measurement of Income and Product in the Oil and Gas Mining Industries," on measures of depletion, an important question for estimates of saving and net investment. The only previous paper in this area had been at the 1948 conference, around the time of a previous period of worry about natural resource exhaustion. The paper by Boskin, Robinson, and Huber in the present volume includes estimates of government-owned land and mineral rights.

Volume 46, from a conference held in 1977 on *Modeling the Distribution and Intergenerational Transmission of Wealth,* edited by James D. Smith, the third in five years devoted to distribution questions, was the closest in that respect to the material of the present volume and involved several of the same authors. Several papers discussed the role of inheritance in the transmission of wealth, mainly dealing with small samples of that part of the population that did inherit rather than with the role of inheritance in the distribution of wealth in society as a whole. Several papers in that meeting discussed historical trends in wealth distribution, and two reported on synthetic distributions. James D. Smith's introduction pointed out the importance of the development of national balance sheets for the early estimates of wealth concentration, providing the aggregates for comparisons with the holdings of wealthy families and in general supplying what were thought of as more solidly based totals and distributions than could be arrived at from surveys. Now, the survey data have been developed so far that their producers are ready to claim, in this volume, that the aggregate data can be improved by using the results of the surveys, instead of the other way around.

The conference on *The U.S. National Income and Product Accounts,* edited by Murray Foss (vol. 47), in 1979 once again returned to the issue of quality adjustments in the measurement of capital goods prices, a topic of long standing with the conference, as was pointed out in the introduction. The paper by Ruggles included a set of complete household accounts covering assets and capital expenditures not treated as capital in the NIPAs and a set of revaluation accounts. The notorious discrepancies in saving estimates between the NIPAs and the FFAs, an issue we wished to investigate at this conference, were mentioned briefly by John Gorman in his discussion of the gross national product data improvement project.

The 1982 conference on *Economic Transfers in the U.S.,* edited by Marilyn Moon (vol. 49), discussed an asset item rarely included in the discussions of wealth distribution up to that time, the value of social security benefits and the corresponding payroll taxes. The 1983 conference on *Horizontal Equity, Uncertainty, and Economic Well-Being,* edited by Martin David and Timothy Smeeding (vol. 50), continued the emphasis on distributional issues and included a paper by Eugene Steuerle tying together wealth data from estate tax returns with income data for decedents and heirs. Hurd and Shoven calculated household balance sheets, including various forms of rights to pensions, social security payments, Medicare and Medicaid, and so on. Several of the papers in this volume addressed the issue of the valuation of pension and social security wealth.

Perhaps the most striking developments in this history are the shift of interest toward distribution questions and the enormous improvement of the basic information on wealth distribution. Simon Kuznets commented in 1939, discussing Merwin's paper in volume 3, on "the daring feats of ingenuity performed by skillful statisticians in their attempts to overcome the absence of basic information." He then went on to ask, "Why was no information collected during these decades on a sufficiently comprehensive scale to make possible an acceptable distribution of income or wealth by size among individuals or families?" Among the factors he cited were the technical difficulties of obtaining information from family units that maintained no formal accounting systems and also the strong faith in the fairness of the economic system and the general attitude that the level of a person's income was the result of his efforts and was not the proper concern of the government. He attributed the development of the first large-scale surveys in the mid-1930s partly to changes in social attitudes: pessimism about future aggregate growth as a solution to social problems led to more interest in distribution and to the acceptance of a greater governmental role in affecting the distribution of consumption. In addition to the change in attitudes, there were also technical developments, including improvements in "the statistical theory that makes it possible to establish in advance the reliability of samples" and improvements in the "organizational machinery for dealing with large scale surveys" (92). Moreover, greater government involvement in distributional questions produced administrative records of certain types of income payments and of government programs to aid the distressed.

In this connection, it is interesting to note that one of the new surveys discussed in this program is the Survey of Income and Program Participation (SIPP), one of the justifications for which was to assess the coverage of government assistance programs.

There has been less obvious change on the side of aggregate saving and investment estimates, although they have undoubtedly improved in quality. One development urged in earlier conferences, the measurement of capital consumption in current prices, has been incorporated into the NIPAs, and the Commerce Department has answered the calls for data on investment in consumer durables and government capital by producing estimates for these outside the NIPAs. However, the saving data, particularly the sectoral estimates, remain a weak element in the accounts. There has been little official interest in incorporating human capital investment or other types of intangible investment into the accounts, the quality change adjustment issue remains controversial and unsettled, and the discrepancies among saving estimates from different sources remain enormous.

Although the topics covered in this volume have much in common with those of past conferences, the papers included here also take a fresh look at several issues from a variety of perspectives. They examine major data sets in detail for their statistical properties and limitations. They discuss questions of current versus capital account measurement of saving, the treatment of pensions and pension wealth, and the scope of saving and wealth measures. Wealth estimates are developed from the new microdata on households, and a number of methodological issues are explored.

An Insider's Look at Saving Data

In this Conference, many of the major bodies of saving data receive the close examination and assessment that can be given only by an insider. The papers by Holloway, by Wilson, Freund, Yohn, and Lederer, by McNeil and Lamas, and by Curtin, Juster, and Morgan provide that kind of background for the NIPAs, the FFAs, the SIPP, and the SCF, respectively.

Thomas H. Holloway reviews the NIPA sources and statistical methods and the conventions that underlie the estimates. He examines the effect of altering some of these conventions on the story told by the official NIPA series and finds that, although there are changes in the levels of both amounts of saving and saving rates, their trends and cyclical behavior are not greatly altered. The statistical revisions of the NIPA estimates of saving have tended mainly to raise them. A point that emerges from Holloway's discussion of alternative conventions regarding sectoring and the scope of saving and investment measures is the desirability of avoiding overemphasis on single measures and of offering enough sectoral detail and estimates of the effects of alternative assumptions to permit users to construct whatever measures they prefer. Paul Wachtel makes the point even more strongly in his discussion.

John F. Wilson, James L. Freund, Frederick O. Yohn, Jr., and Walther Lederer provide a similar review of the household saving estimates from the FFAs. These, even adjusted to the NIPA definition, have typically been higher than NIPA personal saving, often by 50 percent or more in recent years. In the past, NIPA revisions have usually reduced the differences between the FFA and the NIPA saving estimates. The authors explore several potential statistical improvements in the FFAs involving reattributions of financial asset holdings toward sectors other than households that would tend in the opposite direction, that of reducing the FFA household saving estimates. They also discuss the implications for the household account of some of the misreporting of international transactions, the subject of Stephen Taylor's paper, although George M. von Furstenberg, their discussant, offers his own speculations on this account and expresses some skepticism about the suggestions in this paper.

John M. McNeil and Enrique J. Lamas ask whether the SIPP provides useful measures of the relative net worth of various population subgroups and of year-to-year changes in net worth. They conclude that, despite limitations in coverage and underreporting, the SIPP data are useful in studying differentials in median wealth holdings among population groups. However, these limitations, the extensive use of imputations, and the sensitivity of both aggregate measures and concentration measures to the presence of high outliers, correctly or incorrectly reported, preclude the use of SIPP data in measuring the concentration of wealth or changes in wealth. A number of suggestions for changes in method and for validation research are made by Martin H. David in his discussion.

Richard T. Curtin, F. Thomas Juster, and James N. Morgan examine three recent household surveys of household net worth (SCF, PSID, and SIPP) to assess their quality and usefulness, with particular emphasis on the SCF. They conclude that the SCF, because of its heavy oversampling of high-income households, produces the most reliable estimates of wealth distribution and of wealth aggregates. However, all three surveys agree quite well in categories in which the distribution is not highly skewed and for wealth classes below the top one or two. In fact, they are sufficiently confident in the SCF to suggest that, in some categories, the household aggregates from it are more reliable than those in the FFAs. It is only recently that such a claim has been made, and the producers of the FFAs seem quite willing to consider it.

Current Account versus Capital Account Measurement of Saving

Should saving be measured from the current account or from the capital account? For individual households, only the change in wealth is generally available. In the aggregate statistics, by contrast, both methods are available. The NIPAs measure personal saving as income less current expenditures, and the estimate of saving thus includes the effects of measurement errors in both income and expenditures. Since saving is much smaller than either income or current expenditures, even small errors or revisions in those measures can produce very large errors or revisions in estimated saving. The FFAs measure financial saving through financial assets and liabilities (tangible saving is taken from the NIPAs) as the change in wealth other than revaluations. In other words, financial saving is the net acquisition of assets less the net incurrence of liabilities; measured saving thus includes measurement errors in both acquisition and disposition of assets and issuance and retirement of liabilities. Here, too, the household sector is mostly derived as a residual, by subtracting known holdings by businesses and governments from known totals outstanding for most assets.

Despite the status of the NIPA measures as the most widely used and most "official" saving measures, a number of the participants favored the capital account view to obtain what they considered more valid measures of saving. In addition, such measures are much more easily linked to microdata from household wealth surveys, and indeed the latter data may improve the aggregate estimates, as Curtin, Juster, and Morgan observe. Richard and Nancy Ruggles, in a paper that was withdrawn after the death of Nancy Ruggles, also explored the use of the *Statistics of Income* balance sheet data for corporations, the main basis for the nonfinancial corporate sector in the FFAs, to disaggregate the saving of nonfinancial corporations along broad industry lines.

Clark W. Reynolds and Wayne Camard observe that FFA estimates have considerable potential for developing countries in addressing the role of finance in savings mobilization and in understanding the sectoral distribution of saving. Moreover, inconsistencies between capital account estimates, such as those represented by FFAs, and the current-account estimates of the NIPAs may lead to improvements in both sets of estimates, as was the experience in Colombia.

The balancing item in the NIPA foreign transactions account, net foreign investment by the United States, is conceptually equivalent to the current account balance in the balance of payments accounts or the capital account balance in the FFAs. The fact that the world has not kept track of these flows very well has been obvious from the fact that the total of these balances, conceptually zero, has approached a world net deficit of close to $100 billion in some recent years.

Stephen Taylor looks at the implications of the recent IMF study on the world current account discrepancy for estimates of saving in the United States. The international data discrepancies since 1979 have been most pronounced in investment income accounts. They reflect the lack of consistent treatment of reinvested direct investment income, inadequate estimates of positions in interest-bearing assets, and omission of much shipping and other transportation expenses and revenues. U.S. investment income has been severely understated, but it is not clear how much the correction would increase U.S. income and saving measures. The main source of the measurement problems seems to be the enormous increase in international capital flows and in the resulting service payments and receipts. In the words of Michael P. Dooley, the discussant for Taylor's paper, these omissions are "the seeds of destruction for the usability of the data on international transactions" (p. 430).

The Measurement of Aggregate Saving: Conceptual Issues

In addition to the statistical problems encountered in the quantification of the NIPA and FFA saving measures, others have pointed out conceptual inadequacies over the years. For example, Blades and Sturm mentioned some of them in their attempt to compare saving rates internationally, such as the omission from saving of consumer investment in durables, enterprise research and development expenditures, educational expenses, and real capital gains and losses. Various papers at the Conference looked at these proposals (and other issues—nonmarket and illegal transactions, consistent pension treatment, alternative measures of government saving) and attempted to quantify the effects such changes might have on the historical record on U.S. saving rates.

The official saving measures for the United States tend to be the NIPA measures, which are shown in NIPA table 5.1. Personal saving and gross private saving are the most familiar, but certain sectoral concepts are also available—such as government saving and undistributed corporate profits and capital consumption allowances.

The NIPA convention of counting as investment only capital goods purchased by business—including the business of owner occupancy of housing—means that household saving in the form of automobiles and other consumer durable goods is excluded from both personal and private saving. The NIPA convention of counting as saving only saving out of income from current production means that saving measures exclude capital gains and exclude saving that arises from most nonmarket activities. The government surplus or deficit—government saving—reflects the capital formation convention and the pension attribution mentioned above.

Some of the papers propose only limited changes or question present treatment in only minor ways. Holloway's paper discusses the NIPA measures of personal saving and gross private saving; the latter is the preferable measure, in his opinion, because it is not affected by many of the imputations and attributions that make the straightforward interpretation of the personal saving measure as a measure of household saving troublesome. In particular, the distinction between personal and business components of saving by owners of noncorporate business and the treatment of the saving of pension funds, both private and public, make the measure of personal saving different from what one might think of as household saving.

Holloway shows the effects on saving rates of capitalizing consumer durable and government capital expenditures and attributing part of government pension fund saving to households. Others provide a more sweeping critique and propose more radical changes. Patric H. Hendershott and Joe Peek adjust the NIPA measures of personal and corporate saving to correct for what they view as four "measurement"—

really conceptual—errors in the official NIPA estimates. They do not make adjustments to include real capital gains or losses or investment in human capital, except to the extent that the former are incorporated in the interest rate adjustment. Personal saving is adjusted for the difference between income tax payments and actual liabilities, increased to reflect net purchases of government pension assets—including social security—and consumer durables, and reduced to reflect the portion of after tax interest income attributable to inflation. Corporate saving is increased by the portion of after tax interest expense attributable to inflation. Thus adjusted, measures of personal and private saving are only slightly below their post-1950 averages rather than greatly below, as reported in the official estimates. The adjusted measures are more volatile than the NIPA measures in the case of personal saving but less volatile in the case of corporate saving. The inflation premium adjustments remove the negative correlation between personal and corporate saving in the official figures. Frank de Leeuw raises some questions about both the social security and the inflation premium adjustments.

Thomas K. Rymes suggests that current imputations for bank output lack theoretical justification and presents two models of banking and the behavior of monetary authorities with different implications for imputation procedures, for banking output, and for rates of saving in the personal and government sectors. Anna J. Schwartz expresses skepticism about the models and their relevance to imputation. The importance of the issue for saving estimates appears to be small, but the discussion raises questions about the theoretical basis for many customary imputations. In particular, it points to the issue of the extent to which national accounting takes existing institutions for granted or values nonmarket or barter activities in relation to a theoretical norm of competitive markets or some definition of appropriate government policy.

Dale W. Jorgenson and Barbara M. Fraumeni not only broaden the official definition of investment to include human capital but measure the investment in human capital in terms of lifetime labor incomes, including nonmarket incomes, rather than in terms of the cost of such investment, as in the earlier work of Kendrick, Schultz, and others. The result is to depict 70–80 percent of "full investment" as human capital investment and almost all wealth—over 90 percent—as consisting of human wealth, even though the Jorgenson and Fraumeni estimates of nonhuman wealth are much larger than those of other investigators. Their "full gross private domestic product" is more than three times the official gross domestic product, mainly from the addition of the value of time in household production and leisure and investment in human capital.

Michael J. Boskin, Marc S. Robinson, and Alan M. Huber replace the conventional NIPA view of government output, saving, and wealth with an accounting that allows for government capital formation in the form of construction and equipment and for government wealth in these forms and in the form of land, natural resources, and financial assets, and they estimate the output produced by government assets. They also make some calculations of contingent liabilities for employee pensions and social security. They find that, especially for state and local governments, where fixed capital is substantial, government investment (net of depreciation) is often sufficient to turn the government sector as a whole into a net saver despite large deficits as conventionally measured. As Robert Eisner points out in his discussion, they omit the government's role in human capital formation and they omit capital gains and losses. They are, in this respect, considerably less radical than Eisner himself in various writings or Jorgenson and Fraumeni in this volume.

The Treatment of Pensions and Pension Wealth

Pension rights, which constitute a significant fraction of household wealth, were omitted in many early household surveys. When they are included, their valuation presents complex problems for respondents. A special effort was made to have papers at the Conference that would examine such questions as how to value them and the most appropriate way of including them—and the contingent liabilities that they represent—in saving measures. Although most attention was focused on private pension plans, there was some attention to social security wealth, which, because of the uncertainties as to future benefits and obligations, presents the most difficult problems. The valuation concept often used was the present value of future benefits for the current adult population.

The NIPAs, as Holloway pointed out, are inconsistent in their treatment of public employee and private pension plans. They include saving by the latter in personal saving and exclude benefits from personal income while doing the reverse for the former. Holloway quantifies the results of imposing consistent treatment, as do both Hendershott and Peek and Boskin, Robinson, and Huber. The preferred solution, adopted in the FFAs, is to treat both as private. Neither NIPA or FFA personal or household saving includes that of the social security system, and most of the authors who mention it agree that it presents particularly knotty problems. Boskin, Robinson, and Huber discuss it as part of the issue of contingent claims against the government.

Pension wealth has often been omitted from wealth distribution microdata because respondents do not usually know how to value it. Ann A. McDermed, Robert L. Clark, and Steven G. Allen attempt to solve the difficulties posed by respondents' lack of knowledge by using both respondent information and additional information from the pension-provider component of the 1983 SCF survey. They find that the use of pension-provider information raises the estimate of the value of pension wealth, that pension wealth is a significant component of household net worth, and that its inclusion in wealth reduces measured inequality in wealth distribution. Their discussant, Cordelia W. Reimers, is skeptical about the supposed effects on inequality. Edward N. Wolff and Marcia Marley also find that pension wealth, and particularly social security wealth, has grown relative to other forms of household wealth; including it reduces the measured concentration of wealth and changes the historical pattern of wealth inequality since the late 1940s from stability to continuing decline. However, Robert B. Avery, in his discussion, points out that there are many alternative estimates of social security wealth that vary widely, and only one of them was picked as the basis for the imputations to households. He also notes that the extrapolation to 1983 by Wolff and Marley ignores the major changes in the law that took place in 1982.

Wealth Estimates from New Microdata on Households

Two new microdata sets were examined or utilized by several authors. The SIPP appears in four of the papers: McNeil and Lamas; Curtin, Juster, and Morgan; Radner; and Wolff and Marley. The SCF is involved in the papers by Curtin, Juster and Morgan; Radner; McDermed, Clark, and Allen; Hurd and Mundaca; and Wolff and Marley. These papers, for the most part, had different aims and thus examined different aspects of the new data.

Aside from the "insiders'" reports mentioned earlier, Daniel B. Radner discusses wealth data requirements for the analysis of the economic status of households, emphasizing the resources available to households other than the very wealthy and focusing on age groups, especially the aged. Most of his analysis is based on the 1984 wealth supplement to SIPP, which has a number of desirable properties from his point of view, but he compares the SIPP relative means and medians to those from five household surveys and two synthetic estimates, finding that the SIPP results are broadly comparable to those obtained from other surveys. Marilyn Moon, the discussant, suggests the use of resource measures that combine income and wealth as preferable to analyses that treat them as alternative measures of resources available to households.

McDermed, Clark, and Allen use both the respondent and the pension-provider information in the 1983 SCF to study pensions as a component of wealth. Michael D. Hurd and B. Gabriela Mundaca, using data from the 1964 survey of the economic behavior of the affluent, estimate the fraction of household assets from inheritances and from gifts at 15–20 percent and 5–10 percent, respectively. Although much less comprehensive in its information on this question, the 1983 SCF high-income supplement yields results consistent with those from the 1964 survey. While their discussant, Denis Kessler, shares their skepticism about some of the very high estimates of the importance of gifts and bequests, he considers the issue to be still unsettled and suggests that "direct survey estimates provide the weakest evidence" on this question. Wolff and Marley use both the SIPP and the 1983 SCF in their attempt to construct a consistent historical record on the household wealth distribution.

Methodological Matters

In the past, microdata have often been criticized for not producing aggregates that replicated the macro NIPA or FFA data sufficiently well. This time, staff of the Federal Reserve had worked closely to align SCF and FFA totals for certain well-specified household asset positions, and the implications were that the microdata might be the more accurate, particularly for certain classes of assets. In addition, there was some suggestion that direct estimation of FFA household entries might shift residual uncertainty to other sectors.

Several papers address methodological questions of using the information typically available in microdata. McNeil and Lamas and Curtin, Juster, and Morgan describe some of the lessons learned in their respective surveys on imputations, oversampling, and the like. In particular, heavy oversampling at the upper tail seems to be essential for developing a data set that is adequate for studying the distribution of wealth. McDermed, Clark, and Allen use both employer and employee responses to estimate pension wealth and thus implicitly provide a test of the accuracy of the pension information typically provided in household surveys.

Nancy Ammon Jianakoplos, Paul L. Menchik, and F. Owen Irvine use panel data to evaluate the use of cross-sectional data to draw life-cycle inferences. They assess the biases in cross-sectional inferences of life-cycle changes in the level and composition of household wealth by comparing age-wealth profiles based on five cross-sectional surveys of a panel with time-series age-wealth profiles for each of the fifteen age cohorts from the same panel observed over fifteen years. They find that productivity growth and differential mortality cause substantial distortions in age-wealth profiles based on cross-sectional data. Moreover, procedures heretofore used to adjust cross-sectional data for the productivity effect are unreliable and do not correct for the differential mortality effect.

Wolff and Marley assemble a consistent long-run record on household wealth and its distribution for the United States from a variety of sources, including survey data, estate tax returns, and synthetic data sets. In the process, they discuss some of the methodological issues involved in reconciling microdata and published data on household wealth distribution, both with each other and with aggregate balance sheet data. They find that the inclusion of pension wealth and social security wealth changes the historical pattern of inequality since the late 1940s from stability to continuing decline because of the relative growth in such wealth. They also find that estimates of the level of wealth concentration are quite sensitive to the methods used in their construction and to the choice of wealth concepts.

Conclusion

Perhaps the major lesson of the Conference is the advance in the technology of wealth surveys to the point at which their producers no longer feel that they must defer to the producers of aggregate wealth data and the latter are at least partially ready to recognize a state of something like parity in accuracy. The most serious problem with the surveys, only partly cured by the device of heavy oversampling of upper-income and -wealth groups, remains their sensitivity, given the extreme skewness of the wealth distribution, to the inclusion or exclusion of exceptionally wealthy households and the large potential for distortions as the result of incorrect observations. The problem is discussed in the paper by Curtin, Juster, and Morgan and was highlighted by the controversy over the report of the Joint Economic Committee on changes in wealth distribution.

The other clear change in views is the readiness of many scholars to incorporate at least investment in consumer durables and government capital investment into measures of aggregate capital formation and the ease with which that can now be done, given the supplementary information on these topics published by the Department of Commerce. What is probably a neglected issue (although it receives some attention) is the importance of certain assumptions in constructing new estimates. Among the examples mentioned by readers is the assumption in Boskin, Robinson, and Huber that real prices of natural resources would rise indefinitely. Despite its underpinnings in classical theory, this assumption has been challenged by some readings of the long-run movements of the relative prices of natural resource products. Another set of assumptions that has received attention elsewhere, but little here, is that underlying the valuations of time spent in the acquisition of human capital.

There remain a number of topics in the area of saving and wealth measurement that the conference either did not reach or touched on only lightly. For example, there must be more experience than we heard about in a variety of countries with the measurement of saving from NIPA and FFA accounts. Are huge differences typical, and is there some relation that would suggest where the errors lie? We heard relatively little about intangible investment, aside from the paper by Jorgenson and Fraumeni, although there has been a good deal of work in that area, particularly on research and development, its output, and its rate of depreciation or obsolescence. Aside from Taylor's paper on the IMF study of current account surpluses and deficits and some discussion in the paper by Wilson, Freund, Yohn, and Lederer, there was nothing on the measurement of wealth held in the form of international assets, a quite undeveloped area of wealth measurement now given prominence by the reported shift of the United States to the position of a net debtor. There is room for another conference on these issues.

We should not end this introduction without noting, with sadness, the deaths since the date of this conference of three members of the Conference on Research in Income and Wealth who had been active in it for many years. Nancy Ruggles, together with Richard Ruggles, had first contributed to the 1958 Income and Wealth Conference (vol. 25) on *Output, Input, and Productivity Measurement* a paper on "Concepts of Real Capital Stocks and Services," and they had prepared a paper for this meeting on saving by various industry sectors. Unfortunately, the paper had to be withdrawn after Nancy Ruggles' tragic death. Irwin Friend and Raymond Goldsmith, who were unable to attend this conference, both had made important contributions to the subjects discussed here. Irwin Friend's first contribution, at the 1951 Conference (vol. 17) on *Short-Term Economic Forecasting*, was on plant and equipment expenditures, with Jean Bronfenbrenner. Raymond Goldsmith's contributions spanned almost the entire history of the Income and Wealth Conference, beginning with a paper on "The Volume and Components of Saving in the United States, 1933–1937" for the April 1939 Conference (vol. 3). In Goldsmith's case, this and the measurement of wealth were subjects that occupied almost his whole working life.

1 Present NIPA Saving Measures: Their Characteristics and Limitations

Thomas M. Holloway

In public policy debates, it has often been suggested that saving and saving rates in the United States are too low to permit adequate capital formation. The saving measures being considered in these policy debates frequently are those from the national income and product accounts (NIPAs) produced by the Bureau of Economic Analysis (BEA).[1] Because of the policy relevance of NIPA saving measures, it is important that the concepts and measurement procedures be clearly understood and that the limitations of these measures be recognized.

The purpose of this paper is to provide an overview of present NIPA saving measures and to discuss their limitations and possible alternative measures. The paper has four sections. The first section provides an introduction to the NIPA measures considered in the paper and comments on some widely known trends reflected by these measures. The second section discusses NIPA concepts and conventions that are particularly relevant to the measurement of saving, focusing on the production boundary, sectoring, classifications, attributions, and imputations. The third section provides a brief summary of measurement procedures and then reviews the scope and importance of revisions to NIPA saving measures, emphasizing the results from the comprehensive revision of the NIPAs that became available in December 1985

Thomas M. Holloway is Senior Economist, Mortgage Bankers Association of America. He was formerly chief, Special Studies Branch, Government Division, Bureau of Economic Analysis.

The views expressed in this paper are those of the author and do not necessarily reflect the views of his current or former employers. Comments from Frank de Leeuw, David T. Dobbs, Gerald F. Donahoe, John A. Gorman, Jeanette Honsa, Arnold J. Katz, David J. Levin, Thae S. Park, Robert P. Parker, Helen S. Tice, and Joseph C. Wakefield are gratefully acknowledged. Katherine Dent typed the manuscript. Ivy D. Dunson and Jane S. Reeb assisted with the tables and charts.

(hereafter referred to as the 1985 comprehensive revision). The fourth section discusses limitations and criticisms of present NIPA saving measures and describes some alternative measures.

1.1   Introduction and Trends

1.1.1   Introduction to NIPA Saving Measures

In the NIPAs, saving reflects resources freed for investment, where investment is defined as the sum of purchases of fixed capital goods (structures and equipment) by private business and nonprofit institutions, the value of the change in the physical volume of inventories held by private business, and the changes in net claims of U.S. residents on foreigners.

NIPA saving measures appear in NIPA table 5.1, which is published regularly in the *Survey of Current Business* (1985 estimates are reproduced here in table 1.1). Gross saving is gross private saving plus the government surplus or deficit (measured on a NIPA basis) plus capital grants received by the United States (net). In turn, gross private saving is the sum of personal saving, undistributed corporate profits with inventory valuation adjustment (IVA) and capital consumption adjustment (CCAdj), corporate and noncorporate capital consumption

Table 1.1   **NIPA Gross Saving and Investment, 1985 (billions of dollars)**

Measure	Amount
Gross saving	551.5
Gross private saving	687.8
Personal saving	143.3
Undistributed corporate profits with inventory valuation and capital consumption adjustments	107.3
Undistributed profits	49.8
Inventory valuation adjustments	− .6
Capital consumption adjustments	58.1
Corporate capital consumption allowances with capital consumption adjustment	268.2
Noncorporate capital consumption allowances with capital consumption adjustment	169.0
Wage accruals less disbursements	0
Government surplus or deficit (−), NIPAs	− 136.3
Federal	− 198.0
State and local	61.7
Capital grants received by the United States (net)	0
Gross investment	545.9
Gross private domestic investment	661.1
Net foreign investment	− 115.2
Statistical discrepancy	− 5.5

allowances (CCA) with CCAdj (hereafter referred to as capital consumption), and wage accruals less disbursements. The government surplus or deficit is the measure of government saving and is the sum of the surplus or deficit of the federal government and of state and local governments.

Gross investment consists of gross private domestic investment and net foreign investment. To complete the saving picture, net foreign investment must be discussed. In the NIPAs, foreign-sector transactions underlying net foreign investment are treated not as additions to or deductions from gross saving but as uses of gross saving. Alternatively, these transactions could be listed under saving by simply reversing the sign of net foreign investment, calling it net foreign saving, and making the appropriate adjustments to gross saving and investment. Regardless of whether these transactions are treated as saving or investment, net foreign investment less capital grants received by the United States (net) is a measure of whether the United States receives net saving from abroad (if the difference is negative) or is a net lender (if the difference is positive). Because capital grants are very small in most years, net foreign investment alone with the sign reversed reflects most foreign-sector saving. Definitions of many of these saving and investment measures are reported in BEA publications.[2]

Some NIPA saving measures are estimated directly (e.g., capital consumption). However, other NIPA saving measures are defined as differences between large aggregates (e.g., personal saving is the difference between disposable personal income and personal outlays). Consequently, the NIPA concepts, conventions, and methods underlying these aggregates contribute to the determination of saving measures. Some of the more important concepts, conventions, and methods are discussed later in the paper.

1.1.2 Trends in Major NIPA Saving Measures

Table 1.2 shows annual estimates of NIPA saving measures for 1950–85. The lower part of the table shows averages for 5- and 10-year subperiods. Most of the measures are shown as percentages of gross national product (GNP); net private saving is also shown as a percentage of net national product, and personal saving is also shown as a percentage of disposable personal income.[3] Personal saving as a percentage of disposable personal income—the personal saving rate—is the only saving ratio regularly published by BEA. Net private saving is not shown in table 1.1. It is gross private saving less CCA with CCAdj and is a measure of private saving after allowances for capital consumption. No depreciation is calculated for the government sector in the NIPAs; consequently, net and gross government saving are the same.

Table 1.2 NIPA Saving Measures

						Percentage of GNP						
						Capital Consumption Allowances[c]			Government Surplus or Deficit (−)			
Year	Gross Saving	Gross Private Saving	Net Private Saving[a]	Personal Saving	Undistributed Corporate Profits[b]	Total	Corporate	Noncorporate	Total	Federal	State and Local	Other[d]
1950	18.2	15.4	7.2	4.4	2.8	8.2	4.3	3.9	2.8	3.2	−.4	0
1951	17.6	15.8	7.6	5.0	2.6	8.2	4.3	3.9	1.8	1.9	−.1	0
1952	14.9	16.0	7.7	4.9	2.7	8.3	4.4	4.0	−1.1	−1.1	0	0
1953	13.7	15.6	7.3	5.0	2.3	8.3	4.4	3.9	−1.9	−1.9	0	0
1954	13.9	15.8	7.1	4.4	2.6	8.7	4.6	4.1	−1.9	−1.6	−.3	0
1955	16.9	16.1	7.6	3.9	3.6	8.5	4.5	4.0	.8	1.1	−.3	0
1956	18.1	16.8	7.9	5.0	3.0	8.9	4.8	4.1	1.2	1.4	−.2	0
1957	17.1	16.9	7.8	5.0	2.7	9.1	5.0	4.1	.2	.5	−.3	0
1958	14.1	16.9	7.5	5.3	2.2	9.4	5.2	4.2	−2.8	−2.3	−.5	0
1959	16.2	16.6	7.5	4.4	3.1	9.0	5.0	4.0	−.3	−.2	−.1	0
1960	16.3	15.7	6.7	4.0	2.7	9.0	5.0	4.0	.6	.6	0	0
1961	15.5	16.3	7.3	4.7	2.7	9.0	5.0	4.0	−.8	−.7	−.1	0
1962	15.9	16.6	8.0	4.5	3.5	8.6	4.8	3.8	−.7	−.7	.1	0
1963	16.3	16.1	7.7	4.1	3.6	8.5	4.8	3.7	.1	0	.1	0
1964	16.7	17.1	8.8	4.8	3.9	8.3	4.7	3.6	−.4	−.5	.2	0
1965	17.5	17.4	9.3	4.9	4.4	8.1	4.6	3.5	.1	.1	0	0
1966	16.9	17.0	9.0	4.7	4.3	8.0	4.6	3.4	−.2	−.2	.1	0
1967	15.9	17.6	9.4	5.5	3.8	8.3	4.8	3.5	−1.7	−1.6	−.1	0
1968	15.6	16.3	8.0	4.8	3.3	8.3	4.8	3.4	−.7	−.7	0	0
1969	16.5	15.4	7.0	4.4	2.6	8.4	4.9	3.5	1.0	.9	.2	0
1970	15.2	16.2	7.4	5.7	1.8	8.7	5.1	3.6	−1.0	−1.2	.2	.1
1971	15.6	17.3	8.4	6.0	2.4	8.8	5.2	3.7	−1.8	−2.0	.2	.1
1972	16.5	16.8	7.9	5.1	2.8	8.9	5.2	3.7	−.3	−1.4	1.1	0
1973	18.5	18.0	9.3	6.5	2.7	8.7	5.0	3.7	.6	−.4	1.0	0
1974	16.8	17.3	7.9	6.6	1.4	9.3	5.4	3.9	−.3	−.8	.5	−.1

	Net Private Saving as a Percentage of Net National Product	Personal Saving as a Percentage of Disposable Personal Income	Net Foreign Investment as a Percentage of GNP	Addenda: GNP[e]	Net National Product[e]	Disposable Personal Income[e]
1950	7.9	6.1	-.6	288.3	264.6	207.5
1951	8.3	7.3	.3	333.4	306.2	227.6
1952	8.4	7.3	.2	351.6	322.5	239.8
1953	8.0	7.2	-.3	371.6	340.7	255.1
1954	7.7	6.3	.1	372.5	340.0	260.5
1955	8.3	5.8	.1	405.9	371.5	278.8
1956	8.7	7.2	.7	428.2	390.1	297.5
1957	8.5	7.2	1.1	451.0	409.9	313.9
1958	8.3	7.5	.2	456.8	414.0	324.9
1959	8.3	6.3	-.2	495.8	451.2	344.6
1960	7.4	5.8	.6	515.3	468.9	358.9
1961	8.0	6.6	.8	533.8	486.1	373.8
1962	8.7	6.5	.7	574.6	525.2	396.2
1963	8.4	5.9	.8	606.9	555.5	415.8
1964	9.5	7.0	1.2	649.8	595.9	451.4
1965	10.1	7.0	.9	705.1	647.7	486.8
1966	9.8	6.8	.5	772.0	709.9	525.9
1967	10.2	8.0	.4	816.4	749.0	562.1
1968	8.8	7.0	.2	892.7	818.7	609.6
1969	7.6	6.4	.2	963.9	882.5	656.7
1970	8.2	8.1	.5	1,015.5	926.6	715.6
1971	9.3	8.5	.1	1,102.7	1,005.1	776.8
1972	8.6	7.3	-.2	1,212.8	1,104.8	839.6
1973	10.1	9.4	.6	1,359.3	1,241.2	949.8
1974	8.7	9.3	.4	1,472.8	1,335.4	1,038.4

(continued)

Table 1.2 (continued)

					Undistri-buted Corporate Profits[b]	Capital Consumption Allowances[c]			Government Surplus or Deficit (−)			
	Gross Saving	Gross Private Saving	Net Private Saving[a]	Personal Saving		Total	Corporate	Noncor-porate	Total	Federal	State and Local	Other[d]
1975	14.9	19.0	8.9	6.5	2.3	10.1	6.0	4.1	−4.1	−4.3	.3	0
1976	15.9	18.0	8.0	5.4	2.6	10.1	6.0	4.0	−2.2	−3.0	.9	0
1977	16.9	17.8	7.7	4.6	3.1	10.1	6.1	4.1	−1.0	−2.3	1.4	0
1978	18.2	18.2	8.0	4.9	3.1	10.2	6.1	4.1	0	−1.3	1.3	0
1979	18.3	17.8	7.2	4.7	2.5	10.6	6.3	4.3	.5	−.6	1.1	0
1980	16.3	17.5	6.4	5.0	1.4	11.1	6.6	4.5	−1.3	−2.2	1.0	0
1981	17.1	18.0	6.6	5.2	1.4	11.4	6.9	4.5	−1.0	−2.1	1.1	0
1982	14.1	17.6	5.5	4.9	.6	12.1	7.4	4.7	−3.5	−4.6	1.1	0
1983	13.6	17.4	5.7	3.8	1.9	11.6	7.1	4.5	−3.8	−5.2	1.4	0
1984	15.2	17.9	6.9	4.5	2.4	11.0	6.7	4.3	−2.7	−4.5	1.8	0
1985	13.8	17.2	6.3	3.6	2.7	10.9	6.7	4.2	−3.4	−5.0	1.5	0
Period averages:												
1950–59	16.0	16.2	7.5	4.7	2.8	8.7	4.7	4.0	−.2	0	−.2	0
1950–54	15.5	15.7	7.4	4.7	2.6	8.3	4.4	4.0	−.2	−.1	−.2	0
1955–59	16.4	16.7	7.7	4.7	2.9	9.0	4.9	4.1	−.2	.1	−.3	0
1960–69	16.3	16.6	8.2	4.7	3.5	8.4	4.8	3.6	−.3	−.3	0	0
1960–64	16.2	16.4	7.7	4.4	3.3	8.6	4.9	3.8	−.2	−.3	.1	0
1965–69	16.4	16.7	8.5	4.8	3.6	8.2	4.8	3.5	−.3	−.3	0	0
1970–79	16.9	17.7	8.0	5.5	2.5	9.7	5.8	4.0	−.9	−1.7	.9	0
1970–74	16.7	17.1	8.2	6.0	2.2	8.9	5.2	3.7	−.5	−1.1	.6	0
1975–79	17.0	18.1	7.9	5.1	2.7	10.2	6.1	4.1	−1.1	−2.1	1.0	0
1980–85	14.9	17.6	6.2	4.4	1.8	11.4	6.9	4.4	−2.7	−4.1	1.4	0

Percentage of GNP

	Net Private Saving as a Percentage of Net National Product	Personal Saving as a Percentage of Disposable Personal Income	Net Foreign Investment as a Percentage of GNP	Addenda: GNP	Addenda: Net National Product	Addenda: Disposable Personal Income[e]
1975	9.9	9.2	1.4	1,598.4	1,436.6	1,142.8
1976	8.9	7.6	.5	1,782.8	1,603.6	1,252.6
1977	8.6	6.6	-.4	1,990.5	1,789.0	1,379.3
1978	8.9	7.1	-.4	2,249.7	2,019.8	1,551.2
1979	8.0	6.8	.1	2,508.2	2,242.4	1,729.3
1980	7.2	7.1	.5	2,732.0	2,428.1	1,918.0
1981	7.5	7.5	.3	3,052.6	2,704.8	2,127.6
1982	6.3	6.8	0	3,166.0	2,782.8	2,261.4
1983	6.5	5.4	-1.0	3,405.7	3,009.1	2,428.1
1984	7.8	6.3	-2.4	3,765.0	3,349.9	2,670.6
1985	7.0	5.1	-2.9	3,998.1	3,560.9	2,828.0

(*continued*)

Table 1.2 (continued)

	Net Private Saving as a Percentage of Net National Product	Personal Saving as a Percentage of Disposable Personal Income	Net Foreign Investment as a Percentage of GNP	Addenda:		
				GNP	Net National Product	Disposable Personal Income[e]
Period averages:						
1950–59	8.3	6.8	.2	395.5	361.1	275.0
1950–54	8.0	6.8	–.1	343.5	314.8	238.1
1955–59	8.4	6.8	.3	447.5	407.3	311.9
1960–69	8.9	6.8	.6	703.1	643.9	483.7
1960–64	8.5	6.4	.8	576.1	526.3	399.2
1965–69	9.2	7.0	.4	830.0	761.6	568.2
1970–79	8.9	7.8	.2	1,629.3	1,470.5	1,137.5
1970–74	9.0	8.6	.3	1,232.6	1,122.6	864.0
1975–79	8.8	7.4	.1	2,025.9	1,818.3	1,411.0
1980–85	7.0	6.3	–1.1	3,353.2	2,972.6	2,372.3

[a]Net private saving is gross private saving less capital consumption allowances with capital consumption adjustment.

[b]With inventory valuation and capital consumption adjustments.

[c]With capital consumption adjustment.

[d]Consists of wage accruals less disbursements and capital grants received by the United States (net). The values for 1948–51 and 1973 round to zero.

[e]Billions of dollars.

Figure 1.1 shows ratios to GNP of gross saving, gross private saving, net private saving, and government saving. Considering the entire 1950–85 period, the gross saving ratio had considerable amplitude but no trend.[4] The gross private saving ratio had less amplitude and a slightly positive trend; the government saving ratio had about the same amplitude as the gross saving ratio and a negative trend. The relative stability in the NIPA gross private saving ratio has long been noted and is often referred to as "Denison's law" (Denison 1958).[5] The net private saving ratio had a slightly negative trend with greater amplitude than the gross private saving ratio but less than the government saving ratio.

Recent developments diverge in important ways from these trends. The mean of the gross saving ratio for the 1980–85 period was considerably less than the means for any of the earlier periods shown in the lower part of table 1.2. Although the gross private saving ratio had been relatively stable since the mid-1970s and the mean for the 1980–85 period was relatively high by historical standards, the negative government saving ratio was large enough to lead to declines in the gross saving ratio. Like the gross saving ratio, the mean of the net private saving ratio was lower in the 1980–85 period than in any of the earlier periods. The reasons are discussed in connection with figure 1.2.

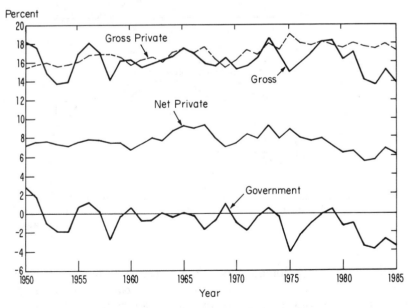

Fig. 1.1   NIPA gross, gross private, net private, and government saving as a percentage of GNP

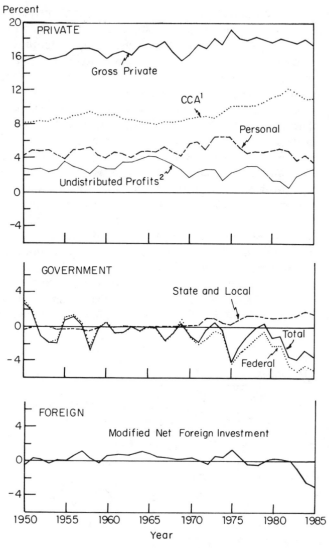

Fig. 1.2   Selected NIPA saving and investment measures, as a percentage of GNP. [1]With capital consumption adjustment. [2]With inventory valuation and capital consumption adjustments.

Figure 1.2 shows components of the measures in figure 1.1 and a related measure for the foreign sector. The top panel reproduces the gross private saving ratio and shows its major components: capital consumption, personal saving, and undistributed corporate profits with IVA and CCAdj. The middle panel reproduces the government surplus or deficit ratio and shows its components: the federal surplus or deficit and the state and local government surplus or deficit. The bottom panel shows the foreign-sector measure discussed earlier: net foreign investment less capital grants received by the United States (net), hereafter referred to as modified net foreign investment.

The additional measures shown in figure 1.2 provide interesting insights into patterns of saving in the United States. Starting with the top panel, the relative stability in the gross private saving ratio did not occur as a result of stability in its components; rather, two of the components—personal saving and undistributed corporate profits—showed significant fluctuations that were often in opposite directions by similar magnitudes. However, the widely publicized declines in the personal saving ratio during many of the years since the mid-1970s were not entirely offset by movements in the undistributed corporate profits ratio. Consequently, the net private saving ratio, which is approximately the sum of these two ratios, had a downward trend since the mid-1970s.[6] The gross private saving ratio remained relatively stable because the capital consumption ratio had an upward trend.[7]

The second panel of figure 1.2 shows the sharp contrast between federal and state-local government budget measures. The cyclical pattern of the federal surplus or deficit ratio was unmistakable and accounted for most of the fluctuations of the government surplus or deficit ratio.[8]

The bottom panel of figure 1.2 shows the significant change in recent years in the modified net foreign investment ratio. Starting in 1983, the ratio was relatively large and negative and reflected the growing part of gross investment financed by foreign saving.[9]

To summarize, these trends convey several messages.[10] First, the gross saving ratio declined to uncharacteristically low levels toward the end of the period. Second, federal dissaving offset an increased percentage of gross private saving. Third, the personal saving ratio peaked in the mid-1970s, then declined to levels similar to those in the early part of the period. Fourth, capital consumption accounted for an increased percentage of gross saving toward the end of the period relative to the early part of the period. Fifth, reliance on foreign saving to finance investment grew toward the end of the period.

These messages, of course, depend on the nature and validity of the underlying saving measures. In turn, the saving measures are determined by numerous concepts and conventions underlying the NIPAs.

1.2 Concepts and Conventions

NIPA saving measures are part of a broader NIPA framework and, as such, reflect the purposes, concepts, conventions, and methods associated with that framework. In this section, some of the concepts and conventions that are especially relevant to NIPA saving measures are discussed. First, the general purposes, scope, and accounting framework of the NIPAs are summarized. Second, some of the sectoring conventions in the NIPAs are discussed. Third, classifications, attributions, and imputations that have important implications for saving measures are discussed.

1.2.1   Purposes, Scope, and Accounting Framework of the NIPAs

Two fundamental purposes of the NIPAs can be identified (Young and Tice 1985; Bureau of Economic Analysis 1985b).[11] The first is to measure current production, its composition, and its distribution.[12] The second is to provide an overview of the processes involved in the production, distribution, and use of the nation's output. Clearly, the NIPAs are built around the concept of current production. Among other things, this focus has important implications for the accounts with respect to what types of activities should be included and what types excluded. Capital gains (and losses) are an important case in point.[13]

Both realized and unrealized capital gains are excluded from the NIPAs on the ground that these gains do not reflect current production. Because there is widespread agreement that capital gains have important effects on economic behavior in general and consumption/saving decisions in particular, the NIPA exclusion is noteworthy. Some alternative measures of saving discussed later go beyond the NIPA framework and include capital gains.

The exclusion of capital gains from the NIPAs follows from the focus on current production. However, the boundary of what exactly constitutes production—the scope of the NIPAs—requires the adoption of conventions. These conventions reflect both conceptual concerns and considerations related to the feasibility and practicality of measurement. For the most part, NIPA production is limited to market transactions. Valuation is at market prices.[14] There are also a few imputations for nonmarket activities that are closely related to market counterparts. Some of the most important imputations are for wages and salaries in kind, the value of services from owner-occupied dwellings, food and fuel produced and consumed on farms, and the value of services provided without charge by financial intermediaries (excluding life insurance carriers). Most other nonmarket activities are excluded from NIPA production.[15]

Another important convention determining the production boundary is the exclusion of illegal activity. The NIPAs exclude activities that are prohibited by federal, state, or local laws. Two of the reasons often given for excluding illegal activities are that they do not contribute to economic welfare and/or that they are difficult to measure (Easterlin 1958; Carson 1984b).[16] Consequently, some activities that by all other relevant criteria would be included in the NIPAs are excluded because of legal prohibition. A classic case was the purchase of alcoholic beverages during Prohibition: personal consumption expenditures for alcoholic beverages was set equal to zero during those years. Exploratory work is underway at BEA to measure illegal activities within the NIPA framework.[17]

The determination of what constitutes production provides guides to establishing an accounting framework for measurement.[18] The skeleton of that framework is provided by the familiar NIPA five-account summary with GNP—a production measure—as the central focus.[19] Appendix A shows the five-account summary. Conceptually, the summary accounts are based on production, appropriation, and saving-investment accounts of four NIPA sectors: business, households and related institutions, government, and foreign.[20] The first of the five summary accounts reports GNP and is a consolidation of the business, household, government, and foreign production accounts and the business appropriation account. The second summary account shows personal income, outlays, and saving and represents the household appropriation account. The third account shows receipts, expenditures, and the surplus or deficit of government and represents the government appropriation account. The fourth account shows foreign transactions and is a consolidation of the foreign appropriation and foreign saving-investment accounts. The fifth summary account shows gross saving and investment and is a consolidation of the business, household, and government saving-investment accounts (NIPA table 5.1, reproduced earlier as table 1.1, is a slightly more detailed representation of the fifth account).

Within this accounting framework, NIPA gross saving is the source of resources for gross private domestic investment (GPDI) and net foreign investment.[21] GPDI represents purchases of private fixed capital goods and the change in business inventories. As alluded to earlier, capital goods include structures and equipment purchased by private business and nonprofit institutions. These purchases include private purchases of new residential structures for either tenant or owner occupancy and net purchases of used capital goods. The detailed components of NIPA saving show the sources of gross saving for this investment.

To make the accounting framework operational, many additional concepts and conventions must be adopted, some of which concern who or what is included in each sector, how transactions are classified within the sectors, and how transactions are attributed to the sectors.

1.2.2 Sectoring

Four sectors were noted above in connection with the NIPA accounting framework: business, households and institutions, government, and foreign. From the standpoint of measuring production, the business sector includes all organizations that produce goods and services for sale at a price intended to cover the costs of production. In addition to corporate and noncorporate entities organized for profit, other entities, such as Federal Reserve banks and government enterprises, are included.[22] Homeowners, in their role as owner occupants, are also included.

The determination of what constitutes the business sector helps define what entities and activities constitute the remaining sectors. The household and institutions sector includes households, which consist of families and unrelated individuals, and nonprofit institutions serving individuals. The only activities of the household and institutions sector that constitute production are the services rendered by nonprofit institutions and by domestic workers employed by households. All the other activities of households, such as purchases of new owner-occupied dwellings, are excluded from the sector because they are classified elsewhere. The government sector includes all federal, state, and local government agencies except government enterprises. Finally, foreign transactions related to production define the rest-of-the-world sector. The rest-of-the-world sector is the difference between production abroad attributed to U.S. factors of production and production in the United States attributed to foreign factors of production.

These few remarks about sectoring with respect to measuring production are suggestive of the complexities involved in classifying entities and activities into sectors. Further complexities emerge with respect to saving measures. The categories of NIPA saving that constitute gross saving do not conform to the sectors noted above with respect to measuring production; rather, the saving measures are defined in appropriation accounts. Consequently, there are many instances of entities classified in one production sector having their saving attributed to another sector.[23] The sum of undistributed corporate profits and corporate CCAs reflects business-sector saving; personal saving reflects household-sector saving; the government surplus or deficit reflects government-sector saving; and net foreign investment with the sign reversed reflects foreign-sector saving. However, there are numerous qualifications. For example, unincorporated business saving from proprietors' income is classified as personal saving, although unincorporated businesses are in the business sector. The saving (surplus or deficit) of government enterprises is classified as government saving, although government enterprises are in the business sector. The reinvested earnings of incorporated foreign affiliates of U.S. corporations included in factor income is in undistributed corporate profits, although these transactions are part of the rest-of-the-world sector. There are many other examples. A brief discussion of NIPA personal saving illustrates some of these sectoring issues and serves as an introduction to a more detailed discussion of classifications, attributions, and imputations.

Personal saving includes the saving of households, nonprofit institutions serving individuals, proprietors, private noninsured pension funds, pension funds operated by life insurance carriers, and private trust funds. Several conventions related to sectoring merit comment.

Nonprofit institutions serving individuals are grouped with households in the NIPAs because they are viewed as associations of individuals and because some of their activities are considered to resemble the activities of households more closely than the activities of other sectors (Denison 1982b).[24] The inclusion of proprietors' income and saving arises primarily because many proprietors do not distinguish between their income and saving in a personal versus business capacity (Denison 1955; Jaszi 1958). Consequently, all their income and saving is attributed to households.

The attribution of the saving of private noninsured pension funds, life insurance carriers, and private trust funds to personal saving (even though all but the last of these entities are in the business sector) also partially reflects the notion that these entities are associations of individuals. Consequently, their saving is viewed to be on behalf of households.

1.2.3 Classifications, Attributions, and Imputations

The discussion of sectoring and remarks about personal saving illustrate the fact that many decisions affect NIPA saving measures. Additional details about classifications, attributions, and imputations highlight some of these decisions and help clarify the nature of the saving measures.

Perhaps the most fundamental classification decision affecting NIPA saving measures concerns what BEA defines as investment.[25] Because investment expenditures are matched by equal changes in saving, the classification of an expenditure as investment has a direct effect on saving.[26] In the NIPAs, investment, or capital formation, is mainly restricted to the business sector, where the operational guideline used in the NIPAs is to measure investment as business expenditures not charged to current expenses (Jaszi 1958, 1971). Capital formation by households in the form of housing is treated as business activity. Capital formation by government is not recognized. Further, some expenditures by business (e.g., for research and development) are expensed by business and treated as current purchases in the NIPAs, but in some ways are conceptually similar to investment expenditures (Blades 1983). Finally, some expenditures expensed by business (e.g., certain expenditures for mining exploration, shafts, and wells) are treated as investment in the NIPAs.

The present NIPA classifications of owner-occupied housing, consumer durable goods, government structures and durable goods, and research and development expenditures merit additional discussion. The major reasons for the present classifications and the roles of attributions and imputations in the treatment of owner-occupied housing are discussed next; criticisms of some of the present classifications are discussed in the final section.

It was noted earlier that all private purchases of new residential structures, including those for owner occupancy, are classified as investment. Under this treatment, owner occupants are classified as unincorporated entities in the business sector. These entities pay all the expenses associated with owning the residential structure and receive imputed space rental for the housing services provided. Imputed space rental is the largest single imputation in the NIPAs.[27] In 1985, it was $286 billion or about 11 percent of personal consumption expenditures. The difference between imputed space rental and expenses, including capital consumption, is imputed rental income. In the case of nonfarm housing, this income is included in rental income of persons; in the case of farm housing, it is included in farm proprietors' income. In 1985, imputed rental income was about −$19 billion, and imputed proprietors' income from farm housing was about $4 billion.

This treatment recognizes that housing provides a long-term flow of services to the owner occupant. If housing were not treated as part of capital formation, only the initial purchase would appear; the subsequent flow of services would be omitted.

In many respects, other consumer durable goods also yield a flow of services over time, but personal consumption expenditures for durable goods are not capitalized. Conceptually, consumer durable goods could be treated exactly the same way as housing. However, major conceptual and statistical difficulties arise in estimating the value of services.[28] In the case of housing, the imputed rental value is based on a viable market analogy with rental housing that allows the determination of the value of services. In the case of other consumer durable goods, the market analogy is frequently much weaker.

Although consumer durable goods remain a current purchase in the NIPAs, BEA regularly publishes estimates of gross and net stocks of these goods.[29] Estimates of capital consumption are available on request. Work was also done at BEA on estimating the service value of consumer durables, but this work is not regularly updated (Katz and Peskin 1980).

Purchases of government structures and durable goods are also classified as current purchases in the NIPAs. As with consumer durable goods, government structures and durable goods could be capitalized and a flow of services could be attributed to them. However, the value of services for government capital is even more difficult to determine than that for consumer durable goods.[30]

To provide information on government capital, BEA regularly publishes estimates of gross and net stocks.[31] Estimates of capital consumption are available on request. Work was also done at BEA on estimating the value of services provided by the stock of government-owned fixed capital, but this work is not regularly updated (Martin, Landefeld, and Peskin 1982).

Research and development expenditures by both business and government are classified as current purchases. In the case of business, the purchases are intermediate; in the case of government and nonprofit institutions, the purchases are final, but they are not part of investment. Two of the reasons for classifying research and development expenditures as current purchases include difficulty in defining what constitutes research and development subject to classification as investment and difficulties in determining service lives, depreciation, and valuation of intangible investment (Jaszi 1973).[32]

These classification conventions have a direct bearing on NIPA saving measures because reclassification of any of these types of expenditures would affect gross saving on a dollar-for-dollar basis. The effects on the components of gross saving would depend on what sector the expenditure was in and the corresponding estimates of capital consumption. The effects of reclassifying some of these purchases are discussed further in the final section.

Classifications, attributions, and imputations related to pensions also play important roles in shaping NIPA saving measures. Because private and public pensions involve significantly different treatments in the NIPAs, it is helpful to discuss them separately.[33]

The NIPA treatment of private pension funds—private noninsured pension funds and funds operated by life insurance carriers—is especially significant in the determination of personal saving because most of the investment earnings and operating expenses of these funds are attributed to persons.[34] Additional smaller effects arise as a result of the related treatments of contributions and benefits.

The attribution to persons of investment earnings by private pension funds is accomplished through imputations. Pension fund reserves are viewed as though they are owned by individuals. Consequently, the investment earnings on these reserves are shown as imputed interest to persons to recognize that these earnings belong to the ultimate beneficiaries.[35] The earnings are attributed in the year they accrue.

To maintain a consistent treatment of private pension funds, an estimate of the operating expenses of these funds is attributed to persons as part of personal consumption expenditures (PCE). Because operating expenses, which exclude benefit payments, are much less than the income items, and because these income items are not subject to personal taxes, private pension funds account for a significant positive contribution to personal saving.[36]

Employer contributions to private pension funds are considered current compensation and are classified as other labor income. This classification also means these contributions are part of personal income and disposable personal income. Because income is recorded at the time of the employer contribution, it is necessary to exclude private pension benefits from income at the time they are received to avoid double counting. Consequently, benefits received do not appear in the NIPAs, although estimates are prepared by BEA and published in a supplemental table.[37] The convention of treating contributions rather than benefits as part of personal income affects personal saving partly through differences in the amounts of contributions and benefits.

Public pension funds are treated differently. The most important types of public pensions are social security, federal civilian retirement, and state and local government retirement. The NIPA treatment of these funds affects the government surplus or deficit and personal saving. The most important NIPA conventions concern the treatments of contributions, benefits, and earnings of the funds. These treatments arise because the saving of these funds is considered to be part of government saving rather than private saving. Both employer and employee contributions to public pension funds are classified as contributions for social insurance. This classification means that they are excluded from personal income and disposable personal income but included in government receipts. Benefits paid are classified as government transfer payments. This means that they are included in government expenditures and in personal income.[38] Thus, public pensions affect the government surplus or deficit through their effects on receipts and expenditures. They affect personal saving through their effects on personal income.

The treatment of the investment earnings by public pension funds is less complicated than the treatment of private funds. In the case of federal pension funds, all funds must be invested in federal government securities until 1988. Therefore, interest on federal pension funds has no effect on federal net interest paid and no effect on the government surplus or deficit.[39] This limitation on investment is a major reason for the present treatment of federal pension funds. Starting in 1988, investment options in federal civilian pension funds will be more flexible and more like state and local government pension funds.

State and local government pension funds, unlike federal pension funds, can be invested in a wide variety of securities, including corporate stocks. Earnings from these securities include both interest and dividends and are recorded as offsets to expenditures.[40] Consequently, the investment earnings of state and local pension funds affect the government surplus or deficit to the extent that these earnings are not from municipal securities.

These treatments of contributions, benefits, and earnings highlight an important distinction between private pension funds and public pension funds. The income to persons from private pension funds is attributed when paid into the funds or when earned in the funds in the case of investment earnings; the income to persons from public pension funds is attributed when transfer payments are received.

Partly because of this difference between income flows, and because of similarities between the objectives of private and public pension funds, it has sometimes been suggested that the treatment of private and public pensions, at least state and local government funds, should be more consistent. This point is explored more later in the paper.

A final point concerning the NIPA treatment of pensions is that there is no attempt to introduce estimates of the discounted present value of unfunded liabilities associated with public pension funds. Estimates of unfunded liabilities are often discussed in connection with social security (Boskin 1986). Such estimates would obviously be extremely sensitive to assumed parameters and could cause very large swings in NIPA gross saving.

1.3   Measurement and Revisions

It was noted earlier that some NIPA saving measures are derived as differences between large aggregates. Where the estimates of the aggregates are derived independently, as in personal saving, revisions in saving measures are more likely to arise. Personal saving is measured as the difference between disposable personal income and personal outlays; government saving (surplus or deficit) is measured as the difference between government receipts and government expenditures; and so forth. As a consequence, relatively small percentage revisions in either of the aggregates can result in very large revisions in saving. For example, at 1985 levels, a 1 percent upward revision in disposable personal income or a 1 percent downward revision in personal outlays would result in a 20 percent upward revision in personal saving and a 0.6 percentage point increase in the personal saving rate, ceteris paribus.

Consequently, it is clear that the precision of the measurement of the aggregates has important consequences for NIPA saving measures. In this section, a few comments about the sources and methods underlying the saving measures are provided. With this background, the discussion turns to revisions in NIPA saving measures. The 1985 comprehensive revision serves as the main example.

1.3.1 Sources and Methods

NIPA estimates rely on a wide variety of source data and methods. Appendix B provides some notes on the sources and methods underlying NIPA saving measures. As the appendix shows, nearly all the NIPA estimates depend on data subject to reporting lags and revisions. Consequently, revisions in the NIPAs must be made periodically to incorporate revisions in the underlying source data.

The appendix indicates that tax return data play a particularly important part in the NIPA estimates of income. Data from the income tax returns of corporations, sole proprietorships, and partnerships are compiled by the Internal Revenue Service (IRS) and reported in the *Statistics of Income* series. Data from payroll tax returns of employers covered under state unemployment insurance programs are compiled by the Bureau of Labor Statistics (BLS) and reported in *Employment and Wages*. Because it is widely recognized that there is misreporting (specifically, underreporting of income and failure to file) in the tax return data, the BEA makes adjustments to correct for it. The revisions in annual estimates discussed next partly resulted from improvements in these adjustments.

1.3.2 Sources of Revisions

The size, frequency, and sources of revisions in economic statistics are obviously very important. If the statistics are subject to large and frequent revisions, their value in economic studies and policy discussions is slight.[41] Revisions can arise for many reasons. First, estimates may be revised to produce series that better reflect current institutions or types of activities. Second, estimates may be revised to incorporate more up-to-date or improved source data. Third, estimates may be revised to incorporate improved statistical methods and estimating procedures.

The size and sources of revisions in annual NIPA saving measures are discussed below. The focus is on the revisions resulting from the 1985 comprehensive revision; however, some revisions from earlier comprehensive revisions will also be discussed briefly.

There are two major types of NIPA revisions: definitional and classificational revisions and statistical revisions. Definitional and classificational revisions are generally changes made to improve the treatment of evolving institutions in the economy and their economic activities. Statistical revisions are generally changes made on the basis of new source data or improved estimating procedures.

For the most part, definitional and classificational revisions are introduced only during comprehensive revisions so that the revisions can be incorporated into historical estimates on a consistent basis. Statistical revisions are made during comprehensive revisions and the regular annual July revisions.

Before turning to the 1985 comprehensive revision, a few examples of definitional and classificational revisions that had important effects on NIPA saving measures from earlier comprehensive revisions serve to illustrate the nature of this type of revision. In the comprehensive revision that became available in January 1976, four definitional and classificational revisions had particularly important effects on NIPA gross saving or its components: the introduction of economic capital consumption, the reclassification of mobile home purchases from PCE to investment, the reclassification of consumer-type durable purchases by landlords from PCE to investment, and the reclassification of outlays for drilling mine shafts from current purchases to investment (Jaszi and Carson 1976).[42]

The use of economic capital consumption in the NIPAs had been advocated for many years because the tax-return-based depreciation estimates used previously had serious shortcomings for economic analysis.[43] Two of the major shortcomings are that tax return depreciation reflects asset lives and depreciation formulas that may not reflect true consumption of fixed capital and that tax return depreciation reflects historical costs and does not reflect replacement costs. The introduction of economic capital consumption, which appeared through the use of an adjustment (CCAdj) to the tax return measures, had important effects on the composition of gross saving but no effect on gross saving itself. In most years covered by the revision, the effects were to increase the estimates of capital consumption, increase undistributed corporate profits, and decrease personal saving.

The reclassification of mobile homes was done because their use as permanent residences had increased significantly from their use for recreational purposes.[44] The reclassification of consumer-type durable purchases by landlords was done to improve consistency with the investment treatment of housing. The reclassification of outlays for drilling mine shafts was done to improve consistency with the investment treatment of outlays for drilling petroleum and natural gas wells, which had been treated as investment in the NIPAs. These reclassifications necessarily increased capital consumption and gross saving. Because the purchases of these items exceeded their capital consumption, the effect of the reclassifications was also to increase both undistributed corporate profits and personal saving.

The effects of all the definitional and classificational revisions combined were to increase capital consumption in most years, increase undistributed corporate profits in most years, and decrease personal saving in all years. In some years, the personal saving rate was revised down in level by nearly a full percentage point.

In the comprehensive revision that became available in December 1980, one major definitional and classificational revision had an important effect on NIPA gross saving and its components: the addition of reinvested earnings of incorporated foreign affiliates to receipts and payments of income on direct investment (Denison and Parker 1980).[45] This definitional revision was made to provide a better treatment of transactions that had become relatively more important and to incorporate improved data that had become available. The main effects were to increase net foreign investment and undistributed corporate profits. These increases, of course, also resulted in increases in gross saving and gross private saving. By the late 1970s, this definitional revision accounted for an upward revision in the ratio of gross saving to GNP of about 0.5 percentage points.

In the 1985 comprehensive revision, three definitional and classificational revisions had effects on NIPA saving measures: the reclassification of replacement railroad track from current purchases to investment, the reclassification of major replacements to residential structures from current purchases to investment, and the reclassification of military shipments financed by "forgiven" loans from government purchases to exports (Bureau of Economic Analysis 1985a; Parker and Fox 1985).

The reclassification of replacement railroad track was done to reflect changes in the accounting treatment adopted by railroads in the early 1980s and to improve consistency within the NIPAs. Outlays intended for replacement of capital in other industries had been treated as NIPA investment. In 1984, the revision increased investment and gross saving by about $2 billion. The major effects were to increase capital consumption in all years and to decrease undistributed corporate profits in most years. Undistributed corporate profits was revised by the difference between outlays for replacement railroad track and the corresponding depreciation estimates. In most years since 1950, outlays were less than the depreciation estimates, and track mileage declined.

The reclassification of major replacements to residential structures also was done to improve consistency within the NIPAs.[46] The revision makes the treatment of residential replacements similar to the treatment of nonresidential replacements. In 1984, the revision increased investment and gross saving by about $14 billion. The major effects were to increase capital consumption and personal saving by substantial amounts in all years and to increase undistributed corporate profits by small amounts in most years. Proprietors' income and rental income of persons, both of which affect personal saving, and undistributed corporate profits were revised by the differences between outlays for major replacements and the corresponding depreciation estimates.

The reclassification of certain military shipments was done to reflect the nature of these transactions more accurately and to eliminate a difference in treatment between the NIPAs and U.S. international transactions accounts.[47] The reclassification involved reclassifying shipments from government purchases to exports and reclassifying forgiven loans from military grants to transfer payments to foreigners. The amounts were less than $1 billion in all years. The main effect was to decrease net foreign investment, the government surplus, and gross saving by equal amounts.

These three definitional and classificational revisions accounted for a significant part of the revisions in NIPA saving measures that occurred during the 1985 comprehensive revision. Statistical revisions accounted for the rest.[48] As previously noted, statistical revisions result from the introduction of new data and methodological changes. Revisions resulting from new data occur mainly because there are lags and revisions in the source data. Source data that become available less often than annually, such as the economic censuses, were incorporated mainly through the use of BEA's 1977 input-output tables. Other sources included the 1980 Census of Housing, the 1977 Census of Governments, the 1978 Census of Agriculture, and preliminary or summary data from the 1982 economic censuses, the 1982 Census of Agriculture, and the 1982 Census of Governments. Regularly used annual data sources are noted in Appendix B.

Methodological changes, the other major factor underlying statistical revisions, often occur in connection with new source data or new research findings. The most important methodological change in the 1985 comprehensive revision affecting saving concerned improved adjustments for misreporting on tax returns. These adjustments are sometimes referred to as "underground economy" adjustments (Bureau of Economic Analysis 1985a).[49]

It has been noted that tax return data from *Statistics of Income* and *Employment and Wages* are a major source underlying NIPA estimates—including NIPA saving measures. In addition to their direct use in the NIPAs, these data enter the NIPAs indirectly because the Census Bureau uses tax return information in connection with the economic censuses and annual surveys based on these censuses.[50] In recognition of underreporting on tax returns, the BEA had, for many years, made adjustments for that underreporting. These adjustments were extended by incorporating new information on failure to file income and employment tax returns, by using new estimates of the extent of underreporting, and by introducing adjustments to the census data used in the NIPAs. Methodological, conceptual, and measurement aspects of the improved adjustments are discussed in Parker (1984a), Bureau of Economic Analysis (1985a), and Parker and Fox (1985).

The most important effects of the improved adjustments were to revise PCE, wages and salaries, and nonfarm proprietors' income up sharply.[51] In 1984, these revisions amounted to about $44 billion in PCE, about $24 billion in wages and salaries, and about $78 billion in nonfarm proprietors' income. Because the revisions in income exceeded those in outlays, the net effect of improved adjustments was to contribute to an upward revision in personal saving. The newly available information did not provide any reason to revise the adjustments to corporate profits or to capital consumption.

Table 1.3 shows total revisions in selected NIPA saving measures and the separate effects of definitional and classificational revisions and of statistical revisions. The estimates primarily reflect revisions from the 1985 comprehensive revision, but the estimates for 1983 and 1984 also reflect the July 1986 revisions.[52] Total revisions are important. In some respects, the type of revision is irrelevant because the total revision indicates whether the initial estimates provided adequate information for decision makers. In all years, gross saving was revised upward. In most years, these revisions reflected revisions in gross private saving; the noticeable exception was 1984, when most of the revision was the result of an upward revision in state and local government saving. Personal saving was revised upward in most years and typically accounted for about half the revision in gross private saving. Except for 1984, the revisions in government saving were relatively small.

The definitional and classificational revisions increased gross saving in all years shown. The revisions in gross saving and gross private saving were nearly identical. The increases mainly resulted from revisions in capital consumption, but increases in personal saving also contributed. The reasons for these revisions were discussed earlier.

The statistical revisions also increased gross saving in most years shown. As would be expected, the statistical revisions show a great deal of variation. In most years, gross private saving and personal saving were revised upward. The improved adjustments for underreporting made important contributions to the direction of these revisions.

The revisions in level provide a view of relative changes among components of gross saving, but they do not provide a view of how large these revisions are relative to the size of the economy. Figure 1.3 shows a comparison of selected saving ratios based on pre–comprehensive revision data (referred to in the chart as unrevised) and on current data (referred in the chart as revised).[53] The top panel shows the gross saving–to–GNP ratio. The second panel shows the gross private saving–to–GNP ratio. For most years, the revised gross and

Table 1.3   Sources of Revisions in Selected NIPA Saving Measures (billions of dollars)

	1950	1955	1960	1965	1970	1971	1972	1973	1974	1975
Total revision:										
Gross saving	1.8	.9	3.1	3.3	5.8	10.3	14.1	16.4	20.1	19.8
Gross private saving	1.8	.8	3.1	3.3	5.9	10.3	14.2	16.3	19.8	20.9
Personal saving	.7	-.4	1.1	.6	1.9	5.6	8.8	10.0	11.6	10.3
Undistributed corporate profits[a]	1.0	1.7	1.8	1.3	3.1	3.6	3.9	4.7	6.8	8.0
Capital consumption allowances[b]	.1	-.4	.1	1.4	.7	.9	1.5	1.6	1.5	2.5
Government surplus or deficit (−)	0	0	0	0	0	-.1	-.1	.1	.4	-1.1
Federal	0	0	0	0	0	0	0	0	-.1	-.1
State and local	0	0	0	0	-.1	0	0	.1	.4	-1.0
Definitional and classificational revision:										
Gross saving	1.3	1.6	2.1	2.1	3.2	3.8	3.9	3.9	5.2	4.8
Gross private saving	1.3	1.6	2.1	2.1	3.2	3.8	3.9	3.9	5.3	5.1
Personal saving	.5	.6	1.0	.7	.7	1.0	.9	.6	1.4	.8
Undistributed corporate profits[a]	0	-.2	-.4	-.3	-.3	-.2	-.2	-.2	-.3	-.4
Capital consumption allowances[b]	.8	1.1	1.5	1.7	2.7	3.0	3.2	3.5	4.1	4.7
Government surplus or deficit (−)	0	0	0	0	0	0	0	0	-.1	-.3
Federal	0	0	0	0	0	0	0	0	-.1	-.3
State and local	0	0	0	0	0	0	0	0	0	0

(continued)

Table 1.3 (continued)

	1950	1955	1960	1965	1970	1971	1972	1973	1974	1975
Statistical revision:										
Gross saving	.5	−.7	1.0	1.2	2.6	6.5	10.2	12.5	14.9	15.0
Gross private saving	.5	−.8	1.0	1.2	2.7	6.5	10.3	12.4	14.5	15.8
Personal saving	.2	−1.0	.1	−.1	1.2	4.6	7.9	9.4	10.2	9.5
Undistributed corporate profits[a]	1.0	1.9	2.2	1.6	3.4	3.8	4.1	4.9	7.1	8.4
Capital consumption allowances[b]	−.7	−1.5	−1.4	−.3	−2.0	−2.1	−1.7	−1.9	−2.6	−2.2
Government surplus or deficit (−)	0	0	0	0	0	−.1	−.1	.1	.5	−.8
Federal	0	0	0	0	0	0	0	0	0	.2
State and local	0	0	0	0	−.1	0	0	.1	.4	−1.0
Addenda:										
Revisions in net foreign investment:										
Total	0	0	.4	.8	1.6	2.0	2.2	2.3	2.5	3.3
Definitional and classificational	0	0	0	0	0	0	0	0	−.1	−.3
Statistical	0	0	.4	.8	1.6	2.0	2.2	2.3	2.6	3.6

	1976	1977	1978	1979	1980	1981	1982	1983	1984
Total revision:									
Gross saving	25.1	26.3	33.8	35.7	39.1	37.7	37.6	26.4	21.5
Gross private saving	27.0	27.6	35.0	38.5	43.0	40.6	33.1	20.5	0
Personal saving	13.3	12.7	20.8	21.4	26.7	22.0	17.9	12.5	12.6
Undistributed corporate profits[a]	9.5	8.6	6.8	7.5	5.6	.9	−9.2	−11.5	−24.4
Capital consumption allowances[b]	4.1	6.3	7.4	9.8	10.7	17.6	24.3	19.5	11.9
Government surplus or deficit (−)	−1.9	−1.3	−1.2	−2.8	−3.8	−3.0	4.5	5.9	21.4
Federal	−.4	−.1	.2	0	−.1	.5	2.3	2.6	5.8
State and local	−1.4	−1.1	−1.4	−2.8	−3.8	−3.5	2.2	3.4	15.6

Definitional and classificational revision:

Gross saving	5.8	6.6	9.1	9.8	10.5	11.3	10.4	11.3	15.0
Gross private saving	6.2	6.6	8.9	9.9	10.5	11.3	10.5	11.6	15.8
Personal saving	1.2	1.0	2.8	2.9	2.8	2.5	1.5	2.3	5.6
Undistributed corporate profits[a]	-.1	0	-.1	.2	0	0	-.3	-.5	-.1
Capital consumption allowances[b]	5.1	5.6	6.2	6.8	7.8	8.7	9.4	9.8	10.4
Government surplus or deficit (−)	-.5	0	.2	-.1	0	0	-.1	-.3	-.8
Federal	-.5	0	.2	-.1	0	0	-.1	-.3	-.8
State and local	0	0	0	0	0	0	0	0	0

Statistical revision:

Gross saving	19.3	19.7	24.7	25.9	28.6	26.4	27.2	15.1	6.5
Gross private saving	20.8	21.0	26.1	28.6	32.5	29.3	22.6	8.9	-15.8
Personal saving	12.1	11.7	18.0	18.5	23.9	19.5	16.4	10.2	7.0
Undistributed corporate profits[a]	9.6	8.6	6.9	7.3	5.6	.9	-8.9	-11.0	-24.3
Capital consumption allowances[b]	-1.0	.7	1.2	3.0	2.9	8.9	14.9	9.7	1.5
Government surplus or deficit (−)	-1.4	-1.3	-1.4	-2.7	-3.8	-3.0	4.6	6.2	22.2
Federal	.1	-.1	0	.1	-.1	.5	2.4	2.9	6.6
State and local	-1.4	-1.1	-1.4	-2.8	-3.8	-3.5	2.2	3.4	15.6

Addenda:

Revisions in net foreign investment:									
Total	3.9	4.9	4.2	4.4	6.7	4.8	5.6	.4	2.7
Definitional and classificational	-.5	0	.2	-.1	0	0	-.1	-.3	-.8
Statistical	4.4	4.9	4.0	4.5	6.7	4.8	5.7	.7	3.5

Note: The revisions are measured as differences between estimates available when the July 1986 *Survey of Current Business* was published and those available when the November 1985 *Survey* was published.
[a]With inventory valuation and capital consumption adjustments.
[b]With capital consumption adjustment.

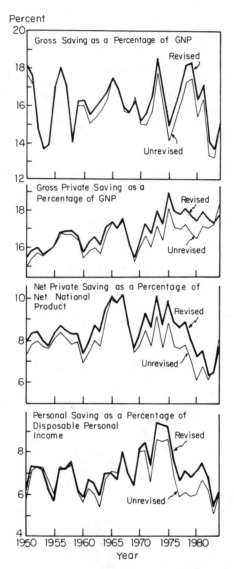

Fig. 1.3   Revised and unrevised NIPA saving measures. *Note:* Revised
estimates reflect those available when the July 1986 *Survey
of Current Business* was published. Unrevised estimates reflect those available when the November 1985 *Survey* was
published.

gross private ratios were higher than the unrevised ratios. The exception was 1984, when the state and local government saving revision affected gross saving but not gross private saving. The revised ratios exceeded the unrevised ratios most during the late 1970s and early 1980s. In addition to level differences, some of the year-to-year changes differed, but most were similar. One difference in changes occurred when the unrevised gross private saving ratio rose from 1982 to 1983, but the revised ratio fell.

In the third panel, the revised net private saving ratio was also higher than the unrevised ratio in most years. As with the gross and gross private ratios, a gap opened between the revised and the unrevised net private saving ratios during the late 1970s and early 1980s. The differences changed sign after 1982.

In the bottom panel, the revised personal saving rate was higher than the unrevised rate in most years and helps explain many of the differences between the revised and the unrevised ratios in the other panels.

A simple decomposition of the revision in the ratios helps attribute the revisions to their major sources. Letting S_r = the revised saving measure (e.g., levels of gross saving, gross private saving, etc.), S_u = the unrevised saving measure, Y_r = the revised base of the ratio (e.g., GNP, disposable personal income), Y_u = the unrevised base of the ratio, $\Delta S = S_r - S_u$, and $\Delta Y = Y_r - Y_u$, then the revision in the ratios can be expressed:

$$(1) \qquad \Delta\left(\frac{S}{Y}\right) = \frac{\Delta S}{Y_r} - \left(\frac{S_u}{Y_u}\right)g,$$

where $g = \Delta Y / Y_r$. Letting ΔS^d = definitional and classificational revisions and ΔS^s = statistical revisions, and noting that $\Delta S = \Delta S^d + \Delta S^s$, equation (1) can be rewritten as:

$$(2) \qquad \Delta\left(\frac{S}{Y}\right) = \frac{\Delta S^d}{Y_r} + \frac{\Delta S^s}{Y_r} - \left(\frac{S_u}{Y_u}\right)g.$$

The numerators of the first two terms are the revisions shown in table 1.3. Table 1.4 shows all the terms in equation (2) under the "factors" heading as well as the total revisions in the ratios. The denominator change reflects the final term in the equation and is entered with a negative sign so the factors can be summed across to equal the total revisions in the ratios.

The decomposition gives an indication of how much of the revisions in the saving ratios was due to definitional and classificational revisions, how much to statistical revisions, and how much to revisions in the base of the ratios.[54] Because GNP, net national product, and disposable

Table 1.4   Sources of Revisions in Selected NIPA Saving Ratios (percentage points)

Year	Gross Saving Ratio[a]				Gross Private Saving Ratio[a]			
		Factors				Factors		
	Total Revision	Definitional and Classificational	Statistical	Denominator Change	Total Revision	Definitional and Classificational	Statistical	Denominator Change
1950	.5	.5	.2	-.1	.5	.5	.2	-.1
1955	0	.4	-.2	-.2	0	.4	-.2	-.2
1960	.3	.4	.2	-.3	.3	.4	.2	-.3
1965	.1	.3	.2	-.3	.1	.3	.2	-.3
1970	.2	.3	.3	-.3	.2	.3	.3	-.4
1971	.6	.3	.6	-.3	.6	.3	.6	-.4
1972	.8	.3	.8	-.3	.8	.3	.8	-.4
1973	.7	.3	.9	-.4	.8	.3	.9	-.4
1974	.9	.4	1.0	-.4	.9	.4	1.0	-.4
1975	.8	.3	.9	-.4	.8	.3	1.0	-.6
1976	.9	.3	1.1	-.5	.9	.3	1.2	-.6
1977	.8	.3	1.0	-.6	.8	.3	1.1	-.6
1978	.9	.4	1.1	-.7	.9	.4	1.2	-.7
1979	.8	.4	1.0	-.6	1.0	.4	1.1	-.6
1980	.9	.4	1.0	-.6	1.0	.4	1.2	-.6
1981	.7	.4	.9	-.5	.8	.4	1.0	-.5
1982	.8	.3	.9	-.4	.5	.3	.7	-.5
1983	.4	.3	.4	-.4	.1	.3	.3	-.5
1984	.1	.4	.2	-.4	-.5	.4	-.4	-.5

Year	Net Private Saving Ratio[b]					Personal Saving Rate[c]		
1950	.6	.2	.4	0	.3	.2	.1	0
1955	.2	.1	.2	-.1	-.3	.2	-.4	-.1
1960	.5	.1	.5	-.1	.2	.3	0	-.1
1965	.1	.1	.2	-.2	-.1	.1	0	-.2
1970	.4	.1	.5	-.2	.1	.1	.2	-.2
1971	.8	.1	.9	-.2	.4	.1	.6	-.3
1972	.9	.1	1.1	-.2	.8	.1	.9	-.2
1973	.9	0	1.2	-.2	.8	.1	1.0	-.3
1974	1.1	.1	1.3	-.2	.8	.1	1.0	-.3
1975	1.0	0	1.3	-.3	.6	.1	.8	-.4
1976	1.2	.1	1.4	-.3	.7	.1	1.0	-.3
1977	1.0	.1	1.1	-.3	.7	.1	.8	-.3
1978	1.1	.1	1.2	-.3	1.0	.2	1.2	-.3
1979	1.0	.1	1.1	-.3	.9	.2	1.1	-.3
1980	1.1	.1	1.2	-.2	1.1	.1	1.2	-.3
1981	.7	.1	.8	-.2	.8	.1	.9	-.3
1982	.2	0	.3	-.2	.6	.1	.7	-.2
1983	-.1	.1	0	-.2	.4	.1	.4	-.2
1984	-.5	.2	-.5	-.2	.2	.2	.3	-.2

Note: The revisions are measured as differences between estimates available when the July 1986 *Survey of Current Business* was published and those available when the November 1985 *Survey* was published.

[a]Percentage of gross national product.
[b]Percentage of net national product.
[c]Percentage of disposable personal income.

personal income were all generally revised upward, the denominator change factor contributed to downward revisions of the ratios in most years. The definitional and classificational revision factor contributed to upward revisions in all years shown, but the magnitudes in most years were considerably less than those related to statistical revisions. The statistical revision factor accounted for most of the revision in the ratios in most years.

In addition to statistical revisions that arise in connection with comprehensive revisions, BEA makes regular annual revisions in July of most years that generally are limited to statistical revisions. In these revisions, estimates for the most recent calendar year and the two preceding calendar years are revised.[55] After the third revision, the estimate for a given year is not revised again until a comprehensive revision. Table 1.5 shows the provisional estimates for 1980 and 1981 of selected NIPA saving measures as percentages of their value from the 1985 comprehensive revision.[56] The table also shows comparable estimates for other selected series related to the saving measures. The estimates have been adjusted to account for definitional and classificational revisions in order to isolate statistical revisions. Because the estimates from the comprehensive revision are better estimates of the true magnitude of the saving measure than the provisional estimates, the percentages show how close the provisional estimates came to the better estimates.

Most of the provisional estimates were less than the estimates from the comprehensive revision. The reasons for these level differences were discussed in connection with the comprehensive revision. Table 1.5 enables the determination of whether the provisional estimates move toward the comprehensive revision estimate through successive revisions. Generally, but not always, they do.[57] In both years, gross saving moved to within 5–6 percent of the comprehensive revision estimate but showed little further revision after the second July revision. Personal saving, capital consumption, and federal saving also moved toward the comprehensive revision estimate. By the third July revision, the federal estimate was almost identical to the comprehensive revision estimate. One saving measure did not fare as well. State and local government saving missed by larger amounts in several of the successive revisions.

The addenda items in the table show some of the major income and outlay items underlying personal saving. These items suggest that part of the reason personal saving moves toward the comprehensive revision estimate is that personal income moves toward its comprehensive revision estimate. This occurs in spite of misses by some of its smaller components.

Table 1.5 Comparison of Selected Provisional NIPA Saving Measures for 1980 and 1981 with Estimates from the 1985 Comprehensive Revision[a]

| | 1980 | | | | | 1981 | | | | |
| | Provisional Estimate as a Percent of Comprehensive Revision Estimate | | | | Comprehensive Revision Estimate (billions of dollars) | Provisional Estimate as a Percent of Comprehensive Revision Estimate | | | | Comprehensive Revision Estimate (billions of dollars) |
	March 1981	First July 1981	Second July 1982	Third July 1983		March 1982	First July 1982	Second July 1983	Third July 1984	
Gross saving	92.7	…	93.6	93.6	445.0	89.5	93.6	94.8	94.9	522.0
Gross private saving	92.7	…	93.8	93.2	478.4	89.3	93.7	94.6	94.7	550.5
Personal saving	76.0	…	79.6	82.5	136.9	69.1	83.2	86.4	87.8	159.4
Undistributed corporate profits[b]	117.5	…	103.2	85.1	37.7	118.3	102.8	103.7	97.9	43.2
Capital consumption allowances[c]	97.1	…	99.1	99.0	303.8	95.0	97.4	97.2	97.4	347.8
Government surplus or deficit (−)	93.3	…	96.2	89.0	−34.5	86.2	94.9	90.6	90.0	−29.7
Federal	99.8	…	100.2	99.8	−61.3	97.6	94.0	97.5	100.8	−63.8
State and local	108.6	…	105.2	114.2	26.8	107.6	93.0	103.5	110.3	34.1
Addenda:										
Net foreign investment	45.4	…	60.0	48.5	13.0	39.6	38.7	37.7	54.7	10.6
Personal income	96.9	…	96.9	97.1	2,258.5	96.6	97.1	97.9	97.6	2,520.9
Wages and salaries	97.9	…	98.8	98.9	1,372.0	98.2	98.9	98.9	98.9	1,510.3
Other labor income	99.1	…	91.9	92.5	138.4	102.5	93.4	95.5	93.1	150.3
Nonfarm proprietors income[b]	67.2	…	60.8	60.0	160.1	72.4	64.9	57.8	60.4	156.1
Personal interest income	93.7	…	96.3	97.3	271.9	91.6	97.7	101.4	98.5	335.4
Outlays	97.8	…	97.7	97.7	1,781.1	98.3	97.8	98.5	98.1	1,968.1
Personal consumption expenditures[b]	97.8	…	97.5	97.5	1,732.6	98.3	97.6	98.3	97.9	1,915.1
Corporate profits[b]	103.0	…	102.5	99.0	177.2	102.2	101.4	102.3	101.0	188.0

[a]Provisional estimates are adjusted for definitional and classificational revisions.
[b]With inventory value adjustments and capital consumption adjustments.
[c]With capital consumption adjustments.

1.3.3   An Assessment of the Revisions

Two important questions to consider in assessing revisions are, Were the revisions large enough to change the prior view of saving patterns? Did the revisions improve the analytic usefulness and quality of the measures? In response to the first question, the trends in current measures discussed earlier were essentially the same as those prior to the 1985 comprehensive revision. However, figure 1.3 did show some differences resulting mainly from revisions in personal saving. Specifically, the personal saving rate rose by considerably more in the early 1970s than had appeared to be the case in the prior estimates. The rate then fell considerably more from the early 1970s to the early 1980s. Consequently, the revised estimates did not differ in indicating direction, but they did differ considerably in magnitude. Because the magnitudes are of considerable importance, the size of the revisions implies that the measures must be used cautiously.

In response to the second question, it is useful to discuss definitional and classificational revisions and statistical revisions separately. The definitional and classificational revisions discussed earlier covered three comprehensive revisions. The incorporation in 1976 of economic capital consumption in place of tax-return-based depreciation clearly improved the analytic usefulness of the NIPAs. The revision provided a much clearer picture of the actual consumption of fixed capital than had been provided before. The other major definitional and classificational revisions affecting saving related to capitalizing items that had been treated as current purchases and to changing the treatment of various foreign transactions. In both cases, the revisions improved the consistency of treatments within the NIPAs. Further, many of these revisions were made to provide a more accurate reflection of what transactors view as investment. Consequently, these revisions improved the analytic usefulness of NIPA investment measures and the accompanying saving measures.

With respect to statistical revisions, new source data improve the quality of NIPA estimates because these new data provide more complete coverage and more detailed information. However, the major statistical revision in the 1985 comprehensive revision resulted from methodological changes concerning improved adjustments for misreporting on tax returns. The improved adjustments represent a significant improvement in NIPA coverage of underground economic activities. Although the initial introduction of these improved adjustments accounted for relatively large statistical revisions, future revisions to the adjustments are not likely to be large.

An evaluation of the improved adjustments is in Parker (1984a); several possible sources of error were discussed. The sources of error mainly concerned the unavailability of information to make additional adjustments, the unavailability of information to evaluate IRS findings on the degree of underreporting, assorted limitations with some of the data used, and limitations in extending the estimates to years not covered in the initial work. The evaluation concluded that the sign of the combined sources of error was indeterminate.

1.4   Limitations and Alternatives

NIPA saving measures and important conventions contributing to them have been criticized on a number of counts. Often, these criticisms are accompanied by suggestions for alternative measures. In this section, some of the criticisms and limitations are discussed along with some possible alternatives. Five groups of issues are discussed: extensions of the NIPA accounting framework, extensions of the NIPA production boundary, more consistent treatments with respect to pensions, current purchases versus capitalization, and adjustments and alternatives to government saving measures. There are obviously some overlaps among the five groups; these interrelations will be noted.

1.4.1   Extensions of the NIPA Accounting Framework

It has been noted that saving in the NIPAs is linked to NIPA concepts of current production, which, for example, exclude capital gains and losses. However, for many types of analyses, saving measures should take these gains or losses into account.[58] One way to address both realized and unrealized capital gains and losses is to develop national (including sector) balance sheets and to calculate changes in net worth.

The development of balance sheets that are entirely consistent with the NIPAs has been considered an important goal for many years.[59] However, at present, only estimates of fixed capital and inventories are available, and complete balance sheets have not been developed. To the extent that net worth and other balance sheet measures have important effects on saving behavior, NIPA saving measures are limited in their usefulness in some behavioral studies.

Others have done additional work on U.S. balance sheets. The work of the Board of Governors of the Federal Reserve System (1987), Ruggles and Ruggles (1982b, 1985), Goldsmith (1985), Eisner (1986), and others may be cited. In all cases, however, there are conceptual and statistical differences between these measures and those that would be entirely consistent with the NIPAs.[60]

Developing balance sheets for the household sector has been viewed as particularly important. The household sector balance sheets that have been constructed by others generally are not consistent with NIPA measures because of various sectoring, attribution, and classification differences. For example, the Ruggleses' integrated economic accounts (IEA) differ in the treatments of nonprofit institutions serving individuals, owner-occupied housing, pension fund attributions, and many other conventions (Ruggles and Ruggles 1982b). Consequently, the relation between IEA saving and changes in IEA household sector net worth may not be indicative of the relation between NIPA personal saving and the corresponding change in net worth from balance sheets entirely consistent with NIPA concepts and conventions. Nevertheless, it is interesting to note that capital gains accounted for about 80 percent of the change in the Ruggleses' household sector net worth measure during the 1947–80 period. In their measure, capital gains were calculated on owner-occupied houses, land, consumer durables, corporate stock, and other equities.

In a recent study by Peek (1986), it is suggested that NIPA personal saving has been a poor indicator of changes in household net worth. Specifically, the declines in the personal saving rate noted earlier were offset by capital gains. If households are primarily concerned about their levels of net worth, then NIPA personal saving is only part of the picture. Because changes in the NIPA personal saving rate may reflect only offsetting changes in capital gains or losses rather than significant changes in desired wealth accumulation, it may be appropriate for BEA to extend the NIPA accounting framework to include balance sheets and estimates of net worth. Unfortunately, there are major data limitations associated with such a project. Additional comments on limitations in NIPA saving measures related to extensions of the accounting framework are provided later in connection with adjustments to government saving measures.

1.4.2 Extensions of the NIPA Production Boundary

There have been numerous criticisms of the present NIPA production boundary and many suggestions for changes. Nearly all extensions would involve some effects on NIPA saving measures, but the magnitudes (even the signs in some cases) are often difficult to determine. Two extensions are discussed briefly below: more extensive coverage of nonmarket activity and the inclusion of illegal activity.

The extension of the NIPA production boundary to include a broader range of nonmarket activities primarily focuses on the household sector and is mainly suggested to improve the NIPAs as measures of economic welfare (Juster 1973; Eisner 1985).[61] The suggested extensions involve imputations of the value of various types of activities. Among the most important are the value of housework and do-it-yourself work. Incorporating these types of imputations would increase aggregate income and outlays equally and have no effect on the level of gross saving. However, the gross saving rate would be reduced. In estimates by Kendrick (1979), these nonmarket activities were valued at about one-fourth of NIPA GNP. Consequently, a saving rate with such expanded GNP in the denominator would be reduced significantly.

The criticisms of adding these types of imputations center on the obvious distortions to the NIPAs as measures of market activity and on the lack of agreement on the statistical procedures to measure non-market activities (Okun 1971; Jaszi 1971). With respect to saving measures, the extension of the production boundary to include these types of activities would make saving rates much more difficult to interpret.

In addition to these imputations, it has been suggested that some expenditures that are now treated as current purchases should be capitalized and an imputed flow of services could be attributed to them. Consumer durable goods are frequently mentioned for this treatment. This change would increase gross saving and is discussed later in connection with current purchases versus capitalization.

Because illegal activities have grown in importance, the extension of the production boundary to include them has been discussed (Adler 1982; Carson 1984a, 1984b). The activities that are viewed as potentially large include trade in narcotics, prostitution, and gambling. Reliable source data on these activities are not available; consequently, estimates of the level of illegal income and outlays are extremely speculative. Based on a survey of studies by Carson (1984a), illegal source income was estimated to be equivalent to 1–7 percent of GNP.

The effects on NIPA saving measures of including illegal activities are not clear. It has been suggested that NIPA personal saving is understated because of the exclusion of illegal activities, but it is more likely that the level of NIPA saving is unaffected.[62] If income were reported in laundered form (e.g., a prostitute reporting part of illegal income as modeling fees on IRS schedule C), then NIPA income could include some of the illegal income. However, in this case, the estimate of PCE for services relies on the same source data and would be misstated by the same amount. It is more likely that both income and outlays for illegal activities are not recorded. In these cases, income and outlays probably would be increased by equal amounts leaving the level of saving unchanged.

Under scenarios in which the level of saving remains unchanged, saving rates would unambiguously decline with the inclusion of illegal activities because the denominators of the ratios would increase. Under a scenario in which the level of saving increases, the saving rate may not increase if the accompanying increases in the denominator are large enough.

1.4.3   More Consistent Treatments with Respect to Pensions

It was noted earlier that pension funds play important roles in NIPA saving measures and that public and private pension funds are treated differently. While social security is dissimilar to private pension funds in many respects, state and local government pension funds and private pension funds are more similar. For this reason, NIPA private saving measures have sometimes been criticized for excluding state and local government pension fund saving, which could be attributed to persons.[63] This treatment would change personal saving and government saving by equal amounts with opposite signs. Disposable personal income would change by an amount equal to the change in personal saving. Gross saving would not be affected. The adjustments to personal saving are shown in equation (3); they do not make changes to the treatment of operating expenses:[64]

$$(3) \qquad \Delta PS = EC + PC + DIV + INT - TP,$$

where

ΔPS = the change in personal saving associated with attributing state and local government pension fund saving to persons;

EC = employer contributions for state and local government employee retirement;

PC = personal contributions for state and local government employee retirement;

DIV = dividends received by state and local government pension funds;

INT = interest earnings received by state and local government pension funds; and

TP = transfer payments to persons from state and local government pension funds.

Table 1.6 shows estimates of the effects on personal saving and personal saving rates. In addition to the state and local government pension attribution, the table also shows a similar attribution of federal civilian pension fund saving.[65] The same operations in equation (3) are used for the federal estimates by substituting "federal" for "state and local" in the descriptions of the variables and omitting the DIV term. The attribution of state and local and selected federal pension fund saving to persons would increase personal saving by about $58 billion in 1985 and result in an increase in the personal saving rate of about 1.9 percentage points.

Figure 1.4 shows estimates of the personal saving rate after attributing selected government pension fund saving to persons. In most years, the state and local attribution accounts for all but about

Table 1.6   Effects of Attributing Saving of Selected Government Pension Funds to Persons

Year	Adjustment to Personal Saving Resulting from the Attribution[a] (billions of dollars)			Personal Saving as a Percentage of Disposable Personal Income after the Attribution[a]			Currently Published Personal Saving as a Percentage of Disposable Personal Income
	Combined Government Pension Funds	State and Local Government Pension Funds	Federal Pension Funds	Combined Government Pension Funds	State and Local Government Pension Funds	Federal Pension Funds	
1960	3.2	2.3	1.0	6.6	6.4	6.1	5.8
1961	3.5	2.5	1.0	7.5	7.3	6.9	6.6
1962	3.7	2.6	1.1	7.4	7.2	6.8	6.5
1963	4.0	2.8	1.1	6.8	6.6	6.2	5.9
1964	4.4	3.2	1.3	7.9	7.6	7.2	7.0
1965	4.6	3.4	1.2	7.9	7.7	7.3	7.0
1966	5.1	3.9	1.1	7.7	7.5	7.0	6.8
1967	6.0	4.8	1.2	9.0	8.8	8.2	8.0
1968	6.5	5.2	1.3	8.0	7.8	7.2	7.0
1969	7.3	5.8	1.5	7.5	7.2	6.6	6.4
1970	9.1	6.9	2.2	9.2	8.9	8.3	8.1
1971	9.9	7.5	2.4	9.7	9.4	8.8	8.5
1972	11.0	8.6	2.4	8.5	8.2	7.6	7.3
1973	11.6	9.5	2.1	10.5	10.3	9.6	9.4

(*continued*)

Table 1.6 (continued)

Year	Adjustment to Personal Saving Resulting from the Attribution[a] (billions of dollars)			Personal Saving as a Percentage of Disposable Personal Income after the Attribution[a]			Currently Published Personal Saving as a Percentage of Disposable Personal Income
	Combined Government Pension Funds	State and Local Government Pension Funds	Federal Pension Funds	Combined Government Pension Funds	State and Local Government Pension Funds	Federal Pension Funds	
1974	12.7	10.8	1.9	10.4	10.2	9.5	9.3
1975	14.4	12.8	1.6	10.3	10.2	9.3	9.2
1976	16.8	15.2	1.5	8.9	8.8	7.8	7.6
1977	18.5	17.2	1.3	7.8	7.7	6.7	6.6
1978	20.2	19.0	1.1	8.3	8.2	7.2	7.1
1979	24.0	22.3	1.8	8.1	8.0	6.9	6.8
1980	27.2	26.0	1.2	8.4	8.0	7.2	7.1
1981	30.2	29.0	1.1	8.8	8.4	7.2	7.5
1982	38.1	36.1	2.0	8.4	8.7	7.5	6.8
1983	45.3	42.4	3.0	7.1	8.3	6.9	5.4
1984	52.7	48.1	4.6	8.1	7.0	5.5	6.3
1985	58.0	51.6	6.4	7.0	8.0	6.5	5.1

Note: Selected government pension funds consist primarily of civilian government employee retirement funds.
[a]Does not include an adjustment for administrative expenses, which would slightly lower the attribution.

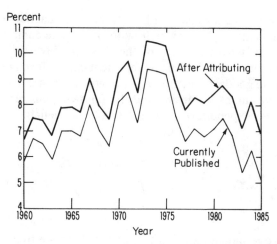

Fig. 1.4   Personal savings as a percentage of disposable personal income, currently published and after attributing saving of selected government pension fund to persons. *Note:* Selected government pension funds primarily consist of civilian government employee retirement funds.

0.1–0.2 percentage points of the difference between the currently published rate and the rate after attributing the pension fund saving. After the attribution, most of the short-term patterns of the personal saving rate would remain the same as those of the currently published rate because state and local pension fund saving has grown smoothly. For this reason, however, the trends over longer periods differ somewhat. The decline since the mid-1970s in the modified rate is a little less pronounced. Consequently, to the extent that state and local pension funds are viewed by the employees in the same way as private pension funds, the decline in personal saving may be less pronounced than the current measures suggest.

1.4.4   Current Purchases versus Capitalization

NIPA saving measures have often been criticized on the ground that they underestimate saving by classifying some purchases that reflect investment as current purchases. Some critics have suggested very broad views of what constitutes investment. Such things as research and development, education, and health care are mentioned (Hawrylyshyn 1974; Eisner 1985). If such items were capitalized, NIPA saving would rise very substantially. For example, Eisner (1985) estimated gross investment in these three items alone at about $850 billion in 1981—considerably more than published NIPA gross saving in that year. However, there are numerous problems with such a broad view of investment (Jaszi 1971, 1973). One of the most important problems is that there is no consensus on how to measure capital consumption or other elements of the service flow for intangible capital.

A somewhat narrower view of the scope of investment is that it should be broadened to include government capital formation and consumer durable goods.[66] The treatment of government capital formation as NIPA investment would involve the following changes to government receipts, expenditures, and the surplus or deficit:[67]

$$\text{(4)} \qquad E^* = E - I_g + V_g - M_g,$$

$$\text{(5)} \qquad R^* = R + V_g - M_g - D_g,$$

$$\text{(6)} \qquad \text{SU}^* = R - E + I_g - D_g,$$

where

E^* = government expenditures adjusted for the treatment of government capital formation as NIPA investment;

E = current government expenditures;

I_g = government investment;

V_g = service value of government capital;

M_g = expenditures for maintenance and repair of government capital;

D_g = capital consumption of government capital;

R^* = government receipts adjusted for the treatment of government capital formation as NIPA investment;

R = current government receipts; and

SU^* = government surplus or deficit adjusted for the treatment of government capital formation as NIPA investment.

Gross saving would change by the amount classified as NIPA investment (I_g), and GNP would change by the difference between service value (V_g) and maintenance and repair expenditures (M_g).

The treatment of consumer durable goods would be analogous:[68]

$$\text{(7)} \qquad \text{DPI}^* = \text{DPI} + V_c - M_c - i_c - D_c,$$

$$\text{(8)} \qquad O^* = O - I_c + V_c - M_c - i_c,$$

$$\text{(9)} \qquad \text{PS}^* = \text{DPI} - O + I_c - D_c,$$

where

DPI^* = disposable personal income adjusted for the treatment of consumer durable goods as NIPA investment;

DPI = current disposable personal income;

V_c = service value of consumer durable goods;

M_c = expenditures for maintenance and repair of consumer durable goods;

i_c = interest paid on credit-financed consumer durable goods;

D_c = capital consumption of consumer durable goods;

O^* = outlays adjusted for the treatment of consumer durable goods as NIPA investment;

O = current outlays;

I_c = investment in consumer durable goods; and

PS^* = personal saving adjusted for the treatment of consumer durable goods as NIPA investment.

Gross saving would change by the amount classified as NIPA investment (I_c), and GNP would change by the difference between service value (V_c) and maintenance and repair expenditures (M_c).

For both government capital and consumer durable goods, estimates of capital consumption are regularly produced by the BEA (Musgrave 1979, 1980, 1986a, 1986b). The service value of government capital (Martin, Landefeld, and Peskin 1982) and of consumer durable goods (Katz 1982) was estimated annually for 1947–79 but is not regularly updated. It is widely recognized that measures of capital consumption and service value for these types of capital are extremely difficult to estimate.

Figure 1.5 shows current saving ratios and saving ratios adjusted for government and consumer durables capitalization.[69] The top two panels show the effects of modifying the treatment of government capital. The top panel shows the government surplus or deficit as a percentage of GNP. The effect of the modified treatment is to move the government saving ratio toward surplus. The movements are especially pronounced during the 1960s. The differences between the gross saving ratios in the middle panel show patterns similar to the differences between the surplus/deficit ratios. The differences become much more narrow toward the end of the period.

The bottom panel of the chart shows the effects of modifying the treatment of consumer durable goods. In most years, the modified personal saving rate is one or more percentage points higher than the currently published rate. The largest differences occur during the early part of the period, when the net stock of consumer durables was growing rapidly.

1.4.5 Adjustments and Alternatives to Government Saving Measures

Unlike other components of gross saving, NIPA government saving measures are unique in that they are often used as indicators of fiscal policy. It is in the context of this use that adjustments to the government saving measures are often suggested. The federal surplus or deficit, in particular, is the focus of most of the attention. Some of the major

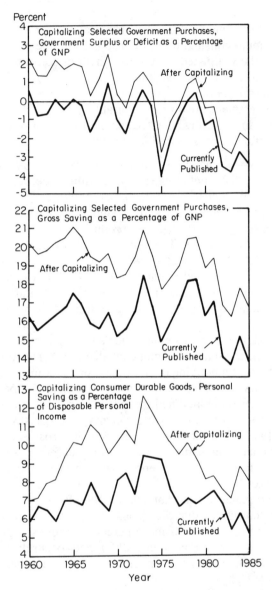

Fig. 1.5 Selected NIPA saving measures, currently published and after capitalizing selected government purchases or consumer durable goods

criticisms concern the cyclical sensitivity of the federal measure, the failure of the federal measure to distinguish between current and capital transactions, the failure of the federal measure to treat the effects of inflation properly, and the failure of the federal measure to include estimates of federal unfunded liabilities (Boskin 1982; Eisner and Pieper 1984; Boskin 1986; Eisner 1986). In many of these cases, the criticisms concern analytic uses of the NIPA measures rather than the measures themselves.

The cyclical sensitivity of the NIPA federal surplus or deficit undermines its usefulness as an indicator of discretionary fiscal policy. The reason is that many of its changes reflect automatic responses to economic fluctuations rather than budget decisions. To overcome this limitation, the cyclically adjusted budget was developed.[70] The cyclically adjusted budget removes automatic cyclical effects from the NIPA federal budget estimates. The resulting cyclically adjusted estimates are regularly published by BEA. Figure 1.6 shows actual and cyclically adjusted estimates of the federal surplus or deficit-to-GNP ratios.[71] The cyclically adjusted measure dampens the variation in the ratio during most of the period but does not have much effect on the trends. A particularly important point is that very little of the rising deficit-to-GNP ratio in the 1980s could be attributed to the business cycle.

The cyclically adjusted budget does not address some of the other criticisms. BEA's decision not to treat government capital formation

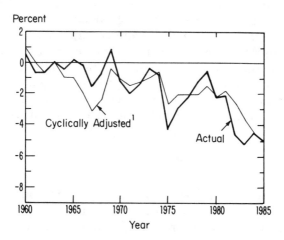

Fig. 1.6   Actual and cyclically adjusted NIPA federal surplus or deficit as a percentage of GNP. [1]Cyclically adjusted federal surplus or deficit as a percentage of middle-expansion trend GNP.

as investment is an example. The other criticisms mentioned relate mainly to limitations in coverage or accounting procedures. Boskin (1982) argued that alternative measures should address unfunded liabilities of social insurance funds, federal loan guarantees, and other items related to future spending commitments. Further, federal balance sheet concepts, such as revaluations of land and mineral rights, can have important policy effects and should be incorporated into federal fiscal measures.

Eisner and Pieper (1984) and Eisner (1986) have suggested that changes in the real value of federal net debt provide a more analytically meaningful view of the effects of fiscal policy than either the actual or the cyclically adjusted federal surplus or deficit. Their measures rely on balance sheet concepts and adjust outstanding federal debt from par to market, from gross to net, and from nominal to real debt. They point out that their measures suggest that federal fiscal policy was much less stimulative during the late 1970s and early 1980s than NIPA saving measures would suggest. Their measures show strong stimulus after 1982.

Along the same lines of research, BEA regularly publishes estimates of cyclically adjusted debt at par value and at market value (de Leeuw and Holloway 1983). In many respects, changes in the cyclically adjusted debt-to-GNP ratio provide the same type of information as the Eisner-Pieper work. The BEA estimates have indicated strong fiscal stimulus in recent years.

In addition to the alternative federal measures estimated by BEA, an alternative state and local measure is also prepared (Levin 1984, 1986). The alternative measure attempts to adjust the NIPA state and local surplus or deficit to reflect more closely what a state or local government finance officer would view as the combined general and special funds surplus or deficit. The alternative measure adjusts the NIPA state and local surplus or deficit by excluding social insurance fund transactions, excluding capital expenditures except those funded from current receipts, and including financial transactions.

1.5   Concluding Remarks

NIPA saving measures are part of a broader economic accounting framework that is primarily designed to measure current production and to show the economic processes associated with the production, distribution, and use of the nation's output. Consequently, NIPA saving measures are shaped by many concepts and conventions governing the broader accounting framework. Within this broader framework, NIPA saving measures show the level and composition of gross saving that frees resources for NIPA gross investment. While such estimates of saving have proven to be highly useful, there are a number of limitations, and, as a result, the estimates have been subject to much criticism.

Some criticisms or possible alternatives, such as those related to inadequate coverage of nonmarket or illegal activities, are directed at the broader NIPA framework and not at saving measures per se. Responding to these criticisms would require significant changes to many entries throughout the NIPAs.

Other criticisms or possible alternatives, such as those related to attributions of pension fund activities or reclassifications of current purchases as investment, focus mainly on how to attribute saving among sectors or what constitutes saving and investment. Responding to these criticisms would require mainly rearranging the present NIPAs and possibly adding a few new entries. However, in some cases, the resulting NIPA measures of output and investment would probably be less useful for analyzing short-run developments in the economy.

Finally, some criticisms or possible alternatives, such as those related to balance sheets or the cyclical sensitivity of government saving measures, focus mainly on extensions, but not alterations, of the present NIPA framework or measures. Responding to these criticisms would require mainly producing additional measures.

Because most of these criticisms or suggested alternatives arise in connection with various analytic uses of NIPA saving measures, it is obvious that present NIPA measures are not appropriate for all uses. Perhaps BEA should respond to these concerns by both emphasizing the limitations of the measures and providing alternative measures as supplements to the present measures. Because alternative uses call for alternative saving measures, it would be desirable for BEA to publish several variant saving measures regularly. Obvious candidates would include variants that treat consumer durables and government capital as investment. Because of uncertainty surrounding the estimation of these variants (e.g., the estimation of the service value of these types of purchases), it would be appropriate to show these variants in special tables rather than integrating them into the NIPAs. This, of course, is the current method of presenting the cyclically adjusted budget and some of the other government saving variants.

With respect to the treatment of government pension funds, perhaps something more would be appropriate. It has been noted that several government pension funds, particularly those administered by state and local governments, are extremely similar to private pension funds whose earnings are attributed to persons. It would be desirable to make additional attributions, at least for the state and local government funds, a part of regular NIPA estimates. The change in treatment could be made as part of the 1990 comprehensive revision.

Appendix A
Summary NIPAs, 1985

The five-account summary, discussed briefly in the main text and accompanying footnotes, provides an overview of the NIPA accounting framework and serves as an organizing framework for more detailed estimates. Table 1.A.1 shows the accounts. The interrelations among the accounts are shown by the parenthetical numbers following individual items. These numbers reflect the location of counterentries elsewhere in the five-account summary.

The role of the five-account summary as an organizing framework for more detailed estimates can be illustrated by example. Account 2 shows personal income and outlays. In the *Survey of Current Business,* NIPA table 2.1 shows a slight variant of account 2; other NIPA tables beginning with "2" provide additional variants or more detailed estimates related to personal income and outlays. In the July 1986 *Survey,* that amounted to nine tables. Complete discussions of the five-account summary are in Jaszi and Carson (1979), Carson and Jaszi (1981), Young and Tice (1985), and Bureau of Economic Analysis (1985b).

Appendix B
Notes on Sources and Methods
Underlying NIPA Saving Measures

The most important components of gross saving are personal saving, undistributed corporate profits with IVA and CCAdj, capital consumption, and the government surplus or deficit. The other measures of saving discussed earlier are simply combinations of these components. To complete the saving picture, net foreign investment also plays an important role for the reasons discussed earlier. The sources and methods underlying these saving and investment measures are discussed in turn.

The components of personal income and outlays underlying personal saving are shown in Appendix A, NIPA summary account 2.[72] On the outlay side, the two largest entries are PCE and personal tax and nontax payments. On the income side, wages and salaries is the largest entry. Other relatively large entries are other labor income, proprietors' income with IVA and CCAdj, personal interest income, and transfer payments. Personal contributions for social insurance is also a relatively large entry that is deducted on the income side.

Annual estimates of these components depend on a large number of data sources. Table 1.B.1 shows some of the major data sources used

Table 1.A.1   Summary NIPAs, 1985

Account 1—NIPA (billions of dollars)

Line			Line		
1	Compensation of employees	2,368.2	27	Personal consumption expenditures (2–3)	2,600.5
2	Wage and salaries	1,965.8	28	Durable goods	359.3
3	Disbursements (2–7)	1,966.1	29	Nondurable goods	905.1
4	Wage accruals less disbursements (3–12) and (5–4)	–.2	30	Services	1,336.1
5	Supplements to wages and salaries	402.4	31	Gross private domestic investment (5–1)	661.1
6	Employer contributions for social insurance (3–20)	205.5	32	Fixed investment	650.0
7	Other labor income (2–8)	196.9	33	Nonresidential	458.2
8	Proprietors' income with inventory valuation and capital consumption adjustments (2–9)	254.4	34	Structures	154.8
			35	Producers' durable equipment	303.4
9	Rental income of persons with capital consumption adjustment (2–10)	7.6	36	Residential	191.8
			37	Change in business inventories	11.1
10	Corporate profits with inventory valuation and capital consumption adjustments	280.7	38	Net exports of goods and services	–78.9
			39	Exports (4–1)	369.8
11	Profits before tax	223.2	40	Imports (4–3)	448.6

(continued)

Table 1.A.1 (continued)

12	Profits tax liability (3–17)	91.8	41	Government purchases of goods and services (3–1)	815.4
13	Profits after tax	131.4	42	Federal	354.1
14	Dividends (2–12)	81.6	43	National defense	259.4
15	Undistributed profits (5–6)	49.8	44	Nondefense	94.7
16	Inventory valuation adjustment (5–7)	–.6	45	State and local	461.3
17	Capital consumption adjustment (5–8)	58.1			
18	Net interest (2–15)	311.4			
19	National income	3,222.3			
20	Business transfer payments (2–20)	20.9			
21	Indirect business tax and nontax liability (3–18)	331.4			
22	Less subsidies less current surplus of government enterprises (3–11)	8.2			
23	Charges against net national product	3,566.5			
24	Capital consumption allowances with capital consumption adjustment (5–9)	437.2			
25	Charges against gross national product	4,003.7			
26	Statistical discrepancy (5–12)	–5.5			
	Gross National Product	3,998.1		Gross national product	3,998.1

Account 2—Personal Income and Outlay Account (billions of dollars)

Line			Line		
1	Personal tax and nontax payments (3–16)	486.5	7	Wage and salary disbursements (1–3)	1,966.1
2	Personal outlays	2,684.7	8	Other labor income (1–7)	196.9
3	Personal consumption expenditures (1–27)	2,600.5	9	Proprietors' income with inventory valuation and capital consumption adjustments (1–8)	254.4
4	Interest paid by consumers to business (2–18)	82.6	10	Rental income of persons with capital consumption adjustment (1–9)	7.6
5	Personal transfer payments to foreigners (net) (4–5)	1.6	11	Personal dividend income	76.4
6	Personal saving (5–3)	143.3	12	Dividends (1–14)	81.6
			13	Less dividends received by government (3–10)	5.2
			14	Personal interest income	476.2
			15	Net interest (1–18)	311.4
			16	Interest paid by government to persons and business (3–7)	173.4
			17	Less interest received by government (3–9)	91.1
			18	Interest paid by consumers to business (2–4)	82.6
			19	Transfer payments to persons	487.1
			20	From business (1–20)	20.9
			21	From government (3–3)	466.2
			22	Less personal contributions for social insurance (3–21)	150.2
	Personal taxes, outlays, and saving	3,314.5		Personal income	3,314.5

(continued)

Table 1.A.1 (continued)

Account 3—Government Receipts and Expenditures Account (billions of dollars)

Line			Line		
1	Purchases of goods and services (1–41)	815.4	16	Personal tax and nontax payments (2–1)	486.5
2	Transfer payments	479.5	17	Corporate profits tax liability (1–12)	91.8
3	To persons (2–21)	466.2	18	Indirect business tax and nontax liability (1–21)	331.4
4	To foreigners (net) (4–6)	13.4	19	Contributions for social insurance	355.7
5	Net interest paid	103.6	20	Employer (1–6)	205.5
6	Interest paid	194.7	21	Personal (2–22)	150.2
7	To persons and business (2–16)	173.4			
8	To foreigners (4–7)	21.3			
9	Less interest received by government (2–17)	91.1			
10	Less dividends received by government (2–13)	5.2			
11	Subsidies less current surplus of government enterprises (1–22)	8.2			
12	Less wage accruals less disbursements (1–4)	–.2			
13	Surplus or deficit (–), NIPAs (5–10)	–136.3			
14	Federal	–198.0			
15	State and local	61.7			
	Government expenditures and surplus	1,265.4		Government receipts	1,265.4

Account 4—Foreign Transactions Account (billions of dollars)

Line			Line		
1	Exports of goods and services (1–39)	369.8	3	Imports of goods and services (1–40)	448.6
2	Capital grants received by the United States (net) (5–11)	0	4	Transfer payments to foreigners (net)	15.0
			5	From persons (net) (2–5)	1.6
			6	From government (net) (3–4)	13.4
			7	Interest paid by government to foreigners (3–8)	21.3
			8	Net foreign investment (5–2)	−115.2
	Receipts from foreigners	369.8		Payments to foreigners	369.8

Account 5—Gross Saving and Investment Account (billions of dollars)

Line			Line		
1	Gross private domestic investment (1–31)	661.1	3	Personal saving (2–6)	143.3
2	Net foreign investment (4–8)	−115.2	4	Wage accruals less disbursements (1–4)	0
			5	Undistributed corporate profits with inventory valuation and capital consumption adjustments	107.3
			6	Undistributed corporate profits (1–15)	49.8
			7	Inventory valuation adjustment (1–16)	−.6
			8	Capital consumption adjustment (1–17)	58.1
			9	Capital consumption allowances with capital consumption adjustment (1–24)	437.2
			10	Government surplus or deficit (−), NIPA (3–13)	−136.3
			11	Capital grants received by the United States (net) (4–2)	0
			12	Statistical discrepancy (1–26)	−5.5
	Gross investment	545.9		Gross saving and statistical discrepancy	545.9

Note: Numbers in parentheses indicate accounts and items of counterentry in the accounts. For example, the counterentry for wage and salary disbursements (2–7) is in account 2, line 7.

Table 1.B.1   Selected Source Data for Current-Dollar Estimates, 1983–85

Source Data	Personal Consumption Expenditures		Wages and Salaries	Other Labor Income	Proprietors' Income[a]	
	Goods	Services			Farm	Nonfarm
Census Bureau annual surveys of merchant wholesale and retail trade	1983–84[r]	...	...	...	...	...
Census Bureau annual survey of services	...	1983–84[r], 1985	...	...	...	1985
Internal Revenue Service tabulations of business tax returns:						
Corporations	...	1983	...	1983	...	...
Sole proprietorships and partnerships	...	1984	...	1984	...	1984
Census Bureau value of new construction put in place	...	...	...	...	...	1985[r]
Census Bureau annual survey of manufacturers	...	...	...	...	...	...
U.S. Department of Agriculture farm statistics	1983–85[r]	1983–85[r]	1983–85[r]	...	1983–85[r]	...

Bureau of Economic Analysis U.S. international transactions accounts	1983–85r	1983–85r	1983–85r	...	...
Office of Management and Budget federal budget data	...	...	1985	...	...
Census Bureau surveys of state and local government	...	...	...	...	...
Bureau of Labor Statistics tabulations of employees covered by state unemployment insurance	...	1983–84r, 1985	1983–84r, 1985	...	...
Bureau of Economic Analysis capital stock statistics	...	...	...	1983–85r	1983–85r

Note: Years shown are the years of the estimates into which the source data are directly incorporated; r = revised.

[a] With inventory valuation adjustments and capital consumption adjustments.

[b] With capital consumption adjustments.

(continued)

Table 1.B.1 (continued)

	Personal Interest Income	Corporate Profits[a]	Capital Consumption Allowances[b]	Government Expenditures Federal	Government Expenditures State and Local	Government Receipts Federal	Government Receipts State and Local
Census Bureau annual surveys of merchant wholesale and retail trade	...	...	...	...	...	...	...
Census Bureau annual survey of services	...	...	...	...	...	...	...
Internal Revenue Service tabulations of business tax returns:							
Corporations	1983	1983	1983	...	...	1983	...
Sole proprietorships and partnerships	1984	...	1984	...	...	...	...
Census Bureau value of new construction put in place	...	...	...	...	1985r	...	...
Census Bureau annual survey of manufacturers	...	...	...	...	...	...	...
U.S. Department of Agriculture farm statistics	1983–85r	...	...	...	...	...	...
Bureau of Economic Analysis U.S. international transactions accounts	1983–85r	1983–85r	...	...	...	1983–85r	...
Office of Management and Budget federal budget data	1984r, 1985	...	...	1984r, 1985	...	1984r, 1985	...
Census Bureau surveys of state and local government	1983–84	...	...	...	1983r, 1984–85	...	1983r, 1984–85
Bureau of Labor Statistics tabulation of employees covered by state unemployment insurance	...	...	...	...	1984r, 1985	...	...
Bureau of Economic Analysis capital stock statistics	...	1983–85r	1983–85r	...	...	...	...

to derive selected components of personal income and outlays; it also shows data sources used to derive other selected NIPA measures discussed later.[73] The table indicates the years for which source data available in July 1986 were used. As the table shows, many of these source data are subject to revision and involve reporting lags. Consequently, BEA estimates based on these data must also be revised periodically to incorporate revisions in the source data.

For PCE, the annual data sources in table 1.B.1 are used to extrapolate benchmark estimates. The PCE benchmark estimates are based on the final demand category of BEA's most current benchmark input-output tables. The input-output tables, in turn, are based primarily on the detailed industry statistics available in the economic censuses.[74] The BEA 1977 input-output table is the most current and was incorporated into NIPA estimates during the 1985 comprehensive revision.

For personal tax and nontax payments, the annual federal estimates are derived mainly from Treasury data on collections of withheld federal income taxes and Federal Insurance Contribution Act (FICA) payments.[75] Estimates of FICA payments are netted. The FICA estimates are derived using Social Security Administration estimates of wages subject to FICA coverage and applying appropriate tax rates. The annual state and local estimates are based on quarterly Census Bureau data on tax collections.[76]

For wages and salaries, the annual estimates are based mainly on quarterly BLS compilations of wages and salaries reported by employers covered under state unemployment insurance tax programs.[77] Federal employee wage and salaries estimates are not available from this source. They are derived mainly from Office of Personnel Management payroll data.

For other labor income, the data sources vary with the items included. The main items are employer contributions to private pensions, to health insurance, and to life insurance. Annual estimates of contributions to private pensions are based mainly on IRS tabulations of the tax returns of sole proprietorships, partnerships, and corporations.[78] Annual estimates of contributions to health insurance funds are derived mainly from data on premiums provided by Blue Cross/Blue Shield, the Health Insurance Association of America, and the Department of Health and Human Services. Annual estimates of contributions to life insurance funds are derived mainly from data on premiums provided by the American Council of Life Insurance and by the Department of Health and Human Services.

For proprietors' income with IVA and CCAdj, annual estimates are based primarily on IRS tabulations of the tax returns of sole proprietorships and partnerships. Because it is recognized that there is significant underreporting of income on these tax returns, adjustments for underreporting are made in estimating nonfarm proprietors' income. These adjustments are developed by BEA primarily on the basis of IRS audit results.

For personal interest income, annual estimates are derived indirectly using a number of interest flows.[79] The estimates are based primarily on IRS tabulations from tax returns of interest paid and received by sole proprietorships, partnerships, and corporations. Additional sources include Treasury data on federal interest paid, federal budget data on federal interest received, census data on state and local government interest paid and received, and IRS and Labor Department data on interest received by private noninsured pension funds.[80] Interest paid by consumers to business is derived primarily by multiplying Federal Reserve data on outstanding consumer credit by BEA estimates of effective interest rates.[81]

For transfer payments, annual estimates of government transfer payments are based primarily on federal budget data, Treasury data, and data from agencies administering the programs, such as the Social Security Administration for part of social security benefits. Annual estimates of business transfer payments are based primarily on insurance industry data and IRS tax return data.

For personal contributions for social insurance, annual estimates for most of the federal component are derived in the same way as employer contributions discussed in connection with personal tax and nontax payments. These estimates depend mainly on Social Security Administration data on taxable wages. The state and local government component estimates are derived mainly from census data on retirement programs and BLS data on disability programs.[82]

Undistributed corporate profits with IVA and CCAdj is the sum of (1) profits before tax less profits tax liability less dividends, (2) the corporate IVA, and (3) the corporate CCAdj. These entries are part of charges against GNP shown in Appendix A, NIPA summary account 1.[83] For the profits, taxes, and dividends entries, annual estimates are based primarily on IRS tabulations of the tax returns of corporations. Annual estimates also depend partly on Federal Reserve data on the net earnings of Federal Reserve banks, census data on state and local corporate profits tax liability, and BEA balance of payments accounts data on rest-of-the-world profits.[84] Like the proprietors' income estimates, the tax return data are adjusted by BEA for underreporting on the basis of IRS audit results.

The corporate IVA estimates are based primarily on census data on manufacturing and trade inventories and BLS producer price index data on commodity prices.[85] The corporate CCAdj estimates are derived primarily using IRS tabulations of tax return depreciation and economic depreciation derived from BEA perpetual inventory method calculations of the capital stock.[86]

Capital consumption appears as part of charges against GNP.[87] The annual estimates are based primarily on the same sources as those discussed in connection with the corporate CCAdj.

The components of receipts and expenditures underlying the government surplus or deficit are shown in Appendix A, NIPA summary account 3. On the expenditures side, the two largest entries are purchases of goods and services and transfer payments. On the receipts side, the three largest entries are personal tax and nontax payments, indirect business taxes, and contributions for social insurance. Only purchases and indirect business taxes have not yet been discussed.

Annual estimates of federal purchases of goods and services, like those for federal transfer payments, are based primarily on federal budget data, Treasury data, and data from agencies concerning their operations.[88] The annual estimates of state and local government purchases are based primarily on census compilations of state and local budget data.

Annual estimates of federal indirect business taxes are based on collections data tabulated by IRS. Annual estimates of state and local government indirect business taxes are based largely on census data.

Net foreign investment appears as part of payments to foreigners in Appendix A, NIPA summary account 4.[89] Annual estimates of net foreign investment are based mainly on census data on merchandise trade and BEA surveys of direct foreign investment income and other services. BEA balance of payments accounts data and Treasury data on international capital flows are also used.

Notes

1. A recent example of a policy discussion involving NIPA saving measures is in Council of Economic Advisers (1986, 46–52).

2. Definitions of some of the components in NIPA table 5.1 and some additional notes about them are provided below (Bureau of Economic Analysis 1986a). The components of gross private saving are defined as follows. Personal saving is "personal income less the sum of personal outlays and of personal tax and nontax payments. It is current saving of individuals (including proprietors), nonprofit institutions serving individuals, private noninsured welfare funds, and private trust funds" (xii).

Undistributed corporate profits with IVA and CCAdj consists of three separate elements: undistributed corporate profits, IVA, and CCAdj. Undistributed corporate profits is corporate profits before tax—sometimes referred to as "book profits"—less corporate profits tax liability less dividends. IVA for corporations is "the difference between the cost of inventory withdrawals as valued in determining profits before tax and the cost of withdrawals valued at current replacement cost" (x). CCAdj for corporations is corporate tax-return-based CCA less estimates of CCA that more accurately reflect economic depreciation (CCA with CCAdj).

CCA with CCAdj is capital consumption "based on the use of uniform service lives, straight line depreciation, and replacement costs" (xi). For the part of CCA with CCAdj related to nonprofit institutions serving individuals, it is "the value of the current services of the fixed capital assets owned and used by these institutions" (xi). In NIPA table 5.1, corporate CCA with CCAdj is shown separately from the corresponding noncorporate measure.

Wage accruals less disbursements is retroactive wages that are measured on a when paid basis rather than a when earned basis.

The components of the government surplus or deficit are defined as follows. The federal surplus or deficit is the sum of federal government receipts less federal government expenditures, both on a NIPA basis. The state and local government surplus or deficit involves the same calculation with state and local government receipts and expenditures.

With respect to foreign transactions, capital grants is a component of gross saving in NIPA table 5.1; net foreign investment is a component of gross investment. Capital grants received by the United States (net) is mainly the allocation of Special Drawing Rights to the United States. Net foreign investment is "U.S. exports of goods and services and capital grants received by the United States (net), less imports of goods and services by the United States, transfer payments to foreigners (net), and U.S. Government interest paid to foreigners" (xii). A recent discussion of foreign transactions in the NIPAs is in Tice and Moczar (1986).

3. Numerous studies use, or start with and adjust, the NIPA personal saving–to–disposable personal income ratio or the net private saving–to–net national product ratio. Examples include von Furstenberg (1981), Auerbach (1982), Hendershott and Peek (1985), Boskin (1986), Bosworth (1986), and Peek (1986).

4. The slope coefficients from linear trends using the measures in figure 1.1 are as follows (t-statistics in parentheses): gross saving, -0.01 (-0.6); gross private saving, 0.06 (6.6); government saving, -0.08 (-3.5); and net private saving, -0.02 (-1.6). The standard errors of the regression, which are percentage points and are used here as an indicator of amplitude, are as follows: gross saving, 1.41; gross private saving, 0.60; government saving, 1.37; and net private saving, 0.90.

5. An attempt to provide theoretical and empirical support for Denison's law is in David and Scadding (1974). Criticisms can be found in Boskin (1986) and Kotlikoff (1984).

6. Wage accruals less disbursements must also be added to personal saving and undistributed corporate profits to equal net private saving exactly. Movements in the personal saving–to–GNP ratio closely parallel those in the more often discussed personal saving–to–disposable personal income ratio.

7. It must be noted that capital consumption and undistributed corporate profits are not independent components of saving because corporate profits are derived, in part, by deducting depreciation charges from receipts. Therefore, there is a dollar-for-dollar inverse relation between the corporate component of capital consumption and undistributed corporate profits, ceteris

paribus. There is a similar relation between capital consumption and personal saving through rental income and proprietors' income.

8. After adjustment to remove cyclical responses, the federal measure still shows a strong trend toward deficit. For a discussion of the issues and estimates of the cyclical effects, see de Leeuw and Holloway (1983) and Holloway (1986).

9. However, the receipt of savings from the rest of the world was not large enough to compensate for the decline in gross saving.

10. These trends are drawn from the 1950–85 period. Over longer periods, there are obvious qualifications. For example, the federal deficit–to–GNP ratio during the 1980s was well below the ratio during World War II.

11. Additional statements, elaborations, and reaffirmations of the purposes of the NIPAs are in Jaszi (1958, 1971, 1986), Jaszi and Carson (1979), and Carson and Jaszi (1981, 1986).

12. While current production and the income generated by that production have welfare implications, the focus of the NIPAs is not on the measurement of economic welfare per se. The many issues related to the measurement of welfare in a NIPA context have been discussed for decades. See, e.g., Jaszi (1958), Easterlin (1958), Eisner (1971, 1985), Gordon (1971), Okun (1971), Adler (1982), Moss (1973), and Juster (1977).

13. Some of the issues related to capital gains are discussed in National Accounts Review Committee (1957), Jaszi (1958), Goode (1976), Ruggles and Ruggles (1982a, 1982b), Hibbert (1983), Hill (1984), and Eisner (1985).

14. National income is a measure of production valued at factor cost.

15. A major problem with the inclusion of nonmarket activities is that valuation is extremely difficult. However, many ingenious attempts have been made to assign values to various types of activities. See, e.g., Kendrick (1979), Katz and Peskin (1980), Martin, Landefeld, and Peskin (1982), and Katz (1983).

16. The exact definition of illegal activity in the NIPAs is reflected by the preceding sentences in the main text but is more complicated than would appear at first glance. Some transactions are illegal for one party but not for the other. For example, it is illegal for illegal aliens to work in the United States, but, prior to 1987, it was not illegal for employers to hire them. In this case, the production of these workers was and is included in the NIPAs. Carson (1984a, 1984b) explores some of the issues further.

The NIPA practice of excluding illegal activities is not the international standard. For example, the System of National Accounts of the United Nations calls for inclusion, although, in practice, the accounts of many countries also exclude them.

17. Carson (1984b) provides a hypothetical example of the NIPA treatment of imported drugs. The growing need to measure illegal activities has been suggested by some economists. See, e.g., Adler (1982).

18. Obviously, there are many other conceptual issues related to the scope and measurement of current production besides those mentioned in the text. Some of the issues include the intermediate vs. final product debates related to government transactions, financial transactions, advertising, and transportation to work; and the more extensive use of imputations to extend the production boundary. For discussion of some of these issues, see Jaszi (1958), Hawrylyshyn (1974), Kendrick (1979), Adler (1982), Ruggles and Ruggles (1982a, 1982b), Berger (1983), and Eisner (1985).

19. The five-account summary was proposed by Jaszi (1958) to replace a six-account summary that showed a separate business account. Jaszi's proposal

was endorsed by the National Accounts Review Committee (1957) and has been used by BEA since 1958. The central focus on GNP was emphasized in Jaszi (1971). For discussions of the evolution of the accounts, see Carson (1975) and Ruggles (1983).

20. Production accounts show production attributable to a sector. Appropriation accounts show sector income, outlays, and saving. Saving-investment accounts show the sector's gross saving, net increase in assets, and net increase in liabilities. Young and Tice (1985) provide a detailed discussion of the relation of the national economic accounting system to conventional accounting statements used by business and government.

21. Using data for 1953, Denison (1955) explains how the ex post saving-investment equality comes about.

22. A more complete listing in addition to those mentioned includes mutual financial institutions, private noninsured pension funds, cooperatives, nonprofit organizations that serve business, federally sponsored credit agencies, and the treatment as business entities of buildings and equipment owned and used by nonprofit organizations serving individuals.

23. Denison (1955, 1982a) has suggested that the most meaningful distinction among categories of NIPA saving is between total government saving and total private saving. However, even this distinction is very sensitive to certain conventions. The NIPA treatment of public pensions, discussed later, is an example.

24. Part of the conceptual justification is that nonprofit institutions, like households, are often final consumers of goods and services.

25. Obviously, many other classification decisions are also important. For example, not classifying realized capital gains as income has important ramifications for NIPA measures. For further discussion related to capital gains, see National Accounts Review Committee (1957) and Eisner (1985).

26. The timing of investment also has implications for NIPA saving measures. For example, construction is recorded in the NIPAs on a "value put in place" basis—i.e., the value of work done during the period. Except for electric utilities, estimates of capital consumption begin when construction begins.

27. Detailed tables of NIPA imputations are published annually in the July *Survey of Current Business*. In the July 1986 *Survey,* NIPA table 8.9 shows the major NIPA imputations, and NIPA table 8.8 shows additional details concerning interest imputations.

28. For a discussion of some of the difficulties, see Jaszi (1971).

29. A discussion of the estimation of the stocks based on the perpetual inventory method is in Musgrave (1979), Young and Musgrave (1980), Bureau of Economic Analysis (1982), and Gorman et al. (1985). Recent time series are in Musgrave (1986a, 1986b).

30. For a discussion of some of the issues, see National Accounts Review Committee (1957).

31. A discussion of the estimation of these stocks is in Young and Musgrave (1980) and Musgrave (1980). Recent time series are in Musgrave (1986a, 1986b).

32. For further discussion concerning the treatment of research and development expenditures, see Juster (1973), Hawrylyshyn (1974), Blades and Sturm (1982), and Blades (1983). Some of the problems mentioned with respect to measuring intangible investment are even more pronounced when human capital is considered. Investments in human capital occur through education, health maintenance, on-the-job training, and the like. Classifying these expenditures as capital expenditures has been suggested but is not done in the NIPAs. Some

of the issues are discussed in Eisner (1971), Kendrick (1971, 1979), Juster (1973), and Jaszi (1971, 1973).

33. Public pensions is defined broadly here to include social security, federal civilian retirement, state and local government retirement, railroad retirement, and military retirement. The treatment of military retirement changed recently. The Defense Authorization Act for fiscal year 1984 established a military retirement trust fund similar to the civil service retirement trust fund. In the 1985 comprehensive revision, a NIPA social insurance fund was created to reflect this law change, and an employer contribution was imputed back to 1929. An equal amount was imputed to expenditures so government saving was not affected. For details, see Bureau of Economic Analysis (1985a).

34. It is assumed in the NIPAs that all the ownership interest in private noninsured pension plans is held by the ultimate beneficiaries. Consequently, all the investment earnings are attributed to persons. In the case of plans operated by life insurance carriers, both ultimate beneficiaries and shareholders may have a claim on the investment earnings if the insurance carrier is a stock corporation. Consequently, most of the investment earnings are attributed to persons, but some may be attributed to shareholders.

35. Imputed interest paid to persons from private pension funds is part of an item published in NIPA table 8.8 in the July 1986 *Survey of Current Business*. The item is imputed interest paid by life insurance carriers and private noninsured pension plans, and it amounted to about $102 billion in 1985—$48 billion by life insurance carriers and $55 billion by private noninsured pension plans. This imputed interest item includes investment earnings in the form of rent, interest, and dividends, but it excludes capital gains. The amounts are not imputed; the imputation arises in attributing these earnings to persons and in treating all the earnings as interest. Only part of imputed interest paid by life insurance carriers is from pension funds. The remainder includes interest on life insurance policies.

36. The operating expenses are not shown separately in BEA publications. However, expenditures for the expenses of handling life insurance, which includes these operating expenses along with other items, are published in NIPA table 2.4 in the July 1986 *Survey of Current Business*. The 1985 estimate was about $34 billion. The nontaxable income components in personal income are discussed in Park (1986).

37. In the July 1986 *Survey of Current Business,* recent estimates appear in NIPA table 6.13 on other labor income by industry and by type.

38. Personal income excludes transfer payments to foreigners.

39. Even though there would not be an effect on the total government surplus or deficit, there would be offsetting effects on the social insurance funds surplus or deficit and the all "other" surplus or deficit. The BEA regularly publishes these separate measures.

40. Realized capital gains are excluded as they are elsewhere in the NIPAs.

41. For general discussions of NIPA revisions and assessments of the estimates, see Jaszi (1963), Cole (1969), Young (1974), Office of Federal Statistical Policy and Standards (1977), and Parker (1984b). Annual NIPA estimates go through a series of revisions. Each July, estimates for the most recent calendar year and the two preceding calendar years are usually revised. Using calendar year 1981 as an example, the first revision (referred to as the first July) would occur in July 1982, the second revision (referred to as the second July) would occur in July 1983, and the third revision (referred to as

the third July) would occur in July 1984. After the third July revision, the estimates would not be revised again until a comprehensive revision occurs. Comprehensive revisions—sometimes referred to as benchmarks—occur about every five years. The latest was completed in 1985.

42. The reclassification of mobile homes involved about 90 percent of these purchases; the other 10 percent had previously been classified as investment in producers' durable equipment.

43. Interest in introducing economic depreciation is expressed in National Accounts Review Committee (1957), Jaszi (1958), Denison (1971), and Jaszi (1971). The statistical implementation is discussed in Young (1975).

44. The 1976 comprehensive revision followed one in 1965. Consequently, it reflected changes over a 10-year period rather than over the typical 5-year period.

45. The new treatment allocated reinvested earnings, which is the difference between net earnings and dividends paid, to investors in proportion to their equity interest. Because reinvested earnings of incorporated foreign affiliates of U.S. direct investors exceeded the reinvested earnings of incorporated U.S. affiliates of foreign direct investors, the revision resulted in an upward revision of net exports, net foreign investment, and undistributed corporate profits.

46. Major replacements include such things as heating systems and roofing.

47. The shipments were mainly to Israel.

48. Discussions of statistical revisions incorporated during the 1985 comprehensive revision are in Donahoe (1984), Bureau of Economic Analysis (1985a), and Parker and Fox (1985).

49. BEA studies concerning the underground economy include Carson (1984a, 1984b), Parker (1984a), and de Leeuw (1985).

50. Specifically, the Census Bureau uses the information to define the universe of large firms and for basic data on small firms. For details, see Parker (1984a).

51. The effects of the improved adjustments for selected years are shown in table 4 in Parker and Fox (1985). Annual estimates of the effects for wages and salaries and nonfarm proprietors' income are shown in table 1 in Park (1986).

52. The revisions are measured as differences between estimates available when the July 1986 *Survey of Current Business* was published and those available when the November 1985 *Survey* was published. The definitional and classificational revisions are from the 1985 comprehensive revision. Consequently, the effects of the July revision appear under statistical revisions.

53. The pre–comprehensive revision data are those published in the November 1985 *Survey of Current Business;* the current data are those published in the July 1986 *Survey.*

54. The revisions in the bases of the ratios are from all sources.

55. July revisions are usually skipped in the year of a comprehensive revision. Further details about the revision schedule are in n. 41 above.

56. No July revision was conducted in 1981.

57. Similar results for many NIPA series using earlier estimates and previous comprehensive revisions are shown in Office of Federal Statistical Policy and Standards (1977).

58. See, e.g., Barro (1978).

59. Some early discussions of the need for balance sheets are in Goldsmith (1955, 1958). Later calls for balance sheets are in Gainsbrugh (1971), Jorgenson (1971), Kendrick (1971), Ruggles and Ruggles (1971, 1982b), and Goldsmith (1971, 1985).

60. For example, the discrepancies between NIPA and flow-of-funds saving measures undermine the statistical relation between NIPA saving measures and Federal Reserve balance sheet estimates. For a discussion of the discrepancies, see Gorman (1983) and de Leeuw (1984).

61. Further discussion of the issues in connection with the System of National Accounts is in United Nations (1977). It should be noted that a focus on welfare measurement could lower measured output instead of raise it if deductions for pollution abatement and the like were large enough.

62. Goldsmith has suggested that both disposable income and personal saving are often understated in the NIPAs. Reference to this position is in von Furstenberg (1981).

63. For example, Bosworth (1986) adjusts a measure of net private saving to include the pension fund activities of state and local governments. The flow-of-funds accounts attribute state and local government pension fund activities to their household sector.

64. The data for EC and PC are published in NIPA table 3.6 and for TP in NIPA table 3.11 in the *Survey of Current Business*. The data for the other terms are unpublished.

65. The adjustments are restricted to federal civilian retirement programs.

66. The view that consumer durable goods should be reflected in NIPA saving measures has been advocated by many economists for many years and is probably the most frequent criticism of the measures. A sampling of the critics include Ando (1971), Eldridge (1971), Kendrick (1971, 1979), Ruggles and Ruggles (1971, 1982a, 1982b), and Hendershott and Peek (1985). Denison (1982a, 1982b) has argued for the present treatment.

67. Using the definitions of the variables shown below equations (4)–(6) in the text, the net return on government capital (N_g) can be defined as

$$N_g = V_g - M_g - D_g.$$

The service value can be written as

$$V_g = N_g + M_g + D_g.$$

Because M_g is currently in actual expenditures in eq. (4), it must be subtracted from V_g to avoid double counting. The change in receipts in eq. (5) is the addition of the net return.

68. Using the definitions of the variables shown below eqq. (7)–(9) in the text, and letting T_c = personal property taxes on consumer durable goods, the net return on consumer durable goods (N_c) can be defined as

$$N_c = V_c - M_c - D_c - i_c - T_c.$$

The service value can be written as

$$V_c = N_c + M_c + D_c + i_c + T_c.$$

To arrive at DPI* in eq. (7), the net return (N_c) is added to personal income, and personal property taxes are subtracted from personal tax and nontax payments. DPI is not affected by changes in the treatment of interest paid on credit-financed consumer durable goods because net interest increases by exactly the amount that interest paid by consumers to business decreases. These latter two interest items are summed with other interest items to derive personal interest income.

To arrive at O^* in eq. (8), several changes are required. Outlays (O) include both PCE and interest paid by consumers to business. PCE is changed by adding the service value (V_c); subtracting expenditures on consumer durable goods (I_c), which are reclassified as investment; and subtracting maintenance and repairs (M_c), which must be done to avoid double counting. M_c is part of both O and V_c (for a similar double counting issue, see n. 67 above). Interest paid by consumers to business is changed by subtracting interest paid on credit-financed consumer durable goods, which is reclassified as net interest.

69. I derived estimates for 1980–85 judgmentally on the basis of movements in selected interest rates and the net stocks of consumer durables and government capital.

Martin, Landefeld, and Peskin (1982) estimate the service value of government capital as the sum of depreciation and net return. They exclude maintenance and repairs because of lack of data. Given this definition of service value, GNP changes by the sum of depreciation and net return. Their net return is based on a constant 7 percent rate of return and the net stock of government capital.

Katz and Peskin (1980) and Katz (1982) estimate the service value of consumer durables as the sum of depreciation, maintenance and repairs, personal property taxes, and net return (defined to include interest paid). Their net return is based on a complex weighted average of rates of return applied to the net stock of consumer durables by type.

In contrast to the approach discussed above for consumer durables, considerably less involved approaches could be used. For example, in the flow-of-funds accounts, consumer durables are treated as investment, but no net return or service value is estimated. Depreciation on consumer durable goods is deducted from gross household saving to estimate net household saving.

70. The cyclical adjustment of the federal budget has a long history. Early cyclically adjusted budgets were based on estimates of potential GNP consistent with full employment or high employment without accelerating inflation. More recent estimates rely on a noncyclical trend for GNP that is more closely linked to the trend in actual GNP. For a discussion of some of the concepts and measurement procedures, see de Leeuw et al. (1980) and de Leeuw and Holloway (1982, 1983).

71. The cyclically adjusted measures are based on middle-expansion trend GNP; this middle-expansion series is used in the denominator of the cyclically adjusted ratio. For details, see de Leeuw and Holloway (1983) and Holloway (1986).

72. For details about many of the sources and methods underlying personal income, taxes, and outlays, see Byrnes et al. (1979). See also Bureau of Economic Analysis (1981).

73. Parts of table 1.B.1 are reproduced from Bureau of Economic Analysis (1986b). In virtually all cases, source data are adjusted for timing, coverage, or other differences to conform to NIPA concepts and conventions.

74. The 1977 input-output tables depend mainly on the 1977 economic censuses. The 1977 tables also use the 1980 census of housing, the 1977 census of governments, and the 1978 census of agriculture.

75. The Treasury data are published in *Monthly Treasury Statement*. Among other adjustments, the BEA adjusts these data for timing differences between employer withholding and Treasury collection.

76. The census data are published in *Quarterly Summary of Federal, State, and Local Tax Revenue*.

77. The BLS data are published in *Employment and Wages*.

78. The IRS data are published in *Statistics of Income: Sole Proprietorship Returns, Statistics of Income: Partnership Returns,* and *Statistics of Income: Corporation Income Tax Returns*.

79. Personal interest income is interest income of persons from all sources. It is derived as the sum of (1) interest paid by business less interest received by business, (2) interest received from abroad less interest paid abroad, (3) interest paid by government to persons and business less interest received by government, and (4) interest paid by consumers to business. A detailed discussion is in Bureau of Economic Analysis (1981).

80. The Treasury data are published in *Monthly Treasury Statement*. The federal budget data are published in *Budget of the United States*. The state and local government data are published in *Governmental Finances*.

81. The Federal Reserve data are published in *Federal Reserve Bulletin*.

82. The census data are published in *Finances of Employee Retirement Systems of State and Local Governments*.

83. Complete documentation on sources and methods for corporate profits is in Bureau of Economic Analysis (1985c).

84. The Federal Reserve data are published in their *Annual Report*. The census data are published in *Quarterly Summary of Federal, State, and Local Tax Revenue*.

85. For a discussion of some of the data and methods related to manufacturing inventories, see Hinrichs and Eckman (1981).

86. The perpetual inventory method calculations are described in Young and Musgrave (1980) and Gorman et al. (1985). The method essentially involves estimating gross stocks by cumulating estimates of gross investment, then subtracting estimates of assets that have completed their service lives. Depreciation estimates are derived by applying depreciation rates (based on the straight-line depreciation formula) to the gross stocks.

87. A discussion of some of the sources and methods underlying capital consumption is in Young (1975) and Gorman et al. (1985).

88. In practice, many of the estimates that comprise federal purchases are derived as residuals. For example, total budget outlays for a program are known from budget documents. Amounts from the program attributed to transfer payments, grants in aid to state and local governments, or other types of expenditures excluding purchases are estimated. These amounts are deducted from the total to estimate purchases.

89. Complete documentation on sources and methods for foreign transactions, including net foreign investment, is in Tice and Moczar (1986). Additional documentation will be published in a forthcoming BEA methodology paper.

References

Adler, Hans J. 1982. Selected problems of welfare and production in the national accounts. *Review of Income and Wealth* 28 (June): 121–32.

Ando, Albert. 1971. An econometrician comments on the national income and product accounts. *Survey of Current Business* 51 (July): 1–3.

Auerbach, Alan J. 1982. Issues in the measurement and encouragement of business saving. In *Saving and government policy,* 79–100. Federal Reserve

Bank of Boston Conference Series, no. 25. Boston: Federal Reserve Bank of Boston.

Barro, Robert J. 1978. *The impact of social security on private saving: Evidence from the U.S. time series.* Washington, D.C.: American Enterprise Institute for Public Policy Research.

Berger, S. 1983. Dividing government product between intermediate and final uses: A comment. *Review of Income and Wealth* 29 (September): 333–34.

Blades, Derek. 1983. Alternative measures of saving. *Organisation for Economic Co-operation and Development Occasional Studies* (June): 66–84.

Blades, Derek, and Peter H. Sturm. 1982. The concept and measurement of savings: The United States and other industrialized countries. In *Saving and government policy,* 1–30. Federal Reserve Bank of Boston Conference Series, no. 25. Boston: Federal Reserve Bank of Boston.

Board of Governors of the Federal Reserve System. 1987. *Balance sheets for the U.S. economy, 1947–86.* Washington, D.C.: Board of Governors of the Federal Reserve System.

Boskin, Michael J. 1982. Federal government deficits: Some myths and realities. *American Economic Review* 72 (May): 296–303.

———. 1986. Theoretical and empirical issues in the measurement, evaluation, and interpretation of postwar U.S. saving. In *Savings and capital formation,* ed. F. Gerard Adams and Susan M. Wachter, 11–43. Lexington, Mass.: D. C. Heath & Co.

Bosworth, Barry P. 1986. Savings and government policy. In *Savings and Capital Formation,* ed. F. Gerard Adams and Susan M. Wachter, 173–87. Lexington, Mass.: D. C. Heath & Co.

Bureau of Economic Analysis. 1981. Special note—Personal interest income. *Survey of Current Business* 61 (September): 4–5.

———. 1982. *Fixed reproducible tangible wealth in the United States, 1925–79.* Washington, D.C.: U.S. Government Printing Office.

———. 1985a. An advance overview of the comprehensive revision of the national income and product accounts. *Survey of Current Business* 65 (October): 19–28.

———. 1985b. An introduction to national economic accounting. Bureau of Economic Analysis Methodology Paper, series MP-1. Washington, D.C.: U.S. Government Printing Office.

———. 1985c. Corporate profits: Profits before tax, profits tax liability, and dividends. Bureau of Economic Analysis Methodology Paper, series MP-2. Washington, D.C.: U.S. Government Printing Office.

———. 1986a. *The national income and product accounts of the United States, 1929–82: Statistical tables.* Washington, D.C.: U.S. Government Printing Office.

———. 1986b. The U.S. national income and product accounts: Revised estimates. *Survey of Current Business* 66 (July): 7–23.

Byrnes, James C., Gerald F. Donahoe, Mary W. Hook, and Robert P. Parker. 1979. Monthly estimates of personal income, taxes, and outlays. *Survey of Current Business* 59 (November): 18–36.

Carson, Carol S. 1975. The history of the United States national income and product accounts: Development of an analytical tool. *Review of Income and Wealth* 21 (June): 153–81.

———. 1984a. The underground economy: An introduction. *Survey of Current Business* 64 (May): 21–37.

———. 1984b. The underground economy: An introduction. *Survey of Current Business* 64 (July): 106–17.

Carson, Carol S., and George Jaszi. 1981. The national income and product accounts of the United States: An overview. *Survey of Current Business* 61 (February): 22–34.

———. 1986. The use of national income and product accounts for public policy: Our successes and failures. Bureau of Economic Analysis Staff Paper, no. 43. Washington, D.C.: U.S. Government Printing Office.

Cole, Rosanne. 1969. *Errors in provisional estimates of gross national product.* New York: Columbia University Press.

Council of Economic Advisers. 1986. *Economic report of the president.* Washington, D.C.: U.S. Government Printing Office.

David, Paul A., and John Scadding. 1974. Private savings: Ultra-rationality, aggregation and "Denison's law." *Journal of Political Economy* 82 (March/April): 225–49.

de Leeuw, Frank. 1984. Conflicting measures of private saving. *Survey of Current Business* 64 (November): 17–33.

———. 1985. An indirect technique for measuring the underground economy. *Survey of Current Business* 65 (April): 64–72.

de Leeuw, Frank, and Thomas M. Holloway. 1982. The high-employment budget: Revised estimates and automatic inflation effects. *Survey of Current Business* 62 (April): 21–33.

———. 1983. Cyclical adjustment of the federal budget and federal debt. *Survey of Current Business* 63 (December): 25–40.

de Leeuw, Frank, Thomas M. Holloway, Darwin G. Johnson, David S. McClain, and Charles A. Waite. 1980. The high-employment budget: New estimates, 1955–80. *Survey of Current Business* 60 (November): 13–43.

Denison, Edward F. 1955. Saving in the national economy: From the national income perspective. *Survey of Current Business* 35 (January): 8–24.

———. 1958. A note on private saving. *Review of Economics and Statistics* 40 (August): 261–67.

———. 1971. U.S. national income and product estimates: Evaluation and some specific suggestions for improvement. *Survey of Current Business* 51 (July): 36–44.

———. 1982a. Comment on Blades and Sturm's "The concept and measurement of savings: The United States and other industrialized countries." In *Saving and government policy,* 39–45. Federal Reserve Bank of Boston Conference Series, no. 25. Boston: Federal Reserve Bank of Boston.

———. 1982b. Comment on Ruggleses' "Integrated economic accounts for the United States, 1947–80." *Survey of Current Business* 62 (May): 59–65.

Denison, Edward F., and Robert P. Parker. 1980. The national income and product accounts of the United States: An introduction to the revised estimates for 1929–80. *Survey of Current Business* 60 (December): 1–26.

Donahoe, Gerald F. 1984. The national income and product accounts: Preliminary estimates, 1977. *Survey of Current Business* 64 (May): 38–41.

Easterlin, Richard A. 1958. Comment on Jaszi's "The conceptual basis of the accounts: A re-examination." In *A critique of the United States income and product accounts,* 127–40. NBER Conference on Research in Income and Wealth. Studies in Income and Wealth, vol. 22. Princeton, N.J.: Princeton University Press.

Eisner, Robert. 1971. New twists to income and product. *Survey of Current Business* 51 (July): 67–68.

———. 1985. The total incomes system of accounts. *Survey of Current Business* 65 (January): 24–48.

_____. 1986. *How real is the federal deficit?* New York: Free Press.

Eisner, Robert, and Paul J. Pieper. 1984. A new view of the federal debt and budget deficits. *American Economic Review* 74 (March): 11–29.

Eldridge, Douglas H. 1971. Congratulations from the National Bureau. *Survey of Current Business* 51 (July): 69–71.

Gainsbrugh, Martin R. 1971. Measuring the nation's wealth. *Survey of Current Business* 51 (July): 72–73.

Goldsmith, Raymond W. 1955. *A study of saving in the United States.* New York: Greenwood Press.

_____. 1958. Saving. In *A critique of the United States income and product accounts,* 448–54. NBER Conference on Research in Income and Wealth. Studies in Income and Wealth, vol. 22. Princeton, N.J.: Princeton University Press.

_____. 1971. Toward a national balance sheet. *Survey of Current Business* 51 (July): 74–79.

_____. 1985. *Comparative national balance sheets: A study of twenty countries, 1688–1978.* Chicago: University of Chicago Press.

Goode, Richard. 1976. *The individual income tax.* Washington, D.C.: Brookings Institution.

Gordon, R. A. 1971. Looking forward after fifty years. *Survey of Current Business* 51 (July): 80–82.

Gorman, John A. 1983. Data needs in flow of funds. In *The U.S. national income and product accounts: Selected topics,* ed. Murray Foss, 409–15. NBER Conference on Research in Income and Wealth. Studies in Income and Wealth, vol. 47. Chicago: University of Chicago Press.

Gorman, John A., John C. Musgrave, Gerald Silverstein, and Kathy A. Comins. 1985. Fixed private capital in the United States. *Survey of Current Business* 65 (July): 36–59.

Hawrylyshyn, Oli. 1974. *A review of recent proposals for modifying and extending the measure of GNP.* Ottawa: Statistics Canada.

Hendershott, Patric H., and Joe Peek. 1985. Household saving: An econometric investigation. In *The level and composition of household saving,* ed. Patric H. Hendershott, 63–100. Cambridge, Mass.: Ballinger Publishing Co.

Hibbert, Jack. 1983. *Measuring the effects of inflation on income, saving and wealth.* Paris: Organisation for Economic Co-operation and Development.

Hill, Peter. 1984. Inflation, holding gains, and saving. *OECD Economic Studies* 2 (Spring): 151–64.

Hinrichs, John C., and Anthony D. Eckman. 1981. Constant-dollar manufacturing inventories. *Survey of Current Business* 61 (November): 16–23.

Holloway, Thomas M. 1986. Cyclical adjustment of the federal budget and federal debt: Revised and updated estimates. *Survey of Current Business* 66 (March): 11–17.

Jaszi, George. 1958. The conceptual basis of the accounts: A re-examination. In *A critique of the United States income and product accounts,* 13–126. NBER Conference on Research in Income and Wealth. Studies in Income and Wealth, vol. 22. Princeton, N.J.: Princeton University Press.

_____. 1963. The quarterly national income and product accounts of the United States, 1942–62. Paper presented at the annual meeting of the International Association for Research in Income and Wealth, Corfu, June.

_____. 1971. An economic accountant's ledger. *Survey of Current Business* 51 (July): 183–227.

_____. 1973. Comment on Juster's "A framework for the measurement of economic and social performance." In *The measurement of economic and social performance,* ed. Milton Moss, 84–99. NBER Conference on Research in Income and Wealth. Studies in Income and Wealth, vol. 38. New York: Columbia University Press.

———. 1986. An economic accountant's audit. *American Economic Review* 76 (May): 411–17.

Jaszi, George, and Carol S. Carson. 1976. The national income and product accounts of the United States: Revised estimates, 1929–74. *Survey of Current Business* 56 (January): 1–38.

———. 1979. The national income and product accounts of the United States: An overview. *Survey of Current Business* 59 (October): 25–34.

Jorgenson, Dale W. 1971. Econometric research and the national accounts. *Survey of Current Business* 51 (July): 99–102.

Juster, F. Thomas. 1973. A framework for the measurement of economic and social performance. In *The measurement of economic and social performance,* ed. Milton Moss, 25–84. NBER Conference on Research in Income and Wealth. Studies in Income and Wealth, vol. 38. New York: NBER.

———. 1977. *Distribution of economic well-being.* NBER Conference on Research in Income and Wealth. Studies in Income and Wealth, vol. 41. Cambridge, Mass.: Ballinger Publishing Co. for the NBER.

Katz, Arnold J. 1982. The value of services provided by the stock of consumer durables, 1947–79: Alternative user cost measures. In *Measuring nonmarket economic activity: BEA working papers.* Bureau of Economic Analysis Working Paper, no. 2. Washington, D.C.: U.S. Government Printing Office.

———. 1983. Valuing the services of consumer durables. *Review of Income and Wealth* 29 (December): 405–28.

Katz, Arnold J., and Janice Peskin. 1980. The value of services provided by the stock of consumer durables, 1947–77: An opportunity cost measure. *Survey of Current Business* 60 (July): 22–31.

Kendrick, John W. 1971. The national accounts: The heart of OBE's statistical program. *Survey of Current Business* 51 (July): 103–4.

———. 1979. Expanding imputed values in the national income and product accounts. *Review of Income and Wealth* 25 (December): 349–63.

Kotlikoff, Laurence J. 1984. Taxation and savings: A neoclassical perspective. *Journal of Economic Literature* 22 (December): 1576–1629.

Levin, David J. 1984. The state and local government fiscal position: An alternative measure. *Survey of Current Business* 64 (March): 23–25.

———. 1986. Alternative measure of the state and local government fiscal position: Revised and updated estimates. *Survey of Current Business* 66 (April): 36.

Martin, Frank, J. Steven Landefeld, and Janice Peskin. 1982. The value of services provided by the stock of government-owned fixed capital, 1948–79. In *Measuring nonmarket economic activity: BEA working papers.* Bureau of Economic Analysis Working Paper, no. 2. Washington, D.C.: U.S. Government Printing Office.

Moss, Milton, ed. 1973. *The measurement of economic and social performance.* NBER Conference on Research in Income and Wealth. Studies in Income and Wealth, vol. 38. New York: NBER.

Musgrave, John C. 1979. Durable goods owned by consumers in the United States, 1925–77. *Survey of Current Business* 59 (March): 17–25.

———. 1980. Government owned fixed capital in the United States, 1925–79. *Survey of Current Business* 60 (March): 33–43.

———. 1986a. Fixed reproducible tangible wealth in the United States: Revised estimates. *Survey of Current Business* 66 (January): 51–75.

_____. 1986b. Fixed Reproducible tangible wealth in the United States, 1982–85. *Survey of Current Business* 66 (August): 36–39.

National Accounts Review Committee. 1957. The national economic accounts of the United States: Review, appraisal, and recommendations. Hearings before the Subcommittee on Economic Statistics of the Joint Economic Committee, Congress of the United States. 85th Cong., 1st sess.

Office of Federal Statistical Policy and Standards. 1977. *Gross national product data improvement project report*. Report of the Advisory Committee on Gross National Product Data Improvement. Washington, D.C.: U.S. Government Printing Office.

Okun, Arthur M. 1971. Social welfare has no price tag. *Survey of Current Business* 51 (July): 129–33.

Park, Thae S. 1986. Relationship between personal income and adjusted gross income: Revised estimates, 1947–83. *Survey of Current Business* 66 (May): 34–40.

Parker, Robert P. 1984a. Improved adjustments for misreporting of tax return information used to estimate the national income and product accounts, 1977. *Survey of Current Business* 64 (June): 17–25.

_____. 1984b. Revisions to the initial estimates of quarterly gross national product of the United States, 1968–83. Paper presented at the Seminar on Provisional and Revised Estimates of Economic Data, Florence, Italy, November.

Parker, Robert P., and Douglas R. Fox. 1985. Revised estimates of the national income and product accounts of the United States, 1929–85: An introduction. *Survey of Current Business* 65 (December): 1–19.

Peek, Joe. 1986. Household wealth composition: The impact of capital gains. *New England Economic Review* (November/December): 26–39.

Ruggles, Richard. 1983. The United States national income accounts, 1947–1977: Their conceptual basis and evolution. In *The U.S. national income and product accounts: Selected topics,* ed. Murray Foss, 15–96. NBER Conference on Research in Income and Wealth. Studies in Income and Wealth, vol. 47. Chicago: University of Chicago Press.

Ruggles, Richard, and Nancy D. Ruggles. 1971. The evolution of national accounts and the national data base. *Survey of Current Business* 51 (July): 152–61.

_____. 1982a. Integrated economic accounts: Reply. *Survey of Current Business* 62 (November): 36–53.

_____. 1982b. Integrated economic accounts for the United States, 1947–80. *Survey of Current Business* 62 (May): 1–53.

_____. 1985. The integration of macro and micro data for the household sector. Paper presented at the annual meeting of the American Economic Association, New York, December.

Tice, Helen Stone, and Louis J. Moczar. 1986. Foreign transactions in the national income and product accounts: An overview. *Survey of Current Business* 66 (November): 23–36.

United Nations. Department of Economic and Social Affairs. 1977. *The feasibility of welfare-oriented measures to supplement the national accounts and balances: A technical report.* New York: United Nations.

von Furstenberg, George M. 1981. Saving. In *How taxes affect economic behavior,* ed. Henry J. Aaron and Joseph A. Pechman, 327–90. Washington, D.C.: Brookings Institution.

Young, Allan H. 1974. Reliability of the quarterly national income and product accounts of the United States, 1947–71. Bureau of Economic Analysis Staff Paper, no. 23. Washington, D.C.: U.S. Government Printing Office.

———. 1975. New estimates of capital consumption allowances revision of GNP in the benchmark. *Survey of Current Business* 55 (October): 14–16, 35.

Young, Allan H., and John C. Musgrave. 1980. Estimation of capital stock in the United States. In *The measurement of capital,* ed. Dan Usher, 23–58. NBER Conference on Research in Income and Wealth. Studies in Income and Wealth, vol. 45. Chicago: University of Chicago Press.

Young, Allan H., and Helen Stone Tice. 1985. An introduction to national economic accounting. *Survey of Current Business* 65 (March): 59–74.

Comment   Paul Wachtel

There are not very many people who can write a paper like this, although there are a great number of people who can profit from it. Only a Bureau of Economic Analysis (BEA) insider like Thomas Holloway can have the store of institutional knowledge and the access to information necessary to prepare a reference work on the national income and product account (NIPA) data. Also, it is refreshing to see a BEA staff member make the judgments and statements of opinion that are often lacking in the formal BEA presentations in the *Survey of Current Business*. Thus, this paper is both enjoyable and useful.

This paper is an insider's account but not an insider's exposé. Holloway does not condemn the procedures used by the BEA or call for any sweeping changes in the definitions employed in the accounts. Nevertheless, a careful reading of the paper provides some good indication of the kinds of changes and improvements that might be made by the BEA in the not too distant future.

Since the paper presents a formidable body of information, it may appear at first glance to be impenetrable. This is not the case because Holloway has prepared a text that is clear and full of informative asides on the workings of the NIPAs. Nevertheless, it will be useful to summarize some of the ideas as I present my own views.

Holloway begins with the definitions of saving that are used in the various official presentations and that appear in most of the ubiquitous discussions of the so-called American saving problem. The concepts employed in the NIPAs are gross saving, gross private saving, and net private saving. In addition, much attention is paid to saving rates—particularly the one published by the BEA, the personal saving rate. Holloway's inspection of the data leads to a few conclusions. (1) Using any of the three economy-wide saving definitions, saving rates really do seem to validate Denison's law or the hypothesis that saving rates

Paul Wachtel is research professor of economics and department chairman at the New York University Graduate School of Business Administration and a research associate at the National Bureau of Economic Research.

are secularly stable.(2) If there is any recent decline in saving rates, it is seen only in the ratio of net private saving to gross national product (GNP), which has had a negative trend since the mid-1960s. This saving rate averaged 8.4 percent in 1965–69 and 6.2 percent in 1980–85. It is also true that the gross saving rate was low in the 1980s because of the large federal government deficits (negative government saving). Private saving was not unusually low in these years. (3) The striking difference in the recent data as compared to earlier years is the large increase in volatility observed recently. (4) The stability of the saving rate is not due to the stability of its parts. For example, personal saving and business saving often move in opposite directions. The negative trend of net private saving noted above occurred because the declines in personal saving were only partly offset by increases in business saving. In the same period, the gross saving rate was steady because capital consumption increased.

I will pause here to interject my own views. The tendency of many economists—students of growth and NIPA accountants—to emphasize overall or aggregate saving measures always puzzles me. Our amazement with Denison's law leads us to overlook the final point that Holloway makes—the heterogeneity of movements among saving components. The components of saving are so disparate and so interrelated that I think we make a big mistake by often focusing on the aggregates.

In my view, we need to have a matrix of saving figures that picks up data from the various NIPA sectors. For example, a matrix for net saving would include rows for each of the NIPA sectors and columns for at least three saving components. That is, there could be rows for the personal, business, government, and foreign sectors and columns for expenditures on physical assets, capital consumption allowances and adjustments, and the sectoral financial surplus.

This framework is similar to a flow-of-funds approach, but only conceptually. Like the flow-of-funds approach, it represents a matrix of activities and sectors. However, I am not advocating that the entries in the matrix be funds flows. I think the conceptual approach is helpful, but I am not suggesting that the NIPAs be made into a financial accounting system. As Holloway reminded me, it is apparent that the flow-of-funds staff at the Federal Reserve has a tougher time developing estimates than does the NIPA staff. Thus, it would be premature to suggest that an attempt be made to integrate the two accounting systems. Instead, my suggestion is that the matrix approach used in the flow-of-funds be adapted to the NIPA system as it now exists.

The NIPA data can be readily used to prepare the saving matrix outlined above. Definitions and data for 1986 are shown in table C1.1, which uses only readily available published data. The references in the

Table C1.1   **U.S. Net Saving Matrix, 1986 (billions of dollars)**

Sector	Investment Expenditures	−	Depreciation	+	Sectoral Surplus	=	Net Saving
Personal	218.3[a]		100.8[b]		13.1		130.6[c]
Business	452.8		355.9		−4.4		92.5[d]
Government	0		0		−147.8[e]		−147.8
Foreign	0		0		143.9[f]		143.9
Discrepancy	0		0		−4.9[g]		−4.9
Total	671.0[h]		456.7[i]		0		214.3
Reconciliation:							
	+ Depreciation						456.7
	= Gross private domestic investment						671.0
	+ Net foreign investment						−143.9
	= Gross investment[j]						527.1
	− Statistical discrepancy						4.9
	= Gross saving[k]						532.0

Note: Data are taken from the July 1987 *Survey of Current Business,* and the notes provide labels when they correspond to NIPA usage. Entries without any references are simply derived from the row or column totals and the other entries. The familiar saving aggregates appear as row or column totals in the matrix. The references in parentheses in the notes that follow are to table and line numbers from the standard tables in the *Survey.*

[a]Residential, (5.2.16).

[b](5.2.17).

[c]Personal saving, (5.1.3)

[d](5.1.2.) − (5.1.3) − (5.2.2).

[e]Government surplus, (5.1.11).

[f]Minus net foreign investment, −(5.1.17).

[g]Statistical discrepancy, (5.1.18).

[h]Gross private domestic investment, (5.2.1).

[i](5.2.2).

[j](5.1.15).

[k](5.1.1).

table notes are to table and line numbers from the standard presentation in the *Survey of Current Business;* the data are from the July 1987 *Survey.* The notes also provide labels for the matrix entries when they correspond to standard NIPA usage. Entries without any references are simply derived from the row or column totals and the other entries. The familiar saving aggregates appear as row or column totals in the matrix.

Existing data could easily be used to refine the presentation shown here. For example, some part of housing expenditure and depreciation should be moved to the business sector. Furthermore, alternative definitions of saving could be incorporated into the matrix. For example, consumer durables could be treated as a capital good using data already prepared by the BEA, and a capital account for the government sector could be added as well. An advantage of the matrix framework is that it could be used to expand the definition of saving and also facilitate the continued presentation of existing concepts.

This matrix presentation is valuable because it shifts our focus from the aggregates and Denison's law to Holloway's point about the heterogeneity of movements among saving components. This is hardly a radical innovation; it simply reorganizes the data in the NIPAs to emphasize components and concepts that are already there and to avoid the presentation that presents the pieces as a buildup to a grand finale called gross saving and investment.

The column of table C1.1 labeled "sectoral surplus" introduces a concept that is new to the NIPAs. It is important because it provides some information about the deficit and surplus sectors in the economy. Contemporary policy discussions are often concerned with whether foreign saving is too large, whether personal saving available to the other sectors is too small, and so on. These sectoral surpluses have varied considerably over time. Table C1.2 summarizes the surpluses as percentages of GNP in the past twenty-five years. I think that these numbers are ultimately more revealing than the standard measures of aggregate saving.

The above discussion raises the question of what is the purpose of the saving aggregate. This is the issue that Holloway logically turns to next. For some purposes, the NIPA gross saving concept is useful; for others, we might want a broader concept that capitalizes all sorts of expenditures and includes unfunded liabilities; and for yet other purposes, we might want an even narrower definition. Holloway starts with an exploration of the conceptual intent of the current accounting scheme.

Some of the issues and arguments set out are well known. The NIPAs are by intent based on current production (capital gains do not enter) and limited to legal market activities. Some of the other issues are less well understood. A most informative part of the paper is Holloway's investigation of the sectoring scheme used in the NIPAs. The NIPAs

Table C1.2	Sectoral Surplus as Percent of GNP			
	Personal	Business	Government	Foreign
1960–64	1.4	− .1	− .2	− .8
1965–69	2.5	− 1.7	− .3	− .4
1970–74	3.2	− 2.3	− .6	− .3
1975–79	2.5	− 1.0	− 1.4	− .2
1980–86	2.3	− .9	− 2.7	1.3

Note: Data are rounded and are averages of annual ratios for years shown.

can be very confusing when one encounters entities classified in one production sector whose saving is attributed to another sector.

For example, unincorporated businesses are in the business sector, but their saving is attributed to the personal sector. Another example involves pension funds. Personal saving includes the saving of households and associations of individuals (which include nonprofit institutions). Thus, the saving of pension funds and life insurance saving are attributed to the personal sector (and they are large parts of the total), although these are business-sector entities.

Pension fund reserves are viewed as owned by individuals, and their investment earnings ($100 billion in 1985) are imputed interest earnings to persons. An estimate of their operating expenses (which does not include benefits paid) is a consumption expenditure. Employer contributions to pension funds are current labor income; thus, benefits paid are not. To compound the confusion, state and local government pension funds are treated entirely differently.

Another set of classification decisions that affect saving measures is the decision to treat certain expenditures as investment. In particular, the arguments for and against the capitalization of business research and development expenditures, consumer durables expenditures, and government capital expenditures are summarized.

Holloway seems to be leaning toward the inclusion of a government capital account (he notes that much of the data are already available, although developing imputed income estimates for government capital presents difficulties), perhaps for the capitalization of consumer durables (data are available, if not entirely reliable), for consistent treatment of public and private pensions (he virtually predicts this change in a future benchmark revision), but against capitalizing intangibles like research and development and unfunded pension liabilities. Thus, he (and, I think, correctly) is not suggesting that the NIPAs be turned into a social accounting framework, but he is willing to make improvements that retain the current production/market activity orientation of the accounts. NIPA saving should not be an attempt to measure changes in all claims on wealth.

The last major topic addressed in the paper is measurement and revision. The issue here is whether the standard data are robust to changes in measurement concepts and/or data revisions. More specifically, does a supposed decline in saving disappear as better data become available or as small conceptual changes are introduced? This is an important topic for the NIPAs in general.

Data revisions of two kinds are made to NIPAs, and Holloway examines both of them. First, there are changes in definition and classification that are made at the time of "comprehensive" revision—about once every five years. Second, there are "annual" revisions—

usually made in July—that introduce improved data measurement for the three prior calendar years. Each year's data are subject to three such revisions as more complete information becomes available.

In either case, it is important to note that saving measures are particularly susceptible to changes introduced by the revision process. Saving is the difference between income and expenditure. Small revisions to income and expenditure can result in large changes in the difference.

Some examples of the changes in classification and definition introduced in recent comprehensive revisions follow: (1) Expenditures on mobile homes was moved from personal consumption expenditure (because it is a car) to investment (because it is a house), which reflected changes in the use of the product (1976). (2) Reinvested earnings of foreign affiliates were added to receipts and payments of income (1980). As a result, net foreign investment, undistributed corporate profits, and gross saving increased. In the 1970s, this increased the ratio of gross saving to GNP by half a percentage point. (3) An "underground economy" adjustment was made to better account for underreporting (1985). Personal consumption expenditures, wages, and proprietors' nonfarm income increased (in 1984 by $44, $24, and $78 billion, respectively). Since income went up by more than consumption, saving increased.

The total revisions (regardless of source) are of interest. Here, the aggregate may be more interesting than the very different parts. The difference between definitional/classificational or statistical revisions is less interesting than the difference between the original data used for analysis and decision making and the revised data, which is presumably the "truth." Thus, the magnitude of the revisions tells us something about the adequacy of the data already used. Does the revision process alter our view of the world? For example, Holloway's figure 1.3 suggests that, prior to comprehensive revisions in 1986, the net private saving–to–net national product ratio trended down from 1965 on. After the revisions, no such trend is apparent.

The final part of the paper examines the effects on our familiar saving measures of feasible data improvements. Holloway presents them in an unjudgmental fashion. I can be a little bolder and will not hesitate to tell you what I think of each one. Holloway mentions five issues: (1) broaden the accounting framework (e.g., include capital gains); (2) broaden the concept of production (e.g., include an imputation for household work); (3) make the treatment of private and public pensions consistent; (4) capitalize more expenditures; and (5) measure government saving differently.

I would not like to see the NIPAs move away from a current market production emphasis, but for many purposes a broader view is valuable. Pat Hendershott and Joe Peek (chap. 5, in this vol.) show that saving behavior is very much related to aspects of saving that are not measured in the income accounts. It is silly to study the NIPA definition of personal saving in isolation without exploring capital gains on housing and equities, inflation effects on liabilities, and the role of unfunded pension wealth. However, this does not imply that the NIPA saving definition should be broadened to account for all these issues. Instead, it would be helpful to develop a national balance sheet that is integrated with the NIPAs and therefore can be used to supplement the standard accounts.

I think this would be a good idea that would enable us to expand, at will, saving definitions to include, for example, capital gains. There are of course several balance sheet accounts available (the work of Robert Eisner, Richard and Nancy Ruggles, and Raymond Goldsmith are well-known examples), but each is inconsistent with the NIPA sectoring in some way. The desirability of an integrated balance sheet is most clear for the household sector, for which our personal saving measure is a poor indicator of the change in wealth because capital gains tend to offset personal saving.

The conceptual boundaries in the NIPAs could be broadened in a number of ways.

1. Include imputations for housework that would increase income and outlays by the same amount and leave saving unchanged. But the saving rate would decline. This change always strikes me as unnecessary for the vast majority of issues for which the accounts are used.

2. Capitalize consumer durables. This is simple to do, and I have always been puzzled why the BEA is so hesitant to take the step. Let me suggest that they provide the necessary data as some addendum items on the tables and leave formal definitions as they are. Adding this to personal saving increases the level but changes the trends only slightly. The increase in the saving rate in the 1960s would be larger because net investment in durables was particularly high at that time.

3. Estimate illegal activity.

4. Make the treatment of private and public pension funds consistent. This is logical, could easily be done, and, as already noted, may well be on the way. Public employee pension funds operate like private pension funds and should not be lumped with social insurance contributions. (The flow-of-funds accounts do put the saving of state and local government pension funds in the household sector.) This change would leave gross saving the same, but it would increase personal saving and reduce government saving. Holloway's figure 1.4 shows the effect of this change in attribution. Saving patterns are pretty much the same, but the decline in personal saving since 1975 is less pronounced.

5. Capitalize government expenditures. This should be no more difficult, arbitrary, or controversial than similar decisions for the private

sector. The government sector of the NIPAs is not the government budget, so capitalization in the accounting scheme has nothing to do with budget policy. The main effect of such a change would be to increase government saving. The small deficits of the 1960s would be surpluses, and the large deficits of the 1980s would be somewhat smaller, although still very large.

6. An interesting but controversial issue is the unfunded liabilities of social insurance funds and, for that matter, of lots of other entities. Imputations for these liabilities could be incorporated into an expanded balance sheet and also counted as saving. However, I, too, would step lightly here because the potential for controversy is great. There would be too much disagreement about how to define these imputations.

7. The last example treated by Holloway struck me as a little odd. Although the BEA does make cyclical adjustments to the government budget deficit in order to generate a standardized measure of fiscal influence, this is not related to the NIPAs at all. The numbers are well prepared (largely by Holloway) and widely used and respected, but these activities of the BEA should stand apart from the NIPAs.

Despite the length of these comments, Holloway and I generally agree with one another. Neither of us advocates change in the current production/market activity focus of the accounts. We do look favorably on some minor changes that affect saving and the addition of some data items that would enable users to alter their saving definitions at will.

The only point of difference is the one that I started with. Holloway seems to favor retaining a single saving measure. I am almost willing to abolish the term. I am interested not in the "saving" of the household sector but in its capital accumulation, its wealth augmentation (including capital gains), and its surplus or the resources it makes available to other sectors of the economy. The concept of saving should not be one dimensional—both our discussions of saving problems and our presentations of the data should be cognizant of this.

2 Measuring Household Saving: Recent Experience from the Flow-of-Funds Perspective

John F. Wilson, James L. Freund, Frederick O. Yohn, Jr., and Walther Lederer

2.1 Introduction

The sharp decline in the personal saving rate as measured by the national income and product accounts (NIPAs) during the past several years, to post–World War II lows, has kindled renewed interest in alternative measures of saving and their relative merits. In particular, saving as measured in the capital accounts prepared by the Flow of Funds Section of the Board of Governors of the Federal Reserve System often has been cited as an alternative to the income/expenditure-based NIPA measure. The measurement of personal saving in the flow-of-funds accounts (FFAs) is not, however, as well understood by many users of these statistics as the income-less-expenditure framework employed in the NIPAs.

The numerical difference between the NIPA and the FFA measures is definitionally the imbalance between estimated sources and uses of funds in the household sector of the FFAs (the so-called household discrepancy—saving plus changes in liabilities less changes in assets). That is, personal saving measured via the capital account route starts with NIPA saving as a source of funds to the sector. Credit market

John F. Wilson is chief of the Flow of Funds Section, Division of Research and Statistics, Board of Governors of the Federal Reserve System. James L. Freund and Frederick O. Yohn, Jr., were staff economists in the Flow of Funds Section at the time this paper was prepared; Freund is now with the Federal Home Loan Bank Board. Walther Lederer is a consultant for the section and has previously served as chief of the Commerce Department's Balance of Payments Division.

The authors wish to express appreciation to Steve Taylor, John Gorman, George von Furstenberg, Robert Lipsey, and Helen Tice for helpful comments on drafts of this paper. Phil Laughlin and Dave Ribar provided valuable research and charting assistance; Rebecca Hughes, Jim Courtney, Theresa Lee, and LaVerne Grant patiently prepared several versions of the manuscript.

borrowing and other increases in liabilities are added as additional sources of funds, and the total is compared with households' estimated net purchases of physical and financial assets. Resulting imbalances typically show higher increases in assets than can be accounted for by measured sources of funds. This usually gives rise to an estimate of personal saving, definitionally the same as in the NIPAs, that is higher than the NIPA measure. Examining possible sources of the household discrepancy thus is important to understanding why these two sets of social accounts produce different results; that is the main objective of this paper.

The remainder of this introduction reviews recent movements in saving measures and provides some detail on sector discrepancies. Section 2.2 describes the discrepancy system in the FFAs, putting the household discrepancy in the context of other balances in the system. The next six sections explore possible explanations for the household discrepancy. Section 2.3 discusses the role of data revisions, especially in the NIPAs. Section 2.4 discusses the role of asset write-offs in commercial banking, nonfinancial business, and the federal government. Section 2.5 discusses the possibilities for direct measurement of household financial positions. Section 2.6 discusses the effect on household accounts of measurement errors in estimates for nonfinancial business sectors. Section 2.7 examines possible links between international transactions and other sector imbalances. Section 2.8 looks at several issues for which the evidence is less complete: transactions in land and tangible assets, new institutions, brokers and dealers, and the underground economy. Section 2.9 summarizes the findings and draws a few conclusions.

It seems worthwhile to underscore at the outset that exactly what constitutes "personal saving" is a matter of definition and therefore open to discussion (cf. Boskin 1986). The FFAs, indeed, have long presented alternatives to the NIPA measure, and there is a considerable literature about other approaches (see, e.g., Holloway chap. 1, in this vol.; and Hendershott and Peek, chap. 4, in this vol.). The present essay, we hope, avoids any tone of advocacy in this matter; its intent is to explore measurement differences between two sets of accounts strictly on the NIPA definition of personal saving.

2.1.1 Recent Movement in Saving Measures

As may be seen in the upper panel of figure 2.1, the dollar value of personal saving as measured by the FFAs (i.e., from capital accounts) has exceeded that measured by the NIPAs (from the income/expenditure perspective) by a considerable margin in recent years, and this has received occasional attention in the financial press (cf. Arenson 1981 and Berry 1985). The gap also can be presented, as in the lower

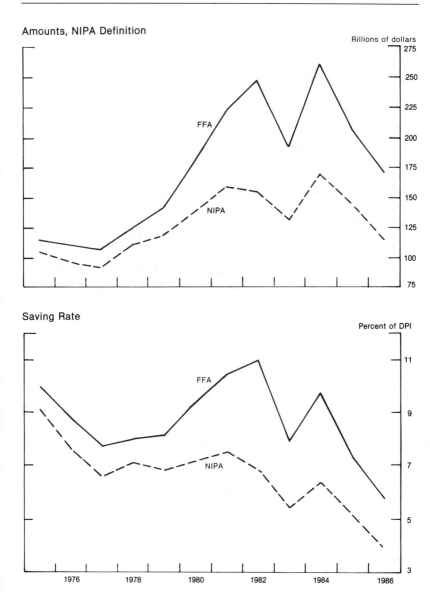

Amounts, NIPA Definition

Billions of dollars

FFA

NIPA

Saving Rate

Percent of DPI

FFA

NIPA

Fig. 2.1   Personal saving in the NIPAs and FFAs

panel, relative to income in the form of the personal saving rate. Both measures indicate that saving by households has weakened considerably relative to income during the current economic expansion. The NIPA saving rate fell to its lowest level since 1947, averaging just 3.8 percent in 1986. The FFA measure also was quite low in historical perspective in 1986, at 5.9 percent, having fallen more than 4 percentage points from a recent peak of 10.9 percent reached in 1982.[1]

The low and falling NIPA saving rate, of course, reflects strong estimated expenditures relative to income. However, additional information can be garnered on household behavior from financial asset and liability changes estimated from the capital account perspective, as described above. In the FFAs, the declining saving rate in recent years reflects in part a surge in household borrowing—presumably to finance consumption spending—relative to estimated acquisition of assets. Lines 1–4 of table 2.1 summarize the elements of capital account saving calculated from the FFAs; figure 2.2 shows these same elements relative to income.

The increased pace of asset acquisition relative to sources of funds (i.e., NIPA saving and borrowing) has augmented measured gross saving in the FFAs in recent years. Household purchases of tangible assets have grown noticeably throughout the current economic expansion—both absolutely and relative to income. Likewise, acquisitions of financial assets have picked up smartly. On the average during the 1984–86 period, households acquired about $460 billion net of financial assets—up on the average by $100 billion from three years earlier. In fact, when measured relative to income, households during this interval acquired financial assets at the most rapid pace in postwar history.

Increases in household assets, however, have been accompanied by rapid growth in credit market borrowing and other financial liabilities. As may be seen in line 3 of table 2.1, during the current economic expansion borrowing climbed from a $95.3 billion rate in 1982 (the recession trough) to around $300 billion in both 1985 and 1986. This represented an increase of more than 200 percent, compared with 44 percent growth in purchases of financial and tangible assets over this four-year period. This disparity held down the growth of gross personal saving as measured by the capital accounts, but saving nonetheless rose by more than $100 billion in dollar terms (table 2.1, line 4).

To make personal saving derived from the FFAs conceptually comparable to the NIPA measure, some accounting adjustments are necessary. These are indicated in lines 5–8 of table 2.1. Capital consumption allowances for all types of tangible goods (housing and consumer durables) must be subtracted to obtain saving on a net basis (line 6). Further, since net consumer durable outlays are not treated as saving in the NIPAs, they must be subtracted (line 7). And because some income components in the FFAs are not included in NIPA personal income, these also must be subtracted (line 7). After these adjustments, line 8 shows the FFA estimate of saving on the same conceptual basis as the NIPA measurement, while line 9 shows the direct NIPA estimate.

Table 2.1 Decomposition of Household Saving from the Flow-of-Funds Perspective (billions of dollars)

		1980	1981	1982	1983	1984	1985	1986
	1. Capital expenditures[a]	342.7	352.0	355.0	427.8	500.2	535.3	581.4
+	2. Acquisition of financial assets	278.9	327.1	351.0	377.0	469.0	490.2	439.0
−	3. Change in liabilities	130.0	124.2	95.3	198.7	237.2	312.7	297.6
=	4. Gross personal saving, FFAs	491.6	564.9	610.7	606.1	732.0	712.8	722.9
−	5. Capital consumption allowances	243.1	263.7	280.3	294.7	310.4	332.8	355.0
=	6. Net personal saving, FFAs	248.5	301.2	330.3	311.4	421.6	380.0	367.9
−	7. Net consumer durables spending	31.9	37.4	37.2	62.7	92.7	102.9	113.6
−	8. Income adjustments[b]	37.1	42.4	46.3	57.9	69.9	71.4	80.3
=	9. Personal saving, NIPA basis; FFA measurement	179.5	221.4	247.0	190.8	259.0	205.7	174.0
	Memo:							
	10. Personal saving, NIPAs	136.9	159.4	154.0	130.6	168.7	143.3	114.0
	11. FFA saving less NIPA	42.6	62.0	93.0	60.2	90.3	62.4	60.0

[a]Residential construction, expenditures on consumer durable goods, and nonprofit plant and equipment.
[b]Credits from government insurance plus capital gains distributions from mutual funds.

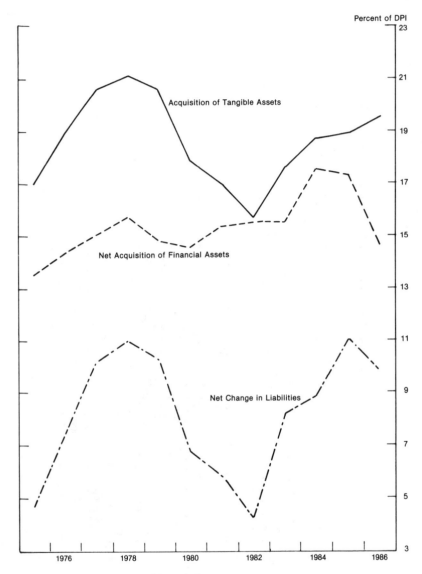

Fig. 2.2   Household capital accounts

For some years the FFA measure of this quantity has been higher than the estimate made by the Commerce Department. This has been especially true since 1980, when the dollar value of the difference about doubled to $40 billion. Commerce analysts, among others, have studied these disparate results (Mann 1987).

2.1.2   Some Detail on Sector Discrepancies

The much-publicized widening of the gap between the NIPA and the FFA measures of personal saving, when stated on the same basis, is entirely equivalent to the much-less-discussed growth of the household sector discrepancy calculated in the FFAs. The (negative) $68 billion average annual rate of this discrepancy over the 1980–85 period represents a four-fold increase from its average during the last half of the 1970s (table 2.2).

The marked negative swing in the household discrepancy has been accompanied by a substantial positive rise in the discrepancy of the nonfinancial corporate sector. Over the past five years, this discrepancy averaged almost $31 billion—some three-and-a-half times its average during the preceding five years. The coincident swelling of these two imbalances, together with their opposite arithmetic signs, has led some observers to attribute much of the growing personal saving gap to a sustained intersectoral misallocation of financial assets, and possibly liabilities, in the FFAs. This hypothesis is, of course, strengthened by the fact—discussed in more detail below—that some asset and liability items for the household sector are, by necessity, measured as residuals between system totals and amounts attributed to other sectors, so that mismeasurement of financial items for other sectors can result in off-setting errors in the household financial accounts.

Looking at the dollar discrepancy figures in the context of the overall scale of the U.S. economy, however, gives a somewhat different impression. Measuring in relation to trend gross national product (GNP) confirms the pronounced expansion of the household sector's discrepancy since 1980 (fig. 2.3, top panel), but on this "deflated basis" the nonfinancial corporate discrepancy has shown only very modest growth on balance during the past fifteen years. Moreover, the pronounced year-to-year fluctuations in the household discrepancy since 1980 have been very poorly correlated with movements in the corporate discrepancy, despite somewhat closer correlation during the 1970s.

As close inspection of table 2.2 makes clear, nominal dollar growth in the nonfinancial corporate discrepancy, even if entirely allocable to movement in the household discrepancy, accounts for less than half the $50 billion rise in the latter. Moreover, the growth of other nonfinancial sectors' discrepancies, although of the correct sign, together amounts to less than 20 percent of the expansion in the household discrepancy. Statistical discrepancies in financial sectors in the FFAs, in contrast, have grown only modestly during the past fifteen years, in large part owing to the more accurate and complete financial data available for most financial entities.

Table 2.2   **Sector Discrepancies: Historical Movements (annual averages in billions of dollars)**

	Household	Nonfinancial Corporate	Foreign	Other Nonfinancial	Financial Sectors	Total System
1970–74	–1.2	5.3	–4.2	3.3	2.7	5.8
1975–79	–15.1	8.4	6.0	7.1	–.6	5.9
1980–85	–68.4	30.7	17.1	12.4	–1.9	–10.1
Memo:						
1980–85 less 1975–79	–53.3	22.3	11.1	5.3	–1.3	–15.9

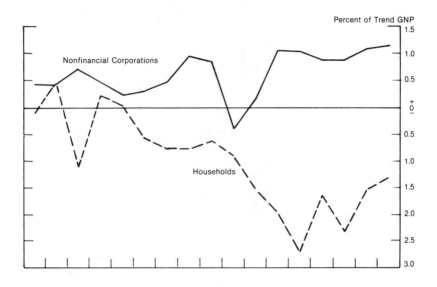

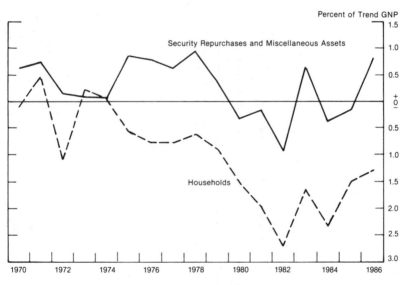

Fig. 2.3   Sector discrepancies relative to GNP

The total system discrepancy in the FFAs also has grown somewhat in absolute terms over the past several years. From a positive average in the 1970s, this discrepancy—which is the sum of all transactions discrepancies, including the NIPA discrepancy—declined rapidly in the 1980s to a negative $10 billion average level. As seen in table 2.3, the $16 billion change in the system discrepancy amounts to a slightly

Table 2.3   Transaction Discrepancies (annual averages in billions of dollars)

	Treasury Currency	Interbank Claims	Security Repos	Demand Deposit Float	Trade Credit	Taxes Payable	Miscellaneous Assets	National Income	Total System
1970–74	–.1	–.8	2.4	1.4	–.8	–.0	1.1	2.5	5.8
1975–79	–.1	–2.5	7.7	.9	–6.1	.2	6.7	–.9	5.9
1980–85	–.2	–.3	–4.8	4.0	–3.9	–.5	–2.8	–1.5	–10.1
Memo:									
1980–85 less 1975–79	.1	2.2	–12.5	3.1	2.2	–.7	–9.5	–.6	–15.9

greater share of the corresponding change in the household discrepancy than does the nonfinancial corporate discrepancy.

On balance, changes in the transaction discrepancies for security repurchase agreements (RPs) and miscellaneous assets have accounted for the bulk of the marked growth in the total system discrepancy (table 2.3). From positive average positions in the 1970s, each of these two discrepancies has swung to sharply negative averages in the 1980s. While their combined (negative) $22 billion change from one period average to the next was partially offset by smaller positive changes in net interbank, trade credit discrepancies and floats, the total system discrepancy underwent a large negative change.

As shown in table 2.4, year-to-year fluctuations in the dollar value of the RP and miscellaneous asset discrepancies have been quite closely correlated with the pronounced movements in the household sector discrepancy; when measured relative to trend GNP (fig. 2.3, bottom panel) this correlation also is visible. Between 1978 and 1981, the RP and miscellaneous assets discrepancies fell, on balance, almost $59 billion, or about three-fourths of the corresponding widening in the household sector discrepancy. As is evident, sectoral and transaction discrepancies are interconnected in the FFAs, so the following section looks at this subject in greater detail as background to how financial measures throughout the accounts may affect household saving measurement.

2.2 Discrepancy System in FFAs

Economic measurements—financial and nonfinancial—are generally imprecise and subject to error from many sources, including conflicting and inconsistent data, sampling and estimation problems, timing differences, and outright misreporting of key information. Thus both the NIPA and the FFA statistics present estimates of key aggregates, such as saving, that are at best approximations of reality, even when definitional differences are eliminated.

The only statistical imbalance presented explicitly in the NIPAs is that between estimates of gross investment and saving (table 5.1 in *Survey of Current Business*), which is carried into the FFAs as the "nonfinancial discrepancy." As a difference between gross sources and uses of funds, this discrepancy is needed in the financial accounts, but in addition there are many others derived from the financial calculations. For illustration, table 2.4, which is published as part of the quarterly FFAs, shows detailed sectoral and transactions imbalances in various parts of the system.

Discrepancies arise (and are acknowledged) in numerous places in the FFA system because of the diffuse and incomplete data sources

Table 2.4   Discrepancies—Summary for Sectors and Transactions: Annual Flows, 1975–86 (billions of dollars)

						Sector Discrepancies						
	1975	1976	1977	1978	1979	1980	1981	1982	1983	1984	1985	1986
1 Total, all sectors	11.9	4.9	-1.5	18.5	-4.2	-27.4	-.7	-18.9	-13.2	-15.3	15.2	28.4
2 Households	-9.6	-14.2	-15.6	-13.7	-22.2	-42.6	-62.0	-93.0	-60.2	-90.3	-62.5	-55.5
3 Nonfinancial corporate business	5.0	8.7	19.3	19.2	-10.1	4.4	33.3	35.6	32.2	34.3	44.6	49.6
4 State and local governments	.6	.7	-4.8	5.9	10.9	8.9	4.7	2.9	5.4	4.6	5.1	1.8
5 U.S. government	2.6	4.3	5.6	4.0	5.7	-.6	10.2	3.2	10.2	11.8	8.2	6.1
6 Foreign	2.4	5.8	-7.8	7.6	22.2	17.1	15.5	29.2	4.7	20.0	16.3	20.2
7 Financial sectors	11.0	-.6	1.8	-4.5	-10.7	-14.6	-2.4	3.2	-5.4	4.3	3.5	6.2
8 Sponsored credit agencies	*	*	*	.1	.2	.5	.7	.3	.1	.1	1.8	.3
9 Monetary authority	–	–	–	–	–	–	–	–	–	–	–	–
10 Commercial banks	8.6	3.8	.1	-2.8	-5.0	-4.1	7.4	6.3	6.3	2.7	-11.9	-11.0
11 Private nonbank finance	2.4	-4.3	1.7	-1.8	-5.9	-11.0	-10.4	-3.4	-11.7	1.5	13.5	16.9
12 Savings and loan associations	*	-.2	-.5	-.2	-.3	.8	-.3	-.8	1.8	1.9	2.5	.9
13 Mutual savings banks	-.1	-.2	-.3	*	*	-.2	-.4	-1.2	-1.7	-.4	-1.7	-4.6
14 Life insurance	-.3	.5	1.3	1.5	-.5	-.1	1.1	-1.3	-.7	1.0	.4	.8
15 Other insurance	-.9	-2.9	-1.6	-.8	1.1	1.9	.7	*	-1.8	1.5	-.5	*
16 Finance, not elsewhere classified	3.6	-1.6	2.7	-2.3	-6.3	-13.3	-11.6	-.2	-9.3	-2.6	12.8	19.8

Transaction Discrepancies

1 Total, all types	11.9	4.7	-1.5	18.5	-4.2	-27.4	-.7	-18.9	-13.2	-15.3	15.2	28.4
2 Treasury currency	-.1	-.1	-.3	*	-.2	-.2	-.2	-.2	-.2	-.1	-.2	*
3 Interbank claims	-3.2	-.9	-7.1	-.5	-1.0	-3.6	-.5	-1.0	-11.6	7.4	7.7	2.3
4 Security RPs	2.6	8.5	6.4	15.9	4.8	10.0	-7.5	-15.9	.4	-19.4	3.3	11.0
Demand deposit mail floats:												
5 U.S. government	.1	-.8	1.5	*	.3	-.6	-1.1	-.4	2.0	1.1	1.2	-.6
6 Other	1.6	.6	1.8	-.5	-.1	2.3	4.1	3.2	.1	8.1	3.8	1.6
7 Trade credit	2.8	-5.0	-8.9	-4.8	-14.4	-10.5	6.9	14.0	-20.3	-13.8	.6	-4.1
8 Profit taxes payable	-1.0	.2	-1.0	1.5	1.5	.6	.7	-2.5	-1.4	-4.5	3.9	-2.6
9 Miscellaneous	11.6	5.9	6.1	4.9	4.9	-19.4	2.1	-16.2	23.2	3.9	-10.6	23.9
10 Nonfinancial	-2.5	-3.6	*	1.9	-.2	-6.1	-5.2	.1	-5.3	1.9	5.6	-3.1
Nonfinancial components:												
11 NIPA discrepancy	2.5	3.6	*	-1.9	.2	6.1	5.2	-.1	5.3	-1.9	-5.6	3.1
12 Private wage accruals less disbursements	-	-	-	-	-	-	-	-	-	-	-	-

Note: * = less than $50 million; - = 0.

that contribute to sector and transactions estimates. In the typical case for economic sectors, the NIPAs provide estimates of nonfinancial sources (saving) and uses (capital investment) of funds, but estimates of financial sources and uses must be pieced together from a variety of other data sources that were not designed to produce a coherent picture of financing activity and in which enumeration of transactions types is highly inconsistent. FFA discrepancies thus make explicit provision for the ensuing uncertainties. For a few sectors for which complete balance sheets are available and for which these balance sheets constitute the sole source of sectoral data, there is no discrepancy. An example is the Federal Reserve System, shown as "monetary authority" in the accounts. For other, mostly financial, entities such as thrift institutions, estimates are largely, but not completely, taken from sectoral balance sheets, so that small discrepancies may still arise in reconciliations of asset/liability flows with control totals. Households and nonfinancial corporations typically show substantial discrepancies. Since sectoral discrepancies in the system are the imbalance between estimated sources of funds and their uses, these results suggest that the accounts typically produce too much corporate saving/borrowing relative to capital expenditures and financial uses of funds, whereas for households the opposite is the case.

Transactions discrepancies, on the other hand, display uncertainty about the size of several kinds of financial markets. Typically, it is not possible to reconcile information drawn from one set of sources about the net issuance of a particular type of financial liability with that from others on the acquisition of the corresponding claims. Often there is better information on the issuance of claims than on their purchase. However, not all forms of transactions show discrepancies in the accounts (cf. table 2.4)). For instance, estimated net issuance of corporate bonds and equities in the system are "exhausted" in each period by explicit allocations of the total to various sectors. That is, given an estimate of the net issuance of bonds as liabilities, net purchase estimates for all but one holding sectors are derived from one or more data sources, and the estimate for the last sector is made as a residual. In such a case, the accounts will not show an explicit "bonds" discrepancy, but that should not be construed as a lack of uncertainty, either about the net amount of bond issuance or its distribution in holdings. The FFAs simply "assign" residual uncertainty to changes in one sector's asset holdings, frequently to households. This assignment reflects an analytic judgment about the kinds of markets in which each economic sector tends to operate, and thus is not a simple arithmetic convenience.

Other transaction accounts make provision for an explicit discrepancy, usually when there is a statistical basis for measuring both asset and liability changes or when the residual cannot be allocated with confidence to one of the named holding sectors. A good example of this, mentioned earlier, is security repurchase transactions. Liabilities of this form originate in a limited range of financial institutions, and the total therefore can be measured fairly well. The range of asset holders is broader and cannot be measured at all well from existing sources, except for commercial banks. Even for other financial institutions, RP assets often are merged together in regulatory reports with some "cash assets" composite, where they cannot be disentangled from deposits or other short-term assets. In such a case, rather than assume that residual RP holdings are by households or another sector in the system, the FFAs make provision for an explicit imbalance, giving rise to a transactions discrepancy.

In the purely arithmetic sense, obviously, either of these two routes could be followed for any kind of transaction; the decision about which should be used has been based on familiarity with individual data sources, analysis, and judgment. Again, as an arithmetic matter, most transactions discrepancies could be mechanically eliminated from the system, or more could be added. Since the system totals of transactions and sector discrepancies are the same, eliminating the former perforce would reduce the latter, but this would not really solve the underlying problems of imprecision in data sources. The resulting uncertainties merely would be buried in ways that would obscure the amounts by which both sectoral and transactions estimates seem questionable.

In a few cases, balance sheet information from several sectors conflicts, leading to a certain "overdetermination" that occasions a transaction discrepancy. An example is the two versions of federal government cash balances at depository institutions. Typically, the federal data (e.g., *Monthly Treasury Statement*) show different balances than banking source data, so the accounts record a transactions "float."

It is well known that the household sector of the accounts is the principal "residual" in the overall set of calculations, in the sense that households do not report directly any element of their assets and liabilities. All information on this sector is derived from statements of other transactors. The Flow of Funds Section staff has relatively more control over household asset than liability estimates because the bulk of the data on saving and other sources of funds are generated elsewhere, inside or outside the Federal Reserve.[2] If, for whatever reason, total liability or asset changes of other sectors are misestimated, household balance sheets become the "dumping ground" for the errors. The typically negative numerical values of the household discrepancy are at least consistent with the notion of persistent underestimates of household saving/borrowing, underestimates of asset acquisitions by other sectors (e.g., corporations), or both. Errors in any or all of the nonfinancial and financial figures contribute equally to this discrepancy, and, in the highly interdependent context of the accounts, it is hardly ever clear which of these components may be the underlying source of a problem.

The fact that the FFAs "assign" certain residual asset holdings to households largely is a matter of arithmetic convenience, but the calculation process should not be interpreted too mechanically. The problem, again, is that, even if there were exact information on the issuance of most financial claims, information on purchases by other sectors than households often is imprecise. Sometimes the problem is more severe. With corporate bonds, for instance, there remains some slack both in the estimates of total issuance and in those of purchases by sectors other than households.[3] Data sources simply are not coherent enough to establish either in such a way that changes in household assets are cleanly derivable from a known total and complete data on all other purchasers.

Against this background, it may be tempting to conclude that the negative household discrepancy results from systematic overstatement of certain asset purchases, but, even if this were the case, it would be difficult to establish where the problems originate in the capital account estimates.[4] In addition, errors can be introduced through problems with the NIPAs and, perhaps, with the balance of payments data, which also are used in the accounts. (We will take up this topic shortly.)

2.2.1 The Household Discrepancy in Relation to System Imbalances

System totals of sectoral and transactions discrepancies are equal in the FFAs, but that total is not the same as the nonfinancial discrepancy from the NIPA accounts: calculation of the FFAs introduces into the national accounts an additional imbalance that is spread across various sectors and transactions forms. From a capital account perspective, this means that a national saving total derived from the FFAs would be slightly different from the NIPA income/expenditure total. The difference between the sector/transactions total and (the negative of) the nonfinancial discrepancy is the sum of the transactions discrepancies that have been defined in the accounts.[5]

It is implied, therefore, that, if the accounts were restructured to eliminate transactions discrepancies completely (toward the form in which corporate and government bonds are handled, e.g.), differences between the "total" FFA discrepancy and the NIPA residual would be wiped out, the balance being absorbed somewhere in the sectoral discrepancies. Clearly, such a solution is more akin to burying the problem than to solving it.

The question thus arises, How sensitive is the household discrepancy to adjustments to the accounts as they are prepared each quarter? Alternatively, as sector and transactions discrepancies are adjusted, what kinds of changes are offset in other sectors or transactions without affecting the system total, and what kinds simply contribute to changes in the system total without effects elsewhere?

The answer to these questions will be put with reference to the household sector as a participant in certain asset/liability markets and as a "residual" purchaser of most assets. The effect in each case depends on the array of named assets and liabilities in which sectors are assumed to transact.[6] Many changes in estimates of major forms of sectoral sources and uses of funds that alter discrepancies in those sectors are simply offset in others, most frequently households, without changing imbalances in the system total. Within the categories of trans- actions discrepancies, this one-for-one substitutability does not exist because forms of transactions do not "overlap" with each other as do elements of sectoral balance sheets. Given a liability total, however, the essence of a transactions discrepancy is some difference between identified holders of that instrument and the total itself. Thus, a change to transactions accounts that moves part or all of that difference into (or out of) a named holder's accounts likewise will produce a sectoral offset that will not affect the system total.

While many kinds of changes to sectoral estimates will affect the household discrepancy, only two transactions types (cf. table 2.4) will potentially have a direct effect on that quantity: demand deposits mail float and trade credit. The former occurs because, as noted, floats represent timing differences between deposit records of different sec- tors; as there are bank records on deposits (albeit without good dis- tinctions between business and households) but none directly from households, some provision is needed for this item. Float is an unal- located asset, so raising/lowering it serves to lower/raise estimates of household deposits and thus changes the sectoral imbalance. Trade credit can have a similar mechanical effect because the nonprofit sub- sector of households has some trade debt (although true households are not holders of trade credit). Thus, there is a potential trade-off between this discrepancy and that in households. Both these items are, however, minor influences. Most of the scope for "adjusting" the household discrepancy and apparent differences with the NIPA saving estimates comes in through efforts to balance out sectoral patterns of discrepancies.

Two points arising from this discussion may perhaps be underscored. First, while household sector financial aggregates are often described as "residuals," this is true only in a narrow arithmetic perspective. Account calculation involves asset/liability estimates in many places;

published results are best conceived as simultaneous solutions for all sectors/transactions in the system taken together. This process involves reference to past history, knowledge of strengths and weaknesses in available data sources, and a certain amount of judgment applied to data that are extraordinarily diffuse and not at all coordinated with each other. Second, sources and uses of funds estimates for most non-financial sectors are largely independent of each other, giving rise to the potential for household and other differences with NIPA saving statistics. Both financial and nonfinancial data are potential digging ground in the effort to reduce sectoral discrepancies. The balance of this paper will provide more detail about possible areas of weakness in both the nonfinancial and the financial calculations that, if overcome, might bring the figures somewhat closer together.

2.3   The Role of Data Revisions

The comparison given in section 2.1 of recent household discrepancies with those of earlier years has overlooked the probably significant effect of future data revisions on current estimates of near-term discrepancies. For example, initial estimates of household-sector discrepancies for the 1975–79 period (table 2.2) were revised down in absolute magnitude by about 25 percent on the average during the four years following the first publication of annual totals.

Revisions to the household—or, for that matter, another sector's—discrepancy reflect the sum of revisions to both income and balance sheet data for the sector. In analyzing such revisions, it is useful to differentiate between revisions to NIPA data incorporated in the FFAs and revisions to financial data. Since federal income tax return data—a principal source of benchmark data for the NIPAs—are available only with a three-year lag, a useful perspective on data revisions is provided by the total or cumulative revision to a data estimate that occurs in the four years following the initial estimate.[7]

As shown in the first column of table 2.5, the $13.5 billion annual average upward revision to the NIPA personal saving estimates for the 1975–79 interval—amounting to about 50 percent of the gap between the two personal saving measures—was due almost entirely to upward revisions to disposable personal income (DPI) estimates for this period. These income revisions, which amount to about 1 percent of the period-average (DPI), reflect unemployment insurance data introduced one year after the original estimate as well as benchmark *Statistics of Income* data introduced three years after the initial estimate. This revision history suggests greater near-term accuracy of the NIPA product-expenditure estimates than in the income estimates.

Relative to the substantial upward revision in the NIPA income statement–based personal saving estimates for the 1975–79 period, balance

Table 2.5   **Revisions to Household Sector's Sources and Uses of Funds (annual averages in billions of dollars)[a]**

| | 1975–79 | | | 1980–82 | | |
	4-Year	Bench-mark	Total	4-Year	Bench-mark	Total
Disposable personal income	13.4	67.2	80.6	8.0	85.2	93.2
Less personal outlays	− .2	49.4	49.2	− 1.0	63.1	62.1
Equals NIPA personal saving	13.6	17.8	31.4	9.0	22.2	31.1
Net capital expenditures	8.8	12.9	21.7	3.3	11.0	14.3
Plus net financial investment	.0	− 2.2	− 2.2	. . .	. . .	− 3.1
Equals FFA personal saving	5.5	8.3	13.8	. . .	. . .	12.6
Household-sector discrepancy[b]	8.1	9.5	17.6	14.2	4.3	18.5
Average revisions as percent of average initial estimates:						
Disposable personal income	1.0	5.1	6.1	.4	4.2	4.6
Personal outlays	0	3.9	3.9	− .1	3.3	3.3
NIPA personal savings	18.8	24.5	43.3	7.6	18.7	26.1
Household-sector discrepancy	24.7	29.0	53.8	16.8	5.1	21.9
Personal saving rate[c]	1.0	1.3	2.4	.4	1.1	1.5

[a]Average of total revision to annual estimate between initial estimate and estimate four years later. The "four-year" effect reflects new data sources; the benchmark effect reflects definitional and other changes made during 1985.

[b]Household discrepancy equals income statement–based estimate of personal saving less balance sheet–based estimate.

[c]Revision to personal saving as a percentage of initial disposable personal income estimates.

sheet–based personal saving estimates from the FFAs were revised by lesser amounts. As shown in the first column of table 2.5, upward revisions to NIPA data on net physical capital acquisitions by households—averaging over $5 billion—caused an increase in the balance sheet–based measure of personal saving, while net financial investment on the average was unchanged. On balance, the NIPA data revisions alone resulted in an almost 25 percent narrowing of the gap between the two alternative saving estimates for this period.[8]

Abstracting from the steady-state differences between the two estimates, the appreciably smaller revision to the FFA-derived personal saving estimates for the 1975–79 period has suggested to some observers that the indirect or balance sheet–based approach provides more accurate near-term estimates of movements in the personal saving rate.[9] Unfortunately, the financial press often has confused this point with the more difficult to interpret issue of the steady-state differences in the levels of the two estimates. Moreover, differences in accounting for consumer durables between NIPA personal saving and the most visible FFA personal saving figure—which, by including net consumer durables, is different from the NIPA measure—have further confused discussions in the financial press (see Murray 1983).

The 1980–82 period, as discussed above, witnessed a rapid expansion of the household sector's discrepancy. This three-year period, the most recent for which *Statistics of Income* benchmark data are now fully incorporated in the NIPAs, also is characterized by a very different data revision experience. However, comparison of this recent period with the 1975–79 four-year revision experience is complicated by the far-reaching benchmark revision to the NIPAs introduced in late 1985 (see Parker and Fox 1985). The effect of these revisions—which included important definitional changes, particularly the capitalization of expenditures on repairs and improvements to owner-occupied housing—are shown for the 1975–79 period in the second column of table 2.5. The upward revisions to both disposable personal income and personal outlays were quite sizable, amounting to almost 5 percent of the respective earlier estimates. On balance, NIPA personal saving also was revised up considerably, somewhat exceeding the data source-related revision.

While these definitional benchmark revisions considerably altered the level of NIPA personal saving, they had only a moderate effect on the gap between the NIPA and the FFA saving measures since the upward revision to the NIPA's net capital expenditure data also is incorporated in the balance sheet-based estimates of personal saving. On balance, the benchmark revisions, together with relatively minor further revisions to net financial investment estimates for households, resulted in an average further reduction in the saving gap of about $8 billion, only slightly more than the effect of the four-year data revision.

For the 1980–82 period, therefore, benchmark definitional revisions are overlaid on revisions attributable solely to incorporation of additional *Statistics of Income* data. This confluence prevents a direct comparison between the observed, or total, four-year revisions for this recent period—shown in column 6 of table 2.5—with the four-year revision experience for the 1975–79 period shown in column 1. The benchmark revision effect for this recent period is readily computed, however, enabling the approximate decomposition of the two revision effects shown in columns 4 and 5.

As in the earlier period, benchmark-related revisions to disposable income for 1980–82 are quite large relative to the corresponding initial estimates. However, the additional data-related revisions inferred for this three-year period are considerably smaller than those for the 1975–79 period, when these revisions averaged about 1 percent of DPI.

As in the 1975–79 period, new data-related revisions to personal outlays were quite small on the average over 1980–82, amounting to about one-tenth of 1 percent of the initial estimate. On balance, these revisions to NIPA personal income and outlays resulted in upward revisions to the income expenditure-based measure of personal saving that averaged less than 8 percent of initial estimates. These moderate data-related revisions to NIPA personal saving data for 1980–82 contrast with the pronounced upward revision experience of the 1975–79 period.

Benchmark-related revisions to personal income and outlays for 1980–82, as estimated in column 5, produced a large upward revision to personal saving estimates, amounting to almost 20 percent of initial saving estimates. Although the overall average revision to NIPA personal saving estimates for 1980–82 in nominal dollars is only slightly smaller than the corresponding 1975–79 figure, as a percent of initial personal saving estimates the recent average revision is less than two-thirds the earlier total revision.

The effect of the benchmark revision also carries over to NIPA net capital expenditure estimates for the 1980–82 period. The effect of this revision on the balance sheet–based measure of personal saving is only partially offset by a modest downward revision to net financial investment estimates. On balance, the average dollar gap between the two personal saving estimates for 1980–82 was narrowed by only about as much as for the 1975–79 period, despite the much larger initial average discrepancy. Indeed, as a percentage of initial discrepancy estimates, the 1980–82 average revision was only about half the 1975–79 average.

In summary, comparison of recent revision experience with the second half of the 1970s suggests an appreciable downward bias to the NIPA's pre-1985 benchmark estimates of both disposable income and personal saving. Based on this earlier experience, introduction of *Statistics of Income* benchmarks and unemployment insurance data for the 1983–86 period might be expected to raise the current very low personal saving rate estimates by up to 1 percentage point on the average while at the same time lowering the household sector's discrepancy in the FFAs by 20–50 percent. It should be clear, in any case, that a substantial fraction of the household discrepancy can in principle be associated with provisional national accounts data and that in some circumstances revisions to nonfinancial elements of the accounts can markedly change the apparent differences between saving estimates.

2.4   The Role of Asset Write-offs

The possible role of asset write-offs in generating sectoral imbalances in the FFAs is a subject that has received little attention. In this area, certain problems may exist in both the NIPA and the FFA statistics. As this section will show, reliable quantifications of the extent to which write-offs affect financial and nonfinancial statistics are not yet possible, but certain directions are indicated, and the problem suggests that further exploration is warranted.

In social accounting, a transfer of purchasing power from one economic sector to another through lending (e.g., loans by banks to business or households) is considered a capital account transaction, not an element of income to the recipient. If such loans go bad and are written off by the lending sector, however, income of the borrowers is raised, in the sense of defaulter's gain. Gross additions to bad debt reserves are charged against operating income for tax purposes by lenders, but for national accounts purposes the actual or estimated amounts of write-offs are used to estimate lenders' income. Likewise, tax rules require defaulters, except in cases of bankruptcy, to add the amount of their defaults to their taxable income. The initial lending-borrowing relation is converted into a current transfer in which the capital account asset-liability balance is converted into offsetting income flows.

The possibility that net asset write-offs play some role in the FFA household discrepancy is suggested both by the negative sign of the discrepancy and by its rising amount since evidence from lending sectors shows increasing amounts of write-offs in the past few years. Because of the way data are assimilated into the FFAs, the source of a problem, if any, would appear to reside in the income/saving relations estimated in the NIPAs.

2.4.1 Commercial Banking

Taking banking as an example, the FFAs employ asset data from bank reports as their primary source of information about claims on sectors of the economy. Borrowing flows are derived by first-differencing claims reported on the loan schedule of successive quarterly Reports of Condition ("call" reports). Assets reported on this schedule are gross of bad debt provisions, but they are net of actual write-offs, so the calculated flows also are net of write-downs. When net write-offs (gross write-offs less recoveries) are positive, as is usually the case, such a procedure somewhat understates the true flow of capital to borrowers. However, if write-off amounts are reported in defaulters' tax statements or attributed by BEA staff using recent regulatory reports, then these amounts should also be reflected in defaulters' income/saving balances. All sources of funds to borrowers that are understated in FFAs because levels data were relied on to derive flows should be compensated by the extra income in the NIPAs for the defaulting sectors from the current account transfers represented by the defaults themselves.[10]

Experience of the past few years indicates that net write-offs of many kinds of loan balances have been rising fairly rapidly. Table 2.6 (drawn from call reports) shows the annual experience of domestically char-

Table 2.6   Net Write-offs at Domestically Chartered Commerical Banks
                   (billions of dollars)

Loan Type	1982[a]	1983[a]	1984	1985	1986
Real estate	.2	.3	.9	1.2	2.1
Domestic depository institutions	.04	.1	− .01	.03	.09
Agricultural loans	N.A.	N.A.	.9	1.4	1.2
Domestic commercial and industrial loans	2.1	2.5	5.7	5.4	6.4
Foreign loans	.5	.9	1.3	1.9	1.8
Individuals	1.1	1.0	1.7	3.1	4.6
Other	N.A.	N.A.	.3	.2	.1
Total	6.6	8.4	10.8	13.2	16.2

Source: Reports of Condition for domestically chartered commercial banks.
[a]Loan-type detail is only for banks with assets greater than $500 million. Detail not available for smaller banks.
N.A. = not available.

tered commercial banks from 1982 through 1986. The amounts are now sizable—over $16 billion in 1986, almost twice the 1983 value. The massive reserve provisions taken by major banks in mid-1987 likely portend further large write-offs. Discussions with BEA staff indicate that, in principle, write-offs by banking organizations are captured in the income/saving statistics, although there seems a possibility that, owing to the lag in financial corporate tax return data or extrapolation of write-off data from earlier experience, the acceleration of recent years may have been missed. This would lead to some understatement of sectoral income and saving. Because of lack of sectoral detail in banks' write-off figures, some uncertainty always attaches to allocation of these defaulters' gains. Write-downs of loans to individuals (consumer loans) clearly are benefits to households, but the sectoral allocation of commercial and industrial loans and real estate loans is not clear. Some part of both go to unincorporated business—ownership of which is attributed to households in the FFAs—but the amounts cannot be determined from the banking data.

Loan problems at U.S. branches and agencies of foreign banks pose an even more intractable problem because the basic report filed by these entities with federal regulators does not include write-off information from which estimates can be derived. At mid-year 1986, "foreign-related" banking in the FFAs had assets of approximately one-sixth those of domestically chartered banks. If the bad debt experience of foreign banks were comparable to that of domestically chartered banks, one might expect annual write-downs in the vicinity of $2.5 billion currently.

2.4.2   Nonfinancial Business

Write-offs of household debts to nonfinancial business is another potential problem area. At mid-1986, consumer credit extended by business to households totaled around $81 billion, about 12 percent of the total of installment plus noninstallment credit owed by households. Fragmentary evidence indicates that write-offs by such businesses, like those by financial institutions, have risen noticeably in the past few years, to around the 3–4 percent range annually, relative to outstanding assets. Again, BEA estimates take account of these (net) charge-offs in putting together the income/saving statistics, but the Internal Revenue Service (IRS)–based statistics on which estimates depend are usually three years old. It is possible that extrapolations of these data fail to capture all the apparent discrepancy.[11]

2.4.3   Federal Government

Finally, charge-offs of loans made or purchased by the U.S. government appear to be a factor contributing to discrepancies in the FFAs, in households and elsewhere. The federal government (excluding sponsored agencies) had a loan portfolio of almost $260 billion, about 12 percent of credit extended by all commercial banking, at the end of 1986. About one-fifth of this was direct mortgage holdings, with the balance in loans to domestic sectors and the rest of the world. Most of this portfolio originated with loans extended directly by the government; the remainder was largely acquired under numerous guarantee programs, sometimes to indemnify private sector institutions when loans they had issued became delinquent. As with banking data, the FFAs use first-differences in government loan-balance data to generate net flows to other sectors of the economy, and the same problems may ensue.

In federal budget accounting, the government's loan extensions or purchases are treated as outlays that, naturally, require financing and contribute to common measures of the federal deficit. This differs from treatment in the NIPAs, under which financial transactions are excluded from the deficit measure. Loan repayments are treated in the budget as negative expenditures that reduce financing needs, while charge-offs of existing loan balances contribute positively to the government's borrowing needs for any given level of assets kept on the books. Repayments and asset write-offs, therefore, reconcile "expenditures" for acquisitions of financial assets to changes in outstandings. Annual Office of Management and Budget budget materials afford at least some insight into the government's bad debt experience on a fiscal year basis.

Table 2.7 illustrates the substantial increase in government writedowns over the past several fiscal years. In fiscal year 1986 alone, the amount of such terminations rose by more than 50 percent, to more than $10 billion. As indicated by the table, available data on federal write-offs are organized by budget function, so exact sectoral allocations are uncertain. The budget data suggest, however, that a substan-

Table 2.7   **Federal Government Loan Write-offs (fiscal years, billions of dollars)**

Budget Category	1980	1981	1982	1983	1984	1985	1986
Student loans	. . .	. . .	.3	.7	.8	1.0	1.5
Veterans Administration	. . .	. . .	.7	1.1	1.1	1.4	1.5
Federal Housing Administration	.1	. . .	1.0	2.1	1.9	2.3	3.0
Farmers Home Administration	. . .	. . .	. . .	. . .	. . .	.1	.3
Commodity Credit Corporation	. . .	. . .	. . .	. . .	. . .	.2	.3
Small Business Administration	.2	. . .	1.2	1.2	1.0	1.0	1.0
Economic Development Revolving Fund	. . .	. . .	. . .	. . .	. . .	.1	.0
Maritime Administration	. . .	. . .	. . .	. . .	. . .	.3	1.2
Exim Bank	. . .	. . .	. . .	. . .	.5	.3	. . .
Other foreign loans[a]	. . .	. . .	.2	.4	.9	. . .	. . .
Other	.5	. . .	.2	.6	1.4[b]	.2	. . .
Total[c]	.9	. . .	3.7	6.1	7.8	6.8	10.3

Source: Office of Management and Budget, *Special Analyses: Budget of the United States Government,* Special Analysis F: Federal Credit Programs, various.

[a]Mostly military sales and the Agency for International Development.

[b]Includes grants to AMTRAK of $0.9 billion.

[c]Total may not equal sum of detail owing to rounding.

tial part of the recent bad debt experience has been with households and noncorporate business.

It appears that the present statistical treatment of federal write-offs contributes to the household discrepancy in the FFAs since the NIPAs currently do not include defaulters' gains on such loans. In the absence of parallel treatment in the NIPAs, accounting for such write-offs in the FFA statistics would require a "capital transfer account" to capture the income transfers from the government to defaulting sectors. Either this approach or the recognition of defaulters' gain on government loans in the NIPAs likely would shave some billions of dollars off the household discrepancy.

2.4.4 Summary

The volume of loan write-offs has been on the rise during the past few years. Since such amounts are deducted from income of lenders, conceptually they should be included as income to borrowers, whether to households or elsewhere in the economy. If they are not, or if the amount of such "extra" income is understated, saving estimates derived from nonfinancial accounts will tend to run low relative to estimates based on capital accounts, as seems to be the case with households. While the data summarized in table 2.8 are only suggestive of the beneficiary sectors, they show that bad debt experience of some major lenders has more than doubled in dollar volume in the last five

Table 2.8   Loan-Loss Reserves (A) or Write-offs (B): Selected Lenders
(billions of dollars)

	1982	1983	1984	1985	1986
Federal government (A)[a]	3.7	6.1	7.8	6.8	10.3
Commercial banks (B):	6.6	8.4	10.8	13.2	16.2
Domestically chartered					
Foreign related[b]	N.A.	N.A.	N.A.	N.A.	N.A.
Savings and loans (A)[c]	.8	1.1	2.4	4.0	N.A.
Farm Credit System (A)	.2	.2	.3	3.0	1.8

[a]Fiscal years.
[b]U.S. branches and agencies of foreign banks.
[c]Federal Savings and Loan Insurance Corporation–insured institutions.
N.A. = not available.

years. However, estimates of "business transfer payments" (to consumers—see NIPA table 1.9) rise only about 50 percent between 1982 and 1986. It seems possible, therefore, that the incorporation of tax return–based benchmark data in the periodic NIPA revisions eventually will capture this sharp upturn in private defaults, raising income/saving estimates in the NIPA statistics and reducing discrepancies between the capital and current account estimates in the FFA statistics. Not all this will accrue to households, of course, but the portion that does should cut the differences somewhat. The likely future recognition in the NIPAs of defaulters' gains on government loans also could reduce this discrepancy.

2.5   Direct Measurement of Households' Financial Position

The Federal Reserve Board's recently published Survey of Consumer Finances (SCF) (see Avery, Elliehausen, and Canner 1984a, 1984b; Avery and Elliehausen 1986; Avery et al. 1986) for 1983 represents the first attempt, since the board's 1963 Survey of Financial Characteristics of Consumers, to measure the complete balance sheet position of households directly. In contrast with earlier consumer finance surveys, the 1983 effort utilized substantial oversampling of wealthy households to compensate for the disproportionate share of many assets held by these households, in an effort to increase the statistical precision of the resulting estimates of total assets.

Although SCF data, as well as estate tax–based estimates of household wealth, have been available for certain points in time, the recent estimation of a separate balance sheet for nonprofit organizations has enabled the first direct comparison of the Flow of Funds Section balance sheet data for individuals—that is, the household sector published in the FFAs less the assets and liabilities of nonprofit organizations and private foundations. While a detailed comparison of these two sets of data is not yet complete, several important findings have emerged (table 2.9).

Even after the special sampling of high-income households, the 1983 survey-based estimates of households' financial asset holdings are substantially below the indirect estimates published in the FFAs. In particular, the SCF estimates confirm that the FFA procedure of "allocating" all mutual fund shares and money-market mutual fund (MMMF) deposits to households overstates their actual holdings of these instruments. For 1983, the difference between the two estimates of MMMF ownership amounted to about $80 billion, somewhat above the Investment Company Institute's estimate of institutional holdings of these assets.

The SCF estimates of individuals' holdings of other deposit assets are also substantially below the FFA indirect estimates for the survey period. Since the total amounts of such deposits can be measured accurately, this survey result tends to support the view that underallocation of financial assets to other sectors has induced overestimates of households' financial assets through the process discussed earlier. In addition, this apparent overestimate of individuals' demand deposits may reflect at least partly an increase in the float associated with consumers' demand deposits that is not captured in the FFAs. It should be noted, however, that the amount of bias in household deposit holdings is not well established. The SCF results are hardly definitive, and reports filed by depository institutions tend to lump business and personal accounts together, so that obligor data are not much use as a cross-check on the survey.

The SCF-based estimates of individuals' equity in unincorporated business also are substantially below the indirect estimates found in the FFAs. For 1983, the $540 billion difference between these two estimates amounts to more than 20 percent of the FFA total equity estimate for unincorporated businesses. This sizable difference may in

Table 2.9   **Comparison of Survey-based and FFA Estimates of Households' Financial Assets (billions of dollars)**

	1963		1983	
	Survey	FFA	Survey	FFA
Checkable and savings deposits	128	276	1,051	1,832[a]
Bonds and mortgages	75	123	566	498
Mutual funds	25	16	125	76
Corporate stock	197	350	970	968[a]
Unincorporated business equity	289	410	1,810	2,365

[a]Excludes estimates of holdings by nonprofit organizations.

part reflect corporate ownership claims on unincorporated business—
a type of corporate asset not currently recognized in the FFAs. This
omission, too, likely has contributed something to overestimates of
households' financial assets in the FFAs.

Some of the asset misallocation problems suggested by comparison
of SCF and FFA estimates of household asset holdings are potentially
soluble through exploitation of other data sources, such as *Statistics
of Income* special tabulations of partnership returns and Investment
Company Institute data on ownership of mutual funds. However, in
concept the direct incorporation of a complete survey-based household
balance sheet in estimating household sources and uses of funds data
published in the FFAs has certain advantages. By eliminating the need
to determine many household asset acquisitions as residuals, this approach could expand the measurement of transactions discrepancies
described above to include most financial instrument accounts. Given
the improved accuracy of survey-based estimates resulting from the
oversampling of high-income households and the potential availability
of regular data on nonprofit organizations, the exploitation of survey-
based household data in the FFAs nonetheless would be dependent on
assurance of continued, regular availability of consumer finance surveys. This appears unlikely in the foreseeable future; thus, the main
contribution of such surveys to improvements in the FFAs may be to
provide occasional reference points that draw attention to problem
areas and provide guidance for further research.

2.6   Estimates for Nonfinancial Business Sectors

As previously discussed, the size of the nonfinancial corporate discrepancy—together with its apparent inverse correlation with the
household discrepancy—has led some observers to conclude that inaccuracies in the FFAs' nonfinancial business sectors may be responsible for much of the divergence between NIPA- and FFA-based
measures of personal saving. Although the relation between these two
discrepancies is not nearly as close as some observers have suggested,
it is important to take into account the sources and potential effects
of nonfinancial business sector inaccuracies in evaluating the relative
merits of the FFA indirect measure of personal saving.

In contrast with the relatively complete figures on financial enterprises, consistent sets of balance sheet data for nonfinancial businesses—both incorporated and unincorporated—are not available. While
Statistics of Income balance sheet data for corporations and partnerships are of some help, sources and uses of funds data for the business

sector are, of necessity, pieced together from a variety of disparate—and potentially inconsistent—financial data.

Within the corporate sector, data on the current portion of the balance sheet—that is, short-term assets and liabilities—are based on the Working Capital data maintained by the Flow of Funds Section. While data for manufacturing, mining, and trade industries drawn directly from the Census Bureau's *Quarterly Financial Reports* are relatively accurate, quarterly estimates for transportation and utilities likely are less accurate since they are based on small sample tabulations benchmarked to annual universe balance sheet data from trade associations and regulatory agencies. Moreover, the rapidly growing "other industries" portion of the Working Capital data—primarily construction and services, for which quarterly data currently do not exist—is benchmarked to *Statistics of Income* data that are available only with a three-year delay.

To the extent that industries covered by the *Quarterly Financial Reports* dominate the Working Capital data, the consistent financial accounting and consolidation standards mandated by the Census Bureau make these data suitable for use in the FFAs. In recent years, however, the share of current financial assets of all nonfinancial corporations accounted for by industries covered by the *Quarterly Financial Reports* has declined appreciably as the services sector of the U.S. economy has grown in importance. By year-end 1985, industries covered by the *Quarterly Financial Reports* accounted for only about two-thirds of the current financial assets of the nonfinancial corporate sector, a considerable decline from the three-fourths share that prevailed in 1975, when the current Working Capital series was established.

Recent work by Flow of Funds Section staff has determined that the rapid growth of the services and construction industries, as well as their quite different balance sheet structure, has been captured quite accurately in the Working Capital data on a year-to-year basis. Given the very different balance sheet structure of this "other" sector, however, quarter-to-quarter estimates likely have been subject to increasing distortion as the "other" sector has gained importance. Indeed, quarterly inaccuracies may be responsible for much of the recent increase and volatility in the trade credit discrepancy, discussed earlier.

In the course of retabulating balance sheet data used to benchmark the Working Capital "other" sector, *Statistics of Income* current asset and liability data for industries covered by the *Quarterly Financial Reports* was compared with the corresponding *Quarterly Financial Reports* data themselves. The magnitude of data differences between these two basic corporate sources—which is unlikely to be attributable solely to consolidation differences—underscores the inherent inconsistencies in assimilating corporate financial data from multiple, loosely related sources.

Because of a lack of detail on specific financial instruments, most components of the Working Capital data do not appear directly in the FFAs. Instead, Working Capital results are used as control totals in allocating independent data on a particular financial instrument between corporate and noncorporate business. For example, the Working Capital category "cash" (and equivalents) covers a range of financial instruments that includes cash, demand deposits, time deposits, and other liquid financial instruments such as commercial paper holdings. This Working Capital cash category thus is used in conjunction with other data, such as the Federal Reserve's Demand Deposit Ownership Survey, to allocate specific assets between corporate and noncorporate holdings.

To the extent that Working Capital control totals are correct, therefore, an underestimate of one component asset hold by business results in an offsetting overestimate of another asset, leaving this sector's and the household discrepancies unchanged. One example of a known misestimation that is not expected to alter the discrepancy is corporate holdings of MMMFs, a liquid asset covered by the Working Capital cash and equivalents control total. In contrast, the omission in the FFAs of corporate holdings of shares in open-ended mutual funds may well affect sector discrepancies since these assets likely are not reported as current assets in the *Quarterly Financial Reports,* just as one corporation's holdings of another's bonds are not included in current assets. This treatment has tended to lead to underestimates of corporate financial asset totals and, thus, to overstate household asset acquisitions, which is consistent with the tendency for account calculations to show rising negative household discrepancies and rising positive corporate discrepancies.

Work is still in progress on corporate financial issues, using additional sources of information that it is hoped will lead to a more accurate, detailed view in the near future. Thus, no judgment can yet be made about the relevance of mutual fund (or bond) holdings in discrepancies of household- and business-sector discrepancies. It should be mentioned, however, that Investment Company Institute data also show mutual fund holdings by other kinds of institutions. The bulk of these are nonprofit institutions that, since they currently are embedded in the FFA household sector, are properly accounted for by the attribution of all mutual funds to "households." Small amounts also appear to be held by other kinds of financial organizations.

In contrast with the corporate sector, measurement errors in financial assets of unincorporated business—while distorting the measurement of households' direct financial asset holdings—will not affect the household discrepancy. Since investment in unincorporated business—calculated as the difference between these businesses' uses and other sources of funds—is entirely attributed to households, an underestimate of unincorporated business assets produces an equal underestimate of investment in such firms, which in the household sources and uses statement exactly offsets the resulting overestimate in households' financial asset acquisitions.

In point of fact, not all equity in unincorporated businesses is held by households. Recent work by the BEA, using special tabulations of partnership tax returns, has shown that an increasing and nonnegligible proportion of partnership income—and hence equity—actually accrues to corporations. While corporate profits data in the NIPAs reflect this corporate participation in partnership ventures, the FFAs' asset data do not, resulting in a potentially sizable overestimate of households' net investment in unincorporated business that also contributes to the household discrepancy. A major revision of the unincorporated business sector, exploiting these tax return data, currently is in process.[12]

In summary, there appear to be several connections between business and household financial calculations in the FFAs that may account for the ''complementarity'' of their sectoral discrepancies. Errors in the nonfinancial corporate part of the calculation are more likely to contribute to the household discrepancy than are those in the noncorporate portion, but the issues are heavily intertwined. As noted, corporate financial data are themselves not well suited to use in the established FFA system, and, while the staff currently is at work on the problem, results are some distance off and, as yet, difficult to predict. It does seem likely, however, that better assimilation of business financial data will lower sources/uses discrepancies in both the business and the household sectors.

2.7 International Transactions: Possible Links to Sectoral Imbalances

Discrepancies in international accounts are, by their nature, unexplained differences between recorded current (nonfinancial) and capital account transactions. Except for translating the U.S. balance of payments discrepancy—as computed by the BEA—into ''national accounts'' terms, the FFAs take this discrepancy as given and outside staff control. In an integrated system such as the FFAs, therefore, it must be expected that any imbalance in international sources/uses statistics will have repercussions elsewhere in the system, contributing to counterpart discrepancies in one or more domestic sectors. The possible connection between the balance of payments and household discrepancies is at least suggested by the former's tendency to become more positive in recent years, while the latter has become more negative. While the exact connections are conjectural, this section of our paper will review certain features of recent U.S. international transactions in an effort to explain how they might be related to the household discrepancy and, thus, to differences between NIPA and FFA measures of personal saving.

International capital transactions can be conducted by domestic households and business enterprises as well as by the government and thus can—in principle—involve purchases of assets as well as liquidation of liabilities by each of these sectors. Certain categories of international capital transactions are reported by those engaged in the transactions and thus can be attributed to specific sectors of the economy. Such transactions include those related to direct investments or borrowing and lending by nonfinancial and financial domestic enterprises. Some clearly can be attributed to the U.S. government. The statistical data used in the compilations of U.S. international transactions by the BEA are based on compulsory reports collected in part by the U.S. Treasury Department and, in part, by the BEA itself.

In contrast, international capital transactions by individuals generally are not subject to compulsory reporting by the parties involved. However, when households purchase or sell foreign securities through U.S. agents (brokers, dealers, etc.), the latter have the obligation to report such transactions. Likewise, if U.S. households invest in short-term foreign obligations, a U.S. financial institution that has custody of these assets would be required to report such custody holdings. But neither U.S. agents who purchase and sell foreign securities nor U.S. financial institutions that hold in custody foreign deposits or other assets report the domestic sectors that are associated with the reported transactions. The allocation of such transactions by sectors, therefore, cannot be done on the basis of the available statistical information. The following comments, based on measured capital flows in 1985, will illustrate how some of these transactions might be related to the household discrepancy.

2.7.1   Reported Transactions in Securities with Foreign Residents

In 1985, net U.S. purchases of foreign securities (stocks and bonds) are reported to have been close to $8 billion. Any allocation of these transactions between the household sector, including nonprofit organizations, and businesses cannot be made on some sort of fixed percentage basis since the shares of households and businesses in the total may vary in different statistical periods. Moreover, the $8 billion net purchases of foreign securities in 1985 could be the balance of net sales by households and much larger net purchases by financial businesses, or vice versa.

The statistical method used in the FFA compilations dispenses with the requirement explicitly to allocate foreign security transactions to particular domestic sectors. Net sales of foreign securities to U.S. residents simply are added to net new issues of domestic securities, and the disposition of this total change in supply among the different categories of purchasers is indicated. Purchasers include households, banks, and other economic sectors, including foreign residents.[13] In this calculation, information about net purchases by the financial organizations as well as about net sales of domestic securities to foreign residents is available. Clearly, as indicated in section 2.6, the estimate for net purchases of households can be distorted by the absence of data on or provision for net purchases by nonfinancial businesses.

Net purchases of $4 billion of foreign stocks in 1985 may have involved transactions by U.S. households as well as transactions by business enterprises. The latter certainly included investments by mutual funds and also acquisitions by U.S. corporations of foreign stocks as preliminary steps toward direct investments. But it would be difficult to judge what the share of households in the total may have been. The increase in acquisitions of foreign securities by mutual funds would suggest, however, that, compared with earlier years, the significance of direct purchases of stocks by households may have been declining and that by 1985 it was relatively small. Net purchases of foreign bonds in 1985 likely also reflected the balance of many cross-currents of transactions. Purchasers in the United States could, of course, include households. It is probable, however, that they were mainly financial organizations, such as insurance companies, pension funds, or mutual funds.

There is a similar allocation problem with inward flows in the international accounts, in which net foreign purchases of U.S. stocks were about $5 billion in 1985. The U.S. sellers could have belonged to either the household sector or the financial or nonfinancial business sector. In view of the large share of financial businesses in the holding and trading of stocks, it may be a fair assumption that businesses were the principal net sellers of stocks to foreign residents. Net foreign purchases of U.S. private bonds were about $40 billion (almost wholly newly issued bonds), which again strongly suggests that the U.S. transactors were predominantly in the business sector.

Combining all statistically reported transactions with foreigners involving long-term private securities, it seems likely, therefore, that the largest part of such transactions in 1985 affected the assets or liabilities of domestic business enterprises, and that the direct effect of these transactions on estimated assets of households was relatively small. But this was not necessarily the case in earlier years. The preference of households to invest in securities through mutual funds rather than directly has strengthened considerably in recent years. Thus, while households may have accounted for a larger share of net investments in foreign securities some years ago, the statistically reported total of such net investments, at least in the early 1980s, was considerably smaller than in 1985. However, there also may have been a considerable amount of transactions in foreign securities that have not been statistically recorded, as will be outlined in the following section dealing with the statistical discrepancy. It will be suggested that past balance of payments discrepancies have some relation to current ones and may also affect the household discrepancy in the FFAs.

2.7.2   Statistical Discrepancy in the International Transactions Account

From 1960 through 1974, with the exceptions of 1966 and 1968, the statistical discrepancy in the U.S. international transactions accounts was negative, indicating that recorded or estimated credits exceeded recorded or estimated debits. The total for the fifteen years was net debits of $22 billion, of which $16 billion was accounted for by the four years 1971–74.

By contrast, for most years from 1975 through 1985 the discrepancy was positive, and the cumulative discrepancy during these eleven years was nearly $196 billion. In the first four years of that period, 1975–78, the discrepancy averaged a little under $7 billion per year. In the last seven years, 1979–85, it averaged $24 billion per year, totaling $168 billion.

The statistical discrepancy in the international accounts can, in principle, arise from deficiences in the estimates of both current and capital account transactions, provided that the counterpart transactions are properly recorded. For instance, if certain services transactions, such as expenditures in the United States by foreign residents on legal fees, are not estimated while at the same time the decline in foreign deposits in U.S. banks reflecting the payments of these fees is statistically recorded, a discrepancy would arise. The credit part of the transactions would be missing, while the debit portion, the decline in foreign balances in U.S. banks, would be recorded. Or, if foreign residents make unrecorded investments in real estate in the United States while at the same time the associated decline in U.S. bank balances held by foreign residents is recorded, a discrepancy likewise would arise because credit transactions are missing.

Small (or, in the extreme, zero) discrepancies in the international accounts do not prove, however, that transactions estimates are free of error. Some transactions may escape recording of both their credit and their debit sides. For instance, earnings on foreign investments by

U.S. residents may be reinvested abroad, and both the earnings and the reinvestments may escape the statistical reporting system. Transactions of this type would, however, result in understatements of the saving estimates in the NIPAs and the FFAs by the same amount. Of course, any given discrepancy in the international accounts may represent a balance between larger missing transactions of households and larger missing transactions of the business sectors.

It is widely thought that missing current account transactions are subject to smaller quarter-to-quarter or year-to-year fluctuations than missing capital account transactions. Missing current account transactions may include some merchandise exports, but most are likely to consist of services transactions, such as legal and consulting fees, or expenditures by foreigners for education, medical purposes, and financial services. They also include income receipts on U.S. investments abroad that have not been statistically captured, particularly assets that had been purchased abroad directly without U.S. intermediaries, foreign purchases of real property in the United States for personal use, and unilateral transfers of funds such as those by immigrants to the United States and taxes paid to the United States by foreign residents. In general, there appears to be a basic upward trend in net credits on missing transactions. In the early part of the 1979–85 period, when the (positive) discrepancy in the international accounts was relatively high, U.S. earnings from financial services may have risen relatively rapidly. In the latter part of that period, however, large borrowings abroad by U.S. corporations may have involved the payment of fees to foreign underwriters, payments that are missing from the international accounts and probably reduced the net receipts on unrecorded current account transactions.[14]

There are estimates—some as high as $10 billion—of the balance of missing services transactions in recent years. Presumably, large amounts of net receipts of income on investments also are missing, particularly in view of the fact that liabilities of foreign banks to U.S. nonbank residents, as reported in IMF and BIS statistics, are about $100 billion larger than assets reported by U.S. sources. If the foreign figures are correct, the U.S. income earned in 1985 that is not reflected in the balance of payments compilations could have been somewhere in the vicinity of $5 or $6 billion. On balance, it is possible to conclude that the positive balance on underestimated and unrecorded current account transactions may have reached somewhere between $7 and $10 billion in 1985. It may also be assumed that nearly all the unrecorded net income from current transactions accrued to business enterprises.

These considerations suggest higher U.S. income/saving figures than shown in the usual statistics. A higher income on investments would have raised incomes as well as saving and net foreign investment and thus increased the saving ratio for the business sector and for the economy as a whole. Larger net incomes from the sale of goods or services to foreign residents would have raised net foreign investments and GNP and thus raised the ratio between investment and GNP. It may have affected the statistical discrepancy within the NIPA calculations and also the statistical discrepancy in the FFA calculations. But it would not have affected the differences between the saving ratios. Thus, it appears unlikely that flaws in current account data are closely associated with the household discrepancy.

Deducting the assumed current account contribution to the total discrepancy in the international accounts leaves the presumed contribution of unreported capital transactions. In the 1980s, these "missing" capital transactions would have averaged net inflows of roughly $16 billion per year. Several types of transactions could be included in these net inflows. As indicated earlier, in the early 1970s large unrecorded net outflows of funds occurred. It is conceivable that some of these funds were repatriated starting around 1980, when interest rates in the United States were high relative to those in other industrialized countries and the exchange rate of the dollar was on the rise. The roughly $15 billion or more of unrecorded funds that may have been invested abroad from 1971 to 1974 could have risen in value by 1980 to more than $50 billion.[15]

Thus, the repatriation of earlier outflows alone would have been sufficient to account for the balance of payments discrepancy for more than three years in the early 1980s. It is unlikely that all these funds were actually repatriated, but a large part of repatriations that did occur may have involved assets of households and affected the household discrepancy. In the FFAs, the acquisition of domestic assets with such funds would have been captured, but the liquidation of foreign assets would not have been recorded, just as the earlier purchase of foreign assets would have been missed. Consequently, the global net acquisition of assets by households would have been overstated for the recent period, which is consistent with a household discrepancy showing larger asset increases than could be explained by measured saving on the NIPA basis.

Borrowing in foreign capital markets by U.S. corporations through syndicated loans or issues of short-term obligations may have been a major development contributing to the international discrepancy in the latter part of the 1980–85 period. These transactions should, according to reporting requirements, have been included in the statistical data, but the coverage of such liabilities on the required forms submitted by nonbank corporations is not very satisfactory. The absence of data on such net borrowings would tend to result in an overstatement of the net acquisition of assets and thus of net saving by (mostly) nonfinancial business. It would not affect, however, the estimates of the acquisition of assets and liabilities and of net saving by households.

Many other types of transactions could have contributed to the large shortfall of credits in the international capital accounts in the latter half of the 1980–85 period. Among these may have been net foreign purchases of U.S. securities through intermediaries that did not report these transactions. In the FFA compilations, any underestimate of net purchases of securities by foreigners leads to an overestimate of net purchases by households.

Other types of transactions that are, in principle, reportable, but may not always be reported, are foreign investments in U.S. commercial real estate, mortgages, and partnership interests. Underreporting by foreigners of such investments may have raised the FFA estimates for net purchases of assets by business enterprises or by households higher than they should have been, and that also applies to estimates of their net saving.

It appears, in summary, that the large rise in the excess of missing credit over missing debit transactions in the international accounts in the 1980–85 period initially may have contributed more to an overstatement of the net increase in assets by households than by business enterprises and that this relation may have been reversed during the later years of that period. The large increase in the statistical discrepancy during that period has contributed, however, to considerable efforts in the last two years to improve the collection of data on international capital transactions. Considerable efforts also have been made to improve the collection of data on international services transactions and thus to reduce that part of the statistical discrepancy that reflects lack of such data or inadequate estimates. So, while the channels between the balance of payments discrepancy and differing measures of household saving are elusive and may change through time, it seems clear from the above hypotheses that such connections exist and do contribute to the measurement problems addressed in this paper. Other factors being equal, progress in reducing discrepancies in international accounts should be accompanied by greater concordance between nonfinancial and financial measures of saving for households and other sectors of the domestic economy.

2.8   Miscellaneous Issues

A variety of miscellaneous influences also may be contributing to the enlarged imbalances between current and capital account approaches to the household sector in recent years. A few of these will be mentioned as examples of, if nothing else, the difficulty of the underlying statistical material.

2.8.1   Transactions in Tangible Assets

The FFAs take account of gross physical investment in the economy, making certain allocations across sectors for which NIPA data do not provide complete information. It is possible that such allocations introduce some element of error to the household accounts, but these are not likely to be a major influence through time. Most transactions in existing tangible assets, however, are not well accounted for, and this may be a source of greater problems. This issue has been addressed as follows (Board of Governors of the Federal Reserve System 1980, 31):

> Like existing-house transactions, purchases and sales of all types of land and existing plant and equipment are omitted from the sector distribution of capital outlays, as are transactions in intangibles such as leaseholds and patents. This omission produces statistical imbalances in the accounts insofar as there are net transfers among sectors in tangible assets, and the basis for omitting such transactions is only the lack of substantial information on the quantities. In general there is probably a net sale of land and intangibles by households and noncorporate business and a net purchase of these assets by corporate business and finance, causing imbalances of opposite sign in the two sets of sector statements. There may have been several billion dollars of such transfers in recent years that are not in the accounts.[16]

An increasing volume of transactions such as these, which would "generate" rising amounts of household financial assets relative to measured sources of funds, would be consistent with the evolution of the household discrepancy in the past several years. Unfortunately, as there are still no statistics on which to base firm estimates, the role of sales of tangibles in household imbalances remains conjectural. [17]

2.8.2   New Institutions

Financial innovation during the past decade has given rise to a host of new, usually specialized, institutions, often set up as subsidiaries of established financial or nonfinancial businesses. Some are caught in existing reporting systems, such as "nonbank banks," but others fall into statistical gaps, and their activities may contribute to imbalances elsewhere in the accounts. As an example, the proliferation of "service corporations" as subsidiaries of savings and loan associations has created an economic subsector for which balance sheet information is still deficient. Such organizations may hold appreciable amounts of some kinds of assets, which are currently residually attributed to households for lack of this information; this data gap adds something to the household imbalance. The emergence of such entities is to some extent reflected in miscellaneous assets of established institutions, like savings and loans, through amounts provided in capitalization of subsidiaries.

As the counterpart subsidiary sector is missing, such financial flows show up in the FFA structure as "miscellaneous unallocated" assets of the parents, contributing to the total system discrepancy as discussed in an earlier section. In contrast, within the commercial banking sector, holding company investments in subsidiary banks (which can be read from both holding company reports and bank call reports) can be included in statements for both parent and subsidiary organizations.

The potential importance of missing subsectors is illustrated by the rapid growth of the service corporations mentioned above. According to annual reports filed with the Federal Home Loan Bank Board, at year-end 1985 balance sheets of these corporations had grown to almost $47 billion, almost three-and-a-half times the size of their 1983 position. Their assets included appreciable holdings of real estate, mortgage loans, and marketable securities, and their liabilities—in addition to capital—included both current notes and long-term debt. While the exact effect of including such organizations in the FFA structure on the household and other imbalances cannot be stated with precision at this time, it seems clear that their omission is a potentially material factor in the accounts. A closer examination is scheduled for the near future.

2.8.3   Brokers and Dealers

The rapid expansion of broker/dealer activities, combined with deterioration of older sources of information, makes this another area for potential research in reducing system discrepancies. It is known, for instance, that brokers/dealers (a category that includes major investment banks) have become quite active in collateralized mortgage obligation issuance, supporting portfolios of mortgages or pass-through securities. For some time, this segment of the accounts has suffered from fragmentary information, and it is also ripe for more detailed exploration, based initially on Securities and Exchange Commission *Annual Reports* and the FOCUS reporting system. Again, the eventual effect of "rebuilding" this sector on other areas of the accounts cannot be foreseen exactly, but the effort must be undertaken in the near future to keep pace with the rapidly changing financial structure of the economy.

2.8.4   Underground Economy

It sometimes has been argued that the capital account approach to saving is more likely to reflect the net accumulation of assets by those engaged in underground activities than is the NIPA approach, which is based on the deduction of consumer expenditures from incomes. A potential underestimate of income from underground activity has been considered to be one factor "explaining" the higher personal saving estimates in the FFAs relative to those shown in the NIPAs.

The main line of this argument is that personal saving from the proceeds of underground activity is likely to be stored in financial and tangible assets recorded in the FFAs and that the NIPAs do not fully account for the income from such activities. On the basis of national accounting principles, however, this argument is of doubtful validity (cf. Parker and Fox 1985). While many scenarios of underground activity can be devised, it is sometimes forgotten that income to one party in such transactions simultaneously is "consumption" expenditure by the other party. Thus, only when NIPA expenditures are estimated on the basis of methods that already implicitly include payments to "underground" sellers of services—for instance, payments for repair and maintenance of residential houses—would the addition of the "underground" income of the seller of such services add to saving. Otherwise, the omission of underground activities from the statistical sources used in the preparation of the NIPAs likely reduces the estimates for income and expenditures by the same amounts, leaving the estimate for personal saving unchanged. From the FFA perspective, there is a similar balancing of sources and uses of funds. Consequently, the omission of underground activities in the NIPAs may not affect the difference between saving estimates in these accounts and those in the FFAs.

There are, of course, numerous facets to the social accounting treatment of underground economy issues; most were covered in a recent, thorough review by BEA staff (Carson 1984; see also de Leeuw 1985). Two main types can be named. First, there are activities such as drug dealing and prostitution that are (usually) illegal and therefore not included in national accounts measures of income and output by definition. That is, neither the income nor the expenditure should be measured in the NIPAs. While capital account measures of sources and uses of funds do not suffer from such scruples, illegal income (and saving) to one party nonetheless is illegal expenditure (reduced saving) to the other, so the NIPA and FFA treatments appear to lead to the same results.

The second type of underground activity is that which is not illegal per se but which tends to involve misreporting by transactors—usually underreporting of income for tax purposes. To compensate for distortions of this sort, the BEA already uses alternative sources and estimating procedures to adjust income for national accounts purposes. To the extent it is successful, the potential bias in the income/saving balance is removed, and NIPA saving figures are adjusted toward values that might be obtained from a purely capital accounts approach. Of course, some potential problems remain. The BEA recognizes that its adjustments are based on "information that is incomplete and, in some cases, of questionable quality" (Carson 1984, 110). It is felt that there is no obvious bias in the procedure, but it is nonetheless worth nothing that NIPA adjustments are based on IRS taxpayer compliance survey information that is generated only irregularly. A judgment—which we do not make here—that NIPA saving measures are downward biased is the same as concluding that upward adjustments to income are insufficient relative to those for expenditures.

More generally, of course, since estimates of personal incomes in the NIPAs are derived separately from estimates of expenditures, such a bias arises only when either or both are flawed, whether or not underground activities are a significant factor in the economy. The direction of such a bias, if any, is uncertain. Consequently, further improvement in NIPA estimating procedures for effects of both above-ground and underground activities could either raise or lower the statistical gap between the NIPA and the FFA personal saving estimates.

2.9 Summary and Conclusion

This paper has documented the sharp increase in the divergence between personal saving as measured in the NIPAs and in the FFAs. The amount of this divergence is shown in the FFAs as the household discrepancy. This particular discrepancy can be understood only in the context of the overall discrepancy system in the FFAs, in which imbalances between assets and liabilities in one sector affect other sectors. As a residual calculation, the household discrepancy is an indirect result of errors in estimating changes in assets and liabilities in a number of other key sectors. But it must be recalled that errors in nonfinancial inputs into the accounts also will contribute to the household discrepancy indirectly. Moreover, the exact magnitude of the household discrepancy is subject to "judgmental" adjustments made in the estimation process.

Looking at empirical developments within the FFA discrepancy system, almost half the recent growth of the household discrepancy can be "attributed" to offsetting growth in the nonfinancial corporate sector. Discrepancy changes in other nonfinancial sectors also help explain some of this growth. However, the growth of the overall system discrepancy—which is the sum of all transaction discrepancies, including the NIPA discrepancy—also is a key element in the growth of the household discrepancy.

The historical record suggests that at least some of the initial differences between personal saving estimates in the NIPAs and the FFAs will be revised away, through periodic revisions in the NIPAs. Still, recent accounting changes in the NIPAs with regard to personal outlays and capital expenditures may affect historical revision relations between the two saving measures in as yet unpredictable ways.

Various areas were explored in some detail in this paper to identify specific problem areas that might be affecting the household discrepancy. In addition to periodic national accounts revisions, other areas of the accounts were also reviewed. Structural and data-related problems in the nonfinancial corporate sector were examined. In addition, possible effects of loan write-off accounting problems were reviewed. While, in general, adjustments to the capital accounts for write-offs are fairly accurate, the compensating income adjustments in the NIPAs appear to be subject to some timing and coverage problems. Any such problems would understate the income-based NIPA saving measures relative to the capital account–based FFA measure. Deficiencies in flow-of-funds data sources—affecting many sectors—were mentioned frequently in this paper, and the possible effect on the household sector was elucidated. Since almost all these sources are beyond the staff's control, prospects for better coordination are uncertain, but directions were indicated for better use of corporate business material, and there is some hope of deeper exploitation of periodic microsurveys of household finances.

Problems in the measurement of U.S. international transactions also were reviewed to see what potential connection they might have to the saving/discrepancy issue. In contrast to earlier experience, it is not felt that unrecorded international capital transactions have been a major problem in recent years. The repatriation of large unrecorded capital outflows of the early 1970s may have been a problem in the early 1980s, but it has not been deemed important recently.

Finally, an assortment of other issues that may be potential contributors to the household discrepancy was mentioned. On the most publicized of these—the role of the "underground economy"—we reach the general conclusion that perhaps too much has been made of this activity as a contributing factor, but it cannot be discounted altogether. With regard to new institutions, structural change, and existing but poorly captured sectors in the FFAs, these are matters of continuing research endeavors by the staff.

Notes

1. Both the NIPAs and the FFAs are revised periodically, so both nonfinancial and financial estimates change from time to time. Data in this paper reflect the status of both sets of accounts as of April 1987 and should be regarded as

illustrative only. The July 1987 NIPA and September 1987 FFA revisions do not greatly change the observations made in the text.

2. The personal saving figure, for instance, is taken over from the NIPAs. Certain additions are made for surpluses of government retirement funds and capital gain dividends of mutual funds, but these are entirely offset in estimates of increased financial assets. The bulk of household liability changes come from estimates of home mortgage and consumer credit borrowing, generated elsewhere at the Federal Reserve Board from lender sources. Other amounts—usually small—are accounted for by estimates of tax-exempt debt, bank loans, etc., which are made by the Flow of Funds Section.

3. One of the persistent problems in account calculation, for instance, is working up net corporate bond issuance figures. Data on gross issuance are more readily obtainable than are estimates for retirements.

4. Some observers appear to have the impression that the FFAs have exact data on household assets (see, e.g., O'Leary 1986). Only a few asset estimates are robust: certain forms of bank deposits, mutual and money-market fund shares, and insurance and pension reserves.

5. The nonfinancial discrepancy enters negatively because, in the NIPAs, it is defined as the difference between uses (gross investment) and sources (gross saving). In the FFAs, discrepancies are defined as sources less uses.

6. These assumptions are under continual review, and the accounts are changed from time to time when necessary. As a later section of the paper notes, provision is being made to expand identified asset holdings in the corporate sector.

7. Since these NIPA historical revisions generally are incorporated in the second-quarter flow-of-funds publication, the four-year revisions discussed below are measured as changes between annual data estimates as contained in respective second-quarter flow-of-funds releases.

8. Of course, the lack of revision to financial figures reflects in part a shortage of benchmarks on which to base retrospective adjustments to early estimates.

9. It should be noted that results of revision studies are sensitive to the choice of both data frequency and revision interval. A recent study (de Leeuw 1984) uses quarterly data to focus on short-term revisions from initial quarterly estimates. From the short-run perspective, de Leeuw found that the NIPA's income, expenditure-based approach provides much more stable estimates of personal saving. Rather than reflecting a fundamental flaw in the Flow of Funds Section estimates, however, this finding underscores the point—stressed in considerable detail in flow-of-funds quarterly publications—that initial FFA estimates of the most recent quarter are highly tentative because of the substantial amount of data available only with a one-quarter lag.

10. The procedure can be shown as follows. Expressing bank assets as A, net new borrowing as B, and net write-offs as W, the growth in bank assets is

$$A_t = A_{t-1} + B_t - W_t.$$

Net loan flows in the FFAs are $\Delta A_t = B_t - W_t$. This understates total sources to borrowing sectors only insofar as write-off amounts are missing from the income statistics. Charges against taxable current income are taken by lending institutions when funds are added to bad debt reserves, not when write-offs themselves are taken. But assuming these two magnitudes move roughly together, only temporary aberrations should result. Transfers to bad debt reserves afford less insight into the proper sectoral allocations of the extra source of funds than do write-offs themselves, which appear in disaggregated form in banking reports.

11. Consumer credit statistics used in the FFAs are prepared by the Mortgage and Consumer Finance Section at the Federal Reserve Board. Like the banking statistics, period flows are derived as first-differences in outstandings reported by surveyed institutions.

12. It bears repeating that the account structure and data illustrations given are as of early 1987, after the preparation of the fourth-quarter 1986 accounts. In the course of the 1987 annual revision, Flow of Funds Section staff made adjustments in structure to address some of the problems mentioned in this section.

13. Household purchases of foreign securities cannot even be inferred residually since information from most other sectors does not distinguish purchases of domestic stocks and bonds from purchases of those of foreign origin but rather gives only a "global" total.

14. Fees related to security issues abroad by U.S. corporations recently have been estimated and included in compilations of U.S. international transactions published in the June 1987 *Survey of Current Business.*

15. This figure is based on the assumption that the outflow of U.S. funds in the early 1970s was equal to the negative statistical discrepancy in the years 1971–74. Actually, the net outflow may have been larger since the statistical discrepancy for these years presumably also reflects some inflows on account of unrecorded services transactions. For simplicity, it was also assumed that these funds were invested and reinvested in assets that yielded between 6 and 8 percent per year and that the funds were invested either in Germany or in another country whose currency moved more or less parallel to the deutsche mark. For the date of presumed repatriation of these investments, two calculations were made—1980 and 1981—leading to the following results. A net outflow of U.S. dollars from 1971 through 1974 of about $15 billion that was repatriated in 1980 would have yielded between $46 billion and $54 billion. The same funds repatriated in 1981 would have yielded between $40 billion and $47 billion, a smaller amount because of the rise of the exchange rate of the dollar.

16. Transactions between the government and business in used assets, however, are captured in the NIPAs.

17. Recent, still unpublished, research at the BEA on asset purchases by businesses may provide a way to quantify this long-standing problem in the accounts.

References

Arenson, Karen. 1981. The low U.S. rate of savings. *New York Times,* 22 December, D–1.

Avery, Robert, and Gregory Elliehausen. 1986. Financial characteristics of high-income families. *Federal Reserve Bulletin* 72 (March): 163–77.

Avery, Robert, Gregory Elliehausen, and Glenn Canner. 1984a. Survey of consumer finances, 1983. *Federal Reserve Bulletin* 70 (September): 679–92.

_____. 1984b. Survey of consumer finances, 1983: A second report. *Federal Reserve Bulletin* 70 (December): 857–68.

Avery, Robert, Gregory Elliehausen, Arthur Kennickell, and Paul Spindt. 1986. The use of cash and transactions accounts by American families. *Federal Reserve Bulletin* 72 (February): 87–108.

Berry, John M. 1985. U.S. savings gap persists. *Washington Post*, 1 December, Fl.

Boskin, Michael J. 1986. Theoretical and empirical issues in the measurement, evaluation and interpretation of postwar U.S. saving. In *Savings and capital formation*, ed. F. Gerard Adams and Susan M. Wachter, 11–43. Lexington, Mass.: Lexington Books.

Carson, Carol. 1984. The underground economy: An introduction. *Survey of Current Business* 64 (May): 21–37; (July): 106–17.

de Leeuw, Frank. 1984. Conflicting measures of private saving. *Survey of Current Business* 64 (November): 17–23.

———. 1985. An indirect technique for measuring the underground economy. *Survey of Current Business* 65 (April): 64–72.

Board of Governors of the Federal Reserve System. Flow of Funds Section. 1980. *Introduction to flow of funds*. Washington, D.C.

Mann, Michael A. 1987. Comparing measures of private saving: An update. Bureau of Economic Analysis Discussion Paper no. 14. Washington, D.C., January.

Murray, Alan. 1983. Widely disparate savings statistics given by Fed, Commerce officials. *Wall Street Journal*, 11 November, 37.

O'Leary, James J. 1986. What is the personal saving rate in the United States? U.S. Trust Company, New York, 9 June.

Parker, Robert P. 1984. Improved adjustments for misreporting of tax return information used to estimate the national income and product accounts, 1977. *Survey of Current Business* 64 (June): 17–25.

Parker, Robert P., and Douglas R. Fox. 1985. Revised estimates of the national income and product accounts of the United States, 1929–85: An introduction. *Survey of Current Business* 65 (December): 1–19.

Comment   George M. von Furstenberg

Does the United States save too little? Martin Feldstein (1977) posed this question over ten years ago, but his affirmative answer did not put the issue to rest. One of the lingering concerns has been whether the data describe the facts adequately enough for reaching a judgment in the first place. A quadrumvirate of authors address this issue with the authority of collectively vast experience in the leading U.S. government agencies for financial statistics and economic data analysis. Specifically, they investigate the suspicion, nourished by the excess of household-sector flow-of-funds accounts (FFA) over national income and product

George M. von Furstenberg is Rudy Professor of Economics at Indiana University.
The author is indebted to Walther Lederer for written advice based on the conference draft of these comments.

accounts (NIPA) personal saving, that households save more than meets NIPA's eye.

Before recapitulating and commenting on some aspects of the authors' work, it may be helpful to point out that they do not intend to evaluate the usefulness of the official data on saving for economic analysis. They do not aim to bridge the conceptual and statistical gaps between saving out of current income and a current-dollar measure of the change in real net worth. Rather, they accept the official definitions and measurement conventions as their frame of reference for pinpointing data gaps and exploring uncertainties of attribution that are encountered within the statistical networks used by the data gathering and reporting agencies. As a result, tricks played by inflation of the kind exposed by Feldstein (1983) and Eisner (1986) are not discussed. What the authors are concerned with exclusively is reconciling nominal flows viewed as sources and uses of funds of various sectors. In particular, their main objective is to elucidate possible factors contributing to the shortfall of reported household sources from uses of funds. This statistical discrepancy, calculated as the difference between sources and uses, averaged −$70 billion annually over the period 1980–85, four times what it was during the last half of the 1970s.

Recapitulation of Some of the Main Points

Under the FFA approach, household-sector saving funds come from NIPA personal saving plus credit market borrowing and other increases in liabilities. These total sources are then compared with total uses, which is the sum of the sector's net increase in physical and financial assets. Since no data reports are taken directly from the household sector, some assets and liabilities are measured through a residual process. Because any net mismeasurement of financial items in other sectors then results in corresponding offsets being entered in the financial account of the household sector, that sector has been called a dumping ground of errors.

The authors sift through the possible errors in the household sector and examine a number of ways of spotting and eventually reducing them.

1. The unexplained rubble on the dumping ground cannot all have arrived from the nonfinancial corporate sector or be due to its overstating the sources of funds from, relative to their uses on, households. Comparing the first six years of the present decade with those of the previous decade, the discrepancy in the nonfinancial corporate sector, while positive to indicate an excess of recorded sources over uses of funds to corporations, has risen less than half as much—$22 billion as against −$53 billion on the annual average—as the negative household

discrepancy it might offset. Furthermore, the authors emphasize that matching a statistical discrepancy in one sector against that of another is arbitrary in a multisector framework unless there are strong prior indications of bilateral relation.

Little insight can thus be gained by pointing to partial offsets between growing sector discrepancies of opposite sign that still left a $-\$23$ billion average annual swing in the overall system discrepancy from $6 billion for 1970–75 to $-\$17$ billion in 1980–85. Changes in the NIPA discrepancy contributed less than $-\$2$ billion to the $-\$23$ billion swing. This could be determined after changing sign on the NIPA discrepancy, which is defined, reversing the FFA discrepancy, as recorded uses (total investment) minus sources (total saving).

2. The small contribution from the NIPA "nonfinancial" discrepancy apart, the entire swing in the system discrepancy toward a global excess of uses over sources is mechanically due to transaction discrepancies. Flow of funds accounting conventions force sources and uses of all credit market instruments to balance—if necessary by assigning unallocated amounts to the household sector. Hence, transaction discrepancies are allowed to surface in only a few selected items for which recourse to assignment has been rejected. Security repurchase agreements, trade credit, and "miscellaneous" are the main swing items. It is unclear why recorded net uses of funds to acquire those items as assets should increasingly have tended to exceed the net sources of funds obtained from issuing these same items as liabilities. The authors only add to the question when they explain that while liabilities for security repurchase agreements and federal funds transactions are measured fairly well because they originate in a limited range of financial institutions, the corresponding asset holdings are more dispersed and less well documented.

Perhaps all the recent discrepancies are still so much in flux that little should be made of them. In the past, revisions have been dramatic. For instance, the estimate of the trade credit discrepancy for 1978, which had been $-\$12.3$ billion (Board of Governors of the Federal Reserve System 1980, S.1) in June 1980, had shrunk to only $-\$4.8$ billion by March 1987 (Wilson et al., chap. 2, in this vol., table 2.4). With trade credit, unlike security repurchase agreements, a negative discrepancy has remained common for good reason. Those who grant trade credit are more likely to be subject to reporting requirements than are those who receive it, and sectoral allocation of the difference is sufficiently uncertain to have convinced the statisticians to let some of it stand.

This example shows that the excess of recorded uses over sources in the FFA financial transactions tables should not be taken to indicate that the missing source component is saving. It could at least as well be borrowing or, more generally, incomplete reporting of financial intermediation.

3. The second major part of the paper, starting with section 2.3, returns to the attempt to analyze and, if possible, reduce the gap between the NIPA and FFA measures of saving by households. This gap is due to recorded acquisition of physical and financial assets minus borrowing exceeding the NIPA measure of personal saving after saving and investment measures have been adjusted for consistency with the FFA concepts. The major adjustments involve recognizing the growth in government insurance and pension reserves as an addition to public liabilities and private assets and recognizing purchases of consumer durables as gross investment. Given these adjustments, revisions raising the estimates of physical and financial assets acquired increase the gap, while upward revisions of household borrowing or NIPA saving reduce it.

In the past, revisions associated with the incorporation of (Internal Revenue Service) *Statistics of Income* data, available with roughly three-year lag, have tended to raise estimates of personal saving by about 1 percent of disposable income. However, upward revisions in the NIPA estimates of net physical capital acquisitions by households have kept the net effect on reducing the gap between the different estimates of saving small.

Another possibility is that the rapid rise in asset write-offs during the last few years has not yet been reflected in the statistics. To recognize defaulters' gain and lenders' loss only when write-offs occur, corporate profits, business transfer payments to households, and factor incomes from the rest of world may be adjusted as necessary to shift the recorded effect away from the time loan loss reserves (bad debt reserves) are credited to the time they are debited and assets are written off. The quality of the adjustment depends on the accuracy and speed with which write-offs are taken into account. Write-offs are treated in the NIPAs as if they were income transfers from lender to borrower that the latter uses to repay debt. Because of this, the sum total of household sources is not distorted when changes in virtually all household liabilities are derived indirectly by differencing intertemporal positions in lenders' balance sheets. Assume, for instance, that the household sector defaults to the corporate sector, say through a declaration of personal bankruptcy. Then the defaulters' gain that is added to personal saving plus the net increase in household liabilities left after any write-offs equals the increase in household borrowing before write-offs. Only to the extent that defaulters' gain is underestimated will there be an underestimate of saving and borrowing combined on the sources side of the household sector that could contribute to the recorded excess of uses over sources.

Adding to that sector's FFA discrepancy from the other side is the practice of allocating all money-market mutual fund shares to households. This substantially overestimates their actual holdings of these instruments and understates the asset acquisitions of corporations. By the same token, any unrecorded net sale of land and intangibles by households and unincorporated businesses to corporate businesses and financial institutions overstates the net acquisition of assets by the former sectors and understates the net uses of funds by the latter.

4. The booking of international transactions creates much further uncertainty in FFAs. Net sales of securities by foreign to domestic residents are allocated to the purchasing sectors along with new domestic issues. The list of purchasers does not include nonfinancial businesses, and households are treated as the residual buyer. To the extent that net U.S. purchases of foreign stocks and bonds are undertaken by households primarily through investments in mutual or closed-end funds, financial corporations appear as the buyer. Households also do not generally issue bonds to foreigners. For these reasons, the effect of international financial transactions on the U.S. household balance sheets has been rated as still small. Nevertheless, household ownership of foreign deposits and securities is likely to have increased dramatically in recent years in ways that may not have been reported fully to the Internal Revenue Service.

Extending the Search for Reconciliation Items Internationally

The swing in the statistical discrepancy in U.S. international transactions from negative values in 1971–74 to increasingly large positive numbers of over $20 billion per annum in most recent years (since 1979) also poses many problems of interpretation. The authors speculate that, if the 1971–74 discrepancies, which indicated an excess of recorded credits (+) over debits (−) in the balance of payments, were due to unrecorded capital exports (−) that came back with interest in the 1980s (+), the changing sign and size of these discrepancies would point to overestimation of uses of funds (and hence of FFA-deduced saving) in the first years of the 1980s and underestimation in 1971–74. Sales of domestic assets by households to other sectors, but not the purchase of foreign assets, would have been recorded in the earlier period, understating household uses of funds and capital exports. More recently, the reverse of this pattern of discrepancies would have been observed, with purchases of domestic assets by households from other sectors recorded, but not their sales of foreign assets, at least not in the United States.

Conjectures of this kind invite some remarks on possible asymmetries elsewhere. It is curious to suggest that acquisitions and subsequent liquidations of claims by U.S. households on other countries with highly developed capital markets and reporting systems—the study mentions Germany or another country whose currency moves more or less parallel to the German currency—would escape detection in the statistical reports of the United States. If these claims have a high probability of not being identified abroad, actual or required reporting systems there would be less revealing than those of the United States, where foreign claims on the home country are assumed to be identified correctly. On the other hand, if the U.S. claims on foreign countries have been identified correctly in those countries, why was the authors' conjecture not hardened by recourse to foreign data? Even if such countries as Germany and Switzerland did not share details of individual transactions with the United States, more might then be found out than the authors let on. Until some such confirming evidence is provided, I cannot find their particular story of capital flight, engineered by U.S. households and then allegedly reversed, altogether persuasive just because it happens to fit the pattern of discrepancies. Rather, I would surmise that the trend toward international diversification of household portfolios has seen no such massive interruptions.

Other stories that relate to the growing excess of household uses over reported sources of funds could have more statistical support. For instance, the liberalization of financial markets in a number of Latin American countries in the 1970s created occasional waves of repatriation of funds from abroad to those countries, primarily from the United States. Funds that originally had arrived through capital flight may not have been identified as claims against the United States, being credited instead to U.S. residents—perhaps friends, relatives, or their proprietorships. On repatriation to foreign countries and transfer to the financial sector above ground, recorded foreign claims on the United States, often in the form of official reserves, thus would rise. With the onset of the international debt crisis after 1981, capital fled from Latin America once again. Assuming the foreign private capital arriving in the United States would, in good part, be (mis)represented as being owned by U.S. residents once again, there would be an overstatement of household uses of funds in the United States that is coupled with an understatement of capital imports. The official claims of Latin American countries on the United States would fall, or their foreign indebtedness to the United States would rise, without a corresponding increase being recorded in foreign private claims on this country.

Thus, it would appear to me that the unrecorded side of international capital flows, "motivated by a flight from economic or political crises *abroad,* by exchange rate expectations or by relatively attractive rates of return in the United States''—a judgment cited approvingly by de Leeuw (1984, 18; emphasis added)—is a stronger suspect than the one suggested by the authors. An overview of different estimates of capital flight in major Latin American countries by Watson et al. (1986, 142) provides some measure of support for this view. In work subsequently published, Lessard and Williamson (1987) have shed more light on the matter.

Looking abroad and not just at home may also be useful in another respect, that of spotting the traces left by the underground economy in FFA discrepancies. Although I commend the kind of caution expressed in several studies of the problem published by Tanzi (1982), imports of misrepresented or concealed goods into the United States are likely to exceed U.S. exports of such goods by a large amount. Furthermore, this hidden import balance, which may have amounted to billions of dollars already years ago in the United States, could have continued to grow rapidly since. Unrecorded net imports may be used to acquire recorded claims on the United States eventually. This can happen, for instance, when Colombian drug smugglers find it useful to convert U.S. dollars into Colombian pesos in the "parallel" capital market. From there, the dollars may surface, being legalized through redeposit in the officially recognized sector. As a result, recorded claims against the United States suddenly appear when it suits Colombian drug lords to convert some of their previously invisible hoards of dollars. At first glance this would seem to be an example of an international timing and coverage discrepancy that does not have any immediate implication for the growing excess of household uses over sources of funds recorded in the United States. In reality, however, the undetected leeching of currency from the United States into foreign hands leads to an overstatement of monetary assets owned by U.S. households. Financial uses are then overstated also because they are determined by differencing estimates of stocks at different points in time.

These examples may be enough to show that there are a few additional leads abroad that could have been explored in the main paper. However, there is no denying that its achievements are already substantial, with a number of problem areas in the NIPAs and FFAs evaluated with impressive clarity and care.

The authors also have pointed to some areas in which the FFA statistics can and soon may be improved in matching up financial assets and liabilities by sector. This would reduce the problem of unallocated balances and the use of the household sector as the dumping ground for many of them. Nevertheless, a very large degree of uncertainty will continue to attach to measures of saving no matter how derived. As the authors have been careful to point out, in double-entry book-keeping, offsetting errors on one side of the accounts or matching omissions on both sides can be quite consistent with approximate balance. Hence, even a negligible statistical discrepancy would not prove the absence of major errors and uncertainties about the data. There is no alternative to improving the data patiently item by item while trying to keep up with innovations in financial instruments. The authors have proved very good and experienced at doing just that.

References

Board of Governors of the Federal Reserve System. 1980. *Introduction to flow of funds*. Washington, D.C.: Board of Governors of the Federal Reserve System.

de Leeuw, Frank. 1984. Conflicting measures of private saving. *Survey of Current Business* 64 (November): 17–23.

Eisner, Robert. 1986. *How real is the federal deficit?* New York: Free Press.

Feldstein, Martin. 1977. Does the United States save too little? *American Economic Review* 67 (February): 116–21.

———. 1983. *Inflation, tax rules, and capital formation*. Chicago: University of Chicago Press for NBER.

Lessard, Donald R., and John Williamson, eds. 1987. *Capital flight and Third World debt*. Washington, D.C.: Institute for International Economics.

Tanzi, Vito. 1982. *The underground economy in the United States and abroad*. Lexington, Mass.: Lexington Books.

Watson, Maxwell, Russell Kincaid, Caroline Atkinson, Eliot Kalter, and David Folkerts-Landau. 1986. *International capital markets: Developments and prospects*. Washington, D.C.: International Monetary Fund.

3 Flow-of-Funds and National Income and Product Account Savings Estimates in Latin America

Clark W. Reynolds and Wayne Camard

3.1 Introduction

This paper will argue that flow-of-funds data have considerable potential for addressing the role of finance in savings mobilization. Some of the data that have been compiled on the flow of funds in Latin America are examined to show that, despite their limitations, they are useful in gaining a better understanding of the sectoral distribution of savings. Attempts at compiling flow of funds in Latin America go back at least as far as the early 1960s in Argentina and Chile and have continued, if intermittently, until the present day. There has not, however, been a concomitant stream of research analyzing the data. As a result—with the exception of Colombia, which continued and improved the preparation of financial accounts, integrating them with the real accounts in the process—most of the countries in Latin America have abandoned their short-lived forays into flow-of-funds accounting. Nevertheless, the studies examined here produce estimates of household savings considerably higher than those of the national income and product accounts (NIPAs).

Flow-of-funds analysis can be useful in understanding the investment uses of savings. It can also be useful in understanding and encouraging saving itself. It is an open question whether the level of investment is constrained by the amount of available savings or whether new savings arise spontaneously to meet the needs of investors. If the rate of savings is the constraint, as is argued by McKinnon (1973), Shaw (1973), and others (owing to an implicit assumption of excess demand for investment

Clark W. Reynolds is a professor of economics in the Food Research Institute and Director of the Americas Program at Stanford University. Wayne Camard is a graduate student in economics at Stanford University.

funds), how much can the savings rate be enhanced by manipulation of the financial environment? The answers to these questions, accepting the premise that marginal savings in the economy goes into a financial asset (essentially true for households), are entwined with the responsiveness of savers/asset holders to the rate of return on their savings. This, presumably, is the principal mechanism through which the needs of borrowers are communicated to actual or potential savers.

Flow-of-funds analysis offers the possibility for innovative research on the relation between real and financial decision making now that it is evident that finance is of importance to the real behavior of economies. It is well suited to deal with questions of choice among competing financial assets by measuring financial flows among asset types and the allocation of net savings. Notwithstanding the pitfalls of financial model building, econometric models such as that of Hendershott (1977) permit an even more sophisticated examination of the effect of interest rate manipulation on portfolio shifting. In addition, the less formal examination of financial flows in response to interest rate and other policies can be highly suggestive as to the potential for voluntary financial savings in the enhancement of real investment.

In order to construct and interpret a set of flow-of-funds accounts (FFAs) successfully, it is necessary to sectorize the economy in a functional way that addresses likely policy questions. "Government" and "rest of world" are natural and easy-to-define categories, though at the fringe the exact definition may be largely a matter of taste. The natural division within the private sector, that between producers and consumers (or firms and households), is particularly difficult in developing countries. Indeed, McKinnon and other analysts frequently use the "firm-household" as their representative agent. Flow-of-funds systems in industrial countries typically differentiate between corporations, noncorporate enterprise, and households. The firm-household would correspond to the aggregation of noncorporate enterprise and households, and in some places this is done. In others, though the process requires some ad hoc estimation, a traditional division between households and firms is made. In still others, the task of sectoring has proved too great, and the private sector is presented as a unitary entity. These issues are taken up in depth in the next section.

3.2 Flow of Funds in Latin America

Pilot flow-of-funds studies were done in the early 1970s in several countries of the Western Hemisphere: Colombia (1962–69), Peru (1965–70), Costa Rica (1961–71), Jamaica (1964–72), and Brazil (1959–69, selected years) (Banco de la República 1971; Comisión Nacional Supervisora de Empresas y Valores 1973; Banco Central de Costa Rica, n.d.; Bank of Jamaica 1974; Banco Central do Brasil 1973). This and the next section of the paper focus on these studies, though work has been done on financial accounts in some other countries as well. As is the case in Argentina, though, the data are not always amenable to the comparison of NIPA and FFA savings data because the FFAs are made to conform to NIPA savings figures (for a discussion of Argentina's FFAs, see Banco Central de la Republica Argentina 1972 and Reynolds 1982). The accounts examined here do allow comparison and also give important components of the countries' national balance sheets (for discussion of national balance sheets, see Goldsmith 1985).

A country's national accounts are commonly divided into several categories: income and product, input-output, and flow of funds are the major divisions. The NIPAs and the FFAs intersect over the measurement of intersectoral capital flows. Sectoral saving minus sectoral investment in the NIPAs should generate a figure for net financial saving that matches the change in the financial assets of that sector in the FFAs. Differences in definitions and in method, though, would ensure that the corresponding figures from the two accounts not match. The fact that some fairly strong and divergent assumptions underlie each set of accounts further guarantees that the figures will be different. However, an integration of the accounts involving reconciliation of divergent estimates can and has been done in some countries, improving the reliability of both sets of accounts.

The flow-of-funds studies that have been done in Latin America were prepared with varying degrees of comprehensiveness. At one end of the spectrum, the Brazilian flow-of-funds study covers little beyond the banking system. At the other end is Colombia, which continues to compile FFAs, and where improvements in methodology have led to a more thorough accounting for all sectors and integration with the NIPAs. With the exception of the Colombian accounts since 1970, some sections of the Brazilian accounts, and the external accounts of Jamaica and Costa Rica, flow-of-funds accounting was performed on a stock-change basis. That is to say, the accounts give outstanding stocks of financial assets and liabilities and infer flows from the changes in the stocks, after making the appropriate valuation changes wherever possible. The cases in which adjustments were or were not made are discussed sector by sector below. Table 3.1, showing the ratio of total financial assets in the economy to gross domestic product (GDP), chronicles the increasing use of financial assets in the economies studied. Almost none of the increase, as table 3.2 indicates, was in monetary holdings; almost all was in more sophisticated assets. Thus, the increased financial interrelatedness in the economy—the extent to which the different sectors of the economy are bound up in financial relations with the rest of the economy, the subject of flow-of-funds study—was

Table 3.1   **Gross Financial Assets (percent of GDP)**

	Brazil	Colombia	Costa Rica	Jamaica	Peru
1961	. . .	. . .	126	. . .	. . .
1962	99	145	128	. . .	. . .
1963	83	130	133	. . .	. . .
1964	. . .	124	148	136	. . .
1965	102	131	157	144	170
1966	83	129	159	. . .	165
1967	. . .	135	159	143	169
1968	116	147	161	156	168
1969	116	157	158	153	178
1970	. . .	. . .	160	169	195
1971	. . .	. . .	178	81	. . .
1972	. . .	. . .	. . .	179	. . .

Sources: Brazil: Banco Central do Brasil 1973, supplementary tables; Banco Central do Brasil, n.d., table 3.13.2.1, p. 510. Colombia: Banco de la República 1971, table 1, p. 14. Costa Rica: Banco Central de Costa Rica, n.d., table II-1, p. 25. Jamaica: Bank of Jamaica 1974, pt. 1, table 3.00, p. 71; Department of Statistics of Jamaica 1973, account 1, p. 17. Peru: Comisión Nacional Supervisora de Empresas y Valores 1973, vol. 1, table 1, p. 18.

Note: Average financial assests/GDP for available years: Brazil (1962–69), 100 percent; Colombia (1962–69), 137 percent; Costa Rica (1961–71), 152 percent; Peru (1965–70), 174 percent; and Jamaica (1964–69), 158 percent.

Table 3.2   **Monetary Holdings (percent of GDP)**

	Brazil		Colombia		Costa Rica		Jamaica		Peru	
	M1	M2	M1	M2	M1	M2	M1	M2	M1	M2
1961	. . .	. . .	. . .	. . .	14	17	. . .	. . .	. . .	. . .
1962	25	29	19	26	15	18	. . .	. . .	. . .	. . .
1963	23	25	17	24	15	18	. . .	. . .	. . .	. . .
1964	. . .	. . .	16	21	16	19	12	31	. . .	. . .
1965	27	29	17	23	15	18	10	29	20	33
1966	22	25	16	22	15	18	13	33	18	30
1967	. . .	. . .	17	22	18	21	13	34	18	29
1968	26	29	17	22	17	21	15	39	18	27
1969	25	28	17	23	18	21	16	43	20	31
1970	. . .	. . .	. . .	. . .	18	21	15	43	. . .	. . .
1971	. . .	. . .	. . .	. . .	20	23	17	48	. . .	. . .
1972	. . .	. . .	. . .	. . .	. . .	. . .	16	50	. . .	. . .

Sources: Brazil: Banco Central do Brasil 1973, supplementary tables; Banco Central do Brasil, n.d., table 3.13.2.1, p. 510. Colombia: Banco de la República 1971, table 1, p. 14, and annex table 1, pp. 82–97. Costa Rica: Banco Central de Costa Rica, n.d., table II-2, p. 26. Jamaica: Bank of Jamaica 1974, pt. 2, app. 1, pp. 22–44; Department of Statistics of Jamaica, *Income and Product Accounts 1975,* account 1, p. 17. Peru: Comisión Nacional Supervisora de Empresas y Valores 1973, vol. 1, table 1, p. 18, and table 20, p. 78.

Note: M1 = currency and demand deposits. M2 = M1 + time deposits.

not due simply to a transactions motive. However, it is important not to compare the figures from table 3.1 across countries. With the exception of the comparatively high ratios for Costa Rica, the rank ordering of financial assets to GDP among the five countries tends to reflect the comprehensiveness of the flow-of-funds data rather than the relative degree of financial intermediation of the country concerned.

Some indication of the strengths and weaknesses of these accounts may become apparent through the following examination of the sectoral treatment accorded the data. Particular attention will be paid to the relation between the flow-of-funds treatment in the Organization of American States (OAS) system and the income and product account equivalents. While the major domestic source of net financial savings for use by other sectors is households, its treatment in the NIPAs is particularly weak. For this reason, corporation, noncorporate enterprise, government, rest of world, and financial system activities will be dealt with largely in terms of their interrelation with households.

3.2.1 Households

In any sort of national accounting framework, the household accounts are the most difficult to capture accurately, and FFAs are no exception. Many of the component figures were arrived at by assigning a fixed share of a particular type of asset to the household sector over time. Sometimes these shares were derived from survey data, but this was not always the case. Estimated holdings of currency and demand deposits in Jamaica and Colombia (before the integration of the accounts) will serve as useful examples. Currency held by households in Jamaica was found by assuming that firms held 5 percent of all currency in circulation, so that the household figure could be arrived at by deducting all other sectors from the national total. In Colombia, a similar method was used, with 10 percent of private-sector currency holdings assigned to firms. In the case of demand deposits, the Colombians calculated a share for official deposits at commercial and public-sector banks using surveys taken by the superintendent of banks in 1968 and 1969. These shares were then deducted from aggregate deposits, and 40 percent of the balance was assigned to families on the basis of a survey taken in 1971. Jamaica had readily available data on official deposits and used surveys from the early 1960s and 1972 to calculate a trend share of the remainder for households; the 1972 share was 46.9 percent.

Until the integrated national accounts for Colombia (which made use of more recent U.N. methodology), the NIPA figure for household saving in the five countries was a residual item derived from an erroneous base. A fundamental assumption in the NIPAs is that investment by households is zero. A precise accounting must include owner/

occupier-built housing as household investment. Purchases of consumer durables, treated as investment in the U.S. FFAs, could be—but are not—counted as well, though the derivation of the stream of services from these consumption investments would be seriously error prone. In short, the NIPAs are measuring net rather than gross investment by households and misattributing some of it as well.

Saving by households in the NIPAs is derived by taking the national accounting estimate of total saving and deducting savings by firms and government. Weaknesses in these other figures will be indicated in the appropriate section, but it is worth pointing out here that the figure for total saving is frequently figured as $S = I + X - M$ where independent estimates of consumption are unavailable to cross-check with the more familiar $S = Y - C$. The result is that inaccuracies in the figure for total investment translate one for one into inaccuracy in the household saving figure. Moreover, while the current account figure is among the most reliable in the income and product account framework, under-invoicing of exports has been a chronic problem in Latin America, resulting in an overstated current account deficit and again a one-for-one understatement of household saving.

In addition, the real accounts are likely to underestimate household saving because of their derivation of it as a residual item that is sensitive to underestimation of investment. The gross investment figure is generally a composite index of a very incomplete set of measures of capital goods production, producers goods imports, cement production as a proxy for construction, land clearing, and the like. It is not built up from physical asset figures or a more comprehensive set of capital formation estimates.

A particularly important weakness of the household accounts is the nearly complete omission (except for Jamaican foreign exchange data for some years, unlikely to be a thorough accounting) of statistics on foreign assets and liabilities. This issue will be discussed more fully later, but some mention here is appropriate. Recent discussions of capital flight in the early 1980s have raised the question of "normal" levels of foreign asset holding; Diaz-Alejandro (1984, 377) speculated that Latin American households typically held 10 percent of their wealth overseas. It would have been useful to be able to test such assertions empirically. This is thus a particularly disheartening omission considering its importance for current policy questions.

3.2.2 Corporations

The transactions of firms are only slightly easier to capture in a national accounting framework than those of households, but this sector presents a particularly thorny problem in the flow-of-funds context. Owners' equity is among the most important components of firms' financial accounts. The way this has been handled in these FFAs has been to record new issues at book value and add retained earnings to the firms' liabilities to shareholders. No attempt was made to capture the market value of the firm, only the flows. However, this major divergence from the stock-differencing methodology hampers meaningful discussion of portfolio preferences based on outstanding asset balances.

An important element on the other side of a firm's balance sheet that is quite difficult to record is the assets generated by sales on credit, whether interfirm suppliers' credits or consumer credit. These figures are entirely missing from Brazil's and Colombia's (early) FFAs and no doubt contributed to Costa Rica's decision to present a consolidated private sector in its FFAs. In Jamaica, survey data from the early 1960s was inflated along with personal consumption expenditures to estimate consumer credit from businesses, but no attempt was made to capture interfirm credit (Department of Statistics of Jamaica 1970). Only Peru, of the five countries studied, estimates this particular figure, but the published accounts do not indicate the precise method used.

Both investment and saving by firms are inaccurately measured in the NIPAs. Capital consumption allowances are thought to be overstated and some investment not captured by the accounts, though any actual investment by households erroneously boosts corporate investment.

3.2.3   Noncorporate Enterprise

This is a difficult sector to capture accurately and is only occasionally of independent analytic interest. Indeed, this is a great stumbling block in the construction of FFAs. Nowhere is it separately reported in either the NIPAs or the FFAs. In practice, noncorporate enterprise is treated in several different ways. Costa Rica leaves the private sector as a single sector. In the cases of Brazil, Colombia (early system), Jamaica, and Peru, it is necessary to estimate the sectoral dividing line between firms and households, and for Colombia (current system) noncorporate enterprise is lumped in with households as a residual. In the revised Colombian methodology, because the social accounts use the corporate balance sheets submitted to the Superintendencia de Sociedades (the government regulators of corporations), corporations are identified separately, and noncorporate enterprises are classed with households. Naturally, this makes the analysis of Colombian household behavior somewhat problematic. This issue will be dealt with more fully in section 3.4.

3.2.4   Government

The figures for net financial saving in the FFAs are generally complete and correct. Indeed, it is precisely this financial measure, commonly referred to as the public-sector borrowing requirement, that is often looked to as the best measure of the government deficit.

Income and product account figures for government saving and investment are highly suspect, as government current expenditures are often disguised as investment. The net figure, thankfully, benefits from the offset of the two errors generated by the reclassification of transactions. There may, however, be discrepancies between the two sets of accounts owing to differing classification of some autonomous governmental or quasi-governmental agencies. More important, the timing of receipts and expenditures may generate year-to-year fluctuations in the difference between the two that can be substantial.

3.2.5   Rest of World

Assets and liabilities of the rest-of-world sector are frequently denominated in foreign currency. This subjects them to valuation changes that appear as flows in the domestic currency representation of the FFAs since the stock-change methodology was used. An adjustment to the figure for outstanding claims needs to be made in order to approximate the true flows. However, the obvious adjustment does not always bring the data into conformity with the flows recorded in the balance of payments (BPAs). It is fortunate that, for at least some countries in the group, devaluation was infrequent during the period of study. Costa Rica, in fact, maintained a completely stable exchange rate for the decade of the study. Peru devalued only once, in 1967. Jamaica, tied to sterling until 1972, moved against the U.S. dollar until that date only in 1967 and 1971. In this case, though, there is a problem of deciding on the currency composition of foreign assets: the usual dollar standard is likely to have been replaced with a dollar-pound mix.

Assets and, especially, liabilities of the rest-of-world sector are prone to omission because of lack of data. In three out of five cases (Brazil, Costa Rica, and Jamaica), the FFA rest-of-world sector relies directly on the capital account of the BPAs. Where the sector is directly estimated, it is possible that foreign-sector assets are reported more fully than liabilities. In such a case, the discrepancy between the FFAs and the NIPAs gives an indication of that component of capital flight that is registered in the capital account of the BPAs. Some countries use a residual from the BPAs, which will embrace part of these omissions, to estimate the relations between the foreign and the domestic private sectors. Export underinvoicing, so far as it can be estimated, provides an additional source from which capital flight estimates can be improved, in this case capturing capital flight through the current account. A combination of these techniques holds the potential for finally getting more accurate figures for this very important phenomenon. Because this is the only account in the NIPA estimates that includes both real and financial flows, it permits an estimate of "errors and omissions." These errors and omissions figures are analogous to and form a part of the discrepancy between real and financial flows that can be estimated fully only through the availability of both real and financial accounts, the only such discrepancy available in routinely compiled data.

3.2.6   The Financial System

A pure financial intermediary would show net financial saving of zero at all times since all its assets are financial and always equal its (all financial) liabilities. In reality, however, financial intermediaries are corporations and do hold some real assets (offices, e.g.). Statistical problems of one sort or another may also contribute to the observed variation in net financial assets of the financial system in the FFAs. The discrepancies are, in most cases, fairly small. Where they are not, they can be interpreted either as a problem related to data collection or as an item belonging properly to the corporate sector. The financial system, insofar as it appears in the NIPAs, is included in that sector, as it should be. It should also be noted here that the monetary authorities are classified as part of the financial system, so that central bank holdings of government debt do in fact show up in the government's intersectoral accounts. Thus, operating losses (or, less commonly, profits) of the central bank, which can be substantial, may also contribute to the discrepancy between the two systems.

This extremely brief introduction to the methods used to compile flow-of-funds statistics in Latin America is a testament to the ingenuity of the creators of these accounts. By concentrating on the weaknesses of the FFAs, we have perhaps left the impression that the accounts are weaker than they in fact are, but a catalog of the accurately recorded figures would obscure the more important issues that need further improvement. The next section will compare the household saving figure from the FFAs (which, as was mentioned earlier, is the weakest section of the accounts) with the corresponding figure from the NIPAs, and it will be seen that the FFAs compare quite favorably with their more established counterparts.

3.3   A Comparison of Household Saving

The importance of attention to financial flows in the estimation of real saving is particularly evident when one explores the household sector in Latin America. In the studies examined, sizable discrepancies appear when FFA estimates are compared with NIPA estimates of household saving. Household savings are always among the weakest figures in the NIPAs, even in industrial countries with well-developed statistical agencies, and the discrepancy between NIPA and FFA estimates can be considerable. In Latin America, NIPA household savings have long been thought to be understated (see Mamalakis 1976), and are subject to substantial upward correction when matched with the comparable figure from FFAs.

Among the five countries examined, only Colombia, Peru, and Jamaica have households as a separate sector in both the NIPAs and the FFAs. For Colombia, we consider here only the years 1963–69, the years of the original OAS study; for years after that, the accounts have been recalculated on the basis of the new U.N. methodology and integrated, eliminating almost all the discrepancy (the earlier estimates of Colombian FFAs appear in Banco de la Republica n.d.-a).

The implications of the accompanying tables are quite striking. The FFAs impute a level of net financial saving to households that is, on the average over the sample periods, significantly higher than that of the NIPAs. The difference amounts to an increase in the ratio of household savings to GDP of 2.2 percent of GDP in Peru (table 3.3), 3.0 percent in Jamaica (table 3.4), and 4.5 percent in Colombia (table 3.5). To illustrate the likely downward bias of the NIPA figures for household saving, savings in the real accounts are actually negative for 1966 and 1969 in Colombia and for 1971, 1972, and 1973 in Jamaica, with con-

Table 3.3   **Peru: Household-Sector Savings: Comparison of FFAs and NIPAs**

	FFA Assets (1)	FFA Liabilities (2)	FFA NFA (1) − (2)	FFA Change in NFA (3)	NIPA Saving (4)	Statistical Discrepancy (3) − (4)
1965[a]	44.3	20.2	24.1	N.A.	1.7	N.A.
1966[a]	55.7	21.6	34.1	10.0	2.7	7.3
1967[a]	61.1	28.0	33.1	− 1.0	5.2	− 6.2
1968[a]	72.9	32.2	40.7	7.6	.0	7.6
1969[a]	83.4	37.7	45.7	5.0	2.8	2.2
1970[a]	105.4	44.1	61.3	15.6	6.2	9.4
1965[b]	38.6	17.6	21.0	N.A.	1.5	N.A.
1966[b]	40.7	15.8	24.9	7.3	2.0	5.3
1967[b]	38.9	17.8	21.1	− .6	3.3	− 4.0
1968[b]	39.2	17.3	21.9	4.1	.0	4.1
1969[b]	39.9	18.0	21.9	2.4	1.3	1.1
1970[b]	43.8	18.3	25.5	6.5	2.6	3.9

Sources: Comisión Nacional Supervisora de Empresas y Valores 1973, vol. 1, table 1, p. 18, table 38, p. 114, and table 43, p. 126; Banco Central de Reserva del Perú 1974, table 5, pp. 18–19.

Note: NFA = net financial assets; N.A. = not available.

[a]Figures given in millions of soles.

[b]Figures given as percentage of GDP.

Table 3.4   **Jamaica: Household-Sector Savings: Comparison of FFAs and NIPAs**

	FFA Assets (1)	FFA Liabilities (2)	FFA NFA (1) − (2)	FFA Change in NFA (3)	NIPA Saving (4)	Statistical Discrepancy (3) − (4)
1964[a]	244.7	91.1	153.6	. . .	. . .	. . .
1965[a]	260.4	97.0	163.4	9.8	10.6	− .8
1966[a]	310.4	111.1	199.3	35.9	11.3	24.6
1967[a]	340.2	126.6	213.6	14.3	19.6	− 5.3
1968[a]	401.7	149.4	252.3	38.7	33.6	5.1
1969[a]	518.5	195.9	322.6	70.3	14.8	55.5
1970[a]	556.1	201.2	354.9	32.3	20.7	11.6
1971[a]	691.6	246.8	444.8	89.9	− 16.8	106.7
1972[a]	777.9	287.3	490.6	45.8	− 49.8	95.6
1964[b]	41.6	15.5	26.1	. . .	. . .	. . .
1965[b]	41.0	15.3	25.7	1.5	1.7	− .1
1966[b]	44.9	16.1	28.9	5.2	1.6	3.6
1967[b]	45.7	17.0	28.7	1.9	2.6	− .7
1968[b]	49.0	18.2	30.8	4.7	4.1	.6
1969[b]	52.2	19.7	32.5	7.1	1.5	5.6
1970[b]	47.5	17.2	30.3	2.8	1.8	1.0
1971[b]	53.9	19.2	34.7	7.0	− 1.3	8.3
1972[b]	54.1	20.0	34.1	3.2	− 3.5	6.6

Sources: Bank of Jamaica 1974, pt. 1, table 3.16, p. 103, and table 3.22, p. 114; Bank of Jamaica, n.d., table 4, p. 15; Department of Statistics of Jamaica 1973, account 1, p. 17, and account 5, p. 21.

Note: NFA = net financial assets.

[a]Figures given in millions of Jamaican dollars.

[b]Figures given as percentage of GDP.

sistently low rates in both countries. The figures for Peru are also quite low, though here it is an FFA figure that suggests dissaving, in this case for 1967.

It is also possible to report a distinct figure for household saving for Brazil from the FFAs (table 3.6), even though the household sector is not broken out of the NIPAs. These data suggest a household saving rate similar to those reported in the FFAs for the other countries, with an average of 4.4 percent of GDP for the four years reported. In principle, it would also be possible to report a net financial savings estimate for businesses on the basis of the FFAs. This could be done by deducting the FFA estimate of household savings from the NIPA figure for private-sector savings. This would, however, be inaccurate. The NIPA figure for private-sector saving is subject to underestimation because of all the "upstream" problems discussed in section 3.2. Deducting from this a substantially correct figure for household saving

Table 3.5   Colombia: Household-Sector Savings: Comparison of FFAs and
                   NIPAs

	FFA Assets (1)	FFA Liabilities (2)	FFA NFA (1) − (2)	FFA Change in NFA (3)	NIPA Saving (4)	Statistical Discrepancy (3) − (4)
1962[a]	17.20	1.68	15.53	N.A.	1.10	N.A.
1963[a]	18.22	1.91	16.31	.78	.61	.17
1964[a]	23.68	2.08	21.60	5.29	.39	4.90
1965[a]	25.10	2.47	22.63	1.03	1.59	−.56
1966[a]	32.50	3.05	29.45	6.82	−.18	7.00
1967[a]	37.14	3.58	33.56	4.11	1.22	2.89
1968[a]	43.01	4.80	38.21	4.65	1.60	3.05
1969[a]	51.12	6.37	44.75	6.53	−.60	7.13
1962[b]	50.3	4.9	45.4	N.A.	3.2	N.A.
1963[b]	41.9	4.4	37.5	1.8	1.4	.4
1964[b]	44.0	3.9	40.2	9.8	.7	9.1
1965[b]	41.3	4.1	37.2	1.7	2.6	−.9
1966[b]	44.2	4.1	40.0	9.3	−.2	9.5
1967[b]	44.7	4.3	40.4	4.9	1.5	3.5
1968[b]	44.6	5.0	39.6	4.8	1.7	3.2
1969[b]	46.1	5.7	40.3	5.9	−.5	6.4

Sources: Banco de la República 1971, table 9, p. 20; Banco de la República, n.d. = g,
table 4, p. 33; Banco de la República, n.d. = h, table 4, p. 6.
Note: NFA = net financial assets; N.A. = not available.
[a]Figures given in billions of pesos.
[b]Figures given as percentage of GDP.

would accordingly leave us with an underestimated figure for firm saving. It bears repeating, especially in the case of Brazil (for which we
report a figure without an alternative source for comparison), that there
are substantial problems with these figures. However, they do consistently point in the direction in which we know the true figures to lie,
thus adding to the information available from NIPAs.

This has important implications for the role of financial policy in a
developing economy. Giving credence to the artificially low personal
saving rate that appears in the NIPAs can lead to an unduly pessimistic
appraisal of the role that households can play in the mobilization of
capital resources. In the same vein, the opportunity costs of financial
repression are likely to be understated, and so the bias of the NIPA
saving figures can lead to an overreliance on restrictive capital market
policies. To know that a well-designed capital market development
program could raise the rate of personal saving by 50 percent is a
different thing when that rate is 2 percent of GDP from what it is when
that rate is 6 percent.

Table 3.6 Brazil: Private-Sector Net Financial Savings

	Private Sector				Private Sector			
	NIPA[a]	FFA[a]	Firms: FFA[a]	Households: FFA[a]	NIPA[b]	FFA[b]	Firms: FFA[b]	Households: FFA[b]
1960	−58	−28	−126	98	−2.1	−1.0	−4.6	3.6
1963	330	−13	−510	497	2.8	−.1	−4.3	4.2
1966	500	−1,559	−4,355	2,796	.9	−2.9	−8.1	5.2
1969	5,110	−7,980	−14,392	6,412	3.8	−6.0	−10.8	4.8

Sources: Banco Central do Brasil 1973, supplementary tables; Fundação Getulio Vargas 1973, tables 5, and 7.

[a]Figures given in millions of cruzeiros.

[b]Figures given in percentage of GDP.

It is to be expected, from the considerations discussed in section 3.2, that the FFAs will provide a more comprehensive coverage of household savings than do the NIPAs. This is because the accumulation of financial assets and liabilities of households is directly covered by the financial accounts (except for informal sector transactions, many of which are interhousehold flows that would net out in the accounts anyway). Also, while the informal sector of the real economy may escape reporting in the NIPAs, the financial flows that they permit may well be captured in the FFAs as changes in financial savings of the producing units (which appear as households). It must be admitted, though, that, in cases in which there is severe financial disintermediation, the portion of the informal credit market that is not captured directly in the FFAs may well assume significant proportions. There also may be some underreporting of consumer credit and other lending from business to households in the FFAs that could exaggerate the net financial savings of households vis-à-vis the real accounts. Under such circumstances, the real account estimates of financial savings could approach—or even exceed—those of the FFAs.

As useful as they are in improving the NIPAs, the significance of these estimates of household saving extends beyond their usefulness for refinement of the statistical source. In general, households are the only net-saving domestic sector in a modern economy. From an economic policy perspective, it is clearly important to know the resources potentially available for deployment, the more so since the FFA estimates permit us to revise the figure for household saving sharply upward. Any attempt to increase the gross saving in the economy must rely on capturing the financial savings of households. The next section will examine more closely the recent experience of Colombia and will show the susceptibility of financial savings of households (albeit firm-households) to both deliberate manipulation and circumstantial adjustment.

3.4   A Case Study of Colombia, 1970–83

As was mentioned earlier, Colombia has integrated its NIPAs with the FFAs for the years since 1970 and has produced flow-based figures up through 1983 with a substantially smaller discrepancy between the real and financial accounts and an improved set of NIPAs. The availability of both sets of accounts at the sectoral level permits one to observe the interaction between real and financial savings of households. This type of information is particularly important in identifying the net effect of financial policy and real economic shocks on voluntary financial savings as a source of actual and potential resources available for accumulation and growth. It illustrates that greater attention to policies favoring the use of funds for investment rather than consumption lending may be critical in permitting financial savings to realize their real accumulation potential.

From a policy perspective, five periods may be identified for Colombia during the seventies and early eighties (Jaramillo 1982; World Bank 1984; Brock 1980). The pattern they show is one in which a heavily repressed economy liberalizes partially, returns to repression, and then liberalizes more fully. The major macroeconomic characteristics of each period are summarized in table 3.7.

3.4.1   1970–72: Financial Repression

During these years, financial policy by and large continued the preliberalization measures of the 1960s, with government ceilings on lending and borrowing rates, credit rationing in the formal financial sector, and financial disintermediation. While in the late 1960s and early 1970s some of the interest ceilings were raised and the country moved from a fixed to a crawling peg exchange rate, Colombia began the 1970s in conditions fundamentally similar to those in many developing countries. Attempts to restrict nominal interest rate responses to inflation led to financial repression, the problems of proliferating informal credit market activity (the "extrabank" market), less than optimal saving rates, and investment inefficiency.

3.4.2   1972–74: First Step to Liberalization

In 1972, although credit markets remained subject to regulation, a new instrument, inflation indexed, was introduced for the express purpose of funding housing finance. This first step was partial at best. This new instrument came to be known by the name of the indexing unit, the UPAC ("unit of constant purchasing power"). While UPACs enjoyed understandable success in attracting voluntary savings into residential construction, much of their growth involved a shift in portfolios out of lessfavored financial instruments. (UPACs are included in "savings

Table 3.7   **Financial Policy Regimes in Colombia, 1970–83**

Period	Financial Policy	Economic Conditions
1970–72	Financial repression	Rapid growth Low inflation
1972–74	First steps to liberalization	Accelerating inflation
1974–76	Liberalization is broadened	"Growth recession," 1975
1977–79	Stabilization and financial repression	Coffee boom
1979–83	Increasing liberalization	Coffee "bust" External deficits

deposits'' in the tables. They show considerable growth as a share of household financial savings over the period [table 3.8], even though financial savings as a share of GDP did not rise significantly [table 3.9].)

3.4.3   1974–76: Liberalization Is Broadened

These were years of more extensive, though still incomplete, financial liberalization. Interest rates were increased across the board, with limits placed on the indexing of UPACs to reduce their preferred status, which had led to considerable diversion of funds out of other assets. Indeed, there was speculation that the UPAC was devised to be a "foot in the door" for broader liberalization. Time and savings deposit rates were raised (though not deregulated) along with yields on government bonds, though the interest on the latter lost its tax exemption.

3.4.4   1977–79: Stabilization and Financial Repression

The fourth period involved the imposition of restrictive credit policies in order to prevent increased export revenues from generating inflation. Improved coffee terms of trade and expansion of the "other economy" (illegal drug exports) caused a considerable increase in dollar earnings. To prevent this expansion of the monetary base from increasing the monetary aggregates and stimulating inflation, the authorities implemented a program that included import and foreign borrowing restrictions, a fiscal surplus, and increased reserve requirements.

Table 3.8   **Colombian Household Financial Investment by Asset Type**

	Investment Shares (percent of annual total)				
Year	Money	Savings Deposits	Equity	Other Long-Term Assets	Other Short-Term Assets
1970	17.5	6.4	19.6	8.6	47.8
1971	12.1	6.3	35.4	23.2	23.1
1972	20.0	11.1	26.4	13.5	28.9
1973	16.7	19.4	18.7	7.7	37.5
1974	7.2	16.1	19.8	6.4	50.5
1975	14.6	24.1	18.6	−6.6	49.3
1976	30.3	21.6	17.2	6.0	24.9
1977	24.8	19.3	13.3	11.0	31.6
1978	17.0	22.2	7.0	31.1	22.6
1979	16.0	20.0	13.2	12.2	38.6
1980	11.8	35.7	12.8	8.8	30.8
1981	8.5	42.2	14.3	13.2	21.8
1982	14.2	25.9	13.5	5.6	40.7
1983	16.6	37.3	13.7	11.8	20.6

Sources: Banco de la República, n.d. = b, table 15a; Banco de la República, n.d. = f, table 16.

Table 3.9   Colombia Firm-Household Data (percent of GDP)

Year	Investment	Saving	Net Real Saving	Net Financial Saving	Asset Increase	Liability Increase
1970	4.7	7.1	2.4	4.5	8.9	4.3
1971	3.9	5.1	1.3	1.2	7.2	6.0
1972	5.7	8.8	3.3	3.5	9.0	5.4
1973	5.4	10.2	4.8	3.9	10.4	6.5
1974	6.3	9.0	2.9	1.9	9.1	7.3
1975	5.6	7.9	2.5	2.7	6.8	4.0
1976	5.2	7.9	2.9	3.5	9.1	5.6
1977	4.5	9.9	5.5	5.4	9.4	4.0
1978	5.0	9.0	4.3	4.5	9.0	4.5
1979	5.3	9.4	4.2	4.5	7.9	3.4
1980	5.0	9.0	4.1	4.0	9.6	5.1
1981	4.9	8.0	3.1	4.6	9.0	4.4
1982	5.0	8.1	2.9	3.4	7.3	3.9
1983	5.3	5.3	3.4	2.8	7.0	4.2

Sources: Banco de la República, n.d.-b, table 1; Banco de la República, n.d.-c, table 1; Banco de la República, n.d.-e, table 1; Banco de la República, n.d.-f. table 1.

As intended, the share of savings flowing into money and savings deposits fell sharply between 1976 and 1979 (table 3.8), but the figures in table 3.9 indicate that net financial saving of households still rose significantly as a share of GDP.

3.4.5   1979–83: Increasing Liberalization

In 1979 and 1980, a number of fundamental changes took place in financial policy; most important were the liberalization of important lending and borrowing rates, the removal of 100 percent marginal reserve requirements, and the introduction of marketable short-term government securities. This caused a considerable increase in both deposit and lending rates from their earlier repressed levels. Though net financial savings of households as a share of GDP remained fairly stable during the period of policy transition from 1979 to 1981, the ensuing years showed a sharp decline (table 3.9). This was almost certainly due to the slowdown in real growth (which had averaged 5.4 percent per year from 1976 to 1980 and fell to 1.6 percent from 1981 to 1983) that accompanied the decline in export revenue. During the period 1981–83, there was a reversal of net foreign savings as the capital account of the balance of payments, which had been negative from 1975 to 1980, became a deficit averaging 4.8 percent of GDP during the period 1981–83 (table 3.10).

Before examining the Colombian FFA data in depth, there are two issues particular to Colombia that need to be discussed: the parallel economy and the sectorization of the accounts. To a considerable degree, the

Table 3.10   **Colombian Saving and Investment**

Year	Investment	Saving	Current Account Deficit [a, b]	Inflation (%)	GDP Growth (%)
1970	20.3	16.3	3.9	6.8	9.3
1971	19.4	13.3	6.2	9.0	6.0
1972	18.1	16.2	2.0	13.4	7.7
1973	18.3	18.3	.0	20.8	6.7
1974	20.8	18.3	2.5	24.3	5.7
1975	17.0	17.1	−.1	22.9	2.3
1976	17.6	19.0	−1.5	20.2	4.7
1977	18.8	21.6	−2.8	33.1	4.2
1978	18.3	20.4	−2.2	17.8	8.5
1979	18.2	19.8	−1.6	24.7	4.1
1980	19.1	19.6	−.5	26.5	2.3
1981	20.6	16.9	3.7	27.5	.9
1982	20.5	15.1	5.4	24.5	1.6
1983	19.9	14.7	5.2	19.8	3.2

Sources: Banco de la República, n.d.-b, table 1; Banco de la República, n.d.-c, table 1; Banco de la República, n.d.-e, table 1; Banco de la República, n.d.-f, table 1; International Monetary Fund 1986 (inflation data only).

[a]Figures given in percentage of GDP.

[b]A minus sign (−) indicates a surplus

drug economy functions like a traditional Latin American enclave and does not grossly distort either the real or the financial accounts. Colombia's informal credit market does include a small-scale consumer loan market. For most informal credit market operations, though, firms are the principle takers and a frequent source of funds, so that these transactions appear in the balance sheets incorporated in the FFA corporate sector. The parallel market is thus not as important a source of error in the FFAs as might be imagined.

In what follows, the sector is referred to interchangeably as the household sector and the firm-household sector. The difference is that, in a great many instances, the household has the option of investing its earnings in the family enterprise rather than a financial asset. McKinnon's (1973) analysis of the "fragmented economy," which chronicles the lack of investment opportunities and savings vehicles in a developing economy, emphasizes the difficulty of separating the family's savings decision from its entrepreneurial investment decision. Given the difficulty, even in industrial countries, of distinguishing noncorporate enterprise from household transactions, the treatment of the two as a single sector in Colombia seems wholly justified.

Household-sector savings as estimated in the earlier NIPAs prior to their integration with the financial accounts can be compared with the postintegration accounts for the years 1970–74. The results support the contention that FFA estimates provide a more comprehensive figure for the residual of household savings over investment than traditional (nonintegrated) NIPAs and that integrated real and financial accounts do an even better job. During these years, the household saving figure under the earlier system averaged 2.7 percent of GDP, a ratio that is somewhat higher than the figures for the 1960s examined in the previous section. But, in the same years (1970–74), the comparable figures in the integrated social accounts is 8.0 percent. The difference between these two figures is reasonably close to the difference of 4.5 percent found by comparing the NIPAs with the FFAs for the 1960s. In short, the initial OAS FFAs, despite the degree of disintermediation in those earlier years, were able to identify a serious downward bias in the NIPA estimates of household saving. Given the critical importance of household saving to the noninflationary finance of public and private investment and debt service, it is imperative that such estimates be as accurate as possible.

If one were to compare the net real saving of the household sector as reported in the NIPAs with the net financial saving from the financial accounts, the difference is almost zero. While a slight statistical discrepancy does exist, it is quite small for most of the years and shows no systematic bias. For only eight years out of fourteen does the financial account figure exceed the corresponding figure of the real accounts, and the average premium is only 0.2 percent of GDP. Thus, the large discrepancy reported for Colombia in section 3.3 for the years prior to the new, integrated account estimates appears to have been entirely corrected by the revised real saving figure, as one would have expected, leaving only a small residual between the two sets of accounts.

What did households do with their savings? One of the main objectives of financial policy from the very beginning of liberalization was to increase real savings and channel them into productive investment and noninflationary finance of the public deficit. It is possible to determine the effectiveness of such efforts once comprehensive real and financial accounts are available. One can derive two types of disaggregation from the financial accounts in order to address such questions. First, asset accumulation may be divided by type of asset, which is done for households in table 3.8. For this purpose, we have divided financial assets into five categories: (1) money, including demand deposits; (2) various forms of savings deposits; (3) equity capital, including partnership investment as well as corporate shares; (4) other long-term assets (having a maturity of more than two years); and (5) other short-term assets. The results show how the composition of household asset portfolios adjusted to real and financial conditions during the period studied. Note that the integrated accounts from Colombia deal with annual flows rather than end-year stocks and reflect only actual intersectoral transactions rather than valuation adjustments (Pinot de Libreros, Vinasco Medina, and Riveros Mora 1982). The difficulties that were examined in section 3.2 in moving from stock measures to flow measures were bypassed. Our second breakdown of financial flows in table 3.11 disaggregates them by institutional sectors of origin and destination. All domestic household transactions are divided into three main sectors: corporations, government, and the financial system. It is an unfortunate limitation of the available data that household transactions with the rest of the world are not presented as independent estimates. The omission of resource flows between households and proprietary firms is equally lamentable.

We look first at the aggregate accumulation of assets and liabilities. We turn next to the examination of asset portfolio adjustment and finally to an examination of intersectoral flows.

The firm-household sector accumulated financial assets at an average rate of 8.5 percent of GDP over our fourteen-year sample period while accumulating liabilities at a rate of just under 5 percent of GDP. In the period 1970–72, prior to liberalization, households acquired financial assets valued at an average of 8.4 percent of GDP while acquiring liabilities in an average amount equal to 5.2 percent of GDP; net financial saving thus averaged 3.2 percent of GDP. Since the years from 1972 to 1980 involved different degrees of partial liberalization, as

Table 3.11   Colombian Household Financial Flows by Sector (percent of total)

	Assets			Liabilities		
Year	Firms	Government	Financial System	Firms	Government	Financial System
1970	23.1	16.1	60.8	35.1	6.5	58.4
1971	32.7	17.0	50.4	22.3	31.9	45.7
1972	30.5	11.2	58.4	30.1	19.4	50.5
1973	32.5	7.5	59.9	36.3	24.8	38.9
1974	27.3	6.3	66.4	30.7	19.5	49.8
1975	32.8	6.9	60.2	2.2	35.4	62.4
1976	31.3	3.9	64.7	33.4	−4.1	70.6
1977	18.7	2.8	78.5	25.0	16.5	58.5
1978	17.0	2.3	80.7	6.8	46.0	47.2
1979	18.4	2.0	79.6	35.4	8.5	56.1
1980	35.8	1.3	62.9	39.5	5.5	55.0
1981	43.1	1.1	55.9	45.9	−.7	54.7
1982	26.1	1.0	72.9	41.6	5.3	53.2
1983	34.3	.9	64.8	19.2	7.4	73.5

Sources: Banco de la República, n.d.-b, tables 26a–42b; Banco de la República, n.d.-c, tables A-1–A 19; Banco de la República, n.d.-e, tables A-1–A-19; Banco de la República, n.d.-f, tables A-1–A-19.

Note: Figures represent shares of net increases in financial assets and liabilities.

described at the beginning of this section, all of which went well beyond the policies of the 1960s and early 1970s, the period is best taken as a whole. Excluding the slow-growth year of 1975, financial assets grew by an average of 9.1 percent of GDP from 1972 to 1980 as against a 5.1 percent growth of liabilities, causing net financial savings to rise to 4.0 percent of GDP (table 3.9), 0.8 percent above the "preliberalization" rate. In the liberalized (but recessionary) period 1981–83, assets grew by only 7.8 percent of GDP, with liabilities also growing at a reduced rate of 4.2 percent of GDP, cutting net financial savings of households back to 3.6 percent of GDP, midway between the two earlier periods.

The implications of these figures are quite interesting. They suggest that a partial financial liberalization did encourage firm-households to acquire more financial assets as a share of income without triggering a boom in consumer lending that would have offset any increase in financial saving. It is important to note in this regard that substantial liberalization, with the exception of UPACs, did not begin until 1974. In fact, the greatest spurt of household borrowing was associated with the UPAC system and consequent boom in housing construction. The years 1973 and 1974 constituted the peak for household borrowing, with new financial liabilities equal to 6.5 and 7.3 percent of GDP, respectively. Hence, net financial saving by households had fallen to 1.9 percent of GDP in 1974 (table 3.9), a full percentage point below the net real saving figure from the NIPAs.

Only after 1976 did net financial saving grow significantly, coinciding as much with the export boom as with financial liberalization per se. It may well be that the coffee boom gave households the wherewithal to finance their purchases out of income rather than taking up loans that were available. Certainly, a rational household would increase its net saving (out of transitory income) during a cyclical boom, irrespective of additional incentives provided by financial liberalization. But the availability of attractive financial assets would certainly provide an incentive to hold those savings in a form that would be more readily available for productive investment (rather than, e.g., inflation hedges). And 1979, the peak of the coffee boom, was also the lowest year in the sample in growth of household liabilities. It looks as though one effect of liberalization was simply to increase the rate of acquisition of both financial assets and financial liabilities. But this also places greater emphasis on policies to direct the use of funds into investment rather than consumption expenditures.

For the final period 1981–83, economic downturn was the dominant characteristic—GDP grew by only 1.6 percent per year from 1981 to 1983. By contrast, from 1970 to 1980 (again excluding 1975) the Colombian economy grew at a rate of 6.1 percent. Public administration, which had shown a surplus in both the real and the financial accounts from 1974 to 1980, moved into deficit, with that deficit reaching 3 percent of GDP by 1983. As we have seen, these events show up clearly in the household FFA aggregates. As could be expected, asset accumulation slows by 1.3 percent of GDP, and liability growth falls by 0.9 percent of GDP, resulting in a fall in net saving of just under half a percentage point of GDP.

Turning now to the composition of this growth in household financial asset holdings (table 3.8), we focus particularly on the effect of increased financial liberalization. As mentioned above, perhaps the most important element of this was the introduction of the UPAC-indexed savings deposit. As it happens, Colombian inflation increased during the 1970s from an average of under 10 percent per year in the period 1970–72 to 24 percent from 1973–83. The result was a shift not so much out of money as out of longer-term assets. This accords well with the observation that the extrabank credit market, which mushroomed during the financially repressed years of the coffee boom, was heavily concentrated in short-term lending.

Though the figures are highly variable from year to year since they reflect marginal shifts in portfolios, the pattern is quite clear. In the process of financial liberalization, while incremental money holdings and "other short-term assets" held a steady share of the total increase in assets, new equity (shares plus partnership investment) fell from 27.1 percent in 1970–72 to 15.1 percent from 1973 to 1983, and "other long-term assets" fell from 15.1 to 9.6 percent of total increases. At the same time, savings deposits (including UPAC deposits) skyrocketed from 7.9 to 22.3 percent of the total. From the boom of the 1970s into the slump of the 1980s, savings deposits grew even further, at the expense of other short-term assets. A slight decline in incremental money holdings, corresponding to the slower rate of income and therefore transactions growth, was the only other significant change into the early 1980s.

These changes in asset holdings had important effects on the sectoral distribution of the increase in firm-household assets as shown in table 3.11. The most significant shift among sectors between 1970–72 and 1973–83 was the sharp decline in household claims against government, from 14.8 percent to 3.3 percent, offset by increases in assets of the financial system from 56.5 percent to 67.9 percent. This represents in part the strong fiscal position of the government in the years of the coffee boom and in part increases in minimum denominations for some public-sector liabilities. The net assets of households against the business sector remained the same 28.8 percent over the two periods. On the liability side, household liabilities to business also showed almost no change (29.2 percent in the first period as against 28.7 percent in the years of liberalization), while liabilities to the financial system rose from 51.5 percent to 56.4 percent of the total increment. This further illustrates that financial opening such as Colombia experienced can effectively increase the amount of financial savings of households available for channeling into investment through the financial system.

The preceding analysis has been conducted from the vantage of the firm-household sector. It might well have been repeated for the corporate sector. Table 3.12, though, shows that corporate saving remained fairly steady throughout the period being examined (reflecting in part the steady rate of capital consumption) and that the investment rate varies mostly with the business cycle (table 3.13). An important reason for this is likely to be the ability of the larger enterprises represented in the corporate sector to get access to credit. Table 3.14 outlines the forms this credit took. Leff (1976, 1978, 1979) and Strachan (1976) discuss the ways in which financial conglomerates (*grupos*) in Latin America ensure themselves a supply of credit. In the Colombian case, Tybout (1980, 1983, 1984) has established a clear link between firm size and credit access. The phenomenal growth of *grupos* through takeovers during the 1970s makes the analysis of the corporate sector accounts even more difficult. Further work on corporation finance at the micro level would be an essential complement to analysis of that sector's aggregate flow of funds.

Table 3.12 **Colombia Corporation Data (percent of GDP)**

Year	Investment	Saving	Real NFS	Financial NFS
1970	11.7	5.4	−5.8	−8.6
1971	11.7	5.5	−5.9	−6.7
1972	9.3	5.1	−3.9	−6.3
1973	7.9	5.2	−2.6	−2.8
1974	11.0	5.4	−5.6	−5.8
1975	8.7	4.1	−4.5	−4.0
1976	9.5	4.7	−4.8	−4.8
1977	7.2	4.8	−4.0	−4.0
1978	9.1	4.5	−4.6	−6.0
1979	9.8	5.5	−4.3	−3.2
1980	9.9	5.4	−4.4	−5.8
1981	10.4	5.4	−4.5	−6.1
1982	15.0	5.0	−7.3	−7.6
1983	9.5	5.2	−4.0	−6.0

Sources: Banco de la República, n.d.-b, table 1; Banco de la República, n.d.-c, table 1; Banco de la República, n.d.-e, table 1; Banco de la República, n.d.-f, table 1.

Note: NFS = net financial saving.

Table 3.13   Colombian Corporate Asset Growth (percent of GDP)

Year	Total	Commercial Credit	Loans	Domestic Equity	M1*	Indexed Accounts	Other Deposits	Foreign Assets
1970	7.7	5.0	1.1	.6	.4	.0	.4	.1
1971	4.4	3.5	.4	.1	.3	.0	.0	.2
1972	7.1	4.4	1.1	.4	.5	.0	.5	.1
1973	9.5	5.4	1.4	.4	.7	.3	.9	−.1
1974	6.7	4.5	1.1	.3	.4	.1	.3	.3
1975	5.2	3.8	1.0	.2	.5	.0	.4	−.3
1976	7.2	4.3	1.4	.2	.8	.1	.3	−.1
1977	11.3	4.1	3.4	.6	.9	.1	.8	−.2
1978	8.8	4.5	1.8	.7	.6	.3	.4	.2
1979	8.7	5.0	1.1	.7	.5	.1	.8	.1
1980	12.3	7.0	1.4	.7	.9	.2	1.9	.2
1981	8.7	4.1	1.4	.6	.8	.2	1.4	−.1
1982	6.2	3.6	.8	.2	1.0	.3	.0	−.1
1983	6.2	3.2	.4	.3	.8	.1	1.1	.0

Sources: Banco de la República, n.d.-b, tables 1, 14a; Banco de la República, n.d.-c, tables 1, 15; Banco de la República, n.d.-e, tables 1, 15; Banco de la República, n.d.-f, tables 1, 15.

*M1 = currency and demand deposits.

Table 3.14   **Colombian Corporate Liability Growth (percent of GDP)**

Year	Total	Commercial Credit	Loans	Domestic Equity
1970	16.3	6.0	5.8	2.9
1971	11.2	2.3	4.3	3.3
1972	13.4	2.0	5.9	3.3
1973	12.3	5.6	3.0	2.7
1974	12.5	3.5	4.8	3.0
1975	9.2	2.7	3.6	1.9
1976	11.9	3.8	5.1	2.1
1977	15.3	3.2	9.1	2.4
1978	14.8	4.5	7.9	1.9
1979	11.9	.7	7.7	2.3
1980	18.1	4.6	9.3	2.3
1981	14.8	3.7	7.5	2.6
1982	13.8	3.9	6.0	1.9
1983	12.3	2.9	6.1	1.9

Sources: Banco de la República, n.d.-b, tables 1, 14b; Banco de la República, n.d.-c, tables 1, 15; Banco de la República, n.d.-e, tables 1, 15; Banco de la República, n.d.-f, tables 1, 15.

3.5 Conclusions

By presenting evidence from the FFAs, NIPAs, and integrated social accounts of several countries from Latin America and one from the Caribbean, it has been possible to illustrate the importance of source and use of funds analysis to an assessment of the effect of real and financial changes on developing countries. Academic attention to financial sector development led to important steps in the direction of financial liberalization in the 1970s. These steps caused a reduction in the degree of financial repression and disintermediation resulting from the imposition of interest rate ceilings, credit rationing, and other controls on financial markets. Evidence has been presented that financial liberalization did in fact increase financial intermediation of household savings.

However, one danger with liberalization is the threat that financial intermediation might inadvertently offset gross financial savings with dissaving by other sectors (for consumption lending and funding of government current expenditures), thus preventing the potential real savings and investment out of income from being fully realized. While the present study is not designed to pursue these inquiries in depth or to deal with issues of financial development policy, it suggests that such an endeavor would be extremely productive, especially in the present period of Third World indebtedness and the need to resort to internal sources of accumulation for recovery, restructuring, and growth.

In addition, the study illustrates the value of flow-of-funds analyses, even of a relatively rudimentary kind, in identifying possible gaps between actual levels of household savings and those reported in NIPAs. The Colombian case is particularly compelling in this regard, as it shows how the increase of several percentage points of GDP in personal savings uncovered by the earlier OAS Capital Markets Project FFAs was in time eliminated by the country's statisticians through the preparation of integrated real and financial flow accounts. It is unfortunate that Colombia is one of the only countries in the earlier OAS project that elected to continue its flow-of-funds accounting and to integrate it into improved national income accounting procedures. The importance of institutional cooperation between the central bank and the national statistical office, in this case, along with the use of U.N. supported advisers cannot be overstated. Unfortunately, however, the use of the resulting estimates has been limited to research by only a few economists, and the data have been relatively ignored outside Colombia.

It is quite likely that the potential for analysis of the relation between financial structure and growth in developing countries is only beginning to be realized, and a considerable increase in attention to such work may lie ahead. This will be especially important as both lending and borrowing countries and international institutions rediscover the importance of financial policies that will attract domestic savings into development finance (Reynolds 1978, 1979; Reynolds and Camard 1988). There are roles to be played by FFAs and by integrated social accounting as instruments of development policy.

References

Banco Central de Costa Rica. Departamento de Investigaciones Económicos. N.d. *Estructura y transacciones del sistema financiero costarricense, análisis preliminar, 1961–1971.* San José: Banco Central de Costa Rica.

Banco Central de la República Argentina. Departamento de Cuentas Monetarias. 1972. *Flujo global de fondos del sistema financiero institucionalizado Argentino, periodo 1967–71 (versión preliminar).* Buenos Aires: Banco Central de la República Argentina.

Banco Central de Reserva del Perú. 1974. *Cuentas nacionales del Peru, 1960–1973.* Lima: Banco Central de Reserva del Perú.

Banco Central do Brasil. N.d. *Anuario estatístico do Brasil, 1971.* Rio de Janeiro: Banco Central do Brasil.

———. Departamento Econômico. 1973. *Fluxo de fundos na economia brasileira—1959/1969, estudio preliminar.* Special supplement to *Boletim* 9. Rio de Janeiro: Banco Central do Brasil.

Banco de la República. Departamento de Investigaciones Económicos. 1971. *Análisis preliminar de las cuentas de flujo de fondos financieros de la economía colombiana, 1962–1969.* Bogota, Colombia: Banco de la República.

————. N.d.-a. *Cuentas de flujo de fondos financieros de la economía colombiana, 1972–1973–1974.* Bogota, Colombia: Banco de la República.

————. N.d.-b. *Cuentas financieras de Colombia, 1970–1980.* Bogota, Colombia: Banco de la República.

————. N.d.-c. *Cuentas financieras de Colombia, 1977–1981.* Bogota, Colombia: Banco de la República. Mimeo.

————. N.d.-e. *Cuentas financieras de Colombia, 1978–1982.* Bogota, Colombia: Banco de la República. Mimeo.

————. N.d.-f. *Cuentas financieras de Colombia, 1979–1983.* Bogota, Colombia: Banco de la República. Mimeo.

————. N.d.-g. *Cuentas nacionales, 1950–1967.* Bogota, Colombia: Banco de la República.

————. N.d.-h. *Cuentas nacionales, 1967–1970.* Bogota, Colombia: Banco de la República.

Bank of Jamaica. 1974. *An introduction to flow of funds accounting.* 2 pts. Kingston: Bank of Jamaica.

————. Research Department. N.d. *Flow of funds accounts of Jamaica, 1974.* Kingston: Bank of Jamaica.

Brock, Phil. 1980. Flow of funds study: Colombia. Stanford, Calif.: Stanford University. Mimeo.

Comisión Nacional Supervisora de Empresas y Valores. Departamento de Estudios Económicos y Financieros. 1973. *Flujo de fondos financieros en el Perú, período 1965–1970.* 2 vols. Lima, Peru: Comision Nacional Supervisora de Empresas y Valores.

Department of Statistics of Jamaica. 1970. *Sources and uses of funds in corporate establishments, 1962–1966.* Kingston: Department of Statistics of Jamaica.

————. 1973. *National income and product, 1972.* Kingston: Department of Statistics of Jamaica.

Diaz-Alejandro, Carlos F. 1984. Latin American debt: I don't think we are in Kansas anymore. *Brookings Papers on Economic Activity,* 335–89.

Fundação Getulio Vargas. Instituto Brasileiro de Economia. 1973. *Sistema de contas nacionais, 1939–1947/1969.* 2d ed. N.p.

Goldsmith, Raymond W. 1985. *Comparative national balance sheets.* Chicago: University of Chicago Press.

Hendershott, Patric. 1977. *Understanding capital markets.* Lexington, Mass.: D. C. Heath & Co.

International Monetary Fund. 1986. *International financial statistics yearbook,* vol. 39. Washington, D.C.: International Monetary Fund.

Jaramillo, Juan Carlos. 1982. El proceso de liberación del mercado financiero Colombian. *Ensayos sobre Política Económica* (Bogota, Colombia), no. 1 (March): 7–19.

Leff, Nathaniel H. 1976. Capital markets in the less developed countries: The group principle. In *Money and finance in economic growth and development,* ed. R. McKinnon, 97–122. New York: Dekker Books.

————. 1978. Industrial organization and entrepreneurship in the developing countries: The economic groups. *Economic Development and Cultural Change* 26:661–78.

_____. 1979. Entrepreneurship and economic development: The problem revisited. *Journal of Economic Literature* 17:46–64.

McKinnon, Ronald I. 1973. *Money and capital in economic development.* Washington, D.C.: Brookings Institution.

Mamalakis, Marcos J. 1976. Negative personal saving in the Chilean national accounts: Artifact or reality? *The growth and structure of the Chilean economy: From independence to Allende,* chap. 13, 315–44.: New Haven, Conn. Yale University Press.

Pinot de Libreros, Marión, Adolfo Vinasco Medina, and Jorge Enrique Riveros Mora. 1982. Metodología de las cuentas financieras de Colombia. *Ensayos sobre Política Económica* (Bogota, Colombia), no. 1 (March):171–211.

Reynolds, Clark W. 1978. Integrating financial planning with macroeconomic planning for efficient foreign debt management. In *LDC external debt and the world economy,* ed. Miguel S. Wionczek. Mexico City: El Colegio de Mexico and Center for Economic and Social Studies of the Third World.

_____. 1979. Bankers as revolutionaries. In *Debt and Less Developed Countries,* ed. Jonathan D. Aronson. Boulder, Colo.: Westview Press.

_____. 1982. Housekeeping during an earthquake: Argentina's flow of funds during the rapid inflation of 1970 to 1978. *Food Research Institute Studies* 18:293–315.

Reynolds, Clark W., and Wayne Camard. 1988. Flow of Funds savings estimates in the Americas: Some uses. Americas Program working paper, Stanford University.

Shaw, Edward S. 1973. *Financial deepening in economic development.* New York: Oxford University Press.

Strachan, Harry W. 1976. *Family and other business groups in economic development.* New York: Praeger Publishers.

Tybout, James R. 1980. *Credit rationing and industrial growth in Colombia: A micro-econometric analysis.* Ph.D. diss., University of Wisconsin—Madison.

_____. 1983. Credit rationing and investment behavior in a developing country. *Review of Economics and Statistics* 66:598–607.

_____. 1984. Interest controls and credit allocation in developing countries. *Journal of Money, Credit, and Banking* 14:474–87.

World Bank. 1984. *Colombia: A country study.* Washington, D.C.: World Bank.

Comment   Nathaniel H. Leff

Introduction

This paper by Clark W. Reynolds and Wayne Camard offers the prospect of new, disaggregated data, based on flow-of-funds analysis, for the study of savings behavior in less-developed countries (LDCs). That prospect is all the more welcome because of the inadequacies of the estimates compiled within the framework of the national income and product accounts (NIPAs). Data limitations, however, hamper the

Nathaniel H. Leff is a professor in the Graduate School of Business, Columbia University.

capacity of the authors to deliver as much as one would like in the way of improved and more reliable savings estimates.

The research is motivated by the assumption that saving is crucial for economic development. Consequently, it would help to have more (and better) data to facilitate understanding of the conditions that promote domestic saving in LDCs. I am sympathetic to this general approach. But it is worth noting that, for many economists, the operational paradigm in the field of economic development no longers accords so central a role to saving and physical capital formation (Krueger 1986). Much more emphasis is now accorded to such conditions as human capital formation, external trade, and foreign-exchange availability. Even within the new paradigm, however, saving remains important for economic development. Here, Reynolds and Camard are correct in noting that the hypotheses presently available to explain savings behavior in developing countries do not have much predictive power.

To illustrate, some Latin American countries have shown upward trends in their aggregate saving ratios during the past three decades. By contrast, other countries in the region have experienced statistically significant negative trends. Available models of saving in developing countries are not very helpful in explaining this observed behavior. Further, the present state of the analytical literature is such that economists have little in the way of tested, practicable advice to recommend to policymakers in Latin America who might be interested in raising domestic saving rates in their countries. In this context, the prospect that flow-of-funds analysis may make available new and better-quality data on savings behavior in individual countries is extremely attractive. More accurate statistical information should help raise the level of analysis. The availability of new, disaggregated data would permit the application in an LDC context of previously unused analytic models. Reynolds and Camard report sparse flow-of-funds data for five Latin American countries (Brazil, Colombia, Costa Rica, Peru, and Jamaica) as well as more complete information for one country, Colombia.

The Flow-of-Funds Results and Their Implications

As careful scholars, Reynolds and Camard take pains to explain the methodological limitations of the flow-of-funds studies that they report. That discussion points to a series of approximations that culminate in doubts concerning the reliability of the results. The authors share these doubts. They must be taken into account in assessing the usefulness of the results.

The paper's main substantive finding is that the flow-of-funds results show household saving to be substantially higher than estimated in the NIPAs for these five countries. This is an important finding; however, it is not entirely clear what to make of it. Part of the disparity may reflect the behavioral porosity of the corporate and household sectors in the LDCs. In such conditions, it is difficult to allocate uniquely to one sector or the other flows that belong to essentially the same agents. To the extent that strong substitution effects exist as between the two components of private saving, the policy implications of higher-than-expected household saving are weakened.

I think it is fair to conclude from this paper that flow-of-funds analysis of saving in LDCs can be a useful complement to the estimates developed in the NIPA framework. The two sets of estimates do not always tell the same story. The paper also suggests new directions for future work on flow-of-funds research in developing countries. First, it may be useful to refocus from the present emphasis on the household sector to an emphasis on saving in the corporate sector. Because of corporate reporting requirements, such a refocusing may mitigate data problems. Further, the availability of flow-of-funds data for the corporate sector would permit application and development of some of the analytic models that have been elaborated to apply corporate finance theory in the special context of the LDCs (Galvez and Tybout 1985; Sundararajan 1985).

In view of the greater richness—in depth and in time—of the flow-of-funds data available for Colombia, greater attention might be given to analyzing financial flows, saving, and investment for that country. Two topics come immediately to mind: the interaction of the individual sectoral components of aggregate saving and their joint responsiveness to changing economic conditions and policy incentives. Apart from the possible analytic and policy benefits from that research, such use of flow-of-funds statistics may also help increase the demand for collecting these data (see below).

It is also fair to learn something from the history of flow-of-funds research in Latin America. Despite the long-standing efforts of those concerned for such research, flow-of-funds estimates are still not prepared on a regular basis for many developing countries. A reason for the absence of this statistical output seems to be the lack of demand for these data on the part of economists in these countries. I expect the future to be like the past in this respect. To the extent that economists in Latin America are not educated to the potential uses of flow-of-funds statistics, they will not demand them. In practice, I do not see any such wave of education on the uses of flow-of-funds data reaching the graduate schools that Latin American economists attend, either in their own countries or in the United States. Consequently, it is unlikely that demand for flow-of-funds statistics will increase significantly. Accordingly, neither will the resources allocated for the preparation of such estimates.

In that event, research to improve the quality of the savings data in Latin America may follow a different route: more surveys to enhance the accuracy of the NIPA estimates. Some of these surveys—in particular those identifying and addressing the weak points in the NIPA estimates—may well be informed by flow-of-funds perspectives. In effect, we may see the fusion of the two approaches in improved NIPAs. This paper can be a milestone in such an evolution.

References

Galvez, Julio, and James Tybout. 1985. Microeconomic adjustments in Chile during 1977–81. *World Development* 13, no. 8 (August).

Krueger, Anne. 1986. Aid in the development process. *World Bank Research Observer* 1, no. 1 (January):57–78.

Sundararajan, V. 1985. Debt-equity ratios of firms and interest rate policy. *International Monetary Fund Staff Papers* 32, no. 3 (September):430–74.

4 Aggregate U.S. Private Saving: Conceptual Measures and Empirical Tests

Patric H. Hendershott and Joe Peek

Many researchers define saving synonymously with the change in real wealth: net worth at the end of the period less net worth (revalued to current prices) at the beginning of the period.[1] Saving, then, would be the change in real resources available for future consumption.[2] While this change is certainly an important variable worthy of serious investigation, the ex post change in real wealth in most periods is largely the result of unexpected wealth changes (stock market gains or losses, housing and land booms, etc.). That is, the change in real wealth is generally dominated by real asset price changes, not planned decisions to increase or decrease the accumulation of wealth.[3]

Alternatively, and more customarily, saving is defined in flow terms as income less consumption and taxes. Given initial wealth and expectations regarding after-tax income and real capital gains, saving and consumption are simultaneously determined. Movements in saving rates, then, lead observers to conclusions regarding the effects of policies on behavior. For example, a decline in the personal saving rate immediately following both the introduction of individual retirement accounts (IRAs) and a sharp increase in real interest rates might lead one to conclude that IRAs have not encouraged saving and that saving is highly interest

Patric H. Hendershott is a professor of finance and the holder of the John W. Galbreath Chair in Real Estate at the Ohio State University and a research associate of the National Bureau of Economic Research. Joe Peek is an associate professor of economics at Boston College and a visiting economist at the Federal Reserve Bank of Boston.

Joe Peek thanks the Federal Reserve Bank of Boston for financial support and George Houlihan and Edward Lyon for their assistance with the graphics. Any opinions expressed are those of the authors, not those of the Federal Reserve Bank of Boston, the Board of Governors of the Federal Reserve System, or the National Bureau of Economic Research.

inelastic. However, if the saving decline were due to mismeasurement, then one or both of these conclusions could be incorrect.

The proper conceptual measurement of personal and private saving is the subject of this paper. The official national income and product account (NIPA) saving series are increased to reflect saving via net purchases of government pension assets (including social security) and consumer durables and decreased by that part of after-tax interest income attributable to inflation. The need for these adjustments is well understood (see, e.g., Blades and Sturm 1982); our intended contribution is the careful implementation of the adjustments and analysis of the resulting adjusted saving series.

The plan of the paper is as follows. We begin with a discussion of the problems in the official measurement of personal and corporate saving and then propose adjustments to correct the official series. Next, the adjusted personal and private saving rates are computed and analyzed. Finally, personal saving equations are estimated on annual data for the 1952–85 period to verify that the proposed conceptual adjustments are consistent with the data, that is, that the estimated coefficients on the adjustments are significantly different from zero and not significantly different from their expected values (plus or minus unity). While such macro relations suffer from aggregation problems, the estimates seem appropriate for the task at hand.[4]

A number of interesting findings are obtained. First, correctly measured personal and private saving rates in recent years (1983–85) are 5 percent (not percentage points) below their averages since 1950, not, as reported in the official statistics, at all-time lows and 20 percent below their post-1950 averages. Second, the personal saving rate has been more volatile over the past thirty-five years than the official data indicate. Third, consistent with Auerbach's (1982) findings, corporate saving has been less volatile. Fourth, the often-observed negative correlation between personal and corporate saving is due solely to measurement error (the negatively correlated inflation premia in the two saving components). Fifth, both personal and private saving have rebounded somewhat in recent years (1983–85), again in contrast to the official series.

4.1 Adjustments to Personal and Corporate Saving

Saving is generally calculated residually as the difference between income received and certain outlays made. For personal saving, income received includes wages and salaries, dividends, rents, interest, and transfers; for business saving, income is profits. Outlays for both include consumption expenditures ("dividends" and "depreciation" for businesses), taxes, and interest paid. For our purposes, it is convenient to define saving as

(1)   SNIA = INC − CEXP − TAX − NINTP,

where SNIA is NIPA saving, INC is income other than interest received, CEXP is consumption expenditures, TAX is tax payments, and NINTP is net interest payments (interest paid less interest received). Thus, measurement errors in income or in any of the terms subtracted from it will be embedded in saving, dollar for dollar. Significant conceptual errors are generally made in the measurement of personal income, consumption, and net interest income of both persons and businesses. Before turning to the adjustments necessary to correct these errors, we explain why and how noncorporate business saving is included in personal saving rather than being aggregated with corporate saving into a broad total business category.

4.1.1 Integration of Households and Noncorporate Businesses

Private saving is the sum of household and business saving, but the components of saving reported in the NIPA are personal and corporate saving. That is, saving of noncorporate businesses is integrated with that of households into personal saving. Thus, corporate and noncorporate business saving are treated decidedly differently.

In the NIPA, two categories of noncorporate nonfinancial business are delineated: (1) sole proprietorships and partnerships and (2) other private business. The first category is further subdivided into farm and nonfarm, the second into real estate and other. The other-private distinction is apparently for household "portfolio" rental activities, such as owning a small duplex or shares in rental or oil and gas partnerships. Such portfolio activities, being analogous to purchases of real estate investment trusts (REITs) and other corporate shares, certainly should be integrated with household personal accounts. However, farm and nonfarm sole proprietorships and partnerships are businesses, and the retention of earnings within these enterprises seems no different from the retention within corporations.[5]

Unfortunately, the division of proprietorship and rental income between wages earned and capital income is unclear. Moreover, given the residual definition of saving as income less outlays, one would need to allocate household expenditures, taxes, and interest paid between personal and business activities. Given the impossibility of separating any of the right-hand-side variables in equation (1) into their personal and business components, "household" and noncorporate business income and expenses are fully integrated, and the resulting saving measure is labeled "personal saving."

Table 4.1 illustrates the effects of integration on the 1985 household balance sheet. The underlying data, which include market values of tangible assets and corporate equity, are from the Board of Governors of the Federal Reserve System (1986). In these data, nonfinancial business activity is divided among corporate, farm (including a small amount of corporate), and nonfarm noncorporate. Longer-term financial asset and liability series have been converted from par to market values (the data in parentheses are par values) using updated bond-price indices from Eisner and Pieper (1984). The first column in the table contains the basic household data (plus nonprofit organizations and personal trusts), the second column the noncorporate data (plus a small amount for corporate farms), and the third column the integrated household-noncorporate accounts. For comparison purposes, the data for nonfinancial corporations (excluding farms) are listed in the fourth column. As can be seen, the basic household sector has about $5 trillion in tangible assets (two-thirds is owner-occupied housing and the land it is on and over three-quarters of the rest is consumer durables), almost $6 trillion in financial assets, nearly $4.5 trillion in corporate and noncorporate equity, and $2.5 trillion in debt ($1.5 trillion of which is mortgages). Household net worth is thus about $13 trillion.

The nearly $2.5 trillion of household noncorporate equity represents claims on over $3 trillion of tangible assets as well as nearly $1 trillion of net debt. Almost half the tangible assets is land, largely for farming, and half the remainder is rental housing. Thus, the merged household-noncorporate balance sheet in column 3 looks far different from the basic household balance sheet.

The balance sheet of nonfinancial corporations differs greatly from that of nonfinancial noncorporate business, owing to the large role of corporations in manufacturing and their small roles in rental housing (less than 5 percent of the stock) and farming (which is in the noncorporate accounts anyway). In addition, corporations have far larger holdings of financial assets than do noncorporate businesses. Noteworthy is the large difference between the net worth of corporations computed residually from the balance sheet ($3,238 billion) and the market value of household corporate equity holdings ($1,906 billion). About half the difference reflects indirect household equity holdings via their life insurance and pension reserves. The other half is the often-noted difference between the replacement cost and the market value of corporate assets (Tobin's q being less than unity).

4.1.2 Conceptual Saving Adjustments

Household retirement transactions with the private sector are accounted for correctly in the computation of saving. A dollar "contributed" to a retirement plan is a dollar of income not consumed and thus

Table 4.1   Balance Sheets of Households and Nonprofits, Noncorporate Businesses, and Nonfinancial Corporations, 1985 (billions of dollars)

	(1) Households and Nonprofits	(2) Noncorporate Businesses and Corporate Farms	(3) (1) + (2)	(4) Nonfinancial Corporations
Tangible assets:				
Owner-occupied housing	2,381	65	2,446	
Consumer durables	1,393		1,393	
Plant and equipment	251[a]	667	918	2,701
Rental housing	60[a]	883	943	47
Inventories		116	116	789
Land:				
Owner occupied	952		952	
Other	65[a]	1,504	1,569	526
Plus Financial assets:				
Demand deposits and currency[b]	303	21	324	78
Other deposit and credit market assets[b]	3,525 (3,506)	53	3,578 (3,559)	933 (933)
Life insurance and pension reserves	1,992		1,992	
Net other assets	107	61	168	173

(*continued*)

Table 4.1 (continued)

	(1) Households and Nonprofits	(2) Noncorporate Businesses and Corporate Farms	(3) (1) + (2)	(4) Nonfinancial Corporations
Plus Equity:				
Corporate	1,949	−43[c]	1,906	−3,238 (−3,234)
Noncorporate	2,388 (2,434)	−2,388 (−2,434)		
Minus Debt:				
Home mortgages	−1,570 (−1,495)[d]		−1,570 (−1,495)	
Other	−982 (−946)	−939 (−893)	−1,921 (−1,839)	−2,009 (−2,013)
	12,814 (12,952)	0	12,814 (12,952)	0

Source: Board of Governors of the Federal Reserve System (1986); and authors' adjustments of book-to-market values for debt instruments (book values are in parentheses).

[a] Assets of nonprofit organizations (largely private schools, churches, and hospitals).

[b] Negotiable order of withdrawal accounts included in other deposits; credit market instruments defined broadly to include security and trade credit.

[c] Equity of noncorporate farms.

[d] Includes $44 billion of other mortgages.

a dollar of saving. Similarly, a dollar of interest earned on retirement accounts and not consumed is a dollar of saving. Finally, a dollar of benefits received and not consumed does not affect measured saving; cumulated wealth is simply being transferred from one asset form to another. Unfortunately, the treatment of government retirement accounts in the official NIPA saving statistics is far different.[6] A dollar contributed to a government retirement plan or social security, or accrued as interest on either, is not included in personal income and thus is not counted as a dollar of saving. Also, all benefits received are classified as income (transfer payments) and thus raise saving, even though a part of benefits are certainly a return of principal or interest. Because contributions and interest earned exceed benefits paid in a growing retirement system, the net result of this asymmetrical treatment is an understatement of income and thus of saving.

Theoretical models of consumption and saving behavior (e.g., the Life Cycle Hypothesis, the Permanent Income Hypothesis, and their derivatives) are stated in terms of the consumption of service flows. These flows, rather than consumption expenditures, are a determinant of household utility. Thus, saving is the deferral of consumption of service flows. To be consistent with theory, only the consumption of service flows should be subtracted from income; the component of consumer expenditures representing net investment in consumer durable goods should properly be considered saving. Official NIPA measures of personal saving, however, are based on the subtraction of all consumption expenditures, rather than of service flows only, and thus understate personal saving.

A major problem with both household and business saving statistics is the measurement of interest income received and paid during inflationary periods. The expectation of net capital losses on fixed-dollar financial assets that are due to inflation leads to the incorporation of an inflation premium in nominal interest rates to compensate investors for the expected losses. Part of household and business stocks of fixed-dollar assets are being converted into flows (the inflation premium component) that are recorded inappropriately as interest income received. Conversely, part of household and business stocks of financial liabilities are being eroded, and the associated inflation premium is wrongly recorded as interest paid. These inflation premia obviously rise with the inflation rate. Because households are net creditors, the overstatement of interest paid is less than the overstatement of interest received. Thus, personal saving is overstated. Because corporations are net debtors, corporate saving is understated.

The above discussion is summarized in table 4.2: row 1 contains the official measure of the various variables used to compute saving, row 2 lists the conceptual error, row 3 indicates the effect of the error on

Table 4.2   **Conceptual Errors in the Calculation of Personal and Corporate Saving**

	Income	Consumption	Net Interest Paid
1. Official series:			
Personal	Personal income less interest received	All consumption outlays	Interest paid less interest received
Corporate	Profits (with IVA and CCA) less interest received	Dividends plus capital consumption	Interest paid less interest received
2. Error:			
Personal	Net government pension purchases excluded	Some outlays are net investment	Some net interest received is return of principal
Corporate			Some net interest paid is erosion of principal
3. Effect of error:			
Personal	Saving understated	Saving understated	Saving overstated
Corporate			Saving understated
4. Correction:			
Personal	Add net government pension purchases	Add net consumer durable outlays	Subtract return of principal
Corporate			Add erosion of principal

Note: IVA = inventory valuation adjustment; CCA = capital consumption allowance.

the saving measures, and row 4 states the required corrections to the official series. Note that business income is defined to include the NIPA capital consumption and inventory valuation adjustments.[7]

One final point. Corporate income taxes are measured on an accrual basis, while personal income taxes are on a cash basis. Because individuals plan consumption and saving over a period of years, not weeks, the appropriate measurement convention is the accrual method (see Peek 1982). Thus, household tax payments need to be converted to an accrual basis.

4.1.3   Actual Consumption, Income, and Tax Adjustments

Some of the adjustments to the official saving series are straightforward. For the personal consumption mismeasurement, net (of depreciation) purchases of consumer durables (SCDUR) are added;[8] for the government employee life insurance and pension adjustment to personal income, net purchases of government life insurance and pension reserves (SGPEN) are added. Each of these series is available from the Federal Reserve flow-of-funds accounts.

As for social security, Blades and Sturm (1982) argue that contributions plus accrued interest less benefits should be added to personal saving.[9] This procedure seems appropriate if social security promises a fair market return. However, if social security is a bad investment, then some of the contribution should be viewed as a tax paid, and, if social security is an extraordinary investment, then households are receiving a transfer payment above and beyond their contribution. More generally, the addition to personal saving should be

$$(1 + \beta) \, \text{CON} + i^m \text{ACCON} - \text{BENE},$$

where CON is current contributions, ACCON is the implicit cumulated stock of contributions and past interest earned, BENE is benefits paid, i^m is the fair market interest rate, and the sign (and magnitude) of β depends on how much the promised return on social security, i^s, exceeds or falls short of the market rate of return:

$$\beta \gtreqless 0 \quad \text{as} \quad i^s \gtreqless i^m.$$

Unfortunately, β and ACCON are not known. Thus, our adjustment for social security is more conjectural than our other adjustments.

Munnell, speculating that households might view social security old-age and survivors insurance (OASI) contributions as saving, added them to official saving (Munnell 1977, fig. 6-1, p. 115). Adding contributions to saving is the correct adjustment if one assumes that the transfer component of contributions, βCON, plus accrued interest at the market interest rate equals benefits received. This equality may have held approximately during the 1950s, 1960s, and 1970s. For example, the equality would hold if contributions equaled benefits (approximately correct since the mid-1950s), accumulated contributions equaled twenty-five times benefits paid, the market interest rate were 0.03, and the return on social security were perceived to be sufficiently above market that twenty-five cents of transfers accompanied every dollar of contributions ($\beta = 0.25$). We adopt this assumption as a working hypothesis and thus add OASI contributions (both employee and employer) to personal saving, denoting the adjustment as SSSEC. The contributions data are from U.S. Department of Health and Human Services (1986, table 15, p. 81).

In the late 1970s and early 1980s, the need to revise benefits downward and contributions upward (lower i^s relative to i^m and thus lower β) became clear. Declining birth rates, increased life expectancy, and likely slower real growth were all contributing factors (McSteen 1985). Legislation in 1983, which advanced scheduled tax-rate increases, taxed half of benefits above a fixed nominal total income level, and raised the retirement age for future retirees, confirmed expectations of a reduced β. To account for a decline in β, we freeze the OASI adjustment at its 1980 real level of $119.5 billion (SSSEC80) for the entire 1981–85 period. The difference between SSSEC and SSSEC80 is roughly $10 billion in 1981–83 and $35 billion in 1984–85.

Figure 4.1 contains SGPEN, SGPEN plus SSSEC (or SSSEC80), and the sum of SGPEN, SSSEC (or SSSEC80), and SCDUR in constant 1982 dollars. Net purchases of government life insurance and pension reserves and social security OASI contributions have risen monotonically from $6 and $10 billion, respectively, in the early 1950s to $60 and $155 billion ($120 billion with the 1980s adjustment) in the mid-1980s. The net durables series has a strong cyclical component as well as an upward trend. On a trend basis, the series has risen, erratically, from $30 billion in the early 1950s (1950 and 1951 data were greatly affected by the outbreak of the Korean War) to $90 billion in the mid-1980s.

The personal income tax timing adjustment (STAX) is the difference between NIPA federal personal income tax payments and federal personal income tax accruals as calculated by the Bureau of Economic Analysis. The latter series is based on individual income tax return data adjusted for liability changes that are due to audits, amended returns, and additional assessments.[10] Most of the difference between payments and accruals (which has fluctuated between −7 and 16 billion 1982 dollars) arises because the net refund for tax year t is included in the liabilities of year t and in the cash payments of year $t + 1$. The

Fig. 4.1   Adjustments to personal saving

major fluctuations in the net refund series are due to differences in the timing and magnitude of the changes in income tax rates and the corresponding withholding schedules.

4.1.4 Inflation Premium Adjustments

A simple specification of the inflation premium is the product of the anticipated inflation rate and the stock of net fixed-income assets (see, e.g., Jump 1980).[11] This specification implies immediate, complete adjustment of interest income to the current anticipated inflation rate. In fact, net interest income included in personal saving did not adjust anywhere near this rapidly during the 1965–79 period of rising inflation. First, binding interest rate ceilings on at least some demand and savings accounts have existed in the United States since the early 1960s. Once these nominal interest rate ceilings became binding, the monetary interest payments on such assets incorporated an additional inflation premium only as rapidly as ceiling interest rates were raised. Second, while additional interest from financial institutions was imputed to individuals when interest rates (inflation) rose, imputed interest responded sluggishly to interest rate increases. Third, a significant part of fixed-coupon household assets and liabilities are long term. For these instruments, coupon receipts/payments adjust to an increase in interest rates only over time as new bonds are issued to replace maturing bonds (yields adjust immediately via a decline in the market price of the instruments). Thus, the inflation component of NIPA interest income and expenses substantially lagged the increase in the anticipated inflation rate. (The adjustment to a decrease in inflation will occur more rapidly to the extent that refinancing results in high coupons being replaced by lower coupons and deposit rate floors do not exist.)

The final problem with the simple specification of the inflation premium as the product of anticipated inflation and the stock of net fixed-income assets is the treatment of tax liabilities incurred on monetary interest income. Taxes are ignored in the specification, but only the net-of-tax inflation premium component is available to individuals to maintain the real value of their net financial assets during an inflationary period. If the real value falls by more than the net-of-tax premium, then an uncompensated real capital loss is incurred.

Similar arguments can be made against such a specification for the inflation premium in business net interest paid. Interest payments increase sluggishly when interest rates rise because some debt is long term. Moreover, interest is fully tax deductible, so the cost of the erosion of outstanding debt is only the net-of-tax inflation premium.

We have constructed inflation premium adjustments for personal and corporate saving that are based on the relevant measures of NIPA interest income and expense. Table 4.3 presents the components of the

Table 4.3   Interest Income Received and Paid, 1985 (billions of dollars)

| | Households: | | Nonfinancial Corporations |
	As Persons	As Business	
Interest received:			
Monetary	310.1	8.4	105.3
Imputed[a]	91.0	0	0
Total	401.1	8.4	105.3
Interest paid	82.6	251.5	219.4

Source: NIPA table 8.8.

[a]Imputed interest from life insurance carriers and private pension plans (an unpublished Bureau of Economic Analysis series: the interest component of NIPA table 8.8, line 50). Because the imputed interest from banks, credit agencies, and investment companies does not enter into the calculation of the saving series, it has been omitted from the table.

interest measures relevant to our adjustments for 1985. Household interest received equals monetary interest received by persons and noncorporate businesses plus imputed interest received by persons from life insurance carriers and private noninsured pension plans. Imputed interest received by persons from banks, credit agencies, and investment companies is omitted because this interest is included in both personal income and consumer expenditures (in the latter as services furnished without payment by financial intermediaries) and thus nets out in the calculation of personal saving. Imputed interest received by noncorporate business and nonfinancial corporations is not included in their net income (and hence in personal income) for the same reason. Interest paid by households includes interest paid by proprietorships and partnerships and that on consumer credit and home mortgages.[12]

In general, the before-tax inflation premium component added to personal saving is calculated as

$$(2) \quad SINFPERBT = (RRECPER - RRECPER50)APER$$
$$- (RPAIDPER - RPAIDPER50)LPER,$$

where APER and LPER, respectively, represent the stocks of household fixed-income assets and liabilities at the beginning of the period, RRECPER and RPAIDPER, respectively, represent the ratios of the household interest series just discussed to APER and LPER, and RRECPER50 and RPAIDPER50 are the 1950 values of RRECPER and RPAIDPER.[13] This procedure allocates any increase in interest income/expense (adjusted for the growth in financial assets/liabilities) to our inflation component measure. It is likely that the inflation premium component in 1950, if any, was extremely small. To the extent that this component was nonzero, our measures differ from the true components by a small constant.

To obtain the after-tax inflation premium, SINFPER, we divide the inflation premium terms into their taxable and nontaxable components and multiply the taxable component by 1 − TXPER, where TXPER is the assumed tax rate on personal interest income/expense.[14] The nontaxable portion is the imputed interest income from life insurance and private pension fund reserves and the interest received on state and local government bonds. The after-tax inflation premium is the sum of the nontaxable and the after-tax taxable terms.

The above equation implicitly assumes that the real interest rate built into interest income was constant during the 1950–85 period.[15] Because an increase in the real interest rate in the early 1980s is well documented (Clarida and Friedman 1983; and Hendershott 1986), we have constructed an inflation premium with a special adjustment for the early 1980s, SINFPER80. This premium allows for the gradual adjustment of interest income to a 3 percentage point increase in real interest rates in 1981. On the basis of an examination of changes in the differences between both RRECPER and RPAIDPER and the Livingston expected inflation data for the 1978–85 period, the SINFPER80 calculation assumes that the real interest rate incorporated in interest receipts and expenses was 1 percentage point higher in 1981, 2 points higher in 1982, and 3 points higher during 1983–85. This is equivalent to adding 1, 2, and 3 percentage points to the values of RRECPER50 and RPAIDPER50 for 1981, 1982, and 1983–85, respectively.

The after-tax inflation premium component netted from corporate saving is calculated directly as

$$(3) \quad \text{SINFCOR} = (1 - \text{TXCOR})[(\text{RPAIDCOR} - \text{RPAIDCOR50})$$
$$\text{LCOR} - (\text{RRECCOR} - \text{RRECCOR50})\text{ACOR}],$$

where TXCOR is the maximum corporate tax rate and the other variables are defined analogously to those used in the personal inflation premium adjustment except that they refer to interest paid/received by nonfinancial corporations on their stocks of liabilities/assets.[16] SINFCOR80 is SINFCOR calculated with the same adjustment to RPAIDCOR50 and RRECCOR50 that was made to RRECPER50 and RPAIDPER50 in the calculation of SINFPER80. The annual series underlying the inflation premium adjustments are listed for 1950–85 in tables 4.4 and 4.5.

Figure 4.2 contains graphs of SINFPER, SINFCOR, SINFPER80, and SINFCOR80, again in 1982 dollars. The upward surge in the series, owing to both rising inflation (interest rates) and growing real (net) stocks of financial assets (households) and liabilities (corporations), is

Table 4.4   Series Used in Calculation of Inflation Premium for Personal Saving

	RRECPER (%)	RPAIDPER (%)	APER (billions of 1982 dollars)	LPER (billions of 1982 dollars)	TXPER (%)	SINFPER80 (billions of 1982 dollars)
1950	3.47213	6.67765	885.569	346.890	30.0000	0
1951	3.62734	6.31558	864.240	393.454	30.3000	1.17095
1952	3.78848	6.53545	860.559	418.250	32.4000	1.60004
1953	3.89554	6.72429	902.713	459.938	31.4000	1.96519
1954	4.02821	6.69979	962.390	501.293	28.4000	3.24317
1955	4.08097	6.93031	1,019.70	554.528	28.5000	2.94494
1956	4.22877	6.81111	1,071.92	628.785	29.2000	4.76539
1957	4.54734	6.97978	1,101.46	667.828	28.9000	6.99265
1958	4.64783	7.08339	1,161.29	699.622	28.6000	7.77630
1959	4.81918	7.31863	1,197.68	740.423	28.7000	8.54296
1960	5.03400	7.39512	1,249.80	800.947	27.9000	10.6701
1961	4.97613	7.25813	1,343.23	865.178	28.1000	11.6896
1962	5.23429	7.34574	1,409.46	922.403	27.3000	14.5868
1963	5.33418	7.41829	1,502.21	989.720	26.9000	16.2594
1964	5.59896	7.56336	1,575.97	1,072.81	24.7000	19.5194
1965	5.72340	7.54045	1,678.31	1,164.62	24.0000	22.6639
1966	5.89077	7.43275	1,745.77	1,248.80	24.3000	26.6974
1967	6.03193	7.44494	1,817.28	1,291.72	25.2000	29.5664
1968	6.13088	7.62368	1,876.79	1,333.80	27.6000	29.6173
1969	6.52220	7.98455	1,925.77	1,375.37	28.8000	32.2455
1970	7.05883	8.21503	1,923.00	1,404.16	27.5000	38.1481
1971	6.99428	8.32244	2,016.38	1,464.93	27.4000	37.6406
1972	6.95614	8.34080	2,102.10	1,585.28	28.3000	37.4130
1973	7.20567	8.35859	2,211.84	1,733.44	29.2000	42.3995
1974	7.73404	8.51718	2,223.77	1,768.64	30.3000	48.9060
1975	7.68269	8.66644	2,215.23	1,737.21	30.0000	47.2946
1976	7.59892	8.83102	2,314.65	1,782.80	30.8000	45.9414
1977	7.69806	8.95511	2,488.39	1,898.76	31.1000	49.6751
1978	8.05590	9.28648	2,570.19	2,037.51	32.5000	52.4066
1979	8.90958	9.88541	2,623.69	2,127.10	33.5000	60.2478
1980	9.96542	10.2795	2,672.13	2,168.89	35.5000	75.7653
1981	11.7073	11.3744	2,680.44	2,113.07	36.6000	87.6004
1982	11.5109	11.9017	2,831.30	2,100.11	33.3000	79.2545
1983	10.2373	11.4400	3,136.94	2,276.92	29.5000	61.9581
1984	10.7530	11.2722	3,321.55	2,512.49	31.6000	79.2944
1985	9.93531	10.9157	3,682.87	2,735.17	31.6000	74.1202

clear. The series rise from under $1 billion to peaks of $104 billion ($88 billion with the real rate adjustment) for households and $41 billion ($36 billion) for corporations. The business premium is generally 25–35 percent of the household premium until 1969. During the 1970–82 period, the business premium ranged between 40 and 48 percent of the household premium, before declining to just under 40 percent in recent years. The relatively high business premium in the 1970–82 period

Table 4.5   **Series Used in Calculation of Inflation Premium for Corporate Saving**

	RPAIDCOR (%)	RRECCOR (%)	LCOR (billions of 1982 dollars)	ACOR (billions of 1982 dollars)	TXCOR (%)	SINFCOR80 (billions of 1982 dollars)
1950	2.85923	1.54279	347.075	197.917	60.4000	.625985
1951	2.82839	1.35521	381.538	238.886	67.4500	.728603
1952	3.03263	1.42381	394.767	247.303	64.6000	1.04571
1953	2.95627	1.37445	419.914	250.884	64.2000	1.01444
1954	3.03899	1.35119	428.224	253.454	52.0000	1.57428
1955	3.10570	1.56251	458.425	260.338	52.0000	1.51578
1956	3.15123	1.53044	506.052	303.910	52.0000	1.89241
1957	3.30919	1.72385	536.142	299.404	52.0000	2.04559
1958	3.51458	1.70430	540.245	297.089	52.0000	2.60809
1959	3.70191	1.95630	568.696	316.513	52.0000	2.88552
1960	3.91519	2.01275	590.017	347.330	52.0000	3.53865
1961	3.85295	1.99045	631.317	347.002	52.0000	3.59599
1962	4.04220	2.05675	666.050	359.618	52.0000	4.27352
1963	4.15746	2.34922	704.165	370.151	52.0000	4.37428
1964	4.21240	2.38181	748.235	396.991	50.0000	4.98240
1965	4.26573	2.33330	796.786	421.355	48.0000	5.84551
1966	4.56703	2.52404	859.137	453.406	48.0000	7.19924
1967	4.90450	2.65485	900.172	470.837	48.0000	8.80650
1968	5.28326	3.14811	939.161	476.881	52.8000	8.92976
1969	6.19463	3.78531	1,000.08	509.028	52.8000	12.2754
1970	7.08312	4.10079	1,026.77	528.638	49.2000	17.3072
1971	6.49681	3.97785	1,103.85	526.300	48.0000	16.4014
1972	6.35713	4.01425	1,172.20	560.103	48.0000	16.4492
1973	7.17331	5.06742	1,241.98	609.957	48.0000	19.2155
1974	8.04000	5.57038	1,277.89	659.666	48.0000	23.3504
1975	8.49088	6.01390	1,128.00	564.570	48.0000	22.2516
1976	8.21072	6.34924	1,122.59	561.059	48.0000	19.5464
1977	8.10676	6.60031	1,203.95	583.771	48.0000	19.9242
1978	9.05009	7.69456	1,233.23	601.642	48.0000	22.9534
1979	10.4931	9.18456	1,269.86	655.776	46.0000	28.1149
1980	12.0062	10.4335	1,291.68	698.363	46.0000	33.2841
1981	14.6499	13.1575	1,253.36	702.177	46.0000	35.8125
1982	14.7015	13.0457	1,280.14	702.145	46.0000	35.0345
1983	12.4382	12.5213	1,380.89	685.095	46.0000	22.4964
1984	13.6668	12.8099	1,426.85	767.649	46.0000	29.1985
1985	12.3820	11.7272	1,583.50	802.422	46.0000	28.1052

reflected much higher interest rates relative to the 1960s and the depressing effect of deposit rate ceilings on household interest earned.

4.2 Official and Adjusted Saving Rates

Our adjusted personal saving series incorporates the five adjustments to SNIA described above. The first four adjustments are added to

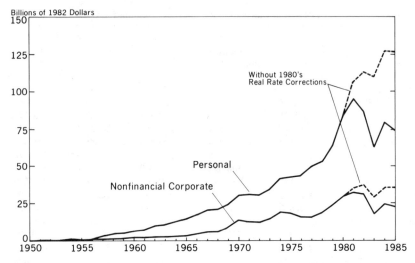

Fig. 4.2   Personal and corporate after-tax inflation premium adjustments

SNIA, while the inflation component is subtracted. Adjusted personal saving is thus

(4)   SADJPER = SNIAPER + SCDUR + SGPEN

$$+ \text{SSSEC80} + \text{STAX} - \text{SINFPER80}.$$

To obtain an adjusted personal saving rate, we divide the adjusted series by adjusted disposable income (and multiply by 100). The adjustments to disposable income are those indicated in the income and net-interest-paid columns of table 4.2 and the tax-timing adjustment. The adjusted income series is calculated as

(5)   YDADJ = YDNIA + STAX + SGPEN

$$+ \text{SSSEC80} - \text{YINF80},$$

where YDNIA is NIPA personal disposable income and YINF80 is the inflation premium adjustment for disposable income. The latter is computed from a relation similar to the after-tax version of equation (2) but with the interest income received/paid (adjusted for the rise in real rates in the 1980s) and asset/liability stock series redefined appropriately. The interest income received/paid series are increased, respectively, by including imputed interest received from banks, credit agencies and investment companies ($63.9 billion in 1985), and interest paid by consumers to business ($82.6 billion in 1985); the asset stock is increased by demand deposit holdings and the liability stock by other debt of households.

Our adjusted corporate saving series includes only the inflation premium adjustment:

(6)   SADJCOR = SNIACOR + SINFCOR80,

where SNIACOR already incorporates the NIPA capital consumption and inventory valuation adjustments. Owing to the inflation premium adjustment, the ratio of adjusted corporate saving to adjusted official disposable income is 15 percent greater, on the average, than the ratio of official corporate saving to official disposable income. However, the standard deviation of the adjusted ratio is 18 percent less. Our adjusted private saving series is the sum of the adjusted personal and corporate saving series:

(7)   SADJPRI = SADJPER + SADJCOR.

The components needed to compute these series are listed for 1950–85 in tables 4.6 and 4.7.

Figures 4.3 and 4.4 present the adjusted and official personal and private saving rates, respectively. The most obvious difference in the adjusted and official series is their average values. Given our additions to official saving, the adjusted personal series is over 6 percentage points greater than the official, on the average, while the adjusted private rate is nearly 7 percentage points greater. Moreover, the differences between the adjusted and the official series are far larger since 1970 than in the 1950s and early 1960s. The trend increase in the differences is the result of trends in our adjustments. The retirement contributions (government employees pension and social security) correction has a strong upward trend, adding 2 percentage points to saving rates in the early 1950s but 7 percentage points in the 1980s. The inflation premium correction also has an upward trend, rising from zero to nearly 4 percentage points of adjusted disposable income (for personal saving) in the early 1980s, before tailing off. No trends exist in the durables and tax-timing adjustments.

The retirement correction and the difference between it and the inflation premium corrections for personal and private saving, respectively, are plotted in figure 4.5. As can be seen, the difference (the net adjustment to saving) raises the official personal and private saving rates from 2 percentage points in the early 1950s to 4 points (5 for private saving) in the mid- and late 1970s, after which the effect is roughly constant.

The adjusted personal saving rate is more volatile than the official rate; its standard deviation is 60 percent greater. Moreover, the adjusted rate contains some broad movements that are not evident in the official rate. In particular, the adjusted saving rate declines from above 14 percent in 1950–51 to below 11 percent in 1958–61 and then rises back to over

Table 4.6   Personal Saving and Its Adjustments (billions of 1982 dollars)

	SADJPER	SNIAPER	SCDUR	SGPEN	SSSEC80	STAX
1950	114.817	48.0916	56.8702	6.87023	10.1794	− 7.19466
1951	117.955	59.7122	41.0072	5.75539	12.0971	.553957
1952	115.865	61.2676	30.6338	7.04225	13.4472	5.07394
1953	120.855	63.4483	35.5172	6.55172	13.6034	3.70000
1954	102.202	56.1644	23.9726	5.47945	17.6815	2.14726
1955	119.875	54.2373	43.0509	6.10170	19.3661	.064407
1956	124.866	70.7641	29.2359	7.97342	20.5050	1.15282
1957	123.204	73.2258	25.4839	7.09677	22.0161	2.37419
1958	114.299	76.8987	11.7089	8.86076	23.9430	.664557
1959	113.494	67.4922	23.8390	8.97833	24.9288	− 3.20124
1960	121.883	63.2219	22.1884	9.72645	33.0274	4.38906
1961	118.923	74.7748	13.5135	10.2102	33.8889	− 1.77478
1962	135.088	76.6272	25.4438	10.3550	35.6775	1.57101
1963	142.367	71.3044	34.4928	11.3044	42.1478	− .623189
1964	164.406	90.2579	43.2665	12.6074	44.9542	− 7.16046
1965	189.125	96.3483	56.7416	13.2022	44.9916	.505618
1966	208.948	98.0926	63.2153	15.2589	56.0763	3.00272
1967	223.330	119.947	56.6489	14.6277	61.5372	.135638
1968	218.500	108.142	68.4478	15.5216	60.3537	− 4.34860
1969	228.330	102.927	63.9024	17.3171	68.1634	8.26585
1970	242.497	134.499	46.3869	20.7459	70.5268	8.48718
1971	260.744	147.661	57.2383	21.1581	75.1069	− 2.77951
1972	290.411	131.477	74.5182	24.8394	80.9015	16.0878
1973	336.499	179.798	83.2323	23.8384	92.8788	− .848485
1974	302.352	176.782	54.6618	23.0347	95.2121	1.56673
1975	304.322	176.689	47.9730	25.5067	95.9729	5.47466
1976	302.464	153.035	68.5303	28.2748	101.217	− 2.65176
1977	305.575	135.982	79.9100	33.7331	104.306	1.31934
1978	326.979	154.126	82.2377	39.0210	105.554	− 1.55245
1979	314.377	151.023	69.0537	31.2020	112.428	10.9182
1980	276.859	158.083	36.8360	40.7621	119.464	− 2.52079
1981	285.723	168.499	39.5349	41.9662	119.464	3.85941
1982	281.839	153.900	37.2000	43.9000	119.464	6.63000
1983	302.453	125.456	60.2306	51.3929	119.464	7.86744
1984	335.047	156.059	85.7539	59.1120	119.464	− 6.04718
1985	324.790	128.061	91.9571	59.4281	119.464	0.0

14 percent in 1966. During the same time span, the official rate moves erratically within a 1.75 percentage point band. The two series also move differently since 1978. The adjusted series declines from nearly 15 percent to below 12.5 percent in 1980–82 and then rises slightly in 1984–85. In contrast, the official rate is nearly constant at about 7 percent throughout the 1978–82 period and then drops to 5.5 percent in 1983–85. That is, the adjusted series is 1 percentage point higher in 1983–85 than in 1980–82 rather than 1.5 percentage points lower.

Figure 4.6 presents the national and government (federal, state, and local) saving rates, both adjusted and unadjusted, as percentages of net

Table 4.7   Other Saving and Income Series (billions of 1982 dollars)

	SADJPRI	SNIACOR	YDADJ	YDNIA	YINF80
1950	146.740	31.2977	801.840	791.985	0.0
1951	150.338	31.6547	836.501	818.705	.610829
1952	150.713	33.8028	867.980	844.366	1.94956
1953	151.525	29.6552	899.911	879.655	3.59890
1954	137.338	33.5616	912.512	892.123	4.91936
1955	171.561	50.1695	964.880	945.085	5.73726
1956	168.951	42.1927	1,009.77	988.372	8.23759
1957	164.927	39.6774	1,033.30	1,012.58	10.7714
1958	148.870	31.9620	1,050.30	1,028.16	11.3275
1959	164.677	48.2972	1,083.96	1,066.87	13.6111
1960	167.671	42.2492	1,121.10	1,090.88	16.9193
1961	165.161	42.6427	1,147.95	1,122.52	16.8920
1962	198.237	58.8758	1,199.76	1,172.19	20.0331
1963	210.219	63.4783	1,234.56	1,205.22	23.4820
1964	241.881	72.4928	1,316.40	1,293.41	27.4121
1965	282.892	87.9214	1,394.58	1,367.42	31.5330
1966	307.428	91.2806	1,470.80	1,432.97	36.5017
1967	315.115	82.9787	1,530.99	1,494.95	40.2550
1968	302.239	74.8092	1,581.21	1,551.14	41.4639
1969	302.069	61.4634	1,648.49	1,601.71	46.9568
1970	301.529	41.7249	1,711.18	1,668.06	56.6385
1971	335.943	58.7973	1,768.93	1,730.07	54.6237
1972	380.522	73.6616	1,864.53	1,797.86	55.1533
1973	430.462	74.7475	1,972.85	1,918.79	61.8059
1974	362.631	36.9287	1,949.07	1,898.35	69.0914
1975	389.242	62.6689	1,987.24	1,930.40	70.1152
1976	396.132	74.1214	2,057.54	2,000.96	70.2597
1977	418.902	93.4032	2,132.37	2,067.92	74.9047
1978	446.436	96.5035	2,227.59	2,169.51	84.9369
1979	421.776	79.2839	2,269.52	2,211.38	96.4107
1980	353.677	43.5335	2,262.69	2,214.78	109.790
1981	367.201	45.6660	2,299.27	2,249.05	115.070
1982	336.874	20.0000	2,327.31	2,261.40	104.079
1983	387.389	62.4400	2,423.99	2,332.47	87.1984
1984	448.427	84.1813	2,537.72	2,470.49	105.299
1985	448.784	95.8892	2,601.90	2,527.26	104.250

national product. The area between the two pairs of national and government saving rate lines represents private saving. Less than half our adjustment to private saving represents a net addition to national saving. For the 1950–85 period, the private saving rate (as a percentage of net national product) is increased by 5.5 percentage points; the national saving rate is increased by only 2.5 percentage points (owing to the consumer durables adjustment). The remaining increase to private saving comes from a 3 percentage point reduction in the government saving rate (2.5 federal and 0.5 state and local). The federal government saving adjustment is composed of the tax-timing adjustment, the social security

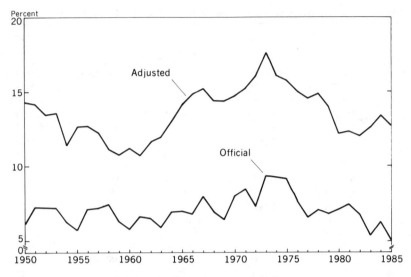

Fig. 4.3   Official and adjusted personal saving rates

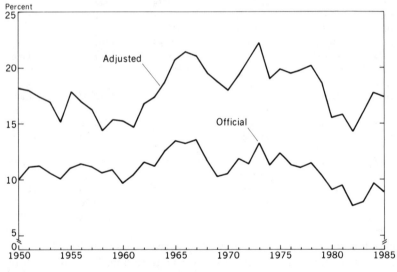

Fig. 4.4   Official and adjusted private saving rates

adjustment, about one-quarter of the government employees pension adjustment (SGPEN), and a portion of the net inflation premium adjustment (SINFPER80 − SINFCOR80). The federal government share of the net inflation premium adjustment oscillates from 80 percent in the 1950s down to almost 50 percent by the early 1970s and then back to 80 percent by 1985. The state and local saving adjustment is composed of the remainder of the SGPEN and net inflation premium adjustments.

Table 4.8 contains average national, private, and federal government saving rates, both official and adjusted, for the 1982–85 period and the three preceding decades, 1952–61, 1962–71, and 1972–81, each of

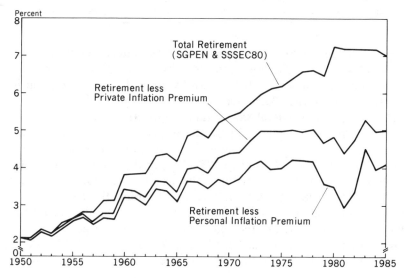

Fig. 4.5   Trend adjustments

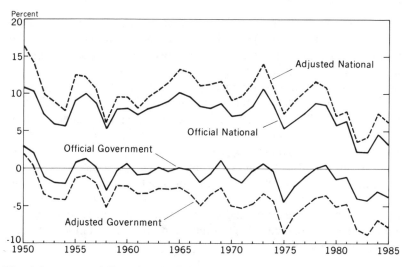

Fig. 4.6   Adjusted and official national and government saving rates

Table 4.8   Official and Adjusted National, Private, and Federal Government
                   Saving Rates (percent of net national product)

	National		Private		Federal Government	
	Official	Adjusted	Official	Adjusted	Official	Adjusted
1952–61	7.50	9.55	8.16	12.33	−.46	−2.25
1962–71	8.48	11.14	9.05	14.48	−.65	−3.18
1972–81	7.64	10.08	8.64	15.12	−2.06	−5.67
1982–85	3.11	5.38	6.88	13.52	−5.43	−8.86

which concluded with a recession.[17] All three official saving rates are reasonably constant for the three decades, although the federal and national saving rates were both down by about 1 percentage point in the 1970s. In contrast, 2 and over 3 percentage point declines occurred in the private and federal saving rates, respectively, in the 1982–85 period, giving a whopping 4.5 percentage point decline in the national saving rate. The component adjusted saving rate series decline in a similar fashion from 1972–81 to 1982–85, but the context of their declines is far different. For one thing, the decline in federal saving is not a one-time aberration but the continuation of a trend; the decrease from 1972–81 to 1982–85 is only slightly greater than the decrease from 1962–71 to 1972–81. On the other hand, the decline in the private saving rate reverses an upward trend. Thus, the 1982–85 rate is 1 percentage point above the 1952–61 rate rather than at an all-time low.

4.3   Personal Saving Equation Estimates

Estimates of equations explaining real per capita personal saving are reported in this section. The primary purpose of the equations is to provide a test, albeit crude, of our proposed personal saving adjustments. If, for example, an adjustment should have a coefficient of minus unity in an equation explaining NIPA saving and the estimated coefficient is positive, this would constitute strong grounds for rejecting our adjustment. The equations are based on a model of planned wealth accumulation that includes measures of wealth, income, capital gains, the gross national product (GNP) gap (all in per capita constant 1982 dollars), the real after-tax interest rate, and the age composition of the population as explanatory variables (for a detailed description of the model, see Hendershott and Peek 1985a). This section begins with a discussion of the variables and estimation procedure, reports the results, and then analyzes their implications for the relation between personal and corporate saving.

4.3.1 The Variables and Estimation Procedure

Our adjusted disposable labor income measure is equal to the NIPA measures of wages and salaries, other labor income, and a proportion of proprietor's income, less labor's share of actual personal income tax liabilities and employee contributions for social insurance, plus the sum of government employees retirement benefits and SGPEN (equal to contributions plus accrued interest on cumulated contributions) and both SSSEC80 and OASI benefit payments (assumed to equal accrued interest on the stock of cumulated OASI contributions). The latter additions are needed to make the income measure consistent with our adjusted saving measure. Transfer payments are set equal to NIPA transfer payments less both government employees retirement benefits and OASI benefits (which we have reallocated to disposable labor income).

Both adjusted real disposable labor income and adjusted real transfer payments are divided into their expected and unexpected components through regression analysis (for specific details, see Hendershott and Peek 1985a). The predicted value from an equation with the variable in question being regressed on a set of predetermined variables is taken as the expected component; the residual series from the regression is taken as the proxy for the unexpected component. We use annual observations for the 1951–85 period. The explanatory variables for real per capita labor income/transfer payments are four lagged values of the dependent variable and one lagged value of each of the following: real government expenditures, the difference (gap) between potential and actual real GNP, the real value of the narrowly defined money supply (M1), the one-year after-tax nominal Treasury bill yield (RAT), an index of marginal personal income tax rates, and the one-year-ahead Livingston expected inflation rate from the December survey (π). The potential GNP measure is the middle expansion trend GNP series calculated by the Bureau of Economic Analysis. All variables except for interest, tax, and inflation rates are per capita.

The real net capital gains data were calculated from the Board of Governors of the Federal Reserve System (1986) as in Hendershott and Peek (1985b). We combined household assets and liabilities (including noncorporate business holdings) into three categories: (1) tangible capital (residential structures, consumer durable goods, land, and the plant and equipment and inventories of nonprofit institutions and noncorporate business); (2) corporate equities, held both directly and indirectly through household life insurance and pension fund reserves; and (3) all other financial assets less liabilities. The real capital gains measures were divided into their expected and unexpected components using a regression procedure similar to that used for the labor income and transfer variables. The capital gains regressions have the ratio of net capital gains to the beginning-of-period stock of assets as the dependent variable. The explanatory variables include four lagged values of the dependent variable, the expected inflation rate, and lagged values of the first-differences of all the explanatory variables in the labor income/transfer equations. For the equities equation, we also include both our adjusted corporate saving variable lagged one period divided by the beginning-of-period stock of corporate equities and the top corporate income tax rate.

Below, we present estimates of personal saving equations with and without our tax-timing, government pension, social security, and inflation premium adjustments. The consumer durables adjustment cannot be employed as a regressor because it is an endogenous decision variable.[18] According to the Life Cycle/Permanent Income Hypothesis, individuals choose their level of consumption (durable plus nondurable) subject to their budget constraint. Not only do they choose the level of their consumption, but they also choose its composition; they can substitute more or less durable services for nondurables and services within their total consumption. In contrast, consumer choice over government employees pension or social security contributions and the inflation premium in interest income is severely limited, and thus these adjustments can be employed as regressors. The hypothesized minus one coefficient on the consumer durables adjustment is *imposed* in our estimation by adding this adjustment to NIPA saving and using this sum as the dependent variable.

Regressors considered, in addition to our saving adjustments and the income and capital gains variables previously described, include the beginning-of-period stock of real household wealth (with financial assets and liabilities converted from par to market values) from Board of Governors of the Federal Reserve System (1986); the share of the population over age sixty-four from the Council of Economic Advisers (1987); the real GNP gap; and the one-year after-tax expected real interest rate from the previous December, calculated as $RAT - \pi$. Both the population share and the real interest rate variables (less their mean values) have been multiplied by expected adjusted real disposable labor income. All the dollar variables are per capita constant 1982 dollar magnitudes.

The rather high correlations between pairs of explanatory variables make it very difficult to pinpoint the individual effects of the variables on personal saving. For example, the pairwise correlations between wealth, expected labor income, expected transfers, share of population over age sixty-four, SINFPER80, SGPEN, and SSSEC80 are each above 0.9. Furthermore, the pairwise correlations of each of these variables with expected capital gains on net financial assets range between -0.88 and -0.92. First-differencing the data substantially reduces the collinearity between pairs of explanatory variables. Consequently, the equations have been estimated using first-differenced data. To simplify the exposition and to preserve degrees of freedom, we have combined the expected and unexpected components of adjusted disposable labor income, which tended to have very similar estimated coefficients. Similarly, because the estimated coefficients on expected transfer payments, expected and unexpected capital gains on net financial assets, and unexpected capital gains on tangible assets tended to be statistically insignificant (and, in many cases, quite erratic) across the various saving equation specifications, they have been omitted from the equations presented in the table. Finally, the one-year after-tax real Treasury bill rate was omitted because it never had a coefficient of either quantitative or statistical significance.[19]

Table 4.9 lists the annual values of the underlying income and capital gains variables employed; table 4.10 contains annual values of the wealth, GNP gap, and share of population over age sixty-four variables as well as the population and price (personal consumption deflator) series used to convert the variables to real per capita values.

4.3.2 The Estimates

Columns 1 and 2 in table 4.11 are estimated with data from the full 1952–85 sample period. The first column explains personal saving (including net durables, SNIAPER + SCDUR) without our proposed adjustments. Only the coefficients on wealth, disposable labor income, population share, and expected gains on tangible assets are statistically significant at the 95 percent confidence level with the predicted sign, although the unexpected transfer payments and GNP gap variables contribute to the explanatory power of the equation. In column 2, our saving adjustments (without the 1980s modifications) are included as additional explanatory variables. Each of the estimated coefficients on the four adjustment variables, except that on SSSEC, is more than two standard errors from zero with the expected sign, and that on SSSEC is nearly two standard errors from zero. Moreover, none of the four estimated coefficients are more than two standard errors away from their predicted values. However, the point estimates of the coefficients on both SGPEN and SINFPER are more than one standard error greater than their predicted values.

Because the equation underlying column 2 makes no special modification for either the 1980s decline in the expected rate of return on social security relative to market interest rates or the 1980s rise in real interest rates, the estimates are suspect. The problem with the 1980s

Table 4.9   Income and Capital Gains Regressors (billions of 1982 dollars)

	Disposable Labor Income	Expected Disposable Labor Income	Unexpected Transfers	Expected Capital Gains on Tangibles	Expected Capital Gains on Equities	Unexpected Capital Gains on Equities
1952	712.033	714.994	-.996596	-23.6644	50.6966	-20.4824
1953	740.798	722.594	-2.74272	18.9905	12.7700	-48.5985
1954	744.181	766.129	2.56290	-23.0304	181.424	61.3535
1955	792.188	801.673	-1.48341	38.7237	132.045	34.5562
1956	835.777	837.259	1.09040	52.2574	-33.4491	58.2429
1957	852.610	858.213	-1.40838	5.60093	70.3883	-223.059
1958	854.143	863.228	8.08566	11.6434	321.562	2.60369
1959	891.756	904.531	-2.98386	48.5902	57.7643	6.90525
1960	921.073	919.437	-1.61325	-40.1458	-47.9675	9.27656
1961	938.973	947.694	5.85560	48.7047	125.827	183.317
1962	985.174	981.883	-2.35641	10.0481	41.4844	-257.679
1963	1,014.77	1,037.76	-.826178	21.7782	107.671	108.101
1964	1,089.24	1,051.74	-2.02050	-5.30211	22.2578	111.837
1965	1,157.50	1,150.41	-2.07097	-36.5888	384.905	-211.248
1966	1,227.97	1,210.73	-.620632	23.1387	74.0213	-301.956
1967	1,271.51	1,273.73	7.11006	-80.8843	275.857	86.2283
1968	1,319.20	1,336.83	-2.70948	35.1256	-59.4526	349.605
1969	1,374.09	1,365.45	-6.76241	-21.3546	-575.661	200.040
1970	1,419.76	1,396.52	-5.19148	-85.5128	-249.114	131.943

1971	1,461.32	1,458.06	−1.85800	34.1214	177.194	14.7430
1972	1,545.53	1,530.34	4.07099	149.965	11.0519	130.596
1973	1,627.99	1,610.79	−.753529	56.3680	−583.386	−44.4732
1974	1,596.42	1,633.24	2.46929	30.1998	−160.863	−409.710
1975	1,603.04	1,597.59	20.4542	7.65396	204.291	35.3645
1976	1,673.66	1,679.58	4.38220	147.518	332.863	−190.838
1977	1,744.50	1,763.60	3.61491	166.509	−95.9255	−72.4244
1978	1,820.08	1,802.54	−2.79025	211.814	−12.5711	−46.3101
1979	1,851.20	1,833.68	1.42846	189.879	125.979	−3.92644
1980	1,829.55	1,850.95	4.04897	140.270	110.858	159.938
1981	1,834.07	1,838.87	−13.3642	−5.92587	−142.723	−16.2415
1982	1,840.05	1,832.49	−1.92113	−311.419	75.5721	46.9768
1983	1,903.60	1,892.92	−3.86014	117.652	224.651	−59.5040
1984	2,021.72	2,012.75	−8.74482	−8.52137	46.3441	−51.2612
1985	2,077.01	2,103.42	5.49889	−73.2014	84.0190	378.951

Table 4.10   Other Variables Used in the Estimations

	Wealth (billions of 1982 dollars)	GNPGAP (billions of 1982 dollars)	Population Over 64 (%)	Personal Consumption Deflator	Total Population (millions)
1952	3,731.63	− 66.9006	8.38004	.284000	157.553
1953	3,828.43	− 59.0993	8.50085	.290000	160.184
1954	3,891.66	16.8994	8.63421	.292000	163.026
1955	4,251.45	− 18.5000	8.75364	.295000	165.931
1956	4,558.41	− 3.59912	8.84413	.301000	168.903
1957	4,716.73	6.90063	8.94735	.310000	171.984
1958	4,627.57	54.3991	9.03810	.316000	174.882
1959	5,076.27	1.69995	9.13682	.323000	177.830
1960	5,219.43	17.9006	9.22948	.329000	180.671
1961	5,270.39	32.0993	9.30312	.333000	183.691
1962	5,664.32	1.10010	9.35842	.338000	186.538
1963	5,536.23	− 6.29931	9.39432	.345000	189.242
1964	5,831.70	− 35.5000	9.44661	.349000	191.889
1965	6,142.55	− 76.2997	9.49599	.356000	194.303
1966	6,450.65	− 120.599	9.54162	.367000	196.560
1967	6,462.38	− 104.500	9.59731	.376000	198.712
1968	6,983.71	− 116.500	9.64844	.393000	200.706
1969	7,489.31	− 88.9001	9.71003	.410000	202.677
1970	7,247.24	6.80004	9.80581	.429000	205.052
1971	7,213.76	30.0998	9.90123	.449000	207.661
1972	7,595.64	− 2.00000	10.0145	.467000	209.896
1973	8,080.00	− 66.6000	10.1577	.495000	211.909
1974	7,750.13	17.1999	10.3159	.547000	213.854
1975	7,368.16	122.200	10.5087	.592000	215.973
1976	7,771.13	63.0993	10.6763	.626000	218.035
1977	8,355.22	5.30004	10.8482	.667000	220.239
1978	8,634.07	− 77.4999	11.0079	.715000	222.585
1979	9,148.14	− 79.5997	11.1679	.782000	225.055
1980	9,564.73	2.69995	11.2867	.866000	227.738
1981	10,009.9	18.0998	11.4001	.946000	230.138
1982	10,167.9	172.499	11.5375	1.00000	232.520
1983	10,049.3	132.000	11.6815	1.04100	234.799
1984	10,615.9	− 4.59985	11.7995	1.08100	237.019
1985	10,831.1	− 23.4006	11.9231	1.11900	239.283

observations can be solved either by eliminating the troublesome 1981–85 observations from the estimation period (col. 3) or by retaining the entire sample period but using the modified measures of the social security (SSSEC80) and inflation premium (SINFPER80) adjustments (col. 4). For the 1952–80 subperiod, each of the estimated coefficients on the saving adjustments is within one standard error of its predicted value, with the exception of that on STAX, which is just slightly more than a single standard error away. All but the inflation premium coefficient differ significantly from zero. Alternatively, when SSSEC80 and

Table 4.11   Personal Saving (including net investment in consumer durables) Regressions, Annual Observations for 1952–85 (first-differences of real per capita data, standard errors in parentheses)

Explanatory Variables	(1)	(2)[a]	(3)[b]	(4)	(5)	(6)	(7)
Tax-timing adjustment (STAX)	...	-1.034 (.232)	-1.276 (.266)	-1.016 (.226)	-1.020 (.225)	-1.00	-1.00
Government pension adjustment (SGPEN)	...	-1.704 (.692)	-1.593 (.721)	-1.613 (.640)	-1.868 (.592)	-1.00	-1.00
Social security adjustment (SSSEC80)	...	-1.023 (.575)	-1.429 (.618)	1.401 (.479)	-1.516 (.464)	-1.00	-1.00
Inflation premium adjustment (SINFPER80)	...	1.926 (.651)	.739 (.884)	1.225 (.398)	1.224 (.396)	1.00	1.00
Wealth	-.0309 (.0152)	-.0411 (.0119)	-.0287 (.0127)	-.0345 (.0105)	-.0382 (.0099)	-.0375 (.0090)	-.0357 (.0087)
Adjusted labor income	.497 (.087)	.599 (.075)	.584 (.075)	.566 (.062)	.552 (.060)	.503 (.050)	.489 (.049)
Unexpected transfers	-.783 (.505)	.134 (.385)	.656 (.422)	.322 (.382)	.298 (.379)	.096 (.312)	.124 (.301)
Percent population over age 64	-3.60 (1.68)	-3.68 (1.39)	-3.05 (1.57)	-2.83 (1.22)	-1.50	-1.50	-1.50
GNP gap	.0693 (.0488)	.0814 (.0351)	.0476 (.0445)	.0958 (.0348)	.0949 (.0346)	.0786 (.0303)	.0997 (.0314)

(continued)

Table 4.11 (continued)

Explanatory Variables	(1)	(2)[a]	(3)[b]	(4)	(5)	(6)	(7)
Expected gains on tangible assets	-.0657 (.0257)	-.0211 (.0213)	-.0318 (.0311)	-.0363 (.0183)	-.0356 (.0182)	-.0387 (.0160)	-.0491 (.0164)
Expected gains on corporate equities	-.0058 (.0137)	-.0239 (.0110)	-.0215 (.0108)	-.0246 (.0099)	-.0288 (.0091)	-.0251 (.0081)	-.0289 (.0081)
Unexpected gains on corporate equities	.0013 (.0131)	-.0092 (.0094)	-.0167 (.0099)	-.0138 (.0091)	-.0146 (.0090)	-.0142 (.0081)	-.0124 (.0079)
Nuclear fear	...	...	...	...	...	...	.00134 (.00073)
R^2	.632	.854	.862	.866	.861	.817	.836
SEE	63.87	43.81	41.93	41.92	41.67	39.88	38.46
DW	2.31	2.06	2.00	1.84	1.87	2.05	2.25

[a]The social security and inflation premium adjustments for this column, SSSEC and SINFPER, do not include the 1980s corrections.

[b]These estimates are for the 1952–80 period.

SINFPER80 are used as regressors and the equation is estimated over the entire 1952–85 sample period, each of the four coefficients differs significantly from zero, and each of the four is within a single standard error of its predicted value. All the estimated coefficients except for those on unexpected transfer payments and unexpected gains on corporate equities are now statistically significant with the expected sign. The introduction of the saving adjustments reduces the standard error of the equation by 35 percent compared to column 1. Whether we omit the 1981–85 observations or modify the social security and inflation premium adjustments, we obtain very similar results. As we move from column 3 to column 4, the sharpest differences are the doubling of the GNP gap coefficient and the sharp declines in both the unexpected transfer payments coefficient and the standard errors of the inflation premium adjustment coefficient and the coefficient on expected gains on tangible assets.

The only problem with the estimates in column 4, in our view, is the magnitude of the population share coefficient. This coefficient implies too large a negative effect of the aging of the population. In fact, a coefficient of -1.5 is as large, in absolute value, as seems plausible (Hendershott and Peek 1985a, 89). Constraining the coefficient to this value (col. 5) makes little difference. The equation standard error is reduced somewhat, and none of the individual coefficients changes by as much as half a standard deviation. The pension adjustment coefficients are now slightly more than one standard error from their expected values.[20]

Column 6 contains estimates with the coefficients on all the saving adjustments constrained to their theoretical values. These estimates imply significant positive labor income (coefficient of 0.50) and GNP gap (0.79) responses, significant negative wealth (-0.038) and expected gains on tangible assets (-0.039) and corporate equities (-0.025) relations, and an almost significant negative response to unexpected gains on equities (-0.014). The unexpected transfer payments coefficient, in contrast, is less than half a standard error from zero.

The final equation in table 4.11 includes Slemrod's (1986) nuclear fear variable. Increased fear of nuclear holocaust would likely reduce the propensity to save. When this variable (scaled by expected real adjusted disposable labor income per capita) is added to our basic equation, the estimated coefficient is significantly greater than zero (t-statistic $= 1.84$).[21] Of the other estimated coefficients, only those on the GNP gap and expected gains on tangible assets change (barely) by as much as half a standard error.[22]

How do the various explanatory variables interact to explain the broad swings in the adjusted personal saving rate discussed earlier, namely, the rise from an average 11.5 percent rate in the 1954–64 period

to nearly 15 percent in the 1966–78 period and then the decline to
12.5 percent in the 1980s? The two upper series plotted in figure 4.7
are the adjusted personal saving rate and the wealth/income ratio. The
negative correlation between the series is obvious. The lower series
is an average of the rate of growth in our real adjusted disposable
income series for the current year and the preceding two. This average
correlates positively with the saving rate and negatively with the wealth
ratio, although the correlations break down somewhat in the 1969–78
decade. The correlations with the saving and wealth ratios indicate
the two channels through which real income growth affects saving:
more rapid growth raises the saving rate both directly because the
marginal propensity to save exceeds the average and indirectly because
the saving rate is negatively related to the wealth/income ratio, which
falls when income grows more rapidly than wealth. The last relevant
part of the explanation concerns movements in the stock market.
Stock market gains averaged (as a share of income) 9.2, −2.9, and
6.0 percent in the 1954–66, 1968–78, and 1980–85 periods. These
gains alter the wealth/income ratio (the negative gains in the middle
period explain the breakdown in the negative relation between income
growth and the wealth ratio) and also have a small direct effect on
the saving rate.

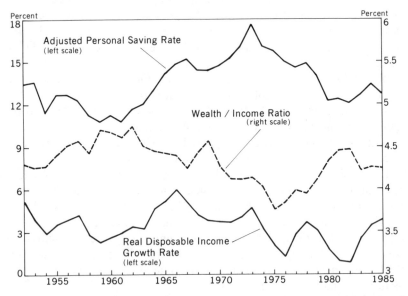

Fig. 4.7   Adjusted personal saving rate, wealth/income ratio, and real
income growth

4.3.3 The Corporate Veil and Denison's Law

A question often asked is, Do households directly alter their saving in response to changes in corporate saving (Feldstein 1973)? The answer usually given is yes, to a significant extent (Howrey and Hymans 1978; and von Furstenberg 1981). That is, the coefficient on corporate saving when it is added to a personal saving equation generally lies between -0.45 and -0.7 and is statistically different from zero. If we regress official NIPA saving on the variables in column 1 plus official NIPA corporate saving, we get a similar result (coefficient of -0.43 with standard error of 0.23). However, this estimate comes from an equation in which both personal and corporate saving are mismeasured. More important, the measurement errors are negatively correlated; personal saving is too high during inflationary periods, and corporate saving is too low. When the series are corrected, that is, personal saving is lowered by the household inflation premium adjustment (and augmented by the other adjustments) and corporate saving is raised by the corporate inflation premium adjustment, the coefficient on corporate saving is positive (0.18 with a standard error of 0.13).

Even earlier, Denison (1958) focused attention on the relative stability of the *gross* private saving rate. He argued that, for many purposes, analysis of the total private saving rate is more appropriate than considering the personal and corporate saving components separately: "Indeed, it was the clear tendency, readily observable even in the dollar figures, for personal saving and corporate saving to move in offsetting fashion that first led me to deal directly with total saving" (p. 264). Later work by David and Scadding (1974) and others confirmed this relation. When official gross saving rates are plotted for the 1952–85 period, the negative correlation between them is, indeed, "readily observable"; moreover, the simple correlation coefficient is -0.31. However, such a relation is not observable between the adjusted saving rates, and their simple correlation coefficient is 0.33. Thus, the often-noted negative correlation between the personal and the corporate saving rates, either gross or net, appears to be due to the negatively correlated inflation premia inappropriately contained in the official saving measures.

The absence of a negative relation between household and business saving, correctly measured, does not mean that households do not respond rationally to corporate real wealth accumulation. If corporations were to generate an additional dollar of retained earnings through wise investments, the market value of corporate equity would rise. If the higher retained earnings were not expected to continue, then the equity value would increase by $1 and households, by our estimates, would consume 1.2 cents (the coefficient on unexpected corporate equity gains) in the current year and 3.6 cents (the wealth coefficient) in subsequent years. If retained earnings were expected to be higher in perpetuity, then the market value of corporate equity would rise by a multiple, say $25, and households would consume thirty cents of the initial $1 (0.012 times $25) and ninety cents (0.036 times $25) in each of the subsequent years.

4.4   Summary and Conclusion

Personal and private saving rates have hit post-1950 lows in the 1980s, according to official saving statistics. The average personal saving rate for 1983–85 was 5.6 percent, less than any year in the 1950–82 period and 20 percent below the average rate for that period. The average private saving rate for 1982–85 was 8.6 percent, less than any year in the 1950–81 period and 23 percent below the average rate for that period.

But the official statistics contain a number of conceptual measurement errors. The major ones are (1) treating net investment in consumer durables as consumption; (2) effectively treating net investment in government retirement plans, especially social security, as taxes; and (3) counting as interest income that part of interest received that is both due to inflation and available to compensate for inflation's erosion of fixed-valued asset stocks. The first two errors cause the official personal and private saving rates to understate the true rates; the last causes an overstatement of both rates, although less for private saving because the private sector is a smaller net creditor than is the personal sector.

The consumer durables correction is highly cyclical and generally raises saving rates by between 1.5 and 4.5 percentage points over the 1952–85 period. The retirement contributions correction, in contrast, has a strong upward trend, adding 2 percentage points to saving rates in the early 1950s but 7 percentage points in the 1980s. The inflation premium correction also has an upward trend, rising from zero to 3.5 percentage points (for personal saving) in the early 1980s, before tailing off. The difference between these trend adjustments raises the official personal and private saving rates by increasing amounts between 1951 and the mid-1970s.

Because of this trend in our adjustments, our adjusted saving rates in the mid 1980s are generally higher than the rates during the 1950–65 period and only slightly below the averages for the entire 1950–85 period. For adjusted personal saving, the rate for each year so far in the 1980s exceeds every year in the 1957–63 period, and the adjusted rate for 1984–85 exceeds the rate in every year in the 1954–64 span. Moreover, the 1984–85 rate is less than half a percentage point below the 1950–83 average, in contrast to the 1.5 percentage points the official rate is below its 1950–83 average. The adjusted personal saving rate was low in 1954–64, high in 1966–78, and then slightly below average in 1980–85.

Basically, the same description holds for the adjusted private saving rate, which recently is only slightly below its 1950–85 average but above its value during most of the 1950s and early 1960s. More specifically, the 1984–85 rate exceeds the rate in every year between 1952 and 1963, except 1955. Furthermore, the adjusted private saving rate in 1984–85 is only a quarter percentage point below the 1950–83 average, in contrast to the 2 percentage point difference in the official private saving rate for the same two periods.

In contrast to personal saving, corporate saving has been less volatile than the official statistics indicate. The official rate has been especially low during high inflation periods (1974–75, 1980–82). When the inflation premium correction is added (some of corporate interest expense is simply compensation for declines in the real value of their debt), these low values are smoothed out. The inflation premium corrections, for both corporate and personal saving, have another interesting effect: they remove the negative correlation between personal and corporate saving. For the 1950–85 period, the official personal and corporate saving rates, where disposable personal income is the denominator, exhibit a correlation of −0.23, but the adjusted saving rates, where adjusted disposable income is the denominator, have a correlation coefficient of 0.17. That is, earlier evidence on households "seeing through the corporate veil" reflected measurement errors in the two series (the negatively correlated inflation premia). Households respond rationally to corporate retentions that raise stock prices and thus wealth; they do not irrationally respond to retentions that are not viewed as increasing wealth.

To summarize, private saving has been relatively robust in recent years, according to our adjusted saving series. While the rate is below peak rates in the 1970s, it is up from its early 1980s low and is close to the average rate for the 1950–82 period. On the other hand, the decrease in federal government saving in the 1982–85 period, rather than being a one-time aberration, is simply the continuation of a trend toward larger negative saving starting in the 1960s.

Notes

1. See, e.g., Auerbach (1985), Kane (1985), and Jianakoplos (1985).
2. As straightforward as this definition is, conceptual and practical difficulties exist in the determination of what constitutes an increase in real resources,

not the least of which is measuring changes in unfunded pension wealth (private and social security), a task requiring heroic assumptions about future legislation, tax treatment, and discount rates (see, e.g., Auerbach 1985; and Hendershott and Peek 1985b).

3. See Hendershott and Peek (1985a).

4. Auerbach and Kotlikoff (1983) illustrate how relations that exist (by construction) in individual household data can "disappear" when macroeconomic relations are estimated on data aggregated over the households.

5. Rather than being retained, capital was withdrawn from these enterprises at an annual rate of $64 billion over the 1982–85 period.

6. For a fascinating analysis of the illogic of government accounting methods, including those for social security, see Kotlikoff (1986).

7. We also considered an accelerated-depreciation adjustment for business saving. When capital purchases are written off faster than capital productivity erodes, taxes on current profits are postponed. In effect, businesses are borrowing interest free to reduce current taxes, and thus saving is overstated. The overstatement of saving is the implicit amount firms are borrowing in order to be able to pay the extra taxes that will come due when economic depreciation on today's investment eventually exceeds tax depreciation. However, the extra taxes come due only to the extent that the business shrinks or depreciation allowances are made less generous in the future. For an ongoing concern that does not expect a shortening of tax lives, the implicit amount borrowed is zero; the deferral is a permanent gift.

8. To be complete, we should also impute income from the use of durables to consumption. However, the same imputation would be made to personal income, leaving saving unaffected.

9. Blades and Sturm (1982) claim to have made this adjustment, but we do not know how accrued interest (either the rate of return on social security or the stock of accumulated contributions to which it is applied) could be calculated.

10. For a more detailed discussion of the tax liabilities series, see Park (1986) and articles cited therein.

11. The inflation adjustment was first addressed by Poole (1972). His measure of the inflation premium in disposable income was constructed as

$$YPREM = \frac{\pi}{RCB} \, YINT,$$

where π, RCB, and YINT represent the anticipated inflation rate, the corporate bond rate, and net interest income, respectively.

12. Because the NIPA convention treats homeowners as businesses, the other private business component of NIPA interest paid includes mortgage interest on owner-occupied housing. This enters the calculation of personal income (and hence personal saving) through the imputed component of personal rental income. NIPA-imputed rental income is calculated as space rent less certain costs incurred by homeowners such as intermediate goods and services consumed, property taxes, and mortgage interest. Thus, given the value of space rent from the product side of the accounts, a dollar increase in mortgage interest payments would reduce imputed rental income by a dollar.

13. In terms of table 4.1, the asset stock equals the integrated household holdings (col. 3) of other deposits and credit market assets plus life insurance and pension fund holdings of the same assets (which are implicit in household insurance and pension reserves), all at market values. The liability stock equals

the market value of the stock of integrated household liabilities (mortgage debt plus other debt).

14. The TXPER series is constructed from data contained in annual issues of the U.S. Internal Revenue Service's *Statistics of Income*. Following Wright (1969), the tax rate is calculated as a weighted average of the marginal personal income tax rate for each adjusted gross income class. The weight for each class is equal to its share of the total interest received by all income classes.

15. This is not meant to suggest that we think the real interest rate was constant; ample empirical evidence exists that the real rate has varied cyclically (e.g., Hendershott and Huang 1985). However, during the 1950–80 period, this variation has been on the order of only 2 percentage points. Moreover, the variation in the rate built into interest income is substantially less given the lags with which this income reflects rate movements. In contrast, interest income incorporates a major (6–8 percentage point) trend increase in expected inflation between 1950 and 1980.

16. In terms of table 4.1, the asset stock equals nonfinancial corporate (col. 4) other deposits and credit market instruments at market value. The liability stock equals the market value of other debt. The after-tax premium can be calculated directly because the nontaxable interest income of corporations is negligible.

17. Because this study is primarily concerned with private saving, the adjustment to federal government saving is incomplete, e.g., government net investment in tangible capital should be included as net investment in consumer durables is included in household saving. We have made only those adjustments to government saving that are required by our adjustments to private saving.

18. We thank Edward McKelvey for emphasizing the general problem of bias in the estimated coefficients on the adjustment variables. Technically, bias will exist if a variable is correlated with the error term. As noted in the text, this is likely to be true for the consumer durables adjustment but not for the other adjustments.

19. While the real after-tax interest rate has a negligible direct effect on personal saving, this rate has a major indirect effect through capital gains on tangible wealth (Hendershott and Peek 1985a).

20. The Federal Reserve series for government employees pension contributions exhibits surprising volatility (especially troubling is a $4.5 billion decline in the state and local component in 1979 followed by a $10 billion increase in 1980). Holloway (chap.1, in this vol.) presents an alternative series excluding military federal employees. When we use his series for state and local employees and the Federal Reserve's federal employee's series (about one-quarter of the total), the estimated coefficient rises by 35 percent, and its standard error increases by 50 percent. The pension coefficient is still nearly three standard deviations from zero and less than two standard deviations from minus unity.

21. The coefficient and its level of significance are much higher when Slemrod's nuclear fear variable is included in an equation explaining official NIPA personal saving without the saving adjustments. When combined with the regressors included in col.1, the coefficient is 0.0049 with a t-statistic of four.

22. Because corporate equities account for such a large proportion of the movement in total household wealth, we reestimated our final equation with wealth separated into two components: corporate equities and noncorporate equity wealth. The noncorporate equity component has the larger effect (-0.0398 vs. -0.0326), but the coefficients are not statistically different (their standard errors are about 0.011).

References

Auerbach, Alan J. 1982. Issues in the measurement and encouragement of business saving. In *Saving and government policy*, 79–99. Conference Series, no. 25. Boston: Federal Reserve Bank of Boston.
————. 1985. Saving in the U.S.: Some conceptual issues. In *The level and composition of household saving*, ed. Patric H. Hendershott, 15–38. Cambridge, Mass.: Ballinger Publishing Co.
Auerbach, Alan J., and Lawrence J. Kotlikoff. 1983. An examination of empirical tests of social security and savings. In *Social policy evaluation: An economic perspective*, ed. E. Helpman, A. Razin, and E. Sadka, 161–81. New York: Academic.
Blades, Derek W., and Peter H. Sturm. 1982. The concept and measurement of savings: The United States and other industrialized countries. In *Saving and government policy*, 1–30. Conference Series, no. 25. Boston: Federal Reserve Bank of Boston.
Board of Governors of the Federal Reserve System. 1986. *Balance sheets for the U.S. economy, 1946–85*. Washington, D.C., October.
Clarida, R. H., and Benjamin M. Friedman. 1983. The behavior of U.S. short-term interest rates since October 1979. *Journal of Finance* 39 (July): 671–82.
Council of Economic Advisers. 1987. *Economic report of the president*. Washington, D.C.: U.S. Government Printing Office.
David, Paul A., and John L. Scadding. 1974. Private savings: Ultrarationality, aggregation, and "Denison's law." *Journal of Political Economy* 82 (March/April): 225–49.
Denison, Edward. 1958. A note on private saving. *Review of Economics and Statistics* 15 (August): 261–67.
Eisner, Robert, and Paul J. Pieper. 1984. A new view of the federal debt and budget deficits. *American Economic Review* 74 (March): 11–29.
Feldstein, Martin. 1973. Tax incentives, corporate saving, and capital accumulation in the United States. *Journal of Public Economics* 2 (February): 159–71.
Hendershott, Patric H. 1986. Debt and equity returns revisited. In *Financing corporate capital formation*, ed. Benjamin Friedman, 35–50. Chicago: University of Chicago Press.
Hendershott, Patric H., and Roger Huang. 1985. Debt and equity yields: 1926–80. In *Corporate capital structure in the United States,* ed. Benjamin Friedman, 17–63. Chicago: University of Chicago Press.
Hendershott, Patric H., and Joe Peek. 1985a. Household saving: An econometric investigation. In *The level and composition of household saving*, ed. Patric H. Hendershott, Cambridge, Mass.: Ballinger Publishing Co.
————. 1985b. Real household capital gains and wealth accumulation. In *The level and composition of household saving*, ed. Patric H. Hendershott, 41–61. Cambridge, Mass.: Ballinger Publishing Co.
Howrey, E. Philip, and Saul H. Hymans. 1978. The measurement and determination of loanable-funds saving. *Brookings Papers on Economic Activity*, no. 3: 655–85.
Jianakoplos, Nancy. 1985. Inflation and the accumulation of wealth by older households, 1966 to 1976. In *The level and composition of household saving*, ed. Patric H. Hendershott, 151–80. Cambridge, Mass.: Ballinger Publishing Co.

Jump, Gregory V. 1980. Interest rates, inflation expectations, and spurious elements in measured real income and saving. *American Economic Review* 70 (December): 990–1004.

Kane, Edward J. 1985. Microeconomic evidence on the composition of household savings in recent years. In *The level and composition of household saving,* ed. Patric H. Hendershott, 101–49. Cambridge, Mass.: Ballinger Publishing Co.

Kotlikoff, Laurence J. 1986. Deficit delusion. *Public Interest* 84 (Summer): 53–65.

McSteen, Martha A. 1985. Fifty years of social security. *Social Security Bulletin* 48 (August): 36–44.

Munnell, Alicia. 1977. *The future of social security.* Washington, D.C.: Brookings Institution.

Park, Thae S. 1986. Federal personal income taxes: Revised and updated estimates of liabilities and payments, 1949–84. *Survey of Current Business* (May): 40–41.

Peek, Joe. 1982. Personal saving and the measurement of income tax liabilities. *Review of Economics and Statistics* 64 (February): 143–47.

Poole, William. 1972. The role of interest rates and inflation in the consumption function. *Brookings Papers on Economic Activity,* no. 1: 211–20.

Slemrod, Joel. 1986. Saving and the fear of nuclear war. *Journal of Conflict Resolution* 30, no. 3: 403–19.

U.S. Department of Health and Human Services. 1986. *Social security bulletin—An annual statistical supplement.* Washington D.C.: U.S. Government Printing Office.

von Furstenberg, George M. 1981. Saving. In *How taxes affect economic behavior,* ed. Henry Aaron and Joseph Pechman, 327–490. Washington, D.C.: Brookings Institution.

Wright, Colin. 1969. Saving and the rate of interest. In *The taxation of income from capital,* ed. Arnold C. Harberger and Martin J. Bailey, 275–300. Washington D.C.: Brookings Institution.

Comment   Frank de Leeuw

Hendershott and Peek (HP) are far from the first to redesign the personal sector, but their approach and their resultant saving measure differ from others'. Most of their adjustments can be viewed as moving personal saving closer to a change-in-wealth concept; the adjustments for consumer durable goods and for the "inflation premium" in interest income are clear examples. They could have moved even closer—for example, by changing the treatment of capital gains on real assets—but they chose not to do so.

Some other redesigners of the personal sector, in contrast, have moved personal saving toward a cash basis—for example, by treating

Frank de Leeuw is chief statistician of the Bureau of Economic Analysis, U.S. Department of Commerce.

owner-occupied housing the way the Bureau of Economic Analysis (BEA) now treats consumer durables rather than (as in HP) the reverse. The paper by Richard and Nancy Ruggles presented at the conference (but not included in this volume) redesigns the personal sector in a still different way, moving in the same direction as HP for consumer durables, moving in the opposite direction for pensions, and making no change in the treatment of inflation-induced capital losses.

I think that experimental redesigns of the personal sector have provided, and will provide, useful insights into consumer behavior. Moreover, I believe that HP's strategy of moving closer, but not all the way, to a change-in-wealth concept of personal saving is likely to be one of the more fruitful redesigns. I do, however, have doubts about some of their specific adjustments. I shall focus on the two that seem to me most problematic, the adjustment for social security and the one for the inflation premium in interest income.

Social Security

A change-in-wealth approach to social security imputes to households a stock of social security wealth equal to the present value of future benefits (for the current adult population). It treats additions to the stock as personal saving and treats subtractions from the stock as personal dissaving. BEA's cash approach, in contrast, treats the main source of additions to the stock, social security taxes, as an exclusion from personal income (and hence from personal saving) and treats the main source of subtraction from the stock, benefit payments, as a part of personal income.

It would seem, therefore, that adjusting the present estimates to a change-in-wealth approach would require adding contributions to personal saving and subtracting benefit payments from personal saving as presently measured. It would also require adjustments to reflect other sources of change in the imputed stock, such as interest earnings or legislated changes in benefit formulas (and it would require adjustments in government saving that are the opposite of those in personal saving).

HP's adjustments do add contributions to personal saving, but they do *not* subtract benefit payments from personal saving. This procedure has the peculiar consequence that, if contributions and benefits rise by identical amounts in some year, personal saving rises (and the federal deficit also rises). In support of this procedure, they argue that benefit payments have been offset by increases in the present value of social security wealth, mainly through legislation increasing benefits. They do not, however, offer any evidence that this equivalence holds even on a trend basis, let alone year by year. In fact, they doubt that it holds since 1980 and use a modified procedure beginning in 1981.

Clearly, HP are on weak ground statistically in making this adjustment. I think they are also on weak ground conceptually. If the Congress this year changes the present value of social security wealth—for example, by a change in the retirement age at which full benefits apply, beginning ten years from now—do we wish to classify that change as a component of this year's personal saving? The implication of HP's reasoning, I believe, is that we do. For most purposes, I would prefer to classify it as a revaluation of wealth, akin to capital gains or losses on real assets—revaluations that we should take account of when we try to understand saving behavior but not build into the saving measure itself.

The Inflation Premium in Interest Income

A change-in-wealth approach to interest income recognizes that, in an inflationary period, a portion of the interest income that persons receive serves merely to offset the decline in the real value of their dollar-denominated assets. That portion does not add to personal wealth and hence should not be included in personal income and saving.

HP estimate the inflation premium in interest income by assuming that the average real interest rate on consumer dollar-denominated assets was a constant, equal to the average nominal rate in 1950, from 1950 through 1980. Their adjustment to interest income amounts to substituting this assumed rate times actual assets for currently estimated interest income. They make a similar adjustment to business saving, substituting an assumed real rate times actual net liabilities for currently estimated interest expense (the business adjustment goes in the opposite direction from the consumer adjustment, but not by an equal amount). For both series, the procedure is modified after 1980 because real rates are thought to have risen.

HP's objective of trying to remove an inflation premium from interest flows seems worthwhile to me, but I have doubts about the actual adjustments they make, for two reasons. The first is the obvious one that real interest rates may not have been constant from 1950 through 1980. Some of the movements of nominal interest rates during that period—for example, the drop in 1967—surely reflect changing real rates rather than a change in the inflation premium. These movements should be reflected in interest income and saving.

The second reason for doubt is that HP's procedure may violate the accounting identity between saving and investment (including net foreign investment). They show adjustments only for the personal and the business sectors, and it is possible that corresponding adjustments for the foreign and the government sectors would produce a complete set of adjustments that sum to zero, as they must if the saving-investment identity is to be preserved. However, it is hard for me to see how the HP methodology would produce this result.

Further Comments

I have some doubts about the regression tests that HP offer in support of the validity of their adjustments. The dependent variables in these regressions are BEA's present measures of saving. The independent variables are of two sorts: variables that cause households to change their saving, such as income growth or rates of return, and the various adjustments that HP advocate. For adjustments that they believe should be added to BEA's measure, they expect to find regression coefficients of -1.0 (for those that they believe should be subtracted, they expect coefficients of $+1.0$). Generally, they find coefficients close to those that they expect.

HP's interpretation of the coefficients is one plausible interpretation, but it is not the only one. The adjustments generally involve removing or adding some piece of presently measured income or outlays; for example, the inflation premium adjustment involves subtracting from saving personal interest income as presently measured (and adding in an alternative measure). An alternative interpretation of the coefficients is that the pieces of income or outlays that enter into HP's adjustments are significant sources of the variance in BEA's measure of personal saving. A regression that included a complete set of pieces of income and outlays—an identity—would produce nothing but coefficients of -1.0 and $+1.0$. HP do not include anything close to a complete set of pieces in their regressions, but their results could still be due to the fact that their adjustments include some of the more variable components of saving.

These questions about the regression results and about some of the adjustments make me much less inclined than HP to refer without qualification to the "conceptual errors" and "measurement errors" of the present series. Nevertheless, I want to stress that in spite of the questions—which it is the function of a discussant to raise—I found this a stimulating paper. Redesigns of the personal sector can contribute to our understanding and can influence official measurement practices. I hope that Hendershott and Peek continue to contribute to this area.

5 The Accumulation of Human and Nonhuman Capital, 1948–84

Dale W. Jorgenson and Barbara M. Fraumeni

5.1 Introduction

The objective of this paper is to present a new system of national accounts for the U.S. economy. The purpose of this accounting system is to provide a comprehensive perspective on the role of capital formation in U.S. economic growth. The distinctive feature of our system is that we include fully comparable measures of investment in human and nonhuman capital. We have implemented this system of accounts for the private sector of the U.S. economy, covering the period 1948–84.

The concept of human capital is based on an analogy between investment in physical capital and investment in human beings. The common element is that present expenditures yield returns over the future. In order to construct comparable measures of investment in human and nonhuman capital, we define human capital in terms of lifetime labor incomes for all individuals in the U.S. population. Lifetime labor incomes correspond to the asset values for investment goods used in accounting for physical or nonhuman capital. We present a summary of our methodology in section 5.2.

The U.S. national income and product accounts (NIPAs) contain a great deal of valuable information on capital formation. For example, these accounts provide data on investment in physical or nonhuman capital that are both comprehensive and detailed;[1] however, the national accounts are closely tied to market transactions, avoiding imputations

Dale W. Jorgenson is Frederic Eaton Abbe Professor of Economics at Harvard University. Barbara M. Fraumeni is an associate professor of economics at Northeastern University.

Brian Alves, Ian Gershengorn, Mun Sing Ho, and Perry Lin provided able research support. The authors are grateful to the National Science Foundation for support of this research.

for nonmarket activities wherever possible. Not surprisingly, investment in human capital is not included in the U.S. national accounts.

The perspective on capital formation provided by the U.S. national accounts is seriously incomplete, as a consequence of the fact that these accounts are limited to market transactions. Our measures of capital formation show that investment in human capital is at least four times the magnitude of investment in nonhuman capital; moreover, the value of wealth in the form of human capital is over eleven times the value of physical or nonhuman capital.

The total product of an economic system includes investment in human and nonhuman capital and consumption of market and non-market goods and services. We define full consumption as the sum of goods and services supplied by market and nonmarket activities. Similarly, we define full investment as the sum of investments in human and nonhuman capital. Finally, we define full product as the sum of investment and consumption. We present measures of full product, investment, and consumption in section 5.3.

Our system of accounts assigns an equal role to consumption and investment as proportions of the national product; however, the relative importance of investment is much greater in our system than in the U.S. national accounts. Full investment is around 50 percent of full product, where human and nonhuman capital are treated on a comparable basis. Full consumption is about half of full product, where both market and nonmarket goods and services are included in consumption.

The value of full product is equal to the value of outlays on the services of human and nonhuman capital. These outlays take the form of labor and property compensation. We define full labor compensation as the sum of market labor compensation for activities involving employment through the labor market and nonmarket labor compensation for activities resulting in investment in education and direct consumption of labor services. Similarly, we define full property compensation as the sum of market and nonmarket property compensation. Finally, we define full factor outlay as the sum of labor and property compensation. We present measures for full factor outlay, labor compensation, and property compensation in section 5.3.

Nonmarket labor compensation is more than 80 percent of labor compensation since full compensation includes the value of nonmarket activities such as investment in education, household production, and leisure time. Full labor compensation is around 90 percent of factor outlay, while property compensation is close to 10 percent of the total. In our system of national accounts, the relative importance of labor compensation is much greater than in the U.S. national accounts.

Both property and labor compensation must be reduced by taxes and increased by subsidies to obtain incomes accruing to individuals. We define full labor income as the sum of market and nonmarket labor compensation after taxes. Similarly, we define full property income as the sum of market and nonmarket property compensation after taxes. Full income is defined as the sum of labor income and property income. We present measures for full income, labor income, and property income in section 5.4.

Receipts accruing to individuals include full income and government transfer payments to persons. Receipts are divided between consumption of market and nonmarket goods and services and saving in the form of human and nonhuman capital. We define full personal consumption expenditures as the sum of market goods and services consumed by households and nonprofit institutions, the services of human capital consumed directly through household production and leisure, and the services of nonhuman capital consumed directly in the form of services of consumers' durables and owner-occupied housing. We define full consumer outlays as the sum of personal consumption expenditures, personal transfer payments to foreigners, and personal nontax payments. We present measures for full consumer outlays and saving in the form of human and nonhuman capital in section 5.4.

Since our system of accounts includes the consumption of both market and nonmarket goods and services, consumer outlays are much greater than in the U.S. national accounts. The market share of consumer outlays averages around 35 percent of total outlays. Similarly, our concept of human and nonhuman saving is much more comprehensive than the concept of saving in the U.S. national accounts. Human saving is between 80 and 90 percent of full saving. Nonhuman saving, the only portion included in the U.S. national accounts, is between 10 and 20 percent of the total.

The proportion of full saving to national expenditure ranges from 45 to 50 percent in our accounting system. This is far greater than the proportion of national saving to national expenditure in the U.S. national accounts. The saving proportion in our accounts rose to a peak in the year 1971 and has been gradually declining since then. The saving rate is lower in 1983 and 1984 than at any previous time in the postwar period.

To integrate our measures of income and expenditure with measures of human and nonhuman wealth, we require concepts of depreciation and revaluation for human and nonhuman capital. We define depreciation of human capital in terms of changes in the lifetime labor incomes of individuals with age. Depreciation on human capital is the sum of changes in lifetime labor incomes with age for all individuals who remain in the population and lifetime labor incomes of all individuals who die or emigrate. Similarly, we define depreciation for nonhuman capital in terms of changes in asset values with age. Depreciation on nonhuman capital is the sum of changes in asset values for all investment goods remaining in the capital stock and the asset values of all investment goods that are retired from the capital stock. We define full depreciation as the sum of depreciation for human and nonhuman capital.

Depreciation is a very large component of saving in the form of both human and nonhuman capital. Depreciation was a fairly stable proportion of full gross saving at around 35 percent until the mid-1960s. Since that time, the relative importance of depreciation has risen steadily to almost 50 percent of saving. By contrast, net saving has declined from nearly 65 percent of saving at the beginning of the postwar period to slightly over 50 percent at the end of the period.

We define revaluation for human capital in terms of changes in lifetime labor incomes from period to period for individuals with a given set of demographic characteristics—age, sex, and education. Revaluation of human wealth is the sum of changes in lifetime incomes for all individuals initially in the population, holding age, sex, and education for each individual constant. Similarly, we define revaluation for nonhuman capital in terms of changes in asset values from period to period for individual investment goods. Revaluation of nonhuman capital is the sum of changes in asset values for all investment goods initially in the capital stock, holding the age of each investment good constant. We define full revaluation as the sum of revaluation for human and nonhuman capital.

We conclude the development of a new system of national accounts for the United States by defining full wealth as the sum of human and nonhuman wealth. The change in wealth from period to period is the sum of investment in human and nonhuman capital, net of depreciation, and the revaluation of human and nonhuman capital. We present measures of full investment, depreciation, revaluation, and changes in wealth in section 5.5 below. Finally, we present measures of full wealth in section 5.5.

Human wealth greatly predominates in the value of wealth, amounting to more than 90 percent of the total throughout the postwar period. The U.S. national accounts do not include wealth accounts. Only investment in the form of physical or nonhuman wealth is included in the national accounts. Wealth accounts consistent with the U.S. national accounts would exclude human wealth altogether. Obviously, the exclusion of investment in the form of human wealth is an extremely important omission.

It is necessary to emphasize that our study is exploratory in character. Unlike the U.S. national accounts, which are firmly rooted in market transactions, our system of accounts involves very sizable imputations for the value of nonmarket activities. This disadvantage must be weighed against the important advantage that we provide a comprehensive view of capital formation. Judgments about the relative importance of investment and consumption, labor and property income, or different forms of saving require information of the type presented in our new system of national accounts.

5.2 Methodology

The implementation of our system of accounts for human capital requires a new data base for measuring lifetime labor incomes for all individuals in the U.S. population.[2] Our system includes demographic accounts that incorporate population data from the U.S. Bureau of the Census. Our demographic accounts include annual estimates of midyear population by sex and age for individuals under seventy-five years of age. Using data from the censuses of population for 1940, 1950, 1960, 1970, and 1980, we have distributed the population of each sex by individual years of age and individual years of educational attainment. The estimation of changes in the numbers of individuals classified by age, sex, and education from year to year requires data on enrollment in formal schooling and on births, deaths, and migration.[3]

The starting point for the measurement of lifetime labor incomes for all individuals in the U.S. population is the data base on market labor activities assembled by Gollop and Jorgenson (1980, 1983). This data base includes the number of employed persons, hours worked, and labor compensation for the United States on an annual basis, cross-classified by sex, age, education, employment class, occupation, and industry. We have derived annual estimates of hours worked and labor compensation required for measuring incomes from market labor activities by summing over employment class, occupation, and industry and by distributing the work force of each sex by individual years of age from fourteen to seventy-four and individual years of educational attainment from no education to one to seventeen or more. We obtain average hourly labor compensation annually for individuals classified by the two sexes, sixty-one age groups, eighteen education groups for a total of 2,196 groups by dividing market labor compensation by hours worked by each group.

The second step in the measurement of lifetime labor incomes is to impute labor compensation and hours devoted to nonmarket activities. Six types of nonmarket activities are commonly distinguished in studies of time allocation—production of goods and services within the household unit, volunteer work outside the household unit, commuting to work, formal education, leisure, and the satisfaction of physiological needs such as eating and sleeping.[4] We classify time spent satisfying physiological needs as maintenance and exclude this time from our measure of time spent in nonmarket activities. We assume that the time available for all market and nonmarket activities has been constant over time and is equal to fourteen hours per day for all individuals.

We allocate the annual time available for all individuals in the population among work, schooling, household production and leisure, and maintenance. Our system of demographic accounts includes the enrollment status for individuals of each sex between five and thirty-four years of age. We estimate the time spent in formal schooling for all individuals by assigning 1,300 hours per year to each person enrolled in school. We allocate time spent in schooling to investment. Similarly, our demographic accounts include employment status for individuals of each sex between fourteen and seventy-four years of age. Hours worked for all employed individuals, classified by sex, age, and education, are included in our data base for market labor activities. We allocate time that is not spent working or in formal schooling directly to consumption. For all individuals, this time is equal to the difference between fourteen hours per day and time spent working or in school.

The third step in the measure of lifetime labor incomes is to impute the value of labor compensation for nonmarket activities.[5] For this purpose, we first obtain average hourly labor compensation for all employed persons classified by sex, age, and education from our data base for market labor activities. Second, we estimate marginal tax rates for all employed persons, again classified by sex, age, and education. We multiply compensation per hour by one minus the marginal tax rate to obtain imputed hourly labor compensation for nonmarket activities other than formal schooling. Since individuals under fourteen years of age do not participate in the labor force, their imputed hourly labor compensation is set equal to zero. Individuals over seventy-four years of age are also assigned zero as their hourly labor compensation.

To estimate lifetime labor incomes for all individuals in the U.S. population, we distinguish among three stages in the life cycle. In the first stage, individuals may participate in formal schooling but not in the labor market. In the second stage, individuals may enroll in school and also work. In the third stage, individuals may participate in the labor market but not in formal schooling. For individuals in the third stage of the life cycle, total labor compensation is the sum of compensation for market labor activities after taxes and imputed compensation for nonmarket labor activities. For individuals in the second stage of the life cycle, total labor compensation also includes imputed labor compensation for schooling. For individuals in the first stage of the life cycle, labor compensation includes only the imputed value of time spent in schooling.

For an individual in the third stage of the life cycle, we assume that expected incomes in future time periods are equal to the incomes of individuals of the same sex and education, but with the age that the individual will have in the future time period, adjusted for increases in real income. We assume that real incomes rise over time at the rate of Harrod-neutral technical change, which we estimate at 2 percent per year. We weight income for each future year by the probability of survival, given the initial age of the individual. We obtain these probabilities by sex from publications of the National Center for Health Statistics. Where necessary, these survival functions, giving probability of survival by age and sex, are interpolated by means of standard demographic techniques. Finally, we discount expected future incomes at a real rate of return of 4 percent per year to obtain the lifetime labor income of an individual of a given sex, age, and education.

For an individual at the second stage of the life cycle, combining formal schooling with the possibility of participation in the labor market, we impute the value of time spent in schooling through its effect on lifetime labor income. For an individual of a given sex and age who is completing the highest level of schooling, grade seventeen or over, lifetime labor income is the discounted value of expected future labor incomes for a person of that sex and age and seventeen or more years of schooling. The imputed labor compensation for the time spent in formal schooling is equal to the difference between the lifetime labor incomes of an individual with seventeen years of education and an individual with the same sex and age and one less year of education, less tuition and fees for that grade of schooling. Total labor compensation is equal to the value of time spent in formal schooling plus labor compensation for market and nonmarket activities other than formal schooling.

For an individual completing grade 16, lifetime labor income is equal to the lifetime labor income of an individual of the same sex and education, but one year older, plus expected labor compensation for one year, discounted back to the present and multiplied by the probability of survival for one year. Expected labor compensation is equal to the probability of enrollment in grade 17 or higher, multiplied by market and nonmarket labor compensation for a person enrolled in that grade, and one minus the probability of enrollment, multiplied by market and nonmarket labor compensation for a person with sixteen years of education, not enrolled in school. As before, the imputed labor compensation for the time spent in formal schooling is equal to the difference between the lifetime incomes of an individual with sixteen years of education and an individual with the same sex and age and one less year of education, less tuition and fees. Using the same approach to defining lifetime labor incomes for individuals completing earlier grades, lifetime incomes and imputed labor compensation for the time spent in formal schooling can be determined for individuals completing fifteen years of education, fourteen years of education, and so on.

For an individual in the first stage of the life cycle, where participation in the labor market is ruled out, the value of labor compensation is limited to the imputed value of schooling. Lifetime incomes for individuals at this stage of the life cycle can be determined for individuals completing one year of education, two years of education, and so on, working back from higher levels of education as outlined above. For individuals too young to be enrolled in school, imputed labor compensation is zero, but lifetime labor incomes are well defined. The value of a newborn entrant into the population is equal to the lifetime labor income of that individual at age zero. Investment in human capital in any year is the sum of lifetime incomes for all individuals born in that year and all immigrants plus the imputed labor compensation for formal schooling for all individuals enrolled in school.

The implementation of our new system of national accounts for the United States begins with the accounting system presented by Fraumeni and Jorgenson (1980). That accounting system includes a production account, an income and expenditure account, an accumulation account, and a wealth account—all in current and constant prices;[6] however, their accounts for capital services, investment, and wealth are limited to nonhuman capital. We have incorporated their estimates for nonhuman capital into our system of U.S. national accounts. We have added estimates of the services of human capital, investment in human capital, and human wealth.

Our system of U.S. national accounts includes a production account that divides the national product between investment and consumption and divides national factor input between the services of human and nonhuman capital. The system also includes an income and expenditure account that divides income between compensation for human and nonhuman capital services and divides expenditures between saving and current consumption. Changes in wealth are divided between investment and revaluation of human and nonhuman capital in an accumulation account. The system is completed by a wealth account incorporating human and nonhuman wealth.

As a basis for comparison of measurements of human capital based on lifetime labor incomes with alternative approaches, we can compare our estimates of human wealth and investment in human capital with those of Kendrick (1976). Like Machlup (1962), Nordhaus and Tobin (1972), Schultz (1961), and others, Kendrick employs costs of education, including earnings forgone by students, as a basis for measuring investment through education. He employs costs of rearing as a basis for measuring investment through addition of new members of the population. Since his estimates of human capital are based on costs of education and rearing rather than lifetime labor incomes, he omits the value of nonmarket activities from his estimates of human capital. Our estimates of human capital are much larger than those of Kendrick. Our estimates of nonhuman wealth are also higher than Kendrick's, and our estimates of total wealth are much higher than his.[7]

5.3   Production

In implementing our production account for the United States, we limit our attention to the private domestic sector of the U.S. economy, following Fraumeni and Jorgenson (1980). The total product of the private domestic sector of the U.S. economy includes investment in human and nonhuman capital and consumption of market and non-market goods and services. We add to consumption of market goods and services, as defined by Fraumeni and Jorgenson, our estimates of consumption of nonmarket goods and services. Similarly, we add to their estimates of investment in nonhuman capital our estimates of investment in human capital.

The value of total product is equal to the value of total factor outlay for the production account. Total factor outlay in the U.S. economy includes market labor compensation for activities involving employment through the labor market and nonmarket labor compensation for activities resulting in investment in education and direct consumption of labor services. We add to market labor compensation, as defined by Fraumeni and Jorgenson (1986), our estimates of the value of non-market labor compensation. We incorporate their estimates of property compensation into our factor outlay account.

We present the production account in current prices for the private domestic sector of the U.S. economy for the year 1982 in table 5.1. We first observe that the value of time spent in household production and leisure, which is assigned to consumption, is larger than the gross private domestic product, as defined by Fraumeni and Jorgenson. The value of investment in human capital is comparable in magnitude to gross private domestic product. Considering the value of time spent in household production and leisure and investment in human capital together, we find that outlay on human capital services is more than twice the size of gross private domestic factor outlay, as defined by Fraumeni and Jorgenson.

Our next objective is to allocate the value of total product for the private domestic sector of the U.S. economy between consumption and investment for the period 1948–84. We first estimate the value of

Table 5.1   **Production Account, Gross Private Domestic Product and Factor Outlay, United States, 1982 (billions of current dollars)**

Product	
1. Private gross national product (table 1.7, line 1 minus line 12)	2,822.1
2. − Compensation of employees in government enterprises (table 6.4, lines 81, 86)	39.6
3. − Rest-of-the-world gross national product (table 1.7, line 15)	51.2
4. − Federal indirect business tax and nontax accruals (table 3.2, line 9)	48.1
5. + Capital stock tax (table 3.1, n. 2)	. . .
6. − State and local indirect business tax and nontax accruals (table 3.3, line 7)	210.8
7. + Business motor vehicle licenses (table 3.5, line 25)	2.1
8. + Business property taxes (table 3.3, line 9)	85.3
9. + Business other taxes (table 3.5, lines 26, 27)	14.8
10. + Subsidies less current surplus of federal government enterprises (table 3.2, line 27)	16.0
11. + Subsidies less current surplus of state and local government enterprises (table 3.3, line 22)	−7.3
12. + Imputation for nonhuman capital services	338.7
13. = Gross private domestic product	2,921.9
14. + Time in household production and leisure	3,944.5
15. + Investment in human capital	4,568.6
16. = Full gross private domestic product	11,435.0

Factor Outlay	
1. Capital consumption allowances (table 1.9, line 2)	383.2
2. + Business transfer payments (table 1.9, line 7)	14.3
3. + Statistical discrepancy (table 1.9, line 8)	−.1
4. + Certain indirect business taxes (product account above, 5 + 7 + 8 + 9)	102.2
5. + Income originating in business (table 1.12, line 14)	2,010.6
6. − Compensation of employees in government enterprises (table 6.4, lines 81, 86)	39.6
7. + Income originating in households and institutions (table 1.12, line 19)	112.7
8. + Imputation for nonhuman capital services	338.7
9. = Gross private domestic factor outlay	2,921.9
10. + Imputations for human capital services (14 + 15 above)	8,513.1
11. = Full gross private domestic factor outlay	11,435.0

Note: All table references are to the NIPA tables in the March 1986 *Survey of Current Business,* with the exception of capital stock tax, which refers to Bureau of Economic Analysis (1966).

investment in human and nonhuman capital for all years. The value of investment in human capital is equal to the value of investment in education and the value of new members of the population resulting from births and migration. Our estimates of investment in nonhuman capital are based on those of Fraumeni and Jorgenson. We present estimates of investment in human capital, investment in nonhuman capital, and full investment in current prices in table 5.2 and in constant prices in table 5.3.

The value of investment in human capital is by far the largest part of full investment, varying from 0.812 to 0.869 as a proportion of investment during the period 1948–84. The share of investment in nonhuman capital fell over the period from 0.166 in 1948 to 0.131 in 1971. The nonhuman share then rose to 0.167 in 1984, almost the same level as in 1948. The price of investment in human capital has risen much more rapidly than the price of investment in nonhuman capital. By

Table 5.2   **Full Investment (billions of current dollars)**

Year	Full Investment	Human Investment	Nonhuman Investment	Human Share	Nonhuman Share
1948	471.0	392.9	78.1	.834	.166
1949	488.4	415.5	72.9	.851	.149
1950	536.5	441.3	95.2	.823	.177
1951	587.8	477.2	110.5	.812	.188
1952	619.9	508.9	111.0	.821	.179
1953	679.9	563.7	116.3	.829	.171
1954	720.7	607.6	113.0	.843	.157
1955	768.1	635.9	132.3	.828	.172
1956	816.7	678.6	138.1	.831	.169
1957	896.4	755.2	141.2	.843	.157
1958	951.4	819.5	132.0	.861	.139
1959	997.4	846.5	150.9	.849	.151
1960	1,034.5	884.7	149.8	.855	.145
1961	1,102.9	952.5	150.4	.864	.136
1962	1,163.8	996.1	167.7	.856	.144
1963	1,209.6	1,031.3	178.3	.853	.147
1964	1,331.1	1,140.5	190.6	.857	.143
1965	1,406.9	1,193.2	213.7	.848	.152
1966	1,504.6	1,268.3	236.3	.843	.157
1967	1,596.1	1,355.7	240.4	.849	.151
1968	1,728.5	1,466.7	261.8	.849	.151
1969	1,864.0	1,582.9	281.0	.849	.151
1970	2,074.1	1,796.2	277.9	.866	.134
1971	2,335.9	2,029.6	306.3	.869	.131
1972	2,413.7	2,068.3	345.5	.857	.143
1973	2,568.9	2,170.2	398.7	.845	.155
1974	2,809.0	2,397.1	411.9	.853	.147
1975	3,143.7	2,722.2	421.5	.866	.134
1976	3,316.0	2,817.4	498.5	.850	.150
1977	3,626.9	3,047.3	579.6	.840	.160
1978	3,794.1	3,121.1	673.0	.823	.177
1979	4,287.2	3,545.2	741.9	.827	.173
1980	4,724.9	3,974.7	750.1	.841	.159
1981	5,129.4	4,289.4	839.9	.836	.164
1982	5,354.4	4,568.6	785.8	.853	.147
1983	5,701.5	4,843.1	858.4	.849	.151
1984	6,153.2	5,123.2	1,030.0	.833	.167

Table 5.3   Full Investment (billions of constant dollars)

Year	Full Investment Quantity	Full Investment Price	Human Investment Quantity	Human Investment Price	Nonhuman Investment Quantity	Nonhuman Investment Price
1949	2,899.1	.168	2,669.1	.156	282.0	.259
1950	3,025.0	.177	2,686.5	.164	353.8	.269
1951	3,144.1	.187	2,756.9	.173	389.3	.284
1952	3,207.0	.193	2,812.6	.181	396.8	.280
1953	3,293.1	.206	2,878.3	.196	414.0	.281
1954	3,349.0	.215	2,956.1	.206	400.5	.282
1955	3,487.9	.220	3,032.9	.210	450.0	.294
1956	3,552.8	.230	3,106.6	.218	446.1	.310
1957	3,658.0	.245	3,226.6	.234	439.3	.321
1958	3,706.2	.257	3,312.7	.247	412.5	.320
1959	3,805.1	.262	3,356.2	.252	458.0	.330
1960	3,872.9	.267	3,438.3	.257	448.9	.334
1961	3,991.1	.276	3,556.0	.268	452.6	.332
1962	4,091.0	.284	3,606.4	.276	495.2	.339
1963	4,209.2	.287	3,694.2	.279	523.0	.341
1964	4,338.5	.307	3,790.0	.301	553.9	.344
1965	4,402.0	.320	3,797.7	.314	604.2	.354
1966	4,443.3	.339	3,786.3	.335	652.6	.362
1967	4,508.5	.354	3,851.1	.352	653.3	.368
1968	4,625.5	.374	3,941.8	.372	679.2	.385
1969	4,767.4	.391	4,072.2	.389	690.9	.407
1970	4,876.0	.425	4,218.3	.426	654.6	.425
1971	5,020.9	.465	4,335.4	.468	682.4	.449
1972	5,010.3	.482	4,268.6	.485	741.0	.466
1973	5,066.4	.507	4,240.4	.512	829.1	.481
1974	5,045.1	.557	4,253.6	.564	792.4	.520
1975	5,046.8	.623	4,323.7	.630	718.7	.587
1976	5,124.4	.647	4,328.4	.651	794.7	.627
1977	5,286.1	.686	4,418.0	.690	868.6	.667
1978	5,385.0	.705	4,447.7	.702	938.0	.718
1979	5,434.5	.789	4,487.8	.790	947.3	.783
1980	5,439.3	.869	4,560.3	.872	878.7	.854
1981	5,468.9	.938	4,575.7	.937	892.9	.941
1982	5,354.4	1.000	4,568.6	1.000	785.8	1.000
1983	5,395.4	1.057	4,543.7	1.066	853.4	1.006
1984	5,501.4	1.118	4,510.4	1.136	1,002.9	1.027

contrast, investment in human capital has grown much more slowly than investment in nonhuman capital. Investment in human capital reached a peak in 1971 that was not surpassed until 1977. The level of investment in human capital in 1984 was below the peak for the period as a whole, which was reached in 1981.

Our final step in allocating the value of total product of the private sector of the U.S. economy between consumption and investment for the period 1948–84 is to estimate the value of consumption for all years. The value of full consumption is equal to the value of consumption of market goods and services plus the value of nonmarket consumption in the form of time spent in household production and leisure. Our estimates of consumption of market goods and services are based on those of Fraumeni and Jorgenson. We present estimates of full consumption, investment, and product in current prices in table 5.4 and

Table 5.4   **Full Gross Private Domestic Product (billions of current dollars)**

Year	Full Product	Full Consumption	Full Investment	Consumption Share	Investment Share
1948	988.4	517.4	471.0	.523	.477
1949	1,037.7	549.3	488.4	.529	.471
1950	1,113.3	576.8	536.5	.518	.482
1951	1,203.0	615.2	587.8	.511	.489
1952	1,262.8	642.9	619.9	.509	.491
1953	1,379.3	699.4	679.9	.507	.493
1954	1,462.0	741.3	720.7	.507	.493
1955	1,531.8	763.6	768.1	.499	.501
1956	1,617.5	800.8	816.7	.495	.505
1957	1,759.1	862.7	896.4	.490	.510
1958	1,877.6	926.2	951.4	.493	.507
1959	1,951.5	954.2	997.4	.489	.511
1960	2,027.8	993.3	1,034.5	.490	.510
1961	2,162.8	1,059.9	1,102.9	.490	.510
1962	2,273.7	1,109.9	1,163.8	.488	.512
1963	2,360.4	1,150.8	1,209.6	.488	.512
1964	2,587.4	1,256.2	1,331.1	.486	.514
1965	2,765.8	1,358.9	1,406.9	.491	.509
1966	2,980.1	1,475.5	1,504.6	.495	.505
1967	3,168.4	1,572.4	1,596.1	.496	.504
1968	3,401.3	1,672.8	1,728.5	.492	.508
1969	3,651.7	1,787.7	1,864.0	.490	.510
1970	4,056.9	1,982.8	2,074.1	.489	.511
1971	4,538.8	2,202.9	2,335.9	.485	.515
1972	4,785.5	2,371.8	2,413.7	.496	.504
1973	5,184.1	2,615.1	2,568.9	.504	.496
1974	5,670.2	2,861.2	2,809.0	.505	.495
1975	6,335.6	3,191.9	3,143.7	.504	.496
1976	6,790.7	3,474.7	3,316.0	.512	.488
1977	7,382.5	3,755.7	3,626.9	.509	.491
1978	7,911.4	4,117.3	3,794.1	.520	.480
1979	8,918.2	4,631.0	4,287.2	.519	.481
1980	9,731.1	5,006.2	4,724.9	.514	.486
1981	10,620.7	5,491.4	5,129.4	.517	.483
1982	11,435.0	6,080.6	5,354.4	.532	.468
1983	12,272.2	6,570.7	5,701.5	.535	.465
1984	13,254.7	7,101.5	6,153.2	.536	.464

in constant prices in table 5.5. The share of consumption in total product is almost the same as the share of investment, falling from 0.523 in 1948 to a low of 0.485 in 1971 and rising to a peak of 0.536 in 1984 at the end of the period. The price of investment has risen more rapidly than the price of consumption. By contrast, investment has grown more slowly than consumption.

Table 5.5   Full Gross Private Domestic Product (billions of constant dollars)

Year	Full Product		Full Consumption		Full Investment	
	Quantity	Price	Quantity	Price	Quantity	Price
1949	5,597.2	.185	2,696.7	.204	2,899.1	.168
1950	5,755.8	.193	2,736.6	.211	3,025.0	.177
1951	5,944.0	.202	2,809.1	.219	3,144.1	.187
1952	6,062.9	.208	2,865.2	.224	3,207.0	.193
1953	6,234.7	.221	2,950.5	.237	3,293.1	.206
1954	6,321.0	.231	2,982.3	.249	3,349.0	.215
1955	6,524.7	.235	3,051.4	.250	3,487.9	.220
1956	6,648.6	.243	3,110.6	.257	3,552.8	.230
1957	6,830.7	.258	3,188.7	.271	3,658.0	.245
1958	6,943.8	.270	3,252.6	.285	3,706.2	.257
1959	7,105.9	.275	3,317.3	.288	3,805.1	.262
1960	7,240.1	.280	3,383.7	.294	3,872.9	.267
1961	7,464.4	.290	3,490.1	.304	3,991.1	.276
1962	7,643.6	.297	3,570.3	.311	4,091.0	.284
1963	7,858.7	.300	3,667.9	.314	4,209.2	.287
1964	8,101.9	.319	3,782.4	.332	4,338.5	.307
1965	8,280.5	.334	3,895.2	.349	4,402.0	.320
1966	8,444.5	.353	4,014.5	.368	4,443.3	.339
1967	8,620.3	.368	4,123.3	.381	4,508.5	.354
1968	8,833.0	.385	4,219.7	.396	4,625.5	.374
1969	9,060.5	.403	4,306.9	.415	4,767.4	.391
1970	9,286.4	.437	4,424.0	.448	4,876.0	.425
1971	9,561.0	.475	4,554.2	.484	5,020.9	.465
1972	9,700.9	.493	4,701.3	.504	5,010.3	.482
1973	9,848.5	.526	4,791.9	.546	5,066.4	.507
1974	9,929.0	.571	4,890.0	.585	5,045.1	.557
1975	10,129.2	.625	5,085.7	.628	5,046.8	.623
1976	10,345.4	.656	5,223.9	.665	5,124.4	.647
1977	10,643.1	.694	5,360.3	.701	5,286.1	.686
1978	10,872.9	.728	5,490.7	.750	5,385.0	.705
1979	11,027.5	.805	5,638.3	.821	5,434.5	.789
1980	11,223.5	.867	5,783.3	.866	5,439.3	.869
1981	11,375.0	.934	5,905.6	.930	5,468.9	.938
1982	11,435.0	1.000	6,080.6	1.000	5,354.4	1.000
1983	11,584.5	1.059	6,189.0	1.062	5,395.4	1.057
1984	11,811.5	1.122	6,310.0	1.125	5,501.4	1.118

We next analyze changes in the structure of full gross private domestic product for the U.S. economy over the period 1948–84. We present growth rates of full product, investment, and consumption for the period as a whole and for eight subperiods in table 5.6. We give growth rates for each measure of output in current and constant prices and a growth rate for the corresponding price index. We also provide growth rates for each output measure in per capita terms.

The growth rate of full investment was at its maximum during the period 1948–53 at 3.19 percent per year. The growth rate of investment per capita was only 0.54 percent per year for the period as a whole and was negative for the last of the eight subperiods. By contrast, the growth rate of full consumption per capita was positive for all eight subperiods with a rising trend, reaching a maximum in the period 1973–79 at 1.87 percent. The growth rate of full product showed little trend through 1960–66 after an initial burst of growth in full product at 2.70 percent per year in 1948–53. Since 1966, the growth rate of full product has gradually declined, exhibiting the much-discussed slowdown in U.S. economic growth.

Our next objective is to allocate the value of total factor outlay for the private domestic sector of the U.S. economy between labor and property services for the period 1948–84. We first estimate the value of outlay on the services of human capital for all years. The value of outlay on the services of human capital is the sum of outlay on market and nonmarket labor activities. Our estimates of market labor outlays are based on those of Fraumeni and Jorgenson. We present estimates of market labor outlay, nonmarket labor outlay, and full labor outlay in current prices in table 5.7 and in constant prices in table 5.8. The share of nonmarket labor outlay has been by far the largest part of labor outlay, varying relatively little from 0.835 at the beginning of the postwar period. The prices of market and nonmarket labor outlay move in parallel throughout the period, as do the corresponding quantities.

We combine our estimates of the services of human capital with estimates of the services of nonhuman capital, which are based on those of Fraumeni and Jorgenson. We present the value of full factor outlay, property outlay, and labor outlay in current prices in table 5.9 and in constant prices in table 5.10. Labor has had a predominant share in full factor outlay, averaging around 90 percent throughout the period. The share of property has averaged close to 10 percent, rising slightly from 0.112 at the beginning of the period to 0.119 at the end of the period. The price of labor outlay has risen relative to the price of property outlay, while capital services have risen relative to labor services. Capital services have grown more rapidly than output throughout the period.

Table 5.6   **Full Gross Private Domestic Product, Rates of Growth, 1949–84**

	1949–84	1949–53	1953–57	1957–60	1960–66	1966–69	1969–73	1973–79	1979–84
Full product:									
Current prices	7.28	7.11	6.08	4.74	6.42	6.77	8.76	9.04	7.93
Constant prices	2.13	2.70	2.28	1.94	2.56	2.35	2.08	1.95	1.29
Constant prices per capita	.84	1.04	.51	.13	1.11	1.25	1.12	1.11	.24
Price index	5.15	4.45	3.87	2.73	3.86	4.42	6.66	7.09	6.64
Full investment:									
Current prices	7.24	8.27	6.91	4.78	6.24	7.14	8.02	8.54	7.23
Constant prices	1.83	3.19	2.63	1.90	2.29	2.35	1.52	1.17	.24
Constant prices per capita	.54	1.52	.86	.10	.84	1.25	.55	.33	-.80
Price index	5.42	5.10	4.33	2.87	3.98	4.76	6.50	7.37	6.97
Full consumption:									
Current prices	7.31	6.04	5.25	4.70	6.60	6.40	9.51	9.52	8.55
Constant prices	2.43	2.25	1.94	1.98	2.85	2.34	2.67	2.71	2.25
Constant prices per capita	1.13	.59	.17	.17	1.40	1.25	1.70	1.87	1.20
Price index	4.88	3.75	3.35	2.72	3.74	4.01	6.86	6.80	6.30

Table 5.7   **Full Labor Outlay (billions of current dollars)**

Year	Full Labor Outlay	Market Labor Outlay	Nonmarket Labor Outlay	Market Share	Nonmarket Share
1948	877.6	144.8	732.8	.165	.835
1949	929.5	144.1	785.3	.155	.845
1950	988.6	156.9	831.7	.159	.841
1951	1,062.7	180.5	882.2	.170	.830
1952	1,123.4	194.1	929.3	.173	.827
1953	1,235.2	208.9	1,026.3	.169	.831
1954	1,316.8	209.9	1,106.9	.159	.841
1955	1,360.7	219.2	1,141.5	.161	.839
1956	1,445.7	234.7	1,211.0	.162	.838
1957	1,585.2	250.6	1,334.6	.158	.842
1958	1,710.0	257.2	1,452.8	.150	.850
1959	1,756.6	270.1	1,486.5	.154	.846
1960	1,832.8	282.7	1,550.1	.154	.846
1961	1,961.8	292.4	1,669.3	.149	.851
1962	2,052.4	309.8	1,742.6	.151	.849
1963	2,118.4	320.5	1,797.9	.151	.849
1964	2,321.5	339.5	1,982.0	.146	.854
1965	2,465.1	363.0	2,102.1	.147	.853
1966	2,655.7	401.7	2,254.1	.151	.849
1967	2,838.7	427.3	2,411.4	.151	.849
1968	3,056.5	470.7	2,585.8	.154	.846
1969	3,296.7	519.1	2,777.6	.157	.843
1970	3,698.9	556.2	3,142.6	.150	.850
1971	4,145.7	594.2	3,551.5	.143	.857
1972	4,342.8	652.7	3,690.2	.150	.850
1973	4,706.6	745.2	3,961.4	.158	.842
1974	5,181.2	816.1	4,365.1	.158	.842
1975	5,763.2	858.8	4,904.4	.149	.851
1976	6,139.3	957.3	5,181.9	.156	.844
1977	6,630.6	1,063.0	5,567.6	.160	.840
1978	7,068.3	1,214.7	5,853.5	.172	.828
1979	8,010.9	1,375.3	6,635.6	.172	.828
1980	8,758.3	1,493.9	7,264.4	.171	.829
1981	9,485.9	1,635.5	7,850.4	.172	.828
1982	10,205.1	1,692.0	8,513.1	.166	.834
1983	10,908.4	1,790.5	9,117.8	.164	.836
1984	11,682.8	1,968.6	9,714.1	.169	.831

To analyze changes in the structure of gross private domestic factor outlay, we present growth rates of full factor output, labor outlay, and property outlay for the period 1948–84 and for eight subperiods in table 5.11. The growth rate of labor input or full labor outlay at constant prices was only slightly greater than the growth of population. The per capita

Table 5.8   **Full Labor Outlay (billions of constant dollars)**

	Full Labor Outlay		Market Labor Outlay		Nonmarket Outlay	
Year	Quantity	Price	Quantity	Price	Quantity	Price
1949	5,739.7	.162	1,000.7	.144	4,743.8	.166
1950	5,808.1	.170	1,031.5	.152	4,783.8	.174
1951	5,939.0	.179	1,087.3	.166	4,862.6	.181
1952	6,042.6	.186	1,108.3	.175	4,945.5	.188
1953	6,150.2	.201	1,100.2	.190	5,059.5	.203
1954	6,253.9	.211	1,084.5	.194	5,176.4	.214
1955	6,381.8	.213	1,119.4	.196	5,270.7	.217
1956	6,509.0	.222	1,144.2	.205	5,373.5	.225
1957	6,675.1	.237	1,141.7	.220	5,539.6	.241
1958	6,786.4	.252	1,099.9	.234	5,687.5	.255
1959	6,885.2	.255	1,140.0	.237	5,748.2	.259
1960	7,031.9	.261	1,166.2	.242	5,868.9	.264
1961	7,208.8	.272	1,150.6	.254	6,057.9	.276
1962	7,329.5	.280	1,183.3	.262	6,147.0	.283
1963	7,476.7	.283	1,191.6	.269	6,284.7	.286
1964	7,620.4	.305	1,196.7	.284	6,422.2	.309
1965	7,708.4	.320	1,238.4	.293	6,470.9	.325
1966	7,779.6	.341	1,275.3	.315	6,507.6	.346
1967	7,919.3	.358	1,286.4	.332	6,635.2	.363
1968	8,101.1	.377	1,322.2	.356	6,781.7	.381
1969	8,331.4	.396	1,371.5	.379	6,963.6	.399
1970	8,535.9	.433	1,353.8	.411	7,183.0	.438
1971	8,728.4	.475	1,328.5	.447	7,397.1	.480
1972	8,784.8	.494	1,384.1	.472	7,400.8	.499
1973	8,867.1	.531	1,443.4	.516	7,425.8	.533
1974	8,990.3	.576	1,458.5	.560	7,533.8	.579
1975	9,132.7	.631	1,405.9	.611	7,726.1	.635
1976	9,269.8	.662	1,461.2	.655	7,808.8	.664
1977	9,493.2	.698	1,527.9	.696	7,965.7	.699
1978	9,674.1	.731	1,632.3	.744	8,041.5	.728
1979	9,851.9	.813	1,672.3	.822	8,179.2	.811
1980	10,037.7	.873	1,692.9	.882	8,344.5	.871
1981	10,150.4	.935	1,718.3	.952	8,431.7	.931
1982	10,205.1	1.000	1,692.0	1.000	8,513.1	1.000
1983	10,254.0	1.064	1,710.4	1.047	8,543.6	1.067
1984	10,324.7	1.132	1,794.2	1.097	8,532.6	1.138

growth rate of labor input was only 0.38 per year for the period as a whole. This growth rate was negative or zero for two of the eight subperiods.

The growth rate of capital input or full property outlay at constant prices exceeded the growth of population by a considerable margin. The per capita growth rate of capital input was 2.02 percent per year. This growth rate was positive throughout the period. The growth rate of total input, full factor outlay in constant prices, is a weighted average

Table 5.9   **Full Gross Private Domestic Factor Outlay (billions of current dollars)**

Year	Full Factor Outlay	Full Property Outlay	Full Labor Outlay	Property Share	Labor Share
1948	988.4	110.8	877.6	.112	.888
1949	1,037.7	108.3	929.5	.104	.896
1950	1,113.3	124.7	988.6	.112	.888
1951	1,203.0	140.3	1,062.7	.117	.883
1952	1,262.8	139.4	1,123.4	.110	.890
1953	1,379.3	144.1	1,235.2	.104	.896
1954	1,462.0	145.2	1,316.8	.099	.901
1955	1,531.8	171.1	1,360.7	.112	.888
1956	1,617.5	171.8	1,445.7	.106	.894
1957	1,759.1	173.9	1,585.2	.099	.901
1958	1,877.6	167.6	1,710.0	.089	.911
1959	1,951.5	195.0	1,756.6	.100	.900
1960	2,027.8	195.0	1,832.8	.096	.904
1961	2,162.8	201.0	1,961.8	.093	.907
1962	2,273.7	221.3	2,052.4	.097	.903
1963	2,360.4	242.0	2,118.4	.103	.897
1964	2,587.4	265.9	2,321.5	.103	.897
1965	2,765.8	300.7	2,465.1	.109	.891
1966	2,980.1	324.4	2,655.7	.109	.891
1967	3,168.4	329.8	2,838.7	.104	.896
1968	3,401.3	344.8	3,056.5	.101	.899
1969	3,651.7	354.9	3,296.7	.097	.903
1970	4,056.9	358.0	3,698.9	.088	.912
1971	4,538.8	393.1	4,145.7	.087	.913
1972	4,785.5	442.7	4,342.8	.092	.908
1973	5,184.1	477.5	4,706.6	.092	.908
1974	5,670.2	489.0	5,181.2	.086	.914
1975	6,335.6	572.3	5,763.2	.090	.910
1976	6,790.7	651.4	6,139.3	.096	.904
1977	7,382.5	752.0	6,630.6	.102	.898
1978	7,911.4	843.2	7,068.3	.107	.893
1979	8,918.2	907.3	8,010.9	.102	.898
1980	9,731.1	972.7	8,758.3	.100	.900
1981	10,620.7	1,134.9	9,485.9	.107	.893
1982	11,435.0	1,229.9	10,205.1	.108	.892
1983	12,272.2	1,363.8	10,908.4	.111	.889
1984	13,254.7	1,571.9	11,682.8	.119	.881

of growth rates of labor and capital inputs and averaged 0.55 per year in per capita terms for the period as a whole.

Comparing the growth rates of input and output, we find that output grew at 2.13 percent per year for the period as a whole and that input grew at 1.84 percent. Input growth has accounted for 86 percent of output growth. This proportion has increased in recent subperiods. For

Table 5.10   Full Gross Domestic Factor Outlay (billions of constant dollars)

Year	Full Factor Outlay		Property Outlay		Labor Outlay	
	Quantity	Price	Quantity	Price	Quantity	Price
1949	6,081.7	.171	399.0	.271	5,739.7	.162
1950	6,170.2	.180	413.5	.302	5,808.1	.170
1951	6,334.3	.190	437.8	.320	5,939.0	.179
1952	6,464.5	.195	457.5	.305	6,042.6	.186
1953	6,586.8	.209	470.4	.306	6,150.2	.201
1954	6,706.3	.218	484.4	.300	6,253.9	.211
1955	6,847.2	.224	496.8	.344	6,381.8	.213
1956	7,001.9	.231	519.0	.331	6,509.0	.222
1957	7,188.8	.245	538.2	.323	6,675.1	.237
1958	7,317.7	.257	554.4	.302	6,786.4	.252
1959	7,423.3	.263	561.7	.347	6,885.2	.255
1960	7,587.1	.267	578.1	.337	7,031.9	.261
1961	7,777.2	.278	591.9	.340	7,208.8	.272
1962	7,910.1	.287	604.0	.366	7,329.5	.280
1963	8,075.3	.292	621.1	.390	7,476.7	.283
1964	8,241.1	.314	640.9	.415	7,620.4	.305
1965	8,357.3	.331	664.0	.453	7,708.4	.320
1966	8,466.7	.352	694.0	.467	7,779.6	.341
1967	8,645.3	.366	727.2	.453	7,919.3	.358
1968	8,857.9	.384	755.5	.456	8,101.1	.377
1969	9,120.3	.400	786.1	.452	8,331.4	.396
1970	9,359.4	.433	819.7	.437	8,535.9	.433
1971	9,577.8	.474	845.7	.465	8,728.4	.475
1972	9,664.5	.495	875.9	.505	8,784.8	.494
1973	9,785.1	.530	914.0	.522	8,867.1	.531
1974	9,953.7	.570	961.4	.509	8,990.3	.576
1975	10,130.2	.625	997.6	.574	9,132.7	.631
1976	10,288.3	.660	1,018.8	.639	9,269.8	.662
1977	10,543.0	.700	1,050.2	.716	9,493.2	.698
1978	10,764.6	.735	1,090.2	.773	9,674.1	.731
1979	10,988.1	.812	1,135.5	.799	9,851.9	.813
1980	11,214.6	.868	1,176.8	.827	10,037.7	.873
1981	11,353.6	.935	1,203.2	.943	10,150.4	.935
1982	11,435.0	1.000	1,229.9	1.000	10,205.1	1.000
1983	11,502.6	1.067	1,248.5	1.092	10,254.0	1.064
1984	11,597.4	1.143	1,271.7	1.236	10,324.7	1.132

example, input growth was 99 percent of output growth in the period 1973–79 and 84 percent in 1979–84.

5.4   Income and Expenditure

In this section, we integrate the estimates of income and expenditure associated with market activities by Fraumeni and Jorgenson (1980) with our estimates of income and expenditure for nonmarket activities.

Table 5.11   **Gross Private National Labor and Property Income, Rates of Growth, 1949–84**

	1949–84	1949–53	1953–57	1957–60	1960–66	1966–69	1969–73	1973–79	1979–84
Full factor outlay:									
Current prices	7.28	7.11	6.08	4.74	6.42	6.77	8.76	9.04	7.93
Constant prices	1.84	1.99	2.19	1.80	1.83	2.48	1.76	1.93	1.08
Constant prices[a]	.55	.33	.41	-.01	.38	1.38	.79	1.09	.03
Price index	5.43	5.02	3.97	2.87	4.61	4.26	7.04	7.11	6.84
Full labor outlay:									
Current prices	7.23	7.11	6.24	4.84	6.18	7.21	8.90	8.86	7.55
Constant prices	1.68	1.73	2.05	1.74	1.68	2.28	1.56	1.76	.94
Constant prices[a]	.38	.07	.28	-.07	.23	1.19	.59	.91	-.11
Price index	5.55	5.39	4.12	3.22	4.46	4.98	7.33	7.10	6.62
Full property outlay:									
Current prices	7.64	7.14	4.70	3.82	8.48	3.00	7.42	10.70	10.99
Constant prices	3.31	4.12	3.37	2.38	3.05	4.15	3.77	3.62	2.27
Constant prices[a]	2.02	2.45	1.59	.58	1.59	3.06	2.80	2.77	1.22
Price index	4.34	3.04	1.35	1.41	5.44	-1.09	3.60	7.09	8.73

[a]This data calculated on a per capita basis.

Following Fraumeni and Jorgenson, we present accounts for the private national sector of the U.S. economy. The income of the private national sector includes compensation for the services of human and nonhuman capital in the private domestic sector, the government sector, and the rest of the world. Income from the services of human capital for the private national sector includes all incomes generated from human capital for individuals in the U.S. population.

The value of income is equal to the value of expenditure for the income and expenditure account. Expenditure in the U.S. economy includes the consumption of market and nonmarket goods and services and saving in the form of human and nonhuman capital. We add to the consumption of market goods and services, as defined by Fraumeni and Jorgenson, our estimates of the value of consumption of nonmarket goods and services. Similarly, we add to estimates of saving in the form of nonhuman capital by Fraumeni and Jorgenson our estimates of saving in the form of human capital.

We present the income side of the income and expenditure account in current prices for the private national sector of the U.S. economy for the year 1982 in table 5.12. We have estimated labor compensation after taxes for individual workers cross-classified by sex, single year of education, and single year of age. Labor compensation after taxes is the sum of labor compensation for all groups of individual workers. For market labor compensation, we estimate personal income taxes attributed to labor income by the methods of Jorgenson and Yun (1986). Income tax not allocated to labor income is allocated to property income to obtain property compensation after taxes. Following Fraumeni and Jorgenson, we treat social insurance funds as part of the private sector of the U.S. national economy. Contributions to social insurance are included and transfers from social insurance funds excluded from labor income. Property income includes the investment income of social insurance funds, less transfers to general government by these funds.

Our next objective is to allocate the value of income for the private national sector of the U.S. economy between labor and property income for the period 1948–84. We first estimate the value of compensation for market and nonmarket labor activities for all years. The value of labor compensation for nonmarket activities is equal to the value of time spent in household production and leisure and the value of time spent on investment in human capital. Our estimates of market labor compensation after taxes are based on those of Fraumeni and Jorgenson. We present estimates of market labor income, nonmarket labor income, and full labor income in current prices in table 5.13 and in constant prices in table 5.14.

The share of nonmarket labor income is far larger than that of market labor income, varying from 0.817 to 0.842 as a proportion of full labor

Table 5.12   **Gross Private National Labor and Property Income, 1982 (billions of current dollars)**

Labor Income	
1.	Private domestic outlay for labor services (table 6.4, line 3, plus our imputation for proprietors)	1,692.0
2.	+ Income originating in general government (table 1.7, line 12)	343.9
3.	+ Compensation of employees in government enterprises (table 6.4, lines 81, 86)	39.6
4.	+ Compensation of employees, rest of world (table 6.4, line 87)	− .1
5.	− Personal income taxes attributed to labor income (our imputation)	263.1
6.	= Private national labor income	1,812.3
7.	+ Nonmarket labor income	8,513.1
8.	= Full private national labor income	10,325.4

Property Income	
1.	Gross private domestic outlay for capital services (our imputation)	1,229.9
2.	+ Corporate profits and net interest, rest of world (table 6.1, line 82)	51.2
3.	+ Investment income of social insurance funds less transfers to general government (table 3.13, lines 7, 9, 18, 20)	33.0
4.	+ Net interest paid by government (table 1.9, line 16 plus line 12, minus table 3.1, line 18, and table 2.1, line 28)	39.0
5.	− Corporate profits tax liability (tables 3.2, line 6, and 3.3, line 6)	63.0
6.	− Business property taxes (table 3.5, lines 24, 25, 26, 27)	102.2
7.	− Personal income taxes attributed to property income (our imputation)	85.4
8.	− Federal estate and gift taxes (table 3.2, line 4)	7.6
9.	− State and local estate and gift taxes (table 3.4, line 11)	2.6
10.	− State and local personal motor vehicle licenses, property taxes, and other taxes (table 3.4, lines 12, 13, 14)	7.3
11.	= Gross private national property income	1,085.1

Note: All table references are to the NIPA tables in the March 1986 *Survey of Current Business.*

income during the period 1948–84. The share of market labor income is nearly constant over the period. The prices of market and nonmarket components of labor income have risen in proportion with a slightly greater increase in the price of nonmarket income since around 1958.

Our final step in allocating the value of income for the private national sector of the U.S. economy between labor and property income for the period 1948–84 is to estimate the value of property compensation for all years. Our estimates of property compensation are based on those of Fraumeni and Jorgenson. We present estimates of full labor income, property income, and income in current prices in table 5.15 and in constant prices in table 5.16. The property share of national income has risen from a minimum of 0.066 in 1974 to a maximum for the period as a whole of 0.107 in 1984.

The price of property income rose less rapidly than the price of labor income until around 1960. The price of property income then fell during

Table 5.13   Full Labor Income (billions of current dollars)

Year	Full Labor Income	Market Labor Income	Nonmarket Labor Income	Market Share	Nonmarket Share
1948	884.2	151.4	732.8	.171	.829
1949	940.5	155.2	785.3	.165	.835
1950	1,000.5	168.9	831.7	.169	.831
1951	1,073.8	191.7	882.2	.178	.822
1952	1,134.6	205.4	929.3	.181	.819
1953	1,246.3	220.0	1,026.3	.177	.823
1954	1,331.6	224.7	1,106.9	.169	.831
1955	1,375.4	233.9	1,141.5	.170	.830
1956	1,460.2	249.2	1,211.0	.171	.829
1957	1,600.7	266.2	1,334.6	.166	.834
1958	1,729.3	276.5	1,452.8	.160	.840
1959	1,775.6	289.1	1,486.5	.163	.837
1960	1,852.8	302.7	1,550.1	.163	.837
1961	1,984.6	315.3	1,669.3	.159	.841
1962	2,076.5	333.8	1,742.6	.161	.839
1963	2,144.6	346.7	1,797.9	.162	.838
1964	2,355.3	373.3	1,982.0	.159	.841
1965	2,500.2	398.1	2,102.1	.159	.841
1966	2,694.1	440.1	2,254.1	.163	.837
1967	2,881.9	470.5	2,411.4	.163	.837
1968	3,100.7	514.9	2,585.8	.166	.834
1969	3,339.0	561.4	2,777.6	.168	.832
1970	3,756.1	613.4	3,142.6	.163	.837
1971	4,216.1	664.5	3,551.5	.158	.842
1972	4,410.1	719.9	3,690.2	.163	.837
1973	4,781.5	820.1	3,961.4	.172	.828
1974	5,258.3	893.1	4,365.1	.170	.830
1975	5,864.1	959.7	4,904.4	.164	.836
1976	6,239.6	1,057.6	5,181.9	.170	.830
1977	6,730.2	1,162.6	5,567.6	.173	.827
1978	7,166.3	1,312.8	5,853.5	.183	.817
1979	8,102.0	1,466.5	6,635.6	.181	.819
1980	8,858.3	1,593.9	7,264.4	.180	.820
1981	9,583.9	1,733.5	7,850.4	.181	.819
1982	10,325.4	1,812.4	8,513.1	.176	.824
1983	11,055.7	1,937.9	9,117.8	.175	.825
1984	11,840.4	2,126.3	9,714.1	.180	.820

the period 1966–69 and resumed its rise during 1969–73. Since that time, the price of property income has been rising more rapidly with a substantial acceleration, relative to the price of labor income, after 1979. The stability of the share of property income through 1980 was the consequence of a steady increase in property income relative to labor income in constant prices. Property income in constant prices

Table 5.14   **Full Labor Income (billions of constant dollars)**

Year	Full Labor Income Quantity	Full Labor Income Price	Market Labor Income Quantity	Market Labor Income Price	Nonmarket Labor Income Quantity	Nonmarket Labor Income Price
1949	5,692.5	.165	948.0	.164	4,743.8	.166
1950	5,774.5	.173	990.4	.171	4,783.8	.174
1951	5,900.3	.182	1,037.5	.185	4,862.6	.181
1952	6,013.7	.189	1,067.7	.192	4,945.5	.188
1953	6,146.3	.203	1,086.4	.202	5,059.5	.203
1954	6,260.3	.213	1,083.1	.207	5,176.4	.214
1955	6,369.1	.216	1,097.5	.213	5,270.7	.217
1956	6,490.3	.225	1,115.8	.223	5,373.5	.225
1957	6,660.5	.240	1,119.6	.238	5,539.6	.241
1958	6,809.8	.254	1,120.4	.247	5,687.5	.255
1959	6,894.3	.258	1,144.4	.253	5,748.2	.259
1960	7,056.7	.263	1,186.6	.255	5,868.9	.264
1961	7,244.0	.274	1,183.7	.266	6,057.9	.276
1962	7,368.1	.282	1,219.1	.274	6,147.0	.283
1963	7,522.8	.285	1,235.8	.281	6,284.7	.286
1964	7,686.1	.306	1,261.6	.296	6,422.2	.309
1965	7,768.0	.322	1,295.7	.307	6,470.9	.325
1966	7,855.2	.343	1,348.3	.326	6,507.6	.346
1967	8,010.2	.360	1,375.8	.342	6,635.2	.363
1968	8,186.9	.379	1,406.0	.366	6,781.7	.381
1969	8,402.5	.397	1,439.7	.390	6,963.6	.399
1970	8,636.6	.435	1,453.6	.422	7,183.0	.438
1971	8,858.5	.476	1,460.1	.455	7,397.1	.480
1972	8,889.5	.496	1,488.3	.484	7,400.8	.499
1973	8,966.5	.533	1,540.9	.532	7,425.8	.533
1974	9,097.8	.578	1,564.2	.571	7,533.8	.579
1975	9,313.6	.630	1,587.3	.605	7,726.1	.635
1976	9,429.8	.662	1,621.3	.652	7,808.8	.664
1977	9,624.0	.699	1,658.6	.701	7,965.7	.699
1978	9,765.6	.734	1,723.4	.762	8,041.5	.728
1979	9,903.9	.818	1,725.1	.850	8,179.2	.811
1980	10,073.8	.879	1,730.9	.921	8,344.5	.871
1981	10,213.6	.938	1,782.2	.973	8,431.7	.931
1982	10,325.4	1.000	1,812.4	1.000	8,513.1	1.000
1983	10,401.6	1.063	1,858.3	1.043	8,543.6	1.067
1984	10,443.1	1.134	1,911.9	1.112	8,532.6	1.138

corresponds to the services of physical or nonhuman capital, while labor income corresponds to the services of human capital.

We next analyze the structure of full private national income over the postwar period. In table 5.17 we present growth rates of full income, labor income, and property income for the period 1949–84 and for eight subperiods. We give growth rates for each measure of income in current

Table 5.15   Full Private National Income (billions of current dollars)

Year	Full Income	Full Property Income	Full Labor Income	Property Share	Labor Share
1948	974.8	90.6	884.2	.093	.907
1949	1,030.7	90.2	940.5	.087	.913
1950	1,096.9	96.4	1,000.5	.088	.912
1951	1,180.3	106.5	1,073.8	.090	.910
1952	1,242.0	107.4	1,134.6	.086	.914
1953	1,356.3	110.1	1,246.3	.081	.919
1954	1,445.2	113.6	1,331.6	.079	.921
1955	1,509.2	133.8	1,375.4	.089	.911
1956	1,592.9	132.7	1,460.2	.083	.917
1957	1,735.0	134.3	1,600.7	.077	.923
1958	1,858.9	129.6	1,729.3	.070	.930
1959	1,926.5	150.9	1,775.6	.078	.922
1960	2,002.8	150.1	1,852.8	.075	.925
1961	2,138.0	153.4	1,984.6	.072	.928
1962	2,247.7	171.2	2,076.5	.076	.924
1963	2,332.8	188.2	2,144.6	.081	.919
1964	2,565.4	210.1	2,355.3	.082	.918
1965	2,739.3	239.1	2,500.2	.087	.913
1966	2,950.6	256.5	2,694.1	.087	.913
1967	3,141.8	259.9	2,881.9	.083	.917
1968	3,364.3	263.6	3,100.7	.078	.922
1969	3,605.2	266.2	3,339.0	.074	.926
1970	4,029.9	273.8	3,756.1	.068	.932
1971	4,517.6	301.6	4,216.1	.067	.933
1972	4,749.3	339.2	4,410.1	.071	.929
1973	5,149.4	367.9	4,781.5	.071	.929
1974	5,632.3	374.0	5,258.3	.066	.934
1975	6,319.3	455.2	5,864.1	.072	.928
1976	6,756.8	517.3	6,239.5	.077	.923
1977	7,331.1	600.9	6,730.2	.082	.918
1978	7,846.5	680.2	7,166.3	.087	.913
1979	8,846.1	744.1	8,102.0	.084	.916
1980	9,666.9	808.6	8,858.3	.084	.916
1981	10,555.8	972.0	9,583.9	.092	.908
1982	11,410.5	1,085.1	10,325.4	.095	.905
1983	12,268.7	1,212.9	11,055.7	.099	.901
1984	13,251.8	1,411.4	11,840.4	.107	.893

and constant prices and in per capita terms. The growth rate of national income in constant prices was positive throughout the period, averaging 1.89 percent per year. The growth rate of property income in constant prices was considerably greater than that of labor income. The growth rate of property income averaged 3.64 percent per year, while the growth rate of labor income averaged only 1.73 percent.

Table 5.16   Full Private National Income (billions of constant dollars)

Year	Full Income Quantity	Price	Property Income Quantity	Price	Labor Income Quantity	Price
1949	6,013.2	.171	338.6	.266	5,692.5	.165
1950	6,110.8	.180	350.6	.275	5,774.5	.173
1951	6,243.7	.189	358.1	.297	5,900.3	.182
1952	6,367.0	.195	367.2	.292	6,013.7	.189
1953	6,511.1	.208	377.8	.291	6,146.3	.203
1954	6,638.8	.218	389.9	.291	6,260.3	.213
1955	6,761.8	.223	402.1	.333	6,369.1	.216
1956	6,896.3	.231	413.8	.321	6,490.3	.225
1957	7,076.3	.245	424.0	.317	6,660.5	.240
1958	7,238.2	.257	436.2	.297	6,809.8	.254
1959	7,333.4	.263	446.0	.338	6,894.3	.258
1960	7,504.8	.267	455.4	.330	7,056.7	.263
1961	7,700.4	.278	464.5	.330	7,244.0	.274
1962	7,836.4	.287	475.9	.360	7,368.1	.282
1963	8,007.2	.291	490.7	.384	7,522.8	.285
1964	8,187.1	.313	506.0	.415	7,686.1	.306
1965	8,295.0	.330	526.7	.454	7,768.0	.322
1966	8,409.4	.351	548.3	.468	7,855.2	.343
1967	8,595.2	.366	574.6	.452	8,010.2	.360
1968	8,806.3	.382	605.4	.436	8,186.9	.379
1969	9,049.6	.398	631.6	.421	8,402.5	.397
1970	9,304.2	.433	651.7	.420	8,636.6	.435
1971	9,553.2	.473	678.9	.444	8,858.5	.476
1972	9,614.8	.494	710.8	.477	8,889.5	.496
1973	9,717.0	.530	736.7	.499	8,966.5	.533
1974	9,881.6	.570	772.6	.484	9,097.8	.578
1975	10,130.2	.624	807.0	.564	9,313.6	.630
1976	10,302.8	.656	867.9	.596	9,429.8	.662
1977	10,540.1	.696	913.0	.658	9,624.0	.699
1978	10,711.6	.733	943.4	.721	9,765.6	.734
1979	10,877.8	.813	971.8	.766	9,903.9	.818
1980	11,076.1	.873	1,001.0	.808	10,073.8	.879
1981	11,257.5	.938	1,043.8	.931	10,213.6	.938
1982	11,410.5	1.000	1,085.1	1.000	10,325.4	1.000
1983	11,552.4	1.062	1,151.1	1.054	10,401.6	1.063
1984	11,655.9	1.137	1.212.6	1.164	10,443.1	1.134

To complete the income and expenditure account for the private national sector of the U.S. economy, we add government transfer payments to persons, other than benefits from social insurance funds, to full national income to obtain national receipts. To allocate the value of receipts between consumption and saving, we first estimate the value of full consumption. Full consumption is the sum of the consumption of market goods and services, as defined by Fraumeni and Jorgenson,

Table 5.17   Full Private National Income Rates of Growth, 1949–84

	1949–84	1949–53	1953–57	1957–60	1960–66	1966–69	1969–73	1973–79	1979–84
Full national income:									
Current prices	7.30	6.86	6.16	4.78	6.46	6.68	8.91	9.02	8.08
Constant prices	1.89	1.99	2.08	1.96	1.90	2.45	1.78	1.88	1.38
Constant prices[a]	.60	.33	.31	.15	.45	1.35	.81	1.04	.33
Price index	5.41	4.90	4.09	2.87	4.56	4.19	7.16	7.13	6.71
Full labor income:									
Current prices	7.24	7.04	6.26	4.88	6.24	7.15	8.98	8.79	7.59
Constant prices	1.73	1.92	2.01	1.93	1.79	2.25	1.62	1.66	1.06
Constant prices[a]	.44	.26	.24	.12	.34	1.15	.66	.81	.01
Price index	5.51	5.18	4.19	3.05	4.43	4.87	7.36	7.14	6.53
Full property income:									
Current prices	7.86	4.98	4.97	3.71	8.93	1.24	8.09	11.74	12.80
Constant prices	3.64	2.74	2.88	2.38	3.09	4.71	3.85	4.62	4.43
Constant prices[a]	2.35	1.08	1.11	.57	1.64	3.62	2.88	3.77	3.38
Price index	4.22	2.25	2.14	1.34	5.82	−3.53	4.25	7.14	8.37

[a]This data calculated on a per capita basis.

and our estimates of the value of household production and leisure. Next, we estimate the value of full savings. Full saving is the sum of saving in the form of nonhuman capital, again as defined by Fraumeni and Jorgenson, and our estimates of saving in the form of human capital. We present estimates of full receipts and expenditures for the year 1982 in table 5.18.

Our next objective is to allocate the value of full receipts for the private national sector of the U.S. economy between consumption and

Table 5.18   **Gross Private National Receipts and Expenditures, 1982 (billions of current dollars)**

	Receipts	
1.	Gross private domestic factor outlay	2,921.9
2.	+ Income originating in general government (table 1.7, line 12)	343.9
3.	+ Compensation of employees in government enterprises (table 6.4, lines 81, 86)	39.6
4.	+ Income originating in rest of world (table 6.1, line 82)	51.2
5.	+ Investment income of social insurance funds (table 3.13, lines 7, 18)	39.9
6.	− Transfer to general government from social insurance funds (table 3.13, lines 9, 20)	6.9
7.	+ Net interest paid by government (table 1.9, line 16 plus line 12, minus table 3.1, line 18, and table 2.1, line 28)	39.0
8.	− Corporate profits tax liability (tables 3.2, line 6, and 3.3, line 6)	63.0
9.	− Business property taxes (table 3.5, lines 24, 25, 26, 27)	102.2
10.	− Personal tax and nontax payments (table 2.1, line 24)	409.3
11.	+ Personal nontax payments (tables 3.4, lines 8, 15)	43.5
12.	= Gross private national income	2,897.5
13.	+ Nonmarket labor income	8,513.1
14.	= Full gross private national income	11,410.7
15.	+ Government transfer payment to persons other than benefits from social insurance funds (table 3.11, lines 1, 3, 29)	99.6
16.	= Full gross private national consumer receipts	11,510.3

	Expenditures	
1.	Personal consumption expenditures (table 1.1, line 2)	2,050.7
2.	− Personal consumption expenditures, durable goods (table 1.1, line 3)	252.7
3.	+ Imputation for nonhuman capital services	338.7
4.	= Private national consumption expenditure	2,136.7
5.	+ Consumption of nonmarket goods and services	3,944.5
6.	= Full private national consumption expenditure	6,081.2
7.	+ Personal transfer payments to foreigners (table 2.1, line 29)	1.3
8.	+ Personal nontax payments (table 3.4, lines 8, 15)	43.5
9.	= Full private national consumer outlays	6,126.0
10.	+ Full gross private national saving[a]	5,384.4
11.	= Full private national expenditures	11,510.3

Note: All table references are to the NIPA tables in the March 1986 *Survey of Current Business*.

[a]See table 5.26, line 14, below.

saving for the period 1948–84. We first estimate the value of consumer outlays for all years. We present estimates of market consumer outlays, nonmarket consumer outlays, and full consumer outlays in current prices in table 5.19 and in constant prices in table 5.20. The value of consumer outlays in nonmarket goods and services predominates in consumer outlays, averaging around 65 percent of outlays over the period 1948–84. The market share of full consumer outlays reached a

Table 5.19   Full Consumer Outlays (billions of current dollars)

Year	Full Consumer Outlays	Market Consumer Outlays	Nonmarket Consumer Outlays	Market Share	Nonmarket Share
1948	522.0	182.1	339.9	.349	.651
1949	553.6	183.8	369.9	.332	.668
1950	585.9	195.6	390.4	.334	.666
1951	620.1	215.1	404.9	.347	.653
1952	647.8	227.5	420.3	.351	.649
1953	702.0	239.3	462.6	.341	.659
1954	747.5	248.3	499.3	.332	.668
1955	770.6	265.0	505.6	.344	.656
1956	808.8	276.3	532.5	.342	.658
1957	868.8	289.5	579.3	.333	.667
1958	933.1	299.8	633.3	.321	.679
1959	962.3	322.3	640.0	.335	.665
1960	1,000.6	335.3	665.3	.335	.665
1961	1,065.6	348.8	716.8	.327	.673
1962	1,115.3	368.8	746.5	.331	.669
1963	1,157.0	390.4	766.6	.337	.663
1964	1,263.0	421.6	841.5	.334	.666
1965	1,366.6	457.6	909.0	.335	.665
1966	1,480.7	495.0	985.7	.334	.666
1967	1,575.7	520.0	1,055.7	.330	.670
1968	1,678.9	559.8	1,119.1	.333	.667
1969	1,797.8	603.1	1,194.7	.335	.665
1970	1,998.8	652.4	1,346.5	.326	.674
1971	2,220.6	698.7	1,521.9	.315	.685
1972	2,390.8	768.9	1,621.9	.322	.678
1973	2,634.3	843.0	1,791.2	.320	.680
1974	2,888.1	920.1	1,968.1	.319	.681
1975	3,213.3	1,031.1	2,182.2	.321	.679
1976	3,510.6	1,146.1	2,364.5	.326	.674
1977	3,800.6	1,280.3	2,520.3	.337	.663
1978	4,162.2	1,429.8	2,732.5	.344	.656
1979	4,685.4	1,595.1	3,090.3	.340	.660
1980	5,064.9	1,775.2	3,289.7	.350	.650
1981	5,550.6	1,989.6	3,561.0	.358	.642
1982	6,126.0	2,181.5	3,944.5	.356	.644
1983	6,635.5	2,360.9	4,274.7	.356	.644
1984	7,184.5	2,593.6	4,590.9	.361	.639

Table 5.20   **Full Consumer Outlays (billions of constant dollars)**

Year	Full Consumer Outlays		Market Consumer Outlays		Nonmarket Consumer Outlays	
	Quantity	Price	Quantity	Price	Quantity	Price
1949	2,727.1	.203	695.9	.264	2,076.9	.178
1950	2,784.7	.210	725.5	.270	2,098.9	.186
1951	2,828.5	.219	751.8	.286	2,110.1	.192
1952	2,885.0	.225	776.1	.293	2,138.2	.197
1953	2,958.2	.237	799.9	.299	2,186.7	.212
1954	3,014.8	.248	816.4	.304	2,226.8	.224
1955	3,091.4	.249	864.6	.306	2,246.1	.225
1956	3,152.1	.257	891.8	.310	2,276.4	.234
1957	3,223.8	.269	915.1	.316	2,324.3	.249
1958	3,295.0	.283	926.6	.324	2,386.5	.265
1959	3,363.7	.286	971.9	.332	2,404.2	.266
1960	3,424.6	.292	992.8	.338	2,443.7	.272
1961	3,523.3	.302	1,020.0	.342	2,515.8	.285
1962	3,606.9	.309	1,061.7	.347	2,554.6	.292
1963	3,701.4	.313	1,103.1	.354	2,605.3	.294
1964	3,815.9	.331	1,169.7	.360	2,648.0	.318
1965	3,932.4	.348	1,242.2	.368	2,687.9	.338
1966	4,044.1	.366	1,305.9	.379	2,733.8	.361
1967	4,152.6	.379	1,351.6	.385	2,796.1	.378
1968	4,258.3	.394	1,400.5	.400	2,852.6	.392
1969	4,358.2	.413	1,446.9	.417	2,905.6	.411
1970	4,487.3	.445	1,501.3	.435	2,980.4	.452
1971	4,621.9	.480	1,538.3	.454	3,077.4	.495
1972	4,771.3	.501	1,623.7	.474	3,144.0	.516
1973	4,875.9	.540	1,680.2	.502	3,194.0	.561
1974	4,964.4	.582	1,673.9	.550	3,285.3	.599
1975	5,151.4	.624	1,739.9	.593	3,406.3	.641
1976	5,312.1	.661	1,826.1	.628	3,483.1	.679
1977	5,460.0	.696	1,908.5	.671	3,550.5	.710
1978	5,584.0	.745	1,989.1	.719	3,596.0	.760
1979	5,729.4	.818	2,039.2	.782	3,691.1	.837
1980	5,841.7	.867	2,058.4	.862	3,783.5	.869
1981	5,962.0	.931	2,106.5	.944	3,855.6	.924
1982	6,126.0	1.000	2,181.5	1.000	3,944.5	1.000
1983	6,256.6	1.061	2,257.0	1.046	3,999.9	1.069
1984	6,398.0	1.123	2,378.5	1.090	4,022.1	1.141

minimum of 0.315 in 1971 and has risen to a maximum of 0.361 in 1984 at the end of the period, a rise of 15 percent; however, there is almost no trend in this share for the period as a whole. The price of nonmarket consumer outlays has increased more rapidly than the price of market outlays. Constancy of the market share has been maintained by a more rapid growth at market consumer outlays in constant prices.

We combine our estimates of saving in the form of human capital with estimates of saving in the form of nonhuman capital, based on those of Fraumeni and Jorgenson, to obtain the value of full saving. We present estimates of saving in the form of human capital, saving in the form of nonhuman capital, and full saving in current prices in table 5.21 and constant prices in table 5.22. The share of saving in the form of human capital greatly predominates, ranging from 0.881 in 1961 to 0.829 in 1984, a very modest decline. The price of saving in the form

Table 5.21   **Full Gross Private National Saving (billions of current dollars)**

Year	Full Saving	Nonhuman Saving	Human Saving	Nonhuman Share	Human Share
1948	460.3	67.4	392.9	.146	.854
1949	483.8	68.3	415.5	.141	.859
1950	518.6	77.3	441.3	.149	.851
1951	566.4	89.2	477.2	.157	.843
1952	600.2	91.3	508.9	.152	.848
1953	660.7	97.0	563.7	.147	.853
1954	704.1	96.5	607.6	.137	.863
1955	745.2	109.3	635.9	.147	.853
1956	791.0	112.4	678.6	.142	.858
1957	873.5	118.3	755.2	.135	.865
1958	933.9	114.4	819.5	.122	.878
1959	971.9	125.4	846.5	.129	.871
1960	1,010.4	125.7	884.7	.124	.876
1961	1,081.2	128.7	952.5	.119	.881
1962	1,141.4	145.3	996.1	.127	.873
1963	1,185.3	154.0	1,031.3	.130	.870
1964	1,312.7	172.2	1,140.5	.131	.869
1965	1,384.0	190.8	1,193.2	.138	.862
1966	1,482.0	213.7	1,268.3	.144	.856
1967	1,580.8	225.1	1,355.7	.142	.858
1968	1,702.7	236.0	1,466.7	.139	.861
1969	1,827.9	245.0	1,582.9	.134	.866
1970	2,056.0	259.8	1,796.2	.126	.874
1971	2,327.6	298.0	2,029.6	.128	.872
1972	2,392.7	324.4	2,068.3	.136	.864
1973	2,553.2	383.0	2,170.2	.150	.850
1974	2,789.8	392.7	2,397.1	.141	.859
1975	3,163.1	440.9	2,722.2	.139	.861
1976	3,306.7	489.3	2,817.4	.148	.852
1977	3,593.1	545.8	3,047.3	.152	.848
1978	3,752.7	631.6	3,121.1	.168	.832
1979	4,236.1	690.9	3,545.2	.163	.837
1980	4,691.4	716.7	3,974.7	.153	.847
1981	5,102.5	813.1	4,289.4	.159	.841
1982	5,384.4	815.8	4,568.6	.152	.848
1983	5,739.7	896.6	4,843.1	.156	.844
1984	6,178.7	1,055.5	5,123.2	.171	.829

Table 5.22   **Full Gross Private National Saving (billions of constant dollars)**

Year	Full Saving		Nonhuman Saving		Human Saving	
	Quantity	Price	Quantity	Price	Quantity	Price
1949	2,864.8	.169	239.5	.285	2,669.1	.156
1950	2,975.7	.174	299.4	.258	2,686.5	.164
1951	3,044.3	.186	301.2	.296	2,756.9	.173
1952	3,073.8	.195	287.4	.318	2,812.6	.181
1953	3,155.4	.209	300.3	.323	2,878.3	.196
1954	3,224.9	.218	298.0	.324	2,956.1	.206
1955	3,373.2	.221	350.3	.312	3,032.9	.210
1956	3,433.0	.230	343.2	.328	3,106.6	.218
1957	3,537.6	.247	336.7	.351	3,226.6	.234
1958	3,589.4	.260	315.6	.363	3,312.7	.247
1959	3,691.5	.263	360.2	.348	3,356.2	.252
1960	3,761.6	.269	353.7	.355	3,438.3	.257
1961	3,873.3	.279	352.8	.365	3,556.0	.268
1962	3,973.6	.287	392.8	.370	3,606.4	.276
1963	4,091.6	.290	419.0	.368	3,694.2	.279
1964	4,229.9	.310	455.7	.378	3,790.0	.301
1965	4,297.6	.322	506.2	.377	3,797.7	.314
1966	4,336.2	.342	549.4	.389	3,786.3	.335
1967	4,402.9	.359	552.1	.408	3,851.1	.352
1968	4,514.8	.377	572.6	.412	3,941.8	.372
1969	4,654.6	.393	582.6	.420	4,072.2	.389
1970	4,789.1	.429	572.9	.453	4,218.3	.426
1971	4,963.6	.469	629.0	.474	4,335.4	.468
1972	4,944.6	.484	676.9	.479	4,268.6	.485
1973	5,003.0	.510	764.6	.501	4,240.4	.512
1974	4,973.5	.561	720.9	.545	4,253.6	.564
1975	5,019.2	.630	696.2	.633	4,323.7	.630
1976	5,076.7	.651	748.6	.654	4,328.4	.651
1977	5,216.0	.689	798.5	.684	4,418.0	.690
1978	5,305.7	.707	857.6	.737	4,447.7	.702
1979	5,350.5	.792	862.2	.801	4,487.8	.790
1980	5,379.2	.872	818.9	.875	4,560.3	.872
1981	5,430.2	.940	854.3	.952	4,575.7	.937
1982	5,384.4	1.000	815.8	1.000	4,568.6	1.000
1983	5,428.9	1.057	886.8	1.011	4,543.7	1.066
1984	5,527.8	1.118	1,028.4	1.026	4,510.4	1.136

of human capital has risen more rapidly than the price of nonhuman saving, but the growth of nonhuman saving in constant prices has been much more rapid than the growth of human saving.

We combine our estimates of full consumer outlays with our estimates of saving in the form of human and nonhuman capital to obtain the value of full expenditures. We present estimates of full consumer outlays, saving, and expenditures in current prices in table 5.23 and in

Table 5.23   **Full Private National Expenditures (billions of current dollars)**

Year	Full Expenditures	Full Consumer Outlays	Full Saving	Outlays Share	Saving Share
1948	982.3	522.0	460.3	.531	.469
1949	1,037.4	553.6	483.8	.534	.466
1950	1,104.5	585.9	518.6	.530	.470
1951	1,186.5	620.1	566.4	.523	.477
1952	1,248.0	647.8	600.2	.519	.481
1953	1,362.6	702.0	660.7	.515	.485
1954	1,451.7	747.5	704.1	.515	.485
1955	1,515.8	770.6	745.2	.508	.492
1956	1,599.7	808.8	791.0	.506	.494
1957	1,742.3	868.8	873.5	.499	.501
1958	1,867.0	933.1	933.9	.500	.500
1959	1,934.2	962.3	971.9	.498	.502
1960	2,011.0	1,000.6	1,010.4	.498	.502
1961	2,146.8	1,065.6	1,081.2	.496	.504
1962	2,256.7	1,115.3	1,141.4	.494	.506
1963	2,342.3	1,157.0	1,185.3	.494	.506
1964	2,575.7	1,263.0	1,312.7	.490	.510
1965	2,750.5	1,366.6	1,384.0	.497	.503
1966	2,962.7	1,480.7	1,482.0	.500	.500
1967	3,156.5	1,575.7	1,580.8	.499	.501
1968	3,381.6	1,678.9	1,702.7	.496	.504
1969	3,625.7	1,797.8	1,827.9	.496	.504
1970	4,054.8	1,998.8	2,056.0	.493	.507
1971	4,548.2	2,220.6	2,327.6	.488	.512
1972	4,783.5	2,390.8	2,392.7	.500	.500
1973	5,187.5	2,634.3	2,553.2	.508	.492
1974	5,677.9	2,888.1	2,789.8	.509	.491
1975	6,376.4	3,213.3	3,163.1	.504	.496
1976	6,817.3	3,510.6	3,306.7	.515	.485
1977	7,393.7	3,800.6	3,593.1	.514	.486
1978	7,914.9	4,162.2	3,752.7	.526	.474
1979	8,921.5	4,685.4	4,236.1	.525	.475
1980	9,756.3	5,064.9	4,691.4	.519	.481
1981	10,653.1	5,550.6	5,102.5	.521	.479
1982	11,510.3	6,126.0	5,384.4	.532	.468
1983	12,375.3	6,635.5	5,739.7	.536	.464
1984	13,363.2	7,184.5	6,178.7	.538	.462

constant prices in table 5.24. The share of consumer outlays slightly predominates in full expenditures for most of the period, ranging from 0.490 in 1964 to 0.538 in 1984. The share of saving has trended downward since 1970. The price of saving has risen relative to the price of consumer outlays, but the growth rate of outlays in constant prices has been considerably greater than the growth rate of saving.

Table 5.24   **Full Private National Expenditures (billions of constant dollars)**

Year	Full Expenditures		Consumer Outlays		Full Saving	
	Quantity	Price	Quantity	Price	Quantity	Price
1949	5,592.9	.185	2,727.1	.203	2,864.8	.169
1950	5,756.8	.192	2,784.7	.210	2,975.7	.174
1951	5,867.3	.202	2,828.5	.219	3,044.3	.186
1952	5,955.5	.210	2,885.0	.225	3,073.8	.195
1953	6,110.0	.223	2,958.2	.237	3,155.4	.209
1954	6,235.4	.233	3,014.8	.248	3,224.9	.218
1955	6,456.3	.235	3,091.4	.249	3,373.2	.221
1956	6,576.9	.243	3,152.1	.257	3,433.0	.230
1957	6,751.8	.258	3,223.8	.269	3,537.6	.247
1958	6,875.7	.272	3,295.0	.283	3,589.4	.260
1959	7,045.2	.275	3,363.7	.286	3,691.5	.263
1960	7,175.9	.280	3,424.6	.292	3,761.6	.269
1961	7,385.8	.291	3,523.3	.302	3,873.3	.279
1962	7,569.1	.298	3,606.9	.309	3,973.6	.287
1963	7,780.8	.301	3,701.4	.313	4,091.6	.290
1964	8,032.8	.321	3,815.9	.331	4,229.9	.310
1965	8,218.8	.335	3,932.4	.348	4,297.6	.322
1966	8,371.8	.354	4,044.1	.366	4,336.2	.342
1967	8,548.3	.369	4,152.6	.379	4,402.9	.359
1968	8,765.7	.386	4,258.3	.394	4,514.8	.377
1969	9,004.4	.403	4,358.2	.413	4,654.6	.393
1970	9,267.8	.438	4,487.3	.445	4,789.1	.429
1971	9,576.2	.475	4,621.9	.480	4,963.6	.469
1972	9,709.0	.493	4,771.3	.501	4,944.6	.484
1973	9,873.1	.525	4,875.9	.540	5,003.0	.510
1974	9,934.8	.572	4,964.4	.582	4,973.5	.561
1975	10,168.4	.627	5,151.4	.624	5,019.2	.630
1976	10,386.6	.656	5,312.1	.661	5,076.7	.651
1977	10,673.7	.693	5,460.0	.696	5,216.0	.689
1978	10,887.9	.727	5,584.0	.745	5,305.7	.707
1979	11,080.0	.805	5,729.4	.818	5,350.5	.792
1980	11,221.6	.869	5,841.7	.867	5,379.2	.872
1981	11,392.7	.935	5,962.0	.931	5,430.2	.940
1982	11,510.3	1.000	6,126.0	1.000	5,384.4	1.000
1983	11,685.5	1.059	6,256.6	1.061	5,428.9	1.057
1984	11,925.9	1.121	6,398.0	1.123	5,527.8	1.118

We next analyze the structure of full private national expenditures by presenting growth rates of full expenditures, consumer outlays, and saving in current and constant prices for the period 1948–84 and for eight subperiods in table 5.25. We also give growth rates of expenditures, outlays, and saving in constant prices per capita. The growth rate of consumer outlays per capita averaged 1.14 percent per year for

Table 5.25   Full Private National Expenditures, Rates of Growth, 1949–84

	1949–84	1949–53	1953–57	1957–60	1960–66	1966–69	1969–73	1973–79	1979–84
Full expenditures:									
Current prices	7.30	6.82	6.15	4.78	6.46	6.73	8.96	9.04	8.08
Constant prices	2.16	2.21	2.50	2.03	2.57	2.43	2.30	1.92	1.47
Constant prices[a]	.87	.55	.73	.22	1.12	1.33	1.33	1.08	.42
Price index	5.15	4.67	3.64	2.73	3.91	4.32	6.61	7.12	6.62
Full consumer outlays:									
Current prices	7.32	5.94	5.33	4.71	6.53	6.47	9.55	9.60	8.55
Constant prices	2.44	2.03	2.15	2.01	2.77	2.49	2.81	2.69	2.21
Constant prices[a]	1.14	.37	.38	.21	1.32	1.40	1.84	1.85	1.16
Price index	4.89	3.87	3.17	2.73	3.76	4.03	6.70	6.92	6.34
Full saving:									
Current prices	7.28	7.79	6.98	4.85	6.38	6.99	8.35	8.44	7.55
Constant prices	1.88	2.42	2.86	2.05	2.37	2.36	1.80	1.12	.65
Constant prices[a]	.58	.75	1.09	.24	.92	1.26	.84	.28	-.40
Price index	5.40	5.31	4.18	2.84	4.00	4.63	6.52	7.34	6.89

[a]This data calculated on a per capita basis.

the period as a whole. Especially rapid growth has characterized the period since 1960, with only modest retardation after 1979. By contrast, the growth rate of saving per capita averaged only 0.58 percent per year for the period as a whole, with rapid growth in 1953–57 and 1966–69 and negative growth from 1979–84.

5.5 Accumulation and Wealth

Our final objective is to integrate our measures of saving in the form of human and nonhuman capital with measures of human and nonhuman wealth. For this purpose, we implement an accumulation account for the private national sector of the U.S. economy. This account includes saving in the form of human and nonhuman capital and depreciation on both forms of capital. Depreciation on human capital is due to aging, deaths, and emigration. Depreciation on nonhuman capital is due to deterioration and retirement of investment goods with age. The difference between saving and depreciation is the net saving of the private national sector.

The accumulation account also includes revaluation of human and nonhuman capital. Revaluation of human capital is due to changes in lifetime incomes for individuals of a given age, sex, and education. Revaluation of nonhuman capital is due to changes in asset values for investment goods of a given age. The change in the value of wealth from period to period is the sum of net saving and revaluation of capital. The value of saving in the form of human and nonhuman capital is equal to the value of capital formation in both forms. We add saving, depreciation, and revaluation in the form of nonhuman capital, as defined by Fraumeni and Jorgenson (1980), to our estimates of saving, depreciation, and revaluation in the form of human capital.

We present the accumulation account in current prices for the private national sector of the U.S. economy for the year 1982 in table 5.26. Human capital saving is very large by comparison with private national saving, which is very similar to the corresponding concept in the U.S. national accounts. Depreciation is a very large proportion of full gross private national saving, which includes human and nonhuman saving. Finally, in 1982, revaluation of human and nonhuman capital was far more important than net saving in the change in private national wealth. Saving in the accumulation account is equal to saving in the income and expenditure account; in the accumulation account saving is equal to capital formation.

Our next objective is to allocate change in wealth for the private national sector of the U.S. economy among revaluation, saving, and depreciation for the period 1948–84. We first estimate the value of saving and depreciation for all years. Our estimates of full gross saving,

Table 5.26   **Gross Private National Capital Accumulation, 1982 (billions of current dollars)**

Saving	
1. Personal saving (table 5.1, line 3)	153.9
2. + Undistributed corporate profits (table 5.1, line 5)	39.6
3. + Corporate inventory valuation adjustment (table 5.1, line 6)	− 10.4
4. + Capital consumption adjustment (table 5.1, line 7)	− 9.2
5. + Corporate capital consumption allowances with capital consumption adjustment (table 5.1, line 8)	235.0
6. + Noncorporate capital consumption allowances with capital consumption adjustment (table 5.1, line 9)	148.2
7. + Private wage accruals less disbursements (table 5.1, line 10)	.0
8. + Personal consumption expenditures, durable goods (table 1.1, line 3)	252.7
9. + Surplus, social insurance funds (table 3.13, lines 11, 22)	6.1
10. + Government wage accruals less disbursements (table 3.2, line 30, and table 3.3, line 25)	.0
11. + Statistical discrepancy (table 1.9, line 8)	− .1
12. = Gross private national saving	815.8
13. + Human capital saving	4,568.6
14. = Full gross private national saving	5,384.4
15. − Depreciation	2,624.8
16. = Net private national saving	2,759.5
17. + Revaluation	10,643.0
18. = Change in private national wealth	13,402.5

Capital Formation	
1. Gross private domestic investment (table 1.1, line 6)	447.3
2. + Personal consumption expenditures, durable goods (table 1.1, line 3)	252.7
3. + Deficit of federal government (table 3.2, line 31)	145.9
4. + Deficit of state and local governments (table 3.3, line 26)	− 35.1
5. − Deficit, federal social insurance funds (table 3.13, line 11)	30.8
6. − Deficit, state and local social insurance funds (table 3.13, line 22)	− 36.9
7. + Wage accruals less disbursement, federal government (table 3.2, line 30)	.0
8. + Wage accruals less disbursement, state and local government (table 3.3, line 25)	.0
9. + Net foreign investment (table 5.1, line 17)	− 1.0
10. = Gross private national capital formation	815.8
11. + Gross private national human capital formation	4,568.6
12. = Full gross private national capital formation	5,384.4

Note: All table references are to the NIPA tables in the March 1986 *Survey of Current Business*.

net saving, and depreciation are given in current prices in table 5.27 and in constant prices in table 5.28. The share of net saving in gross saving has declined from 0.672 in 1964 to 0.503 in 1984. The share of depreciation has risen from 0.328 to 0.497 between these two years. The prices of net saving and depreciation are nearly proportional to each other so that the rise in the share of depreciation is due to a decline in net saving in constant prices from its peak level in 1971.

Table 5.27   **Full Gross Private National Saving (billions of current dollars)**

Year	Full Gross Saving	Full Net Saving	Depreciation	Net Share	Depreciation Share
1949	483.8	306.9	176.8	.634	.366
1950	518.6	327.6	191.0	.632	.368
1951	566.4	358.8	207.6	.634	.366
1952	600.2	379.7	220.5	.633	.367
1953	660.7	421.9	238.8	.639	.361
1954	704.1	451.3	252.8	.641	.359
1955	745.2	480.6	264.5	.645	.355
1956	791.0	508.5	282.4	.643	.357
1957	873.5	571.0	302.5	.654	.346
1958	933.9	614.7	319.2	.658	.342
1959	971.9	640.8	331.1	.659	.341
1960	1,010.4	670.4	340.1	.663	.337
1961	1,081.2	720.2	361.0	.666	.334
1962	1,141.4	762.8	378.6	.668	.332
1963	1,185.3	791.7	393.6	.668	.332
1964	1,312.7	882.7	430.0	.672	.328
1965	1,384.0	923.4	460.6	.667	.333
1966	1,482.0	980.1	501.9	.661	.339
1967	1,580.8	1,037.4	543.4	.656	.344
1968	1,702.7	1,109.1	593.6	.651	.349
1969	1,827.9	1,184.5	643.4	.648	.352
1970	2,056.0	1,339.9	716.1	.652	.348
1971	2,327.6	1,526.0	801.6	.656	.344
1972	2,392.7	1,515.0	877.7	.633	.367
1973	2,553.2	1,585.0	968.2	.621	.379
1974	2,789.8	1,689.6	1,100.2	.606	.394
1975	3,163.1	1,910.2	1,252.9	.604	.396
1976	3,306.7	1,929.9	1,376.9	.584	.416
1977	3,593.1	2,072.2	1,520.9	.577	.423
1978	3,752.7	2,099.5	1,653.2	.559	.441
1979	4,236.1	2,338.4	1,897.7	.552	.448
1980	4,691.4	2,514.9	2,176.5	.536	.464
1981	5,102.5	2,700.7	2,401.8	.529	.471
1982	5,384.4	2,759.5	2,624.8	.513	.487
1983	5,739.7	2,911.5	2,828.3	.507	.493
1984	6,178.7	3,107.6	3,071.0	.503	.497

Table 5.28   **Full Gross Private National Saving (billions of constant dollars)**

	Full Gross Saving		Full Net Saving		Full Depreciation	
Year	Quantity	Price	Quantity	Price	Quantity	Price
1949	2,864.6	.169	1,815.2	.169	1,073.1	.165
1950	2,975.5	.174	1,884.3	.174	1,105.7	.173
1951	3,044.2	.186	1,932.8	.186	1,136.3	.183
1952	3,073.6	.195	1,949.7	.195	1,157.2	.191
1953	3,155.3	.209	2,017.4	.209	1,174.0	.203
1954	3,224.7	.218	2,075.1	.217	1,190.6	.212
1955	3,373.1	.221	2,206.4	.218	1,202.7	.220
1956	3,432.9	.230	2,245.6	.226	1,224.3	.231
1957	3,537.5	.247	2,339.4	.244	1,241.5	.244
1958	3,589.4	.260	2.383.4	.258	1,255.2	.254
1959	3,691.4	.263	2,460.7	.261	1,266.3	.261
1960	3,761.5	.269	2,514.6	.267	1,279.7	.266
1961	3,873.2	.279	2,602.0	.277	1,305.0	.277
1962	3,973.5	.287	2,670.4	.286	1,326.3	.285
1963	4,091.4	.290	2,752.8	.288	1,353.2	.291
1964	4,229.7	.310	2,850.2	.310	1,384.8	.310
1965	4,297.4	.322	2,869.1	.322	1,423.9	.323
1966	4,336.0	.342	2,853.7	.343	1,473.0	.341
1967	4,402.6	.359	2,866.5	.362	1,526.8	.356
1968	4,514.6	.377	2,924.7	.379	1,579.9	.376
1969	4,654.4	.393	3,011.4	.393	1,634.4	.394
1970	4,788.8	.429	3,093.5	.433	1,689.2	.424
1971	4,963.3	.469	3,210.0	.475	1,746.4	.459
1972	4,944.4	.484	3,124.3	.485	1,816.9	.483
1973	5,002.8	.510	3,116.9	.508	1,893.3	.511
1974	4,973.3	.561	3,009.2	.561	1,978.7	.556
1975	5,019.1	.630	2,977.0	.642	2,056.3	.609
1976	5,076.5	.651	2,961.7	.652	2,130.0	.646
1977	5,215.8	.689	3,017.7	.687	2,212.1	.688
1978	5,305.6	.707	3,012.3	.697	2,306.7	.717
1979	5,350.3	.792	2,950.5	.793	2,407.0	.788
1980	5,379.0	.872	2,881.2	.873	2,498.1	.871
1981	5,430.0	.940	2,869.7	.941	2,560.4	.938
1982	5,384.2	1.000	2,759.3	1.000	2,624.8	1.000
1983	5,428.7	1.057	2,743.4	1.061	2,686.0	1.053
1984	5,527.6	1.118	2,773.5	1.120	2,755.1	1.115

Depreciation in constant prices has grown steadily throughout the postwar period.

We have analyzed the structure of full gross private national saving in table 5.29. We present gross saving, net saving, and depreciation in current and constant prices. We also give saving and depreciation in constant prices per capita. The growth rate of net saving in constant prices per capita has been slightly negative for the period as a whole.

Table 5.29 **Full Gross Private National Saving, Rates of Growth, 1949–84**

	1949–84	1949–53	1953–57	1957–60	1960–66	1966–69	1969–73	1973–79	1979–84
Full gross saving:									
Current prices	7.28	7.79	6.98	4.85	6.38	6.99	8.35	8.44	7.55
Constant prices	1.88	2.42	2.86	2.05	2.37	2.36	1.80	1.12	.65
Constant prices[a]	.58	.75	1.09	.24	.92	1.26	.84	.28	−.40
Price index	5.40	5.31	4.18	2.84	4.00	4.63	6.52	7.34	6.89
Full net saving:									
Current prices	6.61	7.96	7.57	5.35	6.33	6.31	7.28	6.48	5.69
Constant prices	1.21	2.64	3.70	2.41	2.11	1.79	.86	−.91	−1.24
Constant prices[a]	−.08	.98	1.93	.60	.66	.70	−.11	−1.76	−2.28
Price index	5.40	5.31	3.87	3.00	4.17	4.54	6.42	7.42	6.91
Full depreciation:									
Current prices	8.16	7.52	5.91	3.91	6.49	8.28	10.22	11.22	9.63
Constant prices	2.69	2.25	1.40	1.01	2.34	3.47	3.68	4.00	2.70
Constant prices[a]	1.40	.59	−.37	−.80	.89	2.37	2.71	3.16	1.65
Price index	5.46	5.18	4.60	2.88	4.14	4.82	6.50	7.22	6.94

[a]This data calculated on a per capita basis.

This growth rate was positive for the periods 1948–53 through 1966–69 and has been negative ever since. The growth rate of gross saving in constant prices per capita was only 0.58 percent per year for the period as a whole and has been negative for the period 1979–84.

The final step in integrating our measures of saving with measures of human and nonhuman wealth is the estimate of revaluation of human and nonhuman capital for all years. We present estimates of saving, depreciation, net saving, revaluation, and change in wealth for the period 1948–84 in table 5.30. Revaluation rose to a peak in 1979 and has declined since then. Both revaluation and change in wealth fluctuate substantially from period to period, reflecting variations in the rate of change of lifetime labor incomes and asset values from period to period. Revaluation has exceeded net capital formation as a proportion of change in wealth in every year since 1963.

We conclude our presentation of a new system of national accounts for the United States with an account for the wealth of the private national sector of the U.S. economy. The value of full wealth is the sum of nonhuman wealth, as defined by Fraumeni and Jorgenson (1980), and our estimate of human wealth. We present estimates of full wealth, human wealth, and nonhuman wealth for the year 1982 in table 5.31. The share of human wealth dwarfs the share of nonhuman wealth. We present estimates of full wealth, human wealth, and nonhuman wealth for the period 1948–84 in current prices in table 5.32 and in constant prices in table 5.33. The share of human wealth in full wealth ranges from 0.943 in 1971 to 0.921 in 1981. The price of human wealth rises more rapidly than that of nonhuman wealth so that constancy of the human share is due to the slower growth of human wealth in constant prices.

We have analyzed the structure of full private national wealth for the U.S. economy in table 5.34. We present growth rates of full wealth, human wealth, and nonhuman wealth in current and constant prices and constant prices per capita for the period 1949–84. The growth rate of human wealth per capita in constant prices has been only 0.49 percent per year during the postwar period. By contrast, the growth rate of nonhuman wealth per capita in constant prices has averaged 1.65 percent per year. The behavior of full wealth closely parallels that of human wealth, which greatly predominates in the total.

Our final objective is to compare our estimates of human and nonhuman wealth with those of Kendrick (1976). We have defined human wealth in terms of lifetime labor incomes for all individuals in the U.S. population. We have also incorporated nonmarket activities into our measures of lifetime income. These two innovations result in important differences between our estimates and those of Kendrick. Kendrick, following the classic studies of Machlup (1962) and Schultz (1961),

Table 5.30   **Gross Private National Capital Accumulation (billions of current dollars)**

Year	Gross Private National Saving	Depreciation	Net Capital Formation	Revaluation	Change in Wealth
1949	483.8	176.8	306.9	729.5	1,036.5
1950	518.6	191.0	327.6	739.5	1,067.1
1951	566.4	207.6	358.8	941.2	1,300.0
1952	600.2	220.5	379.7	623.3	1,003.0
1953	660.7	238.8	421.9	1,400.4	1,822.3
1954	704.1	252.8	451.3	798.5	1,249.8
1955	745.2	264.5	480.6	−63.3	417.3
1956	791.0	282.4	508.5	927.5	1,436.1
1957	873.5	302.5	571.0	1,744.1	2,315.1
1958	933.9	319.2	614.7	1,783.9	2,398.6
1959	971.9	331.1	640.8	−128.3	512.5
1960	1,010.4	340.1	670.4	838.7	1,509.1
1961	1,081.2	361.0	720.2	1,291.4	2,011.6
1962	1,141.4	378.6	762.8	743.3	1,506.1
1963	1,185.3	393.6	791.7	378.1	1,169.9
1964	1,312.7	430.0	882.7	2,360.0	3,242.7
1965	1,384.0	460.6	923.4	2,202.2	3,125.6
1966	1,482.0	501.9	980.1	2,925.1	3,905.2
1967	1,580.8	543.4	1,037.4	2,392.5	3,429.8
1968	1,702.7	593.6	1,109.1	2,312.3	3,421.4
1969	1,827.9	643.4	1,184.5	2,955.1	4,139.6
1970	2,056.0	716.1	1,339.9	5,424.9	6,764.8
1971	2,327.6	801.6	1,526.0	5,542.9	7,068.9
1972	2,392.7	877.7	1,515.0	3,378.8	4,893.8
1973	2,553.2	968.2	1,585.0	7,663.9	9,248.9
1974	2,789.8	1,100.2	1,689.6	5,834.0	7,523.6
1975	3,163.1	1,252.9	1,910.2	6,335.3	8,245.5
1976	3,306.7	1,376.9	1,929.9	6,937.3	8,867.2
1977	3,593.1	1,520.9	2,072.2	5,632.2	7,704.4
1978	3,752.7	1,653.2	2,099.5	11,069.9	13,169.4
1979	4,236.1	1,897.7	2,338.4	13,278.3	15,616.7
1980	4,691.4	2,176.5	2,514.9	5,053.2	7,568.1
1981	5,102.5	2,401.8	2,700.7	10,410.9	13,111.7
1982	5,384.4	2,624.8	2,759.5	10,643.0	13,402.5
1983	5,739.7	2,828.3	2,911.5	10,571.3	13,482.8
1984	6,178.7	3,071.0	3,107.6	12,048.5	15,156.1

employs costs of education, including income forgone by students, as a basis for measuring investment in education. Similarly, he employs costs of rearing as a basis for measuring investment in human capital through the addition of new members of the population. His estimates do not include measures of the returns to investment in education or additions to the population.

Table 5.31   **Private National Wealth, 1982 (billions of current dollars)**

1.	Private domestic tangible assets			12,791.8
2. +	Net claims on the federal, state, and local governments			896.2
	a. Federal, monetary		182.6	
	i) + Vault cash of commercial banks[a]	19.5		
	ii) + Member bank reserves[a]	26.5		
	iii) + Currency outside banks[a]	136.6		
	b. Federal, nonmonetary		644.1	
	i) U.S. government total liabilities[a]	1,133.9		
	ii) − U.S. government financial assets[a]	292.0		
	iii) + Net liabilities, federally sponsored credit agencies[a]	− 5.9		
	iv) + Assets of social insurance funds[b]	65.7		
	v) − U.S. government liabilities to the rest of world[c]	172.0		
	vi) + U.S. government credits and claims abroad[c]	97.1		
	vii) − Monetary liabilities	182.6		
	c. State and local		69.4	
	i) State and local government total liabilities[a]	315.8		
	ii) − State and local government financial assets[a]	246.5		
	iii) + Assets of cash sickness compensation fund (our imputation)	.1		
3. +	Net claims on the rest of world			199.9
	a. Private U.S. assets and investments abroad[c]	716.6		
	b. − Private U.S. liabilities to foreigners[c]	516.6		
4. =	Private national nonhuman wealth			13,887.9
5. +	Private national human wealth			166,990.4
6. =	Full private national wealth			180,878.3

[a]Board of Governors of the Federal Reserve System, *Flow of Funds Accounts,* various issues.

[b]U.S. Department of the Treasury, *Treasury Bulletin,* February issues.

[c]"The International Investment Position of the United States," *Survey of Current Business,* October issues.

In table 5.35, we present estimates of private national human wealth in current and constant prices from the present study and the study by Kendrick (1976). For comparability between the two studies, we have used the same year as a base for the price system as that employed by Kendrick, namely, 1958. Our estimates range from 14.64 to 16.67 times those of Kendrick in current prices and from 13.15 to 18.68 those of Kendrick in constant prices. It is important to note that Kendrick deflates his estimates on the basis of cost indexes for education and rearing of children, while our estimates are deflated by an index of lifetime incomes for all individuals in the U.S. population.

Table 5.32   **Full Private National Wealth (billions of current dollars)**

Year	Full Wealth	Human Wealth	Nonhuman Wealth	Human Share	Nonhuman Share
1949	16,710.1	15,536.7	1,173.5	.930	.070
1950	17,777.2	16,512.9	1,264.3	.929	.071
1951	19,077.2	17,687.9	1,389.3	.927	.073
1952	20,080.2	18,618.4	1,461.8	.927	.073
1953	21,902.5	20,372.5	1,530.0	.930	.070
1954	23,152.3	21,574.4	1,577.9	.932	.068
1955	23,569.7	21,904.1	1,665.5	.929	.071
1956	25,005.7	23,209.8	1,795.9	.928	.072
1957	27,320.9	25,417.2	1,903.7	.930	.070
1958	29,719.4	27,737.3	1,982.2	.933	.067
1959	30,232.0	28,174.9	2,057.1	.932	.068
1960	31,741.0	29,603.6	2,137.4	.933	.067
1961	33,752.7	31,551.9	2,200.8	.935	.065
1962	35,258.8	32,971.7	2,287.1	.935	.065
1963	36,428.7	34,056.3	2,372.4	.935	.065
1964	39,671.4	37,187.6	2,483.8	.937	.063
1965	42,797.0	40,171.4	2,625.6	.939	.061
1966	46,702.1	43,886.3	2,815.8	.940	.060
1967	50,132.0	47,137.4	2,994.6	.940	.060
1968	53,553.4	50,331.7	3,221.7	.940	.060
1969	57,693.0	54,184.1	3,508.9	.939	.061
1970	64,457.8	60,722.1	3,735.7	.942	.058
1971	71,526.6	67,478.3	4,048.3	.943	.057
1972	76,420.4	71,999.6	4,420.8	.942	.058
1973	85,669.3	80,686.5	4,982.7	.942	.058
1974	93,192.9	87,523.0	5,669.9	.939	.061
1975	101,438.4	95,046.5	6,391.9	.937	.063
1976	110,305.6	103,214.4	7,091.2	.936	.064
1977	118,010.0	110,041.7	7,968.2	.932	.068
1978	131,179.4	122,024.2	9,155.2	.930	.070
1979	146,796.0	136,287.5	10,508.5	.928	.072
1980	154,364.1	142,516.4	11,847.7	.923	.077
1981	167,475.8	154,259.9	13,215.9	.921	.079
1982	180,878.3	166,990.4	13,887.9	.923	.077
1983	194,361.1	179,555.3	14,805.8	.924	.076
1984	209,517.2	193,829.2	15,688.0	.925	.075

Our estimates of nonhuman wealth are based on those of Jorgenson and Fraumeni (1980). In table 5.36, we compare our estimates with those of Kendrick in current and constant prices, using 1958 as the base year for the price system. Our estimates are a fairly constant proportion of Kendrick's, amounting to about twice the level of Kendrick's estimates. In table 5.37, we present a comparison of our estimates of full wealth and those of Kendrick in current and constant prices. Since full wealth is dominated by human wealth, we find that our estimates greatly exceed those of Kendrick in both current and constant prices.

Table 5.33   Full Private National Wealth (billions of constant dollars)

	Full Wealth		Human Wealth		Nonhuman Wealth	
Year	Quantity	Price	Quantity	Price	Quantity	Price
1949	96,884.8	.172	91,689.0	.169	5,213.6	.225
1950	98,785.0	.180	93,314.3	.177	5,446.9	.232
1951	100,730.0	.189	95,024.7	.186	5,650.5	.246
1952	102,664.9	.196	96,789.4	.192	5,805.2	.252
1953	104,650.1	.209	98,603.6	.207	5,962.4	.257
1954	106,679.5	.217	100,472.2	.215	6,113.7	.258
1955	108,896.9	.216	102,441.8	.214	6,338.5	.263
1956	111,142.0	.225	104,468.7	.222	6,538.3	.275
1957	113,477.8	.241	106,624.7	.238	6,708.3	.284
1958	115,805.9	.257	108,833.5	.255	6,827.6	.290
1959	118,302.2	.256	111,134.8	.254	7,013.7	.293
1960	120,844.0	.263	113,506.4	.261	7,178.5	.298
1961	123,408.8	.274	115,910.1	.272	7,335.6	.300
1962	126,098.6	.280	118,390.3	.278	7,537.6	.303
1963	128,874.3	.283	120,934.3	.282	7,760.7	.306
1964	131,693.1	.301	123,489.4	.301	8,015.5	.310
1965	134,505.5	.318	125,992.3	.319	8,319.8	.316
1966	137,273.7	.340	128,423.9	.342	8,657.3	.325
1967	140,060.0	.358	130,911.8	.360	8,959.3	.334
1968	142,922.6	.375	133,470.4	.377	9,269.0	.348
1969	145,801.8	.396	136,048.7	.398	9,575.7	.366
1970	148,666.3	.434	138,650.8	.438	9,843.1	.380
1971	151,669.2	.472	141,342.5	.477	10,170.0	.398
1972	154,569.2	.494	143,901.4	.500	10,536.2	.420
1973	157,173.3	.545	146,113.0	.552	10,970.0	.454
1974	159,869.7	.583	148,492.6	.589	11,310.0	.501
1975	162,721.7	.623	151,071.3	.629	11,593.2	.551
1976	165,344.2	.667	153,376.0	.673	11,927.8	.595
1977	168,111.2	.702	155,791.4	.706	12,295.5	.648
1978	170,556.4	.769	157,858.0	.773	12,689.8	.721
1979	173,039.8	.848	159,991.9	.852	13,049.7	.805
1980	175,753.0	.878	162,424.8	.877	13,331.7	.889
1981	178,384.4	.939	164,751.3	.936	13,634.3	.969
1982	180,878.3	1.000	166,990.4	1.000	13,887.9	1.000
1983	183,323.4	1.060	169,120.6	1.062	14,204.0	1.042
1984	185,734.0	1.128	171,121.4	1.133	14,622.0	1.073

5.6 Conclusion

In this paper, we have presented a new system of national accounts for the United States, based on comparable measures of investment in human and nonhuman capital. Our accounting system incorporates four major innovations. First, we have defined human capital in terms of lifetime labor income for all individuals in the U.S. population. Second, we have integrated demographic accounts for the U.S. population with

Table 5.34   Full Private National Wealth, Rates of Growth, 1949–84

	1949–84	1949–53	1953–57	1957–60	1960–66	1966–69	1969–73	1973–79	1979–84
Full wealth:									
Current prices	7.23	6.76	5.53	5.00	6.44	7.04	9.88	8.98	7.12
Constant prices	1.86	1.93	2.02	2.10	2.12	2.01	1.88	1.60	1.42
Constant prices[a]	.56	.27	.25	.29	.67	.91	.91	.76	.37
Price index	5.37	4.87	3.56	2.91	4.28	5.08	7.98	7.37	5.71
Human wealth:									
Current prices	7.21	6.77	5.53	5.08	6.56	7.03	9.95	8.74	7.04
Constant prices	1.78	1.82	1.96	2.08	2.06	1.92	1.78	1.51	1.35
Constant prices[a]	.49	.16	.18	.28	.61	.82	.82	.67	.30
Price index	5.44	5.07	3.49	3.07	4.50	5.05	8.18	7.23	5.70
Nonhuman wealth:									
Current prices	7.41	6.63	5.46	3.86	4.59	7.34	8.77	12.44	8.01
Constant prices	2.95	3.36	2.95	2.26	3.12	3.36	3.40	2.89	2.28
Constant prices[a]	1.65	1.69	1.18	.45	1.67	2.26	2.43	2.05	1.23
Price index	4.46	3.32	2.50	1.60	1.45	3.96	5.39	9.55	5.75

[a]This data calculated on a per capita basis.

Table 5.35   Private National Human Wealth, 1949–69

	Billions of Current Dollars			Billions of 1958 Dollars		
Year	Jorgenson and Fraumeni	Kendrick	Ratio	Jorgenson and Fraumeni	Kendrick	Ratio
1949	15,536.7	938.9	16.55	23,214.7	1,242.9	18.68
1950	16,512.9	991.3	16.66	23,576.8	1,280.5	18.41
1951	17,687.9	1,097.7	16.11	24,051.8	1,322.2	18.19
1952	18,618.4	1,172.6	15.88	24,412.9	1,366.9	17.86
1953	20,372.5	1,236.8	16.47	25,051.4	1,413.3	17.73
1954	21,574.4	1,294.4	16.67	25,551.2	1,460.0	17.50
1955	21,904.1	1,364.2	16.06	26,061.8	1,509.9	17.26
1956	23,209.8	1,462.7	15.87	26,510.7	1,565.6	16.93
1957	25,417.2	1,576.8	16.12	27,104.6	1,623.7	16.69
1958	27,737.3	1,682.6	16.48	27,737.3	1,682.6	16.48
1959	28,174.9	1,786.9	15.77	28,285.0	1,744.7	16.21
1960	29,603.6	1,901.4	15.57	28,928.2	1,615.1	17.91
1961	31,551.9	2,012.8	15.68	29,594.3	1,888.4	15.67
1962	32,971.7	2,137.4	15.43	30,263.3	1,962.5	15.42
1963	34,056.3	2,273.0	14.98	30,927.5	2,041.9	15.15
1964	37,187.6	2,423.9	15.34	31,751.5	2,126.8	14.93
1965	40,171.4	2,594.4	15.48	32,465.6	2,218.8	14.63
1966	43,886.3	2,818.7	15.57	33,172.9	2,323.4	14.28
1967	47,137.4	3,049.7	15.46	33,838.9	2,434.0	13.90
1968	50,331.7	3,344.4	15.05	34,494.0	2,550.1	13.53
1969	54,184.1	3,699.9	14.64	35,164.9	2,674.4	13.15

economic accounts for the private sector of the U.S. economy. Third, we have incorporated the value of nonmarket activities in our measures of labor incomes and human capital. Fourth, we have measured the services of both human and nonhuman capital in a comparable way.

To implement our system of accounts for the United States, we have constructed a new data base for measuring lifetime labor incomes for all individuals in the U.S. population. Our data base includes demographic accounts in each year for the population by each sex, cross-classified by individual years of age and individual years of educational attainment. Our demographic accounts include data on the number of individuals enrolled in formal schooling and births, deaths, and migration. These accounts are based on annual population data from the U.S. Bureau of the Census. We have incorporated data from the decennial census of population to obtain estimates of the population cross-classified by sex, age, and education.

To measure lifetime labor incomes for all individuals in the U.S. population, we begin with the data base on market labor activities assembled by Gollop and Jorgenson (1980, 1983). We have derived estimates of hours worked and labor compensation for each sex by

Table 5.36   **Private National Nonhuman Wealth, 1949–69**

	Billions of Current Dollars			Billions of 1958 Dollars		
Year	Jorgenson and Fraumeni	Kendrick	Ratio	Jorgenson and Fraumeni	Kendrick	Ratio
1949	1,173.5	571.1	2.05	1,512.5	717.6	2.11
1950	1,264.3	621.4	2.03	1,580.4	750.1	2.11
1951	1,389.3	711.3	1.95	1,637.8	789.6	2.07
1952	1,461.8	749.1	1.95	1,682.2	819.6	2.05
1953	1,530.0	771.4	1.98	1,726.5	844.5	2.04
1954	1,577.9	782.2	2.02	1,773.6	868.3	2.04
1955	1,665.5	827.2	2.01	1,836.5	899.8	2.04
1956	1,795.9	898.1	2.00	1,893.9	938.6	2.02
1957	1,903.7	958.2	1.99	1,943.9	971.3	2.00
1958	1,982.2	989.7	2.00	1,982.2	989.7	2.00
1959	2,057.1	1,031.4	1.99	2,036.0	1,005.9	2.02
1960	2,137.4	1,057.6	2.02	2,080.0	1,030.4	2.02
1961	2,200.8	1,077.7	2.04	2,127.4	1,049.4	2.03
1962	2,287.1	1,115.6	2.05	2,189.0	1,072.2	2.04
1963	2,372.4	1,164.3	2.04	2,248.4	1,102.8	2.04
1964	2,483.8	1,222.6	2.03	2,323.6	1,138.2	2.04
1965	2,625.6	1,292.4	2.03	2,409.6	1,183.5	2.04
1966	2,815.8	1,383.4	2.04	2,512.6	1,235.0	2.03
1967	2,994.6	1,475.5	2.03	2,600.1	1,274.6	2.04
1968	3,221.7	1,549.7	2.08	2,684.8	1,300.8	2.06
1969	3,508.9	1,644.1	2.13	2,780.3	1,332.4	2.09

sixty-one age groups and eighteen education groups for a total of 2,196 groups for each year. We impute wage rates for nonmarket activities from wage rates for employed individuals. We allocate the total time endowment for all individuals in the population among work, schooling, household production and leisure, and maintenance. We exclude maintenance through the satisfaction of physiological needs from our accounts for lifetime labor incomes. We assign the value of time spent in household production and leisure to consumption and time spent in schooling to investment.

Our final step in measuring lifetime labor incomes for all individuals in the U.S. population is to project incomes for future years and to discount incomes for all future years back to the present, weighting income by the probability of survival. We combine estimates of lifetime labor incomes by sex, age, and education with demographic accounts for the numbers of individuals to obtain estimates of human wealth, investment in human capital, and human capital services. We have presented these estimates in current prices for the period 1948–84 for all individuals in the U.S. population. Combining these estimates with measures of nonhuman capital services by Fraumeni and Jorgenson

Table 5.37   Full Private National Wealth, 1949-69

	Billions of Current Dollars			Billions of 1958 Dollars		
Year	Jorgenson and Fraumeni	Kendrick	Ratio	Jorgenson and Fraumeni	Kendrick	Ratio
1949	16,710.1	1,510.0	11.07	24,968.0	1,960.5	12.74
1950	17,777.2	1,612.7	11.02	25,381.9	2,030.8	12.50
1951	19,077.2	1,809.0	10.55	25,941.0	2,111.8	12.28
1952	20,080.2	1,921.7	10.45	26,329.6	2,186.5	12.04
1953	21,902.5	2,008.2	10.91	26,932.7	2,257.8	11.93
1954	23,152.3	2,076.6	11.15	27,420.0	2,328.3	11.78
1955	23,569.7	2,191.4	10.76	28,043.6	2,409.7	11.64
1956	25,005.7	2,360.8	10.59	28,562.1	2,504.2	11.41
1957	27,320.9	2,535.0	10.78	29,134.7	2,595.0	11.23
1958	29,719.4	2,672.3	11.12	29,719.4	2,672.3	11.12
1959	30,232.0	2,818.3	10.73	30,350.1	2,750.6	11.03
1960	31,741.0	2,959.0	10.73	31,016.9	2,845.5	10.90
1961	33,752.7	3,090.5	10.92	31,658.6	2,937.8	10.78
1962	35,258.8	3,253.0	10.84	32,362.5	3,034.7	10.66
1963	36,428.7	3,437.3	10.60	33,081.9	3,144.7	10.52
1964	39,671.4	3,646.5	10.88	33,872.3	3,265.0	10.37
1965	42,797.0	3,886.8	11.01	34,587.5	3,402.3	10.17
1966	46,702.1	4,202.1	11.11	35,301.3	3,558.4	9.92
1967	50,132.0	4,525.2	11.08	35,988.6	3,708.6	9.70
1968	53,553.4	4,894.1	10.94	36,701.9	3,850.9	9.53
1969	57,693.0	5,344.0	10.80	37,442.2	4,006.8	9.34

(1980, 1986), we obtain a complete system of national accounts for the United States.

Our new system of U.S. national accounts results in a dramatic change in perspective on the role of wealth, investment, and capital services in economic activity. We have employed the resulting system of accounts to describe economic growth by means of a production account, the allocation of income between consumption and saving by means of an income and expenditure account, and the accumulation of wealth by means of accumulation and wealth accounts. Even as an accounting exercise, our results have important limitations. Perhaps the most significant is the exclusion of the government sector, including public education, from the production account. This is an important gap that we hope to fill.[8]

Our system of accounts could be extended in the direction of a measure of economic welfare, taking the concept of consumption employed in our income and expenditure account as a point of departure. Our concept includes consumption of nonmarket goods and services, including household production and the enjoyment of leisure, as well as market goods and services. This concept of consumption could be augmented by consumption provided by the business sector, but not included in our expenditure account, and diminished by work-related outlays that are included in our account. Our concept could also be increased by government services, excluding instrumental or defensive outlays. Finally, additional imputations could be made for amenities and disamenities associated with changes in the social and physical environment.[9]

Another task that remains is to employ the new accounting framework in exploring the determinants of saving and wealth, including human and nonhuman capital. The production account could be modeled by means of a production function, giving output as a function of inputs of human and nonhuman capital services. The income and expenditure account could be modeled by means of a model of household behavior, generating income from the supply of human and nonhuman capital services, and allocating this income between consumption and saving. Current consumption would enter into an intertemporal utility function that also includes future consumption. Finally, the accumulation and wealth accounts could be modeled by means of a model of portfolio choice.

Notes

1. See, e.g., Gorman et al. (1985) and Bureau of Economic Analysis (1976).

2. Estimates of lifetime labor incomes for men based on market labor activities have been presented in Weisbrod (1961), Miller (1965), Miller and Hornseth (1967), Bureau of the Census (1968, 1974), and Graham and Webb (1979).

3. Demographic accounting is discussed in detail in Stone (1971) and United Nations (1975). This approach and its relation to economic accounts are reviewed by Stone (1981). A system of demographic accounts has been implemented for the United States by McMillen and Land (1980) and by McMillen (1980). The results of this research are reviewed by Land and McMillen (1981).

4. An economic theory of time allocation is presented by Becker (1965). Detailed references to more recent literature on time allocation are given by Murphy (1980). Results of a comprehensive and recent empirical study for the United States are presented by Juster et al. (1978). Kendrick (1979) summarizes the results of an unpublished paper by Wehle (1979), comparing seventeen studies of time allocation for the United States, covering the period 1924–76.

5. Nineteen empirical studies of the valuation of nonmarket labor activities for the United States are surveyed by Murphy (1980). Kendrick (1979) provides recent estimates covering the period 1929–73. An excellent summary of current research on demographic and time use accounting is provided by a recent volume edited by Juster and Land (1981a). Overviews of research in both areas are provided by House (1981), Juster and Land (1981b), and Ruggles (1981), all of which appear in Juster and Land (1981a). Time use accounting has been discussed by Fox and Ghosh (1981), Juster, Courant, and Dow (1981a, 1981b), and Terleckj (1981). Gates and Murphy (1982) presented detailed time use accounts for the United States for 1975–76 based on data collected by the Survey Research Center of the University of Michigan.

6. A system of vintage accounts for nonhuman capital is presented by Jorgenson (1980). This system of accounts has been implemented for the U.S. economy by Fraumeni and Jorgenson (1980). A preliminary form of vintage accounts for human and nonhuman capital has been presented by Jorgenson and Pachon (1983a, 1983b). Additional details are provided by Christensen and Jorgenson (1969, 1970, 1973a, 1973b). Campbell and Peskin (1979) have summarized accounting systems developed by Kendrick (1976, 1979), Ruggles and Ruggles (1970, 1973), and Eisner (1978, 1980). Kendrick's accounting system is similar in scope to our own since it includes production, income and expenditure, accumulation, and wealth accounts. Kendrick's accounting system is also discussed by Engerman and Rosen (1980). Further references to the literature are given by Campbell and Peskin (1979). Ruggles and Ruggles (1982) have recently presented a system of integrated economic accounts for the United States that combines income and product accounts, flow-of-funds accounts, and balance sheets for nonhuman capital.

7. Kendrick's estimates of human capital have been compared with estimates based on lifetime labor incomes for males between the ages of fourteen and seventy-four for the United States, excluding the value of nonmarket activities, for the year 1969 by Graham and Webb (1979). A very detailed survey of nonmarket labor time and its value has been presented by Murphy (1980). Murphy (1982) provides detailed estimates of the value of household work in the United States for 1976.

8. A complete account for the educational sector is needed to estimate rates of return to educational investment. Estimates of investment in education have been presented by Schultz (1961). Rates of return are given by Becker (1975). Kendrick (1976) provides estimates covering the period 1929–69. Detailed references to recent literature are provided by Campbell and Peskin (1979). Gates (1982) provides time-series estimates of education and training costs for 1965–79.

9. Welfare measures of aggregate economic activity for the United States have been presented by Sametz (1968) and Nordhaus and Tobin (1972). Proposals for measuring welfare have been reviewed by Campbell and Peskin (1979), United Nations (1977), and Beckerman (1978). Measurement of environmental amenities and disamenities is discussed by Cremeans (1977) and by Peskin and Peskin (1978). Detailed references to the literature are given by Campbell and Peskin (1979).

References

Becker, Gary S. 1965. A theory of the allocation of time. *Economic Journal* 75, no. 299 (September): 493–517.

———. 1975. *Human capital*. 2d ed. Chicago: University of Chicago Press.

Beckerman, Wilfred. 1978. *Measures of leisure, equality, and welfare*. Paris: Organization for Economic Cooperation and Development.

Board of Governors of the Federal Reserve System. 1976. *Flow of funds accounts, 1946–1975*. Washington, D.C.: Board of Governors of the Federal Reserve System, December.

Bureau of Economic Analysis. 1966. *The national income and product accounts of the United States, 1929–65, statistical tables, a supplement to the Survey of Current Business*. Washington, D.C.: U.S. Government Printing Office.

————. 1976. *The national income and product accounts of the United States, 1929–74, statistical tables, a supplement to the Survey of Current Business.* Washington, D.C.: U.S. Government Printing Office.

————. Various monthly issues. *Survey of Current Business.* Washington, D.C.: U.S. Government Printing Office.

Bureau of the Census. 1940. *Census of Population, 1940.* Washington, D.C.: U.S. Government Printing Office.

————. 1950. *Census of Population, 1950.* Washington, D.C.: U.S. Government Printing Office.

————. 1960. *Census of Population, 1960.* Washington, D.C.: U.S. Government Printing Office.

————. 1968. Annual mean income, lifetime income, and educational attainment of men in the United States, for selected years, 1950 to 1966. In *Current population report.* Series P-60, no. 56. Washington, D.C.: U.S. Government Printing Office.

————. 1970. *Census of Population, 1970.* Washington, D.C.: U.S. Government Printing Office.

————. 1974. Annual mean income, lifetime income, and educational attainment of men in the United States, for selected years, 1956 to 1972. In *Current population report.* Series P-60, no. 92. Washington, D.C.: U.S. Government Printing Office.

————. 1980. *Census of Population, 1980.* Washington, D.C.: U.S. Government Printing Office.

Campbell, Beth, and Janice Peskin. 1979. Expanding economic accounts and measuring economic welfare: A review of proposals. Washington, D.C.: Bureau of Economic Analysis, U.S. Department of Commerce, October.

Christensen, Laurits R., and Dale W. Jorgenson. 1969. The measurement of U.S. real capital input, 1929–1967. *Review of Income and Wealth* ser. 15, no. 4 (December): 293–320.

————. 1970. U.S. real product and real factor input, 1929–1967. *Review of Income and Wealth* ser. 16, no. 1 (March): 65–94.

————. 1973a. U.S. income, saving, and wealth, 1929–1969. *Review of Income and Wealth* ser. 19, no. 4 (December): 329–62.

————. 1973b. Measuring economic performance in the private sector. In *The measurement of social and economic performance,* ed. Milton Moss, 233–351. NBER Studies in Income and Wealth, vol. 38. New York: National Bureau of Economic Research.

Cremeans, John E. 1977. Conceptual and statistical issues in developing environmental measures—Recent U.S. experience. *Review of Income and Wealth* ser. 23, no. 2 (June): 97–116.

Eisner, Robert. 1978. Total incomes in the United States, 1959 and 1969. *Review of Income and Wealth* ser. 24, no. 1 (March): 41–70.

————. 1980. Capital gains and income: Real changes in the value of capital in the United States, 1946–1977. In *The measurement of capital,* ed. Dan Usher, 175–342. NBER Studies in Income and Wealth, vol. 45. Chicago: University of Chicago Press.

Engerman, Stanley, and Sherwin Rosen. 1980. New books on the measurement of capital. In *The measurement of capital,* ed. Dan Usher, 153–70. NBER Studies in Income and Wealth, vol. 45. Chicago: University of Chicago Press.

Fox, Karl A., and Syamal K. Ghosh. 1981. A behavior setting approach to social accounts combining concepts and data from ecological psychology, economics, and studies of time use. In *Social accounting systems,* ed. F. T. Juster and K. C. Land, 132–217. New York: Academic Press.

Fraumeni, Barbara M., and Dale W. Jorgenson. 1980. The role of capital in U.S. economic growth, 1948–1976. In *Capital, efficiency and growth*, ed. G. von Furstenberg, 9–250. Cambridge, Mass.: Ballinger.

―――. 1986. The role of capital in U.S. economic growth, 1948–1979. In *Measurement issues and behavior of productivity variables*, ed. A. Dogramaci, 161–244. Boston: Nijhoff.

Gates, John A. 1982. Education and training costs: A measurement framework and estimates for 1965–79. In *Measuring nonmarket activity*, ed. J. Peskin, 107–35. Washington, D.C.: U.S. Government Printing Office.

Gates, John A., and Martin Murphy. 1982. The use of time: A classification scheme and estimates for 1975–76. In *Measuring nonmarket activity*, ed. J. Peskin, 3–22. Washington, D.C.: U.S. Government Printing Office.

Gollop, Frank M., and Dale W. Jorgenson. 1980. U.S. productivity growth by Industry, 1947–73. In *New developments in productivity measurement and analysis*, ed. John W. Kendrick and Beatrice N. Vaccara, 17–136. NBER Studies in Income and Wealth, vol. 44. Chicago: University of Chicago Press.

―――. 1983. Sectoral measures of labor cost for the United States, 1948–1979. In *The measurement of labor cost*, ed. J. E. Triplett, 185–235. NBER Studies in Income and Wealth, vol. 48. Chicago: University of Chicago Press.

Gorman, John A., John C. Musgrave, Gerald Silverstein, and Kathy A. Comins. 1985. Fixed private capital in the United States. *Survey of Current Business* 65, no. 7 (July): 36–59.

Graham, John W., and Roy H. Webb. 1979. Stocks and depreciation of human capital: New evidence from a present-value perspective. *Review of Income and Wealth* ser. 25, no. 2 (June): 209–24.

House, James S. 1981. Social indicators, social change, and social accounting: Toward more integrated and dynamic models. In *Social accounting systems*, ed. F. T. Juster and K. C. Land, 377–419. New York: Academic Press.

Jorgenson, Dale W. 1980. Accounting for capital. In *Capital, efficiency and growth*, ed. G. von Furstenberg, 251–319. Cambridge, Mass.: Ballinger.

Jorgenson, Dale W., and Alvaro Pachon. 1983a. The accumulation of human and nonhuman wealth. In *The determinants of national saving and wealth*, ed. R. Hemming and F. Modigliani, 302–52. London: Macmillan.

―――. 1983b. Lifetime income and human capital. In *Human resources, employment, and development*, ed. P. Streeten and H. Maier, 29–90. London: Macmillan.

Jorgenson, Dale W., and Kun-Young Yun. 1986. Tax policy and capital allocation. *Scandinavian Journal of Economics* 88 (2): 355–77.

Juster, F. Thomas, Paul N. Courant, and Greg K. Dow. 1981a. A theoretical framework for the measurement of well being. *Review of Income and Wealth*, ser. 27, no. 1 (March): 1–33.

―――. 1981b. The theory and measurement of well-being: A suggested framework for accounting and analysis. In *Social accounting systems*, ed. F. T. Juster and K. C. Land, 23–94. New York: Academic Press.

Juster, F. Thomas, Paul N. Courant, Greg J. Duncan, John Robinson, and Frank P. Stafford. 1978. *Time use in economic and social accounts*. Ann Arbor: Institute for Social Research, University of Michigan.

Juster, F. Thomas, and Kenneth C. Land, eds. 1981a. *Social accounting systems*. New York: Academic Press.

―――. 1981b. Social accounting systems: An overview. In *Social accounting systems*, ed. F. T. Juster and K. C. Land, 1–21. New York: Academic Press.

Kendrick, John W. 1976. *The formation and stocks of total capital*. New York: National Bureau of Economic Research.

————. 1979. Expanding imputed values in the national income and product accounts. *Review of Income and Wealth,* ser. 25, no. 4 (December): 349–64.

Land, Kenneth C., and Marilyn M. McMillen. 1981. Demographic accounts and the study of social change, with applications to post–World War II United States. In *Social accounting systems,* ed. F. T. Juster and K. C. Land, 242–306. New York: Academic Press.

Machlup, Fritz. 1962. *The production and distribution of knowledge in the United States.* Princeton: Princeton University Press.

McMillen, Marilyn M. 1980. The demographic approach to social accounting. Ph.D. Diss., University of Illinois, Urbana-Champaign.

McMillen, Marilyn M., and Kenneth C. Land. 1980. Methodological considerations in the demographic approach to social accounting. In *1979 Proceedings of the social statistics section.* Washington, D.C.: American Statistical Association.

Miller, Herman P. 1965. Lifetime income and economic growth. *American Economic Review* 55, no. 4 (September): 834–44.

Miller, Herman P., and Richard A. Hornseth. 1967. Present value of estimated lifetime earnings. Technical Paper no. 16. Washington, D.C.: Bureau of the Census, U.S. Department of Commerce.

Murphy, Martin. 1980. The measurement and valuation of household non-market time. Washington: D.C.: Bureau of Economic Analysis, U.S. Department of Commerce, March.

————. 1982. The value of household work for the United States, 1976. In *Measuring nonmarket economic activity,* ed. J. Peskin, 23–41. Washington, D.C.: U.S. Government Printing Office.

National Center for Health Statistics. Various annual issues. *Vital Statistics of the United States.* Public Health Service, U.S. Department of Health, Education and Welfare.

Nordhaus, William D., and James Tobin. 1972. *Economic growth.* New York: National Bureau of Economic Research.

Peskin, Henry M., and Janice Peskin. 1978. The valuation of nonmarket activities in income accounting. *Review of Income and Wealth* ser. 24, no. 1 (March): 71–92.

Ruggles, Nancy, and Richard Ruggles. 1970. *The design of economic accounts.* New York: National Bureau of Economic Research.

————. 1973. A proposal for a system of economic and social accounts. In *The measurement of social and economic performance,* ed. Milton Moss. NBER Studies in Income and Wealth, vol. 38. New York: National Bureau of Economic Research.

Ruggles, Richard. 1981. The conceptual and empirical strengths and limitations of demographic and time-based accounts. In *Social accounting systems,* ed. F. T. Juster and K. C. Land, 454–76. New York: Academic Press.

Ruggles, Richard, and Nancy Ruggles. 1982. Integrated economic accounts for the United States, 1947–1980. *Survey of Current Business* 62, no. 5 (May): 1–53.

Sametz, A. W. 1968. Production of goods and services: The measurement of economic growth. In *Indicators of social change,* ed. E. B. Sheldon and W. Moore. New York: Russell Sage Foundation.

Schultz, Theodore W. 1961. Investment in human capital. *American Economic Review* 51, no. 1 (March): 1–17.

Stone, Richard. 1971. *Demographic accounting and model building.* Paris: Organization for Economic Cooperation and Development.

_____. 1981. The relationship of demographic accounts to national income and product accounts. In *Social accounting systems,* ed. F. T. Juster and K. C. Land, 307–76. New York: Academic Press.

Terleckj, Nestor E. 1981. A social production framework for resource accounting. In *Social accounting systems,* ed. F. T. Juster and K. C. Land, 95–129. New York: Academic Press.

United Nations. 1975. *Towards a system of social and demographic statistics.* New York: Department of Economic and Social Affairs, United Nations.

_____. 1977. *The feasibility of welfare-oriented measures to supplement the national accounts and balances: A technical report.* New York: Department of Economic and Social Affairs, United Nations.

U.S. Department of the Treasury. Various monthly issues. *Treasury Bulletin.* Washington, D.C.: U.S. Government Printing Office.

Wehle, Elizabeth S. 1979. Unpaid household work: Methodology and sources. Typescript.

Weisbrod, Burton A. 1961. The valuation of human capital. *Journal of Political Economy* 69, no. 5 (October): 425–36.

Comment   Sherwin Rosen

This pioneering paper is one of the most comprehensive studies ever undertaken for imputing values of human capital investment and of nonmarket production in national income and product accounts. A project of this scope and importance will be studied, discussed, and refined for many years. My comments are focused on a few points to help get the professional dialogue started.

The imputations for nonmarket production are based on the concept of full income familiar from time allocation theory, under which it is maintained that a person can work as much or as little as desired at a fixed hourly wage rate. The proper shadow price for nonmarket time is the (after-tax) alternative *marginal* market value of a unit of time, assumed here to equal the average hourly wage rate. However, most workers are restricted in their choices of hours on existing jobs. Most jobs offer all-or-nothing fixed hours–wage packages, and a change in hours must be implemented by changing jobs. Since the market equilibrium wage-hours locus is probably nonlinear, the average hourly wage rate does not necessarily equal the marginal product of an additional hour of market work required for the imputation. This point is important because the imputed value of nonmarket time is much larger than the value of market time.

Sherwin Rosen is a professor of economics at the University of Chicago and a research associate of the National Bureau of Economic Research.

Most direct studies (e.g., commuting time) suggest that the value of time is significantly smaller than the (after-tax) wage rate. Moreover, the choice of working hours depends on how a person's productivity varies over the time unit. At the optimal choice, the marginal product of an additional work hour is less than or equal to its marginal disutility. This leads to well-known selectivity biases for people who do not work at all. For people who work substantial amounts, the solution probably lies in the region where average productivity is falling and the marginal product is less than the average. Exceptions occur when either fixed costs of market participation or increasing returns to additional work hours in market production are large, but these are unlikely to dominate the data. We do not know enough about this problem to quantify the bias, and the authors can hardly be faulted for that state of affairs. Nonetheless, these qualifications should be kept in mind in interpreting their numbers. It also would be useful to present estimates of the value of nonmarket production by sex because of the enormous changes in fertility and labor-force behavior of women over the period studied. Labor economists think that the most important component of non-market production is the value of housewives' time associated with the rearing of children. It would be interesting to know if the imputations are consistent with this point.

The estimates of human capital investment rival the magnitude of conventional gross domestic product (their table 5.1). To put Jorgenson and Fraumeni's numbers in perspective, consider that there were about 93 million persons aged zero to twenty-five in the population who were eligible for human capital investment as they define it. Then their 1982 estimate amounts to a very large sum of $25,000 worth of investment for each of these people in that year, and this is a lower bound because many of them were not enrolled in school. These numbers are much larger than either Kendrick's (1976) cost-based estimates or Mincer's (1962) internal-rate-of-return estimates. One reason for the difference is that Jorgenson and Fraumeni's estimates include the value of *both* market and nonmarket time. Kendrick and Mincer did not value non-market time, which is more than half the total because it includes such things as weekends and holidays. Market time accounts for about three-eighths of total time in Jorgenson and Fraumeni's table 5.2 calculations, so a more conventional market value estimate would reduce the $2.36 trillion total to $.9 trillion in 1982, still a substantial sum of about $9,500 in that year for each person aged zero to twenty-five in the population. This raises a question related to the first point. Should all nonmarket time be imputed to human capital investment? How is it that invest-ments in specialized market skills affect the productivity of such non-market activities as watching television or reading the newspaper?

These questions have been raised before but are not yet answered in the literature.

Another reason for the large size of the human investment estimates is that they are based on gross discounted full incomes in the zero to twenty-five age groups. The actual procedure is more complicated, but the following artificial example illustrates how it works. Suppose everyone were alike, stayed in school exactly sixteen years, and did not work at all while in school. At age twenty-one, the representative person graduates and enters the labor market, earning, say, a flat $30,000 per year thereafter. This is increased to $80,000 per year by the non-market time value imputation and amounts to about $2 million in present discounted value at age twenty-one using a 4 percent discount rate and ignoring mortality. In this example, investment equals the number of people graduating from grade 16 in a given year times $2 million. The actual method includes births, immigration, and mortality, and it spreads personal investment over the whole schooling period rather than concentrating it on a single age, but the example illustrates the logic. These estimates are gross of the costs of investment: neither the costs of maintenance during working life nor the considerable time and money costs of raising children (including accumulated interest) are considered. Similarly, the human wealth figures in Jorgenson and Fraumeni's table 5.32 are gross discounted lifetime full earnings summed across the entire U.S. population. If costs were netted out, as they are for physical capital, both investment and stock estimates would be much smaller. I hope the authors subsequently will clarify the questions these imputations are supposed to answer.

The revaluation estimates in their table 5.30 are very large (e.g., the 1982 figure exceeds conventional gross national product by a factor of three), and they show substantial variability. The computational algorithms for this and the other price indexes are not presented in enough detail to clarify these sources of variation, yet age-earnings profiles on which they rest are fairly stable over both time and place. The most important variation for human capital valuation is the intercept, not the slope of the profile, and the four censuses of 1950–80 provide a basis for a smooth year-to-year interpolation. The revaluation estimates would show much less variation had it been done in this way. Finally, the depreciation estimates in Jorgenson and Fraumeni's tables 5.27 and 5.28 seem to include gross on-the-job investment as one of its components. It would be of substantial interest to present those estimates separately.

In conclusion, it is worth emphasizing that these comments do not detract from the conceptual and practical importance of this paper. Jorgenson and Fraumeni have done a great service in proving the importance of human capital and nonmarket production for national income accounting. Their estimates will stand as a benchmark and make it difficult for economists to ignore these issues from now on.

References

Kendrick, John W. 1976. *The formation and stocks of total capital*. General Series, no. 100. New York: National Bureau of Economic Research.
Mincer, Jacob. 1962. On the job training: Costs, returns and some implications. *Journal of Political Economy* 70, suppl.: 50–79.

6 Government Saving, Capital Formation, and Wealth in the United States, 1947–85

Michael J. Boskin, Marc S. Robinson, and
Alan M. Huber

6.1 Introduction

In all countries, the public sector owns substantial amounts of capital. Governments also invest as well as consume and make transfer payments. Government capital, like private capital, also depreciates. Most advanced countries attempt to incorporate this information, however imperfectly, in their formal budget documents by generating separate capital and current accounts. The U.S. federal government is the most conspicuous exception.

Government capital formation raises a number of issues important to national economic well-being. For example, net capital formation may be a major component of net national saving or dissaving. It may be more appropriate to finance government capital formation than government consumption by borrowing rather than taxing. Some types of government capital formation are complementary to private activity and enhance productivity, but government investments do not have to meet the same kind of market test as private investment does.[1] We do

Michael J. Boskin is Burnet C. and Mildred Finley Wohlford Professor of Economics at Stanford University and a research associate of the National Bureau of Economic Research. Marc S. Robinson is now at General Motors Research Laboratories but while working on this project was at Stanford University and the University of California, Los Angeles. Alan M. Huber was a John M. Olin Foundation Graduate Research Fellow at Stanford University while working on this project.

The authors are indebted to the Center for Economic Policy Research at Stanford University for support of this research. They are deeply indebted to John Musgrave for generously providing unpublished data and to Paul Pieper for providing data on inventories and par-to-market indices for financial assets and liabilities. This paper was originally presented at the NBER Conference on Research in Income and Wealth, held in Baltimore, Md., 27–28 March 1987. The authors have greatly benefited from the comments of the conference participants, especially Robert Lipsey and Helen Stone Tice, and the numerous valuable suggestions made by their discussant, Robert Eisner.

not have an analogue to the stock market to value it. Thus, measures of government capital and investment may provide particularly useful information that cannot be inferred from other data.

Measuring government capital raises difficult conceptual issues (see, e.g., Eisner and Nebhut 1982). Among these are the questions of what government versus private product is and what capital is.[2] Another set of questions concerns whether to include and how to measure government human capital investment.[3]

Still, separating out capital and current expenditures and generating sensible measures of depreciation and net investment can be important inputs into various kinds of economic analyses. It would enable us to provide a more accurate picture of how government is using the funds that it raises. It could help develop better measures of productivity and capital. It can improve our understanding of fiscal history and highlight emerging fiscal issues, such as the alleged deterioration of the infrastructure. It may be useful in explaining private consumption and saving (Boskin 1988). Most important from the standpoint of this paper, it is a necessary input into comprehensive measures of net national saving and national wealth and into government balance sheets.

One purpose of this paper is to provide estimates of various types of government investment, depreciation, and capital. Our major innovations lie in the estimates of depreciation of fixed reproducible capital, the value of government land, and the value of government mineral rights.

We then use these series, and corresponding ones for the private sector, to obtain values for government consumption and net worth and to adjust gross national product (GNP), net national product (NNP), and national saving and investment figures from the national income and product accounts (NIPAs). Thus, we seek to complement previous studies attempting to extend measures of national income and product to a more comprehensive treatment of the government sector (e.g., Eisner and Nebhut 1982; Goldsmith 1962, 1982; Martin, Landefeld, and Peskin 1982; Kendrick 1976; Eisner and Pieper 1984; and Eisner 1986).

We focus on a particular subset of improvements to the NIPAs and previous studies while ignoring others. For example, we do not examine mandated private activity or uncompensated or undercompensated services; nor do we examine human capital expenditures. This is not because we consider these issues unimportant but because such a focus allows us to concentrate on other issues. Even with this deliberately narrow focus, our estimates of GNP and NNP extended to include the return to government capital substantially exceed the traditional numbers. Our estimates of the combined state-local and federal government capital stock are a large fraction of the analogously computed private capital stock. Government net saving, defined as revenues less consumption rather than by the traditional budget surplus or deficit figures (in accord with the Organization for Economic Cooperation and Development [OECD] and U.N. system of national accounts for other countries), and government net capital formation are substantial. They also vary over time and can be important components of net national saving and net national investment.

The paper is organized as follows. The next section discusses fixed reproducible capital—the methodology, concerns with the traditional estimates of the Bureau of Economic Analysis (BEA), and various estimates and trends of fixed reproducible capital of the federal and state-local governments in the United States. It provides important estimates based on depreciation assumptions that are consistent with empirical estimates for the private sector. The depreciation estimates generate internally consistent capital stock and imputed rent series. It also presents consistent real net revaluation estimates.

Section 6.3 discusses government inventories, presents data on inventory values, including military and nonmilitary as well as a breakdown by level of government, and compares inventory investment with fixed reproducible investment. It also discusses real revaluations for inventories.

In Section 6.4, we provide comparisons of these estimates of government investment and capital stocks to estimates of net investment and capital stocks in the private sector. We update through 1985 and expand the estimates of Hulten and Wykoff (1981) to consumer durables and residential capital. We also compare government and private capital stocks using consistent depreciation assumptions, although they may be controversial ones.

Section 6.5 presents revised saving, investment, and consumption as well as adjusted GNP and NNP estimates. In addition to imputing the rental flow from government capital as current consumption and developing improved estimates of depreciation to estimate net investment and the accrued capital stock, we also make corresponding adjustments for consumer durables purchases. These are substantial in the United States, substantially exceed the depreciation of the durables, and hence contribute an important component to national capital formation (for an elaboration of the important role such adjustments can play in international comparisons—e.g., with Japan—see Boskin and Roberts 1986). The data reveal interesting patterns of government consumption, saving, and net investment. The federal and, even more important, state and local government sectors are major contributors to national capital formation, and their patterns of capital formation have differed substantially over time and relative to the private sector.

Financial assets and conventional liabilities are discussed in section 6.6. It presents the real market values of federal and state-local financial assets and liabilities. It updates and makes minor changes to the work of Eisner and Pieper (1984) and Eisner (1986), which draw on the work of Seater (1981) and Cox and Hirschhorn (1983). In addition to the tangible assets, government units also have substantial financial assets as well as the traditional liabilities, which have drawn so much recent attention.

Section 6.7 updates and corrects estimates of the value of federal mineral rights developed by Boskin et al. (1985) and extends the analysis—albeit on the basis of scanty data—to state and local mineral rights. The value of these rights is quite large and fluctuates substantially, as one might suppose, given the substantial fluctuation in the prices of minerals. In some years, the change in the value of mineral rights exceeds the conventionally measured budget deficit.

Section 6.8 discusses the value of federal and state-local ownership of land. Again, this extends the analysis in Boskin et al. (1985) to the last several years and to the state and local sector. Various methodological issues are discussed. Governments own a substantial fraction of the total acreage of land in the United States and a modest fraction of the total value of land.

Section 6.9 is concerned with contingent liabilities such as loan guarantees, deposit insurance, and government pension liabilities. We do not provide systematic time series on the value of these contingent liabilities but discuss the conceptual issues in valuing them and some data on the outstanding value of loans, guarantees, and insured deposits. The economic consequences of subsidized loans or loan guarantees depend heavily on one's view of credit markets, especially the supply of funds to them (see Gale 1987). Various issues are discussed in defining a sensible estimate of the expected present value of the contingent liabilities flowing from new commitments of subsidized loans and guarantees and deposit insurance.

Section 6.10 discusses the most important set of potential government liabilities, the unfunded liabilities in social security and government pension plans. We refer the reader to other sources for time series on these data, but we discuss a variety of issues surrounding these unfunded liabilities and their sensitivity to various economic and demographic assumptions as well as to political decisions, and we highlight some key recent events in the system.

In section 6.11, we present a preliminary attempt to develop a balance sheet for the government sector of the U.S. economy. After discussing the advantages and numerous limitations of our estimates and government net worth calculations in general, we present balance sheets for federal and state-local governments for selected years. The trends, particularly in federal "net worth," are sometimes dramatic. Looking at tangible and financial assets and conventional liabilities, the federal government had a net worth (in 1985 dollars) of over $1.0 trillion in 1980, substantially higher than in 1970, but had lost two-thirds of it by 1985.

A brief conclusion summarizes the results and emphasizes the large number of caveats we have had to invoke along the way. It also suggests various avenues for future research.

6.2 Fixed Reproducible Capital

Goldsmith (1962) and Kendrick (1976) both estimated the government capital stock as part of their pioneering studies of national wealth. The most recent and comprehensive estimates of fixed reproducible government capital stocks have been made by the BEA.[4] All three studies use the perpetual inventory method to calculate net capital stocks: gross investment is cumulated, and estimated accumulated depreciation is subtracted. Our estimates use the BEA's gross investment series and most of their service life assumptions, but we adopt a different depreciation method.

The BEA assumes straight-line depreciation over the estimated economic service life of each asset.[5] However, within each category of structure or equipment, the BEA allows for a distribution in service lives around the mean, reflecting a retirement distribution.[6] Since the assets with the shortest assumed lives are retired first, the depreciation rate for any category of investment slows down once retirements start to occur. The resulting overall depreciation pattern resembles a geometric decay.

The straight-line assumption made by the BEA is basically arbitrary. A more satisfactory approach to estimating economic depreciation makes use of the observed sales prices of used assets. For the private sector, Hulten and Wykoff (1981) collected data on used asset price from several sources, weighted these price by estimated survival probabilities to account for discarded assets, and estimated the form and rate of economic depreciation. They used a functional form that included all the common assumptions—geometric, linear, or one-hoss-shay—as special cases. Although none of the common forms was accepted statistically, the estimated price-age profiles were found to be close to geometric for the classes of assets considered.[7] They then estimated the constant depreciation rate that provided the best fit.

These results were used to derive depreciation rates for the types of producers' durables and nonresidential structures defined in the NIPAs. There were sufficient data to estimate some types directly. The declining-balance rates, R, found for these categories were used to infer depreciation rates, δ, for the remainder from the definition $\delta = R/T$, where T equals the BEA estimated service life. The average R value for four equipment categories was 1.65, so depreciation rates for other equipment classes were calculated as $\delta = 1.65 / T$. The average R value for two types of structures was 0.91, so depreciation rates assigned to other types of structures were $\delta = 0.91 / T$.

The Hulten-Wykoff depreciation rates are consistent with the observations of Young and Musgrave (1980) and Hulten and Wykoff (1981)
summarizing earlier studies: equipment depreciates faster than straight
line in the early years, while structures depreciate more slowly. These
depreciation rates are certainly significant topics for future research,
but we feel that the Hulten-Wykoff depreciation estimates are the best
available.[8]

In addition to fitting the used-asset-price data more closely, the geometric depreciation assumption has important theoretical advantages.[9]
The depreciation methods and measures used in the NIPAs, the BEA
capital stock series, the important work of Denison (1957, 1962, 1967,
1972, 1974, 1979, 1985), Kendrick (1973), and studies using the NIPA
and/or BEA capital stock data are internally inconsistent. The measures
of capital must employ the same pattern of relative differences of capital
goods of different vintages for both capital stocks and rental prices.
As pointed out originally by Jorgenson and Griliches (1972), the depreciation patterns assumed in these studies cannot be used both to
impute the rental prices and to measure the capital stocks against which
the rental prices are applied to measure imputed rent, gross or net.[10]
The principle disadvantage of geometric depreciation is that retirement
never occurs. Of course, all simple depreciation formulae assume that
depreciation is constant over time and across assets within a category.

Given the empirical evidence and theoretical advantages, we assume
that fixed government capital depreciates geometrically. Lacking evidence on prices for used government assets,[11] we use the market evidence on used private assets gathered by Hulten and Wykoff; that is,
the depreciation rate for government equipment is 1.65/(service life)
and that for each type of structure is 0.91/(service life). With one exception, the BEA-estimated service lives for the various types of government capital are used to infer depreciation rates.[12]

Our estimates of the net investment and net stock of government
fixed reproducible capital in 1985 dollars are shown in table 6.1. We
give our separate estimates for federal and state-local governments in
table 6.2. Both tables give the corresponding estimates for the BEA,
updated by us to 1985 dollars.[13]

We estimate that the net government fixed reproducible capital stock
exceeds $2.7 trillion dollars, having more than doubled in real terms
since World War II. As can be seen in figure 6.1, the broad trends of
our estimates are consistent with those of the BEA, which is not surprising since we use their gross investment data and most of their
service lives. Nevertheless, there are important differences between
the two series regarding both the level and the postwar growth of the
government capital stock. Our 1985 estimate is 19 percent higher than
that of the BEA, while at the end of World War II our value was 8

Table 6.1   **Total Government Fixed Reproducible Capital (billions of 1985 dollars)**

Year	Net Stock		Net Investment	
	BEA	BRH	BEA	BRH
1927	343.4	369.4	13.8	15.3
1928	358.5	386.1	14.7	16.3
1929	373.7	403.1	14.9	16.6
1930	393.6	424.8	19.4	21.3
1931	414.4	447.5	20.3	22.2
1932	429.9	465.2	15.2	17.3
1933	438.1	475.6	8.0	10.3
1934	451.4	491.3	13.1	15.4
1935	465.1	507.4	13.6	16.0
1936	490.0	534.8	24.5	27.0
1937	508.4	555.9	18.1	20.8
1938	531.4	581.6	22.5	25.2
1939	559.9	612.8	28.0	30.7
1940	583.7	639.3	23.5	26.1
1941	657.4	702.5	72.9	62.6
1942	859.6	854.7	199.8	150.8
1943	1,114.1	1,028.4	250.2	171.1
1944	1,292.1	1,189.2	174.5	157.6
1945	1,341.3	1,241.2	48.0	50.8
1946	1,154.3	1,121.8	− 183.5	− 117.1
1947	1,021.7	1,047.6	− 129.7	− 72.8
1948	935.1	1,004.3	− 84.6	− 42.5
1949	896.0	988.2	− 38.3	− 15.8
1950	886.1	986.4	− 9.7	− 1.7
1951	904.3	1,008.6	17.9	22.0
1952	956.9	1,062.5	51.9	53.1
1953	1,007.8	1,114.6	50.1	51.3
1954	1,053.2	1,162.5	43.8	47.0
1955	1,088.0	1,203.1	35.1	40.0
1956	1,119.3	1,241.5	30.7	37.7
1957	1,146.7	1,277.4	27.0	35.2
1958	1,180.4	1,319.9	33.0	41.8
1959	1,218.9	1,367.6	37.9	46.8
1960	1,259.9	1,417.6	40.3	49.2
1961	1,309.5	1,475.8	48.9	57.2
1962	1,358.4	1,533.1	48.1	56.2
1963	1,412.9	1,595.6	53.6	61.4
1964	1,467.8	1,658.7	54.1	61.9
1965	1,523.7	1,723.2	54.9	63.3
1966	1,584.8	1,793.2	60.3	68.7
1967	1,644.3	1,862.3	58.8	67.9
1968	1,704.8	1,932.9	59.7	69.3
1969	1,756.8	1,995.6	51.2	61.6
1970	1,799.6	2,049.6	43.3	53.0

(*continued*)

Table 6.1   (continued)

Year	Net Stock		Net Investment	
	BEA	BRH	BEA	BRH
1971	1,841.1	2,102.8	39.8	52.2
1972	1,883.1	2,156.1	41.5	52.3
1973	1,918.0	2,202.5	34.4	45.6
1974	1,950.6	2,246.8	32.1	43.6
1975	1,981.7	2,289.8	30.5	42.2
1976	2,009.0	2,329.3	26.7	38.7
1977	2,030.0	2,362.8	20.6	33.0
1978	2,063.2	2,408.3	32.5	44.7
1979	2,092.4	2,449.6	28.6	40.5
1980	2,121.5	2,490.9	28.5	40.6
1981	2,144.3	2,525.8	22.3	34.3
1982	2,175.0	2,567.6	30.0	41.0
1983	2,202.2	2,605.8	26.6	37.5
1984	2,236.9	2,650.8	33.9	44.1
1985	2,285.5	2,708.7	47.4	56.8

Sources: Fixed reproducible capital includes equipment and nonresidential and residential structures. The BEA series are constant-cost estimates in 1982 dollars updated to 1985 dollars by our use of price series implicit in the BEA current- and constant-cost estimates of net capital stocks and depreciation flows for each asset category. The same procedure was used to convert our estimates (the series labeled "BRH") from 1982 dollars into 1985 dollars. Our estimates employ the perpetual inventory method and use BEA gross investment data. Given the evidence of Hulten and Wykoff (1981) on the depreciation of private assets, we assume geometric depreciation of government capital with a declining-balance rate for equipment of 1.65/(service life) and for structures of 0.91/(service life). We use BEA estimated service lives, including detailed lives available for some types of capital based on observed usage, to infer depreciation rates, except that we assume a shorter forty-year service life for highways and streets. The 1986 BEA wealth data tape, unpublished BEA data kindly provide by John Musgrave, and several *Survey of Current Business* articles are our principal data sources. For further details on our methods, see text.

percent lower.[14] The BEA's estimate of the postwar growth in net government capital is more than 40 percent below ours.

With the exception of World War II, state and local government capital stocks have been larger than those of the federal government, as shown in figure 6.2. Currently, state and local governments own 69 percent of total government fixed reproducible capital. Except during military buildups, state and local governments provide an even larger fraction of total government investment, as can be seen in figure 6.3. The surges in federal investment roughly coincide with World War II, the Korean and Vietnam wars, and the Reagan defense buildup.

The behavior of the various components of federal and state-local investment and capital sheds light on several policy debates, though we can only touch on them in this paper. Figure 6.4 pictures the division

Table 6.2   **Federal and State-Local Fixed Reproducible Capital (billions of 1985 dollars)**

	Federal				State-Local			
	Net Stock		Net Investment		Net Stock		Net Investment	
Year	BEA	BRH	BEA	BRH	BEA	BRH	BEA	BRH
1927	75.1	80.1	−1.9	−1.3	268.3	289.3	15.7	16.5
1928	73.4	79.1	−1.7	−1.0	285.1	307.0	16.4	17.3
1929	72.3	78.8	−1.1	−.3	301.4	324.3	16.0	17.0
1930	72.1	79.3	−.2	.6	321.6	345.5	19.7	20.7
1931	73.0	81.1	.9	1.7	341.4	366.4	19.4	20.5
1932	75.3	84.2	2.3	3.1	354.7	381.0	12.9	14.2
1933	79.2	88.9	3.9	4.7	358.9	386.7	4.1	5.6
1934	85.0	95.5	5.8	6.5	366.4	395.8	7.3	8.9
1935	92.8	103.9	7.7	8.4	372.4	403.5	5.8	7.6
1936	99.4	111.4	6.6	7.4	390.6	423.4	17.8	19.5
1937	105.2	118.0	5.7	6.6	403.3	438.0	12.4	14.2
1938	111.1	124.7	5.9	6.7	420.3	456.9	16.6	18.5
1939	118.0	132.3	6.9	7.6	441.9	480.5	21.1	23.1
1940	128.2	143.0	10.2	10.6	455.5	496.4	13.3	15.5
1941	195.7	197.5	66.8	54.1	461.7	505.0	6.1	8.5
1942	400.1	349.2	201.9	150.4	459.6	505.5	−2.1	.5
1943	662.5	528.1	258.0	176.1	451.6	500.3	−7.8	−5.1
1944	849.3	694.9	183.1	163.4	442.7	494.4	−8.7	−5.8
1945	906.5	751.8	55.8	55.7	434.7	489.4	−7.9	−4.9
1946	721.2	630.9	−181.9	−118.5	433.1	490.9	−1.5	1.4
1947	581.2	546.4	−137.4	−82.9	440.4	501.2	7.7	10.1
1948	484.2	489.6	−95.4	−55.7	450.9	514.7	10.8	13.2
1949	431.2	456.5	−52.1	−32.4	464.9	531.7	13.8	16.6
1950	404.2	434.7	−26.4	−21.3	481.9	551.6	16.7	19.6
1951	404.9	436.3	.6	1.7	499.4	572.3	17.3	20.3
1952	439.6	469.3	34.3	32.6	517.3	593.3	17.6	20.6
1953	470.5	498.3	30.5	28.7	537.2	616.4	19.6	22.7
1954	488.5	515.5	17.7	17.1	564.7	646.9	26.1	29.9
1955	494.8	524.5	6.3	8.9	593.2	678.6	28.7	31.0
1956	496.5	530.1	1.7	5.6	622.8	711.4	29.0	32.2
1957	492.2	530.9	−4.1	.9	654.5	746.5	31.1	34.3
1958	491.7	535.6	−.5	4.8	688.7	784.3	33.5	37.0
1959	495.4	544.7	3.7	9.0	723.5	822.9	34.1	37.7
1960	501.8	556.3	6.4	11.5	758.1	861.4	33.9	37.7
1961	513.4	572.3	11.4	15.9	796.2	903.5	37.5	41.3
1962	523.2	586.3	9.7	13.9	835.2	946.8	38.3	42.3
1963	534.6	601.5	11.2	15.1	878.3	994.2	42.4	46.4
1964	543.3	614.0	8.6	12.4	924.5	1,044.7	45.5	49.5
1965	549.9	624.6	6.5	10.6	973.9	1,098.6	48.4	52.7
1966	557.4	636.4	7.4	11.8	1,027.5	1,156.7	52.9	57.0
1967	558.2	642.3	.8	5.9	1,086.2	1,220.0	58.0	62.0
1968	557.4	647.0	−.8	4.7	1,147.4	1,285.8	60.5	64.6
1969	554.4	649.9	−2.9	2.8	1,202.4	1,345.7	54.2	58.7
1970	550.2	651.7	−4.2	1.8	1,249.4	1,397.8	47.5	51.2
1971	546.4	654.2	−3.7	2.5	1,294.7	1,448.5	43.5	49.7
1972	548.6	662.1	2.1	7.8	1,334.5	1,493.9	39.4	44.5
1973	547.7	666.6	−.9	4.5	1,370.3	1,535.8	35.3	41.1
1974	544.1	668.2	−3.6	1.6	1,406.6	1,578.6	35.7	42.0

(*continued*)

Table 6.2 (continued)

| | Federal | | | | State-Local | | | |
| | Net Stock | | Net Investment | | Net Stock | | Net Investment | |
Year	BEA	BRH	BEA	BRH	BEA	BRH	BEA	BRH
1975	544.8	673.8	.7	5.6	1,436.9	1,616.0	29.9	36.7
1976	547.3	681.0	2.5	7.1	1,461.7	1,648.2	24.2	31.6
1977	551.0	689.1	3.6	8.1	1,479.0	1,673.7	17.0	24.9
1978	563.2	705.1	12.0	15.8	1,500.0	1,703.2	20.5	28.9
1979	574.8	719.8	11.3	14.4	1,517.7	1,729.8	17.3	26.1
1980	586.3	734.2	11.3	14.2	1,535.2	1,756.7	17.2	26.4
1981	598.3	748.5	11.7	14.1	1,546.0	1,777.2	10.6	20.1
1982	621.6	772.9	22.8	23.9	1,553.4	1,794.7	7.2	17.1
1983	641.9	793.9	19.9	20.6	1,560.3	1,811.9	6.8	16.9
1984	665.9	817.8	23.5	23.5	1,571.0	1,833.0	10.4	20.6
1985	698.7	849.4	31.3	31.1	1,586.8	1,859.3	16.1	25.7

Sources: See source note to table 6.1 and text.

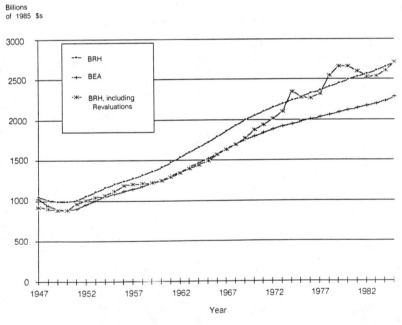

Fig. 6.1 Our (BRH) and BEA estimates of total government fixed reproducible net capital and BRH net estimates, including real net revaluations

Billions
of 1985 $s

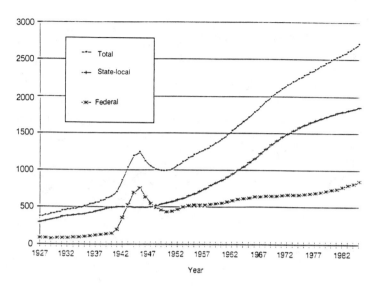

Fig. 6.2   New estimates of government fixed reproducible net capital
                stocks

Billions
of 1985 $s

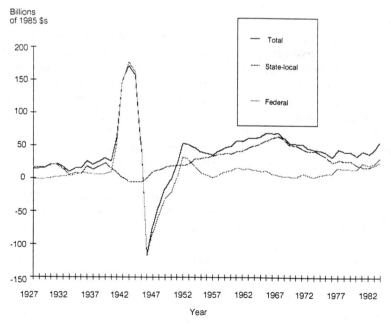

Fig. 6.3   Our (BRH) estimates of government net investment in fixed
                reproducible capital

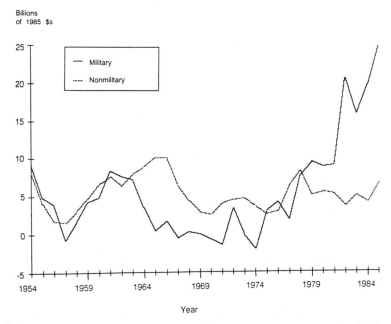

Billions
of 1985 $s

Fig. 6.4   Our (BRH) estimates of federal net investment in fixed reproducible capital

of aggregate federal net investment between military and nonmilitary. For a twenty-five year period beginning in 1954, the military and nonmilitary series track fairly closely, with nonmilitary investment usually slightly larger. Starting in 1979, however, the two series diverge, as military net investment has reached record postwar levels and civilian investment has dropped.

In figure 6.5, we divide net state and local investment into three major categories: educational buildings, highways, and other. The "other" category is primarily other types of structures; equipment is less than 5 percent of the net state and local stock. The three components have a similar pattern: after disinvestment during World War II, all three reach peaks in the late 1960s and drop to troughs in the recent recession. The observed pattern of aggregate net investment, therefore, cannot be attributed solely to the baby boom or the construction of the interstate highway system. The substantial levels of net investment in the highway and other categories, even in recessions, casts doubt on reports of a deteriorating infrastructure.[15]

6.2.1   Real Revaluations of Tangible Fixed Reproducible Capital

The data discussed above and presented in tables 6.1 and 6.2 do not include net revaluations for tangible reproducible capital due to changes

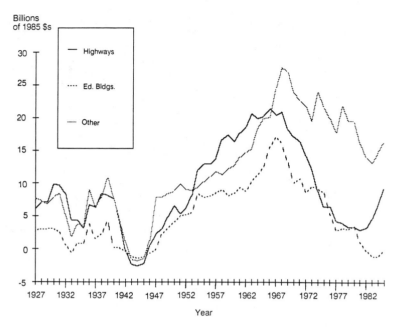

Fig. 6.5   Our (BRH) estimates of state and local net investment in fixed reproducible capital

in capital goods prices relative to the general price level. They deflate current-dollar figures by the BEA implicit deflators for each type of capital. Because real revaluations can be substantial (see Eisner 1980), we present data on real revaluations (in constant 1985 dollars) of federal and state-local tangible fixed reproducible capital in table 6.3. Real net revaluations are defined as the change in the value of capital minus real net investment and minus the change in the value of capital that would just compensate for changes in the general price level. Thus, real net investment (calculated from the specific implicit price deflators for investment goods) plus real net revaluations plus the real capital stock in period $t - 1$ equals the real capital stock in period t (where the real capital stocks are just the current-cost series as deflated by the respective end-of-year GNP deflator).[16]

As table 6.3 reveals, both the federal and the state-local sectors have experienced substantial real capital gains and losses on their corresponding fixed capital stocks. The net revaluations were generally negative in the 1950s and 1960s, positive in the 1970s, and negative in the 1980s. While real revaluations are substantial in absolute dollars and relative to net investment, they are modest relative to the capital stock. For example, the $170 billion and $32 billion real revaluations of state-local and federal capital stocks for 1974 amount to about 10 and 5

Table 6.3   **Real Net Revaluations of Government Fixed Reproducible Capital (billions of 1985 dollars)**

Year	State-Local	Federal	Total
1948	6.7	21.2	27.9
1949	− 10.3	8.2	− 2.1
1950	− 3.0	2.0	− 1.0
1951	33.9	22.8	56.7
1952	7.2	.5	− 6.7
1953	− 22.7	6.5	− 16.2
1954	− 16.4	− 8.1	− 24.5
1955	6.8	8.3	15.1
1956	13.0	14.7	27.7
1957	− 9.2	− 2.4	− 11.6
1958	− 22.0	− 11.1	− 33.0
1959	− 30.3	− 13.5	− 43.8
1960	− 13.5	− 4.2	− 17.7
1961	− 13.3	− 2.5	− 15.8
1962	− 4.6	− 3.6	− 8.3
1963	− 3.6	− .1	− 3.7
1964	− 15.6	− 3.0	− 18.6
1965	− 4.6	− 3.7	− 8.3
1966	4.3	− 1.9	2.4
1967	− 5.5	1.5	− 4.0
1968	− 4.2	− 2.0	− 6.2
1969	12.5	1.7	14.3
1970	39.8	9.7	49.4
1971	12.2	.2	12.4
1972	17.6	7.1	24.6
1973	33.9	4.7	38.7
1974	169.6	31.8	201.4
1975	− 88.8	− 17.0	− 105.8
1976	− 59.3	4.1	− 55.3
1977	22.9	− 2.6	20.3
1978	167.2	13.8	181.0
1979	53.6	18.8	72.4
1980	− 40.6	7.5	− 33.1
1981	− 96.3	− 6.3	− 102.6
1982	− 96.1	− 13.6	− 109.7
1983	− 16.7	− 5.4	− 22.1
1984	27.6	− 3.6	24.0
1985	47.8	− 6.6	41.2

percent of the corresponding stocks but were much larger than net investment. These large real capital gains were offset the following year by real losses approximately half as large. Indeed, cumulating the combined state-local and federal net revaluations from 1948 to 1985 yields a total of about $160 billion, or 6 percent of the estimated 1985 real net stock, excluding revaluations. Thus, while the year-to-year fluctuations are important, the overall cumulative real wealth effect of revaluations has been quite modest, as is evident from figure 6.1. In principle, one would add real net revaluations to real net investment to obtain total net capital formation for each year. Since we often wish to compare gross or net investment spending with borrowing, we adopt the procedure here of separate presentations of real revaluations but do include the values adjusted for revaluations in the balance sheets in section 6.11.

6.3 Government Inventories

The focus of the previous section was on government equipment and structures, but inventories are an important part of government reproducible capital, at least at the federal level. Table 6.4 presents estimates of inventory stocks and investment for both the federal government and the government sector. These are unpublished BEA series updated by us to 1985 dollars.[17]

Table 6.4   **Federal and Total Government Inventory Stocks and Investment (billions of 1985 dollars)**

Year	Federal Stock	Federal Investment	Total Stock	Total Investment	Total Real Revaluations
1926	3.0	.0	3.2	.0	. . .
1927	3.1	.1	3.3	.1	. . .
1928	3.1	.1	3.4	.1	. . .
1929	3.2	.1	3.4	.0	. . .
1930	3.3	.1	3.6	.1	. . .
1931	3.4	.1	3.7	.2	. . .
1932	3.5	.1	3.9	.1	. . .
1933	3.6	.1	4.0	.1	. . .
1934	4.7	1.1	5.1	1.2	. . .
1935	4.8	.2	5.3	.1	. . .
1936	4.2	−.7	4.6	−.7	. . .
1937	4.7	.5	5.1	.5	. . .
1938	7.0	2.3	7.4	2.3	. . .
1939	9.4	2.4	9.8	2.5	. . .
1940	13.7	4.3	14.2	4.3	. . .
1941	28.5	14.8	28.9	14.8	. . .
1942	62.2	33.7	62.6	33.7	. . .
1943	113.9	51.7	114.3	51.7	. . .
1944	173.8	59.9	174.2	59.9	. . .
1945	208.4	34.6	208.8	34.6	. . .
1946	173.5	−34.9	173.9	−35.0	. . .
1947	139.4	−34.1	139.8	−34.1	. . .

(*continued*)

Table 6.4   (continued)

Year	Federal Stock	Federal Investment	Total Stock	Total Investment	Total Real Revaluations
1948	107.5	−31.9	107.9	−31.9	−21.1
1949	91.2	−16.3	91.7	−16.2	−4.5
1950	80.6	−10.6	81.1	−10.6	−9.3
1951	88.2	7.6	88.6	7.6	−3.5
1952	112.4	24.2	112.9	24.2	−6.0
1953	145.8	33.3	146.2	33.3	16.7
1954	162.2	16.5	162.7	16.5	30.2
1955	161.2	−1.0	161.8	−.9	10.1
1956	160.1	−1.2	160.6	−1.2	−7.9
1957	159.1	−.9	159.6	−.9	−11.8
1958	160.2	1.1	160.8	1.2	−4.9
1959	155.5	−4.7	156.3	−4.5	−4.6
1960	150.8	−4.7	151.6	−4.7	−4.9
1961	144.5	−6.3	145.3	−6.3	−4.0
1962	146.5	2.0	147.3	2.0	−6.8
1963	150.7	4.2	151.6	4.3	−3.0
1964	147.2	−3.5	148.2	−3.4	−1.2
1965	139.0	−8.2	140.1	−8.1	−3.3
1966	135.3	−3.6	136.5	−3.5	−8.0
1967	141.9	6.5	143.2	6.6	−4.2
1968	144.6	2.8	146.1	2.9	−4.9
1969	158.8	14.2	160.4	14.4	−5.5
1970	152.5	−6.3	154.4	−6.1	−5.4
1971	147.2	−5.4	149.2	−5.2	−4.7
1972	135.8	−11.4	137.9	−11.3	.2
1973	127.6	−8.2	129.8	−8.1	1.3
1974	132.1	4.5	134.4	4.6	5.7
1975	128.8	−3.3	131.3	−3.0	1.2
1976	127.9	−.9	130.6	−.7	3.1
1977	131.5	3.6	134.5	3.9	3.3
1978	137.1	5.6	140.2	5.7	.8
1979	132.7	−4.5	135.6	−4.6	18.7
1980	132.3	−.4	135.2	−.4	6.6
1981	138.0	5.7	140.8	5.6	−2.6
1982	156.6	18.6	159.5	18.7	−1.5
1983	169.2	12.6	172.7	13.1	−16.9
1984	182.5	13.3	186.1	13.5	−9.1
1985	215.5	33.0	219.4	33.3	−8.1

Source: Unpublished BEA 1982 constant dollar estimates of end-of-year stocks of federal government military, federal government nonmilitary, and state and local government inventories were each updated to 1985 constant dollars by multiplying by the ratio of the 1985 BEA current dollar stock to the 1985 constant (1982) dollar stock for each type. Revaluations are calculated as described in text.

Government inventories are substantial, exceeding $200 billion in 1985, finally surpassing the World War II peak. Almost all the inventories are held by the federal government; for most years, state and local governments had less than 1 percent of the total. Figure 6.6 illustrates that most of these federal inventories are military, such as munitions. Not surprisingly, military inventories are quite volatile.

Nonmilitary inventories have grown, however, from 5 percent of the stock in 1945 to almost 40 percent in 1985. A further breakdown of nonmilitary inventories reveals that, in 1982, more than half were strategic stockpiles of minerals, nuclear materials, helium, and oil (the Strategic Petroleum Reserve).[18] More than two-thirds of the remaining nonmilitary inventories were surplus crops.

Real inventory stocks declined steadily from 1954 through 1980. Since then, inventory investment has taken off, reaching $33 billion in 1985. Inventory changes have a large effect on the level of net federal investment in reproducible capital, as shown in figure 6.7. Net federal investment in structures and equipment has been positive every year since 1950, according to our estimates. When inventories are added in, however, net federal investment becomes negative in five of the last thirty-five years. When inventories increase, as they did in the 1980s,

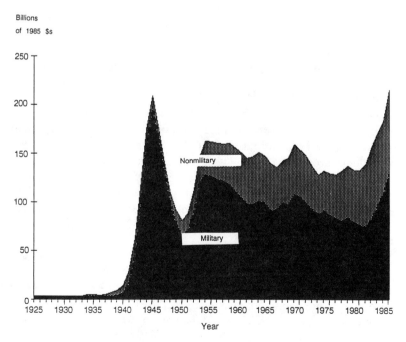

Fig. 6.6   Federal inventory stocks

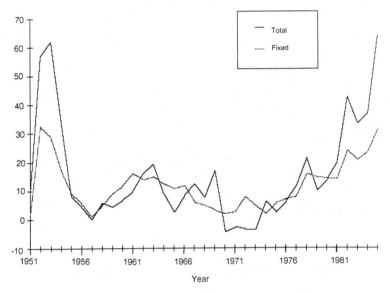

Fig. 6.7   Federal government net investment in reproducible capital: Total and excluding inventories (fixed)

the effect is also large: more than half our estimated $64 billion in net federal investment in 1985 is inventory investment.

6.3.1   Real Inventory Revaluations

As with fixed reproducible capital, real net revaluations may occur for government inventories. Table 6.4 includes a column on estimated real inventory revaluations defined analogously to that for the fixed reproducible capital stock. These data reveal that capital losses on inventories occurred in every year except 1953–55 and 1972–80. Cumulatively, the total real capital loss was approximately $70 billion, about one-third of the value of the net stock excluding revaluations.

6.4   Comparisons with Private Capital

One of the purposes of this paper is to present more comprehensive measures of national product and investment. While we concentrate on government capital, consistency requires adjustments to private capital measures as well. These adjustments also allow a more accurate comparison between private capital and investment and our estimates for the government sector.

Our measures differ from the NIPAs in the treatment of consumer durables and in our depreciation assumptions. As many have noted,[19] expenditures on consumer durables should be treated as investment, while an imputed service flow from these assets should be added to consumption. Accordingly, we add expenditures on consumer durables to gross private domestic investment.

In order to determine private capital stock and net investment, depreciation assumptions must be made. For the various classes of structures and equipment, we generally use the constant depreciation rates that were estimated and imputed by Hulten and Wykoff (1981).[20] For those categories whose service lives, as estimated by the BEA, changed, we imputed depreciation rates using the formulas described in section 6.2. For residential structures, we assumed a depreciation rate of 0.91/ (service life) for the various components, as with most other categories of structures. For consumer durables other than vehicles, we followed Christensen and Jorgenson (1973) in assuming double-declining balance depreciation, and we used the BEA's estimated service lives for the various components.[21] For vehicles, we took the depreciation rates for the corresponding business categories estimated by Hulten and Wykoff.

Our estimates of the various components of the private capital stock are presented for selected years in 1985 dollars in table 6.5. Our value for the total private capital stock in 1985 is $11.0 trillion, which is 16 percent above that of the BEA.[22]

Regardless of whether one takes our estimates or those of the BEA, the government sector clearly owns a large fraction of our national capital stock. As shown in figure 6.8 and table 6.5, total government tangible capital is 27 percent of the size of the private capital stock and 55 percent as large as the stock of private nonresidential structures, equipment, and inventories. A comparison of government and private net investment is made in figure 6.9. Government investment is much less cyclical than private investment and actually exceeded total private nonresidential investment in 1982.

6.5 New Estimates of Adjusted GNP, NNP, Government Consumption, Saving, and Investment

The discussion above highlights the size of the government capital stock and investment. Governments create a large share of the national capital formation, and the failure to include the imputed return on government capital seriously distorts measures of total consumption and income. The inappropriate treatment of consumer durables also distorts our understanding of investment, income, and consumption. These issues are well known (see, e.g., David and Scadding 1974; Boskin 1986; Eisner and Nebhut 1982; Kendrick 1976; and Holloway,

Table 6.5   New Estimates of Net Stocks of Private and Government Reproducible Capital, Excluding Revaluations (billions of 1985 dollars)

Year	Private Nonresidential (1)	Private Residential (2)	Consumer Durables (3)	Total Private = (1) + (2) + (3) (4)	State-Local (5)	Federal (6)	(5) + (6) as % of (1) (7)	(5) + (6) as % of (4) (8)
1928	1,552.0	1,324.1	105.0	2,981.1	307.3	82.2	25.1	13.1
1935	1,495.2	1,336.3	88.8	2,920.3	403.9	108.8	34.3	17.6
1945	1,576.0	1,382.5	96.8	3,055.3	489.8	960.2	92.0	47.5
1955	2,146.9	2,008.2	227.1	4,382.2	679.1	685.8	63.6	31.1
1965	2,861.5	2,816.5	333.4	6,011.4	1,099.7	763.5	65.1	31.0
1975	4,102.1	3,754.0	581.7	8,437.8	1,618.5	802.6	59.0	28.7
1985	5,281.7	4,817.3	899.2	10,998.2	1,863.2	1,064.9	55.4	26.6

Sources: Private nonresidential capital includes our estimates of fixed private nonresidential capital and inventories. Inventory data are from *Economic Report of the President* (1986, table B-17); 1982 constant dollar stocks were updated to 1985 dollars by multiplying by the ratio of 1985 current to constant (1982) dollar stock.

Our estimates of the private fixed nonresidential capital stock may be considered an updating of those in Hulten and Wykoff (1981). We use gross investment data from the 1986 BEA wealth data tape. We assume geometric depreciation patterns and generally use the depreciation rates estimated by Hulten and Wykoff. For asset categories for which depreciation rates were inferred by Hulten and Wykoff from the average relations $d = 0.91$/(service life) for structures and for which the BEA estimated service lives have been revised, as reported in Gorman et al. (1985), we calculated revised depreciation rates. Where there are now multiple service lives for asset subcategories within a type of capital, we have used the subcategory service life closest to the previous single service life for the asset type to infer a single depreciation rate. We convert our constant dollar estimates from 1982 to 1985 dollars by using the price indices implicit in BEA current- and constant-cost estimates for each asset type.

Our estimates of net private residential capital are based on BEA gross investment and service life data and a geometric depreciation rate of 0.91/(service life), which is the average relation for nonresidential structures found by Hulten and Wykoff (1981). Gross investment data are from the 1986 BEA wealth data tape and the BEA detailed industry investment tape. BEA service lives are listed in Gorman et al. (1985).

For consumer durables, our estimates use BEA gross investment data from the 1986 BEA wealth data tape and employ BEA estimated service lives to infer geometric depreciation rates for some assets (see Musgrave 1979). For durables other than vehicles, we assume double-declining balance depreciation. For vehicles, we use the depreciation rates for the corresponding business categories estimated by Hulten and Wykoff. Again, our 1982 dollar estimates are updated to 1985 dollars by using price indices implicit in the BEA current and constant dollar data for each type of consumer durable.

Government reproducible capital includes equipment, inventories, and all structures. See source notes to tables 6.1 and 6.4

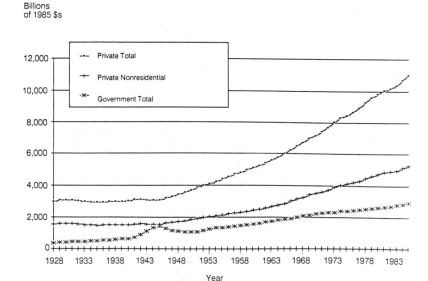

Fig. 6.8   New estimates of net stocks of private and government reproducible capital

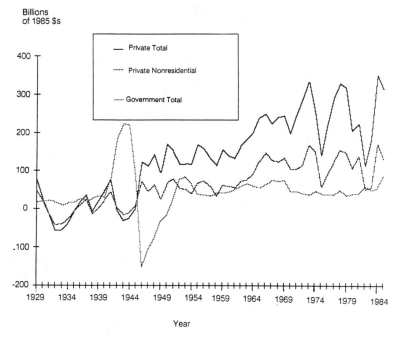

Fig. 6.9   New estimates of net investment in private and government reproducible capital

chap. 1, in this vol.). In this section, we present estimates of GNP and NNP including imputed rent to durables and government capital and adjusted estimates of government and private consumption and saving and investment rates. The advantages of the work reported here, relative to earlier studies, include the following.

1. The estimates of government and private depreciation are consistent with the best available empirical evidence.

2. The depreciation assumptions are internally consistent; that is, the estimates of rental prices of capital services are consistent with the corresponding estimates of capital stock. Unfortunately, the depreciation estimates of the BEA capital stock series and those used in the NIPAs are based on an internally inconsistent set of estimates of depreciation, stemming from Denison (1957). Jorgenson and Griliches (1972) pointed out long ago that the Denison/NIPA approach to estimating depreciation is consistent with the basic economic concept of depreciation only if the relative efficiencies of capital of different ages decline geometrically.

3. We impute a constant 3 percent real rate of return net of depreciation and maintenance to government capital and consumer durables. Given the illiquidity of most government capital and consumer durables, it is unlikely that the service flow from these assets fluctuates with any short-term variation in the real interest rate. A sensitivity analysis showed only very minor changes to variations in the assumed real interest rate.[23]

4. We include an imputed return for government land.

Table 6.6 presents a reconciliation for 1985 of GNP, NNP, private consumption, saving, and investment, and government consumption, saving, and investment based on the adjustments we have made. While real net revaluations might be included in net saving and investment, we do not do so here. First, these estimates are more readily comparable to the traditional figures. Second, we may wish to compare direct investment spending with various variables, not presuming revaluations were being forecast and used in decision making. Further, they are more important for year-to-year variation than cumulatively. Finally, we often compare saving or investment to government borrowing. In the sections that follow, we develop more comprehensive measures of changes in real assets and liabilities. One might well wish to compare, for example, government investment with the change in real net debt (the changes in the real value of financial liabilities in excess of financial assets) or even with an estimate of real "net worth." Again, we adopt the more conventional comparisons in this section, leaving the discussion of these other adjustments to subsequent sections. As can be seen, including the gross rent on government capital and consumer durables increases GNP by more than 10 percent, while including net rent and using our estimates of depreciation increases NNP by about 4 percent.

Table 6.6   **Comparison of Adjusted and Traditional NIPAs for 1985 (billions of 1985 dollars)**

	GNP and NNP	
	Adjusted	Traditional
GNP	3,998.1	3,998.1
Plus rent on government reproducible capital[a]	152.0	. . .
Plus rent on government land	25.5	. . .
Plus rent on consumer durables	317.1	. . .
Equals adjusted GNP	4,492.7	3,998.1
Less depreciation of private capital[b]	380.1	437.2
Less depreciation of government reproducible capital	97.1	. . .
Less depreciation of consumer durables	291.0	. . .
Equals NNP	3,724.6	3,560.9
	Government and Private Consumption	
Total government purchases	815.4	815.4
Plus rent on reproducible capital and land	177.5	. . .
Less government gross investment[c]	199.2	. . .
Equals adjusted government consumption	793.7	815.4
Personal consumption expenditures	2,600.5	2,600.5
Plus rent on consumer durables	317.1	. . .
Less gross investment in consumer durables	347.0	. . .
Equals adjusted private consumption	2,570.7	2,600.5
	Saving	
GNP	4,492.7	3,998.1
Less private consumption	2,570.7	2,600.5
Less government consumption	793.7	815.4
Less adjustments for net transfers and interest paid by government to foreigners and statistical discrepancy	30.8	30.8
Equals gross saving	1,097.6	551.5
Less depreciation of traditional private capital	380.1	437.2
Less depreciation of government reproducible capital	97.1	. . .
Less depreciation of consumer durables	291.0	. . .
Equals net saving	329.4	114.3

(*continued*)

Table 6.6   (continued)

	GNP and NNP	
	Adjusted	Traditional
	Investment	
Gross private investment[c]	639.9	661.1
Plus government gross investment in reproducible capital	187.1	. . .
Plus gross investment in consumer durables	347.0	. . .
Equals gross domestic investment	1,174.0	661.1
Less depreciation of private capital	380.1	437.2
Less depreciation of government capital	97.1	. . .
Less depreciation of consumer durables	291.0	. . .
Equals net domestic investment	405.8	223.9

[a]Rent equals opportunity cost plus depreciation. We assume a constant real interest rate of 3 percent in calculating opportunity cost for government capital and consumer durables. We apply this discount rate to mid-year stocks for year t obtained by averaging the end-of-year stocks for years t and $t - 1$. Because the return on government enterprise capital is, at least in theory, already included in GNP, we do not include imputed rent on government enterprise capital in our expanded measures of government consumption and GNP. For further discussion, see Martin, Landefeld, and Peskin (1982). All depreciation estimates used in the adjusted calculations are the authors', as described in secs. 6.2 and 6.4

[b]This entry includes private equipment and nonresidential and residential structures. Consumer durables are listed separately. Inventories are assumed not to depreciate. The adjusted estimate is from the authors' calculations, while the "traditional" entry is the NIPA capital consumption allowance.

[c]In the adjusted calculations, gross investment data for fixed reproducible capital and consumer durables are from the 1986 BEA wealth data tape, with our conversion to 1985 dollars based on BEA price indices. These series differ slightly from the NIPA series from which they are derived because of adjustments for intersectoral transfers, for instance. Most of the difference between the gross private investment series presented here is in equipment. Government inventory investment is measured as the change in year-end stocks, based on BEA data converted to 1985 dollars. Government gross investment in land is based on estimates of yearly net acquisitions (see sec. 6.8 for a discussion of our land estimates) and does not include revaluations.

Government consumption likewise is slightly different from government purchases of goods and services, as the rent on government capital was about $20 billion smaller than government gross investment. Private consumption, however, is quite close to NIPA personal consumption expenditures, as the estimated rental flow of services from the stock of consumer durables in 1985 (but not in general) is close to gross investment in durables. To total gross investment, we add approximately $190 billion of government investment and almost $350 billion of consumer durable investment. Thus, total gross investment is almost 80 percent larger than gross private investment as traditionally reported in the NIPA. Using our depreciation estimates, both for traditional private investment and for government capital and consumer durables, yields adjusted net national investment of $406 billion, also 80 percent larger than the NIPA figures.

Turning to saving, gross saving substantially exceeds NIPA gross private saving, about $1.1 trillion compared to $551 billion. NIPA net saving of $114 billion is only about one-third of our adjusted net saving.

Corresponding differences would be found in saving, investment, and consumption rates, although recall that NNP and GNP are slightly larger than the NIPA figures, so the proportionate increases would be slightly less. Table 6.7 presents estimates of U.S. saving and investment from 1951 to 1985, using our adjusted accounts, as percentages of adjusted GNP. For the three decades from 1951 to 1980, we present simple averages of annual figures for the decade.[24]

The data reveal some interesting trends in total net saving and total net investment in the United States. Total net saving, while substantially higher than the traditional NIPA figures, has declined substantially relative to the 1950s and 1960s. It declined about 15 percent between the 1950s and 1960s, on the one hand, and the 1970s, on the other, and has deteriorated markedly in the 1980s. By 1985, the third year of an expansion, the total net saving rate, expanded to include government saving and saving in the form of consumer durables, was almost 40 percent below the average for the 1950s and 1960s. Net private saving (also substantially larger than the corresponding NIPA figures because of the inclusion of net saving in consumer durables) was only slightly below historical levels in 1984–85. Net government saving, however, which averages a substantial fraction of GNP in the 1950s and 1960s and a modest fraction in the 1970s, turned negative from 1982 to 1985.

Federal government net saving turned sharply negative and more than offset state and local government saving. Note here that saving is defined to adjust the traditional surplus or deficit figures for net investment. It is interesting to note, for example, that, while the federal government borrowed 4.4 percent of adjusted GNP in 1985, federal government net investment was estimated as 1.4 percent of GNP, about one-third of the deficit figure. Whether the value of these assets the federal government was accumulating is properly measured by purchase price and should be thought of as representing a substantial available set of public assets to offset the growing public liabilities represented by the deficits is a question we do not address here.

The state and local government sector has always been a large net saver. In the period 1951–80, this was primarily because of net investment, for example, in educational buildings. In the 1980s, the

Table 6.7   Adjusted U.S. Saving and Investment, 1951–85 (as a percent of expanded GNP and taken from current dollar calculations)

	1951–60	1961–70	1971–80	1981	1982	1983	1984	1985
Total net saving	11.5	11.4	9.9	8.0	5.2	5.1	7.7	7.2
Net private saving	8.9	9.6	9.3	7.6	6.6	7.5	8.8	8.3
Net government saving	2.6	1.7	.7	.4	−1.4	−2.4	−1.2	−1.1
Federal government saving	1.3	−.0	−1.1	−1.1	−2.8	−4.0	−3.3	−3.0
Federal government net investment	1.4	.4	.5	.7	1.3	.6	.8	1.4
Federal government surplus	−.1	−.4	−1.6	−1.9	−4.1	−4.6	−4.0	−4.4
State-local government saving	1.3	1.7	1.8	1.5	1.4	1.7	2.1	1.9
State-local government net investment	1.4	1.7	1.0	.5	.4	.4	.5	.6
State-local government surplus	−.2	.0	.8	1.0	1.0	1.2	1.6	1.4
Total net investment	11.6	11.3	9.9	8.1	5.2	5.3	7.6	7.1
Net foreign investment	.4	.9	−1.1	−.1	.1	−1.0	−2.0	−1.9
National domestic investment	11.2	10.4	11.0	8.2	5.1	6.2	9.6	9.0
Private domestic investment	8.3	8.3	9.5	6.9	3.4	5.2	8.3	7.1
Government net investment	2.9	2.1	1.5	1.3	1.7	1.0	1.2	1.9
Federal government net investment	1.4	.4	.5	.7	1.3	.6	.8	1.4
State-local government net investment	1.4	1.7	1.0	.5	.4	.4	.5	.6
Memo: Gross national saving	27.6	26.5	26.2	25.4	23.3	22.6	24.6	24.4
Gross private saving	22.1	22.6	23.5	22.9	22.6	22.8	23.7	23.3
Gross government saving	5.5	4.0	2.7	2.5	.8	−.2	.9	1.1
Total capital consumption	16.1	15.2	16.3	17.4	18.1	17.5	16.9	17.2
Private capital consumption	13.2	12.9	14.2	15.4	15.9	15.4	14.8	15.0
Government capital consumption	3.0	2.3	2.1	2.1	2.2	2.2	2.1	2.2
Federal government capital consumption	2.2	1.4	1.0	1.0	1.1	1.1	1.1	1.2
State-local government capital consumption	.8	.9	1.1	1.1	1.1	1.0	1.0	1.0

Note: Our adjustments to NIPA measures to better account for government capital and consumer durables are described in the source note to table 6.5 and in the text. Here we use current dollar data and present our saving, investment, and capital consumption series as percentages of expanded GNP; i.e., NIPA GNP expanded to include rental flows from general government capital and consumer durables. For the three decades from 1951 to 1980, we present simple averages of annual figures for the decade.

Government saving equals the traditionally measured budget balance plus government net investment in reproducible capital and land. Our net investment estimates and the capital consumption figures reported use our estimates of the depreciation of government capital, fixed private capital, and consumer durables; the latter is included here in "private capital consumption."

pattern has changed. Net investment by state and local governments has fallen to one-third of its earlier historical level, perhaps desirably so in view of changing demographics. Counteracting this has been the swing to a very substantial state and local surplus, although the latter is heavily concentrated in pension plans, whose simultaneously accruing liabilities are not accounted for in these data.

Net investment in the United States has been more stable than national saving. Domestic investment was actually a higher fraction of national product in the 1970s than in the 1960s. The net domestic investment rate in 1984–85 was only 14 percent below its level from 1951 to 1980, compared with a 32 percent drop in net saving rates. Making up for much of the savings decline, of course, has been the substantial decline in net foreign investment (due both to a decrease in U.S. investment abroad and an increase in foreign investment in the United States), the other side of the trade deficit. Over 20 percent of domestic investment was financed from abroad in 1984–85.

Government net investment in 1985 was about at the same ratio of national income as it was over the previous three decades, although state and local government net investment had fallen substantially. Federal government net investment heavily reflects the military buildup; in 1985, federal investment was at a level not attained since the 1950s.

It is worth mentioning that gross saving and investment rates were in the low to mid-20 percent range with the expanded definitions, with total capital consumption having risen from 15–16 percent in the 1951–80 period to 17–18 percent in the 1980s. Two-thirds of the difference between the net saving rates in the 1960s and those in the 1980s is attributable to an increased rate of capital consumption. A similar rise is reported in the NIPAs, but the gross saving, gross investment, and depreciation figures are all substantially higher under the expanded definitions.

We present, in table 6.8, estimates of gross and net saving rates on various adjusted bases. We start with the traditional NIPA basis, show the rates on an OECD basis (including government nonmilitary investment but neither government military investment nor consumer durables), and move to broader definitions. While the trends in these rates are important, perhaps at least as important is the fact that traditional comparisons between the United States and other countries are marred by numerous comparability problems, among the most important of which is the differential role played by government relative to private capital formation and net investment, especially military investment, on the one hand and consumer durable purchases on the other. These comparisons are particularly misleading with respect to Japan (see Boskin and Roberts 1986).

Table 6.8   Gross and Net Saving Rates, Selected Years

	Gross National Saving/GNP			
	Exclude Government Nonmilitary Investment and Consumer Durables (NIPA basis)	Include Government Nonmilitary Investment in Fixed Reproducible Capital (OECD basis)	Include Government Nonmilitary Investment in Fixed Reproducible Capital and Consumer Durables	All Government Investment and Consumer Durables
1950	17.8	20.3	24.7	23.9
1960	15.0	18.3	21.9	22.9
1970	13.8	16.8	21.3	21.8
1980	16.4	18.1	23.2	24.0
1985	13.8	15.5	22.2	24.3
	Net National Saving/NNP			
1950	11.7	13.2	14.6	11.8
1960	8.2	10.6	10.9	11.1
1970	6.2	8.2	8.8	8.7
1980	7.7	8.5	8.7	9.2
1985	4.7	5.5	7.0	8.8

Note: These estimates are derived from our 1985 constant dollar adjustment of the NIPAs to account for government capital and consumer durables. Denominators (GNP and NNP for gross and net saving rates, respectively) in each column have been expanded to include the rental flows associated with the types of government investment included in the numerator. The depreciation estimates used are from our calculations, as described earlier. For this reason, the net saving rates reported here in col. 1 differ from those calculated from NIPA data, which obviously use the NIPA capital consumption allowance instead.

As the data in table 6.9 and Figure 6.10 reveal, private consumption as a share of NNP has risen from 62.9 percent in 1950 and 63.7 percent in 1960 to 69.0 percent in 1985. This 6 percentage point rise—about a 10 percent increase—is close to the volume of traditional net private saving. Had private consumption remained at its 1950–60 ratio and the government sector been unchanged, net private saving would have been almost doubled in 1985.

Government consumption, as shown in figure 6.11, remains about 25 percent of NNP throughout the 1950s and 1960s but has since declined to only 21.3 percent by 1985. This aggregate marks a 10 percentage point decline in federal government consumption since the Korean War (despite the growth of the government capital stock) and a 4 percentage point rise in state and local government consumption. The former heavily reflects the growth of federal transfer payments (which by the mid-1970s exceeded purchases of goods and services) and the latter the demographic pressure of the baby boom on government spending on education.

The share of NNP devoted to national consumption has risen from about 86 percent in 1950 to over 90 percent by 1985. Though the consumption ratio has fluctuated substantially, partly for cyclical reasons, the continued upward trend is marked.

While the share of national product devoted to consumption has risen, the government's role in the trend is complex. While direct government consumption has fallen, part of the increase in the private consumption rate undoubtedly reflects the incentives created by growing government transfer payment programs and by tax policies. Thus, the decline in the national saving rate alluded to earlier reflects both the growth of the private consumption ratio, partly resulting from government transfer payment growth, and the decline in the net saving rate of the government sector—indeed, its shift to net dissaver—resulting both from historically large federal deficits and from the decline in state and local government net investment.

Table 6.9   **Private, Government, and National Consumption as Percentage of Expanded NNP, Selected Years**

	Private Consumption/ NNP	Government Consumption/NNP			National Consumption/ NNP
		Total	Federal	State-Local	
1950	62.9	23.5	13.8	9.7	86.4
1960	63.7	25.1	14.4	10.7	88.8
1970	65.4	25.6	12.7	12.9	91.0
1980	67.9	22.0	8.6	13.4	89.8
1985	69.0	21.3	8.7	12.6	90.3

Percentage

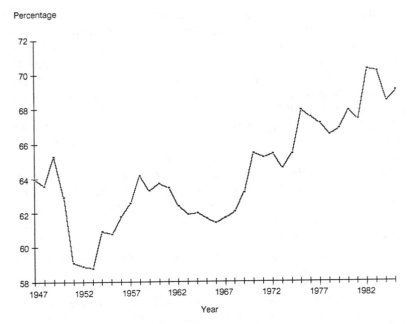

Fig. 6.10   Adjusted private consumption as a percentage of expanded net national product

6.6   Government Financial Assets and Liabilities

The federal debt receives enormous attention from the press and public. Little noticed is that governments also hold substantial financial assets as well as off-budget liabilities. Though, as Boskin (1982) argues, the appropriate definition of deficits depends on the question being asked, the conventional measures of debt and deficits are not accurate answers to almost any of them.

The Federal Reserve's flow-of-funds accounts present balance sheets with financial assets and liabilities for both the federal and the state and local governments. As Eisner and Pieper (1984) point out, these figures should be adjusted to reflect their market, rather than the par, value. They make a series of careful adjustments to the various components on the balance sheet.[25] Eisner (1986) updates the par-to-market conversions and extends them to state and local governments. The conversion factors are particularly large during periods of increasing inflation and interest rates, like 1980.[26]

Financial assets and liabilities in 1985 are presented for both levels of government in table 6.10. We have made only Eisner and Pieper's par-to-market corrections to the flow-of-funds accounts.[27] The federal government had more than $1 trillion in financial assets. More than

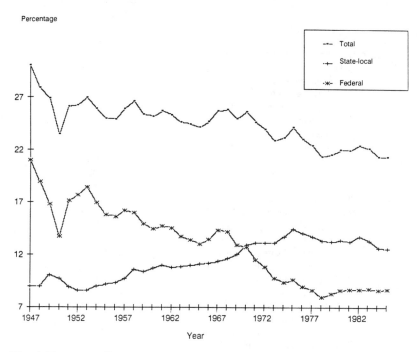

Fig. 6.11   Government consumption as a percentage of expanded net national product

half these were loans, but there was also more than $140 billion in cash, time deposits, and gold. Conventional debt also understates liabilities, which include more than $250 billion in agency debt. State and local government financial assets exceeded $450 billion and were within $100 billion of their financial liabilities. Nearly half of state and local financial assets were federal government liabilities.

Figures 6.12 and 6.13 show the trends in financial assets and liabilities for the two sectors in 1985 dollars. Federal financial liabilities fell rapidly after the war, then changed relatively little in real terms through 1981. At the same time, federal financial assets were gradually rising in real terms. The difference, called by Eisner the "net debt," was less than $600 billion in 1980, only slightly above its postwar low. In the last few years, of course, federal liabilities have exploded, and in 1985 they exceeded the 1945 peak for the first time. Since financial assets grew by only 10 percent, the net debt, as shown in table 6.11, grew by 145 percent.

State and local government financial liabilities grew more rapidly than financial assets through 1971. Liabilities fell sharply in real terms in the late 1970s, while financial assets continued their steady growth, so that net debt in 1985 was $66 billion, less than one-third its peak.

Table 6.10   **Government Financial Assets and Liabilities, 1985 (billions of 1985 dollars)**

	Federal
Financial assets:	
Currency, demand, and time deposits	53.4
Gold	86.4
Foreign exchange and special drawing rights	32.1
U.S. government securities	205.8
Treasury issues	194.3
Agency issues	11.5
Mortgages	224.9
Other loans	317.7
Taxes receivable	10.6
Miscellaneous assets	100.2
Total financial assets	1,031.1
Financial liabilities:	
Treasury currency and special drawing rights certificates	18.0
Demand deposits and currency	182.4
Bank reserves and vault cash	54.1
Credit market instruments	1,954.2
Treasury issues	1,590.1
Agency issues	279.4
Savings bonds	84.7
Insurance, retirement reserves	159.0
Miscellaneous liabilities	92.3
Total financial liabilities	2,460.0
Net debt	1,428.9

	State-Local
Financial assets:	
Currency, demand, and time deposits	78.0
Security repurchase agreements	48.8
U.S. government securities	231.8
Treasury issues	166.3
Agency issues	65.5
State and local obligations	8.3
Mortgages	78.3
Taxes receivable	21.1
Total financial assets	466.3
Financial liabilities:	
State and local obligations	482.6
Short term	18.5
Other	26.8
U.S. government loans	26.8
Trade debt	23.0
Total financial liabilities	532.4
Net debt	66.1

Sources: Par-to-market indices kindly provided by Paul Pieper and described in an appendix to Eisner (1986) were applied to end-of-year 1985 data on government financial assets and liabilities contained in the Federal Reserve flow-of-funds accounts. See text.

Billions
of 1985 $s

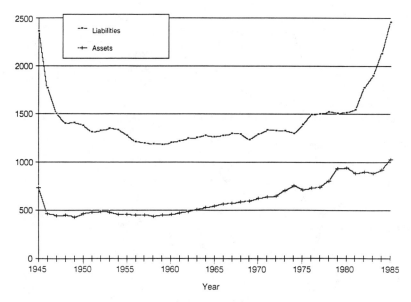

Fig. 6.12   Federal financial assets and liabilities

Billions
of 1985 $s

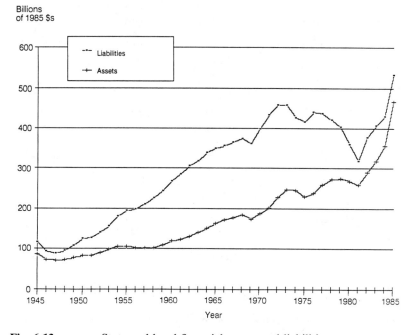

Fig. 6.13   State and local financial assets and liabilities

Table 6.11   **Net Debt and Change in Net Debt for Federal and State-Local Governments (billions of 1985 dollars)**

Years	Federal Net Debt	Change in Federal Net Debt	State-Local Net Debt	Change in State-Local Net Debt
1946	1,309.3	−325.6	20.7	−9.2
1947	1,059.9	−249.4	16.7	−4.0
1948	950.4	−109.5	21.8	5.1
1949	980.6	30.2	29.9	8.2
1950	917.9	−62.7	41.6	11.7
1951	833.5	−84.4	43.2	1.6
1952	842.3	8.8	50.4	7.2
1953	865.6	23.2	57.4	7.0
1954	877.5	11.9	75.2	17.8
1955	817.6	−59.8	89.5	14.4
1956	758.8	−58.8	94.6	5.1
1957	749.3	−9.6	108.2	13.6
1958	753.3	4.0	123.4	15.1
1959	731.9	−21.4	134.1	10.8
1960	749.0	17.1	148.9	14.8
1961	753.3	4.3	163.6	14.7
1962	760.9	7.6	175.4	11.8
1963	744.3	−16.6	177.9	2.5
1964	746.3	1.9	187.4	9.5
1965	719.4	−26.8	187.4	−.0
1966	710.4	−9.0	185.4	−2.0
1967	720.3	9.9	188.6	3.1
1968	704.3	−16.0	191.1	2.6
1969	633.7	−70.6	188.0	−3.1
1970	668.6	34.9	209.8	21.8
1971	697.1	28.5	231.7	21.9
1972	684.4	−12.7	229.9	−1.8
1973	621.5	−62.9	210.8	−19.1
1974	550.6	−70.8	181.0	−29.8
1975	675.1	124.5	187.0	6.1
1976	762.3	87.2	203.2	16.2
1977	764.6	2.4	178.3	−25.0
1978	715.5	−49.1	148.2	−30.0
1979	570.6	−145.0	128.5	−19.7
1980	574.5	4.0	91.2	−37.2
1981	664.0	89.5	59.4	−31.8
1982	882.1	218.1	87.3	27.9
1983	1,015.1	133.0	88.9	1.5
1984	1,215.3	200.2	73.0	−15.9
1985	1,428.9	213.6	66.1	−6.9

Sources: Net debt is defined by Eisner as the excess of government financial liabilities over financial assets. Current dollar series on the estimated market value of government financial liabilities and assets for 1945–84 are taken from Eisner (1986) and converted into 1985 dollars via the GNP deflator. The differences in these series for federal and state-local governments are reported here as net debt. Estimates for 1985 are from table 6.10.

6.7 Government Oil and Gas Mineral Rights

Governments own a large fraction of the mineral rights in the United States. Federal and state governments own all mineral rights on offshore and tidal lands. In addition, all levels own the mineral rights under government land. For consistent accounting, the value of these assets should be counted as wealth, and revenues from government-owned lands should be charged as sales of the assets.

Oil and gas rights are by far the most valuable to the government sector, though other minerals, particularly coal, may be more valuable in some states. For the federal government, we correct, update, and convert to 1985 dollars the estimates of the value of oil and gas rights made by Boskin et al. (1985).[28]

When a government leases the mineral rights in a particular area—rights essentially to as yet undiscovered resources—it has reduced its mineral wealth by transferring claims to part of it to the private sector. In return, the government receives some payment immediately in the form of a bonus, with the rest of the payments deferred as royalties or rental payments. Bonuses are cash payments that are not conditional on the existence or size of the resource and are typically the variable subject to bidding. Royalty payments are fractions, usually fixed in advance, of the gross revenue of the produced output, if any. By the time reserves are "proven," their only value to the government is the present value of royalties they represent.[29]

The method used by Boskin et al. (1985) takes advantage of several institutional and theoretical characteristics of oil and gas production to value federal oil and gas rights with the limited information available.[30] The base-year value of oil and gas rights to the government is the sum of three components: future royalties on proven reserves, future royalties on estimated undiscovered reserves, and future bonuses on unleased land. Fortunately, royalties are historically fixed percentages of the gross revenues. Since the percentage is known, forecasting royalties requires forecasting production and prices. By definition, expected future production, with current prices and technology, is the sum of proven and estimated undiscovered reserves. Since oil and gas are exhaustible resources, there are theoretical, as well as empirical, reasons to expect increasing real prices. Boskin et al. assume that real prices will grow at the real rate of interest since this is both convenient and roughly consistent with historical evidence and theory.[31] Bonuses on unleased land are assumed to be proportional to royalties on undiscovered resources.

Boskin et al. (1985) obtain the value of federal oil and gas rights in other years by making two additional assumptions. First, the quantity of oil and gas reserves changes only with production.[32] Second, the expected future price path at any date is proportional to actual prices at that date.[33] With these assumptions, capital gains or losses are proportional to price changes, and the change in value from year to year is the capital gain less bonuses and royalties received.

The corrected values of federal oil and gas rights, converted to 1985 dollars using the GNP deflator, are given in table 6.12. The magnitudes are enormous, particularly after the second oil shock. The 1980 value

Table 6.12   **Value of Federal Oil and Gas Mineral Rights (billions of 1985 dollars)**

Year	Total	Oil	Gas	Change in Value
1954	247.2	197.1	50.0	
1955	239.0	189.8	49.2	−8.2
1956	234.1	184.5	49.6	−4.9
1957	247.1	196.9	50.2	13.0
1958	239.9	188.1	51.8	−7.2
1959	230.7	176.4	54.3	−9.2
1960	229.5	171.8	57.7	−1.2
1961	231.9	170.5	61.5	2.4
1962	226.8	165.7	61.2	−5.1
1963	223.3	162.4	60.9	−3.5
1964	216.9	158.6	58.3	−6.4
1965	209.8	152.7	57.1	−7.1
1966	202.9	147.8	55.1	−6.9
1967	198.8	144.7	54.0	−4.2
1968	186.6	135.2	51.5	−12.2
1969	182.9	133.6	49.3	−3.7
1970	174.7	128.0	46.7	−8.3
1971	175.0	128.3	46.7	.4
1972	161.6	118.0	43.6	−13.4
1973	166.7	121.6	45.1	5.1
1974	243.0	188.5	54.5	76.3
1975	261.0	189.3	71.6	18.0
1976	273.7	187.7	86.1	12.7
1977	289.3	180.9	108.4	15.6
1978	287.9	173.7	114.1	−1.4
1979	350.7	217.3	133.3	62.8
1980	492.7	328.5	164.2	142.0
1981	618.2	430.3	187.9	125.5
1982	612.2	393.7	218.5	−6.0
1983	571.6	348.7	222.9	−40.7
1984	537.7	327.2	210.5	−33.9
1985	491.5	288.9	202.6	−46.2
1986	334.8	172.2	162.6	−156.7

Sources: The value of oil and gas rights for 1981 was obtained from estimates of proven and undiscovered, but economically recoverable, reserves on federal land, 1981 prices, royalty rates, and historic ratios of bonuses to future royalties. The values for other years were obtained by adjusting for bonuses and royalties paid and price changes. A detailed description of the methodology and underlying assumptions, as well as sensitivity analyses, is given in Boskin et al. (1985). The series was converted to 1985 dollars using the GNP deflator.

is the largest of any single asset on the federal balance sheet, substantially higher than structures, gold, mortgages, or inventories. It is almost as large as the net federal debt in that year. Even after the dramatic drop in world oil prices, we estimate the value of federal oil and gas rights exceeded one-third of a trillion dollars in 1986. As figure 6.14 shows, changes in the value of federal rights can also be large, occasionally exceeding the conventionally measured budget deficit. Some volatility is appropriate since the method is designed to give a contemporaneous estimate of the value of mineral rights.

Before turning to state and local mineral rights, let us add some caveats. Our calculations are sensitive to estimates of undiscovered, economically recoverable reserves. As shown in Boskin et al. (1985), the value of oil and gas rights could be up to 39 percent higher or 29 percent lower if one took the 5 percent or 95 percent bounds calculated by the U.S. Geological Survey (1981). The estimates are also sensitive to the assumptions on price growth.[34]

Since state and local governments do not appear, for the most part, to keep records on either production or reserves on state-owned lands, it is difficult to make estimates of the value of oil and gas rights for them. We have obtained information from three states that account for more than 60 percent of U.S. oil production and a higher fraction of

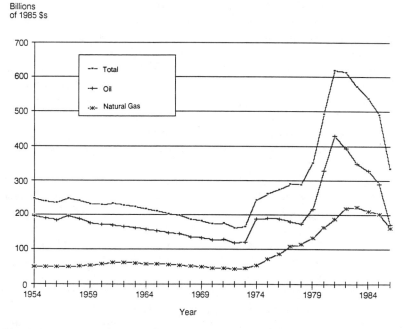

Fig. 6.14   Value of federal oil and gas rights

the value of state-owned oil and gas rights: Alaska, Texas, and California.[35]

By far the most valuable oil and gas rights are owned by the state of Alaska. More than 99 percent of Alaska's production is on state-owned land; this compares to an estimated 6.5 percent for Texas and 1.8 percent for California.[36] Since essentially all Alaska's production is on state-owned land, it is artificial to treat taxes on petroleum differently from royalties. If the severance tax rate were lower, for example, royalty rates could be raised by the same amount without changing production or state revenues. Even the corporate tax on oil companies should be viewed as payment for oil rights; oil companies pay more than 90 percent of corporate income taxes, and the formula for calculating the base was changed to maximize the take from the oil producers.[37] Accordingly, we include all petroleum taxes and royalties as part of the value of rights.

In 1985, Alaska's revenues from petroleum were $3.1 billion, or $4.64 per barrel produced. Alaska had 7.1 billion barrels of proven oil reserves, so, under the price growth assumption of Boskin et al. (1985), these alone were worth at least $32.9 billion in 1985.[38] Alaska was estimated to have 6.9 billion barrels of undiscovered, economically recoverable oil onshore. If this was all on state land, the value of oil rights would have been $65 billion in 1985. Finally, the state was estimated to have 71 trillion cubic feet of natural gas either proven or undiscovered. If the value to the state of 10,000 cubic feet of gas were the same as a barrel of oil, this would make the total value of Alaskan oil and gas rights $98 billion in 1985.[39]

By comparison to Alaska, even Texas looks small. The average royalty rate on state-owned land was 12 percent, and the severance tax rates were 4.6 percent for oil and 7.5 percent for gas.[40] If the reserve-to-production ratio is the same on private and state-owned land, the value of proven reserves of oil and gas on state land in 1985 was $2.2 and $1.6 billion, respectively.[41] If state land contains the same fraction of undiscovered reserves as of production, the total value of Texas's oil and gas rights was roughly $12 billion in 1985.[42]

Since California has much smaller proven and estimated undiscovered reserves, and since the state owns a much smaller fraction of those reserves, the value of California's rights is lower by an order of magnitude. The state collects an average royalty of 16.5 percent. Under Boskin et al.' (1985) assumptions, the value of California's oil and gas rights was $0.8 billion in 1985 if the ratio of both undiscovered and proven reserves to production was the same on private and on state land.

Our estimates of the total value of oil and gas rights in 1985 owned by the three states for which we have data is $110.8 billion. Using the method described by Boskin et al. (1985), we adjust for royalty and bonus payments and price changes to create current dollar estimates for earlier years. Converting the estimate to 1985 dollars using the GNP deflator, we obtain an estimate for state oil and gas rights in 1980 of $125 billion. We wish to stress, however, that data limitations forced several assumptions about the quantity and value of oil and gas reserves, both proven and undiscovered, on state land. In addition, we are limited to three states—the most important omission being Louisiana—and, because of a lack of royalty data, to the 1980s. Our 1980 estimate of the value of state oil and gas rights exceeds our figures for the value of any single category of financial asset on the state and local balance sheet or the value of state and local residential structures, equipment, and inventories combined.

6.8 Government Land

Governmental units own substantial amounts of land in the United States, with the federal government alone holding nearly one-third of the nation's land area. In this section, we present annual estimates of the value of federal and state-local land from 1946 to 1985.[43] The estimates for 1946–51 are taken from Goldsmith (1962) and those for 1952–68 from Milgram (1973). Our contribution is to update these series from 1969 forward. In doing this, we follow Milgram's basic methodology, with some modifications.

Unfortunately, the data available on acreage and market values of government land are incomplete, especially for state and local governments, and not entirely reliable. Like Goldsmith and Milgram, we use these data to update estimates made for 1946 by Reeve et al. (1950), and more current and more rigorously derived benchmark estimates are desirable. These limitations restrict the degree of confidence that can be placed in any estimate of government land values.

The General Services Administration (GSA) publishes estimates of rural and urban acreage owned by the federal government and its original acquisition cost in its annual *Summary Report of Real Property Owned by the United States throughout the World*. These data are compiled from detailed inventory reports submitted by federal agencies. In 1985, the GSA estimated that the federal government owned 723.0 million acres of rural land and 3.7 million acres of urban land, which had a total acquisition cost of $12.9 billion. Given the significant share of national wealth accounted for by land, it is perhaps surprising that there is not a large body of carefully derived data on land prices. We construct a price index for federal rural land that gives equal weight to the U.S. Department of Agriculture's estimated average value of farmland and to stumpage prices paid for timber harvested in national forests. Our price index for federal urban land is based on the average site price per square foot of one-family homes purchased with Federal Housing Administration (FHA)–insured mortgages. We estimate the value of federal urban and rural land in each year by applying our price index for each to the corresponding GSA acreage series.[44]

In table 6.13, we present estimates of federal, state-local, and total government land values for 1946–85. We have used the GNP deflator to convert the estimates drawn from Goldsmith (1962), Milgram (1973), and our calculations into 1985 dollars. We estimate the value of federal land in 1985 at $231.3 billion, with urban land accounting for more than three-fourths of the total value despite the fact that it constitutes only 0.5 percent of total acreage. (For a breakdown of the total federal land stock into rural and urban components, see table 6.14, and, for a chart of government land values, fig. 6.15.) The sizable increase in the federal total from $99.4 billion in 1968 results from an increase of about 160 percent in urban acreage, which is far more valuable than rural land, and from increases in both our land price indices that exceed the general inflation rate. The real value of federal urban land more than triples over 1968–85, and most of the increase occurs in 1970–74 and 1979–81. The rural land series primarily reflects price changes, and it increases gradually until the late 1970s and early 1980s and then decreases sharply. Our 1985 total value estimate is 8 percent lower than the peak attained in 1981.[45]

Less information is available on land owned by state and local governments; there are neither estimates of total acreage nor a breakdown between rural and urban components. Yet the significance of these land holdings is indicated by Milgram's finding that they were more than three times as valuable as federal land in 1968. Thus, it is important to update the previous work on state and local government land also. Here we follow Milgram's methodology almost exactly, partly because a paucity of data constrains us from doing otherwise. We construct one price index for all state and local land that gives equal weight to U.S. Department of Agriculture average farmland values and to the average site price per square foot of homes purchased with FHA–insured mortgages. To estimate acquisitions, we use a Census Bureau data series on state and local governments' "capital outlays for land and existing structures." Lacking other information, we follow Milgram in reducing these values by 10 percent to adjust both for the value of existing structures located on these lands that are purchased for continuing use and for sales of state and local government land, which are not reported separately in the data provided in the Census Bureau's annual *Governmental Finances*. We use this net acquisitions series A_t and our price series P_t to calculate the value of state and local land V_t as

$$V_t = V_{t-1}\left[\frac{P_t}{P_{t-1}}\right] + A_t.$$

Table 6.13   **Estimates of Government Land Values (billions of 1985 dollars)**

Year	Federal	State-Local	Total
1946	40.3	108.8	149.1
1947	42.0	108.2	150.1
1948	42.1	101.8	143.9
1949	43.3	97.4	140.7
1950	53.7	112.2	165.9
1951	59.6	107.7	167.3
1952	47.3	103.8	151.1
1953	46.4	121.6	168.1
1954	48.8	128.4	177.2
1955	50.3	147.4	197.7
1956	53.3	161.3	214.5
1957	55.3	178.6	233.9
1958	57.2	193.2	250.5
1959	61.0	207.1	268.2
1960	66.4	219.1	285.4
1961	73.6	237.3	310.9
1962	77.4	252.1	329.5
1963	82.3	268.8	351.1
1964	86.7	287.4	374.1
1965	90.1	297.8	388.0
1966	94.1	312.3	406.4
1967	98.1	324.5	422.6
1968	99.4	328.0	427.4
1969	112.1	331.6	443.7
1970	111.8	370.5	482.2
1971	132.6	358.9	491.5
1972	144.0	382.1	526.2
1973	167.6	396.8	564.4
1974	177.6	435.1	612.7
1975	175.6	447.9	623.5
1976	182.7	474.8	657.5
1977	200.5	521.4	721.9
1978	217.1	550.0	767.1
1979	217.6	590.0	807.6
1980	226.5	659.3	885.8
1981	252.7	704.6	957.2
1982	233.3	664.6	897.9
1983	238.9	644.4	883.3
1984	244.5	640.6	885.2
1985	231.3	580.5	811.8

Sources: Government land value estimates for 1946–51, 1952–68, and 1969–85 were obtained from Goldsmith (1962), Milgram (1973), and our updating of Milgram's estimates, repectively, with all estimates converted from current dollars into 1985 dollars by the GNP deflator.

Table 6.14   Value of Federal Land: Rural, Urban, and Total (billions of 1985 dollars)

Year	Rural	Urban	Total
1956	20.6	32.7	53.3
1957	19.7	35.6	55.3
1958	19.5	37.8	57.2
1959	22.6	38.4	61.0
1960	25.9	40.5	66.4
1961	30.2	43.4	73.6
1962	31.8	45.6	77.4
1963	33.0	48.6	81.6
1964	35.3	51.4	86.7
1965	37.7	52.4	90.1
1966	39.7	54.5	94.1
1967	42.1	56.0	98.1
1968	43.1	56.3	99.4
1969	50.4	61.7	112.1
1970	47.7	64.0	111.8
1971	44.1	88.4	132.6
1972	50.7	93.4	144.0
1973	55.0	112.6	167.6
1974	61.9	115.7	177.6
1975	54.1	121.5	175.6
1976	62.7	120.0	182.7
1977	73.4	127.2	200.5
1978	83.7	133.1	216.8
1979	83.9	133.7	217.6
1980	73.4	153.1	226.5
1981	76.0	176.7	252.7
1982	56.1	177.2	233.3
1983	60.5	178.4	238.9
1984	58.0	182.4	240.4
1985	49.9	181.4	231.3

Estimated values of state and local government land are found in column 2 of table 6.13. Our 1985 market value is $580.5 billion. As can be seen in figure 6.15, the value of this land grows steadily at a slightly increasing rate between 1968 and 1981. This reflects real increases in average land prices and yearly net acquisitions of 1–2 percent of the stock. Since 1981, the value of state and local land has decreased a total of 18 percent, as a significant decrease in nominal farmland values and a leveling off in urban land values have caused our composite price index to decrease.

6.9   Contingent Liabilities

The federal government and closely allied federally sponsored agencies engage in activities that generate contingent liabilities (and also

Billions
of 1985 $s

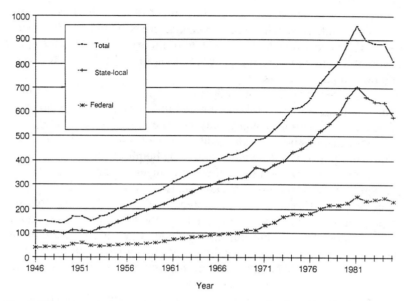

Fig. 6.15   Value of government land

assets) for the government. The most important of these are loans, loan guarantees, and deposit insurance. The recent developments in real estate, agriculture, energy, and less-developed-country loans threaten the solvency of the two major deposit insurance programs—the Federal Deposit Insurance Corporation (FDIC) and the Federal Savings and Loan Insurance Corporation (FSLIC). The agricultural debt crisis has already brought the Farm Credit System, a federally regulated and sponsored financial intermediary, to Congress for emergency financial relief. Agricultural loan guarantees by the Farm Home Administration are in the process of major default and substantial federal payouts. Other federal insurance programs of questionable solvency include the Pension Benefit Guarantee Corporation and social security. We discuss social security in the next section.

The exact nature and extent of these federal liabilities and those of the smaller but often analogous state and local insurance program liabilities are unclear. Various statements have been made that provide estimates of the "maximum" exposure or risk or potential liabilities of the federal government. For example, the federal government publishes annually a document showing total insured deposits. Arthur Anderson and Company (1986) presents estimates of the maximum risk exposure in notes appended to a government balance sheet. But as documented in Boskin, Barham, et al. (1987), the history of deposit insurance has been primarily one in which the uninsured deposits are insured as well. These amount to 30 percent of all bank deposits. But it is also unlikely that a severe financial crisis would result in such payoffs. It is only imaginable in a state of the world in which the entire economy is in chaos and the government is forced to resort to hyper-inflation to pay its debts.

On the other hand, current budgetary treatment of deposit insurance, loans, and guarantees is misleading and inaccurate. There is no sense of accrual accounting, usually only net spending (net of revenues) is reported, there is no separate capital account, and there is no adjustment from par to market value. Still, it is helpful to have some rough idea of the size and nature of these contingent liabilities. Table 6.15 presents postwar time-series data on the total outstanding—at par value—of direct loans, loan guarantees, and federally sponsored enterprise debt. It should be emphasized that the total outstanding figures not only are at par value but also include some double counting as there are secondary guarantees. To avoid the double counting, a rough rule would be that 20 or 25 percent of the total outstanding in the recent years are secondary guarantees.

Each year new commitments amount to a tremendous volume of lending and guaranteeing. For example, in 1986, new commitments of loan guarantees were almost $300 billion. Of this total, the overwhelming bulk were renewing previously extended guarantees that had expired. The total outstanding year-to-year changes reflect the net new commitments. These figures do not include deposit insurance or social security. Of these hundreds of billions in outstanding loans and guarantees, what is a sensible estimate of the contingent liability of the federal government? It is clearly implausible that all the loans will default with probability one, so the total outstanding amounts are a substantial upper bound (although Bartlett 1983 adds them to the regular national debt). While some loans are ultimately forgiven and cost the government the original amount, many are repaid completely. The likely course of future repayments will reflect various factors, including economic conditions such as commodity prices, interest rates, the level of real economic activity, and the like.

It is possible to develop a life-cycle projection of new loan guarantee commitments to determine, on the basis of longitudinal data, the net spending equivalent in present value terms that is likely to occur per dollar of new commitments of loan guarantees and correspondingly for direct loans and agency debt. While in some contingencies the historically based data might prove to be exceedingly inaccurate, it is potentially useful to develop some insight into the historical pattern of

Table 6.15   **Total Outstanding for Direct Loans and Loan Guarantees in Millions of Dollars at Par Value, 1952–86**

Year	Direct Loans, Total Outstanding	Loan Guarantees, Total Outstanding (Gross)	Federally Sponsored Enterprises, Total Outstanding (Gross)[a]
1952	14,020	24,384	2,945
1953	15,656	35,052	3,003
1954	14,740	40,460	3,014
1955	16,088	45,392	3,602
1956	17,116	51,097	4,292
1957	17,503	55,939	5,578
1958	18,454	58,515	5,947
1959	22,458	63,337	7,446
1960	22,579	67,263	9,106
1961	23,932	71,849	9,545
1962	27,264	76,967	11,296
1963	29,459	81,461	11,600
1964	31,326	85,645	13,568
1965	33,054	91,414	15,331
1966	32,997	99,225	19,390
1967	42,208	99,500	19,040
1968	51,799	108,071	22,883
1969	46,856	117,703	26,955
1970	51,078	125,514	37,515
1971	53,156	143,549	38,939
1972	50,149	165,713	43,322
1973	43,891	183,292	54,816
1974	46,132	197,159	71,160
1975	49,777	218,273	84,635
1976	53,404	243,213	90,788
TR	54,220	247,816	93,598
1977	67,637	284,289	101,902
1978	76,526	317,292	129,987
1979	82,972	387,172	163,575
1980	91,663	454,725	195,807
1981	91,287	505,405	231,417
1982	100,220	547,327	275,361
1983	223,000	519,646	261,000
1984	229,300	565,528	314,100
1985	257,400	613,101	369,940
1986	251,600	691,921	453,300

Source: Boskin, Barham, et al. (1987).

[a]The federally sponsored enterprises are the Federal National Mortgage Association, the Federal Home Loan Banks, Federal Land Banks, Federal Home Loan Mortgage Corporation, the Federal Intermediate Credit Banks, Banks for Cooperatives, and the Student Loan Mortgage Association.

actual government spending and support of guarantees and loans. Boskin, Barham, et al. (1987) present an analytic schema and apply it to longitudinal data on cohorts of loan guarantees for government agencies, especially the Small Business Administration, and they estimate that, for each dollar of new commitment, the present value of ultimate spending in support of that commitment is approximately twelve cents. If—and it is a big if—such a figure could be applied to other programs, a rough estimate of the likely value of the ultimate federal government liability based on the value of the loans would be about 12 percent of the figures reported in table 6.15, about $30 billion dollars in support of loans, $80 billion in support of loan guarantees, and perhaps $50 billion in support of federally sponsored enterprises in 1985. There are a variety of reasons to believe that the 12 percent figure may be too low or too high in various circumstances for different kinds of lending activity, but we mention this only because it has become somewhat fashionable either to ignore these contingent liabilities or to report them as the maximum risk exposure or the total value outstanding, as if that figure were readily comparable to, say, the privately held regular national debt. Clearly, that procedure is inappropriate.

Deposit insurance raises similar, though in some ways more subtle and more quantitatively important, issues. First, the nature of the banking deposit insurance system is that the risks are systematically correlated to a much greater extent than in other federal government lending programs. There is a small probability of extremely high payouts. But even defining the maximum exposure of the FDIC or the FSLIC is questionable. The Treasury counts total insured deposits. But that exceeds by a factor of at least fifty the properly measured net worth of the FDIC or the FSLIC. By law, the FDIC and the FSLIC (and several other smaller analogous organizations) have a line of credit at the Treasury, but this line of credit is quite modest. Does the Treasury and/or the Federal Reserve stand behind all insured deposits? All deposits? Or only the amount in the funds plus the standby borrowing authority at the Treasury? Total deposits at insured banks were $1.974 trillion—coincidently, about the size of the privately held national debt—in 1985, whereas the insured amounts were $1.503 trillion. The total assets of the FDIC were $26.4 billion in 1985, and the standby borrowing authority at the Treasury $3 billion.

The FDIC and the FSLIC are technically independent agencies, so they could legally default on their liabilities without giving their creditors a claim on the Treasury. Clearly, the potential liabilities of the FDIC and the FSLIC substantially exceed their assets in bad-case scenarios. What is a sensible expected present value to put forth for such contingent liabilities? Surely, they are substantially less than either the total deposits insured at institutions or the total insured deposits. Formally, we would like to sum the present discounted value of expected payouts in each period to obtain an appropriate loss reserve as the best single number to provide as a contingent liability. This would depend not only on future economic conditions but also on the interpretation of the various rules, laws, and political decisions concerning backing the thrift industry. Rather than present a time series of estimates, we refer the interested reader to Boskin, Barham, et al. (1987) for analytic discussion and report in the balance sheets presented in section 6.11 alternative estimates of these contingent liabilities of the deposit insurance system.

As noted above, state and local governments also have various contingent obligations, including those to state-chartered banks, unfunded pension liabilities, and so on. We raise these issues here but do not attempt to elaborate the analysis.

6.10 Social Security

Because the social security program looms so large in the financial picture of so many, and because, until recently, it has been more or less a pay-as-you-go system, the currently unfunded liabilities of the social security system at any point in time are usually large, subject to substantial variation depending on assumed patterns of economic and demographic trends, and subject to enormous change with seemingly minor (relative to the intense debate over budget deficits and tax reform) changes in rules relating to benefits or taxes. It is not our purpose here to review the voluminous literature concerning the potential effect of social security "wealth" on real economic activity, such as the saving/consumption choice or retirement decisions.[46]

How to define the expected obligations of the social security system is also a subject of much controversy. Under a closed-group approach, the expected future taxes and benefits paid by particular cohorts—for example, all those currently alive or currently above a certain age, such as eighteen—would be calculated, discounted to the present, and compared. The difference between the expected present value of benefits and taxes would be the surplus or deficit. This concept, using current participants as the group, is adapted by Arthur Anderson and Company (1986). Under an open-group concept, the expected present value of benefits and taxes paid over some time period, often taken to be the seventy-five-year long-term actuarial projection period of the Social Security Administration (SSA), would be compared, with the difference being the deficit or surplus. Thus, taxes paid in the early working years of the currently unborn and benefits paid to persons during retirement who are not yet in the labor force would be counted. While seventy-five years is an extremely long time period, and while modest changes in growth rates or demographic assumptions can make huge swings in the expected balances in social security, swings the size of the regular national debt, the time frame is somewhat arbitrary, as are the various assumptions involved.

Table 6.16 presents estimates of the long-term actuarial deficit in the retirement and disability part of social security over the next seventy-five years under alternative economic and demographic scenarios (as developed by Boskin and Puffert 1987 and Boskin 1987). The annual amounts are adjusted for inflation and discounted to the present at a real discount rate of 2 percent (the interest rate assumed earned on social security balances by the Social Security Trustees). As can be seen, in the base case, the SSA's intermediate assumptions for economic and demographic trends over the next seventy-five years, there is a deficit of almost $0.5 trillion, slightly under 0.5 percent of taxable payroll over the period. Under the SSA actuary's optimistic assumptions, there is a $3.4 trillion surplus, while, under the overall pessimistic assumptions, there is a $2.6 trillion deficit. Thus, moving all the economic and demographic projections from intermediate to either optimistic or pessimistic results in a change that is larger than the privately held national debt. But all the assumptions do not have to change for there to be an enormous variation in the expected surplus. For example, leaving all the other assumptions aside and just adopting the high wage growth assumptions of the SSA actuaries results in a surplus of almost $900 billion, a $1.4 trillion increase over the base case. Adopting the low mortality assumption, holding all the other demographic assumptions and economic assumptions to those of the intermediate case, results in a deficit of $1.7 trillion, a $1.2 trillion increase.

The numbers revealed in table 6.16 are substantial, and social security looms large in the lives of many Americans—there are 37 million current beneficiaries and over 100 million taxpayers, the majority of

Table 6.16	OASDI System Finances, Various Economic and Demographic Scenarios, Seventy-five-Year Totals, 1986–2060 (billions of 1986 dollars, discounted to 1986)	
Scenarios	Surplus	Variation of Surplus from Base Case
Base case	−495	0
Overall optimistic for trust fund	3,389	3,884
Overall pessimistic for trust fund	−2,567	−2,072
High wage growth	878	1,373
Low wage growth	−948	−453
High mortality	468	963
Low mortality	−1,700	−1,205
Benefit-ratchet-unfunded	−3,690	−3,195
Pay-as-you-go tax rates	0	495

Source: Boskin and Puffert (1987).

whom pay more in social security taxes than in income taxes. It would be surprising if there were no effects of these variations. However, the seventy-five-year period is somewhat arbitrary. The deficit occurs for a variety of reasons, not the least of which is the passage of the extra large baby boom generation into retirement, followed by the baby bust generation paying high tax rates to finance the benefits of the baby boom. The period beyond the seventy-five-year projections would be one of surplus if the benefits were raised no further and the high tax rates maintained as the ratio of workers to retirees edges upward as the baby bust generation retires.[47]

For a variety of reasons, projections of social security deficits should be taken with a certain degree of caution. Not only are they enormously sensitive to these economic and demographic assumptions, about which reasonable people might disagree, but future social security benefits are also not contractual obligations in the same way as the regularly issued national debt. While the national debt is issued in bonds of nominal dollar value and hence could be altered substantially by unexpected inflation, as emphasized by Eisner (1986), it is unlikely to be repudiated, even in part. Social security benefits and taxes and their difference, on the other hand, are really potential future obligations. They can be changed by congressional action changing the benefit formulae—for example, changing the bend points in the retirement plan as proposed, but rejected, in the early 1980s; taxing all social security benefits, or half of them as was done in 1983; changing marginal tax rates in the income tax, as was done in the Tax Reform Act of 1986; raising the age of eligibility for future social security beneficiaries, as was done in 1983 prospectively for the early twenty-first century, and so on.

Another important issue surrounds the fact that for the first time social security retirement funds are projected to be on a path that deviates systematically from pay-as-you-go finance. Under pay-as-you-go finance, the long-term actuarial deficit in social security is identically zero, as each year's benefits are paid by each year's taxes, although they may not line up so evenly for a particular age group or income group or for families of different marital status. Concern about the long-run deficit really seems to be concern about whether taxes will be raised or benefits reduced when projections create a situation in which the two are likely to diverge systematically. For the old age and survivors insurance system, the real discounted value of the projected surplus peaks around 2020 at almost $800 billion (see fig. 6.16), and several hundred billion dollars would be added by the disability fund. To provide some insight into the possible difference in the social security retirement system's long-run surplus, consider two scenarios: we use the temporary surplus to raise benefits without correspondingly raising taxes later on in the seventy-five-year period, or we revert to pay-as-

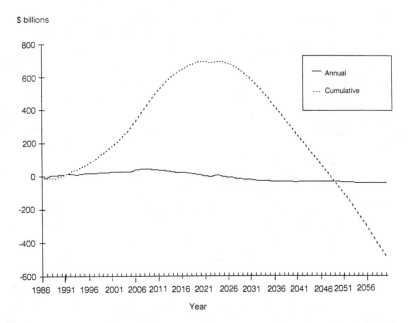

$ billions

Fig. 6.16   Old age and survivors insurance system projected real discounted surplus for base case, annual and cumulative

you-go finance by lowering tax rates during the period of the surplus. As the final two rows of table 6.16 reveal, the long-run actuarial deficit in the retirement part of the system increases to $3.7 trillion under the benefit-ratcheting-up case but is eliminated under the pay-as-you-go tax-rate-reduction case (in which tax rates are reduced during years of surplus and raised during the years of deficits to restore the pay-as-you-go nature of the system).

The hospital insurance system is projected to be in much worse shape than old age, survivors, and disability insurance (OASDI) (see fig. 6.17) because the tax rate for hospital insurance is fixed at 2.9 percent of taxable payroll while health care expenditures are growing, partly for demographic reasons and partly because of differential growth in health care costs versus general inflation. Even if the latter is brought under control, the demographics will cause the expenditures under the hospital insurance part of medicare to rise, so, when compared with slowly growing tax revenues, the deficit must widen. Thus, over the next several decades the options for social security are accruing a surplus in the retirement and disability funds, dissipating it for other uses such as assigning some of the tax proceeds to medicare, and so on.

For all these reasons we prefer to provide the supplemental information concerning social security as additional potential liabilities in

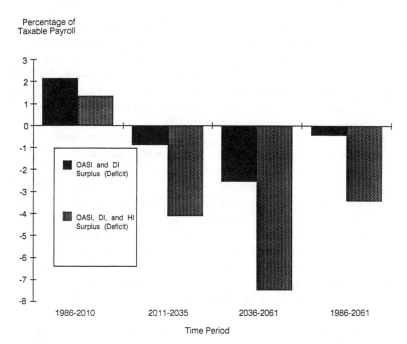

Percentage of
Taxable Payroll

Fig. 6.17   Projected social security finances under intermediate (IIB)
                       assumptions

any balance sheet for the government sector. We do not propose to
add it to the regular national debt.[48]

6.11   Government Balance Sheets

With our estimates of government tangible and financial assets and
liabilities, the temptation to create government balance sheets is irre-
sistible. Before giving in, however, we must stress numerous caveats
and cautions.

While we believe that we have developed improved estimates of
tangible assets, each of the major categories of assets and liabilities
presents conceptual and measurement difficulties. The "net worth"
figures we shall present are, accordingly, subject to substantial error.
Moreover, extremely important classes of liabilities—contingent and
potential—are excluded, at least above the line, because, unlike financial liabilities or assets, they are mostly not traded on a market or easily
quantified with existing data and are subject to large uncertainty. Presenting rough estimates of contingent liabilities on loans, guarantees,
and deposit insurance and potential liabilities in unfunded pension programs (especially social security) "below the line" is not meant to

suggest that they are less important than those included above the line. However, they are subject to different degrees of precision, contractual obligation, and conceptual estimation. Also, they are taken from other sources (although some are by Boskin). Of course, governments have enormous intangible assets, including the power to tax, so a negative net worth would not imply bankruptcy or imminent debt repudiation. Accordingly, our calculations, like similar ones by Eisner and Pieper (1984) and Eisner (1986), should probably be viewed as illustrative of trends rather than as accurate point estimates of net worth.

Further, how to add up various components is by no means obvious. Finance theory tells us we should place greater value on future income streams that are negatively correlated with other sources of income. Thus, if one concludes that the value of government mineral rights will rise substantially when oil prices accelerate sharply, and if this is associated with a deep recession or some other long-lived economic event, these revenues may be systematically negatively correlated with other sources of government revenue; and similar issues arise on the outlay side. The conceptually proper thing would be to apply a risk charge to the various components in the various time periods on the basis of subjective probability distributions of outcomes and estimates of the risk tolerance (the reciprocal of the Arrow-Pratt measure of risk aversion) and to discount those charges to the present. We have not sought to do this here, but we do wish to emphasize that the variability of likely future returns or outlays stemming from various government activities is large, as it is for the private sector, and that there may also be systematic covariance among components that should be taken into account in establishing a balance sheet.

Estimates of the real change in net worth have important, but still limited, uses. The net worth provides some indication of future tax liabilities. When oil was discovered in Alaska, expected future tax liabilities of Alaskan residents dropped dramatically.

Changes in net worth indicate what legacy, in the form of future government service net of tax liabilities, current generations are providing future generations. Of course, this does not imply that the only ethical course is to leave net worth unchanged. If future generations will be richer, or if the current generation has made large sacrifices, as, for example, in World War II, it may be entirely appropriate to pass tax burdens forward.

Changes in net worth are not necessarily a good indicator of fiscal tightness. But information on conventional deficits may usefully be supplemented by various adjustments to government assets and liabilities. Eisner and Pieper (1984) and Eisner (1986) provide some evidence that changes in real net debt are a better measure of fiscal policy than are conventional deficits. Boskin (1988) presents evidence that the private propensity to consume out of the excess of government tangible capital over explicit debt is 0.04, about the same as generally found for private wealth. This suggests that public and private saving are substitutes in the sense that increased government tangible capital increases private consumption and decreases private saving. These studies indicate that the type of data generated in this paper may be of some use in the studies of the effect of fiscal policy on short-run stabilization and/or long-run growth.

Having discussed their usefulness and limitations, we turn to the numbers. In table 6.17, balance sheets for the federal government for 1970, 1980, and 1985 are provided. As throughout this paper, the figures are in 1985 dollars. While real liabilities of the federal government grew by 18 percent between 1970 and 1980, the net debt, owing in part to rising gold prices, fell by 14 percent. Net worth grew by $692 billion, to over $1.0 trillion. While many were bemoaning record deficits, the value of federal assets, especially oil and gas, was growing rapidly. In the 1980s, the picture is very different. Despite large investment in reproducible assets, particularly for the military, the value of federal

Table 6.17   "Balance Sheet" for Federal Government, Selected Years (billions of 1985 dollars)

	1970	1980	1985
Tangible assets[a]	1,063.1	1,661.0	1,787.7
Reproducible assets	776.6	941.8	1,064.9
Residential structures	15.8	27.8	29.5
Nonresidential structures	358.7	469.1	443.1
Equipment	247.4	274.8	376.7
Inventories	154.6	170.1	215.5
Land	111.8	226.5	231.3
Mineral rights	174.7	492.7	491.5
Financial assets	619.7	939.5	1,031.1
Currency, demand, and time deposits	46.8	40.8	53.4
Gold	31.9	203.2	86.4
Foreign exchange—special drawing rights	9.0	20.3	32.1
U.S. government securities	206.4	169.2	205.8
Treasury issues	205.8	157.2	194.3
Agency issues	.5	12.0	11.5
Mortgages	86.7	172.4	224.9
Other loans	173.4	262.6	317.7
Taxes receivable	15.2	9.3	10.6
Miscellaneous assets	50.3	61.7	100.2
Total assets	1,682.8	2,600.5	2,818.8

(*continued*)

Table 6.17   (continued)

	1970	1980	1985
Liabilities			
Treasury currency and special drawing rights certificates	16.0	17.7	18.0
Demand deposits and currency	138.3	158.4	182.4
Bank reserves and vault cash	83.0	61.7	54.1
Credit market instruments	900.2	1,097.3	1,954.2
Treasury issues	654.5	814.8	1,590.1
Agency issues	104.5	193.4	279.4
Savings bonds	141.2	89.2	84.7
Insurance, retirement reserves	92.8	111.4	159.0
Miscellaneous liabilities	58.0	67.5	92.3
Total liabilities	1,288.3	1,514.0	2,460.0
Net debt	668.6	574.5	1,428.9
"Net Worth"	394.5	1,086.5	358.8
Note: Contingent liabilities:[b]			
Loss reserve estimate for loans and guarantees	27.0	90.0	145.0
Deposit insurance	N.A.	30.0	50.0
Potential liabilities (rough est): Unfunded pensions			
Civil service[c]	. . .	575.0	. . .
Military[d]	. . .	525.0	. . .
Social security:			
OASDI[e]	. . .	1,600.0	500.0
Hospital insurance	. . .	2,600.0	2,500.0

Note: N.A. = not available.

[a]Includes real revaluations as discussed in text.

[b]For loans and guarantees, see text. Deposit insurance very rough estimates from Boskin, Barham, et al. (1987) and sources cited therein.

[c]From Leonard (1985).

[d]From Leonard (1987). Estimates are for 1982.

[e]From Boskin (1987) and sources cited therein.

assets increased by about 8 percent (less if 1986 were considered because of falling real oil prices). Meanwhile, federal liabilities reached record levels. The result is that net worth dropped by $727 billion in only five years, unraveling the gains made over the 1970s. Most of this drop occurred after the end of the recession.

State and local government net worth, excluding pension obligations, also grew substantially during the 1970s, as shown in table 6.18. Tangible assets increased by about $1.0 trillion, while net debt fell. Net worth grew by more than 80 percent in real terms. Neither net debt nor tangible assets changed much from 1980 to 1985 so that net worth

Table 6.18   **"Balance Sheet" for State and Local Governments, Selected Years (billions of 1985 dollars)**

	1970	1980	1985
Tangible assets[a]	1,624.4	2,680.3	2,554.5
Reproducible assets	1,253.9	1,896.0	1,863.2
Residential structures	38.6	57.0	56.0
Nonresidential structures	1,161.6	1,765.3	1,723.1
Equipment	52.2	70.3	80.1
Inventories	1.6	3.4	3.9
Mineral rights	[b]	125.0	110.8
Land	370.5	659.3	580.5
Financial assets	188.0	268.2	466.3
Currency, demand, and time deposits	91.2	92.9	78.0
Security repurchase agreements	.0	18.2	48.8
U.S. government securities	69.4	90.1	231.8
Treasury issues	59.8	54.4	166.3
Agency issues	9.6	35.7	65.5
State and local obligations	6.1	7.8	8.3
Mortgages	11.7	40.3	78.3
Taxes receivable	9.6	18.9	21.1
Total assets	1,812.4	2,948.5	3,020.8
Liabilities			
State and local obligations	368.1	326.0	428.6
Short term	34.9	18.6	18.5
Other	333.2	307.3	464.1
U.S. government loans	12.8	9.9	26.8
Trade debt	17.0	23.6	23.0
Total liabilities	397.9	359.5	523.4
Net debt	209.8	91.2	66.1
"Net Worth"	1,414.5	2,589.0	2,488.4
Note: Unfunded pension liabilities[c]	. . .	543.6	. . .

[a]Includes real revaluations as discussed in text.

[b]State and local mineral rights estimates are calculated only for 1980 and 1985 and because of the data limitations are perhaps less reliable than the other items included. Tangible assets and "net worth" for 1970 are understated because of the absence of a mineral rights estimate. For a discussion of contingent liabilities and unfunded pensions, see text.

[c]From R. Inman (1985). Estimates are for 1980 and include teachers retirement systems only; they are therefore a lower bound.

remained about $2.5 trillion. The net worth of state and local governments is still larger, according to our calculations, than the total financial liabilities of the federal government.

Finally, with the provisos mentioned above, we report estimates from other sources of large contingent and potential liabilities. For example, the estimate of the unfunded liability for the retirement and disability part of social security is almost $500 billion under the intermediate economic and demographic projections; for hospital insurance, it is over $2 trillion (see Boskin 1987; and Boskin and Puffert 1987). Federal civil service and military retirement systems unfunded liabilities amounted to over $1 trillion for 1980.

6.12   Conclusion

We have presented new, updated, and adjusted estimates of various components of the government's contribution—positive or negative—to national wealth and its growth in the postwar period. We have invoked numerous caveats along the way and have attempted to highlight what we believe are some important points. We have not gone as deeply into some aspects of these issues as some other previous authors in order to go further in other dimensions of the problem. Our primary substantive conclusions are as follows.

1. The share of national output devoted to consumption has risen substantially, while that devoted to net saving has fallen sharply, in the period 1951–85. The private consumption rate has risen about 6 percentage points, from 63 to 69 percent over this period, while the government consumption rate has fallen slightly. The national saving rate has fallen about 4 percentage points.

2. The federal government consumption rate has fallen dramatically, from 13.7 to 8.7 percent from 1950 to 1985. In the same period, the state and local consumption rate has risen from 9.7 to 12.6 percent.

3. The extension of traditional saving and investment measurement to include consumer durables and government tangible investment raises the national saving rate substantially, as do our depreciation estimates. For example, in 1985, the gross and net saving rates rise from a traditionally measured 13.8 and 3.2 percent to 24.5 and 8.8 percent, respectively, about 1.5 percentage points of the increased net saving rate resulting from our lower estimates of depreciation on conventionally defined business capital.

4. The federal government's assets, tangible and financial, are substantial; throughout the 1970s, they grew much more rapidly than the national debt. By 1980, we estimate federal tangible assets, in constant 1985 dollars, at $1.7 trillion and financial assets at $940 billion compared to liabilities of $1.5 trillion.

5. Since about 1980, the "net worth" news is much worse, as conventional liabilities have grown much faster than assets, causing about a $727 billion decline in federal net worth.

6. The state and local government sector also contributes importantly to government and national wealth. The state-and-local-sector fixed

reproducible capital is about twice the federal amount, $1.9 trillion in 1985 versus $1.0 trillion. The difference between assets and liabilities is also greater, as well as more stable, for state and local governments. The estimated "net worth" of state and local governments was about $2.5 trillion in both 1980 and 1985.

7. Total government reproducible capital amounts to a sizable fraction of corresponding private capital. In 1985, the public capital stock was 55 percent of the private nonresidential capital stock.

8. Government net investment has often been sufficient to turn the government sector into a net saver despite large budget deficits; that is, assets were accruing more rapidly than liabilities.

9. It is important, if difficult, to go beyond traditional structures and equipment investment, and capital stocks. Inventories, mineral rights, and land are quantitatively quite important (over $900 billion in 1985 for the federal government alone) and the most volatile components of government saving. Real revaluations of tangible capital, inventories, land, and mineral rights are frequently substantial.

10. Very large contingent and potential liabilities must be considered, although we prefer not to add them directly to the more contractual obligations. Changes in rules governing social security, for example, can produce changes in potential unfunded liabilities almost as large as the regular privately held national debt. Some previous attempts to incorporate contingent liabilities and unfunded pensions have inappropriately focused on either the maximum risk exposure in the former or a closed-group concept of liabilities for the latter.

In establishing the value of various components and aggregate government assets, liabilities, and net worth, the covariance of the likely revenues or outlays associated with the assets and liabilities with other returns and outlays for the government, and, indeed, other components of national income, must be considered. We have not even begun to do so here. Additional considerations concern the government's power to print money and to tax.

We hope that this study, by focusing attention on the role of the government sector in the generation and formation of national wealth, will join a growing list of important studies enabling us to improve the system of accounts used in reporting economic activity in the United States and in analyzing the performance of the economy. Much research remains to be done before some of the thorny issues addressed here are resolved to the extent that such accounts can stand alongside traditional national income accounts on a daily basis,[49] but the evidence from this and other recent studies suggests that failing to do so may seriously distort our notion of the levels and rates of growth of national saving, capital formation, and other dimensions of economic performance.

Notes

1. The theory of local public goods suggests that there may be at least a partial market test for site-specific investments.

2. Various government-sponsored enterprises that are, at least nominally, private also maintain a specific line of credit at the Treasury. Still more subtle is the treatment of mandated private activity. While the economic "rules of the game," establishing property rights and the like, are made by the government, governments in advanced economies have increasingly required the private sector to engage in various activities and provide various types of benefits. For example, when pollution- and safety-control equipment is mandated by law for automobiles, regardless of whether the activity mandated passes social cost-benefit tests, the expenditures are counted as part of gross private auto sales, although they are close substitutes for the government levying a tax and paying the automobile companies to install them. Various recent proposals would require employers to pay for health insurance coverage for all employees. Quite aside from the effects this might have on wages and/or employment, it would be considered in the data as private compensation of employees, not government taxes and spending.

A related issue is what to do about uncompensated or below-market compensation services "purchased" by the government. For example, a military draft presumably enables the government to hire military personnel at below-market wage rates (for estimates of these uncompensated services in the twenty-five years after World War II, see Eisner and Nebhut 1982). This issue is not confined to the government but extends to the private sector as well. For example, substantial uncompensated volunteer time is given by millions of Americans every year to various charitable causes. This often enables the free- or below-market price dispensation of various services, and, hence, the size of this product is underestimated in the national income accounts. We do not propose magic answers to these problems; we only raise difficult questions and applaud those who have sought to assign plausible orders of magnitude to them.

Another important distinction is between consumption and investment expenditures. Again, accounting rules and various conventions in the private sector make even the traditional private-sector data somewhat suspect. In the booming microelectronics and software industries, much of what an economist might think of as investment—a purchase made to enhance future earnings—becomes totally obsolete before the three-year period elapses that distinguishes investment from consumption expenditures.

3. The government spends substantial amounts on education and health—as does the private sector—and other forms of spending that may include a substantial human capital component. How much of this is investment vs. consumption? Various recent studies have attempted to ascertain this human capital component for both the private and the government sector (see Kendrick 1976; and Eisner and Nebhut 1982). Certainly, the expenditures are quite large, and, if all such expenditures are included, gross investment in human capital is about as large as gross investment in tangible capital. But not all the expenditures is investment, and, of course, the stock of such capital depreciates and obsolesces.

4. Musgrave (1980, 1986) and Bureau of Economic Analysis (1982).

5. For more details on the BEA methodologies, see Bureau of Economic Analysis (1982) and Musgrave (1980).

6. A bell-shaped Winfrey S-3 retirement distribution is used to assign service lives ranging from 45 to 155 percent of the mean service life for each category.

7. Hulten and Wykoff (1981) state that "the age-price profiles estimated using the Box-Cox model were very close, on average, to being geometric in form" (p. 93). The eight NIPA asset categories for which depreciation rates were calculated directly as averages of rates for the assets they study were tractors, construction machinery, metalworking machinery, general industrial equipment, trucks, autos, industrial buildings, and commercial buildings.

8. For further discussion of the strengths and weakness of the estimates and the used-asset-price approach, see Hulten and Wykoff (1981), DeLeeuw (1981), Taubman (1981), and Boskin, Robinson, and Roberts (in press).

9. For additional discussion of the theoretical issues, see Boskin, Robinson, and Huber (1987).

10. For further discussion of this point, see Jorgenson (1986) and Jorgenson and Griliches (1972).

11. For some categories, such as military equipment, there are no private analogues and little or no secondary market. Even for government assets comparable to private categories, depreciation may be systematically different, owing, e.g., to differences in maintenance. Any adjustments to depreciation rate would be quite arbitrary, however, without more information.

12. On the basis of studies (e.g., Jack Faucett Associates 1974; and Kendrick 1976) that estimate or assume a shorter service life than the BEA does, we assume a forty-year service life for highways and streets instead of the BEA's sixty-year life.

13. The BEA's 1982 dollar estimates were updated by the price indices used by the BEA to derive its current and constant dollar estimates. These price indices are implicit in the BEA current- and constant-cost net capital stock, investment, and depreciation data, as found in the 1986 BEA wealth data tape. Separate indices are used for each asset type, and values differ slightly for stocks (end of year) and flows (yearly average).

Thus, we converted the constant-cost net capital stock estimates from 1982 to 1985 dollars for each BEA asset category by multiplying the 1982 dollar net capital stock series by the ratio of the 1985 BEA current-cost net capital stock to the BEA constant-cost (1982 dollars) net capital stock. Similarly, we multiplied the corresponding investment and depreciation flows by the ratio of 1985 current-cost depreciation to 1985 constant-cost depreciation (1982 dollars). This reflects the BEA's use of an end-of-the-year price index for stocks and a yearly average price index for investment and depreciation flows.

We attempted to reproduce the BEA estimates from the gross investment and service life data. We exactly succeeded for several categories, but we were slightly off on others. We believe the differences result from our incomplete data on BEA adjustments for intersectoral transfers. To correct for this and other possible statistical discrepancies, we subtracted the excess of our straight-line estimates over the BEA's from our estimates.

14. The different trend is due to the smaller share of equipment in government investment in the postwar years. For further discussion and detailed estimates, see Boskin, Robinson, and Roberts (in press) and Boskin, Robinson, and Huber (1987).

15. Much of the worry about the infrastructure, however, concerns deferred maintenance. As Hulten and Peterson (1984) point out, maintenance is not counted as investment. If governments spend less on maintenance than the private sector does, our depreciation estimates may be too low. Of course, we are also considering the entire state and local sector. The infrastructure may

well be deteriorating in some areas while substantial investment goes on elsewhere.

16. We have scaled the GNP deflator to equal 1.0 at the end of 1985. Eisner's (1980) definition of real net revaluations seems to be identical to ours. However, he deflates slightly differently. We believe our method corresponds more closely to the definition.

17. The data were kindly provided to us by John Musgrave. We are also grateful to Paul Pieper for his assistance. The BEA 1982 constant dollar estimates of federal government military and nonmilitary, and state and local government, inventories were each updated to constant 1985 dollars by multiplying by the ratio of the 1985 BEA current dollar stock to the 1985 constant (1982) dollar stock for each type. Inventory investment was then calculated as the change in net stock from the previous year.

18. This breakdown was provided to us by Paul Pieper on the basis of BEA data.

19. For a review of the literature on valuing the services of consumer durables, see Katz (1983).

20. Hulten and Wykoff applied their rates only through 1974. Recent work by Hulten, Robertson, and Wykoff (1986) suggests that depreciation did not shift substantially after the oil shocks. Hulten and Wykoff did not attempt to find a depreciation rate for residential capital either.

21. The BEA methodology is described in Musgrave (1979). Kendrick (1976) also used double-declining balance for nonvehicle consumer durables. For a discussion of alternative depreciation assumptions for consumer durables, see Katz (1983).

22. Our depreciation estimates for residential and nonresidential structures are significantly lower than the BEA's, while our estimates of the depreciation of consumer durables are much higher.

23. Martin, Landefeld, and Peskin (1982) consider several methods for calculating the value of services of government capital net of depreciation. The current-cost framework values all vintages of capital at current prices and interest rates. This method would be appropriate if we were using a market value of government capital as set, e.g., in a stock market since the market would demand the same rate of return on all capital of similar risk. With our cost-base capital estimates, such a measure would overstate fluctuations as interest rates change.

A second method used by Martin, Landefeld, and Peskin is a vintage framework, under which investment in any year is assumed to meet a cost-benefit test with an interest rate appropriate to the year. They use a five-year average of nominal interest rates as their proxy for the discount rate used at the time of investment. It seems unlikely, however, that investment decisions vary with fluctuations in interest rates, particularly nominal rates. When inflation rates change, using nominal rates means that the real value of services would vary for the existing capital.

We prefer their third method of assuming a constant real rate of return. They use a 7 percent real rate, but we believe that that is probably above the rate of return actually achieved on government capital. Hence, we use a 3 percent real rate. The calculations, particularly of saving rates, are quite insensitive to the constant real rate chosen.

24. While we have alternative estimates based on different combinations of deflators of the various components, the estimates reported here for comparability with the traditional NIPAs are presented as current dollar estimates for

the corresponding period. The corresponding constant dollar figures are similar but show a smaller rise in private consumption and fall in government consumption.

25. The methodology is described in an appendix to Eisner (1986). Eisner and Pieper build on work by Seater (1981) and Cox and Hirschhorn (1983).

26. The large interest subsidies received by state and municipal bondholders and some borrowers from federal agencies might suggest further refinements of these adjustments if one were willing to contemplate sales of portfolios to the private sector that continued to carry tax advantages.

27. We are grateful to Paul Pieper for providing us with 1985 par-to-market indices.

28. While revising and updating the data, we discovered a programming error underlying table 1 of Boskin et al. (1985). We correct the series in table 6.12. Fortunately, the qualitative conclusions of Boskin et al. (1985) are unaffected by the error, but the revised estimates are about one-third lower.

29. We shall argue below, however, that severance taxes on the production should also be counted as royalties.

30. For a more complete description and discussion of the method, see Boskin et al. (1985). The following persons provided unpublished data or other assistance with this section: L. Cordova of the Minerals Management Service, D. Everitts and H. Gonzalez of the California State Lands Commission, S. Sharlot of the Texas General Land Office, B. Van Dyke of the Alaska Division of Oil and Gas, and C. Logsdon of the Alaska Department of Revenue.

31. Without this assumption, one needs to know the rates of leasing, discovery, and production of the resources. For a justification, see Boskin et al. (1985). We consider alternative assumptions, as did Boskin et al. (1985), below.

32. Since the government receives royalty revenue only on oil actually produced, it seems appropriate for a wealth calculation to use the best estimate of oil reserves rather than have reserves fluctuate with changing geologic predictions. Reserve estimates should change, though, as prices and technology change. Given the assumption of rising real prices, however, oil that is not profitable to produce at current prices will probably become profitable in the future. Even using a reserve estimate made with high real prices—Boskin et al. (1985) use 1981 figures—will probably understate ultimate recovery of oil and gas.

33. Implicitly, this assumes that oil and gas markets are in equilibrium each year.

34. If prices grow more slowly than the interest rate by 1 or 2 percent, and if we assume that 10 percent of proven reserves are produced and 3 percent of undiscovered reserves are proven each year, then the value in 1981 would fall to $494 or $383 billion, respectively.

35. Production figures are from U.S. Department of Energy (1986a). Except for Alaska, most oil and gas on state land is underwater. Louisiana is the only significant omission.

36. The figure for Alaska is based on a phone conversation with the state Department of Revenue (the figure quoted was 99.75 percent). The California and Texas percentages are based on mimeo sheets on "tide and submerged lands" with the Texas figure inferred from royalties, royalty rates, and an assumed price. No information was available on other state-owned land in either state.

37. Alaska changed from using a formula based on fraction of investment and employment in the state to one based on sales when the oil pipeline was completed. Percentage is calculated using figures in State of Alaska (1986).

38. Actually, the figure is even greater since Alaskan revenue increases more than proportionally with the world oil price and Boskin et al. (1985) assume rising oil prices. In part, this is due to the high transportation cost of Alaskan oil. The state is currently forecasting revenues of $1.70 per barrel for fiscal 1987, a drop of 63 percent from the 1985 figure with only a 44 percent drop in the world oil price. This makes calculating the value of oil and gas rights over time even more difficult.

39. Without a gas pipeline, the value of Alaska's gas is problematic.

40. Royalty rates are based on the average of royalty rates on Relinquishment Act lands and State Fee lands weighted by the acreage in each category under lease. Severance tax rates were provided by the U.S. Advisory Commission on Intergovernmental Relations.

41. Reserve figures are from U.S. Department of Energy (1986b). Production on state land is calculated using royalties, royalty rates, and a $26 per barrel price for oil and a $2.60 per thousand cubic feet price for gas.

42. Undiscovered reserve estimates were taken, as usual, from U.S. Geological Survey (1981). Texas figures are approximate since the regions the Geological Survey used were not contiguous with state boundaries.

43. For a discussion of previous estimates of government land values and another version of estimates for the federal government, see Boskin et al. (1985). The following persons provided unpublished data or other assistance with this section: Z. Addison of the Federal Housing Administration, R. Gary of the National Forest Service, B. Daniels of the General Services Administration, J. Jones of the U.S. Department of Agriculture, and W. Sischel.

44. Although there is a clear upward trend in urban acreage from 1.4 million acres in 1968 to 3.7 million acres in 1985, the observations for three years are outliers; i.e., there is a change in the time series of more than 20 percent that is reversed in the following year. These aberrations are due to temporary reclassifications of land between the urban and the rural categories, twice in the Department of the Navy and once in the Interior Department. We have replaced the irregular values for the agencies in these instances with the average of the previous and following years' values.

45. The uncertain nature of government land value estimates is illustrated by using the same price and acreage data in the slightly different formulas used by Milgram (1973). The differences in methodology arise in the treatment of land that has been newly acquired or reclassified as urban or rural. Milgram uses the change in the GSA acquisition cost series to measure total net land acquisitions instead of relying on the GSA acreage series and price data. In contrast to our procedure, Milgram's estimate of total federal land value does not increase when government land is reclassified from rural to urban since the original acquisition cost is unchanged. There is an increase in the value of urban land that is exactly offset by a decrease in the value of rural land. These differences cause Milgram's method to generate much lower estimates of federal land values. The 1985 value for Milgram's method is $133 billion. We prefer our method since reclassification of land from rural to urban as cities expand reflects genuine increases in the value of land. However, the large difference in estimates derived from somewhat different methods suggests that further research remains a high priority.

46. The interested reader might consult Hurd and Boskin (1984), Diamond and Hausman (1984), Feldstein (1974), Barro (1974), and Boskin, Kotlikoff, et al. (1987).

47. However, it will not return to the current ratio as gains in life expectancy result in a permanent increase in the aged dependency ratio.

48. In addition to the social security system's accrued liabilities, the federal government has substantial other accrued pension liabilities as well. These include military, veteran, and civilian retirement and disability compensation plans. Various studies have been done analogous to those on social security, attempting to estimate these liabilities. The pension funds of current military employees and the civil service pension system, while probably subject to revision in years ahead, represent some substantial degree of contractual obligation of the federal government. They amount to well over $1 trillion among them. The unfunded pension liabilities of state and local governments have been, at times, substantial. Again, similar caveats to those mentioned above apply.

49. Attempts to measure either private or government saving, investment, or consumption and, correspondingly, private and government capital should use depreciation methods consistent in treatment of relative vintages of the capital stock, i.e., depreciation methods consistent between formation of the capital stock series and the imputed rental flow series. This is not true of the NIPAs' depreciation or of the depreciation methods and estimates used in most studies of growth accounting. Two recent, important exceptions are Jorgenson, Gollop, and Fraumeni (1987) and the Bureau of Labor Statistics (1983). While it is not our purpose to evaluate the importance of these distinctions in growth accounting, some studies (see Jorgenson 1986) suggest that these differences can be enormously important in partitioning the sources of growth. For our purposes, it is clear that the depreciation series, and therefore the net investment and capital stock series, differ substantially, primarily because of differences in the treatment of structures, relative to NIPA and the BEA capital stock series.

References

Arthur Anderson & Co. 1986. *Sound financial reporting in the U.S. government: A prerequisite to fiscal responsibility.* Chicago: Arthur Anderson & Co.

Barro, R. 1974. Are government bonds net wealth? *Journal of Political Economy* 82 (November/December): 1095–1117.

Bartlett, B. R. 1983. The federal debt: On-budget, off-budget and contingent liabilities. Staff Study for the Joint Economic Committee, Congress of the United States. Washington, D.C.: U.S. Government Printing Office.

Board of Governors of the Federal Reserve System. 1986. *Flow of funds accounts: Financial assets and liabilities year-end, 1962–85.* Washington, D.C.: Board of Governors of the Federal Reserve System.

Boskin, M. J. 1982. Federal government deficits: Myths and realities. *American Economic Review* 72 (May): 296–303.

———. 1986. Theoretical and empirical issues in the measurement, evaluation and interpretation of postwar U.S. saving. In *Savings and capital formation: The policy options,* eds. G. F. Adams and S. M. Wachter. Lexington, Mass.: Lexington Books.

_____. 1987. Future social security financing and national savings. NBER Working Paper, 2256. Cambridge, Mass.: National Bureau of Economic Research.

_____. 1988. Alternative measures of government deficits and debt and their impact on economic activity. In *Economics of public debt,* eds. K. J. Arrow and M. J. Boskin. New York: Macmillan.

_____. In press. *The real federal budget.* Cambridge, Mass.: Harvard University Press.

Boskin, M. J., B. Barham, K. Cone, and S. Ozler. 1987. The federal budget and federal insurance programs. In *Modern developments in public finance,* ed. M. Boskin. Oxford: Basil Blackwell.

Boskin, M. J., L. Kotlikoff, D. Puffert, and J. Shoven. 1987. Social security: A financial appraisal across and within generations. *National Tax Journal* 40, no. 1 (March): 19–34.

Boskin, M. J., and D. J. Puffert. 1987. The financial impact of social security by cohort under alternative financing assumptions. Mimeo. Economics Department, Stanford University.

Boskin, M. J., and J. M. Roberts. 1986. A closer look at saving rates in the United States and Japan. Working paper. Washington, D.C.: American Enterprise Institute.

Boskin, M. J., M. S. Robinson, and A. Huber. 1987. New estimates of state and local government tangible capital and net investment. NBER Working Paper, no. 2131. Cambridge, Mass.: National Bureau of Economic Research.

Boskin, M. J., M. S. Robinson, T. O'Reilly, and P. Kumar. 1985. New estimates of the value of federal mineral rights and land. *American Economic Review* 75 (December): 923–36.

Boskin, M. J., M. S. Robinson, and J. M. Roberts. In press. New estimates of federal government tangible capital and net investment. In *Technology and capital formation,* ed. D. W. Jorgenson. Cambridge, Mass.: MIT Press.

Bureau of Economic Analysis. 1982. *Fixed reproducible tangible wealth in the United States, 1925–79.* Washington, D.C.: U.S. Government Printing Office.

Bureau of Labor Statistics. 1983. *Trends in multifactor productivity, 1948–81.* Bulletin no. 2178. Washington, D.C.: U.S. Government Printing Office.

Christensen, L. R., and D. W. Jorgenson. 1973. Measuring economic performance in the private sector. In *Measurement of economic and social performance,* ed. M. Moss, 233–337. New York: National Bureau of Economic Research.

Cox, W. M., and E. Hirschhorn. 1983. The market value of U.S. government debt: Monthly, 1942–1980. *Journal of Monetary Economics* 11 (March): 261–72.

David, P., and J. Scadding. 1974. Private saving: Ultrarationality, aggregation and Denison's law. *Journal of Political Economy* 82 (March/April): 225–49.

DeLeeuw, F. 1981. Discussion. In *Depreciation, inflation, and the taxation of income from capital,* ed. C. R. Hulten, 126–29. Washington, D.C.: Urban Institute.

Denison, E. F. 1957. Theoretical aspects of quality change, capital consumption, and net capital formation. In *Problems of capital formation,* ed. Franco Modigliani. Conference on Research in Income and Wealth. Princeton, N.J.: Princeton University Press.

_____. 1962. *Sources of economic growth in the United States and the alternatives before us.* New York: Committee for Economic Development.

_____. 1967. *Why growth rates differ.* Washington, D.C.: Brookings Institution.

————. 1972. Final comments. *Survey of Current Business* 52, no. 5, pt. 2 (May): 95–110.

————. 1974. *Accounting for United States economic growth, 1929–1969.* Washington, D.C.: Brookings Institution.

————. 1979. *Accounting for slower economic growth.* Washington, D.C.: Brookings Institution.

————. 1985. *Trends in American economic growth, 1929–1982.* Washington, D.C.: Brookings Institution.

Diamond, P. A., and J. A. Hausman. 1984. Individual retirement and savings behavior. *Journal of Public Economics* 23, no. 112: 81–114.

Economic report of the president, 1986. 1986. Washington, D.C.: U.S. Government Printing Office.

Eisner, R. 1980. Capital gains and income: Real changes in the value of capital in the United States, 1946–77. In *The measurement of capital,* ed. D. Usher, 175–346. Chicago: University of Chicago Press.

————. 1986. *How real is the federal deficit?* New York: Free Press.

Eisner, R., and D. H. Nebhut. 1982. An extended measure of government product: Preliminary results for the United States, 1946–76. *Review of Income and Wealth,* ser. 28 (March): 33–64.

Eisner, R., and P. Pieper. 1984. A new view of federal debt and budget deficits. *American Economic Review* 74 (March): 11–29.

Feldstein, M. 1974. Social security, induced retirement and aggregate capital accumulation. *Journal of Political Economy* 82 (September/October): 905–26.

Gale, W. 1987. Federal lending policies and the market for credit. Mimeo. Economics Department, Stanford University.

Goldsmith, R. 1955. *A study of saving in the United States.* 3 vols. Princeton, N.J.: Princeton University Press.

————. 1962. *The national wealth of the United States in the postwar period.* Princeton, N.J.: Princeton University Press.

————. 1982. *The national balance sheet of the United States, 1953–1980.* Chicago: University of Chicago Press.

Gorman, J. A., J. C. Musgrave, G. Silverstein, and K. A. Comins. 1985. Fixed private capital in the United States. *Survey of Current Business* 65, no. 1 (July): 36–47.

Hulten, C. R., and G. E. Peterson. 1984. The growth of the public capital stock: 1958–82. Washington, D.C.: Urban Institute. Mimeo.

Hulten, C. R., J. W. Robertson, and F. C. Wykoff. 1986. Energy, obsolescence, and the productivity slowdown. Western Economic Association Conference Paper.

Hulten, C. R., and F. C. Wykoff. 1981. The measurement of economic depreciation. In *Depreciation, inflation, and the taxation of income from capital.* ed. C. R. Hulten, 81–125. Washington, D.C.: Urban Institute.

Hurd, M., and M. J. Boskin. 1984. The effect of social security on retirement in the early 70's. *Quarterly Journal of Economics* 99 (November), 767–90.

Inman, R. 1985. The funding status of teachers pensions: An econometric approach. NBER Working Paper, no. 1727. Cambridge, Mass.: National Bureau of Economic Research.

Jack Faucett Associates. 1974. *Capital stock measures for transportation.* Washington, D.C.: Department of Transportation, Assistant Secretary for Policy, Plans, and International Affairs, Office of Transportation Planning Analysis.

Jorgenson, D. W. 1973. The economic theory of replacement and depreciation. In *Econometrics and economic theory,* ed. W. Sellekaerts. New York: Macmillan.

———. 1986. Capital as a factor of production. Harvard Institute of Economic Research Discussion Paper, no. 1276. Cambridge, Mass.: Harvard Institute of Economic Research.

Jorgenson, D. W., F. M. Gollop, and B. M. Fraumeni. 1987. *Productivity and U.S. economic growth.* Cambridge, Mass.: Harvard University Press.

Jorgenson, D. W., and Z. Griliches. 1972. Issues in growth accounting: A reply to E. F. Denison. *Survey of Current Business* 52, no. 4, pt. 2 (May): 65–94.

Katz, A. J. 1983. Valuing the services of consumer durables. *Review of Income and Wealth,* ser. 29 (December): 405–27.

Kendrick, J. W. 1961. *Productivity trends in the United States.* Princeton, N.J.: Princeton University Press.

———. 1973. *Postwar productivity trends in the United States, 1948–1969.* New York: National Bureau of Economic Research.

———. 1976. *The formation and stocks of total capital.* New York: National Bureau of Economic Research.

Leonard, H. 1985. The federal civil service retirement system: An analysis of its financial condition and current reform proposals. In *Pensions, labor, and individual choice,* ed. D. Wise, 399–443. Chicago: University of Chicago Press.

———. 1987. Investing in the defense work force: The debt and structure of military pensions. In *Public sector payrolls,* ed. D. Wise, 47–73. Chicago: University of Chicago Press.

Martin, F., J. S. Landefeld, and J. Peskin. 1982. The value of services provided by the stock of government owned fixed capital, 1948–79. Working Paper, no. 2. Washington, D.C.: U.S. Department of Commerce, Bureau of Economic Analysis.

Milgram, G. 1973. Estimates of the value of land in the United States held by various sectors of the economy, annually, 1952 to 1968. In *Institutional investors and corporate stock—A background study.* ed. R. W. Goldsmith, 341–77. New York: National Bureau of Economic Research.

Musgrave, J. C. 1979. Durable goods owned by consumers in the United States, 1925–1977. *Survey of Current Business* 59 (March): 17–25.

———. 1980. Government-owned fixed capital in the United States, 1925–1979. *Survey of Current Business* 60 (March): 33–43.

———. 1986. Fixed reproducible tangible wealth in the U.S.: Revised estimates. *Survey of Current Business* 66 (January): 51–75.

Reeve, J. E., et al. 1950. Government component in the national wealth. In *Studies in Income and Wealth,* vol. 12, New York: National Bureau of Economic Research.

Seater, J. J. 1981. The market value of outstanding government debt, 1919–1975. *Journal of Monetary Economics* 8 (July): 85–101.

State of Alaska. 1986. *Petroleum production revenue forecast, quarterly report.* Juneau, Alaska: Department of Revenue, December.

Taubman, P. 1981. Discussion. In *Depreciation, inflation, and the taxation of income from capital.* ed. C. R. Hulten, 129–133. Washington, D.C.: Urban Institute.

U.S. Department of Energy. 1986a. *Petroleum supply outlook, 1985.* Washington, D.C.: U.S. Government Printing Office.

———. 1986b. *Reserves of crude oil and natural gas in the United States.* Washington, D.C.: U.S. Government Printing Office.

U.S. Geological Survey. 1981. *Estimates of undiscovered recoverable conventional resources of oil and gas in the United States.* Circular no. 860. Washington, D.C.: U.S. Government Printing Office.

Young, A. H., and J. C. Musgrave. 1980. Estimation of capital stock in the United States. In *The measurement of capital,* ed. D. Usher, 23–82. NBER Studies in Income and Wealth, vol. 45. Chicago: University of Chicago Press.

Comment   Robert Eisner

Boskin, Robinson, and Huber are pioneers in what I hope is a growing band who would enlighten our perceptions of the economy as a whole by bringing the government sector into the mainstream of accounting for saving, capital formation, and wealth. They here offer a number of significant contributions. Among those striking me as most noteworthy are their estimates of the value and fluctuations in the value of government-owned natural resources and their improved estimates of the value of land. I warmly endorse as well their sober and measured view of "contingent liabilities" and of the nature of the government's social security obligations. They have also added helpfully to corrections of naive and simplistic views of the nature of government deficits (and surpluses).

Substantial as are their contributions, it behooves the discussant to suggest things that they also should have done but did not do and things that they might have done differently. Most conspicuous is the exclusion of human capital. After all, a prime role of government is to facilitate the development and preservation of human capital. Government contributes mightily to investments in education, health, and research. The government contribution to capital formation can hardly be measured meaningfully when these are excluded.

A second major exclusion relates to net revaluations or capital gains. If full accounting is not made for the revaluation of government assets and liabilities, the links between saving and capital formation and between income and wealth are lost. As the authors do acknowledge, meaningful discussions of government budget deficits and balance sheets and their effect on the economy cannot take place without recognition of the role of revaluations. They do not, however, endeavor to reconcile the flows of "deficit" and "saving" with balance sheet items for net debt, net worth, and total capital.

Some measure of the importance of government contribution to human capital formation may be found in my estimates (Eisner 1985,

Robert Eisner is the William R. Kenan Professor of Economics at Northwestern University.

1989) that in 1981 the government product going to capital accumulation came to $314.9 billion, of which only $26.7 billion was in natural resource accumulation; the rest was in education and training, health, and research and development. This compared to a total of only $344.5 billion for all business fixed investment (excluding owner-occupied non-farm dwellings). Boskin, Robinson, and Huber do well to add net government investment in tangible assets to the government surplus (perennially a deficit) to get a better measure of government saving, still generally found, at the federal level at least, to be negative. But their measure is very far from being a meaningful indicator of the government contribution to national capital formation. Boskin, Robinson, and Huber are not warranted in labeling the change in government net worth as they measure it, the "legacy in government service net of tax to future generations." They are all the less justified in referring to their measure of gross saving as "government's contribution to national wealth."

I do have some further problems with the authors' measure of fixed reproducible capital, which stems from their depreciation procedures. They take Hulten-Wykoff estimates of declining balance depreciation rates as a percentage of straight line for equipment and for structures and apply these generally to Bureau of Economic Analysis (BEA) estimated service lives for the various types of government capital.

The data used by Hulten and Wykoff (1981) relate to sale prices of used private assets. However ingenious, their approach strikes me as suspect. Assets that are sold may be expected to be worth less to sellers than comparable assets that they retain. Specificity of purpose and function are likely to make them still less valuable to purchasers. And the "lemon principle" is likely to lower further what buyers are willing to pay. The fact that Hulten and Wykoff found a geometric decline in sales price by age of asset hardly confirms that a geometric decline correctly describes the loss of value of assets in place.

The argument of Christensen and Jorgenson (1973) and Jorgenson and Griliches (1972), resurrected by Boskins, Robinson, and Huber, that geometric depreciation is theoretically neater or "consistent" because a geometric decline in efficiency or flow of capital services would then (with constant rates of discount) correspond to geometric declines in value, is not evidence that depreciation is in fact geometric. As Denison (1972) pointed out, the combination of declines in efficiency, obsolescence, and discount rates may well (and probably do) make straight line a reasonable approximation to economic depreciation (see also Eisner 1973). Given straight-line depreciation, it is clearly possible to impute service flows as the sum of depreciation and the return on capital consistent with the rates of discount implicit in the calculation of depreciation.

The effect of Boskin, Robinson, and Huber's depreciation assumption is a somewhat faster depreciation and hence lesser capital stock in government equipment than estimates such as those of Eisner (1986) taken from BEA straight-line-depreciation net stocks but a considerably slower depreciation and hence much larger estimates of net stocks of structures. Which estimates are most appropriate is still another matter because the true lives and rates of obsolescence and decline in efficiency remain critical.

A final caveat relates to Boskin, Robinson, and Huber's measure of government consumption. They define this as total government expenditures for goods and services minus government investment in tangible assets plus the imputed services of government tangible capital. They then offer measures of the total of private and "public" consumption as indicators of the extent to which we are consuming now at the expense of the future. But much of government spending relates essentially to intermediate product or "regrettables" such as defense, police, and transportation, which contribute to final product, if they do, of investment as well as consumption. And Boskin, Robinson, and Huber's government "consumption" very considerably involves services that go to the production of human and other intangible capital that are rather of the nature of investment than consumption.

In similar vein, Boskin, Robinson, and Huber's definition of net government saving tells us little about government—let alone national—capital formation. For government borrowing from the private sector may in fact be used to finance, directly or indirectly, private capital formation. And government borrowing from abroad cannot properly be viewed as a charge against domestic saving without a full accounting for capital gains and losses from both exchange rate changes and other factors. Huge recent declines in the value of the U.S. dollar, for example, generated gains in the dollar value of U.S. holdings abroad that largely counterbalanced our deficits on current account.

The financial deficit of the government, conventionally viewed as public dissaving and still taken by Boskins, Robinson, and Huber as a component of government saving, may actually contribute to capital formation, as noted in Eisner (1986). The deficit, particularly when measured as the increase in real debt of government, generally stimulates more private consumption *and* investment.[1] There is in fact "crowding in" of investment rather than "crowding out." And the current account deficit and capital account surplus with the rest of the world do not, given changes in exchange rates as well as prices, necessarily reflect any decline in our national net worth. It might be well, therefore, to pay less attention to Boskin, Robinson, and Huber's measure of net government saving and more to net government capital formation and, ultimately, to net national capital formation, broadly defined.

Note

1. That proper concerns with regard to government debt must relate largely to its effect on private agents in the economy is a prime reason why I am skeptical as to the usefulness of Boskin, Robinson, and Huber's recommendation, not implemented in their current paper, that the value of state and local debt be reduced to reflect its tax-exempt status. The worth of that debt to its holders is its market value. Further, as the authors acknowledge, it is not clear that state and local governments can and do invest the bulk of the proceeds of their borrowing in assets with a return in excess of their borrowing costs or that whatever arbitrage they can engage in is not already reflected in their balance sheets.

References

Christensen, Laurits R., and Dale W. Jorgenson. 1973. Measuring economic performance in the private sector. In *The measurement of economic and social performance,* ed. Milton Moss, 233–338. New York: National Bureau of Economic Research.

Denison, Edward F. 1972. Final comments. *Survey of Current Business* 52, no. 5, pt. 2 (May): 95–110.

Eisner, Robert. 1973. Comment. In *The measurement of economic and social performance,* ed. Milton Moss, 343–49. New York: National Bureau of Economic Research.

———. 1985. The total incomes system of accounts. *Survey of Current Business* 65, no. 1 (January): 24–48.

———. 1986. *How real is the federal deficit?* New York: Free Press.

———. 1989. *The total incomes system of accounts.* Chicago: University of Chicago Press.

Hulten, C. R., and F. C. Wykoff. 1981. The measurement of economic depreciation. In *Depreciation, inflation, and the taxation of income from capital,* ed. C. R. Hulten, 81–125. Washington, D.C.: Urban Institute.

Jorgenson, Dale W., and Zvi Griliches. 1972. Issues in growth accounting: A reply to Edward F. Denison. *Survey of Current Business* 52, no. 5, pt. 2 (May): 64–94.

7

The Theory and Measurement of the Nominal Output of Banks, Sectoral Rates of Savings, and Wealth in the National Accounts

Thomas K. Rymes

7.1 Introduction

Debate about the treatment of interest and "the banking imputation" in the national accounts, long smoldering, has recently been rekindled (see Haig 1986; Ruggles and Ruggles 1982; Ruggles 1983; Sunga 1967, 1984; Rymes 1985, 1986; and Mamalakis 1987). The debate is important for two reasons. First, the satisfactory integration of money and banking and general equilibrium theory has not yet been achieved (cf. Gale 1983). If money, or, more precisely, the services of money, were a private good, then one would argue that such services would be privately produced and that modern general equilibrium theory would satisfactorily incorporate money into value theory. A growing literature argues that central banks are fifth wheels and that monopoly fiat money exists solely as a device for governments to levy "distorting" taxes. Keynesian monetary theory argues that central banks produce a public good, stability, and that its value enters into the determination of all relative values in a Keynesian momentary general equilibrium. What appears in neoclassical general equilibrium as a set of "distorted" values representing the unfortunate existence of inefficient central banks, in the Keynesian framework is a demonstration that neoclassical general equilibrium value theory cannot be carried over to a monetary economy.

Thomas K. Rymes is professor of economics at Carleton University.

The author would like to thank Shan Lal of Statistics Canada for explaining to him Statistics Canada's imputation procedures and data and Randall Geehan of Carleton University for allowing him to examine data in his possession with respect to the costing of services by Canadian banks. For comments on this paper, the author is indebted to Ehsan Choudhri of Carleton University and Leslie Milton of the Bank of Canada and, for comments on related work, to Angela Redish, University of British Columbia, and Christopher Towe, Bank of Canada. The usual caveats apply to all acknowledgments paid here and elsewhere in the paper.

This theoretical debate is of absolutely vital importance for the second aspect reviewed in this paper: the measurement of the nominal output of banking and rates of saving and wealth at the sectoral and aggregate levels in a monetary economy.

The basic problem that this paper addresses then is what effects on measures of output, rates of saving, and wealth derived from the national accounts are generated by different theoretical approaches associated with the measurement of banking. What measures, derived from monetary theory, can be proposed, and how will such proposals affect measured output, rates of saving, and wealth?

7.2   A Simple National Accounting Illustration of the Banking Problem

A representative statement of revenues and expenses of Canadian banks is shown in table 7.1.

In the national accounts, interest receipts and payments are regarded as part of the distribution of the net returns to capital originating in various activities. If one takes the labour costs and profits before taxes in table 7.1, adds to them interest payments by banks (on the argument that such payments, along with dividends, represent the distribution of the net returns to capital arising in banking), and deducts interest receipts (on the argument that such receipts represent the distribution to banks of the net returns in activities other than banking), one has

Labor costs	2,400
+ Profits before taxes	1,250
	3,650
+ Interest payments	6,920
	10,570
− Interest receipts	10,725
= Net domestic product	− 155

Table 7.1   **Representative Revenues and Expenses, Canadian Banks (millions of Canadian dollars)**

Expenses		Revenues	
Interest payments	6,920	Interest receipts	10,725
Intermediate inputs	1,000	Service charges	845
Labor costs	2,400		
Profits before taxes	1,250		
Taxes	435		
Dividends	227		
	11,570		11,570

Source: Figures are based on data in Revell (1980).

That is, the net (of depreciation) value added or net domestic product originating in banking is negative.

If one estimates net value added or net domestic product originating in the banking activity directly by means of deducting intermediate inputs from gross outputs (where only the service charges are treated as the gross outputs), then the same result occurs. This anomalous result leads national accountants to adopt the so-called banking imputation, which amounts to the assertion that banks do not fully charge depositors and lenders for the services they render and are compensated by paying less interest on deposits than they earn on loans—that is, the banks are delivering an underpriced service, and depositors are loaning their money to the banks in an offsetting underpriced way. It is as if there were a barter arrangement outside the price system between banks and their customers. Then, in line with "usual" national accounting practices, imputations are made.[1]

In Canada (Statistics Canada 1975; 3:201), the imputed value of the service rendered by the banks is in effect the difference between interest flows, and this is added to the gross output of the banks. We then have

Labor costs	2,400
+ Profit before taxes	1,250
	3,650
+ Interest payments	6,920
+ Imputed interest payments	3,805
− Interest receipts	10,725
= Net domestic product	3,650
or Gross output	845
+ Imputed gross output (interest receipts 10,725 − interest payments 6,920)	3,805
= Total gross output	4,650
Less: Intermediate inputs	1,000
= Net domestic product	3,650

Part of the imputed gross output of the banks, that deemed to be purchased by households, is part of consumer expenditures. An equal amount is added to consumer income, in the form of imputed interest receipts. The absolute savings of the household sector is left unchanged. However, since both consumption expenditures and household investment income are increased by the same amounts, then the measured rate of saving is reduced by the imputation. In current practice (which this paper questions), as is shown in table 7.2, the effect for Canada is miniscule.

With respect to the savings of the business sector, which are the undistributed corporate profits and net income of unincorporated

Table 7.2   Incomplete Effects of Interest Imputation on Personal Rate of Saving, Canada, 1975–85 (millions of Canadian dollars)

Year	Personal Disposable Income	Personal Expenditures on Goods and Services	Rate of Saving	Interest Imputation	Rate of Saving (Adjusted)
1975	113.3	97.6	.139	1.3	.141
1976	128.2	111.5	.131	1.5	.132
1977	141.4	123.6	.126	1.6	.128
1978	159.5	137.4	.138	1.8	.140
1979	179.9	153.4	.147	1.9	.149
1980	203.7	172.4	.153	2.0	.155
1981	237.7	196.2	.175	2.4	.176
1982	262.8	212.5	.191	2.6	.193
1983	275.8	232.5	.157	3.4	.159
1984	299.9	251.4	.162	3.4	.164
1985	323.4	274.7	.151	3.7	.153

Source: GNP Division, Statistics Canada. The rate of saving (adjusted) is computed by subtracting imputed interest receipts from disposable income and imputed expenditures on banking services from expenditure on goods and services.

enterprises, there is no effect. The imputation does not affect the undistributed corporate profits of the banks. In Canada, though the imputed gross output produced by banks, beyond that which is treated as the purchases of households, should be deducted, as an intermediate input, from the gross output of nonbanks to obtain their value added, the remaining imputed interest flows from the banks to the nonbanks would leave nonbank corporate profits and the net income of nonbank unincorporated enterprises unchanged. In fact, in Canada the nonconsumer flows of imputed gross outputs and interest distributions are routed through a ''dummy'' banking industry so that measures of value added and gross domestic product originating in the nonbanking sectors in the Canadian national accounts are too high. Total gross domestic expenditures and products are affected, then, only with respect to the imputations that pertain to households' use of the services of banks.[2] If some of the imputed services of the banks are treated as part of government expenditures or as part of private capital formation, total gross domestic expenditures and product and rates of saving would be additionally affected.

To the extent that nonresidents would be deemed to be net purchasers of the services of domestic banks, then aggregate domestic product and expenditures would be further increased by the imputations that would be added to exports. Of course, if Canadians were deemed to be purchasers of banking services produced abroad, then, for households, the imputed expenditures would be added to consumption expenditures and imports, whereas the imputed interest receipts by Canadians would appear as part of exports. It remains the case, however, that the imputations for banking services do not affect the balance of payments on current account or the measures of absolute savings of the rest-of-the-world sector in the national accounts. In fact, in Canada, no imputed expenditures by nonresidents on the output of Canadian banks or imputed expenditures by residents on the output of non-Canadian banks are recorded. Imputed international banking services would, in general, affect merchandise trade balances. Since trade in banking services is an important topic in policy discussions about freedom from nontariff barriers to trade, and since, as I shall argue below, the output of banking services cannot be measured independently of monetary policy, the better measurement of international trade in banking services is a matter of some priority.[3]

The measurement of banking output, obtained by the usual application of the economic theory of the firm producing goods and nonfinancial services and the corresponding national accounting conventions, yields then meaningless results. The various treatments—(1) the standard national accounting imputations, (2) the "spreads" convention (Mintz 1979), and (3) the Ruggles-Sunga treatment of interest receipts and payments as "rentals" received and paid for the use of money and therefore as gross outputs and intermediate inputs of the various activities and not therefore as the distribution of the net returns to capital—while all having different effects on the measurement of the outputs and inputs of banks, and while not affecting measures of absolute savings, do affect measured rates of saving.

The important question is, however, which of the various measures has theoretical support. Is, in fact, the current treatment of banks leading to meaningless results? Are the various palliatives such as the banking imputation really improvements? Do the measures of output, the rate of saving, and wealth that result have theoretical significance and defense?

With respect to stocks, in the national accounts balance sheets, the stock of fiat money, because it is an asset of the private sector and a liability of the public sector, does not appear as a component of overall national wealth.[4]

For the private sector, fiat money in the form of nonprivate circulating currency and reserves of the banking sector with the central bank are considered as part of monetary wealth. (Without this component of wealth, the famous Pigou-Kalecki-Patinkin "real balance effect" would apparently not appear as an ultimate determinant of the overall price level in macroeconomic theory.) Bank deposits (and any private circulating currency) would not be treated as wealth since such assets would be liabilities of the private banks. Yet this distinction between inside and outside money has never been satisfactory (cf. Johnson 1969; and Lucas 1986). Indeed, in a world in which fiat money is created essentially through deposits of the government with the Monetary Authorities that are switched to private banks for reserve creation, the distinction between inside and outside money breaks down. The value of the buildings, computers, and so forth in private and central banks is part of reproducible wealth. Moreover, actual stocks of reproducible wealth will reflect the efficacy with which banking operations are privately and collectively provided. Is it not double-counting to add the capitalized value of the promise of stability in monetary arrangements brought about by central banks, inspectors-general of banks, deposit insurance corporations being effected through private banks, and hence the rest of the economy?

Resolution of these problems awaits a satisfactory general equilibrium theory of banking, to which I now turn. Such a theory must at least explain why private banks do not pay the same rates of interest on deposits as they earn on loans and levy explicit service charges short of the costs of such services provided.

The theory or theories must, that is, explain or predict the national accounting banking problem and the need for the imputation. I present two very simple theories. One I call the neoclassical theory, the other Keynesian. With these two theories in hand, I return to the measurement problems outlined in this introduction.

7.3   On the Neoclassical Theory of the Efficiency of Banking[5]

7.3.1   Introduction

The regulation of banking by Monetary Authorities or central banks leads to Paretian inefficiency. Optimum money supply policies result in banking services being efficiently priced. The regulation by the Authorities determines the relations between interest rates on loans and deposits of banks and between the service charges levied for banking services and the cost of those services (cf. Merrick and Saunders 1985).

7.3.2   An Outline of the Model

The optimum neoclassical monetary growth model is used to portray inefficient pricing by banks. A representative agent, who maximizes intertemporal utility, uses the services of labor not supplied to the representative competitive bank, the services of commodity capital not held by the bank, and the service of the bank as metered by the service of real bank deposits to produce the one commodity output. The output is consumed or is added to the stock of capital or is exchanged for an increase in deposits with the bank, where it appears as an addition to bank capital. All agents taken together have their "real" bank deposits change as the price level changes. Therefore, the flow of bank services or bank output for all banks taken together, given the nominal stock of bank deposits, is a function of the overall price level (Johnson 1972). The services of bank deposits, and therefore the services of banks, are of two kinds. A transaction service is provided such that, for given amounts of nonbank capital and labor, a larger flow of this service of banks will result in a larger final output. A portfolio or store of value service is also performed by banks and bank deposits. Banks pay interest on bank deposits, and, the higher the rate of interest, the greater will be the demand for real bank deposits. For the services provided, in particular, the transaction service, banks levy a service charge, and, the lower the service charge, the greater will be the demand for real bank deposits as agents attempt to obtain more of the transactions services provided by the banks.

All nominal high-powered or fiat money created by the Authorities is randomly distributed among the banks in the form of deposits with the Authorities so that, as an important and restrictive simplification, there is no circulating currency (cf. Friedman and Schwartz 1986; and Selgin 1988).

Banks produce bank services by using labor supplied by the agents, capital obtained from the agents as they substitute real bank deposits for capital, and the services of real high-powered, fiat money or reserves. The services of the reserves stand for the services of the Authorities and can be obtained only through such deposits.

7.3.3   The Competitive Bank

In a deterministic version of the argument, a competitive bank producing primarily transaction services[6] is said to maximize

$$\Pi_B = [\delta_M - (i - p)]M/P + RL/P + (i_H - p - \delta_H)H/P$$
$$- WL_B - \delta K_B + \lambda_1 [M/P - (L/P + K_B + H/P)]$$
$$+ \lambda_2[M/P - M/P(K_B, L_B, H/P)] + x,$$

w.r.t. L/P, M/P, K_B, L_B, H/P, where Π_B = the commodity value of profits; M/P = the commodity value of homogeneous bank deposits; L/P = the commodity value of homogeneous bank loans; H/P = the commodity value of homogeneous bank deposits (reserves or high-powered money) held by the bank with the Authorities; L_B = the flow of labor used by the bank; K_B = the stock of capital used by the bank; δ_M = the service charge paid by depositors, expressed as a rate on deposits, for the services rendered by the bank; i = the nominal rate of interest paid on bank deposits; p = the expected equal to the actual rate of inflation in the money price of the commodity; R = the competitive net rate of return to capital earned on loans; i_H = the nominal rate of interest paid by the Authorities on the bank deposits or reserves with them; δ_H = the service charge paid by the bank, expressed as a rate on deposits or reserves, for the service rendered by the Authorities; W = the commodity rental on labor; δ = the rate of depreciation on the commodity stock of capital; $M/P = L/P + K_B + H/P$ is the balance sheet constraint; $M/P = M/P(K_B, L_B, H/P)$ is the production function; P = the overall price level; and x = the lump-sum changes in high-powered money created by the Authorities.

Competitive banks primarily provide a transaction service obtained by using and holding over any period an average volume of bank deposits. The transactions service of banks is indexed by the services of bank deposits, and these flow services are indexed by the stock of "real" bank deposits. Service charges are, in reality, complex, consisting of a variety of fixed charges and varying charges per debit and credit entries on depositors' accounts.[7] I simplify by expressing the service charge as a rate.

The technology of banking service requires the services of capital and labor and the services of the Authorities, obtained by the banks by holding deposits in turn with the Authorities. Again, the transaction service of the Authorities is indexed by the services of high-powered money, and, again, the flow of services of high-powered money is indexed by the stock of "real" deposits of the banks with the Au-

Table 7.3   Explicit Service Charges Paid to Banks, Canada, 1985

Composite service plans (e.g., Scotia Club)	3.9
Service charges on personal deposits	12.9
Nonpersonal deposit charges	19.2
Night depositories	.3
Guaranties on letters of credit fees	4.5
Funds transfer service fees	2.6
Acceptance fees	5.0
Credit card discounts and fees	19.2
Service charges on mortgages	1.5
Standby loan fees	2.9
Other loan fees	6.3
Safety deposit boxes	2.8
Canada Savings Bonds commissions	3.4
Security investment services fees	1.5
Safekeeping	1.4
Computer service revenue	2.6
Contractual management fees	2.5
Other miscellaneous services	7.4
Total	100.0

Source: GNP Division, Statistics Canada.

thorities just as the services of capital are indexed in neoclassical analysis by their stocks (Fischer 1974). The transaction services rendered by the Authorities could be clearing arrangements or deposit insurance arrangements (cf. Goodhart 1987, 1988) that lead banks to hold reserves with them.

A single bank competes for reserves by attempting to acquire deposits (or borrowing from agents) with the increased deposits taking the form of additional reserves and/or capital stocks. It is assumed that the banking service technology exhibits constant returns to scale. The single bank takes as given the price level, service charges, and all interest rates and knows confidently the steady-state inflation rate. From first-order conditions for profit maximization, we have

$$\frac{W}{\delta_M - (i - p) + R} = \frac{\partial_{M/P}}{\partial_{L_B}} (K_B, L_B, H/P),$$

$$\frac{R + \delta}{\delta_M - (i - p) + R} = \frac{\partial_{M/P}}{\partial_{K_B}} (K_B, L_B, H/P),$$

$$\frac{R - (i_H - p - \delta_H)}{\delta_M - (i - p) + R} = \frac{\partial_{M/P}}{\partial_{H/P}} (K_B, L_B, H/P),$$

which reveal that only if bank deposits earn the competitive rate of return, that is, if $i - p = R$, will the transaction service rental of bank labor and capital be metered by their respective marginal products and only if the Authorities pay the competitive rate of return on reserves, that is, if $i_H - p = R$, will the price of the transactions service provided by the Authorities be metered by the value of the marginal products of such services. We will then have

$$\frac{W}{\delta_M} = \frac{\partial_{M/P}}{\partial_{L_B}} (K_B, L_B, H/P),$$

$$\frac{R + \delta}{\delta_M} = \frac{\partial_{M/P}}{\partial_{K_B}} (K_B, L_B, H/P),$$

$$\frac{\delta_H}{\delta_M} = \frac{\partial_{M/P}}{\partial_{H/P}} (K_B, L_B, H/P).$$

The latter conditions are those required for Paretian efficiency in the provision of banking transactions services.

The zero-profit condition entails

$$[\delta_M - (i - p) + R]M/P = (R + \delta)K_B + WL_B \\ + [R - (i_H - p) + \delta_H]H/P$$

so that, if $R = i - p = i_H - p$, then

$$\delta_M M/P = (R + \delta)K_B + WL_B + \delta_H H/P,$$

or the price of the banking service will equal the marginal cost of providing that service. The link between the Authorities not paying competitive rates on reserves, differences between loan and deposit rates, and service charges not equaling the marginal cost of the provision of banking services is what this paper seeks to establish.

With δ set by technology and δ_H, i_H, and p set by the Authorities, the unknowns to determine are R, δ_M, W, i, and P—the net rate of return to capital, the service charge on bank deposits, the wage rate, the interest rate on bank deposits, and the overall price level.

In the foregoing, the price level is one of the things given to the competitive bank. However, at the market level of analysis, the services of bank deposits and bank reserves and therefore the services of banks and the Authorities cannot be determined independently of the price level. The determination of the price level is the sine qua non of the neoclassical quantity theory of money. In much of the banking literature, the codetermination of the level of output for all banks and the general price level is not investigated because such analysis is generally concerned with single competitive banks (see, e.g., Baltensperger 1980; Elyasiani 1982; Klein 1971; Santomero 1984; Spellman 1982; Tobin 1984; and Hancock 1985). Consideration of the price level, as I shall show, is also vital for the national accounting banking imputation.

From the first-order conditions for capital and real reserves, for any labor input, there will exist portfolio balance relations for different amounts of bank capital and real reserves that ensure that the value of the gross marginal physical product of bank capital equals the competitive gross rate of return or rental on capital and that the value of the gross marginal physical product of real reserves equals the competitive net rate of return or rental on capital plus the service charge, if any, levied by the Authority minus the real rate of interest paid by the Authorities on real reserves. These relations, which were set out in similar form by Keynes (1936, chap. 17), are

$$[\delta_M - (i - p) + R](\partial_{M/P}/\partial_{K_B})\,(K_B, L_B, H/P) = R + \delta,$$

$$[\delta_M - (i - p) + R](\partial_{M/P}/\partial_{H/P})\,(K_B, L_B, H/P) = R - (i_H - p) + \delta_H,$$

and are illustrated in figure 7.1. Figure 7.1 has the following interpretations. If $R = i - p = i_H - p$, then, from the bank capital relation, there are combinations of real reserves or the services of the Authorities used by banks and the services of capital such that the value of the gross marginal product of capital in banking equals the competitive gross rate of return or rental on capital. Those combinations are shown by the curve denoted K_B^*. Similarly, there are combinations of real reserves and real bank capital such that the value of the gross marginal

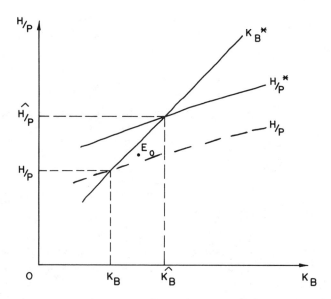

Fig. 7.1   Capital and real reserves for banks

product of the services of Authorities in banking equals the service charge levied by the Authorities. Those combinations are shown by the curve denoted H/P^*.[8] There is one combination of bank capital and real reserves such that portfolio equilibrium would hold, namely, banks would be content to hold capital and real reserve stocks. $\hat{K}_B$ *and* $\hat{H}/P$. If the Authorities then set $i_H - p < R$, then the banks would seek to hold fewer reserves. If the banks were able to generate lower real reserves, then real capital stocks would be earning less than the going rate of return, and both capital and real reserves would be reduced to K_B and H/P, where again portfolio equilibrium would be attained. Since nominal reserves are determined by the Authorities, real reserves cannot be altered unless the price level is changed, and, of course, competitive banks by themselves and together cannot determine the price level.

If the interest rate on deposits was lower, and so, proportionally, was the service charge on bank deposits, then the portfolio balance relations would be unaffected. If the reduction in the service charge was less in proportion than the interest rate on bank deposits, then both curves K_B^* and H/P would shift and intersect at a point such as E_0 in figure 7.1. To show that the change in the interest rates on deposits and the service charge is connected with the change in policy by the Authorities, it is necessary to consider the behavior of the representative agent.

7.3.4   Nonbanks

The representative agent maximizes

$$W = \int_0^\infty U(C_t)e^{-\rho t}dt,$$

where $U(C_t)$ is the instantaneous utility function with the usual properties, $U' > 0$, $U'' < 0$, and ρ is a constant rate of time preference, subject to

$$C[K(t), \tilde{L}(t), M/P(t)] + (i - p - \delta_M)M/P(t)$$

$$+ WL_B(t) - \dot{K}(t) - \dot{M}/P(t) = C(t),$$

where $C(t)$ is consumption; $\dot{K}(t)$ and $M/P(t)$ are investments in commodity capital and real bank deposits; $C[K(t), \tilde{L}(t), M/P(t)]$ is the gross output of the flow of consumption goods as a function of the services of the stock of capital, labor, and the services of the stock of real bank deposits (with again the services of bank deposits indexing the transaction services of banks); $i - p - \delta_M$ is the nominal rate of interest on bank deposits less the confidently expected steady-state rate of inflation less the service charge (as a rate); and $WL_B(t)$ are the wages paid by the banks. The technology $C[K(t), \tilde{L}(t), M/P(t)]$ entails that the production of consumption, now assumed subject to constant returns to scale, is positively related to real bank deposits or the services of banks in the sense that a lower use of the transactions services of banks would necessitate more labor and capital to produce the same level of consumption. In this paper, I ignore bank loans and assume for simplicity that agents demand bank deposits services, will give up capital to the banks for such deposits, and will supply labor to the banks.

The optimum solution entails

$$\partial_C/\partial_{\tilde{L}} (K, \tilde{L}, M/P) = W,$$

$$\partial_C/\partial_K(K, \tilde{L}, M/P) - (\delta + \rho) + \eta_c/c = 0,$$

$$\partial_C /\partial_{M/P}(K, \tilde{L}, M/P) + i - p - (\delta_M + \rho) + \eta_c/c = 0,$$

where η is the elasticity of the marginal utility of consumption with respect to consumption. In the steady state,

$$\partial_C/\partial_K (K, L, M/P) - \delta = \rho = R_K,$$

$$\partial_C/\partial_{M/P}(K, L, M/P) - \delta_M + i - p = \rho = R_M.$$

With normalization on labor, a second portfolio balance diagram is provided in figure 7.2. There are, for $\dot{C} = 0$, combinations of K and M/P such that $\dot{K}$ is also zero. Similarly, again for $\dot{C} = 0$, there are

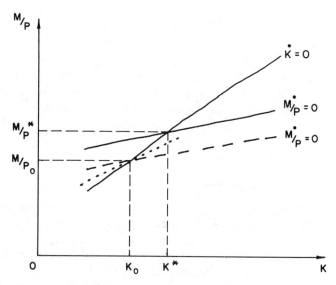

Fig. 7.2   Capital and real deposits for nonbanks

different combinations of K and M/P such that $\dot{M}/P$ is zero. A steady-state combination $(K^*, M/P^*)$ of real nonbank capital and real bank deposits is such that the net marginal rates of transformation between present and permanent consumption through either capital or bank deposits equals ρ, the steady-state rate of return. The steady-state combination depends on $i - \delta_M - p$, the net of the service charge real rate of interest earned on bank deposits. If $i - p$ is equal to ρ, then

$$\partial_C/\partial_{M/P}(K^*, M/P^*) - \delta_M = 0,$$

that is, the amount of K^* and M/P^* would be such that the gross marginal rate of transformation between present and permanent consumption through bank deposits would be equal to the service charge equal to the marginal social cost of producing such services.

The efficient steady-state equilibrium in which the Monetary Authorities pursue the optimal money supply policy, such that $i_H - p = \rho$, that is, the Authorities pay the steady-state competitive real net rate of return on reserves, entails that $i - p = \rho$, that is, the real interest rate on bank deposits will also equal the competitive real net rate of return. Thus, all service charges, expressed as rates, would equal the values of the marginal physical products of the services of real reserves and bank deposits. For bank deposits, then, in steady state we would have

$$\rho = \partial_C / \partial_{M/P}(K^*, M/P^*) + i^* - p - \delta_M^*,$$

such that $\rho = i^* - p$ entails $\partial_C / \partial_{M/P}(K^*, M/P^*) = \delta_M^*$.
Could the same equilibrium exist if $i < i^*$ and $\delta_M < \delta_M^*$ but $i - \delta_M = i^* - \delta_M^*$? The answer is no. A reduction in δ_M entails a reduction in the price of bank services relative to P, the overall price level, so that real effects must follow. A lower overall price level entails real effects such that the contemplated equilibria other than $\rho = i^* - p$ would not exist.

7.4 The Model (and Stability)

If the Authority sets $i_H - p$ less than ρ, the banks' demand for real reserves will be less, and they will attempt to supply fewer real deposits, which results in lower interest rates being paid on bank deposits. Agents in turn would want to hold fewer bank deposits or demand fewer services because of the lower interest rate, which would result in lower service charges. Agents wishing to hold fewer bank deposits are, however, simultaneously wishing to hold more stocks of goods (as are banks), and the price of goods in general will be higher so that the relative price of banking services in terms of the numeraire commodity must be lower. The higher price level is associated with lower amounts of real deposits and reserves.[9] The real deposits and reserves are associated with higher gross marginal rates of transformation between present and permanent consumption through reserves and bank deposits to offset the difference between $i_H - p - \delta_H$ and between $i - p - \delta_M$ and ρ. The lower real reserves and deposits in turn are associated with lower amounts of real capital.

The argument is partially illustrated in figure 7.2. One starts with optimum monetary arrangements and the observed allocations M/P^* and K^*. The Authority then sets $i_H - p < i_H^* - p$. Banks therefore have a negative excess demand for reserves at the existing price level. In competing less for reserves, the banks attempt to supply fewer bank deposits and so generate lower interest rates on bank deposits. The lower interest rates on bank deposits will be associated with agents demanding fewer bank deposits and bank services.

Two effects follow: If service charges could be lower pari passu with interest rates on bank deposits (a possible partial equilibrium result), then the negative excess demand for bank deposits would be eliminated, but the negative excess demand for reserves would remain. The reduction in the service charges will be less, however, because as part of a generalized increase in the excess demand for goods the price of all consumption in general, including bank services, will rise, offsetting to some extent the fall in the nominal price of the services of banks but not preventing a decline in the relative service price of banks. The result is a dashed $M/P = 0$ locus in figure 7.2 and a dotted temporary equilibrium locus that indicates that at the higher overall price level, which equalizes rates of return on capital and real bank deposits,[10] the temporary equilibrium rates of return to capital and real bank deposits would be below ρ, agents will save less, and a new steady-state equilibrium, $M/\overset{*}{P}_0$, K_0, would exist. By the simplifications on the balance sheet $M/P = K_B + H/P$, it follows that in the banking sector there will be a new steady-state equilibrium H/P_0, K_0, such that the volume of the transaction services of banks would be lower.

The inefficient steady state entails that real interest rates on bank deposits are less than ρ with

$$\frac{\partial_C}{\partial_{M/P}} (K_0, M/P_0) - \delta_M = \rho - (i - p) > 0,$$

$$\frac{\partial_{M/P}}{\partial_{H/P}} (K_{B0}, H/P_0) - \delta_H = \rho - (i_H - p) > 0.$$

The Authorities, by setting $i_H - p$ less than ρ, behave as a monopolist constrained by pecuniary behavior to maximize (say) the inflation tax, and the community experiences the associated welfare losses. That behavior by the Authorities shows up not only in the "distortion" of relative interest rates and relative prices but in a "distortion" of the price level (the once-over change in the level of prices is the key to the argument) as compared to that state that results from the optimum money supply policy. It is these "distortions" that lead to the standard observations that interest rates on bank deposits are less than those on bank loans and that the service charges banks levy do not cover the cost of the services provided. Again, the argument depends on the supposed ability of the Authorities to effect changes in $i_H - \delta_H - p$ independently of x, the lump-sum tax transfer mechanism, an ability this paper assumes. This is a requirement for the supernonneutrality results to hold (see Dornbusch and Frenkel 1973).

To recapitulate, then, the levying of a tax by the authorities, that is, their failure to pursue the Friedman-Lucas optimal money supply policy of paying the competitive real rate of return on reserves results in banks earning a higher rate on their loans than they pay on their deposits and in the value of the transactions services provided by the banks being greater than the service charges collected. These are, however, precisely the conditions that give rise to the problem of measuring nominal banking output and that lead national accountants to embrace the banking imputation "resolution" of the problem.

It will be noted that only one "distortion" has been introduced—the failure of the Authorities to pay the competitive real rate of return on reserves. Generalizations and extensions would appear possible. Additional "distortions" would be imposed if the Authorities compelled the banks to hold (binding) legal and varied cash reserve ratios or to set some ceiling to the interest rates banks could pay on deposits or could earn on loans[11]—to name just two examples.

Technical objections to the neoclassical general equilibrium theory of efficient banking (cf. Harkness 1978; Sargent and Wallace 1985; Bewley 1985; Milbourne 1987), while of concern (cf. Rymes 1972), are not as important as the obvious fact that it leaves no room for a theory of central banking. In the neoclassical theory, the failure of central banks or Monetary Authorities to pay competitive interest rates on fiat money results in a "distorting" tax. The Authorities must be constrained (Brennan and Buchanan 1980) to follow optimum money supply policies and must not behave in a discretionary fashion because such behavior may not be effective in affecting real nonmonetary variables such as the volume of unemployment and can lead only to departures, such as inflation or a reduction in $i_H - p$, from efficient monetary arrangements. A central bank, constrained to pay competitive interest rates on reserves and to replicate other competitive conditions, is not a central bank. As Wills (1982, 258) argues: "A system with a mandatory cash base on which the marginal cost of funds is paid is equivalent to an unregulated system." In our simple case, the reserve base is not mandatory, but, even in the case in which the interest rate on reserves is set below the competitive rate, banks will still hold such reserves if such holdings permit them to access the provision of (say) deposit insurance by the Authorities, such insurance potentially obviating the phenomenon of bank runs (see Diamond and Dybvig 1983). The "tax" still applies since a service charge would be and is levied by the Authorities for the service provided.

However, if the reserves did earn the competitive rate of return, it would be possible for the reserves to be privately produced and held and for the Monetary Authorities to provide the insurance service other than through the reserves of the competitive banks. Similarly, the banks could hold their reserves privately, and the Monetary Authorities could provide interbank clearing or transaction services without the need for the banks to hold reserves with the Authorities. Such insurance and clearing services could be provided privately, in which case the rationale for Monetary Authorities or central banks has completely vanished. The services of competitive banks would be efficiently priced, the service charges would cover the costs of the banking services, or the transactions services of bank deposits and the set of prices associated with the transition-production technology would be observed to be but a part of standard monetary general equilibrium analysis (Fama 1980, 1983; Greenfield and Yeager 1983; Hall 1982; King 1983; Yeager

1985). The special problems associated with the measurement of banking output would have disappeared.

All this results from the nonexistence of a satisfactory theory of central banking in the foregoing analysis. I now turn to that crucial problem.

7.5   The Model (and Instability): An Introduction to the Keynesian Theory of Banking

In the analysis so far, global stability in a rational expectations perfect foresight sense has been assumed. Had global instability been assumed, nothing could have been said. What about the rational expectations saddlepoint instability argument? In figure 7.3, I illustrate the problem. In figure 7.3, suppose there exists an optimal steady state, $(K^*, M^*/P)$. Suppose the equilibrium is "disturbed" by a change in the capital stock. If lower, it would appear that, in a temporary equilibrium, as agents tried to go from bank deposits into goods, the rise in the price of goods would so reduce M/P that further decumulation and a further rise in prices would occur. The economy would be off into infinite capital shallowing and ever-higher price levels. If the capital stock were greater, it would appear, for temporary equilibrium to hold, that the price of goods would fall, resulting in further accumulation, and the economy would be off into infinite capital deepening and ever-lower price levels.

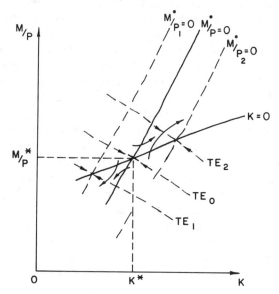

Fig. 7.3   Capital and real deposits for nonbanks: saddlepoint stability

Agents would know, however, that the Authorities would engage in monetary reform to prevent such inefficient outcomes. In the first case, agents would be compensated for the reduction in the real value of their bank deposits; the extent of such expected compensation would be such that agents would seek to hold greater, not less, real cash balances; the initial price level would be lower, not higher; and the temporary equilibrium would be on the stable arm of the saddlepoint equilibrium, labelled TE_0 in figure 7.3. In the second case, the value of bank deposits would be reduced by the monetary reform. Agents, knowing this, would seek to hold fewer real deposits, and the price level would be higher rather than lower, putting the economy in temporary equilibrium again on the stable arm of the saddlepoint equilibrium TE_0 (Sargent and Wallace 1973; Begg 1982; and Sheffrin 1983, 1981).

The unique stable perfect foresight path is not connected with any rules the Authority would follow but is in fact a product of the supposed discretionary power of the Authority to provide the stability.

The saddlepoint instability may arise because of myopic expectations—all agents, for example, may not know exactly what the steady-state rate of inflation must be and are sufficiently misguided to adapt their inflation expectations to the different rates of inflation that would exist along any sequence of temporary equilibria. The saddlepoint equilibria can also arise from the specification of the basic transformation schedules $C(K, \bar{L}, M/P)$ and $M/P(K_B, L_B, H/P)$ so that second-order conditions may not be secure. In figure 7.3, the relative slopes of the portfolio balance relations have been altered to reflect this possibility of a transactions technology that is consistent with instability.

Suppose that the Authority, endeavoring to increase efficiency, raises the real rate paid on reserves and that the real rate of interest net of the service charge on bank deposits increases. Then, as illustrated in figure 7.3, the $M/P = 0$ locus is shifted upward to $M/P_1 = 0$ because the net rate of return on real bank deposits, with $i - p - \delta_M$ higher, would remain at ρ only if real bank deposits were much higher, ensuring that the gross marginal rate of transformation respecting consumption through bank deposits was lower. With no further action by the Authorities, the system would be unstable, off on a programme of infinite capital and real bank deposit accumulation. Action by the Authorities known by the agents to be required for monetary stability entails that the holding of real bank deposits will be penalized. The relevant unique perfect foresight stable path is along the temporary equilibrium locus TE_1. Conversely, if the Authorities caused the banks to pay lower interest rates on deposits, then agents, trying to move out of deposits, would cause prices to rise at an accelerating rate, and the economy as in figure 7.3 would be off into infinite capital shallowing and ever-higher price levels. Again, agents who perceive such a possibility will be expecting monetary reform such that the terminal value of their bank deposits will be greater than under the unstable scenario. The relevant temporary equilibrium locus becomes TE_2. The extent to which reform must occur is such that in the first instance agents would seek to hold less real money and the price level would adjust instantaneously upward. The reason for this is that overall, taking into account the higher rate of interest on deposits and the reduction in the terminal value of the deposits, money is not as attractive to hold. In short, the Authorities have made the holding of money less, not more, attractive. Similarly, in the second instance, the expected increase in the real value of bank deposits more than offsets the lower interest rates, and overall money is more attractive to hold. Again, the Authorities have in fact made the holding of money more, not less, attractive.

An interesting problem emerges. The possibility of a unique perfect foresight path to a steady-state equilibrium depends on the maintenance of stability by the Authorities. The efficiency of monetary arrangements depends not on the maintenance of a competitive real rate of interest on reserves but on the preservation of stability by the Authorities— assuming instability in the saddlepoint sense. What is then meant by the efficiency gains from an optimal money supply rule such as paying competitive real rates on the reserves of the banks? This question is particularly relevant when cognizance is taken of the point that attempted maintenance of optimum rules by the Authorities may contribute to rather than reduce the instability of the economic system. Discretionary behavior by the Authorities, when fully taken into account by private agents, is stabilizing, whereas conduct of policy by rules is disstabilizing.

Under the assumptions of neoclassical monetary growth theory, if global stability is assumed, the failure of the Authorities to follow the rule of paying competitive real interest rates on reserves involves welfare losses. If saddlepoint instability is assumed, no rule will ensure efficiency. In fact, the announcement by the Authorities of a rule will necessitate at some time the announcement of a change in the rule— what some call "time inconsistency" in rules (Calvo 1978)—to enhance the efficiency of the economic system.

More important, if stability is assumed, it is hard to see any role for Monetary Authorities. Optimum money supply policies entail the complete deregulation of the banking activity. Optimum rules and laissez-faire banking are one and the same thing. Once the optimum rules are followed, interest rates on reserves and on deposits equal the competitive real net rate of transformation between present and permanent consumption streams, all services performed by the Authorities and by the banks are efficiently priced, and M would be at the level of the marginal real resource cost of the services of banks. The central bank has no role to play. The problem with banks in the national accounts would, at least on this analysis, not exist.

These conclusions are radically altered if saddlepoint instability in the rational expectations sense is assumed in which the unique sequence of temporary equilibria to steady-state equilibria is a function of the rationally expected discretionary action of the Authorities. Depending on the specification of the service of bank deposits and reserves in production relations, the rule $i_M - p = \rho$ can lead to instability and is corrected into a unique sequence of temporary equilibria if and only if the Authorities change the rule at some time. Then optimum money supply policy rules cannot be followed.

The consequence of Monetary Authorities that act in a discretionary way is that the rules set out for efficiency in the case in which stability was assumed cannot apply. Banks will not earn the going net rate of return on their reserves, interest rates on deposits will not be the same as those earned on loans, and the service charges levied by the banks will not cover the cost of such services. In a world in which the Monetary Authorities play the essential role of ensuring monetary stability, then the sets of interest rates and service charges will generate precisely those characteristics that give rise to the banking problem outlined in the introduction to this paper.

Reserves and, indirectly, bank deposits would earn nonpecuniary liquidity premia (not part of the return on money balances in the neoclassical case) because the real value of the services of money and hence the real value of the money stocks themselves are associated with the provision of the public good, stability, by the Authorities. It is not the service of money that is a public good (cf. Weldon 1971; Laidler 1977) but the service of stability by the Authorities.

7.6 The Problem of Measuring Nominal Private and Central Bank Output

What is the significance of the theoretical discussion for the measurement problems that are also the topic of this paper? Consider the neoclassical argument first. It was observed, under the optimum monetary policy argument, that for bank deposits

$$R = \frac{\partial c}{\partial_{M/P}} (K^*, \bar{L}, M/P^*) + i - p - \delta_M$$

so that, where $i_M - p = R$, then

$$\frac{\partial c}{\partial_{M/P}} (K^*, \bar{L}, M/P^*) - \delta_M = 0,$$

or

$$\delta_M = \frac{\partial_C}{\partial_{M/P}} (K^*, \bar{L}, M/P^*),$$

that is, the rental price of the services of bank deposits or the price of the output of banks equals the value of the marginal product of such services. The banking imputation would not be needed, and the measurement problem associated with banks would not exist.

For nonoptimum monetary policy, however, we have

$$R - (i - p) + \delta_M = \frac{\partial_C}{\partial_{M/P}} (K, \bar{L}, M/P).$$

The theoretical argument says that the nonoptimum value of the marginal product of banking services will be equal to the difference between the competitive net real rate of return and the real interest rate paid on bank deposits (or $R + p - i$, the difference between the competitive net nominal rate of return less the nominal rate of interest paid on bank deposits) plus the service charge rate associated with banking services.

This would appear to be precisely that which results from the application of the banking imputation procedure. If we assume that bank loans earn the competitive rate of return, then the imputed real gross output for banks will be, where M/P is the real value of bank deposits equal to loans,

$$[R - (i - p) + \delta_M]M/P,$$

or the imputed nominal gross output for banks will be

$$[R + p - i + \delta_M]M,$$

which is precisely what national accountants do.

The "real" gross output of the banks,

$$[R - (i - p) + \delta_M]M/P,$$

which results from this imputation, reflects, however, the policy of the Authorities. Given M, the greater the "distortion" tax levied by the Authorities, then, by the preceding argument, the higher will be the price level P (so that on this ground the lower will be the real gross output of the banks) and the lower will be $i - p$ (offset by some possible lesser fall in δ_M because of the rise in the overall price level)—so that on this latter ground the higher will be the real gross output of the banks.

The implication of the analysis is that the measure of output of banks, obtained from the banking imputations, is not independent of the policy of the Monetary Authorities. If other nonbanking industries had their purchases of bank services so measured and treated as intermediate inputs, then such real intermediate inputs in all other nonbanking industries would also reflect the policy of the Authorities.[12]

The imputation based on the neoclassical argument suffers, however, from a grave drawback. Corrections are made for interest rates on deposits and service charges on deposits on the grounds of being too "low," but no account is taken in the imputation procedure for the overall price level being too "high." At the given level of nominal deposits, then, the argument is that "real" bank deposits are too low. Hence, were the imputation applied according to the neoclassical theory, the real value of bank deposits would have to be increased so that the imputed gross output in banks would have to be greater. This argument is based on the revision of interest rates and prices that are the components of the imputation and that would be reflected in the revision of prices in the temporary equilibrium accompanying the adoption of efficient policies by the Authorities. It is not the revisions in interest rates and prices that will be associated with the full equilibrium adjustments in the economy. If correct, though, it means that the present banking imputation results in an underestimate of banking output and value added. It is conjectured that the effects of such revised imputations on measured rates of saving would be significant.

There are further implications associated with the neoclassical analysis. One of the inputs into the production of the bank's transaction service is the services of the reserves or the services of the central bank. The neoclassical analysis implies that an imputed measure of the gross output of the central bank can also be derived.

Consider again the optimum money supply argument. We would have

$$\delta_M \frac{\partial_{M/P}}{\partial_{H/P}} (K_{B^*}, L_B, H/P^*) - \delta_H = 0,$$

or

$$\delta_H = \delta_M \frac{\partial_{M/P}}{\partial_{H/P}} (K_{B^*}, L_B, H/P^*),$$

or the rental price on reserves would equal the real value of the marginal product of real reserves or the service of the Authorities. Otherwise, we would have

$$R - (i_H - p) + \delta_H = [\delta_M - (i - p) + R]\frac{\partial_{M/P}}{\partial_{H/P}} (K_B, L_B, H/P)$$

so that, even if no interest was paid on reserves and no service charge was levied for the services rendered by the Authorities, the nominal interest rate, $R + p$, would be a measure of the price of gross output of the Authorities.

In general, the imputed real gross output of central banks would be

$$[R - (i_H - p) + \delta_H]H/P,$$

or the nominal gross output would be

$$[R + p - i_H + \delta_H]H.$$

Since the burden of the neoclassical argument is that a central bank or Monetary Authority can be treated as if it were a private bank—particularly so if the optimum monetary policy were pursued and Authorities charged for any services rendered—then it follows that the banking imputation can be applied to central banks or Monetary Authorities as well. The banking imputation applied to Monetary Authorities, just as when it is applied to private banks, would result in measures of "real" gross output that would imperfectly reflect the policy being carried out by such Authorities.[13]

In the Keynesian case, if the banking imputations were employed, then the price of the gross output of the banks would meter not just the value of the marginal physical product of the transaction service of banks but also the liquidity premium attached to bank deposits for a service not produced by the banks, except indirectly through their holding of reserves, the liquidity premium being a measure of the confidence with which the Authorities are expected to perform their function of preserving monetary stability. The "failure" of the Authorities to pay full interest on reserves (i.e., $R > i_H - p$) in the Keynesian case would not represent the imposition of a "distorting" tax but would reflect the "price" banks would pay for the provision of monetary stability by the Authorities obtained through the holding of reserves. Similarly, the "failure" of the banks to pay full interest on deposits (i.e., $R > [i - p]$) in the Keynesian case again would not represent the indirect imposition of a "distorting" tax by the Authorities but would reflect the "price" nonbank agents would "pay" for the provision of monetary stability by the Authorities, obtained indirectly through the holding of bank deposits, since they, in turn, access that provision directly through the holding of reserves.

In the case of the Keynesian theory of central banking and the resulting liquidity premia on "money," application of the national accounting banking imputation confounds the measure of the rental price on banking services with the liquidity premia that results from the provision of the public good, monetary stability, by the Monetary Authorities.

From the theoretical viewpoint, the Keynesian analysis entails liquidity premia being imbedded in all relative prices since in modern monetary economies all activities employ, directly and indirectly, as intermediate inputs, the services of private banks, which incorporate indirectly the provision of monetary stability by the Monetary Authorities. There is no way to "price" the provision of monetary stability by the Authorities, but the various liquidity premia are imbedded in the structure of relative prices with no operational way of separating, say in the case of the rental price of banking service, $\partial_C/\partial_{M/P}(K, L, M/P)$, the value of the marginal product of banking services from the liquidity premium on bank deposits.

In general, therefore, the output of banks—in particular, the transaction services of banks—cannot be defined or measured independently of the conception and measurement of the output of the Monetary Authorities, which given the nature of the output cannot be measured in the ex post manner applicable to the national accounts.

7.7   Relation to Measures of Rates of Saving and Wealth

The limited application of the banking imputation results in a lower rate of saving for the personal sector, though, as is shown in table 7.2, the effects are negligible.

Governments can as well be treated as (collectivities of) households. Governments hold deposits with private banks and central banks. (In fact, these government accounts, particularly switches between them, are part of the day-to-day operations of directionary monetary policy and are the mechanism by which increases in fiat money are brought into existence.) Government deposits with private banks are the means by which governments tap the transactions services provided by banks, and, since they are in this respect identical to households, the banking imputation would result in an increase in imputed government expenditures and imputed investment income. One could similarly argue that government deposits with the central bank are devices by which the government accesses the transactions services being provided by the central bank, and an imputation could be made for those deposits as well. Again, government expenditures and income would be further equally increased. Each level of imputation would reduce the rate of saving of the government sector.

The results then of the banking imputation is that the rate of saving of both households and governments is decreased.[14] There remains the fundamental objection to the application of the imputation procedure, even assuming the applicability of the neoclassical general equilibrium theory of banking, namely, that for each and every variant of nonoptimum money supply policies there will be a different price level. It is understood that different nominal money supplies entail, by the underlying quantity theory of money, different proportionate price levels. Beyond that—and this is the major point—if one assumes that each variant left nominal stocks of money unchanged, it would still be the case that the price levels would differ. The greater the departure from optimality, the higher would be the overall price level.

To summarize, the greater the departure of money supply policies from optimum, the greater, other things being equal, will be the banking imputation. The greater the banking imputation, the lower would be "after imputation" rate of saving of households and governments.

By the very nature of the problem, the attempted measurement of banking output must recognize that such output can be ascertained only within the confines of a general equilibrium framework of banking and monetary analyses. The neoclassical theory set out provides such a framework. That theory immediately suggests that, while the standard imputation recognizes that interest rates and service charges on deposits are too low, it should be additionally recognized that the "overall" price level is too "high." If the banking imputation took into account that, the more extensive were the difference in rates on loans and deposits, the more the price would be too "high," then the imputed gross output of banks would be much higher than results from the present limited imputation, and measured rates of saving for the personal (and government) sector would be even less. Such a result would be in accord with the foregoing neoclassical theory, which predicts that, the more efficient the money supply policy conducted by the Monetary Authorities, the greater would be the rate of saving, at the temporary (and steady-state) level of analysis. Thus, the augmented banking imputation would be fully supported by neoclassical general equilibrium banking and monetary theory.

The Keynesian theory recommends, however, against the banking imputation. The immeasurable liquidity premium on private bank deposits, a component of the service of bank deposits, arises because banks specialize in, or are required to hold, the holding of bank deposits with the central bank. The private banks then have direct access to the services connected with provision of monetary stability by the Authorities, and nonbank agents have, through their bank deposits, indirect access to such services. Since these services are public in nature and cannot be produced privately, no price can be found for them. The Keynesian framework rejects the argument that one can impute a measure of the gross output of central banks, that is, a measure of the value of the marginal product of real deposits with the central bank, held either by private banks or government, since the crucial output of the central bank, the preservation of monetary stability, is not measurable (Acheson 1986).

The crucial distinction between the Keynesian general banking and monetary general equilibrium and neoclassical theories can be seen by asking what treatment would be suggested if, for example, all banks were nationalized and became de jure, instead of de facto, agents of the central bank. The rejection by the Keynesian argument of the imputation means that government expenditures in the extended government sector would merely be redefined to include the expenditures on labor and materials undertaken by the bank (cf. Haig 1986). Estimates of the rate of saving in the personal and government sectors would not be affected by the banking imputations since such imputations would not be made.

It was shown earlier that wealth measurement encountered the problem of the distinction between inside and outside money. My discussion of the banking imputation problem permits some advance as well in that discussion.

If the "money" in the neoclassical framework were outside, then the wealth of the private sector would be

$$H/P^* + K_B^* + K^* = M/P^* + K^*,$$

where the efficient monetary policy is pursued, and

$$H/P + K_B + K = M/P + K,$$

where it is not, with all components of such national wealth being lower the further away from optimality the monetary policy would be. No double-counting would be involved since, in the optimum policy case, the present value of the services being rendered by the Authorities (e.g., deposit insurance or clearing arrangements) would be equal to the value of the deposit claims against the Authorities. The capital stock held by the banks would be part of the overall capital stock, $K_B + K$, with K being the stock of capital in all nonbank activities.

It was pointed out that the nominal addition to reserves, rather than being injected into the economy via the lump-sum transfers, x, could be brought about by the switching of government deposits with the central bank to the private banks. It will be remembered that circulating currency is being ignored. In this case, there would be no outside money—that is, for the banks, real reserves as assets would always be offset by real government deposits as liabilities. The components of a national wealth statement by sector, ignoring irrelevant items, would be

Government

Deposits with private banks	Government "bonds" held by the
Deposits with the central bank	central bank

Central Bank

Government "bonds"	Deposits of the government
	Deposits of the private banks

Private Banks

Deposits with the central bank	Deposits of the government
Bank capital	Deposits of the nonbank agents

Nonbanks

Deposits with private banks   Net worth
Nonbank capital

so that, with the deposits of the private banks with the central bank equal to the deposits of the government with the banks, the net worth of the private sector consists only of nonbank and bank capital.

This accounting treatment of the inside money case neglects, of course, the fact that government deposits with the private banks are not a liability that would affect bank behavior in the same sense as the existence of private deposits does. (Canadian bankers have, e.g., argued that they should not be required to hold reserves behind government deposits.) Recognition that the government deposits-reserves mechanism is part of the mechanism by which the Monetary Authorities seek to preserve monetary stability enhances the validity of the Keynesian argument to the effect that, even in the case of "outside" money, that money is not part of national wealth. Rather, it is the expectation of monetary stability that constitutes the monetary component of wealth. It will be captured in the value of nonbank and capital, $K_B + K$, and to add H/P to obtain a measure of private national wealth would involve double-counting.[15]

7.8   Extensions and Conclusion

7.8.1   Extensions

Two extensions to the argument would appear necessary. First, the argument has assumed one homogeneous bank deposit. If Monetary Authorities impose different reserve requirements on different deposits in recognition that banks produce nonhomogeneous banking services with different deposits also being associated implicitly with different transactions and portfolio services, the foregoing analysis would predict different interest rates and service charges (e.g., savings nonchequable deposits would pay higher real rates and have lower service charges since such deposits would perform a greater flow of portfolio services and relatively limited transactions services such as currency withdrawals). A much richer theoretical model than I have presented would be necessary to illustrate and predict such arguments. Also, many other dimensions of banking, such as monitoring and verification costs (cf. Chant 1987) and a more intricate transactions technology, would have to be explored. The essential connection between banking services and the Monetary Authorities must, however, be maintained. It would appear, from the Keynesian viewpoint, that it is the discretionary behavior of the Authorities that provides much of the rationale for the existence of fiat money. Second, there are other financial intermediaries, other than banks per se, that provide differentiated banking services in the sense that some of them may have more indirect access to the services of the Monetary Authorities of a more indirect nature than the banks. In table 7.4, the distribution of deposit interest paid to persons by deposit-taking intermediaries shows that banks are becoming perhaps relatively less important in the provision of transactions services. A needed extension of the preceding theoretical argument is to include transactions services provided by country banks such as trust companies and by those intermediaries that, in the limit, would not be classed as banks.

While providing but one measure of the changing importance of banks in Canada, it must be remembered that the data in table 7.4 are drawn from a decade in which some would say there was a major increase in competition in Canadian banking with a sharp increase in numbers of banks following Royal Assent to the Bank Act in 1980 and important changes in central bank policy with the addition and subsequent disowning of gradual monetarism and monetary targeting from 1975 to 1982.

7.8.2   Conclusion

Two extremely simple general equilibrium theories of banking have been examined with arguments that Monetary Authorities are seen as taxing the community by not following efficient monetary policies in the Friedman-Lucas sense or providing the services, by themselves and indirectly through private agents such as banks, of the public good monetary stability. Both arguments, as developed, predict that banking

Table 7.4   **Distribution of Deposit Interest to Persons, Canada, 1975–85: Major Deposit-Taking Intermediaries**

Year	Banks	Quebec Savings Banks	Trust Companies	Mortgage Loan Companies	Credit Unions
1975	.554	.016	.236	.049	.145
1976	.551	.014	.239	.043	.152
1977	.489	.015	.276	.046	.175
1978	.486	.013	.251	.073	.176
1979	.533	.013	.235	.057	.162
1980	.546	.012	.220	.054	.168
1981	.592	.010	.199	.057	.142
1982	.543	.010	.214	.085	.147
1983	.434	.013	.269	.125	.160
1984	.450	.012	.255	.132	.151
1985	.405	.015	.273	.145	.163

Source: GNP Division, Statistics Canada.

statistics lead to the apparent need for the banking imputation. In this connection, the significance of these two arguments for measures of banking output, rates of saving, and wealth are examined. The neoclassical argument lends partial support to the current imputation procedures but reveals that such procedures suffer from an important defect, which leads to the result that banking output is understated and rates of savings in the personal and government sectors are overstated—and potentially substantially overstated. The less and less efficient is the monetary policy, the greater and greater are these measurement effects. The neoclassical argument tends to include fiat money as a component of private wealth, though, the more and more it is recognized that the fiat money is created by the inside money route, the more and more the neoclassical argument approaches that provided by the Keynesian theory of private and central banking. That theory provides no support for the imputation and arguments associated with it and would, in comparison with the neoclassical argument, result in higher rates of saving of the personal and government sectors. The Keynesian theory concludes as well that it is the policy of the promotion of monetary stability that contributes to wealth, that to add outside money to private national wealth would be to engage in double-counting since the real components of wealth, reproducible capital in the banking and nonbanking sectors, already include the wealth-creating effects of the promotion of monetary stability.

Notes

1. In this case, the imputations are radically different from those customarily made in national accounting. In the case of other imputations, (1) a set of equivalent or nearly equivalent market prices is available that permits the "pricing" of services such as farm production consumed on farms and the rents earned on owner-occupied houses (Rymes 1979), and (2) the case for the imputations is that changes in the distribution of resources between market and nonmarket institutional forms would, unless the imputations were made, result in undue variations in measured output. The banking problem is unique. The uniqueness is that (1) there is apparently not a set of equivalent or nearly equivalent prices that permits the pricing of banking output since there is no apparent market counterpart and (2) the invariance argument fails as well.
A sophisticated version of the invariance argument is that the barter-type arrangements between banks and depositors said to be implicit in the fact that banks underprice services they are rendering to depositors and depositors underprice services they are rendering to banks arise because of the payment of taxes on interest receipts. A household depositor will pay less in taxes if his deposit interest receipts are smaller and so will provide service to the banks at less than market prices to minimize taxes. The bank will compensate the depositor by reducing the service charges on bank deposits or what it is charging

for its service to depositors. The version fails to take account of the different interest rates—service charges on different bank deposits—and the fact that the nonuse of the price system induced by income taxes would not hold for transactions between banking and other industries.

2. In the Canadian input-output accounts, the imputed intermediate output of the banks is, in fact, treated as part of the intermediate inputs of the nonbank industries.

3. The Ruggles-Sunga treatment of interest flows has fundamental ramifications for the national accounts that are not discussed here. Their treatment of interest on the national debt would result, however, again in a reduction in the overall national rate of saving.

4. For the Canadian economy, standard measures of national wealth will include net claims on the rest of the world so that net holdings of fiat monies of other companies do appear as part of Canadian wealth.

5. I have presented overviews of these arguments in my other work on the imputation problem (Rymes 1985, 1986). A full statement of the theoretical framework is necessary to assess the wider measurement problems considered in this paper. Earlier versions of this section of the paper have been presented to the Departments of Economics at Monash University, the Australian National University, Carleton University, McGill University, the University of Strathclyde, Manchester University, the Churchill College Seminar in Economic Theory, and the 1986 meeting of the Canadian Economics Association. I am grateful to Courtney Wright, Ian Harper, Ted Seiper, John Pitchford, Nicholas Rowe, Steve Ferris, Randy Geehan, Jack Weldon, James Pickett, Ian Steedman, Partha Dasgupta, Jack Revell, John Chant, Jack Galbraith, Keith Acheson, and Leslie Milton for critical and helpful comments.

6. In an appendix to this paper supplied on request, the case of a competitive bank providing both transactions and explicit portfolio services is set out.

7. In Fischer's (1983) analysis, while the banks cannot produce their services without acquiring the services of real reserves obtained by holding deposits with the Monetary Authorities, individual agents can obtain the services of banks without holding bank deposits. In my formulation, the crucial transaction service supplied by a bank can be obtained only by holding and using a certain volume, on the average, of bank deposits. I do not deal with services such as safety deposit box rentals, the making up of pay packets, etc. as some of these, e.g., travel services, may have nothing to do with the banking service. Table 7.3 lists the various explicit service charges paid to banks in Canada in 1985, along with their relative importance.

8. The respective slopes of K_B^* and H/P^* in fig. 7.1 are based on the second-order conditions for the bank's maximization problem.

9. If the overall price level is defined to include the nominal price of the services of banks, then, of course, an index number problem is involved in what is meant by "real" bank deposits and reserves. I ignore this complication in this paper.

10. Agents seek to hold fewer bank deposits and more stocks of commodities. There is a temporary equilibrium higher-price level such that, since real bank deposits are lower, the net rate of return on bank deposits rises because of the increase in the gross marginal physical product of real bank deposits and the net rate of return to capital falls until such rates are equalized. Since the net rate on capital has fallen, it is now below the efficient steady-state rate.

11. The latter is a type of "distortion" not practiced in Canada since the 1967 revision of the Bank Act (see Freedman 1983). That the failure of the Authorities to pay interest on reserves is a tax on transactions intermediated

by banks is also argued by Wills (1982), though Wills pays no attention to the general equilibrium effects on service charges and the overall price level.

12. In any given year, the nominal gross output of the banks would be

$$[R - (i - p) + \delta_M]M$$

so that changes in the nominal gross output would reflect changes in R, i, p, δ_M, and M. A Laspeyres index of the "real" gross output of the banks would be

$$\frac{R_0 - (i_0 - p_0) + \delta_{M0}}{R_0 - (i_0 - p_0) + \delta_{M0}} \cdot \frac{M_1/P_1}{M_0/P_0}$$

and a Paasche index would be

$$\frac{R_1 - (i_1 - p_1) + \delta_{M1}}{R_1 - (i_1 - p_1) + \delta_{M1}} \cdot \frac{M_1/P_1}{M_0/P_0},$$

where the expressions are in general vectors and the indexes are aggregators. For examples of some of the other problems involved in measuring the "real" output of banks, see Gorman (1969) and Geehan and Allen (1978).

13. A reallocation of value added from private banks to the central bank would be involved. For instance, if actual service charges were insurance premiums received by Monetary Authorities, such as the Canada Deposit Insurance Corporation (CDIC), all that would be involved, if the CDIC were treated as a government business enterprise in the Canadian system of national accounts, would be a particular distribution of value added within the finance industry. Similarly, with respect to the imputed service charges on reserves, they would be part of the gross output of the central bank, deemed to be a government business enterprise, and part of the intermediate inputs of the private banks.

In Canada, an imputation for central banking output is made by splitting the expenditures on labor and other inputs by the central bank between the personal and government sectors and adding the personal component to imputed expenditures in the personal sector. The theoretical argument for this Canadian treatment is not clear.

14. In Canada, only expenditures and interest income from private financial intermediaries are imputed to the government sector (no imputed expenditures on the Bank of Canada's output is made). In the years 1981–85, the ratio of government to personal expenditures for these imputations is about 7 percent. The effects on the rate of saving for the government sector are quite insignificant, given the incomplete nature of the imputations.

15. It is argued (cf. Patinkin 1972) that outside money is the value of the government's monopoly right to issue currency. Such arguments beg the question of the need for the Authorities in the first place.

References

Acheson, Keith. 1986. Bureaucratic theory retrospect and prospect. Carleton Economic Papers no. 86–08. Ottawa: Carleton University.

Baltensperger, E. 1980. Alternative approaches to the theory of the banking firm. *Journal of Monetary Economics* 6 (January): 1–37.

Begg, David K. H. 1982. *The rational expectations revolution in macroeconomics: Theories and evidence.* Oxford: Philip Alan.

Bewley, Truman. 1985. A difficulty with the optimum quantity of money. *Econometrica* 6 (September): 1485–1504.

Brennan, Geoffrey, and James M. Buchanan. 1980. *The power to tax: Analytical foundations of a fiscal constitution.* Cambridge: Cambridge University Press.

Calvo, Guillermo A. 1978. On the time consistency of optimal policy in a monetary economy. *Econometrica* 46 (November): 1411–28.

Chant, John. 1987. *Regulation of financial institutions.* Technical Report no. 45. Ottawa: Bank of Canada, January.

Diamond, Douglas W., and Philip H. Dybvig. 1983. Bank runs, deposit insurance, and liquidity. *Journal of Political Economy* 91, 401–20.

Dornbusch, R., and J. A. Frenkel. Inflation and growth: Alternative approaches. *Journal of Money, Credit and Banking* 5 (February): 141–56.

Elyasiani, Elyas. 1984. The multiproduct depository firm, interest-bearing transaction balances, interest bearing reserves, and uncertainty. *Bulletin of Economic Research* 36 (November): 173–93.

Fama, Eugene F. 1980. Banking in the theory of finance. *Journal of Monetary Economics* 6: 39–57.

———. 1983. Financial intermediation and price level control. *Journal of Monetary Economics* 12 (July): 1–28.

Fischer, Stanley. 1974. Money and the production function. *Economic Inquiry* 12 (December): 517–33.

———. 1983. A framework for monetary and banking analysis. *Economic Journal Conference Papers* 93 (March): 1–16.

Freedman, Charles. 1983. Financial innovations in Canada: Causes and consequences. *American Economic Review Papers and Proceedings* 73 (May): 101–06.

Friedman, Milton, and Anna Schwartz. 1986. Has government any role in money? *Journal of Monetary Economics* 17 (January): 37–62.

Gale, Douglas. 1983. *Money: In disequilibrium.* Cambridge: Cambridge University Press.

Geehan, Randall, and Len Allen. 1978. Measuring the real output and productivity of savings and credit institutions. *Canadian Journal of Economics* 11 (November): 669–79.

Goodhart, C. A. E. 1987. Why do banks need a central bank? *Oxford Economic Papers* 39 (January): 75–89.

———. 1988. *The evolution of central banks.* (Cambridge, Mass.: MIT Press.)

Gorman, John A. 1969. Alternative measures of the real output and productivity of commercial banks. In *Production and productivity in the service industries,* ed. V. R. Fuchs. New York: National Bureau of Economic Research.

Greenfield, Robert L., and Leland B. Yeager. 1983. A laissez faire approach to monetary stability. *Journal of Money, Credit and Banking* 15 (August): 302–15.

Haig, Brian. 1986. The treatment of interest and financial intermediaries in the national accounts of Australia. *Review of Income and Wealth* 32 (December): 409–24.

Hall, Robert E. 1982. Monetary trends in the United States and the United Kingdom: A review from the perspective of new developments in monetary economics. *Journal of Economic Literature* 20 (December): 1552–56.

Hancock, Diana. 1985. The financial firm: Production with monetary and nonmonetary goods. *Journal of Political Economy* 93 (October): 859–80.

Harkness, Jon. 1978. The neutrality of money in neoclassical growth models. *Canadian Journal of Economics* 11 (November): 701–13.

Johnson, Harry G. 1969. Inside money, outside money, income, wealth and welfare in monetary theory. *Journal of Money, Credit and Banking* 1 (February): 30–45. (Reprinted in Harry G. Johnson, *Further Essays in Monetary Economics.* London: Allen and Unwin, 1972.)

————. 1968. Problems of efficiency in monetary management. *Journal of Political Economy* 76 (September/October): 971–90. (Reprinted in Harry G. Johnson, *Further Essays in Monetary Economics.* London: Allen and Unwin, 1972.)

Keynes, J. M. 1936. *The general theory of employment, interest and money.* In *The collected writings of John Maynard Keynes.* Cambridge: Cambridge University Press.

King, Robert G. 1983. The economics of private money. *Journal of Monetary Economics* 12 (July): 127–58.

Klein, Benjamin. 1978. Money, wealth and seigniorage. In *Redistribution through the financial systems,* ed. K. E. Goulding and T. F. Wilson. New York: Praeger Publishers.

Klein, Michael A. 1971. A theory of the banking firm. *Journal of Money, Credit and Banking* 3 (May): 205–18.

Laidler, David. 1977. The welfare costs of inflation in neoclassical theory—Some unsettled questions. In *Inflation theory and anti-inflation policy,* ed. E. Lundberg. Boulder, Colo.: Westview Press.

Lucas, Robert E., Jr. 1986. Principles of fiscal and monetary policy. *Journal of Monetary Economics* 17 (January): 117–34.

Mamalakis, M. J. 1987. The treatment of interest and financial intermediaries in the national accounts: The old ''bundle'' versus the new ''unbundle'' approach. *Review of Income and Wealth* 33 (June): 169–92.

Merrick, John J., Jr., and Anthony Saunders. 1985. Bank regulation and monetary policy. *Journal of Money, Credit and Banking* 17 (November): 691–717.

Milbourne, Ross. 1987. Does paying interest on bank reserves improve welfare? Kingston, Ont.: Department of Economics, Queen's University, May. Mimeo.

Mintz, Jack M. 1979. *The measures of rates of return in Canadian banking.* Hull, Que.: Canadian Government Printing Centre.

Patinkin, Don. 1972. Money and wealth. In *Studies in monetary economics.* New York: Harper and Row.

Revell, J. R. S. 1980. *Costs and margins in banking: An international survey.* Paris: Organization for Economic Cooperation and Development.

Ruggles, Richard. 1983. The United States national income accounts, 1947–1977: Their conceptual basis and evolution. In *The U.S. national income and product accounts: Selected topics,* ed. Murray F. Foss. Studies in Income and Wealth, vol. 47. Chicago: University of Chicago Press.

Ruggles, Richard, and Nancy Ruggles. 1982. Integrated economic accounts for the United States, 1947–1980. *Survey of Current Business* 62 annex (May): 13–16.

Rymes, Thomas K. 1972. The logical impossibility of optimum money supply policies. Carleton Economic Papers, no. 1972–15. Ottawa: Carleton University.

————. 1979. The treatment of homeownership in the CPI. *Review of Income and Wealth* 25 (December): 393–412.

———. 1985. Inflation, non-optimal monetary arrangements and the banking imputation in the national accounts. *Review of Income and Wealth* 31 (March): 85–96.

———. 1986. Further thoughts on the banking imputation in the national accounts. *Review of Income and Wealth* 32 (December): 425–41.

Santomero, Anthony M. 1984. Modeling the banking firm. *Journal of Money, Credit and Banking* 16 (November): 576–602.

Sargent, Thomas J., and Neil Wallace. 1973. The stability of models of money and growth with perfect foresight. *Econometrica* 41 (November): 1043–48.

———. 1985. Interest on reserves. *Journal of Monetary Economics* 15 (May): 279–90.

Selgin, George A. 1988. *The theory of free banking: Money supply under competitive note issue.* Totawa, N.J.: Royan & Littlefield.

Sheffrin, Steven M. 1983. *Rational expectations.* Surveys of Economic Literature. Cambridge: Cambridge University Press.

Spellman, Lewis J. 1982. *The depository firm and industry: Theory, history and regulation.* Toronto: Academic Press.

Statistics Canada. 1975. *National income and expenditure accounts.* Ottawa: Information Canada.

Sunga, P. 1967. The treatment of interest and net rents in the national accounts framework. *Review of Income and Wealth* 13 (March): 26–35.

———. 1984. An alternative to the current treatment of interest as transfer in the United Nations and Canadian systems of national accounts. *Review of Income and Wealth* 30 (December): 385–402.

Tobin, James. 1982. The commercial banking firm: A simple model. *Scandinavian Journal of Economics* 74: 495–530.

Weldon, J. C. 1971. Theoretical penalties of inflation. In *Inflation and the Canadian experience,* ed. N. Swan and D. Wilton. Kingston: Queen's University.

Wills, H. R. 1982. The simple economics of bank regulation. *Economica* 49 (August): 249–59.

Yeager, Leland B. 1985. Deregulation and monetary reform. *American Economic Review Papers and Proceedings* 75 (May): 103–7.

Comment   Anna J. Schwartz

The focus of the paper is on the theoretical justification for bank imputation. Two contrasting general equilibrium theories of banking are presented, each of which predicts the apparent need for banking imputation. One theory lends partial support to the current imputation procedures; the other provides no support. In this connection, the significance of the two theories for measures of banking output, rates of saving, and wealth is examined.

Neither of Professor Rymes's models seems to me to have anything to do with the need for bank imputation. My first question is how he

Anna J. Schwartz is a research associate emerita of the National Bureau of Economic Research and in 1987–88 was president of the Western Economic Association.

explains the need for bank imputation in Canada before 1935. Canada had no central bank until that year, so there is no basis either for a so-called neoclassical model in which the central bank does not pay the competitive rate of return on bank reserves or for a so-called Keynesian model in which the monetary authorities are providing monetary stability. Commercial banks in Canada had no required reserves before 1935 but maintained prudential reserves of about 10 percent of their deposits that became the required reserve ratio under the Bank of Canada.

Income is imputed to the banking industry, not because the authorities fail to pay interest on reserves, and not because of the monetary policy followed by the authorities, but for the same reason that food produced and consumed on farms is added to the national income, namely, that in both cases the aim is to include income in kind in the national income and not simply income associated with monetary payments.

In the case of banking, there are two questions. First, is there income in kind, that is, are barter transactions being engaged in that would bias the income account if not allowed for? Second, why are those barter transactions carried out? It is easier to answer the second of these questions than the first. In U.S. commercial banking, at least since the Banking Act of 1933, barter transactions have occurred because of the prohibition of payment of interest on demand deposits. This is a major incentive to engage in barter transactions, as is also the incentive to avoid taxation on interest paid. Even if interest were permitted to be paid on demand deposit accounts, individuals could benefit by accepting a lower interest rate on deposits in return for services rendered without charge because that would reduce the income reported on their income tax returns and hence reduce the tax they have to pay.

In Canada, there was no prohibition on the payment of interest on demand deposits, so this reason for the emergence of barter would not exist. However, the tax reason would certainly be present. It seems to be in operation currently where interest is permitted to be paid on household demand deposits, but how much is paid depends on the volume of services rendered free of charge.

So far as the failure to pay interest on reserves is concerned, that is currently viewed as tax. As a tax, it affects the allocation of resources but gives no particular reason for the imputation of income. A tax on tobacco, for example, is not viewed as a reason for the imputation of income to the tobacco industry. However, as in the case of banking, it might lead to a strong incentive to engage in barter, in which case there might be noncash items of income that should be included. The tax implicit in the nonpayment of interest on reserves has the same effect as any other tax of raising the relative price of the item taxed and reducing the quantity, but again that is no reason to impute any items of income any more so than we do in other areas where taxes are imposed.

With respect to the models, since they have nothing to do with the imputation of income to financial enterprises, have they any interest in their own right? There is nothing particularly interesting or novel about the so-called neoclassical model. I do not understand Rymes's argument that it is a shortcoming of the neoclassical model that it leaves no room for a central bank. If, as he notes, reserves can be held privately by banks, insurance and clearing services can be provided privately, with the result that competitive bank services would be efficiently priced, service charges would cover banking costs, and problems of measuring bank output would vanish, why is that a shortcoming? If this were the outcome, why is a central bank essential?

Turning to the Keynesian general equilibrium model of banking that Rymes has fashioned, what is the basis for his assumption that there is saddlepoint instability in the economy that monetary authorities offset? According to the model, agents *know* that authorities will engage in monetary reform to prevent inefficient outcomes. Suppose we grant these assumptions. Rymes's argument that banking imputation is not needed in this case is unsustainable. If the wedge between what banks earn on loans and what they pay on deposits measures the price that banks and agents willingly pay for monetary stability services that the authorities provide, imputation is surely required to measure the monetary value of these services. Rymes's answer is that the wedge is immeasurable because the services are public in nature, not producible privately. Are not many government services not producible privately yet measurable by the cost the government incurs in providing those services? All sorts of arbitrary rules have had to be used to distinguish between those government activities that are to be regarded as intermediate goods and those that are to be regarded as providing final services. The cost of rendering these services is included in the national income except insofar as they are regarded as intermediate goods, in which case they are implicitly included in the sales prices of the final products for which these services are regarded as intermediate goods.

Now drop the assumptions that agents know that monetary authorities will provide the service of monetary stability and know instead that what the authorities will provide is likely to be monetary instability. Consider the two examples of monetary authority actions that Rymes himself has suggested will be destabilizing but he contends the authorities will then take actions to undo, if and when they result in any damage. We have recently had a demonstration of agents moving out of deposits in the face of accelerating price levels. Agents who purchased money-market funds, instead of keeping deposits, paid a cost that was imbedded in the market rate of return. Imputation would provide for deducting that cost as an expense. U.S. firms that now rely on sweeping and overnight repos to have their demand deposits recorded as zero on a daily basis incur a cost in engaging in this activity to avoid those deposits that pay no interest. In the Keynesian model that Rymes proposes, once one does not take for granted, as he does, that authorities will invariably provide monetary stability, the case for imputation is restored.

Finally, I do not accept Rymes's argument against treating outside money as wealth in the private-sector accounts. He argues that bank reserve assets cancel when matched with government deposits as commercial bank liabilities and that such shifts of government deposits from the central bank to commercial banks are the principal way in which inside money is created. His facts are wrong. Reserves are a much larger magnitude than government deposits at commercial banks, and, in this country, transfers of government deposits from central banks to commercial banks are dwarfed by open-market purchases and sales by the Federal Reserve in accounting for inside money creation. But, even if Rymes were right about the magnitudes of reserves and government deposits, he tells us nothing about currency held by the public—the much larger component of the monetary base than reserves. What offset is there for currency that would make their inclusion in private sector wealth unacceptable?

Rymes's paper suggests that research is needed to investigate the motives that have led to the use of barter in financial transactions and their importance, how these motives are likely to be affected by the deregulation of banks, and how the volume of income imputed to financial intermediaries in this country after 1933 compared to that before that time.

Reply   Thomas K. Rymes

Though I have profited from Dr. Schwartz's comments, she does not understand the basic points of my paper. Before dealing with her comments, I reiterate one of its main neoclassical contentions.

Though he is absolutely not responsible for anything said in this reply, the author is indebted to Ehsan Choudhri for very helpful discussions on his paper, Dr. Schwartz's comments, and his reply.

Employing the usual neoclassical assumption of global stability, I investigate the consequence of the failure of the Monetary Authorities, in a world of near-costless fiat money[1] and in the context of an otherwise costless price system (cf. McManus 1975), to pursue the Friedman-Lucas optimum money supply policy. In my model, in which the fiat money is only reserves voluntarily held by competitive banks, the failure takes the form, as is well known, of the nonpayment of the competitive real net rate of return on such reserves. (It is understood that this encompasses the usual inflation tax argument.) The model is the optimal neoclassical monetary growth model with the banking sector introduced in the manner (though necessarily emended) of Fischer (1983). With profit-maximizing firms and wealth-maximizing individuals, the results of the failure that are of interest for this paper are that the rate of interest paid on deposits will be less than the competitive net real rate of return and that the service charges paid for the service rendered by the banks will be less than the value of the marginal product of the transaction service provided by the banks through bank deposits so that the service charges will not cover the costs of such services.

The latter is exactly the measure of the Paretian inefficiency introduced into the economy by the failure of the Monetary Authorities to follow the Friedman-Lucas rule. (In a model in which the banks are ignored, this inefficient equilibrium is commonly described by the condition that the value of the marginal physical product or utility of the services of real money balances [cf. Friedman 1969] will exceed the social marginal costs of providing such services.) The two conditions are exactly the conditions that give rise to the apparent necessity for the banking imputation in the national accounts.

Should the Authorities follow the Friedman-Lucas rule, however, the banks, more anxious to acquire reserves, will bid up interest rates on deposits, individuals will bid up service charges because the bank deposits that are the source of the services are more attractive to hold and to use, and, in accordance with the theoretical framework being employed, the overall price level, which must include the price of the service provided by the banks, will be lower. The result will be that the rate of interest on deposits will equal the going rate of return and that the service charges will meter the value of the marginal physical product of bank deposits and the marginal costs of providing such services. Not only will the full efficiency associated with the Friedman-Lucas rule be captured, but there would also apparently be no need for the banking imputation.

It is important to note that the only source of inefficiency in my model is the failure of the Authorities to pay the going rate of return on reserves. Should the Authorities require banks to hold reserves in excess of those voluntarily held (e.g., there could be binding legal cash reserves ratios), the tax levied on reserves by the failure to pay the going rate of return will be increased, and I conjecture that the observed differences in interest rates and between service charges and the costs of transaction services will also be increased.[2]

The discussion so far permits me to deal with some of Schwartz's points. By Monetary Authorities, I do not necessarily mean central banks per se. Indeed, Monetary Authorities can take on a variety of institutional forms. The pre-1935 period in Canada to which she refers as offering evidence against my hypothesis is characterized, through the operations of the Finance Act, by Canada's chartered banks holding *some* non-interest-bearing reserves (see Bordo and Redish 1987); however, the Canadian monetary system for most of that time would not be characterized as having a near-costless fiat standard. If income taxes are offered as another explanation of banking data that seem to call for the banking imputation, then, since Schwartz offers the earlier period in Canada as evidence inconsistent with my hypothesis, a difficulty for her exists in that Canada did not have an income tax until 1917. For many years after that, I would not want to argue that income taxes on interest income were such as to generate the barter-type arrangements she claims lie behind the banking statistics. There are other objections to her assertions. How are the taxes on interest income supposed to result in a reduction in the accompanying service charges for those deposits held by businesses; that is, why should businesses enter into such barter-type arrangements with the banks? Why are interest rates higher in general on those deposits with lower reserve requirements, an observation that seems more consistent with extensions of my basic model, as noted in my paper, than Schwartz's observations about income taxes. I am quite willing to admit, however, and subject to the qualifications noted, that income taxes may play some role, but I should continue to argue that a principal reason for the problem is the pursuit of inefficient policies in the Friedman-Lucas sense by the Monetary Authorities. I quite agree with Schwartz that an additional reason is the prohibition of interest payments on deposits, but such prohibition I regard as part of inefficient regulation and supervision by the Monetary Authorities.[3] Indeed, arguments to the effect that Monetary Authorities should be constrained constitutionally to behave according to the Friedman-Lucas rule are, in my view, the ultimate ones for the deregulation of financial intermediation and a particular manifestation of the argument that free banking, that is, private banking without inefficient regulation by the Monetary Authorities, will result in "unbundling" and the Pareto-efficient pricing of the services banks render.

Contrary, then, to Schwartz's assertion that the optimal neoclassical monetary growth model has nothing to do with the banking statistics problem, I maintain that it is central. She admits that there is a tax, that the existence of such a tax may lead to barter, and that, because of the barter, imputations should be made. Yet she then turns around and argues that, since it is a tax like any other tax, there are no reasons to impute any more than we do where other taxes lead people and firms to engage in tax-minimizing activities. The inefficient monetary supply rule "tax" is, I should argue, so essentially different in its general equilibrium effects on the general level of prices that it must be treated differently and is treated differently if the argument about the general equilibrium effects on the competitive banking system is correct and if the banking imputation is done.[4] I therefore reject her assertion that the neoclassical monetary growth model with the banking system modeled explicitly with the Monetary Authorities failing to follow the Friedman-Lucas rule has "nothing to do with the imputation of income to financial enterprises." Rather, I would have thought that it is rewarding to have a theory that predicts, other things being equal, that the interest rate and service charges data for a competitive banking system give rise to the seeming need for the banking imputation and the resulting effects on the rates of saving and the conceptions of monetary wealth as measured in national accounting dealt with in my paper. Schwartz may be right that there are other reasons why such data require the imputations, but her assertions and casual evidence in no way lead to nonconfirmation of my argument. I confess to enormous simplicity in the theoretical structure presented, but the simple general equilibrium model of banking I advance is at least one of the usual ways of attempting to understand a problem in economics.

I return now to my argument. It is the essence of the assumption of stability in the neoclassical optimum monetary supply model that the Monetary Authorities must be constrained to follow the Friedman-Lucas money supply policy rule. If they do, then the resulting outcome will, it is argued, match that set out in my paper and in Schwartz's comments, namely, that, among other things, competitive bank services would be efficiently priced and no banking imputation would be necessary. Monetary Authorities constrained to follow a rule, however, do not engage in discretionary policy. Indeed, should the Authorities do so, the argument is that that would return us to the situation associated with the inefficiencies of Authorities *not* following the Friedman-Lucas rule. I failed to make clear that the neoclassical theory has no room for a Pareto-improving discretionary Monetary Authorities.[5]

I assumed stability in examining the neoclassical case. I also argue that a Keynesian central banking theory entails the need for discretionary monetary policy. I provide a potential rationale for that policy and collective Monetary Authorities by assuming saddlepoint instability. The discretionary policy modeled entails the abandonment of the efficient rule and, I conjecture, the reemergence of banking data necessitating imputation. The imputation would be an attempt, in effect, to value the service of monetary stability provided by the Authorities. I know of no way this can be done. If I do not misunderstand Schwartz, she seems to be arguing that that service is properly valued by including in national income the value of the wages and salaries and intermediate inputs used by the authority, and she seems to be saying I am arguing against his procedure. I am not, but the procedure she sets out is not an imputation for the service of monetary stability any more than the value of wages and salaries and intermediate inputs used by the Supreme Court of Canada is a measure of the value of the public goods provided by the Court.

It is the essence of the saddlepoint instability case that it provides a rationale for the existence of discretionary monetary policy. I do not believe I took for granted that the Authorities would always be successful. What the rational expectations model does in this case is provide for the possibility of discretionary policy. Schwartz has been critical of Monetary Authorities who have failed to provide the services of monetary stability (cf. Friedman and Schwartz 1963, esp. chap. 7), but it is quite unsatisfactory to admit the possibility of saddlepoint instability and argue also that Monetary Authorities will always fail in the conduct of discretionary policy. It is equally unsatisfactory to assume stability and to argue that Monetary Authorities will be tempted to act in a discretionary and disstabilizing fashion. If one sees no role for Monetary Authorities, one will want, I suppose, to constrain them by constitutional rules for stable money (cf. Dorn and Schwartz 1987). If one admits, however, the possibility of a role for Monetary Authorities, then one must state clearly what it is. I do point out, then, that rules may not be sufficient to ensure stable money and that discretion may be necessary, and I specify the consequences for banking data, the measurement of banking output, and the other empirical concerns of my paper. I do not know what theory of central banks, save perhaps that they are mischievious, Schwartz has.

With the aid of the analysis in my paper, consider the scenario set out by Schwartz. The Monetary Authorities have failed to contain unstable inflation. The inefficiencies associated with the inflation tax would then be experienced, that is, the fall in real wealth as exhibited in my figure 7.3, because the Authorities fail to engage in the discretionary policy that ensures stable temporary equilibria. My argument in this case would be that the banking data would appear as those requiring the imputation. I leave it to the reader to imagine what the imputation, recommended by Schwartz in this case, could possibly mean.

Two final points. I specifically stated in my paper that I was ignoring circulating currency. I have already stated why. If the Monetary Authorities have prohibited banks from issuing private currencies and have instead replaced private note issue with non-interest-bearing Authority currency, thereby enhancing the inefficiency of the money supply rule, I do not understand Schwartz's argument that this should be regarded as an addition to wealth. The point about wealth measures I was trying to make is very simple. If the government purchases goods with money, then the additions to the money supply are indeed costly. It is not then the near-costless fiat money case I am considering. If the government replaces bonds with money, then the Ricardian equivalence theorems would raise questions about the money supply being part of net wealth. The mechanism for the creation of money, the switching of government accounts, was introduced merely to illustrate the idea that, in the case of potential instability, monetary wealth surely consists in the confidence of the community in the ability of the Authorities to maintain a stable monetary environment (cf. Klein 1978) and not in any "outsidedness" of money. That some arbitrarily defined concept of outside money should determine what is the wealth of the community in the context in which it depends on the discretionary conduct of policy seems simply beside the point.

A general theory of imputation in the national accounts and the effects that they have on the meaning of the measures of output, rates of saving, and wealth has yet to be written. Most theories would appear to have something to do with the costliness of the use of price systems and then are undertaken apparently only when otherwise anomalous results would "significantly" appear.

I have, in that context, set out a very simple but abstract argument based on the barest bones, as I understand it, of the general equilibrium theory of private and central banking that is beginning to emerge. My argument might be wrong, and much I have no doubt missed. I regard Schwartz's comments as helping me to sharpen the argument, but I wish she had directed her comments to the central theoretical concern of my paper.

Notes

1. Friedman and Schwartz (1986) note that the emergence of currencies based on a pure fiat standard is a key development in the world monetary system. It is that world with which I am essentially concerned. By near costless, I mean that I ignore the cost of production of fiat money but take costs of running the reserves system as being positive.

2. In my paper, I did not consider circulating currency such as banknotes. Why? There is nothing in the theoretical framework permitting me to ascertain whether banknotes should be issued by the Authorities as monopoly issue or whether competitive banks, though holding reserves in the form of deposits

with the Authorities, would issue bank notes on which, as history would seem to suggest has happened (cf. Goodhart 1988, chap. 4), interest might be paid. It would appear, though, that the sole issue by the Authorities of non-interest-bearing circulating currency notes is yet another way of requiring the banks (and individuals) to hold non-interest-bearing monies and constitutes yet another tax on reserves and another departure from the Friedman-Lucas rule, thereby exacerbating the effects I discuss.

3. As Schwartz notes, in Canada there is no prohibition of the payment on interest on deposits (cf. Freedman 1983). Up to the decennial revision of the banking legislation in Canada in 1967, however, chartered banks were prohibited from charging interest rates above 6 percent on consumer loans. When that regulation began to bind, the banks resorted to the same sort of subterfuges that the banks in the United States have done to undercut the limitation on interest rates on deposits (cf. Klein 1974).

4. For an argument about the essential difference in the "inflation tax," see Lucas (1986, 123), who argues, "Liquidity is not 'another good' nor, indeed, a 'good' at all. It is the *means* to a subset of goods that an income tax has already taxed once."

5. The theory of central banking contained in Goodhart (1988) purports to show that, because of free-rider and moral hazard problems associated with costly information in the provision of banking, a nonprofit Monetary Authority will "evolve" to meet the needs of competitive banks; that is, the Authority will be a way in which the private banks agree to constrain their opportunistic behavior so as to capture all the feasible gains from trade in banking. Goodhart argues that this Monetary Authority will be a government body. So far as I can see, no logical reason, arising out of the transactions cost theory of institutional form, is provided as to why that Authority could not be one contained within the private sector. That is, there is nothing in Goodhart's argument that would obviate (say) the Canadian Bankers' Association from taking on the role of the Monetary Authority. The essence of Goodhart's Monetary Authority is, however, that it engages in no discretionary monetary policy.

References

Bordo, Michael D., and Angela Redish. 1987. Why did the Bank of Canada emerge in 1935? *Journal of Economic History* 47 (June): 405–17.

Dorn, James A., and Anna J. Schwartz, eds. 1987. *The search for stable money.* Chicago: University of Chicago Press.

Fischer, Stanley. 1983. A framework for monetary and banking analysis. *Economic Journal Conference Papers* 93 (March): 1–16.

Friedman, Milton. 1969. The optimum quantity of money. *The optimum quantity of money and other essays.* London: Macmillan.

Friedman, Milton, and Anna J. Schwartz. 1963. *A monetary history of the United States, 1867–1960.* Princeton, N.J.: Princeton University Press.

———. 1986. Has government any role in money? *Journal of Monetary Economics* 17 (January): 37–62.

Goodhart, C. A. E. 1988. *The evolution of central banks.* Cambridge, Mass.: MIT Press.

Klein, Benjamin. 1974. Competitive interest payments on bank deposits and the long-run demand for money. *American Economic Review* 64 (December): 931–49.

————. 1978. Money, wealth and seigniorage. In *Redistribution through the financial systems,* ed. K. E. Goulding and T. F. Wilson. New York: Praeger Publishers.

Lucas, Robert E., Jr. 1986. Principles of fiscal and monetary policy. *Journal of Monetary Economics* 17 (January): 117–34.

McManus, John. 1975. The costs of alternative economic organizations. *Canadian Journal of Economics* 7 (August): 334–50.

8 World Payments Imbalances and U.S. Statistics

Stephen Taylor

8.1 Introduction

Between 1978 and 1982, the world's balance of payments statistics went off balance in ways that received a good deal of publicity and that presented difficulties to analysts who tried to work with global views of economic activity. The problem showed itself most plainly in current-account balances, which for all the countries of the world together should always add to zero since each transaction receipt of one economy is also a transaction payment by another economy. Any nonzero balance in the world current account represents inconsistencies among the country statistics included and incomplete coverage for the world as a whole. After 1978, the current-account net balance for the world changed from a net debit of roughly $10–20 billion, which prevailed through most of the 1970s, to a net debit of more than $100 billion by 1982, a level that has been maintained more or less ever since. Starting around 1979, that is, the data began showing a bias toward current-account deficits that could be seen as a global system error without clues as to specific countries or regions that were the locus of such excess deficits. It was a condition that could produce policy biases possibly perverse and destabilizing, and it was unsettling to anyone concerned with such matters.

By 1984, the International Monetary Fund (hereafter referred to as the Fund) and other public bodies had concluded that the statistical problem was serious enough to justify an explicit and visible effort at finding causes and remedies for these imbalances. At the end of 1984, the Fund formed a working party to carry out the project and give a

Stephen Taylor is retired from the Federal Reserve Board, where he was an assistant director and chief of the Flow of Funds Section.

report to the managing director by the end of 1986 explaining what the group could discover by then. The working party included members from the Fund's Research Department and Bureau of Statistics and also from the Organization for Economic Cooperation and Development (OECD), the Bank for International Settlements (BIS), and several national statistical offices around the world. The group represented a well-structured set of viewpoints and information on the matter. A small professional staff was set up at the Fund for the project headed by Samuel Pizer, who had come to the Fund from the Federal Reserve Board for the purpose.

The final report of the working party was given to the managing director in December 1986.[1] As a member of the technical staff I am summarizing in this paper some of the major findings of the group on sources of the discrepancy, particularly in relation to the United States. The next section gives the sizes of the imbalances that the working party encountered, and the third section summarizes the principal findings of the group as to the sources of the problem and the nature of remedies proposed by the working party. The fourth section gives findings in the report about U.S. statistics in their relation to the world discrepancies.

The fifth and sixth sections go beyond the scope of the working party's report, which was limited entirely to statistical problems of current-account transactions. The fifth section describes briefly problems in the world's capital account statistics that are connected with current-account discrepancies. It then combines tentative suggestions for capital account revision with the proposed current-account revisions to suggest a new view of the world's balance of payments statement as a whole. The sixth section concludes the paper with some comments on the effects that revisions in balance of payments accounting would have on national income and product accounting. These comments raise some questions on defining geographic coverage of an economy that should be discussed in the ongoing U.N. project of revising the system of national accounts (SNA).

8.2   State of the World Balances

Table 8.1 gives the set of world balances that the working party put its attention to. These are world totals published by the Fund in part 2 of the 1985 edition of its *Balance of Payments Statistics Yearbook*. The categories of balance in the table conform to the Fund's *Balance of Payments Manual* (International Monetary Fund 1977) in definition, and country statistics that are combined into the table have been fitted into these categories by the Fund as closely as possible. The note to table 8.1 mentions some omissions from the coverage—mainly Eastern

Table 8.1   Selected Balances of World Current-Account Transactions (in billions of U.S. dollars)

	1978	1979	1980	1981	1982	1983	1984
Trade balance	18.1	20.3	28.2	24.9	-2.0	9.8	11.0
Service balance	-24.7	-29.3	-49.2	-80.6	-100.9	-78.7	-96.4
Shipment	-24.2	-27.4	-32.0	-34.6	-33.8	-31.8	-33.5
Other transportation	-1.7	-1.3	-3.4	-6.2	-4.4	-3.4	-1.1
Travel	-.3	-1.9	-.9	.7	1.5	3.2	4.5
Reinvested earnings on direct investments	6.7	11.8	11.2	10.4	7.5	9.9	5.8
Other direct-investment income	-4.6	.1	-7.6	-10.7	-11.3	-11.5	-11.7
Other investment income	-6.2	-7.3	-11.2	-22.3	-35.9	-32.0	-41.6
Other official transactions	-4.0	-9.6	-11.4	-18.3	-24.0	-18.2	-20.5
Other private transactions	9.6	6.4	6.2	.4	-.4	5.1	1.8
Private transfers	4.5	5.9	7.0	5.7	3.8	6.7	3.7
Current account (excluding official transfers)	-2.1	-3.0	-14.0	-50.1	-99.1	-62.2	-81.6
Official transfers	-17.5	-16.3	-20.8	-18.9	-14.8	-12.9	-14.2
Current account (including official transfers)	-19.7	-19.4	-34.7	-69.0	-113.9	-75.1	-95.8
Memo: Service balance as a percentage of service payments	5.8	5.4	7.1	10.4	12.8	10.9	12.7

Source: Balance of Payments Statistics Yearbook, pt. 2, (IMF 1985).

Note: Does not include estimates of certain current transactions of the Soviet Union and other nonmember countries of Eastern Europe as reported in the *World Economic Outlook*. International organizations do not supply comparable data, and some economies are not included in the statistics on certain transactions.

Europe and international organizations—and estimates for these groups are part of the explanation of the world balances that appear in the table.

Other presentations of world current-account balances are available from, for example, the OECD and the Fund's own Research Department, and these other versions have somewhat different figures for the world net balances. They all show about the same explosion in debit balance after 1978, however, and the Fund's *Yearbook* version has many advantages in underlying detail and staff study that made it the most useful form of the problem for the working party to examine. The report is hence a commentary on that specific form of world accounts, as produced by the Fund's Bureau of Statistics, a point that is worth making early here.

Most of the growth in discrepancy from 1978 to 1982 occurred in services—$75 billion (table 8.1, row 2), of which $36 billion was in the investment income components, and the working party was asked to pay particular attention to the problems of investment income that had suddenly come to light. "Other" transactions, both official and private, accounted for another $30 billion of the $75 billion increase, and shipping and other transportation showed a $12 billion growth. The trade balance discrepancy has been surprisingly small in relation to the gross totals of world trade, and it has shown no particular trend recently that has contributed to the recent discrepancy rise.[2] Hanging over the trade balance, though, are some still-unanswered questions about shipping, other transportation, and "other" services that may reflect inconsistent classifications with counterparts in trade. If this turns out to be the case, corrections will affect the trade balance, and the question may become more important than it now is. Unrequited transfers had a sizable debit balance over the years in the table, but it did not grow enough to be part of the problem of current-balance increase over 1978–83.

8.3 Adjustments to the Balances

Table 8.2 summarizes in a comprehensive form the major findings of the working party, as presented in the final December 1986 report. It gives the amounts of adjustment that the group can propose now to improve matters and preliminary estimates of the regional distribution of those adjustments. The table is entirely for the year 1983, and, moving from top to bottom, it gives regional distributions of each of the published balances, the working party's adjustments spread regionally, and the adjusted results at the bottom of the table. The columns of the table cover all categories of current account except trade; the trade balance was not part of the working party's assignment and is omitted from the table. At the far right is a summary column with a

Table 8.2 Allocation of Services and Transfer Discrepancy, by Country Groups, 1983 (in billions of U.S. dollars)

	Income on Investments				Shipment and Transport	Other Services	Transfers	Total Current Account, Excluding Merchandise
	Reinvested Earnings	Other Direct-Investment Income	Non-Direct-Investment Income	Total				
Reported data:[a]								
Industrial countries	11.7	4.9	-6.6	10.0	-6.0	19.6	-30.3	-6.7
Middle East oil exporters	-.1	-6.3	24.8	18.4	-13.4	-37.0	-14.2	-46.2
Major offshore banking centers	.1	-.2	.6	.5	1.3	6.4	-.1	8.1
Other developing countries	-1.7	-9.9	-50.7	-62.3	-17.1	.9	38.3	-40.2
Eastern European countries	...	...	...	...	...	...	...	...
International organizations	...	...	...	...	...	...	...	...
Unallocated	...	...	...	...	...	...	...	...
Total	9.9	-11.5	-32.0	-33.6	-35.2	-10.0	-6.2	-84.9
Adjustments:								
Industrial countries	-5.3	4.4	13.9	13.0	1.0	...	...	14.0
Middle East oil exporters	-.1	4.0	2.0	5.9	7.6	...	-2.0	11.5
Major offshore banking centers	-1.9	-3.7	6.0	.4	2.5	...	...	2.9
Other developing countries	-3.1	.6	5.5	3.0	10.4	...	3.4	16.8
Eastern European countries	...	...	-3.7	-3.7	.8	...	...	-2.9
International organizations	...	...	3.1	3.1	...	...	...	3.1
Unallocated	...	...	5.9	5.9	6.7	-7.0	7.0	12.6
Total	-10.4	5.3	32.8	27.7	29.0	-7.0	8.4	58.1

(continued)

Table 8.2 (continued)

Adjusted data:	Income on Investments				Shipment and Transport	Other Services	Transfers	Total Current Account, Excluding Merchandise
	Reinvested Earnings	Other Direct-Investment Income	Non-Direct-Investment Income	Total				
Industrial countries	6.4	9.3	7.3	23.0	-5.0	19.6	-30.3	7.3
Middle East oil exporters	-.2	-2.3	26.8	24.3	-5.8	-37.0	-16.2	-34.7
Major offshore banking centers	-1.8	-3.9	6.6	.9	3.8	6.4	-.1	11.0
Other developing countries	-4.8	-9.3	-45.2	-59.3	-6.7	.9	41.7	-23.4
Eastern European countries	...	...	-3.7	-3.7	.8	...	...	-2.9
International organizations	...	...	3.1	3.1	...	-7.0	7.0	3.1
Unallocated	...	...	5.9	5.9	6.7	...	...	12.6
Total	-.5	-6.2	.8	-5.9	-6.2	-17.0	2.2	-26.8

Note: Details may not add to totals because of rounding.

[a]*Balance of Payments Statistics Yearbook*, pt. 2, (IMF 1985).

set of adjustments that reduces the 1983 debit balance from $85 billion to $27 billion remaining to be explained and eliminated. Most of the adjustments used for 1983 were also worked out for the period from 1979 to 1984, and results for the other years were similar to those in table 8.2 for 1983.

It is important to point out that not all the $58 billion of adjustments in table 8.2 can be attributed to specific countries in ways that can be brought into country statistical procedures. There is an "unallocated" row in the table that contains particular debits and credits that are known to be missing from the system but for which there is no usable evidence on the countries involved. The regional totals also include some adjustments that can be allocated to specific regions but not to countries within the regions. The table thus overstates somewhat the steps that might be taken right now in statistical procedures to improve matters by either the country or the Fund, but there is nevertheless a sizable agenda for improvements to work out between the Fund and the countries, and the working party has several recommendations on proceeding to this next step.

Reinvested earnings, or reinvested direct-investment income, causes statistical trouble in several ways at the world level. Only a few countries estimate the item at all, and the important ones are net investor countries, notably the United States, the United Kingdom, Germany, and the Netherlands. The reinvested-earnings discrepancy is, as a result, a net credit balance—$10 billion in 1983—rather than a debit, and reducing it only worsens the total current-account problem. Nevertheless, table 8.2 shows almost all the $10 billion removed, using the following principal steps.

1. The United States includes in this item a revaluation element to reflect effects of exchange rate changes on dollar equivalents of overseas balance sheets stated in foreign currencies. In recent years this has been a large, changeable, and conspicuous source of discrepancy in the world current account. For 1983 it was a $7 billion debit, and from 1984 to 1985 it changed by more than $12 billion, from an $8 billion debit to a $4 billion credit, when the dollar turned around and started downward. No other country includes exchange rate effects in its balance of payments, and this U.S. procedure plainly produces a floater that goes directly to the current-account total balance. The working party recommends that the U.S. data exclude any such capital gains and losses—as they are excluded from the U.S. income and product accounts—and that at most they may be included as memo items on the U.S. country page of the *Yearbook*.

2. The United States includes in reinvested income an estimate for retained earnings of foreign branches that is also not matched by other

countries, which put branch earnings entirely in "other" direct-investment income. Part of the table 8.2 adjustments ($3 billion) shifts the U.S. earnings as credits to the second column, improving both balances without affecting the current-account total balance.

3. Finally, geographic information from the four major investor countries mentioned above is used to insert contra entries on reinvested earnings into the accounts of partner countries that had reported nothing or obviously incomplete amounts for this item. This was a big adjustment—$13 billion of net debits for 1983—and is plainly self-balancing since it uses one country's estimates for both sides of a transaction. At the same time it is an example of improving the system by using information for a country that comes from international or other-country sources, a practice the working party also uses in other adjustments and recommends for wider country consideration in national estimates.

Because of the great void in reporting reinvested earnings that was pointed out by the working party, the report strongly recommends that this item be omitted from the world tabulations that the Fund publishes in part 2 of the *Yearbook*—until a good many more countries can be persuaded to send in data. Omitting the item does not change the balance in the country's statement because for each country the reinvested-earnings part of current account is automatically matched by an equal and opposite item in direct-investment flows in capital account. There is no actual payment of funds, and omitting both entries has no effect on the country's error and omissions. Without better reporting, the item is more confusing than helpful in using the world data and should be removed for now.

Other direct-investment income, in the second column of table 8.2, has been a more intractable problem than reinvested income, and only about half the imbalance could be eliminated for reasons discovered in the project. The shift of U.S. branch office reinvested earnings to this column that was mentioned above gives a $3 billion credit for 1983, and an adjustment for U.S. treatment of finance subsidiaries in the Netherlands Antilles adds almost another $3 billion. These Antilles subsidiaries had until recently a special tax position that gives U.S. borrowers a lower-cost access to Eurobond markets than direct U.S. issues in those markets. The practice produced a sizable asymmetry in world figures for investment income, however. While countries that bought the Antilles Eurobonds reported the bond income as interest receipts (if they reported it at all), the payments that were made by U.S. borrowers were treated as negative direct-investment income of U.S. companies by balance of payments compilers at the Commerce Department. In the middle, the Antilles simply omitted the subsidiaries from their own balance of payments accounts, and the result was a mismatch between form of payment and form of receipt within the world current account. The working party shifted the U.S. entries to the third column of table 8.2, "non-direct-investment income," to match income credits from lender countries.

The Fund's version of direct-investment income also includes a Saudi Arabia debit of $4 billion that is labeled by the Saudis in their own balance of payments as "oil-sector-investment income." The nature of this $4 billion is altogether obscure, but it is much larger than the corresponding net receipts of $117 million that are reported by the United States, the United Kingdom, and Germany, so it appears that the $4 billion does not belong in this category, whatever its nature. In table 8.2, it is removed in the second column and not reinserted elsewhere in the table, and it is thus an adjustment that carries over to the current-account total.

With some other adjustments that offset those for the United States and Saudi Arabia, the working party was not able to eliminate more than half the published discrepancy in this direct-investment income item. A good deal more needs to be done, and some of the remaining problems are already known through bilateral country comparisons that show large inconsistencies. To some extent, these inconsistencies come from differences in definition of direct-investment relations and in definition of foreign and domestic companies. Reconciling these differences can take a great deal of time even at the international level, and persuading countries to adopt consistent rules in their own work is a larger job since the changes that are needed can also affect national income and product accounts.

Non-direct-investment income, the third column of table 8.2, is the category that most conspicuously went off balance after 1978, rising from a net debit of $6 billion in 1978 to one of $36 billion in 1982 and $42 billion in 1984 (all these amounts as shown in the 1985 *Yearbook*). On a comparable basis, the 1985 discrepancy was $51 billion. The years 1979–83 saw a good deal of inflation—10 percent yearly in the Fund's world gross domestic product (GDP) deflator, and a sharp rise in financial claims across borders—a 13 percent yearly growth, and large swings in interest rates. It appeared that statistical procedures were not able to track interest and dividends well enough to cope with the new scale of international financial relations. What had been a minor defect in balance of payments measurement suddenly became a glaring problem and a source of uncertainty. As mentioned earlier, the working party was given particular instruction to look at this item, and it was a major subject of study by the group and its technical staff. Table 8.2 shows that as a result of that work the report was able to explain almost all the $32 billion net debit for 1983, and the explanations proved to be equally effective for the other years of the 1979–84 period.

Two adjustments were straightforward—to include entries for interest transactions by Eastern European countries not covered in the Fund's world figures and for international organizations such as the World Bank and the Fund itself that were also omitted from the Fund's totals. These two adjustments roughly offset each other on a net basis, however, as table 8.2 shows. (In part 2 of the 1986 *Balance of Payments Statistics Yearbook,* international institutions are introduced to the world totals for the first time, although only for investment income receipts and expenses, with the offset in errors and omissions. As a result, the imbalance in this item is now considerably smaller than it was in the 1985 version, but it does not yet reflect the offsetting Eastern Europe position.)

The big adjustments against the $32 billion discrepancy came not from better geographic coverage, however, but rather from independent tests of the quality of the data already in the system. These tests were made separately for income from international holdings of bonds and stocks and for income from the various forms of bank positions cross-border vis-à-vis other banks, central banks, and nonbanks. A starting point for the tests was a detailed questionnaire on investment income that the working party sent to about sixty countries asking for national information on types of investment income receipts and payments and also for whatever stock data the countries had on international financial positions. These questionnaires yielded some significant revisions of data in relation to the Fund's published version, and those revisions are included in the table 8.2 adjustments. From the detail in the questionnaires, though, specific comparisons could also be made between country figures on income and estimates based on independent information outside the country. It was this procedure that yielded most of the $32 billion of adjustments in table 8.2.

For bonds and equities, the results were very approximate because useful information on the structure of international security markets is scarce and informal. There are no systematic tabulations by official or industry groups on the outstanding amounts of securities held internationally that generate the income flows, and the working party had to put together estimates of its own, primarily by cumulating gross new issues for several years in the form that the OECD publishes in its *Financial Statistics* publications. There are several steps too detailed to go into here in producing appropriate stock figures, but the final result in this exercise was an estimate for cross-border bond holdings not involving banks of $340 billion for the end of 1983 and a corresponding equity total of $250 billion. Comparisons of these market-based totals with the questionnaire totals of security stocks reported by countries implied that about 20 percent of securities are missing from country data as liabilities and that something over 40 percent are missing as assets. This finding led to the conclusion that income debits and credits are understated in the same proportions and should be adjusted upward to balance the system. The total adjustment amounts to a $9 billion net credit for 1983, almost one-third of the total imbalance in this column of table 8.2 for the year.

There is a problem here in geographic distribution because, although the OECD data on gross issues give a clear enough country identification of debtors, we have no statistical basis whatever from market data for locating holders of securities. The securities industry believes widely that most cross-border securities are held in industrial countries, and that belief is used in the adjustments that were made for underreporting of income on securities. This is a case, however, in which the report, in table 8.2, attributes missing flows to a region—industrial countries—but has no basis for going farther in country identification.

The other source of independent data that were used to assess the investment income discrepancy is the collection of cross-border banking information that is compiled by the BIS and the Fund.[3] The core of these data is a great body of detail reported by banks in about thirty industrial countries and offshore financial centers on the geographic location of borrowers from and depositors in these banks. The banks reporting in the system account for a large part of the world totals of international banking claims that the Fund reports. As a result, the cumulated positions in the tables vis-à-vis a particular country such as the United States give a measure of that country's international banking position that is independent of the country's own statistical system and that can be compared with national estimates of the amounts.

The BIS-Fund data divide the reported bank positions between interbank claims on the one hand and nonbank borrowings and "deposits" (actually, all forms of claim) on the other. The interbank positions from the data are in general closely consistent with national data, with the exception of offshore financial centers, which do not always include in national totals all the foreign banking business that appears in BIS-Fund figures.[4] Most of the $6 billion adjustment for "major offshore banking centers" entered in the third column of table 8.2 introduces the foreign branch earnings to offshore center balance of payments, but most of that is also offset in the second-column entry as a direct investment debit for those branches vis-à-vis their parents.

On nonbank positions, however, the BIS-Fund geographic detail that appears in "International Banking Statistics" (IBS) indicates strongly that country figures tend to understate both claims on foreign banks and income from those claims on banks. Although liabilities to foreign banks are also understated in country figures, the bias is generally weaker than in assets. The net effect of substituting IBS-based income credits and debits for country versions produces a total net credit adjustment for all countries of over $20 billion for 1983 to be included in the third column of table 8.2. This amount, together with the $9 billion net credit adjustment for bonds and equities, accounts for most of the total $33 billion adjustment in the table.[5]

The nonbank position data underlying these bank-derived adjustments come, to repeat, from the geographic detail reported by banks in about thirty countries that accounted for most of the international banking industry at the time. Most, but not all, of the "unallocated" adjustment of $5.9 billion in table 8.2 arises from the difference between the total of nonbank geographic detail reported and the total of nonbank positions vis-à-vis all banks of all countries in the IBS totals. That difference appears as "unallocated" in IBS tables, and the $5.9 billion adjustment is a rough estimate of income not reported on those unallocated positions. The unallocated positions have been rising fairly fast in IBS, primarily because IBS is expanding its coverage of financial institutions beyond the conventional group of banks that report geographic detail. The positions of these added institutions—for example, thrifts and development banks—must be put into the unallocated item even for industrial countries that have reported to the BIS for many years. The unallocated adjustments can be used in explaining the world discrepancy, but, plainly, to get better country figures that will reduce the discrepancy requires a greater extent of geographic detail in the IBS body of financial institutions. The usefulness of the IBS figures even in their present form is a persuasive basis for asking countries to widen their reporting scope.

The growth of the discrepancy in investment income after 1977 raised suspicions widely that the discrepancy was related to the growth of offshore banking and also perhaps to capital flight from Latin American and Asian countries. The Fund gave the working party explicit instruction to look into the offshore centers as a source of statistical problems, and a section of the report is concerned with the centers and with innovations in financial instruments as a source of the troubles.

The use of IBS-type data took care of a major portion of this question, however, insofar as IBS measures offshore centers adequately and insofar as capital flight tends ultimately to take the form of claims on banks. IBS coverage of offshore centers was vital for this purpose.[6] Another important part of the IBS tabulation for this question is the special treatment of Swiss data in the Fund's version of IBS data: a good deal of money (about $100 billion in 1983) is held in trust accounts of Swiss banks for owners outside Switzerland and reinvested in deposits in other banking centers, and in IBS tabulations these "other" centers report such deposits as interbank liabilities to Swiss banks. Switzerland, meanwhile, omits them entirely from reports it sends to the BIS as either assets or liabilities, a practice that results in a discrepancy of that amount in BIS totals of interbank claims as assets and as liabilities. In order to balance the figures and to show a little better what is going on, the Fund's form of IBS adjusts the Swiss numbers to include the interbank claims as assets and also to show Swiss bank liabilities to foreign nonbanks for the amounts deposited in the trust accounts. The Swiss National Bank publishes a geographic distribution of the holders of those accounts.

The geography for offshore centers and for Swiss trust accounts seems to go far toward covering capital flight flows that come into organized financial markets, and, in the table 8.2 adjustments, nothing further is included to reflect capital flight. Several analysts have estimated capital flight residually for important developing countries, using a residual method that is based on cumulations of reported international flows for each country over a run of years. In the procedure, the cumulation of capital inflows is treated as a measure of external debt, and cumulated current-account deficits and recorded capital outflows are viewed as known uses of funds from that debt. The excess of debt over deficits and recorded outflows is treated as unrecorded capital outflows, often called "capital flight" (see, e.g., Dooley 1986). For individual countries, these cumulated residuals have been a good deal larger than assets measured by the working party from IBS and security market data. However, when the working party tried this procedure for all developing countries as a group using twenty-year cumulations, the resulting total of private assets was not far from the amounts shown in IBS, and most of the difference can be explained.

The inconsistency here between the results on a country basis and the aggregate form has not been explained, and there is more to investigate on capital flight measurements. For the working party's purposes, though, the larger totals could not be fitted into global statistics on financial markets and, more operationally, were not needed to balance the investment income accounts. It is possible and perhaps even likely that cross-border financial positions are a good deal larger than the IBS-based and security market–based amounts used by the working party, through claims that are nominally "resident" in the country in which they are invested and through holding-company and other relations that never enter statistical systems. The working party was not able to look into such possibilities on a basis that produces usable data. Instead, the group focused on those procedures that could bring published balance of payments data into consistency with one another and with existing statistics on cross-border claims.

The adjustments in table 8.2 for the last three columns are more tentative and sketchy than are those for investment income, which was the principal subject for the working party's program. In *shipment and transport*, the world discrepancies were in the range of a $30 billion debit but had not changed much over the years from 1978. The report concludes that the principal reason for this imbalance is a combination of missing shipping revenues and missing port receipts. These two gaps arise for separate reasons, but they are both plainly present, and they seem to be of about the right size to take care of most of the problem. The missing shipping revenues are mainly for three merchant fleets—those of the Soviet Union, Greece, and Hong Kong—that are excluded from the Fund's world totals for various reasons. The gap here seems to be related to operators of the fleets rather than registry under flags of convenience such as Liberia. Foreign registry of a country's fleet does not appear to cause problems for countries that include shipping in their balance of payments figures. None of these conclusions can be very firm, though, because the world statistics on shipping that might be the outside test of balance of payments figures have no standardized concepts of ownership and operator identity that can be related to the Fund's concepts. Shipping statistics need much more development before they provide the kind of data base that this problem needs.

Missing fleet revenues are matched by missing costs of operating those fleets, which should be in transport credits of countries selling fuel and services to the fleets. It is clear from the Fund's figures, however, that many countries are understating port receipts by large amounts. Table 8.2 includes some tentative and putative adjustments for missing fleets and missing port receipts in the fifth column, but they are not yet the basis for reshaping country figures that the subject needs.

The column for *other services* has only a single adjustment to reflect debits by international organizations that belong in the world totals but have not been included in Fund publications. This category has a large imbalance that is only made larger by the adjustment. Much the largest entry in the Fund's world table for this item is an official debit for Saudi Arabia—$25 billion for 1983—that is roughly the size of the world imbalance in official services. The content of this item is not known, and without explanation no adjustment is possible. The credit entries against this Saudi debit may be in other current-account categories, or there may in fact be none in this system.

The *transfers* adjustments consists mainly of the receipts by international organizations of contributions from supporting governments that are already in transfers debits. With this and some smaller adjustments for specific countries, the world imbalance in transfers can be made small.

8.4   Effects of the Findings on U.S. Statistics

The United States is a large economy with long borders and long coastlines, and, over the recent years when the world discrepancies have been growing, the United States has been running a very large discrepancy in its own balance of payments—about $25 billion net credit annually. One can easily expect that U.S. statistical problems and procedures are in some way related to the world imbalances, and the earlier section on direct-investment income mentions explicitly some effects of the U.S. numbers. When the U.S. components of the table 8.2 adjustments are sorted out, however, the total effect of U.S. figures is no more than in line with the U.S. share of world trade and could from some viewpoints be judged to be less than that.

Table 8.3 displays the main U.S. components of the adjustments from the "industrial countries" row of table 8.2. All are in the invest-ment income categories, but not all of them affect the total current-account balance. Moreover, items 6–8 have an ambiguous position in the table because they are amounts that the United States reports that

Table 8.3   **Adjustment Proposed for U.S. Investment Income (1983 flows in billions of dollars)**

	Direct-investment Income		Other Investment Income	Effect on Current Account
	Reinvested Earnings	Other		
1. Remove capital gains	7.0			7.0
2. Reestimate bank income:				
Credits			7.7	
Debits			−3.7	
Net effect			4.0	4.0
3. Reestimate security income:				
Credits			2.5	
Debits			−2.1	
Net			.4	.4
4. Shift reinvested branch earnings	−3.1	3.1		. . .
5. Shift Antilles earnings		2.8	−2.8	. . .
First total of adjustments	3.9	5.9	1.6	11.4
6. Reinvested earnings not reported by other country	−7.9			−7.9
7. Other income not reported separately by other country		−1.8	1.8	. . .
8. U.S. transactions with nonreporting countries		−1.9		−1.9
Second total of adjustments	−4.0	2.2	3.4	1.6

Source: Final report of working party and unpublished tables underlying the report.

are omitted as contraentries by other countries. Those three items are included to show the full relation of U.S. reporting to the world balances without regard to the source of the inconsistency.

The first item in the table is the adjustment mentioned earlier to eliminate U.S. capital gains components that are evidently unique in the world figures. This adjustment alone reduces the 1983 world imbalance on investment income from $34 to $27 billion, but it is a volatile item, and after the dollar exchange rate started downward in 1985 its effect on discrepancies had an opposite sign.

The second item results from replacing Treasury-Commerce data for cross-border positions of U.S. nonbanks with foreign banks with the corresponding amounts reported by foreign banks in IBS. The IBS figures are much larger for both assets and liabilities, as table 8.4 shows, and the income adjustments in table 8.3 are the differences that result from applying 1983 interest rates to year-average levels of the IBS positions.[7] The revision in asset and income credit is larger than the liability revision, and there is a net contribution of $4 billion to reduce the income and current-account discrepancies. The third item is a similar but much smaller adjustment for portfolio security assets and liabilities.

Items 4 and 5 are explicitly mentioned earlier as shifts between categories that do not affect the current-account total, and these plus items 1–3 reflect the total of the report's specific recommendations about U.S. data. These items remove $11 billion, one-third of the world debit balance in investment income. Most of that is from the capital gains adjustment, however, which changes sign in later years and results in very different relations.

The other items in table 8.3—lines 6–8—are problems not with U.S. reporting but rather with the lack of corresponding figures in other countries' reporting in the world tables. About $7.9 billion of U.S. net reinvested earnings in 1983 were not reported by the countries listed in U.S. geographic detail. If the Fund were to accept the working party's recommendation to remove reinvested earnings, at least tem-

Table 8.4   **U.S. Nonbank Positions with Foreign Banks (1983 year end in billions of dollars)**

	Assets	Liabilities	Net Assets
Reported by United States to working party on investment income questionnaire	52.8	20.6	32.2
Reported by foreign banks in IBS	167.9	58.0	109.9
Excess of IBS over U.S. data	125.1	37.4	77.7

Note: IBS = "International Banking Statistics" published by the Fund in *International Financial Statistics.*

porarily, from the standard world tables in part 2 of the *Balance of Payments Yearbook,* the U.S. credit would disappear from world current balances, along with $4 billion of net credits reported by the few other countries that show this category. Item 6 in table 8.3 reflects such a change, while item 7 shifts across categories to match credits and debits, and item 8 reflects the absence of some British colonies in the Fund's world numbers. These changes make U.S. figures more "symmetrical" with reporting by other countries, and with them the total U.S. effect on the discrepancy almost vanishes for 1983. This is not the case in later years, however.

From this work so far, then, the only substantial finding about U.S. figures that could affect statistical practices in this country is that U.S. claims on foreign banks, net of liabilities to banks, are considerably larger than reported by the United States—almost $80 billion in 1983. Although the effect of this on the world current account is plain enough, as in table 8.3, it is by no means clear how a shift to that larger number would change U.S. national accounts since the effect depends partly on whether the income is repatriated. Whatever use is made of the income, the revision would raise U.S. gross national product (GNP), personal income, and personal saving. To the extent that the income is left abroad for reinvestment, however, offsets to the income revision appear in increased capital outflows in balance of payments and larger financial investments by households in flow-of-funds accounts; there is no effect on statistical discrepancies in either balance of payments or household-sector statements.[8] Only repatriated income would carry through to affect those discrepancies.

No one need actually judge statistically as to the disposition of this U.S. income from foreign sources, however, and that is just as well since the question is inherently moot. The shift to an IBS-based measure of income, rather, would be part of a broader revision that also inserts IBS measures of U.S. nonbank positions into the calculation of U.S. capital account flows in place of the Treasury data that are now used. The effect is a joint revision for current and capital accounts together producing a discrepancy revision that implicitly "answers" the income disposition question. A shift to IBS sources for U.S. balance of payments raises questions for the United States that go well beyond the working party's concern, such as how to deal with the short history in IBS nonbank positions and the extent to which IBS figures overlap securities data covered by other Treasury reports. It remains to be seen what the full effect of the shift would be.

For U.S. statistics, the question remains of how it could happen that cross-border nonbank positions vis-à-vis banks could be so much larger—$80–$100 billion, net—than the $32 billion reported by the United States for 1983. How, that is, did the money get out there, in light of the reasonably well-behaved set of international statistics for the United States before the problems that began in the late 1970s? We do not know the answer, and there is a wide set of possibilities that ranges from underreported current-account balances to capital gains on earlier investments abroad. A few simple assumptions can explain a large part of the difference, however, without going far from the published statistics, and, although such an explanation has no more validity than others, it illustrates what might have happened.

The procedure consists of no more than applying to the U.S. statistics the same capital flight calculations that have been used so often for developing countries. We start from the premise that the current-account balance is measured "correctly"—in a particular sense that hinges on the use of the answer—and take the statistical discrepancy to be a net measure of unrecorded capital flows either outward or inward. From the 1950s to 1974, the United States tended to have negative discrepancies that averaged $400 million annually for 1950–59 and $850 million annually for 1960–74, except for the infamous 1971, when it was almost $10 billion of unrecorded outflow. The simple cumulated sum of these discrepancies from 1950 to 1974 is a $26 billion net debit in the U.S. accounts. If we treat these as capital flows, in the limited sense that they come out of the recorded transactions as shown, and if we assume further that that money is invested and reinvested abroad at roughly reasonable interest rates, then the $26 billion easily compounds to a total of about $90 billion by the end of 1983, which is not far from the $78 billion net excess in table 8.4. The $90 billion result assumes that the positive discrepancies after 1974, which cumulate to $145 billion from 1975 to 1983, are not a return to the United States of these earlier outflows. These later amounts can be some combination of unrecorded foreign capital inflows and understated current-account balances, but the earlier outflows remain abroad in the calculation and constitute part of U.S. positions in the Fund's IBS tables. Arithmetic like this is not the basis for actually revising any statistics, even when it is ringed by considerations of detail that might look realistic. It illustrates only that, on this particular question, there can be ways to reconcile the U.S. accounts as they exist with international statistics unrelated to U.S. sources.

8.5 The Capital Account Problem

The last few paragraphs are the first mention in this paper of the relation of current-account statistical problems to capital account flows. If there is a world discrepancy of $100 billion in current-account flows in a year, however, then there is also an offsetting $100 billion of other discrepancy divided between world net totals of capital account flows and errors and omissions. For the one problem there is the other, but the Fund's working party concentrated its work and its recommendations almost entirely on current account, as requested by the Fund in establishing the project. Table 8.5 is the principal reference in the working party report to the offsets to current account. It shows plainly the abrupt expansion after 1976 in both capital account discrepancies and the errors and omissions total, with capital account offsetting about two-thirds of the growth in current-account imbalances.

The capital account discrepancy fits well with the investment income debit balance in current account: along with understatement of income credits, the accounts have an understatement of investment capital outflows. Finding the categories of flow that are biased, however, is more difficult in capital account than in current because the Fund's standard structure of balance of payments categories is much less suited for matching credits and debits in capital account than in current. The categories include, for example, separate items for bank and nonbank asset and liability flows. However, both bank and nonbank transactions are partly with foreign banks and partly with foreign nonbanks, and neither category is a consistent set of debits and credits that can add to zero across countries.[9] This is very different from current-account

Table 8.5   **Main Sectors of World Balance of Payments Accounts (in billions of U.S. dollars)**

	Cumulated 1964–76	Cumulated 1977–83	Cumulated 1977–83 Adjusted[a]
Current account[b]	−38	−347	−407
Of which: Investment income[b]	. . .	−110	−170
Capital movements (including reserve transactions)[b]	34	237	297
Of which: Increase of liabilities	892	2,670	2,621
Of which: Increase of assets	−858	−2,433	−2,324
Errors and omissions	4	111	111
Of which: Credit entries	34	285	285
Of which: Debit entries	−30	−174	−174

Source: Unpublished tabulations by the Fund's Bureau of Statistics.

Note: Negative signs indicate debits.

[a]Adjusted to exclude reported reinvested earnings from the investment income account because they are recorded asymmetrically and introduce a net credit entry that tends to conceal the extent of the actual discrepancy.

[b]Balances of reported transactions, which in principle should be zero for the world as a whole.

structure, under which, for example, shipping payments to foreign carriers fall reasonably into the same category as shipping receipts from foreign customers.

Even so, some conclusions about capital account come out of the Fund group's work on investment income, which has a direct link to capital account measurement. Tables 8.6 and 8.7 sketch some adjustments to capital account that illustrate what might be done, and table 8.8 is then a final statement about the condition of world balance of payments measurements, at least for 1983. These three tables were put together at the end of the project by Dietrich Hartenstein of the Bundesbank, who was a member of the working party's technical staff. They are not included in the report to the Fund, but they constitute a useful agenda for future work on both current and capital account.

Table 8.6 is based on the assumption that shortfalls in measuring investment income imply similar shortfalls in measuring capital flows. The

Table 8.6   **Derivation of Nonreported Capital Flows (in billions of dollars, 1983)**

	Total	Industrial Countries	Other Countries[a]
Actual flows:			
Nonbanks' bank deposits[b]	−49.9	−20.1	−29.8
Nonbanks' bank borrowings[b]	25.5	4.0	21.5
Security assets[c]	−85	−68	−17
Security liabilities[c]	85	76.5	8.5
Nonreporting in percent:[d]			
Nonbanks' bank deposits	. . .	60	85
Nonbanks' bank borrowings	. . .	20	20
Security assets	55	55	55
Security liabilities	20	20	20
Nonreporting in U.S. dollars:			
Nonbanks' bank deposits	−38	−12	−26
Nonbanks' bank borrowings	5	1	4
Security assets	−47	−37	−10
Security liabilities	17	14	3

[a]Including unallocated positions but excluding major offshore banking centers.
[b]Derived from IBS data. However, now allowance could be made for valuation changes.
[c]Data and regional distribution according to chap. 4 of the final report.
[d]Percentages according to chap. 4 of the final report, taking into account that reporting of new flows (increase of deposits, purchases of bonds) is even worse than reporting on amounts outstanding.

Table 8.7   **Adjustments to World Balance of Payments Accounts with Respect to Investment Income (in billions of dollars, 1983)**

	Total	Industrial Countries	Other Countries[a]
Investment income (current account):[b]			
Reinvested earnings	−10	−5	−5
Other direct-investment income	5	4	1
Nondirect-investment income	33	14	19
Total	28	13	15
Capital flows:			
Reinvested earnings	10	4	6
Nonbanks' bank deposits[c]	−38	−12	−26
Nonbanks' bank borrowings[c]	5	1	4
Securities (net)	−30	−22	−8
Major offshore banking centers	−5	. . .	−5
Eastern Europe	−5	. . .	−5
Total	−63	−29	−34

[a]Including international organizations and Eastern Europe.
[b]For derivation, see chaps. 3 and 4 of the final report.
[c]Including unallocated accounts but excluding major offshore banking centers, Eastern Europe, and international organizations.

same information used for income adjustments in table 8.2 for deposits, loans, and portfolio securities is then the basis for estimating missing amounts of capital flows in these instruments, at the bottom of table 8.6. As mentioned earlier, these adjustments cannot be fitted to specific row items in Fund publications, but the totals are there to work with. Table 8.7 combines those adjustments with others related to investment income to produce a total identified revision to capital account for 1983 of $63 billion. The revision in reinvested earnings in current account is automatically offset in capital account, and the other changes shown in the table are mentioned in the description of table 8.2.

Table 8.8, then, is the final summary of adjustments that combines the current-account changes in table 8.2 (and in the report to the Fund) with Hartenstein's estimates for capital account revisions. The $63 billion of capital flow adjustments from table 8.7 virtually eliminates the 1983 imbalance in capital account and appears in "adjustments 1" along with current-account changes from table 8.2 (and along with a residual $3 billion unidentified in capital account). These changes produce a revised set of world accounts, in the center panel of table 8.8, that consists only of current-account discrepancies matched in errors and omissions for the world totals and with balanced capital flows for the two country groups. "Adjustments 2," the next panel, premises that at that point the regional capital account balances are correct and

Table 8.8   **Overall Results of World Balance of Payments Adjustments (in billions of dollars, 1983)**

	Total	Industrial Countries	Other Countries[a]
Reported flows:[b]			
Current account	−75	−18	−57
Capital flows[c]	66	−5	71
Errors and omissions	9	23	−14
Adjustments 1:			
Current account (table 8.1)	58	14	44
Capital flows (table 8.7)[c]	−66	−29	−37[d]
Adjusted flows:			
Current account	−17	−4	−13
Capital flows[c]	0	−34	34
Errors and omissions	17	38	−21
Adjustments 2:			
Current account	17	38	−21
Errors and omissions	−17	−38	21
Final flows:			
Current account	0	34	−34
Capital flows[c]	0	−34	34
Errors and omissions	0	0	0

[a]Including international organizations and Eastern Europe.
[b]*Balance of Payments Statistics Yearbook* (IMF 1985).
[c]Including changes in official reserves.
[d]Includes $3 billion of nonidentified capital outflows.

on that basis states that further corrections of current account, not yet known or specified, will eliminate not only remaining imbalances but remaining errors and omissions as well.

The table proceeds from there to a bottom panel that says that correcting those remaining problems will result in a world statement for 1983 that consists of a $34 billion current-account surplus for industrial countries against the rest of the world and a matching capital flow to the rest of the world. This is an upward revision in current-account balance of $52 billion for industrial countries and $23 billion for the rest of the world relative to the amounts published in the 1985 *Yearbook*.

As mentioned, table 8.8 is a statement of work still to be done. "Adjustments 2" are both large and unknown, and "Adjustments 1" are still lacking a usable identification of countries for some items, even as between the United States and other industrial countries. Shipping, other services, and transfers can be adjusted only in a sketchy way with the information available and need a much closer look than has been possible so far.

The matter now lies, most appropriately, in the hands of the Fund, which has received the working party's report and its recommendations. These recommendations range widely, from improving relations with country statistical offices to reorganizing the Fund's *Balance of Payments Manual,* and as a set they are a reasonably explicit statement of work to be done. At the head of the Fund's agenda, however, should be a detailed look by its own staff at the broad quantities of table 8.8 across countries and across time. There is a good deal of work to be done here in spreading out world balances, testing assumptions, establishing a history for the table, and reconciling the flows of the table with existing bodies of stock data such as IBS that are separate from the flow data.

All this should be done before discussion of country data problems with individual statistical offices. There is a close interlock between current- and capital account data problems for most countries, and the two sides need to be worked out jointly. At least as important is a detailed Fund statement of the condition of the statistics at a world level that will show which problems matter most for analysis and policy and will be the basis for establishing priorities in the work.

The Fund has the statistical base, country knowledge, and operating incentive to be in a most favored position globally for stating the problem and working through it. Up to now, the Fund has published its world figures on balance of payments as something of a footnote—part 2—to its annual *Balance of Payments Statistics Yearbook* and has taken the totals and balances largely as they come from country reports and staff estimates of missing items. The last eight years show that that is no longer an adequate procedure. The world figures now need a more specifically active role by Fund staff than they have had so far, most specifically with procedures for a substantial review of country data that can result in replacing country figures by better information when it exists. This is never done at present, and the proposal to do so is a major recommendation to the Fund.

As mentioned earlier, the capital account counterparts to world current-account imbalances are much less plain in the present form of the Fund's tables than are the current-account balances because of the accounting structure imposed on them. Capital account categories in the Fund's *Balance of Payments Manual* are defined mainly in terms of sectors—official, banks, nonbanks—rather than markets and cannot be used in international financial market analysis or even for consistency checking in statistics. The *Manual*'s chapters on capital account are a small part of the publication and are far too simplified for today's financial practices. A part of the Fund's agenda for modernizing its balance of payments program is surely to put attention to capital account on a scale that the subject now deserves. Imminent SNA revisions make such a review all the more urgent.

8.6   Relation to National Accounting Systems

It seems appropriate, in an Income and Wealth Conference volume, to mention, at least, the connection and possible effect the working party's report might have on national accounts around the world and in total. Current accounts are, after all, part of national income and product accounts, and the full balance of payments statement is part of flow-of-funds accounting. More broadly, these changes are proposed in a world that is at least quadruple entry in its bookkeeping within one or another form of SNA. The connection is simple in principle, but it is also complicated enough in its detail to make a thorough description far too tedious to work through here.

The accounts that we are dealing with here can be laid out as a matrix with country balance of payments statements as columns and the Fund's categories—both current account and a reorganized or homogenized or summarized form of capital account—as rows. The rows add horizontally to a final column, variously called "all countries" or "world," depending on context, that carries the full collection of world imbalances that the working party has been looking into. The net vertical sum in this last column is world-total errors and omissions, which is also the horizontal sum across countries of errors and omissions. The structure here is exactly that of a flow-of-funds matrix, and each column is in fact a flow-of-funds accounting for a country in which all domestic relations have been consolidated out.

Every change proposed in the report for the current-account section of the matrix affects at least four cells and perhaps subtotals and groupings of rows such as GNP and national saving and investment. Shifts of a country's flows from one row to another within current account typically have little or no effect, while a statement that a country has the wrong number for an income flow alters a good many domestic figures and discrepancies as well as the imbalances in the Fund's world totals. The working party proposed a set of current-account changes that altogether come to $50 billion of net credits affecting the GNP of various countries—much less for GDP—and another $8 billion for transfers. Capital account changes associated with these and separate from them have not been worked out except in the suggestions of table 8.7, and the effects on country errors and omissions and on national income and product account discrepancies are also still to be calculated.

Although the full results are not known yet, this is a useful context for mentioning one policy-related aspect of the working party's exercise, namely, the scope of a country's transactions for balance of payments analysis. Some of the adjustments in table 8.2 are for international organizations, and these are plainly a column in the world matrix that was missing from the Fund's totals in 1985 and that belongs there parallel with geographic countries. Other economic groups were also missing, however, including holders—or holdings—of at least $300 billion of international claims and the owners—or operations—of the Greek merchant shipping fleet. In both cases, these amounts were not known to and not included by any reporting country. It is possible, as illustrated in the report, to use information from Switzerland and other investor havens to get the addresses on the accounts of such claims and to allocate international assets to the countries named in the account addresses. Such a procedure affects the national accounts of the named countries accordingly, but there is an important question whether any knowledge is added by the practice of attributing to countries assets or activities that have effectively moved into international markets separate from all conventional country connections. In such cases the urge to balance the accounts as presently constructed seems to have obscured rather than clarified matters.

The report raises this question and suggests that the money or income can appropriately be identified with a country if it is somehow available for the country's international financing, either through domestic investment conditions that can attract it home or by some form of commandeering. The problem here is that, if commandeering is any kind of a possibility, the expatriate money surely goes underground as tightly as it can to avoid being available. On the other hand, domestic conditions that are attractive enough for a reflow of national capital will also attract fully foreign funds, perhaps at least as well, and the meaning of availability then broadens to embrace an entire world financial market. In either condition, the meaning of a country's funds held abroad is ambiguous, and the report concludes that there is a gray area here that calls for judgment.

The problem here may be in attaching concepts based on nation-state traditions to a world where there are many states but only poorly delineated nations and where in fact much economic activity is truly international and without significant national connections. Major international banks seem to be in this condition, along with more mature multinational corporations. Statisticians tend to insert data for these banks and businesses rather arbitrarily into one or another national total without regard for the operating relations among the parts of these firms or with their host countries. There is at the same time a great deal of individuals' wealth that is as international as the business activity but much less well known and largely ignored in country statistics.

For neither business nor individuals is the present treatment helpful analytically. It may be time now, when SNA structure is being reconsidered, to set up such internationalized activity in the accounts in a more realistic form, namely, as separate columns in the world matrix parallel to international agencies and to geographic states. Such columns need their own balance of payments statements vis-à-vis all other columns, and they need GNP, GDP, and saving and investment measurements of their own. Defining the group statistically needs thoughtful consideration from several viewpoints, but one starts from the concept that it consists of all the money in international markets that conventional national statistics do not claim for one or another geographic state. Working this out is another natural function for the staff of the Fund, using the statistical base they have and can develop in relation to table 8.8. One role such a synthetic sector group can serve for the Fund is to act as intermediary between the country-reported statistics that the Fund much prefers to use and the alternative global views that are inflicted on the Fund by independent information and imbalances.

Appendix A
Terms of Reference of the Working Party on the Statistical Discrepancy in World Balance of Payments Accounts

The Working Party will investigate the principal sources of discrepancy in global balance of payments statistics, consider various ways in which statistical practices might be amended, and make recommendations.

It is understood that the principal focus of the group's activities will be the Investment Income and Financial Services accounts, and that particular attention will be given to the role of the offshore centers. In carrying forward its work in this area the group will be assisted by a technical staff, of up to five professionals, that will be provided by the Fund and will be based in Washington.

The Working Party may also consider other sources of discrepancy in balance of payments accounts, if these appear to be of significant importance and amenable to investigation. In undertaking work in these areas, the Working Party may call on the assistance of the Fund staff, the OECD secretariat or other agencies, within the limits of the resources available.

The Chairman of the Working Party will determine, in consultation with other members, the program of work and the timing of meetings. The final report of the Working Party will be presented to the Managing Director no later than December 1986, and an interim report will be presented no later than December 1985.

Appendix B
Members of the Working Party on the Statistical Discrepancy in World Balance of Payments Accounts

Chairman:
> Mr. Pierre Esteva, Ministry of Finance, Paris, France

Members:
> Dr. Gunter Baer, Bank for International Settlements, Basle, Switzerland

> Mr. Max Baltensperger, Swiss National Bank, Zurich, Switzerland

> Mr. Andrew Crockett, International Monetary Fund, Washington, D.C.

> Mr. Werner Dannemann, International Monetary Fund, Washington, D.C.

> Mr. Piero Erba, Statistical Office, Eurostat, Luxembourg

> Mr. Michael Feiner, Organisation for Economic Cooperation and Development, Paris, France

> Dr. Mohammed Haider Ghuloum, Central Bank of Kuwait, Safat, Kuwait

> Dr. Lin See-Yan, Bank Negara Malaysia (Central Bank Malaysia), Kuala Lumpur, Malaysia

> Mr. Marius van Nieuwkerk, De Nederlandsche Bank N.V., Amsterdam, Netherlands

> Mr. Samuel Pizer (director, Technical Staff), International Monetary Fund, Washington, D.C.

> Dr. Kurt Senff, Deutsche Bundesbank, Frankfurt, West Germany

> Mr. Jack Wells, Central Statistical Office, London, England

> Mr. Yoneyoshi Yasugi,[10] Bank of Japan, Tokyo, Japan

> Mr. Ernesto Zedillo, Director General de Ficorca, Mexico, D.F., Mexico

Rapporteur:
> Mr. D. Keith McAlister, International Monetary Fund, Washington, D.C.

Members of the Technical Staff:
> Chester L. Callander

> Edna E. Ehrlich (Federal Reserve Bank of New York)

> Dietrich Hartenstein (Deutsche Bundesbank)

> Samuel Pizer (director)

> Robert L. Sammons

> Stephen P. Taylor

> Keith McAlister (liaison with Bureau of Statistics, International Monetary Fund)

Secretarial Staff:
  Martha J. Haldeman
  Alice McPhillips

Notes

1. For the final published report, see International Monetary Fund (1987).

2. Some of the discrepancy in trade arises from a timing float between recording of shipments as exports and as imports, and the Fund's Research Department includes estimates of the float component of the discrepancy in their *World Economic Outlook* publications (e.g., International Monetary Fund 1986c, 70, table A30). The timing asymmetry and the residual asymmetry are both more volatile than the total trade balance discrepancy and are negatively correlated with each other, but the components are as small as the total and also without trend relative to the volume of trade. Trade is not part of the direct problem whether or not the timing adjustment is accurate.

3. The BIS maintains its banking data on a quarterly basis and publishes them quarterly in *International Banking and Financial Market Developments,* along with a commentary (e.g., Bank for International Settlements 1986). The Fund incorporates BIS geographic detail into a broader coverage and somewhat different definition of banking, and the results appear in the Fund's monthly *International Financial Statistics,* in the world tables at the front as "International Banking Statistics" (IBS). The relation between the two forms of statistics and between them and other types of banking statistics is described in several publications (e.g., International Monetary Fund 1986b). The working party's report includes an appendix that describes the data in detail.

4. Comparing BIS-Fund data with national banking statistics can require a good deal of specific knowledge for any country on the nature of banking data and the structure of financial institutions. This is true even in comparing IBS pages with country pages within *International Financial Statistics.*

5. The $33 billion total is, to be sure, a net sum of credits less debits, and giving proportions of such a net sum, as in the text, is not proper. Credit adjustments, however, far outweigh debits in the sum in this case.

6. It is important to mention that offshore reporting of geographic detail for nonbanks was thin before December 1983 and only at that date became substantial enough to contribute significant information to the problem. The BIS shows a major break in series at December 1983, one that the user should cross only with much caution. The Fund made a different choice by estimating nonbank geography back to 1981 on a basis consistent with the new series and showing nothing before 1981 on nonbank geography. Both treatments show plainly the lack of history that could put present conditions into perspective.

7. The asset difference in table 8.4 appears to be a minimum. The IBS figure probably omits most amounts invested abroad by banks on behalf of customers, about $34 billion at 1983 year end, and the difference could be that much larger than table 8.4 shows.

8. If the income is spent abroad on consumption, we can hope that the spending is picked up in the foreign travel component of personal consumption already, and the revision will have the same effect as repatriated income.

9. The working party's income questionnaire shows that a closer match is possible for many countries by bringing more capital account detail into the standard structure.

10. Succeeded Mr. Kozo Tsukagoshi, Bank of Japan, in July 1985.

References

Bank for International Settlements. 1986. *International banking and financial markets developments*. Basle: Bank for International Settlements, May.

Dooley, Michael P. 1986. *Capital flight: A response to differences in financial risks*. Washington, D.C.: International Monetary Fund, Research Department. Typescript.

International Monetary Fund. 1977. *Balance of payments manual*. 4th ed. Washington, D.C.: IMF.

———. 1985. *Balance of payments statistics yearbook*. Washington, D.C.: IMF.

———. 1986a. *Balance of payments statistics yearbook*. Washington, D.C.: IMF.

———. 1986b. *The Fund's international banking statistics*. Washington, D.C.: IMF.

———. 1986c. *World economic outlook*. Washington, D.C.: IMF, October.

———. 1987. *Report on the world current account discrepancy*. Washington, D.C.: IMF, September.

Comment   Michael P. Dooley

The emergence of a statistical discrepancy in the adding up property of current accounts in international payments statistics has been an important problem for analysis of international economic conditions. Analysis of economic development, exchange rate determination, and international debt problems all require information concerning net flows of goods and services among countries and groups of countries. As Mr. Taylor clearly shows, the attempts to reconcile recorded payments for purchases of goods and services with recorded receipts in recent years have consistently shown that some countries have on balance received but not recorded receipts. Thus, some countries' current-account deficits have been smaller (or their surpluses larger) than national statistics suggest. Moreover, these discrepancies have been so large that they call into doubt even broad analyses of net resource transfers among groups of countries.

Michael P. Dooley is chief, External Adjustment Division, Research Department, International Monetary Fund.

The report of the task force of which Taylor was a member provides a very detailed report on the major sources of the statistical discrepancy. Roughly speaking, this report identifies the types of transactions that account for most of the discrepancy, although the report provides only limited geographic breakdown as to which countries' or groups of countries' current accounts were most affected. Taylor supplements this material by providing educated guesses concerning the regional breakdowns for the unrecorded receipts.

Perhaps the most interesting aspect of the exercise is the evidence that financial transactions account for a substantial part of the difficulty. It is well known that the scale of gross capital flows among countries is many times greater today than it was only a few years ago. What is less appreciated is the fact that interest and dividend payments on such positions have become an important part of "service" payments appearing in the current account. In particular, Taylor shows that creditors seem to report income receipts that are substantially less than payments reported by debtors. Moreover, if the natural assumption is made that unreported receipts in turn become unreported financial claims that in time will generate even more unreported income, we have the seeds of destruction for the usability of the data on international transactions. As Taylor suggests, damage could be limited by utilizing data for cross-border stocks appearing on the books of financial institutions to benchmark the investment income and capital flow data.

The unwillingness of investors to report income on their foreign investments may not be difficult to understand. Indeed, one of the attractions of foreign financial positions may be that income is relatively easily concealed. Procedures set out in the task force report for adjusting data for countries that are known to be creditors, perhaps on the basis of debtors' data on stocks of debt or payments flows, would seem necessary in order to restore greater confidence in the data on international transactions.

9 Year-Apart Estimates of Household Net Worth from the Survey of Income and Program Participation

John M. McNeil and Enrique J. Lamas

9.1 Introduction

The difficulty of collecting accurate data on wealth in a household survey has long been recognized. The modern history of wealth surveys began with a 1946 survey sponsored by the Federal Reserve Board (FRB) and continued with the annual surveys of consumer finances conducted by the Survey Research Center at the University of Michigan during the period 1947–70. In the 1960–61 Survey of Consumer Expeditures, sponsored by the Bureau of Labor Statistics (BLS), data on assets and liabilities were collected one year apart, enabling the BLS to calculate the net change in assets and liabilities. In 1963 and 1964, the FRB sponsored what might be viewed as the most ambitious effort ever to obtain wealth and saving estimates from a household survey. The 1963 survey collected very detailed asset and liability data from a sample of approximately 2,500 households (Projector and Weiss 1966). The households were visited again one year later to obtain the data that were used in producing estimates of household saving (Projector 1968). A special feature of the 1963–64 survey was a design that sampled high-income households at a higher rate than other households. Other household surveys that collected a significant amount of data on household wealth included the FRB's 1977 Consumer Credit Survey (Durkin and Elliehausen 1978), the 1979

John M. McNeil is a senior poverty and disability statistics analyst in the Housing and Household Economic Statistics Division, U.S. Bureau of the Census. Enrique J. Lamas is Chief, Poverty and Wealth Statistics Branch, Housing and Household Economic Statistics Division, U.S. Bureau of the Census.

This paper reports the general result of research undertaken by the Census Bureau staff. The views expressed are attributable to the authors and do not necessarily reflect those of the Census Bureau.

Survey of the President's Commission on Pension Policy (Cartwright and Friedland 1985), and the 1979 Income and Survey Development Program (Pearl and Frankel 1982; Radner 1984).

More recently, data from two major wealth surveys have received a considerable amount of attention. The 1983 Survey of Consumer Finances (SCF) was conducted by the University of Michigan's Survey Research Center and was sponsored by several federal agencies, including the Federal Reserve Board. The survey collected data from a basic representative sample of about 3,800 families and from a special high-income sample of 438 families. Estimates are available from a sampling frame that excludes the high-income families and from a frame that includes them (Avery et al. 1984a, 1984b; Avery and Elliehausen 1986). The survey received a good deal of attention when the results were used to estimate the change in wealth inequality (Joint Economic Committee 1986). The second major survey was the Survey of Income and Program Participation (SIPP). SIPP is an ongoing panel survey sponsored by the Bureau of the Census. Each panel remains in sample for two and a half years, and interviews are conducted every four months. The source of the data for the SIPP wealth report was the asset and liability questions that were asked in the fourth wave of the 1984 panel.[1] The interviews were conducted during the period September–December 1984, and the sample of 20,000 households was the largest for any survey containing a detailed set of wealth questions. SIPP wealth data have been presented in a report and in several papers (U.S. Bureau of the Census 1986; Lamas and McNeil 1984, 1985, 1986).

The design of the first four panels of SIPP calls for the collection of wealth data twice each panel. The same questions that were asked in wave 4 of the 1984 panel were repeated one year later in wave 7. This design allows us to examine changes in net worth over a one-year period. The major purpose of this paper is to present the wave 4 and wave 7 estimates and to offer some conclusions about what the comparisons show about the reliability of the estimates.

Asset and liability data are collected in SIPP because a certain amount of asset data is required to determine program eligibility, because such information makes the SIPP data base more useful to those who want to model the effect of tax and transfer policies, and because net worth provides a dimension of economic status that is not fully captured by income. The design of the asset questions is based on the core questions about income recipiency. In some sense, the marginal cost of SIPP asset questions is small because the ownership of various categories of assets is established in the core of each wave as part of the method of measuring income. Information about the value of certain major assets is collected as a composite amount. For example, the amount held in the following four forms is collected as a single figure: regular savings accounts, money-market deposit accounts, certificates of deposit, and interest-earning checking accounts. Another single-amount question is asked about four other assets: money-market funds, U.S. government securities, municipal or corporate bonds, and other interest-earning assets, excluding mortgages and U.S. savings bonds. The assets are grouped in this way to measure income, and the grouping is maintained to minimize the cost of the additional questions about asset value. For other assets, amounts were collected for each type, including stocks and mutual fund shares, own home, rental property, other real estate, mortgages held from the sale of property, regular checking accounts, U.S. savings bonds, and other financial assets.

The major asset categories not covered in SIPP are pension plan assets, cash surrender value of life insurance, and consumer durables other than vehicles. SIPP does collect information on whether persons are covered by or vested in a pension plan and information on the face value and type of life insurance policies.

The next section compares SIPP and SCF estimates of net worth. The third section compares SIPP net worth estimates from waves 4 and 7. The fourth section compares SIPP estimates with those from the flow-of funds-accounts (FFAs). The fifth section examines the change in SIPP net worth at the individual household level. The sixth section fits a saving model to the SIPP data. The seventh and final section responds to several points raised by the discussant, Martin H. David.

9.2   Comparison of SIPP and SCF Estimates of Net Worth

Because the 1983 SCF was designed as a wealth survey, it provides a useful reference for examining some of the basic wealth estimates from SIPP. There are minor differences between SIPP and SCF in the timing of the survey (SIPP interviews were conducted from September to December 1984 and SCF interviews from February to July 1983) and in the coverage of the household population (SCF did not obtain data for secondary unrelated individuals or for unrelated subfamilies). The major differences have to do with the amount of detail collected and, perhaps most important, with the availability of a high-income sample for the SCF. The comparisons in table 9.1 distinguish between SCF estimates based on the representative sample and those based on the merged sample. The SCF representative sample was selected in approximately the same manner as the SIPP sample was. The SCF merged sample combines the high-income sample with the representative sample. The comparisons in table 9.1 show SCF data as published in the *Federal Reserve Bulletin* as well as revised estimates (Avery and Elliehausen 1986). The revisions essentially reflect the correction of a very large error on a single questionnaire.

Table 9.1   Comparisons of SIPP and SCF Estimates of Net Worth (in dollars)

| | SCF before Revision[a] | | SCF after Revision[b] | | |
| | Representative Sample | Merged Sample | Representative Sample | Merged Sample | SIPP |
Net Worth					
Excluding equity in motor vehicle and own business:					
Mean	66,050	N.A.	N.A.	N.A.	65,801
Median	24,574	N.A.	N.A.	N.A.	N.A.
Including equity in motor vehicles and own business:					
Mean	N.A.	133,502	103,463	119,898	78,574
Median	N.A.	30,553	N.A.	N.A.	32,455

Note: The SCF estimates include forms of wealth not included in the SIPP estimates, including the cash value of life insurance and the value of employer-sponsored thrift, profit-sharing, stock option, and tax-deferred savings plans. In addition, the SCF and the SIPP differ in their measures of business equity. The SCF estimate includes equity in nonpublic businesses in which the person had no management responsibilities. The SIPP questionnaire had no specific questions on such arrangements and probably did not count most of the wealth held in this form. N.A. = not available.

[a]From the September and December 1984 *Federal Reserve Bulletin.*
[b]Obtained from the Federal Reserve Board.

The first row in table 9.1 shows mean net worth when motor vehicle and business equity are excluded. This is a measure of net worth that was published in the *Federal Reserve Bulletin,* and we have chosen to show it here because it offers an opportunity to examine the effect of business equity on the SIPP and SCF estimates. The SIPP and SCF estimates shown in the first row are very close. The second row is based on a more comprehensive measure of net worth and shows the following. (1) The SCF merged sample estimate of mean net worth is much higher than the SCF representative sample estimate (about 16 percent higher). (2) The SCF revision had a large effect on the estimate of net worth (it lowered the estimate of the mean by about 11 percent and the estimate of total net worth by about $1.1 trillion). (3) When business equity is included, the SIPP estimate of mean net worth is much lower than the SCF figures, but the SIPP estimate of median net worth is higher than the SCF estimate even when the comparison is with the SCF estimate that would be expected to produce the highest figure (the merged sample before revision).

Judged on the basis of a comparison of medians, the SIPP wealth estimates are clearly no worse than the SCF estimates and might be considered slightly better. This conclusion is reinforced when one considers that the SCF estimates include forms of wealth that are not included in the SIPP estimates.[2] A comparison of means seems to show a much different result, but the measurement issues are complex, and the comparison must be approached with caution. Two major measurement issues are the stability of measures of business equity and the effect of including 438 high-income families in the SCF sample. Table 9.1 shows that the SIPP and SCF estimates of mean net worth are virtually identical when equity in own business is excluded from the net worth measure and when the SCF estimate is based on the representative sample (the SIPP estimate was $65,801 and the SCF estimate $66,050). When business equity is included, the difference between the SIPP and SCF estimates becomes sizable. The SIPP estimate of mean net worth when business equity is included is $78,574, and the SCF revised estimate based on the representative sample is $103,463. The SCF revised estimate rises to $119,898 when it is based on the merged sample.

The data in table 9.1 show that relatively high SCF estimates of business equity and the addition of 438 high-income families to the SCF sample result in SCF estimates of mean net worth that are substantially above the SIPP estimates. Does this mean that the SCF estimates are superior to the SIPP estimates? The proper answer to this question is that the choice of the data set depends on the intended use of the data. Because of its larger sample size, and because it produces an estimate of median net worth that is slightly higher than any SCF estimate, it seems reasonable to select the SIPP data set when comparing the wealth status of various subgroups of the population. The dramatic effect a single questionnaire can have on mean values makes it prudent to use medians rather than means when making comparisons among demographic, social, or ethnic groups. In fact, the very large effect of "outliers" raises questions about any analysis that depends on means or aggregates. Curtin, Juster, and Morgan (chap. 10, in this vol.) describe the problems of "outliers" and cite three cases in the SCF sample and one case in the SIPP sample. The first SCF case they cite is the case that led to the major revision in the SCF estimates. An entry of $200,000,000 was subsequently changed to $2,000,000 on the basis of information obtained in 1986. The original value, when weighted, had accounted for approximately 10 percent of U.S. household wealth. Curtin, Juster, and Morgan also cite an SCF case in which reported net worth was about $1 billion. This case was not included in the final SCF sample because of a lack of information on income, but its inclusion would have approximately doubled the SCF estimate of total U.S. household wealth. The SIPP case involved a questionnaire showing a business equity of $50,000,000. This case was not included in the final SIPP file because the 1984 wealth data appeared to be inconsistent with other data obtained for this household, including information on wealth holdings in 1985.

The message for data users is that household survey estimates of aggregate and mean wealth are potentially highly unstable. We advise caution when using either the SCF or the SIPP if conclusions are to be based primarily on cross-section or time-series differences in aggregate or mean wealth.

We do regard household survey estimates of median wealth as useful and valid. This judgment is based on comparisons of medians between SIPP and SCF and between the SIPP estimates from the wave 4 and 7 interviews.

9.3   Comparison of SIPP Net Worth Estimates from Wave 4 and Wave 7

Tables 9.2 and 9.3 provide basic estimates of median, mean, and aggregate household net worth for both wave 4 and wave 7. The data have been weighted to represent all U.S. households. The wave 7 figures have been adjusted by the change in the consumer price index to allow for a constant dollar comparison. Over the twelve-month period, the estimates show a $818 decline in household median net worth (from $32,455 to $31,637), a $34 decline in mean net worth (from $78,574 to $78,540), and a $121 billion dollar increase in aggregate net worth (from $6.825 trillion to $6.946 trillion). These estimates of change, however, are not statistically significant.

When comparing net worth estimates, either in the cross section or over time, both sampling and nonsampling errors must be taken into consideration. The standard errors for each of the net worth estimates in table 9.2 are shown in parentheses. For the population subgroups shown in the table, the relatively large sample size of SIPP produces standard errors small enough so that it is possible to identify those race, age, family-type, and income groups with relatively high or low levels of net worth. The data also show a certain stability in the net worth estimates between wave 4 and wave 7. For example, consider the following ratios of median net worth: the white to black ratio was twelve to one in both wave 4 and wave 7; the old to young (sixty-five and over to under thirty-five) ratio was eleven to one in both waves; the married-couple family to female householder family ratio was nine to one in wave 4 and eleven to one in wave 7; and the highest-income quintile to lowest-income quintile ratio was about twenty to one in both wave 4 and wave 7. Table 9.2 shows very few statistically significant year-to-year changes in net worth. The three changes that were significant at the 95 percent confidence level are marked with a single asterisk, and the one change that was significant at the 90 percent

Table 9.2   Median and Mean Household Net Worth by Selected Household Characteristics: Wave 4 and Wave 7 (in constant dollars, with standard errors in parentheses)

	Median Net Worth			Mean Net Worth		
Characteristic	Wave 4	Wave 7	Wave 7 Minus Wave 4	Wave 4	Wave 7	Wave 7 Minus Wave 4
All households	32,455 (685)	31,637 (677)	−818	78,574 (1,951)	78,540 (1,747)	−34
Race and Hispanic origin:						
White	38,915 (798)	37,472 (716)	−1,443**	86,153 (2,222)	86,068 (1,984)	−85
Black	3,342 (247)	3,241 (312)	−101	20,180 (1,009)	21,292 (1,360)	1,112
Hispanic origin	4,871 (936)	4,573 (806)	−298	35,827 (3,626)	33,917 (3,976)	−1,910
Age of householder:						
Under 35 years	5,622 (303)	5,129 (284)	−493	22,548 (1,076)	21,575 (892)	−973
35–44 years	35,311 (1,344)	34,507 (1,184)	−804	68,555 (2,528)	73,454 (4,034)	4,899
45–54 years	56,461 (1,764)	51,431 (1,965)	−5,030*	114,491 (8,268)	98,046 (5,705)	−16,445*
55–64 years	73,454 (2,006)	70,455 (2,044)	−2,999	132,279 (5,536)	129,686 (5,668)	−2,593
65 years and over	60,061 (1,629)	58,145 (1,828)	−1,916	104,596 (5,239)	112,773 (4,203)	8,177

(continued)

Table 9.2   (continued)

Characteristic	Median Net Worth			Mean Net Worth		
	Wave 4	Wave 7	Wave 7 Minus Wave 4	Wave 4	Wave 7	Wave 7 Minus Wave 4
Type of household:						
Family:	40,653	39,647	−1,006	90,319	90,394	75
	(904)	(874)		(2,603)	(2,301)	
Married couple	49,715	48,599	−1,116	101,689	102,523	834
	(1,076)	(1,017)		(3,166)	(2,796)	
Female householder	5,620	4,522	−1,098	37,379	35,424	−1,955
	(841)	(839)		(2,117)	(2,201)	
Male householder	20,269	22,537	2,268	66,960	62,711	−4,249
	(3,351)	(3,385)		(8,097)	(6,171)	
Nonfamily	14,295	13,650	−645	47,820	48,104	284
	(1,032)	(928)		(1,740)	(1,897)	
Income quintile:[a]						
Lowest	4,119	3,916	−203	27,802	27,899	97
	(618)	(573)		(1,273)	(1,481)	
Second lowest	18,692	17,171	−1,521	46,499	43,813	−2,686
	(1,370)	(1,616)		(1,593)	(1,807)	
Middle	24,695	24,673	−22	53,672	59,307	5,635*
	(1,364)	(1,423)		(1,674)	(2,493)	
Second highest	39,262	37,934	−1,328	72,263	72,895	632
	(1,403)	(1,322)		(2,197)	(2,055)	
Highest	82,199	84,118	1,919	173,432	177,128	3,696
	(1,941)	(1,970)		(7,840)	(6,941)	

[a]Income quintile groups are approximate.

*Change is statistically significant at the 95 percent confidence level.

**Change is statistically significant at the 90 percent confidence level.

Table 9.3   **Number of Households and Aggregate Household Net Worth: Wave 4 and Wave 7**

| Characteristic | Number of Households (in thousands) | | Aggregate Net Worth (in billions of constant dollars) | | |
	Wave 4	Wave 7	Wave 4	Wave 7	Wave 7 Minus Wave 4
All households	86,871	88,443	6,825.8	6,946.3	120.5
Race and Hispanic origin:					
White	75,419	76,629	6,497.6	6,595.3	97.7
Black	9,515	9,862	192.0	210.0	18.0
Hispanic origin	4,173	4,339	149.5	147.2	−2.3
Age of householder:					
Under 35 years	25,788	25,742	581.5	555.4	−26.1
35–44 years	17,404	18,162	1,193.1	1,334.1	141.0
45–54 years	12,605	12,838	1,443.2	1,258.7	−184.5
55–64 years	12,924	13,191	1,709.6	1,710.7	1.1
65 years and over	18,151	18,510	1,898.5	2,087.4	188.9
Type of household:					
Family:	62,864	63,651	5,677.8	5,753.7	75.9
Married couple	50,690	51,168	5,154.6	5,245.9	91.3
Female householder	9,861	10,081	368.3	357.1	−11.2
Male householder	2,312	2,402	154.8	150.6	−4.2
Nonfamily	24,008	24,792	1,148.1	1,192.6	44.5
Income quintile:					
Lowest	17,374	17,689	483.0	493.5	10.5
Second lowest	17,374	17,689	807.9	775.0	−32.9
Middle	17,374	17,689	932.5	1,049.1	116.6
Second highest	17,374	17,689	1,255.5	1,289.4	33.9
Highest	17,374	17,689	3,013.2	3,133.2	120.0

confidence level is marked with a double asterisk. As we examine the data more closely, we are likely to conclude that these "significant changes" probably reflect measurement problems.

Sampling error becomes more important as the base of the estimate declines. Table 9.4 shows the mean net worth of households by income quintile cross-classified by household type and age of householder for both wave 4 and wave 7. The data show a positive relation between income and wealth for most types of households by age groups, and there is evidence that net worth increases with age for most types of households by income groups, but the standard errors for most of the cells are very large. Many of the cross-section comparisons have to be carefully qualified, and little can be said about year-to-year changes.

Table 9.4   **Mean Net Worth by Type of Household and Income Quintile: Wave 4 and Wave 7 (in constant dollars, with standard errors in parentheses)**

Type of Household, Age of Householder, and SIPP Wave	All Income Levels	Income Quintile				
		Lowest	Second Lowest	Middle	Second Highest	Highest
Married couple:						
Wave 4	$101,689	52,326	54,407	59,266	74,669	183,238
	(3,166)	(4,731)	(2,706)	(2,214)	(2,557)	(9,206)
Wave 7	102,523	42,484	53,781	67,196	75,648	184,779
	(2,796)	(4,056)	(3,491)	(3,405)	(2,434)	(7,945)
Under 35 years:						
Wave 4	30,343	18,504	13,997	19,939	27,178	61,909
	(1,553)	(6,679)	(2,125)	(1,661)	(2,081)	(5,321)
Wave 7	30,845	9,048	13,462	19,123	27,807	67,126
	(1,449)	(2,189)	(1,549)	(1,703)	(1,960)	(5,119)
35–54 years:						
Wave 4	107,213	68,563	51,441	53,402	67,944	163,256
	(5,352)	(11,340)	(7,777)	(3,820)	(3,720)	(11,296)
Wave 7	104,605	55,721	56,133	52,459	67,026	163,372
	(4,740)	(11,108)	(9,964)	(4,231)	(3,540)	(10,230)
55–64 years:						
Wave 4	164,271	77,528	90,780	89,917	115,849	287,941
	(7,997)	(12,771)	(9,330)	(5,534)	(6,993)	(20,506)
Wave 7	161,462	77,445	93,918	109,482	114,293	269,943
	(8,333)	(12,378)	(13,028)	(12,458)	(6,078)	(21,011)
65 years and over:						
Wave 4	146,699	50,881	74,359	119,440	185,849	436,525
	(11,295)	(6,698)	(3,167)	(6,621)	(10,948)	(80,775)
Wave 7	160,444	38,489	69,950	137,733	199,255	455,827
	(8,454)	(3,825)	(3,438)	(10,177)	(10,201)	(47,729)
Female householder:						
Wave 4	44,781	21,652	42,310	51,090	78,570	143,098
	(1,502)	(1,038)	(1,970)	(3,138)	(6,012)	(15,652)
Wave 7	44,442	21,865	38,717	53,408	79,410	149,102
	(1,540)	(1,148)	(2,133)	(3,264)	(5,865)	(17,361)
Under 35 years:						
Wave 4	8,865	2,698	6,639	9,508	16,480	41,907
	(1,421)	(1,009)	(1,093)	(1,261)	(2,745)	(19,577)
Wave 7	8,074	2,157	5,555	9,443	17,839	42,211
	(1,081)	(754)	(836)	(1,384)	(3,252)	(16,067)

Table 9.4   (continued)

Type of Household, Age of Householder, and SIPP Wave	All Income Levels	Income Quintile				
		Lowest	Second Lowest	Middle	Second Highest	Highest
35–54 years:						
Wave 4	41,054	12,934	25,616	39,045	63,799	137,549
	(2,954)	(1,804)	(3,411)	(3,843)	(7,798)	(22,561)
Wave 7	32,975	8,440	23,480	39,123	47,624	94,722
	(2,111)	(1,344)	(3,512)	(4,028)	(5,272)	(14,152)
55–64 years:						
Wave 4	67,726	30,547	64,733	74,896	107,080	176,998
	(4,725)	(3,487)	(6,932)	(9,694)	(18,844)	(31,822)
Wave 7	70,392	26,678	53,355	90,437	113,190	239,248
	(5,107)	(2,928)	(6,487)	(9,544)	(14,247)	(46,158)
65 years and over:						
Wave 4	67,511	33,161	75,057	116,133	190,602	286,882
	(2,910)	(1,737)	(3,248)	(8,692)	(16,975)	(52,578)
Wave 7	71,619	35,576	77,999	116,539	197,768	336,788
	(3,377)	(2,091)	(4,625)	(9,401)	(19,412)	(62,715)
Male householder:						
Wave 4	48,835	19,132	33,966	36,356	49,684	133,977
	(2,853)	(1,943)	(3,683)	(4,095)	(5,940)	(14,209)
Wave 7	47,788	29,538	30,166	40,212	49,077	125,592
	(3,007)	(5,080)	(2,562)	(6,926)	(4,505)	(15,039)
Under 35 years:						
Wave 4	18,924	6,283	9,360	14,509	18,625	63,377
	(2,648)	(1,827)	(1,903)	(3,469)	(3,223)	(16,999)
Wave 7	13,737	8,640	5,361	12,096	17,840	37,987
	(1,349)	(2,383)	(1,136)	(1,371)	(2,789)	(8,995)
35–54 years:						
Wave 4	53,838	16,348	34,035	38,495	47,777	117,638
	(5,214)	(4,313)	(6,784)	(8,767)	(8,296)	(17,735)
Wave 7	52,456	32,055	34,564	51,858	46,991	98,354
	(6,330)	(10,215)	(5,818)	(19,814)	(5,238)	(19,657)
55–64 years:						
Wave 4	85,694	28,144	65,020	58,368	135,394	195,686
	(11,059)	(6,846)	(13,630)	(11,309)	(49,255)	(38,220)
Wave 7	82,483	41,447	42,773	66,086	101,327	205,365
	(10,777)	(17,038)	(8,053)	(17,669)	(26,111)	(39,769)
65 years and over:						
Wave 4	90,067	30,438	68,667	116,933	138,529	509,985
	(9,282)	(3,676)	(11,618)	(17,221)	(21,088)	(91,559)
Wave 7	93,830	42,082	68,106	101,944	179,205	525,739
	(9,589)	(11,225)	(6,811)	(11,389)	(27,227)	(88,702)

Nonsampling errors in the form of reporting errors and nonresponse may be more important than sampling errors. Reporting errors can have a very large effect on estimates, and it is difficult to determine when a serious reporting error has occurred. The controversy surrounding the Joint Economic Committee's report on changes in wealth inequality underlines the dramatic effect a single observation can have on estimates of mean and aggregate net worth. Every household survey faces this problem, and in wave 4 of SIPP we encountered a case that we considered a problem case. One of the sample households in that wave reported a business equity of $50,000,000. A review of the other entries on the questionnaire raised doubts about the accuracy of that figure, but the evidence was not conclusive. We decided to wait until we could examine the responses to the wave 7 questionnaire before making a final decision on the value to adopt for wave 4. The wave 7 responses convinced us that the wave 4 data were incorrect, and the final value adopted for wave 4 was set equal to the wave 7 response: $2,000,000. Given that the household weight was about 6,500, the decision reduced the potential wave 4 estimate of total business equity by approximately $300 billion.

There is a particular kind of reporting error that is frequently important in panel surveys. The error, called time-in-sample bias, is present in Current Population Survey rotation group estimates of income and labor force activity and may very well be present in SIPP estimates. Whether this type of error has a serious effect on SIPP estimates of year-to-year change in net worth can be examined as data from the 1985 and other panels become available.

The problems of noninterviews and nonresponse can be serious for household surveys. Noninterviews occur when a person or household refuses to participate in the survey or when the person or household cannot be located in order to conduct an interview. Approximately 11 percent of the households eligible for the first wave interview were noninterviews in wave 4. The figure was about 17 percent in wave 7. These noninterview rates compare favorably to the rates in other wealth surveys. Nonresponse occurs when a respondent does not know the answer to a question, and questions about the value of assets and debts are difficult to answer in the setting of a relatively brief household interview. The problem is compounded when interviews are conducted with proxy respondents, and the SIPP survey design allows for the interview to be conducted with a "knowledgeable" relative if the sample person is not available at the time of the household interview. Nonresponse also occurs when a respondent refuses to answer a question. This is relatively rare in SIPP, but some of the "don't know" responses may, in fact, be polite refusals. When SIPP questionnaires are processed, missing information is imputed using a procedure that searches for a donor with similar characteristics and then sets the missing value equal to the value reported in the questionnaire of the donor. It is important to realize that the wave 4 and wave 7 data were processed independently. Except for the single case described above, we did not use information from one wave to fill in missing information or modify responses in the other wave. The importance of this feature of the processing system will become apparent later, when we examine estimates for matched households.

Table 9.5 shows the proportion of total value that was imputed for selected assets. In wave 4, imputations accounted for nearly 40 percent of the value of stocks and mutual fund shares and the value of own businesses. About 30 percent of the value of rental property was imputed and about 20 percent of the wealth held in own homes, other real estate, and individual retirement accounts (IRAs). The wave 7 imputation rates were generally similar except for a large increase in the amount of imputation for the value of own business. The rate was approximately 50 percent in wave 7.

In order to test the theory that knowledge of their earlier response would lead respondents to give improved estimates of change, information about wave 4 responses was given to half the sample at the time of the wave 7 interview. This feedback procedure was similar to the procedure used in the 1964 FRB survey (Projector 1968). Tables 9.6 and 9.7 show median and mean net worth figures by whether the household was in or out of the feedback sample. When the various subgroups are examined, it is difficult to discern any regular effect of the feedback procedure. For example, among the fifty-five- to sixty-four-years-of-age group, those in the feedback sample reported a smaller change than did those in the nonfeedback group, but the relation was reversed for the sixty-five years and over age group.

The comparison of wave 4 with wave 7 shows a certain stability in the basic relations. The net worth data in table 9.8 illustrate this stability, and the comparison with the income data shows that net worth data are an important addition to our usual set of income tables. Black

Table 9.5 **Sum of Imputed Values as a Percentage of Total Values: Selected Assets**

Asset	Wave 4	Wave 7
Stocks and mutual fund shares	38.3	39.0
Own business	38.7	49.9
Own home	18.7	16.8
Rental property	28.9	27.8
Other real estate	18.6	14.9
IRAs	18.3	19.2

Table 9.6   **Median Household Net Worth in Wave 4 and Wave 7 by Whether Household Was in Feedback Sample in Wave 7 (in constant dollars)**

Characteristic	In Feedback Sample in Wave 7			Not in Feedback Sample in Wave 7		
	Wave 4	Wave 7	Wave 7 Minus Wave 4	Wave 4	Wave 7	Wave 7 Minus Wave 4
All households	32,944	32,357	−587	32,048	30,890	−1,158
Race and Hispanic origin:						
White	39,268	37,557	−1,711	38,533	37,388	−1,145
Black	3,661	3,418	−243	3,112	3,137	25
Hispanic origin	7,477	7,863	386	2,926	2,963	37
Age of householder:						
Under 35 years	5,719	5,516	−203	5,544	4,781	−763
35–44 years	34,389	33,279	−1,110	36,044	35,647	−370
45–54 years	55,166	49,881	−5,285	57,457	52,450	−5,007
55–64 years	73,065	72,658	−407	73,901	67,298	−6,603
65 years and over	62,763	59,019	−3,744	57,427	57,280	−147
Type of household:						
Family:	40,800	39,694	−1,106	40,523	39,597	−926
Married couple	49,273	46,916	−2,357	50,121	50,076	−45
Female householder	6,041	5,941	−100	5,350	4,105	−1,245
Male householder	19,612	22,031	2,419	20,718	22,769	2,051
Nonfamily	15,996	14,977	−1,019	12,702	11,620	−1,082
Income quintile:[a]						
Lowest	4,380	4,738	358	3,932	3,271	−661
Second lowest	20,083	20,602	519	17,393	13,987	−3,406
Middle	26,278	24,580	−1,698	23,192	24,720	1,528
Second highest	37,706	35,700	−2,006	40,588	40,015	−573
Highest	85,008	86,170	1,162	80,078	82,346	2,268

[a]Income groups are approximate.

households, for example, receive about 7 percent of aggregate income but own only 3 percent of total net worth. On the other hand, families with a householder sixty-five and over received about 13 percent of total income and owned about 30 percent of total net worth. When we examine year-to-year changes in net worth, the results are less encouraging. Among most population subgroups, the change in net worth was not statistically significant. Perhaps more important, those changes that passed the test of statistical significance seem more likely to reflect measurement problems than real economic change. It is difficult to understand, for example, why households with a householder forty-

Table 9.7   **Mean Household Net Worth in Wave 4 and Wave 7 by Whether Household Was in Feedback Sample in Wave 7 (in constant dollars)**

Characteristic	In Feedback Sample in Wave 7			Not in Feedback Sample in Wave 7		
	Wave 4	Wave 7	Wave 7 Minus Wave 4	Wave 4	Wave 7	Wave 7 Minus Wave 4
All households	80,025	79,161	− 864	77,223	77,964	741
Race and Hispanic origin:						
White	87,573	86,059	− 1,514	84,834	86,075	1,241
Black	19,945	24,609	4,664	20,397	18,383	− 2,014
Hispanic origin	35,982	39,320	3,338	35,662	28,128	− 7,534
Age of householder:						
Under 35 years	22,247	22,683	436	22,832	20,565	− 2,267
35–44 years	65,930	66,245	315	70,793	79,674	8,881
45–54 years	118,462	103,397	− 15,065	110,883	93,274	− 17,609
55–64 years	130,773	127,859	− 2,914	133,770	131,494	− 2,276
65 years and over	111,240	115,478	4,238	98,155	110,075	11,920
Type of household:						
Family:	93,241	91,068	− 2,173	87,646	89,784	2,138
Married couple	104,257	102,039	− 2,218	99,319	102,969	3,650
Female householder	39,338	38,912	− 426	35,591	32,479	− 3,112
Male householder	76,000	65,141	− 10,859	59,083	60,673	1,590
Nonfamily	46,549	49,895	3,346	49,060	46,341	− 2,719
Income quintile:[a]						
Lowest	26,100	29,552	3,452	29,449	26,233	− 3,216
Second lowest	45,171	43,717	− 1,454	47,766	43,904	− 3,862
Middle	54,167	58,362	4,195	53,214	60,150	6,936
Second highest	71,064	70,406	− 658	73,317	75,065	1,748
Highest	185,715	182,931	− 2,784	165,794	171,703	5,909

[a]Income groups are approximate.

five to fifty-four years of age should have experienced a 9 percent drop in median net worth during a twelve-month period.

9.4   Comparison with FFA Estimates

The categories used to collect asset data in SIPP, along with information about the number of owners and the values of the assets, are shown in table 9.9. The wave 4 and wave 7 data are generally similar, although there is some suggestion of a decline in asset ownership (most of the changes in the ownership rate for individual assets were not

Table 9.8   Percentage Distribution of Aggregate Income and Aggregate Net
                   Worth among Selected Household Groups: Wave 4 and Wave 7

Characteristic	Aggregate Income		Aggregate Net Worth	
	Wave 4	Wave 7	Wave 4	Wave 7
All households	100.0	100.0	100.0	100.0
Race and Hispanic origin:				
White	90.5	90.1	95.2	94.9
Black	7.0	7.4	2.8	3.0
Hispanic origin	3.8	3.7	2.2	2.1
Age of householder:				
Under 35 years	26.1	24.8	8.5	8.0
35–44 years	24.4	24.6	17.5	19.2
45–54 years	19.3	18.8	21.1	18.1
55–64 years	16.9	18.0	25.0	24.6
65 years and over	13.2	13.7	27.8	30.1
Type of household:				
Family:	83.1	82.8	83.2	82.8
Married couple	73.2	73.1	75.5	75.5
Female householder	7.2	7.0	5.4	5.1
Male householder	2.7	2.7	2.3	2.2
Nonfamily	16.9	17.2	16.8	17.2
Income quintile:				
Lowest	4.1	4.0	6.7	6.8
Second lowest	9.9	9.8	11.5	10.6
Middle	15.8	15.3	12.7	14.2
Second highest	23.1	22.8	18.6	20.0
Highest	47.2	48.1	49.8	48.4

statistically significant, but in ten out of twelve asset categories the measured change was negative). The value of home equity was by far the largest asset category, accounting for nearly $3 trillion out of the aggregate net worth figure of approximately $7 trillion.

The SIPP asset categories are not directly comparable to the categories used by the FRB in their FFA estimates. First, SIPP does not cover all the assets that are included in the FFA estimates. We have mentioned that SIPP excludes pension wealth, the cash value of life insurance, and the value of consumer durables other than vehicles. Cash holdings should be added to the list. There is some ambiguity as to the coverage of estates and personal trusts. SIPP does not have specific questions on these assets, and it seems likely that most of this form of wealth is absent from the SIPP estimates. A second difference between SIPP and the FFAs is the inclusion of holdings of the nonprofit

Table 9.9 Percentage of Households Owning and Mean and Aggregate Value (in constant dollars) of Asset by Type: Wave 4 and Wave 7

Asset Type	Percentage of Households Owning		Mean Net Value of Asset		Aggregate Net Value of Asset (in billions of dollars)	
	Wave 4	Wave 7	Wave 4	Wave 7	Wave 4	Wave 7
Interest-earning assets at financial institutions[a]	71.8	71.2	15,806	15,788	985.3	993.4
Other interest-earning assets[b]	8.5	9.3	28,946	32,051	212.9	265.0
Regular checking accounts	53.9	52.8	922	865	43.2	40.4
Stocks and mutual fund shares[c]	20.0	19.8	26,834	29,762	466.8	521.9
Own business or profession[d]	12.9	12.5	63,012	59,731	705.5	660.4
Motor vehicles	85.5	84.8	5,442	5,099	404.0	382.6
Own home	64.3	64.1	50,475	51,692	2,818.6	2,932.3
Rental property	9.8	9.3	71,982	68,555	610.3	563.0
Other real estate	10.0	10.2	34,437	35,185	298.6	317.4
U.S. savings bonds	15.0	14.9	2,490	2,214	32.5	29.2
IRA or Keogh accounts	19.5	21.6	8,877	10,015	150.6	191.1
Other financial assets[e]	7.0	6.5	55,788	50,924	337.1	292.7
Addendum: Unsecured debt	67.1	61.5	4,123	4,493	240.5	244.5

[a]Includes passbook savings accounts, money-market deposit accounts, certificates of deposit, and interest-earning checking accounts.

[b]Includes money-market funds, U.S. government securities (other than savings bonds), municipal or corporate bonds, and other interest-earning assets (other than mortgages held).

[c]Excludes stock held in own company by self-employed persons.

[d]Includes value of corporate stock for persons employed by self-owned corporations. The value of this stock was $271.1 billion in wave 4 and $229.8 billion in wave 7. For purposes of comparisons with FFA data, these values should be added to "stocks and matched fund shares" and subtracted from "own business or profession."

[e]Includes mortgages held from sale of real estate, amount due from sale of business, unit trusts, and other financial investments.

sector in the latter accounts. A rough estimate of the 1984 assets of this sector was $530 billion. A third difference is population coverage; SIPP excludes the institutional and military populations. Finally, it should be noted that the FFA household-sector estimates are essentially the residuals that remain after allocations are made to other sectors and are not free from measurement error.

Table 9.10 compares SIPP and FFA estimates for 1984 by attempting to combine and adjust the categories where necessary. Two categories that are common are equity in own home and motor vehicle equity. The SIPP estimate of home equity is far greater than the FFA estimate ($2.8 trillion vs. $1.9 trillion). The SIPP estimate of $0.4 trillion for vehicle equity was slightly less than the FFA estimate of $0.5 trillion.

In order to compare holdings of financial assets, we must add together two categories from the FFA estimates—"deposits and credit market instruments" and "corporate equities"—shown in table 9.11, adjust this sum for personal trust and nonprofit-sector holdings, and compare the adjusted sum to the sum of certain SIPP categories.

The SIPP categories that make up the estimate of financial assets include stock and mutual fund shares, interest-earning assets, regular checking accounts, savings bonds, IRA and Keogh accounts, other financial assets, and the amount of corporate stock included in the SIPP category "own business or profession" (certain corporate stock is counted in this category because of the design of the questionnaire). Table 9.10 shows that the FFA estimate of financial assets was $3.4 trillion, compared to a SIPP estimate of $2.5 trillion. The final category to be compared is equity in noncorporate business. The FFA estimate for this category was $2.5 trillion. The SIPP estimate, obtained by

Table 9.10   Comparison of SIPP and FFA Estimates of Household Wealth (in trillions of dollars)

Category	SIPP (wave 4)	FFA (fourth quarter 1984)
1. Equity in own home	2.8	1.9
2. Equity in motor vehicles	.4	.5
3. Financial assets	2.5[a]	3.4[b]
4. Equity in noncorporate business	1.0[c]	2.5

[a]Sum of stock and mutual fund shares ($0.5 trillion), interest-earning assets ($1.2 trillion), regular checking accounts ($43 billion), savings bonds ($33 billion), value of IRA and Keogh accounts ($0.2 trillion), other financial assets ($0.3 trillion), and the amount of corporate stock included in the SIPP category of "own business or profession" ($0.3 trillion).

[b]Sum of deposits and credit market instruments ($3.3 trillion) and corporate equities ($1.5 trillion) less estimated value of estates and personal trusts ($0.9 trillion) and nonprofit sector assets ($0.5 trillion).

[c]Sum of equity in own business or profession ($0.8 trillion) less value of corporate stock included in this category ($0.3 trillion) plus equity in rental property ($0.6 trillion).

Table 9.11   FFA Estimates of Household- and Nonprofit-Sector Net Worth: Fourth Quarter 1984 and Fourth Quarter 1985 (in constant dollars)

Characteristic	Value of Asset or Liability (in billions)			Value of Asset or Liability per Household		
	1984	1985	Difference	1984	1985	Difference
A. Equity in own home	1,927.5	1,810.8	−116.7	22,188	20,474	−1,714
B. Equity in motor vehicles	473.3	511.8	38.5	5,448	5,787	339
C. Deposits and credit market instruments[a]	3,321.0	3,557.9	236.9	38,229	40,228	1,999
D. Corporate equities[a]	1,493.0	1,880.7	387.7	17,186	21,265	4,079
E. Equity in noncorporate business[a]	2,510.8	2,396.0	−114.8	28,903	27.091	−1,812
F. Consumer debt, excluding mortgages and automobile debt[a]	512.4	571.0	58.6	5,898	6,456	558
G. Sum of A–E minus F	9,213.2	9,586.2	373.0	106,056	108,388	2,332
Addendum: Pension fund reserves	1,435.3	1,659.0	223.7	16,522	18,758	2,236

[a]Includes amounts held in personal trusts and by nonprofit organizations.

adding together own business or profession (less the corporate stock included in this category) and equity in rental property, was $1.0 trillion.

If the FFA estimates are taken at face value, it would appear that SIPP seriously underestimates wealth held in the form of financial assets and business equity and seriously overestimates wealth held in the form of home equity. On the basis of comparisons with other household survey estimates of home equity and of validation studies of survey estimates of home value (Wolters and Woltman 1974), we think it unlikely that the SIPP estimate of home equity is seriously biased. We conclude that the FFA estimate of home equity is not a good reference figure. Validation studies of survey estimates of financial assets show that the failure to report ownership of financial assets is a serious problem (Ferber et al. 1968, 1969), and the evidence seems strong that the SIPP estimates of holdings in the form of financial assets have a serious downward bias. Finally, the SIPP estimate of business equity is well below the FFA estimate. Again, it seems likely that the SIPP estimate has a serious downward bias, but a definitive conclusion could be reached only after some form of validation study.

The above comparison leaves out the SIPP category "other real estate" (about $0.3 trillion). Some of the assets in this category are vacation homes; some probably belong in the "own business" category.

9.5   Changes in Net Worth at the Individual Household Level

The discussion thus far has been concerned with the comparison between cross-section estimates. Because SIPP is a panel survey, it is possible to measure changes in net worth at the individual household level. In order to do so, we began with households as they existed on the wave 7 file and matched back to the wave 4 file. We considered a match to exist if the householder in the wave 7 household was present as a householder or spouse of householder in the wave 4 file. We classified the matched household as "having no change in composition" if each wave 7 adult was present in the wave 4 household and each wave 4 adult was present in the wave 7 household. The "matched household" file produces estimates that are not strictly comparable to the wave 4 and wave 7 files taken separately. Some households were not present in wave 7 because of a sample cut that occurred between the two waves.

In interpreting these matched results shown in tables 9.12 and 9.13, it should be remembered that the imputation procedures used for wave 4 and wave 7 were independent. The imputation procedures give cross-section results that are reasonable, but the estimates of change produced by two independent procedures cannot be expected to be reasonable.

Table 9.12   Matched Households: Change in Net Worth From Wave 4 to Wave 7 by Imputation Status and by Change in Composition Status of the Household (in current dollars)

| | | Percentage with Specified Change in Net Worth from Wave 4 to Wave 7 | | | | | | | Mean Difference between Wave 4 and Wave 7 ($) |
| | | Decrease | | | Decrease or Increase: Less Than $1,000 | Increase | | | |
Characteristic	Number	$10,000 or More	$5,000 to $9,999	$1,000 to $4,999		$1,000 to $4,999	$5,000 to $9,999	$10,000 or More	
No imputation:									
Total	34,380	14.6	5.9	13.2	22.8	15.3	8.3	19.9	2,686
No change in composition:									
Married-couple family	16,556	15.0	6.5	12.9	13.4	15.3	10.2	26.7	5,329
Female family householder	3,451	6.9	2.5	11.3	49.1	15.6	5.7	8.9	2,224
Male family householder	615	7.2	2.7	10.1	30.2	15.6	12.2	22.0	5,947
Nonfamily householder	9,187	11.3	5.8	13.5	32.1	15.7	7.0	14.6	2,361
Change in composition:									
Married, husband present in wave 4:									
Widowed in wave 7	155	27.6	9.7	.0	7.7	18.8	4.0	32.2	12,593
Separated or divorced in wave 7	380	27.3	8.7	29.7	16.8	11.9	4.7	.9	−11,481
Some imputation:									
Total	50,672	30.4	6.2	8.1	8.1	9.0	6.2	31.8	−38
No change in composition:									
Married-couple family	27,726	28.9	5.6	7.3	5.6	8.2	6.6	37.6	6,962
Female family householder	3,534	26.0	6.0	10.9	17.7	11.7	4.6	23.1	2,593
Male family householder	923	30.9	6.4	8.6	6.9	9.7	9.7	27.8	−23,240
Nonfamily householder	9,605	27.5	7.8	8.9	12.8	10.1	6.6	26.4	3,462

(continued)

Table 9.12 (continued)

Characteristic	Number	Decrease			Decrease or Increase: Less Than $1,000	Increase			Mean Difference between Wave 4 and Wave 7 ($)
		$10,000 or More	$5,000 to $9,999	$1,000 to $4,999		$1,000 to $4,999	$5,000 to $9,999	$10,000 or More	
Change in composition: Married, husband present in wave 4:									
Widowed in wave 7	248	34.8	2.9	11.4	12.2	3.8	8.4	26.4	−8,499
Separated or divorced in wave 7	514	39.4	4.4	18.3	8.4	12.5	4.6	12.5	−46,151
No imputation, feedback form used:									
Total	16,752	14.1	5.2	13.2	22.8	16.5	8.9	19.3	1,947
No change in composition:									
Married-couple family	8,149	13.6	6.7	12.3	14.4	16.3	10.4	26.2	5,846
Female family householder	1,499	7.9	1.7	13.2	48.8	17.2	5.6	5.5	−1,001
Male family householder	301	8.1	5.4	10.8	33.1	13.9	10.7	18.0	4,879
Nonfamily householder	4,656	12.2	3.5	14.1	31.3	17.5	8.7	12.8	95
Change in composition: Married, husband present in wave 4:									
Widowed in wave 7	93	36.5	5.6	...	7.2	25.5	...	25.1	a
Separated or divorced in wave 7	168	23.8	15.2	24.6	21.0	4.9	10.5	...	a

No imputation, feedback form not used:								
Total	17,628	15.2	6.6	13.2	22.7	14.1	7.8	20.5	3,387
No change in composition:									
Married-couple family	8,406	16.3	6.3	13.4	12.4	14.4	10.0	27.2	4,828
Female family householder	1,951	6.2	3.1	9.9	49.3	14.3	5.7	11.5	4,701
Male family householder	314	6.3	. . .	9.5	27.4	17.4	13.7	25.8	6,973
Nonfamily householder	4,531	10.5	8.2	12.8	32.9	13.8	5.3	16.5	4,689
Change in composition:									
Married, husband present in wave 4:									
Widowed in wave 7	61	14.1	15.8	. . .	8.5	8.5	10.1	43.0	a
Separated or divorced in wave 7	212	30.1	3.6	33.8	13.5	17.4	. . .	1.6	−13,892
No imputation:									
Income quintile in wave 4:									
Lowest	8,538	7.2	4.8	11.5	49.5	13.0	5.1	8.9	2,050
Second lowest	7,225	12.0	6.0	15.2	23.9	20.5	7.6	14.8	3,485
Middle	6,828	14.6	6.3	17.2	13.8	18.3	10.2	19.7	2,164
Second highest	6,577	19.7	6.5	12.8	9.7	14.1	11.0	26.2	2,422
Highest	5,213	24.2	6.3	8.7	5.6	9.4	8.6	37.3	3,634

[a] Base less than 200,000.

Table 9.13   **Matched Households: Mean Net Worth in Wave 4 and Wave 7 by Imputation Status and Selected Household Characteristics (in current dollars, with standard errors in parentheses)**

Characteristic	Number (in thousands)	Wave 4	Wave 7	Wave 7 Minus Wave 4
		No Items Imputed in Either Wave 4 or Wave 7		
		Mean Net Worth		
All households	34,380	49,754 (539)	52,440 (568)	2,686
Composition change status:				
No change in composition:				
Married-couple family	16,556	66,493 (941)	71,821 (967)	5,328
Female family householder	3,451	18,174 (770)	20,397 (961)	2,223
Male family householder	615	37,283 (2,599)	43,229 (2,578)	5,946
Nonfamily householder	9,187	36,249 (788)	38,609 (874)	2,360
Change in composition:				
Married, husband present in wave 4:				
Widowed in wave 7	155	115,456 (17,856)	128,049 (23,455)	12,593 (8,105)
Separated or divorced in wave 7	380	27,076 (1,901)	15,594 (1,196)	−11,482
Race and Hispanic origin:				
White	29,582	54,883 (607)	58,084 (643)	3,201
Black	4,072	11,853 (472)	11,562 (489)	−291
Hispanic origin	1,932	18,513 (1,192)	20,030 (1,227)	1,517
		One or More Items Imputed in Either Wave 4 or Wave 7		
All households	50,671	101,118 (1,326)	101,080 (1,116)	−38
Composition change status:				
No change in composition:				
Married-couple family	27,726	122,946 (2,232)	129,908 (1,852)	6,962
Female family householder	3,534	53,450 (1,656)	56,042 (1,995)	2,592
Male family householder	923	105,721 (7,543)	82,481 (4,795)	−23,240

Table 9.13   (continued)

Characteristic	Number (in thousands)	One or More Items Imputed in Either Wave 4 or Wave 7		
		Mean Net Worth		
		Wave 4	Wave 7	Wave 7 Minus Wave 4
Nonfamily householder	9,605	63,945 (1,155)	67,407 (1,507)	3,462
Change in composition: Married, husband present in wave 4:				
Widowed in wave 7	248	95,169 (8,010)	86,670 (8,611)	−8,499
Separated or divorced in wave 7	514	78,352 (6,768)	32,201 (2,526)	−46,151
Race and Hispanic origin:				
White	44,268	110,202 (1,505)	109,676 (1,257)	−526
Black	5,282	25,919 (548)	30,668 (1,136)	4,749
Hispanic origin	2,184	48,417	48,396	−21
		No Items Imputed in Either Wave 4 or Wave 7		
Age of householder:				
Under 35 years	12,652	16,982 (390)	16,567 (319)	−415
35–44 years	6,708	47,854 (1,075)	50,812 (1,083)	2,958
45–54 years	3,971	74,978 (2,470)	79,515 (2,611)	4,537
55–64 years	4,285	85,723 (1,934)	92,552 (2,105)	6,829
65 years and over	6,765	75,342 (1,292)	79,846 (1,420)	4,504
Income quintile in wave 4:				
Lowest	8,538	17,249 (453)	19,299 (526)	2,050
Second lowest	7,225	33,859 (712)	37,345 (889)	3,486
Middle	6,828	45,893 (887)	48,057 (958)	2,164
Second highest	6,577	65,316 (1,369)	67,739 (1,384)	2,423
Highest	5,213	110,448 (2,371)	114,082 (2,440)	3,634

(*continued*)

Table 9.13   (continued)

| | One or More Items Imputed in Either Wave 4 or Wave 7 | | |
| | Number (in thousands) | Mean Net Worth | | |
Characteristic		Wave 4	Wave 7	Wave 7 Minus Wave 4
Age of householder:				
Under 35 years	13,516	39,807 (838)	31,592 (647)	−8,215
35–44 years	10,306	84,698 (1,447)	102,139 (2,809)	17,441
45–54 years	8,563	134,401 (5,062)	116,509 (3,170)	−17,892
55–64 years	8,189	153,140 (3,007)	157,856 (3,375)	4,716
65 years and over	10,098	129,532 (3,945)	133,883 (2,575)	4,351
Income quintile in wave 4:				
Lowest	8,428	43,490 (856)	47,220 (1,377)	3,730
Second lowest	9,775	55,774 (836)	62,307 (1,433)	6,533
Middle	10,186	63,839 (949)	71,291 (1,161)	7,452
Second highest	10,432	86,417 (1,246)	94,975 (1,769)	8,558
Highest	11,851	224,480 (5,263)	202,339 (3,970)	−22,141

Table 9.12 shows the percentage distribution of various household groups by their change in net worth from wave 4 to wave 7. For all matched households without imputations, about 15 percent had a decline of $10,000 or more, 20 percent had an increase of $10,000 or more, 23 percent had an increase or decrease of less than $1,000, and the rest had declines or increases in the $1,000–$9,999 range. It is difficult to determine the extent to which these estimates reflect real changes and the extent to which they represent measurement problems. We can start by considering that only 2 percent of households have annual incomes of $100,000 or more. For 98 percent of households, then, a change in net worth of $10,000 is a very large change. If asset prices were stable, a $10,000 increase in net worth would mean that more than 10 percent of current income had been saved. We know, of course, that asset prices were not stable during our reference period. The value

of the average share of stock listed on the New York Stock Exchange increased by 12 percent from late 1984 to late 1985. Our data from SIPP, however, show that only about 20 percent of households owned stock and that the average value of stock portfolios was about $27,000 in late 1984. Given these considerations, it seems likely that the measured changes in the net worth of individual households has a large error component.

Table 9.12 shows estimates for households with no change in composition and for a certain set of households that did have a change in composition. Households without a change in composition had, on the average, an increase in net worth. Married-couple households had an average increase of $5,329, for example, although 34 percent had a decrease of $1,000 or more, and 15 percent had a decrease of $10,000 or more. The universes for two groups of households that did have a change—wave 7 widows who were married, spouse present in wave 4, and wave 7 divorced or separated women who were married, spouse present in wave 4—are quite small. The data show an average net worth increase of $13,000 for the widows and an average decrease of $11,000 for the divorced and separated.

The "some imputation" panel of table 9.12 shows net worth change data for households that had one or more net worth items imputed in either wave 4 or wave 7. As discussed earlier, the fact that the wave 4 and wave 7 imputation procedures were independent essentially eliminates these households as a data source for analyzing changes in the net worth of individual households. About 62 percent of the households in this group had a change of $10,000 or more. Unfortunately, there are more households in the "imputed" group than in the "nonimputed" group. Sixty percent of all matched households had one more imputed net worth item in either wave 4 or wave 7.

There is some evidence that the feedback procedure reduces the estimates of change. The "no imputation, feedback form used" panel of table 9.12 presents data for those matched households with no imputation who were in the feedback sample. The mean difference in net worth for this group was $1,947, versus $3,387 for matched, nonimputed households who were not in the feedback sample. The proportion of feedback sample households with changes of $10,000 or more was 33 percent for the feedback sample and 36 percent for the nonfeedback sample.

The data in the last panel of table 9.12 show a reasonable relation between income level and change in net worth. One would expect that large changes would be more common for high-income than for low-income households, and the data support this expectation. Approximately 37 percent of households in the highest-income quintile had an increase of $10,000 or more, 24 percent had a decrease of $10,000 or more, and 6 percent had a change of less than $1,000. In comparison, 9 percent of households in the lowest quintile had an increase of $10,000 or more, 7 percent had a decrease of $10,000 or more, and 50 percent had a change smaller than $1,000.

9.6   Fitting a Savings Model

We have used the SIPP data to fit a simple model of savings in which the change in net worth is a function of the level of total net worth and income at the beginning of the period, the change in income during the period, and certain characteristics of the householder, including age, marital status, and race and ethnicity. The set of observations was limited to those households without a change in composition who had no imputed net worth items.

The results of regressing the change in net worth on the independent variables are summarized in table 9.14. The regression was significant and had an R^2 of 0.08. The income variables had a significant positive effect on savings (the value of their coefficients were more than twice as large as the standard errors), wave 4 net worth had a negative and

Table 9.14   Savings Regression Results for Savings Regression Model

Independent Variable	Coefficient Value	Standard Error
Wave 4 net worth	−.15*	.01
Wave 4 income level	4.55*	.43
Change in income	6.35	.44
Age of householder:[a]		
Under 35 years	−15,301.94*	2,271.51
35–44 years	−12,055.77*	2,481.98
45–54 years	−4,477.93	2,799.11
65 years and over	273.76	2,407.95
Married, spouse present[b]	2,639.80	1,479.36
Black[c]	−4,261.40	2,178.16
Other[c]	−936.43	4,826.76
Spanish[d]	−2,427.58	3,014.06
Constant	9,435.24	

Note: $R^2 = .08$.

[a]Control group is 55–64 years of age.

[b]Control group is other than married, spouse present.

[c]Control group is white.

[d]Control group is non-Hispanic.

*Significant at the .05 significance level.

significant coefficient, the age groups "less than 35 years" and "45–54 years" had a significant negative effect, and the other variables were not significant. These regressions are consistent with the results obtained by Projector when she regressed 1963 savings on 1963 disposable income and December 1962 net worth. In that study, the coefficient of income was positive, the coefficient of net worth was negative, and the R^2 was 0.04 (Projector 1968).

9.7 Reply to Comment

In his discussion of this paper, Martin H. David has provided an extremely valuable critique of household wealth surveys in general and the SIPP survey in particular. We agree with many of his points, but we also note that the measurement of household wealth per se has not been viewed as a primary purpose of SIPP. We hope that some of the suggested changes can be adopted, but changes that are costly or that impinge on other aspects of the survey are unlikely to occur. In the area of survey procedures, David recommends that an effort be made to interview the household member who is best able to provide financial information. He also recommends that the questionnaire be modified to obtain data on assets held in trust for children, on business investments in which the person does not play an active management role, and on certain other assets not presently covered. A third major recommendation is to ask respondents to examine records when possible. All these recommendations seem useful.

David makes a strong case for conducting validation studies. He notes that previous studies identified the problem of false negatives as a major factor in the tendency of survey estimates to fall short of independent estimates. He suggests that information from validation studies could be used to correct for false negatives (change some of the "no" responses) and would provide a basis for imputing amounts to persons who refuse to answer questions on ownership or value.

We agree completely with his statement that the wealth data should be subjected to longitudinal editing and imputation procedures if the data file is to be used to examine changes in wealth. We have attempted to circumvent this problem in some of our analysis by restricting the universe to cases that did not require imputation in either of the two waves, but this approach sacrifices large amounts of data.

The implementation of any of these changes will depend on a review of the evidence concerning their likely benefit and a comparison of the likely benefit with the likely cost. For example, the suggestion that an attempt be made to interview the household member who is most knowledgeable about finances would be accepted only if it could be demonstrated that the cost was small in terms of field resources, response rates, and the quality of other types of data.

9.8   Conclusions

The major purpose of this paper was to present an evaluation of SIPP data on household wealth. The major aspect of the evaluation was comparison of the net worth levels of individual households as reported in interviews conducted one year apart. Other methods of evaluation included comparisons with SCF and FFA estimates. The major findings include the following.

1. A comparison of median net worth estimates from wave 4 and wave 7 shows that SIPP estimates of the relative wealth holdings of various population subgroups are remarkably stable.

2. Household survey estimates of aggregate and mean net worth are very sensitive to "outliers" (cases with very high values). These outliers may represent response errors or marking errors, or they may, in fact, be an accurate estimate of the holdings of an individual. In the latter case, the outlier may or may not be multiplied by an appropriate weight when the raw survey data are converted to estimates of the wealth of U.S. households.

3. The problem of outliers is so severe that analyses and evaluations of household survey wealth data that are based solely on aggregate or mean estimates are subject to serious questions about validity.

4. The large differences between wave 4 and wave 7 in the holdings of individual households is additional evidence that household wealth estimates are subject to large reporting or marking errors.

The finding that SIPP produces stable estimates of median net worth suggests that SIPP provides important new data on population subgroup differences in net worth. The relatively large sample size and an estimate of median net worth that is larger than the SCF estimate means that SIPP is the preferred data set for this purpose. The value of SIPP net worth estimates is enhanced by the rich array of demographic, social, and economic data collected during the life of the panel (e.g., personal history characteristics, program participation status, and employer benefit recipiency).

We concur with Martin David that certain questionnaire and procedural changes would improve the quality of SIPP wealth data, but we are cautious about the desirability of major changes. We note that differences between household surveys in estimates of mean and aggregate net worth are strongly influenced by outliers. In the absence of validation studies, we are not prepared to accept an increase in estimated mean or aggregate wealth as evidence that a better source of data has been obtained.

Notes

1. The first wave of interviews with the 1984 panel households was conducted in October, November, and December 1983 and January 1984. In general, a wave is a complete set of interviews with the sample households and is completed over a four-month period.
2. For a description of these forms of wealth, see the note to table 9.1.

References

Avery, Robert B., and Gregory E. Elliehausen. 1986. Financial characteristics of high income families. *Federal Reserve Bulletin* (March): 163–277.

Avery, Robert B., Gregory E. Elliehausen, Glenn B. Canner, and Thomas A. Gustafson. 1984a. Survey of consumer finances, 1983. *Federal Reserve Bulletin* (September): 679–92.

———. 1984b. Survey of consumer finances, 1983: A second report. *Federal Reserve Bulletin* (December): 857–68.

Cartwright, William S., and Robert B. Friedland. 1985. The President's Commission on Pension Policy Household Survey, 1979: Net wealth distributions by type and age for the United States. *Review of Income and Wealth* (September): 285–308.

Durkin, Thomas A., and Gregory E. Elliehausen. 1978. 1977 Consumer Credit Survey. Washington, D.C.: Board of Governors of the Federal Reserve System.

Ferber, Robert, J. Forsythe, H. W. Guthrie, and E. S. Maynes. 1968. Validation of consumer financial characteristics: Common stock. *Journal of the American Statistical Association*, 415–32.

———. 1969. Validation of a national survey of consumer financial characteristics: Savings accounts. *Review of Economics and Statistics*, 436–44.

Joint Economic Committee. U.S. Congress. 1986. The concentration of wealth in the United States. Washington, D.C.: U.S. Government Printing Office, July.

Lamas, Enrique J., and John M. McNeil. 1984. The measurement of household wealth in the Survey of Income and Program Participation. *1984 Proceedings of the Social Statistics Section, American Statistical Association* (August): 484–89.

———. 1985. Household asset ownership and wealth holdings in 1984: Data from the Survey of Income and Program Participation. Paper presented at the meeting of the American Economic Association, New York City, December.

———. 1986. Factors associated with household net worth. Paper presented at the meeting of the American Economic Association, New Orleans, December.

Pearl, Robert, and Matilda Frankel. 1982. Composition of the personal wealth of American households at the start of the eighties. Urbana: Survey Research Laboratory, University of Illinois.

Projector, Dorothy S. 1968. Survey of changes in family finances. Washington, D.C.: Board of Governors of the Federal Reserve System.

Projector, Dorothy S., and Gertrude S. Weiss. 1966. Survey of financial characteristics of consumers. Washington, D.C.: Board of Governors of the Federal Reserve System.

Radner, Daniel. 1984. The wealth and income of aged households. *Proceedings of the Social Statistics Section, American Statistical Association* (August): 490–95.

U.S. Bureau of the Census. 1986. Household wealth and asset ownership: 1984. Ser. P-70, no. 7. Washington, D.C.: U.S. Government Printing Office.

Wolters, Charles, and Henry Woltman. 1974. Special study on value of home. 1970 Census, Prelinimary Evaluation Results Memorandum, no. 48, addendum 1. Washington, D.C.: U.S. Bureau of the Census.

Comment   Martin H. David

What's New?

The McNeil and Lamas paper reports on a measurement design that is new in a number of regards. It is the largest sample for wealth measurement that has been studied in the United States. It is an ongoing effort that will generate annual wealth estimates at least to 1988 because those data collections are in the pipeline. The most interesting innovation is the use of conditioning from a prior interview to aid the recall of the respondent in the "feedback experiment."

Most of the results from these measurements were predicted by previous methodologists working in the field of wealth measurement. All the problems were uncovered in the pilot wealth measurement of the Income Survey Development Program (ISDP; Radner and Vaughn 1987). The Bureau of the Census was publicly advised by its advisory committees (in 1982 and 1983) that a program of wealth measurement must be accompanied by a strong program of validation research and methodological studies if the results were to be credible. That advice still holds—my remarks will concentrate on why we need validation research and why methodological studies will pay off.

Features of the SIPP design

Several features of the Survey of Income and Program Participation (SIPP) design must be noted before I comment on the nature of the data collected.

1. For married couples, jointly held property, income, debt, and wealth is reported by the first spouse to be interviewed. Otherwise, the person who is the owner is to report for himself, except that 35 percent of all reports are given by proxies. No attempt is made to

Martin H. David is professor of economics at the University of Wisconsin—Madison. He is currently directing SIPP-ACCESS, an on-line facility for extracting data from the Survey of Income and Program Participation, including the wealth data reported here.

identify the member of the household who specializes in financial matters and who is most likely to be informed about nonearned income.

2. The data are collected from a sample that is defined one year prior to the first wealth measurement. Aging of the population implies that some wealth exits the sample as people move into retirement and nursing homes. This loss does not occur in cross-sectional samples.

3. The conduct of prior interviews conditions respondents. After the first wave, income from assets is elicited in four steps. (a) Receipt of income from property reported in the previous wave is recalled, and the respondent is asked to verify that receipt. (b) The respondent is asked whether receipt of that income continued in the current reference period. (c) The respondent is shown a card describing fourteen types of property income and is asked whether receipt of any of those types was initiated during the period. (d) At a later stage of the interview, questions on the amount of income and the amount of the asset balance are asked for groups of interest-bearing asset items for which recipiency was previously reported.

4. Assets held in trust for children, control over wealth through powers of attorney, and wealth held in irrevocable trusts are nowhere recorded.

5. Respondents are not asked to check records before reporting income or asset amounts.

6. Ownership of a self-employed business enterprise is elicited through a sequence of questions related to "working." Passive partnership interests, other than rent-producing interests, are elicited from a residual category in the list of fourteen asset types mentioned in point 3c above.

What Have We Learned?

Validation Studies of Savings and Common Stock

In their validation studies of common stock holdings and savings account, Ferber et al. (1969a, 1969b) indicate five types of response by the owners of the accounts sampled (see table C9.1). False negatives (group 3) accounted for 20 and 33 percent of the respondents in the two studies. Refusals of amounts have validated means 20 and 80 percent higher than those of reporters (a response likely to be characterized by nonignorable selection). Noninterviews show differences in the two studies, with refusers having substantially larger savings than reporters and noncontacts having somewhat larger share holdings.

The implications of these findings are that it is necessary to find ways to alter false negative reports in addition to imputation and that it may be necessary to use data from validation studies to impute holdings of item refusals rather than using the hot deck imputation from reporters.

Table C9.1

Group	Interviewed?	Ownership	Amount
1. Complete	Yes	Report	Reported
2. Presence	Yes	+ Report	N.A.
3. False negatives	Yes	− Report	N.I.U.
4. Refused:			
a) Interview	Yes	N.A.	N.A.
b) Answers to financial questions	No	N.I.U.	N.I.U.
5. No contract	No	N.I.U.	N.I.U.

Note: N.A. = not ascertained.
N.I.U. = not in universe.

Motivation of Respondents and Use of Records

Extensive work by Ferber (1966), Maynes (1965), Horn (1960), and Claycamp (1963) has established that asking the respondent to check records results in more precise information. While it is obvious that use of a record will increase accuracy for the records retrieved, it is not so obvious that use of records will also reduce the proportion of false negatives. Evidence appears favorable for this latter effect. Lansing, Ginsburg, and Braaten (1961) and Cannell, Miller, and Oksenberg (1981) explain this phenomenon as a process of conditioning the respondent to what is expected of a respondent who is fulfilling the objectives of the survey. Both argue that high-quality response depends on cognitive recognition of the information that is desired in concert with positive motivation to perform the mental work that is required to recall the information.

The experimental work of Cannell, Miller, and Oksenberg (1981) on survey design is a model of what needs to be done to improve the adequacy of financial data reporting. Their experiments include the use of a "contract" to establish an obligation to report, specific instructions incorporated into the question as to the type of response that is needed, and programmed reinforcement of responses that adequately answer the question. (By way of contrast, the SIPP questionnaire approaches the problem of reporting amounts by confounding the reports of several types of assets in one response, when the respondent may think of those assets as distinct and separate classes. This increases the potential for response error [Sudman and Bradburn 1974].)

In related work, Bradburn and Sudman (1980) make it clear that longer, open-ended questions and devices to assure confidentiality of responses assist in reducing the response distortions that arise from revealing threatening information. While economists are not likely to think of reports of balance sheet items as threatening, psychological research has established that respondents are more reluctant to give out such information than other intimate facts pertaining to their sex life and mild law-breaking behavior (Cannell and Henson 1974).

Evidence of Reporting Adequacy

Few results in the validation research give easily measured correlates of response insufficiency. Three are worthy of further work: respondent rounding of reports, respondents' failure to keep records of money spent, and respondent learning of parental income amounts no earlier than age sixteen (or never). Lansing, Ginsburg, and Braaten (1961) find that each of these three attributes is associated with failures to report savings accounts or inaccuracy as to amount.

Incentives and Panels

Received wisdom is that the mean square error of measurement falls as the number of contacts in a panel increases. Ferber (1966, 212; 1964), Lansing, Ginsburg, and Braaten (1961, 186), and Lansing and Morgan (1971) all affirm a view that attrition of noncooperative respondents early in a panel and the opportunity to check measurements made at a prior time will enhance the precision of a panel relative to cross-sectional results.

How Does SIPP Perform on Asset Measures?

I consider Ferber's five categories in reverse order.

Categories 4–5: Noninterview

McNeil and Lamas report the Bureau's household noninterview rate (11 percent for wave 4). I believe that this is misleading, as the households that are formed in the year since the area probability sample was drawn are added to both the numerator and the denominator of this fraction. These household "splits" do not constitute independent drawings and will have a high intraclass correlation with the original sample members. They do not therefore contribute to representation in the same way as the losses experienced through attrition subtract from representation. Even so, the noninterview rate is undoubtedly less than that of the Survey Research Center, and this fact makes it important to use the SIPP capabilities for wealth measurement.

Category 3: False Negatives

The only evidence for this problem comes from a comparison of ISDP asset data to income aggregates. The amount of dividends and interest, after longitudinal imputation, appears to be near the relevant benchmark aggregate (Vaughn, Whiteman, and Lininger 1984, table 8). The interest and dividend income imputed to assets (which were themselves imputed to the extent of 23–66 percent [U.S. Bureau of the

Census 1986, table D-2]) amounts to 69 percent of the aggregate. While imputation rates on SIPP are 13–42 percent for the same asset types, it is not clear that any changes in the mode of eliciting ownership of property income sources reduced the false negative problem. This area is an area in which validating studies such as David et al. (1986) need to be done to assess both the quality of reporting and the appropriateness of imputations.

Categories 2 and 4b: Item Nonresponse

Point 3 above, explaining the design, suggests that insufficient effort is made to identify new sources of property income that develop in the course of the panel and that insufficient effort is made at any time in the survey to identify partnership interests that involve silent partners.

Category 2: Item Nonresponse

Curtin, Juster, and Morgan (chap. 10, in this vol.) tabulate the available percentages of nonresponse to recipiency and amount questions. (It would be valuable to have the complete tabulation. It would be even more valuable to differentiate refusals from other types of nonresponse, given the significance of noncooperation as evidence of threat, while incomplete response can occur for a variety of reasons, including deficiencies in questionnaire design, processing, and enumerator ability.) It appears that SIPP item nonresponse levels are larger than those for the Survey Research Center's cross-sectional samples.

The high rates of item nonresponse to amount questions must be correlated with the failure of SIPP to locate the financial recordkeeper in many households (point 1 above). It is a mark of the deficient design of SIPP that nearly one-seventh of respondents fail to report amounts in savings accounts. At a minimum, something could be done to classify the amounts in these accounts into orders of magnitude. The 40 percent of respondents who fail to report debt on stocks and bonds indicates that either respondent motivation or cognition of the desired information is wanting.

A second mark of the deficiency of the design is that McNeil and Lamas's table 9.4 implies that one-quarter of all asset values have been imputed in wave 4. Sixty percent of all matched households in their table 9.11 have at least one wealth item imputed; for the highest income quintile, the proportion is 70 percent. While these imputations may not dominate the values of net worth for most households, the prospect is profoundly unsettling.

What Steps for the Future?

This extended discussion of methodological work on survey design provides a road map for future work with SIPP. Five steps appear to be high priority for redesign of the wealth measurement. First, the rules for choosing respondents should elicit property income information from the informed members of the household. To ease the cognitive task of assembling that information, I believe the children's assets should also be included so that a parent does not need to make some abstract legal distinctions to report completely.

Second, the prompts for property income following the first wave need to be developed. Most respondents confronted with a list of fourteen items will not pay equal attention to all parts of the list. As a result, some types of income will be missed.

Third, records should be requested and reinforcement given to the responses that exhaustively report an entire portfolio. Qualitative followups should be given to persons who cannot supply exact amounts to establish orders of magnitude.

Fourth, more questions eliciting income from partnership ventures should be included.

Fifth, a carefully orchestrated set of validation studies based on samples of individuals owning assets drawn from the accounts of institutions should be pursued. Armed with calibration functions derived from such studies, the Bureau would be in a position to make sensible imputations to those who refuse to participate and whose nonresponse is likely to be nonignorable (cf. Ferber 1965).

Analysis of the Wealth Data

Equally informative work can be done to exploit the data already available. The SIPP contains the basis for longitudinal imputation. Simple models of the change in asset holding and asset amount can be used to impute item nonresponse that is missing in one period (because a proxy interview was taken) but available in a second (because the interview was taken with the informed respondent). This work is already underway (Kalton and Miller 1986), but the methods should be applied to imputation across years for the wealth data.

A second device that is worth exploiting is the reinterview information that is recovered at every wave of SIPP. Since the recipiency of the prior wave is validated in the current wave, error-correcting functions can be generated, and false negatives can be identified. This will again be important when the respondent in the prior wave was a proxy and the respondent in the current wave reports for herself.

A third device that will assist in better estimation is to use the distributional information in SIPP to estimate the tail, as was done by Aigner and Goldberger (1970). While this technique can never replace a high-income sample, it can stabilize the estimates of the means and produce more informed data for policy analysis.

Analysis of Year-to-Year Change in Wealth

Lamas and McNeil (1986) have fit descriptive regressions to the 1984 asset data. They now report the change in wealth from the year-to-year matched cases. These two efforts are necessarily related. Two points need to be made.

In the interval since Projector (1968), the life-cycle model has been elaborated (e.g., Blinder 1974, 31–33) and leads us to a somewhat different specification. The intertemporal consumption allocation will be a function of inheritance, the human capital endowment, interest rates, and two subjective measures—the rate of time preference and the taste for bequests. This specification differs from the permanent income specifications of the 1960s, and McNeil and Lamas may find it more productive. It would imply, for example, that lifetime earnings should appear on the right-hand side of the equation, and these earnings should be better measured in the SIPP panel than in the two-wave panel used by Projector. It also implies unmeasured individual effects that can be identified only through analysis of panel data on identical individuals.

The more important point comes from Solon (n.d.) and Rogers (1986). Both speculate on the problem created by measurement error that is correlated over time. In panel surveys, we have an opportunity to exploit the data to discover some properties of that correlation. Consider the model underlying McNeil and Lamas's table 9.12:

$$(1) \qquad W(7) = aW(4) + bY(7) + cY(4) + dz + f + \epsilon_{it} + (1 - a)\mu_i \,,$$

where $W(t)$ is wealth at time t, $Y(t)$ is income for the four months prior to t, and z is a vector of personal characteristics. If $a = 1$, the nuisance parameter describing personal tastes disappears, and unbiased estimates of the parameters b, c, and d can be estimated.

If wealth and income are measured with error, we have

$$(2) \qquad \begin{aligned} W^{\phi}(t) &= W(t) + u, \\ Y^{\phi}(t) &= Y(t) + v. \end{aligned}$$

If, in addition, u and v are autocorrelated, the hope that might exist for eliminating μ_i is dashed, and consistent estimation of the parameters is not generally possible. Consider, for example, the simpler problem of estimating the autocorrelation of W, θ_w. Let θ_u represent the autocorrelation of the measurement errors. Then the estimator of θ_w,

$$\operatorname*{plim}_{n} r_w = \theta_w - [\sigma_u^2(\theta_w - \theta_u)/(\sigma_u^2 + \sigma_w^2)].$$

Unless θ_u and σ_u are measured, it is likely that θ_w cannot be estimated. Such measurements can be made as part of the ongoing SIPP wealth measurements. While this may appear to be a counsel of despair, it does recognize the dominant message of these remarks—there is correlated error in the measurement of wealth data. Attempts to obtain estimates of that error will make it possible to extract important behavioral parameters from such data as we are now discussing.

The potential for much more informative wealth information from SIPP exists.

Appendix

Review of McNeil-Lamas Tables

Table 9.1

The change estimated reflects different samples; furthermore, identical individuals will be one year older and may have changed marital status and income quintile. Thus, care should be exercised in interpreting these estimates of net change over time. The age group that shows the largest loss is the group that is at highest risk for divorce and for paying college expenses. It will be interesting to see whether this explains the significant differences.

Tables 9.4 and 9.11

These estimates suggest that at least one-fourth of the net worth is imputed.

Table 9.5

This table presents results of the feedback. It is difficult to see any effect (particularly in the absence of sampling errors). However, one might imagine a significant improvement in a small subsample: households in which the same respondent supplied information in both interviews and households characterized by complex property ownership (older or higher-earnings groups). The jury is still out on what benefit we get from this type of experiment.

Tables 9.8 and 9.9

These tables display data for comparison to the flow-of-funds accounts (FFAs). Two comments are in order. The estimates can be improved by estimating the upper tail of the distribution with a Pareto function (Aigner and Goldberger 1970). This would reduce the problem of sampling variability that arises from small proportions of very wealthy people. Second, the FFAs do not produce flawless measures, and it is widely recognized that the sectoral definition does not mesh with the household population. The best indication we have of the difficulties of the comparison is in the housing estimates. Kish and Lansing (1954) show that homeowners give unbiased estimates of house value. (While this finding is old, it has not been refuted.)

Table 9.10

This table highlights change in net worth at the micro level. The presentation by income quintile for the complete data cases is most noteworthy. Change in net worth of less than $10,000, or less than 10 percent of initial net worth levels, falls dramatically with income level. This is an indication of response error. It would be useful to see the same table for the cases in which the feedback technique was used and respondents reported for themselves.

Table 9.12

This table replicates the Projector savings regression, including a lagged adjustment to net wealth levels and a linear relation between current income and desired net wealth. The result offers promise since the explanatory power is higher and the coefficient on net worth suggests a more plausible rate of adjustment.

References

Aigner, Dennis, and Arthur S. Goldberger. 1970. Estimation of Pareto's law. *Journal of the American Statistical Association* 65:712–23.

Blinder, Alan S. 1974. *Toward an economic theory of income distribution.* Cambridge, Mass.: MIT Press.

Bradburn, Norman M., and Seymour Sudman. 1980. *Improving interview method and questionnaire design.* San Francisco: Jossey-Bass.

Cannell, Charles F., and Ramon Henson. 1974. Incentives, motives, and response bias. *Annals of Economic and Social Measurement* 3:307–17.

Cannell, Charles F., Peter V. Miller, and Lois Oksenberg. 1981. Research on interviewing techniques. In *Social Methodology, 1981.* San Francisco: Jossey-Bass.

Claycamp, Henry J. 1963. *The composition of consumer savings portfolios.* Urbana: Bureau of Economic and Business Research, University of Illinois.

David, Martin H., R. J. Little, Robert Triest, and Michael Samuhel. 1986. Alternative methods for CPS income imputation. *Journal of the American Statistical Association* 81:29–41.

Ferber, Robert. 1964. Does a panel operation increase the reliability of survey data? *Proceedings of the Social Statistics Section of the American Statistical Association,* 210–16.

———. 1965. The reliability of consumer surveys of financial holdings: Time deposits. *Journal of the American Statistical Association* 60:148–63.

———. 1966. *The reliability of consumer reports of financial assets and debts.* Urbana: Bureau of Economic and Business Research, University of Illinois.

Ferber, Robert, J. Forsythe, H. W. Guthrie, and E. S. Maynes. 1969a. Validation of a national survey of consumer financial characteristics: Savings accounts. *Review of Economics and Statistics* 51:436–44.

———. 1969b. Validation of consumer financial characteristics: Common stock. *Journal of the American Statistical Association* 64:415–32.

Horn, W. 1960. Reliability survey: A survey on the reliability of response to an interview survey. *Het PTT-bedriff* 10:105–56.

Kalton, Graham, and Michael E. Miller. 1986. Effects of adjustments for wave nonresponse on panel survey estimates. *Proceedings of the Survey Research Section of the American Statistical Association.*

Kish, Leslie, and John B. Lansing. 1954. Response errors in estimating the value of homes. *Journal of the American Statistical Association* 49:520–38.

Lamas, Enrique J., and John M. McNeil. 1986. Factors associated with household net worth. Bureau of the Census SIPP Working Paper. Washington, D.C.: Bureau of the Census.

Lansing, John B., Gerald P. Ginsburg, and Kaisa Braaten. 1961. *An investigation of response error.* Urbana: Bureau of Economic and Business Research, University of Illinois.

Lansing, John B., and James N. Morgan. 1971. *Economic survey methods.* Ann Arbor, Mich.: Survey Research Center, Institute for Social Research.

Maynes, E. S. 1963. The anatomy of response errors: Consumer saving. *Journal of Marketing Research* 2:378–87.

Projector, Dorothy S. 1968. *Survey of changes in family finances.* Washington, D.C.: Board of Governors of the Federal Reserve System.

Radner, Daniel B., and Denton R. Vaughn. 1987. Wealth, income, and the economic status of aged households. In *International comparisons of the distribution of household wealth,* ed. Edward N. Wolff. New York: Oxford University Press.

Rogers, Willard L. 1986. Comparisons of alternative approaches to the estimation of simple causal models from panel data. In *International symposium on panel data,* ed. Greg Duncan. New York: John Wiley.

Solon, Gary. n.d. The value of panel data in economic research. In *International symposium on panel data,* ed. Greg Duncan. New York: John Wiley. Forthcoming.

Sudman, Seymour, and Norman M. Bradburn. 1974. *Response effects in surveys.* Chicago: Aldine Publishing Co.

U.S. Bureau of the Census. 1986. Household wealth and asset ownership: 1984. Ser. P-70, no. 7. Washington, D.C.: U.S. Government Printing Office.

Vaughn, Denton R., T. Cameron Whiteman, and Charles A. Lininger. 1984. The quality of income and program data in the 1979 ISDP Research Panel: Some preliminary findings. *Review of Public Data Use* 12:107–131.

10 Survey Estimates of Wealth: An Assessment of Quality

Richard T. Curtin, F. Thomas Juster, and
James N. Morgan

10.1 Introduction

This paper examines the three most recent surveys of household net
worth and provides an assessment of their probable quality, their potential usefulness for analysis, and their different strengths and weaknesses. For the most part, we concentrate on the two surveys produced
at the University of Michigan's Survey Research Center (SRC)—the

Richard T. Curtin is an associate research scientist at the Survey Research Center,
Institute for Social Research, University of Michigan, Ann Arbor. F. Thomas Juster is
a professor of economics and a research scientist at the Survey Research Center, Institute
for Social Research, University of Michigan, Ann Arbor. James N. Morgan is a professor
of economics and a research scientist (emeritus) at the Survey Research Center, Institute
for Social Research, University of Michigan, Ann Arbor.

This paper owes a substantial debt to the federal agency sponsors and staff who
supported the collection of the household wealth surveys that are analyzed here. In
particular, the authors appreciate the help, interest, and financial support of the Board
of Governors of the Federal Reserve System, the Office of the Assistant Secretary for
Planning and Evaluation in the Department of Health and Human Services (the two
major sponsors of the 1983 Survey of Consumer Finances [SCF]), and the National
Science Foundation (the major sponsor of the Panel Study of Income Dynamics [PSID]).
The Department of Health and Human Services was the major supporter of the PSID
from 1973 until 1977 and an important supplementer since then.

The authors are especially grateful for the work done by Robert Avery, Greg Elliehausen, and Arthur Kennickell of the Federal Reserve Board staff, who not only devoted
a great deal of painstaking effort to cleaning the 1983 SCF data and estimating imputed
values but also provided the data that underpin secs. 10.6 and 10.7 of the paper. Fritz
Scheuren of the Internal Revenue Service staff was extensively involved in the design
and implementation of the high-income supplement to the 1983 SCF. Jack McNeil of the
U.S. Census Bureau gave us a good deal of help and guidance in interpreting the Survey
of Income and Program Participation data. The authors also wish to express their appreciation to the staff—Richard Barfield, for much of the statistical analysis in the paper,
and Esther Kerr, for preparation of the manuscript. Needless to say, the analysis and
conclusions in the paper are the sole responsibility of the authors.

1983 Survey of Consumer Finances (SCF) and the 1984 Wealth Supplement to the Panel Study of Income Dynamics (PSID)—but do pay some attention to the 1984 Wealth Supplement to the Survey of Income and Program Participation (SIPP). This differential concentration results mainly from the fact that the SIPP wealth data are the subject of a separate paper at the conference as well as from the fact that we have a comparative advantage in examination and analysis of the SCF and PSID data.

The general plan of the paper is to provide an assessment of the wealth surveys in terms of five characteristics that relate to quality: the sample and questionnaire design; the derived distribution of wealth holdings, especially the upper tail; the size of measurement errors; the incidence of item nonresponse and imputed values; and the comparison of survey estimates with independent information on national wealth. First, section 10.2 provides a description of the basic designs of the surveys. We discuss the basic sample designs, which have a great many features in common but also have specialized features; response rates and their interpretation in terms of probable quality; and the designs of the questionnaires themselves in terms of level of detail, definitions of variables, and the use of single or multiple household respondents. The major differences turn out to be the special design features of the SCF, especially the high-income supplement to that survey; the oversampling of low-income households and the longitudinal characteristics of the PSID; and the enormous difference in level of detail (and cost) between PSID and either SCF or SIPP. The PSID was a very low-cost wealth survey compared to the other two and contained substantially less detailed information on the composition of household net worth.

Section 10.3 provides some descriptive statistics for all three household wealth surveys. We start with a basic description of the composition and amount of wealth holding as estimated by the three surveys and of the distribution of the three samples by amounts of net worth reported in the surveys. These data are not quite comparable since the SIPP data available on the public use tape are top coded (truncated) in several of the net worth categories. The striking feature of these comparisons is the substantial similarity in the amounts and distribution of wealth holding across the three surveys—provided one ignores households with extremely high wealth (in excess of $0.5 million). This is not true for all types of assets, but it is certainly the dominant feature of these comparisons. Because of differences in both the estimated distributions and the estimated average wealth of relatively wealthy households, the three surveys produce substantially different estimates of total net worth for the United States as a whole—SCF shows by far the largest total, with PSID next and SIPP lowest. It appears that much of the difference in estimates of total wealth among the three surveys is due to differential estimates of wealth held in the form of common stock or business assets—types of wealth that are heavily concentrated in the population. The higher SCF wealth totals are also due in part to the oversampling of very wealthy households, resulting in a presumably more accurate representation of the wealth of such households in the total. It has been known for many years that survey estimates of wealth will typically underestimate the wealth of wealthy households unless special efforts are made to provide an adequate representation of such households in the sample design; SCF explicitly did so, while neither SIPP nor PSID was so designed.

Section 10.4 uses a model-based approach to analyze the probable measurement error in the three household surveys. Basically, we set up a version of a standard life-cycle/permanent income model of wealth holdings, in which net worth or the various components of net worth are related to income and age and to a variety of factors presumed to be associated with lifetime earnings (occupation, education, marital status, race, and sex). The basic idea is that residuals from such a model are a combination of misspecification, omitted variables, and measurement error and that differences in the explanatory power of the same model run across different surveys give some insight into the probable size of the measurement error component. We also experiment in this section with various truncations designed to reduce the weight of very high values in the analysis.

In addition to the overall assessment of the quality of net worth data measured in this way, this section also provides as many comparisons as possible between the net worth components measured in the three surveys. Complete comparability is not possible, simply because the level of aggregation differs quite a lot among the surveys. For the most part, we can compare all the net worth components for SIPP and SCF since both measure net worth with a fair level of disaggregation. We can make some global comparisons between PSID net worth categories and both SIPP and SCF, although the comparisons are not always precise because the asset definitions in PSID are not totally commensurate with those used in the other surveys.

By and large, the results of this set of analyses are quite favorable to SCF, and moderately favorable for PSID, relative to SIPP. We think there are well-defined reasons for these differences, and we relate them to differences in survey characteristics discussed in the previous sections.

Section 10.5 discusses quality as reflected by the incidence of imputed values. All survey data contain item nonresponse, and either such observations can be dropped from the analysis, or values for the missing item can be imputed. All three household wealth surveys have done extensive imputations, using somewhat different procedures. In this section, we examine the incidence of imputations, in terms of both percentage of cases for which values had to be imputed and percentage of assets or liabilities that represent imputed values rather than respondent-provided values. What turns up here is that imputed values are very high for certain types of assets in all data sets (e.g., the cash value of life insurance reserves), are relatively low for other asset types (e.g., checking or savings accounts), and differ quite a lot among the three surveys—imputations are clearly lower for SCF than for SIPP, but it is difficult to compare PSID with the other two because of the difference in aggregation.

In this section, we also examine the "outlier" problem involved in measuring household wealth from sample surveys. The basic SCF data provide several good illustrations of outliers—observations whose inclusion in the survey total with the original weight provides conclusions that run counter to common sense or ordinary observation. This issue arises in several of the net worth components derived from the SCF data, and we discuss various types of adjustment that are suggested in the literature. We also provide an analysis of the sensitivity of both the aggregate estimates and the model-based estimates to various ways of handling outliers.

Section 10.6 of the paper uses data from the Federal Reserve Board's flow-of-funds accounts (FFAs) to make some aggregate comparisons with SCF estimates. This section, as well as much of the analysis on imputations, draws heavily on Avery, Elliehausen, and Kennickell (1987), in which FFA and SCF comparisons are provided. We do some adjustment of the results from the Avery, Elliehausen, and Kennickell paper and also provide a general view of what aggregate comparison between the SIPP and PSID surveys and the FFA data would look like, given that we have comparisons involving all three surveys and a comparison of one survey with aggregate FFA data from 1983.

A principal conclusion in this section is that many of the differences between the aggregate FFA data and the SCF data seem to reflect inadequacies of the FFAs rather than bias or measurement errors in the surveys. This is especially true for estimates of real estate, concerning which there is well-documented evidence that survey estimates of home equity and housing values represent unbiased population estimates of the mean, although with substantial measurement error in individual cases. Other FFA estimates that differ substantially from the survey estimates are also highly suspect, for example, FFA estimates of saving and checking accounts are quite likely to overestimate the holdings of such accounts by households and to underestimate holdings of such accounts by business. Overall, the surprising message is that the survey estimates of wealth are remarkably close to the aggregate

FFA data and that many of the larger differences are more likely to be attributable to errors in the FFA data than to errors in the survey data. That conclusion runs counter to much previous thinking about the reliability of survey-based estimates of household wealth.

Section 10.7 examines the data on pension rights obtained as part of the SCF survey. Estimates were obtained directly from households of the expected value of their entitlements to pension benefits from either their current or their previous employers; counterpart data were also obtained directly from the pension providers about the pension rights that would accrue to employees with certain characteristics. These two sources of data can be directly compared in the SCF data to assess the quality of respondent data—an important topic since the general view is that respondents possess little if any information about their pension rights. The SCF found mixed, but encouraging, results. While nearly all households knew whether or not they were covered by a pension plan, the majority of those covered did not know what benefit amount they would receive at retirement. Among those that did give estimates, however, the differences between the household and pension provider data were surprisingly small. The median values differed by less than 20 percent, and the correlation between the two was reasonably high. Moreover, imputations of missing benefit amounts, based solely on other household data, proved to be a close match to the pension provider data.

The final section of the paper, section 10.8, provides an overall assessment of data quality in the three household surveys and some recommendations. The recommendations are designed to illuminate decisions about resource allocation as it relates to the collection of data on household wealth. Here, we are concerned about the trade-offs between data quality and data costs, and our conclusions probably run counter to what has been widely believed by students of survey measures of household wealth. Briefly, we conclude that, for analyses in which net worth is needed as an independent variable, relatively inexpensive measures of household net worth can be obtained with sufficient reliability to make them valuable as an analytic variable. The evidence here comes mainly from the surprisingly strong performance of the PSID data, which represents a very short module on a survey designed primarily for other purposes. The analysis indicates that these estimates are of surprisingly high quality, relative to the quality obtainable with much more intensive survey methods and much higher costs per case. On the other hand, if one wants to analyze the characteristic of wealth and wealth holdings, the types of measures obtained on PSID are simply not adequate, and here we focus on the comparison between SCF and SIPP estimates.

10.2   Alternative Sources of Survey Data

Between 1983 and 1985, three national surveys obtained information on household assets and debts: the 1983 SCF, the 1984 PSID, and the 1984 SIPP. Although the overall objectives of these research projects differed, as did some of the major elements of the sample design and measurement strategies, they nonetheless share a substantial number of common elements. Each study focuses on similar measures of economic well-being, each used nationally representative household sample surveys, and each relied on self-reported information on holdings of assets and debts.

The 1983 SCF, conducted by the SRC at the University of Michigan, continued a longstanding research program first begun in 1946.[1] Although this survey was usually conducted annually from the late 1940s through the 1960s, during the past dozen years it has been conducted only twice: in 1977 and 1983. The 1983 survey was unique. Like the others in the series, it focused on household wealth, collecting detailed information on the amount and types of financial and nonfinancial assets and liabilities. But it also collected data on entitlements to pension benefits, and the nationally representative base sample was supplemented by a sample of high-income households in order to improve representation of the upper tail of the wealth distribution. This design is comparable to only one prior household wealth survey—the 1962 Survey of Financial Characteristics of Consumers (SFCC), which also incorporated a high-income supplemental sample (Projector and Weiss 1966).

In addition to the supplemental high-income sample, the SCF included a second supplemental sample of pension providers. In view of the importance of pension entitlements for the analysis of wealth as well as saving behavior, the 1983 SCF was designed to incorporate interviews with all pension providers that included SCF family members as participants. Since respondent data on pension coverage were also collected, the independent pension provider data offer an opportunity to assess the accuracy of these self-reports. Interviews were conducted with the household sample from April to July 1983 and with the pension providers from September to December 1983.

The PSID, conducted by the SRC, was begun in 1968, and reinterviews have been conducted in each subsequent year.[2] The PSID was designed for the analysis of the dynamics of change in the economic well-being of individuals and families over time. Because of research and public policy interests in issues related to poverty, the base representative cross-section sample was supplemented by a sample of low-income households. Following all those who move out of sample families and weighting to account for people moving into sample families provide representative (weighted) samples each year. The annual interviews include core questions on income, employment, and family composition as well as special supplements. The questions on holdings of assets and debts were included in the seventeenth annual interview wave, conducted from March to September 1984.

The SIPP was designed to obtain information over time on the level and change in the economic well-being of individuals and households (U.S. Bureau of the Census 1986). Although information on participation in federal transfer programs was of special interest, the data can be used to address a wide array of research interests. The SIPP was designed as a panel survey, consisting of nine interview waves at four-month intervals over a period of two and a half years. In addition to the core survey content on income and labor force participation included in each interview wave, various questionnaire supplements have been included. Questions on ownership of assets and debts were included in the fourth interview wave, conducted between September and December 1984, as well as in the seventh wave.[3]

10.2.1   Base Samples

Each of the three studies used comparable sampling methods. All three are multistage area probability samples, designed to be representative of the noninstitutionalized resident population. Both the SCF and the PSID base samples were drawn from the SRC's master sampling frame. The base sample design gave all households an equal and known probability of selection. The SIPP sample was drawn from an updated listing prepared for the 1970 decennial census. All three base samples were stratified by geographic area, with clusters of housing units selected at the final stage.

Small differences in population coverage among the three samples exist. The SIPP sample included residents of Alaska and Hawaii, while the SCF and the original PSID samples did not. Although the census samples include group living quarters while SRC samples do not, for the purposes of the wealth analysis the SIPP data base excluded all persons living in group quarters (dormitories, rooming houses, religious group dwellings). All three base samples excluded U.S. citizens residing abroad. Some additional coverage differences were related to the inclusion in the SIPP sample of housing units on military bases (not barracks). Although similar definitions of "housing unit" (SCF) and "living quarters" (SIPP) were used, data on primary and secondary family units are continued separately for the PSID when leavers return home but combined as household totals in SCF and SIPP. To correct for this difference, the PSID data presented in this paper have been adjusted to reflect the combined total where a secondary family unit was present.

10.2.2 Supplemental Samples

The PSID low-income supplemental sample, as well as the SCF high-income supplemental sample, was originally drawn by federal agencies. In both cases, before the actual names and addresses were released to SRC, permission from the potential respondents was sought by the federal agency. Only information for respondents who agreed to participate was forwarded to SRC.

The PSID supplemental sample was initially drawn by the Census Bureau from the 1966–67 Survey of Economic Opportunity. From this base, selection for inclusion in the PSID was limited to households with incomes of less than twice the official poverty level whose head was under age sixty in 1967. When respondents were asked for their approval for the Census Bureau to forward their name and address to the PSID for interviewing, approximately 75 percent responded in the affirmative.

The SCF supplemental sample of high-income households was drawn by the Internal Revenue Service from the 1980 Statistics of Income data file. An income cutoff criterion of $100,000 in adjusted gross income was used to determine eligibility for inclusion in the sample. Respondents were chosen at random within income strata, with differential selection probabilities based on the proportion of estimated wealth holdings within each strata. Each person selected as a potential respondent was sent a letter seeking permission to release his or her name and address to SRC. For individuals who indicated their willingness to participate in the survey, the only information forwarded to SRC was the name and address. No financial information for specific individuals, or the sample as a whole, has been provided by the Internal Revenue Service, and no identifiable financial information collected by SRC has been released to anyone. Despite the safeguards devised to insure confidentiality, only 9 percent of the persons contacted agreed to participate in the study. It is important to note that, owing to concerns about privacy, no follow-up letter was sent after the initial mailing (the use of a follow-up letter usually results in higher response rates).[4] As we note later, it is hard to know how the 9 percent response rate for this supplemental sample should be interpreted: declining to volunteer is not the same as refusing to be interviewed.

The SCF also included an additional supplemental sample of pension plans and providers. The sample for the study of employer-sponsored pension benefit plans was derived in three interdependent stages. The overall research design was based on the use of the SCF to identify, in turn, which households were covered by employer-sponsored pensions, which pension providers and plans covered these employees, and which benefit formulas and requirements governed these pension entitlements. The SCF questionnaire obtained detailed information on employment for the household head and spouse. All respondents or spouses with work experience were questioned about pension coverage on their current job as well as vested pension entitlements from prior employers. Households that reported pension coverage were asked to identify the provider of the pension—in most cases, their employers.

All the pension providers that were identified were pooled, and a sample listing was generated. A telephone interview was conducted with each of the pension providers. Each pension provider was asked to identify the pension plans that covered workers in a specific occupational classification and work location. Each pension provider was asked to mail copies of all official plan documents that covered SCF respondents to SRC. All necessary information on entitlement formulas and benefit requirements was coded from official plan documents by a trained staff of specialists. To estimate the dollar amount of pension entitlements, the provisions and benefit formulas obtained from the pension providers were combined with the household interview data on the respondent's income and employment history.

10.2.3   Panel Procedures

All three studies incorporate panel designs. For the SCF survey, however, the asset and debt questions were included in the first wave of interviews, and so for practical purposes it can be viewed as a single cross-section survey.[5] Although the PSID and SIPP panels differ greatly in terms of length, both share similar panel designs. The PSID follows all members of the original sample of families as well as any new family units that those original families spawned over time. As children leave home or adults separate to establish their own households, new families are "born" and remain part of the panel as long as they include a member or child of a member of the original base sample. Families drop out of the panel through death or combination with other panel families or are eliminated because no eligible sample member remains. This design produces an unbiased, weighted sample of families over time and thus remains representative with respect to its original sample design. The 1968 interview samples included 2,930 families in the base cross-section sample and 1,872 families in the low-income supplement. Overall, the size of the panel has increased from 4,802 families in 1968 to 6,918 in 1984.

The SIPP was designed to follow all members of the original sample of households that were age fifteen and older at the time of the first interview. In each subsequent SIPP wave, all members of the original households were eligible for reinterviews. Original sample members who left the household were also contacted, and information was obtained on them and all other members of the "new" household. Members of the "new" households that were not part of the original sample were included as part of the data base only while they resided with original sample members. Since the SIPP panel calls for interviews over only a two-and-a-half-year period, the limitation to persons age fifteen or older has little practical effect.

10.2.4   Sample Size and Response Rates

The SCF was a personal interview survey. Most respondents were contacted at home for the interview, although many of the high-income respondents preferred to be contacted at an office location where records and, in some cases, accountants and other financial advisers could be consulted. The respondent selected within the household was either the head in a single-adult household, or the most knowledgeable spouse in married-couple households. The SCF data base included 4,262 completed household interviews—3,824 cross-section and 438 high-income interviews. The overall response rate was 73 percent, with a response rate of 71 percent for the cross-section portion. For high-income respondents who granted SRC permission to contact them, the response rate was 95 percent. About 4 percent of the cross-section cases were judged to be of uniformly poor quality in regard to financial data and were deleted from the analysis.

For the pension provider supplement, 1,886 households with 2,261 people reported being covered by one or more pension plans. Of these, 1,735 households covering 2,061 people gave permission and the necessary information to contact their pension provider. Consequently, 91 percent of all covered employees in the original SCF sample were included in the pension study sample base. Among all eligible pension providers, 86 percent were successfully contacted. These providers covered 91 percent of all eligible sample members, indicating a higher success rate among providers who covered multiple sample members. Once contacted, 85 percent of the providers provided sufficient information to ensure accurate coding. When each of these stages is taken into account, the overall coverage rate was 73 percent for all eligible sample members and 73 percent for all eligible pension providers. The overall coverage rate for households was somewhat higher (75 percent), as was the coverage rate for all eligible pension plans (75 percent).

Almost all the 1984 PSID interviews were conducted by telephone (92 percent), and the respondent was most frequently the family head (81 percent)—defined as the husband for married couples. One distinctive aspect of the PSID is that small annual payments are made to the respondents to complete interviews ($10) and to provide updated address information ($5). The PSID data base included 6,918 completed interviews. This represented a 97 percent response rate from the prior year's base, as has been true for most years. Given that this was the seventeenth interview wave, and because panel attrition was much higher in the first few years, the cumulative response rate as a proportion of the original sample base was just 44 percent. Studies have shown that the cumulative loss has not meant an increase in bias. A detailed study of panel attrition over the first fourteen years found no systematic evidence of nonrepresentativeness of the PSID data (Becketti et al. 1983; Duncan, Hill, and Ponza 1984).

The SIPP survey conducted personal interviews with each individual age fifteen or older living in selected households. Data were then aggregated to the household level for analysis. The fourth wave of SIPP included 20,900 completed household interviews, with a cumulative response rate of 85 percent, averaged across the four rotation groups. In both the SCF and the PSID surveys, asset and debt information was obtained for the household as a unit, whereas the SIPP survey ascertained whether the assets and debts were held separately by individuals within the household or were jointly owned by household members. Jointly held assets and debts were reported by either spouse in SIPP, depending on who was the first to be interviewed. Most of the SIPP interviews appear to have been conducted with the wife in husband/ wife households, in contrast to both PSID and SCF, in which the most knowledgeable adult (usually the husband in husband/wife households) was the respondent.

10.2.5   Weights

In order to provide for unbiased population estimates, each survey devised a set of weights. In general, the procedures used to construct the weights were similar and included adjustments for differential selection probabilities and nonresponse rates. Although the procedures for assigning relative weights were similar, the variation in the weights differs substantially among the surveys.

The SCF weights were devised to integrate the cross-section and high-income supplement. These weights are based on the separate selection probabilities for each subsample and the joint probability for respondents that were eligible for selection in both samples. Weights were also adjusted to reflect the overall household nonresponse rate as well as the differential nonresponse rates across the seventy-four primary sampling units in the national sample. In addition, poststratification adjustments were made to the final weights, to bring the sample distribution in line with population demographics as measured in the 1980 census.

Weights for the PSID were devised to combine the two samples, taking into account the original probabilities of selection for each subsample and the joint selection probabilities and adjusting for those who refused to participate and other sources of nonresponse. The PSID weights have also been adjusted for movement of nonsample individuals into sample families and for presumed or actual mortality. The PSID weights do not include any poststratification adjustments to force the distribution of selected variables to correspond to an external estimate of the population—although comparisons indicate a close match without such adjustments.

Weights for the SIPP data represent three factors: the selection probability, nonresponse adjustments, and poststratification adjustments using independent information on the estimated population size, by age, race, and sex. In addition, the weights were adjusted so that husband and wife were given equal weights.

10.2.6 Questionnaire Format

A major methodological difference across the three projects involved the type and number of questionnaire items used to measure wealth. The measurement of household wealth requires the valuation of a wide array of assets and debts. Each study divided the various assets and debts into a manageable number of mutually exclusive and exhaustive categories. The SCF used much more narrowly defined categories and frequently obtained balances on an account-by-account basis within those categories. The PSID and SIPP surveys, in contrast, used many fewer and much more broadly defined categories. (This difference in the level of detail reflects the fact that the measurement of net worth was a major focus of the SCF and a supplementary objective for the other two projects.) Given that the amount of information that must be provided by respondents is extensive, more accurate reporting is believed to be obtained by using greater detail in the measures. In the case of assets and debts, much of the information is recorded and comes to the attention of respondents on an "account" basis. Thus, the SCF asked respondents about each checking or savings account separately and asked about each mortgage, installment, or credit card debt separately.

The difference between the SCF and the PSID in the number of questionnaire items is quite dramatic: what the PSID covers in ten questions the SCF used more than 100 questions to elicit. The SIPP survey was between these two extremes but much closer to the PSID. The PSID used three categories of financial assets (liquid assets, stocks, and bonds), three categories of tangible assets (primary residence, other properties, and vehicles), and three categories for ownership of businesses (including farms), pension entitlements, and household debts.

Across the three surveys, the greatest difference in the number of questionnaire categories involved financial assets. The PSID used just three questionnaire categories of financial assets for which dollar amounts were determined: checking and savings accounts, money-market funds, certificates of deposit, government savings bonds, and Treasury bills (including funds in individual retirement accounts [IRA] and Keogh accounts); stocks, mutual funds, investment trusts (including funds in IRA and Keogh accounts); and bonds, rights in trusts or estates, life insurance cash value, and collectibles held for investment purposes. The SIPP survey used eight financial asset categories to obtain dollar holding of financial assets:[6] regular and passbook savings accounts, money-market deposit accounts, certificates of deposit and other savings certificates, and negotiable order of withdrawal (NOW), super NOW, and other interest-earning checking accounts; money-market funds, U.S. government securities, municipal and corporate bonds, and other interest-earning assets; checking accounts (non–interest earning); stocks and mutual fund shares; U.S. savings bonds; IRA accounts; Keogh accounts; and other financial assets. The SCF used more than twenty questionnaire categories to measure financial asset holdings, and, for some of the categories, separate balances were determined for each account in the category: checking, NOW, share draft, super NOW, super share draft, cash management, sweep accounts (five accounts); IRA accounts; Keogh accounts; all savers certificates; seven- to ninety-day savings certificates, six-month money-market certificates, repurchase agreements; small saver, four-year, or other savings certificates; money-market mutual funds, money-market deposit accounts (three accounts); passbook, statement savings, share, or Christmas club accounts (five accounts); U.S. savings bonds; federal government bonds and bills; state, county, and municipal bonds; corporate and foreign bonds; tax free mutual funds; other mutual funds; stocks in company for which family member works; stocks held in investment clubs or partnerships; other publicly traded common or preferred stocks; call money accounts; trusts or managed investment accounts; life insurance cash value; and other financial assets.

The three studies more often used similar categories to define tangible assets—primary residence, vehicles, and other properties. But even here the studies differed in the types of questions asked. For example, the SCF study asked respondents to identify each vehicle they owned by its make, model, and year of manufacture as well as the amount of any outstanding debt on each vehicle. Using the vehicle's make, model, and year of manufacture, the asset value of each vehicle was estimated from "blue books," and then the amount of outstanding debt was deducted. The net value of each vehicle was then summed for household totals. In sharp contrast, using just one question, the PSID asked respondents not only for one dollar figure that covered all household vehicles ("everything on wheels") but also that this figure be given net of any debt owed on those vehicles. The same was true for the measurement of debt. In comparison to the many detailed questions on household debts included in the SCF questionnaire, the PSID used one question to determine the total amount of all outstanding debt, aside from mortgages and vehicle loans. The SIPP was similar to the SCF in the method of measuring vehicle equity and similar to the PSID in the method of measuring debt.

10.3 Descriptive Statistics and Patterns

10.3.1 Introduction

In this section, we provide a general overview of the SCF, PSID, and SIPP survey data. The descriptive statistics cover the incidence and mean holdings of various types of assets in the three surveys within various net worth categories, and the section concludes with an extensive analysis of the age and income patterns of asset holding in the SCF and PSID surveys.

10.3.2 Incidence of Asset Holding

Table 10.1 provides comparative statistics for the three surveys on the incidence of asset holdings of various types—housing equity, common stock and mutual fund shares, liquid assets, farm and business equity, equity in other real estate, and net worth. The most striking feature of these data is the commonality across the three surveys, even though there are some differences in definition with consequent minor effects on incidence. Some of the principal anomalies tend to be explained by minor differences in survey technique and definition. For example, SCF is much lower than the others in the estimated proportion of households reporting zero liquid assets and much higher in the estimated proportion reporting very small amounts of liquid assets (under $5,000). But that difference is almost certainly due to the relatively greater detail in the SCF survey on different types of checking and saving accounts within households. Similarly, PSID has fewer households reporting zero holdings of common stock than the other two surveys, but that is largely a consequence of the fact that PSID includes stock held in IRA and Keogh accounts in their common stock category while the others treat such holdings separately.

Table 10.1 Comparison of Wealth Distributions in Three National Surveys (percentage of households in size category)

Size Category	Net Worth			House Equity			Liquid Assets		
	PSID	SIPP	SCF	PSID	SIPP	SCF	PSID[a]	SIPP	SCF
Zero or negative	10.3	10.9	8.0	38.5	38.2	36.3	18.3	18.8	11.9
$1–$4,999	13.0	15.1	17.0	2.2	2.9	3.4	34.5	48.8	51.7
$5,000–$9,999	7.1	6.4	6.1	4.3	3.4	4.0	12.2	8.8	10.0
$10,000–$24,999	11.5	12.3	12.3	11.9	11.9	12.3	13.9	10.4	12.8
$25,000–$49,999	14.7	14.6	15.3	19.2	19.2	19.5	6.3	6.5	6.7
$50,000–$99,999	17.7	19.8	17.8	18.1	18.8	17.3	6.8	5.5	4.4
$100,000–$249,999	17.8	16.1	14.6	5.3	6.8	6.1	2.7	1.3	1.9
$250,000–$499,999	5.7	3.5	5.0	.4	.6	.9	.2	.1	.4
$500,000 or more	2.2	1.3	3.8	.0	.0	.2	.1	.0	.1
All	100.0	100.0	100.0	100.0	100.0	100.0	100.0	100.0	100.0

Size Category	Common Stock and Mutual Fund Shares			Farm/Business Equity			Other Real Estate Equity		
	PSID[b]	SIPP	SCF	PSID	SIPP	SCF	PSID	SIPP	SCF
Zero	74.6	81.6	79.7	88.4	90.3	85.7	79.4	83.2	79.1
$1–$4,999	9.0	9.5	10.1	1.2	2.7	1.4	2.1	2.2	2.3
$5,000–$9,999	4.7	2.6	3.0	.5	1.0	1.1	1.7	2.0	2.8
$10,000–$24,999	3.3	2.9	2.7	1.7	1.6	2.6	5.2	3.6	4.3

(continued)

Table 10.1 (continued)

	Common Stock and Mutual Fund Shares			Farm/Business Equity			Other Real Estate Equity		
	PSID[b]	SIPP	SCF	PSID	SIPP	SCF	PSID	SIPP	SCF
$25,000–$49,999	3.5	1.4	1.6	1.3	1.3	2.3	3.5	3.4	4.6
$50,000–$99,999	3.1	1.0	1.3	2.0	1.1	2.1	4.6	2.9	3.6
$100,000–$249,999	1.4	.6	.8	3.8	1.1	2.5	2.8	2.0	2.0
$250,000–$499,999	.3	.2	.5	.5	.4	1.2	.5	.5	.8
$500,000 or more	.2	.2	.4	.5	.1	1.1	.3	.1	.5
All	100.0	100.0	100.0	100.0	100.0	100.0	100.0	100.0	100.0

Note: Net worth is defined equivalently in PSID and SCF; the SIPP definition excludes rights in investment trusts, life insurance cash surrender values, and "collectibles"—antiques, coin and stamp collections, etc. None of the surveys defines net worth to include household tangible asset holdings except for houses and cars (and collectibles in PSID and SCF). That is, household durables and furnishings are not included as part of net worth, although debt used to acquire such assets is included in liabilities in all three surveys. House equity is defined equivalently—market value of house less mortgages. Liquid assets is defined to include checking accounts, money-market funds and brokerage call accounts, savings accounts and credit union shares, certificates of deposit, and government savings bonds in all three surveys. In addition, PSID definitions include IRA and Keogh accounts held in liquid asset form as well as Treasury bills. Common stock and mutual fund shares is defined as publicly traded stock and mutual fund shares in all three surveys. PSID includes IRAs and Keoghs held in the form of stock. PSID and SIPP data are net of brokers' loans; SCF is not. Farm business equity is defined equivalently as the market value of the household's equity in owned businesses or farms less any debt owed on those assets. Other real estate equity is defined equivalently as the market value of real estate holdings other than the respondent's own home, including seasonal residences, less any debt on the real estate assets. Both SCF and PSID include land contracts held by the respondent as a rental real estate asset, while SIPP does not.

[a]Includes IRAs and Keoghs held in liquid asset form.
[b]Includes IRAs and Keoghs held in the form of stock.

There are two important differences among the surveys that show up in table 10.1. First, there is a substantial difference between SIPP and the other two surveys in the proportion of households reporting holdings of "entrepreneurial" types of assets—equity in farms or businesses and equity in real estate other than the respondent's own home. For both of these types of assets, as well as for holdings of common stock and mutual fund shares, the great bulk of households report nonownership. For farm and business equity, 90 percent of SIPP households do not report any equity, while, for SCF, almost 86 percent report zero equity; PSID is in the middle. But that means that fewer than 10 percent of SIPP households report some equity in farm or business holdings, while almost 15 percent of SCF households report such ownership—a difference of close to 50 percent in incidence. The same kind of difference shows up in reports of equity in real estate other than the respondent's own home; about 83 percent of SIPP households report zero equity, compared to about 79 percent of SCF and PSID households—a 25 percent difference in incidence. These relatively large percentage differences eventually show up in very substantial absolute differences among the three surveys in estimated aggregate holdings of such assets.

Second, there is a substantial and persistent difference in the incidence of very large asset holdings of all types reported in SCF compared to either PSID or SIPP. As noted in the discussion above on sample design, SCF does not leave the proportion of high-income households, and presumably high-wealth households, entirely to the chance occurrence of selection probabilities applied to the population generally but uses data from IRS files on income distribution to add a high-income and high-wealth supplement to the cross-section probability sample. The SCF is thus likely to have a less biased set of high-income and high-wealth households than either the PSID or the SIPP, unless response rates are independent of income and wealth—a proposition known to be false from a long history of surveys of household wealth. (There may, of course, be biases because of the low response rate in the high-income supplement.) We discuss that issue at greater length below. For the moment, the reader should simply note that, in almost every asset category, SCF has a much larger (weighted) proportion of households in the highest wealth category.

10.3.3   Mean Values of Wealth Holding

Tables 10.2, 10.3, and 10.4 summarize the wealth data from the three household surveys, showing mean values of various asset and liability categories for households distributed across what is roughly a logarithmic scale of net worth size categories. There are some differences in the definition of net worth in the three surveys as well as some differences in the degree to which the data available to us represent original values reported by respondents instead of values truncated at some arbitrary level. The truncation problem applies only to SIPP: except for common stock, the SIPP tape that we used for the analysis is top coded at the level of $500,000. We note below an inadvertent omission from the top-coding rule applied by SIPP, which produces one very large value in business and farm equity that appears on our tape, but generally the SIPP data will show lower totals than either PSID or SCF because of the top coding.

Further, SIPP appears not to include rights in investment trusts, which both the other two surveys include as elements of household wealth; nor does SIPP include life insurance cash surrender values or "collectibles" as part of household wealth. Both the other two surveys include these assets, at least in principle. In addition, the PSID data may have a double-count of rights in investment trusts. In the global questions used in the PSID, one category was specified to include

Table 10.2   Mean SCF Net Worth Components by Size Category, 1983 (N = 4,103, weighted estimates, mean value in dollars)

Net Worth Size Category	Vehicle Equity	House Equity	Liquid Assets	IRAs, Keoghs	Common and Mutual Fund Shares	Other Real Estate Equity
Zero or negative	407	142	467	13	26	. . .
$1–$4,999	1,282	308	601	16	177	26
$5,000–$9,999	2,401	2,440	1,800	87	123	303
$10,000–$24,999	2,643	8,939	3,010	256	364	813
$25,000–$49,999	3,232	23,277	4,266	463	737	2,229
$50,000–$99,999	4,257	43,292	9,584	777	1,505	5,793
$100,000–$249,999	5,928	64,759	25,632	2,709	6,596	20,627
$250,000 $499,999	7,759	94,627	40,556	7,448	20,972	56,419
$500,000 or more	11,617	204,865	93,059	20,155	267,365	322,772
All	3,675	34,602	12,303	1,781	12,587	19,550
Memo: Percentage of total in open-end class	11.9	22.4	28.6	42.8	80.3	62.4
Total assets or liabilities (billions of dollars)[a]	308	2,904	1,032	149	1,056	1,640

Table 10.2   (continued)

Net Worth Size Category	Farm/ Business Equity	Bonds	Investment Trusts	Other Assets	Other Debts	Net Worth
Zero or negative	43	4	1	89	3,172	− 1,979
$1–$4,999	26	244	16	244	1,027	1,915
$5,000–$9,999	109	. . .	40	1,094	1,199	7,180
$10,000–$24,999	401	44	123	1,849	1,675	16,768
$25,000–$49,999	1,072	101	304	2,743	1,508	36,917
$50,000–$99,999	3,136	113	416	4,235	2,045	71,062
$100,000–$249,999	15,324	1,161	1,036	9,086	2,500	150,367
$250,000–$499,999	83,970	16,709	4,400	12,693	2,475	343,078
$500,000 or more	562,578	70,458	150,711	38,762	24,233	1,718,109
All	28,488	3,748	6,208	4,956	2,711	125,188
Memo:						
Percentage of total in openend class	74.6	71.0	91.7	29.6	33.8	51.9
Total assets or liabilities (billions of dollars)[a]	2,391	314	521	425	227	10,505

Note: Vehicle equity is defined as the blue book value of first, second, and third cars owned by respondents, less installment debt on these vehicles, plus the value of other wheeled vehicles (motorcycles, motor homes, recreational vehicles, campers, etc.). *House equity* is defined as the market value of the respondent's home less mortgages on the home. *Liquid assets* is defined as sum of checking accounts, money-market funds, broker call accounts, savings accounts, credit union shares, certificates of deposit, and government savings bonds. *IRAs, Keoghs* is defined as the value of IRA and Keogh retirement accounts. *Common stock and mutual fund shares* is defined as the value of common stock and mutual fund holdings in publicly traded corporations. *Other real estate equity* is defined as the respondent's equity in real estate holdings other than his or her own home—value of property less market value of mortgages, including land contracts as part of real estate holdings. *Farm/business equity* is defined as the market value of the respondent's equity in farms and businesses, including proprietorships, partnerships, and closely held corporations, less any debt outstanding on these assets. *Bonds* is defined as the market value of respondent's holdings of publicly traded bonds—corporate, federal government, state and local, and foreign. *Investment trusts* is defined as the respondent's share of investment trusts. *Other assets* includes personal loans owed to the respondent, gas and oil leases, and the value of "collectibles"—tangible assets such as antiques, stamp or coin collections, etc. *Other debts* includes open-end and closed-end credit, except for automobile debt, mortgages on principal residence, debt on other real estate holdings, and debt on farm or business asset holdings. *Net worth* is the sum of the ten asset categories shown here less other debts.

[a]Estimated on the basis of 83.9 million households.

common stock, IRAs, Keoghs, and "investment trusts." The intent of the question was apparently to ask about REITs—real estate investment trusts or mutual stock funds. But some respondents may easily have interpreted the question to mean managed trust accounts generally. In the catchall asset question in PSID, "other assets," the question

Table 10.3   Mean PSID Net Worth Components by Size Category, 1984 ($N = 6,600$, weighted estimates, mean value in dollars)

Net Worth Size Category	Vehicle Equity	House Equity	Liquid Assets	Common Stock and Mutual Fund Shares	Other Real Estate Equity	Farm/ Business Equity	Other Assets	Other Debt	Net Worth
Zero or negative	763	32	353	62	48	290	69	5,682	-4,063
$1–$4,999	1,587	296	676	41	87	26	74	930	1,857
$5,000–$9,999	3,339	1,536	2,313	270	172	134	449	1,182	7,031
$10,000–$24,999	4,328	7,639	3,346	545	859	379	739	1,268	16,569
$25,000–$49,999	4,974	21,947	5,048	1,084	2,542	831	1,684	1,501	36,610
$50,000–$99,999	6,624	39,464	11,519	3,551	6,640	2,737	3,389	1,571	72,353
$100,000–$249,999	9,925	58,502	31,577	12,990	18,930	17,729	7,990	1,518	155,496
$250,000–$499,999	13,600	97,772	53,268	35,537	60,751	64,250	20,269	1,856	343,591
$500,000 or more	21,817	125,736	87,828	139,750	234,770	423,314	275,265	2,025	1,309,964
All	5,831	29,989	14,036	8,269	13,633	16,739	9,553	1,854	96,201

Memo:

Percentage of total in open-end class	8.1	9.1	13.6	36.8	37.5	55.0	62.7	2.4	29.5
Total assets of liabilities (billions of dollars)[a]	503	2,573	1,204	709	1,170	1,436	820	159	8,254

Note: *Vehicle equity* is defined as the differences between the value of all the respondent's "wheeled vehicles" and any debt outstanding on such assets. *House equity* is defined as the market value of the respondent's home less any mortgages on that home. *Liquid assets* is defined as the value of holdings of checking accounts, savings accounts, money-market funds, certificates of deposit, government savings bonds, Treasury bills, and IRAs and Keoghs held in liquid asset form. *Common stock and mutual fund shares* is defined as the value of the respondent's holdings of common stock, mutual fund shares, IRAs and Keoghs held in the form of common stock or mutual fund shares, and investment trusts, less any debt on these assets. *Other real estate equity* is defined as the market value of the respondent's holdings of real estate other than their own home less any debt owed on these properties. Includes land contract as a real estate asset. *Farm/business equity* is defined as the value of the respondent's equity in business or farm assets less any debt on those assets. *Other assets* includes the value of the respondent's holdings of bonds, rights in investment trusts, life insurance cash surrender values, and "collectibles," less any debt owed on these assets. *Other debt* includes any debt owed by the respondent except for debt on vehicles, housing, brokerage accounts, real estate other than own home, business or farm debt, or debt on other assets and would include such things as credit card debt, debt on open lines of credit, and installment and noninstallment debt except for vehicles. *Net worth* is the sum of the seven asset categories listed here less other debt.

[a]Estimated on the basis of 85.8 million households.

Table 10.4   Mean SIPP Net Worth Components by Size Category, 1984 (*N* = 18,603, weighted estimates, mean value in dollars)

Net Worth Size Category	Vehicle Equity	House Equity	Liquid Assets	IRAs, Keoghs	Common Stock and Mutual Fund Shares	Other Real Estate Equity	Farm/ Business Equity	Other Assets	Other Debt	Net Worth
Zero or negative	958	758	429	89	58	303	−38	180	6,604	−3,865
$1–$4,999	1,858	312	576	59	39	47	57	88	1,095	1,940
$5,000–$9,999	3,926	2,383	1,753	245	182	389	252	261	2,076	7,315
$10,000–$24,999	4,322	9,262	3,062	387	335	794	477	422	2,242	16,819
$25,000–$49,999	4,379	24,781	5,206	664	579	1,797	788	724	2,223	36,696
$50,000–$99,999	5,707	45,314	11,790	1,431	1,745	4,602	1,948	1,516	2,215	71,838
$100,000–$249,999	7,798	75,598	29,140	3,883	6,768	18,439	8,839	4,633	2,718	152,380
$250,000–$499,999	10,583	96,840	49,408	6,414	30,362	72,823	58,654	16,083	4,189	336,978
$500,000 or more	13,863	112,455	78,418	10,663	209,785	168,833	435,216	184,612	10,388	1,203,457
All	4,743	31,037	11,161	1,451	5,393	9,060	9,752	4,232	2,775	74,054

Memo:

Percentage of total in open-end class	3.8	4.7	9.2	9.6	50.9	24.4	58.4	57.1	4.9	21.3
Total assets or liabilities (billions of dollars)[a]	410	2,683	965	125	466	783	843	365	240	6,401

Note: *Vehicle equity* is defined as the blue book value of respondent's holdings of vehicles less installment debt on such items. *Housing equity* is defined as the market value of the respondent's home less any mortgages. *Liquid assets* is defined as interest-earning assets held at banks and interest-earning assets held at other institutions plus checking accounts and government bonds (except for IRAs, Keoghs, and Treasury bills, liquid assets are defined equivalently here as they are in table 10.2 and 10.3). *IRAs, Keoghs* is defined as the value of the respondent's holdings of IRA and Keogh retirement accounts. *Common stock and mutual fund shares* is defined as the respondent's equity in holdings of publicly traded common stock or mutual fund shares. *Other real estate equity* is defined as the value of the respondent's holdings of real estate other than own home less any mortgages owed on these properties. This category does not include land contracts as a housing equity. *Farm/business equity* is defined as the value of the respondent's holdings of business and farm assets less any debt on these assets. *Other assets* includes bonds, loans owed to the respondent, and mortgages held by the respondent. *Other debt* includes open-end and closed-end consumer credit other than debt on vehicles and on common stock and mutual fund shares. *Net worth* is defined as the sum of the eight asset categories here less other debt.

[a]Estimated on the basis of 86.4 million households.

explicitly asks about "rights in investment trusts." Thus, respondents could have counted investment trust rights in both places, although the distribution of PSID assets suggests that most of the investment trust data show up in the "other assets" category and might not have been included in a major way in the "common stock, etc." category.

Finally, the three surveys do not refer to precisely the same time period. Interviewing for SCF was done in the spring of 1983, PSID data were obtained in the spring of 1984, and the SIPP data were obtained in the fall of 1984. These time-period differences should mean that, other things being equal, SIPP totals would be expected to be the highest of the three, PSID next, and SCF perceptibly lower. To some extent, the differences in timing tend to offset some of the differences in coverage—SIPP omits a couple of net worth categories and should therefore be lower than the others, but SIPP was conducted later than the other two and therefore would tend to show higher values. Our reading of the data is that the net differences between the surveys in coverage and timing are only a minor part of the observed differences.

What is most apparent from the data in tables 10.2, 10.3, and 10.4 is the general similarity in the distributions of various types of assets and liabilities and the striking differences among the three in the representation of very wealthy households. The data show a substantially higher level of mean net worth for the open-end wealth class for SCF compared to either PSID or SIPP in virtually every asset category and for PSID compared to SIPP in most categories. The combined effect of a higher mean value for asset holdings in the open-end class, coupled with the higher incidence of households in that category in SCF noted earlier, means that the overall population wealth estimates obtained from SCF are substantially larger than either SIPP or PSID; PSID is somewhat higher than SIPP. The importance of the open-end category for estimation of aggregate wealth is underlined by the memo item in the three tables, in which we show the proportion of total wealth holdings for particular types of asset that are attributable to asset holdings in the open-end category. For net worth as a whole in the SCF survey, more than 50 percent of the total is in the open-end class. For the other two surveys, the comparable proportions are 30 percent (PSID) and 21 percent (SIPP). That difference accounts in large part for the fact that mean net worth in the population as a whole is estimated at roughly $125,000 for SCF, a bit over $96,000 for PSID, and about $74,000 for SIPP.

In terms of specific types of assets and liabilities, the general tendency just discussed applies to all asset categories except vehicle equity. Here, SCF shows somewhat smaller numbers than either SIPP or PSID. The explanation seems to be in the method of data collection and evaluation used for vehicle equity. Both PSID and SIPP have very broad definitions of vehicles: the category includes "everything on wheels"—boats, airplanes, trailers, recreational vehicles, campers, and so on. The SCF category is a bit more restrictive. In addition, PSID asked about the value of cars and other wheeled vehicles directly and in fact asked directly about equity in such items. In contrast, SCF and SIPP asked about make and model year, imputed values from blue book data, and then subtracted debt obtained from another set of questions about installment loans on these items. The overall thrust of these differences is to make the SCF estimate of vehicle equity a bit more conservative then either of the other two.

For other categories, the dominant difference is in the SCF open-end class mean values, which are substantially and consistently higher than either of the other two data sources. This is especially true for net worth categories where wealth is heavily concentrated—common stock, equity in real property other than own home, equity in noncorporate business, bonds, and investment trust accounts. The difference between SCF and the other surveys is not so large where assets are more evenly distributed, such as vehicles, houses, and liquid assets.

A summary of the differences between the three surveys in estimates of aggregate net worth and the composition of net worth is shown in table 10.5. For vehicle equity, house equity, liquid assets, and IRAs and Keoghs, the three surveys are quite close to each other. Aside from the last category (IRAs and Keoghs), these are assets that tend to be widely distributed among the population, and thus the estimated

Table 10.5   **Estimates of Aggregate Net Worth and Major Components (billions of dollars)**

	SCF	PSID	SIPP
Vehicle equity	308	503	410
House equity	2,904	2,573	2,683
Liquid assets	1,032	1,204	965[a]
IRAs, Keoghs	149	[b]	125
Common stock and mutual fund shares	1,056	709	466
Other real estate equity	1,640	1,170	783
Farm/business equity	2,391	1,436	843
Other assets	1,260	820	365
Other debt	227	159	240
Net worth	10,505	8,254	6,401[c]

[a]Includes corporate, municipal, and tradable federal government bonds, which are included in "other assets" in both SCF and PSID data. The SCF total for such bonds is $314 billion (see table 10.2).

[b]Included partly in liquid assets, partly in common stock.

[c]Total from SIPP file without top coding at the $500,000 level is approximately $6.8 trillion (data from U.S. Census Bureau).

size of the aggregates is not very sensitive to the representation of very wealthy households in the sample. In sharp contrast, for holdings of common stock the SCF estimate is more than double the SIPP estimate, with PSID about in the middle. The SCF estimate of equity in real estate other than own home shows similar characteristics—SCF more than twice SIPP, with PSID in between. For equity in farms and businesses, the SCF estimate is almost triple the SIPP estimate, while PSID is almost double the SIPP figure. And for "other assets," which includes bonds and investment trusts, the SCF estimate is more than three times as large as SIPP, while PSID is more than twice as large as SIPP.

As noted earlier, these large differences in total wealth are primarily accounted for by the large differences among the three surveys in the proportions of households owning very large amounts of wealth and the average amount of wealth held by such households. But what characteristics of the three surveys account for these differences in reported wealth holdings? In principle, all three surveys are based on probability samples of the U.S. population, and they should contain roughly equal distributions of population characteristics like income, age, race, marital status, education, and so on. However, response rates on a wealth survey are not independent of these population characteristics and in particular are not independent of income (and wealth) levels. The normal expectation is that very high-income households will tend to be underrepresented in population samples, simply because nonresponse is apt to be much higher in such households and a nonresponse correction cannot be made. In addition, over and above any underrepresentation of high-income households, population samples are apt to provide poor estimates of the mean values of wealth holding for those (underrepresented) sample elements with very high incomes; that is, not only will conventional probability samples underrepresent high-income households generally, but they are also likely to miss the true distribution within the high-income class. It was precisely that difficulty that underlies the importance of adding a high-income supplemental sample if a wealth survey is to have any prospect of capturing the true distribution of wealth in the society.

Note that two issues are involved. First, does the sample represent the size of the upper tail of the income distribution with reasonable accuracy? Second, do the parts of the sample in the upper tail of the income distribution adequately represent the true distribution of the population in that region? The three surveys differ dramatically in this regard, both in the degree to which they represent high-income households at all and in the sampling error (and probable bias) of wealth holdings among very high-income households. In addition, the public use SIPP data file will underestimate the size of the open-end income class because income (as well as most wealth categories) is top coded (truncated). As noted below, the effect of top coding on the estimated distribution of income in the SIPP file is substantial.

Table 10.6 summarizes the information from the three surveys on the actual numbers of households, and the weighted proportions of the population, estimated to be in the various income classes. The weighted data take account of the sharply differential selection probabilities for high-income households in the three wealth surveys. Two estimates are shown for SCF. The first, SCF-CS, shows the income distribution for the cross-sectional part, which ought to be no different from PSID or SIPP. The second, SCF-F, shows the combined distribution for the cross-sectional and high-income parts of the SCF, which ought to be equivalent to SCF-CS when weighted but will have substantially more cases in the very high-income classes. It is these differences that appear to account for the large differences shown in tables 10.2, 10.3, and 10.4.

The data indicate substantial differences in the estimated distribution of income in the three surveys and even more substantial differences in the number of cases in the open-end income categories available to estimate mean wealth in those categories. The key income categories are the last two—households with incomes from $96,000 to $192,000 and those with incomes higher than $192,000. All three surveys have over 1 percent of households in the $96,000–$192,000 category, with SCF and SIPP having about 1.7 percent of the population there and PSID about 1.1 percent. Both SIPP and SCF-F have reasonable sample sizes in these categories—several hundred cases in both—while PSID has only fifty-five and SCF-CS only sixty-three. In the open-end income category—over $192,000—SIPP estimates the population as less than one-tenth of 1 percent, PSID about two-tenths of 1 percent, SCF-CS about five-tenths of 1 percent, and SCF-F about eight-tenths of 1 percent. In terms of the number of cases actually available to estimate

Table 10.6   **Comparison of Income Distribution in Three Wealth Surveys**

Income Class (hundreds of dollars)	Number of Cases				Weighted Proportion of Total			
	SIPP	PSID	SCF-CS	SCF-F	SIPP	PSID	SCF-CS	SCF-F
Under $10.8	4,433	1,724	996	996	23.5	23.0	26.5	26.4
$10.8–$23.9	5,695	2,051	1,223	1,223	31.0	29.3	33.3	33.2
$24–$47.9	5,956	2,054	1,069	1,072	32.4	33.0	29.3	29.3
$48–$95.9	2,168	703	298	328	11.3	13.4	8.6	8.6
$96–$191.9	335	55	63	191	1.7	1.1	1.8	1.6
$192 or more	16	11	13	294	.1	.2	.5	.8
Total	18,603	6,598	3,665	4,103	100.0	100.0	100.0	100.0

mean values of wealth in that income class, SIPP has only sixteen cases, PSID eleven, and SCF-CS thirteen; SCF-F has 294 because of the substantially higher selection probability in SCF-F for this income class. As already noted, top coding on the SIPP tape means that the open-end income category is underestimated.

While the difference between SCF and the other three surveys in the sample sizes in the high-income classes is clearly due to differential sampling weights, there appear to be large differences in the cross-sectional surveys that cannot be attributed to differential sampling fractions. Table 10.6 shows the weighted proportion of households in the open-end income class as 0.1 for SIPP, 0.2 for PSID, and 0.5 for SCF—all extremely small and based on tiny numbers of actual cases. However, the top coding on income reflected in the public use data tape makes a substantial difference here: the true proportion of SIPP households in the open-end income class (above $192,000) is actually about four-tenths of 1 percent rather than the one-tenth of 1 percent shown above. Since most of these cases must have come from the next highest income class, the true distribution of the SIPP sample in the two highest income classes is 2.0 percent, divided 1.6 percent in the $96,000–$192,000 class and 0.4 percent over $192,000 (pers. com. from census staff). The SCF estimates about 2.4 percent in these classes, divided 1.6 percent and 0.8 percent, while PSID is lower than either, with 1.3 percent in the two highest income classes, divided about 1.1 percent and 0.2 percent. Thus, SIPP and SCF are reasonably close to each other, and both are substantially larger than PSID.

This result is puzzling since the data in tables 10.2, 10.3, and 10.4 tell us that, first, the principal difference in the three surveys lies in the (weighted) proportions of households in the open-end wealth class and in the estimated mean value of wealth holdings in that class and, second, that SCF has both more households and higher average wealth in that class than PSID, which in turn has more than SIPP. But that difference apparently cannot be explained by counterpart differences among the three in the weighted proportions of households in the very high-income classes. The SCF/PSID difference can be explained in that way, but the difference between both and SIPP cannot—SIPP has an income distribution in the upper tail that is more like SCF than PSID and actually has more (weighted) households in that part of the income distribution than PSID. Thus, the differences between the three surveys must in large part represent differences in reported asset holdings for households with comparable income (and presumably other) characteristics.

A speculative interpretation that accords with survey folklore is that interviewer/respondent interactions are the cause. SCF interviewing was done by people who knew that there were a lot of wealthy households in the sample (because of the high-income supplement) and who expected such households to be willing to be interviewed. PSID interviewing was done by many of the same people since the SRC field staff conducted both interviews. In addition, the rapport between PSID interviewers and respondents must be quite good since the same interviewers had been talking to many of the same households over a long period of time.

In contrast, SIPP interviews were conducted by people who had rarely conducted wealth surveys in the past and who may well have had the normal expectation of interviewers about the prospects of successfully interviewing wealthy people—that such interviews would be difficult and that most such respondents would either refuse or be uncooperative. Moreover, the SIPP respondent was often the wife in husband/wife households rather than the head of household (defined as the principal wage earner), designated on PSID, or the "most knowledgeable adult," specified on SCF. For wealthy households, that probably matters a good deal since knowledge of the household's assets—especially assets like net worth of a business, the value of a large common stock portfolio, and the value of investment real estate holdings—will often be sketchy unless the respondent is the person who controls that part of the household's saving and investment decisions. Expectancy theory (that people will behave as they are expected to behave) and cognition theory (that you cannot report accurately what you do not know) both predict that SIPP wealth data will be lower than either SCF or PSID, other things being equal.

This interpretation—that the differences between SCF and PSID are largely due to the differential representation of very wealthy households while the differences between SCF or PSID and SIPP are due largely to underreporting of the asset holdings of wealthy households—assumes that neither the coverage differences among the three surveys nor the effect of top coding in the SIPP survey can account for the observed differences. While there are some coverage differences that would explain why the SIPP estimates are lower, they are not large enough to account for much of the observed difference. As noted, SIPP does not include the cash surrender value of life insurance reserves or the value of "investment collectibles"—antiques, art, and so on—in net worth and may not have included rights in investment trusts. Both SCF and PSID included those types of assets, at least in principle. In addition, the PSID data may contain some double-counting of rights in investment trusts. But those differences could not under any circumstance account for more than about one-third of the overall difference between PSID and SIPP and about one-sixth of the difference between SCF and SIPP.

While the top coding on the SIPP public use tape clearly accounts for some of the difference between SIPP and the other two surveys, it cannot account for much of it. The evidence is of two sorts. First, we know from informal communication with the Census Bureau that the net total worth of the SIPP data without top coding is less than 10 percent larger than the public use tape used for this paper. That is simply not enough to account for anything like the observed difference. Second, we do have two asset categories in which top coding was not applied to the public use tape—stock and mutual fund shares and (inadvertently) some of the estimates on the SIPP tape for equity in farm and business assets. For both these categories, the differences between SIPP and the two surveys are very large, and they cannot be accounted for by top coding. We are thus left with the interpretation that part of the difference in the net worth total for the three surveys is attributable to differences in the representation of high-income households in the three surveys, but a major part of the difference must be attributed to differential success in obtaining net worth estimates from wealthy households.

The sensitivity of the aggregate wealth data to adequate representation of the small number of very wealthy households in the population would be even more visible in these data if we were able to classify households by other variables that relate to large wealth holdings. While trying to represent the upper tail of the income distribution is clearly the single most important factor in determining the adequacy of a wealth survey, the age of the respondent must also be highly relevant: asset holdings, after all, are the cumulative consequences of initial wealth, saving rates, and rate of return on both. Older households have a much longer period of time over which to allow initial wealth holdings to grow and to allow annual savings to grow. Thus, holding income constant, older households will have much larger wealth holdings than younger households, at least until retirement. But it is clearly impossible to provide meaningful data on the joint distribution of very high income and age in either the SIPP or the PSID surveys—one has little confidence in estimates of mean wealth holdings obtained from samples of sixteen and eleven, and one simply cannot provide meaningful estimates of wealth holdings for SIPP or PSID respondents in the highest income category cross-classified by age. That can be done for SCF respondents since there are several hundred households in the open-end income category. Table 10.7 shows that distribution for SCF respondents, indicating mean income and mean wealth holdings by age for the 293 SCF respondents with incomes above $192,000; the importance of age is evident.

Although there are major differences between the three surveys in aggregate wealth estimates, in the estimated degree of wealth concentration, and in the distribution of wealth among types of assets, all of which relate to differences in the representation of very wealthy households, one should not lose sight of the commonality of results for the

Table 10.7   **SCF Respondents with Incomes Greater than or Equal to $192,000**

	Age Class						
	<35	35–44	45–54	55–64	65–69	70–74	75+
Weighted mean income (thousands of dollars)	363	345	355	387	437	438	562
Weighted mean wealth (thousands of dollars)	986	1,585	4,239	3,330	4,613	3,496	6,461
N	4	38	69	95	43	21	23

great bulk of the U.S. population in these three surveys. For households with less than $250,000 in net worth, a category comprising over 90 percent of all households, almost all net worth is in the form of housing equity, vehicle equity, and liquid assets. There is very little difference among the three wealth surveys in estimates for these three types of assets. Thus, the wealth data for all three are virtually interchangeable for analyses that focus on, for example, the saving, asset accumulation, labor supply, spending, and fertility behavior of all but the wealthiest 5–10 percent of the population.

10.3.4   Income and Age Distribution of Wealth Holdings

Tables 10.8 and 10.9 provide a more detailed view of the composition of asset and debt holdings obtained by SCF and PSID. Both tables show mean values for the two surveys by income class and age class. The patterns are basically similar for the two except where the highest income classes are concerned, where SCF mean values are consistently much higher. Thus, the message here is fundamentally the same as the message in the earlier tables—adequate representation of high-income and high-wealth classes is crucial to an understanding of wealth and the wealth distribution, and, the better the representation of such households, the better the survey. More precisely, without representation obtained from something other than a conventional probability sample design, accurate assessment of wealth holding in the United States is an impossible task using household survey techniques.

These data have a number of features that are worth noting. First, the exceptional level of detail available on SCF permits examination of the characteristics of wealth holdings in the U.S. population in a way not possible with either of the other two surveys. The PSID, as noted earlier, has only very global net worth components, while SIPP is between the two but closer to PSID than to SCF.

The striking feature of table 10.8, where the SCF data are displayed, is the pattern of relative concentration among the population of various types of assets and liabilities. That concentration is best shown by the last column in the table, which shows the fraction of total asset holding

Table 10.8   SCF Net Worth Data by Income and Age Class, 1983: Mean Values in Thousands of Dollars

Net Worth Category	A. Income Class (percentage of population)							Percentage of Total in Open-End Class
	<$10.8 (26.4)	$10.8– $23.9 (33.2)	$24.0– $47.9 (29.3)	$48.0– $95.9 (8.6)	$96.0– $191.9 (1.6)	≥$192 (0.8)	All (100)	
Real estate:								
Gross value of home	16.0	29.5	55.6	97.6	192.4	370.3	44.9	6.9
Gross value of other property	3.1	6.2	16.1	62.6	123.0	857.7	22.2	32.5
Gross value of land contracts	.1	1.1	1.5	2.6	10.2	18.5	1.4	11.2
Total property	19.2	36.8	73.2	162.8	325.6	1,245.5	68.5	15.3
Mortgages on home	1.7	5.3	15.3	28.2	37.9	64.0	10.3	5.2
Mortgages on other property	a	.8	3.1	14.6	26.7	110.4	3.8	24.5
Mortgages on land contracts	...	.1	.3	.7	1.1	2.2	.2	8.3
Total mortgages	1.7	6.2	18.7	43.5	65.7	176.6	14.3	10.3
Equity in home	14.2	24.2	40.2	69.4	154.5	306.3	34.6	7.4
Equity in other property	3.2	5.4	13.0	48.0	96.3	747.3	18.4	32.8
Equity in land contracts	.1	1.0	1.2	2.0	9.1	16.3	1.2	11.7
Total equity in property	17.5	30.6	54.4	119.4	259.9	1,069.9	54.2	16.6

Financial assets:

Checking accounts	.5	1.0	1.3	3.1	7.3	26.1	1.4	15.1
Money-market funds and broker call accounts	.2	1.5	2.7	7.8	32.4	93.1	3.3	23.5
Saving accounts and credit union shares	.6	1.9	3.0	5.5	8.6	10.6	2.4	3.7
Certificates of deposit	1.2	4.0	5.3	10.4	19.7	46.1	4.8	8.0
Government savings bonds	.1	.2	.5	.6	.9	6.8	.4	15.8
Total Liquid Assets	2.6	8.6	12.9	27.4	69.0	182.6	12.3	12.4
Other bonds	a	.4	.9	9.6	42.1	219.1	3.7	48.6
Common stock and mutual fund shares	.3	1.6	4.2	21.8	151.4	769.9	12.6	51.3
IRAs or Keoghs	.1	.7	1.4	5.0	19.4	45.9	1.8	21.6
Trust accounts	.2	.4	1.8	3.4	24.6	573.6	6.2	77.5
Cash value of life insurance	1.0	1.8	4.4	6.8	13.5	33.4	3.2	8.6
Personal loans and gas, oil leases	a	.1	.1	.5	3.9	21.2	.4	49.7
Total other financial assets	1.7	5.0	12.8	47.1	255.0	1,661.2	27.9	49.9
Total financial assets	4.3	13.6	25.7	74.5	324.0	1,843.8	40.2	38.4

Business assets:

Net equity in business or farm (no management interest)	1.4	.8	1.7	12.9	40.0	208.2	4.6	37.8
Net equity in business or farm (management interest)	5.0	5.9	15.2	53.8	210.1	970.9	23.9	34.1
Total business equity	6.4	6.7	16.9	66.7	250.1	1,179.1	28.5	34.7

(continued)

Table 10.8 (continued)

				A. Income Class (percentage of population)				
Net Worth Category	<$10.8 (26.4)	$10.8–$23.9 (33.2)	$24.0–$47.9 (29.3)	$48.0–$95.9 (8.6)	$96.0–$191.9 (1.6)	≥$192 (0.8)	All (100)	Percentage of Total in Open-End Class
Other tangible assets:								
Automobiles (gross)	1.6	3.7	6.2	8.9	11.2	14.3	4.5	2.7
Debt on automobiles	.3	.9	1.7	2.4	1.6	1.2	1.1	.9
Equity in automobiles	1.3	2.8	4.5	6.5	9.6	13.1	3.4	1.8
Other tangible assets	.6	.9	1.3	3.9	8.1	38.9	1.6	25.5
Total assets (gross)	32.1	61.7	123.2	316.8	918.9	4,322.7	143.3	25.3
Debt:								
Revolving charge debt	.3	.4	.9	1.5	2.1	31.5	.9	28.2
Credit cards	.1	.3	.5	.6	.4	.4	.3	1.0
Open lines of credit	.2	.2	.4	.9	1.7	31.1	.6	42.0
Closed-end consumer debt	.8	2.0	3.0	5.4	13.3	51.0	2.9	14.9
Installment debt	.4	1.4	2.6	4.4	4.5	10.5	1.9	4.6
Automobiles	.3	.9	1.7	2.4	1.6	1.2	1.1	.9
Other	.1	.5	.9	2.0	2.9	9.3	.8	...
Noninstallment debt	.3	.6	.4	.9	8.7	40.5	.9	35.7
Total consumer credit	1.1	2.5	4.0	6.9	15.4	82.5	3.8	18.2
Real estate debt	1.7	6.2	18.7	43.5	65.7	176.6	14.3	10.3
Total debt	2.9	8.7	22.7	50.4	81.1	259.0	18.1	12.0
Net worth	29.3	53.0	100.4	266.4	837.8	4,063.7	125.2	27.2

B. Age Class (percentage of population)

	<35 (30.4)	35–44 (19.5)	45–54 (15.7)	55–64 (15.0)	65–69 (6.7)	70–74 (5.4)	75+ (7.2)	All (100)
Real estate:								
Gross value of home	20.4	52.5	66.2	61.7	60.3	44.3	32.5	44.9
Gross value of other property	5.6	16.0	29.8	32.6	83.8	18.7	15.9	22.2
Gross value of land contracts	.3	.9	1.5	2.8	4.0	1.3	1.6	1.4
Total property	26.3	79.4	97.5	97.1	148.1	64.3	50.0	68.5
Mortgages on home	10.2	18.4	13.8	7.5	3.7	1.1	.4	10.3
Mortgages on other property	1.9	5.0	8.0	4.5	2.9	.2	1.0	3.8
Mortgages on land contracts	.2	.2	.2	.6	.2	...	.1	.2
Total mortgages	12.3	23.6	22.0	12.6	6.8	1.3	1.5	14.3
Equity in home	10.2	34.2	52.4	54.2	56.6	43.2	32.1	34.6
Equity in other property	3.8	11.0	21.8	28.1	80.9	18.5	14.9	18.4
Equity in land contracts	.2	.7	1.3	2.2	3.8	1.3	1.5	1.2
Total equity in property	4.2	45.9	75.5	84.5	141.3	62.0	48.5	54.2
Financial assets:								
Checking accounts	.5	1.1	1.4	2.6	2.9	2.5	2.0	1.4
Money-market funds and broker call accounts	.6	2.5	4.2	5.1	8.9	5.2	4.6	3.3
Savings accounts and credit union shares	1.0	2.3	2.6	2.6	4.2	2.9	5.2	2.4

(continued)

Table 10.8 (continued)

	\<35 (30.4)	35–44 (19.5)	45–54 (15.7)	55–64 (15.0)	65–69 (6.7)	70–74 (5.4)	75+ (7.2)	All (100)
				B. Age Class (percentage of population)				
Certificates of deposit	.7	1.6	3.0	7.7	13.8	12.7	12.1	4.8
Government savings bonds	.1	.2	.3	.9	.6	.2	.7	.4
Total liquid assets	2.7	7.7	11.5	18.9	30.4	23.5	24.6	12.3
Other bonds	.2	1.6	3.2	6.8	13.9	8.7	5.9	3.7
Common stock and mutual fund shares	1.1	4.7	13.4	24.1	33.7	33.9	21.0	12.6
IRAs or Keoghs	.3	1.2	2.0	5.3	4.3	1.2	.2	1.8
Trust accounts	1.1	1.3	26.1	5.1	5.3	3.4	3.1	6.2
Cash value of life insurance	2.5	3.9	3.7	4.8	3.2	2.6	1.0	3.2
Personal loans and gas, oil leases	a	.1	.8	.7	1.0	.1	.1	.4
Total other financial assets	5.2	12.8	49.2	46.8	61.4	49.9	31.3	27.9
Total financial assets	8.1	20.5	60.7	65.7	91.8	73.4	55.9	40.2
Business assets:								
Net equity in business or farm (no management interest)	.7	3.8	6.0	6.0	10.8	4.6	11.7	4.6
Net equity in business or farm (management interest)	5.3	18.3	51.4	45.8	33.9	19.9	4.9	23.9
Total business equity	6.0	22.1	57.4	51.8	44.7	24.5	16.6	28.5
Other tangible assets								
Automobiles (gross)	3.7	5.4	6.1	5.3	4.2	2.9	1.8	4.5
Debt on automobiles	1.2	1.6	1.5	.9	.4	.1	a	1.1

Equity in automobiles	2.5	3.8	4.6	4.4	3.8	2.8	1.8	3.4
Other tangible assets	1.2	2.0	2.4	2.4	.8	1.0	.8	1.6
Total assets (gross)	45.3	129.4	214.1	222.3	289.6	176.1	125.1	143.3
Debt:								
Revolving charge debt	.5	1.3	1.3	1.9	.3	.1	a	.9
Credit cards	.3	.5	.4	.3	.1	.1	a	.3
Open lines of credit	.2	.8	.9	1.6	.2	a	a	.6
Closed-end consumer debt	2.7	4.7	3.1	3.0	.9	.4	1.4	2.9
Installment debt	2.0	3.0	2.4	1.7	.6	.2	.1	1.9
Automobiles	1.2	1.6	1.5	.9	.4	.1	a	1.1
Other	.8	1.4	.9	.8	.2	.1	.1	.8
Noninstallment debt	.6	1.7	.7	1.3	.3	.2	1.3	.9
Total consumer credit	3.2	6.0	4.4	4.9	1.2	.5	1.4	3.8
Real estate debt	12.3	23.5	22.0	12.6	6.8	1.2	1.5	14.3
Total debt	15.5	29.6	26.4	17.5	8.0	1.7	2.9	18.1
Net worth	29.8	99.8	187.7	204.8	281.6	174.4	122.2	125.2

Note: The "net worth" categories here are self-explanatory. A possible exception is "other tangible assets," which include "collectibles," such as stamp and coin collections, antiques, art, etc.

[a]Less than $50.

Table 10.9   PSID Net Worth Data by Income and Age Class, 1983: Mean Values in Thousands of Dollars

	A. Income Class (percentage of population)							Percentage of Total in Open-End Income Class
Net Worth Category	< $10.8 (23.0)	$10.8–23.9 (29.3)	$24–47.9 (33.0)	$48–95.9 (13.4)	$96–191.9 (1.1)	≥ $192 (0.2)	All (100)	
Home equity	11.0	20.0	33.2	65.7	136.7	122.6	30.0	1.0
Real estate equity	2.8	6.1	14.0	37.6	95.5	186.5	13.6	3.3
Business and farm equity	3.7	5.8	15.0	46.5	73.5	892.2	16.7	13.0
Stocks and mutual funds	.8	3.4	7.1	20.7	150.1	105.1	8.3	3.1
Liquid assets	5.1	11.2	15.4	24.8	66.5	174.6	14.0	3.0
Other assets	1.4	2.5	12.1	28.3	46.7	66.5	9.6	1.7
Vehicle equity	1.5	4.1	7.4	11.8	18.1	14.5	5.8	.6
Other debt	1.3	1.2	1.9	3.7	6.5	4.9	1.8	.7
Total net worth	25.0	52.0	102.4	231.9	580.6	1,556.0	96.2	4.0

B. Age Class (percentage of population)

	<35 (31.9)	35–44 (18.7)	45–54 (13.5)	55–64 (15.0)	65–69 (5.4)	70–74 (5.7)	75+ (9.8)	All
Home equity	9.3	33.0	47.5	47.8	46.2	34.5	29.0	30.0
Real estate equity	2.9	15.2	23.1	20.5	31.3	11.7	13.3	13.6
Business and farm equity	5.2	32.4	28.0	24.5	12.0	8.7	4.0	16.7
Stocks and mutual funds	1.6	5.6	11.7	16.7	13.0	11.2	13.1	8.3
Liquid assets	3.5	10.2	14.6	20.2	31.9	23.1	30.1	14.0
Other assets	1.7	5.8	5.7	25.7	6.2	3.1	28.8	9.6
Vehicle equity	4.2	7.6	8.2	7.3	7.1	4.2	2.5	5.8
Other debt	2.3	2.3	3.1	1.0	1.0	.4	.3	1.8
Total net worth	26.1	107.7	135.8	161.8	146.6	96.1	120.4	96.2

Note: Definitions used here are the same as described in table 10.3.

of each type represented by holdings of those in the open-end income class—above $192,000. Among the most concentrated categories are trust accounts (77.5 percent owned by households with incomes over $192,000), common stock (51.3 percent), bonds (48.6 percent), equity in business and farms (34.7 percent), equity in real estate other than own home (32.8 percent), and "other tangible assets" (25.5 percent). Some of the debt categories are also highly concentrated in the open-end income class—over one-third of the noninstallment debt (items like personal loans) and more than 40 percent of the debt incurred on open lines of credit. Among the least concentrated wealth categories are savings accounts (3.7 percent of the total in the open-end income category), mortgages on principal residence (5.2 percent), gross value of principal residences (6.9 percent), certificates of deposit (8.0 percent), and cash value of life insurance (8.6 percent). Most of the debt categories are also widely distributed among the population: automobile debt and credit card debt have only about 1 percent of the total in the open-end income class. The comparable PSID data in table 10.9, which contains much less detail because the PSID categories are much more aggregated, show income and age patterns that are similar for income classes below $96,000 but quite different for income classes above that level—with much less concentration of holdings.

A summary of the distributional characteristics of the three wealth surveys is shown in table 10.10, where a comparison of the mean asset holding by income class is provided for roughly equivalent asset categories. These data show dramatically that the major difference between the surveys shows up in the mean value of heavily concentrated assets held by households in the two (occasionally three) highest income classes. The best comparison here is between PSID and SCF, where the mean values of asset holdings are often very close for the first four income classes—up through the $48,000–$95,900 class. But, for net worth held in the form of equity in real estate other than own home, the mean value in SCF for the highest income class is almost four times as large as for PSID. For common stock, mutual fund shares, IRAs, and Keoghs, the SCF open-end mean is about eight times as high. For other assets (which includes bonds and rights in investment trusts), the SCF mean value in the open-end income class is more than ten times higher than the PSID mean value. And, for net worth as a whole, SCF shows a mean value almost three times as high as PSID. Even for assets that are much more evenly distributed among the population—home equity, for example—SCF showed an average value almost three times as high in the open-end income class.

These comparisons are striking testimony to the fact that because of nonresponse bias the characteristics of a probability sample in a very high-income class may be quite unlike the true characteristics of

Table 10.10 Comparison of Selected SIPP,[a] PSID, and SCF Mean Net Worth Components by Income Class: Mean Values in Thousands of Dollars

	Income Class						Percentage of Total in
Net Worth Category	< $10.8	$10.8–$23.9	$24–$47.9	$48–$95.9	$96–$191.9	≥ $192	All	Open-End Income Class
Home equity:								
SIPP	17.2	25.0	35.0	56.9	82.1	99.1	31.0	.3
PSID	11.0	20.0	33.2	65.7	136.7	122.6	30.0	1.0
SCF	14.2	24.2	40.2	69.4	154.5	306.3	34.6	7.4
Real estate equity:								
SIPP	3.3	5.2	9.1	23.5	59.8	71.8	9.1	.7
PSID	2.8	6.1	14.0	37.6	95.5	185.5	13.6	3.3
SCF	3.2	6.4	14.2	50.0	105.4	763.6	19.5	32.5
Business/farm equity:								
SIPP	3.6	3.8	5.0	13.4	264.3[b]	63.2	9.8	.5
PSID	3.7	5.8	15.0	46.5	73.5	892.2	16.7	13.0
SCF	6.4	6.7	16.9	66.7	250.1	1,179.1	28.5	34.7
Common stock and mutual fund shares, IRAs, Keoghs:								
SIPP	1.1	2.1	5.9	22.3	62.5	531.5	6.8	8.8
PSID	.8	3.4	7.1	20.7	150.1	105.1	8.3	3.1
SCF	.4	2.3	5.7	26.8	171.4	816.8	14.4	47.9

(*continued*)

Table 10.10 (continued)

Net Worth Category	Income Class						All	Percentage of Total in Open-End Income Class
	< $10.8	$10.8–$23.9	$24–$47.9	$48–$95.9	$96–$191.9	≥ $192		
Liquid assets:c								
SIPP	4.7	9.8	11.9	20.4	46.4	87.7	11.2	.7
PSID	5.1	11.2	15.4	24.8	66.5	174.6	14.0	3.0
SCF	2.6	8.6	12.8	27.4	68.9	182.7	12.3	12.4
Net worth:								
SIPP	31.2	49.3	72.0	151.2	600.2	865.6	74.0	1.0
PSID	25.0	52.0	102.4	231.9	580.6	1,556.0	96.2	4.0
SCF	29.3	53.0	100.4	266.4	837.8	4,063.6	125.2	27.2
Memo: SIPP data without top coding (plus other minor adjustments)	29.1	50.6	77.1	179.2	463.0	904.1	78.1	4.6

Note: Definitions for SCF and PSID are the same as those found in table 10.8 (SCF), table 10.3 (PSID), and table 10.4 (SIPP). Net worth does not equal the sum of the six asset categories listed since net worth includes both other assets and other debt, which are not shown here.

aThe SIPP data are top coded (truncated) at $500,000, except common stock and business and farm equity. The effect on the data is to reduce SIPP net worth by about 10 percent; the effect on the mean values in high-income classes could be substantial.

bThe SIPP outlier in our data tape is in this cell. One case accounts for roughly 80 percent of the total and mean value.

cPSID includes some components not in the SCF or SIPP definitions—IRAs and Keoghs in liquid asset form and Treasury bills.

that class. Thus, despite the exceptionally close match, or so it seems to us, between PSID and SCF in the income classes below $48,000 and often in the income classes between $48,000 and $192,000, PSID is not able to represent wealth holdings in the crucial income class in table 10.10—households with more than $192,000. The reader will recall that PSID has only eleven households in that category, in contrast to the almost 300 in the SCF group.

Table 10.10 also indicates the principal reason why SIPP is so much lower in net worth than either PSID or SCF. It is not, as discussed earlier, because the public use SIPP file is top coded. Rather, it seems to be due to the fact that SIPP was much less successful than either PSID or SCF in collecting wealth data from households with large holdings of entrepreneurial type assets—business or farm equity or equity in real estate other than own home.

The divergence between SIPP and the other two surveys in these asset categories is not limited to the very high-income classes. Rather, SIPP begins to diverge sharply from the others in the $24,000–$47,900 income class, and the divergence grows in the higher-income classes. In contrast, SIPP is much more like PSID and SCF in estimates of holdings of conventional financial assets—common stock and liquid assets—although both SIPP and PSID have substantially lower estimates of mean holdings in the two highest income classes than SCF. In short, table 10.10 suggests that SIPP does pretty well on housing equity, common stock, and liquid assets, although along with PSID it has high-income class means that are much too low. It does much worse on holdings of entrepreneurial assets than either, and PSID in turn does much worse than SCF on the entrepreneurial holdings of very wealthy households.

While it is clear enough that PSID and SIPP cannot possibly represent the asset holdings of very wealthy households, the SCF data are also a bit suspect in that regard, although for different reasons. The problem is not that there are insufficient households at the upper end of the income and wealth distribution in the SCF sample to get a good estimate of mean wealth holdings but rather that we have no way of knowing what kind of bias might be contained in the SCF high-income supplement because of the way the sample was drawn. Technically, the response rate for the high-income supplement was of the order of 9 percent. But this is clearly a poor estimate of the true but unobservable response rate since it does not indicate that 91 percent of eligible households refused to provide information or could not be located—as response rates ordinarily would be interpreted. Rather, households had to volunteer to be included in the wealth survey, and we have no way of knowing what fraction of households would have agreed to participate if names and addresses of eligible households had simply been supplied to the SRC and attempts made to contact these households by SRC interviewers. No doubt the response rate would not have been as high as obtained in the SCF cross-section sample—roughly 73 percent—but it seems clear a priori that the response rate would not have been 9 percent. We simply do not know enough about the true characteristics of high-income and high-wealth households to be able to tell whether the 1983 SCF representation of these households provided a reasonable picture of them. Considerations of privacy prevented using IRS data on the incomes of respondents and nonrespondents.

The data in table 10.10, as well as the earlier data in tables 10.2 and 10.8, give some reason for uneasiness about the SCF data. Whether measured by the importance of the open-end net worth category in total wealth (table 10.2) or by the importance of the open-end income category in total wealth (tables 10.8 and 10.10), the SCF data give a totally different picture of wealth concentration than either PSID or SIPP. We are quite prepared to believe that the PSID and SIPP data are much too low in these categories, but we have no solid basis for concluding that SCF has "gotten it right," so to speak. That issue is crucially dependent on whether SCF has the right weights in the open-end income class and on whether the SCF mean wealth values in that class are unbiased. Given the unusual nature of the SCF high-income sample, one cannot feel very confident about either.[7]

An interesting feature of the SCF data is that they provide the first indication of a topic discussed later—the "outlier" problem in survey measures of wealth. The most visible place where an outlier can be found in the SCF data is in row 2 of panel B in table 10.8—other real estate, defined as real estate holdings other than the respondent's own home. The pattern of mean real estate holdings by age has a sharp bump in the sixty-five to sixty-nine age group, going from just under $30,000 to over $80,000 and then back to under $20,000. It turns out that the estimated mean value of $83,800 for the sixty-five to sixty-nine age group is due almost entirely to a single case—an observation with $50 million of estimated holdings in other real estate and a relatively high weight in the SCF sample. That single case accounts for about three-fifths of the total wealth holding reported in that age category, and without that case the average value would drop from $83,800 to roughly $35,000. What should be done with cases of this sort is technically unclear, although various devices have been proposed to moderate the influence of outliers on the statistical properties of distributions. In some of the analysis below, we do adopt strategies to moderate the influence of outliers in the SCF data and discuss the topic at greater length in section 10.7.

10.4 Wealth Models and Measurement Error

The data discussed so far permit only limited direct inferences about data quality. Somewhat stronger inferences can be obtained by asking whether there are differences in the degree to which these three estimates of wealth can be explained by wealth models; more precisely, we can examine the residuals from a wealth model to make inferences about the size of measurement error in the three surveys. Our strategy is to fit a conventional life-cycle model of wealth accumulation to each of the three data sets, to estimate explained variances and standard errors from that model, and to use these statistics as indicators of data quality on the assumption that the observed model statistics result from a combination of misspecification and measurement error and that whatever misspecification exists ought to be roughly constant across the three data sources.

The typical analysis of this sort is based on one data set and uses the amount of explained variance and the standard error to test the model. Our design is based on multiple data sources that appear to measure the same phenomenon and involves some unusual types of differences—especially differences that relate to the alternative sample designs.

Two different sources of measurement error are of concern:[8] measurement errors in the dependent variables (net worth and its components) and measurement errors in the independent variables (income, age, education, sex, race, and marital status). Measurement errors in the dependent variables reduce the amount of explained variance in regression models. Measurement errors in the independent variables bias coefficients toward zero and thus also lower explained variance. In contrast to the substantial differences in the type and number of variables that measure assets and debts, all three surveys used similar questions to determine the household's economic and demographic characteristics. We therefore assume that the overall differences in explained variance reflect differential measurement error in the wealth variables rather than in the independent variables.[9] This assumption appears most appropriate for comparisons of SCF with SIPP. For the PSID sample, most of the independent variables have been subject to repeated verification and updating in each of the seventeen interview waves. Thus, the PSID may have relatively less measurement error in the independent variables when compared to either SCF or SIPP, tending to raise the amount of explained variance for PSID relative to SCF and SIPP without necessarily indicating lower measurement errors in the wealth variables. The extent of the differential, if any, in measurement errors in the independent variables is not known.

These same concerns apply to the use of the error variance of the regression estimate as a measure of data quality. Although explained and error variance are simultaneously determined by regression models and thus do not represent independent information, the R^2 figures are independent of the measurement scales, whereas the estimated error variances are not. Thus, comparisons of the proportion of explained variance across the three surveys are implicitly corrected for differences in sample means and variances. In contrast, the use of the standard error of the estimate for comparison focuses directly on differences in the observed variances and can be influenced by scale effects.

The model that we fit to each of the three sources of data is a conventional life-cycle model of wealth accumulation. The independent variables are income, age, education, occupation, race, sex, and marital status. The dependent variable is either net worth or one of the components of net worth. All the independent variables are categorical, while the dependent variable is continuous. Essentially, the equation we fit is a form of dummy variable regression called multiple classification analysis (MCA), in which the regression coefficients are deviations in each category from the overall mean, adjusted for the effects of other variables in the regression.

To estimate regressions in this form with either net worth or net worth components as the dependent variable, some transformation of the dependent variable is essential because of the strong likelihood of heteroscedastic residuals. The obvious transformation is to convert the dependent variable to logarithmic form, which assumes that the residuals are proportional to the original variable—a not unreasonable assumption. An alternative transformation is to use natural numbers but to truncate the dependent variable—a procedure that assumes that heteroscedasticity is a problem only for observations above the truncation point.

We examined the effect of various truncation rules on the model statistics, with the results shown in table 10.11. The dependent variable is net worth, the independent variables are as indicated above (age, income, occupation, etc.), and the truncation rule ranges from $0.5 million to infinity. Only the ends of that scale are displayed for PSID and SIPP, while a full range of values is shown for SCF (means, standard deviations, and the standard errors of estimates are in thousands of dollars).

These results demonstrate conclusively that the standard errors in natural numbers for these three surveys, even with quite severe truncation, will differ substantially because of scale factors—SCF simply has larger net worth numbers (weighted) than the other two surveys, and even the substantial difference in the explanatory power of the models in favor of the SCF does not produce a lower standard error

Table 10.11   **Effects of Truncation from Statistical Estimates from Wealth Surveys**

Survey	Net Worth Truncated at:	Model Statistics[a]			
		Mean	S.D.	$\bar{R}^2$	SEE
SCF	500 thousand	78.1	117.8	.536	80.2
SCF	2 million	99.9	236.5	.563	156.3
SCF	5 million	109.4	336.9	.533	230.2
SCF	6 million	110.8	358.2	.519	248.5
SCF	10 million	114.5	430.8	.462	316.0
SCF	20 million	118.7	549.3	.367	436.9
SCF	∞	123.6	799.0	.226	702.8
PSID	500 thousand	78.6	110.0	.42	83.7
PSID	∞	96.2	308.3	.16	282.2
SIPP	500 thousand	64.6	92.3	.36	73.8
SIPP	∞	73.8	471.1	.04	461.6

[a]The samples used for these calculations differ slightly from those shown in sec. 10.3. None of the differences would affect the results.

of the regression estimate. The results also show once again that the differences in mean wealth, and implied aggregate wealth, for the three surveys are almost entirely accounted for by the differential importance of the high-wealth category: when net worth is truncated at $500,000, the three surveys are quite close on the estimates of mean net worth in the population. These results for net worth models apply quite generally to models of net worth components estimated in dollar values for the three surveys.

We interpret the model results where the dependent variable is a natural number as indicating that part of the criteria for quality ought to be whether the mean and standard error represent the population adequately to begin with. Since the evidence suggests that SCF is the only one of the three surveys with a reasonable representation of the upper end of the wealth and income distribution, its mean and standard deviation are both larger and more valid than the other two. The fact that a wealth accumulation model does not push the standard error below that of the other two surveys is simply a consequence of the fact that the SIPP and PSID standard errors are too small to begin with.

Given the results of estimating these models in truncated natural numbers, we focus on models with the dependent variable transformed into logs. Negative values and zero values are assigned a small positive integer. For most of the net worth components, the proportion of households who do not own the asset is extremely large; hence, we show estimates using TOBIT—a technique appropriate for estimating a truncated dependent variable—along with estimates using ordinary least squares (OLS). All the regressions are weighted, which is essential given the sample designs in the three surveys. In addition, some of the coefficients turned out to be sensitive to a few extreme values, and we have trimmed the weights on several SCF cases, redistributing the weight to cases in the same income range.

In addition to the problem of differences in scale affecting the estimated residuals, we also need to be concerned with differences in the importance of imputations, which can also affect both model fit and estimates of model error. Although the imputation methods vary, they commonly take the form of using regression methods or the equivalent to impute an asset value in cases in which the respondent reports ownership of the asset (or debt) but is unable or unwilling to provide an estimate of its value. Since the regression model used for imputation is probably very similar to the life-cycle wealth accumulation model used in this section, survey data with large amounts of imputation will produce, other things being equal, a larger proportion of explained variance than survey data with less imputation—the imputation method will tend to increase both total variance and explained variance equivalently, and residual variance will therefore be lower. Since the imputation methods used in the three surveys were not identical, and since a variety of methods were actually used, it is unclear how much of a bias this imparts to the results: it probably biases the SIPP data relative to both PSID and SCF since more imputation was needed on SIPP. PSID has fewer imputations to make but uses subgroup means, which reduces error variance a little more than Census hot deck imputations.

Table 10.12 shows the results of applying the model technique to all the possible comparisons that can be made between the three surveys. Since PSID contains relatively global measures of the various net worth components, we have matched the appropriate set of SCF components to the PSID definition. For SIPP, the level of detail most readily available to us is also relatively global for a good many categories, and we have done an alternative matching job using the SIPP categories on our data tape with the appropriate SCF components. In some cases (equity in housing and equity in farm and business assets), all the surveys define the variables in the same way. For other asset categories, there are minor differences in definition, and some comparisons cannot be made at all (e.g., common stock is not measured in PSID except as part of a broader category.)

In table 10.8, we show data source, type of net worth variable, model statistics (adjusted R^2 and standard error for the OLS regressions, log likelihood and standard error for the Tobit estimates). Estimates are shown for the log form of the dependent variables for reasons discussed above. Both to achieve greater comparability and to get around the problem that Tobit-type estimates will often not iterate to a solution when weighted data are used, we standardized on sample size with a Monte Carlo technique—simple random samples with a target N of 5,000 were selected with probabilities proportional to weights. Five such simple random samples were selected for SCF (denoted SCF-1 to SCF-5 in table 10.12); for PSID and SIPP, only one such sample was drawn. The basic information on data quality can be inferred from the model statistics: other things being equal, a higher $\bar{R}^2$ (or a smaller log

Table 10.12 Fit and Standard Error Statistics, Measurement Error Models of Wealth Data

Data Source	Pseudo N	OLS R^2	OLS SEE	Log Likelihood	TOBIT SEE
			Net Worth		
SCF-1	4,976	.508	1.71	−9,766	1.86
SCF-2	5,042	.493	1.69	−9,867	1.81
SCF-3	4,970	.503	1.67	−9,687	1.81
SCF-4	4,949	.513	1.69	−9,666	1.84
SCF-5	4,810	.506	1.64	−9,301	1.76
PSID	4,922	.494	1.74	−9,726	1.92
SIPP	5,097	.396	1.85	−10,397	2.04
			Housing Equity		
SCF	4,976	.368	2.36	−9,570	3.46
PSID	4,922	.372	2.30	−9,497	3.37
SIPP	5,097	.290	2.46	−10,211	3.60
			Real Estate Equity		
SCF-1	4,976	.149	2.21	−4,904	7.11
PSID-1	4,922	.150	2.18	−4,743	7.07
SCF-2	4,976	.130	2.15	−4,528	7.53
SIPP-2	5,097	.095	1.98	−4,090	7.84
			Business and Farm Equity		
SCF	4,976	.250	1.93	−3,430	7.90
PSID	4,922	.417	1.61	−2,752	6.81
SIPP	5,097	.419	1.20	−2,088	5.77
			Liquid Assets		
SCF	4,976	.500	1.52	−8,842	1.77
PSID	4,922	.417	1.70	−9,138	2.04
SIPP	5,097	.373	1.76	−9,390	2.21

(*continued*)

Table 10.12   (continued)

| Data Source | Net Worth | | | | |
	Pseudo N	OLS R^2	OLS SEE	Log Likelihood	TOBIT SEE
			Common Stock		
SCF	4,976	.232	1.61	−4,081	4.84
PSID	4,922	.194	1.89	−4,852	5.19
SIPP	5,097	.138	1.53	−3,804	5.38
			IRAs		
SCF	4,976	.212	1.29	−3,277	4.50
SIPP	5,097	.181	1.41	−4,013	4.67

Note: The dependent variables in the regression are generally defined as above in the relevant tables (i.e., table 10.1–10.4 and 10.8–10.10). There are some differences: net worth is not defined precisely the same in the three surveys, as already indicated in the notes to tables 10.2–10.4; common stock in SIPP is defined as equity in common stock rather than gross holdings; and the SCF definition of common stock is gross holdings. The PSID definition of other real estate equity does include land contracts, and the SCF definition was accordingly matched—denoted by SCF-1 and PSID-1. For real estate, SIPP does not include equity in land contracts as part of other real estate holdings, and the SCF definition was modified to accord with SIPP—denoted by SCF-2 and SIPP-2. Liquid assets in SIPP are defined to include interest-earning assets held at banks and interest-earning assets held at other financial institutions. It thus excludes non-interest-earning checking accounts and government savings bonds. For PSID, liquid assets are defined to iclude IRAs and Keoghs. The SCF definition of liquid assets is between the two.

likelihood in absolute terms) indicates that the data are of higher quality, and a lower standard error indicates less measurement error and thus higher quality.

Some of the differences in both the model fit and the standard errors are illuminating. For example, there is very little difference among the three surveys in the apparent quality of the data on liquid assets. The SCF has a slightly higher explained variance and slightly lower standard error than either PSID or SIPP (for slightly different definitions of liquid asset holdings), and the same pattern holds for both OLS and Tobit estimates. For housing equity, a comparable story emerges: here, PSID has a slightly better fit and a lower standard error than SCF, and SIPP is a bit worse in both fit and error, but the differences are small. For net worth, SCF is a shade better than PSID on both fit and error statistics, while SIPP is not quite as good on either criteria.

The generalizations that emerge from table 10.12 are fairly straightforward. Simply in terms of criteria relating to the direction of differences and the number of categories in which one survey has better or worse fit or error statistics than the others, both SCF and PSID appear to be a bit better than SIPP on quality criteria, while SCF and PSID are roughly equivalent. For example, of twenty-eight possible comparisons involving SCF and SIPP (two fit statistics, two error statistics, and seven categories), SCF is better than SIPP in twenty of the twenty-eight. On similar criteria, PSID is better than SIPP in fourteen of twenty possible comparisons, while SCF is better than PSID in twelve of the possible comparisons and worse on twelve. That this comparison is not entirely satisfactory is best shown by the results for the business and farm equity category, for which all three surveys define the variable in the same way. Here, SCF is distinctly worse than either PSID or SIPP, on both OLS and Tobit estimates and for both fit and standard error. But the descriptive data discussed earlier, as well as the aggregate comparison to be discussed below, clearly indicate that neither PSID nor SIPP has any reasonable representation of household wealth in the form of business and farm equity, while SCF clearly does. But the variables used in this analysis are unable to explain the pattern of SCF holdings, while they are more effective in explaining the (much poorer) measurements in PSID and SIPP. In effect, the results for this category suggest that there continues to be a scale effect, which will sometimes operate to the detriment of a survey that captures the appropriate dimension of household holdings in a particular wealth category, and that neither conversion to logs nor Tobit estimates represent a solution to that problem.

The pattern of age and income effect (not shown in table 10.12) are of some interest in themselves. In the basic data shown earlier, the age profile of asset holding was one that could be viewed as largely consistent with many versions of the life-cycle model. Net worth as a function of age tended to peak in the age bracket around fifty-five to sixty-four and declined steadily thereafter. The decline was especially marked in the SIPP data base but was substantial in SCF and moderate in PSID. However, correcting for factors that reflect important cohort differences as well as for factors that influence permanent income over and above current income (education, occupation, race, sex, and marital status), none of the three surveys shows much tendency for net worth to decline at all, even up to age seventy-five and above. The SIPP survey, which showed a marked decline with age in the descriptive data, now shows a monotonic rise with age throughout the entire range, and PSID, which earlier showed a very mild decline, now shows consistent increases. There is a slight tendency in the SCF data for log net worth to decline in the oldest age group, but not before then.

The income coefficients also tell what is by now a familiar story. In the income classes below $48,000, and sometimes in the classes below $192,000, the parameters for the three surveys are not systematically different for most of the net worth categories. In the income category above $192,000, and sometimes in all the categories above $48,000, the SCF income coefficient is considerably larger. The differences are especially marked for net worth categories in which wealth is highly concentrated—stock, business and farm equity, and real estate equity—and are much less marked in net worth categories (like housing equity and liquid assets) in which wealth is more dispersed.

The appropriate generalization about data quality from table 10.12 seems quite straightforward and is surprising in only one respect. The evidence suggests that the quality of the data in SCF, as reflected by the explained variance of the models as well as by the standard errors, is a bit better than the apparent quality of the PSID data and that both are consistently better than the SIPP data. Given the presence of the high-income supplement in the SCF survey, and despite the uncertain nature of the response rate from high-income households in SCF, one would have expected the quality of the SCF data to be higher than either of the other two surveys. The PSID, after all, used an experimental and very short module in which a few questions about net worth were included as part of an ongoing survey, while SIPP also had a net worth module imbedded in a survey whose major purposes and functions were otherwise. Neither PSID nor SIPP had any real prospect of being able to measure the wealth holdings of quite wealthy households, and neither should have been expected to do very well on that count. What is surprising to us is the remarkably strong performance of PSID relative to SIPP. Most of what we know about survey design would have suggested the reverse—that the greater attention to the details of household assets and liabilities found in the SIPP survey would have resulted in better estimates of assets and liabilities and of net worth. But that does not appear to have been the case.

10.5 Imputations and Outliers

Another measure of data quality has to do with the incidence of imputed value in the various surveys. The analysis here is quite straightforward, although the imputation method differed somewhat among the three surveys. In SIPP, imputations were done according to traditional Census Bureau techniques. A "host" observation was identified by matching along a number of characteristics, and the host's values imputed along with a disturbance term—the hot deck technique. For SCF, imputations were done in a variety of ways and using a great many types of methods. The process is described in Avery, Elliehausen, and

Kennickell (1987). In this paper, we basically reproduce the conclusions and data from that study, along with a few additional calculations. Generally speaking, the most common method appears to have been regression with a variance-preserving feature, although direct imputation using other variables on the survey was commonly used in many cases, and other more individualistic procedures appear to have been used as well. For PSID, much simpler imputation methods were used. Either mean values of similar subgroups or the midpoints of range estimate provided by respondent were the only methods employed, the former for relatively few cases.

Two types of imputation questions can be asked. First, what was the incidence of nonresponse with respect to the presence or absence of a particular type of asset or liability? Second, given that an asset or liability was reported to be owned, what was the incidence of imputation for amount where the respondent reported ownership but could not or would not provide an estimate of size?

The data from all three surveys are quite consistent with respect to imputations for the presence or absence of an asset or a liability. As table 10.13 indicates, such imputations were rare across the three wealth surveys. However, the situation differs quite a lot with respect to the relative importance of imputation for amounts, given that ownership was reported. Here imputations were about as frequent in PSID as in SCF and were more frequent in SIPP. For both SCF and PSID, the proportion of assets or liabilities represented by imputed value compared to the total amount of assets and liabilities ranged from relatively small amounts (e.g., 7.4 percent for checking accounts in SCF) to relatively large amounts (e.g., 75.9 percent for life insurance reserves in SCF). Imputed values were relatively large proportions of total values for equity in real estate other than own home, for equity in farm and business assets, and for equity in common stock. Imputations were of lesser importance for such categories as liquid assets, savings accounts, and IRA and Keogh accounts. Interestingly enough, as Avery, Elliehausen, and Kennickell (1987) document, the imputation percentages were substantially *lower* for the high-income part of the SCF sample than for the cross-section part, doubtless owing to the fact that the high-income part of the SCF sample consisted of volunteers.

A better comparison of the three surveys, therefore, would be to contrast the cross-section imputation for SCF with the PSID and SIPP imputation. Here, the SCF-CS imputation percentages are somewhat closer to those shown in SIPP, although SIPP is still appreciably higher. Incidentally, it is worth noting that the SIPP imputation percentages are substantially better than they had been in SIPP's predecessor—the Income Survey Development Program (ISDP), begun in the late 1970s. The ISDP had much higher imputation percentages than SIPP, and one

Table 10.13   Item Nonresponse Rates for Three Wealth Surveys (percentage of households or amounts)

Asset/Debt Category	Nonresponse on Ownership				Nonresponse on Amount of Asset/Debt, Given That the Asset/Debt Is Owned						
	SIPP	PSID	SCF-CS	SCF-HY	SIPP	PSID*	PSID	SCF-CS*	SCF-CS	SCF-HY*	SCF-HY
Principal residence	N.A.	N.A.	.1	.0	N.A.	N.A.	N.A.	4.4	7.8	.8	1.4
Other real estate	.9	.2	.1	.0	33.5	16.0	14.4	9.9	9.2	1.2	3.0
Publicly traded stock	1.2	.2	1.3	1.7	41.5	23.6	20.2	11.6	25.4	4.4	6.7
Bonds and trusts	N.A.	N.A.	.7	2.4	25.9[a]	N.A.	N.A.	25.1	24.7	6.3	6.2
Checking accounts	1.9	↑	.1	.5	13.3	↑	↑	7.4	9.6	3.5	4.7
Savings accounts	1.7	↑	.2	.7	16.8	↑	↑	13.7	14.1	3.3	4.8
Money market accounts	2.1	↑	.2	.3	N.A.	↑	↑	15.7	18.3	4.3	9.3
Liquid assets	…	.2	…	…	…	22.1	11.4	…	…	…	…
Certificates of deposit	2.2	→	1.3	.0	N.A.	→	→	23.6	25.6	8.2	9.0
IRAs, Keoghs	1.2	→	.3	.3	N.A.	→	→	8.7	11.9	1.5	2.1
Savings bonds	N.A.	→	.1	.2	24.9	→	→	10.1	17.4	1.0	4.6
Life insurance cash value	N.A.	N.A.	2.4	.5	N.A.	N.A.	N.A.	75.9	71.7	41.2	33.5
Business/farm equity	N.A.	.2	.1	.5	37.9	20.9	23.8	17.6	37.2	19.9	17.6
Automobiles	N.A.	N.A.	.0	.0	N.A.	8.5[b]	6.3[b]	N.A.	N.A.	N.A.	N.A.
Auto debt	N.A.	N.A.	.7	.0	N.A.	N.A.	N.A.	N.A.	4.6	N.A.	1.7
Consumer debt	N.A.	N.A.	.2	.4	N.A.	N.A.	N.A.	N.A.	5.6	N.A.	3.7
Mortgage debt on home	N.A.	N.A.	.3	.5	N.A.	N.A.	N.A.	N.A.	9.6	N.A.	3.6
Other mortgage debt	N.A.	N.A.	1.0	.0	N.A.	N.A.	N.A.	8.2	8.2	N.A.	3.9

Note: Asset/debt categories are self-explanatory. The SIPP nonresponse data are taken from U.S. Bureau of the Census (1986, app. D). The PSID data are calculated directly from the data tape by the authors. Nonresponse on amount of assets or debts, given that the assets or debts are owned, included all respondents who did not give an estimate of market value when asked about the amount. Most of these respondents subsequently provided range responses—indicating the amounts were higher than X and lower than Y—from which imputations were made. For the SCF data, the asterisked columns are taken from Avery, Elliehausen, and Kennickell (1987) and are weighted by amounts. The SCF columns without asterisks were calculated by the authors. Arrows indicate assets included in liquid assets category.

[a]Bonds only.

[b]Equity in vehicles.

can expect that the SIPP imputation rates will drop as a fraction of total asset and liability values as the program proceeds.

Finally, we should note that the PSID imputations shown in table 10.13, and the text discussion above, overstate the incidence of imputations in PSID. When a PSID respondent reported that he or she did not know the value of an asset held by the household, he or she was asked a series of questions designed to bound the amount. The questions were of the form, "Is [net worth component] higher or lower than X?" If lower, "Is it lower than Y?" ($Y < X$). If higher, "Is it higher than Z?" ($Z > X$). Midpoints of the resulting ranges were then used to impute values. Only a few gave not even a range and had to be assigned the mean of a congruent subgroup (1 percent for most assets).

10.5.1   The "Outlier" Problem in Wealth Surveys

With rare exceptions, household survey estimates of means, variances, and aggregates are untroubled by what is called in the literature the "outlier" problem. For example, if one is trying to estimate the average value of houses in the United States, the standard deviation of housing values, and the aggregate value of the housing stock, the fact that there are a few houses worth several million or even tens of millions of dollars is not especially troublesome. In a sample selected at random with selection probabilities that depend on the relation between the sample size and some known external universe, neither the mean, the variance, nor the estimate of aggregate stock would be much influenced by whether or not a few very expensive houses were caught in the sample. The reason is that even very expensive houses are only higher than the mean by a factor of ten or so—there are no really extreme cases.

In contrast, suppose we try to estimate the mean, variance, and total weight of the universe consisting of several million gnats and one elephant. If we know nothing about where the elephant is located and thus must sample randomly, it will matter quite a lot whether our sample contains all gnats or happens to catch the elephant. If the elephant weighs as much as all the gnats combined and we are trying to estimate the mean, variance, and aggregate weight in the population, we will estimate a value that is roughly half the size of the true value if we do not catch the elephant, and we will estimate an average weight that is roughly too high by the inverse of the selection probability if we do catch the elephant. Concretely, if there are 80 million gnats in the universe and one elephant and we are picking a sample of 4,000, we have a selection probability of (approximately) one in 20,000. If we catch only gnats, we estimate the total poundage of this strange universe to be half as large as it should be; if we catch the elephant, we estimate the poundage to be roughly 20,000 times too high. Evidently, if we draw a very large number of samples—say, 40,000 or 50,000 samples of 4,000 units each—the mean value of all the samples has at least some prospect of representing the true value in the universe, although it obviously does not have to. We may easily have too few or too many samples that include the elephant and thus still be pretty far off.

Of course, if we can produce a stratified random sample, in which the probability of selection is proportional to the importance of the relevant dimension (weight) in the universe, then, provided we know where the elephant can be found, we can sample with selection probability equal to unity where the elephant is known to be located and come up with a precisely accurate estimate of total weight, mean weight, and variance.

It is often the case that we are trying to use a sample to estimate some characteristic of the universe while knowing only certain very general properties of the universe—such as how many people there are in total. If the characteristic we are trying to sample is wealth, the possibilities of catching an elephant obviously exist. Consider a probability sample designed to measure wealth, with an N of 4,000 and a selection probability of roughly one in 20,000, and observe what would happen if one or more of the famous Hunt family were to fall into the sample. Assuming that the typical Hunt has assets of $1 billion, with a selection probability of one in 20,000, a Hunt in the sample would produce an estimated aggregate wealth for that single case of 1 billion times 20,000, or 20 trillion. Since the FFA data tell us that household net worth is on the order of 10 trillion in the aggregate, give or take a few trillion, that would tend to create a problem.

Although the distribution of net worth is not so highly skewed as in the universe of all gnats and one elephant, and we are not likely to find one or more of the Hunts to be a respondent in any probability sample of the population, net worth is distributed in a sufficiently skewed fashion that an outlier problem is quite likely to arise. The solution suggested in the statistical literature is to trim the weights when an outlier is identified.[10] The argument basically is that we ought to be doing a stratified selection probability if we are sampling a highly skewed distribution like net worth, and, if we cannot do so for technical reasons, we can certainly impose the restriction that the universe cannot contain 20,000 billionaires if we happen to catch one in a sample of 4,000 households. The reason we know that the universe cannot contain 20,000 billionaires is because of external data; the Forbes 500 does not have 20,000 members, for example. Thus, the recommended solution is (1) examine the case carefully to make sure that it does not represent a keypunching or coding error or a misreading by the interviewer and,

(2) if the data values are legitimate, recognize that the case cannot represent the selection probability that it was given originally and trim the weight substantially—down to one in an extreme case.

Are there outliers in the three wealth surveys discussed in this paper? The answer is unambiguous: yes, there clearly are. Four such cases are discussed briefly.

10.5.2   Case 1

In the original SCF data tape, there was a case deriving from the high-income sample with reported net worth of approximately $200,000,000 and a weight of roughly 5,000. Virtually all the assets in this case were in the form of equity in "owned farm or business." The total value of such assets, given the wealth value and the weight, amounted to approximately $1 trillion ($200,000,000 multiplied by roughly 5,000). That single case accounted for about one-third of the total value of farm and business equity in the SCF sample and approximately 10 percent of total household net worth in the United States. Examination of the details of the questionnaire did not suggest (at least not to us) that the data were obviously wrong—they were certainly a bit suspect, but they could well have been right. Subsequent data, obtained as part of the regular 1986 reinterview, suggested that the $200,000,000 was a misreport by either the interviewer or the respondent: it was certainly not a keypunching error since the questionnaire had $200,000,000 written unambiguously on it, not $2,000,000. But the 1986 data, coupled with some questions routinely asked about changes between 1983 and 1986, suggested that the $200,000,000 was in fact $2,000,000. The data value in the 1983 survey was correspondingly changed, and the outlier problem disappeared.

10.5.3   Case 2

In working with the SIPP data tape, we became suspicious of the possible existence of an outlier because the relation between the overall mean and the overall standard deviation of the sample suggested that the standard deviation was much too large, given the mean, compared to the other wealth data sets we were looking at. We ran a search for outliers in the data tape and discovered a $50,000,000 net worth case, again dominantly in the form of business equity, associated with a weight that was somewhat above average for SIPP—about 6,600, whereas the average weight was about 4,000. That case alone accounted for roughly $335 billion of net worth (roughly $50,000,000 multiplied by roughly 6,600) and represented more than one-third of the total SIPP value of farm and business equity and about 5 percent of total household net worth. Discussions with the Census Bureau people in charge of SIPP indicated that they were aware of the case, that their reinterview data suggested that the value on our tape was almost certainly in error, and that the newest tape had a correction. (We also discovered, in the course of the conversation, that the SIPP tape was supposed to be truncated at $0.5 million in that category, that for technical reasons the truncation rule did not work on the particular variable that the $50,000,000 appeared in, and that the Census Bureau was in the process of recalling the offending tapes and replacing them with ones with the truncation rule firmly in place).

10.5.4   Case 3

This may be the most interesting of the lot. As we indicated earlier in the paper, a number of observations were dropped from the SCF sample because of large amounts of missing data, especially on financial variables such as assets, liabilities, and income. One of the cases that was dropped from the sample for such reasons was a cross-section case with a reported net worth of close to $1 billion. The reason the case was dropped was that the questionnaire contained virtually no income information, although there were lots of net worth data. Examination of the details of the questionnaire suggests, at least to one of us, that the case is probably genuine: when you have that much in assets, the whole notion of income becomes a bit unreal. When you need money, you wire one of your accounts to send you some. That case, which was in the SCF cross-sectional sample with an average weight, would have added $20 trillion, more or less, to measured household net worth—roughly double the total amount of net worth currently measured on the SCF. We differ somewhat about how to handle that case. At least one of us is inclined to put the case back in as legitimate and trim the weight substantially to the lowest-weight figure presently in the SCF file.

10.5.5   Case 4

Besides the outliers we have already noted in SCF, the data clearly suggest the existence of another outlier. As discussed above, in the line under property assets in table 10.8, one can observe a sharp bump in the age distribution of average property values—roughly from $30,000 to $80,000 and back to $20,000. Fully three-fifths of the total value of property holdings in that age class is due to a single case—a $50,000,000 holding of property for a respondent with a weight of approximately 5,000. There is nothing in the observation to suggest that the data are invalid. But one would not like to see statistical analyses conducted on an age distribution that include that kind of value plus that kind of weight. What we have done for the analysis in most of section 10.4 above is to trim the weight on that case down to the smallest weight given to any high-income household and then reallocate the difference in weight to all the remaining high-income households. We did that with one other case in which the combination of net worth times weight seemed excessive, and the analysis in section 10.4 reflects those weight adjustments. The overall effect, incidentally, on average survey values is not small—instead of a mean net worth of about $125,000, as reported in table 10.4, the trimmed sample has a mean net worth of about $120,000, roughly a 4 percent reduction.

10.6   Aggregate Comparisons

A dimension of wealth survey quality that is often of great interest to economists is the degree to which a household wealth survey can reproduce what is thought to be the total national wealth and thus enable analysts to examine the distribution of a net worth figure known to be a reliable estimate of the aggregate. Traditionally, the standard view among virtually all analysts of both aggregate and survey data is that household wealth surveys cannot be used to capture the wealth in the upper tail of the wealth distribution and hence that survey estimates of wealth will always be a substantial underestimate of the wealth actually held by households. That judgment is based on experience with attempts to compare survey wealth estimates with external aggregates—conventionally, estimates derived from the FFA statistics. In this section, we reexamine that question, again drawing heavily on data from Avery, Elliehausen, and Kennickell (1987), who examine the issue in some detail.

It is useful to understand the reasons why survey estimates of wealth have always been suspect as to their aggregate characteristics. It is known (from casual rather than systematic observations as well as from IRS data) that the distribution of wealth is extremely skewed, with a large fraction of wealth being held by a very small proportion of total households. In the United States as well as most other countries, there is no universe of wealth holding that could be sampled efficiently to produce a survey-based estimate of total wealth—that is, it is not known precisely how wealth is distributed and how one can access households in a sample survey so as to ensure adequate representation of the very small proportion of households who are likely to account for a great deal of total wealth. In the absence of such a sample frame, surveys have typically relied on conventional area probability sampling techniques, which ought in principle to represent the entire population, including the very wealthy.

The problem is that nonresponse is known to be much higher among the very wealthy than among other households, but sampling statisticians have no precise way to estimate nonresponse rates as a function of income or wealth level by observing nonresponse rates in a conventional area probability sample. Thus unless special provisions are taken to ensure the appropriate proportion of high-income/high-wealth households in a survey sample, it is bound to be true that wealth estimates derived from surveys will be much too low.

The way that problem has been overcome in the past, at least in part, has been to try to augment an area probability sample with a sample of high-income households derived from an external universe—the IRS universe of tax returns. While wealth is not an observable variable in such a universe, it is reasonable to presume that large amounts of wealth are associated with large amounts of income and to use the IRS income statistics to produce a sample of households that are known to have high incomes and can be presumed to have high wealth. That strategy was used in the 1962 SFCC and was also followed (with some unfortunate modifications) in the 1983 SCF. Broadly speaking, the strategy is to select a sample of very high-income households with a known probability of selection, using the IRS files on income, and to include those addresses along with a conventional cross-sectional sample. Interviewers do not know whether the households they are visiting have come from an area probability sample or from an IRS tax-filing sample, but the survey designers know the appropriate weight to be given to the IRS high-income sample since they know the total distribution from which the high-income sample was drawn. Since the cross section will yield some high-income households, the procedure is meant to ensure that the combined weight of the high-income supplement, plus the households from the cross section who fall into the high-income category by chance, yields a total weight sufficient to include high-income households with the proper proportions.

Note that this procedure does not ensure that the household survey will measure household wealth with a high degree of accuracy. Nonresponse is apt to be quite high among households in the high-income supplement, however derived (Projector and Weiss 1966). While one can correct for nonresponse, one cannot correct for nonresponse bias, and, if the asset holdings of the very wealthiest households in an IRS income group are larger for nonrespondents than for respondents, the survey estimates will still contain a substantial downward bias. Thus, there are serious problems, which some judge to be insurmountable, in using household surveys to estimate aggregate household wealth.

10.6.1   FFA Data

While it is certainly true that wealth surveys have their difficulties in estimating the aggregate properly, it is also true that the external aggregate data often used as a benchmark for "truth"—the FFA data— have problems of their own. While FFA aggregate statistics across all sectors can be judged to be reliable with a high degree of accuracy, how those flows are partitioned among various sectors is a much chancier proposition. For example, the total amount of savings accounts is known with a high degree of accuracy for the economy as a whole. But some of those savings accounts are held by nonfinancial corporate business, some by financial institutions, some by state and local governments, some by federal governments, some by noncorporate business, some by closely held corporate business, some by foreigners, and some by households. Unfortunately, the estimates for the total amount of household savings accounts are derived from the FFAs largely as residuals—the total minus estimates for all the other sectors. The same is true for most of the other household assets and liabilities in the FFAs. For some of these, the match between the asset category and the household sector is quite close—home mortgages are well defined in the FFA statistics, and virtually all home mortgage debt is owed by households. But, for most assets and liabilities, the match is not nearly as close, and one has to rely on accurate sectoring in the FFA data.

The analysis below concentrates entirely on the SCF data. The aggregate match between PSID and SIPP data can easily be inferred, given the discussion earlier about the differences in the three surveys in mean levels of wealth and the mean values of various wealth components.

Substantial adjustments must be made in the data for any household survey before they can be compared with appropriate FFA estimates. For example, the SCF data include estimates of wealth held in the form of investment trusts, and these are not treated as household assets in FFA data. Thus, trusts were eliminated from the household survey numbers. Next, although the household survey estimates of farm and business equity include the value of assets in closely held corporations as well as assets held in farm, business, and professional proprietorships and partnerships, the comparable FFA category includes only the latter—assets held in the form of noncorporate proprietorships and partnerships. Thus, assets in the form of closely held corporate stock must be eliminated from the estimates of business and farm equity in the household wealth survey. It is unclear just where closely held corporations are counted in the FFA data. They are clearly part of household assets, just as publicly traded corporate stocks and bonds are household assets. But such assets are not counted in FFA estimates of the value of common stock, which appear to be based entirely on holdings of publicly traded stock. It is possible that part of these assets shows up in liquid asset holdings in the FFA accounts. Third, assets reported as "other real estate equity" in the household survey must be redistributed among various FFA categories—some go to owner-occupied housing (seasonal residences), others go to noncorporate business, and still others appear to be assets owned by closely held corporations. Other adjustments need to be made in both the household survey data and in the FFA numbers to make the two conceptually comparable. All these adjustments are detailed in Avery, Elliehausen, and Kennickell (1987).

Table 10.14 presents the data provided by Avery, Elliehausen, and Kennickell in somewhat reorganized form, combining some asset categories for which the survey estimate appeared to misclassify assets relative to their (probably more appropriate) classification as reflected in the FFA data. Comparisons are shown for the 1983 SCF survey data.

The results are interesting and, in several respects, surprising. Overall, the 1983 SCF appears to provide a remarkably close match to the

Table 10.14   1983 SCF Implied Aggregate Data Compared to FFA Aggregate Data

	1983 SCF Full Sample	1983 SCF Cross Section	1982 FFA	SCF-F/ FFA	SCF-CS/ FFA
				Ratios	
Assets	9,202	8,416	8,658	1.06	.97
Liquid assets	1,062	1,002	1,899	.56	.53
Currency and checking accounts	273	250	305		
Savings accounts	639	649	1,321		
Money market fund shares	122	78	207		
Savings bonds	27	26	67		
Fixed income assets	370	225	326	1.13	.69
Federal bonds	115	84	238		
State and local bonds	208	97	89		
Corporate and foreign bonds	47	44	. . .		
Variable price assets	1,052	655	1,044	1.01	.63
Publicly traded stock	924	548	968		
Mutual funds	128	107	76		
Other assets	582	495	336	1.73	1.47
Life insurance reserves	371	323	233		
Mortgage assets	211	172	103		
Tangible assets	6,136	6,037	5,050	1.21	1.20
Owner-occupied real estate	4,284	4,110	2,703	1.58	1.52
Noncorporate business equity	1,853	1,928	2,347	.79	.82
Debts	1,354	1,279	1,406	.96	−.91
Home mortgages	996	975	1,065		
Installment credit	252	240	270		
Other debt	106	64	71		
Net worth	7,848	7,137	7,252	1.08	.98

Note: Data taken from Avery, Elliehausen, and Kennickell (1987). We have reorganized their categories somewhat, but the basic data are exactly the same, except for a few minor inconsistencies in their table 6. We have assumed that their component numbers were correct and have modified the totals to accord with the sum of the components where there were discrepancies. The discrepancies were minor and do not affect any of the results.

overall total of net worth shown in the FFA data. That close aggregate match is a consequence of two major offsetting errors—the survey estimates of the housing stock are substantially higher than the FFA estimates, and the survey estimate of liquid assets held in the form of checking accounts, savings accounts, money-market fund shares, and government savings bonds are substantially lower than the FFA estimate. The two are quite close together for estimated holdings of common stock and mutual funds shares, of bonds (provided one combined corporate, federal, state and local, and foreign bonds into a single category), and of debt; the match is especially close for mortgage and installment debt. For noncorporate equity in farms and businesses, the match is reasonably close. Relative to comparisons of the same sort based on the 1962 SFCC, the 1983 SCF provides a much closer match to the FFA data: the 1962 data show FFA estimates higher for almost all categories than the survey data, with the exception of the stock of housing, for which the SFCC numbers were a bit higher.

We find these results curious. First, the evidence strongly suggests that the survey estimate of the value of the residential housing is a better estimate of the value of housing stock than the FFA estimate. Two types of evidence can be advanced. First, a record check study comparing household estimates of house value with actual sale prices for the same housing property was conducted in 1974 by the U.S. Bureau of the Census (Wolters and Woltman 1974). The study showed that the median price difference between household estimates of property value and sale prices was a little over $800 for property selling at about $27,000—an estimated difference of about 3 percent. In this study, the household estimates were lower than the actual property values as reflected by selling prices. Other studies suggest the same conclusion and indicate that, if anything, household estimates are likely to be a bit low because older households typically tend to underestimate the value of their housing properties relative to younger households—presumably because many of their houses were purchased many years ago and appropriate adjustments for housing price indexes are difficult to make if the time span between date of purchase and survey date is very long (Rodgers and Herzog 1987).

Second, estimates of housing value contained in surveys done in the 1960s (the 1963 SFCC), with housing value estimated from the 1983 SCF, show rates of increase in housing value that are very close to the rates of increase shown by housing valuations reported on the relevant decennial censuses, and the rates of price appreciation shown in the 1983 SCF are quite close to the price appreciation rate in housing price indexes (Avery, Elliehausen, and Kennickell 1987).

It is also reasonably clear why FFA estimates of the stock of residential housing might be low relative to market value estimates. The

FFA estimates are derived from a replacement cost model of the stock of residential housing plus an adjustment for land prices. The replacement cost model presumably uses the same data (house price construction indices) as have been shown to be consistent with the survey estimates of housing value, but the land price adjustment is particularly difficult to make and may well be seriously biased downward.

On balance, we read the evidence as suggesting that the survey numbers for residential housing stock are right (and, if anything, underestimates) but that the FFA numbers are much too low. It is also true that all three surveys examined in this paper show quite similar estimates of the value of residential housing stock. Since the methodologies are all about the same, that is hardly surprising.

The other major discrepancy between the survey estimates and the FFA estimates is in the liquid asset category, where the survey numbers on liquid asset holdings—checking and savings accounts, money-market fund shares, government saving bonds, and so on—are much lower than the FFA numbers. There are some technical reasons why the survey numbers would be expected to be lower—they do not, for example, include holdings of currency, while the FFA numbers do. But that cannot account for anything like the difference between the two. In particular, conceptual differences cannot begin to account for the differences between SCF and FFA in estimates of savings accounts, where the largest discrepancy appears.

In considering likely explanations of the difference between the SCF and the FFA estimates of liquid assets, it is worth noting that SCF and FFA are remarkably close in their estimates of the value of common stock and bonds and in estimates of both mortgage and installment debt. Moreover, it is worth noting that all three surveys examined here—SCF, PSID, and SIPP—have roughly the same liquid asset totals, although the three are very different for estimates of common stocks and bonds, where SCF numbers are much higher than the other two.

Our tentative conclusion is that the SCF numbers on liquid asset holdings are more likely to be correct than are the FFA numbers, although there are some technical differences between household survey estimates and such aggregate estimates as FFAs, which tend to narrow the observed discrepancy. That conclusion runs counter to the conventional wisdom, which has always regarded survey estimates of wealth as much less reliable than aggregate estimates derived from the records of financial institutions.

Our conclusion, which we recognize as largely informed conjecture, is based on three considerations. First, we would have thought that if households could estimate any of their financial asset holdings with reasonable accuracy, assuming that they were willing to be candid about their holdings, they could certainly estimate liquid asset holdings a lot more easily and accurately than common stock or bonds. In particular, they could estimate holdings of savings accounts more easily than almost any other asset. Both stocks and bonds involve difficult valuation problems from the point of view of a respondent, although those problems are less onerous these days, when investors are apt to get monthly statements from their brokerage houses or investment advisers. But we can think of no reason why households would have difficulty in estimating their holdings of savings accounts.

Second, there are plausible reasons for supposing that the FFA numbers on liquid asset holdings are overestimated because of the difficulty of distinguishing households from business holdings.[11] We noted above that the FFA data did not appear to have any place to represent the substantial value of business assets in the form of closely held corporations since the corporate stock estimates in FFA are derived almost entirely from estimates of the value of traded stock. But many closely held corporations, as well as noncorporate businesses, must have part of their asset values in the form of liquid assets, and these are quite likely to be hard to disentangle from household assets.

Finally, there is a substantial conceptual difference between FFA estimates of some liquid assets—particularly checking accounts—and household estimates based on surveys. It is likely that households provide an estimate of their current checkbook balance when asked about checking account holdings. But FFA estimates include the "float"—checks that have been debited in the check writer's own account but not yet debited by the bank. Aggregate financial data derived from the balance sheets of banks will thus show larger asset holdings than survey respondents who report their checkbook balances by subtracting checks that have been written but not yet debited. The magnitude of the float can be substantial—Avery, Elliehausen, and Kennickell (1987) estimate it at a quarter of total checking account balances. Since this estimate does not include "mail float" (checks written but not yet deposited), the true discrepancy attributable to float is even larger. Unfortunately, this explanation is of virtually no help in explaining the very large discrepancy in savings account holdings, unless households systematically misclassified their checking and savings account balances to overestimate the first and underestimate the second.

In sum, we have some reason to believe that FFA estimates are conceptually constructed so as to be larger than survey estimates, some reason to believe that FFA estimates of household liquid assets are contaminated by some unknown proportion of business assets, and no plausible story as to why consumers should be able to estimate holdings of common stock but unable to estimate holdings of liquid assets.

Overall, we read the evidence in table 10.14 as casting at least as much doubt on the credibility of the FFA data as on the credibility of the aggregate survey data on household wealth. For the category for which we know that the household measurements are most likely to be unbiased—the stock of housing—the survey numbers differ substantially from the FFA numbers. For asset categories for which we think that households probably have a difficult time making reliable estimates and for which the FFA numbers should be pretty good—publicly held stocks and bonds—the match is quite close. And for assets for which we judge that the household data should be more reliable than they are for common stocks and bonds—for example, liquid assets—the FFA numbers are substantially discrepant from the survey, and we have some reason to believe that conceptually comparable FFA numbers would be lower than the ones in table 10.14. Finally, for the data on consumer credit, the two match closely, especially for mortgages and consumer installment credit.

It is also interesting to note that the 1983 SCF appears to have done much better than the 1962 SFCC in matching FFA data in almost every asset category. That in itself is surprising since we have always thought that the 1962 SFCC was by far the most detailed and comprehensive consumer wealth survey ever done—including the 1983 SCF. For example, in the 1962 survey, estimates were obtained from the accountants of wealthy individuals about every asset and liability held by that household, including lists of shares of common stocks and their market value as of the survey date. In the 1983 SCF, respondents were asked a global question about how much publicly traded stock they owned—a procedure that sounds to us much less likely to yield accurate estimates than the 1962 SFCC procedure (although for some households that question was apparently answered by their accountants).

Perhaps the answer is that in 1983 households generally were much more knowledgeable about their assets and liabilities, if for no other reason than that they now continually receive information returns in conjunction with tax legislation that keeps them much better informed than consumers used to be about the value of various assets and liabilities. In addition, it may be that households are a good deal more sophisticated about the possible misuse of information by survey organizations and are more prepared to be candid about their holdings, provided they are willing to be interviewed at all. And, of course, survey organizations are a lot more sophisticated now than they used to be—all one has to do is compare any of the 1950s or 1960s versions of the SCF with the 1983 version to see the difference. We now expect respondents to give us precise dollar magnitudes, and interviewers are trained not to take "don't know" for an answer without trying pretty hard to extract a number from a hesitant or reluctant respondent. Those conjectures, of course, go under the heading of sheer speculation.

Given the data in table 10.14, it follows that the aggregate match between the PSID and the SIPP data is substantially less good than the aggregate match for the SCF data, although the three surveys are in substantial agreement on housing stock and liquid assets. But, for financial assets, not only are the aggregate values in PSID and SIPP a good deal lower than they are in SCF, but the difference in dates suggests that the reverse should be true if all three surveys provided equally accurate measurements of aggregate wealth—SCF is the earliest of the three surveys, PSID was conducted about one year later, and SIPP was conducted about eighteen months later. A rough adjustment based on differences in FFA estimates of household net worth would add about 10 percent to the wealth holdings in SCF to make it roughly comparable in time to either PSID or SIPP.

10.7 Pension Assets

Entitlements to private and public pensions are the most important assets that have been omitted from the analysis presented so far in this paper. These entitlements are an increasingly important asset for individual families. They are also an important component of aggregate household wealth—private pension reserves accounted for 12 percent of outstanding household net worth in the Federal Reserve Board's 1982 FFAs. Rights to social security as well as other public entitlement programs are also excluded. As a consequence, the estimated wealth holdings included in this paper underestimate household wealth to a significant extent.

Pension reserves have been excluded from wealth estimates not because of the lack of recognition of their importance but rather because of the difficulty of obtaining reliable estimates from household surveys. In fact, the PSID, SIPP, and SCF surveys each contained questions on pension entitlements. Data quality concerns are based on both the ability of respondents to provide accurate information and the wide array of assumptions necessary to estimate pension wealth. Even with a reliable household measurement model, difficult issues remain on how to estimate a reliable current dollar value for entitlements to future income streams.

Wealth surveys use a "balance sheet" approach to assess the various types of assets and liabilities held by households, with each component monetized at its current market value. Unlike most assets held by households, pension benefits usually represent not ownership of an asset "stock" but rather an entitlement to a "flow" of future benefits. The valuation problem is not limited to plans whose benefits are defined as future income flows since even defined contribution plans (where the household usually has assets with a known value) often make benefits payable only after a certain age and may exclude the option of "lump sum" withdrawals at any time.

Three sets of assumptions are required to convert entitlements to benefit flows into stocks of wealth by discounting the expected stream of future benefit amounts to their present value. The first involves the appropriate discount rate to use in present value calculations. The second involves the personal and employment characteristics required to calculate vested entitlements for individual respondents. These assumptions are required because pension entitlements are defined with reference to two dates—the date the individual retires or terminates active participation in the pension plan, and the date at which benefit payments begin. The third involves the current and future financial viability of the pension plan itself as well as the effect of public policy and government regulation on plan benefits. Vested participants face a risk that the pension plan will be unable to meet its financial commitments when their entitlements are due. Government policies, such as funding standards and benefit guarantees, also influence the type and extent of risk faced by participants. Moreover, since benefits from employer-sponsored pensions are often integrated with social security payments, future changes in social security benefit provisions may change net benefit amounts.

10.7.1 Methods Experiment

The SCF pension study combined information from both household members and pension providers to estimate pension benefits. Respondent data played two crucial roles in the research design. First and foremost, the sample of pension providers was based on respondent reports of pension coverage. Systematic errors in self-reported pension coverage would undermine the representativeness of the derived pension provider sample. Second, even if the correct pension provider and plan formulas were identified, respondent data such as length of service, salary level, and other employment characteristics are required to calculate benefit amounts. Systematic errors in the employment information given by respondents would bias the resulting estimates of pension entitlements.

Given the importance of several crucial pieces of respondent information in this design, a separate methodological study was conducted (Duncan and Mathiowetz 1984). A small industrial firm in the Midwest provided access to official records, which included the name, address, and telephone number of all current employees as well as information on the employment and earnings history used to calculate pension entitlements. Differences between respondent reports and offical records were used to estimate the degree of measurement error. The respondent information for which accuracy was most important for the success of this research design involves pension coverage, job tenure, and wages. Inaccuracies in respondent reports of pension coverage would bias the derived pension provider sample, by being either incorrectly included or incorrectly excluded. Tenure and wages are the two most frequently used variables in pension plan formulas. Inaccuracies in the respondent information on these variables would bias the estimated benefit amounts calculated from the plan formulas. The questionnaire items on pension entitlements included in the validation study were based on those used in the SCF and PSID studies.

Among the 371 respondents in the experimental study, 97 percent correctly reported the status of their pension coverage. When asked about vesting status, 90 percent reported the correct number of years counted toward pension benefits, plus or minus one year. Respondents were more likely to underreport work tenure by more than one year (9 percent) than overreport by more than one year (1 percent). The validation study also found very little evidence of response bias in the questions on the respondents' prior years' wages. Respondent reports of annual earnings differed by less than 1 percent on the average from employer records, but this reflected the net effect of larger, offsetting errors—the mean absolute difference was 7 percent. These results indicate that the crucial information necessary for this research design can be reliably estimated using household surveys. The study also indicated that whether the respondent was vested was correctly reported by 89 percent. Questions asking for more detailed information on pension plans were much more frequently answered incorrectly— whether respondents were covered by more than one plan, whether it was a multiemployer plan, and so forth.

10.7.2 SCF Pension Data

In addition to the survey data on financial and tangible assets and liabilities, SCF also included survey questions about pensions on both the respondent's present job and past jobs and about the probable amount of future pensions that such rights entailed. In addition, SCF also obtained independent estimates from the pension providers (usually the employer) from whom household members were expecting to draw pensions in the future. Thus, we can compare estimates of pension rights obtained directly from households with estimates of pension rights obtained from pension providers. The latter were obtained by ascertaining the characteristics of the pension plan in which respondents had pension rights and producing an estimate of future pension benefits predicated on assumptions that were consistent with those used in the household part of the survey.

The decision to distinguish between respondent information that could be reported reliably (coverage, tenure, and income) from that which could not (benefit amounts) was clearly reflected in item nonresponse rates. The SCF question on pension coverage had a 1.1 percent missing data rate, but the question on the amount of pension expected at retirement had a missing data rate of 61 percent. Thus, while nearly all respondents could report coverage, most respondents did not know the retirement benefit amount.[12] Still, 39 percent of the respondents did give an estimate of their expected retirement benefit. To assess the accuracy of these expectations, the benefit amounts that respondents reported in the household survey were compared with the amounts calculated using the actual plan provisions given in the pension provider data base. For these comparisons, calculations for both the household and the pension provider data bases were based on the same set of economic and behavioral assumptions. It is important to note that the questionnaire items focused on the expected pension benefit amount at retirement. As a consequence, the comparison was based on the assumption that the respondent remained working until the date he or she expected to retire or quit.

Given the very high level of missing data on the questions concerning benefit amounts, a second set of comparisons was also made. As with all other survey variables, pension amounts were imputed for respondents with incomplete or missing data. These imputations were done before the information from the pension provider survey was available. Consequently, the amount calculated from the pension provider survey can also be compared with the imputed amounts to assess the adequacy of those imputation procedures. The imputation procedure was limited to respondents age forty or older and used a regression technique with the predicted benefit amount expressed as a proportion of final wages.

When the pension provider data were used to estimate pension benefits, the initial pension benefit amount was 32 percent of final wages. In comparison, the respondent data without imputations amounted to 27 percent of final wages, and with imputations the proportion rose to 34 percent. This same pattern—the raw respondent data yielding the lowest estimates and the pension provider estimate being just below the imputed respondent estimate—was found among subgroups defined by sex, education, and occupation. Using the pension provider data, the estimated initial annual pension benefit was $12,096, compared with respondents' own estimates of $10,057 and with $12,696 when imputation was used with the respondent data. Thus, respondent data, without imputation, were about 17 percent lower than the benefit amounts determined from pension provider data; the imputations to the respondent data resulted in a 5 percent overestimate of pension benefits. These same general results held across sex and education groups and, as shown in table 10.15, indicate that respondent reports of pension entitlements are likely to be underestimates but that imputation procedures appear to remedy this shortfall.[13]

Table 10.15   **Comparison of Respondent and Pension Provider Reports of Pension Entitlements**

		Reported by Respondent		Imputed from Respondent	
	Pension Provider ($)	Amount ($)	Ratio to Provider Data	Amount ($)	Ratio to Provider Data
All	12,096	10,057	.83	12,696	1.05
Sex:					
Male	14,039	11,667	.83	15,061	1.07
Female	8,574	6,706	.78	8,747	1.02
Education:					
College	23,292	19,912	.85	24,853	1.07
No college	8,744	7,305	.84	9,113	1.04

Note: All pension amounts are the median initial annual benefits.

For the analysis of wealth, asset ownership is usually taken to be the equivalent to the legal entitlement to future pension benefits, and legal entitlements are restricted to those benefits that have accrued as of a given date, as if the participant would "quit tomorrow." For most types of behavioral analyses, however, discretionary saving decisions would be expected to be more sensitive to the level of expected retirement benefits, not the level of the current entitlement. Whether expected benefits or current entitlements are used makes a big difference. When the pension provider data were used to estimate the benefits respondents would receive if they retire when planned, the average pension benefit would represent about one-third of final wage, which would begin at age sixty-two, on the average. If, on the other hand, all respondents were assumed to "quit tomorrow," the annual pension benefit would average 22 percent of their current 1983 wage. Thus, even though the average number of work years was only one-third less under the "quit tomorrow" assumption, the estimated yearly pension benefit in current dollars was reduced by two-thirds. Moreover, under the "quit tomorrow" assumption, 38 percent of those that would have been eligible for full pensions at their planned retirement date would not be vested and would thus have no entitlement to future pension benefits.

10.8   Conclusions and Recommendations

The basic question posed by this paper is, What is a reasonable estimate of the probable quality of data on household wealth collected by means of surveys, using as evidence the three wealth surveys conducted during the 1980s?

An assessment of quality must take into account sample and questionnaire design, response rates and nonresponse bias, ability to represent the important upper tail of the income and wealth distribution, the size of measurement error, the importance of item nonresponse and imputations, and the degree to which the household survey adequately represents national wealth. We read the evidence as consistent with a number of generalizations.

1. Measured against the standards set by previous household wealth surveys, all three of these data sets stand up quite well. They do not differ substantially among themselves when it comes to measuring total wealth and the distribution of wealth in the great bulk of the U.S. population.

2. The unique design characteristics of the SCF give it the highest overall potential for wealth analysis of the three data sets examined. The SCF has the right kind of sample design to measure both the overall distribution of wealth and the total national wealth. Its level of detail makes it more useful than the other two for examination of the detailed characteristics of wealth holdings and wealth distribution. Its response rates and potential nonresponse bias are generally worse than the other two, although that may be offset by the fact that it may have less nonresponse bias among very wealthy households. Its overall distributional characteristics seem clearly better than the other two. Its measurement error characteristics are at least as good as the other two, and probably better. It has less item nonresponse and thus less need for constructing imputed values. And it is clearly the best match to external control totals on national wealth.

3. Comparing PSID to SIPP, one gets a mixed picture, but, in general, PSID had the advantage. Although its basic sample design is less well suited to measuring wealth than SIPP (because it oversamples low-income families, for whom wealth holdings are relatively unimportant), its general descriptive characteristics, taking SCF as the benchmark, look to be closer to actual population characteristics than are those of SIPP. Although PSID is not able to describe the details of wealth holding nearly as well as SIPP because of its highly aggregated nature, its measurement error characteristics look to be consistently better than are those of SIPP. The PSID has a lower item nonresponse rate than SIPP and thus less need to construct imputed values, and it appears to be a somewhat closer match to external control totals.

Overall, we judge that the quality of these three wealth surveys is remarkably high, given past experience with attempts to measure household wealth by way of survey techniques. Partly because of differences in sample design—in particular, in the representation of high-income and therefore high-wealth households—and partly because of what appears to be more successful implementation, it appears to us that the SCF and PSID data have better quality characteristics than do the SIPP data.

The most efficient sample design for a wealth survey depends on whether one has in mind using wealth as an independent variable in a model or as the dependent variable and the subject of major interest. If one is interested in wealth as an independent variable to model some other aspect of household behavior, the PSID design seems about right—a small number of relatively highly aggregated questions, involving little response burden and quite moderate cost.

For studies in which saving or net worth itself is the major object of interest, the SCF design has more of the right characteristics than either PSID or SIPP, but even the SCF design is clearly suboptimal. An efficient net worth survey should sample dollars of net worth with equal probability of selection. The SCF uses about one-quarter of the sample to estimate the upper half of the wealth distribution and the remaining three-quarters to estimate the lower half. An optimally efficient design would roughly double the sample size in the upper half of the wealth distribution and reduce it correspondingly in the lower half.

The SIPP design falls between these two and is not optimal for either. There are insufficient high-wealth households in SIPP to provide an efficient estimate of national wealth or to enable a detailed analysis of the distribution of net worth or its composition in the population at large. And SIPP appears to have substantially more detail than is needed to produce estimates of net worth useful as an independent variable in analysis.

The conclusion that a small number of highly aggregated net worth questions can produce wealth data of about the same quality as a substantially more intensive survey effort needs to be tested on a sample that does not have the strongly longitudinal character of PSID. It is possible that the exceptionally good results from the PSID wealth module are due to the fact that these households have been continually interviewed over a long span of time, often by the same interviewers. Testing the PSID design of a wealth survey on a small probability sample is clearly worthwhile, and one would not have confidence in our conclusions unless that were done.

The increasing importance of pension assets makes their continued exclusion from wealth analysis less acceptable on data quality criteria. The potential for bias that is due to this "omitted" variable is likely to rise along with upcoming changes in the age distribution of the population. The analysis indicates that some aspects of pension entitlements can be reliably measured in household surveys and that others cannot. It is important to note that sufficient information on pension characteristics (whether covered, years covered, and wage information) can be reliably obtained and, when combined with data on wage replacement rates (by industry and occupation) can be used to impute benefit amounts. Such a procedure would be most suitable when the pension entitlements are used as independent variables in analysis models.

An important area in which a household wealth survey can significantly improve our knowledge about the economy is in the relative importance of noncorporate enterprises (partnerships and proprietorships), closely held corporations, and corporate enterprises. The household wealth survey data indicates that the first two of these categories are surprisingly large in the economy as a whole, but the survey estimates are based on small and possibly atypical samples of households with such assets. The aggregate data available from FFA on this issue are clearly unsatisfactory, and it may be that the best way to improve measures of economic activity, as well as wealth, is to start with the household survey and obtain detailed follow-up information from households with equity in proprietorships, partnerships, and closely held corporations.

Notes

1. Findings from the 1983 SCF are summarized in the *Federal Reserve Bulletin* (September and December 1984 and March 1986), as were the findings from the surveys conducted in the late 1940s and 1950s—then as now, the Federal Reserve Board has been the primary sponsor of these surveys. See also the annual volumes entitled *Surveys of Consumer Finances,* published by the SRC, from 1960 to 1970.

2. For information on the PSID, see the volumes entitled *Five Thousand American Families—Patterns of Economic Progress, PSID Procedures and Tape Codes,* and *User Guide to the Panel Study of Income Dynamics,* all published by the SRC. Basic data from all SRC surveys and many government surveys are available from Michigan's Inter-university Consortium for Political and Social Research.

3. For one-quarter of the sample (one of the four rotation groups), no interviews were taken in the second interview wave, making it the third rather than the fourth interview in which the asset and debt questions were first included.

4. No information was made available to SRC that indicated the adequacy of the name and address information used in the mailing, making it impossible to determine whether the lack of a response indicated a refusal or simply a letter that did not reach its proper destination.

5. The second SCF interview was conducted in 1986. All family heads were recontacted, as were any spouses that left to establish separate households.

6. The SIPP survey obtained more detailed information on account ownership than on dollar holdings. SIPP obtained ownership information on each asset type included in the category for the first two financial asset categories listed in the text, but obtained information on dollar holding only for the entire category.

7. An investigation of the potential bias in the high-income sample is being jointly conducted by SRC and IRS. The study is designed to yield sufficient information to assess the survey findings, yet ensure that the confidentiality of both data sources are maintained.

8. The discussion here is limited to the consequences of random measurement error. There is in addition correlated measurement error, which considerably complicates the analysis. Basically, we ignore that issue.

9. That assumption is most plausible for the demographic variables—age, sex, race, occupation, education and marital status. It is less plausible for income, where we can be reasonably certain that PSID has less measurement error than SCF. It is also plausible that SIPP has less measurement error than SCF for income in low to moderate-income households, but SIPP may well have more measurement error than SCF for high-income households.

10. The other major option is to delete the case from analysis. Opinions differ on whether outliers contain useful information. The trimming of the weights preserves any such information, while the deletion of the case does not.

11. A similar interpretation of the differences between survey and FFA estimates of household deposit accounts is given in Wilson et al. (chap. 2, in this volume).

12. The other SCF questions needed to calculate benefits from the pension formulas have relatively low missing data rates—5.9 percent for job tenure and 12.7 percent for wages. For these cases, the imputed tenure and wage variables were used in the pension formulas.

13. The success of the imputation procedures was related to the similarities in pension formulas. The average pension plan provided about 1.2 percent of the worker's final wage for each year covered, with a standard deviation of 0.7 percent. There were only relatively small variations in the mean per year replacement rate across major demographic subgroups, ranging from 1.0 to 1.3 percent. Consequently, regression imputations based on job tenure and income levels performed adequately.

References

Avery, R., G. Elliehausen, and A. Kennickell. 1987. Measuring wealth with survey data: An evaluation of the 1983 Survey of Consumer Finances. Paper presented at the twentieth conference of the International Association for Research in Income and Wealth, Rocca di Papa, Italy, August.

Becketti, S., W. Gould, L. Lillard, and F. Welch. 1983. *Attrition from the PSID*. Santa Monica, Calif.: Unicon Research Corp.

Duncan, G., D. Hill, and M. Ponza. 1984. *How representative is the PSID? A response to some questions raised in the Unicon report*. Ann Arbor, Mich.: Survey Research Center, University of Michigan.

Duncan, G., and N. Mathiowetz, with C. Cannell, R. Groves, D. Hill, L. Magilavy, and M. Ponza. 1984. *A validation study of economic survey data.* Ann Arbor, Mich.: Survey Research Center, University of Michigan.

Five thousand American families—Patterns of economic progress, vols. 1–10. 1974–82. Greg J. Duncan. James N. Morgan, and others, ed. Ann Arbor, MI: Institute for Social Research.

A panel study of income dynamics: Study design, procedures, available data, 1968–1972 interviewing years, waves 1–4, vol. 1. 1972. Ann Arbor, MI: Institute for Social Research.

A panel study of income dynamics: Tape codes and indexes, 1968–1972 interviewing years, waves 1–4, vol. 2. 1972. Ann Arbor, MI: Institute for Social Research.

A panel study of income dynamics: Procedures and tape codes, 1973 interviewing year, wave 6, a suppl. 1973. Similar volumes through 1984 interviewing years, wave 17, a suppl. 1986. Ann Arbor, MI: Institute for Social Research.

A panel study of income dynamics: Procedures and tape codes, 1985 interviewing year, wave 18, a suppl., vol. 1 and 2. 1988. (Hereafter, two volumes each year, the second a complete alphabetic index covering all years.)

Projector, D., and G. Weiss. 1966. *Survey of financial characteristics of consumers.* Washington, D.C.: Federal Reserve Board.

Rodgers, W. L., and A. R. Herzog. 1987. Interviewing older adults: The accuracy of factual information. *Journal of Gerontology* 42:387–94.

U.S. Bureau of the Census. 1986. *Household wealth and asset ownership: 1984.* Current Population Reports, ser. P-70, no. 7. Washington, D.C.: U.S. Government Printing Office.

User guide; Panel study of income dynamics. 1984. Ann Arbor, MI: Inter-University Consortium for Political and Social Research, Center for Political Studies, Institute for Social Research, Spring. Last updated May 1985.

Wolters, C. S., and H. W. Woltman. 1974. 1970 census: Preliminary evaluation results, memorandum no. 48, and addendum no. 1. Washington, D.C.: Social and Economics Statistics Administration, Bureau of the Census, U.S. Department of Commerce, October.

Comment   Eugene Smolensky

This session is not about wealth and its distribution but about gathering some kinds of wealth data—those on household wealth. The emphasis is on the 1983 Survey of Consumer Finances (SCF) and the 1984 special wealth supplement to the Panel Study of Income Dynamics (PSID), with an occasional snipe at the Survey of Income and Program Participation (SIPP). The three data sets are compared on four characteristics and with a set of national aggregates. The basic message is, My God, but the Institute for Social Research does do a hell of a job, despite what you armchair data consumers might think—and on the cheap too.

Eugene Smolensky is dean of the Graduate School of Public Policy at the University of California, Berkeley.

The worst part of it is that there is a strong chance that the authors are right.

Most of the effort in the paper is devoted to tracing differences among the data sets to technical issues in survey design and implementation—topics that have been at the center of concerns of the Conference on Income and Wealth since at least volume 13 but that are not in the mainstream of economists' concerns today. It is a kind of nostalgic trip. These issues include sample design, particularly the role of over-sampling; response rates; questionnaire design; top coding; the outlier problem; the most knowledgeable respondent problem; imputations; measurement error; and trade-offs between cost and quality. Imputations, top coding, and measurement error get quite extensive treatment.

In addition to the technical issues, the paper contains an extended comparison of the data reported in the three surveys and a comparison of the SCF with the data in the flow-of-funds accounts (FFA), which rests heavily on the work of Avery, Elliehausen, and Kennickell (1987). Obviously, Curtin, Juster, and Morgan have done a great deal of conscientious work, and the paper is very long. Most of my comments, unfortunately, suggest that it will have to be quite a bit longer.

There are at least two important omissions.

1. There are no comparisons with the usual sources of household wealth data—particularly sources concerning the distribution of wealth. There are no comparisons with the Consumer Expenditures Surveys (CEX), our only source of continuing data on household wealth. There are no comparisons with wealth estimates derived by capitalizing income from property, and there are no comparisons with estimates derived from estate data. (The last is addressed by Avery, Elliehausen, and Kennickell, but they are puzzled by what they find.) These comparisons would tell us more about the other data and methods than they would about the three surveys under review here, but it would be a great service to the profession to know something more about the data and methods that are the workaday stuff of workaday economists. I will return to this theme, particularly to the CEX, in a moment.

2. An omission of another sort relates to the lack of formal tests. We are asked to accept that things are similar or different by eyeballing some columns. What would be more important than formal tests of statistically significant difference would be to think of these alternative data sets as inputs in studies and to ask if the differences matter when making a policy decision or an analytic one.

Section 10.4 is an important exception. There the authors have the ingenious notion of fitting the same statistical model of lifetime accumulation of wealth to each of the three data sets as a way to analyze measurement error. The idea is that misspecification will be the same across the three data sets and that substantial differences in the correlation coefficient or in the standard errors of estimate therefore ought to be telling us something about differential measurement error. But the authors in fact have trouble interpreting what they find, and it is abundantly clear that the precise errors in variables model that is being relied on and the way that model would be affected by measurement error in these surveys need to be precisely known. The model and its error structure are simply going to have to be written down and its sensitivity to selectivity explored analytically since measurement error is correlated with income and with age, since, consequently, measurement error is larger for some assets than others, and since those assets are best measured in the SCF.

I would like to draw an inference from the comparison of the SCF and the FFAs. The authors find that the two are remarkably close in their aggregates but that this results from two large and offsetting differences in the subcomponents. The SCF is very high on house values and very low on liquid assets. The authors argue that self-reported house values are more appropriate than FFA estimates of replacement value, made via a depreciation and land rent adjustment to ancient benchmarks. Surely, the authors must be right about this, certainly in this era in which there has been extraordinary inflation since the benchmarks were established. The low liquid assets reported by households are a puzzle since presumably that is the sort of asset households know most about. So FFA must be wrong again, and the error is probably in assigning too little to small businesses and closely held corporations. Again, FFA probably relies on old benchmarks. If these arguments are right, they relate to a more general concern about our statistical collection effort. If, whenever we look at an FFA number, it is wrong, can we also presume that the FFA numbers we have not looked at carefully are also wrong? If so, does that mean that, when SCF agrees with the FFA, the SCF number is also wrong? Do two rights make a wrong? It may be. Many of our time series are in danger now of being badly out of step with our evolving economy. The data collectors are always loathe to change an ongoing series, and for good reason, but now they lack the time, the trained manpower, and the money as well as the inclination to do anything different. Household surveys, however, are nearly always state of the art. It is becoming easier and easier for me to believe, therefore, what is truly the central message of this paper—if you want to know anything about this economy, you had better resurvey, and, when you resurvey, you had better oversample.

This line of argument takes me back, as promised, to the CEX. Here we have an ongoing survey, but one in which there are natural times at which to change the questionnaires or even the sampling frame. Ranging over income and expenditures as well as net worth, these data now offer what is becoming increasingly unavailable—data that link across the range of independent variables that analysts not directly involved in the survey design will need to understand the variables in uses not of prime concern to the survey designers.

Nowadays you might want to answer such questions as, What does it mean to talk about changes in the distribution of wealth across families when about one child in five has a parent—the wealth-holding natural father, in all probability—residing in a different household? To what extent is the rapid convergence in income for young blacks and young whites and the divergence of income between old whites and their grandchildren going to affect wealth accumulation and its distribution? How tight in any case is the connection between income and wealth accumulation? Where are those random capital gains going? How much of domestic wealth is still held by domestic households? How frequently are the growing number of "involuntary entrepreneurs," to use Bronfenbrenner's felicitous phrase for describing people who go into business because they cannot find jobs, financing their businesses with personal debt? I am sure that each reader could immediately add three questions that he or she would want a graduate student to use the CEX to answer, if only we knew what to make of the asset and liability data of that survey.

The hope, probably forlorn, that the CEX net worth data are usable springs from the same evolving weakness in our statistical superstructure that I mentioned a minute ago. With the recipient unit, tax incentives across income sources, inflation and capital gains, and international capital flows all changing very quickly now, data routinely collected and tied to pre-1973 benchmarks are increasingly incredible. So we go out and survey—and the surveyors are now awash with projects and money. But these surveys are tightly targeted, so we get good data on one series and little or no related data on the variables that will inform our understanding of the target data set. Just as an example, how good is the income data in the SCF?

Reference

Avery, R., G. Elliehausen, and A. Kennickell. 1987. Measuring wealth with survey data: An evaluation of the 1983 Survey of Consumer Finances. Paper presented at the twentieth conference of the International Association for Research in Income and Wealth, Rocca di Papa, Italy, August.

11 Using Panel Data to Assess the Bias in Cross-sectional Inferences of Life-Cycle Changes in the Level and Composition of Household Wealth

Nancy Ammon Jianakoplos, Paul L. Menchik, and F. Owen Irvine

11.1 Introduction

The purpose of this paper is to confront the issue of the bias engendered by using cross-sectional data sets to estimate time-series relations. We focus on two issues: (1) the extent to which inferences about how the level of wealth changes as households age drawn from a single cross section misrepresent the actual pattern of wealth accumulation over time by individual households and (2) the extent to which the reallocations of wealth among various types of assets and liabilities by households of different ages observed in cross sections differ from the actual reallocations of assets and liabilities over time by individual households. Although it is well known that bias is likely to exist in these situations, and although different researchers have employed alternative adjustments in trying to ameliorate the bias, ours is the first attempt to measure this bias by contrasting results obtained by using cross sections and time series of individual households from the same data set.

Bias from using cross-sectional data to make time-series inferences is a topic of interest because cross-sectional estimates of age-wealth profiles have been used frequently to confirm or contradict the validity of the life-cycle hypothesis of saving (Modigliani 1986). The important paper by Shorrocks (1975) suggests that the age-wealth relation observed in a cross section can have little to do with what the profile

Nancy Ammon Jianakoplos is an assistant professor of economics at Michigan State University. Paul L. Menchik is a professor of economics at Michigan State University. F. Owen Irvine is an associate professor of economics at Michigan State University.

The order of the authors' names was determined randomly. All the authors contributed equally. Financial support for this paper was provided in part through grants from the Department of Health and Human Services and Michigan State University. Rob Wassmer provided prompt and efficient computer programming assistance.

would look like over time. First, Shorrocks constructed an example showing that, if every cohort member had increased his savings monotonically until death but different cohorts had different age-wealth profiles owing to different lifetime resources, the profile inferred from cross-sectional data would show the characteristic "hump" contrary to the actual monotonic longitudinal pattern of wealth accumulation. This bias, resulting from differences in accumulation across cohorts, can be thought of as the "productivity effect." Second, Shorrocks considered and attempted to adjust for another shortcoming of cross-sectional wealth studies, the problem of differential mortality. If the poor (like the good) die young, then in a cross section the relatively rich are overrepresented among the elderly. This oversampling of the wealthy imparts an upward bias to the observed age-wealth profile, while the previously mentioned productivity effect would cause a downward bias in the age-wealth profile.

Although it has been known that life-cycle inferences based on cross-sectional estimates are possibly biased, cross sections are still utilized throughout the literature owing to a lack, until recently, of alternatives such as panel data sets. Scholars have tried to "correct" the bias in cross sections by adjusting the data for hypothesized cohort differences, often using ad hoc techniques (Mirer 1979) or by adding lifetime earnings as a conditioning or explanatory variable (King and Dicks-Mireaux 1982). Whether such manipulations of cross-sectional data actually yield results that would be obtained from longitudinal data is a question yet to be answered. For example, is there any similarity between the age-wealth profile obtained by Mirer in his regression and that which would be observed as the subjects actually aged? Does the age profile of wealth divided by an estimate of permanent income in a cross section look anything like the profile of that same variable over time as a representative individual ages?

We construct age-wealth profiles from cross sections of our panel and then compare them to age-wealth profiles obtained by following the same households over time. This comparison allows us to identify and demonstrate the biases yielded by use of the cross-sectional approach. We also point out additional biases that may contaminate results obtained using panel data. Although our evidence indicates that using cross-sectional data to estimate age-wealth profiles and changes in the composition of household wealth over time is subject to substantial bias, we make no claim that the degree of bias is generalizable to other issues in which cross-sectional estimation procedures are used to test hypotheses that are longitudinal in nature.

The next section describes the data we use in our empirical analysis. In the following section, we discuss in more detail the problems associated with using cross-sectional data to make life-cycle inferences and the shortcomings of using panel data. In the next two sections, we present the results of our empirical investigation of the differences between using cross-sectional and panel data in studying age-wealth profiles and portfolio reallocation. The final section contains a summary of our results and our conclusions.

11.2   Data

In our empirical analysis, we utilize data from the National Longitudinal Surveys (NLS) of men aged forty-five to fifty-nine in 1966. These surveys, sponsored by the U.S. Department of Labor, were conducted at intervals from 1966 through 1981 using an initial panel of 5,020 households. Although these households do not represent the entire population, the age-wealth profiles of these households should, according to the life-cycle hypothesis, exhibit the greatest curvature during the ages observed in these surveys. We use the dollar value of household assets and liabilities reported in the 1966, 1971, 1976, and 1981 surveys. All dollar amounts are in 1976 dollars, deflated by the gross national product deflator for personal consumption expenditures.

Our empirical analysis employs three categories of variables constructed from the NLS data: measures of household nonhuman wealth (and its components), earnings variables, and the age of the respondent. WEALTH is defined as the sum of net residential housing assets, net farm assets, net business assets, net investment real estate, deposits in financial institutions, U.S. savings bonds, holdings of stock and bonds, personal loans made to others, and unsecured personal debt. Our analysis excludes annuity wealth, the capitalized value of income streams such as pensions.

In our analysis of household portfolio composition, we grouped net residential housing and farm assets (HOUSE/FARM) together (since the value of the farm frequently includes the value of the house on the farm). We also grouped net business assets and net investment real estate assets together as a variable called BUSINESS/LAND. Deposits in financial institutions, U.S. savings bonds, and personal loans made were grouped together as a variable called FINANCIAL. The amount of wealth held as bonds and stocks constitutes the STOCK/BOND variable. The number of usable observations of household wealth from each survey is reported in table 11.1.

Trend earnings (TREARNAT) is the average of the respondent's wage, salary, self-employment, and farm income (Y_i) discounted to age sixty-two using the following formula:

(1) $\text{TREARNAT} = (1/n)\Sigma[Y_i\,(1 - \text{TRATE}_i)]$

$$[(1.02)\exp(62 - \text{AGE}_i)],$$

where n is the number of observations of earnings included in the average, TRATE is an estimate of the respondent's combined federal

Table 11.1   Comparison of Sizes of NLS Samples Using Household Wealth Data

Sample	Table Where Sample Statistics Presented	Observations in Survey Year (N)				
		1966	1969	1971	1976	1981
Complete reporter survivors:						
15-YEAR CRS 1966–81[a]	11.6	1,691	1,691	1,691	1,691	1,691
5-YEAR CRS 1966–71[b]	11.7	3,372		3,372		
5-YEAR CRS 1971–76[c]	11.8			2,683	2,683	
5-YEAR CRS 1976–81[d]	11.9				2,170	2,170
Complete reporter until death[e]	11.10	2,707	2,478	2,354	2,010	1,691
Survivors, including partial reporters with reentry[f]	11.11	2,288	2,223	2,274	2,221	2,474
Usable data, no reentry[g]	11.5	4,546	3,571	3,103	2,294	1,691
Usable data with reentry[h]	11.12	4,546	3,812	3,656	2,953	2,474
Samples of other NLS users:						
Ohio State University Center for Human Resource Research "key" variable		4,028	3,499	3,076	2,639	2,081
Diamond and Hausman (1980, 7)		4,028	2,958	2,628	2,246	
Sobol (1979, table 1)		4,001	3,499	3,076		

[a]This sample consists of all respondents who provided both usable wealth and usable age data in each of the five surveys. Consequently, respondents in this sample must have survived through 1981.

[b]This sample consists of all respondents who provided both usable wealth and usable age data in both the 1966 and the 1971 surveys.

[c]This sample consists of all respondents who provided both usable wealth and usable age data in both the 1971 and the 1976 surveys.

[d]This sample consists of all respondents who provided both usable wealth and usable age data in both the 1976 and the 1981 surveys.

[e]This sample consists of all respondents who provided both usable wealth and usable age data in each survey until they died or survived through 1981. Thus, this sample adds to the 15-YEAR CRS sample those respondents who reported usable data in every survey but died before 1981.

[f]This sample consists of all respondents who provided both usable wealth and usable age data in any particular survey as long as they also provided these data in the 1981 survey.

[g]This sample consists of all respondents who provided both usable wealth and usable age data in any survey as long as they also provided these data in every preceding survey. Sample statistics are not presented for this sample, but it is the basis for the analysis in table 11.5.

[h]This sample consists of all respondents who provided both usable wealth and usable age data in a particular survey whether or not they reported these data in prior or subsequent surveys.

and state average income tax rate, and AGE is the respondent's age in the year of the survey. The NLS provides ten potential reports of the respondent's earnings. The reported earnings were included in the average only if the respondent was younger than sixty-two or met certain criteria relating to full-time hours and weeks of work for the same employer after age sixty-one. The average was computed only if there were at least two valid observations on earnings. This trend earnings variable is obviously related to the household's permanent income. We also computed a measure, AVERAGE EARNINGS, using the same procedure, except that we did not discount earnings to age sixty-two. Earnings measures could be constructed for 4,327 households.

Each respondent's age in the survey year was computed on the basis of his reported year and month of birth. A few respondents (forty-four) indicated ages outside the forty-five- to fifty-nine-year range of the sample. These households were excluded from all analysis because the sample was not selected to be representative of these cohorts.

Since WEALTH was constructed by summing asset and liability categories, households with incomplete or missing asset and liability data were excluded from our analysis of household wealth, but not completely from our analysis of sample attrition. The determination of whether asset and liability data were incomplete considered three situations in the data: (1) whether asset and liability values coded as missing should be considered zero; (2) whether asset and liability values coded as zero should be considered missing; and (3) whether asset and liability values had been coded correctly.

Some asset and liability values were coded as unavailable or unknown on the NLS data tape. In an effort to preserve as much data as possible, we presumed missing asset and liability values were equal to zero except when other information invalidated this presumption. We examined missing asset and liability data in one survey relative to responses in the other surveys. On the basis of comparisons of these values, we considered household wealth data to be incomplete in those surveys where the missing category had been a large proportion of household wealth (greater than 20 percent of net worth) in other surveys when the category was reported. In addition, if most categories of assets and liabilities were not reported in a specific survey, household wealth was considered incomplete in that year.

Longitudinal checking of the data also helped us identify some households who failed to report the existence of some assets and/or liabilities. For example, in the case in which the survey indicated that the respondent had not moved for three consecutive surveys and that the respondent reported owning a house of approximately equal value in all three surveys (allowing for house price appreciation) but reported the mortgage debt outstanding on the house only in the first and last survey, we considered household wealth incomplete in the middle survey because of the unreported mortgage debt.

Comparing asset, liability, and income data across surveys also lead us to suspect that some data were entered incorrectly on the data tape. For example, when wage and salary data in successive surveys were $10,100, $12,500, $1,400, $13,500, and $16,000, and when there was no indication that the respondent was unemployed or changed jobs over the interval, we suspected that wage and salary data in the third year could very likely be $14,000 rather than $1,400. We forwarded to the Center for Human Resource Research (CHRR) at The Ohio State University, which has responsibility for public distribution of the NLS data, lists of ninety-nine households for which we suspected income data had been incorrectly coded and 173 households for which we suspected asset or liability data had been incorrectly coded. The CHRR contacted the Census Bureau, which maintains the original survey forms, and received verification that, for seventeen and thirty-three households, respectively, on our lists of suspicious income and wealth reporters, data had been incorrectly transcribed from the survey form to the computer tape. For the remaining cases, the possibility remains that the survey taker incorrectly entered the data on the survey form.

Table 11.1 reports the number of usable observations of household wealth we have for each survey and compares these numbers to the number of observations used in other studies based on these NLS data. Many other researchers have used the wealth variable constructed by the CHRR, which is included on the NLS data tape. The CHRR created this variable by summing the same asset and liability categories as we have, but using different criteria for usable data. The CHRR series is comparable to our sample of "usable data allowing reentry." Our sample includes between 10 and 20 percent more observations than the CHRR series, depending on the survey year. On the basis of the number of observations available in 1966, Diamond and Hausman (1980) appear to have used the CHRR series in 1966 but only those observations in 1969, 1971, and 1976 of households that had reported usable data in 1966. This concept is very similar to our sample of "usable data with no reentry." Again, our sample is as much as 20 percent larger in some survey years. Other studies using the NLS Survey of Mature Men, such as those by Kotlikoff (1979) and Munnell (1976), required usable values for other variables in addition to wealth and, therefore, used much smaller-sized subsamples of the data.

11.3   Pitfalls of Cross-sectional and Panel Data

In the last few years, economists have hotly debated the degree to which the predictions of the life-cycle hypothesis of saving are consistent with actual asset holdings over the life cycle. Using cross-sectional samples of wealth holdings, authors have tried to confirm or contradict the predicted "humped" age-wealth profile implied by the well-known life-cycle model of saving (Modigliani and Brumberg 1954). Some of the research used cross-sectional data from estate duty files (Atkinson and Harrison 1978; Brittain 1978), but most studies have used cross-sectional surveys (e.g., Mirer 1979).

The use of cross-sectional data to test hypotheses about events oc-curing over time has been criticized generally by economists (Irvine 1981), and the use of cross-sectional estimates of life-cycle age-wealth profiles has been specifically criticized by Shorrocks (1975). As dis-cussed earlier, Shorrocks identifies two sources of bias (working in opposite directions) that confound the estimation of the age-wealth profile using cross-sectional data. First, owing to differential mortality (the poor die younger, the rich die older), the estimated age-wealth path is steeper than would be observed if the same individuals were followed over time. With death being a nonrandom sampler, the older households in an observed cross section are wealthier. Second, younger birth cohorts have higher income on the average since the real income in the economy grows over time. This makes an age-wealth profile constructed using cross-sectional data appear flatter than that which would be observed over time.

Our data on cohorts allow us first to estimate the size of the pro-ductivity effect and the amount of differential mortality. After docu-menting these, we construct cohort age-wealth profiles that are free from biases caused by productivity or mortality.

11.3.1   Productivity Effect

In table 11.2, both the mean and the median values of AVERAGE EARNINGS are reported for each birth cohort in our sample. On the average, median AVERAGE EARNINGS of a cohort is 1.9 percent greater than the next youngest cohort, while mean AVERAGE EARN-INGS is 1.3 percent greater than the next youngest cohort. Hence, the NLS data confirm the existence, on the average, of a productivity effect that raises the earnings of cohorts over time. However, note that the rate of growth of income is not smooth. For example, median earnings of the 1909 cohort is 13.2 percent greater than that of the 1908 cohort, while median earnings of the 1918 cohort is 4 percent below the median earnings of the 1917 cohort. Mirer attempted to correct cross-sectional household wealth data for this productivity effect by inflating the wealth of each successive cohort in his sample by 2 percent. The 2 percent adjustment is in line with the difference in median earnings observed in our sample.

Table 11.2   **Average Earnings by Cohort (1976 dollars)**

Cohort Birth Year	Median Average Earnings	Ratio of Cohort Median Earnings over Next Older Cohort	Mean Average Earnings	Ratio of Cohort Mean Earnings over Next Older Cohort
1921	10,885	1.053	11,867	1.017
1920	10,333	.994	11,672	1.038
1919	10,390	1.054	11,249	1.040
1918	9,855	.963	10,817	.993
1917	10,232	1.040	10,889	.997
1916	9,835	1.001	10,917	.988
1915	9,827	1.082	11,052	1.126
1914	9,079	1.015	9,818	1.027
1913	8,948	.993	9,561	.933
1912	9,015	1.081	10,251	1.064
1911	8,343	.963	9,630	1.037
1910	8,665	.952	9,282	.949
1909	9,102	1.132	9,779	1.003
1908	8,039	.948	9,753	.967
1907	8,483		10,091	
Average		1.019		1.013

Source: Computed from National Longitudinal Surveys of Mature Men.

Note: Earnings are the sum of wage, salary, business, and farm income for respondents who were younger than sixty-two at the survey date or who, if over sixty-two, met criteria relating to full-time hours and weeks of work for the same employer after age sixty-one. Average earnings are the arithmetic average of all observations on earnings for the 4,327 households reporting earnings in at least two surveys.

11.3.2   Differential Mortality Effect

The data in table 11.3 verify that there is a strong differential mortality effect. The respondents who reported usable household wealth figures in the 1966 survey were ranked according to their position in the distribution of wealth among other members of their birth cohort in 1966. The proportion of each wealth decile that had died by 1981 is given in table 11.3. For the youngest cohort, those born in 1921 (the first column), we find that 13.4 percent of the poorest respondents in percentile 1–20 died, while only 6.3 percent of the wealthiest respondents in percentile 90–100 died. Hence, for this cohort, the poorer households were more than twice as likely as the richest 10 percent to die. For the oldest cohort, those born in 1907, 49.1 percent of the poorest respondents died, compared to only 18.5 percent of the wealthiest respondents. The ratio of the death rate for the wealthiest 10 percent to that of the poorest 20 percent by cohort is given in the last row of table 11.3. As one can see, this ratio generally increases with the age of the cohort, averaging 2.946 across all the cohorts. Hence,

Table 11.3   **Reason for Attrition by Percentile of 1966 Cohort Wealth**

Reason for Attrition	Cohort Birth Year (fraction of initial cohort)				
	1921	1920	1919	1918	1917
Percentile 1–20:					
Died	.134	.269	.315	.266	.277
Refused	.090	.119	.110	.109	.169
Bad data	.090	.075	.068	.031	.092
Other	.194	.194	.178	.156	.138
Percentile 21–40:					
Died	.147	.197	.113	.143	.172
Refused	.132	.061	.127	.127	.109
Bad data	.176	.333	.155	.286	.266
Other	.074	.045	.085	.032	.078
Percentile 41–60:					
Died	.149	.091	.137	.095	.188
Refused	.134	.091	.164	.143	.156
Bad data	.209	.242	.233	.206	.172
Other	.075	.076	.055	.032	.078
Percentile 61–70:					
Died	.059	.152	.167	.091	.219
Refused	.059	.152	.250	.061	.156
Bad data	.147	.121	.194	.485	.219
Other	.029	.091	.028	.061	.063
Percentile 71–80:					
Died	.133	.091	.139	.100	.094
Refused	.233	.061	.167	.133	.219
Bad data	.200	.333	.250	.233	.156
Other	.033	.030	.083	.067	.000
Percentile 81–90:					
Died	.086	.061	.028	.094	.219
Refused	.114	.152	.111	.281	.156
Bad data	.200	.303	.250	.281	.219
Other	.000	.091	.000	.000	.031
Percentile 91–100:					
Died	.063	.000	.000	.100	.091
Refused	.188	.219	.121	.033	.091
Bad data	.250	.375	.455	.433	.455
Other	.031	.125	.061	.033	.061
Percentile 1–100:					
Died	.120	.142	.148	.140	.189
Refused	.129	.112	.145	.127	.149
Bad data	.174	.242	.203	.248	.211
Other	.078	.097	.081	.060	.075
Total	.502	.594	.577	.575	.624

(*continued*)

Table 11.3   (continued)

Reason for Attrition	Cohort Birth Year (fraction of initial cohort)				
	1921	1920	1919	1918	1917
Ratio of percentiles 1–20 to percentiles 91–100:					
Died	2.149	. . .	. . .	2.656	3.046
	1916	1915	1914	1913	1912
Percentile 1–20:					
Died	.284	.352	.443	.354	.404
Refused	.045	.070	.033	.046	.035
Bad data	.060	.070	.082	.046	.070
Other	.119	.099	.148	.092	.175
Percentile 21–40:					
Died	.182	.271	.274	.190	.143
Refused	.076	.086	.097	.111	.161
Bad data	.227	.214	.161	.190	.179
Other	.076	.057	.048	.016	.054
Percentile 41–60:					
Died	.258	.286	.203	.175	.339
Refused	.091	.100	.102	.175	.071
Bad data	.197	.271	.288	.206	.196
Other	.045	.014	.034	.016	.000
Percentile 61–70:					
Died	.147	.257	.172	.250	.111
Refused	.206	.114	.172	.063	.185
Bad data	.118	.286	.276	.219	.333
Other	.088	.057	.000	.094	.000
Percentile 71–80:					
Died	.031	.143	.167	.167	.241
Refused	.188	.114	.133	.200	.207
Bad data	.250	.314	.200	.167	.276
Other	.031	.086	.000	.033	.000
Percentile 81–90:					
Died	.242	.143	.167	.161	.250
Refused	.121	.143	.100	.065	.107
Bad data	.152	.200	.233	.452	.286
Other	.061	.086	.067	.000	.000
Percentile 91–100:					
Died	.138	.059	.194	.133	.034
Refused	.069	.088	.194	.100	.069
Bad data	.448	.500	.290	.367	.310
Other	.034	.029	.000	033	.172

Table 11.3   (continued)

Reason for Attrition	Cohort Birth Year (fraction of initial cohort)				
	1916	1915	1914	1913	1912
Percentile 1–100:					
Died	.202	.243	.255	.217	.241
Refused	.101	.097	.106	.108	.110
Bad data	.190	.240	.205	.207	.209
Other	.070	.060	.053	.041	.064
Total	.563	.640	.619	.573	.624
Ratio of percentiles 1–20 to percentiles 91–100:					
Died	2.056	5.986	2.287	2.654	11.702

	1911	1910	1909	1908	1907	All
Percentile 1–20:						
Died	.484	.389	.426	.462	.491	.350
Refused	.032	.037	.093	.038	.055	.075
Bad data	.081	.019	.000	.058	.036	.059
Other	.161	.148	.130	.135	.109	.141
Percentile 21–40:						
Died	.344	.407	.321	.412	.327	.240
Refused	.049	.056	.094	.020	.102	.093
Bad data	.197	.204	.208	.157	.184	.213
Other	.115	.037	.019	.059	.102	.058
Percentile 41–60:						
Died	.164	.358	.245	.327	.314	.207
Refused	.082	.132	.113	.135	.118	.129
Bad data	.295	.226	.264	.154	.196	.227
Other	.033	.019	.094	.077	.039	.047
Percentile 61–70:						
Died	.400	.296	.259	.208	.400	.218
Refused	.033	.111	.074	.167	.240	.129
Bad data	.200	.259	.333	.167	.120	.227
Other	.033	.037	.037	.042	.040	.055
Percentile 71–80:						
Died	.133	.296	.269	.160	.269	.153
Refused	.100	.111	.269	.120	.077	.155
Bad data	.400	.370	.154	.440	.308	.262
Other	.033	.000	.077	.040	.077	.042

(*continued*)

Table 11.3   (continued)

Reason for Attrition	Cohort Birth Year (fraction of initial cohort)					
	1911	1910	1909	1908	1907	All
Percentile 81–90:						
Died	.267	.074	.074	.259	.240	.150
Refused	.133	.148	.111	.037	.120	.126
Bad data	.367	.370	.185	.259	.240	.278
Other	.033	.000	.000	.074	.080	.035
Percentile 91–100:						
Died	.233	.160	.160	.200	.185	.119
Refused	.000	.080	.000	.040	.037	.094
Bad data	.367	.400	.440	.440	.370	.397
Other	.067	.000	.040	.080	.111	.049
Percentile 1–100:						
Died	.303	.315	.275	.324	.337	.224
Refused	.059	.090	.106	.074	.101	.110
Bad data	.247	.228	.204	.203	.186	.215
Other	.079	.045	.064	.078	.081	.068
Total	.688	.678	.649	.680	.705	.616
Ratio of percentiles 1–20 to percentiles 91–100:						
Died	2.074	2.431	2.662	2.308	2.651	2.946

Source: Computed from the National Longitudinal Surveys of Mature Men.
Note: Sample consists of 4,546 households that reported valid age and wealth data in the 1966 survey.

on the average, the poorer respondents died nearly three times more frequently than the richest respondents, controlling for age. Evidence from our sample certainly confirms Shorrocks's assertion that the poor die young.

We have also examined the death rates between samples by cohort. Higher death rates are, of course, observed between later surveys since the respondents are aging. Aggregating across cohorts, table 11.4 gives the death rates between samples by initial wealth level. Again, we see the poorer respondents dying more frequently between surveys.

11.3.3   Sample Attrition

Panel data offer the advantage of being able to track the behavior of individual cohorts over time. However, over time there is sample attrition. As panel members drop out, the representativeness of the sam-

Table 11.4	Mortality Rates by Percentile of 1966 Wealth				
1966 Wealth Percentile	Deaths between (fraction of remaining cohort):				1966–81 (fraction of initial cohort)
	1966–69	1969–71	1971–76	1976–81	
1–20	.07	.06	.18	.19	.35
21–40	.05	.04	.11	.13	.24
41–60	.04	.03	.11	.15	.21
61–70	.06	.04	.09	.10	.22
71–80	.04	.03	.08	.10	.15
81–90	.04	.02	.06	.11	.15
91–100	.03	.02	.04	.09	.12
1–100	.05	.03	.11	.14	.22

Source: Computed from the National Longitudinal Surveys of Mature Men.
Note: Sample consists of 4,546 households that reported valid age and wealth data in the 1966 survey.

ple with respect to the underlying population may be affected. In table 11.5, data are presented that summarize attrition in the NLS sample between surveys. About two-thirds of the attrition is due to failure to interview the respondent, and about one-third is due to the respondent reporting unusable data ("bad data").

As the next to bottom row indicates, from 38 to 69 percent of the noninterviews were caused by death of the respondent since the last survey date. Even though death is not random (as documented above), the remaining observed sample would be representative of the living members of the cohort if death were the only cause of attrition.

Other forms of attrition, to the extent that they are not randomly distributed across the cohort, however, may cause the observed panel sample to be unrepresentative of the living cohort. Looking again at table 11.3, which classifies households by cohort and wealth percentile, we see in the right-hand column that more of the poorest respondents were lost owing to other reasons (moved, temporary absence, etc.). On the other hand, the percentage of respondents lost because they refused to be interviewed increased with wealth level up to decile 71–80. Even more striking is the fact that the percentage lost because they reported bad data increases dramatically with wealth. This percentage ranges from 5.9 for the bottom 20 percent to about 22 for respondents with moderate wealth to a high of 39.7 for the wealthiest 10 percent of the households. Hence, attrition due to either refusing to answer or giving bad data when interviewed rises dramatically with initial wealth level. Assuming the initial sample was selected so as to be representative of the living cohort in 1966, this attrition due to refusal/bad data makes the observed cohort in later samples unrepresentative of the

Table 11.5   **Reasons for Sample Attrition**

	Survey Year				
	1966	1969	1971	1976	1981
Number of observations with usable wealth and age data	4,546	3,571	3,103	2,294	1,691
Number of attritors[a]		975 (21%)	468 (13%)	809 (26%)	603 (26%)
Reason for attrition:[b]					
Bad data		372 (38%)	249 (53%)	270 (33%)	142 (24%)
Noninterview		603 (62%)	219 (47%)	539 (67%)	461 (76%)
Reason for noninterview:[c]					
No reason		16 (3%)	6 (3%)	10 (2%)	3 (1%)
Moved		45 (7%)	17 (8%)	10 (2%)	5 (1%)
Nonmover		37 (6%)	14 (6%)	6 (1%)	5 (1%)
Temporary absence		16 (2%)	10 (5%)	9 (2%)	4 (1%)
Institutionalized		11 (2%)	11 (5%)	14 (2%)	18 (4%)
Refused		227 (38%)	37 (17%)	135 (25%)	96 (21%)
Dead		229 (38%)	124 (56%)	344 (64%)	319 (69%)
Dropped from sample		22 (4%)	0 (0%)	11 (2%)	11 (2%)

Source: Computed from the National Longitudinal Surveys of Mature Men.

Note: Sample consists of all respondents who provided both usable wealth and usable age data in any survey as long as they also provided these data in every preceding survey.

[a]Numbers in parentheses give percentage of participants in previous survey.

[b]Numbers in parentheses give percentage of attritors.

[c]Numbers in parentheses give the percentage of participants not interviewed.

living cohort members. The observed sample of any cohort in later years contains too few wealthy respondents. For example, using the members of the 1914 cohort who reported usable data in 1976 to calculate the wealth of the 1914 cohort will probably understate the wealth of the living members of the 1914 cohort since attrition due to bad data/refusal was higher among the wealthier deciles. This result is consistent with other research that finds that wealthy people are less likely to respond or respond fully to surveys of financial information (Lillard, Smith, and Welch 1986; Projector and Weiss 1966; Ferber 1965; Ferber et al. 1969).

11.3.4   Construction of Cohort Age-Wealth Profiles

We want to construct age-wealth profiles that are representative of individual behavior over time. In particular, we want to avoid biases that are introduced by the productivity effect, by the differential mortality effect, and by differential attrition. These profiles are of interest not only because they provide some additional evidence on the life-cycle hypothesis but, more important, because they will be used to assess the bias in age-wealth profiles based on cross-sectional data (the focus of this paper).

Productivity-effect biases are avoided by observing the same-aged respondents over time. The NLS data allow us to track the wealth of individuals in fifteen different cohorts as they age from 1966 through 1981. However, one should not simply use the available data from each cohort in each year, calculate the median wealth (or mean wealth), and plot median wealth against age. Such cohort-specific age-wealth profiles would still be subject to biases caused by differential mortality and differential attrition.

By plotting the median wealth of a cohort over time, the implicit assumption is that the median person is the "representative individual" from the cohort. However, as the cohort ages, a larger percentage of the poorer households die. This differential mortality removes more individuals from the lower part of the wealth distribution and, hence, causes the median of the remaining respondents to be a wealthier person. Ceteris paribus, this differential mortality would bias cohort age-wealth profiles to show more wealth accumulation over time. For example, in the extreme case in which every individual simply maintained his initial wealth level over time, the differential mortality of the poor would lead one to observe median wealth increasing with the age of the cohort. Fortunately, one can correct for this differential mortality bias in constructing cohort age-wealth profiles by limiting one's sample to those respondents who survived to the end of the panel. In this way, mortality effects are removed from the sample.

As we saw earlier, however, sample attrition was not caused just by death, but also resulted from respondents' refusal to participate, reporting bad data, or other reasons (moving, etc.). Hence, limiting the sample to those respondents who survive to the end of the panel (1981 in our case) does not produce a sample of the same individuals over time. At any given sample date, some households refuse, report bad data, or are otherwise unavailable. In fact, reentry is possible in that a person may report good data in 1966, unusable data in 1969, and good data again in 1971, 1976, and 1981. If all this attrition (and reentry) were uncorrelated with wealth, little bias would be caused. But as we documented earlier, the frequency of bad data/refusal increased substantially with initial wealth. This leads to more of the richer households being missing from the cohort sample over time. This differential attrition tends to lower the median wealth of the observed distribution, ceteris paribus. One can correct for this differential attrition bias by limiting one's sample to respondents who reported usable data over every interval for which analysis is conducted. However, as explained below, this procedure may affect the representativeness of the remaining sample.[1]

For our analysis of cohort age-wealth profiles over the entire fifteen-year survey interval, we limit our sample to those cohort members who both survived to 1981 and reported usable data in all five surveys. In this way, we eliminate biases caused by differential mortality and differential attrition. By tracking the wealth accumulation of these "fifteen-year complete reporting survivors" (15-YEAR CRS), we are indeed tracking the behavior of the same individuals over time. There are 1,691 households included in this sample. Dividing them into fifteen age cohorts, we are able to construct age-wealth profiles that are representative of the behavior of individuals in these cohorts (but not necessarily the aggregate cohort). We concentrate on age-wealth profiles based on median wealth since the majority of studies have focused on the median individual. However, in table 11.6, we report the mean, median, twenty-fifth, seventy-fifth, and ninetieth percentile wealth of each cohort at each survey date in terms of 1976 dollars for those interested in behavior at other points on the wealth distribution.[2]

Before examining these age-wealth profiles, we should point out possible limitations of using this 15-YEAR CRS sample. To be included in the 15-YEAR CRS sample, the household must have survived until 1981 and reported complete data in every survey. These are very stringent requirements. Studying table 11.1 indicates that the requirement that the respondent live to 1981 reduced the potential sample size by as many as 1,016 households in 1966, but by only 319 households in 1976. Our earlier analysis of differential mortality suggests these were mainly poorer households. The further requirement that the respondent provide usable data in all surveys eliminated 500–600 more households that were partial reporters. These tended to be mainly richer households. Since these effects are somewhat offsetting, it is not clear whether the median wealth of a cohort in our 15-YEAR CRS sample is representative of the living members of the cohort. In either case, it is likely that the very poor and the very rich are underrepresented in the 15-YEAR CRS sample. Hence, 15-YEAR CRS cohort age-wealth profiles are not necessarily representative of the entire NLS mature men sample

Table 11.6   **WEALTH by Cohort for 15-YEAR CRS Sample (1976 dollars)**

Age in 1966 (N):	WEALTH in Survey Year					Age in
Sample Statistic	1966	1969	1971	1976	1981	1981
45 (158):						60
Mean	27,856	35,436	35,060	52,894	68,598	
Median	16,004	20,492	22,204	31,938	39,201	
Twenty-fifth percentile	3,151	7,899	8,186	10,300	16,046	
Seventy-fifth percentile	31,509	43,070	42,974	53,700	88,016	
Ninetieth percentile	66,219	78,987	76,398	117,000	143,873	
46 (131):						61
Mean	30,390	34,244	34,315	43,392	60,274	
Median	13,847	17,884	21,010	28,500	32,837	
Twenty-fifth percentile	1,658	1,490	3,411	3,000	4,739	
Seventy-fifth percentile	27,570	31,244	37,517	50,000	63,643	
Ninetieth percentile	61,360	70,045	79,127	103,000	119,838	
47 (150):						62
Mean	33,295	35,920	38,986	50,158	59,868	
Median	13,553	15,100	18,349	25,353	31,303	
Twenty-fifth percentile	2,488	522	2,046	5,700	10,291	
Seventy-fifth percentile	34,624	39,270	45,157	61,050	74,475	
Ninetieth percentile	66,750	78,689	72,052	110,050	139,066	
48 (131):						63
Mean	25,755	29,179	33,475	40,379	46,120	
Median	14,378	12,665	16,508	21,500	27,420	
Twenty-fifth percentile	2,156	2,666	4,229	6,026	7,583	
Seventy-fifth percentile	33,333	40,238	43,656	48,200	59,580	
Ninetieth percentile	50,415	67,697	75,716	89,500	81,900	
49 (115):						64
Mean	32,206	33,151	34,521	45,752	46,044	
Median	14,096	17,884	19,782	26,453	29,262	
Twenty-fifth percentile	4,146	3,204	6,821	5,500	5,484	
Seventy-fifth percentile	39,138	39,195	41,610	55,000	62,288	
Ninetieth percentile	77,944	78,912	72,033	104,000	119,634	
50 (135):						65
Mean	29,732	31,353	36,297	43,227	49,315	
Median	14,594	14,203	18,690	23,000	30,806	
Twenty-fifth percentile	166	0	2,046	1,600	4,401	
Seventy-fifth percentile	32,803	36,662	41,337	57,000	58,226	
Ninetieth percentile	79,270	82,951	73,670	103,750	124,577	
51 (121):						66
Mean	37,171	36,186	37,303	42,758	48,447	
Median	12,438	17,511	17,735	17,000	21,286	
Twenty-fifth percentile	249	355	614	3,000	4,062	
Seventy-fifth percentile	35,489	44,411	45,634	52,000	55,518	
Ninetieth percentile	66,667	71,535	85,471	86,000	96,276	

(*continued*)

Table 11.6   (continued)

Age in 1966 (N):	WEALTH in Survey Year					Age in
Sample Statistic	1966	1969	1971	1976	1981	1981
52 (108):						67
Mean	33,040	35,789	36,783	45,083	54,203	
Median	15,744	18,350	19,987	24,930	25,051	
Twenty-fifth percentile	5,058	3,690	4,195	6,850	8,633	
Seventy-fifth percentile	36,029	44,330	47,272	49,600	58,565	
Ninetieth percentile	81,260	90,909	88,677	117,000	118,483	
53 (131):						68
Mean	31,282	35,329	38,240	43,177	44,770	
Median	14,096	17,437	20,464	22,000	27,759	
Twenty-fifth percentile	539	37	873	2,000	7,448	
Seventy-fifth percentile	36,070	43,219	47,749	60,000	60,934	
Ninetieth percentile	66,335	76,602	89,495	101,500	98,172	
54 (103):						69
Mean	26,978	31,258	34,526	43,307	41,285	
Median	14,262	18,629	19,100	20,700	17,603	
Twenty-fifth percentile	3,463	4,396	4,775	3,500	1,625	
Seventy-fifth percentile	33,831	45,455	43,656	51,000	50,102	
Ninetieth percentile	76,285	80,626	83,083	120,000	91,401	
55 (87):						70
Mean	48,957	64,248	51,895	51,676	60,032	
Median	17,579	21,495	20,464	23,000	29,824	
Twenty-fifth percentile	2,861	5,961	6,194	4,100	1,726	
Seventy-fifth percentile	36,318	50,820	52,183	58,350	64,320	
Ninetieth percentile	119,403	133,383	121,419	135,000	174,001	
56 (80):						71
Mean	37,063	43,189	49,817	52,558	47,745	
Median	10,116	14,233	15,229	21,800	23,697	
Twenty-fifth percentile	382	1,341	231	300	1,050	
Seventy-fifth percentile	34,163	33,368	45,574	52,050	45,566	
Ninetieth percentile	82,090	96,982	107,231	102,200	87,339	
57 (91):						72
Mean	40,830	43,613	45,121	53,019	67,914	
Median	17,413	21,013	22,374	31,000	30,467	
Twenty-fifth percentile	4,146	4,620	7,640	8,200	6,838	
Seventy-fifth percentile	64,365	55,216	51,842	59,950	64,997	
Ninetieth percentile	109,453	96,982	106,557	137,000	159,106	
58 (80):						73
Mean	35,078	40,965	41,223	42,234	46,356	
Median	16,750	18,257	21,146	22,113	21,165	
Twenty-fifth percentile	1,658	558	3,070	4,242	5,077	
Seventy-fifth percentile	38,943	52,161	46,385	49,000	56,161	
Ninetieth percentile	98,673	110,656	91,406	97,200	102,924	

Table 11.6   (continued)

Age in 1966 (N): Sample Statistic	WEALTH in Survey Year					Age in 1981
	1966	1969	1971	1976	1981	
59 (70):						74
Mean	36,828	27,901	27,330	31,407	30,001	
Median	13,433	12,444	13,438	22,880	20,650	
Twenty-fifth percentile	166	0	2,729	8,000	3,047	
Seventy-fifth percentile	43,947	31,133	29,795	44,000	40,623	
Ninetieth percentile	87,107	70,790	61,051	79,000	70,346	

Source: Computed from the National Longitudinal Surveys of Mature Men.
Note: WEALTH is the sum of net residential housing assets, net farm assets, net business assets, net investment real estate assets, deposits in financial institutions, U.S. savings bonds, holdings of stocks and bonds, and personal loans made to others less unsecured personal debt. The sample consists of 1,691 respondents who provided both usable wealth and usable age data in each of the five surveys.

or even of all living members of the cohort at any given date. The respondents who die before 1981 may very well have differently shaped age-wealth profiles (especially if they expect to die); we document below that their median wealth levels are lower. Also, the partial reporters may have differently shaped age-wealth profiles; we document below that their median wealth is higher. It is also possible that the twentieth or the ninetieth percentile age-wealth profiles differ from the median age-wealth profile. The usefulness of the median 15-YEAR CRS cohort age-wealth profiles is that they allow us to assess the amount of productivity and differential mortality bias present in age-wealth profiles based on cross-sectional data over a fifteen-year span.

To make our analysis more complete, over shorter five-year intervals we have constructed 5-YEAR CRS samples. Inclusion in the 5-YEAR CRS 1966–71 sample required only that a household survive until 1971 and report complete data in both the 1966 and the 1971 surveys. These requirements yielded a sample of 3,372 households, compared to the 1,691 members of the 15-YEAR CRS sample. Likewise, the 5-YEAR CRS 1971–76 and 5-YEAR CRS 1976–81 samples required that households survive to at least 1976 and 1981, respectively, and report complete data in the two adjacent surveys. These samples include 2,683 and 2,170 households in the 5-YEAR CRS 1971–76 and 1976–81 samples, respectively. When these larger samples are compared to the 15-YEAR CRS sample, median cohort wealth was lower in 1966, about the same in 1971, and higher in 1976. However, the larger samples definitely include more wealthy individuals, making the mean wealth across all households larger in the larger samples. The mean and median wealth of cohorts in these larger 5-YEAR CRS samples as well as measures of wealth at other points in the distribution are reported in tables 11.7–11.9.[3]

Table 11.7   WEALTH by Cohort for 5-YEAR CRS 1966–71 SAMPLE
(1976 dollars)

Age in 1966 (N): Sample Statistic	WEALTH in Survey Year		Age Range between Surveys	Number Dissaving
	1966	1971		
45 (269):			45–50	79
Mean	29,073	42,395		
Median	14,925	22,920		
Twenty-fifth percentile	2,920	6,821		
Seventy-fifth percentile	32,753	42,701		
Ninetieth percentile	68,823	77,763		
46 (247):			46–51	81
Mean	38,651	45,318		
Median	14,212	17,735		
Twenty-fifth percentile	1,607	3,553		
Seventy-fifth percentile	31,426	38,199		
Ninetieth percentile	72,139	89,359		
47 (267):			47–52	88
Mean	32,393	37,555		
Median	12,023	15,621		
Twenty-fifth percentile	1,161	1,988		
Seventy-fifth percentile	31,509	41,814		
Ninetieth percentile	71,476	84,686		
48 (236):			48–53	77
Mean	29,931	38,226		
Median	15,527	20,396		
Twenty-fifth percentile	2,805	6,139		
Seventy-fifth percentile	36,310	47,886		
Ninetieth percentile	62,521	85,266		
49 (234):			49–54	78
Mean	37,748	39,206		
Median	12,089	17,889		
Twenty-fifth percentile	3,317	5,457		
Seventy-fifth percentile	32,007	38,199		
Ninetieth percentile	70,481	78,445		
50 (240):			50–55	77
Mean	35,780	42,733		
Median	14,449	18,349		
Twenty-fifth percentile	1,721	3,823		
Seventy-fifth percentile	32,529	41,491		
Ninetieth percentile	80,805	76,057		

Table 11.7   (continued)

Age in 1966 (N): Sample Statistic	WEALTH in Survey Year		Age Range between Surveys	Number Dissaving
	1966	1971		
51 (260):			51–56	83
Mean	35,390	44,276		
Median	12,438	17,572		
Twenty-fifth percentile	637	2,077		
Seventy-fifth percentile	32,007	43,349		
Ninetieth percentile	73,218	90,041		
52 (225):			52–57	76
Mean	42,922	38,788		
Median	15,423	18,267		
Twenty-fifth percentile	2,471	4,502		
Seventy-fifth percentile	37,479	47,749		
Ninetieth percentile	83,250	89,291		
53 (246):			53–58	89
Mean	32,178	43,999		
Median	15,838	20,471		
Twenty-fifth percentile	1,119	873		
Seventy-fifth percentile	38,640	47,749		
Ninetieth percentile	81,260	109,141		
54 (212):			54–59	71
Mean	41,563	37,478		
Median	14,887	19,100		
Twenty-fifth percentile	2,926	4,775		
Seventy-fifth percentile	33,167	40,928		
Ninetieth percentile	56,385	82,435		
55 (202):			55–60	65
Mean	44,681	49,653		
Median	15,672	20,293		
Twenty-fifth percentile	663	2,729		
Seventy-fifth percentile	44,113	53,956		
Ninetieth percentile	107,794	121,419		
56 (182):			56–61	61
Mean	33,045	38,929		
Median	11,941	13,957		
Twenty-fifth percentile	829	153		
Seventy-fifth percentile	28,192	40,928		
Ninetieth percentile	66,874	83,083		

(continued)

Table 11.7 (continued)

Age in 1966 (N): Sample Statistic	WEALTH in Survey Year		Age Range between Surveys	Number Dissaving
	1966	1971		
57 (203):			57–62	66
Mean	35,295	41,956		
Median	17,413	20,464		
Twenty-fifth percentile	3,317	4,775		
Seventy-fifth percentile	38,972	43,656		
Ninetieth percentile	109,453	117,190		
58 (187):			58–63	67
Mean	48,911	48,332		
Median	16,252	19,236		
Twenty-fifth percentile	1,658	2,080		
Seventy-fifth percentile	43,947	45,703		
Ninetieth percentile	120,232	98,226		
59 (162):			59–64	65
Mean	60,984	53,131		
Median	14,902	16,508		
Twenty-fifth percentile	539	1,364		
Seventy-fifth percentile	43,947	36,767		
Ninetieth percentile	96,186	98,909		

Source: Computed from the National Longitudinal Surveys of Mature Men.

Note: WEALTH is the sum of net residential housing assets, net farm assets, net business assets, net investment real estate assets, deposits in financial institutions, U.S. savings bonds, holdings of stocks and bonds, and personal loans made to others less unsecured personal debt. The sample consists of 3,372 respondents who provided both usable wealth and usable age data in the 1966 and 1971 surveys.

Table 11.8 **WEALTH by Cohort for 5-YEAR CRS 1971–76 Sample (1976 dollars)**

Age in 1966 (N): Sample Statistic	WEALTH in Survey Year		Age Range between Surveys	Number Dissaving
	1971	1976		
45 (223):			50–55	61
Mean	46,856	60,225		
Median	24,523	32,000		
Twenty-fifth percentile	9,550	10,200		
Seventy-fifth percentile	50,750	61,000		
Ninetieth percentile	88,677	147,000		
46 (198):			51–56	62
Mean	40,634	48,033		
Median	18,691	25,000		
Twenty-fifth percentile	5,593	4,150		
Seventy-fifth percentile	38,452	50,500		
Ninetieth percentile	95,498	124,675		

Table 11.8   (continued)

Age in 1966 (N): Sample Statistic	WEALTH in Survey Year		Age Range between Surveys	Number Dissaving
	1971	1976		
47 (224):			52–57	59
Mean	39,347	50,083		
Median	17,156	22,813		
Twenty-fifth percentile	2,456	5,708		
Seventy-fifth percentile	43,452	61,065		
Ninetieth percentile	89,632	130,500		
48 (200):			53–58	71
Mean	37,718	44,384		
Median	19,202	22,300		
Twenty-fifth percentile	6,821	7,650		
Seventy-fifth percentile	45,634	51,350		
Ninetieth percentile	80,491	92,120		
49 (186):			54–59	66
Mean	40,995	46,192		
Median	19,100	26,477		
Twenty-fifth percentile	6,821	8,000		
Seventy-fifth percentile	41,883	56,420		
Ninetieth percentile	88,677	93,800		
50 (207):			55–60	63
Mean	41,027	45,848		
Median	20,600	24,500		
Twenty-fifth percentile	3,547	6,100		
Seventy-fifth percentile	43,656	59,050		
Ninetieth percentile	81,855	103,750		
51 (199):			56–61	74
Mean	37,112	43,677		
Median	18,505	23,000		
Twenty-fifth percentile	4,775	5,025		
Seventy-fifth percentile	45,634	51,000		
Ninetieth percentile	88,267	97,000		
52 (191):			57–62	72
Mean	38,527	44,175		
Median	17,599	22,700		
Twenty-fifth percentile	3,411	5,000		
Seventy-fifth percentile	47,783	50,000		
Ninetieth percentile	96,180	109,000		
53 (193):			58–63	67
Mean	41,300	44,607		
Median	21,555	24,000		
Twenty-fifth percentile	1,637	5,000		
Seventy-fifth percentile	46,385	57,676		
Ninetieth percentile	103,001	101,500		

(continued)

Table 11.8   (continued)

Age in 1966 (N): Sample Statistic	WEALTH in Survey Year		Age Range between Surveys	Number Dissaving
	1971	1976		
54 (167):			59–64	65
Mean	31,600	38,272		
Median	18,690	20,700		
Twenty-fifth percentile	4,025	4,685		
Seventy-fifth percentile	40,246	47,400		
Ninetieth percentile	81,310	95,700		
55 (160):			60–65	60
Mean	52,022	50,008		
Median	21,112	21,950		
Twenty-fifth percentile	3,822	3,900		
Seventy-fifth percentile	54,263	55,678		
Ninetieth percentile	125,512	118,800		
56 (127):			61–66	40
Mean	39,885	44,612		
Median	15,280	21,100		
Twenty-fifth percentile	409	1,500		
Seventy-fifth percentile	40,928	50,700		
Ninetieth percentile	76,398	76,000		
57 (149):			62–67	57
Mean	45,548	51,947		
Median	23,874	29,940		
Twenty-fifth percentile	7,149	6,770		
Seventy-fifth percentile	51,842	59,950		
Ninetieth percentile	131,651	138,000		
58 (139):			63–68	67
Mean	51,445	47,529		
Median	22,419	21,600		
Twenty-fifth percentile	3,070	3,000		
Seventy-fifth percentile	51,160	50,000		
Ninetieth percentile	144,611	117,500		
59 (120):			64–69	46
Mean	44,444	45,981		
Median	16,781	22,480		
Twenty-fifth percentile	3,895	7,900		
Seventy-fifth percentile	38,848	44,000		
Ninetieth percentile	89,905	85,875		

Source: Computed from the National Longitudinal Surveys of Mature Men.

Note: WEALTH is the sum of net residential housing assets, net farm assets, net business assets, net investment real estate assets, deposits in financial institutions, U.S. savings bonds, holdings of stocks and bonds, and personal loans made to others less unsecured personal debt. The sample consists of 2,683 respondents who provided both usable wealth and usable age data in the 1971 and 1976 surveys.

Table 11.9   **WEALTH by Cohort for 5-YEAR CRS 1976–81 Sample (1976 dollars)**

Age in 1966 (N): Sample Statistic	WEALTH in Survey Year		Age Range between Surveys	Number Dissaving
	1976	1981		
45 (195):			55–60	60
Mean	64,277	80,190		
Median	34,340	40,691		
Twenty-fifth percentile	15,000	17,332		
Seventy-fifth percentile	61,000	91,401		
Ninetieth percentile	147,000	160,799		
46 (165):			56–61	47
Mean	54,876	71,561		
Median	28,600	32,498		
Twenty-fifth percentile	4,750	7,448		
Seventy-fifth percentile	53,500	64,658		
Ninetieth percentile	165,000	163,372		
47 (187):			57–62	60
Mean	53,484	66,275		
Median	26,125	32,498		
Twenty-fifth percentile	8,700	11,510		
Seventy-fifth percentile	61,800	79,215		
Ninetieth percentile	140,000	152,877		
48 (168):			58–63	57
Mean	45,369	50,034		
Median	25,350	29,079		
Twenty-fifth percentile	7,350	9,510		
Seventy-fifth percentile	51,850	64,355		
Ninetieth percentile	95,000	100,413		
49 (152):			59–64	69
Mean	51,878	54,896		
Median	30,000	35,206		
Twenty-fifth percentile	11,250	8,673		
Seventy-fifth percentile	58,100	70,379		
Ninetieth percentile	107,000	129,113		
50 (176):			60–65	63
Mean	45,104	53,596		
Median	24,450	31,144		
Twenty-fifth percentile	6,736	9,411		
Seventy-fifth percentile	60,750	66,960		
Ninetieth percentile	108,000	132,701		

(continued)

Table 11.9   (continued)

Age in 1966 (N): Sample Statistic	WEALTH in Survey Year		Age Range between Surveys	Number Dissaving
	1976	1981		
51 (160):			61–66	64
Mean	43,496	47,916		
Median	25,700	23,731		
Twenty-fifth percentile	5,112	6,280		
Seventy-fifth percentile	51,900	58,870		
Ninetieth percentile	88,525	97,224		
52 (139):			62–67	66
Mean	47,587	55,932		
Median	25,000	26,405		
Twenty-fifth percentile	7,702	8,125		
Seventy-fifth percentile	50,000	60,528		
Ninetieth percentile	117,000	135,410		
53 (157):			63–68	65
Mean	52,839	57,011		
Median	29,935	33,852		
Twenty-fifth percentile	8,000	9,248		
Seventy-fifth percentile	66,000	64,031		
Ninetieth percentile	156,000	140,149		
54 (124):			64–69	55
Mean	45,742	43,513		
Median	22,250	20,311		
Twenty-fifth percentile	4,843	3,216		
Seventy-fifth percentile	54,634	54,232		
Ninetieth percentile	122,600	94,617		
55 (120):			65–70	61
Mean	56,206	60,089		
Median	26,500	29,469		
Twenty-fifth percentile	5,525	4,063		
Seventy-fifth percentile	68,750	66,690		
Ninetieth percentile	127,500	177,725		
56 (109):			66–71	51
Mean	60,681	52,871		
Median	26,800	30,467		
Twenty-fifth percentile	6,000	5,416		
Seventy-fifth percentile	60,000	55,518		
Ninetieth percentile	135,000	117,129		
57 (114):			67–72	49
Mean	55,319	65,701		
Median	34,500	32,498		
Twenty-fifth percentile	10,900	11,713		
Seventy-fifth percentile	63,400	67,244		
Ninetieth percentile	150,000	159,106		

Table 11.9   (continued)

Age in 1966 (N): Sample Statistic	WEALTH in Survey Year		Age Range between Surveys	Number Dissaving
	1976	1981		
58 (108):			68–73	51
Mean	49,970	53,248		
Median	28,400	28,282		
Twenty-fifth percentile	6,664	6,669		
Seventy-fifth percentile	52,500	60,968		
Ninetieth percentile	120,000	113,067		
59 (96):			69–74	43
Mean	42,540	53,036		
Median	24,200	24,746		
Twenty-fifth percentile	8,930	6,770		
Seventy-fifth percentile	48,788	51,795		
Ninetieth percentile	107,900	107,921		

Source: Computed from the National Longitudinal Surveys of Mature Men.

Note: WEALTH is the sum of net residential housing assets, net farm assets, net business assets, net investment real estate assets, deposits in financial institutions, U.S. savings bonds, holdings of stocks and bonds, and personal loans made to others less unsecured personal debt. The sample consists of 2,170 respondents who provided both usable wealth and usable age data in the 1976 and 1981 surveys.

Age-wealth profiles for each of the 1907–21 cohorts based on the 15-YEAR CRS sample are represented in figures 11.1–11.15 by squares. The other points marked with crosses form the age-wealth profiles that are obtained by adding to the 15-YEAR CRS sample those households who reported usable data in each survey up until their death. These data are reported in table 11.10. This adds 1,016 households in 1966, 787 households in 1969, 663 households in 1971, and 319 households in 1976. The 1981 point is based on the same households and hence is the same. Comparison of the two age-wealth profiles in figures 11.1–11.15 illustrates the effect of differential mortality. The profile that includes respondents who die before 1981 lies below the 15-YEAR CRS age-wealth profile. This downward bias is generally larger for the oldest cohorts since their death rate is larger. In the portions of age-wealth profile that slope up (e.g., in the figures for the 1908, 1914, and 1919 cohorts), this bias can work to steepen the implied age-wealth profile.

In figures 11.16–11.30, the age-wealth profiles of each cohort based on the 15-YEAR CRS sample are again represented by squares. The other points marked by crosses constitute the age-wealth profile one obtains from a sample consisting of the 15-YEAR CRS sample plus those households who survived until 1981 but did not report usable

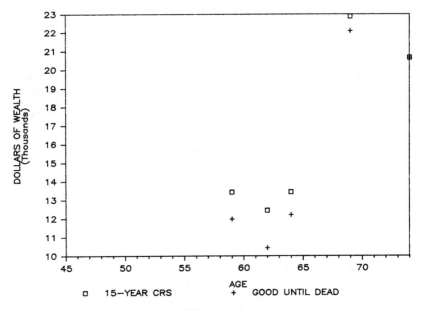

Fig. 11.1   1907 cohort median WEALTH

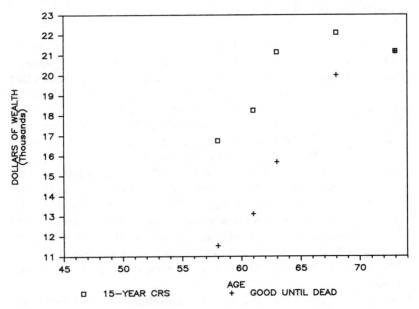

Fig. 11.2   1908 cohort median WEALTH

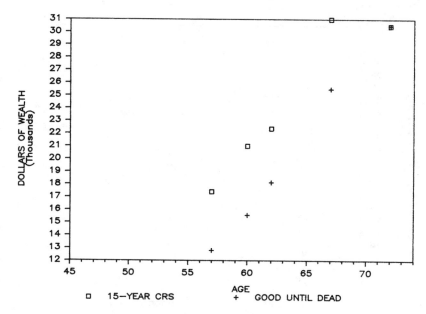

Fig. 11.3   1909 cohort median WEALTH

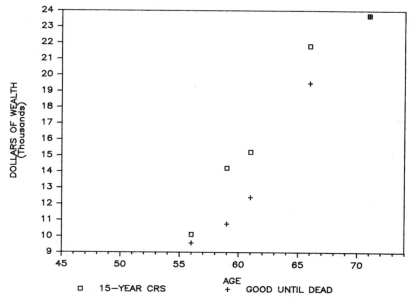

Fig. 11.4   1910 cohort median WEALTH

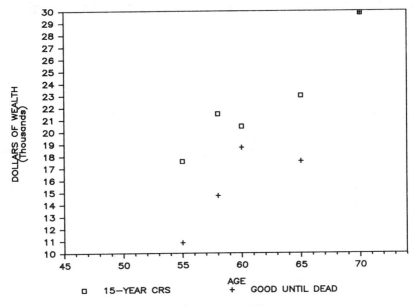

Fig. 11.5   1911 cohort median WEALTH

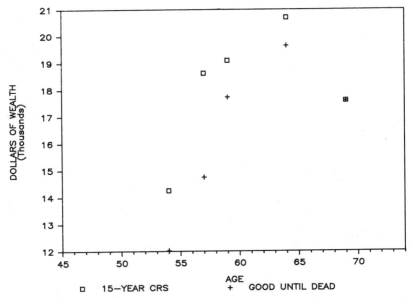

Fig. 11.6   1912 cohort median WEALTH

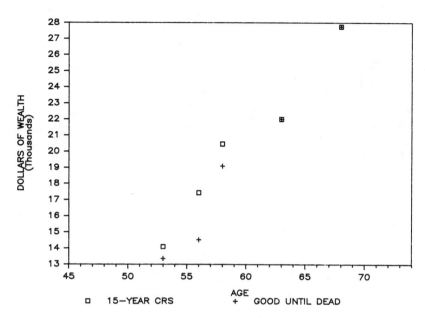

Fig. 11.7   1913 cohort median WEALTH

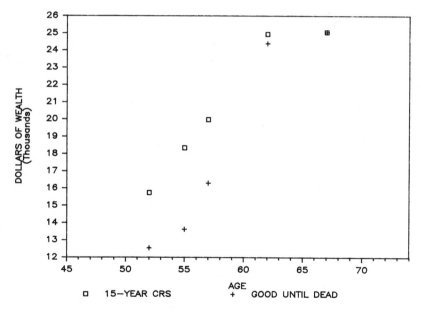

Fig. 11.8   1914 cohort median WEALTH

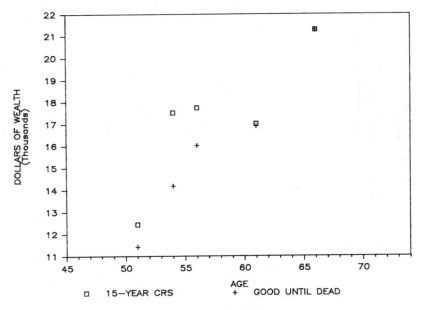

Fig. 11.9　　　　　1915 cohort median WEALTH

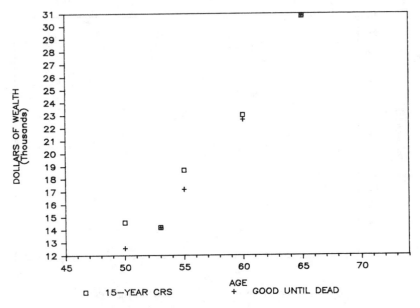

Fig. 11.10　　　　1916 cohort median WEALTH

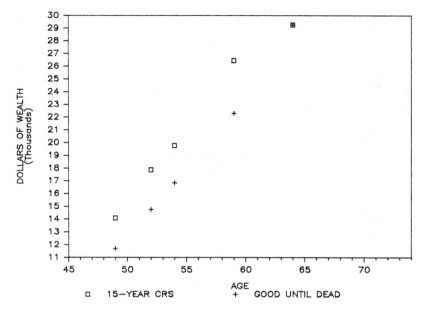

Fig. 11.11   1917 cohort median WEALTH

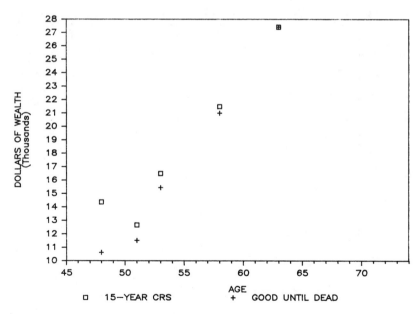

Fig. 11.12   1918 cohort median WEALTH

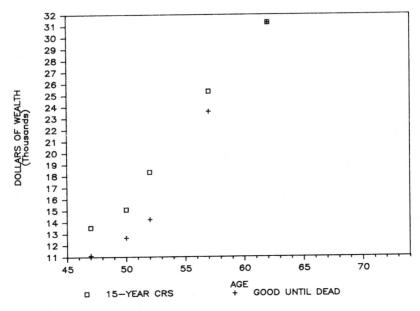

Fig. 11.13   1919 cohort median WEALTH

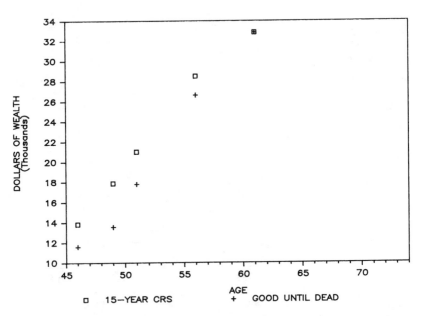

Fig. 11.14   1920 cohort median WEALTH

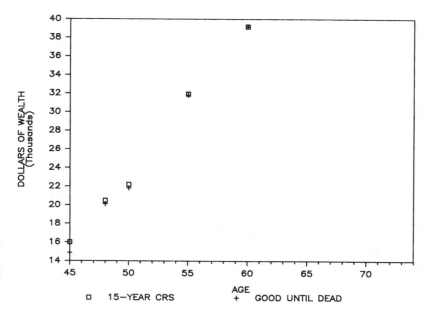

Fig. 11.15   1921 cohort median WEALTH

Table 11.10   **WEALTH by Cohort for Complete Reporter until Dead Sample (1976 dollars)**

Age in 1966: Sample Statistic	WEALTH in Survey Year					Age in 1981
	1966	1969	1971	1976	1981	
45:						60
Mean	25,866	32,889	33,586	52,125	68,598	
Median	14,870	20,119	21,828	31,800	39,201	
Twenty-fifth percentile	2,892	6,707	6,958	10,200	16,046	
Seventy-fifth percentile	31,260	40,127	42,633	53,700	88,016	
Ninetieth percentile	56,385	69,300	69,782	114,000	143,873	
N	198	196	192	173	158	
46:						61
Mean	24,798	29,796	30,544	40,969	60,275	
Median	11,609	13,565	17,799	26,625	32,837	
Twenty-fifth percentile	116	112	1,842	2,000	4,739	
Seventy-fifth percentile	23,134	28,838	34,925	49,500	63,643	
Ninetieth percentile	50,083	67,101	65,765	102,500	119,838	
N	177	163	161	142	131	
47:						62
Mean	26,995	30,650	33,836	47,198	59,868	
Median	11,103	12,668	14,257	23,600	31,303	
Twenty-fifth percentile	493	298	682	3,600	10,291	
Seventy-fifth percentile	28,690	32,720	37,790	57,250	74,475	
Ninetieth percentile	58,043	63,897	69,577	110,000	139,066	
N	203	191	182	165	150	

(continued)

Table 11.10   (continued)

Age in 1966: Sample Statistic	WEALTH in Survey Year					Age in 1981
	1966	1969	1971	1976	1981	
48:						63
Mean	23,595	28,820	34,361	42,773	46,120	
Median	10,614	11,524	15,449	21,000	27,420	
Twenty-fifth percentile	580	1,639	1,985	5,786	7,583	
Seventy-fifth percentile	31,385	39,046	44,686	49,000	59,580	
Ninetieth percentile	51,244	69,747	80,491	92,740	81,900	
N	175	166	160	148	131	
49:						64
Mean	27,981	28,138	30,497	42,087	46,044	
Median	11,692	14,773	16,849	22,300	29,262	
Twenty-fifth percentile	1,741	1,490	2,644	4,000	5,484	
Seventy-fifth percentile	32,007	34,277	37,074	49,500	62,288	
Ninetieth percentile	67,993	61,848	66,849	91,000	119,634	
N	175	162	156	135	115	
50:						65
Mean	35,887	30,024	33,505	41,920	49,316	
Median	12,570	14,203	17,190	22,650	30,806	
Twenty-fifth percentile	111	0	1,091	1,600	4,401	
Seventy-fifth percentile	30,000	36,066	39,563	54,450	58,226	
Ninetieth percentile	74,461	76,453	71,351	103,750	124,577	
N	200	187	177	158	135	
51:						66
Mean	29,499	28,262	30,502	39,834	48,477	
Median	11,418	14,189	16,031	16,900	21,286	
Twenty-fifth percentile	0	185	614	4,610	4,062	
Seventy-fifth percentile	28,358	31,297	38,779	51,000	55,518	
Ninetieth percentile	61,028	63,338	75,034	86,000	96,276	
N	204	189	185	143	121	
52:						67
Mean	29,097	32,049	34,536	42,486	54,203	
Median	12,542	13,636	16,303	24,390	25,051	
Twenty-fifth percentile	498	745	1,637	4,000	8,633	
Seventy-fifth percentile	33,002	38,003	43,656	50,000	58,565	
Ninetieth percentile	75,622	90,909	88,677	117,000	118,483	
N	184	167	158	137	108	
53:						68
Mean	29,125	32,699	36,768	40,763	44,771	
Median	13,350	14,531	19,100	22,000	27,759	
Twenty-fifth percentile	249	0	273	2,000	7,448	
Seventy-fifth percentile	33,167	40,238	44,884	57,000	60,934	
Ninetieth percentile	63,433	74,888	89,495	99,000	98,172	
N	198	186	182	155	131	
54:						69
Mean	22,996	27,893	30,181	37,981	41,285	
Median	12,023	14,754	17,735	19,650	17,603	

Table 11.10   (continued)

Age in 1966: Sample Statistic	WEALTH in Survey Year					Age in 1981
	1966	1969	1971	1976	1981	
Twenty-fifth percentile	912	1,565	2,183	700	1,625	
Seventy-fifth percentile	31,551	36,513	36,835	47,850	50,102	
Ninetieth percentile	53,068	75,261	79,400	97,650	91,401	
N	171	159	149	128	103	
55:						70
Mean	39,691	50,734	49,538	47,683	60,032	
Median	10,863	14,754	18,732	17,600	29,824	
Twenty-fifth percentile	124	0	1,637	1,000	1,726	
Seventy-fifth percentile	33,167	44,709	52,183	55,000	64,320	
Ninetieth percentile	89,055	114,605	129,604	120,000	174,001	
N	178	151	138	117	87	
56:						71
Mean	28,967	31,156	36,302	46,252	47,745	
Median	9,577	10,768	12,415	19,500	23,697	
Twenty-fifth percentile	265	596	0	0	1,050	
Seventy-fifth percentile	27,197	26,826	36,289	47,850	45,566	
Ninetieth percentile	57,877	80,701	67,531	85,500	87,339	
N	163	140	130	100	80	
57:						72
Mean	31,864	35,482	39,746	48,372	67,915	
Median	12,791	15,574	18,152	25,500	30,467	
Twenty-fifth percentile	1,388	2,310	2,985	4,256	6,838	
Seventy-fifth percentile	37,355	46,528	43,656	55,100	64,997	
Ninetieth percentile	93,118	105,067	111,119	130,000	159,106	
N	164	148	140	116	91	
58:						73
Mean	32,602	41,731	38,599	43,312	46,357	
Median	11,531	13,115	15,689	20,000	21,165	
Twenty-fifth percentile	332	0	802	1,750	5,078	
Seventy-fifth percentile	34,992	35,768	39,973	45,000	56,161	
Ninetieth percentile	87,065	84,948	79,809	84,400	102,924	
N	162	144	132	103	80	
59:						74
Mean	31,580	26,525	25,007	33,569	30,001	
Median	11,990	10,432	12,212	22,100	20,650	
Twenty-fifth percentile	0	0	289	8,000	3,047	
Seventy-fifth percentile	33,997	30,432	29,393	42,000	40,623	
Ninetieth percentile	72,637	76,006	67,531	79,500	70,346	
N	155	129	112	90	70	

Source: Computed from the National Longitudinal Surveys of Mature Men.

Note: WEALTH is the sum of net residential housing assets, net farm assets, net business assets, net investment real estate assets, deposits in financial institutions, U.S. savings bonds, holdings of stocks and bonds, and personal loans made to others less unsecured personal debt. The sample consists of those respondents who provided both usable wealth and usable age data in every survey until they died or survived through 1981.

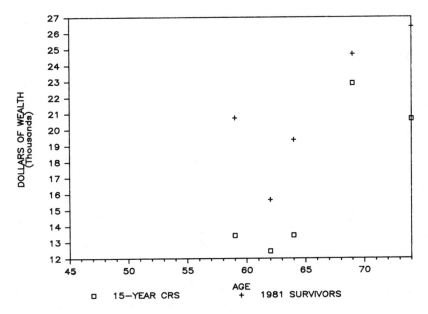

Fig. 11.16   1907 cohort median WEALTH

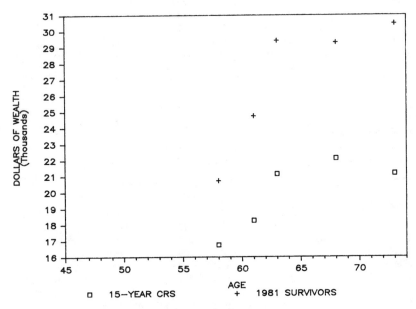

Fig. 11.17   1908 cohort median WEALTH

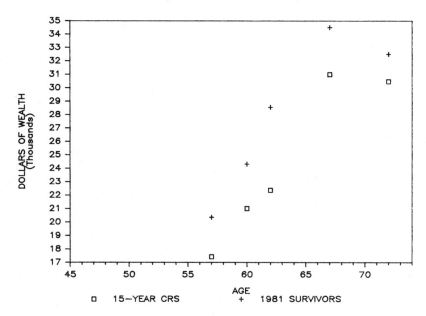

Fig. 11.18   1909 cohort median WEALTH

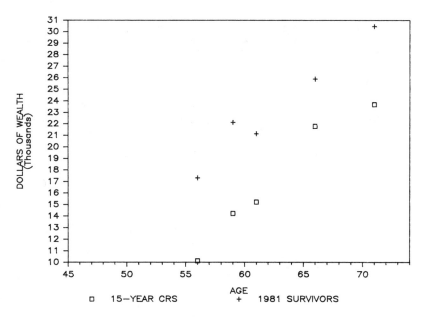

Fig. 11.19   1910 cohort median WEALTH

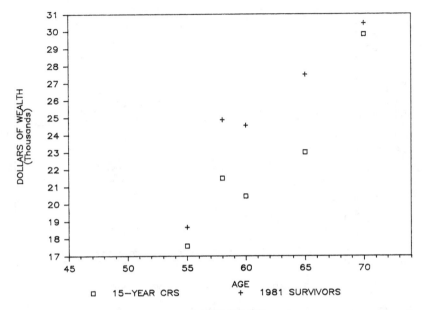

Fig. 11.20   1911 cohort median WEALTH

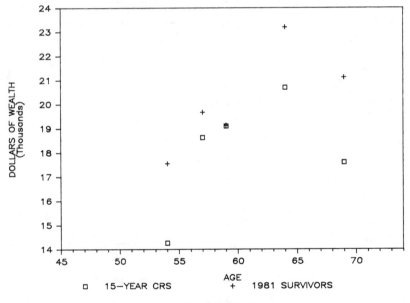

Fig. 11.21   1912 cohort median WEALTH

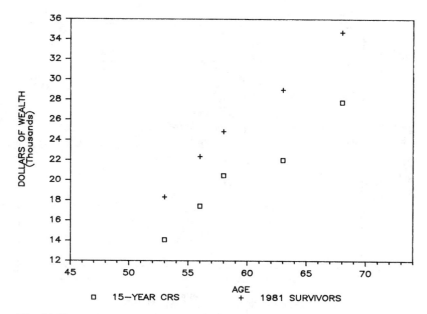

Fig. 11.22   1913 cohort median WEALTH

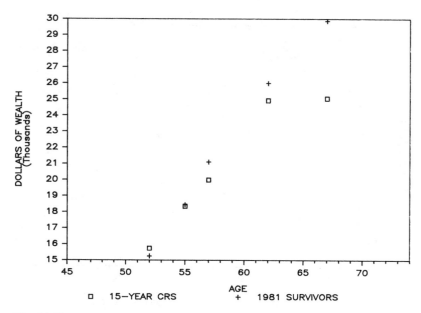

Fig. 11.23   1914 cohort median WEALTH

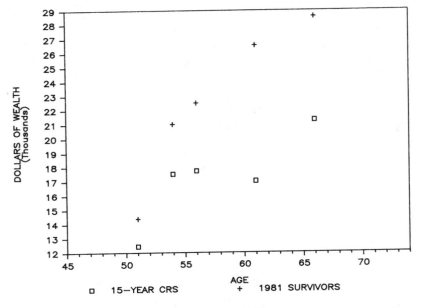

Fig. 11.24   1915 cohort median WEALTH

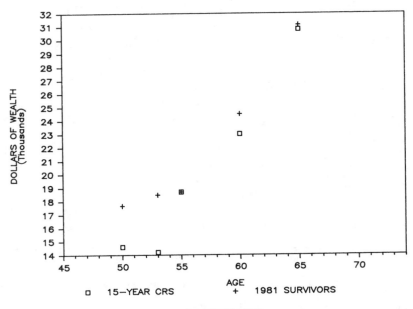

Fig. 11.25   1916 cohort median WEALTH

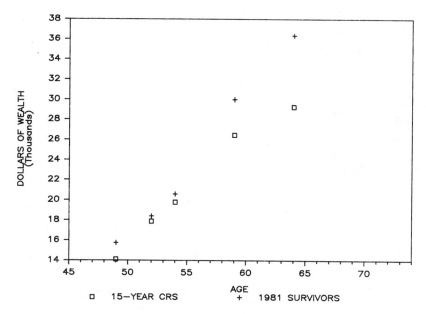

Fig. 11.26   1917 cohort median WEALTH

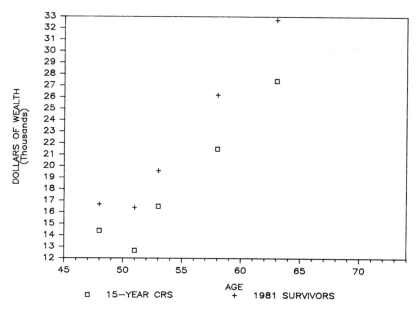

Fig. 11.27   1918 cohort median WEALTH

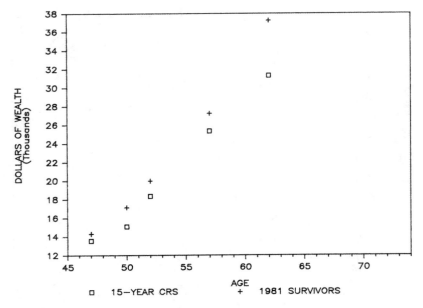

Fig. 11.28 1919 cohort median WEALTH

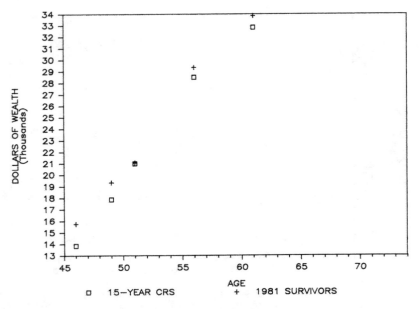

Fig. 11.29 1920 cohort median WEALTH

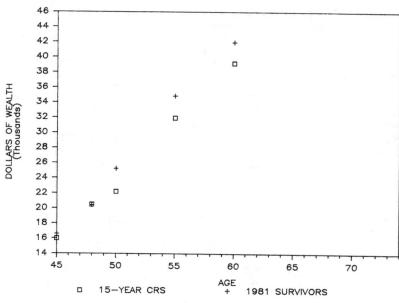

Fig. 11.30   1921 cohort median WEALTH

data in one or more of the 1966, 1969, 1971, or 1976 samples; that is, this age-wealth profile is based on the usable data from all households who survived until 1981. Data for this "survivors, including partial reporters with reentry" (SURVIVOR) sample are reported in table 11.11. These data do not contain any differential mortality effect. Rather, the difference between the age-wealth profiles based on the SURVIVOR sample and on the 15-YEAR CRS sample illustrates the effects of differential attrition (and reentry). Generally, the SURVIVOR age-wealth profile lies above the 15-YEAR CRS sample age-wealth profile. This is consistent with the fact that attrition due to bad data/refusal is more frequent among the rich. The size of this differential attrition effect varies considerably across cohorts; however, it is definitely larger in the older cohorts. As an examination of the figures for the 1907, 1908, 1910, and 1914 cohorts illustrates, it can have an effect on the shape of the age-wealth profile. In comparing points along any cohort's age-wealth profile from the SURVIVOR sample, one must remember that between surveys there is exit and entry of households; therefore, the points for the cohort are not based on the same households. This differential attrition and reentry could easily bias the age-wealth profile; hence, a comparison of shapes is probably inappropriate.

We have illustrated that differential mortality tends to bias downward (and sometimes steepen) cohort age-wealth profiles while differential attrition tends to raise cohort age-wealth profiles. These two biases

Table 11.11   **WEALTH by Cohort for Sample of Survivors, Including Partial Reporters with Reentry (1976 dollars)**

| Age in 1966: | WEALTH in Survey Year | | | | | Age in |
Sample Statistic	1966	1969	1971	1976	1981	1981
45:						60
Mean	28,566	36,915	46,987	66,770	78,832	
Median	16,584	20,417	25,239	34,850	41,977	
Twenty-fifth percentile	4,398	8,942	9,959	15,658	18,957	
Seventy-fifth percentile	30,680	40,238	49,836	64,000	88,016	
Ninetieth percentile	66,219	78,987	88,677	153,000	162,492	
N	204	201	205	200	219	
46:						61
Mean	37,894	37,457	40,271	55,142	76,970	
Median	15,755	19,353	21,078	29,350	33,852	
Twenty-fifth percentile	4,643	4,471	6,821	5,900	10,190	
Seventy-fifth percentile	35,987	34,277	42,394	57,100	86,662	
Ninetieth percentile	93,367	85,693	107,776	165,000	165,877	
N	182	175	175	171	197	
47:						62
Mean	35,967	39,003	44,055	54,457	66,529	
Median	14,324	17,139	19,986	27,244	37,238	
Twenty-fifth percentile	2,620	2,832	3,820	9,000	11,456	
Seventy-fifth percentile	40,216	45,395	51,842	62,060	82,092	
Ninetieth percentile	74,337	89,419	103,683	142,500	156,398	
N	190	186	191	190	208	
48:						63
Mean	32,380	35,031	38,721	50,159	57,852	
Median	16,683	16,393	19,612	26,188	32,702	
Twenty-fifth percentile	3,483	4,471	6,139	7,500	9,827	
Seventy-fifth percentile	39,221	44,113	46,931	54,100	68,923	
Ninetieth percentile	75,870	78,241	87,653	98,350	114,421	
N	180	173	172	170	190	
49:						64
Mean	52,558	42,089	44,733	51,633	64,169	
Median	15,755	18,406	20,600	30,000	36,357	
Twenty-fifth percentile	4,975	4,322	7,367	10,600	12,187	
Seventy-fifth percentile	42,786	41,729	45,020	59,000	72,038	
Ninetieth percentile	100,539	99,106	88,677	107,000	130,569	
N	159	150	161	154	173	
50:						65
Mean	35,385	44,553	45,403	44,794	55,276	
Median	17,662	18,480	18,690	24,500	31,144	
Twenty-fifth percentile	1,078	2,981	3,411	7,372	9,343	
Seventy-fifth percentile	36,650	43,964	43,656	60,000	67,705	
Ninetieth percentile	83,458	99,851	80,491	103,800	135,410	
N	180	187	181	181	198	

Table 11.11   (continued)

Age in 1966: Sample Statistic	WEALTH in Survey Year					Age in 1981
	1966	1969	1971	1976	1981	
51:						66
Mean	45,796	58,055	58,956	45,031	61,628	
Median	14,386	21,013	22,510	26,550	28,571	
Twenty-fifth percentile	1,824	1,164	3,956	5,200	8,490	
Seventy-fifth percentile	41,501	49,553	52,251	52,000	64,320	
Ninetieth percentile	77,114	105,067	110,505	91,750	134,394	
N	177	164	173	166	189	
52:						67
Mean	31,213	36,402	41,128	51,169	59,425	
Median	15,257	18,443	21,112	26,000	29,875	
Twenty-fifth percentile	4,809	5,216	4,952	7,851	9,479	
Seventy-fifth percentile	36,899	44,747	50,102	50,500	61,611	
Ninetieth percentile	75,622	90,909	124,829	123,000	155,721	
N	143	145	148	144	158	
53:						68
Mean	35,040	42,304	48,175	52,343	60,755	
Median	18,325	22,355	24,829	28,975	34,699	
Twenty-fifth percentile	3,259	1,639	3,683	8,000	10,021	
Seventy-fifth percentile	45,357	46,498	54,570	66,000	67,705	
Ninetieth percentile	88,557	120,715	118,145	156,000	141,842	
N	168	157	165	159	176	
54:						69
Mean	31,147	40,574	39,604	47,111	51,581	
Median	17,546	19,672	19,127	23,200	21,124	
Twenty-fifth percentile	4,312	5,589	6,446	5,000	3,385	
Seventy-fifth percentile	39,303	58,006	47,749	58,000	61,070	
Ninetieth percentile	82,919	99,851	90,144	130,000	115,098	
N	133	129	130	126	139	
55:						70
Mean	53,204	81,384	66,541	57,055	66,532	
Median	18,673	24,888	24,557	27,500	30,467	
Twenty-fifth percentile	3,400	7,526	6,194	5,525	7,109	
Seventy-fifth percentile	44,113	55,440	56,480	70,000	74,475	
Ninetieth percentile	107,794	152,012	129,604	135,000	174,001	
N	129	123	129	124	142	
56:						71
Mean	42,344	60,148	56,057	59,430	51,824	
Median	17,330	22,132	21,146	25,900	30,467	
Twenty-fifth percentile	3,267	2,235	2,729	6,000	6,821	
Seventy-fifth percentile	44,569	58,122	54,570	59,250	55,857	
Ninetieth percentile	96,352	112,364	109,413	121,500	117,129	
N	116	118	113	112	128	

(*continued*)

Table 11.11   (continued)

Age in 1966: Sample Statistic	WEALTH in Survey Year					Age in 1981
	1966	1969	1971	1976	1981	
57:						72
Mean	40,197	48,097	47,151	54,667	62,929	
Median	20,357	24,330	28,554	34,500	32,498	
Twenty-fifth percentile	5,804	8,383	10,505	10,450	12,187	
Seventy-fifth percentile	54,726	58,831	60,113	63,050	64,320	
Ninetieth percentile	111,111	128,167	131,992	150,000	158,429	
N	114	108	120	116	125	
58:						73
Mean	60,620	50,696	58,325	50,288	60,957	
Median	20,730	24,739	29,413	29,300	30,467	
Twenty-fifth percentile	3,483	2,385	7,776	6,828	7,038	
Seventy-fifth percentile	59,701	58,867	57,981	53,000	74,475	
Ninetieth percentile	127,363	127,720	136,426	118,750	117,806	
N	112	111	114	110	123	
59:						74
Mean	71,742	41,145	48,664	42,269	70,009	
Median	20,730	15,648	19,372	24,700	26,405	
Twenty-fifth percentile	4,519	5,663	5,484	8,960	10,359	
Seventy-fifth percentile	47,788	52,744	54,570	47,500	52,810	
Ninetieth percentile	193,035	103,577	120,055	107,900	115,775	
N	101	96	97	98	109	

Source: Computed from the National Longitudinal Surveys of Mature Men.

Note: WEALTH is the sum of net residential housing assets, net farm assets, net business assets, net investment real estate assets, deposits in financial institutions, U.S. savings bonds, holdings of stocks and bonds, and personal loans made to others less unsecured personal debt. The sample consists of those respondents who provided both usable wealth and usable age data in any survey as long as they provided these data in the 1981 survey.

can be eliminated by examining cohort age-wealth profiles based on respondents who both survive to the end of the period under analysis and report usable data in every survey during this period, that is, our 5-YEAR and 15-YEAR CRS samples.

11.4 Assessing the Bias in Age-Wealth Profiles Based on Cross-sectional Data

As Shorrocks and others have pointed out, age-wealth profiles based on cross-sectional data suffer from both a productivity bias, which tends to flatten the profile, and a differential mortality bias, which tends to steepen the cross-sectional age-wealth profile. Using the NLS data, we have constructed cross-sectional age-wealth profiles based on the

1966, 1969, 1971, 1976, and 1981 samples. Presumably, these suffer both productivity and differential mortality biases. To assess the extent of these biases, we compare the cross-sectional profiles with the cohort age-wealth profiles that suffer from neither of these biases (the cohort profiles based on the 15-YEAR CRS sample as described in the previous section). This will be done first through figures and then through simple age-wealth regressions.

The cross-sectional age-wealth profiles for 1966, 1971, 1976, and 1981 are plotted in figure 11.31. The 1969 profile is flat, as is the 1966 one. Hence, we observe three flat profiles, one (1981) that slopes down to the right, and one (1976) that is U-shaped. Since the previously examined cohort age-wealth profiles generally slope up at early ages, flatten, and sometimes turn down at later ages, the flat and downward slopes observed on the cross-sectional age-wealth profiles suggest that the downward productivity bias dominates the differential mortality effect bias.

In figure 11.32, the youngest three cohorts are plotted against the 1966 cross section. Clearly, the flat shape of the 1966 cross-sectional profile is not consistent with the rapid wealth accumulation being done by these cohorts. Similar conclusions are drawn from figure 11.33, which shows the 1969 cross-sectional profile and the 1917 and 1918 cohort age-wealth profiles. Figure 11.34 shows that the 1916 cohort

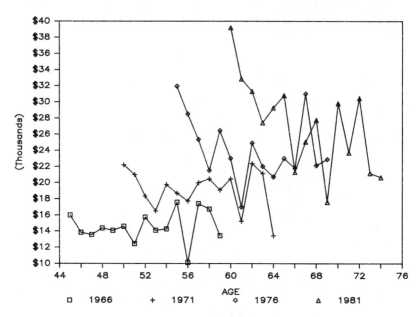

Fig. 11.31   Median WEALTH of 15-YEAR CRS—1966, 1971, 1976, and 1981 cross sections

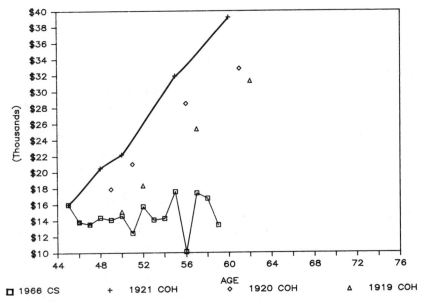

Fig. 11.32   Median WEALTH of 15-YEAR CRS—1966 cross section and 1919, 1920, and 1921 cohorts

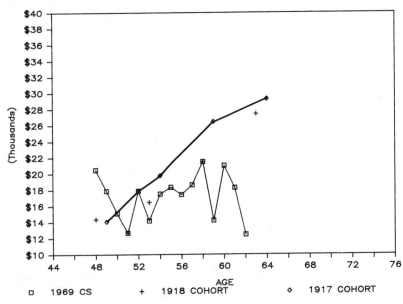

Fig. 11.33   Median WEALTH of 15-YEAR CRS—1969 cross section and 1917 and 1918 cohorts

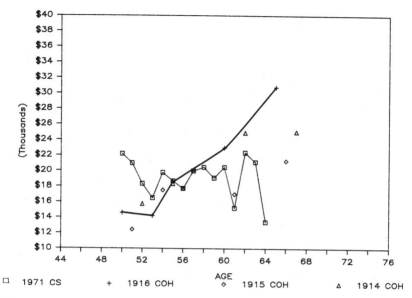

Fig. 11.34   Median WEALTH of 15-YEAR CRS—1971 cross section and 1915, 1916, and 1917 cohorts

also rapidly accumulates wealth between ages fifty-one and sixty-five; this is inconsistent with the flatness of the age-wealth profile from 1971, which also covers these ages. On the other hand, figure 11.34 also shows that the 1915 and 1917 cohorts, which have flatter profiles, are more consistent with the 1971 profile. In figure 11.35, the U-shaped 1976 profile is inconsistent with both the accumulation by the 1911 and 1913 cohorts and the hump-shaped age-wealth profile of the 1912 cohort. In figures 11.36 and 11.37, we see that the downward-sloping 1981 profile is inconsistent with age-wealth profiles of the four older cohorts, which are generally humped shaped. Hence, plotting the correct (longitudinally based) cohort age-wealth profiles against the cross-sectional age-wealth profiles (which overlap the ages covered) leads to the general conclusion that cross-sectional profiles generally take on grossly incorrect shapes.

The data for all the age-wealth profiles in figures 11.31–11.37 come from table 11.6, which reports sample statistics for the 15-YEAR CRS sample. The cohort profiles are obtained by plotting each cohort's median wealth accumulation from 1966 through 1981, which appears across the rows of table 11.6. A cross-sectional profile is obtained by plotting the median wealth taken from a column of table 11.6. The fact that the cross-sectional profiles tend to be flat or downward sloping as mentioned above suggests that the productivity bias outweighs the differential mortality bias.

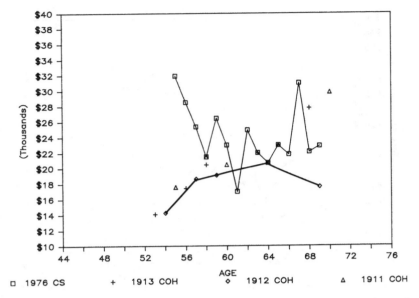

Fig. 11.35   Median WEALTH of 15-YEAR CRS—1976 cross section and 1911, 1912, and 1913 cohorts

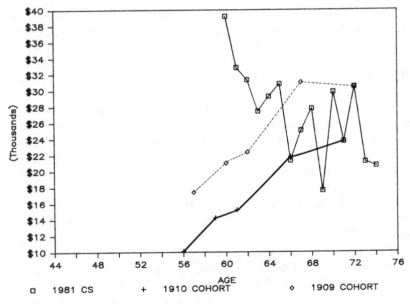

Fig. 11.36   Median WEALTH of 15-YEAR CRS—1981 cross section and 1909 and 1910 cohorts

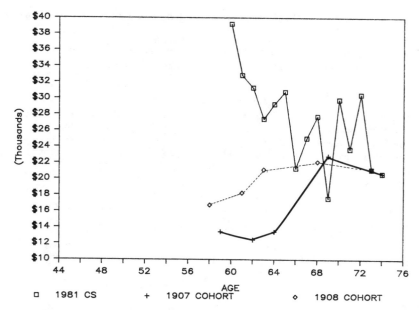

Fig. 11.37   Median WEALTH of 15-YEAR CRS—1981 cross section and 1907 and 1908 cohorts

The hypothesis that this productivity bias is large is supported by the fact that it is quite evident in our most comprehensive sample, that is, the "usable data with reentry" sample. These data, reported in table 11.12, include all households that reported usable data. Consequently, the number and identity of respondents in each cohort change from year to year owing to refusal to respond or to provide usable data and owing to attrition from the sample due to death or other reasons. In other words, these cohort age-wealth profiles, while free from productivity bias, are subject to differential mortality and differential attrition biases. The cross-sectional profiles still have the productivity bias in them. Shorrocks's point about bias due to productivity gain is illustrated quite clearly in table 11.12. If we follow, say, the median wealth by cohort (moving across a row), we see clear and distinct increases with age (albeit far larger for younger than for older cohorts). Looking at individual cross sections (down a column), we observe no clear pattern, showing that the cross sections are biased downward by the productivity effect. For a direct comparison that features an exact age overlap, compare the sequence of medians of the age forty-five cohort (which reveals their experience as they age to sixty) with the 1966 cross section, which has ages forty-five to fifty-nine. Median wealth rises from $15,500 to nearly $42,000 in the cohort but from $15,500 to only about $17,000 in the cross section.

Table 11.12   **WEALTH by Cohort for Usable Data with Reentry Sample (1976 dollars)**

Age in 1966: Sample Statistic	WEALTH in Survey Year					Age in 1981
	1966	1969	1971	1976	1981	
45:						60
Mean	29,204	35,753	45,715	61,563	78,832	
Median	15,506	20,119	23,874	34,140	41,977	
Twenty-fifth percentile	3,317	7,452	7,094	11,000	18,957	
Seventy-fifth percentile	33,167	42,623	47,749	63,000	88,016	
Ninetieth percentile	66,219	81,967	84,857	140,000	162,492	
N	331	285	286	242	219	
46:						61
Mean	37,801	35,511	45,599	51,924	76,970	
Median	13,847	15,499	18,213	25,500	33,852	
Twenty-fifth percentile	768	3,353	5,334	4,390	10,190	
Seventy-fifth percentile	30,514	32,787	41,201	52,500	86,662	
Ninetieth percentile	91,211	83,458	95,498	154,000	165,877	
N	329	278	267	224	197	
47:						62
Mean	37,775	35,999	38,710	49,479	66,529	
Median	13,267	14,791	16,440	23,000	37,238	
Twenty-fifth percentile	1,327	1,043	2,968	6,000	11,456	
Seventy-fifth percentile	31,509	38,003	43,452	61,050	82,092	
Ninetieth percentile	71,891	79,136	95,498	126,100	156,398	
N	357	301	288	241	208	
48:						63
Mean	28,715	34,152	37,399	46,368	57,852	
Median	14,403	16,097	19,714	24,000	32,702	
Twenty-fifth percentile	2,488	3,726	6,139	8,250	9,827	
Seventy-fifth percentile	36,487	43,964	47,476	51,850	68,923	
Ninetieth percentile	66,335	83,160	85,266	95,000	114,421	
N	312	270	255	224	190	
49:						64
Mean	40,136	37,115	42,482	51,538	64,169	
Median	12,604	15,797	17,735	29,000	36,357	
Twenty-fifth percentile	3,648	3,577	4,366	10,000	12,187	
Seventy-fifth percentile	36,318	34,277	39,973	58,500	72,038	
Ninetieth percentile	81,758	78,912	79,945	105,000	130,569	
N	317	255	255	207	173	
50:						65
Mean	41,506	47,597	48,888	48,923	55,279	
Median	14,594	18,480	19,100	25,100	31,144	
Twenty-fifth percentile	1,286	3,726	4,297	8,000	9,343	
Seventy-fifth percentile	33,665	43,964	43,656	64,000	67,705	
Ninetieth percentile	81,758	95,678	81,855	109,000	135,410	
N	324	295	274	230	198	

Table 11.12   (continued)

Age in 1966: Sample Statistic	WEALTH in Survey Year					Age in 1981
	1966	1969	1971	1976	1981	
51:						66
Mean	40,421	45,016	44,213	43,151	61,628	
Median	14,925	17,756	18,008	24,500	28,571	
Twenty-fifth percentile	1,526	1,313	2,947	5,925	8,490	
Seventy-fifth percentile	38,972	42,996	45,634	50,150	64,320	
Ninetieth percentile	91,542	87,779	90,041	91,050	134,394	
N	349	292	283	216	189	
52:						67
Mean	40,356	35,604	40,866	43,203	59,425	
Median	14,895	14,818	18,281	23,700	29,875	
Twenty-fifth percentile	1,493	2,854	4,502	5,000	9,479	
Seventy-fifth percentile	37,479	40,238	47,749	50,000	61,611	
Ninetieth percentile	83,333	103,577	106,262	104,000	155,721	
N	300	260	249	211	158	
53:						68
Mean	37,528	36,604	45,730	51,929	60,754	
Median	18,305	17,884	21,555	27,000	34,699	
Twenty-fifth percentile	2,828	969	1,828	5,730	10,021	
Seventy-fifth percentile	40,630	44,709	48,840	65,500	67,705	
Ninetieth percentile	83,582	105,067	113,233	137,500	141,842	
N	312	265	261	206	176	
54:						69
Mean	40,596	35,213	40,743	39,685	51,581	
Median	14,925	17,884	19,727	21,000	21,124	
Twenty-fifth percentile	1,990	3,353	6,446	4,685	3,385	
Seventy-fifth percentile	36,111	44,709	43,656	48,300	61,070	
Ninetieth percentile	66,750	95,082	90,041	109,500	115,098	
N	280	229	226	178	139	
55:						70
Mean	41,361	51,155	50,124	56,572	66,532	
Median	14,926	17,813	20,464	22,100	30,467	
Twenty-fifth percentile	995	1,565	3,411	4,300	7,109	
Seventy-fifth percentile	43,449	47,362	54,843	58,500	74,475	
Ninetieth percentile	98,673	134,128	129,604	136,000	174,001	
N	280	236	221	173	142	
56:						71
Mean	35,003	38,566	38,635	56,837	51,824	
Median	15,091	15,052	15,450	23,000	30,467	
Twenty-fifth percentile	2,488	2,086	546	6,350	6,821	
Seventy-fifth percentile	35,158	36,811	43,520	57,990	55,857	
Ninetieth percentile	79,602	96,870	77,080	121,200	117,129	
N	298	229	203	152	128	

(*continued*)

Table 11.12   (continued)

Age in 1966: Sample Statistic	WEALTH in Survey Year					Age in 1981
	1966	1969	1971	1976	1981	
57:						72
Mean	37,056	54,099	43,561	56,069	62,929	
Median	17,081	17,884	20,737	28,500	32,498	
Twenty-fifth percentile	3,317	4,471	5,901	7,500	12,187	
Seventy-fifth percentile	38,972	50,224	47,442	59,950	64,320	
Ninetieth percentile	109,453	138,599	122,783	138,000	158,429	
N	263	213	216	161	125	
58:						73
Mean	51,292	47,950	49,175	48,176	60,957	
Median	17,247	17,884	20,464	22,813	30,467	
Twenty-fifth percentile	1,658	466	2,729	3,250	7,038	
Seventy-fifth percentile	45,605	47,988	47,749	52,500	74,475	
Ninetieth percentile	120,232	114,426	122,783	111,000	117,806	
N	255	208	199	152	123	
59:						74
Mean	58,671	47,081	53,281	49,981	70,009	
Median	17,123	15,115	17,053	23,250	26,405	
Twenty-fifth percentile	829	943	2,729	8,600	10,359	
Seventy-fifth percentile	44,776	47,958	41,201	47,000	52,810	
Ninetieth percentile	106,136	100,596	99,318	107,900	115,775	
N	255	196	173	136	109	

Source: Computed from the National Longitudinal Surveys of Mature Men.

Note: WEALTH is the sum of net residential housing assets, net farm assets, net business assets, net investment real estate assets, deposits in financial institutions, U.S. savings bonds, holdings of stocks and bonds, and personal loans made to others less unsecured personal debt. The sample consists of those respondents who provided both usable wealth and usable age data in any survey whether or not they reported these data in prior or subsequent surveys.

The cohort and cross-sectional age-wealth profiles plotted in figures 11.1–11.30 are based on the 15-YEAR CRS sample of households, which both survived through 1981 and provided usable data in every year. Since inclusion criteria for the 15-YEAR CRS sample are stringent and limit the sample to 1,691 households, we decided to check these results with those obtained using the 5-YEAR CRS samples. From those households in the 5-YEAR CRS 1966–71 sample, we constructed a 1966 cross-sectional age-wealth profile. For each cohort, we constructed a five-year segment of its age-wealth profile by comparing the median wealth of all cohort households in this sample. These cohort segments are free from differential mortality, productivity, and attrition biases. Some can be matched with a similar five-year segment from the 1966 cross section. The five-year segment from the cross section is constructed by taking the median wealth of individuals five years apart in age. It is thus subject to biases introduced by productivity and differential mortality. For the 1966 cross section, ten segments are plotted against ten cohort segments in figure 11.38. For example, the left-most lines compare the forty-five to fifty range on the cross-sectional profile (dashed line) to the 1921 cohort (solid line), which ages from forty-five to fifty from 1966 to 1971. From table 11.7, we see that the 1921 cohort's median wealth rose from $14,925 to $20,920 over this period, whereas the cross-sectional wealth declines from $14,925 for forty-five-year-olds to $14,449 for fifty-year-olds. These data and figures confirm what we observed earlier, that the younger cohorts accumulate wealth at considerably faster rates than the flat 1966 cross-sectional age-wealth profile suggests.

Figure 11.39 makes similar comparisons using the 5-YEAR CRS 1971–76 sample. In this case, segments of the 1971 cross section are compared to cohort segments constructed for 1971–76. Again, the cohort segments are steeper than the relatively flat 1971 cross section; this again illustrates the biases in the cross-sectional profile. Notice also that the cohort segments for ages ending in the early sixties are less steep; this is consistent with the flattening out of the fifteen-year cohort age-wealth profiles plotted in figures 11.1–11.15. This flattening is observed even more in figure 11.40, which uses the 5-YEAR CRS 1976–81 sample to plot the cohort segments as they age from 1976 to 1981 against the 1976 cross-sectional segments. Two of the four segments for ages ending in the late sixties are downward sloping, indicating cohort dissaving. Again, we conclude that the 1976 cross-sectional

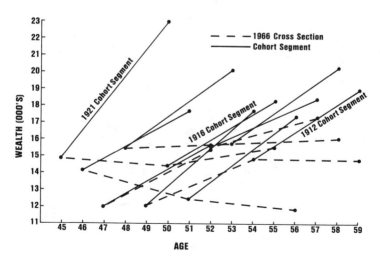

Fig. 11.38   Median WEALTH of 5-YEAR CRS 1966–71 sample

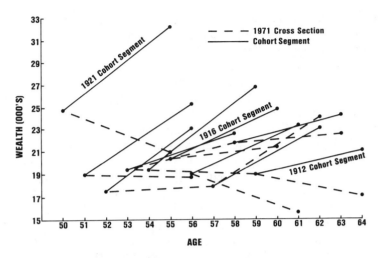

Fig. 11.39   Median WEALTH of 5-YEAR CRS 1971–76 sample

segments are not consistent with the cohort segments. The respective cross-sectional segments do not capture the rapid accumulation by the younger cohorts or the reduced saving or dissaving by the older cohorts.

Comparison of cohort segments based on the larger 5-YEAR CRS samples with the respective cross-sectional profiles supports our earlier conclusion based on the 15-YEAR CRS sample that the cross-sectional profiles are seriously biased by the presence of productivity and differential mortality effects.

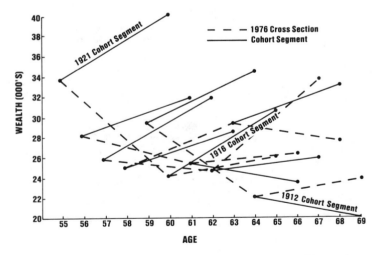

Fig. 11.40   Median WEALTH of 5-YEAR CRS 1976–81 sample

Another way to describe age-wealth profiles is to run a simple regression with wealth as the dependent variable and with AGE and AGE-SQUARED as the independent variables:

(2)   WEALTH = a_1 + a_2 AGE + a_3 AGE-SQUARED.

We estimated these for each cross section and each cohort. Generally, the estimated coefficients of both AGE and AGE-SQUARED had very large standard errors and, hence, did not test to be statistically different from zero. The standard errors were reduced by the deletion of AGE-SQUARED as an independent variable. These regressions are reported in table 11.13. As one can see, the coefficient on age is positive and statistically significant in the equation estimated over the 1966 cross section, statistically insignificant in the equations estimated over the 1969, 1971, and 1976 cross sections, and negatively signed and statistically significant in the equation estimated over the 1981 cross section.

Table 11.13   **Regression Results, Dependent Variable WEALTH:**
WEALTH = b_0 + b_1 AGE

Sample	$\hat{b}_0$	S.E.	$\hat{b}_1$	S.E.	$\bar{R}^2$	SSR (10^{12})	N
1966 cross section	− 5,390	20,804	751	406	.0014	8.2811	1,691
1969 cross section	1,799	24,945	641	460	.0006	10.6290	1,691
1971 cross section	8,497	22,590	523	402	.0004	8.1097	1,691
1976 cross section	62,406	27,864	− 274	455	− .0004	10.0410	1,691
1981 cross section	124,661	35,992	− 1,094	544	.0018	14.8500	1,691
1921 cohort	− 98,020	28,512	2,752	550	.0296	5.3114	790
1920 cohort	− 61,952	31,301	1,948	592	.0148	4.2340	655
1919 cohort	− 55,806	36,948	1,855	686	.0084	7.4548	750
1918 cohort	− 40,852	26,326	1,389	480	.0112	2.7817	655
1917 cohort	− 22,775	24,232	1,099	434	.0094	1.7513	575
1916 cohort	− 39,801	30,836	1,374	542	.0080	3.7744	675
1915 cohort	− 7,375	34,830	829	602	.0015	3.7353	605
1914 cohort	− 43,200	31,363	1,437	533	.0115	2.3309	540
1913 cohort	− 15,489	26,354	907	440	.0049	2.3430	655
1912 cohort	− 28,138	27,425	1,050	451	.0085	1.5164	515
1911 cohort	36,809	68,220	301	1,103	− .0021	6.4756	435
1910 cohort	1,765	63,569	708	1,012	− .0013	4.6029	400
1909 cohort	− 63,441	45,208	1,785	708	.0117	2.9206	455
1908 cohort	886	43,949	624	678	− .0004	2.0669	400
1907 cohort	43,910	29,694	− 201	451	− .0023	.7002	350

Source: Computed from the National Longitudinal Surveys of Mature Men.

Note: The underlying sample is the 15-YEAR CRS, the 1,691 respondents who provided both usable wealth and usable age data in each of the five surveys. WEALTH is the sum of net residential assets, net farm assets, net business assets, net investment real estate assets, deposits in financial institutions, U.S. savings bonds, holdings of stocks and bonds, and personal loans made to others less unsecured personal debt.

These signs merely confirm the shapes of the cross-sectional age-wealth profiles reported in figure 11.31.

Also reported in table 11.13 are equations estimated on data from each individual cohort. The slope coefficients on AGE are generally positive but decline in size the older the cohort. Most of the estimated coefficients on AGE for the youngest ten cohorts test to be statistically different from zero at the 5 percent level by a one-tailed t-test. Only one of the five oldest cohorts has a statistically significant coefficient on AGE. The decline in size of the coefficient on AGE and the decline in its statistical significance presumably reflects the tendency of the older cohorts' age-wealth profiles to flatten out and even decline at older ages (as we observed in figures 11.1–11.15).

Formal F-tests of whether the estimated cohort coefficients are statistically different from the coefficients estimated on each cross section are reported in table 11.14. Each cross section was tested against those cohorts whose observed ages overlapped with at least 50 percent of the ages observed in the cross section. The asterisks indicate that the F-statistic exceeds the 5 percent critical value of 2.99. The conclusion one draws as to whether the estimated cohort age-wealth profiles are consistent with the estimated cross-sectional age-wealth profiles clearly depends on which cross section and which cohort one compares. Rejections are obtained most frequently for the youngest three and the oldest three cohorts. The 1976 and 1981 cross-sectional age-wealth profiles appear to be inconsistent with the estimated age-wealth profiles of most cohorts. Given how poorly all these equations fit, bear in mind that failure to reject does not mean acceptance of the hypothesis that the coefficients are the same.

Overall, these regression estimates suggest that age-wealth profiles estimated on cross-sectional data are likely to be inconsistent with the age-wealth profile one would estimate using cohort data. This is the same conclusion we reached in comparing plots of cohort and cross-sectional age-wealth profiles.

11.4.1 Evaluation of Possible Fixups of Cross-sectional Profiles

Faced with Shorrocks's criticisms, previous researchers with only cross-sectional data available have attempted a variety of fixups. Most have involved transforming the dependent variable through the use of some assumption about how it is distorted. We will evaluate two commonly proposed fixups. The first involves dividing observed wealth by an estimate of the household's permanent income (as King and Dicks-Mireaux did in their often-cited 1982 paper). The second involves scaling up the older households' wealth by an assumed productivity growth factor (as Mirer [1979] did).

Table 11.14   ***F*-Tests of the Equality of Cross-sectional and Cohort Regression Coefficients, Dependent Variable WEALTH: WEALTH = b_0 + b_1 AGE**

	F-Statistic		*F*-Statistic
1966 cross and:		1976 cross and:	
1921 cohort	9.312*	1919 cohort	3.799*
1920 cohort	2.938	1918 cohort	5.345*
1919 cohort	3.422*	1917 cohort	2.970
1918 cohort	.764	1916 cohort	3.956*
1917 cohort	.232	1915 cohort	1.859
1916 cohort	.469	1914 cohort	3.120*
1915 cohort	.189	1913 cohort	3.398*
1914 cohort	.523	1912 cohort	5.233*
		1911 cohort	2.441
1969 cross and:		1910 cohort	.760
1921 cohort	9.167*	1909 cohort	3.964*
1920 cohort	2.759	1908 cohort	.983
1919 cohort	3.432*	1907 cohort	5.075*
1918 cohort	.874		
1917 cohort	.239	1981 cross and:	
1916 cohort	.606	1914 cohort	7.228*
1915 cohort	.055	1913 cohort	8.636*
1914 cohort	.511	1912 cohort	10.384*
1913 cohort	.267	1911 cohort	1.016
1912 cohort	1.279	1910 cohort	2.536
1911 cohort	5.341*	1909 cohort	6.166*
		1908 cohort	4.410*
1971 cross and:		1907 cohort	9.612*
1921 cohort	12.128*		
1920 cohort	3.747*		
1919 cohort	4.719*		
1918 cohort	1.139		
1917 cohort	.437		
1916 cohort	.823		
1915 cohort	.220		
1914 cohort	.921		
1913 cohort	.324		
1912 cohort	1.562		
1911 cohort	5.304*		
1910 cohort	.680		
1909 cohort	2.240		

Source: Computed from the regression results in table 11.13.

Note: Critical *F*-statistics: 2.99 (5 percent), 4.60 (1 percent). Degrees of freedom are 2 and 1,967 or greater.

*Statistically significant at the 5 percent level.

King and Dicks-Mireaux (1982) construct a measure of permanent income based on the predicted value of household earnings obtained from a nonlinear earnings equation. Their data include only one observation on household earnings. The explanatory variables in their earnings equation are a set of demographic characteristics for each household. This technique explains less than 26 percent of log earnings. Their measure of permanent income is the predicted value of the earnings equation plus half the residual. They then estimated an equation like (3) below, with the log of wealth scaled by their estimate of permanent income as the dependent variable:

(3)   ln(WEALTH/PERMANENT INCOME)

$$= a_1 + a_2 \text{ AGE} + a_3 \text{ AGE-SPLINED} + \ldots$$

This transformation is an attempt to correct for the productivity bias. As independent variables they included a spline on AGE, a farm dummy, the number unemployed, the number of adults, the number of persons with life insurance, and the log of social security and pension wealth, each scaled by their permanent-income measure. They also included a Mills ratio since they estimated the equation only for households with greater than $2,500 of wealth.

We are interested in investigating whether scaling wealth by permanent income makes cross-sectional age-wealth profiles similar in shape to age-wealth profiles based on cohort data. Our permanent-income measure, TREARNAT, for each household is better than that used by King and Dicks-Mireaux in that it is based on multiple observations of the respondents' earnings (see sec. 11.2). Since we are using all households in the 15-YEAR CRS sample, including those with negative and zero wealth, our dependent variable is simply WEALTH/TREARNAT rather than the logarithm of this ratio. Figures 11.41 and 11.42 contain plots of the 1966, 1971, 1976, and 1981 median WEALTH/TREARNAT - AGE profiles. Comparing these to figure 11.31, we see that the transformation has imparted a considerable upward slope to the 1966, 1971, and 1976 cross-sectional profiles and reversed the downward slope of the 1981 cross-sectional profile.

Are these transformed cross-sectional age-wealth profiles consistent with observed cohort age-wealth profiles? Regressions of WEALTH/TREARNAT on AGE and a constant are reported in table 11.15. All the cross-sectional regressions now have positive and statistically significant coefficients on age. As in the earlier regressions (table 11.13), the youngest ten cohorts have positively signed, statistically significant coefficients on AGE, while the oldest five cohorts have smaller, statistically insignificant coefficients on age. Again, this insignificance presumably reflects the flattening and decumulation of wealth at older ages

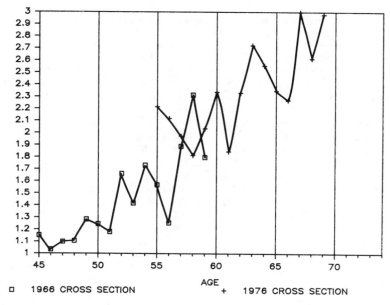

Fig. 11.41   Median WEALTH/TREARNAT—15-YEAR CRS sample

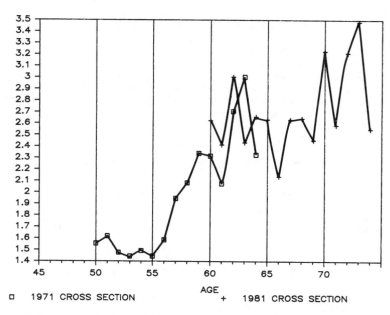

Fig. 11.42   Median WEALTH/TREARNAT—15-YEAR CRS sample

Table 11.15   Regression Results, Dependent Variable WEALTH/TREARNAT: WEALTH/TREARNAT = b_0 + b_1 AGE

Sample	$\hat{b}_0$	S.E.	$\hat{b}_1$	S.E.	$\bar{R}^2$	SSR	N
1966 cross section	−11.725	3.107	.291	.061	.0133	167,463	1,625
1969 cross section	−12.985	3.711	.303	.069	.0113	213,222	1,625
1971 cross section	−12.216	3.317	.281	.059	.0131	158,501	1,625
1976 cross section	−12.949	4.313	.282	.071	.0091	225,968	1,625
1981 cross section	−7.426	4.313	.182	.065	.0042	193,120	1,625
1921 cohort	−5.104	1.294	.150	.025	.0431	10,798	785
1920 cohort	−4.103	1.314	.123	.025	.0369	6,578	615
1919 cohort	−5.064	1.741	.152	.032	.0284	15,464	725
1918 cohort	−2.698	1.514	.094	.028	.0164	8,786	640
1917 cohort	−2.360	3.222	.103	.058	.0039	30,417	570
1916 cohort	−3.340	1.584	.107	.028	.0199	9,962	675
1915 cohort	−1.915	2.164	.089	.037	.0080	13,479	585
1914 cohort	−5.823	3.909	.172	.066	.0110	32,920	515
1913 cohort	−3.521	2.847	.122	.048	.0086	26,100	640
1912 cohort	−.945	2.116	.072	.035	.0068	7,674	475
1911 cohort	3.833	6.332	.027	.102	−.0022	54,502	430
1910 cohort	14.478	20.704	−.092	.330	−.0024	440,553	380
1909 cohort	−8.812	14.094	.245	.221	.0005	253,456	430
1908 cohort	−.115	4.093	.075	.063	.0012	15,332	370
1907 cohort	7.124	6.317	−.052	.096	−.0024	21,727	290

Source: Computed from the National Longitudinal Surveys of Mature Men.

Note: The underlying sample is the 15-YEAR CRS, the 1,691 respondents who provided both usable wealth and usable age data in each of the five surveys and, in addition, those for whom TREARNAT could be computed, resulting in a sample of 1,625. WEALTH is the sum of net residential assets, net farm assets, net business assets, net investment real estate assets, deposits in financial institutions, U.S. savings bonds, holdings of stocks and bonds, and personal loans made to others less unsecured personal debt. TREARNAT is the average of the respondent's after-tax wage, salary, self-employment, and farm income discounted to age sixty-two.

by these cohorts. Formal *F*-tests of whether the estimated cohort coefficients are statistically different from the coefficients estimated on each cross section are reported in table 11.16. The *F*-statistics are generally larger here than they are in table 11.14. The conclusion one draws as to whether the estimated cross-sectional age-wealth profiles are consistent with the estimated cohort age-wealth profiles again depends on which cross section and which cohort are compared. Rejections are obtained most frequently for the older and middle cohorts. The WEALTH/TREARNAT age-wealth profiles are most consistent with the rapid accumulation by the three youngest cohorts. Overall, these *F*-tests suggest that the correction is a failure. Age-wealth profiles estimated on transformed cross-sectional data are likely to be inconsistent with similar equations estimated on transformed cohort data.

Looking further at the table 11.15 regressions, one observes that the cross-sectional slope coefficients on AGE are all considerably larger

Table 11.16 *F*-Tests of the Equality of Cross-sectional and Cohort Regression Coefficients, Dependent Variable WEALTH/TREARNAT
WEALTH/TREARNAT = $b_0 + b_1$ AGE

	F-Statistic		*F*-Statistic
1966 cross and:		1976 cross and:	
1921 cohort	2.919	1919 cohort	1.506
1920 cohort	5.128*	1918 cohort	2.084
1919 cohort	2.631	1917 cohort	1.408
1918 cohort	7.686*	1916 cohort	2.479
1917 cohort	3.013*	1915 cohort	1.923
1916 cohort	8.474*	1914 cohort	.992
1915 cohort	5.619*	1913 cohort	1.393
1914 cohort	1.471	1912 cohort	2.957
		1911 cohort	3.491*
1969 cross and:		1910 cohort	11.913*
1921 cohort	1.933	1909 cohort	2.788
1920 cohort	2.683	1908 cohort	1.766
1919 cohort	1.466	1907 cohort	5.734*
1918 cohort	4.879*		
1917 cohort	2.024	1981 cross and:	
1916 cohort	5.889*	1914 cohort	1.320
1915 cohort	3.962*	1913 cohort	.261
1914 cohort	.853	1912 cohort	.988
1913 cohort	3.485*	1911 cohort	3.445*
1912 cohort	5.447*	1910 cohort	9.803*
1911 cohort	2.501	1909 cohort	7.738*
		1908 cohort	.678
1971 cross and:		1907 cohort	3.113*
1921 cohort	1.630		
1920 cohort	2.044		
1919 cohort	1.322		
1918 cohort	4.118*		
1917 cohort	1.801		
1916 cohort	5.021*		
1915 cohort	3.347*		
1914 cohort	.640		
1913 cohort	2.500		
1912 cohort	5.098*		
1911 cohort	3.550*		
1910 cohort	10.893*		
1909 cohort	.951		

Source: Computed from the regression results in table 11.15.
Note: Critical *F*-Statistics: 2.99 (5 percent), 4.60 (1 percent). Degrees of freedom are 2 and 1,851 or greater.
*Statistically significant at the 5 percent level.

than the coefficients on AGE in the cohort regressions. This suggests that many of the F-test rejections result because the cross-sectional profiles are too steep. This steepness may be due to the fact that the differential mortality effect is still present in the cross-sectional profiles. Scaling wealth by permanent income is an attempt to correct for the productivity effect. It does nothing to correct for the fact that the median wealth of the older cohorts is biased upward by the poor dying young.

Mirer (1979) proposes another sort of adjustment that attempts to eliminate the productivity effect in a cross-sectional sample. He proposes to multiply each household's wealth (other than that of the youngest cohort) by a factor $(1 + g)^A$, where A is the difference between the cohort's age and the age of the youngest cohort. This is based on the assumption that, if income and hence "wealth grows at the rate g, then the typical profile of any given cohort is $(1 + g)$ times as high as that for the cohort which is one year older" (440). Mirer assumed that g was 2 percent per year. Transforming our data by the same 2 percent growth rate yields the cross-sectional age-wealth profiles for 1966, 1971, 1976, and 1981 plotted in figures 11.43 and 11.44. Comparing these to the unadjusted cross-sectional age-wealth profiles we examined earlier (fig. 11.31), one sees that the obvious occurs: the previously flat 1966 and 1971 profiles now slope up somewhat, the U-shaped 1976 profile

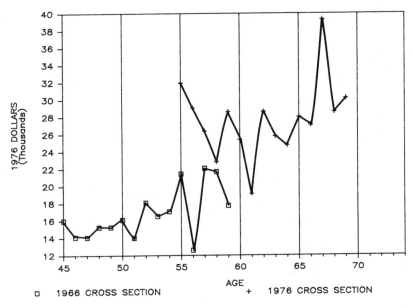

Fig. 11.43   Median TRANSFORMED WEALTH—15-YEAR CRS sample

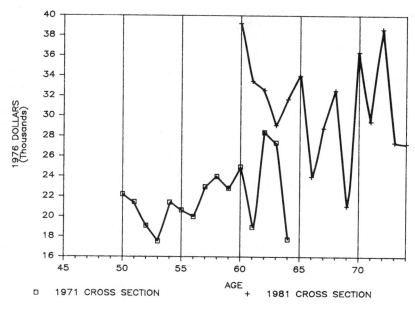

Fig. 11.44   Median TRANSFORMED WEALTH—15-YEAR CRS sample

is now less pronounced, and the previously downward-sloping 1981 profile has become much flatter.

Remembering the shapes of the age-wealth profiles reported for each cohort in figures 11.1–11.15, one might guess that the Mirer transformation makes the 1966 and 1971 cross-sectional profiles more consistent with the correct cohort age-wealth profiles. Formal F-tests based on regressions of TRANSFORMED WEALTH on AGE and a constant reported in table 11.17 confirm that this is true (results of F-tests are reported in table 11.18). On the other hand, the frequency of rejection of the hypothesis that the 1976 and 1981 cross-sectional coefficients are the same as the individual cohort coefficients is about the same. Hence, we conclude that the Mirer transformation might or might not transform a cross-sectional age-wealth profile into one that looks like a true longitudinal cohort profile. It all depends on which cross section one selects for comparison. It also heavily depends on the growth rate, g, assumed. Mirer reports that his results are quite sensitive to changes in g. Clearly, our conclusion as to the similarity of a transformed cross-sectional profile to a cohort profile also depends heavily on the growth rate assumed. With panel data, one can estimate the growth rate. With one cross section, as many researchers have had, the growth rate must be assumed. By varying the growth rate assumed, the researcher can considerably alter the age-wealth profile produced. Hence, it is our conclusion that this is an unreliable fixup method.

Table 11.17   **Regression Results, Dependent Variable TRANSFORMED WEALTH: TRANSFORMED WEALTH = b_0 + b_1 AGE**

Sample	$\hat{b}_0$	S.E.	$\hat{b}_1$	S.E.	$\bar{R}^2$	SSR (10^{12})	N
1966 cross section	−44,990	23,673	1,617	462	.0066	10.723	1,691
1969 cross section	−43,128	28,729	1,566	530	.0046	14.098	1,691
1971 cross section	−37,992	25,782	1,445	458	.0053	10.563	1,691
1976 cross section	7,455	31,410	722	513	.0006	13.228	1,691
1981 cross section	60,606	40,364	−26	610	−.0006	18.676	1,691
1921 cohort	−98,020	28,512	2,752	550	.0296	5.3114	790
1920 cohort	−61,952	31,301	1,948	592	.0148	4.234	655
1919 cohort	−55,806	36,948	1,855	686	.0084	7.4548	750
1918 cohort	−40,852	26,326	1,389	480	.0112	2.7817	655
1917 cohort	−22,775	24,232	1,099	434	.0094	1.7513	575
1916 cohort	−39,801	30,836	1,374	542	.008	3.7744	675
1915 cohort	−7,375	34,830	829	602	.0015	3.7353	605
1914 cohort	−43,200	31,363	1,437	533	.0115	2.3309	540
1913 cohort	−15,489	26,354	907	440	.0049	2.343	655
1912 cohort	−28,138	27,425	1,050	451	.0085	1.5164	515
1911 cohort	36,809	68,220	301	1,103	−.0021	6.4756	435
1910 cohort	1,765	63,569	708	1,012	−.0013	4.6029	400
1909 cohort	−63,441	45,208	1,785	708	.0117	2.9206	455
1908 cohort	886	43,949	624	678	−.0004	2.0669	400
1907 cohort	43,910	29,694	−201	451	−.0023	.7002	350

Source: Computed from the National Longitudinal Surveys of Mature Men.

Note: The underlying sample is the 15-YEAR CRS, the 1,691 respondents who provided both usable wealth and usable age data in each of the five surveys. WEALTH is the sum of net residential assets, net farm assets, net business assets, net investment real estate assets, deposits in financial institutions, U.S. savings bonds, holdings of stocks and bonds, and personal loans made to others less unsecured personal debt. TRANSFORMED WEALTH is WEALTH multiplied by the factor 1.02^x, where x is the difference between the cohort's age and the age of the youngest cohort.

In summary, these fixups for the productivity effect appear to be unreliable. Also, they do not correct for the differential mortality effect. We conclude that there is no substitute for having panel data. Inferences from cross sections about time-series age-wealth profiles are unreliable.

11.5   Assessing the Bias in Household Portfolio Reallocation Over Time Based on Cross-sectional Data

Although far more studies have examined the relation between age and total wealth, the effect of age on the composition of household wealth has been the subject of a number of recent investigations (see, e.g., Kane 1980, 1985; Shorrocks 1982; and Dicks-Mireaux and King 1982). Because assets differ in the degree of liquidity and risk as well as other characteristics, one might hypothesize that a household's demand for particular classes of assets varies as the household ages. For

Table 11.18   ***F*-Tests of the Equality of Cross-sectional and Cohort Regression Coefficients, Dependent Variable TRANSFORMED WEALTH TRANSFORMED WEALTH = $b_0 + b_1$ AGE**

	F-Statistic		*F*-Statistic
1966 cross and:		1976 cross and:	
1921 cohort	2.265	1919 cohort	.907
1920 cohort	.078	1918 cohort	3.373*
1919 cohort	.150	1917 cohort	1.926
1918 cohort	2.471	1916 cohort	2.848
1917 cohort	1.304	1915 cohort	2.065
1916 cohort	2.080	1914 cohort	2.215
1915 cohort	1.388	1913 cohort	4.868*
1914 cohort	1.596	1912 cohort	7.327*
		1911 cohort	.345
1969 cross and:		1910 cohort	.632
1921 cohort	2.928	1909 cohort	1.240
1920 cohort	.191	1908 cohort	3.314*
1919 cohort	.356	1907 cohort	11.423*
1918 cohort	1.902		
1917 cohort	1.016	1981 cross and:	
1916 cohort	1.772	1914 cohort	4.120*
1915 cohort	1.186	1913 cohort	6.599*
1914 cohort	1.264	1912 cohort	8.516*
1913 cohort	3.172*	1911 cohort	.188
1912 cohort	5.161*	1910 cohort	2.192
1911 cohort	1.555	1909 cohort	3.468*
		1908 cohort	5.149*
1971 cross and:		1907 cohort	12.509*
1921 cohort	4.843*		
1920 cohort	.538		
1919 cohort	.923		
1918 cohort	1.485		
1917 cohort	.780		
1916 cohort	1.382		
1915 cohort	1.008		
1914 cohort	1.113		
1913 cohort	3.276*		
1912 cohort	5.853*		
1911 cohort	1.582		
1910 cohort	.452		
1909 cohort	.348		

Source: Computed from the regression results in table 11.17.

Note: Critical *F*-statistics: 2.99 (5 percent), 4.60 (1 percent). Degrees of freedom are 2 and 1,967 or greater.

*Statistically significant at the 5 percent level.

example, households might demand assets with more liquidity to finance consumption spending in the absence of labor income when they retire.

In regressions estimated using cross-sectional data, both Shorrocks (1982) and Dicks-Mireaux and King (1982) found a significant relation between age and portfolio shares for certain classes of household assets. Kane (1985) used three cross sections of households surveyed in 1962, 1970, and 1977 to look at the change in the percentage of wealth held in various asset categories by household type between survey dates. He made two types of comparisons: (1) between households in the same age class in different surveys (for example, 55 to 64 years old in both 1962 and 1970) and (2) between households in the same age cohort between surveys (e.g., fifty- to fifty-nine-year-olds in 1962 become fifty-eight- to sixty-seven-year-olds in 1970). On the basis of comparisons of the second type, he inferred that the rate of home-ownership, in particular, at first increases with age and then declines after late middle age while mortgage debt declines "as a household ages" (Kane 1985, 134).

Just as in the case of the age-wealth profile, there is the potential for both a mortality effect and a productivity effect to cause cross-sectional inferences made about changes in the composition of household wealth as households age, such as those just described, to differ from those obtained using panel data. In addition, inferences about household portfolio reallocation as a household ages made by comparing mean portfolio shares of households in a cross section may be misleading because of cohort-specific asset preferences. Finally, comparison of mean household portfolio shares across surveys mixes up changes that are the result of portfolio reallocation by existing asset owners with those that result from net entry or exit into ownership of a particular type of asset. The remainder of this section discusses each of these potential biases in cross-sectional data.

The discussion of differences between portfolio shares based on cross-sectional versus longitudinal data which follows is subject to a number of caveats. The large dispersion around the means of the portfolio shares makes statistical tests of differences in the means across age classes unlikely to indicate statistically significant differences in portfolio shares. Our comparisons of differences in the reallocation of household portfolios between cross sections and panels of survivors might possibly be modified if this analysis were conducted using a finer breakdown of asset and liability categories or considered assets separately from liabilities, rather than using net values. Differences might also be perceptible if we controlled for differences in household wealth within age classes.

11.5.1   Differential Mortality and Productivity Effects

Differential mortality by wealth class (i.e., the poor die young) can lead to bias in using cross sections to make inferences about changes in the composition of an individual household's portfolio over time if holdings of certain types of assets are disproportionately concentrated in particular wealth classes. As we observed in table 11.3, the poor in our sample have a higher mortality rate than do the wealthier members of the sample. Table 11.19 reports the number of households by cohort in each percentile range of the distribution of 1966 cohort wealth that owned assets in each of four categories—HOUSE/FARM, BUSINESS/LAND, FINANCIAL, and STOCK/BOND—as a percentage of all households in that age-wealth class.

The only category of asset that is widely owned by households in all but the lowest deciles is HOUSE/FARM. Over 90 percent of the households above the fortieth percentile own HOUSE/FARM assets, on the average. Table 11.19 shows that a larger percentage of the wealthier

Table 11.19   Asset Ownership in 1966 by Percentile of 1966 Wealth Cohort

Asset Type	Birth Year Cohort (fraction of initial cohort)				
	1921	1920	1919	1918	1917
Percentile 1–20:					
HOUSE/FARM	.119	.060	.041	.063	.062
BUSINESS/LAND	.060	.045	.027	.016	.000
FINANCIAL	.343	.134	.178	.250	.200
STOCK/BOND	.030	.030	.000	.000	.000
Percentile 21–40:					
HOUSE/FARM	.809	.591	.563	.714	.766
BUSINESS/LAND	.147	.182	.197	.143	.141
FINANCIAL	.647	.606	.676	.524	.563
STOCK/BOND	.059	.045	.070	.079	.031
Percentile 41–60:					
HOUSE/FARM	.896	.894	.959	.905	.938
BUSINESS/LAND	.194	.106	.205	.302	.156
FINANCIAL	.701	.606	.699	.714	.656
STOCK/BOND	.075	.091	.096	.127	.094
Percentile 61–70:					
HOUSE/FARM	.971	.879	.917	.939	.906
BUSINESS/LAND	.265	.333	.167	.364	.188
FINANCIAL	.765	.848	.750	.636	.813
STOCK/BOND	.324	.182	.194	.091	.250

(*continued*)

Table 11.19   (continued)

Asset Type	Birth Year Cohort (fraction of initial cohort)				
	1921	1920	1919	1918	1917
Percentile 71–80:					
HOUSE/FARM	.933	.818	.972	.933	.938
BUSINESS/LAND	.267	.364	.306	.400	.438
FINANCIAL	.833	.909	.833	.867	.875
STOCK/BOND	.333	.152	.333	.200	.281
Percentile 81–90:					
HOUSE/FARM	.914	.970	.972	.906	.969
BUSINESS/LAND	.486	.545	.417	.563	.500
FINANCIAL	.857	.848	.750	.906	.906
STOCK/BOND	.429	.333	.139	.375	.406
Percentile 91–100:					
HOUSE/FARM	.906	.969	.941	1.000	.970
BUSINESS/LAND	.531	.781	.676	.633	.727
FINANCIAL	.938	.875	.971	.933	.939
STOCK/BOND	.563	.594	.588	.600	.515
Percentile 1–100:					
HOUSE/FARM	.736	.670	.691	.711	.730
BUSINESS/LAND	.234	.267	.240	.286	.245
FINANCIAL	.676	.615	.638	.629	.637
STOCK/BOND	.195	.158	.156	.165	.171
	1916	1915	1914	1913	1912
Percentile 1–20:					
HOUSE/FARM	.030	.085	.066	.046	.070
BUSINESS/LAND	.090	.000	.016	.046	.018
FINANCIAL	.179	.099	.115	.200	.193
STOCK/BOND	.000	.000	.000	.000	.000
Percentile 21–40:					
HOUSE/FARM	.652	.629	.677	.714	.696
BUSINESS/LAND	.121	.157	.129	.127	.071
FINANCIAL	.470	.600	.548	.587	.536
STOCK/BOND	.030	.029	.048	.063	.054
Percentile 41–60:					
HOUSE/FARM	.924	.957	.932	.873	.857
BUSINESS/LAND	.227	.271	.220	.222	.304
FINANCIAL	.667	.657	.627	.683	.607
STOCK/BOND	.121	.100	.119	.095	.107
Percentile 61–70:					
HOUSE/FARM	.971	.971	.966	.938	.963
BUSINESS/LAND	.353	.257	.172	.281	.296
FINANCIAL	.765	.629	.862	.906	.630
STOCK/BOND	.147	.114	.103	.281	.148

Table 11.19 (continued)

Asset Type	Birth Year Cohort (fraction of initial cohort)				
	1916	1915	1914	1913	1912
Percentile 71–80:					
HOUSE/FARM	.938	.943	.967	.967	.931
BUSINESS/LAND	.375	.543	.433	.233	.483
FINANCIAL	.906	.800	.933	.700	.862
STOCK/BOND	.375	.286	.267	.300	.103
Percentile 81–90:					
HOUSE/FARM	.970	.914	.967	1.000	.964
BUSINESS/LAND	.606	.429	.400	.484	.500
FINANCIAL	.848	.971	.900	.871	.929
STOCK/BOND	.424	.400	.400	.161	.250
Percentile 91–100:					
HOUSE/FARM	1.000	.941	.968	.933	.897
BUSINESS/LAND	.690	.618	.613	.733	.655
FINANCIAL	.931	.912	.903	.867	.862
STOCK/BOND	.690	.618	.484	.533	.379
Percentile 1–100:					
HOUSE/FARM	.703	.709	.719	.704	.699
BUSINESS/LAND	.284	.269	.235	.248	.273
FINANCIAL	.602	.600	.616	.624	.596
STOCK/BOND	.187	.166	.159	.156	.121

	1911	1910	1909	1908	1907	All
Percentile 1–20:						
HOUSE/FARM	.048	.037	.037	.058	.036	.058
BUSINESS/LAND	.016	.000	.037	.038	.000	.028
FINANCIAL	.032	.259	.241	.173	.073	.178
STOCK/BOND	.000	.000	.000	.000	.000	.004
Percentile 21–40:						
HOUSE/FARM	.525	.796	.679	.647	.633	.672
BUSINESS/LAND	.148	.167	.245	.118	.102	.147
FINANCIAL	.492	.500	.642	.471	.531	.563
STOCK/BOND	.049	.037	.057	.039	.061	.050
Percentile 41–60:						
HOUSE/FARM	.885	.906	.906	.885	.902	.909
BUSINESS/LAND	.295	.283	.264	.308	.255	.238
FINANCIAL	.738	.736	.679	.654	.588	.668
STOCK/BOND	.066	.132	.075	.096	.098	.099

(*continued*)

Table 11.19   (continued)

Asset Type	Cohort Birth Year (fraction of initial cohort)					
	1911	1910	1909	1908	1907	All
Percentile 61–70:						
HOUSE/FARM	.933	.852	.889	.917	1.000	.934
BUSINESS/LAND	.400	.333	.259	.417	.320	.290
FINANCIAL	.733	.667	.815	.708	.680	.749
STOCK/BOND	.167	.074	.148	.250	.080	.172
Percentile 71–80:						
HOUSE/FARM	.933	.963	.923	.880	.923	.931
BUSINESS/LAND	.433	.370	.308	.520	.385	.390
FINANCIAL	.700	.704	.808	.840	.731	.823
STOCK/BOND	.300	.222	.308	.240	.308	.268
Percentile 81–90:						
HOUSE/FARM	.967	1.000	.889	.963	.920	.952
BUSINESS/LAND	.500	.444	.667	.481	.560	.503
FINANCIAL	.800	.815	.889	.926	.800	.868
STOCK/BOND	.400	.222	.333	.593	.200	.338
Percentile 91–100:						
HOUSE/FARM	.933	1.000	.920	.920	.963	.951
BUSINESS/LAND	.633	.480	.560	.720	.667	.650
FINANCIAL	.967	.920	.920	.920	.852	.915
STOCK/BOND	.667	.240	.560	.520	.556	.545
Percentile 1–100:						
HOUSE/FARM	.664	.727	.683	.684	.686	.701
BUSINESS/LAND	.286	.251	.287	.305	.264	.264
FINANCIAL	.569	.607	.653	.598	.539	.615
STOCK/BOND	.174	.109	.158	.188	.147	.161

Source: Computed from the National Longitudinal Surveys of Older Men.

Note: Sample consists of 4,546 households that provided valid age and wealth data in the 1966 survey. HOUSE/FARM is the sum of net residential housing and net farm assets. BUSINESS/LAND is the sum of net business and net investment real estate assets. FINANCIAL is the sum of deposits in financial institutions, U.S. savings bonds, and personal loans made to others. STOCK/BOND is the value of stocks and bonds owned. WEALTH is the sum of net residential assets, net farm asssets, net business assets, net investment real estate assets, deposits in financial institutions, U.S. savings bonds, holdings of stocks and bonds, and personal loans made to others less unsecured personal debt.

households own BUSINESS/LAND, FINANCIAL, and STOCK/BOND assets than poorer households. In the case of STOCK/BOND, for example, almost no household in the poorest twenty percentiles owns STOCK/BOND, while over half the households in the top decile own stock. Thus, cross sections could give the impression that the share of wealth in stock increases with age, whereas the larger proportion of stocks in the portfolio of older households could be the result of the fact that there are more rich households among the older households in a cross section. None of the studies mentioned above that found a relation between age and household portfolio composition made adjustments for differential mortality in cross sections.

Table 11.20 reports portfolio shares for households in the "usable data with reentry" sample (the total wealth of these households is reported in table 11.12). We grouped our households into three age classes spanning five cohorts in each survey. Comparisons of portfolios going down a column are the kind made when using a single cross section. Comparisons across columns are the kind made when comparing data from several cross sections surveyed at different times. Neither of these comparisons corrects for the effect of differential mortality. Table 11.21, on the other hand, reports portfolio shares for our 15-YEAR CRS sample and, therefore, corrects for the mortality bias since the portfolio shares across rows of table 11.21 are portfolio shares for the same households in each of the four surveys.[4]

Comparisons across rows of table 11.21 and comparable rows of table 11.20 illustrate the differential mortality bias in table 11.20. For example, in table 11.20, it appears as though the youngest cohort increased its HOUSE/FARM share by 2.2 percent from 1966 to 1981, whereas table 11.21 indicates that households in this cohort actually decreased their HOUSE/FARM shares by 2.7 percent. For the other two cohorts, table 11.20 shares overstate the amount of increase in the cohort's HOUSE/FARM share by 1.4 percent and 2.7 percent, respectively, over the 1966–81 period. Row 1 in table 11.20 suggests that the youngest cohort's share of STOCKS increased by 0.2 percent over the 1966–81 interval, whereas table 11.21 indicates that this cohort's share actually declined by 0.7 percent over the same period. Failure to correct cohort data for differential mortality clearly can lead to wrong conclusions about the reallocation of a cohort's portfolio over time.

Productivity has increased over time, making younger cohorts wealthier than older ones. As indicated in table 11.19, portfolio shares are influenced by the level of household wealth. Differences in cohort wealth resulting from the growth in productivity over time in the economy may, therefore, impart a bias in inferences made using changes in mean portfolio shares in a cross section to describe portfolio reallocation as a household ages. Comparing the rows and columns of table 11.21 illustrates the productivity bias inherent in cross-sectional data. For example, reading across the first row, one observes that the youngest cohort reduces its HOUSE/FARM share by 2.1 percent by the time it reaches age fifty-five to fifty-nine (in 1976). In contrast, reading

Table 11.20   **Mean Portfolio Shares by Age Group, Usable Data With Reentry Sample (fraction of WEALTH)**

Asset Type	Survey Year			
	1966	1971	1976	1981
	Age (N)			
	45–49 (1,509)	50–54 (1,228)	55–59 (1,047)	60–64 (891)
HOUSE/FARM	.630	.624	.645	.652
BUSINESS/LAND	.113	.134	.115	.108
FINANCIAL	.183	.161	.194	.170
STOCK/BOND	.033	.045	.034	.035
	50–54 (1,419)	55–59 (1,163)	60–64 (944)	65–69 (781)
HOUSE/FARM	.608	.610	.643	.672
BUSINESS/LAND	.111	.110	.096	.081
FINANCIAL	.151	.205	.191	.182
STOCK/BOND	.033	.037	.028	.028
	55–59 (1,194)	60–64 (885)	65–69 (691)	70–74 (571)
HOUSE/FARM	.600	.696	.631	.661
BUSINESS/LAND	.133	.101	.076	.062
FINANCIAL	.185	.153	.209	.203
STOCK/BOND	.035	.036	.036	.025

Source: Computed from the National Longitudinal Surveys of Older Men.

Note: Sample consists of all respondents who provided valid age and wealth data in any survey whether or not they reported these data in prior or subsequent surveys. In the 1966, 1971, 1976, and 1981 surveys, which report zero WEALTH, 424, 379, 271, and 231 households are excluded, respectively. These calculations also exclude one respondent in 1971 who reported a 19,900 percent house share in 1971. HOUSE/FARM is the sum of net residential housing and net farm assets. BUSINESS/LAND is the sum of net business and net investment real estate assets. FINANCIAL is the sum of deposits in financial institutions, U.S. savings bonds, and personal loans made to others. STOCK/ BOND is the value of stocks and bonds owned. WEALTH is the sum of net residential assets, net farm assets, net business assets, net investment real estate assets, deposits in financial institutions, U.S. savings bonds, holdings of stocks and bonds, and personal loans made to others less unsecured personal debt.

down the first column suggests a much larger reduction (6.8 percent) in HOUSE/FARM share as individuals age from age forty-five to forty-nine to age fifty-five to fifty-nine. Likewise, reading across row 2 in table 11.21, one finds that, as this cohort aged from age fifty to fifty-four to age sixty to sixty-four, it increased its HOUSE/FARM share by 0.8 percent from 1966 to 1976, whereas reading down the second column (the 1971 cross section) suggests an average 2.9 percent reduction in HOUSE/FARM shares by households as they aged from age fifty to fifty-four to age sixty to sixty-four. What we observe here is

Table 11.21   **Mean Portfolio Shares by Age Group, 15-YEAR CRS Sample (fraction of WEALTH)**

	Survey Year			
Asset Type	1966	1971	1976	1981
	Age (N)			
	45–49 (684)	50–54 (684)	55–59 (684)	60–64 (684)
HOUSE/FARM	.586	.575	.565	.559
BUSINESS/LAND	.078	.106	.091	.083
FINANCIAL	.192	.15	.194	.168
STOCK/BOND	.036	.041	.031	.029
	50–54 (598)	55–59 (598)	60–64 (598)	65–69 (598)
HOUSE/FARM	.538	.531	.546	.588
BUSINESS/LAND	.092	.075	.086	.067
FINANCIAL	.162	.227	.181	.175
STOCK/BOND	.028	.029	.024	.019
	55–59 (408)	60–64 (408)	65–69 (408)	70–74 (408)
HOUSE/FARM	.518	.546	.540	.552
BUSINESS/LAND	.110	.101	.070	.055
FINANCIAL	.159	.181	.184	.207
STOCK/BOND	.034	.030	.026	.015

Source: Computed from the National Longitudinal Surveys of Older Men.

Note: Sample consists of the 1,691 respondents who provided valid age and wealth data in each of the five surveys. HOUSE/FARM is the sum of net residential housing and net farm assets. BUSINESS/LAND is the sum of net business and net investment real estate assets. FINANCIAL is the sum of deposits in financial institutions, U.S. savings bonds, and personal loans made to others. STOCK/BOND is the value of stocks and bonds owned. WEALTH is the sum of net residential assets, net farm assets, net business assets, net investment real estate assets, deposits in financial institutions, U.S. savings bonds, holdings of stocks and bonds, and personal loans made to others less unsecured personal debt.

clearly a productivity bias in the cross-sectional data. Productivity and home ownership have risen over time, so, when we read down the column, we are observing the portfolio shares of older (poorer) cohorts who own less housing wealth.

11.5.2   Cohort Effect

In addition to the effect of differential mortality, cohort-specific asset preferences may cause cross-sectional inferences to differ from those made using panel data. Macroeconomic events, such as depressions, inflations, and wars, occurred at different stages of the life cycle for each cohort. To the extent that these macroeconomic events influenced the asset preferences of cohorts, changes in the composition of household wealth between households of different ages in a cross section reflect differences between the cohorts rather than life-cycle differences in wealth composition. For example, members of one cohort may not increase the share of stock in their portfolios as they age between forty-five and fifty-five years old because members of this cohort lived through the stock market crash of 1929, while members of another cohort may increase the share of stock in their portfolios as they age between forty-five and fifty-five years old because the stock market offered them a profitable return on their investments.

Kane's (1985) comparison of households in different cohorts at the same age in different surveys addresses this issue. Differential mortality is not an issue in these comparisons since households are compared at the same age and, thus, all have survived to that point. Table 11.22 makes the same type of comparison using households in our "usable data with reentry" sample. The portfolio shares in this table are the same as those in table 11.20, except that the portfolio shares of each (five-year) cohort in successive surveys are shifted down one row. As we read across a row in table 11.22 with the cohorts arranged in this manner, we observe different cohorts passing through the same age classes. All three of our cohorts are observed when they are aged fifty-five to fifty-nine and sixty to sixty-four. Two of our cohorts are observed when they are aged fifty to fifty-four and sixty-five to sixty-nine. Comparisons of the portfolio shares held by each of the cohorts in the same age interval provide information about cohort-specific asset preferences. Inspection of the means across cohorts does not reveal any systematic differences. The lack of any conclusive evidence of cohort-specific asset references may be the result of the narrow range of cohorts for which we have data.

Table 11.22   **Comparison of Mean Portfolio Shares of Different Cohorts at the Same Age (fraction of WEALTH)**

	Survey Year			
Asset Type	1966	1971	1976	1981
	Age (N)			
	45–59 (1,509)			
HOUSE/FARM	.63			
BUSINESS/LAND	.113			
FINANCIAL	.183			
STOCK/BOND	.033			

Table 11.22   (continued)

Asset Type	Survey Year			
	1966	1971	1976	1981
	50–54 (1,419)	50–54 (1,228)		
HOUSE/FARM	.608	.624		
BUSINESS/LAND	.111	.134		
FINANCIAL	.151	.161		
STOCK/BOND	.033	.045		
	55–59 (1,194)	55–59 (1,163)	55–59 (1,047)	
HOUSE/FARM	.6	.61	.645	
BUSINESS/LAND	.133	.11	.115	
FINANCIAL	.185	.205	.194	
STOCK/BOND	.035	.037	.034	
		60–64 (885)	60–64 (944)	60–64 (891)
HOUSE/FARM		.696	.643	.652
BUSINESS/LAND		.101	.096	.108
FINANCIAL		.153	.191	.17
STOCK/BOND		.036	.028	.035
			65–69 (691)	65–69 (781)
HOUSE/FARM			.631	.672
BUSINESS/LAND			.076	.081
FINANCIAL			.209	.182
STOCK/BOND			.036	.028
				70–74 (571)
HOUSE/FARM				.661
BUSINESS/LAND				.062
FINANCIAL				.203
STOCK/BOND				.025

Source: Computed from the National Longitudinal Surveys of Older Men.

Note: Sample consists of all respondents who provided valid age and wealth data in any survey whether or not they reported these data in prior or subsequent surveys. In the 1966, 1971, 1976, and 1981 surveys, 424, 379, 271, and 231 households, respectively, which report zero WEALTH are excluded. These calculations also exclude one respondent in 1971 who reported a 19,900 percent house share in 1971. HOUSE/FARM is the sum of net residential housing and net farm assets. BUSINESS/LAND is the sum of net business and net investment real estate assets. FINANCIAL is the sum of deposits in financial institutions, U.S. savings bonds, and personal loans made to others. STOCK/ BOND is the value of stocks and bonds owned. WEALTH is the sum of net residential assets, net farm assets, net business assets, net investment real estate assets, deposits in financial institutions, U.S. savings bonds, holdings of stocks and bonds, and personal loans made to others less unsecured personal debt.

11.5.3   Ownership Effect

Cross-sectional inferences of changes in portfolio composition over time can also be misleading for a reason that is not tied to aging but that might be termed an ownership effect. Changes in the mean portfolio share of an age class between surveys can be the result of existing asset owners altering the shares they hold or the result of changes in the number of asset owners. Comparisons between cross sections do not allow one to distinguish between these two possibilities. With panel data, however, we can differentiate between these effects.

Tables 11.23–11.25 report the mean and median values of portfolio shares for the four types of assets categories for households in the 15-YEAR CRS sample. Each table compares the portfolio shares in surveys five years apart. Table 11.23, for example, reports portfolio shares from the 1966 and 1971 surveys. The top-most set of shares is calculated for all households. These are the type of portfolio shares that could be calculated using two cross sections, but corrected for mortality bias, since all the households in this sample survived until 1981. It would also be possible to report these shares by cohort and, therefore, control for cohort-specific asset preferences. Since our previous analysis of this issue did not indicate that there was a systematic difference in asset preferences among these cohorts, we have not conducted this type of analysis. We have reported both the mean and the median portfolio shares to illustrate the point that the holding of certain assets such as STOCK/BOND and BUSINESS/LAND is highly concentrated; the medians for these shares, representing the holdings of the "representative" household, are therefore zero.

The set of portfolio shares at the bottom of tables 11.23–11.25 is like those that could be obtained from two cross sections for those households in each survey that held each asset type. When making inferences concerning changes in the means and medians of these portfolios, one cannot tell whether the mean, for example, went up because existing owners of the asset increased the relative share of the asset in their portfolios or whether more households took a position in the asset or whether both events contributed to the change.

Using panel data, however, we can separate the role of each of these effects. The second set of portfolio shares in tables 11.23–11.25 is for those households that owned assets of the type specified in both of the surveys being compared. Changes in these portfolio shares between surveys indicate how existing owners of the asset type rearranged their holdings of this asset. The third set of portfolio shares is for those households that owned the asset in the initial survey but sold off or by some other means completely moved out of the particular asset type. These shares indicate the relative size of the asset in the leavers portfolio. The next-to-bottom set of portfolio shares is for those households

Table 11.23   **Comparison of Mean and Median Household Portfolio Shares in 1966 and 1971, 15-YEAR CRS Sample (fraction of WEALTH)**

Asset Type	1966			1971		
	Mean	Median	N	Mean	Median	N
All households:						
HOUSE/FARM	.553	.625	1,690	.553	.625	1,690
BUSINESS/LAND	.094	.000	1,690	.091	.000	1,690
FINANCIAL	.184	.035	1,690	.174	.056	1,690
STOCK/BOND	.034	.000	1,690	.033	.000	1,690
Households with asset in 1966 and 1971:						
HOUSE/FARM	.772	.857	1,126	.754	.814	1,126
BUSINESS/LAND	.333	.388	287	.379	.343	287
FINANCIAL	.255	.125	924	.266	.149	924
STOCK/BOND	.205	.136	207	.205	.116	207
Households with asset in 1966 only:						
HOUSE/FARM	1.090	1.000	59	.000	.000	59
BUSINESS/LAND	.417	.259	139	.000	.000	139
FINANCIAL	.322	.058	180	.000	.000	180
STOCK/BOND	.143	.051	93	.000	.000	93
Households with asset in 1971 only:						
HOUSE/FARM	.000	.000	93	.910	.974	93
BUSINESS/LAND	.000	.000	148	.335	.231	148
FINANCIAL	.000	.000	209	.315	.115	209
STOCK/BOND	.000	.000	137	.114	.056	137
Households with asset in 1966 or 1971:						
HOUSE/FARM	.788	.861	1,185	.766	.822	1,219
BUSINESS/LAND	.360	.364	426	.364	.310	435
FINANCIAL	.266	.121	1,104	.275	.143	1,133
STOCK/BOND	.186	.109	300	.169	.086	344

Source: Computed from the National Longitudinal Surveys of Older Men.

Note: Sample consists of the 1,691 respondents who provided valid age and wealth data in each of the five surveys. These calculations exclude one respondent in 1971 who reported a 19,900 percent house share in 1971. HOUSE/FARM is the sum of net residential housing and net farm assets. BUSINESS/LAND is the sum of net business and net investment real estate assets. FINANCIAL is the sum of deposits in financial institutions, U.S. savings bonds, and personal loans made to others. STOCK/BOND is the value of stocks and bonds owned. WEALTH is the sum of net residential assets, net farm assets, net business assets, net investment real estate assets, deposits in financial institutions, U.S. savings bonds, holdings of stocks and bonds, and personal loans made to others less unsecured personal debt.

Table 11.24   **Comparison of Mean and Median Household Portfolio Shares in 1971 and 1976, 15-YEAR CRS Sample (fraction of WEALTH)**

Asset Type	1971			1976		
	Mean	Median	N	Mean	Median	N
All households:						
HOUSE/FARM	.553	.625	1,690	.552	.619	1,690
BUSINESS/LAND	.094	.000	1,690	.084	.000	1,690
FINANCIAL	.184	.056	1,690	.187	.063	1,690
STOCK/BOND	.034	.000	1,690	.027	.000	1,690
Households with asset in 1971 and 1976:						
HOUSE/FARM	.761	.816	1,172	.744	.813	1,172
BUSINESS/LAND	.355	.323	307	.328	.293	307
FINANCIAL	.273	.150	942	.290	.185	942
STOCK/BOND	.191	.099	231	.154	.080	231
Households with asset in 1971 only:						
HOUSE/FARM	.891	.984	47	.000	.000	47
BUSINESS/LAND	.386	.286	128	.000	.000	128
FINANCIAL	.287	.091	191	.000	.000	191
STOCK/BOND	.125	.056	113	.000	.000	113
Households with asset in 1976 only:						
HOUSE/FARM	.000	.000	75	.813	.883	75
BUSINESS/LAND	.000	.000	122	.341	.207	122
FINANCIAL	.000	.000	197	.222	.084	197
STOCK/BOND	.000	.000	88	.117	.061	88
Households with asset in 1971 or 1976:						
HOUSE/FARM	.766	.882	1,219	.748	.817	1,247
BUSINESS/LAND	.364	.310	435	.331	.265	429
FINANCIAL	.275	.143	1,133	.278	.169	1,139
STOCK/BOND	.169	.086	344	.144	.074	319

Source: Computed from the National Longitudinal Surveys of Older Men.

Note: Sample consists of the 1,691 respondents who provided valid age and wealth data in each of the five surveys. These calculations exclude one respondent in 1971 who reported a 19,900 percent house share in 1971. HOUSE/FARM is the sum of net residential housing and net farm assets. BUSINESS/LAND is the sum of net business and net investment real estate assets. FINANCIAL is the sum of deposits in financial institutions, U.S. savings bonds, and personal loans made to others. STOCK/BOND is the value of stocks and bonds owned. WEALTH is the sum of net residential assets, net farm assets, net business assets, net investment real estate assets, deposits in financial institutions, U.S. savings bonds, holdings of stocks and bonds, and personal loans made to others less unsecured personal debt.

Table 11.25   **Comparison of Mean and Median Household Portfolio Shares in 1976 and 1981, 15-YEAR CRS Sample (fraction of WEALTH)**

Asset Type	1976			1981		
	Mean	Median	N	Mean	Median	N
All households:						
HOUSE/FARM	.552	.619	1,690	.568	.667	1,690
BUSINESS/LAND	.084	.000	1,690	.071	.000	1,690
FINANCIAL	.187	.063	1,690	.180	.039	1,690
STOCK/BOND	.027	.000	1,690	.022	.000	1,690
Households with asset in 1976 and 1981:						
HOUSE/FARM	.747	.812	1,199	.765	.833	1,199
BUSINESS/LAND	.319	.283	288	.322	.270	288
FINANCIAL	.287	.182	900	.273	.169	900
STOCK/BOND	.161	.085	202	.156	.071	202
Households with asset in 1976 only:						
HOUSE/FARM	.818	.881	48	.000	.000	48
BUSINESS/LAND	.357	.251	141	.000	.000	141
FINANCIAL	.242	.119	239	.000	.000	239
STOCK/BOND	.115	.051	117	.000	.000	117
Households with asset in 1981 only:						
HOUSE/FARM	.000	.000	56	.756	.964	56
BUSINESS/LAND	.000	.000	86	.312	.226	86
FINANCIAL	.000	.000	162	.361	.132	162
STOCK/BOND	.000	.000	66	.093	.043	66
Households with asset in 1976 or 1981:						
HOUSE/FARM	.748	.817	1,247	.764	.846	1,255
BUSINESS/LAND	.331	.265	429	.320	.256	374
FINANCIAL	.278	.169	1,139	.287	.167	1,062
STOCK/BOND	.144	.074	319	.140	.066	268

Source: Computed from the National Longitudinal Surveys of Older Men.

Note: Sample consists of the 1,691 respondents who provided valid age and wealth data in each of the five surveys. These calculations exclude one respondent in 1971 who reported a 19,900 percent house share in 1971. HOUSE/FARM is the sum of net residential housing and net farm assets. BUSINESS/LAND is the sum of net business and net investment real estate assets. FINANCIAL is the sum of deposits in financial institutions, U.S. savings bonds, and personal loans made to others. STOCK/BOND is the value of stocks and bonds owned. WEALTH is the sum of net residential assets, net farm assets net business assets, net investment real estate assets, deposits in financial institutions, U.S. savings bonds, holdings of stocks and bonds, and personal loans made to others less unsecured personal debt.

that did not have a position in a particular asset in the initial survey but moved into the asset by the later survey. These portfolio shares indicate the size of the holdings of the new asset relative to the total household portfolio of the new entrants.

Comparisons between rows of tables 11.23–11.25 indicate that in many cases mean portfolio shares of all households between cross sections increase (decrease) and the mean shares of existing owners (reported in the second row) also increase (decrease). In some instances, however, there are differences between the change in mean shares of all households and the change in the mean of existing asset owners. In these cases, inferences about household portfolio reallocation as households age based on cross-sectional data are misleading.

For example, on the basis of the change in portfolio shares of those owning HOUSE/FARM in each survey (row 2), the inference could be drawn that households on the average reduced the share of HOUSE/ FARM in their portfolio between 1966 and 1971 and between 1971 and 1976 but increased the HOUSE/FARM share between 1976 and 1981. However, row 1 for all households does not show decumulation between 1966 and 1976 because, in comparing row 4 to row 3, we see that more households entered the housing market than left in each of the first two five-year intervals compared. The same sort of comparisons regarding the portfolio share of STOCK/BOND indicate that, while the mean portfolio share of all households owning stock in both 1971 and 1976 trended downward, there was net new entry in this period. Between 1976 and 1981, the mean portfolio share across all households (row 1) in BUSINESS/LAND decreased; however, existing owners of these types of assets increased the share of these holdings in their portfolios. The all-household mean BUSINESS/LAND SHARE decreased on the average because there was a net exodus of households holding positions in these assets.

Overall, these examples illustrate that changes over time in the mean holdings of an asset by all households do not necessarily reflect reallocations in individual portfolios. There does not appear to be a reliable way to predict under what circumstances the mean change in the portfolio shares in the cross section will differ from the mean change in the portfolio shares of existing asset owners. Consequently, using cross-sectional data to make inferences regarding household portfolio reallocations over time is a very unreliable procedure.

11.6 Summary and Conclusions

In this paper, we have used panel data to assess the biases that are present in cross-sectional inferences of life-cycle changes in the level and composition of household wealth. We first constructed cross-sectional estimates of individual household age-wealth profiles and portfolio shares from five NLS surveys considered separately. We then compared these to time-series observations of age-wealth profiles for the fifteen cohorts sampled in the NLS panel. These comparisons of the cross-sectional estimates and the cohort time-series observations provided evidence of the biases present in making inferences about changes in individual household wealth and portfolio composition over time on the basis of cross sections.

Graphic comparisons of cohort age-wealth profiles with the cross-sectional profiles indicated that cross-sectional profiles are seriously biased by the presence of productivity and differential mortality effects. The productivity effect imparts a downward bias to cross-sectional age-wealth profiles, while the differential mortality effect produces an upward bias. The productivity effect appears to outweigh the differential mortality effect in our sample. Consequently, the cross-sectional profiles suggest that there is less accumulation as people age than a true time-series-based profile would show.

Comparisons of simple regression equation estimates of age-wealth profiles estimated using cross-sectional data with those estimated using cohort data suggest that whether cross-sectional age-wealth profiles are consistent with cohort age-wealth profiles depends on which cross section and which cohort one compares. There do not appear to be any systematic differences between cross-sectional and cohort age-wealth profiles that could be used to correct the cross-sectional profiles.

We evaluated two procedures previously used to correct cross-sectional profiles for the productivity bias. One method, used by King and Dicks-Mireaux, scales household wealth by a measure of permanent income. The other method, used by Mirer, scales wealth by a cohort growth-rate factor. Comparisons of cross-sectional age-wealth profiles adjusted in these ways with actual cohort profiles indicate that these fixups are unreliable and, in addition, do not correct for the differential mortality effect.

On balance, our evidence with regard to the bias in using cross-sectional data to make inferences about the reallocation of household portfolios over time suggests that time-series inferences based on cross sections can be misleading. Differential mortality does appear to impart bias into comparisons of changes in portfolio shares between the same age class viewed in successive cross sections relative to changes in portfolio shares of the same members of an age class over time. An examination of how wealth composition varies with age for cohorts versus cross sections suggested that the cross sections suffer from a productivity bias, which can lead to incorrect inferences about how wealth composition changes with age. We found little evidence of differences in cohort-specific asset preferences for the ages covered by our sample. Data covering a greater number of cohorts might alter this conclusion. Finally, we found evidence that comparisons of sample means between cross sections do not necessarily reflect changes that result from the reallocation of portfolio shares by existing asset owners because the change in means between cross-sections is affected by changes that reflect net entry or exit of households from positions in certain assets.

Given the existence of the substantial biases in cross-sectional age-wealth profiles that we have documented here and the lack of any reliable methods to correct these biases in cross sections, we must conclude that there are no substitutes for panel data in the analysis of household life-cycle wealth accumulation and portfolio allocation. By providing observations on the same households over time, panel data avoid the productivity bias found in cross-sectional data. By limiting members of a cohort sample to those who survived over the entire time period under analysis, one can also correct for the differential mortality effect present in cross sections. However, since attrition occurs in panel data for reasons other than death, one should also correct for this differential attrition bias.

On the basis of the evidence presented in this paper, we believe it would be appropriate to stamp a warning label on research that uses cross-sectional data to make inferences about changes in the behavior of household wealth over time much as the surgeon general puts a warning on cigarette packages. Our suggested warning label would read, "Inferences based on cross-sectional data concerning the behavior of household wealth or the composition of household wealth over time probably are biased by the presence of differential mortality effects, cohort-specific productivity effects, or differential asset-ownership effects." While we recommend the use of panel surveys since these data enable researchers to avoid the biases mentioned above, we also urge users to make adjustments in longitudinal samples to avoid bias resulting from differential rates of sample attrition.

Notes

1. Since the age-wealth profile of men who provide usable data every year may differ from those who do not, this technique may impart selectivity bias into our estimates (under the assumption that the objective of the research is to make inferences about all surviving men, not just those who were willing to be good reporters).

2. To the extent that any sample is representative of the living members of the underlying population, following mean values indicates whether the cohort

is saving or dissaving in the aggregate—dollar weighting vs. people weighting (as in the median).

3. An important aside that is revealed by tables 11.7–11.9 is that, when the mean wealth changes, the median does not necessarily change in the same direction. Note that, even when the mean or median wealth of a cohort decreases, this does not imply that the wealth of a majority of the households in the cohort necessarily also decreased. The number of households in each cohort who dissaved is noted in the last column of tables 11.7–11.9.

4. As mentioned before, the 15-YEAR CRS sample excludes many of the very rich and very poor households. Just as in the case of age-wealth profiles, to the extent that portfolio reallocation is related to wealth, the pattern of portfolio reallocation observed in the 15-YEAR CRS sample may differ from the pattern observed in larger samples such as those in the 5-YEAR CRS, which include more wealthy and poor households.

References

Atkinson, A. B., and A. J. Harrison. 1978. *Distribution of personal wealth in Britain*. Cambridge: Cambridge University Press.

Brittain, J. 1978. *Inheritances and the inequality of material wealth*. Washington, D.C.: Brookings Institution.

Diamond, Peter A., and J. Hausman. 1980. Individual savings behavior. Paper prepared for the National Commission on Social Security, May. Mimeo.

Dicks-Mireaux, Louis, and Mervyn A. King. 1982. Portfolio composition and pension wealth: An econometric study. NBER Working Paper, no. 903. Cambridge, Mass.: National Bureau of Economic Research, May.

Ferber, R. 1965. The reliability of consumer surveys of financial holdings: Time deposits. *Journal of the American Statistical Association* 60:148–63.

Ferber, R., John Forsythe, Harold W. Guthrie, and E. Scott Maynes. 1969. Validation of consumer financial characteristics: Common stock. *Journal of the American Statistical Association* 64:415–32.

Irvine, I. J. 1981. The use of cross-section microdata in life cycle models: An application to inequality theory in nonstationary economies. *Quarterly Journal of Economics* 96 (May): 301–16.

Kane, Edward J. 1980. Consequences of contemporary ceilings on mortgage and deposit interest rates for households in different economic circumstances. In *The government and capital formation*, ed. George M. von Furstenberg, 401–41. Cambridge, Mass.: Ballinger Publishing Co.

———. 1985. Microeconomic evidence on the composition of household savings in recent years. In *The level and composition of household saving*, ed. Patric H. Hendershott, 101–49. Cambridge, Mass.: Ballinger Publishing Co.

King, M. A., and L. Dicks-Mireaux. 1982. Asset holdings and the life cycle. *Economic Journal* 92 (June): 247–67.

Kotlikoff, L. J. 1979. Testing the theory of social security and life cycle accumulation. *American Economic Review* 69 (June): 396–410.

Lillard, Lee, James P. Smith, and Finis Welch. 1986. What do we really know about wages? The importance of nonreporting and census imputation. *Journal of Political Economy* 94, no. 5, pt. 1 (June): 489–506.

Mirer, T. W. 1979. The wealth-age relationship among the aged. *American Economic Review* 69 (June): 435–43.

Modigliani, Franco. 1986. Life cycle, individual thrift, and the wealth of nations. *American Economic Review* 76 (June): 297–313.

Modigliani, F., and R. E. Brumberg. 1954. Utility analysis and the consumption function: An interpretation of cross-section data. In *Post-Keynesian economics*, ed. Kenneth K. Kurihara, 388–436. New Brunswick, N.J.: Rutgers University Press.

Munnell, Alicia H. 1976. Private pensions and saving: New evidence. *Journal of Political Economy* 84, no. 5 (October): 1013–32.

Projector, D., and G. Weiss. 1966. *Survey of financial characteristics of consumers.* Washington, D.C.: Federal Reserve Board.

Shorrocks, A. F. 1975. The age-wealth relationships: A cross-section and cohort analysis. *Review of Economics and Statistics* 57 (May): 155–63.

———. 1982. The portfolio composition of asset holdings in the United Kingdom. *Economic Journal* 92 (June): 268–84.

Sobol, Marion Gross. 1979. Factors influencing private capital accumulation on the 'eve of retirement.' *Review of Economics and Statistics* 61 (November): 585–93.

Comment   B. K. Atrostic

This is a meticulously researched and thoroughly documented paper. The research uses longitudinal data to explore the empirical importance of theoretical biases—differential mortality, attrition bias, and differential productivity—on the shape of age-wealth profiles. A parallel analysis examines the related question of whether these potential biases are empirically important in measuring changes in portfolio composition over time. The empirical importance of any of these biases in measures of age-wealth and portfolio profiles and what their net effect might be have been subjects of debate and objects of a series of proposed "fixups." Notably lacking in this literature, however, were empirical estimates either of total bias or of the bias contributed by any of these factors separately. Filling this gap is a major contribution of this research. This research also provides important information for public policy: current pension and retirement policies, for example, are based in large measure on stylized facts of life-cycle wealth derived from aggregated data, most commonly from the aggregated cross-sectional data that are subject to the potential biases.

The longitudinal nature of the data Jianakoplos, Menchik, and Irvine choose for this research permits direct comparisons of age-wealth and portfolio profiles created by treating the data first as a series of repeated cross-sections and then as a longitudinal data file. These comparisons

B. K. Atrostic is a financial economist with the Office of Tax Analysis, U.S. Department of the Treasury.

show that each potential source of bias in repeated cross-sectional data matters for modeling the life-cycle path of wealth and portfolio composition. Moreover, for neither age-wealth profiles nor portfolio composition are the differences between cross-sectional and longitudinal changes predictable. This is an important empirical result because the adjustments made by the standard fixups are valid only if the direction and magnitude of the biases can be predicted. If the research shows that the biases vary in ways that are difficult to predict, the usefulness of the standard fixups and, thereby, the usefulness of repeated cross-sectional data are limited. The authors apply the standard fixups to the aggregated cross-sectional data and compare the resulting life-cycle profiles to those computed from aggregated longitudinal data. They find the fixed up repeated cross-sectional approximations to be poor fits to longitudinal profiles and to be sensitive to assumptions (starting year, growth rates, etc.) required by the various fixups. They suggest, only partly in jest, that research using cross-sectional data to make inferences about changes in the behavior of household wealth over time should bear a warning label.

Jianakoplos, Menchik, and Irvine in some sense erect a straw man—the robustness of aggregate cross-sectional data for drawing inferences about individual behavior over time—and, predictably, demolish it. It is well understood that for other life-cycle behaviors, such as earnings and labor force participation, aggregated cross-sectional data can yield misleading inferences about the time path of individual behavior. Finding the same lack of correspondence between aggregate cross-sectional and longitudinal wealth measures should come as no surprise. It is, however, a considerable inconvenience for wealth research. Unlike labor force and demographic data that often are collected in monthly or annual cross sections and for which many longitudinal surveys exist, wealth data are collected infrequently and rarely in longitudinal form or over a long time period.[1]

The authors' complete reporting of data, data-handling techniques, and necessary caveats about limitations of their techniques and data make their conclusions more compelling. They do more than assert that they examined the data carefully. What they did and why it mattered are explained in detail. Their description of how they reviewed responses for consistency in creating their *own* wealth measure from data, rather than relying on the measure created by the National Longitudinal Survey (NLS), is especially illuminating. By reviewing the data, the authors found miscodes serious enough to require the Census Bureau to recode some observations. Additional discussion of the differences between the authors' measure and the NLS measure, perhaps replicating one basic table using the NLS measure, would help readers evaluate the importance of careful data review.

The amount of miscoding the authors found in a widely used data set (albeit in a little-used variable) properly makes the reader uneasy about miscodes in other data sets. Indeed, Avery, Elliehausen, and Kennickell 1987 and McNeil and Lamas (chap. 9, in this volume) both note miscode problems in wealth measures in the Survey of Consumer Finances and the Survey of Income and Program Participation (SIPP), respectively, but imply that miscodes are relatively random and therefore cancel out, at least in cross-sectional comparisons. Readers made skeptical by Jianakoplos, Menchik, and Irvine are unlikely to be reassured because they generally have no way to assess the quality of data handling in empirical work. The tendency of research presentations to focus on theory, econometrics, and results (together with space constraints) leaves little room for data description. But careful documentation of data development is especially important in reporting results derived from data that are proprietary, little known, little known in a new application area, or too complicated and expensive for others to replicate readily. The NLS data are complex, and the wealth measures are less well known and less used than the labor force data. By providing nearly all the summary data available to them, the authors permit their readers to form independent conclusions. Sufficient information is given in the twenty-five tables to reconstruct any of the forty-four figures. The tables themselves always include sample sizes and summary statistics (e.g., standard errors of coefficients and of the equations, and sample sizes, in tables reporting regressions) or sample statistics (mean, median, and three percentile values, in tables reporting various cohort wealth measures), allowing the reader to evaluate conclusions in the text. Work as careful and clear as this is as valuable as it is rare.[2]

The authors convincingly argue that wealth research cannot be based on aggregated, repeated cross-sectional data alone: the fixups do not work.[3] At the same time, McNeil and Lamas demonstrate that collecting longitudinal wealth data is not in itself a panacea because annual longitudinal wealth data from the SIPP are dominated by nonsampling and nonresponse errors. How best to develop the data needed for life-cycle wealth research from existing and future sources clearly demands further research on issues such as sample design, imputation procedures, the timing of surveys, and nonresponse adjustments.

But that research, while vital, is unlikely to resolve the dilemma the authors raise because that dilemma arises as much from uses of data as from sources. Their evaluation compares the life-cycle profiles generated by alternative aggregations of their longitudinal microdata to profiles generated by aggregated cross-sectional data. The more promising use of longitudinal microdata, however (and the more powerful argument for incurring its costs), is in estimating carefully specified models of individual life-cycle behavior to test alternative theories. How the authors would resolve the dilemma they raise is unclear only because the wealth data so painstakingly computed and reviewed are not used in this paper to model a microdata-based paradigm of life-cycle wealth and portfolio behavior. That work clearly is next on the authors' research agenda, however, and there is every reason to await the results expectantly.

Notes

1. The Panel Survey of Income Dynamics does contain longitudinal wealth data over a relatively lengthy period (Curtin, Juster, and Morgan, chap. 10, in this volume). The Survey of Consumer Finances (described in Avery, Elliehausen, and Kennickell 1987) and the Survey of Income and Program Participation (described in McNeil and Lamas, chap. 9, in this volume), while rich in wealth data, have each just produced their first pair of longitudinal wealth observations, over three- and one-year intervals, respectively.

The National Longitudinal Survey of older men is an exception particularly well suited to the research questions raised in this study. During the fifteen-year survey period, the individuals' ages correspond closely to those for which the ''hump'' in the hypothesized life-cycle age-wealth profile should be most pronounced because the rate of growth of earnings should have slowed at the same time that a spending down of wealth due to retirement (in the absence of strong bequest or precautionary motives) would have begun. The fifteen-year age range represented by individuals in each survey and the fifteen-year observation period on each individual provide the authors with sufficient information to explore cohort effects and differential mortality, sample attrition, and productivity effects.

2. The absence in general of such clear explication of data sources and data handling has led to eroding credibility for empirical work. This erosion prompted the *American Economic Review* to publish ''Replication in Empirical Economics'' (Dewald, Thursby, and Anderson 1986) as the lead article in the September 1986 issue and to preface the article with the following statement of editorial policy: ''It is the policy of the *American Economic Review* to publish papers only where the data used in the analysis are clearly and precisely documented, are readily available to any researcher for purposes of replication, and where details of the computations sufficient to permit replication are provided'' (v).

3. All sources appear to agree about the usefulness, quality, and consistency of national wealth estimates based on alternative cross-sectional wealth data sources (see Avery, Elliehausen, and Kennickell 1987; Curtin, Juster, and Morgan, chap. 10, in this volume; and McNeil and Lamas, chap. 9, in this volume). For alternative views about the usefulness of SIPP cross-sectional data for various policy purposes, see Curtin, Juster, and Morgan (chap. 10, in this volume) and Radner (chap. 12, in this volume).

References

Avery, R., G. Elliehausen, and A. Kennickell. 1987. Measuring wealth with survey data: An evaluation of the 1983 Survey of Consumer Finances. Paper presented at the twentieth conference of the International Association for Research in Income and Wealth, Rocca di Papa, Italy, August.

Dewald, William G., Jerry G. Thursby, and Richard G. Anderson. 1986. Replication in empirical economics. *American Economic Review* 76:587–603.

12 The Wealth of the Aged and Nonaged, 1984

Daniel B. Radner

12.1 Introduction

This paper discusses and illustrates the use of wealth data for the analysis of the economic status of households. Selected estimates of wealth for 1984 from the Survey of Income and Program Participation (SIPP) are used as illustrations. The particular focus is on the wealth of age groups, with a special interest in the aged. Comparisons of the amounts and composition of wealth of the aged and nonaged (and of more detailed age groups) are presented. The emphasis is on the economic resources available to households other than the very wealthy. The degree of concentration of wealth, the subject that wealth data traditionally have been used to examine, is not discussed. Thus, this paper reflects a somewhat different perspective on the use of wealth data.

The estimates from SIPP presented here are not intended to provide a complete description of the wealth of age groups. Rather, they are illustrations of several types of useful wealth estimates that can be made from household survey data. For example, one interesting question that can be examined with these data is how many of the aged have both low income and low wealth and therefore would be unable to pay for high medical expenses or to adjust to income loss.

This paper focuses on the amounts of resources available to units of different ages at a particular time. There is no direct concern with

Daniel B. Radner is an economist in the Office of Research and Statistics, Office of Policy, Social Security Administration.

The author is greatly indebted to Sharon Johnson, who prepared the estimates, and to Benjamin Bridges and Selig Lesnoy for their helpful comments. Any opinions expressed are those of the author and do not necessarily represent the position of the Social Security Administration.

life-cycle issues of saving and accumulation. However, past saving behavior clearly affects the amount of resources available at a specific time,
and the interpretation of the economic status of the aged from the estimates shown here is affected by life-cycle considerations. Within an
age group and at a particular income level, a unit with more wealth would
ordinarily be considered to be better off than a unit with less wealth (assuming that "needs" are the same). Because of life-cycle factors, it is
not obvious that the aged are better off than the nonaged if they have
more wealth than the nonaged. For example, aged households have had
much more time than younger households to accumulate wealth.

A complete assessment of the economic status of the aged (and other
age groups) requires data about both their wealth and their income.
Economic status is usually assessed using data on income, with an
occasional examination of wealth. It is relatively rare that both income
and wealth are considered. Although the focus in this paper is on
wealth, the use of income and wealth data together is discussed.

Detailed age groups are examined because the broad aged and nonaged groups often used are not homogeneous. For example, it is useful
to distinguish between younger aged households (in this paper, head
aged sixty-five to seventy-four) and older aged households (head aged
seventy-five or older). Those two groups differ substantially in many
characteristics, such as labor force participation, marital status, and
average income. Nonaged households also differ greatly by age. For
example, households with head aged twenty-five to thirty-four have
very different characteristics from households with head aged forty-
five to fifty-four, particularly with respect to average income.

Amounts of wealth, the distribution of wealth, the composition of
wealth, and the joint distribution of wealth and income in 1984 are
examined for age groups. Although data needs for analyzing changes
in wealth over time are mentioned, estimates of change in wealth are
not presented.

12.1.1   Types of Wealth Estimates

Three basic types of wealth estimates have been made by researchers.[1] First, estimates have been made from data on wealth collected in
household surveys. These surveys typically collect a wide range of
information that can be used in conjunction with the wealth data. The
collection of information on wealth is the focus of some surveys (e.g.,
the 1962 Survey of Financial Characteristics of Consumers [SFCC]).
But, in other surveys (e.g., SIPP), wealth is a relatively minor part of
the survey. In most cases, data are obtained for households or family
units. Ordinarily, the entire wealth distribution is covered. Wealth data
from surveys are often considered to be of doubtful accuracy, and

estimates of the upper tail of the wealth distribution usually are particularly poor. Sometimes, a specific effort is made to obtain good data for the upper tail (e.g., by means of a high-income sampling frame). The 1983 Survey of Consumer Finances (SCF) used a high-income frame based on income tax return information to improve estimates of high-wealth units (Avery and Elliehausen 1986). Nonresponse and response error, however, are still serious problems in all parts of the distribution in household surveys.

Second, estimates have been made using information from estate tax returns. Multipliers derived from mortality rates are applied to the information for decedents in those returns to produce estimates of the wealth of the living (e.g., Smith 1974; Schwartz 1983). Only limited socioeconomic information is available in this type of data, and the data are for persons. Estate tax data generally are limited to the upper tail of the wealth distribution because the estate tax (currently) does not apply below a relatively high exempt amount. The wealth data in specific estate tax returns are considered to be relatively accurate. The precision of estimates from estate tax returns has been questioned, however, because of uncertainty about the accuracy of the multipliers used.

Finally, "synthetic" estimates have been made. In this type, estimates of wealth are produced, at least in part, from nonwealth data (e.g., Wolff 1983; Greenwood 1983). Asset income flows have been capitalized into amounts of wealth. Regression analysis has been used to impute amounts of assets for which income flows do not exist. Different data sources have been matched together (sometimes using statistical matching) to construct microdata files from which synthetic estimates can be made. Generally, a wide range of socioeconomic information is available, and the entire wealth distribution is covered. Estimates for households or family units can be made. The accuracy of this type of estimate has been questioned because of the many assumptions required. For example, the proper capitalization rates and regression models are not known and must be approximated. Where statistical matching is used, there is uncertainty about the accuracy of estimated joint distributions.

As noted, the accuracy of each of these types of wealth estimate has been questioned. Because household survey data generally are weakest in the upper tail and estate tax data focus on the upper tail, some analysts have suggested combining data from the two sources to produce improved estimates (e.g., Radner 1975). Synthetic estimates also have a role. In addition to their usefulness as independent estimates, synthetic estimates are also useful for facilitating consistency checks. For example, are survey estimates of financial assets consistent with reasonable capitalization rates for asset income?

12.1.2   Desired Characteristics of the Data

The particular focus of this paper has implications for the characteristics of the wealth data that are needed. There is no direct interest in the upper tail of the wealth distribution. How rich the rich are is not of interest here. The emphasis is on the middle and lower portions of the wealth distribution. The lack of interest in the upper tail makes the concerns here different from the usual concerns about the data. Thus, a household survey that did not do a good job of capturing the upper tail of the wealth distribution could be of use for the type of analysis discussed in this paper.

Several requirements for the characteristics of the wealth data are discussed below. First, the wealth data must be sufficiently accurate. Although wealth data obtained in household surveys often have been criticized as inaccurate, the problems with accuracy probably are worst in the upper tail of the distribution. The data for the remainder of the distribution also have serious problems; item nonresponse rates can be substantial, and answers given can be inaccurate.[2] The types of estimates presented here are less sensitive to errors in the data than the measurement of inequality or the change in inequality because the upper tail is not important here.[3]

A second requirement is that the wealth data should be reasonably current. For example, the 1962 SFCC is too old to be used for analysis of the current situation. Of course, older data can be useful to examine changes over time.

Third, a data source that covers the entire wealth distribution (or the entire distribution except for the upper tail) is needed. Thus, data sources such as estate tax returns that are confined to the upper tail are not appropriate.

Fourth, wealth data are needed for all age groups of the population. This follows from the fact that both the aged and the nonaged are examined and compared. This requirement means that data sources that are confined to particular age groups (e.g., the Social Security Administration's Retirement History Study [Irelan 1972]) are not appropriate.

Fifth, it is necessary that several types of information other than wealth be available for the unit. Information on income is crucial, and information on socioeconomic characteristics (e.g., unit size, sex, marital status, and age of the unit head) is very important. Data from estate tax returns are inappropriate for this reason also.

Sixth, the wealth data should be available for units other than persons. Families and unrelated individuals (often called family units) or households are the most useful units. Data from estate tax returns do not meet this criterion.

Seventh, the data need to be comprehensive enough so that a reasonable definition of net worth can be formed. Although information on limited sets of assets can be useful, it is not sufficient. Also, asset-type detail is needed so that alternative definitions of wealth can be examined. For example, for some purposes, net worth excluding home equity or only liquid assets might be examined. Some household surveys do not meet this criterion.

Eighth, the data source should contain a sufficient number of observations so that age groups and other classifications can be examined. Of particular importance here is enough observations to separate the aged into subgroups. In some household surveys, sample sizes are too small to meet this criterion.

Several household surveys, including SIPP, meet the first seven criteria. The eighth criterion, sample size, is met best by SIPP among the household surveys. Some synthetic estimates meet all the criteria except one: existing synthetic estimates are relatively old.

Two other characteristics are also important, although they are not directly relevant for this paper. The first concerns social security wealth and pension wealth. Although these types of assets are not examined in this paper, they are important for some kinds of analyses. Thus, it is useful for the data source to have information from which those asset types can be estimated. Second, a longitudinal component to the data would be of great use in the examination of changes in wealth over time, although data on change in wealth are often considered to be of limited accuracy. Also, a consistent time series would be very valuable.

12.1.3   Appropriate Types of Estimates and Comparisons

Because the upper tail is not of interest, the focus of this paper also has implications for the types of estimates and comparisons that are of the most use. First, mean amounts of groups of units that include the upper tail should be used as little as possible. Such estimates can be affected substantially by the upper tail. In general, medians are much more appropriate than means. Second, estimating the overall inequality of wealth is not of interest. Such estimates are very sensitive to the estimates for the upper tail. Third, if the accuracy of data sources on wealth is assessed by comparing wealth aggregates from the data source to control aggregates, as is often the case, then the upper tail of the distribution should be removed from both sides of the comparison, if possible. Because aggregate amounts of some asset types are highly concentrated in the upper tail (e.g., corporate stock), a substantial adjustment to the control aggregate is necessary if the upper tail is excluded. Of course, comparisons of aggregates are only crude tests of the accuracy of the estimates. Even if the aggregate were correct, the estimated distribution could be very inaccurate.

12.1.4   Plan of the Paper

Section 12.2 describes several existing sources of data on wealth and compares selected estimates of the age-wealth cross-sectional relation. Estimates of the wealth of age groups in 1984 are presented in section 12.3. The sensitivity of the age-wealth relation to the wealth concept used, median net worth by age and net worth quintile, and the size and composition of the wealth held by the middle 60 percent of the wealth distribution in each age group are examined. Section 12.4 presents estimates of the relation between wealth and income for age groups in 1984. Median amounts of wealth by size of income, the wealth of aged households by size of income, the ratio of wealth to income, and the percentage in each age group with relatively low income and low wealth are discussed. A summary and conclusions are presented in section 12.5.

12.2   Comparison of Selected Estimates

It is useful to compare different estimates of the age-wealth relation to see how similar they are and to see how the estimates from the 1984 SIPP compare to other estimates. Seven data sources are described briefly; then published estimates of the age-wealth relation from those data sources are compared. The comparisons presented here are intended to give only a general idea of the consistency among the different estimates.

12.2.1   Selected Data Sources

The 1984 SIPP collected information on wealth, income, and socioeconomic characteristics in interviews conducted in September through December of 1984 (U.S. Bureau of the Census 1986b).[4] The reference point for asset and liability amounts was the last day of the month that preceded the interview. The estimates are for households; persons in group quarters are not included. The estimates are based on information for about 19,000 households. As noted earlier, the collection of wealth data was not the principal purpose of SIPP. A probability sample that represented the U.S. household population was used; there was no oversampling of high-income or high-wealth units. Net worth, as defined in the estimates shown here, includes home equity, vehicle equity, business equity, financial assets, real estate, and individual retirement accounts (IRAs) and Keogh accounts, minus debts. The value of household durables, equities in pension plans, and the cash value of life insurance are not included in the estimates.

The 1983 SCF obtained information on wealth, income, and socioeconomic characteristics (Avery et al. 1984a, 1984b; Avery and Elliehausen 1986). The survey contained two portions, a multistage probability sample and a high-income frame. Estimates are shown here for the probability sample alone and for the probability sample plus the high-income frame. The estimates shown here for the probability sample are based on information for about 3,700 family units, while the estimates that include the high-income frame are based on about 4,100 family units. The high-income supplement was obtained by drawing about 5,000 family units from tax information. Interviews were completed with 438 of those family units (9 percent). Net worth, as defined in the estimates including the high-income supplement, includes home equity, real estate, business equity, financial assets, and retirement assets (which includes IRAs, Keogh accounts, the cash value of life insurance, and employer-sponsored thrift, profit-sharing, and tax-deferred savings plans), minus debts. The net worth concept used for the estimates that do not include the high-income frame excludes the cash value of life insurance and at least some business equity. Both definitions exclude automobile equity, the value of household durables, and pension and social security wealth.

The 1979 Income Survey Development Program (ISDP) file contains information on wealth, income, and socioeconomic characteristics for almost 7,000 households (Radner and Vaughan 1984; Pearl and Frankel 1984). The sample was nationally representative, and both low-income and high-income households were oversampled, but only slightly. The estimates shown here are primarily from wave 5 of that multiwave survey. Net worth, as shown in these estimates, includes home equity, vehicle equity, market value of household durables, business equity, financial assets, and real estate, minus unsecured debt. Social security and private pension wealth, trusts, and the equity value of life insurance are not included in the estimates shown here.

The 1962 SFCC is regarded by some as the best wealth survey ever undertaken in the United States. This survey contains wealth, income, and socioeconomic information on more than 2,500 family units (Projector and Weiss 1966). Oversampling was used to provide a better estimate of the upper tail of the wealth distribution. Wealth, as defined in the estimates shown here, includes home equity, automobile equity, business equity, liquid assets, and real estate and other investment assets. Unsecured debt was not subtracted; therefore, the concept used was wealth, not net worth. The cash surrender value of life insurance policies and equities in annuities and retirement plans were not included in the estimates shown here.

The President's Commission on Pension Policy's household survey collected information on assets and liabilities, income, employment, various demographic characteristics, pensions, and attitudes about retirement in September 1979 (Cartwright and Friedland 1985). Personal interviews were completed with about 3,600 households. The sample was a multistage area probability sample; there was no oversampling of the upper part of the distribution. Estimates were presented for units that differ from those presented for other surveys; the units are similar to Census families and unrelated individuals except that family members age eighteen or older in general are considered to be separate units. Estimates are presented for about 4,300 of these "family units." In these estimates, net wealth includes home equity, personal property, vehicle equity, business equity, liquid and investment assets, miscellaneous assets, and the imputed present value of employer-based pensions, IRAs, Keogh plans, and annuities.

The Greenwood synthetic estimates were made using data from income tax returns, estate tax returns, and a household survey (Greenwood 1983). The basic microdata file used was constructed by statistically matching survey information from the Current Population Survey and income tax returns from the 1973 Individual Income Tax Model. Corporate stock, debt instruments, and real estate held were estimated primarily by capitalizing amounts from income tax return data. Then net wealth was estimated by regression analysis for a sample of 1972 estate tax returns, using the capitalized corporate stock, debt instrument, and real estate amounts. The regression parameters were used to assign an amount of net wealth to each family unit in the basic file. Net wealth, as used in these estimates, is based on a more comprehensive definition than is used in most surveys. In addition to the usual assets, personal possessions and the value of equity in retirement funds, annuities, and life insurance are included in the definition.

Wolff's synthetic estimates for 1969 are based on the Measurement of Economic and Social Performance (MESP) microdata file (Wolff 1983). This file contains information on income, asset holdings, debt, and socioeconomic characteristics for more than 60,000 households. Three statistical matches and two sets of imputations were used in constructing the file. Using a statistical match, each household in a 1970 decennial census sample that was estimated to have taxable income was assigned federal individual income tax return information. Information on owner-occupied housing was available in the census data. Other assets and liabilities were imputed to each household. Estimates of some asset values were obtained by capitalizing income flows. Imputation techniques using outside information were used for other asset types. The estimated values were then adjusted to produce consistency with national balance sheet estimates of the household sector. Household disposable wealth, as defined in the estimates shown, includes home equity, household durables (including automobiles) and inventories, liquid and investment assets (including trust equity), business equity, real estate, the cash value of insurance, and a small amount of cash value for pensions.

The eight estimates described above differed in many respects. The years to which the estimates referred ranged from 1962 (SFCC) to 1984 (SIPP). Thus, any changes in the distribution of wealth by age during this twenty-two-year period should be reflected in the estimates from these data sources. However, both the ISDP and the Pension Commission survey contained data for 1979, and the data from SIPP (1984) and the SCF (1983) are only one year apart.

The definitions of "net worth" differ among the data sources. Assets such as consumer durables, vehicle equity, and the cash value of life insurance are included in the estimates from some data sources but not in the estimates from others. The Pension Commission survey included the present value of retirement assets. Unsecured debt was not deducted in the estimates from the SFCC. Because of the differences in definitions of "net worth," the estimates from these data sources presented below should be used only for rough comparisons. For the purposes of this paper, only rough comparisons are needed.

12.2.2 Estimates of the Age-Wealth Relation

Eight selected estimates of relative mean net worth for age groups are shown in table 12.1. These estimates are from the seven different data sources described; as noted above, the definitions of "net worth" used are not strictly comparable. Also, the wealth-holding units and years are not comparable in some cases. The fifty-five to sixty-four age group is used as the base for these relative means. Six of the estimates are from household surveys, while the other two (Greenwood 1973; and Wolff 1969) are synthetic estimates.

The estimates of relative means are not very similar. The fifty-five to sixty-four age group has the highest mean for three estimates (SIPP, ISDP, and SFCC), although the SFCC might show a peak at an older age if more age detail were available. The two SCF estimates peak in aged age groups, while the Pension Commission estimate peaks in the forty-five to fifty-four age group. The two synthetic estimates peak in the aged age group.

The ranges of relative means for specific age groups are quite broad. For the sixty-five and over age group, the range is from 0.73 to 1.24. The range for the forty-five to fifty-four age group is from 0.68 to 1.04, and the range for the thirty-five to forty-four age group is from 0.42 to 0.83. Even if the comparison is confined to SIPP, SCF, ISDP, and SFCC (data sources for which relative medians are available in table 12.2), differences are still substantial, although smaller. The ranges then are 0.75–1.24 for the sixty-five and over group, 0.68–0.96 for the forty-five to fifty-four group, and 0.42–0.61 for the thirty-five to forty-four group.

When relative medians are examined (table 12.2), the differences are quite a bit smaller. Those estimates are available only for SIPP, SCF,

Table 12.1   Selected Estimates of Relative Mean Net Worth by Age

Age of Head	SIPP 1984	1983 SCF Excluding High-Income Frame	1983 SCF Including High-Income Frame	ISDP 1979	SFCC 1962	Pension Commission 1979	Greenwood 1973	Wolff 1969
Under 35	.17	...	.13	...	...	.33	...	...
Under 25	...	.04	...	.08	...	...	.20	.28
25–34	...	.17	...	.23	...	...	.50	.43
35–44	.53	.43	.42	.61	.49	.83	.76	.58
45–54	.88	.68	.96	.75	.69	1.04	.91	.76
55–64	1.00	1.00	1.00	1.00	1.00	1.00	1.00	1.00
65 and over	.80	...	1.24	.75	.95	.73	1.06	1.02
65–74	...	1.05	...	...	...	...	...	...
65–69	.96	...	...	.85	...	...	...	...
70–74	.79	...	...	.81	...	...	...	...
75 and over	.69	.61	...	.62	...	...	...	...
All ages	.60	.55	.66	.59	.65	.63	.78	.72
Mean, all ages (thousands of current dollars)	78.7	66.0	133.5	62.4	21.0	54.0	37.7	46.0

Sources: SIPP: U.S. Bureau of the Census (1986b, table 3). SCF, excluding high-income frame: Avery et al. (1984b, table 7). SCF, including high-income frame: Avery and Elliehausen (1986, table 2). ISDP: Radner and Vaughan (1984, table 2). SFCC: Projector and Weiss (1966, table A8). Pension Commission: Cartwright and Friedland (1985, table 2). Greenwood: Greenwood (1983, table 2). Wolff: Wolff (1987, table 5).

Note: Net worth is defined differently in many of these estimates; see the text for details. Age 55–64 is used as the base for the relative means.

Table 12.2   **Selected Estimates of Relative Median Net Worth by Age**

		1983 SCF			
Age of Head	SIPP 1984	Excluding High-Income Frame	Including High-Income Frame	ISDP 1979	SFCC 1962
Under 35	.08	. . .	.05	. . .	.08
Under 25	. . .	0	. . .	.07	. . .
25–34	. . .	.07	. . .	.24	. . .
35–44	.48	.52	.58	.58	.53
45–54	.77	.79	.79	.76	.83
55–64	1.00	1.00	1.00	1.00	1.00
65 and over	.82	. . .	.80	.75	.77
65–74	. . .	.90	. . .	. . .	. . .
65–69	.90	. . .	. . .	.92	. . .
70–74	.82	. . .	. . .	.88	. . .
75 and over	.75	.65	. . .	.55	. . .
All ages	.44	.44	.47	.50	.51
Median, all ages (thousands of current dollars)	32.7	24.6	30.6	25.8	6.7

Sources: SIPP: U.S. Bureau of the Census (1986b, table 5). SCF, excluding high-income frame: Avery et al. (1984b, table 7). SCF, including high-income frame: Avery and Elliehausen (1986, table 2). ISDP: Radner and Vaughan (1984, table 2). SFCC: Projector and Weiss (1966, table 8).

Note: Net worth is defined differently in many of these estimates; see the text for details. Age 55–64 is used as the base for the relative medians.

ISDP, and SFCC. In every case, the peak is in the fifty-five to sixty-four age group. The ranges are substantially smaller than they are for relative means: 0.75–0.82 for the sixty-five and over group, 0.76–0.83 for the forty-five to fifty-four group, and 0.48–0.58 for the thirty-five to forty-four group. Except for the youngest (under thirty-five) and oldest (seventy-five and over) age groups, the estimates are quite similar. This correspondence is reassuring, but it is far from proof of the accuracy of the estimates. The correspondence could result from offsetting errors or differences, or these surveys could have the same biases and all be inaccurate. These comparisons do show that the estimates of the age-wealth relation from the 1984 SIPP are at least roughly similar to the estimates from other surveys.

12.3 Wealth of Age Groups

In this section, a broad overall picture of wealth by age is presented. The middle of the wealth distribution is emphasized. Median and mean net worth, medians for selected definitions of wealth, median net worth by net worth quintile, and the composition of the net worth of the middle 60 percent of the net worth distribution in each age group are examined using SIPP data for 1984. The focus here is on a comparison of the wealth of aged and nonaged units.

12.3.1   SIPP Data

Before the estimates are examined, a brief description of the SIPP wealth data is needed. One of the strengths of the SIPP data is the relatively large number of observations available for a survey that includes wealth data. The estimates shown in the remainder of this paper were made from a public use microdata file from wave 4 of the 1984 SIPP panel. These estimates are based on information for 18,701 households. Each age (of head) group shown in this paper includes more than 1,000 observations (table 12.3).[5] Thus, each quintile within an age group includes more than 200 observations. There are more than 3,900 households with an aged head, and the seventy-five and over age group contains almost 1,600 observations. This survey contains enough observations to be useful for the analysis of many subgroups of the aged.

The net worth concept used in the detailed tables in this paper is defined to be wealth minus unsecured debt. Wealth consists of the following five items: equity (market value minus debt) in owner-occupied homes; equity in motor vehicles; equity in business, professional practice, or farm; equity in rental property, vacation homes, and other real estate; and financial assets.[6] The financial assets category includes passbook savings accounts, money-market deposit accounts, certificates of deposit, interest-earning checking (e.g., negotiable order of withdrawal [NOW]) accounts, money-market funds, U.S. government securities, municipal or corporate bonds, stocks and mutual fund shares, U.S. savings bonds, IRAs and Keogh accounts, regular checking accounts, mortgages held for sale of real estate, amount due from sale

Table 12.3   Sample Size and Weighted Number of Households by Age, 1984

Age of Head	Number of Observations	Millions of Households
Under 25	1,342	5.7
25–34	4,161	20.1
35–44	3,592	17.4
45–54	2,885	12.6
55–64	2,787	12.9
65 and over	3,934	18.2
65–74	2,336	10.7
65–69	1,251	5.7
70–74	1,085	5.0
75 and over	1,598	7.5
All ages	18,701	86.9

of business or property, other interest-earning assets, and other financial assets. It should be noted that social security wealth and pension wealth are not included in wealth.

Unsecured debt includes credit card and store bills; doctor, dentist, hospital, and nursing home bills; loans from financial institutions and individuals; and educational loans. Although the value of household durables is not included in wealth, debt incurred to purchase those items is included in unsecured debt.

It is useful to comment on the accuracy of the wealth data contained in the 1984 SIPP. Most of the information about accuracy that does exist is in the form of comparisons between SIPP aggregates and control aggregates.[7] The Bureau of the Census has compared aggregates from the 1984 SIPP with Federal Reserve Board balance sheet data (U.S. Bureau of the Census 1986b, table D-3). They find that home equity is overstated in SIPP by 30 percent and that vehicle equity is overstated by 43 percent. On the other hand, equity in business and rental property, and financial assets are understated by about 25 percent. Unsecured debt is underestimated by about 35 percent. Although comparisons between survey wealth aggregates and wealth control aggregates are usually considered to be difficult and subject to substantial error, the pattern shown for SIPP is cause for some concern.

Item nonresponse rates are also a cause for concern. The market value of stock and mutual fund shares had a nonresponse rate of 41 percent (U.S. Bureau of the Census 1986b, table D-2). The item nonresponse rate for amount in checking accounts was 13 percent. Other financial assets shown by the Bureau of the Census had item nonresponse rates between those two figures. Missing values were imputed by the Bureau of the Census. It should be noted that nonresponse rates for asset ownership (as opposed to amounts) were very low; the highest rate shown was 2.2 percent for certificates of deposit (U.S. Bureau of the Census 1986b, table D-1).

12.3.2   Medians, Means, and Selected Definitions of Wealth

In this section, two important points that affect the analysis of wealth are illustrated. The first point is that whether medians or means are used makes an important difference for many analyses. As noted earlier, medians are more appropriate for the type of analysis discussed in this paper. Second, the definition of wealth used also makes an important difference. Amounts of wealth and the relation between the wealth of the aged and that of the nonaged are affected substantially by the choice of the definition.

Because of the skewed shape of the net worth distribution within each age group, mean net worth exceeds median net worth for every age group (table 12.4). Median net worth is quite low (below $10,000)

Table 12.4   Median and Mean Net Worth by Age, 1984

	Thousands of Dollars		Relative Values	
Age of Head	Median	Mean	Median	Mean
Under 25	2.2	7.2	.03	.06
25–34	8.1	24.8	.11	.21
35–44	35.5	62.4	.49	.54
45–54	56.4	98.7	.78	.85
55–64	72.5	115.6	1.00	1.00
65 and over	59.5	90.8	.82	.79
65–74	62.0	99.4	.86	.86
65–69	65.6	107.2	.90	.93
70–74	59.5	90.6	.82	.78
75 and over	54.6	78.4	.75	.68
All ages	32.5	69.2	.45	.60

for the under thirty-five age groups but rises to a peak of $72,500 in the fifty-five to sixty-four age group. Mean net worth is below $10,000 only for the under twenty-five age group and rises to a peak of $115,600 in the fifty-five to sixty-four age group. It is clear that median and mean amounts of net worth for each age group are quite different and that the choice between the two is important where dollar amounts are used. Of course, mean amounts are far more sensitive to values in the extremes of the wealth distribution and therefore are less appropriate here.

The ratio of mean to median net worth ranges from 1.44 for the seventy-five and over age group to 3.32 for the under twenty-five age group. In general, there is a downward trend in that ratio as age rises. Relative medians exceed relative means for most aged groups, although the differences are not large. Relative means are greater than relative medians for the younger age groups. Medians are focused on in this section.

The sensitivity of the age-wealth relation to the definition of wealth used is shown in tables 12.5 and 12.6. Table 12.5 shows medians and table 12.6 relative medians. For net worth, the medians for the aged groups are in a range of $11,000, from $54,600 for the seventy-five and over age group to $65,600 for the sixty-five to sixty-nine age group. There is a decline in median net worth as age increases within the aged group. The aged medians are roughly similar to the median for the forty-five to fifty-four age group and below the median for the fifty-five to sixty-four group. These relations are evident in table 12.6, which shows relative medians.[8]

When vehicle equity is excluded from net worth, the median falls by relatively small amounts (by $2,200–$6,000). The youngest age group now has a median of zero, and the peak is still in the fifty-five to sixty-four age

Table 12.5   **Median Amounts, 1984 (in thousands of dollars)**

			Definition of Wealth			
Age of Head	Net Worth	Net Worth, Excluding Vehicle Equity	Net Worth, Excluding Vehicle and Home Equity	Financial Assets minus Debt	Wealth	Financial Assets
Under 25	2.2	0	0	0	3.4	0.3
25–34	8.1	3.9	0	0	10.2	0.8
35–44	35.5	30.7	1.8	0.4	38.4	2.2
45–54	56.4	50.4	5.7	1.8	60.7	4.1
55–64	72.5	66.6	15.5	8.0	73.9	10.0
65 and over	59.5	55.8	14.9	10.5	60.0	10.9
65–74	62.0	59.3	15.0	11.0	62.5	11.7
65–69	65.6	61.4	16.2	12.0	66.2	13.0
70–74	59.5	55.6	13.3	10.5	60.0	10.7
75 and over	54.6	51.3	14.3	10.0	54.6	10.1
All ages	32.5	28.4	2.6	1.1	35.0	2.6

Note: Medians are for everyone in the age group.

Table 12.6   **Relative Medians for Alternative Definitions of Wealth, by Age, 1984**

Age of Head	Net Worth	Net Worth Excluding Vehicle Equity	Net Worth Excluding Vehicle and Home Equity	Financial Assets Minus Debt	Wealth	Financial Assets
Under 25	.03	0	0	0	.05	.03
25–34	.11	.06	0	0	.14	.08
35–44	.49	.46	.12	.06	.52	.22
45–54	.78	.76	.37	.23	.82	.41
55–64	1.00	1.00	1.00	1.00	1.00	1.00
65 and over	.82	.84	.96	1.31	.81	1.09
65–74	.86	.89	.97	1.38	.85	1.17
65–69	.90	.92	1.05	1.50	.90	1.30
70–74	.82	.83	.86	1.31	.81	1.07
75 and over	.75	.77	.93	1.25	.74	1.01
All ages	.45	.43	.17	.14	.47	.26

Note: Age 55–64 is used as the base.

group ($66,600). Relative medians rise very slightly for the aged groups and fall substantially for the youngest groups.

When home equity is excluded from net worth minus vehicle equity, there is a much larger effect. However, that effect differs widely among the age groups. The youngest group (which already has a median of zero) shows no change, and the twenty-five to thirty-four group shows a decline of only $3,900. In contrast, the fifty-five to sixty-four group shows a fall of $51,100. All age groups under fifty-five now have medians under $10,000, while all age groups are under $20,000. The peak is now in the sixty-five to sixty-nine group at $16,200. The relation as age rises is not smooth, with an increase through the fifty-five to sixty-four group followed by small increases and decreases. Relative to the median for the fifty-five to sixty-four age group, medians rose substantially for most aged groups and fell substantially for the thirty-five to fifty-four age groups. It should be noted that mean amounts for this definition (not shown) are several times the medians. For example, the mean for the sixty-five and over group is $48,700, while the median is only $14,900.

A less comprehensive definition is financial assets minus unsecured debt. Declines in moving to that definition from net worth excluding vehicle and home equity range from zero for the youngest groups to $7,500 for the fifty-five to sixty-four group. All nonaged groups now have medians under $10,000, and the highest median for any age group is only $12,000 (for age sixty-five to sixty-nine). There is a smooth rise in medians until the peak, then a smooth decline. Relative to the median for the fifty-five to sixty-four age group, medians rose substantially for the aged groups and fell for the thirty-five to fifty-four age groups. Mean amounts are still several times the medians, with the mean for the sixty-five and over group ($36,300) about three and a half times the median for that group.

Two definitions in which unsecured debt is not subtracted are now examined. The wealth medians are slightly above the net worth medians, with the differences ranging from less than $100 to $4,300. The relative values for wealth are very similar to those for net worth. The financial asset medians are slightly above the financial asset minus debt medians, with the aged groups showing small differences. The peak is still in the sixty-five to sixty-nine age group. Relative medians differ from those for financial assets minus debt. When only financial assets are considered, the relative medians are substantially higher for the under fifty-five groups and lower for the aged groups. For example, the relative median for the sixty-five and over group falls from 1.31 to 1.09.

In summary, medians for the aged rose slightly relative to medians for nonaged groups when vehicle equity was omitted from net worth and rose more sharply when home equity was also omitted. When the definition was changed to financial assets minus debt, medians for the aged rose very sharply relative to medians for the nonaged. Relative medians for all age groups are similar for wealth and net worth. Relative medians for the aged are relatively lower for financial assets than for financial assets minus debt. It can be seen from tables 12.5 and 12.6 that the choice of a definition of wealth can make an important difference in comparisons of the aged and nonaged.

12.3.3   Median Net Worth by Net Worth Quintile

Median net worth by age and net worth quintile (within age group) is shown in table 12.7. Median net worth is very low in the bottom quintile for all age groups, ranging from minus $1,300 in the under twenty-five group to $2,400 in the fifty-five to sixty-four group. In the second quintile, the median for each age group is below $36,000. In every age group, the median for the second quintile is less than half the overall median for the age group. In contrast, the top quintile shows medians above $150,000 for all age groups thirty-five and over.

Within each quintile, the age pattern is roughly similar—low amounts at the young ages, a peak in the fifty-five to sixty-four group, and declines among the aged groups. It is interesting to note that, for each of the top four quintiles, median net worth declines within the aged group as age rises. The decline between the sixty-five to sixty-nine and the seventy-five and over age groups is 26 percent for the second quintile, 17 percent for the third quintile, 15 percent for the fourth quintile, and 18 percent for the top quintile.

Table 12.7   **Median Net Worth by Age and Net Worth Quintile, 1984 (in thousands of dollars)**

Age of Head	Net Worth Quintile				
	1	2	3	4	5
Under 25	− 1.3	.2	2.2	5.6	18.1
25–34	− .6	1.7	8.1	23.1	65.6
35–44	0	11.3	35.5	66.6	152.1
45–54	.5	23.3	56.4	97.8	205.3
55–64	2.4	35.3	72.4	118.9	245.4
65 and over	.8	26.7	59.5	99.3	200.1
65–74	.8	29.0	62.0	103.8	209.6
65–69	1.1	32.6	65.6	108.7	219.7
70–74	.5	24.4	59.4	96.5	197.6
75 and over	.7	24.0	54.6	92.5	181.1
All ages	0	7.5	32.5	71.7	166.9

Note: Quintiles are defined within each age group.

The medians for all groups under age fifty-five rise relative to the median for the aged as net worth increases. For example, the median for the thirty-five to forty-four age group rises from zero in the bottom quintile to 76 percent of the median for the aged in the top quintile, and the median for the forty-five to fifty-four age group rises from 68 percent of the median for the aged in the lowest quintile to 102 percent in the top quintile.

12.3.4 Wealth of the Middle 60 Percent of Households

In this section, the asset types held, the mean amounts of those assets, and the percentage composition of net worth are examined for the middle 60 percent of the net worth distribution of each age group. Households in the top and bottom net worth quintiles are excluded because the focus here is on "typical" households in each age group (i.e., households that do not have extreme amounts of net worth). Estimates of amounts for the age group as a whole can be affected by a few very high amounts and by negative amounts. Some roughly comparable estimates for entire age groups appear in a Bureau of the Census report (U.S. Bureau of the Census 1986b).

The percentages of households holding various components of net worth are shown in table 12.8. Compared with nonaged households, aged households show a higher percentage with home equity but lower percentages with vehicle equity, business equity, and unsecured debt. Home equity is held by 84 percent of the aged group. This is higher than the percentages shown by the under forty-five age groups and lower than the percentages shown by the forty-five to sixty-four age groups (90–91 percent). Only 10 percent of the under twenty-five group and 42 percent of the twenty-five to thirty-four group have home equity. Within the aged group, the percentage with home equity declines from 89 percent in the sixty-five to sixty-nine age group to 81 percent in the seventy-five and over group. Even the seventy-five and over age group has a higher percentage than the under forty-five age groups. The percentages with home equity for the middle 60 percent are above the percentages for the entire age group (not shown) for all age groups thirty-five and over. For example, the entire sixty-five and over group shows 73 percent with home equity, compared to 84 percent for the middle 60 percent.

Vehicle equity is held by 76 percent of aged households. This figure is below the percentage for each nonaged age group. The percentage within the aged group falls from 88 percent in the sixty-five to sixty-nine age group to 63 percent in the seventy-five and over age group. The percentage with business equity is very low among the aged and reaches a peak of only 11 percent in the forty-five to fifty-four age group. Real estate reaches a peak of 22 percent in the fifty-five to

Table 12.8 Percentage Holding Specific Asset Types, Households with Medium Net Worth, by Age, 1984

Age of Head		Type of Asset or Debt				
	Home Equity	Vehicle Equity	Financial Assets	Business Equity	Real Estate	Unsecured Debt
Under 25	10	82	72	2	1	58
25–34	42	96	85	6	6	78
35–44	79	96	92	10	14	81
45–54	90	98	93	11	20	79
55–64	91	94	93	9	22	66
65 and over	84	76	93	3	12	38
65–74	87	86	92	3	14	44
65—69	89	88	92	3	16	46
70–74	84	82	93	4	12	40
75 and over	81	63	94	1	10	30
All ages	71	91	90	8	12	69

Note: Medium net worth is defined as the middle 60 percent of the net worth distribution in each age group.

sixty-four age group and is somewhat lower among the aged (10–16 percent). The percentage with unsecured debt is highest in the twenty-five to fifty-four age groups (78–81 percent) and falls to 38 percent in the sixty-five and over group. Only 30 percent of the seventy-five and over age group has unsecured debt.

Financial assets are held by more than 90 percent of all groups age thirty-five and over. The percentages of the middle 60 percent holding selected components of financial assets are shown in table 12.9. Savings accounts are held by roughly two-thirds of all households, with relatively little variation among age groups. Money-market accounts are more prevalent among the aged (23 percent) than among the non-aged, as are certificates of deposit (38 percent for the aged). Interest-earning checking accounts show less variation among age groups, with the aged showing a slightly higher percentage (29 percent) than the nonaged. Stocks and mutual funds are most prevalent in the thirty-five to sixty-four age groups (21–22 percent), but the aged percentage is not much lower (17 percent). U.S. savings bonds are also most prevalent in the thirty-five to sixty-four age groups (19–20 percent); 12 percent of the aged hold such bonds. The fifty-five to sixty-four age group shows the highest percentage with an IRA (40 percent), while only 6 percent of the aged have an IRA. The sixty-five to sixty-nine age group shows 12 percent with an IRA, but only 3 percent of the seventy-five and over group have an IRA. In summary, aged households show higher percentages than nonaged households for money-market accounts, certificates of deposit, and interest-earning checking accounts and lower percentages for U.S. savings bonds and IRAs.

Mean amounts of the various asset types are shown for the middle 60 percent in table 12.10. These means are for all households in the middle 60 percent of the age group, not just for those with the specific asset type. For each age group, mean amounts of vehicle equity, business equity, and real estate are all quite low—below $7,000. The sum of these three asset types minus unsecured debt is below $11,000 for each age group. For aged households, the sum is $6,200, compared with means of $35,200 for home equity and $20,900 for financial assets. Thus, in an absolute sense, these asset types are not very important for the middle 60 percent. However, it should be noted that vehicle equity is relatively important for the under thirty-five age groups.

The relative importance of each asset type for each age group can be seen in table 12.11. Financial assets are more important for aged households than for nonaged households, while home equity is slightly less important for the aged than for the nonaged. Home equity is at least 55 percent of net worth for each age group thirty-five and over. The percentage declines from a peak of 67 percent in the thirty-five to forty-four age group as age rises. The percentage accounted for by

Table 12.9   Percentage Holding Selected Financial Assets, Households with Medium Net Worth, by Age, 1984

				Type of Asset			
Age of Head	Savings Accounts	Money-Market Accounts	Certificates of Deposit	NOW Accounts[a]	Stocks or Mutual Funds	U.S. Savings Bonds	IRA
Under 25	52	2	2	14	4	9	2
25–34	63	6	7	21	13	13	10
35–44	71	11	12	23	21	19	18
45–54	72	13	18	23	21	19	29
55–64	71	21	30	27	22	20	40
65 and over	67	23	38	29	17	12	6
65–74	67	25	39	29	17	14	8
65–69	67	26	37	30	19	15	12
70–74	67	23	40	28	17	13	4
75 and over	66	21	39	29	18	13	3
All ages	67	12	17	23	17	16	16

Note: Medium net worth is defined as the middle 60 percent of the net worth distribution in each age group.

[a]Includes all interest-bearing checking accounts.

Table 12.10 Mean Amounts of Specific Asset Types, Households with Medium Net Worth, by Age, 1984 (in thousands of dollars)

Age of Head	Net Worth	Home Equity	Vehicle Equity	Financial Assets	Business Equity	Real Estate	Unsecured Debt
				Type of Asset or Debt			
Under 25	2.8	.4	2.4	.9	0	0	.9
25–34	11.5	5.9	3.8	2.8	.4	.6	1.9
35–44	38.7	25.9	5.0	6.5	1.2	2.6	2.6
45–54	60.2	39.7	6.3	11.1	2.0	4.6	3.4
55–64	76.3	46.2	5.8	19.4	1.5	5.5	2.1
65 and over	62.3	35.2	3.2	20.9	.4	3.1	.5
65–74	65.7	37.9	4.0	20.8	.5	3.3	.7
65–69	70.2	40.3	4.5	21.7	.8	4.0	1.0
70–74	61.0	34.8	3.6	20.0	.4	2.8	.5
75 and over	57.5	31.5	1.9	21.5	.2	2.7	.3
All ages	38.3	23.9	4.5	8.7	1.0	2.3	2.1

Note: Medium net worth is defined as the middle 60 percent of the net worth distribution in each age group. Mean amounts are for all households in the group, not just for those holding the asset.

Table 12.11   Percentage Composition of Net Worth, Households with Medium Net Worth, by Age, 1984

				Type of Asset or Debt			
Age of Head	Net Worth	Home Equity	Vehicle Equity	Financial Assets	Business Equity	Real Estate	Unsecured Debt
Under 25	100	14	84	31	1	1	32
25–34	100	52	33	24	3	5	17
35–44	100	67	13	17	3	7	7
45–54	100	66	10	18	3	8	6
55–64	100	61	8	25	2	7	3
65 and over	100	57	5	34	1	5	1
65–74	100	58	6	32	1	5	1
65–69	100	57	6	31	1	6	1
70–74	100	57	6	33	1	5	1
75 and over	100	55	3	37	0	5	1
All ages	100	62	12	23	3	6	5

Note: Medium net worth is defined as the middle 60 percent of the net worth distribution in each age group.

financial assets is highest in the seventy-five and over age group (37 percent) and lowest in the thirty-five to forty-four age group (17 percent). Within the aged group, there is a small shift from home equity to financial assets between the sixty-five to sixty-nine and the seventy-five and over age groups. Home equity is roughly four times as important as financial assets for the thirty-five to fifty-four age groups but is less than twice as important for the aged. These percentages are quite different when the entire age group (not just the middle 60 percent) is used. For the aged, home equity (42 percent) and financial assets (41 percent) are of about equal importance in that case.

In summary, home equity and financial assets dominate the net worth of the middle 60 percent of aged households. Financial assets are relatively more important for aged households than for nonaged households. Vehicle equity and unsecured debt are important primarily for younger households.

12.4   Wealth of Age and Income Groups

In assessing the economic well-being of households, the relation between income and wealth is very important. Both income and wealth should be taken into account when economic well-being is examined. In most cases, income alone is used as the classifier for assessing economic status.

Several different methods of using income and wealth data together have been used by researchers. Perhaps the most widely used type of method converts the stock of wealth into a flow and adds that flow to the flow of income. In that method, wealth is converted into an annuity for the expected remaining life of the unit (e.g., Murray 1964; Weisbrod and Hansen 1968; Taussig 1973; Wolfson 1979). Moon (1977) has applied this method to the aged. In a variant of the simple annuity approach, the annuity allows the unit to reach the same utility level as its optimal consumption path, rather than the highest constant consumption path (Nordhaus 1973; Irvine 1980; Beach 1981).

Comparing different age groups using the annuity approach has been criticized on the grounds that the method does not take into account the likelihood that the incomes of young units will rise and that those units ordinarily will be able to increase their wealth as they age (Projector and Weiss 1969). Some researchers have tried to take this into account essentially by estimating future earnings (Nordhaus 1973; Taussig 1973; Irvine 1980).

Some researchers have combined income and wealth by converting income flows into stocks of wealth and adding that wealth to other types of wealth. For example, in looking at the aged, Hurd and Shoven (1982) capitalized several sources of income and added those values to estimates of wealth. Also, for limited purposes, some researchers have taken a simpler approach to combining income and wealth and summed current income and liquid assets (David 1959; Steuerle and McClung 1977) or income and net worth (Steuerle and McClung 1977).

Radner and Vaughan (1984, 1987) and Radner (1984), in looking at a short time horizon, did not combine income and wealth. They considered income and wealth jointly as a two-dimensional classification and examined such characteristics of the joint distribution as the percentage of each age group that had relatively low wealth and relatively low income.

In this section, the amounts of wealth held by different relative income groups within age groups are examined. It should be noted that this is a purely descriptive exercise. Double counting of income and assets is not a concern here; such concerns are important in an analytic use of the data. Thus, income includes asset income and wealth income-producing assets in the estimates shown here.

The income classifications used require some explanation. The income definition is total household money income for the four-month period preceding the interview. (In some of the estimates, this four-month income is "annualized" by multiplying it by three.) The income amounts are adjusted for household size using an equivalence scale based on the scale implicit in the U.S. poverty thresholds.[9] Then, within each age group, households are separated into quintile groups based on the size of their adjusted total money income. There is a presumption that, within each age group, households in higher-income quintiles are "better off" than those in lower-income quintiles. The wealth of households in these different income quintiles is examined. Although all age groups are examined, there is more emphasis on the aged than the nonaged.

12.4.1   Median Amounts

Table 12.12 shows median net worth by adjusted income quintile and age. Aged households with low income typically have small amounts of net worth. Median net worth is only $13,400 for the bottom income quintile of aged households. This is far below the overall median of $59,500 for aged households. The second income quintile of aged households shows a median ($31,200) that is only 52 percent of that overall median. Median net worth for the aged rises as income rises, reflecting the substantial correlation between income and net worth. All other age groups also have low medians for the bottom income quintile. Median net worth is below $8,000 for the bottom income quintile for each age group under age fifty-five. For the under thirty-five age groups, median net worth is low for all income groups. The bottom three income quintiles show peaks in the fifty-five to sixty-four age group, but the

Table 12.12   **Median Net Worth by Adjusted Income Quintile and Age, 1984 (in thousands of dollars)**

	Income Quintile				
Age of Head	1	2	3	4	5
Under 25	0	1.3	2.5	3.8	4.8
25–34	.6	5.3	8.8	12.5	25.4
35–44	5.0	24.1	37.9	45.2	78.5
45–54	7.9	38.8	58.0	71.9	115.0
55–64	20.0	54.1	67.0	89.1	163.7
65 and over	13.4	31.2	61.2	82.5	153.4
65–74	8.7	40.6	63.9	85.5	163.8
65–69	13.0	43.7	65.5	89.5	178.1
70–74	6.9	35.0	57.5	90.3	142.2
75 and over	16.7	25.2	56.6	79.0	143.5
All ages	3.3	20.9	33.2	47.8	87.8

Note: Income quintiles are based on income adjusted for household size and are defined within age groups.

seventy to seventy-four age group has the highest median in the fourth income quintile, and the sixty-five to sixty-nine age group has the highest median in the top quintile.

Table 12.13 shows median financial assets by adjusted income quintile and age. Of course, these medians would be expected to be far below the medians shown in table 12.12, primarily because home equity is excluded here, and that is the case. The bottom quintile of aged households has a median of only $400, and the second quintile has a median

Table 12.13   **Median Financial Assets by Adjusted Income Quintile and Age, 1984 (in thousands of dollars)**

	Income Quintile				
Age of Head	1	2	3	4	5
Under 25	0	.1	.3	.6	1.4
25–34	0	.3	.8	1.7	5.2
35–44	.1	.8	2.1	4.3	12.8
45–54	0	1.7	3.9	7.4	24.5
55–64	.1	4.0	10.0	18.2	46.5
65 and over	.4	3.2	15.0	24.2	63.3
65–74	.1	4.0	12.4	25.5	63.9
65–69	.2	5.6	10.2	31.0	68.0
70–74	.1	3.0	12.5	26.0	60.7
75 and over	.6	2.7	13.0	30.0	62.7
All ages	0	1.0	2.5	4.8	16.8

Note: Income quintiles are based on income adjusted for household size and are defined within age groups.

of only $3,200. These amounts are too small to cover substantial unexpected expenses. In the bottom income quintile, median financial assets is below $1,000 in every age group. The second quintile shows a peak of $5,600, and the highest median in the third quintile is $15,000. It is only the aged in the fourth quintile and age groups forty-five and over in the top quintile that show medians of over $20,000. In the top four income quintiles, the aged have high medians compared to most nonaged groups.

12.4.2   Wealth of Aged Households

Tables 12.14–12.16 show the composition of the wealth of the age sixty-five and over group by adjusted income quintile. In table 12.14, the majority of each income quintile has home equity, with a peak of 85 percent in the top quintile. There is a substantial rise in the percentage as income rises. The percentage with vehicle equity also rises sharply as income rises; only 41 percent of the bottom quintile have that asset. Business equity is held by less than 10 percent in each quintile. The percentage with real estate also shows a strong rise as income increases, with a peak of 30 percent in the top quintile. The percentage with unsecured debt shows a relatively small increase as income rises, with a range from 32 to 45 percent.

The percentage with financial assets exhibits a strong increase as income rises, with most of the increase occurring between the first and the third quintiles. Table 12.15 shows the percentage of aged households holding selected financial assets. The percentage holding each of these assets rises sharply as income rises. Savings accounts are held by 39 percent of the bottom quintile and 76 percent of the top quintile. Savings accounts are the only financial asset shown here that is held by a substantial proportion of the bottom income quintile. The percentages

Table 12.14   **Percentage Holding Specific Asset Types, by Adjusted Income Quintile, Age 65 and Over, 1984**

Income Quintile	Type of Asset or Debt					
	Home Equity	Vehicle Equity	Financial Assets	Business Equity	Real Estate	Unsecured Debt
1	56	41	65	2	7	32
2	64	56	84	2	9	34
3	76	79	94	3	16	38
4	82	88	97	4	20	45
5	85	93	99	8	30	45
Total	73	71	88	4	16	39

Note: Income quintiles are based on income adjusted for household size and are defined within the age group.

Table 12.15   **Percentage Holding Selected Financial Assets, by Adjusted Income Quintile, Age 65 and Over, 1984**

Income Quintile	Savings Accounts	Money-Market Accounts	Certificates of Deposit	NOW Accounts[a]	Stocks or Mutual Funds	U.S. Savings Bonds	IRA
				Type of Financial Asset			
1	39	6	12	10	2	2	1
2	54	12	28	19	9	6	3
3	68	23	42	30	17	12	5
4	74	32	44	38	25	16	10
5	76	47	55	53	51	21	21
Total	63	24	36	30	21	11	8

Note: Income quintiles are based on income adjusted for household size and are defined within the age group.
[a]Includes all interest-bearing checking accounts.

Table 12.16   **Percentage Composition of Net Worth, by Adjusted Income Quintile, Age 65 and Over, 1984**

Income Quintile	Net Worth	Type of Asset or Debt					
		Home Equity	Vehicle Equity	Financial Assets	Business Equity	Real Estate	Unsecured Debt
1	100	72	4	15	1	9	1
2	100	60	4	27	3	7	1
3	100	51	4	34	2	10	1
4	100	46	5	35	2	13	1
5	100	30	3	51	3	12	1
Total	100	42	4	41	3	11	1

Note: Income quintiles are based on income adjusted for household size and are defined within the age group.

of the bottom and top quintiles, respectively, that hold specific types of financial assets are: 6 and 47 percent for money-market accounts, 12 and 55 percent for certificates of deposit, 10 and 53 percent for interest-earning checking accounts, 2 and 51 percent for stocks and mutual funds, 2 and 21 percent for U.S. savings bonds, and 1 and 21 percent for IRAs. The second income quintile holds primarily savings accounts and certificates of deposit. U.S. savings bonds and IRAs are not very prevalent, even among households in the top income quintile.

Table 12.16 shows the composition of net worth.[10] This table is affected to a degree by problems in estimating the upper tail of the wealth distribution. Home equity accounts for more than half of net worth for each of the bottom three income quintiles. Home equity is also the most important component for the fourth quintile, but financial assets are the most important in the top quintile. For the aged group as a whole, home equity and financial assets are about equally important because of the dominance of the top quintile. Vehicle equity, business equity, and unsecured debt are not very important in any quintile. Real estate is slightly more important at higher income levels than at lower levels.

12.4.3   Ratio of Wealth to Income

Another way of examining the importance of wealth is to look at the ratio of wealth to income. Table 12.17 shows the ratio of median financial assets to median annualized income by age and adjusted income quintile. The bottom quintile of each aged group shows a low ratio (0.08 for all the aged), and the ratios for the second quintile are only

Table 12.17   **Ratio of Median Financial Assets to Median Annualized Income, by Adjusted Income Quintile and Age, 1984**

Age of Head	Income Quintile					
	1	2	3	4	5	Total
Under 25	0	.01	.02	.03	.04	.02
25–34	0	.02	.04	.06	.12	.04
35–44	.01	.04	.07	.11	.23	.08
45–54	0	.08	.13	.18	.39	.13
55–64	.02	.28	.43	.54	.79	.42
65 and over	.08	.41	1.22	1.32	1.90	.87
65–74	.02	.43	.89	1.28	1.79	.82
65–69	.03	.53	.66	1.38	1.79	.82
70–74	.02	.37	1.01	1.48	1.89	.86
75 and over	.13	.42	1.30	1.99	2.19	.99
All ages	0	.07	.12	.16	.33	.12

Note: Income quintiles are based on income adjusted for household size and are defined within age groups.

in the 0.37–0.53 range. These estimates confirm the earlier findings that lower-income aged households typically have only small amounts of financial assets. The top quintile in the aged groups demonstrates ratios in the 1.79–2.19 range. All quintiles in all nonaged groups show median financial assets less than median annualized income. For the youngest age groups, the ratios are quite small; the ratios are below 0.25 in all quintiles under age forty-five.

A second way of examining the age-wealth-income relation is by looking at the distribution of households by their ratio of wealth to income. Here, the ratio of financial assets to income is used. Those distributions by age are shown in table 12.18. The most important result in this table is the large dispersion present in the ratios for aged households. For the aged group as a whole, 25 percent had ratios under 0.10 (including zero), 26 percent had ratios from 0.10 to 1.00, 15 percent had ratios from 1.00 to 2.00, and one-third of the group had ratios of 2.00 or more. The percentages for the aged do not differ much within the aged group. In contrast, the youngest groups show far less dispersion. Only 2 percent of the under twenty-five age group had financial assets exceeding annualized income, and only 5 percent had financial assets that were more than half of income. For that age group, 26 percent had no financial assets, and 55 percent had a positive ratio less than 0.10. The forty-five to sixty-four age groups show less dispersion than the aged but more than the youngest age groups.

Table 12.19 shows the distribution of aged households by the ratio of financial assets to annualized income, by adjusted income quintile.

Table 12.18   Percentage Distribution of Households by the Ratio of Financial Assets to Annualized Income, by Age, 1984

		Ratio						
Age of Head	Zero Financial Assets	Under .1	.1–.3	.3–.5	.5–1.0	1.0–2.0	2.0 and over	Total[a]
Under 25	26	55	11	3	3	1	1	99
25–34	19	48	18	6	4	2	2	99
35–44	13	41	19	8	9	5	3	100
45–54	13	32	19	9	12	7	6	100
55–64	12	21	13	10	14	13	17	100
65 and over	12	13	10	6	10	15	33	100
65–74	13	14	10	7	11	16	30	100
65–69	12	14	10	7	11	18	28	100
70–74	14	14	9	6	10	14	32	100
75 and over	11	12	10	6	10	14	37	100
All ages	15	34	16	7	9	8	11	100

[a]A few households with zero or negative income are not shown.

Table 12.19   **Percentage Distribution of Households by the Ratio of Financial Assets to Annualized Income, by Adjusted Income Quintile, Age 65 and Over, 1984**

Income Quintile	Zero Financial Assets	Ratio						Total[a]
		Under .1	.1–.3	.3–.5	.5–1.0	1.0–2.0	2.0 and Over	
1	35	18	12	6	6	9	13	99
2	16	17	11	7	11	12	25	100
3	6	13	10	7	10	16	38	100
4	3	11	10	7	14	17	39	100
5	1	6	7	6	11	23	47	100

Note: Income quintiles are based on income adjusted for household size and are defined within the age group.

[a]A few households with zero or negative income are not shown.

When the aged group is separated into income quintiles, substantial dispersion is still present in each quintile. This suggests that using income data alone is not likely to capture the major effects on well-being of holdings of financial assets. Not surprisingly, the percentage distributions differ greatly by income quintile. For the bottom quintile, 53 percent had either zero financial assets or a positive ratio under 0.10. That percentage falls sharply to 7 percent in the top quintile. Only 22 percent of the bottom quintile had a ratio of at least 1.00, but 70 percent of the top income quintile had a ratio of at least 1.00.

12.4.4   Low Income and Low Wealth

Another way of taking account of both income and wealth is to examine a portion of their joint distribution. In particular, the portion of the joint distribution that includes relatively low income and relatively low wealth is considered here. Two different definitions of wealth, net worth and financial assets, are used, and the results for the two are compared. Relatively low income is defined as being in the bottom income quintile of the all-ages distribution, after adjustment for size of unit. Relatively low net worth (financial assets) is defined as being in the bottom two net worth (financial asset) quintiles of the all-ages distribution, after adjustment for size of unit.

The bottom two quintiles are used for net worth and financial assets because those distributions are so skewed. The bottom quintile contains very small amounts, and the amounts in the second quintile are still not very large. In terms of amounts adjusted for size of unit, the upper bound of the bottom net worth quintile is only $1,423, and the upper bound of the second net worth quintile is $11,760.[11] The corresponding bounds for financial assets are $50 and $753, respectively. It can be seen that these are not very large amounts. The upper bound of the bottom quintile of annualized income (adjusted for size of unit) is $7,212. The percentage of households in each age group with low income and low wealth is shown in table 12.20. For all ages, 13.2 percent of households had low income and low net worth. In general, the pattern is high percentages at young and old ages and lower percentages at ages in between.[12] The percentages range from a low of 8.4 percent for the fifty-five to sixty-four age group to 24.6 percent for the under twenty-five age group. Aged households show 13.3 percent, with a range from 10.2 percent for the youngest aged (aged sixty-five to sixty-nine) to 15.3 percent for the oldest aged (aged seventy-five and older).

The percentages for aged households show that, despite high median net worth compared to most other age groups, a relatively high percentage of aged households have low income and low net worth. This relatively high percentage results primarily from the high percentage of aged households in the bottom income quintile (table 12.20). For the aged, 28.0 percent were in the bottom income quintile, but only 48 percent (13.3/28.0) of those were also in the bottom two net worth quintiles. In contrast, 94 percent of households in the youngest age group in the bottom income quintile were also in the bottom two net worth quintiles.

Table 12.20   **Percentage of Households with Low Income and Low Wealth, by Age of Head, 1984**

Age of Unit Head	With Low Income and Low Net Worth[a]	With Low Income and Low Financial Assets[b]	In Bottom Income Quintile
Under 25	24.6	23.4	26.3
25–34	16.8	16.9	19.1
35–44	11.8	13.5	16.8
45–54	9.2	11.2	14.3
55–64	8.4	11.9	17.3
65 and older	13.3	14.9	28.0
65–74	12.0	14.1	23.1
65–69	10.2	12.0	19.1
70–74	14.0	16.5	27.7
75 and older	15.3	15.9	35.0
All Ages	13.2	14.6	20.0

[a]Low income is defined as the bottom income quintile for all ages, and low net worth is defined as the bottom two net worth quintiles for all ages, in both cases after adjustment for size of unit.

[b]Low income is defined as the bottom income quintile for all ages, and low financial assets is defined as the bottom two financial asset quintiles for all ages, in both cases after adjustment for size of unit.

The results for low income and low financial assets show a less pronounced relation to age, although the general pattern is similar. The percentage for all ages is slightly higher than for net worth (14.6 percent). The range for financial assets is smaller, from 11.2 percent for the forty-five to fifty-four age group to 23.4 percent for the under twenty-five age group. Aged households show 14.9 percent with low income and low financial assets, which is slightly above the percentage found when net worth was used. Thus, in the bottom income quintile, the proportion of aged households with low financial assets (53 percent) is slightly higher than the proportion with low net worth. Aged households have higher median financial assets than net worth relative to other age groups. Despite this, the percentage of aged households with low income and low financial assets is higher than for most other age groups.

This examination of a portion of the joint distribution of income and wealth has shown that, despite the relatively high median amounts of wealth held by the aged, the proportion of aged households with both low income and low wealth is not relatively low. The relatively high percentage of aged households in the bottom income quintile is an important factor here.

12.5 Summary and Conclusions

This paper reflects a somewhat different perspective on the use of wealth data. The emphasis is on analyzing the economic status of ordinary (nonrich) units. Also, there is a particular interest in age groups, with the emphasis on the aged. Selected estimates of wealth for 1984 from SIPP are presented. These estimates are illustrations of several types of useful wealth estimates that can be made from household survey data.

Types of wealth estimates are discussed, and the characteristics of wealth data that are important for the analysis of economic status are examined. Estimates of the age-wealth cross-sectional relation are compared for five household surveys and two synthetic estimates. These estimates differ in definition of wealth, wealth-holding unit, and time period. Although relative mean amounts from the different data sources differ widely, relative medians are quite similar. Estimates of relative medians from the 1984 SIPP are similar to those from the other data sources examined.

Estimates of net worth from the 1984 SIPP show that the mean far exceeds the median in each age group. When home equity and vehicle equity are excluded from net worth, all age groups show medians of under $17,000, with the peak in the sixty-five to sixty-nine age group. Medians for financial assets minus debt also peak in the sixty-five to sixty-nine age group ($12,000). When net worth quintiles within age groups are examined, median net worth is very low in the bottom quintile in each age group.

An examination of the middle 60 percent of the net worth distribution in each age group shows that, except for the under twenty-five group, home equity is by far the most important asset for each age group. Home equity accounts for 57 percent of the net worth of the aged, while financial assets account for 34 percent.

When wealth is examined for income quintiles (based on income adjusted for household size) within age groups, median net worth is low for the bottom income quintile for each age group. Median financial assets is low for the bottom three quintiles in every age group. For the bottom income quintile in the aged group, home equity constitutes 72 percent of net worth, and financial assets account for 15 percent. For the top income quintile of the aged group, home equity accounts for only 30 percent, while financial assets account for 51 percent of net worth.

Ratios of median financial assets to median annualized income are below 1.00 for all income quintiles in each nonaged group. The ratio exceeds 1.00 for higher-income aged households. Large dispersion in the distribution of the ratio of financial assets to annualized income is found for aged households. That dispersion is still substantial within each income quintile of the aged. More than 80 percent of households in the under twenty-five age group have financial assets that are less than 10 percent of their annualized income. For the aged, the corresponding figure is 25 percent. For the aged, that percentage ranges from 53 percent for the bottom income quintile to only 7 percent in the top income quintile.

When the percentage of households in each age group with relatively low income and relatively low wealth is examined, a pattern of high percentages at young and old ages, with lower percentages at ages in between, is found. Aged households show 13.3 percent with low income and low wealth, which is about equal to the percentage for all households and is greater than the percentage for most nonaged age groups. When financial assets is used instead of net worth, the results are similar.

Thus, data on wealth from the 1984 SIPP show that many aged households have little wealth to use in emergencies. This is similar to findings from the 1979 ISDP and from other data sources. Also, a great deal of dispersion in amounts of financial assets was found among the aged, even within income quintiles. This finding suggests that using income data alone does not capture important aspects of the distribution of well-being among the aged.

Wealth data from household surveys were the most appropriate for the analysis in this paper. Although wealth data from a household survey can be very useful for many purposes, such data still have many problems, such as high nonresponse rates and substantial response error. Much further research on the estimation of the distribution of wealth using survey data and other methods is needed.

Notes

1. For a recent discussion of types of wealth estimates and data on wealth, see Smith (1987).
2. For discussions of the accuracy of survey data on wealth, see, e.g., Ferber (1966) and Ferber et al. (1969).
3. For example, estimates of the change in inequality presented in a Joint Economic Committee (1986) report were questioned because of doubts about the accuracy of one high-wealth observation.

In public use household survey microdata files (such as used in this paper), amounts are often top coded to prevent disclosure. Also, the amounts are restricted by the size of amounts that could be coded in the survey. Such problems are far less important if the upper tail of the distribution is excluded from the analysis.

4. This was wave 4 of the 1984 panel in this multiwave survey. For detailed information about the organization of the survey, see U.S. Bureau of the Census (1986b).
5. The age of the household reference person is used. For convenience, in this paper that person is referred to as the head.
6. In addition to this technical definition of wealth, at times the term wealth is used in this paper in a broad sense (e.g., when data requirements for the analysis of wealth are discussed).
7. Another paper in this volume, Curtin, Juster, and Morgan (chap. 10), compares distributional estimates from the 1984 SIPP with those from the 1983 SCF and the 1984 Panel Study of Income Dynamics.
8. The inclusion of other asset types in net worth also can affect the age-wealth relation. The 1979 ISDP contained an estimate of the value of consumer durables. Unpublished tabulations from that file showed that moving from a definition of net worth that excluded consumer durables to one that included consumer durables produced small increases in the relative medians for age groups under age forty-five and a small decrease in the relative median for the sixty-five to seventy-four age group.

In a recent paper, Wolff (1987) examined mean wealth by age group for alternative broad definitions of wealth. The most comprehensive definition included pension and social security wealth and human capital.

9. The scale is derived from the 1984 weighted thresholds (U.S. Bureau of the Census 1986a, table A-2). A one-person household (all ages) is used as the base. Each household's income (or, in one estimate, wealth) is divided by the appropriate scale value to obtain adjusted income. The scale values used are as follows: one person (under age sixty-five), 1.023; one person (age sixty-five and over), 0.943; two persons (under age sixty-five), 1.323; two persons (age sixty-five and over), 1.190; three persons, 1.568; four persons, 2.010; five persons, 2.381; six persons, 2.692; seven persons, 3.050; eight persons, 3.403; and nine persons or more, 4.026.

10. The mean amounts of net worth underlying this table (in thousands of dollars) are $26.7 in quintile 1, $45.3 in quintile 2, $70.6 in quintile 3, $99.7 in quintile 4, and $211.4 in quintile 5.

11. If the adjusted amounts are converted to unadjusted amounts, the upper bound of the second net worth quintile is, e.g., $11,090 for an aged one-person household, $13,994 for an aged two-person household, and $23,638 for a four-person household.

12. This pattern is similar to that found by Radner and Vaughan (1984, 1987) using data from the 1979 ISDP.

References

Avery, Robert B., and Gregory E. Elliehausen. 1986. Financial characteristics of high-income families. *Federal Reserve Bulletin* 72, no. 3 (March): 163–77.

Avery, Robert B., Gregory E. Elliehausen, Glenn B. Conner, and Thomas A. Gustafson. 1984a. Survey of Consumer Finances, 1983. *Federal Reserve Bulletin* 70, no. 9 (September): 679–92.

———. 1984b. Survey of Consumer Finances, 1983: A second report. *Federal Reserve Bulletin* 70, no. 12 (December): 857–68.

Beach, Charles M. 1981. *Distribution of income and wealth in Ontario: Theory and evidence*. Ontario Economic Council Research Studies. Toronto: University of Toronto Press.

Cartwright, William S., and Robert B. Friedland. 1985. The President's Commission on Pension Policy household survey, 1979: Net wealth distributions by type and age for the United States. *Review of Income and Wealth,* ser. 31, no. 3 (September): 285–308.

David, Martin. 1959. Welfare, income, and budget needs. *Review of Economics and Statistics* 41 (November): 393–99.

Ferber, Robert. 1966. *The reliability of consumer reports of financial assets and debts*. Studies in Consumer Savings, no. 6. Urbana: Bureau of Economic and Business Research, University of Illinois.

Ferber, Robert, John Forsythe, Harold W. Guthrie, and E. Scott Maynes. 1969. Validation of a national survey of consumer financial characteristics: Savings accounts. *Review of Economics and Statistics* 51 no. 4 (November): 436–44.

Greenwood, Daphne. 1983. An estimation of U.S. family wealth and its distribution from microdata, 1973. *Review of Income and Wealth,* ser. 29, no. 1 (March): 23–44.

———. 1987. Age, income, and household size: Their relation to wealth distribution in the United States. In *International Comparisons of the Distribution of Household Wealth,* ed. Edward N. Wolff. Oxford: Oxford University Press.

Hurd, Michael, and John B. Shoven. 1982. Real income and wealth of the elderly. *American Economic Review* 72 (May): 314–18.

Irelan, Lola M. 1972. Retirement history study: Introduction. *Social Security Bulletin* 35 (November): 3–8.

Irvine, Ian. 1980. The distribution of income and wealth in Canada in a lifecycle framework. *Canadian Journal of Economics* 13 (August): 455–74.

Joint Economic Committee. 1986. The concentration of wealth in the United States (trends in the distribution of wealth among American families). Washington, D.C.: U.S. Congress, July.

Moon, Marilyn. 1977. *The measurement of economic welfare (its application to the aged poor).* Institute for Research on Poverty Monograph Series. New York: Academic Press.

Murray, Janet. 1964. Potential income from assets: Findings of the 1963 Survey of the Aged. *Social Security Bulletin* 27 (December): 3–11.

Nordhaus, William D. 1973. The effects of inflation on the distribution of economic welfare. *Journal of Money, Credit, and Banking* 5:465–504.

Pearl, Robert B., and Matilda Frankel. 1984. Composition of the personal wealth of american households at the start of the eighties. In *The collection and analysis of economic and consumer data: In memory of Robert Ferber,* ed. Seymour Sudman and Mary A. Spaeth. Champaign: Bureau of Economic and Business Research and Survey Research Laboratory, University of Illinois.

Projector, Dorothy S., and Gertrude S. Weiss. 1966. *Survey of financial characteristics of consumers.* Washington, D.C.: Board of Governors of the Federal Reserve System.

———. 1969. Income–net worth measures of economic welfare. *Social Security Bulletin* 32 (November): 14–17.

Radner, Daniel B. 1975. Discussion. *1975 Proceedings of the American Statistical Association, Business and Economic Statistics Section,* 43–44.

———. 1984. The wealth and income of aged households. *1984 Proceedings of the American Statistical Association, Social Statistics Section,* 490–95.

Radner, Daniel B., and Denton R. Vaughan. 1984. The joint distribution of wealth and income for age groups, 1979. Office of Research, Statistics, and International Policy Working Papers, no. 33. Washington, D.C.: Social Security Administration, March.

———. 1987. Wealth, income, and the economic status of aged households. In *International comparisons of the distribution of household wealth,* ed. Edward N. Wolff. Oxford: Oxford University Press.

Schwartz, Marvin. 1983. Trends in personal wealth, 1976–1981. *SOI Bulletin* 3, no. 1 (Summer): 1–26.

Smith, James D. 1974. The concentration of personal wealth in America, 1969. *Review of Income and Wealth,* ser. 20, no. 2 (June): 143–80.

———. 1987. Recent trends in the distribution of wealth: Data, research problems, and prospects. In *International Comparisons of the Distribution of Household Wealth,* ed. Edward N. Wolff. Oxford: Oxford University Press.

Steuerle, Eugene, and Nelson McClung. 1977. Wealth and the accounting period in the measurement of means. In *The Measure of Poverty.* Technical Paper, no. 6. Washington, D.C.: Department of Health, Education, and Welfare.

Taussig, Michael K. 1973. *Alternative measures of the distribution of economic welfare.* Princeton, N.J.: Industrial Relations Section, Department of Economics, Princeton University.

U.S. Bureau of the Census. 1986a. *Characteristics of the population below the poverty level: 1984.* Current Population Reports, ser. P-60, no. 152 (June). Washington, D.C.: U.S. Government Printing Office.

———. 1986b. *Household wealth and asset ownership: 1984.* Current Population Reports, ser. P-70, no. 7 (July). Washington, D.C.: U.S. Government Printing Office.

Weisbrod, Burton A., and Lee W. Hansen. 1968. An income–net worth approach to measuring economic welfare. *American Economic Review* 58 (December): 1315–29.

Wolff, Edward N. 1983. The size distribution of household disposable wealth in the United States. *Review of Income and Wealth,* ser. 29, no. 2 (June): 125–46.

––––––. 1987. The effects of pensions and social security on the distribution of wealth in the U.S. In *International Comparisons of the Distribution of Household Wealth,* ed. Edward N. Wolff. Oxford: Oxford University Press.

Wolfson, Michael C. 1979. Wealth and the distribution of income, Canada, 1969–70. *Review of Income and Wealth,* ser. 25 (June): 129–40.

Comment   Marilyn Moon

Daniel Radner's interesting paper on wealth data offers a number of insights into this difficult-to-measure source of well-being for households and families. Moreover, the abundance of data presented here offers other researchers a valuable source of information. I suspect many people will spend a great deal of time, as I have, perusing the tables and developing their own stories to fit these data.

Radner offers up a number of ways to view the data and carefully guides the reader through some of them. In particular, he focuses attention on relative wealth measures: looking at variations across age groups with age group fifty-five to sixty-four as the base. These numbers offer some interesting insights into comparisons among alternative data sources, between means and medians, and among different components of net worth.

First, Radner uses these ratios to raise some very sobering glimpses at differences in estimates derived from various data bases. Cross-age comparisons are very sensitive to the measure in use. While the patterns of wealth holding remain reasonably constant, the actual dispersion, as well as the overall means, varies greatly. At first glance, it seems possible to pick and choose among data sets to support whatever claim about the age inequality of wealth one wishes to argue.

Second, Radner compares differences in ratios based on the median and the mean value of net worth. As expected, median ratios are less spread out across the distribution for those over age fifty-five but show greater variation for younger families. Radner chooses to use medians rather than means to avoid letting the upper tail of the distribution dominate his analysis. Such a strategy is certainly the more appropriate for comparing "average" families by age group.

Marilyn Moon is director of the Public Policy Institute of the American Association of Retired Persons.

Our conventional wisdom on cross-age differences also seems to be borne out: net worth shows a steady increase up to the age fifty-five to sixty-four category and then declines monotonically after that. But the disaggregation of net worth into its various components adds some additional dimensions to the story. When home equity is excluded, families above the age of sixty-five do better than when the measure is for net worth as a whole. In fact, the sixty-five to sixty-nine-year-olds have the highest median equity holdings of any age group. When only financial assets are considered, older families do even better, exceeding the fifty-five to sixty-four-year-olds in every case. Subtracting unsecured debts from financial assets leaves families under age forty-five with virtually zero median holdings, while those aged seventy-five and over have holdings 25 percent above the fifty-five to sixty-four-year-olds. The very old are largely debt free.

The author devotes much of his time to describing the data sets and the findings, leaving the reader the job of interpretation. Even here, however, he could do more. For example, Radner could discuss what new information the Survey of Income and Program Participation (SIPP) offers that contrasts with other studies. He should also raise the caveats that one must observe in interpreting these results and spend more time on underreporting issues. Is this truly only a problem for those who are well off? If so, and he is interested in those with more modest holdings, then this is not a major problem.

A number of other areas are certainly worthy of further discussion and may serve to breathe more life into some of the numbers. Consider, for example, his table 12.1. While there are many reasons why the different data sets discussed may give varying results, I was struck by how sensible some of these differences seem to be. Mid-life families (aged thirty-five to fifty-four) display the most interesting differences across the various surveys. But this is as it should be. The Pension Commission data, which include pension wealth in net worth, raise substantially the ratio of net worth for the mid-life families.

Also note the findings from the Survey of Financial Characteristics of Consumers (SFCC). The SCFF was taken twenty years earlier than the 1983 Survey of Consumer Finances (SCF) and the SIPP. Wealth was more concentrated in 1962 among older families, and mid-life families had fewer resources than they have in the 1980s.

Do these findings ring true? I would say yes. Improved pension coverage and the rise in the value of housing due to inflation in the 1970s should have resulted in improvements for families still in their prime working years. These effects seem to be borne out by the data. Such intuitive checks of reasonableness are important if we are to have faith in these complicated sets of findings.

Another set of numbers that I find particularly interesting is the quintile net worth figures by age (table 12.12). Here, I was struck by how unevenly distributed wealth is for older groups as compared to younger ones. Over our lifetimes, a lot of sorting obviously goes on. This particular finding ought to inspire a good deal of future research. It would also be very useful to report the dollar values for the income quintile breaks for each age group to know what to make of these differences. The reader is left with the feeling that just a little more information could tell us a great deal.

I share Radner's strong sense that, although wealth data are historically bad at capturing the numbers for those at the upper tail of the distribution, nonetheless a number of interesting applications are still possible. Indeed, for the very well off, the question seems merely to be, How much do they have? For lower- and middle-income families, on the other hand, wealth may serve as an important adjunct to income for meeting basic consumption needs. But I would have liked to see a more careful discussion of the exact questions that can be reasonably examined within this constraint. The implicit issue raised, I believe, is whether income comparisons across age groups are insufficient and whether, if wealth is included, our views of the relative status of age groups will change. The next step then is to begin to question what we assume people do with their wealth at all ages.

At this point, I feel compelled to quibble with Radner. His basic approach is to contrast income and wealth rather than to try to meld these two very different sources of economic well-being. Combining stocks and flows obviously poses considerable problems. To what extent are dollars of income equivalent to dollars of wealth? Radner recognizes that others have taken different approaches: generally, the decision has been whether to convert stocks into flows or vice versa to make the two sources of well-being consistent. For cross-age group comparisons—the issue of interest here—these two approaches have very different implications. An annuity approach whereby stocks are implicitly converted to flows biases the analysis in favor of higher economic status among the old since net worth is divided across shorter life expectancies. The stock approach, in contrast, favors the young. Families with workers can expect many years of future earnings that can be capitalized. Within age groups, however, either approach will yield meaningful comparisons. But, even across age groups, such comparisons have some validity if we are interested in how well-being is distributed.

Radner approximates this type of approach by looking at wealth quintiles and then at average net worth and financial assets by income quintile. But such measures do not tell us how many people change rank order within age groups. That is, we cannot tell much about how well correlated income and assets are by age group. Such information is particularly interesting to those who wish to discuss how wealth is used to supplement income in achieving economic well-being. This, I believe, is the inherent question that Radner poses in his paper, and I would, consequently, have liked for him to go into more depth.

The closest Radner comes to addressing this questions is in table 12.17 of the paper. There are some intriguing numbers here as well. Radner considers the ratio of net worth to income by income quintile by age. Here, for the oldest households, the ratios decline in the highest quintile, suggesting that wealth is less concentrated among this age group. In contrast, the ratios of net worth to income for the lowest income quintile of the age fifty-five to sixty-four age group are relatively high. To better understand the implications of these findings, it would again be useful to have the quintile income breaks for each age group rather than having to try to extrapolate from other numbers. That is, the lowest quintile of the age fifty-five to sixty-four age group probably has a much higher dollar cutoff than do those over age sixty-five. If so, this would help explain the high ratio for those at the bottom of the income distribution for this age range. The higher the income of those in the lowest quintile, the more likely is the household to have some net worth.

As usual with an interesting paper, rich in data, the author cannot possibly draw out all findings and inferences. Radner's paper instead gives us all the tools; he has packed his paper with valuable numbers that will undoubtedly remain a crucial reference for many future researchers interested in income and wealth.

13 Pension Wealth, Age-Wealth Profiles, and the Distribution of Net Worth

Ann A. McDermed, Robert L. Clark, and
Steven G. Allen

13.1 Introduction

The primary objective of this study is to develop improved estimates
of pension wealth. This will help determine how large pension wealth
is relative to other components of wealth and how consideration of
pension wealth affects measures of the distribution of income and wealth.
Data limitations have prevented a comprehensive investigation of pension wealth relative to other components of household wealth. The
1983 Survey of Consumer Finance (SCF) provides a unique opportunity to examine this issue because it contains detailed information on
household finances and both nonpension wealth, obtained from household interviews, and pension wealth, which can be calculated from
pension plan parameters obtained from employers.

We present two sets of estimates reflecting different models of the
pension contract. Under the implicit contract model of Ippolito (1985),
mean pension wealth is approximately $100,000, which represents
42.7 percent of mean net worth of households with pension coverage.
Under the explicit contract model of Bulow (1982), the estimates of

Ann A. McDermed is an assistant professor of economics and business at North
Carolina State University. Robert L. Clark is a professor of economics and business at
North Carolina State University. Steven G. Allen is a professor of economics and business at North Carolina State University and a research associate of the National Bureau
of Economic Research.

The authors gratefully acknowledge the receipt of the respondent portion of the Survey
of Consumer Finances (SCF) from Robert Avery of the Federal Reserve Board and the
pension-provider portion of the SCF from the Survey Research Center, University of
Michigan. They have benefited from helpful discussions concerning these data with
Robert Avery, Olivia Mitchell, Richard Ippolito, Cordelia Reimers, Alan Gustman, and
Thomas Steinmeier.

pension wealth are much lower; however, mean pension wealth is still approximately $50,000. When pension wealth is incorporated into estimates of the distribution of total wealth, measured inequality is reduced.

The next section of the paper defines pension wealth for defined contribution and defined benefit plans, the latter valued by both the legal and the projected earnings methods. Section 13.3 defines pension saving. Section 13.4 asks which method should be chosen to measure pension wealth. Section 13.5 reports estimates of pension wealth and saving from the SCF. Section 13.6 examines the relations among wealth, pension wealth, and age. Section 13.7 looks at the effect of including pension wealth in the distribution of wealth. Section 13.8 compares these results with those of other studies and draws some conclusions.

13.2   What Is Pension Wealth?

A worker covered by a defined benefit pension plan exchanges labor services for current earnings and the promise of future income in the form of pension benefits. The value of future pension benefits depends on the nature of the labor contract, survival probabilities, market interest rates, and government regulations. Two methods of calculating pension wealth have been proposed. These are the legal method developed by Bulow (1982) and the projected earnings method outlined in Ippolito (1985). This section defines pension wealth and examines the life-cycle pattern of pension wealth implied by pension coverage when wealth is calculated using these methods. The final part of this section describes pension wealth for workers covered by defined contribution plans, under which there is less ambiguity about the nature of the pension contract.

13.2.1   Legal Method of Calculating Pension Wealth: Defined Benefit Plans

Under the legal method of determining pension wealth, the employment contract is assumed to be valid for a single period. Of course, the contract may be renewed, but the worker acts as if he will be terminated at the end of each period. Therefore, he is willing to pay for only those pension benefits that the firm is legally required to pay if the worker leaves the firm at the end of the current period.

For any specific worker, pension wealth is calculated by finding the annual benefit that a worker would receive if he left the firm today. This benefit depends on the plan benefit formula, the extent to which the worker is vested in the plan, and, for most plans, the worker's current years of service and earnings history. Despite leaving the firm, the worker must wait until he has reached the retirement age specified in the plan actually to receive any benefits. Once started, benefits usually continue for the remainder of the worker's life. Thus, the wealth value of these benefits is found by determining the expected discounted value of a life annuity beginning at the retirement age. Pension wealth is illiquid in the sense that it cannot be sold in total or in part, but individuals may be able to borrow against this asset.

Even in this strict legal interpretation of the pension contract, there is some uncertainty as to whether the worker will receive the full value of his pension wealth. The worker could die prior to reaching the retirement age and receive no pension benefits. If the worker is married, the surviving spouse may be eligible for survivorship benefits based on the vested benefits of the worker. The firm could terminate the plan due to financial difficulties. The federally established insurance system, the Pension Benefit Guaranty Corporation, does not fully guarantee vested benefits. Finally, the real value of these future benefits depends on the rate of inflation and any postretirement increases in benefits. Despite these risks associated with the determination of legal pension wealth, we believe that pension wealth calculated in this manner should be a useful, approximate lower-bound estimate of true pension wealth.

Coverage by a pension plan produces a predictable pattern of pension wealth accumulation over the life of an individual. The magnitude of pension wealth depends on plan generosity and worker characteristics and, therefore, will vary across workers. Using the legal method, pension wealth is very low during the early working years because workers have lower earnings and little credited service and must wait many years to receive benefits. However, pension wealth rises rapidly as long as the worker remains with the firm. The growth in pension wealth is due to increased years of service, higher earnings, and a reduction in the number of years until retirement. Each of these factors accelerates the growth rate of pension wealth over time, and, as a result, the rate of growth of pension wealth will exceed the rate of growth of earnings as job tenure increases. This continues until the worker reaches the age of eligibility for retirement benefits.

If the worker remains on the job past the normal retirement age, his pension wealth in most plans will decline with continued work, and the rate of decline will accelerate with advancing age (Clark and McDermed 1986; Kotlikoff and Wise 1985). This results from the fact that most firms do not provide an actuarial increase in benefits with postponed retirement. In addition, approximately half of all pension participants are in plans that cease to credit wage and service accruals after the normal retirement age. Thus, the annual benefit may be frozen at the normal retirement age, and, with continued employment, the worker will have fewer years to receive benefits producing the decline in pension wealth.

We have constructed a simulation model to illustrate this life-cycle pattern of wealth accumulation for a worker covered by a pension plan. The worker is assumed to have been hired at age twenty-five with total compensation equaling $20,000. Total compensation, which is divided into earnings and pension compensation, grows at a rate of 5.5 percent per year. This is based on an assumed real rate of growth of 1.5 percent per year and an inflation of 4 percent per year. Pension compensation, the growth in pension wealth associated with the employment contract, is the change in pension wealth with additional service and higher earnings. It does not include the change in pension wealth associated with aging that is independent of the employment contract.

The normal retirement age is sixty-five, and the plan offers no early retirement benefits. There are no postretirement adjustments in benefits, and the plan has immediate and full vesting. The plan continues to credit fully increases in earnings and service as long as the worker remains with the firm. The benefit is determined by multiplying 0.015 times years of service times average earnings in the last five years. The market interest rate is 6 percent, and workers are assumed to face mortality probabilities as shown in the 1981 U.S. Life Table for white men (U.S. Department of Commerce 1984).

The results of the simulations are shown in table 13.1. Starting with zero pension wealth at age twenty-five, the worker's wealth rises slowly at first and reaches $13,945 at age forty. At this age, pension wealth represents about one-third of annual earnings. Between the ages of forty and sixty-five, pension wealth grows by over 100 percent per five years of work. The rate of growth of pension wealth declines slightly with age during this time. At age sixty-five, pension wealth totals $613,518, or 3.7 times annual earnings. Deflating this value to age twenty-five dollars indicates a real pension wealth at age sixty-five of $128,000. In this example, increases in earnings and service continue to raise pension wealth after age sixty-five but at a rate slower than prior to the worker reaching the age of eligibility for full pension benefits.

Several additional points need to be emphasized concerning the life-cycle pattern of pension wealth. First, a vested worker leaving a firm does not lose any of his accumulated pension wealth. However, if earnings do not rise with the job change, the worker will accumulate less additional pension wealth with the new employer than if he had remained on his initial job. Even if the worker has the same earnings and both employers have the same pension plan, wealth accumulation will be slower for the job changer because years of service at the previous job will not be credited in the pension at the new job. Second, after the worker retires, pension wealth falls systematically with advancing age due to declines in life expectancy. Unanticipated increases in the rate of inflation will also lower the pension wealth of retirees.

Table 13.1   Employee Compensation and Pension Wealth: Legal Method

Age	Tenure (years)	Earnings ($)	Pension Compensation ($)	Pension Compensation as Percentage of Total Compensation	Pension Benefit ($)	Pension Wealth ($)	Pension Savings ($)
25	0	19,959	41	.21	0	0	0
30	5	25,737	402	1.54	1,654	1,530	630
35	10	33,318	845	2.47	4,293	5,340	1,045
40	15	42,946	1,704	3.82	8,323	13,945	2,294
45	20	55,016	3,339	5.72	14,269	32,325	4,833
50	25	69,873	6,395	8.39	22,772	70,361	9,922
55	30	87,684	11,995	12.03	34,543	147,571	20,035
60	35	108,267	22,010	16.89	50,251	302,288	40,040
64	39	126,191	35,199	21.81	65,945	532,487	70,231
65	40	164,680	5,586	3.28	70,304	613,518	81,030
70	45	246,141	−23,610	−10.61	127,045	934,312	75,257

Source: Data are based on a simulation of compensation for a male worker who remains with a firm throughout his work life. He is assumed to have been hired at age 25 with total annual compensation (earnings plus pension compensation) equal to $20,000. Total compensation grows at 5.5 percent per year. The worker is covered by a pension with a normal retirement age of 65 and a benefit formula of .015 times average earnings in last five years times years of service. The market interest rate is 6 percent.

13.2.2   Projected Earnings Method of Determining Pension Wealth: Defined Benefit Plans

An alternative method of calculating pension wealth assumes that the worker and the firm enter into a long-term, implicit contract. The worker promises to remain with the firm until retirement and to perform at the agreed level of effort. The firm promises to continue to employ the worker as long as he fulfills the terms of the contract. To enforce the contract, a firm requires that workers pay for a pension value that is conditional on their remaining with the firm. The "stay pension" exceeds the pension to which workers are legally entitled, which we will call the "leave pension." Firm reputation in the labor market is assumed to be sufficient to keep the firm from reneging on its obligations.

In this model of the labor contract, workers are paid total compensation equal to their value of marginal product in each period. Compensation consists of earnings and pension compensation. The difference between this model and the legal method is that pension compensation is based on pension wealth that is conditional on the worker remaining with the firm until retirement. In each period, pension wealth is based on the plan benefit formula, current years of service, and projected earnings in the final working years just prior to retirement.

Since projected future earnings are typically greater than current earnings, the "stay pension" wealth based on projected earnings will exceed the "leave pension" wealth, which is the value derived using the legal method. Under an implicit contract, workers pay for the stay pension, but, if they quit their jobs or are laid off, they receive only the leave pension. This difference represents a capital loss in pension wealth associated with termination of employment. Thus, pension wealth based on the projected earnings method entails an additional form of risk for the worker, that is, the risk of job termination. This estimate of pension wealth should be an upper-bound estimate of the worker's true pension wealth.

Pension wealth based on the projected earnings method of calculation also follows a predictable life-cycle pattern. As long as the worker remains with a single firm, wealth rises until the age of eligibility for benefits. Compared to pension wealth based on the legal method, wealth is higher early in the work life because it is based on projected final earnings rather than actual earnings but rises more slowly with job tenure because projected final earnings do not change over time. Pension compensation drops sharply at the normal retirement age and may become negative if the worker remains with the firm. The decline after the normal retirement age is due to the ending of the implicit, long-term contract. The worker may remain with the firm after this date but is assumed to be covered by an explicit, year-by-year contract. This results in benefits and pension compensation based on the legal method and actual earnings received after the termination of the implicit contract.

If the worker leaves a job, his pension wealth drops sharply from the stay pension to the leave pension. The magnitude of this capital loss rises during the initial working years, peaks in the late forties or early fifties, and then declines. Of course, at the normal retirement age, there is no loss from leaving because the worker has completed the terms of the contract.

A simulation example can be used to illustrate the life-cycle pattern of wealth accumulation using the projected earnings method. Using the same pension and worker characteristics as described above, pension wealth at various ages is shown in table 13.2. After completing one year of work, pension wealth is $2,822. This value rises with additional years of work, and the rate of increase rises slightly with job tenure. Pension wealth is more than one year of earnings by age forty, when wealth is $51,752. Pension wealth grows by about 70 percent per five years of employment, growing to $690,677 at age sixty-five. Even though the two simulations assume that the worker has the same total compensation in each year, pension wealth at age sixty-five differs slightly. This result is from the small difference in annual earnings between the ages of sixty and sixty-four. Annual earnings are endogenously determined by the algorithm and differ throughout the work life.

Also shown in table 13.2 is the capital loss associated with leaving the job. This loss in pension wealth rises from $21,346 at age thirty-five to $105,082 at age fifty-five. The loss in pension wealth associated with job termination declines to zero at age sixty-five. A series of simulations illustrating the potential capital loss over the work life for various industry, occupation, and plan size groups are shown in Allen, Clark, and McDermed (1986).

13.2.3 Pension Wealth in Defined Contribution Plans

Pension wealth for workers covered by a defined contribution plan is equal to the value of the funds in their accounts. Each pay period, a firm using a defined contribution plan contributes a specified sum into a pension account for its workers. Employer contributions may be augmented by contributions by the employee. The funds are invested and increase over time with additional contributions and the compounding of rate of return on the funds. Future benefits are determined entirely by the magnitude of the pension fund at retirement. The firm's liability ends each period with the contribution. Thus, pension wealth at each age is equal to the value of the pension fund. Calculation of current pension wealth does not require any projection of future earnings or rates of inflation. This value is not affected by potential job

Table 13.2 Employee Compensation and Pension Wealth: Projected Earnings Method

Age	Tenure (years)	Earnings ($)	Pension Compensation ($)	Pension Compensation as Percentage of Total Compensation	Pension Benefit ($)	Pension Wealth ($)	Capital Loss ($)
25	0	18,670	1,330	6.65	0	1,330	1,330
30	5	24,353	1,786	6.83	1,562	10,717	9,272
35	10	31,762	2,401	7.03	4,074	26,414	21,346
40	15	41,415	3,234	7.24	7,969	51,752	38,399
45	20	53,982	4,373	7.49	13,853	91,835	60,452
50	25	70,303	5,964	7.82	22,564	155,076	85,357
55	30	91,432	8,247	8.27	35,245	255,654	105,082
60	35	118,664	11,612	8.91	53,434	418,048	96,610
64	39	145,802	15,587	9.66	73,290	623,494	31,700
65	40	173,397	−3,130	−1.84	79,146	690,677	0
70	45	253,590	−31,059	−13.96	134,412	988,489	0

Source: Data are based on a simulation of compensation for a male worker who remains with a firm throughout his work life. He is assumed to have been hired at age 25 with total annual compensation (earnings plus pension compensation) equal to $20,000. Total compensation grows at 5.5 percent per year. The worker is covered by a pension with a normal retirement age of 65 and a benefit of .015 times average earnings in last five years times years of service. The market interest rate is 6 percent.

changes. As such, the wealth of the worker is not subject to risks concerning job change, but the worker does bear all rate of return risks.

13.3   What Is Pension Saving?

Pension saving is the change in pension wealth from one year to the next. It includes pension compensation as well as the change in pension wealth resulting from aging. The two methods of calculating pension wealth predict somewhat different patterns of savings. Using the legal method, the dollar value of pension saving rises rapidly with increased job tenure. In addition, prior to the normal retirement age, the ratio of pension saving to total compensation also rises rapidly. Table 13.1 shows that, in our simulation example, pension savings rise from $1,045 at age thirty-five to $81,030 at age sixty-five. Using the projected earnings method, the dollar value of pension saving and the ratio of pension saving to total compensation increase with job tenure but at a slower rate than that implied by the legal method. For example, pension saving at age thirty-five is $3,435 and rises to $67,183 at age sixty-five (results are not shown in table 13.2).

13.4   Which Method Should Be Used to Measure Pension Wealth?

Both the legal and the projected earnings methods have been proposed as the appropriate procedure for estimating pension wealth. Which method best captures the nature of the pension contract? Because they yield different predictions concerning labor market behavior, the competing hypotheses can be tested. Primarily, these different predictions concern the rate of growth of earnings and the propensity of workers covered by pensions to quit. The predictions of the projected earnings method seem to conform to the reality of observed labor market influences of pensions.

Under the projected earnings method, workers stand to lose pension wealth if they leave their current employers, which is consistent with the lower quit rates observed for workers covered by pensions (Mitchell 1982; Allen, Clark, and McDermed 1986; Ippolito 1987). The legal method predicts that the growth rate of earnings for workers covered by pensions should be lower than that for other workers, whereas the projected earnings method predicts that pension coverage has no effect on the growth of earnings. The evidence (Ippolito 1985; Clark and McDermed 1988) is consistent with the latter interpretation. Another implication of the legal method is that there should be large decreases in earnings when workers become vested or become eligible for early retirement (Kotlikoff and Wise 1985). There is no evidence of such earnings behavior. In addition, many firms provide ad hoc postretirement benefit increases that can be justified only in terms of an implicit labor contract (Allen, Clark, and Sumner 1986).

Despite this tentative conclusion that the available evidence tends to support the implicit contracting theory of pension, we have calculated pension wealth using both the methods described in this paper. The legal method provides an approximate lower-bound estimate of pension wealth, and the projected earnings method provides an upper bound. By comparing the range of these estimates, we should have a reasonable estimate of the true magnitude of pension wealth.

13.5 Household Wealth and the SCF

The 1983 SCF is the latest in a series of surveys sponsored by the Federal Reserve Board (FRB) to measure the wealth holdings of households in the United States. The survey contains comprehensive data on the assets and liabilities of a representative sample of U.S. households. Additional personal and employment characteristics are included in the survey (Avery, Elliehausen, and Canner 1984a, 1984b). These data are sufficient to construct employment histories for most respondents and their spouses. The actual data tape used in this study is an early copy provided by the FRB. In addition to the household responses to the SCF, this tape also contains a series of variables constructed by the researchers at the FRB. Our analysis relies on their estimate of nonpension net wealth as well as their imputations for missing responses.

The SCF consists of two samples: a representative cross-sectional sample consisting of 3,665 usable households and a special high-income sample containing 438 households. In this paper, we report results based on the combined samples and employ weights provided by the FRB that convert the combined sample to a representation of the U.S. household population as measured by the 1980 census.

The 1983 SCF sought to gather sufficient data to allow analysts to construct the first accurate measures of pension wealth. To this end, there are numerous questions on the survey pertaining to the type and level of pension benefits. Respondents were asked whether they were covered by a pension and, if so, whether it was a defined benefit or defined contribution plan. They were asked the expected future value of benefits from a defined benefit plan and the date when they expected to begin receiving them. For defined contribution plans, they were asked the current value of their accounts. Respondents were asked about other types of thrift and profit-sharing plans. They were also asked about any pensions on past jobs from which they expected to receive a benefit. People currently receiving pension benefits were asked the annual value of their benefits. From these questions alone, a measure of pension wealth can be constructed. This approach has been used to estimate pension wealth from the Retirement History Study by Quinn (1985) and from the President's Commission on Pension Policy by Cartwright and Friedland (1985).

The distinctive feature of the SCF, however, is that data were also gathered from the pension plan sponsor concerning the plan characteristics. These data were separately coded onto a pension-provider tape, which we received from the Survey Research Center of the University of Michigan in conjunction with a Department of Labor contract. These data consist of detailed plan characteristics on the normal benefit formulas and how they apply to various types of workers. Formulas for deferred vested participants, maximum benefits, and social security offsets were also included.

To determine the value of pension benefits on respondents' and spouses' present jobs, we used these specific benefit formulas in conjunction with required respondent characteristics. The methodology used to calculate pension benefits and pension wealth is described below. This methodology is used only for persons covered by a defined benefit plan on their current jobs. The treatment of defined contribution plans on current jobs and the value of benefits on past jobs is described in a separate section.

13.5.1 Calculation of Pensions Benefits from Defined Benefit Plans on Current Jobs

The calculation of pension benefits for defined benefit plans from the pension-provider data required that the benefit formulas as coded in the data be converted to computational algorithms. Most plans had several normal retirement and deferred vesting formulas that applied to different types of workers or applied to different periods of employment. These formulas were often linear combinations and frequently required one to assess relative values from alternative combinations of formulas. Eight of the plans had formulas that were integrated with formulas from other plans. These plans were eliminated from the analysis.

The next step was to apply the algorithms to particular individuals. Work and salary histories were constructed from the household data. The value of years of service used in the algorithms was determined from current job tenure as reported by respondents. Salary histories and earnings projections were based on two alternative assumptions about real earnings growth: a constant 5.5 percent annual growth rate, reflecting 1.5 percent economy-wide real wage growth and 4 percent inflation (CGE), and the FRB estimate of expected annual occupation-specific real wage growth controlled for industry, age, race, and sex (FGE). The FRB estimate also assumes that earnings grow 5.5 percent per year in addition to the occupation-specific component. Specifically, each person was assigned age-related earnings growth rates for ages younger than thirty-five, thirty-five to fifty-four, and fifty-five and over. These rates vary across the sample by race, sex, industry, and occupation. FRB estimates of these occupation-specific rates were not available for the high-income sample.

Legal pension wealth based on an explicit labor contract is calculated from benefits the worker would receive if the worker left the firm today. Workers who are vested and leave a job are legally entitled to receive a benefit based on the deferred vested benefit formulas rather than on the normal benefit formulas. Thus, all benefits using the legal method of determining pension wealth are based on the deferred vested benefit data and assume that the person begins benefits at the worker's expected retirement age. Vesting status was determined from worker characteristics provided in the respondent data and vesting requirements reported in the pension-provider data. For salary-based formulas, earnings histories of the appropriate length were constructed for each of the assumptions described above. Service years were current job tenure in 1983. Workers who were not currently vested were assumed to have zero legal pension wealth.

For the projected earnings method, workers were assumed to remain with their current employers until their expected retirement ages as given in the respondent interviews. Therefore, projected earnings wealth was based on the normal retirement formulas provided by the firm. If the worker was not eligible for normal benefits at the reported retirement age, the worker was assumed to retire at the earliest age of eligibility for normal benefits. Benefits in this method were based on earnings projected to retirement and current years of service. Projected earnings wealth was calculated under each of the two assumptions about earnings growth.

Each plan was checked to see if it had a maximum benefit formula or was integrated with social security. If the plan had a maximum benefit, then the benefit as calculated was restricted to this maximum. Social security integration is done either by excess formulas that pay a higher fraction of earnings above the social security wage base than for earnings below it or by reducing the pension benefit by some fraction of the social security benefit.

For the excess method, we projected the social security maximum taxable earnings to grow at 5.5 percent per year (this is the assumption used in the intermediate projections of the Social Security Administration). We then calculated the average wage base that firms can legally use in conjunction with the excess method. The plan formula indicates whether this level or some other level will be used. We assumed that the excess formula will not be revised during the respondent's work life.

The offset plans required us to calculate the social security benefit that the worker expects to receive at retirement. Social security reductions were based on projected social security benefits at the expected retirement age. We assumed that the current social security offsets in the pension benefit formulas would apply when the worker retired. Using the two growth assumptions, earnings were projected to rise from their current level until retirement. This work history was then used to calculate the worker's social security primary insurance amount (PIA).

We assumed that the social security benefit formula would not be revised but that, as in 1983, the bend points of the formula would rise with the rate of growth of taxable earnings. Earnings prior to age sixty were indexed by the maximum taxable earnings at age sixty-two, while earnings after age sixty-two were indexed by the rate of growth of prices. The social security benefit calculated by this method was then introduced into the benefit formula. In most plans, the offset is some fraction of the social security benefit that varies with earnings or years of service subject to a maximum offset. In this analysis, we have ignored the future changes in social security that were adopted in 1983.

13.5.2 Calculation of Pension Benefits for Defined Contribution Plans and for Past Jobs

In defined contribution plans, the firm and/or the employee contribute a specified amount each pay period into an employee account. Benefits at retirement are based on the amount of funds in the account. At any point in time, pension wealth is the value of the employee's account. While there are data on the pension-provider tape for defined contribution plans, this information is less useful in determining future pension benefits. We could have used these data along with assumptions concerning past contribution rates, rates of growth of earnings, and rates of return to the pension fund to estimate the current value of the pension account.

Instead, we relied on answers to questions on the respondent tape concerning the current value of the pension account. It is likely that most of the people covered by defined contribution plans receive some type of annual statement concerning the current value of their pension accounts. The estimate of this form of pension wealth requires only this knowledge; it specifically does not require the respondent to forecast future rates of growth in wages and prices; nor does it necessitate any evaluation of the prospects of leaving the firm. Therefore, we take the respondent's own evaluation of current pension wealth as the best estimate of its true value. All missing values concerning the funds in the defined contribution accounts were imputed by researchers at the FRB. Since we are interested in pension wealth, we did not convert the value of the pension account into any implied future benefit.

Many respondents and their spouses expect to receive benefits from pensions on previous jobs. For the most part, the pension-provider tape does not contain information on the plan characteristics of pensions on past jobs. However, individuals were asked about the pension benefits they expected to receive from past jobs. We assumed that the respondents gave the value of benefits that they expected to receive at retirement. For past jobs, this may be a reasonably accurate estimate. Having already left the job, the nominal benefit at retirement will not be affected by any further work; nor will it be influenced by future earnings or inflation. Departing workers may also have been told the benefit to expect in their exit interviews with the firm. If respondents answered that they were covered by a pension on their current jobs but did not know either coverage or expected benefits from past jobs, we assigned them their pension wealth from their current job alone.

13.5.3   Missing Values for Pension Benefits

Some respondents reported that either they or their spouse were covered by a pension on their current jobs, but there are no data for these plans on the pension-provider tape. For these workers, we imputed the value of their pension benefit. A pension benefit equation was estimated for persons covered by a pension on their present job and for whom we had calculated a benefit using the procedure described above. The results from four regression equations are shown in table 13.3. The equations are for two benefits using the legal method and

Table 13.3   Pension Benefit Equations for Persons Currently Working and Covered by a Defined Benefit Plan

	Legal		Projected	
Variable	CGE[a]	FGE[b]	CGE[c]	FGE[d]
Intercept	−9.44***	−6.89***	1.61	1.72
	(1.51)	(2.11)	(1.11)	(1.37)
Construction	.43	.31	−1.11***	−1.13***
	(.91)	(1.11)	(.35)	(.41)
Manufacturing	−.45	−.63	−.51**	−.43*
	(.33)	(.41)	(.21)	(.23)
Transportation, communications	−.49	−.58	−.37	−.18
	(.36)	(.45)	(.23)	(.27)
Wholesale and retail trade	−1.04***	−.90*	−.07	.14
	(.41)	(.50)	(.26)	(.30)
Finance, insurance, real estate	−1.57***	−1.48***	−.50*	−.52
	(.42)	(.55)	(.28)	(.33)

Table 13.3   (continued)

Variable	Legal		Projected	
	CGE[a]	FGE[b]	CGE[c]	FGE[d]
Personal and repair services	− .52 (.60)	− .79 (.76)	− .80 (.31)	− .63 (.36)
Professional services	− .09 (.35)	− .21 (.44)	.07 (.22)	.24 (.24)
Public administration	.06 (.36)	.02 (.45)	.11 (.23)	.26 (.25)
Managers, administrators	− .35* (.18)	− .67*** (.23)	.19 (.15)	.07 (.17)
Sales and clerical	− .19 (.17)	− .39* (.22)	− .15 (.13)	− .20 (.15)
Craftsmen, protective services	− .33* (.19)	− .33 (.23)	− .22 (.15)	− .15 (.17)
Operatives, laborers	− .32* (.19)	− .54** (.24)	− .64*** (.13)	− .52*** (.15)
Log (age)	.76*** (.27)	.74** (.35)	− 1.37*** (.18)	− 1.17*** (.21)
Log (tenure)	.97*** (.13)	1.03*** (.17)	.87*** (.05)	.90*** (.06)
Log (salary)	1.26*** (.11)	1.02*** (.16)	1.05*** (.09)	.92*** (.11)
R^2	.63	.53	.52	.46

Source: Benefit data are from the pension-provider portion of the SCF for all persons covered by a defined benefit plan on their current job. Other variables for each individual are from the household portion of the SCF.

Note: Dependent variable is the natural logarithm of pension benefit as calculated by each of two methods using one of two earnings growth assumptions. The omitted industrial group is agriculture, forestry, fishing, and mining. The omitted occupational group is professional, technical, and kindred workers. Standard errors are in parentheses.

[a]Pension benefit is calculated using the legal method assuming a constant 5.5 percent growth in annual earnings.

[b]Pension benefit is calculated using the legal method assuming the individual specific growth rate in earnings derived by the FRB.

[c]Pension benefit is calculated using the projected earnings method assuming a constant 5.5 percent growth in annual earnings.

[d]Pension benefit is calculated using the projected earnings method assuming the individual specific growth rate in earnings derived by the FRB.

*Coefficient is statistically significant at the 10 percent confidence level.

**Coefficient is statistically significant at the 5 percent confidence level.

***Coefficient is statistically significant at the 1 percent confidence level.

two benefits using the projected earnings method. The benefits for each method are based on our two assumptions concerning the rate of growth of earnings. The FGE benefit equations are estimated using respondents only from the cross-sectional sample since salary projections were not made by the FRB for the high-income sample.

These benefit equations are interesting in their own right. To our knowledge, they are the first estimates of pension benefits based on a large sample of data combining actual worker and plan characteristics. Explanatory variables include a series of industry and occupational dichotomous variables along with age, job tenure, and salary. The relatively few statistically significant differences among the industry and occupational coefficients is somewhat surprising; however, it should be remembered that we controlled for salary and tenure differences.

When benefits are estimated using a constant 5.5 percent per year growth in earnings (CGE), the elasticity of benefits with respect to job tenure is slightly less than one, while the elasticity of benefits with respect to salary is slightly greater than one. These values hold for both the legal and the projected methods of calculating benefits. The relative values of these two elasticities is reversed in the equations that are based on the FRB earnings growth assumptions; however, all eight of the estimates for these two variables are relatively close to one. Only the parameter estimate for salary in the legal CGE equation and the parameter estimate for tenure in the projected earnings CGE equation are statistically significantly different from one at the .05 level of significance.

If the benefit formula were a simple multiplicative, earnings-based formula, then both the tenure and the salary elasticities should be one. The existence of social security offsets tends to make benefits rise by more than a proportional percentage in response to salary increases, while maximum benefits would tend to make the tenure and salary elasticities less than one. The negative age elasticities in the equations for projected benefits follow from the construction of the benefit. Holding salary and tenure constant, the projected benefit will be lower for older workers as long as the growth rate of earnings is positive.

Benefits from defined benefit pensions on the current job for persons with missing values were imputed from these regression equations and the individual and firm characteristics. Persons with missing data concerning the value of benefits from past jobs are given the mean value of this type of pension benefit for similar types of workers.

13.5.4 Summary of Pension Benefit Data

There are 2,304 households in the sample who are covered by a pension on a current or past job. This represents 56.2 percent of the unweighted households and 54.8 percent of the weighted households.

Of these households, 1,592 have at least one family member who is a participant in a defined benefit plan on his current job. We were able to derive pension benefits using the plan-specific data for 889 of these households. Therefore, we imputed pension benefits for 703 households. Pension-provider data were not available for these households because the interviewers were unable to locate the firm, there were no summary plan descriptions available, or for some other reason the firm interview was not completed.

Pension wealth from defined contribution plans was determined for 236 households, and pension wealth from past jobs was derived for 740 households. A household could, of course, have wealth from one or more of these sources. Persons with thrift plans or profit-sharing plans are not included in these counts; however, the value in these accounts as given by the respondents is included in pension wealth.

13.5.5 Calculation of Pension Wealth

For defined benefit plans, we converted the value of the pension benefit into a wealth value calculating the value of a life annuity beginning at the age of expected retirement as indicated by the respondent. Benefits were assumed to remain fixed in nominal terms, and the interest (or discount) rate was set at 6 percent. The 1981 mortality rates by race and sex were used to determine survival probabilities. Pensions were assumed to have no death benefits. As noted above, respondents with defined contribution plans were assumed to have accurately reported their pension wealth. Pension wealth is the sum of all defined contribution and defined benefit values from current and past jobs as well as withdrawable amounts in thrift-type accounts.

13.5.6 Calculation of Pension Savings

Pension savings is calculated only for persons who are currently working on a job and are participating in a defined benefit pension plan. For these workers, pension savings was calculated by estimating current pension wealth as described above and subtracting this value from pension wealth one year later. Pension wealth in the succeeding year was calculated by increasing job tenure by one year and increasing the salary average based on the two estimates of earnings growth. This method combines the gain in wealth attributable to an additional year of work (pension compensation) and the gain in wealth due to surviving an extra year and being closer to retirement age. We have not calculated similar values for persons covered by defined contribution plans. For these workers, savings equal new contributions and the return to the pension fund. Neither have we calculated savings for persons with pensions on past jobs. Savings from a pension on a past job is solely attributable to surviving an extra year and being closer to the retirement age.

13.6 Wealth, Pension Wealth, and Age

Since the early development of life-cycle saving theory, economists have predicted that household wealth will tend to be relatively low early in life, rise during the middle years, and then decline during the final years of life. Evidence on the life-cycle accumulation of wealth has typically been from cross-sectional data and has focused exclusively on nonpension wealth. In this section, we present a comprehensive assessment of pension wealth along with nonpension wealth using data from the 1983 SCF. It is important to remember that these data represent wealth at a particular point in time for different cohorts of households and are not a true measure of the effect of aging for a single cohort.

13.6.1 Nonpension Wealth

Our measure of nonpension wealth is a variable that was created by researchers at the FRB. It represents the net value of all paper and other financial assets, equity in the respondent's home and other property, the net value of vehicles and boats, and net worth of any businesses or farms. This measure is compiled by examining the response to numerous questions concerning family assets and liabilities and is intended to represent the standard concept of net household wealth.

Estimates of nonpension net wealth are shown in table 13.4 for all households in the SCF along with separate estimates for households with pension wealth and those without pension wealth. For all three

Table 13.4   **Mean Nonpension Wealth by Age and Pension Status (dollars)**

Age	All Households	Households with Pensions	Households without Pensions
Younger than 25	6,342	10,292	4,842
25–34	31,735	29,731	34,412
35–44	82,181	75,993	94,179
45–54	188,503	188,170	189,122
55–64	196,492	208,896	177,111
65–74	222,514	293,829	163,652
Older than 74	119,639	200,270	87,220
All households	118,419	132,047	101,862
Number of households in sample	4,103	2,304	1,799

Source: Weighted household wealth data from the SCF.

samples, mean nonpension wealth is less than $10,300 for households with respondents under the age of twenty-five. It rises to $30,000 and above for households aged twenty-five to thirty-four. Nonpension wealth then more than doubles across each of the next two ten-year age groups. This form of wealth continues to increase slightly across the next two groups before declining sharply for the oldest age group. For all age groups except those aged forty-five to fifty-four, these estimates are between fifty and seventy-eight percent higher than estimates of net worth presented by Avery, Elliehausen, and Canner (1984b), which estimates excluded the value of consumer durables such as automobiles and home furnishings, the cash value of life insurance, and equity in small businesses and farms.

Studies by Munnell (1974, 1976) and Feldstein (1974, 1982) initiated a debate on the effect of social security and private pensions on the magnitude of private savings. A number of studies followed these early papers, but, to date, this literature has produced no clear picture concerning the elasticity of private savings with respect to pension savings. The data that we have constructed from the SCF will provide a useful new source for testing these hypotheses. As of yet, we have not attempted to estimate savings response to pension coverage and pension savings. The data in table 13.4 indicate that the mean nonpension wealth of persons with pension wealth is not lower than that of persons with no such wealth. In fact, nonpension wealth is considerably higher for households with pension wealth than for those without pension wealth for all ages over fifty-five; however, Z-statistics indicate that nonpension wealth for households covered by a pension is not statistically different for any of the age groups from the wealth of those not covered by a pension.

13.6.2   Pension Wealth and Total Net Wealth: Legal Method

Estimates of legal pension wealth using the two earnings growth assumptions are presented in table 13.5. At all ages, the two estimates are very similar. Holding constant the interest rate, it seems reasonable to conclude that legal pension wealth is relatively insensitive to the earnings growth rate assumption within a fairly wide range of growth rates. This is due to two effects. First, some pension wealth is from past jobs or defined contribution plans, and therefore our earnings assumption, does not enter into the calculation of pension wealth. Second, most plans use relatively few years of earnings to determine the salary average in the benefit calculation. Thus, the earnings histories based on the different growth assumptions are not very different.

As expected, legal pension wealth is quite small early in life, rises rapidly during the working years, and declines with advancing age. For workers younger than twenty-five, mean pension wealth is approximately

Table 13.5   Wealth Estimates: Legal Method (dollars)

	Pension Wealth Households with Pensions		Net Worth						Percentage of Households with Pension
			All Households		Households without Pensions	Households with Pensions			
Age	CGE	FGE	CGE	FGE		CGE	FGE		
Younger than 25	1,951	2,007	6,879	6,894	4,842	12,243	12,299		27.5
25–34	6,899	6,850	35,612	35,584	34,412	36,659	36,609		57.2
35–44	20,383	24,481	98,924	98,329	94,179	101,371	100,469		66.0
45–54	70,764	63,451	230,128	225,362	189,122	258,934	251,621		65.0
55–64	121,183	116,498	270,380	267,523	177,111	330,079	325,395		61.0
65–74	55,060	55,066	247,411	247,413	163,652	348,888	348,894		45.2
Older than 74	25,522	25,651	126,958	126,995	87,220	225,792	225,921		28.7
All households	47,541	45,180	143,837	142,541	100,261	179,642	177,281		54.8

Source: Weighted pension wealth data derived for households in the SCF and weighted nonpension wealth from the household portion of the SCF.

$2,000. Wealth triples across each of the next two ten-year age groups, to stand at over $60,000 for the cohort aged forty-five to fifty-four. Pension wealth then almost doubles for the next cohort so that wealth is over $115,000 for the cohort aged fifty-five to sixty-four. After sixty-five, pension wealth declines sharply.

Net worth is the sum of nonpension and pension wealth for each household, and the mean values are shown in the last five columns of table 13.5. The middle of these columns represents net worth for households without pensions. For these families, total net worth is identical to nonpension wealth. Net worth is also presented for all households and for households with some pension wealth. Net worth for households with some pension wealth exceeds the net wealth of the no pension households at all ages. Between the ages of fifty-five and seventy-four, wealth of the pension households is almost twice that of the nonpension households.

13.6.3   Pension Wealth and Net Worth: Projected Earnings Method

Pension wealth under the projected earnings method is shown in table 13.6. The CGE pension wealth is over $14,000 for households with heads younger than age twenty-five using the projected earnings method, compared to only $1,900 with the legal method. Instead of tripling across the first two age groups, the projected pension wealth only doubles. Slower growth is also observed across the middle working years. Wealth for the oldest age groups is virtually identical for the two methods. This follows from the fact that most of these households are currently receiving benefits and are not still working.

There are greater differences between the CGE and the FGE estimates under the implicit contracting model than were observed with legal pension wealth. This follows from the longer forward projection of earnings in the implicit contract model as compared to the relatively short backward projections done in conjunction with the legal method. These differences vary between 22 and 28 percent for households under the age of forty-five but are less than 4 percent for households aged fifty-five to sixty-four. Since most people are retired after the age of sixty-five, the wealth estimates for these two assumptions are approximately equal at these older ages.

Since pension wealth is higher using the projected earnings method, net worth is also higher with this method, compared to the legal method. The CGE wealth for all households rises from $10,000 for households under the age of twenty-five to approximately $120,000 for those aged thirty-five to forty-four. Net worth peaks for households aged fifty-five to sixty-four at about $358,000 and then declines for the older households. The implicit contract method of evaluating pension wealth results

Table 13.6 **Wealth Estimates: Projected Earnings Method (dollars)**

| | Pension Wealth, Households with Pensions | | Net Worth | | | | | |
| | | | All Households | | Households without Pensions | Households with Pensions | |
Age	CGE	FGE	CGE	FGE		CGE	FGE
Younger than 25	14,862	12,177	10,432	9,693	4,842	25,154	22,469
25–34	22,923	17,785	44,792	41,848	34,412	52,683	47,544
35–44	57,083	44,530	119,837	111,555	94,179	133,072	120,519
45–54	152,315	79,684	283,277	235,941	189,122	340,485	267,853
55–64	264,702	255,286	357,887	352,146	177,111	473,598	464,183
65–74	54,344	53,249	247,087	246,592	163,652	348,173	347,078
Older than 74	24,122	23,631	126,556	126,415	87,220	224,392	223,901
All households	98,291	78,792	171,696	160,992	100,261	230,392	210,893

Source: Weighted pension wealth data derived for households in the SCF and weighted nonpension wealth from the household portion of the SCF.

in much higher net worth for persons with pension wealth at all ages compared to households with no pension wealth.

13.6.4 Pension Wealth as a Percentage of Total Wealth

The data presented in tables 13.4–13.6 illustrate that pension wealth is relatively small early in life and grows until the retirement years. This pattern of wealth accumulation is similar to that for nonpension wealth. Table 13.7 shows the mean value for pension wealth as a percentage of mean total wealth by the age of the household head. The first part of the table shows that, for all households younger than twenty-five, legal pension wealth is about 8 percent of total wealth, as compared to over 34 percent for the projected earnings method. Legal pension wealth as a percent of total wealth rises with age until the fifty-five to sixty-four age group, for which pension wealth represents 27 percent of total wealth. For the projected earnings method, pension wealth varies between 22 and 35 percent of total net worth

Table 13.7   **Pension Wealth as a Percentage of Total Wealth**

| | All Households | | | |
| | Legal | | Projected | |
Age	CGE	FGE	CGE	FGE
Younger than 25	7.8	8.0	39.2	34.6
25–34	11.1	11.0	29.3	24.3
35–44	16.9	16.4	31.4	26.3
45–54	20.0	18.3	35.0	22.0
55–64	27.3	26.6	45.1	44.2
65–74	10.1	10.1	9.9	9.8
Older than 74	5.8	5.8	5.5	5.4
All households	18.1	17.4	31.4	26.9
	Households with Pensions			
Younger than 25	15.9	16.3	59.1	54.2
25–34	18.8	18.7	43.5	37.4
35–44	25.0	24.4	42.9	36.9
45–54	27.3	25.2	44.7	29.7
55–64	36.7	35.8	55.9	55.0
65–74	15.8	15.8	15.6	15.3
Older than 74	11.3	11.4	10.8	10.6
All households	26.5	25.5	42.7	37.4

Source: Weighted pension wealth data derived for households in the SCF and weighted nonpension wealth from the household portion of the SCF.

for all ages prior to fifty-five and increases to over 44 percent of total net worth for the fifty-five to sixty-four group.

Looking only at households with pensions, pension wealth is, of course, a larger proportion of total net worth. In these households, the fraction of wealth that is due to pension wealth is about 16 percent for the youngest households for the legal method. This ratio rises with household age until the fifty-five to sixty-four age group, for which the proportion of wealth due to pensions reaches approximately 37 percent. The fraction of total net worth due to pension wealth using the projected earnings method is more variable. The ratio drops from 59 percent for the youngest households to 54 percent for households aged forty-five to fifty-four before rising slightly for those aged fifty-five to sixty-four.

13.6.5   Pension Savings

These data also permitted us to calculate pension savings or the change in pension wealth. This was done only for persons who were currently working and covered by a defined benefit plan. Pension savings was calculated by finding the change in pension wealth from last year to this year. These values are reported in table 13.8 for both the earnings growth assumptions and both the legal and projected earnings methods of evaluating pension wealth. Legal pension savings are very low at the youngest ages and rise steeply until retirement. Savings under the implicit contract model are larger at all ages, but they increase at a slower rate across the age groups.

In summary, both of these methods of calculating pension wealth clearly indicate that pension wealth is an important component of total wealth. Ignoring pension wealth substantially understates total wealth

Table 13.8   Pension Savings among Households Participating in a Defined Benefit Plan (dollars)

Age	Legal		Projected	
	CGE	FGE	CGE	FGE
Younger than 25	244	284	2,658	1,881
25–34	303	321	1,972	1,420
35–44	1,044	1,060	5,997	4,570
45–54	2,224	2,263	5,340	4,372
55–64	4,747	4,888	6,940	5,738
65–74	4,623	4,451	3,829	3,210
Older than 74	0	0	0	0
All households	1,994	2,017	4,512	3,573

Source: Pension savings data as derived using pension wealth from the pension-provider portion of the SCF.

and can lead to incorrect inferences concerning the distribution of wealth. This latter point is examined in the next section.

13.7   Distribution of Wealth

The preceding sections have described the magnitude of pension wealth by age of the head of household. This analysis indicated that pension wealth is a major component of the net worth of households, with slightly over half the households having some pension coverage. The effect of including pension wealth in an analysis of the distribution of household wealth is an unresolved question. Tables 13.9–13.17 present income distribution data for nonpension wealth, pension wealth, and net worth. These tables show the wealth value at various percentile rankings for each distribution by age of the head of household. For example, the zeroth percentile represents the minimum value in the wealth distribution, the fiftieth percentile is median wealth, and the hundredth percentile is the maximum wealth value. We present distributions for both the legal and the projected earning methods of calculating pension wealth, using the CGE assumptions.

Table 13.9 shows the nonpension wealth for all households by age groups. These data indicate that the median nonpension wealth in the United States in 1983 was $38,300. The values at the various percentiles illustrate the same age-wealth pattern as observed for the mean wealth values in table 13.4.

Tables 13.10 and 13.11 show the nonpension wealth distribution for households with and without pension coverage. These data, along with the mean values shown in table 13.4, indicate that median households with pension coverage have more nonpension wealth than median households with no pension coverage. Median nonpension wealth for all households with pension coverage is $51,600 but is only $18,000 for households without pension coverage. The wealth distribution of households with pensions is more compact, as indicated by the range of the distributions. Households with pensions have higher minimum values and lower maximum values of wealth than do households without pensions. On balance, households with pension coverage have greater nonpension wealth, and this wealth seems to be more equally distributed than the wealth of households without pension coverage.

Tables 13.12 and 13.13 show the distribution of pension wealth for households with pension coverage as estimated using the CGE assumptions. Using the legal method, household pension wealth is zero for unvested workers on current jobs and without pension wealth from other jobs. Over 10 percent of all households and 25 percent of the younger households are in this category. Using the projected earnings method, pension wealth is zero only during the first year of employment.

Table 13.9   **Nonpension Wealth Distribution by Age: All Households (thousands of dollars)**

Age	0 Percent	10 Percent	25 Percent	50 Percent	75 Percent	95 Percent	100 Percent
Younger than 25	−23.2	−3.7	−.7	.2	5.7	33.2	167.4
25–34	−52.0	−2.5	.0	7.1	33.8	148.0	15,497.0
35–44	−44.8	−.2	7.9	41.2	104.4	809.6	53,572.5
45–54	−9.9	.1	21.1	63.0	205.3	2,689.7	71,993.0
55–64	−73.4	1.0	27.8	88.7	409.5	5,149.5	86,820.5
65–74	−40.0	2.9	25.6	78.4	370.2	4,729.8	51,079.0
Older than 74	−2.7	.2	7.3	44.3	137.5	4,594.4	35,033.1
All households	−73.4	−.4	3.1	38.3	123.0	2,231.7	86,820.5

Source: Weighted household wealth data from the SCF.

Table 13.10   Nonpension Wealth Distribution by Age: Households with Pensions (thousands of dollars)

Age	0 Percent	10 Percent	25 Percent	50 Percent	75 Percent	95 Percent	100 Percent
Younger than 25	−23.2	−4.3	−1.4	1.8	16.2	33.2	167.4
25–34	−52.0	−2.6	.0	11.7	35.9	110.7	2,632.9
35–44	−44.8	.3	12.9	45.3	101.8	704.6	6,471.8
45–54	−9.9	3.4	30.6	74.1	212.0	3,484.6	58,690.6
55–64	−6.0	13.1	48.2	104.9	554.8	5,418.2	32,142.3
65–74	−3.3	15.7	47.0	114.0	687.9	5,165.8	51,079.0
Older than 74	−2.7	8.7	36.8	90.1	210.3	7,279.7	25,127.3
All households	−52.0	.0	12.8	51.6	145.4	2,764.0	58,690.6

Source: Weighted household wealth data from the SCF.

Table 13.11 Nonpension Wealth Distribution by Age: Households without Pensions (thousands of dollars)

Age	0 Percent	10 Percent	25 Percent	50 Percent	75 Percent	95 Percent	100 Percent
Younger than 25	−11.0	−3.7	−.6	.1	3.3	35.2	132.9
25–34	−39.9	−2.4	−.1	2.0	30.3	192.0	15,497.0
35–44	−11.8	−.9	.1	30.4	120.5	1,366.6	53,572.5
45–54	−7.9	.0	2.6	42.1	203.8	1,997.6	71,993.0
55–64	−73.4	.0	5.4	51.2	260.1	4,397.1	86,820.5
65–74	−40.0	.5	12.0	56.2	225.7	2,654.6	41,530.2
Older than 74	−1.7	.0	3.2	29.9	91.2	2,926.8	35,033.1
All households	−73.4	−.7	.1	18.0	92.0	1,563.4	86,820.5

Source: Weighted household wealth data from the SCF.

Table 13.12   Pension Wealth Distribution by Age: Households with Pensions, Legal CGE (thousands of dollars)

Age	0 Percent	10 Percent	25 Percent	50 Percent	75 Percent	95 Percent	100 Percent
Younger than 25	.0	.0	.0	.2	2.0	9.0	29.1
25–34	.0	.0	.0	1.8	7.3	35.8	141.9
35–44	.0	.0	2.0	11.6	29.2	152.0	1,158.8
45–54	.0	.0	12.4	39.8	114.3	492.8	5,338.2
55–64	.0	7.3	33.0	80.7	195.3	879.1	17,289.3
65–74	.7	7.0	19.5	44.3	122.6	552.6	3,564.7
Older than 74	.8	2.6	6.3	20.9	42.1	245.7	900.0
All households	.0	.0	2.2	17.7	66.6	383.2	17,289.3

Source: Weighted pension wealth data derived from the pension-provider portion of the SCF.

Table 13.13   **Pension Wealth Distribution by Age: Households with Pensions Projected Earnings CGE (thousands of dollars)**

Age	0 Percent	10 Percent	25 Percent	50 Percent	75 Percent	95 Percent	100 Percent
Younger than 25	.0	.0	.7	3.0	6.7	109.2	270.9
25–34	.0	.9	3.5	9.1	24.2	104.1	330.3
35–44	.0	2.5	8.9	25.5	73.1	300.5	5,941.1
45–54	.0	4.0	19.8	59.4	162.1	905.0	94,079.9
55–64	.0	10.2	32.4	86.9	230.7	1,261.4	44,678.6
65–74	.7	7.0	19.6	44.8	116.1	560.2	5,381.7
Older than 74	.8	2.6	6.3	20.9	42.1	245.7	900.0
All households	.0	2.1	8.7	30.6	100.3	486.2	94,079.9

Source: Weighted pension wealth data derived from the pension-provider portion of the SCF.

Table 13.14   Net Worth Distribution by Age: All Households, Legal CGE (thousands of dollars)

Age	0 Percent	10 Percent	25 Percent	50 Percent	75 Percent	95 Percent	100 Percent
Younger than 25	−21.7	−3.6	−.6	.3	6.3	34.5	169.4
25–34	−51.2	−1.9	.0	9.6	39.6	165.8	15,497.0
35–44	−44.6	.0	13.2	51.3	130.7	1,013.2	53,572.5
45–54	−7.9	2.5	33.7	103.0	292.3	3,039.6	71,993.0
55–64	−73.4	5.5	51.7	160.8	572.6	5,896.7	86,820.5
65–74	−40.0	8.1	34.6	98.2	414.8	5,162.2	51,627.4
Older than 74	−1.9	.2	8.5	52.0	143.6	4,594.4	35,033.1
All households	−73.4	.0	6.6	49.8	169.2	2,463.2	86,820.5

Source: Weighted pension and nonpension wealth data derived from the SCF.

Table 13.15   Net Worth Distribution by Age: All Households, Projected Earnings CGE (thousands of dollars)

Age	0 Percent	10 Percent	25 Percent	50 Percent	75 Percent	95 Percent	100 Percent
Younger than 25	−21.7	−2.8	−.5	.4	8.5	49.7	269.0
25–34	−51.3	−1.1	.7	15.3	52.6	206.0	15,497.0
35–44	−44.6	.5	20.2	67.7	164.4	1,063.5	53,572.5
45–54	−7.9	3.2	40.3	116.1	353.2	3,553.8	95,071.3
55–64	−73.4	7.0	51.9	161.0	595.9	6,184.7	86,820.5
65–74	−40.0	8.1	34.6	100.0	408.3	4,923.3	51,627.4
Older than 74	−1.9	.2	8.5	52.0	143.6	4,594.4	35,033.1
All households	−73.4	.0	9.6	57.9	195.9	2,557.6	95,071.3

Source: Weighted pension and nonpension wealth data derived from the SCF.

Table 13.16   Net Worth Distribution by Age: Households with Pension, Legal CGE (thousands of dollars)

Age	0 Percent	10 Percent	25 Percent	50 Percent	75 Percent	95 Percent	100 Percent
Younger than 25	−21.7	−3.6	−2.2	3.8	19.2	34.3	169.4
25–34	−51.3	−1.4	3.0	18.3	45.6	152.1	2,703.4
35–44	−44.6	6.1	25.5	63.5	133.2	796.4	7,630.6
45–54	−2.2	23.1	57.3	128.9	343.2	3,904.3	58,919.7
55–64	−.8	48.8	102.3	234.0	882.6	6,418.9	34,586.7
65–74	9.4	38.7	79.1	158.3	827.4	5,570.5	51,627.4
Older than 74	−1.9	20.3	57.6	115.4	230.0	7,537.2	25,544.3
All households	−51.3	4.0	24.8	84.5	229.5	3,214.0	58,919.8

Source: Weighted pension and nonpension wealth data derived from the SCF.

Table 13.17 Net Worth Distribution by Age: Households with Pensions, Projected Earnings CGE (thousands of dollars)

Age	0 Percent	10 Percent	25 Percent	50 Percent	75 Percent	95 Percent	100 Percent
Younger than 25	−21.7	−1.6	.4	7.7	27.8	156.4	269.0
25–34	−51.3	1.9	8.9	27.4	66.4	207.0	2,731.8
35–44	−44.6	12.3	35.1	87.9	181.0	920.4	12,412.9
45–54	−3.6	30.5	76.4	144.1	436.2	4,008.2	95,071.3
55–64	.3	50.3	107.8	270.0	926.7	6,667.0	44,699.2
65–74	9.4	38.7	79.1	159.0	827.4	5,968.5	51,627.4
Older than 74	−1.9	20.3	57.6	115.4	230.0	7,537.2	25,544.3
All households	−51.3	9.1	33.8	99.2	277.3	3,340.3	95,071.3

Source: Weighted pension and nonpension wealth data derived from the SCF.

Therefore, only a small proportion of households will have no pension wealth under this criterion.

Median legal pension wealth for all households with pension coverage is $17,700, and the wealth at the ninety-fifth percentile is $383,200. This compares to a median projected earnings pension wealth of $30,600 and a value of $486,200 at the ninety-fifth percentile. These numbers indicate that approximately 42 percent of the pension wealth of a household at the middle of the wealth distribution is contingent on continued employment at the present job. The wealth loss associated with job termination is $12,900 out of the $30,600 in pension wealth shown by the projected earnings method.

Tables 13.14 and 13.15 give the distribution of total net worth for households using the legal and projected earnings methods of determining pension wealth. Adding legal pension wealth to other wealth raises the median net worth for all families from $38,300 (table 13.9) to $49,800 (table 13.14). Using the projected earnings method, median net worth increases to $57,900. Including pension wealth in the analysis primarily raises the wealth of households between the twenty-fifth and the ninety-fifth percentiles of the nonpension wealth distribution. For the most part, very poor and very rich households have relatively little pension wealth.

Tables 13.16 and 13.17 show the net worth distribution for households with pension coverage. These data can be compared to the distribution in table 13.10 to assess the effect of pension wealth on the wealth distribution of only those households with pension coverage. Median wealth for these households is raised from $51,600 ignoring pension wealth to $84,500 using the legal method and $99,200 with the projected earnings method. The effect of including pension wealth has similar effects on the distribution of wealth by age as described above for all households.

These preceding analyses clearly indicate the importance of pension wealth as a component of net worth. Tables 13.9–13.17 show the increased wealth at various percentiles of the wealth distribution. These numbers seem to indicate that most pension wealth accrues to wealth holders between the twenty-fifth and the ninety-fifth percentile. If true, the inclusion of pension wealth in an examination of the distribution of net worth should decrease the degree of inequality in the wealth distribution.

Table 13.18 shows this effect by reporting the proportion of nonpension wealth and net worth that is held by the top 5 percent and the top 1 percent of the wealth distribution. The top 5 percent of all households own 57.9 percent of nonpension wealth but only 52.5 percent of net worth when pensions are evaluated using the legal method and 55.0 percent of net worth using the projected earning

Table 13.18   Measurement of Wealth Distribution

Age	Nonpension Wealth			Net Worth: Legal CGE			Net Worth: Projected CGE		
	Percentage of Wealth Held By:			Percentage of Net Worth Held By:			Percentage of Net Worth Held By:		
	Top 5 Percent	Top 1 Percent	Gini Coefficient	Top 5 Percent	Top 1 Percent	Gini Coefficient	Top 5 Percent	Top 1 Percent	Gini Coefficient
Younger than 25	55.5	25.4	.891	53.3	23.6	.875	53.7	25.3	.860
25–34	47.8	22.5	.799	43.5	20.2	.769	39.1	17.1	.730
35–44	41.9	20.3	.706	37.7	18.8	.688	34.5	16.2	.646
45–54	62.2	40.3	.800	54.6	34.3	.739	57.4	40.2	.761
55–64	50.7	27.2	.745	43.6	23.3	.686	55.2	38.2	.751
65–74	56.1	35.0	.782	52.5	32.6	.749	52.7	32.9	.749
Older than 74	50.9	35.7	.763	49.3	34.0	.750	49.1	34.1	.749
All households	57.9	35.5	.806	52.5	31.1	.777	55.0	36.2	.783

Source: Weighted pension and nonpension wealth data derived from the SCF.

method. Similar declines in the relative holdings of the wealthiest 5 percent of households occur for each age group shown in the table.

Using the legal method, the relative wealth of the top 1 percent drops from 35.5 percent of wealth excluding pensions to 31.1 percent of net worth when pension wealth is included in the analysis. By contrast, when pension wealth is evaluated using the projected earnings method, the inclusion of pension wealth actually increases the proportion of total wealth held by the wealthiest 1 percent of households.

The overall effect of including pensions in the wealth distribution is shown in table 13.18 and figures 13.1 and 13.2. The Lorenz curves are constructed by plotting the cumulative wealth holdings of the population. We restrict the values of the curve to be equal to or greater than zero. Thus, the Lorenz curve coincides with the axis until cumulative positive wealth is greater than the total negative wealth of the poorest households. This procedure maintains the traditional restriction on the Gini coefficient to range between zero and one.

The Gini coefficient for nonpension wealth for all households is 0.806. Including legal pension wealth lowers this value to 0.777, while the Gini coefficient for net worth including projected pension wealth is 0.783. These data confirm that including pension wealth tends to reduce measured inequality in the wealth distribution. This result is shown in the graphs of the Lorenz Curves in figures 13.1 and 13.2. In both figures, including pension wealth shifts the curve in toward the line of equity. Allowing the Lorenz curve to fall below the horizontal axis to reflect negative net worth raises the Gini coefficients but does not alter the conclusion that pension wealth reduces measured inequality.

13.8   Conclusions and Comparison to Earlier Studies

This paper has provided a detailed examination of the value of pension benefits. Two methods of calculating pension wealth were described and shown to bound the true value of pension wealth. Each method was applied to data from the 1983 SCF to derive pension wealth for the U.S. population. For all households with pension coverage, mean pension wealth under the projected earnings method was $98,291 and represented 43 percent of total net worth. At the median of the distribution, pensions represent 31 percent of net worth. Using the legal method of calculating pension wealth lowers these values so that mean pension wealth represents 26 percent of mean net worth while median pension wealth is 21 percent of median net worth.

There are very few studies against which these findings can be compared. The results of two such studies are reviewed below. Quinn (1985) estimated the combined pension and social security wealth for households in the Retirement History Survey (RHS) in 1973 and compared

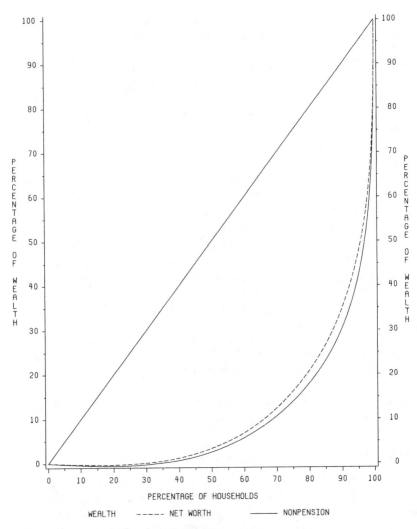

Fig. 13.1   Distribution of wealth: legal method

this to their total wealth. He assumed no postretirement adjustments and estimated pension and social security wealth under interest rate assumptions of 2, 5, and 10 percent. The results at the 5 percent assumption are most comparable to those reported in this study. His sample is limited to households whose head is between age sixty-two and sixty-seven. The RHS reports the expected pension benefit for each person covered by a pension. Quinn's estimate of pension wealth is the present value of this benefit starting at the earliest age of eligibility, adjusted for survival probabilities. Quinn's estimates are in-

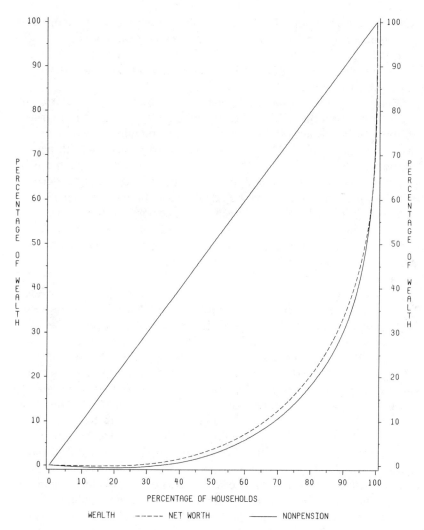

Fig. 13.2   Distribution of wealth: projected earnings

creased by 124 percent (the change in the consumer price index (CPI) and the return on three-month Treasury bills) to make them comparable to our 1983 data.

Quinn found that median wealth without social security and pensions in 1973 was $61,869 for married men, $21,056 for nonmarried men, and $12,790 for nonmarried women. At the 5 percent interest rate assumption, median wealth with social security and pensions was $238,762 for married men, $141,277 for nonmarried men, and $76,653 for nonmarried women. The proportion of this wealth in pension rights was roughly

12.9 percent for married men, 11.9 percent for nonmarried men, and 13.4 percent for nonmarried women (calculated from midpoints of the intervals in table 3 of Quinn 1985). Thus, pension wealth averaged $30,800 for married men, $16,811 for nonmarried men, and $10,286 for nonmarried women.

Mean nonpension wealth is considerably larger for the most comparable group in the SCF—$196,492 for the fifty-five to sixty-four age group. Pension wealth is also much larger using our derived values of wealth. Under the legal (CGE) method, mean pension wealth across all households aged fifty-five to sixty-four is $73,922; under the projected (CGE) earnings method, it is $161,468. These values are derived by multiplying mean pension wealth shown in tables 13.5 and 13.6 by the proportion of persons covered by a pension. Both estimates are much larger than Quinn's estimate for married men. This could be attributable to growth in pension coverage or more generous benefit formulas. Another possibility is that survey respondents systematically underestimate their benefits.

We have not yet examined the data on expected benefits provided by the SCF respondents. Avery, Elliehausen, and Gustafson (1985) report a mean value of pension wealth (including thrift assets) of $43,511 for households with married heads fifty and over and of $27,985 for those with unmarried heads. In all but 8 percent of the households, the age of the head is sixty-five or lower, so the most comparable estimate in our results is once again for the fifty-five to sixty-four age group. Even under the legal method, our estimates are much higher than those obtained by Avery, Elliehausen, and Gustafson from the household responses, suggesting the possibility of significant underreporting.

Cartwright and Friedland (1985) used pension benefit data from a survey done for the President's Commission on Pension Policy in September 1979. Their estimates are largely based on individual responses to the questionnaire. When this information was not available, they imputed benefits from either the Department of Labor's EBS-1 forms or the employer survey. Private pensions were discounted at a rate of 7 percent (3 percent real, 4 percent inflation) and public pensions at a rate of 3 percent (all real). Individual retirement accounts, Keoghs, and annuities are included in the estimates. For nonvested workers, the probability of vesting was imputed from a cross-sectional logit equation. Their estimates are increased by 37.2 percent below to reflect the change in the CPI between 1979 and 1983.

The average household in the Pension Commission Survey had $4,503 of retirement assets, representing 6 percent of net worth. In contrast, our estimates of pension wealth for the average household under the CGE assumptions are $26,052 under the legal method and $53,863 under the projected earnings method. Mean retirement wealth (table 13.19)

Table 13.19   **Retirement Wealth: Pension Commission Survey**

| Age | Mean Retirement Wealth ($) | | Ratio of Households with Retirement Wealth | Ratio of Retirement Assets to Net Wealth All Households |
	All Households	Households with Retirement Wealth		
Under 25	1,547	7,032	.22	.04
35–44	3,906	9,766	.40	.04
45–54	9,922	21,112	.47	.08
55–64	14,175	28,929	.49	.12
65 and over	1,858	30,975	.06	.02

Source: Cartwright and Friedland (1985).

varied by age group in a pattern that was very comparable to that observed in tables 13.5 and 13.6. To compare mean retirement wealth to those for households with pensions in tables 13.5 and 13.6, we divided the mean retirement wealth for all households by the ratio of households with retirement wealth. The corresponding estimates for households with retirement wealth are shown in the second column of table 13.19. Except for the under thirty-five group, the estimates in table 13.19 are much smaller than our estimates in tables 13.5 and 13.6. The gap between these two sets is largest (in relative terms) for the fifty-five to sixty-four age group. Shown in the last column of table 13.19 are ratios of retirement assets to net wealth estimated for each age group using table A8 in Cartwright and Friedland (1985). Again the ratios in table 13.19 are much lower for every age group than the corresponding estimates in table 13.7.

In conclusion, several key findings of this study should be indicated.

1. Pension wealth is a large and important component of household wealth. Pension wealth follows the expected life-cycle pattern of increasing with age up until retirement and then declines.

2. Our results are larger than those reported by Quinn (1985) or by Cartwright and Friedland (1985), both in terms of the absolute magnitude of pension wealth and the ratio of pension wealth to net worth.

3. Nonpension wealth of older households with pension coverage is considerably larger than the wealth of older households without pension coverage.

4. Pension wealth reduces measured inequality in the distribution of wealth.

5. A key omission of this study is social security wealth. Calculating social security wealth for these households is a research priority. Including social security wealth should further reduce wealth inequality. The distribution of social security wealth is an interesting issue in itself.

6. The inclusion of pension wealth into a measure of net worth will bring the life-cycle pattern of net worth more into conformity with the predictions of the life-cycle savings hypothesis. First, during the working years, the inclusion of pension wealth results in a more rapid rise in net worth between ages thirty-five and sixty-five. Second, during the retirement years, the inclusion of pension wealth will accelerate the decline in net worth. Consider the example of a household with $200,000 of nonpension wealth, along with a pension of $1,000 per month for the head, whose is age sixty-five. The wealth value of the pension is $101,370 at sixty-five but declines to $38,980 at eighty solely owing to the decline in life expectancy. Even if nonpension wealth remains constant, the decline in pension wealth lowers net worth from $301,310 to $238,986, or a decline of 21 percent in fifteen years.

References

Allen, Steven, Robert Clark, and Ann McDermed. 1986. Job mobility, older workers and the role of pensions. Final Report for Department of Labor Contract no. J-9-M5-0049. Washington, D.C.: Department of Labor.

Allen, Steven, Robert Clark, and Daniel Sumner. 1986. Post-retirement adjustments of pensions. *Journal of Human Resources* 21:118–37.

Avery, Robert, Gregory Elliehausen, and Glenn Canner. 1984a. Survey of consumer finances, 1983. *Federal Reserve Bulletin* 70(9): 679–92.

———. 1984b. Survey of consumer finances, 1983: A second report. *Federal Reserve Bulletin* 70(12): 857–68.

Avery, Robert, Gregory Elliehausen, and Thomas Gustafson. 1985. Pensions and social security in household portfolios: Evidence from the 1983 Survey of Consumer Finances. Research Papers in Banking and Financial Economics. Washington, D.C.: Board of Governors of the Federal Reserve System.

Bulow, Jeremy. 1982. What are corporate pension liabilities? *Quarterly Journal of Economics* 97:435–52.

Cartwright, William, and Robert Friedland. 1985. The President's Commission on Pension Policy household survey, 1979. *Review of Income and Wealth* 31:285–308.

Clark, Robert, and Ann McDermed. 1986. Earnings and pension compensation: The effect of eligibility. *Quarterly Journal of Economics* 101:341–61.

———. 1988. Do employment contracts alter earnings profiles? Faculty Working Paper no 121. Raleigh: Department of Economics and Business, North Carolina State University.

Feldstein, Martin. 1974. Social security, induced retirement, and aggregate capital accumulation. *Journal of Political Economy* 82:905–26.

———. 1982. Social security and private savings: Reply. *Journal of Political Economy* 90:630–42.

Ippolito, Richard. 1985. The labor contract and true economic pension liabilities. *American Economic Review* 75:1031–43.

———. 1987. Why federal workers don't quit. *Journal of Human Resources* 22:281–99.

Kotlikoff, Laurence, and David Wise. 1985. Labor compensation and the structure of private pension plans. In *Pensions, labor and individual choice,* ed.
David Wise, 55–85. Chicago: University of Chicago Press.

Mitchell, Olivia. 1982. Fringe benefits and labor mobility. *Journal of Human
Resources* 17:286–98.

Munnell, Alicia. 1974. *The effect of social security on personal savings.* Cambridge, Mass.: Ballinger Publishing Co.

———. 1976. Private pensions and savings: New evidence. *Journal of Political
Economy* 84:1013–32.

Quinn, Joseph. 1985 Retirement income rights as a component of wealth.
Review of Income and Wealth 31:223–36.

U.S. Department of Commerce. 1984. *Statistical Abstract of the United States,
1985.* 105th ed. Washington, D.C.: Bureau of the Census.

Comment   Cordelia W. Reimers

McDermed, Clark, and Allen's goal in this paper is to add private
pension wealth (but, it should be noted, not social security wealth) to
household net worth and to show how this affects the distribution of
net worth by age of the household head. It has been notoriously difficult
to get good estimates of private pension wealth for individuals of all
ages from household surveys because people usually do not know their
pension benefits unless they are near retirement. (Indeed, one of the
best predictors of propensity to retire in the next two-year period is
ability to answer a question about the size of pension benefits.) These
authors exploit a better source of information: the 1983 Survey of
Consumer Finance (SCF). This survey asked pension providers for
plan characteristics, enabling the authors to calculate expected pension
benefits, and pension wealth, after making a number of assumptions.

My comments will discuss, first, these basic decisions the authors
had to make; next, what is in the paper and some of their findings;
and, finally, what is controversial about it. Some assumptions are necessary in order to estimate a person's expected future pension benefit
stream and to convert this into an amount of pension wealth accrued
to date.

For defined contribution plans (10 percent of those with pensions in
the SCF sample), current pension wealth is simply the current value
of the person's pension account. There is no need to calculate benefits
or discount them. But, for defined benefit plans, the authors must
estimate the expected benefits accrued so far, convert them to a life
annuity beginning at retirement age, and discount the purchase back

Cordelia W. Reimers is professor of economics at Hunter College and the Graduate
School of the City University of New York.

to the current year, allowing for mortality risk. (However, they do not discount for the risks of job termination, plan termination, or inflation after retirement.)

The problem of estimating the expected benefit accrued to date is a thorny one. Two key issues are highlighted in the paper. First, is the labor contract a one-period, renewable one or an implicit lifetime contract to age sixty-five? Second, how do earnings grow over time?

If the contract is for only one period at a time, the expected benefit is just what has actually accrued to date—what the employer is obligated to pay if the worker is terminated today. Under this "legal" method of calculating benefits, the benefit increases with each year on a job because of increasing years of service and higher earnings. If the contract is long term, on the other hand, the expected benefit is what the worker would get if he or she stayed with the firm until retirement. Since this typically depends on the earnings in the last few years before retirement, it is called the "projected earnings" method. There is still the question of how much of this ultimate total benefit accrues each year. The authors assume that pension wealth increases each year only because there is an additional year of service in the formula since there is no change in the final earnings figure used in the calculation. This in effect assumes that rights to the ultimate total benefit are acquired at a constant rate over the life of the contract. While arguing that the evidence about the relation of quits and earnings behavior to pension coverage and vesting favors the projected earnings method, the authors show results using both it and the legal method.

The second key issue is what growth rate of earnings to use in calculating either the past earnings history (for the legal method) or future earnings (for the projected earnings method). Again, McDermed, Clark, and Allen show results under two assumptions: a constant earnings growth rate (CGE) of 5.5 percent per year, due to economy-wide real wage growth of 1.5 percent and inflation of 4 percent, and the Federal Reserve Board's computed age-race-sex-industry-occupation-specific growth rates that are included in the SCF data tape (FGE). These FGE growth rates average 5.5 percent overall but decline with age. The CGE assumption implies a linear age-log earnings profile, while the FGE assumption conforms better to the observed concavity of age-log earnings profiles.

The FGE assumption about earnings growth yields lower pension wealth estimates than does the CGE assumption, under both assumptions about the nature of the labor contract. On the one hand, FGE assumes earnings have grown faster than 5.5 percent up to the current age. This yields lower average past earnings when benefits are calculated by the legal method. On the other hand, under the FGE assumption, earnings grow more slowly than 5.5 percent at later ages. This results in lower final earnings when benefits are calculated by the projected earnings method.

In the paper, McDermed, Clark, and Allen first present simulations of life-cycle accumulation of pension wealth for a hypothetical individual under a one-period versus a long-term labor contract, assuming a constant 5.5 percent rate of growth of total compensation (i.e., earnings plus pension compensation). They then use the 1983 SCF to estimate actual pension wealth and total wealth of a cross section of households under the four combinations of assumptions: one-period versus long-term labor contract (i.e., legal vs. projected earnings method) and linear versus concave age-log earnings profile (i.e., CGE vs. FGE). Despite the effort to collect information from pension providers, 44 percent of the people with defined benefit plans on their current job had missing data on the plan's characteristics. The authors therefore estimated pension benefit regressions to impute the missing information, again using the four alternative assumptions about the labor contract and earnings growth rate.

These regressions may be one of the most useful parts of the paper to other researchers who need to impute pension benefits. Given data on age, job tenure, salary, industry, occupation, and plan type, one can use these regression equations to predict a person's pension benefit. (I only wish race and gender had been included, too.) These equations should be more accurate than those one can estimate from the National Longitudinal Survey (NLS) or the Retirement History Survey (RHS) because they are based on provider information about the plan rather than on the worker's guess and because the sample used to estimate the equations is not biased toward people who are about to retire.

Having estimated pension and total wealth, the authors show the cross-sectional distributions, by age of the household head, of nonpension wealth, pension wealth, total net worth, pension/net worth ratio, and annual pension savings, for households with and without pensions and for all households under all four assumptions. Comparison of these tables reveals the effect of including pension wealth on the wealth distribution. First, wealth is increased, of course, but primarily between the twenty-fifth and the ninety-fifth percentiles. Second, households with pensions have higher nonpension wealth than those without pensions. This would suggest that pensions increase inequality. But, third, including pension wealth reduces the Gini coefficient, which suggests just the opposite—that pensions reduce inequality. This apparent contradiction highlights an issue to which I return below: the inherent limitations of Lorenz curves and Gini coefficients in this type of analysis.

Fourth, as other researchers have found, the cross-cohort wealth distribution has a peak at age fifty-five to sixty-four. We should not too easily conclude from this that the distribution of wealth over an individual's life cycle has a similar shape without knowing the effect of the shift in gender of household heads as age rises in the cross section owing to differential mortality of men and women. Perhaps the lower wealth of households with heads over age sixty-five reflects the increasing number of female heads and women's relative poverty rather than dissaving by the elderly.

The paper concludes with a comparison of these results with a few other studies of the distribution of pension wealth. McDermed, Clark, and Allen find much higher estimates of nonpension and pension wealth in the SCF than are reported in other studies that used the NLS or the RHS. The SCF is more thorough in asking about all types of assets, including life insurance and consumer durables, and includes provider information about pension plans. Apparently, people tend to underestimate their benefits when answering survey questions.

This paper is carefully done, uses better data than has hitherto been available, and gives a clear picture of the consequences of including private pensions in the distribution of household wealth, given the assumptions adopted by the authors. However, the paper is controversial in certain respects. I shall focus on three: the failure to discount adequately for risk, the assumed time path of pension accrual under an implicit lifetime labor contract, and the misleading use of Lorenz curves and Gini coefficients.

The first controversy involves a basic conceptual issue: how to assign a present value to a stream of future income that cannot be alienated from the recipient. We want to count pensions in household wealth because they presumably affect savings behavior and labor supply behavior and because they are an aspect of inequality of access to goods and services. But pensions are different from conventional assets and so may not have the same effects on either behavior or inequality. If all goes well and the person actually receives the anticipated real benefits, of course the pension is as good as a bond or a rental property. But all may not go well. In particular, their illiquidity and the types of risk to which they are subject mean that pensions are a much less valuable form of wealth than marketable assets yielding the same future income stream. Perhaps the right way to evaluate pension wealth is to imagine that a person could sell his or her pension rights and to ask what the market value would be. Does the fact that this would be a very low number—that in fact no such market has developed—suggest something about the discount factor for risk?

This line of reasoning concludes that pension wealth is seriously overestimated in this paper, even using the legal method and the FGE earnings growth rates. As the authors recognize, their pension wealth figures calculated by the projected earnings method are upper-bound estimates because they discount only for mortality risk, not for the risks of job termination, plan termination, and unanticipated inflation after retirement. However, they consider the legal method estimates to be a lower bound. Surely, these too should be discounted for the risks of employer bankruptcy, plan termination, and inflation. The fact that pension rights are not marketable and that one cannot even borrow against them much before retirement suggests that the risk discount factor is quite large.

One could quibble with many of the other assumptions that the authors had to make, such as immediate vesting, no survivors' benefits, no early retirement benefits, no postretirement changes in benefits, a nominal interest rate of 6 percent, and an inflation rate of 4 percent. But this would hardly be fair since one inevitably must assume something about these matters and since these assumptions are as sensible as any. Some speculation about the way these assumptions affect the results would have been useful. But these are minor issues compared with the lack of discounting for risk.

The authors' implicit assumption about the accumulation path of pension wealth under the projected earnings method is also questionable. Under a lifetime labor contract, the expected pension will depend on final earnings and total years of service at retirement. If we take seriously the assumption of a lifetime labor contract, this final pension wealth fund could be built up from zero over the duration of the job by a variety of time patterns of accumulation, bounded from below by the time path of pension wealth as calculated by the legal method. The choice of any particular path is essentially arbitrary, yet the estimated age profile of pension wealth depends critically on this choice. In this paper, it is assumed without discussion that pension wealth grows in a straight line. But there could be other assumptions, which would alter the age distribution of pension wealth under the projected earnings method.

Next, there are the seemingly contradictory findings about the effect of pensions on the distribution of wealth. Apparently, pensions increase inequality, at least in the lower part of the distribution, since those households with low nonpension wealth do not have pensions either. But this is missed by the Lorenz curves and Gini coefficients, which show pension wealth reducing inequality. The problem is that many households have negative wealth; the lower tail of the wealth distribution is made up of these net debtors. Because Lorenz curves and Gini coefficients are completely insensitive to changes in the distribution of negative wealth, they cannot properly summarize or compare distributions that include net debtors. They could be used to depict the distribution of wealth among the subset of households that have nonnegative wealth, but, since including pensions changes the composition of this subset, Gini coefficients cannot fully capture the effect of pensions on this distribution either. In any case, their use in this paper is misleading; we should not accept the conclusion that private pensions reduce the inequality of wealth.

Finally, I wish the authors had explored the gender difference in pension wealth and had shown the distributions by gender as well as age of household head. As noted above, this might shed some light on the peak at age fifty-five to sixty-four as well as on gender differences in wealth. I hope a future paper as careful, clear, and thorough as this one will investigate the effects of gender, too.

14   The Importance of Gifts and Inheritances among the Affluent

Michael D. Hurd and B. Gabriela Mundaca

14.1 Introduction

Although the life-cycle hypothesis of consumption (LCH) has for many years been the standard model for theoretical and empirical analysis of consumption behavior, recently a number of studies have cast doubt on its empirical accuracy. In cross-sectional data, wealth is often found to increase with age even at advanced ages (Mirer 1979; Menchik and David 1983; Kurz 1984). These results are taken to mean that even the very elderly continue to save, which is not consistent with the LCH under uncertainty about the date of death. According to Danziger et al. (1982), "The elderly not only do not dissave to finance their consumption during retirement, they spend less on consumption goods and services (save significantly more) than the nonelderly at all levels of income. Moreover, the oldest of the elderly save the most at given levels of income" (210).

White (1978, 1984) and Darby (1979), among others, have simulated the paths of consumption and earnings of representative consumers. They find that, under plausible assumptions about the form of the utility function, the difference between the two paths, which is life-cycle savings, can account for only a fraction of the wealth held by households.

In a widely cited paper, Kotlikoff and Summers (1981) estimated, using historical data, the consumption and earnings paths of the 1974 population. From these paths, they calculated a number of estimates of life-cycle savings, which depended on various assumptions about

Michael D. Hurd is a professor of economics at the State University of New York at Stony Brook and a research associate of the National Bureau of Economic Research. B. Gabriela Mundaca is a graduate student at the State University of New York at Stony Brook.

interest rates and intergenerational transfers. Their best guess is that only 20 percent of the assets held by the household sector came from life-cycle saving.

These and other empirical results have generated interest in a model in which utility is derived both from consumption and from bequests; that is, consumers have a bequest motive for saving (Menchik and David 1983; and Modigliani 1986). This would explain the cross-sectional results: it seems plausible that, if the bequest motive is strong enough, even the very elderly will continue to save. It would explain the simulations and the Kotlikoff and Summers findings: if only 20 percent of the wealth held by households comes from life-cycle saving, the other 80 percent must have come from bequests.

The extent of a bequest motive has important implications for theoretical and empirical work and for economic policy. We give several examples of the latter. Increases in social security benefits will have substantially different effects on capital formation according to the strength of a bequest motive: with a strong bequest motive, the elderly will tend to save the increase; otherwise, they will consume it. The response of consumers to bond versus tax financing will depend on the bequest motive. The demand for government-sponsored indexed annuities will vary with the strength of a bequest motive.

When the date of death is uncertain, people will leave bequests under the LCH even if they have no bequest motive. To understand the strength of a bequest motive, one needs to study savings decisions in a model that allows for both uncertainty and a desire to leave bequests. One could, then, separate intended from unintended bequests. Our goal in this paper is more modest. We aim to present data that will suggest the strength of the bequest motive. The first and most important result is an estimate of fraction of assets from intergenerational transfers. Our estimate can be compared with that of Kotlikoff and Summers. The comparison is important because their result has been widely, if somewhat mistakenly, interpreted to be strong evidence against the LCH. Our method of estimation is very different from theirs. They estimated intergeneration transfers as the difference between household assets and life-cycle savings; we directly estimate the fraction of assets from gifts and bequests.[1] While a finding that a large fraction of household assets comes from bequests does not prove that people have a bequest motive, it certainly suggests that at least part of bequests are intended and that one ought to study models that emphasize intergenerational transfers. A finding that only a small fraction of assets come from intergenerational transfers would cast doubt on the Kotlikoff and Summers result; furthermore, it would be consistent with the LCH when the date of death is uncertain.

Our second result documents motives for saving as reported by individuals. While it may not be possible to develop a formal test for a bequest motive from these kinds of data, they do suggest how individuals view their own reasons for saving. One would imagine that, if individuals have a strong bequest motive, they would report a desire to leave a bequest as a reason for saving.

Our main source of data is the 1964 survey of the economic behavior of the affluent (Barlow, Brazer, and Morgan 1966). Respondents were asked the fraction of their assets from inheritances and gifts. We also use the 1983 Survey of Consumer Finances with the high-income supplement, which, while not as detailed as the 1964 data, does have some information on intergenerational transfers.

Using the 1964 data, we estimate that 15–20 percent of household wealth came from inheritances and about 5–10 percent from gifts. Even in households with very high incomes, very few people say that a large fraction of their assets were inherited or given to them. It is not creditable that anything approaching 80 percent of the wealth held by the people in the sample could be the result of intergenerational transfers.

14.2 Results from 1964 Survey on the Economic Behavior of the Affluent

The survey was conducted in the spring of 1964 by the University of Michigan Survey Research Center (SRC). The probability of selection into the sample was roughly proportional to 1961 income. Completed interviews were eventually obtained for 957 high-income households (income over $10,000) and ninety-four low-income households. In the population, about 90 percent of households are low-income households. Sampling weights allow one to estimate population averages. Extensive questions were asked on variables such as the source of assets, attitudes toward risk, philanthrophy, extent of portfolio management, economic reactions to taxes, and work patterns. In this paper, we are most interested in the questions on size of portfolio, sources of wealth, objectives of saving, and extent of bequests.

In table 14.1, we present information about the distribution of portfolio size by income class and the population weights of each income class. Portfolios include holdings of fixed-yield assets (savings accounts, corporate bonds, preferred stock, savings bonds, government bonds, notes and bills, mortgages, and land contracts), common stocks and mutual fund shares, and interests in real estate and unincorporated businesses (including farms but excluding owner-occupied housing). The major wealth components that are missing are housing, consumer durables, claims to pension and retirement funds, and (possibly) consumer debt. Because the underlying questions from which the portfolio size was calculated gave only intervals for the various assets, the portfolio classification has overlapping intervals. Some examples will show the difficulty of finding total assets. Someone who has less than $10,000

Table 14.1   Distribution of Portfolio Size by Income Class (percentage of income class)

	1961 Income					
Portfolio Size (1964)	Less than $10,000	$10,000– $15,000	$15,000– $25,000	$25,000– $50,000	$50,000– $100,000	More than $100,000
Less than $1,000	28 (26)	11 (19)	3 (6)	1 (2)	1 (1)	0 (0)
Less than $30,000	39 (37)	24 (41)	16 (34)	2 (4)	1 (1)	0 (0)
$10,000– $300,000	29 (27)	56 (94)	53 (114)	38 (85)	14 (26)	4 (6)
More than $100,000	4 (4)	8 (13)	25 (54)	47 (105)	52 (96)	37 (60)
More than $500,000	0 (0)	1 (2)	3 (7)	13 (29)	33 (60)	60 (98)
Total	100 (94)	100 (169)	100 (215)	100 (225)	100 (184)	100 (164)
Income class weight	.903	.067	.020	.008	.002	< .0005

Source: Authors' calculations from the 1964 survey on the economic behavior of the affluent.
Note: Figures in parentheses represent the number of households in each income class.

in each of the three asset categories (but has positive holdings in each category) will have less than $30,000 in total assets. Someone who has $10,000–$100,000 in one asset category but none in the others cannot be said to have less than $30,000; yet he cannot be said to have more than $30,000. That is, his assets are in the range $10,000–$100,000. Someone who has from $10,000 to $100,000 in each of the three asset categories will have from $30,000–$300,000 in total assets. Someone who has more than $100,000 in one of the assets categories and less than $100,000 in the others will have more than $100,000 in total assets. Altogether, there are forty-two possible combinations. To make a usable asset variable, the SRC calculated an indicator of total assets that takes values in the intervals shown in table 14.1.

As would be expected, the fraction of households with large asset holdings in an income class rises with income class. Among those in the highest income classes, the fraction having large wealth holdings is substantial: in the highest income class, 60 percent had more than $500,000 in assets. In the lowest income class, which represents about 90 percent of all households, 67 percent of the households had portfolios of less than $30,000. Even in the next income class, which goes up to the ninety-seventh income percentile, only about 65 percent of the income class had portfolios greater than $30,000. The table confirms in a qualitative way a highly skewed wealth distribution. However, because there is not a good way to assign mean values to the two largest portfolio intervals, the calculation of a wealth distribution can be, at best, only approximate.

In table 14.2, we give information about the fraction of total assets received as gifts. Unlike the asset variable, this fraction apparently refers to total assets. Although gifts become increasingly important as income rises, even in the highest income class only 6 percent of the respondents said gifts accounted for more than 50 percent of their assets. The more usual situation is found in the first income class, which accounts for about 90 percent of the households: 88 percent of the households in that income class either had less than $1,000 in assets or received no gifts. We note that the fraction of missing values rises with income class: apparently, the very well to do are less willing to be interviewed. This, of course, has the potential to bias estimates of population averages. In this case, however, even if the missing values are assigned the highest fraction, the fraction of households with more than 50 percent of assets in gifts is still small. The general impression from this table is that, for almost everyone, the amount of wealth transferred through gifts is unimportant.

Table 14.3 has information about the importance of inheritances. The data are responses to the question, "Now, speaking about the inheritance, about what fraction of your total assets today does it account for?" In general, inheritances appear to be more important than gifts. For example, the unweighted fraction having 15 percent or more in inheritances was 17 percent, compared with 8 percent for gifts. Even in the lowest income class, 15 percent of households have received some inheritance. However, it is still the case that most people even in the high income classes received no inheritances. The magnitude of most inheritances apparently is not large. For example, in the highest income class, which represents less than 0.05 percent of all households, just 8 percent of households have more than 50 percent in inheritances. Even assigning all the missing values to the highest category raises the figure to just 15 percent.

Although, of course, one cannot directly aggregate gifts and inheritances from the data in tables 14.2 and 14.3, it seems inconceivable that anything approaching 50 percent of wealth could have come to households through gifts and bequests. The general impression is that the total fraction must be considerably less than 50 percent.

In tables 14.4 and 14.5, we give data on the fraction of assets from gifts and inheritances, but cross-classified by asset level. Even in the highest asset category, gifts are not an important source of wealth: only 2 percent said they had received more than 75 percent of their wealth from gifts. The frequency of missing values rises with asset level, but assigning the missing values to the highest gift category certainly does

Table 14.2   **Distribution of Fraction of Wealth Received as Gifts by Income Class (percentage of income class)**

Percentage Received as Gift	1961 Income						Unweighted Total
	Less than $10,000	$10,000–$15,000	$15,000–$25,000	$25,000–$50,000	$50,000–$100,000	$100,000 and Above	
None or no assets	88 (83)	87 (147)	81 (174)	76 (171)	77 (142)	71 (117)	79 (834)
Less than 5 percent	3 (3)	3 (5)	5 (10)	6 (13)	5 (9)	5 (9)	5 (49)
5–14 percent	4 (4)	4 (7)	5 (11)	8 (19)	5 (10)	8 (13)	6 (64)
15–49 percent	1 (1)	3 (5)	4 (9)	7 (16)	7 (12)	6 (10)	5 (53)
More than 50 percent	3 (3)	2 (3)	3 (8)	3 (6)	2 (4)	6 (10)	3 (34)
Missing	0 (0)	1 (2)	1 (3)	0 (0)	4 (7)	3 (5)	2 (17)
Total	100 (94)	100 (169)	100 (215)	100 (225)	100 (184)	100 (164)	100 (1,051)
Income class weight	.903	.067	.020	.008	.002	< .0005	

Source: Authors' calculations from the 1964 survey on the economic behavior of the affluent.

Note: Figures in parentheses represent the number of households in each income class.

Table 14.3 Distribution of Fraction of Wealth Received as Inheritance by Income Class (percentage of income class)

Percentage Received as Inheritance	Less than $10,000	$10,000–$15,000	$15,000–$25,000	$25,000–$50,000	$50,000–$100,000	$100,000 and Above	Unweighted Total
None or no assets	85 (80)	65 (109)	56 (121)	57 (128)	48 (89)	52 (85)	58 (612)
Less than 5 percent	3 (3)	5 (9)	10 (21)	14 (31)	17 (31)	15 (24)	11 (119)
5–14 percent	4 (4)	10 (16)	13 (28)	10 (21)	11 (21)	9 (15)	10 (105)
15–49 percent	4 (4)	10 (16)	9 (19)	8 (17)	11 (21)	9 (15)	9 (92)
More than 50 percent	2 (2)	8 (14)	10 (22)	8 (18)	9 (16)	8 (13)	8 (85)
Missing	1 (1)	3 (5)	2 (4)	4 (10)	3 (6)	7 (12)	4 (38)
Total	100 (94)	100 (169)	100 (215)	100 (225)	100 (184)	100 (164)	100 (1,051)
Income class weight	.903	.067	.020	.008	.002	< .0005	

Source: Authors' calculations from the 1964 survey on the economic behavior of the affluent.
Note: Figures in parentheses represent the number of households in each income class.

Table 14.4   Distribution of Fraction of Wealth Received as Gifts by Portfolio Size (percentage of portfolio category)

Percentage Received as Gift	Portfolio Size (1964)				
	Less than $1,000	Less than $30,000	$10,000–$300,000	More than $100,000	More than $500,000
Zero or no assets	100	86	83	77	66
	(54)	(101)	(292)	(257)	(130)
Less than 5 percent	0	6	3	5	7
	(0)	(7)	(11)	(18)	(13)
5–14 percent	0	4	6	6	9
	(0)	(5)	(22)	(19)	(18)
15–24 percent	0	1	2	3	4
	(0)	(1)	(6)	(9)	(7)
25–49 percent	0	2	2	3	5
	(0)	(2)	(7)	(11)	(10)
50–74 percent	0	1	3	3	3
	(0)	(1)	(10)	(11)	(5)
75 percent or more	0	0	0	1	2
	(0)	(0)	(1)	(2)	(4)
Missing	0	0	1	2	5
	(0)	(0)	(3)	(5)	(9)
Total	100	100	100	100	100
	(54)	(117)	(352)	(332)	(196)

Source: Authors' calculations from the 1964 survey on the economic behavior of the affluent.

Note: Figures in parentheses represent the number of households in each portfolio category.

not change the general impression that gifts cannot explain a substantial fraction of assets.

Although inheritances are more important than gifts, they still do not seem to be the source of a great deal of wealth. In the highest asset class, 42 percent said they had received no inheritances; just 16 percent said inheritances accounted for more than 50 percent of assets. Again, it is difficult to see in these data that gifts and inheritances could account for even half of assets.

To estimate the fraction of assets from gifts and inheritances, we would like to take, in each income class, a weighted average of the fraction of assets in gifts, where the weights would be total assets. This would be average wealth received from gifts in the income class. Then, using the income class weights, we could calculate average gifts in the population. In a similar way, we could calculate average assets in each income class and average assets in the population. The two numbers would provide an estimate of the fraction of assets received as gifts.

Table 14.5   **Distribution of Fraction of Wealth Received as Inheritances by Portfolio Size (percentage of portfolio category)**

Percentage Received as Inheritance	Portfolio Size (1964)				
	Less than $1,000	Less than $30,000	$10,000– $300,000	More than $100,000	More than $500,000
Zero or no assets	100	76	61	54	42
	(54)	(89)	(214)	(173)	(82)
Less than 5 percent	0	9	10	15	13
	(0)	(10)	(34)	(50)	(25)
5–14 percent	0	8	11	10	13
	(0)	(9)	(39)	(32)	(25)
15–24 percent	0	2	4	5	6
	(0)	(2)	(15)	(16)	(12)
25–49 percent	0	3	4	7	3
	(0)	(3)	(15)	(23)	(6)
50–74 percent	0	1	6	4	8
	(0)	(1)	(21)	(14)	(15)
75 percent or more	0	2	1	4	8
	(0)	(2)	(4)	(13)	(15)
Missing	0	1	3	3	8
	(0)	(1)	(10)	(11)	(16)
Total	100	100	100	100	100
	(54)	(117)	(352)	(332)	(196)

Source: Authors' calculations from the 1964 survey on the economic behavior of the affluent.
Note: Figures in parentheses represent the number of households in each portfolio category.

Our data, however, do not allow such a precise calculation: for the fraction in gifts, we have only a range; for the asset level, we have in some cases a range and in others an open-ended interval. Our method is to assign the midpoint of the reported gift range and a point in the reported asset interval. Assigning the midpoint of the gift interval surely overstates the average gift fraction in the interval because the distribution of gift fractions is highly skewed toward zero. The point we assign for assets is certainly arbitrary and surely misstates the assets of any individual, especially those in the open-ended asset categories. However, a large fraction of the individuals in the open-ended asset categories are in the income classes that have very small weight, so the error in the population fractions is probably small.[2]

The questions on the fractions of assets in gifts and inheritances have an ambiguity: it is not clear whether a respondent reports the value of his gifts, at the time he received them, as a fraction of his assets today or the value to which his gifts have grown as a fraction of his assets.[3] Because we do not have a convincing way to decide between them, we present estimates based on both interpretations. For the first interpretation, we calculate, using an average Baa corporate interest rate over the postwar period, the present value of the gift from information on the reported date of the gift. In table 14.6, this is called the average present value of the gift. For the second interpretation, we take the fraction as reported in the data. In table 14.6, this is called the simple average of the gift. There is a substantial difference between the two averages, roughly a factor of two because many people reported they received the gifts before 1949. For these people, we used twenty-five years, which, at our interest rate of 4.3 percent, increases the value of the gifts by a factor of almost three. The estimates of gifts mostly increase with income class, reaching rather substantial values in the higher classes. The weighted averages show that the top 10 percent of the income distribution has about 63 percent of gifts as measured by the present value. No one in the highest income class (five observations) reported any gifts.

Estimated inheritances are reported in table 14.7. They are substantially larger than gifts. They increase sharply with income class. The difference between the present value and the simple estimates is about two. The receipt of inheritances is even more skewed than the receipt of gifts: the top 10 percent of the income distribution received about 82 percent in both present value and simple value of the total inheritances. The third income group accounts for the largest fraction of inheritances.

Table 14.6   **Gifts by Income Class**

1961 Income	Weight	Average		Weighted Average	
		Present Value	Simple	Present Value	Simple
Less than $5,000	.565	0	0	0	0
$5,000–$10,000	.338	2.32	1.33	.78	.45
$10,000–$15,000	.067	3.15	1.80	.21	.12
$15,000–$25,000	.020	25.3	13.8	.51	.28
$25,000–$50,000	.008	38.1	16.7	.31	.13
$50,000–$100,000	.002	98.6	35.0	.20	.07
$100,000–$150,000	.00027	167	61.5	.05	.02
$150,000–$500,000	.00019	234	84.3	.04	.02
$500,000–$1,000,000	.00002	265	84.4	.01	.00
More than $1,000,000	.00001	0	0	0	0
Gifts per household				2.11	1.09

Source: Authors' calculations from the 1964 survey on the economic behavior of the affluent.

Note: Gifts in thousands of dollars.

Table 14.7   **Inheritances by Income Class**

1961 Income	Weight	Average		Weighted Average	
		Present Value	Simple	Present Value	Simple
Less than $5,000	.565	.04	.01	.02	.01
$5,000–$10,000	.338	2.77	1.56	.94	.53
$10,000–$15,000	.067	30.8	21.4	2.06	1.43
$15,000–$25,000	.020	50.5	23.5	1.01	.47
$25,000–$50,000	.008	94.4	38.8	.76	.31
$50,000–$100,000	.002	258	108	.52	.22
$100,000–$150,000	.00027	197	93.9	.05	.03
$150,000–$500,000	.00019	343	132	.07	.03
$500,000–$1,000,000	.00002	220	102	.00	.00
More than $1,000,000	.00001	51.3	16.1	.00	.00
Inheritances per household				5.43	3.03

Source: Authors' calculations from the 1964 survey on the economic behavior of the affluent.

Note: Inheritances in thousands of dollars.

We estimate total assets per household to be $27,300. Thus, our estimates of the fractions of assets from gifts and inheritances is

	Present Value (%)	Simple (%)
Gifts	7.7	4.0
Inheritances	19.9	11.1
Total	27.6	15.1

It is not clear which of these numbers to compare to the 80 percent figure of Kotlikoff and Summers. Although Kotlikoff and Summers refer to their estimate as the magnitude of intergenerational transfers, it is probably closer to an estimate of the magnitude of bequests. This is because, in their method, gifts do not appear as intergenerational transfers as long as the giver is alive: if the giver is alive, his accumulation of life-cycle savings is, in principle, recorded in the data, and the gift is recorded in the assets of the household sector. Therefore, the gift is part of life-cycle savings, not part of intergenerational transfers. After the giver's death, his life-cycle accumulation is no longer recorded, and the gift is no longer explained as life-cycle savings. Were Kotlikoff and Summers able to account for this, their 80 percent figure would be even higher.

Our two estimates of bequests, while quite different from each other, are far below the 80 percent estimate of Kotlikoff and Summers. Even our estimates of total intergenerational transfers are very much less. Although one could argue about the precise weights applied to the fractions from gifts and inheritances and, in particular, the values assigned to the open-ended asset categories, it is inconceivable that any reasonable weights could raise the transfer fraction to anything approaching 80 percent. This, of course, can be seen almost directly from the earlier tables. However, we did do some sensitivity analysis of our assignment of asset values. For example, when we assigned 15, 150, and 250 (thousands) rather than 10, 50, and 200 to asset categories 2, 3, and 4, the average asset holdings increased substantially, but the percentage of assets from gifts and inheritances decreased to 22.2 percent in the present value averages and 12.0 percent in the simple averages.

There is no particular reason to choose between the present value estimates and the simple estimates because both show that the fraction of wealth from intergenerational transfers is moderate. We tend to favor the simple estimates, for reasons to be discussed later.

In table 14.8, we show our estimates of the assets in each income class and the percentage of assets from gifts and inheritances. Average assets are $27,300, the sum of weighted assets. The upper 10 percent of the income distribution had, according to these estimates, about 40 percent of assets; the upper 1 percent had about 15 percent of assets.

Table 14.8   **Assets and Percentage of Assets from Gifts and Inheritances by Income Class**

1961 Income	Weight	Assets		Percentage from Gifts and Inheritances	
		Unweighted	Weighted	Present Value	Simple
Less than $5,000	.565	10.3	5.82	.4	.1
$5,000–$10,000	.338	31.4	10.61	16.2	9.2
$10,000–$15,000	.067	63.4	4.25	53.6	36.6
$15,000–$25,000	.020	127	2.54	59.7	29.4
$25,000–$50,000	.008	306	2.45	43.3	18.1
$50,000–$100,000	.002	601	1.20	59.3	23.8
$100,000–$150,000	.00027	787	.21	46.2	19.7
$150,000–$500,000	.00019	1,110	.21	52.0	19.5
$500,000–$1,000,000	.00002	1,094	.02	44.3	17.0
More than $1,000,000	.00001	1,314	.01	3.9	1.2
Assets per household			27.3		

Source: Authors' calculations from the 1964 survey on the economic behavior of the affluent.

Note: Assets in thousands of dollars.

The percentage of wealth in gifts and inheritances is substantial in the high income classes; accordingly, if wealth were more concentrated among the high-income groups, the average percentage would, of course, rise. Again, it is hard to see that the average percentage could approach the 80 percent of Kotlikoff and Summers.

We now present some other indicators of the importance of gifts and bequests. We take them to be supportive of the results we have already given.

In a separate question, respondents were asked if they had ever received any money or property as a gift or inheritances from parents or others. Nine percent said they had received gifts, 31 percent said inheritances, and 7 percent said both (Barlow, Brazer, and Morgan 1966, 227). These are weighted averages over the top 10 percent of the income distribution. They are quite consistent with the distributions in tables 14.2 and 14.3. They show that, even among the affluent, inter-generational transfers are by no means universal.

The respondents were asked about the source of most of their assets. In table 14.9, we give two distributions of the answers to this question. The weighted distribution is over the top 10 percent of incomes; the unweighted distribution is over the entire sample, ignoring the sampling weights. In the unweighted distribution, 6 percent say gifts or inheritances. In table 14.2, about 3 percent of the high-income group (income over $10,000) say that gifts were more than half of wealth; in table 14.3, about 9 percent say that inheritances accounted for more than half of wealth. Thus, the fraction having "most" of their assets from gifts and inheritances in table 14.9 is smaller than the fraction implied

Table 14.9   **Distribution of Source of Most of Assets (percentage)**

	Unweighted	Weighted
Gifts or inheritances	6	6
Savings out of income	37	49
Appreciation of assets	14	7
Gifts or inheritances and savings	3	7
Gifts or inheritances and appreciation	5	4
Savings out of income and appreciation	24	15
Gifts or inheritances, savings, and appreciation	5	3
Not reported	1	1
Assets less than $1,000	5	8

Sources: Unweighted column from the authors' calculations from the 1964 survey on the economic behavior of the affluent. Weighted column from Barlow, Brazer, and Morgan (1966, 227)—high-income households only.

by tables 14.2 and 14.3. The fraction in table 14.9 saying gifts or inheritances, or gifts or inheritances and appreciation, is about 11 percent, which is very close to the fraction implied by tables 14.2 and 14.3. This lends mild support to the view that the fractions in tables 14.2 and 14.3 include appreciation from the gift or inheritance and that, therefore, the calculations of transfers that use simple sums rather than present values are more accurate. The general impression from table 14.9 is that, over the households in the top 10 percent of the income distribution, the great majority of their assets resulted from savings out of income and appreciation.

The results already given concern the fraction of assets from gifts and inheritances. We now give some information on what individuals say their motives for saving are. In table 14.10, the column labeled "primary" gives the respondents' primary reason for saving and columns 2 and 3 the secondary and tertiary reasons. These distributions are not weighted according to the probability of sample selection, so they are dominated by the answers of very high-income families. The last column gives, over the top 10 percent of the income distribution, a weighted average of the fraction of households that mentioned one

Table 14.10   **Purposes for Saving by Ranking of Importance (percentage)**

	Primary	Secondary	Tertiary	Weighted Percentage Mentioning
Retirement	28	14	2	53
Children's education	16	7	1	31
Buy a house	1	1	0	3
Give to charitable organization	1	2	1	1
Travel	3	3	2	11
Buy stocks, business, real estate, equipment	10	2	1	10
Bequeath or provide for family in case of death	18	10	2	23
Emergencies	9	16	10	35
Pay bills	2	3	3	10
None given	3	36	76	0
Not available, other	9	5	2	13
Total	100	100	100	a

Sources: Authors' calculations from the 1964 survey on the economic behavior of the affluent, except col. 4, which is drawn from Barlow, Brazer, and Morgan (1966, 198)—high-income households only.

[a]Adds to more than 100 because some give more than one reason.

of the reasons. We see that retirement is given most often as a reason for saving. The interpretation of the fraction of households saving for bequests is ambiguous in the context of intergenerational transfers because at least part of the saving is to provide for the wife at the husband's death. Even so, only 23 percent of the respondents mentioned such a saving motive. Again, the general impression from this table is that saving for bequests is not an important motive.

The respondents were asked if they had given any large gifts "within the last couple of years." Over the high-income households, 8 percent had given to individuals, 7 percent to churches or charitable organizations, and 4 percent to both.[4] The types of individuals given to were children (7 percent), other (2 percent), and children and others (1 percent). The fraction giving to grandchildren rounded to 0 percent. The reasons for the gifts were taxes (4 percent), beneficiary needed (2 percent), and other (5 percent). Since the time period is not well specified, the interpretation is ambiguous. It does appear that most giving is very conventional, to children and organizations. In these data, as in other data, there is little evidence that the family provides an annuity for the elderly should they live past their life expectancy.

Our impression from these data is that, while a substantial number of people receive gifts and inheritances, the amounts received are not large even among the very well to do. Our best estimate of the fraction of household wealth due to intergenerational transfers is about 20 percent. For most families, inheritances are more important than gifts, even though over this period there were, for wealthy individuals, substantial tax advantages for inter vivos giving.

14.3 Results from the 1983 Survey of Consumer Finances

The 1983 Survey of Consumer Finances of 3,824 households was supplemented by 438 high-income households.[5] Although extensive questions were asked about income and assets, details on the sources of assets and attitudes toward saving are considerably fewer than in the 1964 data. In particular, the data cannot be used to estimate the fraction of wealth that came from intergenerational transfers. We can, however, make a rough comparison with some of our results from the 1964 data, and with the Kotlikoff and Summers results.

In table 14.11, we give the response of households to the following question: "Overall did most of your (family's) savings come from your regular income, or did it come originally from gifts and inheritances, or other sources?" Even at high income levels the great fraction of households said that most of their savings came from earnings (including pensions and social security). For example, of the households in the top 10 percent of the earnings distribution only about 6 percent

Table 14.11   **Source of Most of Savings**

				1982 Income			
Source	Missing	$0– $10,000	$10,000– $25,000	$25,000– $50,000	$50,000– $64,000	$64,000– $200,000	$200,000 or More	Total
Earnings	81	72	81	86	84	87	79	81
Gifts and inheritances	6	8	7	7	6	6	9	7
Investment income	2	1	2	2	5	2	5	2
Earnings and other	2	1	2	2	3	3	5	2
Other, missing	5	4	3	2	1	1	1	3
No savings	5	13	5	2	1	0	0	5
Total	100	100	100	100	100	100	100	100
	(647)	(762)	(1,192)	(943)	(148)	(304)	(265)	(4,261)
Income class weight	. . .	.167	.369	.355	.059	.05	.05	1.00

Source: Authors' calculations from the 1983 Survey of Consumer Finances.

Note: Except for the last row, the entry in each column is the percent in each income class. Figures in parentheses represent number of households in each income class.

said most of their assets came from gifts and inheritances. Even if one adds in another 3 percent for "earnings and other," which includes gifts and inheritances, the fraction of the high-income households having most of their assets from intergenerational transfers is only 9 percent. The impression certainly is that saving from earnings is by far the most important way to accumulate assets.

The survey asked people their reasons for saving. The question did not ask people to choose among given categories; rather it was open-ended. The primary reasons given by the respondents are given in table 14.12 and the secondary reasons in table 14.13. Apparently the specific reason "bequests" was not given by the respondents was that it is not listed as a separate category.

Saving for emergency ("rainy days," for "security") was mentioned by the greatest fraction of households at all income levels. In the top 10 percent of the income distribution, about 40 percent mentioned retirement either as a primary reason or secondary reason. Responses that could be interpreted to mean saving for bequests might be saving "for the children," "get ahead, for the future," and, possibly, "make investments." But even the sum of these categories does not add up to a large fraction of households. For example, in the $50,000 to $200,000 income group, which is approximately the top 10 percent of the income distribution, about 12 percent mentioned "for the children" or "get ahead, for the future" as either a primary or secondary reason for saving. Adding "make investments" would include about 21 percent of families. Thus, even a very broad interpretation of the meaning of the questions finds a modest fraction of families that save for bequests.

In table 14.14 we report the percent of households that expect a large gift or inheritance. Overall, the percent is small, about 13 percent; in the top 10 percent of the income distribution the percent is larger, about 21 percent, but still far below what one would expect were gifts and inheritances an important part of the source of most households' assets.

14.4 Conclusions

In the 1964 data, even in the top 10 percent of the income distribution, very few households said more than half their assets were from gifts or inheritances: about 3 percent from gifts and 9 percent from inheritances or about 12 percent from intergenerational transfers (tables 14.2 and 14.3). Although the 1983 data are much less precise, this result was roughly confirmed: in the upper 10 percent of the income distribution, at most 9 percent of the households said most of their assets came from intergenerational transfers (table 14.11). If anything, the general impression from comparing tables 14.9 and 14.11 is that saving from earnings has become more important.

Table 14.12   Primary Reason for Saving

Reason	Missing	$0–$10,000	$10,000–$25,000	$25,000–$50,000	$50,000–$64,000	$64,000–$200,000	$200,000 or More	Total
Education	6	6	6	8	12	11	5	7
Purchase durables/house	10	11	13	13	8	7	3	11
In case of illness	9	20	11	8	6	4	3	10
Make investments	3	1	2	2	1	10	18	4
Retirement	21	7	15	19	27	25	22	17
Emergencies	28	24	33	32	34	29	30	30
To get ahead; future	6	4	6	7	3	6	8	6
For the children/family	3	4	2	2	1	1	3	2
No saving	4	7	2	2	0	2	2	3
Bills, travel, other	11	15	9	6	7	6	8	10
Total	100	100	100	100	100	100	100	100
	(647)	(762)	(1,192)	(943)	(148)	(304)	(265)	(4,261)
Income class weight	. . .	.167	.369	.355	.059	.05		1.00

Source: Authors' calculations from the 1983 Survey of Consumer Finances.

Note: Except for the last row, the entry in each column is the percent in each income class. Figures in parentheses represent the number of households in each income class.

Table 14.13   Secondary Reason for Saving

Reason	Missing	$0–$10,000	$10,000–$25,000	$25,000–$50,000	$50,000–$64,000	$64,000–$200,000	$200,000 or More	Total
				1982 Income				
Education	4	3	5	8	7	7	7	6
Purchase durables/house	8	9	10	11	6	7	3	9
In case of illness	9	14	12	10	7	5	2	10
Make investments	3	1	1	2	4	5	8	2
Retirement	9	3	6	9	14	16	11	8
Emergencies	7	6	9	10	14	10	6	8
To get ahead; future	2	2	3	2	5	3	7	3
For the children/family	3	2	2	2	3	3	9	3
No saving	3	6	4	2	1	0	1	3
Bills, travel, other	9	9	10	10	11	10	5	9
None given	43	44	39	34	28	33	41	39
Total	100	100	100	100	100	100	100	100
	(647)	(762)	(1,192)	(943)	(148)	(304)	(265)	(4,261)
Income class weight	. . .	.167	.369	.355	.059	.05		1.00

Source: Authors' calculations from the 1983 Survey of Consumer Finances.

Note: Except for the last row, the entry in each column is the percent in each income class. Figures in parentheses represent the number of households in each income class.

Table 14.14   **Expect Ever to Receive Large Inheritance**

				1982 Income			
	Missing	$0–$10,000	$10,000–$25,000	$25,000–$50,000	$50,000–$64,000	$64,000–$200,000	$200,000 or More	Total
Yes	8	7	13	18	22	21	16	13
No	87	90	85	80	76	78	83	84
Other	4	3	1	1	3	1	1	2
Total	100	100	100	100	100	100	100	100
	(647)	(762)	(1,192)	(943)	(148)	(304)	(265)	(4,261)
Income class weight	. . .	.167	.369	.355	.059	.05		1.00

Source: Authors' calculations from the 1983 Survey of Consumer Finances.

Note: Except for the last row, the entry in each column is the percent in each income class. Figures in parentheses represent the number of households in each income class.

In both surveys, the reasons for saving seem mostly to be for emergencies, for retirement, and for education. Rather than specifying consumption models in which a bequest motive is important, as called for by Kotlikoff and Summers, these data suggest that, if one wants to modify the LCH, the modification should include a precautionary motive for saving.

Notes

1. Following Kotlikoff and Summers (1981), we do not include in intergenerational transfer amounts spent on consumption and education of the children when they are young.

2. We assigned the following values for the gift and inheritance intervals that are given in tables 14.2–14.5: 0, 0.025, 0.1, 0.2, 0.375, 0.625, and 0.8. For the portfolios, which are given in tables 14.1, 14.4, and 14.5, we assigned the following values (in thousands): 0.5, 10, 50, 200, and 1,500.

3. The question about gifts was, "Speaking of the gifts, about what fraction of your total assets do they account for?" The question about inheritances was, "Now, speaking about the inheritance, about what fraction of your total assets today does it account for?"

4. These and the other percentages in this paragraph are weighted percentages over high-income households. The numbers come from Barlow, Brazer, and Morgan (1966, 233–35).

5. Information about the sample can be found in Avery et al. (1984).

References

Avery, R., G. Elliehausen, G. Canner, and T. Gustafson, 1984. Survey of Consumer Finances, 1983. *Federal Reserve Bulletin* 70 (September): 679–92.

Barlow, R., H. Brazer, and J. Morgan. 1966. *Economic behavior of the affluent.* Washington, D.C.: Brookings Institution.

Danziger, S., J. van der Gaag, E. Smolensky, and M. Taussig. 1982. The life cycle hypothesis and the consumption behavior of the elderly. *Journal of Post Keynesian Economics* 5 (Winter): 208–27.

Darby, M. 1979. *The effects of social security on income and the capital stock.* Washington, D.C.: American Enterprise Institute for Public Policy Research.

Kotlikoff, L., and L. Summers. 1981. The role of intergenerational transfers in aggregate capital accumulation. *Journal of Political Economy* 89 (August): 706–32.

Kurz, M. 1984. Capital accumulation and the characteristics of private intergenerational transfers. *Economica* 51 (February): 1–22.

Menchik, P., and M. David. 1983. Income distribution, lifetime savings and bequests. *American Economic Review* 73: 672–90.

Mirer, T. 1979. The wealth-age relation among the aged. *American Economic Review* 69 (June): 435–43.
Modigliani, F. 1986. Life cycle, individual thrift, and the wealth of nations. *American Economic Review* 76, no. 3 (June): 297–313.
White, B. 1978. Empirical tests of the life cycle hypothesis. *American Economic Review* 68 (September): 547–60.
White, B. 1984. Empirical tests of the life cycle hypothesis: Reply. *American Economic Review* 74 (March): 258–59.

Comment   Denis Kessler

Michael Hurd and Gabriela Mundaca's paper is an important contribution to the ongoing debate on the importance of bequests in wealth accumulation. For a long time, the most commonly held view was that inherited wealth represents only a small fraction of the wealth owned by households. Most of the assets held at a given time were considered to result from the past saving of the existing cohorts of consumers. The prevailing opinion was that consumers behave according to the basic life-cycle model (see Modigliani 1988). Life-cycle saving—accumulated primarily for future consumption when retired—was assumed to be the main source of wealth accumulation.

The consensus was broken by the publication of Kotlikoff and Summers (1981), which argued that the bulk of wealth accumulation is due to intergenerational transfers. On the basis of estimates from U.S. data covering the twentieth century, Kotlikoff and Summers claimed that life-cycle saving accounts for only one-fifth of existing wealth. These results—if valid—have important theoretical consequences since they cast doubt on the life-cycle hypothesis of savings behavior and lead to a new view in which intergenerational transfers play the dominant role.

Two opposing positions are now distinguishable. Both of them lead to the law of the 20/80. The traditional position is that life-cycle wealth accounts roughly for 80 percent of existing wealth, whereas the new position takes exactly the opposite stand since it considers that bequests represent 80 percent of existing wealth. The debate is crucial for all researchers involved in understanding consumer behavior and also for policymakers. It has both efficiency and equity implications (see Kessler and Masson 1988). In their interesting contribution, Hurd and Mundaca strongly defend Modigliani's position by providing evidence against Kotlikoff and Summers' position.

Denis Kessler is a senior research fellow at the Centre National de la Recherche Scientifique (France). He heads the Centre d'Etudes et de Recherche sur l'Epargne, le Patrimoine et les Inégalités and teaches economics at the University of Paris, X.

There are indeed different ways to assess the quantitative importance of bequests in wealth accumulation. To date, three main paths have been explored. The first approach uses data from surveys in which households give estimates of the share of bequests in the assets they hold. The second approach uses the so-called flow-of-bequests method, where the objective is to find a relation between the annual flow of bequests and the stock of inherited wealth. The third approach employs a simulation model to derive the share of bequests indirectly as the difference between an independant estimate of total wealth and an estimate of aggregate life-cycle wealth.

Hurd and Mundaca follow the first approach in analyzing two households surveys, the well-known 1964 survey on the economic behavior of the affluent conducted by the University of Michigan Survey Research Center and the 1983 Survey of Consumer Finances with the high-income supplement. The authors reach six main conclusions from the analysis of these survey data.

1. Households were asked in the 1964 survey what fraction of total assets were received as gifts. The data show clearly that "although gifts become increasingly important as income rises, even in the highest income class only 6 percent of the respondents said gifts accounted for more than 50 percent of their assets".

2. As far as inheritances are concerned, the survey data show that inheritances appear to be more important than gifts. Although the frequency of inheritors is higher, the magnitude of most inheritances apparently is not large. In the highest income class (0.05 percent of households), the percentage of households having more than 50 percent in inheritances is just 8 percent.

3. Computations are made to estimate the fraction of total assets from gifts and inheritances. This is a rather delicate task owing to the way the data were collected. Two estimates are presented. The first one (R1) is the ratio of inheritance or gifts to estimated wealth, and the second (R2) is the ratio of the present value of inheritance or gifts to estimated wealth. The fraction of assets from gifts varies from 4.0 percent (R1) to 7.7 percent (R2), and the fraction from inheritances varies from 11.1 percent (R1) to 19.9 percent (R2). The ratio (inheritances plus gifts)/estimated wealth varies from 15.1 percent (R1) to 27.6 percent (R2). Those figures lead the authors to conclude that estimates of bequests are far below the 80 percent estimate of Kotlikoff and Summers.

4. For the top 10 percent of the income distribution, only 9 percent of respondents declared that they had received gifts, 31 percent inheritances, and 7 percent both gifts and inheritances. When asked about the source of wealth, only a minority declared gifts or inheritances.

5. Conversely, respondents declared that retirement was the primary reason for saving. Only one-fifth of them mentioned the bequest motive.

6. The results are consistent with those of the 1983 Survey of Consumer Finances. Even rich households declared that most of their savings came from earnings and not from bequests.

These findings lead Hurd and Mundaca to conclude that the life-cycle model is valid and that it is useless to specify consumption models in which a bequest motive is important. This conclusion appears a little harsh.

Hurd and Mundaca's contribution raises a lot of interesting issues and questions. Let me start with a general remark.

Despite these new findings, the debate on the importance of inheritance in wealth accumulation is still unresolved. The available evidence does not allow us to make a definitive statement on this general issue. The analysis of historical evidence, the study of age-wealth profiles, the examination of annuity markets, and the outcomes of simulation models do not lead to firm conclusions. All direct estimates coming from household surveys appear to show that households consider that bequests received represent a small fraction of their total assets. However, among all the approaches that can be followed to assess the quantitative importance of bequests, I think that direct survey estimates tend to provide the weakest evidence. The reason is that survey data suffer from important biases, in particular recall bias, underreporting, and nonresponse. In addition, there is even a specific bias in this issue. As Modigliani himself puts it, "It is not inconceivable that respondents would tend to underestimate systematically and significantly the extent to which their wealth was bestowed on them by others rather than representing the fruits of their own effort" (Modigliani 1988). We are here in the presence of a kind of moral hazard problem.

There is indeed in the data provided by Hurd and Mundaca some evidence of such a problem, which is due to the fact that people declare more easily to have given than to have received. The authors mention that "the respondents were asked if they have given any large gifts 'within the last couple of years.' Over the high-income households, 8 percent had given to individuals, 7 percent to churches or charitable organizations, and 4 percent to both". From table 14.2, we find that 78 percent of households with income higher than $10,000 have never received any gifts or hold no assets. It is hard to reconcile the fact that 12 percent of households declare to have given within the last couple of years and only 22 percent of households declare to have ever received a gift.

Hurd and Mundaca compare their household survey estimates of the fraction of intergenerational transfers in assets with estimates offered by Kotlikoff and Summers in their well-known 1981 article. In this article, Kotlikoff and Summers, using a simulation model, concluded that the share of inherited wealth accounted for 81 percent of total assets, a figure quite different from the 20 percent of Hurd and Mundaca. But the debate has evolved since then, and the gap between the Kotlikoff and Summers estimate and the traditional Modigliani estimate has been largely explained and reduced. When considering the various estimates stemming from the household survey method, the flow-of-bequests method, and the simulation method, the gap among them lies in particular in the definition of intergenerational transfers (and especially the nature of educational expenditures), the problem of accumulated interest on past inheritances, and the treatment of durables (see Blinder 1988).

Moreover, the Kotlikoff and Summers estimate is largely the outcome of the specific shapes of the consumption and income profiles of the cohorts they examine. Both profiles are almost identical up to age forty-five, and therefore the need for life-cycle accumulation to even out consumption expenditures is eliminated over half the life span.

When comparing the results of a household survey and those of a simulation model, great care must therefore be given to all the various elements, such as differences in methods, hypotheses, cohorts effects, and definitions, that may explain the apparently very wide gap in results. In regard to the household survey approach followed by Hurd and Mundaca, five observations may be offered.

1. The authors seem to overlook age effects. Most of the people living at a certain period of time have not yet inherited. Inheritances are linked to mortality rates, and the age of receipt is likely to be about fifty. The inheritance frequency among the general population given by the authors is therefore biased. This, of course, is less true for gifts that are not linked to mortality rates. One should therefore consider only people that are no longer in a position to inherit from their parents since most bequests come from parents. Inherited wealth is a strictly increasing function of age. Life-cycle wealth first increases and then decreases with age. So, if you consider the ratio of inherited wealth to the sum of inherited wealth and life-cycle wealth, it would first decrease until retirement and then increase after retirement. Therefore, it would be very interesting to have the data computed by age groups to check if this ratio exhibits this specific pattern.

2. Hurd and Mundaca seem to have overlooked the age effects, but they have also neglected cohort effects. The relative size of inheritances and gifts in total assets depends, of course, on the growth rate of income. The higher this rate, the lower the fraction of inherited wealth. It is therefore important to take into account the possible cohort effects when assessing the fraction of inherited wealth in total assets. Cohort effects are indeed likely to be large.

3. Concerning the question of capitalization of inheritances, the authors give both the present value of inheritances and gifts and their value at time of receipt. Capital income on inheritances and gifts should be considered as part of inherited wealth. So one should consider only present values. But, in computing these present values, Hurd and Mundaca use the Baa bond index. By choosing this index, they underestimate the fraction of inherited wealth in total assets. It is likely that the rate of return (including capital gains) on inherited wealth is certainly higher than the Baa index, especially considering the higher-income groups of the population. From the 1983 Survey of Consumers Finances, we know, for instance, that high-income earners and high-wealth holders are likely to take more risks and therefore obtain higher returns than are low-income households (Avery and Elliehausen 1986). The fraction of inherited wealth is very sensitive to the rate of return assumptions (as we can see by comparing the difference between estimates based on value at time of receipt and estimates based on present value estimates). By choosing a rate of return twice the Baa index, the fraction of inherited wealth could easily approach 0.40. To make better assumptions, more information on the structure of inherited wealth is needed.

4. In assessing the importance of inherited wealth in total assets held, Hurd and Mundaca consider only the direct effects. However, indirect effects might be important. It is hard to consider that inherited wealth is entirely independent of life-cycle wealth and that those two components of wealth could be simply added, as implicitly assumed in the methods chosen. There can be multiplicative effects whereby inheritance by itself boosts the accumulation of wealth. Let me give two examples. For example, adding inherited wealth to life-cycle wealth can increase portfolio diversification. Someone receiving a gift at, say, age thirty can use it as collateral and have greater access (and cheaper) to credit and therefore accumulate more wealth then someone who has to save before going into debt. Indirect effects are likely to be large and, if taken into account (and eventually measured), would tend to increase the role of bequests in wealth accumulation.

5. Some of the data provided by Hurd and Mundaca raise other questions. For instance, when computing the wealth/income ratio of the sample from table 14.1 (using the means chosen by the authors in their n. 2 for wealth and means for income of $5,000, $12,500, $20,000, $37,500, $75,000, and $150,000), one finds a ratio of seven, which is much higher than the usual ratio of three implied by the standard life-cycle theory. Such a wealth/income ratio implies very high savings rates or significant bequests. In the same table, two households appear to have a very high wealth/income ratio (120) that is very unrealistic.

In the 1983 survey, when asked about the reasons for saving, only 5 percent of households declared that they did not save. The percentage of zero savers appears too small, especially because these figures implicitly include dissavers since they are not specifically included elsewhere. Again, these data do not seem to support the argument of the paper that people neither receive large bequests nor leave bequests.

In conclusion, let it be clear that my questioning the approach followed and the results obtained by Hurd and Mundaca does not mean that I believe that the ratio of inherited wealth in total assets approaches 80 percent, as stated by Kotlikoff and Summers. It means that this question still deserves a lot of attention because of its policy implications. Great care should be given to the definitions of intergenerational transfers. There is an urgent need for drawing up an accounting framework able to capture all intergenerational transfers, from the old to the young (through inheritances, gifts, loans, and educational expenditures), from the young to the old (through social security, public debt, etc.), whether private or public, whether in human capital or nonhuman capital. Such an accounting framework would help us to measure the importance of intergenerational transfers and assess their efficiency and equity implications.

References

Avery, R. B., and G. E. Elliehausen. 1986. Financial characteristics of high income families. *Federal Reserve Bulletin* 72, no. 3 (March): 163–77.

Blinder, A. S. 1988. Comments on F. Modigliani's "Measuring the contribution of intergenerational transfers to total wealth," and L. Kotlikoff and L. Summers, "The contribution of intergenerational transfers to total wealth: A reply." In *Modelling the accumulation and distribution of wealth,* ed. D. Kessler and A. Masson, 68–76. Oxford: Oxford University Press.

Kessler, D., and A. Masson. 1988. Introduction. In *Modelling the accumulation and distribution of wealth,* ed. D. Kessler and A. Masson, 1–18. Oxford: Oxford University Press.

Kotlikoff, L., and L. Summers. 1981. The role of intergenerational transfers in aggregate capital accumulation. *Journal of Political Economy* 89 (August): 706–32.

———. 1988. The contribution of intergenerational transfers to total wealth: A reply. In *Modelling the accumulation and distribution of wealth,* ed. D. Kessler and A. Masson, 53–67. Oxford: Oxford University Press.

Modigliani, F. 1988. Measuring the contribution of intergenerational transfers to total wealth. In *Modelling the accumulation and distribution of wealth,* ed. D. Kessler and A. Masson, 21–52. Oxford: Oxford University Press.

15   Long-Term Trends in U.S. Wealth Inequality: Methodological Issues and Results

Edward N. Wolff and Marcia Marley

15.1   Introduction

Our paper has two primary objectives. First, we discuss some of the methodological issues involved in reconciling microdata and published data on household wealth distribution both with each other and with aggregate balance sheet data on household wealth. Second, on the basis of selected measures, we attempt to construct a reasonably consistent time series on the size distribution of household wealth for the period 1922–83 from estate file and survey data. In so doing, this paper builds on previous research on household wealth, including the work of Lampman, Smith, Schwartz, Goldsmith, Ruggles and Ruggles, and Musgrave. Our major purpose is to extend and improve this body of wealth data by reconciling and aligning the different sources on wealth concentration in order to improve comparability. We estimate alternative measures of wealth concentration and inequality on the basis of different sources and different imputation techniques. We also present alternative estimates based on different concepts of household wealth, including expected retirement wealth.

Several principal findings emerge from our work. First, from the estate data series, we find that wealth concentration is very high, with the top 1 percent of wealth holders owning at least one-fourth of total wealth from 1922 to 1983, though its share has fallen over the period.

Edward N. Wolff is a professor of economics at New York University and managing editor of the *Review of Income and Wealth*. Marcia Marley is a research associate at the C. V. Starr Center for Applied Economics at New York University.

The authors would like to thank Robert Avery for his helpful comments, Philip Rothman for his research assistance, Stephanie Valchar for her assistance, and the C. V. Starr Center for Applied Economics for its financial support.

This decline in twentieth-century wealth inequality is consistent with that found by other researchers, including Lampman (1962), Williamson and Lindert (1980), and Smith (1987). Second, from the examination of both the estate data series and household survey data, we find that the estimates of household wealth concentration are quite sensitive to the methods used in their construction and to the choice of wealth concept, particularly the inclusion of expected social security wealth. The paper's results illustrate the importance of including expected retirement benefits in measurements of wealth inequality.

Third, we find that the downward trend in wealth inequality from the estate data series remains robust to many different choices of adjustment procedures and wealth concepts. However, there are two factors that influence the trend in measured inequality. The first is the addition of expected social security wealth, which increases the decline in concentration over the sixty-year period. The second factor is the transformation of the estate data series, which is based on the individual as the unit of observation, into corresponding household estimates of concentration. The household-based series shows less of a decline in inequality during and after World War II. Fourth, there are large discrepancies between the concentration estimates derived from the estate data series and those derived from household survey data that are not due to differences in wealth definition or imputation assumptions. More work needs to be done in ascertaining the relative reliability of the estate data and household survey data.

Fifth, adjustments for missing values and underreporting in the 1962 Survey of Financial Characteristics of Consumers (SFCC) and the 1983 Survey of Consumer Finances (SCF) do not significantly alter the estimates of overall wealth inequality. This result seems particularly germane to the 1962 and 1983 household surveys, which have a rich representation of the top of the wealth distribution, and should not be generalized to all household wealth surveys, particularly those that do not oversample the wealthy. On the other hand, imputations for assets not included in the 1962 and 1983 surveys—in particular, consumer durables, household inventories, and expected retirement wealth—result in a significant reduction in the level of inequality.

The remainder of the paper is divided into five sections. In the next section, we discuss alternative concepts of household wealth. The traditional concept of household wealth includes only assets (and liabilities) that are fungible and that have a readily available market value. In this section, we broaden the concept of wealth to include not only traditional components but also claims against future income streams. Such claims include pension and social security entitlements as well as trust income. We also argue that, because of data limitations, empirical measures of household wealth often do not correspond precisely to those implied by theoretical models of household wealth. In this section, we discuss the correspondence between such empirical measures and those implied from behavioral models, such as the life-cycle or liquidity constraint model.

In the third part, we present new estimates of aggregate household balance sheet data for the period from 1922 to 1983. Our estimates are based on figures compiled by Goldsmith, Brady, and Mendershausen (1956), Goldsmith (1962), Goldsmith, Lipsey, and Mendelson (1963), Ruggles and Ruggles (1982), the Department of Commerce (principally, John Musgrave's data on household durables and housing), and the Federal Reserve Board flow-of-funds data. These sources are not entirely consistent in their choice of wealth concept, definition of assets and liabilities, or methodology. We have made adjustments to the published data where possible to improve comparability. In this section, we also present estimates of net worth and gross assets based on alternative wealth definitions. A more detailed description of the adjustments made for each asset category is given in Appendix A. Our adjusted aggregate household balance sheet data are available for the years 1922, 1929, 1939, 1945, 1949, 1953, 1962, 1969, 1972, 1979, 1981, and 1983. These correspond to the years for which distribution data are available. In addition, we have included Goldsmith's aggregate estimates for the years 1900, 1912, and 1933.

In the fourth part of the paper, we develop a time series of wealth concentration estimates for the years indicated above. We compare our adjusted concentration estimates for top wealth holders derived from estate tax data with other sources such as household survey data and synthetic data bases. Our data sources are as follows: (1) 1922–53, selected years: Lampman's (1962) estimates of the wealth of the top wealth holders, which are based on estate tax return records; (2) 1958–76, selected years: estimates from Smith and Franklin (1974) and Smith (1984, 1987) of the wealth of the top percentiles, which are based on estate tax returns; (3) 1962: our adjustments to the original survey data from the SFCC; (4) 1969: Wolff's (1983) MESP synthetic database;[1] (5) 1973: Greenwood's (1987) calculations, which are based on a synthetic database of her creation; (6) 1979: the published results of the Income Survey and Development Program (ISDP) data base and the 1979 President's Commission on Pension Policy survey; (7) 1981: Schwartz's (1983) estimates of top wealth holders' wealth, which are based on estate tax returns; (8) 1983: our adjustments to the original survey data from the SCF; and (9) 1984: published sources for the Survey of Income and Program Participation (SIPP).

As with the aggregate household balance sheet data, we made several transformations and adjustments to the size distribution data in order to increase consistency within the estate tax data series and to compare estimates from different data sources. In this section, we summarize the data adjustments and report different series on the shares of the top percentile of wealth holders. A more detailed explanation of the adjustments and imputations made to the size distribution data is given in Appendix B. In order to ascertain the sensitivity of estimates of both concentration levels and trends, we have analyzed the effect of different wealth definitions and imputation procedures on Lampman's and Smith's estimates as well as on the survey data.

Several comparisons are undertaken in this section. First, we compare concentration estimates based on different wealth concepts, such as traditional wealth and broader measures that include retirement wealth, for both the estate data series and the estimates derived from household survey data. Second, we transform Lampman's estate data estimates for the period 1922–53 to represent the top percentile and half percentile of the population in order to compare the results with Smith's estimates. Third, our adjusted estimates are then compared with the original published estimates. Fourth, as a test of the reliability of the reported trends in concentration, we do a preliminary transformation of the estate data from an individual base to a household base and compare the resulting household trend with the time trends based on the individual data. Fifth, for the various adjustments and transformations enumerated above we then compute upper and lower bounds on wealth concentration to test how sensitive the results are to the different assumptions made and to the various wealth definitions used.

The fifth section focuses on wealth inequality estimates derived from the 1962 SFCC and the 1983 SCF. Our major interest is the sensitivity of these estimates, particularly the Gini coefficient and the shares of top wealth holders, to adjustments for underreporting and missing assets. We base the underreporting correction on a comparison of asset and liability totals derived from each of the two surveys and the respective aggregate household balance sheet estimates. An asset-by-asset comparison between the survey and the aggregate estimates provides an index of underreporting. For the 1962 data, corrections for zero entries are based on comparisons between the wealth entries from the survey data and income flows from the Internal Revenue Service's *Statistics of Income* that correspond to the wealth entry (such as dividends and corporate stock). For the 1983 data, we use proportional adjustment of each asset and liability in the microdata to correspond to the aggregate balance sheet total.

We also consider the effects of including measures of expected pension and social security wealth on the estimated household wealth inequality. For 1962 and 1983, we provide estimates of the distribution of retirement wealth and augmented household wealth based on the microdata for these years. Alternative estimates of retirement wealth and the distribution of augmented household wealth are devised, according to varying assumptions about the future growth in pension and social security benefits.

In the last part of the paper, we consider two general issues. First, how sensitive are estimated time trends in household wealth inequality to alternative imputation, correction, and adjustment procedures? Second, how do inequality estimates and trends in these estimates differ in regard to different definitions of household wealth, particularly with respect to the inclusion of social security and pension wealth?

15.2 Alternative Definitions of Household Wealth

As with other economic concepts, there is no single measure of household wealth that can fulfill all possible uses of the concept. In this section, we develop five alternative operational measures of household wealth. These wealth measures are explained below and summarized in table 15.1. The first of these, W1, is defined as the cash surrender value (CSV) of tangible and financial assets (less liabilities).

Table 15.1   Definitions of the Various Wealth Concepts Used

W1	W1 is defined as the cash surrender value (CSV) of total assets less liabilities and is a measure of the wealth currently available to the household or individual. The assets include owner-occupied housing, other real estate, all consumer durables, demand deposits and currency, time and savings deposits, bonds and other financial securities, corporate stock, unincorporated business equity, trust fund equity (see below), the CSV of insurance, and the CSV of pensions. Liabilities include mortgage debt, consumer debt, and other debt. Trusts are measured at their actuarial value, which represents between 40 and 60 percent of the total reserves of trusts, depending on the year. For an explanation of "actuarial value," see sec. 15.2 of the text. Pensions are measured at their CSV, which represents a very small percentage, around 5 percent, of their total reserves. All other tangible and financial assets and liabilities are measured at full value.
W2	W2 is a broader measure of wealth than W1 and is defined as W1 plus the full reserves of trust funds less their actuarial value included in W1.
W2*	W2* is a slight modification of W2 and is defined as W2 plus household inventories.
W3	W3 incorporates an extended concept of pension wealth and is defined as W2 plus the total value of pension reserves less the CSV of pensions (which is included in W1 and W2).
W4	W4 is one proxy for life-cycle wealth and is equal to W3 plus the expected present value of future social security benefits.
W5	W5 represents another proxy for life-cycle wealth and is equal to W4 plus the expected present value of future pension benefits less the full reserve value of pensions (included in W4). This measure has been provided only for 1962 and 1983 and is based on household survey data.
W5*	W5* is defined as W5 plus household inventories.

The second measure, W2, is a slightly broader concept and is defined as W1 less the CSV or actuarial value of trusts plus the full reserve value of trusts. As is apparent, the difference between W1 and W2 is in the treatment of trusts. W1 measures trusts at their actuarial value or CSV, while W2 assigns the full value of trusts to their beneficiaries. In the case of trusts over which the beneficiary has complete control, the CSV is identical to the full equity value of the trust. However, in the case of second- or third-party trusts, in which the beneficiary and owner are different, the trust has no CSV to the beneficiary. In this case, the beneficiary is assigned the so-called actuarial value of the trust, which is defined as its full value discounted over the expected lifetime of the second and/or third parties. This approach is used in Smith's work on estate tax data. The actuarial value is included in W1, while the full trust equity is included in W2.

Both W1 and W2 measure pensions at their CSV, which has historically been very small. Our third measure, W3, is defined as W2 less the CSV of pensions plus the total value of pension reserves. In W3, pension reserves are imputed to both current and future beneficiaries, and thus pension reserves are treated in analogous fashion to trust equity. Our fourth measure, W4, is defined as W3 plus the expected present value of future social security benefits. Our last measure, W5, is defined as W4 less the reserve value of pension wealth plus the present value of future expected pension benefits.

Measures W1–W3 are all based on actual accumulations of wealth. The difference among them is in the alternative treatment of accumulated assets over which individuals do not have full control. Aggregate household balance sheet data differ in their treatment of these assets. The flow-of-funds data and Goldsmith's estimates include the full value of both trusts and pension funds, as in our W3. On the other hand, Ruggles and Ruggles' estimates include only the CSV of pensions but the full value of household trusts, as in our W2. Our measures W4 and W5 differ from the first three measures by imputing to households retirement wealth that does not correspond to any accumulated reserves. These measures are useful insofar as household behavior may be affected by perceived social security or pension wealth.

All five measures of household wealth are operational in that they can be estimated from available data. However, the relation of these measures and the wealth concepts implied by the behavioral models is not always delineated clearly. A narrow cash surrender wealth concept, such as W1, is the appropriate one for analyzing behavior if there are significant liquidity constraints or if there is a very short planning horizon by households. Some researchers have used a liquid asset concept, which is defined as either total financial wealth or some subset such as savings and checking accounts. The rationale for this even more narrow wealth concept is not clear. While it is true that tangible assets are not perfect substitutes for financial assets, the ease and frequency with which home owners use the equity in their homes to finance purchases suggest that home equity also has a high degree of liquidity.

There is no behavioral model of which we are aware that corresponds to our W3 measure. If we include pension reserves, then we should include some form of expected social security payments, even though social security does not represent a stock of savings as do pensions. We have introduced W3 in order to separate out the effects of pensions on both aggregate wealth and the concentration of household wealth.

The most common model used for analyzing savings behavior is the life-cycle model, in which household accumulation is primarily for retirement, and the planning horizon is one's lifetime. A life-cycle wealth variant should include all expected transfers, social security as well as pensions. Empirical proxies to life-cycle wealth have often been constructed by adding expected discounted retirement wealth to one of the balance sheet wealth concepts. For example, Feldstein (1974) added a measure of expected discounted social security wealth to balance sheet wealth for his consumption studies. Our W4 measure falls into this category. We use a corrected version of Feldstein's aggregate series as our estimate of social security wealth in W4.[2] It should be stressed here that estimates of both individual and aggregate social security wealth are very sensitive to the assumptions used in their construction. In particular, differences in the discount rate, the mortality rates, the retirement age, the assumed rate of growth in real earnings over time, and the assumed rate of growth of future social security benefits can substantially affect estimates of individual social security wealth, aggregate social security wealth, and the distribution of social security wealth. Here, we make the most conservative assumptions in our estimate of social security wealth in order to analyze broad trends in its concentration over time. For further discussion of these issues, see section 15.5.2 below and Wolff (1987a).

Another wealth concept motivated by the life-cycle model is W_{LC}, defined as the expected discounted value of marketable (fungible) household wealth. Corresponding to this is augmented life-cycle wealth, AW_{LC}, defined as the sum of W_{LC} and the expected discounted present value of retirement wealth. The motivation for this becomes clear when we consider Feldstein's (1974) algorithm for calculating social security wealth, which we call life-cycle social security wealth, SS_{LC}. Assume, for simplicity, that everyone retires at age sixty-five.[3] Then, for a worker of age a:

$$SS_{LC} = e^{-d(65-a)}SS_{65,a} \, ,$$

where d is the discount rate, and $SS_{65,a}$ is the stream of expected social security benefits discounted to age sixty-five (and also discounted on the basis of survival probabilities). The equivalent life-cycle fungible wealth concept is

$$W_{LC} = e^{-d(65-a)}EW_{65,a}$$

where $EW_{65,a}$ is the expected fungible wealth at age sixty-five for some-one currently of age a.

With a few simplifying assumptions, including that the expected annual rate of return to wealth r^* (assumed to be constant over the period) is equal to the discount rate d, W_{LC} can be represented as

$$W_{LC} = \alpha Y_a \int_a^{65} e^{g^*(t-a)}dt + W_a ,$$

where α is the savings rate (assumed to be constant over the period), Y_a is income at current age a, W_a is current marketable wealth, and g^* is the expected annual growth rate of income (also assumed to be constant).

Thus, the difference between W_{LC} and W_a is positive as long as there is a positive income growth rate. This is also the case for AW_{LC}, which is greater than our W4 or W5 wealth measures:[4]

$$AW_{LC} - W4 = W_{LC} - W_a = \alpha Y_a \int_a^{65} e^{g^*(t-a)}dt.$$

The magnitude of the difference between AW_{LC} and W4 can be significant. For example, let us assume the following values for a representative household: $a = 50$, $Y_a = \$20,000$, $g^* = r^* = d = .03$, $\alpha = .05$, and $W_a = \$50,000$. Then the difference between AW_{LC} and W4 is $19,000, or 38 percent of W_a. This difference increases inversely with age.

From the above discussion, it is clear that adding a life-cycle retirement wealth concept to a current balance sheet wealth measure yields a total wealth measure that is smaller than the measure AW_{LC}. In addition, estimates of inequality based on W4 or W5 will likely show less inequality than those based on AW_{LC}. The reason is that social security wealth is distributed more equally than fungible wealth, as we shall see below, and W_a is smaller than W_{LC}. Though estimates for AW_{LC} do not exist, this concept is closer to a life-cycle variable than W4 or W5 are. A full life-cycle concept would include all expected discounted income and capital gains as well as inherited wealth. Unfortunately, this measure cannot be calculated with any reasonable degree of accuracy.

15.3 Aggregate Household Balance Sheets for Selected Years, 1922–83

In order to construct wealth concentration estimates for the period from 1922 to 1983, corresponding aggregate household balance sheet figures were required. While there are several historical time series available on aggregate household wealth, none covers the entire period. Moreover, the sources available are not entirely consistent with each other, thus necessitating several adjustments to make them comparable.

We relied on the following sources in our work. (1) For 1900–1958, full household balance sheet estimates are available in Goldsmith, Brady, and Mendershausen (1956) and Goldsmith, Lipsey, and Mendelson (1963). The figures from these sources will be referred to in this paper and in Appendix A as the Goldsmith data. These are the only sources available for nontangible assets for the period from 1900 to 1946. (2) For 1925–85, Musgrave (1986) provides estimate of tangible assets for every year in this period. (3) For 1946–85, complete balance sheet data are contained in the 1986 flow-of-funds accounts (FFAs). However, the FFA household sector includes not only households but also trusts and nonprofit organizations. For tangible assets, this can be corrected since the FFA source is Musgrave, who reports separate estimates for the more narrowly defined household sector. For nontangible assets, other adjustments must be made. (4) For 1946–80, Ruggles and Ruggles (1982) provide aggregate balance sheet data for the narrowly defined household sector for all assets and liabilities. The Ruggles and Ruggles estimates are based on imputations to the FFA household balance sheet data to separate out nonprofit organizations and trust funds. They also use a wealth concept that includes only the cash surrender value of pensions and insurance and is thus consistent with our W2.

Our aggregate household balance sheet estimates combine data from the above sources. For tangible assets, we rely on Musgrave (1986) for the period from 1925 to 1983. Our 1922 figures are estimated from Musgrave's data. The rationale for using Musgrave's data rather than the Goldsmith data for the period prior to 1949 is, first, that Musgrave provides a consistent series over the entire period, from 1925 to 1983, and, second, that Musgrave's numbers are based on revised and improved data that were not available to Goldsmith in 1963. For nontangibles, we base our estimates on Goldsmith's data for years prior to 1949, on Ruggles and Ruggles (1982) for most financial assets over the period from 1949 to 1980, and on FFA data for all assets in 1981 and 1983 as well as some nontangible assets for the 1949–80 period. The reason for our use of the Ruggles and Ruggles data instead of the FFA data for financial assets is that Ruggles and Ruggles provide a separate trust category, whereas the FFAs include the financial assets, particularly stocks and bonds, held by trusts as part of the household sector. In our analysis of estate tax data and household survey data, a separate asset category for trust funds is required. There are several reasons for this. One is that the treatment of trusts in the estate data is problematic (see sec. 15.4). Another is that trusts are recorded separately in household survey data.

In order to create a consistent aggregate balance sheet series, a number of adjustments were required to these basic data sources. Fortunately, for the years between 1946 and 1958, household balance sheet data were available from all four sources: Musgrave, Goldsmith, Ruggles and Ruggles, and the FFAs. Major discrepancies were found between Goldsmith and Musgrave for tangible assets (for residential structures, e.g., differences ranged between 10 and 31 percent) and between Goldsmith on the one hand and Ruggles and Ruggles and the FFAs on the other for financial assets (differences of up to 80 percent for some assets). These discrepancies were traced to the following causes. First, there are several differences in the categorization of assets between Goldsmith on the one hand and Ruggles and Ruggles and the FFAs on the other. These differences do not affect the wealth totals, only the composition among asset categories. Second, there are some differences in the definition of household wealth. Goldsmith's total wealth concept corresponds to our W3, which includes total pension reserves, whereas Ruggles and Ruggles' definition corresponds to our W2, which includes only the cash surrender value of pensions. Third, there are several methodological differences. For example, Goldsmith attributes all the agricultural sector's net worth to the household sector, whereas Ruggles and Ruggles assume that a small percentage of this represents corporate business rather than unincorporated business, and this would be included in the household sector only through corporate stocks. Fourth, a large part of the difference in estimates is attributable to the revisions in the basic data since Goldsmith's study.

Our adjustments were done in two stages. In the first, we corrected for definitional differences in the asset categories between the various sources and our own classification scheme. In our scheme, we divided the asset categories into three broad groups: tangible, financial fixed claim, and equities. Liabilities were separated into mortgage debt, consumer debt, and other debt. This corresponds to Wolff's (1987b) categories, and it represents only a slight aggregation of the Ruggles and Ruggles classification scheme. However, some substantial realignment of Goldsmith's categories was required.

In the second stage, we adjusted for differences in methodology between Goldsmith on the one hand and Ruggles and Ruggles and the FFAs on the other, especially with respect to the items to be included in each asset category. Goldsmith differs from the other two in regard to the following assets: farm equity, unincorporated business equity, trusts, insurance, and pensions. Moreover, Ruggles and Ruggles include household inventories, which consist of such items as clothing and food, in their tangible asset category. In 1983, the value of these inventory assets was roughly $253.8 billion, or roughly 2 percent of the total value of household assets of $11.8 trillion. We eliminated the household inventory category from our final balance sheet since it is not available for the early years and does not represent fungible wealth. We also added expected social security payments for our wealth concept W4, which is not included in any of the original sources. Our adjustment procedures are summarized in Appendix A by asset category.

Differences in total household net worth between our estimates and those of Goldsmith and Ruggles and Ruggles vary by year and wealth concept. In regard to Goldsmith's figures, our total net worth figure for W3 differs from his by between 3 and 6 percent, depending on the year, while for W2 the difference varies between 7 and 8 percent. Our total wealth figure for W2 differs from that of Ruggles and Ruggles by between 2 and 6 percent, whereas for W3 the difference ranges from 4 to 12 percent. For W4 and W5, the percentage differences between our estimates and those of Goldsmith and Ruggles and Ruggles are much larger.

The accuracy of our aggregate estimates depends both on the reasonableness of our assumptions in realigning Goldsmith's data with Ruggles and Ruggles and the FFAs and on the accuracy of the original sources. We have assumed, in general, that the techniques and assumptions made in the aggregate sources are correct. For one important category, owner-occupied housing, we were able to compare the aggregate household balance sheet estimates with those derived from household survey data. These latter numbers were obtained from the U.S. census of housing for years 1950, 1960, 1970, and 1980 and from the 1962 SFCC and the 1983 SCF (see table 15.2). Housing values in the census data are recorded in a limited number of groups, with the last consisting of an open-ended interval. We estimated an aggregate value of owner-occupied housing for the census data in each year first by fitting a Pareto distribution to the upper tail of the distribution of housing values to obtain the mean for the open-ended category and then by aggregating across each house value category. For the 1962 SFCC and the 1983 SCF, we calculated the total value of owner-occupied housing from the microdata. The estimates from the surveys are compared to our balance sheet estimates in table 15.2. The estimated aggregates from the household survey data vary between 30 percent lower than the FFA totals in 1950 and 25 percent higher than the FFA totals in 1983. The estimates from the census data are always lower than the FFA figures, while estimates derived from the 1962 and 1983 surveys are higher.

It is often assumed that for financial assets, such as stocks and bonds, the aggregate estimates are more reliable than survey estimates because of nonreporting and underreporting in the upper tail of the wealth distribution. For real estate, the opposite is often assumed—namely,

Table 15.2   Value of Owner-occupied Housing and Land: A Comparison of
               Aggregate Values Derived from Household Survey Data with
               Aggregate Balance Sheet Estimates

Year	Household Survey Data (billions of dollars)[a]	FFA Balance Sheet Data (billions of dollars)[b]	Percentage Difference
1950	130.8	177.0	30.0
1960	353.4	372.9	5.4
1962	473.9	419.8	− 12.1
1970	626.8	689.9	9.6
1980	2,234.3	2,568.9	13.9
1983	3,777.8	2,937.6	− 25.0

[a]For 1950, 1960, 1970, and 1980, the figures are drawn from the corresponding census of housing (vol. 1, pt. 1) for that year: 1950, table 16; 1960, table 8; 1970, table 5; and 1980, table 5. The 1962 figure is based on our own calculations from the SFCC and the 1983 figure on our own calculations from the SCF.
[b]The FFA balance sheet figures are drawn from FFA household sector (Board of Governors 1986).

that the survey estimates are more reliable than the aggregate balance sheet estimates. For liquid financial assets, such as bank deposits, there is some controversy over whether the FFA methodology produces more reliable estimates than those obtained from surveys. Curtin, Juster, and Morgan (chap. 10, in this vol.) argue that for such liquid assets the FFA values overestimate the true value owing to the FFA treatment of the household accounts as a residual—that is, what is left over after estimates are made for the other sectors of the economy (such as corporations, the government, and financial institutions). Their evidence is based on the intuition that households should know the value of their bank accounts better than the value of other financial assets, such as stocks and bonds. Thus, if the survey's estimate for stocks is reasonably close to the aggregate balance sheet value, as is the case for the 1983 SCF, but only 30 or 40 percent for liquid assets, then the FFA household values for liquid assets are very likely overestimated. While this may be true for surveys that contain a large representation of the wealthy, such as the 1983 SCF, it is not clear that survey estimates are generally better than those from the FFAs, particularly when the survey is more subject to underreporting, missing values, and underrepresentation of top wealth holders. In conclusion, comparisons between aggregate household wealth estimates derived from reliable macrodata and microdata sources suggest that the aggregate balance sheet sources used in this paper may slightly underestimate real estate assets and overestimate liquid assets.[5]

Results from our adjusted balance sheet estimates are presented in table 15.3 and figure 15.1. Table 15.3 shows our estimates of total net

Table 15.3   **Household Balance Sheet Totals for Assets and Net Worth, Using Wealth Definitions W1–W4, 1922–83 (billions of dollars)**

Wealth Version	1922 Total Assets	Net Worth	1929 Total Assets	Net Worth
W1	309.3	292.5	465.5	425.7
W2	315.4	298.6	475.7	435.9
W3	315.7	298.9	477.2	437.4
W4	315.7	298.9	477.2	437.4
	1939		1945	
W1	370.3	342.2	637.2	608.3
W2	382.2	354.1	652.6	623.7
W3	387.6	359.5	663.3	634.4
W4	434.0	405.9	856.5	827.6
	1949		1953	
W1	854.4	793.0	1,140.8	1,033.7
W2	866.8	805.4	1,159.2	1,052.1
W3	886.1	824.7	1,194.8	1,087.7
W4	1,125.5	1,064.1	1,600.8	1,493.7
	1958		1962	
W1	1,632.9	1,454.3	1,927.8	1,671.8
W2	1,662.6	1,484.0	1,967.8	1,711.8
W3	1,731.7	1,553.1	2,071.6	1,815.6
W4	2,317.8	2,139.2	2,811.5	2,555.5
	1965		1969	
W1	2,381.2	2,039.2	3,104.2	2,649.3
W2	2,428.6	2,086.6	3,158.9	2,704.0
W3	2,575.7	2,233.7	3,366.3	2,911.4
W4	3,250.0	3,183.0	4,727.2	4,272.3
	1972		1976	
W1	3,907.8	3,314.9	5,550.2	4,687.9
W2	3,983.2	3,390.3	5,629.6	4,767.3
W3	4,293.3	3,700.4	6,073.4	5,211.1
W4	6,055.6	5,462.7	8,748.9	7,886.6
	1981		1983	
W1	9,996.4	8,422.6	11,251.2	9,401.7
W2	10,118.2	8,544.4	11,425.3	9,575.8
W3	11,012.2	9,438.4	12,675.9	10,826.4
W4	15,873.0	14,299.2	18,117.7	16,268.2

Source: The figures are based on our own computations. For details, see App. A. Also note that the figures here may not correspond exactly to those in table 15.A.1 because of rounding error.

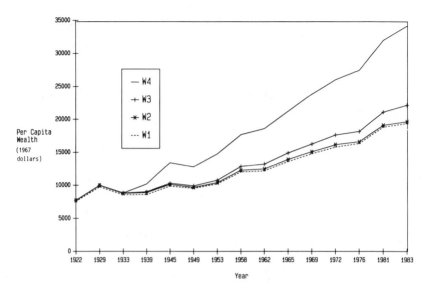

Fig. 15.1   Real household per capita wealth for wealth concepts W1–
W4, 1922–83. *Source:* Calculated from the aggregate wealth
data in table 15.3.

worth and total assets for wealth measures W1–W4 for selected years.[6]
The estimates in table 15.3 are in nominal values. In figure 15.1, real
per capita wealth is shown for all four wealth measures over the period
1922–83. From the table and the figure, it is clear that, while both
pension and social security wealth grew over the period, social security
wealth made the most significant difference in the movement of total
wealth over time. The percentage increase in net worth between wealth
definitions W3 and W4 in 1976 was 51 percent, compared with a 2
percent increase between W1 and W2 and a 9 percent increase between
W2 and W3 for the same year. Figure 15.1 illustrates that per capita
real wealth increased substantially over the period and that social security wealth and pension wealth were significant in raising average
wealth. This suggests that empirical work on average or aggregate
household wealth should pay particular attention to the effects of expected social security benefits on the results. Whether this wealth growth
also increased the national well-being depends on how it was distributed.

15.4   The Concentration of Wealth, 1922–83

Information available on household wealth distribution for the twentieth century is based mainly on estate data for the very wealthy collected from national estate tax records for selected years between 1922
and 1982 and cross-sectional household surveys for selected years start-

ing in 1953. In addition, there are synthetic data bases, such as Wolff's 1969 MESP sample (Wolff 1980) and Greenwood's 1973 database (Greenwood 1983), which have been constructed using income tax data merged with census files, estate files, and other sources.

In table 15.4 and figure 15.2, we report Lampman's and Smith's original concentration estimates for the top 0.5 percent of the population from 1922 through 1976.[7] These estimates show a high concentration of wealth throughout the period. Over 20 percent of total wealth was owned by the top 0.5 percent in each of these years except 1949

Table 15.4   **Lampman's and Smith's Original Estimates of the Share of Total Household Net Worth Held by the Top 0.5 Percent of Individual Wealth Holders**

	1922	1929	1933	1939	1945	1949	1953
Lampman's estimates	29.8	32.4	25.2	28.0	20.9	19.3	22.7
	1958	1962	1965	1969	1972	1976	
Smith's estimates	21.4	22.2	25.4	21.8	21.9	14.4	

Sources: 1922–53: Lampman's (1962, 202) so-called basic variant for the wealth holdings of the top 0.5 percent. 1958–76: Smith (1984, 422).

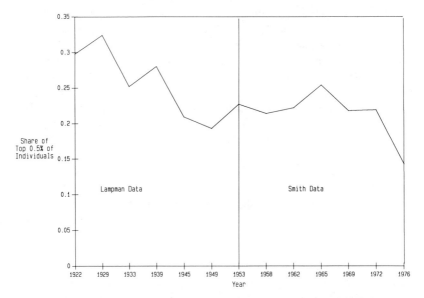

Fig. 15.2   Lampman and Smith estimates of the share of total wealth held by the top individual wealth holders, 1922–76. *Source:* Table 15.4.

and 1976. However, table 15.4 and figure 15.2 also indicate a significant decline in concentration over the century, from a maximum share of 32.4 percent for the top 0.5 percent in 1929 to 14.3 percent in 1976. In particular, there was a substantial decline in the top wealth holders' share during World War II and another large fall in the mid-1970s, as indicated in Smith's results.

This section explores the sensitivity of the concentration results in table 15.4 to the following factors: (1) differences between Smith's and Lampman's imputation assumptions; (2) adjustments to the aggregate balance sheet series; (3) the addition of retirement wealth (W3 and W4); (4) changes in the number of household units and the composition of wealth between household members; and (5) differences in the data and methodology used (in particular, a comparison of estate data estimates with those from household surveys and other sources).

15.4.1   Unadjusted Concentration Estimates from Estate Data

The estate files represent the wealth of the deceased. The wealth estimates for the living population are derived using the estate multiplier method, which divides the population by age and sex and weights the deceased in each group by the reciprocal of the survival probability for each group. The survival probabilities used are higher than those for the population at large, owing to the longer expected life span of the wealthy. This method represents a point estimate that can have a very large variance, particularly for the young, since there are very few in the sample. In fact, the multipliers for those under fifty approach 2,000. Estate estimates have been criticized by Atkinson (1975) and Shorrocks (1987) as overestimating the decline in inequality. The reason is that estate estimates are based on the individual rather than the household unit and over the century marital customs and relations have changed. Married women now inherit more wealth and have higher wealth levels than they did in 1900 or 1930. This reduces individual concentration even if household wealth inequality does not change. For example, between 1929 and 1953, Lampman reported that the percentage of married women among top wealth holders increased from 8.5 to 18 percent.

The estate files used by Lampman and Smith do not include all assets, and the authors used different assumptions concerning pensions and trusts. For example, in Smith's estimates, pensions are included only at their CSV, and a large percentage of trusts, those that were not directly under the control of the deceased, are measured at their actuarial value since that is how they are measured in the estate files. Thus, Smith's wealth definition corresponds to a narrower "available" wealth concept, as in our W1. On the other hand, Lampman used a wealth measure that includes the full value of pensions as well as trusts

(W3). Because of the fraction of trusts not included, Smith's reported concentration estimates are biased downward in relation to Lampman's. Another asset, life insurance, is overstated in the estate files, a problem that both Lampman and Smith recognized and made adjustments for. Another difference is that Lampman's concentration estimates reported in table 15.4 are based on Goldsmith's estimates of aggregate household wealth. In contrast. Smith's estimates are based on Ruggles and Ruggles aggregate data.[8] Also, Lampman used Goldsmith's end-year aggregates, whereas Smith used a mid-year aggregate estimate.[9] Finally, neither Smith nor Lampman included expected social security benefits in their wealth estimates.

15.4.2   Adjusted Concentration Estimates from Estate Data

In order to derive a more consistent series on household wealth concentration than the one presented in table 15.4 and to include social security wealth, we made a series of adjustments to the Lampman and Smith figures. First, we used our adjusted aggregate household balance sheet totals to derive the concentration estimates. Second, imputations were provided for the assets that were left out of the estate files— trusts, pensions, and social security wealth. For them, we made several alternative assumptions, creating upper and lower bounds for the top wealth holders' holdings in each asset category. These imputation assumptions and results are discussed in Appendix B. In the tables in this section, we report only selected concentration results from the alternative scenarios that we devised. Other imputation assumptions yielded estimates that either were not substantially different (less than 2 percentage points) from those reported in table 15.5 or fell between the bounds shown in the table.

For each wealth definition, W1–W4, table 15.5 presents our adjusted concentration shares for top wealth holders from the estate data estimates as well as concentration estimates for the top 0.5 and 1.0 percent of households from household survey data. In addition to the Lampman and Smith data, we included Schwartz's (1983) estate data estimates. In the original Lampman data, for the period 1922–53, estimates were made for a different proportion of the population in each year. His sample was all wealth holders with total assets above $60,000. Thus, the fraction of population represented in the sample and reported in table 15.5 varied over the period, from a low of 0.3 percent in 1929 to a high of 1.0 percent in 1958. In table 15.5, the percentage of the population represented in the Lampman data is reported in row 1 of table 15.5, followed by the corresponding wealth shares for this population percentage for wealth concepts W1–W4.

Comparisons among the concentration estimates for wealth definitions W1–W4 in table 15.5 illustrate the sensitivity of the estimated

Table 15.5   **The Share of Total Net Worth and Total Assets of Top Wealth Holders Using Different Wealth Definitions: Our Adjusted Series**

	Estimates from Estate Data[a]					
Wealth Definition	1922, 0.5%	1929, 0.3%	1939, 0.6%	1945, 0.7%	1949, 0.8%	1953, 1.0%
Percentage of net worth:						
W1	26.8	27.3	27.2	22.3	21.9	26.6
W2	28.4	29.1	29.8	24.4	23.2	28.4
W3	28.0	28.5	28.8	23.7	22.6	27.4
W4	28.0	28.5	25.9	18.9	18.4	21.3
Percentage of total assets:						
W1	28.9	29.1	28.9	23.5	21.2	26.5
W2	30.3	30.7	31.3	25.5	23.8	28.1
W3	29.9	30.2	30.4	24.8	23.2	27.3
W4	29.9	30.2	27.5	19.9	19.1	21.6

	1958		1962		1965	
	0.5%	1.0%	0.5%	1.0%	0.5%	1.0%
Percentage of net worth:						
W1	20.8	25.9	23.0	29.1	25.4	31.3
W2	22.7	27.7	25.0	31.1	27.7	33.6
W3	21.5	26.6	23.4	29.5	25.7	31.5
W4	16.4	20.7	17.5	22.4	18.9	23.6
Percentage of total assets:						
W1	20.3	25.4	22.4	28.4	24.2	29.9
W2	22.0	27.0	24.2	30.1	26.2	31.9
W3	21.0	26.0	22.8	28.8	24.5	30.2
W4	16.4	20.7	17.6	22.5	18.7	23.4

	1969		1972		1976	
	0.5%	1.0%	0.5%	1.0%	0.5%	1.0%
Percentage of net worth:						
W1	22.5	28.2	21.8	27.6	12.6	17.3
W2	24.5	30.2	24.0	29.8	14.6	19.1
W3	22.6	28.3	21.9	27.6	13.2	17.8
W4	16.4	20.9	15.8	20.3	9.8	13.4
Percentage of total assets:						
W1	21.7	27.3	21.0	26.8	12.8	17.3
W2	23.4	29.0	23.0	28.6	14.4	18.9
W3	21.8	27.4	21.2	26.8	13.3	17.7
W4	16.4	21.0	15.9	20.5	10.1	13.8

Table 15.5   (continued)

	Estimates from Estate Data[a]	
	1981	
Wealth Definition	0.08%	2.0%
Percentage of net worth:		
W1	19.7	28.4
W2	21.2	29.7
W3	19.5	27.8
W4	14.0	20.4
Percentage of total assets:		
W1	19.6	28.1
W2	20.8	29.3
W3	19.4	27.6
W4	14.5	21.0

	Estimates from Household Survey Data[b]			
	1962		1983	
	0.5%	1.0%	0.5%	1.0%
Percentage of net worth:				
W1	22.4	31.0	23.2	31.2
W2	24.8	33.2	24.9	32.7
W3	23.2	31.4	22.0	29.2
W4	16.7	22.7	15.1	20.5
Percentage of total assets:				
W1	20.1	27.8	20.6	28.2
W2	22.2	29.9	22.0	29.5
W3	21.0	28.5	19.9	26.9
W4	15.6	22.3	14.3	19.7

Sources: The estate date sources are, for 1922–53, Lampman (1962); for 1953–76, Smith (1984, 1987); and, for 1981, Schwartz (1983). The adjustments and imputations to these are explained in detail in App. B. The household survey data sources are, for 1962, the SFCC database; and, for 1983, the SCF database. The concentration estimates are from our own calculations. The adjustments and procedures are explained in section 15.5. The figures differ slightly from those in section 15.5 because of different assumptions concerning trust and pension holdings, which are necessary for consistency between the estate data and the survey data estimates.

[a]Data are broken down by year and percentage of population.

[b]Data are broken down by year and percentage of households.

shares of top wealth holders to the different imputation assumptions and to the inclusion of retirement wealth. The difference arising from alternative assumptions in the treatment of trusts is captured by wealth concepts W2 and W1. W2 represents an upper bound for trust holdings since for its calculation it is assumed that the top 1 percent owned 100 percent of total trust assets, while W1 represents a reasonable lower bound since it evaluates trusts at their much lower actuarial value and assumes that all the trust holdings of the wealthy were included in the estate file. In contrast, Lampman assumed that only about 10 percent of total trusts were included in the basic estate data, and Smith estimated that the actuarial value represented 54 percent of all trusts.[10] Our concentration estimates for W1 correspond to the wealth definition used by Smith. Those for W2 give the highest concentration ratio because of the assumption that 100 percent of trusts are held by the top 1 percent and the inclusion of the full value of trusts in W2. In addition, W2 excludes retirement wealth, except for the CSV of pensions, which constitutes a negligible fraction of total wealth. The results from table 15.5 indicate that the share of wealth held by the top wealth holders differs by about 2 percentage points from the upper- and lower-bound assumptions concerning trusts.

The extent to which wealth concentration is lessened when retirement wealth is included in the household balance sheet is indicated by concentration estimates for W3 and W4. W3 includes full pension reserves, which are reported in the aggregate data sources. However, one major difficulty is that there is very little information concerning the percentage of total pensions owned by the top wealth holders. We made alternative assumptions about this share, ranging from a maximum of 15 percent to a minimum of 3 percent for the top 1 percent of wealth holders. The different assumptions had little effect on total wealth concentration. In the W3 estimates reported in table 15.5, we assumed that the share of total pension wealth held by the top percentile of wealth holders declined over the twentieth century because of the growth of pensions over the period. The addition of pension wealth has had a minor effect on concentration, owing to its relatively small size in relation to total assets. On the other hand, the addition of social security wealth (in W4) significantly lowered the degree of inequality because of its relatively large magnitude. The share of net worth of the top percentile dropped between 4 and 8 percentage points from the inclusion of social security wealth. This represents a decline of 20–33 percent in the share of total net worth held by the top 1 percent.

In order to analyze time trends in our concentration estimates, we standardized the concentration shares from Lampman and Schwartz shown in table 15.5 to the top 0.5 and 1.0 percent of the population using the Pareto distribution. This technique assumes that the Pareto distribution is representative of the wealth distribution at the upper tail for each year. The technique and assumptions are explained in the second section of Appendix B. The standardized results are reported in table 15.6 and illustrated in figure 15.3.

The difference in the share of the top 0.5 percent between the original Lampman and Smith estimates, shown in table 15.4, and our W1 estimates in tables 15.5 and 15.6 primarily reflects differences in the Goldsmith and Ruggles and Ruggles aggregate wealth estimates for the household sector and our revised figures.[11] Our concentration estimates for W1 (for the top 0.5 percent) are lower than Lampman's figures, while for W2 the shares are higher. Our new concentration estimates for W1 based on Smith's data are higher than his original estimates in some years and lower in others. In general, the aggregate adjustments changed the concentration results from 1 to 2 percentage points.

A comparison among the four wealth measures, W1–W4, in table 15.6 confirms the results from table 15.5. While the addition of retirement wealth to conventional wealth reduces measured concentration, the effect of adding pension wealth is relatively small, while the effect of including social security wealth is significant and relatively constant over time since its introduction.[12] Our adjustments to the estate estimates did not account for underreporting of assets or nonfiling in the estate data. Both omissions bias the reported concentration results downward. The extent of this bias is discussed below, in the comparisons between estate and survey data (see table 15.8 below).

15.4.3   Long-Term Trends in Wealth Inequality: Individual versus Household-based Data

With the previous adjustments to the estate data, we examined the sensitivity of the level of concentration to different wealth aggregates and imputations and adjustments. These adjustments did not significantly alter the trend in concentration. The results from table 15.6 and figure 3 indicate that concentration was at a peak during the period from 1922 through 1939, declined significantly during World War II, then increased between 1949 and 1965, declined slightly in 1972, and then fell in 1976 to a record low, which was only partially recovered by 1981.

A large permanent decline in concentration during the 1970s is not substantiated by the household survey data (reported in table 15.5). A comparison of the 1962 and 1983 survey data for the top 1 percent of households indicates similar concentration levels in the two years. One possible reason for this discrepancy is the difference in the unit of observation between estate and survey data. Estate files record wealth for the individual, while surveys are based on household units. As mentioned earlier, the increased tendency to divide wealth equally

Table 15.6   **Estimated Shares of Total Assets of the Top 0.5 and 1.0 Percent of the Population for Alternative Definitions of Wealth, 1922–81**

	Proportion of Total Assets[a]					
	1922		1929		1939	
Wealth Definition	0.5%	1.0%	0.5%	1.0%	0.5%	1.0%
W1	28.8	37.1	31.7	35.8	26.7	35.9
W2	30.3	38.3	33.2	37.2	29.1	38.1
W3	29.9	37.9	32.7	36.7	28.3	37.1
W4	29.9	37.9	32.7	36.7	25.6	33.4
	1945		1949		1953	
	0.5%	1.0%	0.5%	1.0%	0.5%	1.0%
W1	20.6	27.0	18.2	23.9	21.2	26.5
W2	22.6	28.9	20.2	25.7	22.9	28.1
W3	21.9	28.1	19.6	25.0	22.2	27.3
W4	17.7	22.4	16.3	20.5	17.9	21.6
	1958		1962		1965	
	0.5%	1.0%	0.5%	1.0%	0.5%	1.0%
W1	20.3	25.4	22.4	28.4	24.2	29.9
W2	22.0	27.0	24.2	30.1	26.2	31.9
W3	21.0	26.0	22.8	28.8	24.5	30.2
W4	16.4	20.7	17.6	22.5	18.7	23.4
	1969		1972		1976	
	0.5%	1.0%	0.5%	1.0%	0.5%	1.0%
W1	21.7	27.3	21.0	26.8	12.8	17.3
W2	23.4	29.0	23.0	28.6	14.4	18.9
W3	21.8	27.4	21.2	26.8	13.3	17.7
W4	16.4	21.0	15.9	20.5	10.1	13.8
	1981					
	0.5%	1.0%				
W1	16.0	22.0				

Sources: For the Lampman and Schwartz data (years 1922, 1929, 1939, 1945, 1949, 1953, and 1981), we estimated the share of the top 0.5 and 1.0 percent of wealth holders using the Pareto distribution. The technique is explained in App. B.

Note: The 1981 figure is computed for W1 only.

[a]Data are broken down by year and percentage of population.

between household members will reduce the estate concentration estimates without changing household wealth concentration. In table 15.7 and figure 15.4, we do a preliminary analysis of the sensitivity of the trends in concentration to changes in the unit of observation. The reported concentration estimates in table 15.7 represent the estimated

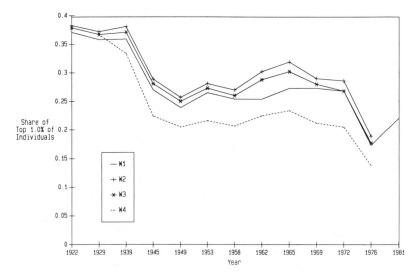

Fig. 15.3   Share of total wealth held by top individual wealth holders for wealth concepts W1–W4, 1922–81, our estimates. *Source:* Table 15.6.

Table 15.7   **Lower-Bound Estimate of the Share of Wealth Held by the Top 1 Percent of Households from Alternative Definitions of Wealth, 1922–76**

Wealth Definition	Proportion of Total Assets					
	1922	1929	1939	1945	1949	1953
W1	24.0	29.1	22.7	18.6	16.8	20.0
W2	25.5	30.7	25.3	20.7	18.8	21.7
W3	25.2	30.2	24.5	20.1	18.3	21.1
W4	25.2	30.2	22.2	16.2	15.2	17.0
	1958	1962	1965	1969	1972	1976
W1	18.5	20.5	22.1	20.0	18.5	11.3
W2	20.0	22.1	23.9	21.6	20.2	12.7
W3	19.1	20.9	22.4	20.7	18.6	11.7
W4	15.0	16.1	17.1	15.4	14.0	9.0

Source: The household shares are derived from estate tax data on the wealth of individual wealthholders. For details, see App. B.

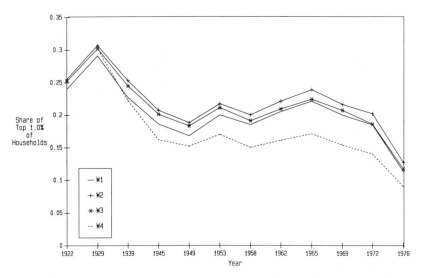

Fig. 15.4   Share of total wealth held by the wealthiest households for wealth concepts W1–W4, 1922–76, lower-bound estimates. *Source:* Table 15.7.

top 1.0 percent of households rather than the top 1.0 percent of individuals, as reported in table 15.6.

In order to change the estate data to a household base, certain assumptions were required about the division of wealth within households. For the values shown in table 15.7, we assumed that all married women in the sample of top wealth holders married wealthy men in the sample, while the remaining married men had wives with zero wealth (our assumption 1 in App. B). Married men represented from 55 to 59 percent of the sample, while married woman represented between 9 and 18 percent. This assumption results in the lowest number of households formed from the individuals in the sample and thus the highest level of household wealth concentration with regard to married women. However, it produces a very low estimate of the total wealth held by the top 1.0 percent of households because of the assumption that the married men in the sample married women with zero wealth. This method is explained in more detail in Appendix B, as are alternative transformation assumptions.

The results from 15.7 and figure 15.4 indicate that a proportion of the decline in individual wealth concentration over the period 1922–53 was due to changes in the wealth of married women. The share of total assets of the top 1.0 percent of households declined 4 percentage points over this period, in contrast to a 10 percentage point drop in the share of the wealthiest 1 percent of individuals. The years 1929 and 1949 appear to be outliers, with 1929 a peak and 1949 a trough. During the period from 1958 to 1976, we estimated on the basis of Smith's data that the percentage of married women among the wealthy remained relatively constant at 18 percent.[13] Thus, for Smith's data, there is no significant difference in the concentration estimates between the top 1 percent of households and the top 1 percent of individuals.

While some of the decline in wealth concentration found by Lampman appears to be due to changes in the wealth status of married women, the sharp drop in inequality found in Smith's results cannot be explained by our transformation of the estate data to the household unit. There are several other possible explanations. First, the 1976 estate estimates could be incorrect, especially with respect to stock holdings. The 1976 results suggest not only a significant drop in the value of stocks but also a substantial fall in the percentage of stock held by the top 1.0 percent of the population, from 57.4 percent in 1972 to 37.6 percent in 1976. If this drop represented a portfolio shift, then some other asset should have increased. However, this did not happen. Second, a large increase may have occurred in the volume of stocks that were owned primarily by the less wealthy. However, there is no evidence of this from other sources. Third, there was a sharp fall in the price of stock shares relative to that of real estate in the 1970s. However, the relative price shift was not significant enough to account for the magnitude of the fall in wealth concentration between 1972 and 1976. The last possibility is that there was an increase in the degree of underreporting of all assets in the estate data. There is no obvious reason for such an increase in the 1970s, although in the early 1980s this was probably the case, owing to the large increase in the gift exclusion in estate tax returns.

15.4.4   Comparison of Inequality Estimates from Various Data Sources

The estate data are not corrected for underreporting or the transferring of wealth through gifts. In order to examine the extent of any underreporting, we compare the estate estimates to household survey estimates for 1962 and 1983 (see table 15.8). The concentration estimates for the latter are based on the 1962 SFCC and the 1983 SCF, both of which have been adjusted to correspond to the aggregate household balance sheet totals for each asset (the adjustments are discussed in sec. 15.5 below and in Wolff [1987b]). The estate data figures are our estimates of the share of the top 1 percent of households derived from Smith's data. For 1962, we have estimates from both sources. The household concentration estimates from the 1962 SFCC are significantly higher, by about 7 percentage points, than those derived from estate data. One possible reason for this difference is the conservative assumption used in converting the estate data to a household base. If

Table 15.8   **A Comparison of Shares of Top Wealth Holders Based on Estate Tax and Household Survey Data (percentage of total assets)**

Wealth Definition	Estate Data				Survey Data	
	1962	1972	1976		1962	1983
Top 1.0 percent of households:						
W1	20.5	18.5	11.3		27.8	28.2
W2	22.1	20.2	12.7		29.9	29.5
W3	20.9	18.6	11.7		28.5	26.9
W4	16.1	14.0	9.0		22.3	19.7

	Estate Data			
	1962	1972	1976	1981[a]
Top 1.0 percent of individuals:				
W1	28.4	26.8	17.3	22.0
W2	30.1	28.6	18.9	
W3	28.8	26.8	17.7	
W4	22.5	20.5	13.8	

Sources: For households, estate estimates are taken from table 15.7 and survey estimates from table 15.5. For individuals, estate estimates are taken from table 15.6.

[a]The 1981 figure is computed for W1 only.

we, instead, assume that all married men in the estate sample of top wealth holders had married women with wealth, the concentration estimates would have been higher, but not enough to account for the difference (see App. B). Another possible reason for the discrepancy between the estate and the survey estimates is that there is a serious underreporting problem in the estate data. A recent article by Marley (1987) supports the results found here that there are large differences between the estate and the survey concentration estimates that cannot be ascribed to differences in the unit of observation (individual vs. household) or to differences in wealth definitions. The results in tables 15.7 and 15.8 indicate the need for further work to be done on the effect of the unit of observation (household vs. individual) on measures of wealth inequality as well as the need for further reconciliation between estate data estimates and household survey estimates of wealth inequality.

In table 15.9, we report some concentration estimates from other sources. The results suggest that many surveys do not sufficiently oversample the rich to capture the upper tail of the distribution. For example, the 1979 ISDP survey captured only 66 percent of net worth, and the 1979 Pension Commission survey estimated an aggregate household wealth that was only 52 percent of our total net worth. In com-

Table 15.9   **Share of Total Net Worth of Richest Households: Estimates from Other Sources, 1969–84**

	1969 MESP Data Base[a]	1973 Greenwood Data Base[b]	1979 ISDP Survey[c]	1979 Pension Survey[d]	1984 SIPP Survey[e]
Percentage of richest households	1.0	1.0	1.5	1.0	1.9
Percentage of net worth, based on sample totals	N.A.	32.6	26.0	16.2	26.0
Percentage of net worth, based on national balance sheet totals	30.8	24.0	17.0	8.4	N.A.

Note: N.A. = not available.

[a]From Wolff (1983), which is based on the MESP file, a synthetic data base created by matching income tax return data to the 1970 census public use sample.

[b]From Greenwood (1987). The data base is derived from a synthetic match of income tax returns with the 1973 Current Population survey.

[c]From Radner and Vaughan (1987), which is based on the ISDP. The share of wealth of the top 1.5 percent of households is estimated using a Pareto distribution.

[d]From Cartwright and Friedland (1985), which is based on the Pension Commission survey.

[e]From Lamas and NcNeil (1986), which is based on the SIPP. The estimates shown above were provided to us by John McNeil.

parison, the (unadjusted) 1962 SFCC captured 79 percent and the (unadjusted) 1983 SCF 89 percent of aggregate net worth.[14] The resulting concentration estimates from each survey vary with the degree of underreporting and bias in the sample. The 1979 ISDP sample captured a higher proportion of aggregate wealth and also had a higher proportion of wealthy individuals than the Pension Commission survey of the same year. Consequently, the reported inequality based on the ISDP is higher. The top 1.5 percent held 26 percent of total wealth in the ISDP, while the top 0.96 percent owned 16.2 percent in the Pension Commission survey. The concentration estimates from the 1984 SIPP (table 15.9) and the 1983 SCF (table 15.8) provide an indication of the extent of the problem of inadequate coverage in some wealth surveys. On the basis of the 1984 SIPP file, Lamas and McNeil (1986) estimate that the share of wealth held by the top 1.9 percent was 26 percent, compared to 34.5 percent for the top 1 percent from the unadjusted 1983 SCF data. The reliability of these two surveys is discussed in Curtin, Juster, and Morgan (chap. 10, in this vol.).

Inequality estimates from synthetic databases that combine several sources may also be subject to biases, from both the underlying data sources and the methodology employed. Results from two such databases are reported in table 15.9. The first are from the 1969 MESP database, created from a synthetic match of Internal Revenue Service

(IRS) tax records to the 1970 census one in 1,000 public use sample and the capitalization of selected income flows to corresponding asset types (e.g., dividends to stock shares). Asset and liability values were then aligned to the Ruggles and Ruggles national balance sheet totals for the household sector. The methodology is described in detail in Wolff (1980, 1982, 1983). Various problems arise from the imputation procedures used. Two are worth noting here. The first is that the tax unit differs from the household unit, and the second is that a not insignificant fraction of families in the United States are not subject to federal income tax and thus do not file tax returns. Both problems create biases in the matching procedure. From the MESP database, it was estimated that the share of the top 1 percent of households was 30.8 percent of total household net worth, a figure that was slightly greater than the corresponding estimate of 29.3 percent for 1962 (see sec. 15.5 below).

The second source is Greenwood's synthetic database, which is based on income tax records that were merged with the 1973 Current Population Survey file. Imputations of asset values were based on an analysis of estate tax records. The methodology is explained in Greenwood (1983, 1987). In this case, there appear to be some sampling problems. Her estimated aggregate wealth was 74 percent of our balance sheet figure. Her estimates of total financial securities and stocks, assets held largely by the wealthy, were actually higher than our balance sheet estimates, while the total value of real estate, an asset concentrated in the middle class, was only 80 percent of our balance sheet total (see Greenwood 1987, 126). Greenwood calculated that the top 1 percent owned 32.6 percent of total wealth in 1973, a share that is probably overestimated as a result of the underestimation of total assets. An alternative estimate of 24.0 percent is given in row 3 of table 15.9, calculated by dividing Greenwood's estimated wealth of the top 1 percent by our balance sheet total for the household sector.

The conclusions from our analysis of twentieth-century concentration are several. First, the concentration estimates for the early years were slightly reduced when we adjusted for inconsistencies in the aggregate data and when we included pension funds. With the exception of social security, the effect on the top wealth holders' share of different versions of wealth and/or different asset assumptions is no more than 2–3 percentage points. However, the inclusion of social security wealth does make a significant difference on the concentration estimates—up to a maximum reduction of 8 percentage points. Second, preliminary adjustments for changes in number of households and married women among the top wealth holders indicate that the drop in concentration during and after World War II is considerably less than indicated from estimates based on individual shares. Third, when we include the concentration estimates based on household survey data for 1962 and 1983, we find that the level of wealth inequality in 1983 was about the same as in 1962. The estate data series, on the other hand, shows a large decline in concentration between 1962 and 1976, followed by an increase in 1981, though the inequality level in 1981 is considerably less than it was in 1962. The reason for the apparent difference in results is not clear, though underreporting in the estate data may have increased during the period. A more extensive analysis is required, both in comparisons of inequality estimates between survey and estate data and in ascertaining the degree of bias introduced in estate data by gift transfers (presently limited to $10,000 a year per person) and unreported trusts. Fourth, the results reported in tables 15.8 and 15.9 suggest that inequality estimates are particularly sensitive not only to the inclusion of retirement wealth but also to the quality and representativeness of the data source used.

15.5   Household Survey Estimates for 1962 and 1983

In this section, we investigate the sensitivity of estimates of wealth inequality based on household survey data to adjustments for missing assets, underreporting, and different definitions of household wealth. Several measures of wealth inequality are used, including the Gini coefficient, the shares of the top wealth holders, and quintile shares. Estimates for 1962 are based on the SFCC, and those for 1983 are based on the SCF. Particular attention is paid to the effects on the distribution of household wealth of including measures of expected pension and social security wealth in the household portfolio. As in sec. 15.4, we find that estimates of wealth inequality are quite sensitive to imputations for missing assets such as consumer durables and household inventories and to the inclusion of retirement wealth. They are less sensitive to adjustments made for underreporting.

15.5.1   Adjustment Procedures for the 1962 SFCC

Table 15.10 presents a comparison of household balance sheet totals from the original SFCC data with those from national balance sheet data (for a description of the national balance sheet estimates used in the paper, see sec. 15.3 and App. A). The total of all assets in the national balance sheet data is $2,005.7 billion. The SFCC database includes all the national balance sheet assets except other (i.e., nonvehicle) consumer durables, inventories, insurance CSV, and pension CSV. The national balance sheet total for only assets included in the SFCC is $1,741.2 billion. The original SFCC asset values total to $1,410.1 billion, or 81 percent of the national balance sheet total for corresponding assets. Real estate and unincorporated business equity are quite

Table 15.10   Comparison of National Balance Sheet and Survey Data Estimates of Total Household Wealth, 1962 and 1983

	1962 (end-year)			1983 (mid-year)		
	National Balance Sheet Data	SFCC	Ratio of SFCC to National Balance Sheets	National Balance Sheet Data	SCF	Ratio of SCF to National Balance Sheets
Assets	2,005.7	1,410.1	.70	11,165.0	11,847.7	1.06
Tangible assets	782.5	643.3	.82	4,356.0	6,012.2	...
Owner-occupied housing	419.8	473.9	1.13	2,937.6	3,777.8	1.29
Other real estate	104.3	114.4	1.10	...	1,721.4	...
Cars	74.5	55.0	.74	413.7	375.5	.91
Other consumer durables[a]	127.8	...	...	760.6	137.5	...
Inventories	56.1	...	...	244.1	...	...
Fixed claim assets	415.3	265.0	.64	2,618.1	1,623.6	.62
Demand deposits and currency	69.8	23.7	.34	326.9	122.2	.37
Time and savings deposits[b]	207.3	104.7	.51	1,832.3	1,061.8	.58
Financial securities[c]	138.2	117.4	.85	458.9	439.6	.96

Equities	807.9	501.8	.62	4,190.9	4,211.9	1.01
Corporate stock	361.0	222.8	.62	1,134.7	1,026.8	.90
Unincorporated business equity	281.1	224.7	.80	2,361.8	2,298.3	.97
Trust fund equity	85.2	54.3	.64	331.1	461.3	1.39
Insurance (CSV)	75.6	...	...	213.1	273.5	1.28
Pensions (CSV)	5.0	...	...	60.9	121.5	1.99
Miscellaneous assets[d]	...	...	...	89.3	30.5	...
Liabilities	256.0	218.5	.85	1,749.6	1,509.7	.86
Mortgage debt	163.8	146.5	.89	1,116.0	963.4	.86
Insurance debt	⎫ 92.2	...	...	633.6	546.3	.86
Other debt	⎭	72.0	...			
Net worth	1,749.7	1,191.6	.68	9,415.4	10,338.0	1.10

Source: For the 1983 SCF tabulations, we used the 1987 Federal Reserve Board tape version of this data set, which includes imputations for missing values from nonresponses (for details, see Avery, Elliehausen, and Kennickell [1987]). The national balance sheet figures are based on our own estimates. For details on sources and methods, see App. A.

Note: All figures are in billions of current dollars.

[a] This includes boats, antiques, precious metals, jewelry, art, and miscellaneous durables in the 1983 SCF.

[b] This includes certificates of deposit, individual retirement accounts, Keoghs, money-market funds, and U.S. savings bonds in 1983.

[c] This includes mortgage assets in both years and U.S. savings bonds in 1962 but excludes U.S. savings bonds in 1983.

[d] Miscellaneous assets in the SCF include other investments, consisting of money lent to friends and relatives, and the CSV of company savings plans, including thrift, profit-sharing, stock options, and employee stock option plans. The national balance sheet miscellaneous asset category includes only the FFA miscellaneous financial asset entry, which is not directly comparable to the SCF entry.

close between the two sources. The SFCC values are significantly below the corresponding national balance sheet estimates for the following asset categories. 1) Demand deposits and currency are undervalued by two-thirds. One should note that currency is not included in the SFCC data. 2) Time and saving deposits are undervalued by almost half. 3) Corporate stock is undervalued by almost 40 percent. 4) Trust fund equity is undervalued by over one-third.

The total of all liabilities in the national balance sheet data is $256.0 billion. This estimate probably includes the debt on life insurance, which is excluded from the SFCC tape data. The total of all liabilities represented in the SFCC is $218.5 billion. In the SFCC published tables (Projector and Weiss 1966, table A14), debt on life insurance is given as $3.6 billion. Adding this to the value of the liabilities found on the SFCC tape yields a figure of $222.1 billion as the SFCC estimate of total liabilities, which is 15 percent lower than the national balance sheet.

The estimate of net worth from the national balance sheet data is $1,485 billion if only comparable assets are included. The SFCC estimate is $1,192 billion. Thus, the national balance sheet estimate is 25 percent greater than the SFCC net worth estimate if only comparable assets are used.

In order to align the SFCC data with the national balance sheet totals, each asset or liability in the SFCC is adjusted either by a constant proportion or in more complex fashion, depending on the degree of error and the availability of outside information.[15] The undervaluation of assets in the survey data could be due to two types of errors—the underreporting of asset ownership and the underreporting of asset values. Moreover, the degree of underreporting of either type could differ by income class. In order to ascertain the type of underreporting present in the SFCC and whether this underreporting varied by income class, we compared SFCC asset information (percentage ownership and mean value) by income class to corresponding income flow information from income data (the percentage of households receiving income from the asset and mean income received).

The income data were obtained from *Statistics of Income* (Internal Revenue Service 1965). Thus, the percentage of households who reported dividends in the *Statistics of Income* figures was compared to the percentage who reported corporate stock holdings in the SFCC. It is then possible to increase the percentage of households holding each asset type in the SFCC by income class if the percentage of units reporting the corresponding income flow is greater in the *Statistics of Income* figures. Moreover, it is also possible to adjust for underreporting of asset values in the SFCC differentially by income class if average yields, defined as the ratio of the income flow in the *Statistics of Income* data to the asset value in the SFCC, differ substantially by income class. These asset comparisons between the SFCC and the *Statistics of Income* data along with our adjustment factors are reported in table 15.11.

For almost all asset types, the percentage of households reporting the asset in the SFCC was greater than or equal to the percentage of units reporting the corresponding income flow in the *Statistics of Income* data. Thus, adjustment for nonreporting of assets is not required. The one exception was trust funds. The adjustment for trusts is explained below. Moreover, for many asset types, average yield figures were fairly uniform across income classes. For these, we used the same adjustment or scaling factor for each income class. The scaling factor was defined as the ratio of the national balance sheet total to the SFCC total for that asset (the reciprocal of the third column of table 15.10). On the other hand, for stocks, unincorporated business equity, and other financial assets, the average yield figures varied considerably by income class. For these assets, the adjustment factor varied correspondingly by income class. The details of the adjustments for underreporting (if any) and imputations for missing assets are explained below by asset category and summarized in table 15.11.[16]

1. The owner-occupied housing figures in the SFCC are not adjusted. The SFCC total is a little larger than the national balance sheet figure. The likely reason is that SFCC households report the estimated market value of their homes, while the national balance sheet data, which are based on a perpetual inventory accumulation of the value of residential investment in new construction, are biased downward. Though the balance sheet technique attempts to include price changes, it is possible that it does not fully capture the change in both construction costs and land values.

2. For the same reason, the other real estate figures in the SFCC are not adjusted.

3. Automobiles are adjusted through scaling up by a factor of 1.355.

4. Other consumer durables are not included in the SFCC. Their value is imputed to each household on the basis of a regression equation estimated from the 1969 MESP data base (for more details, see Wolff [1980]), which is as follows:

$$OTHRDUR62 = 2871.4 + .08644\,INC62 - (.3271 \times 10^{-6})\,(INC62)^2$$
$$- 7.1401\,AGEHEAD + 811.32\,MARRIED - 240.31\,FEMHEAD$$
$$+ 189.51\,URBANRES,$$

where OTHRDUR = value of other consumer durables in 1962 dollars; INC62 = income of the household unit in 1962 dollars; AGEHEAD = age of head of unit; MARRIED = 1 if head is married, 0 otherwise;

Table 15.11   Reconciliation of SFCC Asset Categories with Corresponding Income Flows

	Bonds and Bond Interest				Corporate Stock and Dividends			
1962 Family Income Class	SFCC, Percentage of Units Owning Bonds[a]	SOI, Percentage of Units Reporting Interest[b]	Estimated Yield[c]	Adjustment Factor	SFCC, Percentage of Units Owning Stock[d]	SOI, Percentage of Units Reporting Dividends[e]	Estimated Yield[f]	Adjustment Factors
Under $3,000	12–16	13.5	.006	1.83	7	5.1	.083	1.30
$3,000–$4,999	20–30	17.0	.018	1.59	8	6.0	.121	2.10
$5,000–$7,499	30–41	23.3	.003	1.83	15	6.9	.078	1.30
$7,500–$9,999	40–61	32.6	.001	1.83	19	10.5	.056	1.30
$10,000–$14,999	51–84	49.2	.018	1.59	32	20.8	.079	1.30
$15,000–$24,999	43–88	68.3	.044	1.43	52	46.7	.109	1.94
$25,000–$49,999	51–100	78.2	.060	1.03	83	69.4	.060	1.30
$50,000–$99,999	69–100	84.9	.026	1.43	88	85.7	.078	1.30
$100,000 or more	75–100	88.1	.109	1.03	97	94.4	.075	1.30
All units	28–45	23.5	.010	...	16	9.3	.078	1.30

	Unincorporated Business Equity and Unincorporated Business Income				Trust Fund Equity and Trust Income			Adjustment Factors	
	SFCC, Percentage of Units Owning Unincorporated Business Equity[g]	SOI, Percentage of Units Reporting Income from Unincorporated Business[n]	Estimated Yield[i]	Adjustment Factor	SFCC, Percentage of Units Owning Trusts[j]	SOI, Percentage of Units Reporting Trust Income	Estimated Yield[k]	Percentage of Units	Value
Under $3,000	12	16.51	.129	2.10	...	.4	.088	...	1.10
$3,000–$4,999	12	16.38	.311	2.10	1	.5	2.298	...	1.10

$5,000–$7,499	17	13.38	.307	2.10	1	.5	.001	...	1.10
$7,500–$9,999	18	14.38	.414	2.10	1	.6	.082	...	1.10
$10,000–$14,999	22	19.31	.404	2.10	3	1.3	.198	...	1.10
$15,000–$24,999	26	41.44	.344	2.10	5	3.7	.042	...	1.10
$25,000–$49,999	64	63.81	.254	2.10	4	7.1	.002	+ 3.19	1.10
$50,000–$99,999	70	68.67	.112	1.00	5	11.5	.018	+ 6.5	1.10
$100,000 or more	35	70.63	.112	1.00	15	22.3	.018	+ 7.3	1.10
All units	17	16.88	.238	...	1	.7	.016	...	...

Note: SOI = Statistics of Income data.

[a] Projector and Weiss (1966, table A9, A10, A12). This category includes U.S. savings bonds, marketable securities other than stock and state and local bonds, mortgage assets, company savings plans, and loans to individuals. Percentage range indicates lowest and highest possible percentage owning the asset. Mean computed from midpoint of percentage range.

[b] Includes interest on time and savings deposits.

[c] Interest on bonds is calculated from *Statistics of Income* and SFCC data under the assumption that interest on time and savings deposits averaged 2.8 percent. The estimated yield is the ratio of mean bond interest to mean bonds by income class.

[d] Projector and Weiss (1966, table A10).

[e] Dividends after exclusion.

[f] Defined as the ratio of *Statistics of Income* data dividends to SFCC stock holdings.

[g] Projector and Weiss (1966, table A8).

[h] Includes partnership income.

[i] Defined as ratio of *Statistics of Income* data unincorporated business income (excluding losses) to SFCC unincorporated business equity.

[j] Projector and Weiss (1966, table A9).

[k] Defined as the ratio of *Statistics of Income* data trust income to SFCC trust equity.

FEMHEAD = 1 if head is female, 0 otherwise; and URBANRES = 1 if unit's residence is in an urbanized area. The total value for other consumer durables developed from this equation is then adjusted proportionately to conform to the national balance sheet total.

5. Inventories such as food and clothing are not included in the SFCC. The ratio of inventory holdings to family income is computed from the 1960–61 Consumer Expenditure Survey.[17] These ratios are applied to each household on the basis of family income and then adjusted by a scalar to conform to the balance sheet total.

6. Demand deposits and currency are adjusted by the factor 2.945.

7. Time and savings deposits are adjusted by the factor 1.980.

8. State and local government bonds are proportionately adjusted by the factor 1.441.

9. Corporate and U.S. government bonds and instruments and other financial assets are adjusted differentially by income class. The percentage reporting interest income (including interest on both savings and time deposits and financial securities) in the *Statistics of Income* data falls either below the range or within the range of households in the SFCC reporting that they owned other financial assets (see table 5.11). Therefore, it is unlikely that there is an underreporting problem in the SFCC with regard to the number of households who report holding these financial assets. However, the estimated yields, although volatile, seem extremely low. Total interest reported in the *Statistics of Income* data ($7.16 billion) divided by total national balance sheet savings deposits plus other financial assets ($329.2 billion) is only 2 percent. Bank rates were about 2.8 percent in 1962, and bond rates were about 5 percent. Thus, it appears that IRS interest was severely underreported. Despite underreporting problems in the IRS data, it appears from comparisons of estimated yields across income levels that SFCC financial assets are underreported more for lower-income than upper-income groups, and therefore our adjustment factors vary accordingly.

10. Corporate stock is also adjusted differentially by income class. As shown in table 15.11, the percentage reporting stock in the SFCC is uniformly greater than the percentage reporting dividends in the *Statistics of Income* data. It should be noted that reported dividends are underreported in the *Statistics of Income* data since they are net of the exclusion allowance. Moreover, many forms of stock pay no dividends. Despite this, the comparison suggests that there is no significant underreporting in percentage of holders in the SFCC. The yield figures show no clear pattern by income class. However, there are two income classes with yields significantly higher than the average, which suggests greater than average underreporting of asset values in these two income classes. Thus, these income classes are assigned higher than average adjustment factors.

11. Unincorporated business equity also has different adjustment factors by income class. As shown in table 15.11, the overall percentage reporting business equity in the SFCC is identical to the percentage reporting business income in the *Statistics of Income* data, and the percentages are also similar within income class. However, the estimated yields are particularly high for lower-income groups. All the adjustment is therefore done in the bottom seven income classes.

12. Trust fund equity is the only asset whose ownership appears to be underreported in the SFCC (table 15.11). The corresponding income category is income from estate and trusts. Since estates are included, the percentage reporting this income item should be higher in the *Statistics of Income* data than in the SFCC. However, not all trust funds may generate income. In any case, for lower-income groups, the percentage reporting trusts is uniformly greater in the SFCC than in the *Statistics of Income* data. For the upper three income groups, the opposite was the case. As a result, for these three income classes, the percentage owning trusts was increased in the SFCC. These additional household units in the top three income classes are assigned the mean asset value in the SFCC. The yield numbers vary quite erratically, so the adjustment factor assigned to each income class is the same.

13. The CSV of life insurance and pensions does not appear on the SFCC tape. However, tabulations of both the mean value of each asset and the percentage of households owning each by income class appear in Projector and Weiss (1966, table A31). This information is used to impute these two assets to households in the SFCC tape, and the results are adjusted by a scalar to conform with the national balance sheet totals.

14. Mortgage debt is adjusted proportionately by a factor of 1.118 to conform with the national balance sheet total.

15. Life insurance debt does not appear on the SFCC tape, but tabulations of mean value and percentage of households with this liability by income class are found in Projector and Weiss (1966, table A14). This information is used to impute life insurance debt, and the results are proportionately adjusted to conform with the aggregate totals.

16. Other debt is added to life insurance debt, and the sum is scaled by a factor of 1.07.

15.5.2 Imputation of Social Security and Pension Wealth for Wealth Concept W5 in the 1962 SFCC and the 1983 SCF

As noted in section 15.1, for wealth concept W5, pension wealth is defined as the present value of discounted future pension benefits. In similar fashion, social security wealth is defined as the present value of the discounted stream of future social security benefits. Future entitlements from both pensions and the social security program depend on many factors, such as the health (and survival) of a company, productivity growth and other macroeconomic factors, and future legislation. Estimating the value of such forms of wealth depends on relatively crude assumptions about the future state of the economy.

The imputation of both pension and social security wealth involves a large number of steps, which we will summarize here (technical details can be obtained directly from the authors). For retirees (r), the procedure is straightforward. Let PB be the pension benefit currently being received by the retiree. If it is assumed that pension benefits remain fixed in nominal terms over time for a particular beneficiary (as was generally true in 1962, though less true in 1983), then

$$PW_r = \int_0^{LE} PBe^{-it}dt,$$

where LE is the conditional life expectancy, and i is the (nominal) discount rate, for which the ten-year Treasury bill rate is used. For current social security beneficiaries,

$$SSW_r = \int_0^{LE} SSBe^{(g'-i^*)t}dt,$$

where SSB is the currently received social security benefit, g' the expected rate of growth of mean social security benefits over time for retirees, and i^* the real discount rate.[18]

Among current workers (w), the procedure is more complex. For pension wealth in 1962, a two-stage imputation is necessary. The first stage assigns pension coverage among workers. From Skolnik (1976) and Kotlikoff and Smith (1983, table 3.1.1), the total number of covered workers is estimated for 1962. From the President's Commission on Pension Policy (1980a, 1980b), information is obtained on relative coverage rates by income class, industry of employment, age, and sex of worker. On the basis of these data, pension coverage is randomly assigned among workers in such a way that the totals match known coverage rates by these characteristics.[19] In the second stage, accumulated earnings (AE) from the start of working life to the present are estimated for each covered worker. These are based on human capital earnings functions, which are imputed separately by sex, race, and schooling level. Past earnings are accumulated on the basis of real growth in average earnings, and the discount rate is the average yield on high-grade corporate bonds.

Covered workers in a given age cohort are then assigned a percentile ranking n based on the distribution of AE for their cohort. Their expected pension benefit, EPB, is then given by

$$EPB_n = PB_n e^{g''(65-A)}$$

where PB_n is the nth percentile among pension benefits of beneficiaries of age sixty-five, g'' is the expected rate of growth of average pension benefits, and A is current age. Then pension wealth for current workers in the nth percentile is given by

$$PW_{w,n} = \int_0^{LD} EPB_n e^{\,g''t} e^{-i(t + A_r)} dt,$$

where $A_r = 65 - A$ is the years to retirement, and $LD = LE - 65$.

The calculation of the 1983 pension wealth for current workers was much easier since pension coverage and expected pension benefits are provided in the Federal Reserve tape for current workers.

The imputation of social security wealth among current workers is analogous to that of pension wealth. For the 1962 data, coverage is assigned on the basis of employment status. Workers are again assigned a percentile ranking n on the basis of the accumulated earnings for their age group. Then, the expected social security benefit at retirement (at age sixty-five), ESSB, is given by

$$ESSB_n = SSB_n e^{g(65 - A)},$$

where SSB_n is the nth percentile of social security benefits among beneficiaries of age sixty-five. Then

$$SSW_{w,n} = \int_0^{LD} ESSB_n e^{gt} e^{-i^*(t + A_r)} dt,$$

where g is the expected rate of growth in mean real social security benefits for new retirees.

The procedure for calculating social security wealth from the 1983 data is identical, except that information on social security coverage for current workers is already provided.

15.5.3   Results for the 1962 SFCC

Table 15.12 presents results on the concentration of different components of household wealth for both the original (unadjusted) data and the data adjusted to align with the national balance sheet totals and other outside information. Each row shows the concentration of that entry based on holdings in that asset or liability alone. Thus, the share of the top 1 percent of stocks is based on the highest holdings of stock shares. The striking result is the differences in the degree of concentration for the different components of wealth. Trust funds, corporate stock, unincorporated business equity, financial securities, and other (mainly investment) real estate are the most highly concentrated; bank deposits are less concentrated; and owner-occupied housing and vehicles are the most equally distributed. In general, the results from tables 15.10 and 15.12 indicate that highly concentrated assets are also those that are significantly underreported. The last set of columns of table 15.10 shows concentration estimates for the adjusted data. The adjustment process has almost no effect on the concentration levels of individual assets, with the possible exception of unincorporated

Table 15.12   Concentration of Unadjusted and Adjusted Household Wealth By Component, 1962

	Original Data			Adjusted Data	
	Share of Top 1 Percent	Percentage of Households with Item	Gini Coefficient for Holders	Share of Top 1 Percent	Gini Coefficient for Holders
Assets					
Owner-occupied housing	28.7	100.0	.713	26.8	.675
Other real estate	8.2	57.0	.354	8.2	.354
Vehicles	50.5	11.3	.658	50.5	.658
Other consumer durables	7.4	73.9	.472	7.4	.472
Inventories	...	...	...	1.8	.098
	...	...	...	4.9	.284
Demand deposits and currency	34.6	100.0	.808	34.6	.808
Time and savings deposits	23.6	58.5	.729	23.6	.729
State and local government bonds	100.0	0.4	.749	100.0	.749
Other financial securities	50.4	39.5	.824	52.5	.832
Corporate stock	71.9	16.1	.858	69.7	.853
Unincorporated business equity	53.5	16.2	.758	46.7	.725
Trust fund equity	99.7	1.4	.914	99.7	.923
Insurance (CSV)	...	...	...	14.8	.175
Pensions (CSV)	...	...	...	3.8	.398
Liabilities	15.4	66.1	.623	16.1	.621
Mortgage debt	10.2	32.6	.383	10.2	.383
Other debt	34.7	58.2	.694	34.7	.699
Net worth	32.4	100.0	.772	29.3	.715

business equity, which shows a modest decline in inequality from the adjustment procedure. However, the two assets missing from the SFCC, other consumer durables and household inventories, are much less concentrated than any other asset. Their inclusion in the household portfolio should have a pronounced equalizing effect.

These implications are confirmed by the results of table 15.13. The first row indicates that the Gini coefficient for original, unadjusted household wealth is 0.772 and that the share of the top percentile is 32 percent. The change in inequality that results from adding an asset to the household portfolio is a function of three factors: (1) the degree of concentration of the asset, (2) the relative magnitude of the asset; and (3) its covariance with other components of net worth (see, e.g., Wolff 1987a). The addition of other consumer durables (a category that comprises 6 percent of total balance sheet assets and is distributed equally) to original unadjusted net worth causes the Gini coefficient to decline from 0.77 to 0.70. This decline is primarily due to the increasing shares of the bottom two quintiles. The further addition of household inventories has a similar effect, with the Gini coefficient declining from 0.70 to 0.68.

The adjustment and alignment of the original components of household wealth in the SFCC to the national balance sheet causes an increase in the Gini coefficient from 0.77 to 0.79 (row 5). Most of the increased concentration occurs in the upper quintile, as might be expected, since the most underreported items were those held by the upper part of the distribution. The addition of the CSV of life insurance and pensions to the household portfolio causes relatively little change since these items are quite small. However, the addition of other consumer durables to produce wealth measure W2 causes a sharp reduction in measured inequality, and the further addition of household inventories (W2*) causes another reduction in measured inequality.[20] The net effect of including missing items and aligning with the national balance sheets is a reduction in measured inequality, and the reduction is quite substantial, with the Gini coefficient falling from 0.77 (row 1) to 0.72 (row 8). Most of the change is due to gains by the bottom two quintiles, and, indeed, the share of the top percentile was reduced relatively little. Finally, rows 4 and 9 compare unadjusted and adjusted estimates of what might be called "fungible net worth"—W2 less all consumer durables. The distributional estimates are almost identical, 0.798 compared to 0.805. For fungible wealth, alignment makes almost no difference in measured concentration.

Row 10 presents results on the distribution of social security and pension wealth. Because of data limitations, we are unable to separate the two components. Retirement wealth is distributed considerably more equally than marketable wealth. In particular, the shares of the

Table 15.13   Inequality Measures for Different Concepts of Household Wealth, Based on Both Unadjusted and Adjusted Data, 1962

	Gini Coefficient	Share of Top 1 Percent	Share of Top 5 Percent	Quintile Shares				
				Top	Second	Third	Fourth	Bottom
Unadjusted estimates:								
1. Original wealth components	.772	32.4	52.5	78.2	14.4	6.2	1.4	-.3
2. Row 1 plus other durables	.701	29.5	48.0	72.7	15.0	7.6	3.2	1.5
3. Row 2 plus inventories	.679	28.4	46.5	70.9	15.2	8.1	3.9	1.9
4. Row 1 less autos	.798	33.9	54.5	80.3	14.0	5.7	.6	-.6
Measures adjusted to align with the national balance sheets:								
5. Original components only	.793	33.3	54.6	80.9	12.9	5.3	1.2	-.3
6. Row 5 plus CSV of Insurance and pensions	.782	32.2	53.2	79.8	13.4	5.7	1.4	-.3
7. W2 = row 6 plus other durables	.731	31.8	50.1	75.9	13.8	6.6	2.6	1.0
8. W2* = W2 plus inventories	.715	29.3	48.9	74.4	14.1	7.1	3.1	1.3
9. W2 less all durables	.805	33.4	55.0	81.7	12.9	5.2	.8	-.5
Augmented measures of household wealth with retirement wealth:								
10. Social security plus pension wealth only:[a]								
$g = .0$	.504	8.0	22.7	52.9	22.9	14.3	8.3	1.7
$g = .01$	.482	7.9	21.4	50.6	23.4	15.2	9.0	1.8
$g = .02$	.466	7.8	20.3	48.8	24.1	16.0	9.4	1.8
$g = .03$	.458	7.6	19.4	47.6	24.6	16.5	9.5	1.7
11. W5* = W2* plus social security and pension wealth:								
$g = .0$	.624	23.8	40.8	65.8	16.8	9.5	5.4	2.5
$g = .01$	.607	22.9	39.5	64.3	17.2	9.9	5.9	2.7
$g = .02$	.586	21.9	38.0	62.5	17.6	10.5	6.4	3.1
$g = .03$	.563	20.6	36.1	60.3	18.1	11.2	7.1	3.3

Source: Results are based on the 1962 SFCC.

[a] This panel shows the distribution of retirement wealth only. The quantile shares are based on the size distribution of families ranked by their retirement wealth, not net worth. If ranked by net worth, the top 1 percent would hold about 2 percent of total retirement wealth. Because of data limitations, we are unable to separate pension from social security wealth. The parameter g is the assumed rate of growth of mean real social security benefits.

upper percentile and quintile of retirement holdings are substantially lower and the shares of the middle three quintiles considerably higher than the corresponding shares for other types of assets. Moreover, the higher the assumed growth rate in social security benefits over time (the parameter g), the greater is measured equality. The reason for this is that raising g increases the equality in social security wealth between younger and older age cohorts. Moreover, the higher g is, the greater is the magnitude of retirement wealth since the present value of the future benefit stream is increased. For $g = 0.0$, total retirement wealth is 23 percent of balance sheet assets, while, for $g = 0.03$, the ratio becomes 42 percent.

In row 11, we show results on the distribution of W5*, defined as the sum of W2* plus pension and social security wealth.[21] For all values of g, the addition of retirement wealth to traditional wealth causes a marked reduction in measured inequality. Moreover, the higher the value of g, the greater the reduction in measured wealth inequality since the magnitude of retirement wealth increases and its concentration declines. For $g = 0.0$, the Gini coefficient for W5* is 0.62, and, for $g = 0.03$, the Gini coefficient is 0.56.

15.5.4   Adjustment Procedures for the 1983 SCF

The 1983 SCF contains richer detail on asset and liability holdings than the 1962 SFCC does. As in the SFCC file, there were also a considerable number of missing value problems and inconsistencies in the original survey data. The Federal Reserve Board devoted substantial and careful effort to overcoming the problems of item nonresponse and internal data inconsistencies, as it did in the case of the 1962 SFCC. The imputation procedures are described in detail in Avery, Elliehausen, and Kennickell (1987). For consistency with the 1962 SFCC data that we used, we base all the tabulations and data results reported here on this fully imputed version of the 1983 SCF.

Table 15.10 presents a comparison of balance sheet totals derived from the SCF and the national balance sheet data. The underreporting patterns are very similar to the 1962 SFCC, except for corporate stock, unincorporated business equity, and trust fund equity. Owner-occupied housing and vehicles appear well covered in the SCF, as do investment real estate and unincorporated business equity. Demand deposits (including currency) and time deposits (including money-market funds, certificates of deposits, and related liquid assets) are significantly underreported—almost to the same extent as they were in the 1962 SFCC. Financial securities, including bonds and mortgage assets, are well captured in the survey, as they were in the SFCC.

Ninety percent of corporate stock is captured in the SCF, a substantially higher share than in the 1962 survey. The total value of trust funds is considerably higher in the SCF than the balance sheet value. This contrasts with a 64 percent coverage rate in the 1962 data. The total value of life insurance CSV from the survey exceeds the national balance sheet total, though this result may be partly due to a misalignment between insurance savings and time deposit savings. Total pension CSV from the survey is more than double our national balance sheet estimate, though this may be a result of our national balance sheet estimation procedure for this category. Finally, liabilities are well covered in the SCF—almost to exactly the same extent as they were in the 1962 SFCC. On net, the 1983 SCF appears to have done a better job capturing household wealth than the 1962 SFCC did.

There is some debate on the issue of alignment of the 1983 SCF survey results to the national balance sheet totals. For example, Curtin, Juster, and Morgan (chap. 10, in this vol.) argue that the 1983 SCF results are more reliable than the FFA data and, as a result, imply that no alignment should be done. For example, they claim that the apparent low coverage rate of time deposits and savings accounts in the SCF vis-à-vis the FFAs is actually a result of different estimation techniques in the FFA data. A similar argument was also made by Avery, Elliehausen, and Kennickell (1987). Irrespective of the merits of their argument, our interest here is in estimates that are consistent between the 1962 and the 1983 household surveys. As a result, it seemed that the best way to obtain this was to align both surveys to a single source that was, at least, internally consistent, namely, the national balance sheets for the household sector.

For owner-occupied housing, other real estate, vehicles, unincorporated business equity, trust fund equity, and pension CSV, SCF coverage appears quite adequate, and no alignment was done.[22] For other asset and liability components, alignment to the national balance sheet totals was performed. This was effected by using a proportional adjustment factor for each of the underreported items in the balance sheet, with three exceptions. First, time and savings deposits and insurance CSV were aligned as a single category since the latter was overreported with respect to the national balance sheet total and the two classifications can be easily confused by the respondent. Second, mortgage debt was constrained to be no greater than the maximum of either its reported value or 80 percent of the gross value of the real estate. Third, nonmortgage debt was constrained to be no greater than the maximum of either its reported value or 50 percent of the total value of gross assets. In the 1983 SCF, there was partial reporting of nonvehicle consumer durables, though the total was less than one-fourth of the balance sheet total. We used the same regression technique to impute the missing portion of the nonvehicle consumer durable category, as we did for the 1962 data, with the total for this category (including the portion reported in the 1983 SCF) aligned to the national balance sheet figure of $760.6 billion. Household inventories were imputed in the same manner as for the 1962 data.[23]

Table 15.14 shows the concentration of each asset and liability component after alignment to the national balance sheet totals. The distribution of other consumer durables, household inventories, demand deposits and currency, trust funds, mortgage debt, and other debt remained largely unchanged between 1962 and 1983 (cf. table 15.12). However, there are some important changes between the two years. First, the percentage of families owning their own home climbed from 57 to 64, and inequality of home values among home owners increased from a Gini coefficient of 0.35 to one of 0.43. However, these two

Table 15.14   **Concentration of Household Wealth by Component, Based on Adjusted Data, 1983**

	Share of Top 1 Percent	Percentage of Households with Item	Gini Coefficient for Holders
Assets	28.6	100.0	.703
Owner-occupied housing	11.2	63.4	.427
Other real estate	55.5	18.9	.750
Vehicles	6.8	84.4	.442
Other consumer durables	2.2	100.0	.144
Inventories	7.5	100.0	.271
Demand deposits and currency	29.6	100.0	.795
Time and savings deposits	25.8	74.1	.771
Financial securities	68.9	7.7	.747
Corporate stock	74.3	20.7	.891
Unincorporated business equity	63.0	14.2	.789
Trust fund equity	96.8	4.0	.933
Insurance (CSV)	30.8	34.1	.686
Pensions (CSV)	65.7	10.9	.788
Miscellaneous assets	63.4	11.2	.754
Liabilities	23.4	69.8	.683
Mortgage debt	13.4	37.1	.455
Other debt	41.9	63.6	.795
Net worth	30.4	100.0	.728

Source: Results are based on the 1987 Federal Reserve Board tape for the 1983 SCF. This version contains imputations for missing values from nonresponse and corrections of inconsistencies in the data (for details, see Avery, Elliehausen, and Kennickell [1987]).

Note: The results are shown after the data are aligned to national balance sheet totals.

effects are offsetting, so that the overall Gini coefficient for owner-occupied housing (for home owners and non–home owners) remained at 0.63 in the two years. Second, the fraction of families owning other real estate grew from 11 to 19 percent, while the Gini coefficient among owners remained unchanged. Third, the percentage of families owning vehicles increased from 74 to 84, and the Gini coefficient among owners fell from 0.47 to 0.44.

Fourth, the proportion of families with time deposits rose from 59 to 74 percent, and the Gini coefficient for this asset increased slightly from 0.73 to 0.77. Fifth, the percentage of families owning corporate stock increased from 16 to 21, while the Gini coefficient among owners rose from 0.85 to 0.89. The net result was no change in the overall Gini coefficient for corporate stock.[24]

Table 15.15 shows the estimates of overall household wealth inequality before and after alignment to the national balance sheet totals. The pattern of results is similar to those based on the 1962 SFCC. Based on unadjusted wealth figures, the inclusion of other consumer durables and household inventories in the household portfolio causes a substantial reduction in measured inequality, in this case from a Gini coefficient of 0.79 (row 1) to one of 0.73 (row 3). As with the 1962 data, alignment to the national balance sheet totals of the original wealth components in the SCF had less of an effect on measured inequality than did adding other consumer durables and inventories. However, the direction of change is different for the 1983 data. In this case, the Gini coefficient declines slightly from 0.79 (row 1) to 0.78 (row 5). The total effect of both the imputation of missing assets and the alignment to the national balance sheet totals is to cause a decline of the Gini coefficient from 0.79 to 0.74 (row 6) and a fall of the share of the top percentile from 35 percent of total wealth to 31 percent.

Row 9 shows results on the distribution of pension wealth PW, defined as the expected value of the flow of future pension benefits, based on the rank ordering of families by the value of PW. The Gini coefficient for pension wealth is 0.84, considerably greater than that for traditional wealth W2* (row 7). However, part of the higher inequality is due to the fact that only 34 percent of families in 1983 held this asset. Among pension wealth holders only, the Gini coefficient for PW is 0.56. As with the 1962 data, social security wealth is distributed considerably more equally than W2*. For g (the assumed rate of growth of real social security benefits) = 0.02, the Gini coefficient for social security wealth is 0.51 (row 10), compared to 0.73 for W2*. There is a slight increase in the concentration of total retirement wealth between 1962 and 1983. The Gini coefficient for the sum of pension wealth and social security wealth (for g = 0.02) is 0.47 for the 1962 data (row 10 of table 15.13), compared to 0.50 for the 1983 data (result not shown). Moreover, the

Table 15.15 Inequality Measures for Different Concepts of Household Wealth, Based on Both Unadjusted and Adjusted Data, 1983

	Gini Coefficient	Share of Top 1 Percent	Share of Top 5 Percent	Quintile Shares				
				Top	Second	Third	Fourth	Bottom
Unadjusted estimates:								
1. Original wealth components	.788	34.5	56.2	80.3	12.6	5.6	1.5	−.0
2. Row 1 plus other durables	.740	32.4	53.0	76.6	13.1	6.5	2.7	1.1
3. Row 2 plus inventories	.729	31.8	52.1	75.7	13.3	6.8	2.9	1.3
4. Row 1 less autos	.806	35.7	57.9	82.0	12.2	5.1	1.1	−.3
Measures adjusted to align with national balance sheets:								
5. Original components only	.781	32.8	54.6	79.8	12.9	5.7	1.6	−.0
6. W2 = row 5 plus other durables	.739	30.9	51.8	76.5	13.4	6.5	2.6	1.0
7. W2* = W2 plus household inventories	.728	30.4	51.0	75.6	13.6	6.8	2.9	1.2
8. W2 less all durables	.800	34.0	56.3	81.5	12.5	5.2	1.1	−.3

(*continued*)

Table 15.15 (continued)

	Gini Coefficient	Share of Top 1 Percent	Share of Top 5 Percent	Quintile Shares				
				Top	Second	Third	Fourth	Bottom
Augmented measures of household wealth with retirement wealth:								
9. Pension wealth[a]	.844	19.8	48.8	90.3	9.7	.0	.0	.0
10. Social security wealth[b]								
$g = .0$	.557	7.3	25.2	58.3	21.3	12.8	7.0	.6
$g = .01$	.528	7.5	25.1	55.0	21.9	14.2	8.2	.7
$g = .02$	.509	8.0	25.4	52.9	22.3	15.0	9.1	.8
$g = .03$	.503	8.6	25.7	52.2	22.4	15.2	9.4	.9
11. W5* = W2* plus social security and pension wealth:								
$g = .0$	.607	20.6	39.1	64.2	17.3	10.3	5.8	2.4
$g = .01$	.592	20.0	37.9	63.0	17.4	10.5	6.2	2.9
$g = .02$	.572	19.0	36.4	61.7	17.4	10.8	6.7	3.3
$g = .03$	.550	17.8	34.7	60.2	17.4	11.2	7.4	3.8

Source: Results are based on the 1987 Federal Reserve Board tape for the 1983 SCF. This version contains imputations for missing values from nonresponse and corrections of inconsistencies in the data.

[a]This panel shows the distribution of pension wealth only. The quantile shares are based on the size distribution of families ranked by their pension wealth.

[b]This panel shows the distribution of social security wealth only. The top percentile and quintile shares are based on the size distribution of families ranked by their social security wealth. If ranked by net worth, the top 1 percent would hold about 3 percent of total social security wealth. The parameter g is the assumed rate of growth of mean real social security benefits.

magnitude of retirement wealth relative to traditional wealth grew considerably over the period, from 38 percent of W2* in 1962 to 88 percent in 1983.

As with the 1962 data, the addition of pension and social security wealth to traditional wealth (W2*), our W5* wealth measure, causes a marked reduction in estimated inequality. For $g = 0.02$, the Gini coefficient falls from 0.73 (row 7) to 0.57 (row 11). The decline is greater than in 1962 because of the increased magnitude of retirement wealth relative to traditional wealth.

Our final table, table 15.16, summarizes the effects of imputations for missing assets and alignment to the national balance sheet totals on measured wealth inequality (the Gini coefficient). The major effect stems from the inclusion of missing assets in the 1962 and 1983 survey data. The addition of missing consumer durables (and pension and insurance CSV for the 1962 data) to the original components of household wealth to produce W2 results in a decline of the Gini coefficient of about 9 percent, and the inclusion of household inventories to create W2* causes a further drop of 2–3 percent. The imputation of pension wealth PW and social security wealth to produce W5* results in another decrease of the Gini coefficient of 0.13–0.16 points (for $g = 0.02$). Alignment, on the other hand, causes only a modest change in measured inequality. The change in the Gini coefficient for the various wealth concepts is in the range of 0.02–0.04 points for the 1962 data and between 0.0 and 0.01 for the 1983 data. This is also true for fungible wealth, defined as W2 less all consumer durables. In addition, the direction of change is not necessarily the same among different wealth surveys. In the two cases considered here, alignment increases measured wealth inequality when applied to the 1962 SFCC but reduces it slightly for the 1983 SCF.[25]

Table 15.16   **Summary Table of the Effects of Imputations for Missing Assets and Alignment to National Balance Sheet Totals on Gini Coefficients for Household Wealth, 1962 and 1983**

Wealth Concept	1962		1983	
	Before Alignment	After Alignment	Before Alignment	After Alignment
Original components only	.77	.79	.79	.78
W2 components	.70	.73	.74	.74
W2* components	.68	.72	.73	.73
W5* components ($g = 0.02$)	. . .	.59	. . .	.57
WF[a]	.80	.81	.81	.80

[a]WF is fungible wealth, defined as W2 less all durables.

15.6 Conclusion

The long-run record based on original and unadjusted estate data (individual based estimates) shows a decline in wealth concentration in the United States from the late 1920s to the late 1940s, a slight increase in the 1960s, a sharp drop in the 1970s, followed by a minor increase in 1981. These trends are robust to corrections for inconsistencies in the national balance sheet data and in wealth definitions and to most other adjustments. However, two factors do have an effect on the above concentration trends. First, including social security wealth in the household portfolio increases the decline in inequality over the period 1939–81. Second, changing the unit of observation in the estate data, from individual to household, reduces the decline in wealth concentration over the period 1922–53, although it does not alter the drop in the 1970s. The smaller decline in inequality over the period prior to 1953 in the household estimates vis-à-vis the individual series can be explained by changes in wealth-holding patterns among married women.

The decade of the 1970s presents a puzzle. On the basis of estate tax data from Smith, there was a precipitous fall in wealth inequality between 1972 and 1976, as mentioned above. Unfortunately, there were no household surveys conducted during the 1970s that are comparable in terms of coverage of upper wealth groups to the 1962 SFCC and the 1983 SCF. However, on the basis of the three sources available—Greenwood's synthetic database, with our figures for total household wealth; the 1979 ISDP; and the 1979 Pension Commission survey—there appears to be a sizable decline in household wealth inequality between the 1960s and the 1970s. However, as noted in the text above, both 1979 results have to be interpreted very cautiously since the wealthy are thinly sampled. From Schwartz's 1981 estate estimates, concentration appears to have risen slightly between 1976 and 1981. Also, the 1983 SCF wealth estimates indicate that wealth inequality in 1983 was as high as it was in 1962. These sources taken together suggest that there was a wealth inequality trough during the 1970s—that is, a period of relatively low wealth inequality—and a reversal during the 1980s. Yet this result must be interpreted cautiously because of the various problems with the data.

Though trend patterns in the estate data are not sensitive to the choice of data and the adjustment procedures used, estate estimates of concentration levels are quite sensitive to these factors. Adjustments in the aggregate balance sheet data and the treatment of trust and pension funds makes a difference of 2–4 percentage points in the share of the top percentile. The inclusion of social security wealth in the estate wealth estimates causes a 4–8 percentage point drop in the share of the top 1 percent of wealth holders.

Results from the household survey data (1962 SFCC and 1983 SCF) indicate a similar wealth distribution in the two years, 1962 and 1983, the only period for which reliable survey data are available in the United States. The original unadjusted survey estimates indicate a small increase in inequality, from a Gini coefficient of 0.77 in 1962 to one of 0.79 in 1983. Adjustments to the survey data negated this trend. Gini coefficients for 1962 and 1983 are quite close, 0.715 and 0.728, respectively, after adjustments for missing assets and alignment to national balance sheet totals. Adding retirement wealth to the adjusted traditional net worth, our W5* concept, results in a slight decline in inequality between 1962 and 1983, from a Gini coefficient of 0.59 to one of 0.57 (for $g = 0.02$). This decline is relatively modest given the rapid growth in social security wealth over the period. The apparent reason is that the growth in social security is offset by the rapid growth of pension wealth, which is distributed quite unequally.

As with the estate data, adjustments and imputations to the survey data have more effect on the level of inequality than the trend. However, for the 1962 and 1983 surveys, alignment to national balance sheet totals appears to make relatively little difference, a maximum change in the Gini coefficient of 0.04, while imputations for missing assets have a sizable effect on inequality. The inclusion of missing consumer durables causes a 0.05–0.07-point change in the Gini coefficient and the inclusion of household inventories an additional 0.01–0.02-point decline. The addition of pension and social security wealth causes an even sharper decrease in the Gini coefficient, of 0.13–0.16 points. Finally, if we exclude consumer durables, inventories, and retirement wealth, then inequality measures of "fungible net worth" are quite insensitive to adjustment procedures. Thus, the unadjusted 1962 and 1983 survey data provide reliable concentration estimates of this component of household wealth.

A last point of caution concerns the combining of inequality estimates from different sources. Preliminary comparisons in this paper suggest that estate tax data and household survey data can produce very different point estimates of wealth inequality for the same year. One possible conclusion is that the estate estimates are substantially underreported. Further comparisons of these two important sources of U.S. wealth information need to be done in order to ascertain the relative reliability of each data source.

Appendix A
Sources and Methods in the Construction of Aggregate Household Balance Sheets, 1900–1983

This appendix summarizes the procedures used to adjust the original sources of household balance sheet data to create our new set of estimates. The discussion is by asset type. A more detailed description, including tables comparing the different sources by asset category, is available in Wolff (1989).

The discussion is organized by asset and liability component. For our new series for selected years between 1900 and 1983 for wealth concept W2, see table 15.A.1.

Note on Sources

1. For brevity, we use the term "Goldsmith data" to refer to estimates from either Goldsmith, Brady, and Mendershausen (1956) or Goldsmith, Lipsey, and Mendelson (1963). All household balance sheet data except for trust accounts come from Goldsmith, Lipsey, and Mendelson (1963, 42–85, 118–19, under the "nonfarm household" and "agricultural headings"). Data for personal trusts for the pre-1945 years are from Goldsmith, Brady, and Mendershausen (1956, 42–53) and for the 1945–59 period from Goldsmith, Lipsey, and Mendelson (1963, 120).

2. FFA data are taken from Board of Governors (1986). We use data from the category "households, personal trusts and nonprofit organizations" (11–15) and also from the "farm business" and "nonfarm noncorporate business" sectors (16–20).

3. The "Musgrave data" are taken from his revised estimates of tangible wealth in Musgrave (1986, table 10, p. 65, and table 18, p. 73).

4. Data from Ruggles and Ruggles (1982) are taken from their table 2.40, which provides end-of-year values for household-sector capital accounts.

Notes on Methods

Assets

Tangible Assets

Real Estate: Owner-occupied Housing, Tenant-occupied Housing, and Residential Land. For the period 1925–83, the values for "owner-occupied housing" and "tenant-occupied housing" are taken from Musgrave's (1986) annual estimates of net structures. Musgrave's data cover the period 1925–84 and are the source for the FFA tangible assets.

Table 15.A.1 National Balance Sheet Estimates for the Household Sector, 1900–1983, Based on Wealth Concept W2 (billions, current dollars)

	1900	1912	1921	1922	1929	1933	1939	1945	1949	1953
Assets	81.4	159.7	286.4	315.5	475.8	325.5	382.2	652.6	866.8	1,159.4
Tangible assets	28.2	47.4	91.3	108.1	148.5	108.7	132.0	195.0	332.5	477.9
Real estate	22.2	33.8	63.2	78.6	109.7	81.7	101.9	148.8	245.9	334.9
Consumer durables	6.0	13.6	28.1	29.5	38.8	27.0	30.1	46.2	86.6	143.0
Fixed claim assets	11.7	25.0	64.6	69.0	91.8	83.4	79.9	183.0	200.9	244.9
Demand deposits and currency	1.5	2.6	8.0	9.4	7.8	10.4	13.9	47.8	52.7	62.5
Other deposits	3.5	8.7	18.6	19.6	32.1	26.8	30.1	53.9	63.9	86.8
Federal securities	.6	.4	5.3	10.5	4.4	4.9	6.7	54.6	55.0	57.9
State and local government securities	.4	1.1	3.5	3.6	5.4	6.8	5.2	8.6	4.1	7.3
Other securities	5.7	12.2	29.2	25.7	42.1	34.5	24.0	18.1	25.2	30.4
Equities held	41.6	87.3	130.4	138.5	235.4	130.9	170.3	274.6	333.4	436.6
Corporate stock	10.2	28.2	43.0	50.7	128.8	50.9	63.1	97.0	89.9	133.0
Unincorporated business equity	28.2	51.3	69.9	69.3	73.0	46.9	60.6	112.4	162.7	205.4
Trust fund equity	1.9	4.5	10.8	11.5	19.2	16.0	22.4	29.0	32.9	39.1
Insurance (CSV)	1.3	3.3	6.7	7.0	14.3	17.0	23.9	35.6	46.9	57.2
Pension (CSV)	.0	.0	.0	.0	.1	.1	.3	.6	1.0	1.9
Liabilities	4.1	7.7	N.A.	16.8	39.8	27.3	28.1	28.9	61.4	107.1
Mortgage debt	2.3	3.6	N.A.	7.5	16.6	13.1	14.1	17.2	35.3	62.5
Other debt	1.7	4.1	N.A.	9.3	23.2	14.2	14.0	11.7	26.1	44.6
Net worth (W2)	77.4	152.0	N.A.	298.7	436.0	298.2	354.1	623.8	805.4	1,052.3

(continued)

Table 15.A.1 (continued)

	1958	1962	1965	1969	1972	1976	1979	1981	1983
Assets									
Tangible assets	1,662.6	1,967.6	2,428.7	3,158.9	3,983.2	5,629.5	8,255.7	10,118.1	11,425.8
Real estate	629.3	736.4	846.7	1,211.5	1,570.8	2,526.1	4,016.6	4,971.2	5,390.1
Consumer durables	447.3	534.1	610.6	867.8	1,146.1	1,873.3	3,091.3	3,874.7	4,183.2
Fixed claim assets	182.0	202.3	236.1	343.7	424.7	652.8	925.3	1,096.5	1,206.9
Demand deposits and currency	323.8	415.3	523.3	715.6	939.9	1,428.4	1,988.2	2,364.5	2,834.4
Other deposits	67.9	69.8	86.5	105.2	138.9	184.6	250.3	291.3	346.1
Federal securities	139.7	207.3	286.4	381.0	564.4	876.7	1,201.3	1,534.7	1,841.7
State and local government securities	60.9	67.5	67.4	98.4	82.7	144.1	227.4	240.7	280.5
Other securities	14.8	18.3	24.9	35.5	32.7	48.5	49.5	62.9	106.6
Equities held	40.5	52.4	58.1	95.5	121.2	174.5	259.7	235.0	259.5
Corporate stock	709.5	815.9	1,058.7	1,231.8	1,472.5	1,675.0	2,250.9	2,782.4	3,201.2
Unincorporated business equity	314.0	361.0	529.4	626.9	745.9	622.6	745.9	935.9	1,210.6
Trust fund equity	258.1	281.1	311.2	348.3	397.7	678.5	1,054.2	1,300.6	1,359.9
Insurance (CSV)	63.1	85.2	115.0	132.8	183.1	192.8	229.8	295.8	348.2
Pension (CSV)	70.7	83.2	95.3	112.9	129.5	157.8	186.0	203.0	216.7
	3.6	5.5	7.7	10.9	16.3	23.4	35.0	47.1	65.8
Liabilities	178.6	256.0	342.0	454.9	592.9	862.3	1,336.3	1,573.8	1,849.5
Mortgage debt	112.9	163.8	214.5	276.3	358.0	540.1	856.8	1,024.0	1,179.5
Other debt	65.7	92.2	127.5	178.6	234.9	322.2	479.5	549.8	670.0
Net worth (W2)	1,484.0	1,711.6	2,086.7	2,704.0	3,390.3	4,767.2	6,919.4	8,544.3	9,576.3

Sources: Authors' computations.

Note: N.A. = not available.

The 1922 figures are based on extrapolating time trends estimated using regression analysis for the 1925–29 period. We used Goldsmith's data for residential structures only for 1900 and 1912. We preferred Musgrave's figures for the 1922–58 period over Goldsmith's both because we wished to maintain consistency with later years and because we believe Musgrave's estimates to be more reliable since the underlying worksheets have been considerably updated and revised since Goldsmith's work. As a result, the 1900 and 1912 estimates are not consistent with the rest of the series for tangible assets. Goldsmith's figures were significantly lower than Musgrave's, between 10 and 31 percent, for every year in which the two series overlapped.

There were some definitional differences between our real estate categories and those from Goldsmith, the FFAs, and Ruggles and Ruggles. Goldsmith included both residential structures and nonresidential structures in the real estate sector, and his land estimate included both types of property. We transferred his estimate of nonresidential structures to the "unincorporated business equity" category (below) for the years 1900–1945. On the other hand, Ruggles and Ruggles and the FFAs included tenant-occupied housing under unincorporated business, which we transferred to the "real estate" category.

Our "residential land" estimate includes both tenant and owner-occupied land. For the Goldsmith years, we first subtracted non-residential land from his total land estimates and transferred it to "unincorporated business equity." We used Goldsmith's estimates of owner-occupied land and estimated tenant-occupied land by assuming that the proportion of tenant-occupied to owner-occupied land was the same as the ratio of tenant-occupied to owner-occupied structures. For the 1949–83 period, we used the FFA estimates for owner-occupied land. There were substantial differences between the Ruggles and Ruggles estimates and the FFA estimates for this category, with the ratio between the two ranging from 0.64 to 1.00 with no systematic trend. There is no apparent explanation for the differences. As for the Goldsmith years, we estimated tenant-occupied land for the 1949–83 period by assuming that the proportion of tenant-occupied to owner-occupied land in each year was the same as the ratio of tenant-occupied to owner-occupied structures. The amount of tenant-occupied land was then subtracted from the total for the "unincorporated business equity" category.

Consumer Durables: Motor Vehicles and Other Consumer Durables. For both the "motor vehicles" and the "other consumer durables" categories, we used Musgrave's data, which, like the residential structures series, are complete for the period from 1925 to 1984. For the 1922 value, we extrapolated from the estimated 1925–29 time trend.

Fixed Claim Assets:

Demand Deposits and Currency; Deposits in Other Financial Institutions; Federal Securities; State and Local Securities; and Corporate and Foreign Bonds, Mortgages, Open Market Paper, and Other Instruments.

For these categories, we used Goldsmith's data for the 1900–1945 period and the Ruggles and Ruggles series for the 1949–80 period. As noted above, the FFA data for the "household sector" include personal trusts and nonprofit organizations and thus could not be used for this period. Since the Ruggles and Ruggles data end in 1980, we had to estimate values for all five categories for 1981 and 1983. For the three bond and security categories ("federal securities," "state and local securities," and "corporate and foreign bonds, mortgages, open market paper, and other instruments"), we computed the average ratio of the Ruggles and Ruggles estimates to the FFA data over the 1946–80 period and multiplied the FFA figures for 1981 and 1983 to obtain estimates for the narrowly defined household sector. This ratio for federal securities and the corporate bond category showed an upward trend approaching 1.0 by the end of the period. This implied that trust and nonprofit organization holdings of these two categories were zero in 1980. Since this seemed unlikely, we decided to ignore the trend component in this ratio and relied, instead, on the average value of this ratio over the postwar period. For the two liquid asset categories ("demand deposits and currency" and "deposits in other financial institutions"), we used a trend regression of the ratio between the Ruggles and Ruggles figures and the corresponding FFA figures to estimate the 1981 and 1983 values.

There were no major definitional differences between the Goldsmith and the Ruggles and Ruggles fixed claim asset categories. In order to maintain consistency with our definition of farm assets held by the household sector, we shifted a small amount of assets from Goldsmith's farm equity estimates into the household-sector categories "deposits in other financial institutions," "federal securities," and "corporate and foreign bonds, mortgages, open market paper, and other instruments." These adjustments are explained in the "farm equity" section below. There are large percentage differences for "state and local securities" between Goldsmith and Ruggles and Ruggles. These are usually offset in absolute terms by the discrepancies in the corporate bond category. For the overlapping years (1949, 1953, and 1958), Goldsmith's estimates are higher for state and local securities, from $2 to $6 billion. Except for 1958, the Ruggles and Ruggles figures are higher for the corporate bond category. These differences are small relative to total assets, and, since we had no independent information, no correction was made to either series. While Goldsmith's balance sheets are well documented, Ruggles and Ruggles do not provide detailed documentation on how they adjusted the FFA asset categories.

Equities

Corporate Stock. We used Goldsmith's and Ruggles and Ruggles' corporate stock estimates in our household balance sheet. While there are substantial differences for the overlapping years between the Goldsmith and the Ruggles and Ruggles estimates, there was no discernible trend in the percentage differences. Thus, we made no correction to either Ruggles and Ruggles' estimates or Goldsmith's numbers in this category. As noted above, the FFA household balance sheets include the nonprofit sector and personal trusts as well as households. As a result, the FFA values provide an upper bound to corporate stock holdings among households. Both the Goldsmith and the Ruggles and Ruggles estimates of household corporate stock are below the FFA values for all years. Our 1981 and 1983 values were estimated using a trend regression of the ratio of the Ruggles and Ruggles values to the corresponding FFA figures.

Farm Equity. We used Goldsmith's data for the 1900–1949 period and the FFA figures for the 1953–83 period. The Ruggles and Ruggles series and the FFA data are similar once adjustments are made for definitional differences. Before our adjustments, there were large differences, both in relation to total assets and in percentage terms, between the Goldsmith estimates and both the Ruggles and Ruggles and the FFA values for farm equity. Goldsmith's estimates are approximately one-third higher than the Ruggles and Ruggles figures for each year.

There are two reasons for this discrepancy. First, after examining the respective farm-sector balance sheets, it was apparent that Goldsmith included all the residential household assets of a farm family in the farm equity category. Ruggles and Ruggles included only those assets associated with the farm business, and all others owned by farm families were included in the household sector. In particular, Ruggles and Ruggles included the value of consumer durables, owner-occupied housing, and savings accounts owned by the farm family in the respective asset categories of the household sector instead of as part of farm equity. The FFA approach is closer to that of Ruggles and Ruggles, except that the FFA includes owner-occupied farm housing in farm equity. Second, Ruggles and Ruggles did not attribute all the farm sector's net worth to households but rather assigned part of it to the corporate sector, whereas Goldsmith assumed no corporate ownership of farms. In 1958, a year for which we have farm balance sheets from both sources, Ruggles and Ruggles transferred 92 percent of total farm equity to the household sector and 8 percent to the corporate sector. We adjusted Goldsmith's farm equity estimates as well as the FFA data to be consistent with Ruggles and Ruggles' approach. After the above adjustments, the percentage differences between the Goldsmith, the FFA, and the Ruggles and Ruggles data were significantly reduced, between 0.0 and 8.0 percent for the overlapping years (1949–58) compared with over 30 percent for the unadjusted data.

Unincorporated Business Equity. For the 1900–1945 period, we used Goldsmith's data with adjustments for differences in definitions already mentioned above in the discussion of tenant-occupied housing and land. For subsequent years, we used the FFA series, under the assumption that the holdings of trust funds and nonprofit organizations of this asset were negligible. One reason that we did not use Ruggles and Ruggles' estimates for this category is that, even after correcting for differences in concept, Ruggles and Ruggles' numbers are still 6–15 percent lower than the FFA or the Goldsmith estimates for the 1949–58 period.

Trust Fund Equity, Wealth Definitions: W1 and W2. Trust funds are reported differently in Goldsmith's balance sheets than in they are in those of Ruggles and Ruggles. Goldsmith distributed trust funds across all financial categories, an approach similar to that of the FFA, although the estimates in Goldsmith, Brady, and Mendershausen (1956) include separate trust estimates for each asset category and Goldsmith, Lipsey, and Mendelson (1963) include a separate trust balance sheet for 1945–58. Ruggles and Ruggles recorded a separate category for trust funds. The FFA did not separate out this category from household assets and did not report on estimate for trusts in any year. We prefer the Ruggles and Ruggles approach of separating out trust funds because of the extreme concentration of this asset and our desire to separate out the actuarial concept from the full trust value. Thus, we subtracted from Goldsmith's categories an estimated amount for trust funds. The difference between Goldsmith's and Ruggles and Ruggles' estimates of total trust equity ranged from 1.0 to 13.0 percent for the years 1949–58. However, we have no information on the source for the Ruggles and Ruggles trust estimates, and no further correction was possible to increase consistency between Goldsmith's and Ruggles and Ruggles' trust estimates.

Our W1 wealth measure includes only the actuarial value of trusts (see table 15.1 for wealth definitions). The actuarial value of trust funds was obtained by reducing the aggregate trust values by the appropriate proportion. The percentage reduction was based on the analysis of Smith and Franklin (1974). For further explanation, see the first section of Appendix B. Our W2 measure includes the full trust value reported by Goldsmith and Ruggles and Ruggles.

Insurance Equity. In the calculation of insurance equity, there were also substantial differences between the various sources in terms of concept. Insurance equity here refers to the combined value of government employee insurance and private insurance plans. Ruggles and Ruggles use a CSV concept, whereas the FFAs include the full reserves or equity of life insurance in the category. Ruggles and Ruggles estimated the CSV of life insurance as approximately 90 percent of the FFA total insurance reserves for every year. Goldsmith, like the FFAs, reported the full insurance reserves in his household estimates. In comparing the estimates from the different sources, we found that Goldsmith's private insurance reserves were substantially higher than the reserves of both the government and the private insurance systems reported in the FFAs. Between 1946 and 1958, the ratio of the FFA total reserves to Goldsmith's private reserves declined from 0.97 to 0.79. The higher Goldsmith numbers are due to the inclusion in his insurance category of both the insurance companies' pension funds and the total net assets of the insurance companies (Goldsmith et al. 1963, 5, 18). These items were not included in the FFA or the Ruggles and Ruggles estimates. These two additional components in the Goldsmith category increased over time, reaching 45 percent of the FFA private life insurance reserves in 1958. In our insurance category, we used the narrower FFA definition and included life insurance pension reserves in the pension category. We thus adjusted Goldsmith's figures by netting out these two extra components. In addition, we followed Ruggles and Ruggles' convention in including only the CSV of life insurance reserves in this category.

Pensions. Goldsmith differed from Ruggles and Ruggles and the FFAs also with respect to what should be included in the pension category. Ruggles and Ruggles and the FFAs include only pension reserves of the private and government pension systems. Goldsmith's concept was much broader and included such items as the reserves of the unemployment insurance system and those of the OASI system (see Goldsmith 1963, 7). Our first adjustment to the Goldsmith figures was to eliminate nonpension reserves from his category.

As with life insurance, Ruggles and Ruggles used a cash surrender concept. The CSV of pensions equaled about 5 percent of total pension reserves for any year. Goldsmith, on the other hand, included the full pension reserves in his household balance sheet. For our W1 and W2 wealth concepts, we follow Ruggles and Ruggles in using the CSV of

pensions. The W3 and W4 wealth measures use the full pension reserves reported in Goldsmith's data and the FFAs. The W5 definition
includes the present value of pension benefits, which can be more or
less than the total value of pension reserves.

The difference between these pension measures has increased in
magnitude as pension wealth has increased. For example, in 1983, total
pension reserves were $1,316.4 billion, representing 9.3 percent of net
worth, while the CSV was $65.8 billion, or less than 1 percent of net
worth. The present value of pension benefits was also calculated for
1983 on the basis of the SCF as part of our W5 measure. The aggregate
value varied between $3,416 and $5,942 billion, depending on the assumptions used. The W5 wealth measure was not incorporated in the
time-series estimates presented in sections 15.3 or 15.5 since the calculation requires microdata. However, the W5 measure is included in
the household survey results reported in section 15.5.

Expected Social Security Payments, W4 and W5 only

Aggregate estimates of expected social security benefits are not available from any of the balance sheet sources. Feldstein (1974) calculated
annual aggregate social security estimates for his analysis of U.S. saving
over the period 1929–71. Feldstein's estimates were corrected and
updated by Leimer and Lesnoy (1982). For our W4 estimates, we assume that expected social security benefits were zero before 1936, and,
from 1936 through 1976, we use Leimer and Lesnoy's fixed ratio estimates, which end in 1977.[26] The fixed ratio assumption produced the
smallest aggregate estimates among the alternative social security series calculated by Leimer and Lesnoy.

Our 1981 and 1983 social security estimates, for the W4 wealth definition, are from two sources: (1) a time trend extrapolation of the
Leimer and Lesnoy series and (2) estimates calculated from the 1983
SCF survey. The aggregate social security estimates from the 1983
survey varied between $3,735 and $7,578 billion for real growth rates
in mean social security benefits (g) of 0–3 percent. (The assumptions
and methodology for the 1983 survey estimates of expected retirement
benefits are explained in sec. 15.5 of the paper.) The time trend regression forecasts of expected social security benefits, based on Leimer
and Lesnoy's series, are $6,000 billion for 1983 and $4,861 billion for
1981. In our W4 series, we use the survey estimate of $5,441.8 billion
(for $g = 0.02$) for 1983 and the time trend regression forecast for 1981.
We are currently calculating estimates for social security wealth for
1981–83 based on Leimer and Lesnoy's algorithms, but these estimates
are not available yet.

Liabilities

Mortgages, Consumer Debt, and Other

There are no major differences in these categories between Gold-smith's work and that of Ruggles and Ruggles and the FFAs. We used Goldsmith's data for the 1900–1945 period and the FFA and the Ruggles and Ruggles estimates for 1949 and subsequent years. For the over-lapping years, the difference between Goldsmith's and Ruggles and Ruggles' estimates is quite small, ranging between 1 and 5 percent.

Appendix B
Adjustment and Imputation Methods in the Construction Of Estimates of the Shares of Top Wealth Holders

This appendix discusses the assumptions used in deriving the esti-mates of both individual and household wealth concentration reported in section 15.4. It is divided into two parts. The first treats the ad-justments and imputations made to the original estimates of Lampman, Smith, and Schwartz on the share of top wealth holders based on estate tax data. In addition, adjustments made to household survey data to obtain consistency with the estate tax estimates are also discussed. These results are reported in table 15.5. The second part of this Ap-pendix explains the transformations to the estate tax data, the standard-ization of the concentration estimates for the top 0.5 and 1.0 percent of the population, and the conversion of the estate data from individual wealth estimates to household estimates.

Adjustments to Original Estate Tax and Household Survey Data

The original data sources used for the construction of our series on the share of top wealth holders reported in table 15.5 are Lampman (1962), Smith and Franklin (1974), and Smith (1984, 1987)—which we collectively refer to as the "Smith data"—and Schwartz (1983) for the estate data and the 1962 SFCC and 1983 SCF adjusted survey data described in section 15.5. Lampman's estimates of top wealth holders' wealth are for the years 1922, 1929, 1939, 1945, 1949, and 1953. Smith's data cover the years 1958, 1962, 1965, 1969, 1972, and 1976. Schwartz's wealth estimate is for 1981.

The adjustments described in this section were undertaken in order to provide a more consistent concentration series from the estate and survey data and to provide concentration estimates for our four wealth definitions, W1–W4. Our adjustments consisted of imputations for trusts, pensions, and, in the W4 wealth definition, social security. We made no adjustments for differences in the estimation of life insurance values among Lampman, Smith, and Schwartz.

Our adjustments to trusts, pensions, and social security are explained below under each asset category. For trusts and pensions, there is a brief description of the methodology used by Lampman and Smith in deriving their concentration estimates. This is followed by an explanation of our adjustments and imputations to the estate sources as well as any adjustments made to the survey data in order to increase comparability between the estate and survey estimates presented in table 15.5. A summary of the data sources and methods used by Lampman, Smith, and Schwartz in deriving their wealth estimates for the various asset categories is given in table 15.B.1.

Trusts

In the original estate data, trust holdings are distributed among the various asset categories (such as stocks, bonds, and real estate) rather than treated as a separate entry. As explained in the text, remainder trusts, which made up a large percentage of trusts, are valued in the estate files at their actuarial value rather than full market value.[27] On the other hand, the aggregate balance sheet data report trusts at full market value. We use both concepts in our estimates. The W1 wealth concept uses the estate actuarial approach, while the W2–W4 wealth measures are based on the full value of trusts.

Procedures Used by Lampman and Smith

Lampman and Smith used different approaches to reconcile the aggregate balance sheet figures with the estate file data. In what Lampman called his "basic version," no adjustments to the original estate data were made. For his so-called total wealth variant, Lampman augmented the reported trust values in the estate data to reflect the full market value of trusts. In order to derive concentration estimates for his total wealth variant, Lampman assumed that the actuarial amount of trusts included in the estate files was approximately 10 percent of their market value. He also made the following assumptions concerning the top wealth holders' percentage of the aggregate market value of trusts: in 1922, 1929, and 1933, the top wealth holders' share was 66 percent; in 1939, 75 percent; in 1949, 80 percent; and in 1953, 85 percent.[28] Smith's approach was the opposite. He used the actuarial concept for trust valuation and reduced the aggregate household balance sheet totals to

Table 15.B.1   Summary of Data Sources and Adjustments for Trusts, Pensions, and Social Security Wealth

Data Source and Years	Summary of Methodology by Asset Type		
	Trusts	Pensions	Social Security
Estate data: Lampman: 1922, 1929, 1939, 1945, 1949, 1953,	Basic wealth variant: no adjustment to estate data	Basic wealth variant: no adjustment to estate data	No estimate
	Total wealth variant: used market value of trusts concept. Top wealth holders' share of total trusts was imputed. Used Goldsmith's aggregate value of total pensions for concentration estimates	Total wealth variant: used full pension reserve concept. Top wealth holders' share of pension reserves was imputed. Used Goldsmith's aggregate value of total pensions for concentration estimates	

(*continued*)

Table 15.B.1 (continued)

	Summary of Methodology by Asset Type		
Data Source and Years	Trusts	Pensions	Social Security
Smith: 1958, 1962, 1965, 1969, 1972, 1976,	No adjustment to estate data; reduced Ruggles and Ruggles' aggregate values to reflect the lower actuarial value in the estate data	No adjustment to estate data; used Ruggles and Ruggles' aggregate CSV of pensions for concentration estimates	No estimate
Schwartz: 1981[a]	No adjustment to the estate data	No adjustment to the estate data	No estimate
Household survey data:			
SFCC: 1962; SFC: 1983	Used market value of trusts concept. For explanation of adjustments for underreporting and missing values, see sec. 15.5	Used the CSV concept and also imputed expected pension benefits (W5) Method is explained in sec. 15.5	Estimated expected social security benefits

Note: This table includes only the adjustment procedures used by the original sources in deriving their estimates of wealth inequality. Our adjustment procedures and assumptions used for trusts, pensions, and social security wealth in order to derive our own estimates of wealth concentration, reported in table 15.5, are explained in the first section of App. B.

[a]Schwartz also estimated the wealth of top shareholders for 1982 from the estate files. The 1982 results are not included here because they were not received in time to do the calculations.

be consistent with the lower actuarial value in the estate files. On the basis of his analysis of the 1965 estate file, Smith assumed that the actuarial value represented 54.3 percent of the aggregate market value of trusts and reduced the balance sheet aggregates by this percentage for each year.[29]

Our Adjustments and Imputations for Wealth Concepts W1–W4

Our concentration estimates for wealth version W1 were based on Lampman's "basic version" and Smith's and Schwartz's concentration estimates, all of which included only the actuarial value of trusts in the estate files. The corresponding household aggregate totals for trust funds were reduced by 40–55 percent, depending on the year, on the basis of Smith's analysis of the 1965 data.

Our wealth definitions W2–W4 incorporated the full balance sheet value of trusts. We adjusted the published estate wealth holdings of Lampman and Smith to be consistent with this broader trust definition. First, for each asset category in the balance sheet, we subtracted an estimate of the portion of that asset included in trust funds from the balance sheet total for that asset. For Lampman's data, we based our adjustments on the asset composition of trusts reported in Goldsmith, Lipsey, and Mendelson (1963). For the Smith data, we used the percentage composition of asset holdings by trust funds that he estimated to adjust Ruggles and Ruggles' aggregate trust fund totals. Table 15.B.2 lists the estimated percentage composition of trust funds used to adjust the aggregate household balance sheet totals for each asset.

Second, we estimated upper and lower bounds for the proportion of total trusts owned by the top wealth holders. To compute the upper bound, we assumed that the top 1 percent owned 100 percent of total trusts and that the top 0.5 percent owned 95 percent in every year.

Table 15.B.2   Composition of Trusts Used for Adjusting Top Wealth Holders' Shares for Wealth Concepts W2–W4 (percentages)

	Lampman Years (1922–53)	Smith Years (1958–76)
Real estate	3	2
Cash	2	3
Bonds	20	22
Stocks	70	71
Debt instruments	3	2
Miscellaneous assets	2	0

Sources: The percentage composition for the Lampman years is a weighted average of the yearly composition 1945–59 in Goldsmith, Lipsey, and Mendelson (1963, table III-1a, p. 120). The percentage composition for the Smith years is based on his own calculations from the 1965 Internal Revenue Estate tax file (Smith 1984, 428).

These assumptions were used in the construction of the concentration estimates for W2 reported in the text. The lower-bound assumption was that the top 1 percent owned 80 percent of total trusts and that the top 0.5 percent owned 75 percent in every year. Another alternative assumption that was made was that there was a decreasing trend in the percentage of trusts owned by the wealthy between 1922 and 1983. The lower-bound series and the decreasing-trend series both produced concentration results that fell between the W1 estimates and the upper-bound estimates reported for W2. Thus, the difference between the share estimates of W2 and those of W1 represents the sensitivity of the inequality estimates to alternative trust imputation assumptions. For the W3 and W4 wealth concepts, we assumed that the top 1 percent owned 90 percent and that the top 0.5 percent owned 85 percent of trusts in every year.

The concentration results based on the 1962 SFCC and the 1983 SCF for wealth concepts W1–W4, reported in tables 15.5 and 15.8, used the same assumptions about trusts as explained above for the reported estate series estimates for wealth concepts W1–W4 rather than the estimates based directly on the two surveys. Thus, for the W3 and W4 survey estimates, it was assumed that the top 1 percent owned 90 percent of trust wealth; for W2, it was assumed that they owned 100 percent; and, for W1, the lower actuarial value was used. The reason for this approach is to increase comparability between the survey and the estate tax estimates. The actual estimated trust share of the top 1 percent of wealth holders based on the survey data is 90 percent for the 1962 SFCC and 84 percent for the 1983 SCF.

Pensions

Procedures Used by Lampman and Smith

As was the case with trusts, Lampman and Smith used different valuation methods for pensions. Lampman used the full pension value, based on total pension reserves, and added a constant fraction of total pension reserves to the estimated wealth holdings of the top wealth holders in the estate file. In particular, he assumed that the top wealth holders' share of pensions was approximately 10 percent of total private holdings and 5 percent of total public pension funds in each year. Smith, on the other hand, used the CSV of pension funds, which was already included in the estate file, so that no imputation assumptions were needed.

Our Adjustments and Imputations for Wealth Concepts W1–W4

We used three different valuation techniques for pensions. In wealth concepts W1 and W2, we used, as Smith did, the CSV of pensions.

For W3 and W4, we used the full reserve value of pension funds. Our W5 concentration estimates, calculated for the household survey data and reported in section 15.5, used a different measure, the present value of expected future pension benefits.

For the estate data, we assumed that the CSV of pensions was already included in the estate files. For the household survey data estimates, the CSV of pensions was computed as a constant fraction of the full pension reserves assigned to the top percentiles (see below). The overall concentration shares were not very sensitive to alternative imputations of CSV of pensions because the total CSV value of pensions amounted to only a very small percentage of total household wealth.

We employed the same method in estimating the pension shares of the wealthy as we did for trusts. We calculated reasonable upper and lower bounds and checked the sensitivity of the estimates to the imputation assumptions. For three alternative scenarios, we assumed that the top 1 percent owned a declining proportion of total pension wealth over the 1922–83 period. We based this trend assumption on the growth of actual pension plans over the period and the results from the 1983 SCF. Based on the 1983 SCF and the definition of pension wealth used for wealth concept W5, we found that the share of total pension wealth held by the top wealth holders was very low, with the top 1 percent of households owning between 2.7 and 3.2 percent, depending on the assumed growth rate of future pension benefits.[30] On the basis of this, we assumed that, as a lower bound, the share of pension reserves held by the top 1 percent of wealth recipients declined from 5 to 3 percent over the 1922–83 period. For an upper bound, we assumed that the top 1 percent's share of pension wealth fell from 15 to 10 percent between 1922 and 1983. For our W3 and W4 concentration series, as reported in tables 15.5–15.8, we assumed that the top 1 percent's share declined from 9 to 5 percent over the 1922–83 period. We also estimated several constant proportion scenarios in which the top 1 percent owned either 5 or 3 percent of pension reserves in each year. Our alternative imputation assumptions resulted in, at most, a 1 percentage point difference in the share of total wealth held by the top 1 percent. The survey concentration results for W3 and W4 reported in tables 15.5 and 15.8 used the same assumptions as described above for the W3 and W4 estate estimates.

Social Security (W4 only)

The concentration estimates reported by Lampman, Smith, and Schwartz did not include any imputations for social security wealth. For our W4 series, we made such imputations. To be consistent with the aggregate social security wealth series that we used (see App. A), the top wealth holders' social security holdings should reflect their expected discounted stream of future benefits. Such imputations were performed for 1962 and 1983, based on the household survey data for those years (see sec. 15.5). However, such direct imputations were not possible for the estate data and, as in case of the trust and pension imputations, certain assumptions were made about the share of total social security wealth held by the top wealth holders. The household survey estimates provide information on the social security shares of the top wealth holders. From the 1962 survey data, we calculated that the top 1 percent of households owned between 2.0 and 2.3 percent of total expected retirement benefits (pension and social security) and that the top 5.0 percent of households owned between 7.3 and 8.4 percent. Our 1983 calculations indicated that the top 1 percent owned between 2.2 and 2.8 percent of expected social security wealth.[31] For our W4 series, we assumed that the top 1 percent owned 5 percent of social security wealth over the 1939–58 period and that this percentage declined from 4 to 3 percent during the period from 1962 to 1983. These shares are slightly higher than the estimates from the two household surveys indicate.

Transformations of the Estate Data Series

As noted in the text, Lampman, Smith, and Schwartz reported concentration estimates for different sample sizes in computing the wealth of top wealth holders. Lampman reported the proportion of the population with gross assets above 60,000 dollars. Smith reported wealth concentration estimates for the top 0.5 and 1.0 percent in each year. Schwartz reported wealth for those with gross assets above $300,000 and $1,000,000. Lampman's population percentage varied from 0.3 to 1.0 percent over the 1922–53 period, while Schwartz's results for 1981 represented 0.8 and 2.0 percent of the population. In table 15.6, we standardized Lampman's and Schwartz's estimates to represent the top 0.5 and 1.0 percent of the population in order to compare their concentration estimates with those of Smith. This required an assumption concerning the functional form of the distribution of wealth.

In tables 15.7 and 15.8, we transformed the estate series from the individual to the household unit in order to estimate the effect of household composition on the concentration trends reported in tables 15.4–15.6 and to compare the estate estimates with the survey estimates. Our assumptions and procedures are explained below.

Extrapolation using the Pareto Distribution

We assumed that wealth above mean wealth followed a Pareto distribution. We fit the Pareto distribution to the estate data concentration estimates for each year. We used the following cumulative density and mean wealth equation to estimate the parameters, α and β, for each year.

(A1) $$P(X > W_0) = \int_{W_0}^{\infty} f(X)dx,$$

where $P(X > W_0)$ is the percentage of the population with wealth above W_0, $f(X) = r(X)\beta$, and $r(X)$ is the Pareto density function. The function $r(X)$ is given by

$$r(X) = \alpha \, \bar{W}^{\alpha} X^{-(\alpha+1)}, \quad X > \bar{W}, \alpha > 1,$$

where $\bar{W}$ is mean wealth, and $\beta = \text{prob}(X > W)$. The mean of the distribution above W_0 is then given by

(A2) $$E(X|X > W_0) = [\int_{W0}^{\infty} xf(x)dx] \, / \, [\int_{W0}^{\infty} f(x)dx].$$

For Lampman's sample, W_0 was \$60,000.

In order to test the sensitivity of the estimated parameters to the lower bound of the support of the Pareto distribution, we estimated α and β from frequency distributions derived from the 1962 SFCC and the 1983 SCF for the top percentiles. The estimated value of α varied from 1.37 to 1.60 as the lower bound increased. As a check on our point estimates for the Lampman years, we inserted different values for α. Varying α between 1.37 and 1.90 altered the estimated concentration shares of the top 1 percent of wealth holders less than 0.5 of a percentage point. This is due to the fact that the estimate of β shifts with changes in α.

Individual to Household Estimates

In tables 15.8 and 15.9, we report shares for the top 1 percent of households, which we estimated from the estate data on individual wealth holdings. These were calculated in two steps. We first estimated the number of households represented by the individual top wealth holders and then, using the Pareto distribution, standardized to the top 1 percent of households. The latter step was comparatively straightforward. The extrapolation technique to the top 1 percent of households was the same as the population standardization explained above except that for Smith's data we had to estimate the lower wealth bound (W_0) for his published results. The first step required assumptions concerning the number and wealth of households represented by Lampman's and Smith's individual top wealth holders. Since we had no information on the number or the wealth of the households represented, we made assumptions concerning the number of households represented, keeping the wealth level of these "households" the same as the estimated wealth in Lampman's and Smith's individual samples. This was also done by Williamson and Lindert (1980). We tried two alternative assumptions concerning the number of households represented.

Assumption 1, which was used to calculate the concentration estimates reported in table 15.7, corresponds to the minimum number of households among the top individual wealth holders. We assumed that all married women had married men within the top wealth holders sample. The married women composed from 9 to 18 percent of the sample of top wealth holders, while married men accounted for over 50 percent. Assumption 1 yields a low estimate of the wealth concentration of households compared to individuals because it assumes that the remaining married men wed women with zero wealth. Part of the difference between the survey and our household concentration estimates (table 15.8) is due to the underestimation of married men's wealth in converting the individual estate series into household estimates.

Assumption 2 yields even lower concentration results and, as a result, seems less believable. For it, we assumed that each individual top wealth holder corresponds to a household. This is tantamount to assuming that every married wealthy individual wed a spouse with zero wealth, and this assumption thus runs the risk of overestimating the number of households represented in the sample. Both assumption 1 and assumption 2 result in wealth shares for the top 1 percent of households that are lower than the corresponding shares of the top 1 percent of individuals. Therefore, our conclusion that there is less of a downward trend in the household concentration series than in the individual series for the Lampman years holds, even if the level of the estimates is not reliable.

An alternative set of assumptions was also used in which both the number of households and the level of wealth held by the sample of top wealth holders are altered. For example, in a variant of assumption 1, we assumed that the remaining married men married women with positive wealth levels. These alternative assumptions yield higher levels of concentration than those reported in tables 15.7 and 15.8. However, there is no information on the amount of wealth to allocate to the spouses. An extension of the work in section 15.4 is to investigate the sensitivity of inequality estimates to changes in the unit of observation (household vs. individual) and to changes in household size. This is more accurately done with the survey data than with the estate data since information exists on household size and composition necessary to adjust the survey household estimates to individual wealth estimates.

A recent paper by Marley (1987) transforms the household distribution of wealth from the 1962 and 1983 surveys into individual wealth distributions under alternative assumptions concerning the division of wealth among household members. Results indicate that wealth inequality estimates from the individual based survey distributions are higher than are estimates from the estate data.

Notes

1. MESP is an acronym for the Measurement of Economic and Social Performance, the name of the project in which the data set was created.

2. Our aggregate social security wealth measure is taken from Leimer and Lesnoy's (1982) revision of Feldstein's original series. We use their fixed ratio version since it yields the smallest value of social security wealth among the alternatives.

3. Also, for simplicity, we shall ignore pension wealth.

4. The assumptions are made to simplify the expression of W_{LC}. For example, if r^* does not equal d, then discounted net interest after age sixty-five must be included in the calculation of W_{LC}. Relaxing the assumptions does not change the result that AW_{LC} is greater than W4, provided that there is positive real income growth over the period from age a to age sixty-five.

5. A comparison of aggregate wealth totals for 1962 and 1983 from national balance sheet data and household survey data is also discussed in sec. 15.5 below, in which we use the aggregate balance sheet figures to adjust the survey estimates for missing values and underreporting.

6. The W4 measure uses the Leimer and Lesnoy (1982) total social security wealth series, which ends in 1978. Our 1981 figure for total social security wealth is estimated using regression analysis. The variables used are described in App. A. The 1983 figure is computed directly from the SCF. For details, see sec. 15.5.

7. The estate estimates provide information for only the top wealth holders. There is not an exact mapping between estimates of the share of top wealth holders and more inclusive inequality measures such as the Gini coefficient.

8. Although we tried several alternative groupings, we could not reproduce exactly Smith's reported aggregate numbers using Ruggles and Ruggles' published numbers. The largest discrepancy was in his miscellaneous asset category.

9. We used the end-year aggregates reported in sec. 15.3 because mid-year calculations were not possible for the 1922–45 period.

10. However, some trusts were not included at all in Smith's estate files. Thus, his numbers are below the "true" actuarial values. Lampman, on the other hand, assumed that there was extensive gift transfer to avoid taxes and adjusted the trust figures upward.

11. Table 15.6 reports concentration figures for total assets, whereas table 15.4 reports them for net worth.

12. It should be noted that the shares for W4 reported in tables 15.5 and 15.6 depend both on the net growth assumptions used in calculating aggregate social security wealth and on the assumed share of social security wealth held by the top 1 percent of wealth holders. The assumptions underlying the W4 concentration estimates are explained in Apps. A and B.

13. This result is based on a comparison of Lampman's 1953 results and Schwartz's 1976 and 1981 estimates. In 1953, married women represented 18 percent of the sample. In 1976, they composed 16.8 percent and, in 1981, 18 percent.

14. The 1979 ISDP results are from Radner and Vaughan (1987). The 1979 Pension Commission survey estimates are from Cartwright and Friedland (1985). The 1962 SFCC and 1983 SCF are from sec. 15.5 of this paper.

15. It should be noted that there were no missing value problems in our SFCC tape version since imputations for missing values had already been performed by the Federal Reserve Board.

16. It should be noted that the use of uniform adjustment factors (overall or by income class) leads to an understatement of the actual variance of these holdings within the population. However, in previous work, sensitivity analyses were conducted on the 1969 MESP file, in which a random error term was added to the average adjustment factor for each asset. The results showed that the inclusion of such an error term had very little effect on estimates of the Gini coefficient and other measures of overall wealth inequality in the population. For details, see Wolff (1982).

17. The source is U.S. Bureau of Labor Statistics (1978, table 127, p. 359). Household inventory items include (1) food purchased for home use, (2) tobacco, (3) alcoholic beverages, and (4) clothing and clothing materials.

18. Separate imputations were performed for husband and wife, and an adjustment in the social security benefit was made for the surviving spouse. The real discount rate i^* was estimated as the ten-year Treasury bill rate less the average annual rate of inflation (as measured by the consumer price index) over the previous ten years.

19. For simplicity, it is assumed that pension vesting is immediate.

20. We define a new measure of household wealth, W2*, as W2 plus household inventories. This is a more standard definition of traditional household wealth than is W2. Since household inventories are lacking in the estate data, we used W2 for this series.

21. Results are similar for W5, the sum of W2 and pension and social security wealth.

22. Indeed, the converse issue arises for some of these categories: namely, should their reported values be adjusted downward to align with the national balance sheet totals? We assumed, as we did for the 1962 SFCC, that there is no apparent incentive for respondents to overreport the value of their assets. Moreover, it is likely that respondent market value estimates of some items such as owner-occupied housing and other real estate would be better than aggregate estimates based on perpetual inventory techniques. Therefore, as in the case of the 1962 SFCC, we made no adjustment for these items.

23. The imputations for inventories were based on U.S. Bureau of Labor Statistics (1978).

24. It was not possible to compare either the distribution of financial securities between the two years since savings bonds were included in the 1962 category but excluded in the later year or the distribution of insurance CSV or pension CSV between the two years because these items were imputed in the 1962 data.

25. The effect of alignment is relatively modest for these two data bases because the degree of underreporting of wealth among the rich is not as significant as it is in other wealth surveys. For example, Curtin, Juster, and Morgan (chap. 10, in this vol.) report significant differences in coverage, particularly

of the upper wealth strata, between the 1983 SCF, on the one hand, and the 1984 Panel Study of Income Dynamics and the 1984 Wealth Supplement to the SIPP, on the other hand. Also, table 15.9 of this paper indicates large variations in the reliability of different wealth surveys. Thus, for those surveys with poor coverage of the upper wealth strata, alignment to aggregate national balance sheet totals is likely to alter estimated wealth inequality significantly.

26. The Leimer and Lesnoy series are in 1972 dollars and were converted to nominal values in our W4 estimates.

27. For a more detailed explanation, see Smith (1984).

28. Lampman's estimates of the percentage of trusts owned by the top wealth holders increased over time because the percentage of top wealth holders in the estate tax sample increased from 0.3 to 1 percent of the population over this period.

29. Smith and Franklin (1974) compared the capitalized income from trusts reported on the income tax returns filed for 1965 (the only year for which these data were available) to the aggregate household balance sheet total for trusts.

30. In this case, pension wealth was defined as the present value of future pension benefits. For the 1962 survey, it was not possible to separate out pension from social security benefits.

31. The percentage of retirement wealth held by the top wealth holders varies, depending on the growth rate assumption used for future social security benefits. The methodology used in calculating expected retirement wealth for the two household surveys is explained in sec. 15.5 of the paper.

References

Atkinson, A. B. 1975. The distribution of wealth in Britain in the 1960's—The estate duty method reexamined. In *The personal distribution of income and wealth,* ed. James D. Smith. NBER Studies in Income and Wealth, no. 39. New York: Columbia University Press.

Avery, Robert B., Gregory E. Elliehausen, and Arthur B. Kennickell. 1987. Measuring wealth with survey data: An evaluation of the 1983 Survey of Consumer Finances. Paper presented at the twentieth conference of the International Association for Research in Income and Wealth, Rocca di Papa, Italy, September.

Board of Governors of the Federal Reserve System. Flow of Funds Section. 1986. *Balance sheets for the U.S. economy, 1946–1985.* Washington, D.C.: Board of Governors of the Federal Reserve System.

Cartwright, William S., and Robert B. Friedland. 1985. The President's Commission on Pension Policy household survey 1979: Net wealth distribution by type and age for the United States. *Review of Income and Wealth,* ser. 31 (September): 285–308.

Feldstein, Martin S. 1974. Social security, induced retirement and aggregate capital accumulation. *Journal of Political Economy* 82 (October): 905–26.

Goldsmith, Raymond W. 1962. *The national wealth of the United States in the postwar period.* Princeton, N.J.: Princeton University Press.

Goldsmith, Raymond W., Dorothy S. Brady, and Horst Mendershausen. 1956. *A study of saving in the United States.* Princeton, N.J.: Princeton University Press.

Goldsmith, Raymond W., Robert E. Lipsey, and Morris Mendelson. 1963. *Studies in the national balance sheet of the United States.* Princeton, N.J.: Princeton University Press.

Greenwood, Daphne. 1983. An estimation of U.S. family wealth and its distribution from microdata, 1973. *Review of Income and Wealth,* ser. 29 (March): 23–43.

————. 1987. Age, income, and household size: Their relation to wealth distribution in the United States. In *International comparisons of the distribution of household wealth,* ed. Edward N. Wolff. New York: Oxford University Press.

Internal Revenue Service. 1965. *Statistics of Income, 1962: Individual Income Tax Returns.* Publication no. 79 (1-65). Washington, D.C.: U.S. Government Printing Office.

Kotlikoff, Laurence J., and Daniel E. Smith. 1983. *Pensions in the American economy.* Chicago: University of Chicago Press.

Lamas, Enrique J., and John M. McNeil. 1986. Factors associated with household net worth. Paper presented at the meeting of the American Economic Association, New Orleans, LA, December.

Lampman, Robert J. 1962. *The share of top wealthholders in national wealth, 1922–56.* Princeton, N.J.: Princeton University Press.

Leimer, Dean R., and Selig D. Lesnoy. 1982. Social security and private saving: New time-series evidence. *Journal of Political Economy* 90 (June): 606–21.

Marley, Marcia. 1987. Sensitivity of U.S. wealth inequality to population unit, data source and wealth definition. Paper presented at the meeting of the American Statistical Association, San Francisco, Calif., August.

Musgrave, John C. 1986. Fixed reproducible tangible wealth in the United States: Revised estimates. *Survey of Current Business* 66 (January): 51–75.

President's Commission on Pension Policy. 1980a. Pension coverage in the United States. Washington, D.C. Mimeo.

————. 1980b. Preliminary findings on a nationwide survey on retirement income issues. Washington, D.C. Mimeo.

Projector, Dorothy, and Gertrude Weiss. 1966. Survey of financial characteristics of consumers. Technical Papers. Washington, D.C.: Board of Governors of the Federal Reserve System.

Radner, Daniel B., and Denton R. Vaughan. 1987. Wealth, income and the economic status of aged households. In *International comparisons of the distribution of household wealth,* ed. Edward N. Wolff. New York: Oxford University Press.

Ruggles, Richard, and Nancy Ruggles. 1982. Integrated economic accounts for the United States, 1947–1980. *Survey of Current Business* 62 (May): 1–53.

Schwartz, Marvin. 1983. Trends in personal wealth, 1976–1981. *Statistics of Income Bulletin* 3 (Summer): 1–26.

Shorrocks, Anthony F. 1987. U.K. wealth distribution: Current evidence and future prospects. In *International comparisons of the distribution of household wealth,* ed. Edward N. Wolff. New York: Oxford University Press.

Skolnik, Alfred. 1976. Private pension plans, 1950–74. *Social Security Bulletin* 39 (June): 3–17.

Smith, James D. 1984. Trends in the concentration of personal wealth in the United States, 1958–1976. *Review of Income and Wealth,* ser. 30 (December): 419–28.

————. 1987. Recent trends in the distribution of wealth in the U.S.: Data research problems and prospects. In *International comparisons of the dis-*

tribution of household wealth, ed. Edward N. Wolff. New York: Oxford University Press.

Smith, James D., and Stephen D. Franklin. 1974. The concentration of personal wealth, 1922–1969. *American Economic Review* 64 (May): 162–67.

U.S. Bureau of Labor Statistics. 1978. *Consumer Expenditure Survey: Integrated diary and interview survey data, 1972–73.* Bulletin no. 1978. Washington, D.C.: U.S. Government Printing Office.

Williamson, Jeffrey G., and Peter A. Lindert. 1980. Long-term Trends in American wealth inequality. In *Modeling the distribution and intergenerational transmission of wealth,* ed. James D. Smith. Chicago: University of Chicago Press.

Wolff, Edward N. 1980. Estimates of the 1969 size distribution of household wealth in the U.S. from a synthetic database. In *Modeling the distribution and intergenerational transmission of wealth,* ed. James D. Smith. Chicago: University of Chicago Press.

———. 1982. Effect of alternative imputation techniques on estimates of household wealth in the U.S. in 1969. In *Accumulation et repartition des patrimoines,* ed. D. Kessler, A. Masson, and D. Strauss-Kahn. Paris: Economica.

———. 1983. The size distribution of household disposable wealth in the United States. *Review of Income and Wealth,* ser. 29 (June): 125–46.

———. 1987a. The effects of pensions and social security on the distribution of wealth in the United States. In International comparisons of the distribution of household wealth, ed. Edward N. Wolff. New York: Oxford University Press.

———. 1987b. Estimates of household wealth inequality in the U.S., 1962–1983. *Review of Income and Wealth,* ser. 33 (September): 231–56.

———. 1989. Trends in aggregate household wealth in the U.S., 1900–1983. *Review of Income and Wealth,* ser. 35 (March).

Comment   Robert B. Avery

Wolff and Marley have embarked on an ambitious enterprise: first, to align a number of sources to produce a historically consistent time series of aggregate U.S. household wealth from the 1920s to date and, second, to compare the evidence on wealth concentration over the same time period. Not surprisingly, their paper is quite long and cannot be easily evaluated in a few simple comments.

In my view, the primary contribution of their paper is their careful and painstaking attempt to build a set of consistent series of household wealth. Because these series depend critically on numerous small de-

Robert B. Avery is associate professor at Cornell University. He was a Senior Economist in the Research and Statistics Division of the Board of Governors of the Federal Reserve System when this paper was written.

The opinions expressed here do not necessarily reflect those of the Board of Governors of the Federal Reserve System or its staff. Special thanks to Arthur Kennickell for helpful comments.

cisions, I have chosen to comment principally on some of the key decisions rather than the conclusions based on the series.

Four different measures of aggregate wealth are tabulated for twenty points in time ranging from 1900 to 1983. The four wealth measures differ according to their treatment of trust assets (cash surrender value [CSV] vs. full equity value), private pension assets (CSV vs. current value of pension reserves), and the inclusion of social security wealth (measured by the present value of future benefits). Most of the data for the authors' tabulations are drawn from Goldsmith, Lipsey, and Mendelson (1963) for prewar figures, and the Federal Reserve Board's flow-of-funds accounts (FFAs) and Ruggles and Ruggles (1982) for postwar data. Data on household durables are also taken from Musgrave (1986) and social security wealth estimates from Leimer and Lesnoy (1982).

Most of the adjustments the authors made involve resectoring of the published data—that is, changes in the classification of assets rather than changes in value totals. Some of these changes are substantial, as pointedly demonstrated by a comparison of values for 1949, 1953, and 1958, years for which data from Goldsmith, Lipsey, and Mendelson, Ruggles and Ruggles, and the FFAs are all available. The three sources differ in their projected totals for virtually every asset, and differences are not small, ranging from 3 to 47 percent. The magnitude of these differences—many of which can be only partially corrected through resectoring—suggests that great caution should be exercised in using specific asset series drawn from different sources. Moreover, although definitional problems will tend to be offsetting, they almost surely do affect net worth calculations.

Unfortunately, Wolff and Marley give little sense of either the precision of their calculations or the robustness of their estimates to the meshing rules that they use. The reader is given little feeling of how sensitive conclusions about such issues as the long-run trend in real per capita wealth are to these decisions.

Their treatment of social security wealth is a case in point. In their paper, Leimer and Lesnoy propose twenty different social security wealth series that range in value from $1.3 to $4 trillion in 1976. This range amounts to almost 50 percent of the total value of all other household wealth at that time. Wolff and Marley, apparently arbitrarily, select one measure. Moreover, they choose a measure of *gross* social security wealth, which some might argue is inconsistent with the concept of *net* worth. They also use a "time trend extrapolation" to extend the Leimer and Lesnoy series, which ends in 1977, to 1983. This procedure ignores the major overhaul of social security that took place in 1982, which surely affected social security wealth. Since Wolff and Marley attribute the majority of the increase in real per capita wealth in the last fifty years to social security, it would be very useful to know how sensitive their conclusions are to these decisions.

The second portion of the paper deals with wealth concentration. Wolff and Marley use data from the Internal Revenue Service (IRS) estate tax multiplier series to estimate the wealth holdings of the top 1 percent of the population for years ranging from 1922 to 1981. Since published data for the estate tax series are given for individual wealth holdings above certain dollar amounts (e.g., the wealth of individuals with gross assets of more than $60,000), Wolff and Marley have to make certain assumptions to convert these figures to percentages of total household wealth. They fit a Pareto distribution to the reported data and use the estimated distribution to determine the wealth holdings of the top 0.5 and the top 1 percent of households. Clearly, the estate tax series is virtually the only source that can be used to examine changes in concentration over a long period of time. However, as has been pointed out elsewhere, several concerns arise with its use. The estate tax series is defined for individuals, whereas some concept of a household is generally thought to be the relevant unit for measuring changes in society's well-being over time. Wolff and Marley acknowledge this problem and propose several different methods for combining individual estate tax filers into households. Their estimates, however, are lower bounds. Moreover, the authors do not allow for changes over time in the rules allocating wealth within households. Work that my colleagues and I have done with the 1983 Survey of Consumer Finances (SCF) and the 1962 Survey of Financial Characteristics of Consumers (SFCC) suggests that the effect of such assumptions can be large.[1] Working with household data, we have found that the percentage of wealth held by the top 1 percent of individuals can vary by more than 5 percentage points, depending on whether wealth within the household is allocated to maximize or minimize concentration. This range is almost as large as the computed change in the Wolff and Marley series from 1922 to 1972. While I am a strong supporter of the estate tax multiplier data, I believe that more work needs to be done on the allocation of taxable assets between household members (and between generations)—and changes in these allocations over time—before we can make definitive statements about long-run trends in concentration.[2]

The final portion of the paper looks at the issue of wealth concentration using household survey data. Most of their discussion focuses on the 1962 SFCC and 1983 SCF and parallels work that I have done with my colleagues Arthur Kennickell and Gregory Elliehausen (see Avery, Kennickell, and Elliehausen 1988). Not unexpectedly, we made some different assumptions from Wolff and Marley on which I would like to focus my remarks.

Although both the SCF and the SFCC were very complex surveys, they are not complete. In addition, there are missing values for many variables in both data sets. Several items, such as businesses and life insurance, were not fully imputed in the original public use tape of the

SFCC, and complete pension and social security data were not collected in that survey. The original SCF tape contained missing values for many variables. In the paper presented at the conference, Wolff and Marley used fairly simple algorithms to impute missing values. The most complicated of their procedures involved assigning the observed mean value by income class to missing items. Assets such as pensions or durable goods were assigned as mean predictions from very simple regressions based on demographic and employment variables.

Our own work suggests that, while variation in imputation procedures may not affect estimates of mean holdings of many assets and liabilities very much, this is not true for every asset category (or for income). Moreover, concentration measures are not invariant to the imputation procedures used. Most state-of-the-art imputation procedures attempt to estimate and preserve both the first and the second moments of variables with missing values. Filling in missing values with means reduces the variance of variables and reduces the density in the extreme tails. The holdings of the top 1 percent of the population, the group looked at by Wolff and Marley, are very likely to be biased downward by this procedure. In the present version of their paper, Wolff and Marley have recomputed their tables for the 1983 SCF using our imputations, which took full account of second moments. Nevertheless, simplistic imputations remain for a number of variables, such as durable goods, social security, and pensions. Their imputations for the 1962 SFCC also lack any adjustment for second moments.

A more serious problem with Wolff and Marley's methodology is their decision to align the household survey data with aggregate estimates, presumably to give a better measure of the overall wealth of each household. Survey-based totals are compared to aggregate estimates (FFAs, etc.) on a variable-by-variable basis. If the survey total exceeds the aggregate total by, say, 10 percent, then the holding of that variable for each survey respondent is reduced by 10 percent. Survey responses are inflated when survey totals are less than the aggregate.

Underlying the Wolff and Marley adjustment is the presumption that response bias affects every holder of an asset proportionately and is unrelated to bias in other answers. I believe that very few survey experts would agree with this view. It is clear that much of the "bias" in survey reporting involves missectoring—that is, respondents misclassify assets, calling a money-market account a checking account and so forth. Our detailed work in this area shows that survey-based estimates for bonds, for example, match FFA-based estimates quite closely in total but miss substantially in allocating bonds between federal, municipal, and other categories. This suggests that some respondents may not know what kind of bond they have but that they can report its value accurately. The Wolff and Marley procedure would probably cause no great harm if sectoring problems were random. However, they probably are not. More sophisticated respondents may be less likely to misclassify assets; however, respondents with a lot of different holdings may have more opportunity to do so. If misclassifications are not random, the Wolff and Marley procedures could very likely bias concentration estimates. As an example, suppose that a narrowly held asset, Treasury bills, tends to be misclassified as a broadly held asset, U.S. savings bonds. The Wolff and Marley procedure would inflate the value of all reported Treasury bills and deflate the value of all reported savings bonds. The net worth of less wealthy households will be decreased, on the average, because they hold savings bonds but do not hold Treasury bills. Wealthy households will gain by the same reasoning, thus distorting the share of wealth estimated for the top wealth holders.

The Wolff and Marley alignment procedure also rests critically on the assumption that aggregate estimates of asset and liability categories are themselves measured accurately and that they measure the same things as the survey estimates. Our work suggests that neither of these assumptions may be realistic. The household-sector holdings of many assets are computed as the balancing residuals in the FFAs and thus are sensitive to measurement errors in every sector. Drawing the line between true households and small businesses, trusts, and nonprofits, for example, is inexact at best. Our work suggests that the survey estimates of deposit holdings and installment loans can be bought into much closer alignment than appears at first glance. Much of this adjustment, however, is to the FFA numbers, not just the survey estimates. At the very least, our work suggests that, if one wanted to align the survey data, the process would involve a much more complicated, variable-by-variable, analysis than that done by Wolff and Marley.

I fear that some of my comments may leave an overall view that I am negative about the Wolff and Marley paper. On the contrary, I believe that they have made a tremendous effort on a difficult and complex task. While I believe that much work remains for them, and for others, they have made a bold start.

Notes

1. See Avery, Elliehausen, and Kennickell (1988).
2. There are a number of other issues related to the estate tax multiplier series that I raised at the conference, particularly the "preaudit" nature of the series, differences between the value of assets at death and for the living, and the effect of the 1976 and 1981 tax law changes on returns filed for those years.

Subsequent work by Fritz Scheuren and Janet McCubbin at the IRS suggests that differences between pre- and postaudit figures may not be large. This effort, which is part of an ongoing project, shows great promise in shedding light on a number of issues related to the series.

References

Avery, Robert B., Gregory E. Elliehausen, and Arthur B. Kennickell. 1988. Measuring wealth with survey data: An evaluation of the 1983 Survey of Consumer Finances. *Review of Income and Wealth* ser. 34, no. 4 (December).

Goldsmith, Raymond W., Robert E. Lipsey, and Morris Mendelson. 1963. *Studies in the national balance sheet of the United States.* Princeton, N.J.: Princeton University Press.

Leimer, Dean R., and Selig D. Lesnoy. 1982. Social security and private saving: New time-series evidence. *Journal of Political Economy* 90 (June): 606–21.

Musgrave, John C. 1986. Fixed reproducible tangible wealth in the United States: Revised estimates. *Survey of Current Business* 66 (January): 51–75.

Ruggles, Richard, and Nancy Ruggles. 1982. Integrated economic accounts for the United States, 1947–1980. *Survey of Current Business* 62 (May): 1–53.

Contributors

Steven G. Allen
Department of Economics and
  Business
North Carolina State University
Box 8110
Raleigh, NC 27695-8110

B. K. Atrostic
Office of Tax Analysis
U.S. Department of the Treasury
Room 4044 Main Treasury Bldg
15th and Pennsylvania Ave. NW
Washington, DC 20220

Robert B. Avery
Consumer Economics and Housing
135 Martha Van Rensselaer
Cornell University
Ithaca, NY 14853

Michael J. Boskin
National Bureau of Economic
  Research
204 Junipero Serra Boulevard
Stanford, CA 94305

Wayne Camard
Americas Program
Room 306, Food Research Institute
Stanford University
Stanford, CA 94305-6084

Robert L. Clark
Department of Economics and
  Business
North Carolina State University
Box 8110
Raleigh, NC 27695-8110

Richard T. Curtin
Survey Research Center
Institute for Social Research
The University of Michigan
Ann Arbor, MI 48106-1248

Martin H. David
Department of Economics
University of Wisconsin
1180 Observatory Drive
Madison, WI 53706

Frank de Leeuw
Bureau of Economic Analysis
U.S. Department of Commerce
Washington, DC 20230

Michael P. Dooley
External Adjustment Division
Research Department
International Monetary Fund
19th and H Streets, NW
Washington, DC 20431

Robert Eisner
Department of Economics
Northwestern University
Evanston, IL 60201

Barbara M. Fraumeni
Department of Economics
Northeastern University
Lake Hall, #301
360 Huntington Avenue
Boston, MA 02115

James L. Freund
Office of Policy and Economic
    Research
Federal Home Loan Bank Board
1700 G Street, NW
Washington, DC 20552

Patric H. Hendershott
Department of Finance
The Ohio State University
Hagerty Hall
1775 College Road
Columbus, OH 43210-1309

Thomas M. Holloway
Mortgage Bankers Association of
    America
1125 15th Street, NW
Washington, DC 20005

Alan M. Huber
National Bureau of Economic
    Research
204 Junipero Serra Boulevard
Stanford, CA 94305

Michael D. Hurd
Department of Economics
State University of New York at
    Stony Brook
Stony Brook, NY 11794-4384

F. Owen Irvine
Department of Economics
Michigan State University
East Lansing, MI 48824-1038

Nancy Ammon Jianakoplos
Department of Economics
Michigan State University
East Lansing, MI 48824-1038

Dale W. Jorgenson
Department of Economics
Littauer Center 122
Harvard University
Cambridge, MA 02138

F. Thomas Juster
Survey Research Center
Institute for Social Research
The University of Michigan
Box 1248
Ann Arbor, MI 48106-1248

Denis Kessler
Centre National de la Recherche
    Scientifique
42 Bd Raspail
75007 Paris, France

Enrique J. Lamas
Housing and Household Economic
    Statistics Division
U.S. Bureau of the Census
Room 408, Iverson Mall
Washington, DC 20233

Walther Lederer
Flow of Funds Section
Board of Governors of the Federal
    Reserve System
20th and Constitution Avenue, NW
Washington, DC 20551

Nathaniel H. Leff
Graduate School of Business
Columbia University
403 Uris Hall
New York, NY 10027

Robert E. Lipsey
Queens College and The Graduate
    Center
City University of New York
Flushing, NY 11367

Ann A. McDermed
Department of Economics and
    Business
North Carolina State University
Raleigh, NC 27695-8110

John M. McNeil
Chief, Poverty and Wealth Statistics
    Branch
Housing and Household Economic
    Statistics Division
U.S. Department of Commerce
Bureau of the Census
Room 408, Iverson Mall
Washington, DC 20233

Marcia Marley
Department of Economics
New York University
269 Mercer Street, 7th Floor
New York, NY 10003

Paul L. Menchik
Department of Economics
Michigan State University
East Lansing, MI 48824-1038

Marilyn Moon
Public Policy Institute
American Association of Retired
    Persons
1909 K Street, NW
Washington, DC 20049

James N. Morgan
Survey Research Center
Institute for Social Research
University of Michigan
Ann Arbor, MI 48106-1248

B. Gabriela Mundaca
Department of Economics
State University of New York
Stony Brook, NY 11794

Joe Peek
Department of Economics
Boston College
Chestnut Hill, MA 02167

Daniel B. Radner
Department of Health and Human
    Services
Social Security Administration
4301 Connecticut Avenue, NW
Suite 211
Washington, DC 20008

Cordelia W. Reimers
Department of Economics
Hunter College
695 Park Avenue
New York, NY 10021

Clark W. Reynolds
Director, Americas Program
Room 306, Food Research Institute
Stanford University
Stanford, CA 94305-6084

Marc S. Robinson
Senior Research Scientist
Societal Analysis Department
General Motors Research
    Laboratories
Warren, MI 48090

Sherwin Rosen
Department of Economics
The University of Chicago
1126 East 59th Street
Chicago, IL 60637

Thomas K. Rymes
Department of Economics
Carleton University
Ottawa, Ontario
Canada K1S 5B6

Anna J. Schwartz
National Bureau of Economic
    Research
269 Mercer Street, 8th Floor
New York, NY 10003

Eugene Smolensky
Graduate School of Public Policy
University of California
2607 Hearst Avenue
Berkeley, CA 94720

Stephen Taylor
2510 24th Street, N.
Arlington, VA 22207

Helen Stone Tice
Bureau of Economic Analysis
 (BE-1)
U.S. Department of Commerce
Washington, DC 20230

George M. von Furstenberg
Department of Economics
Indiana University
Bloomington, IN 47405

Paul Wachtel
Chairman, Department of
 Economics
Graduate School of Business
 Administration
New York University
100 Trinity Place
New York, NY 10006

John F. Wilson
Chief, Flow of Funds Section
Division of Research and Statistics
Board of Governors of the Federal
 Reserve System
20th and Constitution Avenue, NW
Washington, DC 20551

Edward N. Wolff
Department of Economics
New York University
269 Mercer Street, 7th Floor
New York, NY 10003

Frederick O. Yohn, Jr.
Flow of Funds Section
Board of Governors of the Federal
 Reserve System
20th and Constitution Avenue, NW
Washington, DC 20551

Author Index

Subject Index